Growing Up in America

Growing Up

in America

Historical Experiences

EDITED AND INTRODUCED BY

Harvey J. Graff

Wayne State University Press
DETROIT 1987

Copyright © 1987 by Wayne State University Press,
Detroit, Michigan 48202. All rights are reserved.
No part of this book may be reproduced without formal permission.
91 90 89 88 87   5 4 3 2 1

Library of Congress Cataloging-in-Publication Data

Growing up in America.

  Includes bibliographical references and index.
  1. United States—Social conditions. 2. Adolescence
—History. 3. Children—United States—History.
4. Family—United States—History. I. Graff, Harvey J.
HN57.G76 1987   305.2'35'0973   87-23095
ISBN 0-8143-1899-1 (alk.)
ISBN 0-8143-1900-9 (pbk.)

Thomas L. Webber, "The Setting: Growing Up in the Quarter Community," is
reprinted from *Deep Like the Rivers: Education in the Slave Quarter Community,*
1831–1865, by Thomas L. Webber, by permission of W. W. Norton & Company,
Inc. Copyright © 1978 by W. W. Norton & Company, Inc.

For the children of today,
in hopes for tomorrow;
in solidarity with the Children's Defense Fund's solitary struggles

Contents

Acknowledgments

Several persons merit special thanks for their contributions to the design and execution of this book. Graduate students in the Arts and Humanities Program at the University of Texas at Dallas, who field-tested much of this material in the form of a seminar syllabus, were firm critics. Robert Mandel and the staff of Wayne State University Press responded with enthusiasm and professional competence. Those authors willing, indeed eager, to allow republication of their work were more supportive of the larger project than perhaps they recognized. Most of all, I wish to thank my graduate assistant, Patricia Hill, an apprentice historian in her own right, for her help in the preparation of the manuscript for publication.

Introduction

Compare our response to children and to adults: we give to the existence of children the value we give to the intentions of adults.

John Berger, *G* (1972)

Hoary convention decrees that one look back fondly upon the years spent growing up. The family nest, brimming with affection, symbolized things as they should be: warm, secure, and caring. Such nests surely existed, beyond the conventional generalities, but one suspects that they were not the norm. In the home, or the society that prolongs it, the ideal appears to be less one of harmony than of unity imposed from outside or above. Family relations are adversary relations. . . . The family sheltered less tenderness than tension, suffering, and more or less covert violence.

Eugen Weber, *France: Fin de siècle* (1986)

To assert that "the history of growing up" is a historical orphan is at once to understand its recent prominence as a significant area of scholarly interest *and* its lack of legitimate definition and status. In its focus on "growing up," this anthology spans and connects the usually segregated and balkanized research fields of the histories of childhood, adolescence, and youth.[1] In so doing, it seeks to reorient study and interpretation, and makes an explicit argument that this fragmentation obscures the best way to understand historical patterns of these critical early phases of the human life course. Typically, children are studied without interest in the completion of that developmental stage and its relations to the next; similarly, adolescents and youth are segregated.[2] The promise of the new attention to the history of the life course is compromised and lost. For all the raging debates about the so-called boundaries of life course division—for example, the ages at which adolescence or youth commence and end, and the historical time period in which adolescence emerges in recognizable form—implicit boundaries preclude our viewing growing up in its developmental totality.

Yet the interests of historians—and their peers in the humanities and the social sciences—in the early phases of the life course show no sign of lessening. At least since the publication of Philippe Ariès's seminal *Centuries of Childhood* in 1960 (with English translation in 1962), the flow of articles and books has been incessant.[3] These topics—childhood, adolesence, and youth—along with closely related research on the family, women, education, social and socializing institutions, and social policies—are major growth industries, and not only within the academy. In fact, in the wake of Ariès's *Centuries of Childhood* and, to a lesser extent, Lloyd DeMause's *Journal of Psychohistory* (formerly *History of Childhood Quarterly*) and his edited volume *The History of Childhood* (1974),[4] the historical basis and background have become standard reference points in writings about children, adolescence, and youth by nonhistorians. A sign of interdisciplinary development, this can be as much a problem as a mark of progress.[5] Recognition of both and their expansion is another task of this volume.

We have certainly learned a great deal about these traditionally neglected topics. Their centrality to historical development, social change and continuity, and cultural life is now undoubted. The last two decades' writings show a healthy pluralism of interpretations and approaches. Both are well reflected in the selections that follow.

Yet the fields, with their burgeoning literatures, remain unwieldy and surprisingly undefined.[6] A major symbol and symptom of this is the lack of standard historical interpretations, as well as the nature of continuing controversies.[7] This is especially true with respect to the *nature* and the *historical meanings* of childhood and youth as human experiences and core elements of society and culture.

Several approaches dominate research. One may be categorized as the *psychohistorical,* which ranges from the proposed "psychogenic" theory of Lloyd DeMause and his followers in the *Journal of Psychohistory* to the Erik Erikson–influenced ego psychology of John Demos and the more diffuse cultural psychology of Philip J. Greven and the studies on American childhood recently collected by Hiner and Hawes.[8] A second approach is the *sociocultural,* represented well in the books by Joseph F. Kett, John R. Gillis, and, in England, John Springhill.[9] A third may be called the *transitions in the life course* approach, conceptualized principally by Glen Elder, Jr., and sponsored in historical research in large measure by Tamara K. Hareven.[10] To these we should add related studies in social and demographic history, many but not all with a quantitative base—some from urban and community history, some from family history, some from histories of discrete social, gender, ethnic, or racial groups.[11] A fourth major approach lies in studies of the development of social, especially educational, *institutions and social policies* aimed at the young and their presumed problems.[12] Of course, these approaches are not wholly exclusive; nevertheless, they often remain separated from one another.

The selections included in this volume represent these major approaches and illustrate their range of approaches, methods, and interpretations. They are a rich roster. They also reveal, when read closely and compared with each other and with related work, the state of the field and its limitations to date. Together, they may also offer some potential for surmounting the lacunae.

A historical approach to growing up must build upon research to date, but also recognize the fragmentations that delimit the field and the set of generally common problems and conceptual complications that disparate studies share. Consider these key characteristics for a *new* history of growing up:

1. The central place and presence of the young themselves, either individually or collectively, within the histories of childhood, adolescence, and youth: a question of approach, sources and evidence, and interpretation;

2. An integrated view of "growing up" in terms of (a) social, cultural, economic, demographic, and psychological processes and dynamic; and (b) passages and transitions between the several phases that constitute childhood, adolescence, and youth: an issue of conceptualization and theoretical assumptions;

3. Recognition of (historically variable) conflict in its many dimensions as central to growing up and its personal, psychological, social, institutional, economic, cultural, and political relations;

4. The nature and extent of dependency as a central, often defining characteristic of the young, historically variable and shifting with notions and experiences of the child, the adolescent, and the youth;

5. Coexistence of central tendencies and patterns of growing up in discrete historical times and places, often but not always in the form of norms, *and* major but patterned variations according to gender, social class and social origins, ethnicity, race, geographic location, place, and age itself;

6. Regular divergence among normative theories of growing up; parental and adult goals, behaviors, and expectations; and the conduct and thinking of the young themselves;

7. The historicity—the historically variable and historically defined nature—of growing up, and its correlative, the demand that understanding of growing up (its nature and variations) comes only from its firm grounding in historical context.

These attributes demarcate the outlines for a synthetic historical approach to growing up; they confront existing weaknesses and limitations and offer means to overcome them. In so doing, they offer a vehicle for the comprehension, evaluation, and synthesis of the materials presented in this collection, along with the larger field.

By the place of the young themselves, I refer to an obvious but often neglected need for the direct analysis and appearance of young persons themselves—as both actors and subjects—in the history of growing up. John Gillis perhaps has been the most insistent in reminding us, in his two editions of *Youth and History,* that the young make their own histories within "traditions of youth." This essential recognition need not ignore the fact that constraints on the actions of the young always coexist, and often conflict, with opportunities and traditions. We must be wary, nevertheless, of studies that neglect the actions, perceptions, responses, options, and sometimes the actual presence of children and youth.[13] The shifting recourse to traditions and their selective reinterpretation, and the patterns of actions over against constraints, are central to the historical experiences of growing up.

The second element is a sharpened, more inclusive conceptualization and context for growing up itself. On the one hand, this serves to remind us that "growth" is never only intrinsically developmental and often not narrowly or normatively psychological, while not neglecting the import of the psychological and subjective component. On the other hand, we emphasize that growth—including, incidentally, physical growth and sexual maturation—is historically defined and historically variable.[14] Moreover, scholarly debates—controversies that overlap with, and both influence and are infected by, public policy issues—about the beginning and end points of life course stages, or "boundaries," deflect attention from the at least equally consequential question of growing up as totality and the transitions or passages between childhood, adolescence, and youth.

In this respect consider that as recently as 1971, historian David Rothman asked, "Do age groups in fact have histories?" A decade later, a rush of studies implicitly answered the question affirmatively. Yet, in 1981, Lawrence Stone commented, "Far more controversial is the dating of the emergence of the concept of adolescence as a clearly defined period of life after puberty during which a young person remains in a position of dependence. [Pioneering child psychologist G. Stanley] Hall saw it emerge only in the late nineteenth century. [Historians John] Demos and Gillis place it in the early nineteenth century, [historian Joseph F.] Kett puts it later, and others—including myself—much earlier." Stone continues: "The dispute seems to be more about boundaries and definitions than about concrete social realities, and the difference between 'youth' and 'adolescence' to be mainly one of terminology."[15]

Yet a third student implicitly disputes Stone's interim settlement and underscores the persisting conceptual conundrums. In *History of Bourgeois Perception,* Donald Lowe asserts:

> In bourgeois society, youth becomes yet another age separating childhood from adulthood. Previously, youth had been not so much an age, but a semidependent status in society, when one had already left the family to become an apprentice, a servant, a page, or a student elsewhere, but had not yet gotten married or set up an independent household. It had been, in effect, an intermediate space between family and society at large. But industrialization and urbanization both strengthened and prolonged the bourgeois family. Bourgeois youth now reverted from that intermediate space into the family. One stayed at home longer after childhood, and had to go to school to acquire the necessary virtues of rationality and discipline, in preparation for the mature, adult world.[16]

Lowe, incidentally, places this development, an epochal one, prior to the late nineteenth- and early twentieth-century "phenomenon of adolescence." More generally, he properly underscores that not only does growing up have a history, is itself historical, but also that that history differs for different young persons. The recent sociological and social psychological guise of homogeneous or converging youth or youth cultures is as ahistorical as it is contemporarily misleading. Moreover, as adolescence shifted, so too did childhood and youth. Thus, overattention to the formal concepts (whose meaning and transformations always must be grasped) can lead into mazes of semantic, chronological, and terminological morasses. That, in relation to social realities and their experiences, can be misleading and counterproductive. Conceiving growing up as connected series of transitions, across even divergent paths of development, is a major advance. Among its innovations is a closer link between historical scholarship and current research in life span and generational-gerontological social psychology and life course sociology.[17]

The third issue—the centrality of conflict to experiences of growing up—is potentially the most innovative, if also the most dangerous and susceptible to confusion and abuse. Recognition of conflict—broadly viewed—derives from a psychological perspective widely cast, but is not limited to psychological processes and reactions alone. As Mihaly Csikszentmihalyi and Reed Larsen write in *Being Adolescent:* "Youth cannot rely either on the instructions contained in their genes or on unchanging adult models as guides for living. They cannot just relax and wait for the passage of time to turn them into adults. Maturation is not a preprogrammed process that unfolds automatically; a young person has to learn habits of thought, action, and feeling that are often difficult and unnatural. *This is a process which, not surprisingly, is cause for much tension and conflict.*"[18]

To an extent whose significance is insufficiently appreciated, the history of growing up—and not merely the twentieth-century episodes of "restless" youth—is a history of conflicts and shifting struggles for maturity and autonomy and development. These conflicts embrace, in diverse ways in different times and places for varying groups of the young, those of generations, peer groups, families, sexes, social classes, ethnic and racial groups, private and public spheres, institutions and the law—the state, professional experts and their quests for recognition and authority, as well as those within the developing person him or herself. As historian Anne Digby recently commented, with respect to just the family: "Images of the family and of the role of children within it are often contradictory and confused. At one extreme the family unit may be depicted as warm and loving: its supportive atmosphere nurturing its members and helping them to come to terms with their problems. At the opposite extreme the family may be seen as a more negative, even destructive force: its claustrophobic inner life inhibiting independent growth and its authoritarian parent control constraining the individuality of children."[19] Contradictions join with conflicts in the making and remaking of growing up. The nature, extent, and variability of conflicts and tensions—and the means of their resolution and the broad social forces that influence the terms of struggle—join to shape the nature, extent, boundaries, length, and experiences of dependency, the fourth factor in our list and, potentially, the central defining element within the history of growing up.[20]

Growing up, misleading appearances aside, is neither an idiosyncratic, individual experience nor a homogeneous generation-wide commonality. As the wide-ranging tales of boys and girls, Anglos and blacks, rich and poor, urban, small town, and rural, and ethnically varied episodes related in the chapters below confirm, there are indeed major historical patterns and trends within the histories of growing up.[21] Time itself is one central variable in their determination, but at least as important are the social origins of young persons. Identification and understanding of the principal paths of growing up, their comparison and contrast, are among the central tasks of the student of childhood, adolescence, and youth.

A necessary corollary for the presence of the young in grasping their history is the need to distinguish them—actor and subject both—from adults, and their concerns and behavior from the shifting currents of child-rearing, psychological, pedagogical, and behavioral theories and from adult-shaped social expectations. Adult testimony, while never to be ignored, should not be taken in isolation or without caution as descriptive of the young. Far more often it is prescriptive. Generational distinctions emerge as equally powerful as those of the other major variations in gender, class, ethnicity, race, and geography, in the making and remaking of growing up historically. As art and cultural critic and novelist John Berger perceived in the quotation that begins this introduction: "Compare our response to children and to adults: we give to the existence of children the value we give to the intentions of adults." Failure to make such key qualifications is hardly a complication of historical work alone. The consequences include a long history of failing social policies.[22]

Stressing the historicity of growing up, while hardly novel to students of history, remains necessary for social scientists, educators, policy makers, and concerned citizens. Growing up and some of its characteristics, of course, feature central elements of biological and biosocial-psychological universality—from physical maturity to sexual development—as the essays in Part I of this anthology indicate. Even those basic elements have changed over time. Moreover, the ways in which specific historical societies and cultures come to interpret and respond to these features and formulate the *rites de passage* that define culturally while also interpreting and expressing its content and concerns are historical developments. In this respect, one may say that growing up is at once a human universal and a cultural invention. Adolescence, with its sometimes curious intellectual history, is perhaps the best example of this.[23] Sorting out these changing relations is the proper task of a historical social and cultural biology (as opposed to the recent faddish sociobiology).[24] Parenthetically, it is no cliché to note that typically a culture expresses its central values, concerns, and conflicts in its approaches to the rearing and raising of the young and responses to their perceived problems. The history of growing up thus provides a key to unlocking the nature of historical civilization.

It is more than likely that the "modern" sense of growing up as "inherently" problematic—for an individual as for one's society—and the corollary of expectations, institu-

tional arrangements, social-psychological theories, and regular "discovery" of social problems arising from growing up are themselves recent historical inventions. This sense of
growing up as problematic developed as part of the formation of and adaptation to
modern social arrangements wrought in the transformation of capitalist social relations
during the past two centuries. As an increasing number of scholars appreciate, the
consequences of this conjunction of behavior and social mythology can be severe. Generational division and often dramatically incomplete and inappropriate social policy formulation are only two sides of the results.[25] The present, we must all grasp, is here emphatically the product of the past. Its contradictions and conflicts are at least as important as its
social progress. From this basis alone we may fairly confront the future of growing up.

That future has come to bedevil contemporary interpreters. Today's impassioned cries
pivot on perceptions of "endangered children," "erosion of childhood," "children without childhood," and "broken promises."[26] The writings from which these shrill fears
emanate range from the silly and superficial to the deeply felt and occasionally useful.
Although many of them pretend to draw on the recent historical literature, their distance
from its sense of complexity and variability is sometimes immense. In part this stems
from the repeated, almost reflexive reference to Ariès's *Centuries of Childhood* without
recognition of its limitations as a source and its deeply conservative ideological bias.[27]
And, in part, it also derives from the persisting limits of interdisciplinary communication
despite almost a generation of pleas that human development can be understood only on
an interdisciplinary basis.

In an important sense, one motivation for the publication of this volume is to make
available for the use of nonhistorians—as well as students of the past—a carefully selected
set of highly relevant historical studies. The success of this particular venture, in part,
depends on the extent to which it reaches and is assimilated by students of psychology,
sociology, education, social policy, and related areas. In this respect, let us note its special
features:

1. The selections that follow, taken collectively, offer a fairly complete and detailed
overview of the historical experience of growing up in the United States (and North
America) from the colonial era to the present. Most of the main trend lines and principal
patterns of divergence are present.

2. The presentation, to facilitate that task, is broadly chronological. Yet the selections
may be reordered to highlight themes, trends, and topics, from class to gender, ethnicity,
institutionalization or deviance, among others. The volume is designed flexibly for multiple use.

3. Within the organization, selections typically emphasize experience and its variations. Social thought and theory, adult expectations, norms, and responses to the young
are clearly incorporated, but in the perspective of the more discrete patterns and paths of
the historical experience of growing up. Thus, gender, social class, ethnicity, geographic
location, race, and the like are principal concerns. Collective patterns—plural paths of
growing up—rather than individual lines are emphasized in a social perspective.

4. To advance this goal and to offer the most advantageous setting for comprehending the historical experiences of growing up, case studies of the young in particular
settings dominate. In part this reflects the richness of the studies and of the histories they
illuminate; in part this derives from an approach to a firmly grounded understanding
from which contrasts and comparisons, generalizations, and new questions may develop.

5. This organization also highlights the variety of approaches, methods, and sources

available for use in studying and interpreting the configurations, parameters, and transformations of growing up. They merit readers' attention, comparison, and criticism.

6. The selections also promote a comparative viewpoint by highlighting the principal lines of diversity and plurality of experiences within even one national and regional setting.

7. The collection as a whole offers important examples of controversy—as in the cases of the place of children in colonial America, the impact of gender on growing up, the boundaries of adolescence, and the historical legacy. Whereas I generally have chosen to emphasize newer approaches and interpretations, the range of their differences and the key areas for further inquiry are not at all slighted.

8. As a whole, *Growing Up in America* stresses the relevance of history for contemporary understanding and policy/problem approaches. The present as an outcome of this past and the range of alternatives that that history offers to us will, I hope, be clear to the perusers of this material. Only then may we, as students, scholars, and citizens, face the future of growing up.

Notes

1. See, in general, Joseph M. Hawes and N. Ray Hiner, eds., *American Childhood: A Research Guides and Historical Handbook* (Westport, Conn.: Greenwood Press, 1985), for most recent and complete bibliography. No effort is made here to duplicate that reference work. The notes to this introduction provide citations to important critical and general works; full references are included for each of the selections that follows. Together they provide an excellent guide to the secondary literature. See also, Part I, below; Hiner and Hawes, eds., *Growing Up in America: Children in Historical Perspective* (Urbana: University of Illinois Press, 1985); Carolyn Steedman, Cathy Urwin, and Valerie Walkerdine, eds., *Language, Gender and Childhood* (London: Routledge and Kegan Paul, 1985); Lloyd DeMause, ed., *The History of Childhood* (New York: Psychohistory Press, 1974); John Gillis, *Youth in History: Tradition and Change in European Age Relations, 1770–Present,* 2d ed. (New York: Academic Press, 1981); John Springhill, *Coming of Age: Adolescence in Britain, 1860–1960* (Dublin: Gill and Macmillan, 1986); Joseph F. Kett, *Rites of Passage: Adolescence in America, 1790 to the Present* (New York: Basic Books, 1977); Harry Hendrik, "The History of Childhood and Youth," *Social History* 9 (1984):87–96; John Demos, *Past, Present, and Personal* (New York: Oxford University Press, 1986); Linda Pollock, *Forgotten Children: Parent-Child Relations from 1500 to 1900* (Cambridge: Cambridge University Press, 1983); John Gillis, "Youth in History: Progress and Prospects," *Journal of Social History* 7 (1974):201–7; Konrad H. Jarausch, "Restoring Youth to Its Own History," *History of Education Quarterly* 15 (1975):445–56; Steven Kern, "The History of Childhood," *Journal of the History of the Behavioral Sciences* 9 (1973):406–12; Daniel Calhoun, "On the Psychohistory of Childhood," *History of Education Quarterly* 14 (1974):371–77; N. Ray Hiner, "The Child in American Historiography," *Psychohistory Review* 7 (1978):13–23; Harvey J. Graff, "The History of Childhood and Youth: Beyond Infancy?" *History of Education Quarterly* 26 (1986):95–109; Graff, "Early Adolescence in Antebellum America: The Remaking of Growing Up," *Journal of Early Adolescence* 5 (1985):411–26; special issues of *Journal of Early Adolescence* 5, no. 4 (Fall 1985) and *William and Mary Quarterly* (Jan. 1982); Michael Anderson, "The Emergence of the Modern Life Cycle in Britain," *Social History* 10 (1985):69–87; Paul Thompson, "The Family and Child-Rearing as Forces for Economic Change," *Sociology* 18 (1984):515–30; P.E.H. Hair, "Children in Society, 1850–1980," in *Population and Society in Britain, 1850–1980,* ed. Theo Barker and Michael Drake (New York: New York University Press, 1982), 34–61; Pat Thane, "Childhood in History," in *Childhood, Welfare and Justice,* ed. Michael King (London: Batsford, 1981), 6–25; C. John Sommerville, "Bibliographic Note: Toward a History of Childhood and Youth," *Journal of Interdisciplinary History* 3

(1972):439–47. I am currently engaged in writing a new social history of growing up in Anglo-America, c. 1750–1920.

2. Consider the titles of major works, including many of those cited in n. 1, above. Hiner and Hawes's collection *Growing Up in America* is subtitled *Children in Historical Perspective* but includes adolescents and youths without attention to definitional or boundary issues. See also below.

3. *Centuries of Childhood: A Social History of Family Life* in translation by Robert Baldick was published by Knopf. For recent, retrospective evaluation of Ariès and his impact, and citations to uses of the book, see Adrian Wilson, "The Infancy of the History of Childhood: An Appraisal of Philippe Ariès," *History and Theory* 19 (1980):132–53; Richard T. Vann, "The Youth of *Centuries of Childhood*," *History and Theory* 21 (1982):279–97; David Herlihy, "Medieval Children," in *Essays in Medieval History,* ed. B. K. Lackner and K. R. Philp (Austin: University of Texas Press, 1978), 109–42; Natalie Zemon Davis, "The Reasons of Misrule: Youth Groups and Charivaris in Sixteenth-Century France," *Past & Present,* no. 50 (1971):41–75; Ross W. Beales, Jr., "In Search of the Historical Child," *American Quarterly* 27 (1975):379–98; Charles Tilly, "Population and Pedagogy in France," *History of Education Quarterly* 13 (1973):113–28.

4. *History of Childhood* was published by DeMause's own Psychohistory Press in 1974 with a paperbound edition later from Harper and Row.

5. See studies cited in n. 3, above, as well as Linda Pollock's *Forgotten Children.* The persisting reference to Ariès without awareness of historical criticism represents a real problem for students of growing up in the social sciences.

6. See Graff, "The History of Childhood"; Hawes and Hiner's two recent collections; articles in Parts I, II, and III, below; and studies cited in n. 1, above.

7. See, e.g., Lawrence Stone, "Family History in the 1980s," *Journal of Interdisciplinary History* 12 (1981):51–87; and idem, *The Family, Sex, and Marriage in England, 1500–1800* (New York: Harper and Row, 1977); Demos, *Past, Present, and Personal;* articles by Demos, Beales, and Kett, below. Female growing up represents a special example of neglect combined with cavalier assumptions.

8. See, e.g., Lloyd DeMause, ed., *The History of Childhood;* John Demos, *The Little Commonwealth* (New York: Oxford University Press, 1970); Philip Greven, *The Protestant Temperament: Patterns of Child-Rearing, Religious Experience, and the Self in Early America* (New York: Knopf, 1977); Demos, *Past, Present, and Personal;* Hiner and Hawes, eds., *Growing Up.*

9. Joseph F. Kett, *Rites of Passage: Adolescence in America, 1790 to the Present;* John Gillis, *Youth and History,* 2d ed., 1981; Springhill, *Coming of Age;* articles that appear below.

10. Among Elder's voluminous writings, see the two examples included in this anthology: "Adolescence in Historical Perspective" and "Children in the Family Economy"; Tamara Hareven, ed., *Transitions: The Family and the Life Course in Historical Perspective* (New York: Academic Press, 1978). This influence appears in studies below by Katz and Davey and especially by Modell, Furstenberg, and Hershberg.

11. See Michael B. Katz, *The People of Hamilton, Canada West: Family and Class in a Mid-Nineteenth-Century City* (Cambridge, Mass.: Harvard University Press, 1975); Michael B. Katz, Michael J. Doucet, and Mark J. Stern, *The Social Organization of Early Industrial Capitalism* (Cambridge, Mass.: Harvard University Press, 1982); Mary P. Ryan, *Cradle of the Middle Class: The Family in Oneida County, New York, 1790–1865* (New York: Cambridge University Press, 1981), as well as selections from this work and related examples in this volume.

12. See especially W. Norton Grubb and Marvin Lazerson, *Broken Promises: How Americans Fail Their Children* (New York: Basic Books, 1982); Edith Abbott's classic two-volume edition of documents and the more recent updated three-volume collection *Children and Youth in America,* ed. Robert Bremner (Cambridge, Mass.: Harvard University Press). For interpretive sketches, see also Eileen Boris and Peter Bardaglio, "The Transformation of Patriarchy: The Historical Role of the State," in *Families, Politics, and Public Policy,* ed. Irene Diamond (New York: Longmans, 1983); Richard Busacca and Mary P. Ryan, "Beyond the Family Crisis," *democracy* 2 (1982):79–92; Eli Zaretsky, "The Place of the Family in the Origins of the Welfare State," in *Rethinking the Family,* ed. Barrie Thorne with Marilyn Yalom (New York: Longmans, 1982), 188–224; Michael Zuckerman, "Children's Rights: The Failure of Reform," *Policy Analysis* 2 (1976):371–85; as well as several of the articles below. There are many monographic studies too.

13. Gillis, *Youth in History.* For extremes, see on one side C. John Sommerville, *The Rise and*

Fall of Childhood (Beverly Hills, Calif.: Sage, 1982), for absence of children; on the other side the dangers of loss of context appear in David Nasaw, *Children of the City at Work and at Play* (Garden City, N.Y.: Doubleday, 1985). In their introduction to *Growing Up in America,* Hiner and Hawes tend to emphasize "subjective experience" to the exclusions of other key elements.

14. See the classic work of J. M. Tanner, for example, the accessible summary "Sequence, Tempo, and Individual Variation in the Growth and Development of Boys and Girls Aged Twelve to Sixteen," *Daedalus* 100 (Fall 1971); Peter Laslett, "Age at Menarche in Europe since the Eighteenth Century," in *The Family in History,* ed. T. K. Rabb and R. I. Rotberg (New York: Harper and Row, 1973), 28–47. Robert Fogel, along with a number of economic historians in the United States and England, is engaged in a massive research project on changes in health, height, and weight over time.

15. Rothman, "Documents in Search of a Historian: Toward a History of Children and Youth in America," *Journal of Interdisciplinary History* 2 (1971):367 (reprinted in Part I, below); Stone, "Family History in the 1980s," 69.

16. Donald Lowe, *History of Bourgeois Perception* (Chicago: University of Chicago Press, 1982), 52. See also studies of adolescence, below.

17. See also Graff, "Early Adolescence" and "The History of Childhood and Youth"; Elder on the life course.

18. *Being Adolescent: Conflict and Growth in the Teenage Years* (New York: Basic Books, 1984), 11–12.

19. Anne Digby, *Madness, Morality and Medicine: A Study of the York Retreat, 1796–1914* (Cambridge: Cambridge University Press, 1985).

20. See the studies of Kett and Katz and Davey reprinted below, as well as their books, cited above.

21. Here I note the major omissions—due to the lack of sophisticated studies—of native American and Hispanic children, adolescents, and youths.

22. For confusion between the young and adult perceptions and expectations, see, e.g., Sommerville, *Rise and Fall;* John Walvin, *A Child's World: A Social History of English Childhood, 1800–1914* (Harmondsworth: Penguin, 1982); Richard Rapson, ed., *The Cult of Youth in Middle-Class America* (Lexington, Mass.: D. C. Heath, 1971). For creative efforts using oral history, see Paul Thompson, *The Edwardians* (Bloomington: Indiana University Press, 1975); Thea Thompson, *Edwardian Childhoods* (London: Routledge and Kegan Paul, 1981); the English journal *Oral History,* especially the "Family History" issue, 3, no. 2 (1975). North American oral history lags behind, but see Neil Sutherland's important work in progress for British Columbia. For innovative use of diaries and autobiographies, see David Vincent, *Bread, Knowledge and Freedom* (London: Europa, 1981); John Burnett, ed., *Destiny Obscure: Autobiographies of Childhood, Education and Family from the 1820s to the 1920s* (Harmondsworth: Penguin, 1982); Deborah Gorham, *The Victorian Girl and the Feminine Ideal* (Bloomington: Indiana University Press, 1982). Again, North American work lags behind.

23. See Part I of this volume; Katz et al., *The Social Organization,* chap. 9; Demos, *Past, Present, and Personal,* esp. chap. 5; the work of psychologist Joseph Adelson, e.g., *The Invention of Adolescence* (New Brunswick, N. J.: Transaction, 1985); and the seminal contribution of Paul Goodman, as well as the interesting work of Kenneth Keniston.

24. Linda Pollock's *Forgotten Children* provides an interesting effort in this respect.

25. See studies below; Katz et al., *Social Organization;* Lazerson and Grubb, *Broken Promises;* Christopher Lasch, "Origins of the Asylum" in his *The World of Nations* (New York: Vintage, 1973); Kett, *Rites of Passage;* the many relevant and important writings of Paul Goodman.

26. For examples, see Marie Winn, *Children without Childhood* (New York: Pantheon, 1983); Valerie Polakow Suransky, *The Erosion of Childhood* (Chicago: University of Chicago Press, 1982); Neil Postman, *The Disappearance of Childhood* (New York: Delacorte, 1982); Vance Packard, *Our Endangered Children* (Boston: Little, Brown, 1983), among a large and growing number of such writings.

27. See the articles of Vann and Wilson on Ariès and the uses made of that seminal work, cited above.

Approaches

Introduction

Part I of *Growing Up in America* constitutes a special but absolutely necessary point of origin. Here, we confront—from the multiple lenses of sociologists, social psychologists, psychologists, and historians—broadly based essays on overarching issues and questions of approach, conceptualization, theory, method, source, and practice in viewing and reviewing the contours and configurations of growing up. The range is distinctive in these four bold pieces. Points held in common as well as sharp divergence mark these essays, each of which not only attracted major interest upon first publication but also continues to be cited frequently.

Especially noteworthy is the use of history and historical material in the writings of the three nonhistorians—Elder, Eisenstadt, and Keniston. Readers should take them as: (1) overviews of the subject and its most significant issues; (2) critical inquiries into how best to approach the many themes and challenges of growing up; (3) position papers, attempting to mark out key ground and challenge readers, and traps and fallacies to avoid; and (4) baselines from which to confront and integrate the substance of the five parts to follow. Important in their own right, these programmatic pieces take on an added salience in terms of the larger quest to grasp and understand the historical experience of growing up in America.

Glen Elder's "Adolescence in Historical Perspective" combines a survey of major social science approaches to adolescence in the twentieth century with a strong plea for mutual interaction among historians and sociologists and psychologists. His is an exceptionally important voice in a growing chorus of those who recognize the absolute need for such interdisciplinarity and for the thoroughgoing historicization of social science on issues of human development. Elder has pioneered the "transitions in the life course" approach, whose influence is marked in many of the essays that follow. Elder also gives examples from his own unique work on transitions in the life course of Americans in the twentieth century and the impact of the Great Depression on their lives.

Sociologist S. N. Eisenstadt's often-cited "Archetypal Patterns of Youth" marks a watershed in approaches to youth. In a sharp challenge to narrow focuses on recent experience of youth as unique, he attempts to distinguish the larger-term, indeed the humanly universal, characteristics of "coming of age" from the temporally bound developments. His is a voice influential for a quarter of a century, and he poses questions that all students of growing will continue to confront.

Kenneth Keniston's work, of which "Psychological Development and Historical Change" is an important example, occupies a similar place—but from the viewpoint of the interaction between history and human psychology. Psychological dimensions of growing up are at once among the most central but are also likely to attract some of the most cavalier statements. Keniston presents a strong case for the need to confront them in the context of historically grounded lives. These issues feature strikingly, if not always in Keniston's own perspective, in key essays reprinted below.

Finally, David Rothman offers to us in the form of an essay review, "Documents in Search of a Historian: Toward a History of Children and Youth in America," a critical set of observations that all students of growing up history need to face. In this collection, he offers an interesting complement and contrast to the views of the social scientists, and we should raise questions about points of compatibility and intersection that offer a springboard to us as well as points of disagreement that equally belong on the agenda for study. Among these are the roles of context and historical change and continuity especially with respect to family, institutions, and social developments.

From Part I we clarify our initial assumptions as well as gain insight into the range of the inquiry and complexity of the path whose journey this volume represents. From this section we should develop an agenda or a list of key questions to pose to the authors whose work follows, and their sense of historical development, their approach to change and continuity and variance in patterns of childhood, adolescence, and youth. That is the goal of the encounter with Elder, Eisenstadt, Keniston, and Rothman. Compare them with the views that are expressed in Parts II through VI. I recommend returning to them regularly as readers work through the material and juxtaposing each section with the range of these approaches and interpretive sketches.

1. Adolescence in Historical Perspective

Adolescence is intimately linked to matters historical: the evolution of social age categories, the emergence of youth-related institutions, the impact of social change in lives. The developmental foci of all these involve the relationship between historical variation and life patterns. Adolescent experience may be shaped directly by historical events, as in the 1960s, and indirectly through the life histories that young people bring to this stage. After years of neglect, this perspective is beginning to appear not only on the agenda of those involved in developmental research,[1] but also in the promising outline of a life-course framework that relates history and social structure in the human biography. Fruitful applications of this framework are seen in the notable growth since the 1960s of genuine archival studies on youth in history, a scope of inquiry that extends from the preindustrial age to the present. This chapter examines these developments in terms of their contribution to an analytical perspective that locates adolescence and young people in historical time, in the social order, and in the life span.

These developments began to crystallize in the troubled decade of the 1960s; and reflect the intellectual currents and problematic issues of these years. In combination, they represent a line of demarcation between the atemporal theme of postwar research on youth and an expanding recognition of the interdependence between social history and life history. Though historical change has long been noted as a determinant of life patterns (Thomas & Znaniecki, 1918–1920; Kuhlen, 1940), this observation left no enduring imprint on research until the 1960s. At this point, we see thoughtful efforts across disciplines that suggest ways of viewing social change in lives. Warner Schaie (1965) proposed a methodology for assessing the effect of historical change on development; Norman Ryder (1965), in social demography, outlined a cohort historical perspective on social change in the life course; and historians (see Thernstrom, 1965) specified the potential interpretative errors in research that ignores historical facts. Intergenerational tensions also posed questions that could only be answered from an understanding of the diverse historical origins of parents and offspring, a problem identified many years ago by Kingsley Davis (1940).

Though path-breaking in many respects, these analytic ventures toward history have only recently made a difference in the actual study of adolescence and youth (Nesselroade & Baltes, 1974; Elder, 1974; Gillis, 1974). By and large, the contemporary literature on adolescence is distinguished by the absence of historical facts and considerations. Adolescents are seldom viewed within the life course and historical context; longitudinal studies pay little attention to the implications of social change (Elder, 1975a). These deficiencies stand out among contemporary textbooks on adolescence. For example, Muus's *Theories of Adolescence* (1975) includes only one section that bears on adolescence as a socially defined age division, and it makes no reference to analytical developments that place this stage within the life course and historical time. However rudimentary, these developments raise questions of critical importance for any study of human development. In what sense can we presume to understand the psychosocial development of youth without systematic knowledge of their life course and collective experience in specific historical times?

As a point of departure, I begin the chapter with a brief overview of its two central themes: (1) the life course as an emergent perspective that incorporates the historical dimension and (2) the burgeoning field of historical research on youth. With this as background, I turn to various age-based concepts of adolescence and their distinctive features. These concepts and the problem foci of historical periods have shaped the study of American adolescence and young people since the 1920s. This development is portrayed in terms of key studies, their strengths and limitations, and three age concepts (developmental, social, and historical) in the life-course framework. I conclude by reviewing selected themes in historical research, findings, and analytical contributions. The objective is not to provide a survey of research and knowledge on youth in history, which is available in other sources (Gillis, 1974; Kett, 1977), but to suggest something of the possibilities of an analytical perspective on the life course that brings historical considerations to the study of adolescence.

The Life Course and Historical Research

The life-course perspective represents developments over the past decade in understanding the bond between age and time (Riley, Johnson, and Foner, 1972; Elder, 1975b). Three temporal modalities have been identified:

1. The lifetime of the individual—chronological or developmental age as a rudimentary index of stage in the aging process.

2. Social time in the age-patterning of events and roles throughout life (e.g., entry into formal schooling, departure from home, first job, and marriage)—a pattern structured by age criteria in norms, roles, and institutions.

3. Historical time in the process of social change—birth-year, or entry into the system, as an index of historical location and membership in a specific cohort.

The lifetime perspective focuses on the inevitable and irreversible process of aging; social time, on age differentiation in the sequence and arrangement of life events and roles; and historical time, on cohort membership, differentiation, and succession, with their implications for life patterns. We derive the meaning of each temporal dimension from correlated variables; in the case of historical time, from knowledge of events, circumstances, and mentalities of the period.

Each temporal perspective is associated with a distinctive tradition of research and theory:

1. Lifetime—John Dollard's (1949, p. 3) use of life histories to assess the growth of a person in a cultural setting; Charlotte Bühler's (1935) concept of the biological cycle of life; and the general field of life-span development (Goulet & Baltes, 1970).

2. Social time—analyses of age strata and hierarchies by Ralph Linton (1942) and Talcott Parsons (1942), as well as S. N. Eisenstadt's (1956) pioneering synthesis of ethnographic materials on age-based differentiation and youth groups.

3. Historical time—most notably Karl Mannheim's (1928/1952) influential essay on the emergent mentalities of generations (age cohorts in conventional terminology) and generation units or subgroups.

Important continuities within the framework of social time are illustrated by assessments of the "traditions of youth," from Willard Waller's (1932/1965) insightful essay on age-graded student traditions to David Matza's (1964) thoughtful essay on American youth and John Gillis's (1974) historical exploration of European age relations. Life transitions constitute another prominent theme across time, from Leonard Cottrell's (1942) propositional inventory on age-status adjustments to Modell, Furstenberg, and Hershberg's (1976) study of social change in the transition to adult roles. On historical time, a number of Mannheim's conceptual distinctions ("fresh contact with social change," stratification of experience, and the psychology of subgroups) influenced theoretical approaches in studies of student unrest and movements in the 1960s (Bengtson & Laufer, 1974; Braungart, 1975, pp. 255–289).

More than ever before, the life span defines the analytic scope of these areas of inquiry. Socialization, behavioral adaptation, and development are represented as lifelong processes that relate life stages in the human biography, from childhood to old age. Thus in the study of aging, life-span theoretical interests have fostered studies that extend beyond such age categories as adolescence (Baltes & Schaie, 1973; Baltes, 1977; Huston-Stein & Baltes, 1976). According to programmatic statements, the objective of these studies is to describe and explain age-related behavior change from birth to death as well as to specify temporal linkages through the identification of antecedent-consequent relations. For the most part, this explanatory aim remains an ideal. It has not been implemented by research on diverse life paths through the dependency years and their psychological effects.

Life-span issues in the sociocultural tradition (social time) are expressed in the literature on careers and by studies of orientations toward adult careers—marriage, parenthood, work—in the field of adolescence. But only in the past decade have career orientations and paths been viewed in terms of temporal distinctions from an articulation of social age (Clasen, 1972), the timing of events and their synchronization across multiple careers, and the role of age standards in self-assessments of career progress. Norman Ryder (1965) and Riley, Johnson, and Foner (1972) have linked historical change to the life course, a connection not developed in Mannheim's essay, "The Problem of Generations." The current trend is toward a more inclusive perspective on the life course, one that builds on all three temporal foci; locates individuals in age cohorts and thus, according to historical time, depicts their age-differentiated life pattern in relation to historical context; and represents the interplay between life paths and development. Evidence of this development is seen in the establishment in October 1977 of a Social Science Research Council Committee on the Life Course.

According to this perspective, adolescence (or the broader category of youth) can be fully understood only when viewed within the life course and its historical setting. Each generalized stage, or age category, is constructed from norms and institutional constraints that establish a basis for identity and specify appropriate behavior, roles, and timetables. Cultural norms that differentiate age categories also structure modes of interdependence among them; one's rights implies another's obligations in cross-age (e.g., children vs. adolescents) and intergenerational relationships. The interlocking careers of parents and offspring relate young-adult status and childhood, middle age and adolescence, old age and maturity. The experience of adolescence is shaped by what one has been and by what is foreseen, by the problems of middle-aged parents and by those of the very young. Cross-age linkages are basic elements of an evolving life course.

A normative model of the life course includes event schedules that serve as guidelines for the life course, alerting individuals or cohorts to the appropriate timing and sequencing of social transitions. In theory, these schedules define appropriate times for school entry and departure; for leaving home and establishing an independent domicile; for economic independence, marriage, and parenthood. An informal system of rewards and negative sanctions ensures, for example, consciousness of the relationships between age and status or the consequences associated with being early, on time, or late in role performance and accomplishments. Referring to preindustrial Europe, Gillis (1974, p. 4) notes that despite the apparent disarray of age norms "premature entry into the marriage market was bound to provoke public censure, while remaining unmarried past a certain age made 'old maids' of girls and confirmed bachelors of boys." During the 1960s in midwestern America, Neugarten, Moore, and Lowe (1965) observed a high level of consensus among middle-class adults on age norms (usually above 80%) across some 15 age-related characteristics, including the timing of marriage. This study and a partial replication in a Japanese city (Plath & Ikeda, 1975) show generalized sensitivity to age norms from early adulthood to old age. However, age norms and perceptions of age status constitute an undeveloped field of inquiry. Normative assertions are frequently made without adequate empirical evidence.

Beyond generalized age categories, the life course reflects the degree of social differentiation in complex societies, their plural age structures, timetables, and constraints across institutional domains—family, education, workplace, military. Status passage over the life course entails the assumption of concurrent multiple roles—from those of son or daughter, age-mate, and student during years of dependency to adult lines of activity in major institutional sectors. One's life course thus takes the form of interlocking career lines, each defined by a particular event sequence and timetable, for example, the temporal pattern of events and transitions in schooling and its relation to the timetable of family life and to the anticipated claims of military service, marriage, and work. Problems of life management arise in large measure from the competing demands of multiple careers.

Relevant to this point is Goode's observation that an individual's set of obligations is "unique and overdemanding" (1960). Since all demands cannot be met within the same time frame, a manageable course requires strategies that minimize conflicts and strain, for example, the selection of compatible lines of action, the scheduling and deferring of obligations, or appeals to shared values or authorities to rationalize priorities. The pressures of these demands, most notable when youth are entering lines of adult activity, bring to mind Erikson's observations on role confusion. This psychic state becomes most acute, according to Erikson (1959), when the adolescent is exposed to a "combination of experiences which demand his simultaneous commitment to *physical intimacy* (not by any means overtly sexual), to decisive *occupational choice,* to energetic *competition,* and to *psychosocial self-definition*" (p. 123).

With a multi-dimensional concept of the life course, we are able to represent the diverse pathways that link childhood to the adult years and explore developmental problems and processes that arise from their interdependence. This concept parallels the organismic concept of "developmental lines," such as intellectual, moral, and sexual, "each of which may be in or out of phase with the others" (Keniston, 1970, p. 636; see also 1971). Variations in the timing and sequencing of events and decisions during late adolescence acquire psychological significance through investigation of their implications for coherent or discordant patterns of development. Completion of education, marriage, and economic independence are commonly viewed as indications of the lower boundary of adulthood, yet the timing of these events spans a wide age range, up to 10 years or more. Leaving school, departing from home, marriage, and economic independence come early for some young people and relatively late for others (Modell, Furstenberg, & Hershberg, 1976). The order and spacing of these events also vary widely. Marriage may occur before the completion of formal education, especially when schooling is prolonged, whereas early teen-age pregnancy typically precedes marriage and economic independence. For the individual, such variations pose important implications for social identity, personal integration, and life chances. The full meaning of a transition is derived from knowledge of this life course and related situational change.

Historical placement of adolescence and young people inevitably generates questions regarding the social and cultural milieu of time and place. What are the historical events and forces that have relevance for life chances and psychosocial development? How were generalized trends in demographic, economic, and cultural change expressed in this setting, giving form and substance to the biographies of youth, their life stage, collective experience, and future? The birth-year of youth directs inquiry toward their historical origins and experiences as they move through time in an age cohort. At points of rapid change, the historical experience of successive cohorts varies through exposure to different events (such as wartime mobilization for persons born before and after World War II) and by exposure to the same event at different points in the life course.

Cohort differences in life stage at times of drastic change suggest variations in adaptive options relative to the event, in resulting experience, and thus in the process by which the event is expressed in life patterns. World War II entailed military obligations for American males who were born in the early 1920s and experienced adolescence in the depressed 1930s. By contrast, younger men, who were born at the end of the 1920s, experienced this war as adolescents on the home front, following a childhood shaped by the Great Depression. We derive the psychosocial meaning of cohort membership and of particular cohort attributes from knowledge of this differential experience. Cohort attributes (e.g., relative size and composition) are themselves a product of historical change, business cycles, institutional change, mass migration.

From this vantage point, youth cohorts represent a connection between social change and life-course patterns, historical time and lifetime. Within each cohort, processes of socialization and role allocation (via schools, etc.) serve as linkages between the young and social options—the labor requirements of industry, citizenship obligations in war and peace. Social change threatens the fragile character of these linkages as disparities emerge between youth characteristics and available options, for example, large cohorts who have come of age in a period of declining opportunities. Some analysts, for example, have viewed the rise of National Socialism in terms of the large German youth cohorts that encountered depressed opportunities in the 1930s after a history of wartime deprivations (Loewenberg, 1972; cf. Merkl, 1975). Likewise, a mood of fear (Scully, 1977) has been noted among the large postwar cohorts of university students in Europe who face declining opportunities for commensurate employment. American student unrest and protests in the 1960s, a decade of extraordinary growth of the youth population, generally support Herbert Moller's historical assessment (1968) over three centuries—that periods of social and revolutionary change are characterized by youth cohorts of ascending size. The historical dialectic between successive cohort flows and the social order tells us much about the socialization, opportunities, and actions of young people in concrete situations. It is this interplay that underscores the inadequacy of approaches that have focused on the age structure without attention to demographic factors or that have theorized about adolescent development in an historical vacuum.

A cohort is said to be distinctively marked by the life stage it occupies when historical events impinge on it (Ryder, 1965), but exposure to an event is not likely to be uniform among its members. For example, father-absence represents an important connection between World War II and the lives of young people: military service altered the socialization of children by removing fathers from the family over a two- to three-year period. However, deferments of one kind or another kept some fathers at home throughout this conflict. With such variation, the war's impact on a cohort of youth can be assessed by comparing psychological development under conditions of father-absence and father-presence (see Carlsmith, 1973). The hypothesis of life-stage variation (change has differential consequences for persons of unlike age) cautions against generalization from this comparison to other groups and favors a comparative design in which the developmental effects of war-caused father-absence are assessed in successive cohorts, for example, birthdates of 1930–1933, 1934–1937, 1938–1941.

This intracohort approach permits direct analysis of historical factors and explication of the process by which they are expressed in the lives of youth. The process is shaped in part by what families and offspring bring to events, their cultural heritage and expectations, their material resources and social position. Class, ethnic, and residential variations may identify subgroups that differ in how they "work up" historically relevant experience. Thus middle- and working-class families brought different resources to the Great Depression, resources that shaped both their response to economic misfortunes and the effect of the Depression on their children (Elder, 1974). Likewise, father-absence in World War II occurred in contexts (defined by marital harmony or conflict, financial security or strain) that influenced the meaning of the event and its impact on the welfare of family members (Hill, 1949). More recent examples include differences between college and noncollege youth of the 1960s in attitudes and actions relative to the Vietnam War (Braungart, 1975). As stressed by Mannheim's essay (1928/1952), historical differentiation within cohorts may stem from three sources of variation: exposure to events, interpretations of them, and subsequent modes of response.

Up to this point, we have emphasized historical facts that differentiate and explain the experience of youth cohorts or subgroups. Instead of asking whether there are behavioral variations across successive cohorts, investigation is guided by the rationale that expects such variation in the first place. Given known variations among and within cohorts, the research problem concerns their relevance for life experience. Developmental questions are posed by an understanding of historical realities and their plausible life-course effects, proximal and enduring. This approach is not synonomous with cohort studies and a large number bear only superficial resemblance to historical analysis—to the assessment of historical facts that give explicit meaning to the life experience of youth cohorts (for a review, see Bengtson & Starr, 1975). Estimates of developmental variation across cohorts point to the influence of social change (Baltes, Cornelius, & Nesselroade, 1977), but global reference to change leaves unspecified what aspects of change produced this outcome and the processes involved.

Without any doubt, the most notable advance on knowledge of social change in youth experience has come from the work of social historians, especially those of the new generation who have applied the procedures and techniques of social science to studies of the "inarticulate"—the ordinary folk who left no personal record of their lives, for example, letters, diaries, genealogies, and so on. Archival data for this research is largely based on institutional records—government censuses, welfare and property lists, marriage certificates, parish registers, school censuses, employment rolls, From Newark, New Jersey of the mid-nineteenth century (Bloomberg, 1974) to Manchester, New Hampshire of 1900–1930 (Hareven, 1975), the studies of historians show an attention to historical facts that warrants emulation if historical time is to acquire substantive and theoretical meaning in research on youth.

A major turning point toward historical research on youth occurred with the publication of Philipe Ariès's impressionistic history of childhood and youth in France (*Centuries of Childhood*, 1965) and Bernard Bailyn's *Education in the Forming of American Society* (1960). Due to research limitations at the time, both volumes could offer only tentative characterizations of institutional, ideological, and demographic changes in life stages, timetables, and pathways from birth to adult status. Among other issues Ariès's dating of male adolescence in the late eighteenth century, according to military conscription and advanced schooling, has been challenged by more recent work (see N. Z. Davis, 1975, pp. 97–123). Nonetheless, his path-breaking study and the research agenda outlined by Bailyn identified questions and unknowns that have influenced the course of subsequent inquiry, for example, on the emergence of mass schooling or the interaction of family, educational, and industrial change. Since the early 1960s the historical literature on youth has grown exponentially, with a scope that extends from the colonial era (Demos, 1970; Greven, 1970; Smith, 1973) into the twentieth century (Modell, Furstenberg, & Hershberg, 1976). Robert Bremner's multivolume anthology (1970–1974) of documents on American children and youth also spans this time frame. Two synthetic works on youth in history provide extensive bibliographies of American and European research: (1) Joseph Kett's survey (1977) of American youth, which is based largely on the social commentaries of upper-class adults; (2) John Gillis's (1974) analytical study of historical change in the position and traditions of youth in England and Germany.

In historical settings, the life experience of American youth has been depicted through assessments of family and kinship (Hareven, 1978), the most rapidly expanding field in social history; by studies of educational change and reform in the nineteenth century and their interplay with family patterns, demographic and economic change, and ideologies (Tyack, 1975; Kaestle & Vinovskis, 1976); and by studies of "child-saving" ideology and institutional realities (the juvenile court) through the progressive era (Platt, 1969; Schlossman, 1977). With skillful use of archival data and methodologies, historians have moved beyond social concepts of youth and age vocabulary to the actual structure and content of the transition from childhood to full adult status. Their studies have enlarged our perspective on adolescence and its emergence as a concept in late nineteenth-century America by stressing the variable properties of the stage of youth across time and place, a view consistent with Eisenstadt's (1956) observation that a period of youth between childhood and adulthood exists to some extent in all known societies and historical periods. Its variation reflects the degree to which roles are assigned on the basis of age criteria, the prevalence of groups based on age, and the exigencies of demographic/ economic conditions.

As in sociology, intensive study of age by historians has led to conceptual distinctions that are part of a life-course framework—the social timetable of events and roles, multiple career lines and transitions, the relation between age cohorts and age strata. Research themes include the changing normative and demographic properties of childhood and youth from the preindustrial age to the twentieth century (Gillis, 1974); nineteenth-century institutional change in life-course differentiation and the extension of age-graded schooling (Meyer et al., 1977); strain arising from change toward a broader social base in the composition of student cohorts among early nineteenth-century colleges (Allmend-inger, 1975); change since 1860 in the timing of marriage and its life-course implications (Modell, Furstenberg, and Strong, 1978); and age patterns in the life course and psychological development in Plymouth Colony (Demos, 1970). Examples of this historical research will be discussed in a later section of the chapter.

Since the writings of G. Stanley Hall, *Adolescence* (1904), concepts of adolescence and its study have reflected the various lines of inquiry that come together on the life course—developmental, social-structural, historical. As a life stage, adolescence has been defined in terms of observed or attributed characteristics of the developing organism— the physical and physiological changes during puberty, the stage of formal operations in cognitive development and moral judgment. Hall used late nineteenth-century knowledge of man's evolution in formulating his developmental concept of adolescence and life stages generally—law of recapitulation, saltatory rather than continuous development (Grinder, 1969; Ross, 1972); Harold Jones (1939), Director of the well-known Oakland Growth Study of Adolescents, emphasized the biological parameters of adolescence; and, more recently, Jerome Kagan (1971) has argued that developmental knowledge warrants postulation of a psychological stage called "early adolescence," a stage defined by the emergence of a new cognitive competence among 12-year-olds in the ability to "examine the logic and consistency of existing beliefs" (p. 998).

Historically, developmental concepts of life stages have provided rationales for corresponding social timetables and mechanisms of socialization (Demos & Demos, 1969; Skolnick, 1975; Lüscher, 1975). But the problematic record of their social expression— for example, from the Judge Lindsay doctrine of love-oriented treatment to the punitive realities of the juvenile court (Schlossman, 1977)—offers a valuable reminder of the distance between a concept and its implementation. In this regard, Rothman (1971) correctly warns that just because the concept of adolescence as a developmental stage "was invented only at the end of the nineteenth century is no indication that the *actual* experience of the young had changed" (p. 367).

Developmental variations and social attributes on the individual level may generate different status classifications as to life stage. Thus Keniston's (1970) observations on an emerging category of youth in postwar America refer to a psychological stage that "cannot be equated with a particular age-range." The developmental themes of this stage (e.g., vacillating moods of estrangement and power, ambivalence toward self and social institutions) identify young people who do not "necessarily join together in indentifiable groups, nor do they share a common social position" (pp. 648–649). By making explicit the distinction between youth as a developmental age and a social age, Keniston's essay leads beyond aspects of each domain to problems involving their relationship, to the social and developmental implications of inconsistent placement on psychological and social criteria, for example, the "youthful" person who is socially defined as an adult. Problems of this sort have been explored by Erikson (1964) and by Berger (1971) in a study of life styles.

The literature on adolescence over the past half century is distinguished by relatively separate lines of research on the developmental and social properties of adolescence. The former typically viewed adolescent experience in terms of ontogenetic development with minimal attention to sociocultural influences, whereas sociological research neglected developmental facts in the study of age categories, subcultures, generational relations, and youth movements. Despite the separation, there has always been a degree of interchange and debate between proponents of each perspective. Thus the presumed turmoil and conflicts of adolescence in the developmental perspective of G. Stanley Hall were challenged (1) by evidence of cross-cultural variation through the anthropological studies of Margaret Mead (1928) and (2) by historical specification in Kingsley Davis's (1940) analysis of rapid change in generational conflict. Some lessons from this interplay are manifested in the life-course approach of the 1960s and 1970s. Social conditions and issues at the time gave visibility to the historical dimension of lives, institutions, and their temporal interdependence. In addition to its developmental and social features, the study of adolescence slowly acquired an historical feature, one shaped by matters of time, place, and by the life histories of its members.

One way to view this development is through an examination of studies that reveal the strengths and limitations of a single concept of adolescence, whether developmental, social, or historical. We begin with a brief consideration of historical times in research themes from the 1920s to the 1970s and pursue this topic in greater depth from the vantage point of concepts of adolescence and their problem foci. Then we cover developmental and social themes through the 1940s, the 1950s' perspective on adolescence in the course of societal development, and the introduction of historical questions to the study of adolescence and youth in the 1960s. This brings us to specific examples of life-course analysis in historical research on youth.

Historical Times and the Study of Adolescence: 1920s to the 1970s

Child development emerged as a scientific field of inquiry in the United States during the 1920s, and we see a pale shadow of this beginning in the accumulation of studies of adolescents by the 1930s (Hollingsworth, 1928). Social needs or concerns were prominent in the development of research on children (Sears, 1975, p. 4) and in the study of adolescents, especially among sociologists. In the 1920s, rapid change through urbanization and immigration focused attention on the costs of social disorganization; the sociological research of Clifford Shaw and his colleagues depicted the juvenile delinquent as disaffiliated, lacking social bonds, supports, and controls (Finestone, 1976). Problems of employment and family disorganization gained prominence in the 1930s (Elder, 1974) in addition to questions regarding the impact of movie attendance and the radio on young people. Between the Depression and the 1970s, research on families and youth continued to reflect public issues of the times (Elder, 1978), from social change in World War II (rural to urban migration, absent fathers, employed mothers) to massive population and institutional growth in the postwar era and the civil strife of the 1960s.

Educational developments since the turn of the century stand out in the evolution of adolescence and its extension to a category of older youth: the rapidly expanding enrollment of young people (ages 14 to 17) in the high-school grades up to 1940 and a pronounced increase during the postwar era in the proportion of youth (ages 18 to 21) enrolled in higher education (Figure 1). Only one-third of American youth, ages 14 to 17, were attending high school by 1920, but this figure is six times the rate of 1890. In the city of Middletown, the Lynds (1929) found that the high school had become the locus of youth activity and peer association: "The high school, with its athletics, clubs, sororities and fraternities, dances and parties, and other 'extracurricular' activities, is a fairly complete social cosmos in itself—a city within a city" (p. 211). The first major assessment of the social world of high school was authored by Willard Waller (1932/1965) in the 1930s,[2] followed some 10 years later by another classic, August Hollingshead's (1949) empirical investigation of high-school youth in Elmtown. With the proportion of youth in high school climbing above 80% in the 1950s, it is not surprising that the literature of the decade includes major studies of adolescent subcultures and peer influence, such as James Coleman's *The Adolescent Society* (1961).

Two important implications emerge from the trend toward universal high-school education, and both are represented in the literature on adolescents: (1) increasing age segregation and (2) social inequality in student access to school rewards and life opportunities. From Hollingshead to Coleman and the Presidential Science Advisory Commission's report, *Youth* (1973), we see emphasis on the forms and dysfunctions of age segregation relative to the transition between childhood and adult life. Hollingshead's *Elmtown's Youth* (1949) focused on class origins in the collective experience and life chances of youth at a time when the high-school student body was still heavily weighted toward the sons and daughters of the middle class. This problem gained significance in the postwar era as successive high-school cohorts recruited even larger proportions of students from the lower strata, accentuating issues of social privilege and status deprivation in the school environment (Trow, 1961). During this era, theory viewed juvenile delinquency as an adaptation to the disparity between the "American dream" and the constraints of social position. The image of the juvenile delinquent was that of a young male who had been sold a bill of goods, but lacked the approved means of acquiring those goods; in Finestone's words, (1976) the image of a "frustrated social climber" (p. 12). Arthur Stinchcombe (1964) provides a superior example of this conceptual approach in his study, *Rebellion in a High School*.

Though far more numerous in the 1950s than at the turn of the century, American youth had become a smaller proportion of the adult population, an aging trend characteristic of modernizing societies. There were more adults per youth to serve as *socializers* in the 1950s than in 1900, thus indicating a decline in the burden of *socialization* and status placement. This trend reversed dramatically in the 1960s, owing to the postwar baby boom, and coincided with a noteworthy increase in the proportion of older youth in schools of higher learning. The size and broader composition of college cohorts in this decade implies an emerging life stage beyond traditional adolescence—a stage of youth or studentry (Parsons & Platt, 1972, pp. 236–291). Problems once identified with early adolescence and high school—age segregation and status deprivation—acquired prominence on the college campus through student mobilization and protests on civil-rights issues (Braungart, 1975). This development suggested to some (Gillis, 1974) the beginning of the end of an insular, protracted stage (adolescence?) of semidependency and social disability. Youth problems among older adolescents and college students in the 1960s

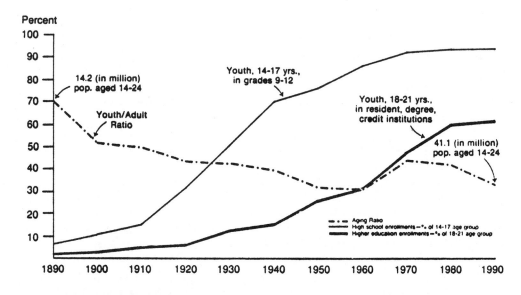

Figure 1. Secular trends in population aging and enrollment rates for secondary and higher education, United States, 1890–1990.

focused attention on the transition to adulthood[3] (PSAC, 1973; Heyneman, 1976), placing early adolescence in the shadows. Joan Lipsitz (1977) aptly refers to younger adolescents in the 1970s as "growing up forgotten," a theme also stressed by a recent National Institute of Mental Health (NIMH) Conference on Early Adolescence (May 1976).

Despite the imprint of historical conditions on research foci over the past decades, these conditions seldom became variables in the study of adolescence and youth. Indeed, by far the largest share of research through the 1940s centered on the developmental perspective of adolescence and paid little attention to the social and historical contexts of young people. Critiques of this literature by sociologists and anthropologists offered correctives by stressing the social character of life stages, but they often did so without regard for developmental variations, their interaction with the social environment, and historical forces. In retrospect, one gains some appreciation of these conceptual limitations from the incompleteness of the work and thus of analytical distinctions that are now part of a life-course perspective on adolescence. We shall illustrate this point by reference to Adolescence (1944) the 43rd Yearbook of the NSSE—National Society for the Study of Education—(see also Dennis, 1946, pp. 633–666); Hollingshead's Elmtown study (1949); and prominent social views of adolescence in the 1950s.

Developmental and Social Themes in the Study of Adolescence

Adolescence as a "biological phenomenon" defines a primary theme of contributions to Adolescence (1944), a perspective that reflects research priorities at the time as well as the influence of Harold Jones (Chairman of the NSSE 43rd Yearbook Committee) and his pioneering, longitudinal study of physical growth and development at the Institute of Child Welfare (now Human Development), Berkeley, California. Half of the contributions portray the course of physical and physiological change; the development of physical, motor, and mental skills; and asynchronies across developmental lines. But even in these chapters, assumptions about age-graded expectations informed assessments of the psychosocial implications of physical growth, for example, in the case of maturation rates that depart from social expectations. Lack of time-series data ruled out consideration of one of the most important biological developments viewed in relation to the age structure: a pronounced upward trend in the height and weight of youth since at least the 1850s and a decline in the average age of menarche—approximately four months per decade over this period (Tanner, 1962, p. 152; Laslett, 1971). Nevertheless, the lag between developmental maturity and commensurate options was commonly acknowledged by analysts of the 1930s and 1940s as a prime source of adolescent emotional and social problems (K. Davis, 1944). In their classic monograph, *Frustration and Aggression* (1939), John Dollard and associates viewed this lag in terms of sources of adolescent frustration—the taboo on sexual activity, constraints on employment. The adolescent "gives every indication of being strongly instigated to perform the varied goal-responses appropriate to his new capacities, but tends to find that these responses are interfered with by adult restrictions" (pp. 96–97).

The biological theme of the yearbook exemplified a view of adolescence that August Hollingshead (1949) challenged through his investigation of adolescents in the class structure of Elmtown, a midwestern community studied in 1941–1942. After sorting through the available literature, heavily biased toward physical manifestations, Hollingshead stressed the primacy of environments that give meaning to physical facts (see also Mead, 1928). Whatever the connection of physical and physiological facts to adolescence and behavior, Hollingshead (1949) argued that "their functional importance for the maturing individual is defined by the culture" (p. 6). In social terms, the noteworthy feature of the adolescent years is not puberty, the growth spurt, or maturational processes in general, but rather how society views the maturing individual. Adolescence represents a social stage in which the individual is regarded as neither a child nor an adult in status, roles, or functions.

A full understanding of these facts in lives entails knowledge of the culture and social structure, but the underlying assumption throughout *Elmtown's Youth* is that adolescent behavior is far more contingent on position in the social structure than upon age-related biopsychological phenomena. Just as psychologists had ignored or oversimplified the cultural environment relative to developmental processes, Hollingshead excluded physical characteristics from analysis in relation to age-expectations and class subcultures. The questions he posed on cultural variation in causal linkages between pubertal growth phenomena and adolescent behavior were not subjected to empirical test. Nevertheless, a number of implicit premises on development informed the study. As the gap between development and social options suggests, the social character of adolescence also acquires meaning from knowledge of the human organism, its developmental timetable and processes.

Elmtown's Youth offers a vivid portrait of social stratification (age, sex, and class) in the life experience and chances of young people. It documents the control functions of age and class patterns in adolescent behavior and provides a firm reminder of adolescence as a variable in social and physical space within the course of lives. Four social properties of adolescence were singled out for special attention:

- The social ambiguity and status contradictions of this life stage ("an ill-defined no man's land").
- Competition and conflicts among youth-training institutions.
- Age segregation as a social control mechanism.
- Class variations in the transition to adult status.

Field work in the community disclosed few widely shared concepts regarding the lower or upper boundaries of adolescence, other than the span of years encompassed by secondary school and the assumption of adult roles. Inconsistent age norms in legal codes, from employment to matrimony and criminal law, underscored the ambiguous position of young people who were neither children nor adults; a "contrast" category defined by what it is not. Expressions of general developmental trends (institutional differentiation and specialization) took the form of: (1) multiple, youth-training agencies with competing claims on the adolescent's time and commitments and (2) an elaborate system of age segregation that sought to ensure "proper" development by isolating youth from the adult world of their parents—an isolation most typical of the middle-class student in school. On a theme that reappears in the 1950s and 1960s, Hollingshead (1949) cites the essentially negative character of a system that turned youth away from adult realities; "by trying to keep the maturing child ignorant of this world of conflict and contradictions, adults think they are keeping him 'pure' " (p. 108).

Hollingshead's study provides only a small sample of the wide variation in American youth experience at the time of World War II, but it offers a uniquely valuable picture of the institutional changes that have shaped adolescence as a social stage, in particular, the extension of schooling and its pronounced class variation among youth. As a category of dependents set apart from the adult world and childhood, adolescence had relevance mainly to the sons and daughters of middle- and upper-middle-class families. They were most likely to be members of the student body of the local high school (with its youth culture) and to pursue a college education and delay marriage. Offspring of the lower strata typically left school before the ninth grade with the prospect of unstable, menial employment as well as early marriage and childbearing. The harsh realities of adult disadvantage came early to the experience of these young people.

But other realities, World War II and a background in the Great Depression, also impinged on the life chances of youth in all class strata in Elmtown. Hard times in the 1930s generally encouraged school persistence and led to the postponement of adult entry (marriage, full-time employment) among older youth, but it also brought younger adolescents into the world of adultlike tasks through the labor-intensive and financial needs of deprived households (Elder, 1974). World War II produced a striking contrast in the balance of young labor supply and demand; military service and work absorbed the older segment of youth and a substantial number of adolescents of high-school age left school early for lucrative jobs (Magee, 1944). These historical conditions did not enter the analysis of Elmtown's youth. Civilian mobilization and the likelihood of military service were not part of the wartime experience of these adolescents, as we see it described; nor was any assessment made of their Depression experience as children. In these respects, at least, the youth of Elmtown appear in a "timeless" realm. Though Hollingshead effectively placed adolescents in the social structure, he failed to locate them in historical time and thus according to events that may have shaped their development course and life chances.

Adolescence in Societal Development

Social views of adolescence in the 1950s generally correspond to that of *Elmtown's Youth:* we see historical change in the social position of adolescents, but not in the particular events of life histories. The general theme is long-term structural change, especially its contemporary manifestations (Eisenstadt, 1956; Coleman, 1961; Parsons, 1964), that is, the expanding role of formal education, adult-directed youth groups, and peer groups in socialization. These reflect structural change that diminished the family's role in upbringing and enlarged the gap between family experience and the requirements of adult life.

Discontinuities between family experience and adult life generate problems for the adult community and young people. The problem for adults and social institutions is to link youth to adult roles through appropriate socialization and mechanisms of role allocation, such as the schools. For young people, the problem entails matters of independence, sexual relations, decisions on future options, and the establishment of their identity. These conditions give rise to organized, adult-directed agencies or groups that presumably serve the collective interests of society and also generate a propensity for peer association among youth. Functional specialization of the family is thus expressed in a more differentiated socialization environment.

As suggested by Hollingshead's study of Elmtown, the family of small-town America represented a major force in this multifaceted environment. However, postwar change suggested a shift in relative contributions to socialization, from family to school and peers. Two related developments, in particular, gave a sense of reality to the image of "adolescents in a world of their own": (1) increasing school size and (2) functional differentiation, for example, the growth of junior high schools. The major demographic change between 1940 and 1960 occurred in the average size of student cohorts, not in the proportion of youth enrolled in high school. Between the 1930s and 1960s, the estimated average size of high schools more than doubled—from 682 to 1539 in 1967. Small student bodies (less than 400) could still be found in the 1950s among towns with less than 10,000 residents, but these urban places were far less numerous than before the war. During the 1950s, the average high school in large suburbs (10,000+) and large cities (50,000+) ranged above 1000 students (Garbarino, 1977). This figure was, of course, much higher in metropolitan centers, often exceeding 3000 in places such as Chicago and New York. If large schools enhanced the power of youth groups, they may have done so in part by offering less to the individual student in social rewards, such as less recognition from peers, that is greater anonymity (Barker & Gump, 1964), or less opportunity, when compared to students in small schools, to assume leadership or responsible positions.

The large school phenomenon was coupled with noteworthy structural and functional changes in educational environment. Both the lower and upper reaches of secondary education were in transition to new forms and functions: the lower grades through physical separation of sixth and seventh graders (Blyth, Simmons, & Bush, 1977); the upper grades of high school through functional ties to higher education (Trow, 1961). Though junior high schools date back to 1918, it was only in the early 1950s that separate or combined junior and senior high schools became more prominent as an organizational type than the eight-year elementary school and the four-year high school. The tipping point between these organizational types, either as an historical development or as a change with profound social implications, arrived with little notice. The emerging school structure established a more standard marker for the lower boundary of adolescence and linked early adolescence, with its developmental changes, to an age-segregated phase of schooling. The transition to secondary school in this new system placed students in a larger, more heterogeneous setting at an earlier age, posing issues of social acceleration with the erosion of parental control.

Analytic themes on youth of the 1950s generally mirror some implications of this change, in particular the ascendance of the peer group in an age-segregated society. Major appraisals of peer influence were published or initiated during this decade, including David Riesman's *The Lonely Crowd* (1950), which depicts the emergence of other-directed peer groups in the upper middle class; S. N. Eisenstadt's *From Generation to Generation* (1956), a scholarly analysis of ethnographic materials on age groups and relationships: Albert Cohen's influential treatise on delinquent subcultures, 1955; Calvin Gordon's study, *The Social System of the High School* (1957); James Coleman's major work on youth in 10 midwestern high schools, *The Adolescent Society* (1961); and Ralph Turner's research on adolescent ambition in the subcultures of high schools, *The Social Context of Ambition,* 1964. In combination, these studies brought fresh awareness to the dysfunctions of age segregation and social inequality in the transition of youth to adult roles.

The transfer of control over socialization from family to school and peers is most vividly described in Riesman's provocative essay, which some (Lipset & Lowenthal, 1961) regard as "one of the most significant and successful sociological contributions of our time" (p. v). The essay covers an exceedingly broad canvass on relations among historical change, social structure, and character, but considerable attention is given to the emergence of other-directed peer groups in the upper middle class. Bureaucratization and growth of a service-oriented economy are linked to other-directed personality among the young through adaptations of socialization to structural requirements, in particular the emergence of prolonged schooling and youth groups.

Affluent parents may select appropriate environments for their offspring by choice of residence, but control over what is "best" resides with school and peers, who help locate the young in the social order. Parents in this stratum function mainly as stage managers or facilitators for their child's experience. Lacking clear standards on upbringing, they seek the counsel of magazines, other parents, and the peer groups of their sons or daughters. The young learn how the parental role should be played from television and peers and use this knowledge to achieve their ends. In postwar America, children of the upper middle class may have been "loved" toward maturity, but they were no longer "brought up" as were the products of inner-directed homes.

For parents and offspring, success is being popular, accepted, making friends—a standard that enhances the peer group's control over valued rewards and its power to enforce conformity. Through group sanctions, competition for individual prominence is replaced by competition for peer acceptance. Social pressures enforce taste standardization and fashion skills in consumption, defining peers as the behavioral model and measuring rod for all endeavors. In the world of the other-directed, parents have abdicated their responsibilities and authority to their children's peer group. As Riesman

(1961) puts it, "if adults are the judge, these peers are the jury, and as in America, the judge is hemmed in by rules which give the jury a power it has in no other common-law land, so the American peer-group, too, cannot be matched for power throughout the middle-class world" (pp. 70–71).

However insightful, this characterization has been faulted on a number of grounds, from its simplistic image of parent-youth relations to the lack of empirical support from studies carried out in the 1950s. In Parson's judgment (1964), the major weakness of Riesman's depiction of peer influence is that he "tends to 'reify' the peer group, as if it were the overwhelmingly predominant factor in socialization and constituted a kind of microcosm of the emerging adult 'other-directed' society" (p. 221). Empirical studies of the 1950s (Bowerman & Kinch, 1959; Douvan & Adelson, 1966) show a more differentiated picture in which adolescent orientations to parents and peers vary according to issues and family patterns. Strong ties to peers do not necessarily imply weak ties to parents. The task is to specify situations and areas in which peers are most likely to function as allies or adversaries of parents in youth socialization. Thus Bowerman and Kinch observed that greater dependence on peers than parents for support and guidance was most probable under conditions of parental indifference, rejection, and lack of understanding. Important studies from the 1950s to the present (Kandel & Lesser, 1972; Jennings, Allerbeck, & Rosenmayr, 1976) have consistently documented the central role of family in the lives of young people.

The disparity between Riesman's assessment and empirical work reflects in part a common tendency in the postwar years of social change: that of describing youth behavior in terms of inferences that are based on institutional change, as in schooling. Though postwar change indicates constraints and options relative to parent and youth behavior, it does not specify actual patterns of behavior. A differentiated environment of socialization does not tell us how parents and youth work out relationships and choices within this setting. Moreover, the self-reports of youth do not enable us to determine the character of generational patterns; perceptions of parents are not a reliable gauge of parental values, attitudes, and behavior. Dependence on this data source represents a major limitation of James Coleman's (1961) study of the presumed cleavage between the adult world and the isolated cultural setting of adolescents in high school: that the adolescent in high school is "cut off" from the rest of society and maintains only "a few threads of connection" with significant others and realities in the adult community.

Across 10 high schools in the Chicago area, Coleman (1961) found that a sizable percentage of adolescents were more reluctant to break with a friend than to receive parental or teacher disapproval; that student leaders, in the liberated climate of large high schools, were more inclined than followers to side with peers (against the perceived wishes of parents) on issues involving social participation and club membership; that students placed greater emphasis on popularity, social leadership, and athletics than on academic excellence; and that the anti-intellectual climate of youth groups generally discouraged intellectual accomplishment. The overall impression seems to be one of stronger peer than parental influence and a cultural cleavage between the adolescent and adult communities. However, Coleman's questions frequently set up a forced opposition between parents and peers (with no option to favor both), and he did not have parent information from which to assess value differences between the generations. The leading student groups may not have prized "academic brilliance" above all else, but they were headed, in large measure, for the rewards of higher education.

Judging from the literature, distinctive features of adolescence in the 1950s were not perceived in organismic development, which had changed little since the 1930s, but rather in emerging social form and content. Countless pubertal youth, who would have been grouped with younger children in past times, were identified with secondary school; a large proportion found themselves segregated in physical space from both older and younger students. With steadily expanding numbers of adolescents continuing their education beyond high school, a more prolonged stage of semi-independence acquired generalized significance. The correspondence between these social changes and problem foci is striking. Equally apparent is the inattention to demographic processes and historical facts in lives: the ascending size and changing composition of youth cohorts, from Depression births to the postwar baby boom; specific historical experiences that varied across these cohorts and may have differentiated their developmental course and life chances. High-school cohorts around 1950 were smaller than those at the end of the decade and encountered major historical events (depression, war, recovery) at different points in their lives. Neither studies of adolescent development nor research on adolescent subcultures or generational relations considered the potential implications of such variation for the explanation, interpretation, and generalization of findings.

The skeptic may question the utility of a research strategy that takes demographic or historical factors into account (Do such differences make a difference?), and one finds little hard evidence to support a convincing response. Nevertheless, an historical perspective would have sensitized James Coleman to factors that distinguished his adolescent sample of 1957 from older and younger cohorts. Most of the students in Coleman's "adolescent society" were born in the early 1940s (World War II) and thus were exposed in large numbers to the deprivations of father-absence and the stress of family readjustments on father's return. Though socially accepted, the temporary absence of fathers (two or more years) markedly altered family relationships, placing mothers in a dominant, instrumental role, and establishing fertile conditions for conflict when the returning veteran attempted to resume old family roles (Hill, 1949). Especially relevant to Coleman's generational theme are Lois Stolz's (1954) empirical observations on the father-son relations of war-born children: that sons born during the war experienced a more stressful relation with fathers who served in the military than those born after the war to veterans. Even several years after the father's return to the family, their relations with war-born sons were characterized by greater emotional distance and strain.

No one knows whether such effects persisted into the high-school years, though Carlsmith's study (1973) of Harvard students is suggestive along this line. Carlsmith compared students born during the war with a control group of men from homes in which the father was present, and found that men who experienced father-absence during the war were more likely to describe their ideal self as more like mother. They also shared fewer interests with males in general, displayed a more feminine cognitive style (see also Nelson & Maccoby, 1966), and projected a more delayed pattern of career establishment after college. Although the father-absent students appeared well adjusted to the college environment, Carlsmith concluded that they "feel somewhat less secure about their future roles as adult men." In combination, these studies are much too fragmentary to warrant generalizations regarding war-caused father-absence, but their findings obviously bear on the generational concerns of Coleman. They are also at least suggestive of the developmental implications of one historical event in the lives of males in this cohort.

From Generation to Cohort and History

I have suggested that developments in the 1960s marked a turning point toward historical considerations in the study of adolescence and youth, from the emergence of a life-course perspective that placed lives in historical context to the growth of genuine historical research on young people, their families, and settings. However, other analysts have detected no appreciable change in this direction. As recently as the early 1970s, Seeley (1973) claimed that the literature on adolescence is devoid of a "sense of society and a sense of history," of recognition that adolescence represents "a crucial articulation point or period in the historic as well as the ontogenetic process," a period that spans "the stage of the acted-upon-by history (the child) and the actor in and upon history (the adult)" (pp. 21, 23). Seeley provides numerous examples of these deficiencies, and concludes with a special plea for "the study of what is to be seen in the simultaneously dual perspective of history and life history" (p. 28).

Seeley's criticism is well supported by even a casual search of the literature, but so also is the thesis of a turning point in the 1960s toward the dual perspective he advocates; periods of change are generally characterized by a mixture of old and new and by a lag between innovation and implementation. Analytic themes in the turbulent 1960s reflect a mixture of continuity and change relative to the prior decade; continuity in the prevalence of generational analysis from a social age perspective; and change through greater awareness of historical, demographic, and cultural variations in adolescent experience. New questions were posed by the public issues and problems of this extraordinary decade, its tensions, outbursts, and social movements along racial-ethnic, class, and generational lines. Queries as to the timing of youth unrest (Why the 1960s rather than the 1950s?) focused attention on the diverse historical childhoods of young and old—on Depression hardship in parental lives and postwar affluence among the young.

Studies during the 1960s more frequently identified adolescents and college youth by their membership in a particular age cohort and its subgroups, with guidance from Karl Mannheim's essay on "The Problem of Generations" (Bengtson & Laufer, 1974) and a perspective on age patterns in the life course. Historical analysis and cultural diversity in *Youth* (1975), the 74th NSSE Yearbook, provide a noteworthy record of these developments and the change that has occurred in the study of young people since *Adolescence* (1944), the 43rd NSSE Yearbook. In contrast to the latter's emphasis on physical development, *Youth* is characterized by historical, institutional, and cultural themes; historical change in sex roles; the psychohistory of college youth; comparisons of youth cohorts; demographic and institutional change; cultural differentiation (black, Mexican-American, rural youth); and class or income strata.

In addition to advances in the sociological study of age, some developmentalists began to question research designs that were uninformed by matters of social change and that dealt only with a segment of the life span. Path-breaking essays by Warner Schaie (1965) and Paul Baltes (1968) gave visibility to: (1) the lifelong character of behavioral development, its multidimensionality and plasticity relative to environmental change and (2) the interpretive problems that arise from the ambiguous meaning of age differences, as an outcome of historical change, life situation, or both. These early insights of what is now recognized as life-span developmental psychology (Baltes & Schaie, 1973), along with methodological strategies for disentangling the multiple properties of age, constitute an important step toward placing adolescence within the intersection of social and life history. In sociology and psychology, such efforts to articulate the relation between age and time gradually linked three age concepts—developmental, social, and historical—in a perspective that places adolescence in the life course and history.

To some extent, this perspective can be viewed as a critique of theoretical models that prevailed in the 1950s and continued to shape questions and research on youth unrest in the 1960s. Whether developmental or sociological, age-specific analyses were ill suited to an understanding of the antecedents and outcomes of youth behavior. Theory on adolescence in societal development linked generational strains to periods of rapid change and directed inquiry away from the discordance between youth, as a collective or cohort, and the larger social, economic, and political system. A large number of studies in the 1960s were guided by the *expectation* of parent-youth conflict and value differences in student unrest, an expectation that received little empirical support (Andersson, 1969; Kandel & Lesser, 1972; Bengtson & Laufer, 1974). One overview of the literature concludes that "any major differences that might exist between youth and older generations are more apt to be differences *within* the adult group, which are being manifested in the youth group, than between parents and their adolescent children" (Timpane et al., 1976, p. 48). Observed variations in generational relations and social transmission proved wholly insufficient for explaining the emergence of collective patterns among youth, their timing, location, and diversity in form and substance.

This orientation to youth behavior in the 1960s was influenced by Kingsley Davis's theory of parent-youth conflict (1940), a theory that is based on a comparative analysis of societies at different stages of development. Davis sought an answer to the question of why modern industrial societies were characterized by "an extraordinary amount of parent-adolescent conflict," when compared to premodern societies. Against the background of certain universals (e.g., differential upbringing, status, and aging patterns between parents and youth), Davis identified four major sets of variables that seemed to accentuate the likelihood of generational conflict and also distinguished between historical societies and regions at varying levels of development:

- Rate of social change.
- Degree of structural differentiation and complexity.
- Level and form of cultural variation.
- Mobility, both social and geographic.

Though not meant to account for generational variations in modern societies, Davis's theory did serve as a point of departure for analysts who questioned the explanatory value of rapid change for an understanding of youth behavior in the 1960s. For example, Seymour Lipset (1976) concludes that Davis's account is unsatisfactory because it does not "explain why certain epochs of rapid change lead to student activism, while others do not" (p. 15). In part, the theory fails because it conceptualizes change within the framework of long-range development; it is too global to specify modes of change and their consequences in specific historical settings of modern societies. Theoretical requirements in the modern setting require a more differentiated concept of social change in type, rate, and configuration, as well as assessments of the process by which change finds expression in lives.

In drawing upon Davis's essay, Lipset implicitly assumes a generalized model of causal chains that lacks conceptual precision and verification within industrial societies:

$$\text{rapid change} \rightarrow \text{parent-youth conflict} \rightarrow \text{student activism}$$

Very little is known about the process that links types of rapid change to specific youth outcomes, but it is clear that an understanding of this process requires knowledge of the change and its implications for adaptations in concrete situations (Elder, 1974). Even more uncertain is the presumed link between generational conflict and student activism; as noted, the literature of the 1960s provides little empirical support for this connection. Generational conflict may take a variety of forms under different circumstances; it represents only one potential link between rapid change and youth behavior.

In retrospect, the emerging life-course approach of the 1960s identifies at least three problems or limitations in a purely generational approach to social change in youth experience:

1. The ambiguous meaning of generational differences.
2. The imprecision of generational membership as an index of historical location.
3. Neglect of the relationship between youth and options, cohorts and the social order.

Generational differences in values may reflect the disparity in life stage between parents and offspring, since values are shaped by the imperatives of life situations, or they may indicate socialization differences that are linked to cohort membership and historical times (Bengtson, 1975). Since historical location and life stage are jointly determined by age, both factors and related experience could account for parent-adolescent conflicts over sexual behavior, material concerns, financial responsibility, and so on.

This point is illustrated by one result from a study of three generations in the Los Angeles area (Bengtson & Lovejoy, 1973). Financial support was ranked more highly as a value by the parent and grandparent generations than by the younger generation. Life-stage differences between the generations are suggested as a plausible explanation: that financial constraints and pressures enhanced the importance of this item among the older generations. However, an equally plausible case could be made for a historical explanation, with special reference to experiences in the Great Depression. One solution to this interpretational problem stems from the premise that social change differentiates the experience of persons who share a common historical location. For example, not all families in the Depression suffered heavy income losses. When historical experience is not uniform among lineages with the same age differential, it represents a testable explanation for differences between parents and offspring.

A search for historical factors that account for generational differences requires knowledge of each generation's historical location relative to events and change. However, members of a generation do not occupy anything resembling a common location in the historical process, owing to variations in the timing of births. An age range of 20 years, as in Bengtson and Lovejoy's (1975) sample of parents and grandparents, is far too broad to permit analysis that relates events to lives. The oft mentioned Depression-background of parents of youth in the 1960s was in fact highly differentiated. Some parents encountered the Depression as adolescents, others as young children; a large number were spared hardships altogether. By dividing the age range of a parent generation into birth cohorts and thus across descending generations, generational membership acquires historical precision and enables study of the social transmission of historical experience. *Generational cohorts* facilitate contemporary explorations of Kingsley Davis's research problem—that of rapid change in parent-offspring relations. Consider, for example, the differential experience of two generational cohorts with birth dates before the Great Depression (1920, 1929). Members of the oldest cohort (1920) entered the Depression as preadolescents, were old enough to play a major role in the economy of deprived households, and left high school during the early phase of war mobilization. By contrast, some members of the younger cohort (1929) experienced a more prolonged phase of family hardship, beginning in the early years of childhood and extending to the 1940s. These differences, among others, suggest a number of implications for the parental values of these cohorts in the postwar era.

Whether placed in historical context or not, the microenvironment of generational relations had little to offer for understanding the distinctive collective features of adolescence and youth in the 1960s, in particular, the ascending size of youth cohorts, with their institutional consequences and impact on youth experience. As noted in Figure 1, young Americans, ages 14 to 24, increased by an unparalleled 52% between 1960 and 1970. Most of the increase was absorbed by the military and schools, transforming college campuses into a more conducive environment for student mobilization against the Vietnam War. Change of this sort began to inform studies of youth in the mid-1960s (Musgrove, 1965; Moller, 1968) and brought a neglected dimension to the familiar concept of institutional change when there is social discontinuity between family experience and adult life. The nature of this discontinuity, and the resulting problems for institutions and youth, vary according to economic and demographic conditions. This principle is illustrated by the contrasting institutional problems and life chances associated with the small cohort of Depression-born youth who came of age in the early 1950s and the relatively large cohort that entered a depressed labor market in the early 1970s. Musgrove's historical analysis (1965) suggests that the status and rewards of youth have varied with their relative size in the population, and he concludes that youth in the 1960s, as in the 1970s, are likely to pay a price for their "comparative abundance in the previous twenty years" (p. 81). Large youth cohorts in the 1960s and the prevalence of student protests on large university campuses (Scott & El-Assal, 1969) generally conform to Herbert Moller's historical thesis (1968): that periods of social change and youth unrest are characterized by cohorts of ascending size.

Some developmental implications of membership in a large youth cohort are suggested by Roger Barker's concept of an "overmanned behavior setting" (1968), a setting in which people far outnumber options and only a small number (the elite in background and talent) have access to challenging parts in the drama. This is a setting that exaggerates traits commonly attributed to adolescence as a social category—a no-man's-land without self-defining, productive roles; a position of marginality and low integration relative to the larger community. Observing a historical decline in the prevalence of undermanned settings for Americans, Barker (1968) points out the broader implications of the trend through an idea that links this type of environment to a way of life—the free frontier, people of abundance, a land of opportunity. It is the idea that "there has been a superabundance of goals to be achieved and an excess of tasks to be done in relation to the nation's inhabitants, and that these have been important influences in the American society and people" (p. 189). This idea may still have a future with the pronounced decline in fertility since the 1960s, though much depends on the economy.

Apart from the effect of cohort size, youth unrest in the 1960s was also viewed in terms of a mismatch between the social and developmental characteristics of cohorts and available options. Strains may arise when change provides options and demands that do not correspond with the modal dispositions or skills of particular cohorts, or when developmental change through socialization is not coupled with parallel change in the social order. Consistent with Mannheim's writings on the mentalities of generation or cohort units, variations in life history among members of cohorts in the 1960s were associated with variations in exposure to specific events (e.g., an administrative decision on a college campus), in the personal meaning or relevance of the events, and in responses to the events, collective and otherwise. Thus studies found differences in social and political attitudes between segments of the youth cohort, for example, non-college versus college (Lipset, 1976), to be as large or larger than those observed between youth and older-age groups. Conflict between the development of youth and social institutions is suggested by research that characterized youth of the counterculture as products of socialization within the upper middle class (see Flacks, 1971). Relevant to this point is Hampden-Turner's (1970) observations on coming to this country from England. He was struck by the contrasting position of developmental and humanistic themes in American education and childrearing, on the one hand, and in the commercial-political world, on the other. "It has long seemed to me only a matter of time before the developmental themes in American life confronted the repressive themes, and before those students nurtured in the better homes and schools came to regard the opportunities offered by business and government as an insult to their actual levels of psychosocial development" (Hampden-Turner, p. 364).

Cohort research on youth and social institutions depicted the young as actors responding to and shaping their life situations, not merely as products of institutional change and socialization. Though Gillis (1974) is correct in noting an underrepresentation of youth's own "response to change," compared to the molding influence of institutions (p. ix), such bias was far less apparent in the literature of the 1960s than in prior decades. Youth behavior in the 1960s had much in common with W. I. Thomas's (Elder, 1978) account of responses to situational change: that of persons "working out adaptations to the times that find meaning, if not a plan of action, in customary understanding and values" (p. 519). The actions of young people in this decade were less an outgrowth of new ideas than of old ideas (e.g., civil rights) operating in new or changing situations. From surveys of age groups in Western Europe during the early 1970s, Inglehart (1977) identified postwar economic growth and rising levels of education among successive youth cohorts as prominent factors in the shift from interests centered on "material consumption and security toward greater concern with the quality of life" (p. 363). However, such preferences are subject to the imperatives of changing historical circumstances. Yankelovich's (1974) surveys of American college students between 1969 and the recession year of 1973 show a significant increase among the cohorts in the priority assigned to economic security as a job criterion and to continued support for sexual freedom and civil liberties, but there is a decline in regard for patriotism and religion as central values. Both historical change and cohort properties may account for this change; determination of its meaning and consequences in lives and institutions await thorough study in longitudinal samples (see Fendrich, 1974) and cohort comparisons over multiple data points.

Up to now, we have identified research themes in the 1960s that represent both continuity and change relative to prior decades in studies of adolescence and youth; continuity through generational analysis and its limitations for historical research; and change through the study of youth cohorts, their characteristics, historical settings, and relation to institutions and social options. In generational analysis, the family constitutes a link between historical change and the lives of young people; the impact of change may occur through social transmission or through a breakdown in this process. However, generational status (parent or child) does not place individuals in a precise historical setting, nor does it confer membership in an age group that encounters historical events at the same point in the life span. Youth are characterized as individuals without shared experience in specific historical times. The focal point of generational analysis—parent-youth relations—tended to shift inquiry away from the problematic interplay between youth cohorts and social institutions and the relation of this interplay to both continuity and discontinuity between the generations. Though modest in number and accomplishments, studies of youth cohorts drew attention to this interplay and, with efforts to elaborate the bond between age and time, introduced a temporal and processual dimension to views of adolescence and youth, a perspective that depicts adolescent experience in terms of interactions between historically defined cohorts, their developmental histories, and life stage in the social structure.

This view of adolescence suggests a number of unexplored questions on change or continuity both in the cultural properties of this life stage as well as their consequences for the life course of youth. Consider, for example, the hypothesis that structural features of adolescence (dependency, status uncertainty, loose integration) are expressed in identities or life styles that have persisted across successive youth cohorts. Matza (1964) refers to a set of conventional life styles (academic, sports, moral scrupulosity) and rebel identities (delinquency, bohemianism, radicalism) as "traditions" of youth that have "grown into traditional styles which have been assumed and put aside by one cohort after another" (p. 199). With counterparts and carriers in the larger society, these "traditions" are said to represent adaptations of youth to an emerging social position. The nature of this position would of course vary according to the particular history and characteristics of youth cohorts under changing conditions; this variation implies differing adaptive requirements, for example, cohorts in the Great Depression and the postwar years of prosperity. Sources of "life-style" continuity and change from cohort to cohort are poorly understood, and little is known about the expression of traditional identities in new forms (but see Gillis, 1974) that are more responsive to the times.

Another question concerns normative variation by demographic and economic change in age-graded expectations and the phenomenology of age status. Within the family these expectations may be thought of in terms of independence standards or guidelines—the ages at which the young are expected or permitted to engage in certain behavior. What factors account for change in these standards from one parent cohort to another? Are they subject to change as material conditions vary from good to hard times? Behavioral observations tend to produce more questions than answers along this line. For example, adolescents in the Great Depression frequently assumed positions of family responsibility, suggesting a downward extension of adult expectations, but the depressed labor market also encouraged school persistence and delayed marriage and childbearing (Zachry, 1944, pp. 336–337). The postwar years offer a similar contradiction. They have been described as a period when youth dependency was prolonged, and the extension of formal education generally supports this interpretation. However, this period was also marked by a substantial decline in age at first marriage (Modell, Furstenberg, & Strong, 1978), an event that many regard as the prime indicator of adult status. In the 1960s, we see an increasing tendency to delay marriage and childbearing within a continuing upward trend in the proportion of youth in higher education. The normative meaning of this change is largely unknown (see Jordan, 1976; Goldstein, 1976).

Apart from these unknowns, research on demographic change in the 1960s suggested one noteworthy connection between cohort size and normative factors in the lives of adolescents—by increasing membership in all categories, expanding youth cohorts heightened the visibility of adolescent deviance and its problematic aspects, raising public concern and the likelihood of social intervention. The sheer numerical increase of youth relative to adults had much to do with public concern over juvenile delinquency, deprived youth, student radicals, and teen-age parenthood. Furstenberg (1976) observes that it was only in the 1960s that "public concern about the problem of teenage parenthood became manifest" (p. 8), as seen in the popular literature, government programs, and clinics for young mothers. He attributes this normative change to a convergence of developments, including the large adolescent cohorts of the 1960s and the general issue of overpopulation. There were more adolescent girls of childbearing age than ever before. An increasing proportion of teen-age births were children born out of wedlock (from 15 to 30%, 1960–1970), owing partly to the pregnancy risks of a trend toward earlier sexual experience and a rising pattern of later marriage. Throughout the decade, concern over unplanned childbearing and its social disadvantage led to a broad range of intervention programs; well over 100 programs offering educational and health services were in operation by 1970.

Demographic and normative factors are well represented in Furstenberg's important study of adolescent childbearing; one of the clearest examples of how analytic developments on historical time and the life course began to shape problem foci in adolescent research during the 1960s. The project was launched in 1966 as a traditional, short-term evaluation of a service program for teen-age mothers (before age 18, $N = 323$) in predominantly low-income, black neighborhoods of Baltimore. Like other research on the subject, this initial study focused on the causes of adolescent parenthood and births out of wedlock and paid no attention to historical trends, demographic trends, or to the differentiated life course of the young mother. But events (lack of funds, etc.) soon offered Furstenberg a chance to rethink the study in the light of emerging ideas on the life course and to recast it as a longitudinal investigation of the career of early parenthood and of adaptations to an ill-timed event. Apart from the approved timing of parenthood, early parenthood is "off schedule" in relation to the young mother's social maturation, schooling, and prospects for economic support. Marital postponement, kin support in childcare, the rescheduling of schooling and work, and fertility control represented potential options for managing the deprivations, tensions, and disorder associated with an unplanned birth at an early age. In order to carry out this study, Furstenberg selected a matched sample of the former classmates of the teen-age mothers who had not become pregnant in adolescence. Interviews were conducted with both groups in 1970 and 1972.

Furstenberg located the adolescent girls in his study within the course of postwar developments (rising levels of teen-age childbearing, births out of wedlock). In doing so, he placed the analysis in a context that suggests broader implications, that is, What are the life outcomes and social consequences of the trend in illegitimate births? At the same time, he properly notes distinctive features of his cohort and its historical time, which limit generalizations to other cohorts and times, such as change in the availability of birth-control devices for adolescents. However, the major contribution of the study is seen in its concept of multiple, interlocking career lines and its creative application to the adaptations of unwed adolescent mothers. A specific sequence of events leads to an illegitimate birth, and at each decision point the outcome can be averted: premarital sexual experience or not, contraceptive use or not, pregnancy or not, birth or abortion or marriage. Birth of a child out of wedlock is followed by a number of potential options: abandonment of the child or putting the child up for adoption; marriage or single parenthood; more illegitimate births; educational and vocational decisions; entry into the welfare system or economic independence. Decisions at each stage of the career entail different explanatory processes. Variables that influence early sexual experience differ from those that bear on the use of contraceptives. A full model of unwed motherhood links these separate explanations into a life-course perspective.

The consequences of unplanned parenthood vary according to the form of this career and its relation to other career lines—marital, occupational, and educational. Problems of synchronization and life management stem from this event, and are expressed in coping strategies; judicious planning and use of resources, the rearrangement of event schedules, and educational aspirations play a key role in enabling some adolescent mothers to minimize the disadvantage of an early birth in their life chances and in the development of their children. By following the young mothers into their early 20s, we discover how erroneous some popular impressions of early parenthood have been; in particular, the belief that it leads inevitably to a life of deprivation. On the contrary, diversity in life pattern and prospects stands out as the more prominent theme in their experiences. Though most of the women grew up in disadvantaged homes, their life situations some five years after the birth of their first child reflect a wide range of advantage and hardship. Many questions are left unanswered, as one might expect, and provide an agenda for subsequent work. But most importantly, this study of the life paths of teen-age mothers suggests a fruitful way to investigate the historical, social, and developmental features of adolescence in the life course.

Youth in Historical Time and Social Change

Historical considerations during the 1960s appear in theoretical formulations and methodological designs, in the reformulation of old questions, and in the appraisal of puzzling findings. The use of archival resources to trace out the effects of historical change in lives, cohorts, and institutions is largely missing from this picture. Indeed, questions regarding such effects serve to underline the scarcity of firm knowledge on the past and on the causal processes linking Depression, War, and postwar developments to life situations during the 1960s. In retrospect, this deficiency represents one consequence of a strategy long prominent in sociological work on change: the objective, as Abrams points out (1972), "was not to *know* (italics added) the past but to establish an idea of the past which could be used as a comparative base for the understanding of the present" (p. 28). In the absence of reliable knowledge on the historical record, such ideas often told us more about concepts of the present and the limitations of global theories and grand designs.

Over the past decade, genuine archival research on young people has made us more aware that limited understanding of the present has roots in countless unknowns of the past[4] and that many presumptions regarding social change have been misleading or false. Consider a popular account of family change that has influenced interpretations of youth socialization since the 1920s: a "decline version" that stressed "the great withering away of functions," resulting from urbanization and industrialization (Elder, 1978). Separation of the productive activities from households and the general process of functional specialization (in education, etc.) diminished the family's role in upbringing, hence the conclusion regarding a long-term decline in parental control. The insights of historical research (Smith & Hindus, 1975; Lipschutz, 1977) yield a far more complex picture of fluctuating trends and patterns of time and place, social stratum, mode of control, and life stage.

Well before industrialization, in the agrarian world of seventeenth- and eighteenth-century Andover, Mass., Philip Greven's (1970) study documents a substantial change, from father to son across four generations, in the son's control over his own life course of marriage and work. By and large, yeoman fathers in the first generation exercised firm control over the time of adult independence through the division of their estate. The division occurred relatively late in the father's life, thereby delaying the son's marriage and financial autonomy. By the third and fourth generations, we see a decline in paternal control and greater willingness to assist sons in making their own way, a change stemming from the increasing scarcity of land (favoring impartable inheritance) and greater economic opportunities away from homestead and kin, especially in neighboring towns and villages. Men of the fourth generation were most likely to launch families and an independent worklife at a relatively early age. During the same time period, another study of a New England community (Smith, 1973) has described a shift in control over marriage from parents to offspring by the mid-nineteenth century.

Further erosion in parental control is commonly attributed to industrialization, with special reference to the removal of work and father from household. But a contrary view is suggested by an increasing tendency during the last half of the nineteenth century for young people to remain in the family well beyond puberty (Katz, 1975): a noteworthy reversal of a long-standing parental practice in preindustrial society of sending children out to live as a member of another household between puberty and marriage. This change, which began to equate adolescent dependency with family residence, has been attributed to a number of factors that converged at the time—the decline of apprenticeship training, extension of mass schooling to the secondary years, the rise of domestic sentiments, and the appeal of homelife. Whatever the cause in residential change, its potential implications include a strengthening of generational ties. Indeed, Bloomberg (1974) concludes that perhaps "the most pronounced change in family roles caused by industrialization was in enhancing the powers of parents and decreasing the independence of teenage boys" (p. 13).

Parental control is merely one aspect of a more general historical question on social change in the life course of youth. Historians and sociologists have begun to explore this question from the vantage point of constraints (institutional, demographic, and economic) and their implications for the life course, especially the timing and configuration of events in the transition to adult status. Three studies illustrate different applications of this approach: Michael Katz's intensive study (1975; Katz & Davey, 1978) of youth and their life paths to adulthood before and during early industrialization (1851–1971) in the city of Hamilton, Canada; a comparative study (Modell, Furstenberg, & Hershberg, 1976) of the changing pattern of events in the transition to adult status between late nineteenth-century America and 1970; and a longitudinal investigation of one historical event, economic deprivation during the 1930s in the life patterns of predepression birth cohorts—an Oakland, California, cohort with birthdates of 1920–1921 (Elder, 1974) and a Berkeley cohort, 1928–1929 (Elder & Rockwell, 1979). The problem foci of these studies imply a processual view of lives, though only the Depression project is based on a longitudinal-data archive. Even so, Modell and associates employ their cross-sectional data (mainly based on census schedules) to good effect in suggesting implications for individual life patterns. Katz has linked some data at different points (1851 and 1861) to form life records on individuals, but his analysis relies primarily on cross-sectional information.

The time frame of the Hamilton study is uniquely suited for an examination of how the lives of youth—middle and working class, native and foreign born—were altered by events during the early stage of industrialization. Between 1851 and 1871, Hamilton was transformed from a small commercial center of 14,000 (hit hard by a depression in the late 1850s) to an industrial-commercial center of 26,000. In this period, the city fathers modernized the school system, segregating youth from children; improved local transportation and public services; and witnessed a threefold increase in the number of large firms (10 or more employees). Hamilton's industrialization (from heavy industry to apparel firms) did not include the development of textile mills, with their opportunities for the employment of women and children. Quantifiable data on youth and families were obtained from census manuscripts in 1851, 1861, and 1871. To explore the life-course changes among youth across these points, Katz focused on the temporal configuration of residence, education, work, and marriage. These events, he suggests (1975), "interacted with one another in a way that gave to the experience of people whom today we would call adolescents a distinctly different pattern from that which it has since assumed" (p. 156).

For many years, an image of early nineteenth-century youth depicted an early and abrupt transition to adulthood; complete independence followed a relatively short period of dependency as boys left home at ages of 15 or younger and entered the world of adults. Both Katz (1975) and Joseph Kett (1977) challenge this belief with evidence suggesting an intervening stage of semi-independence or partial autonomy. According to Kett, this state is characterized by a disorderly pattern of events in which age is only loosely correlated with status; boys moved back and forth between school, where they were defined as children, and work, which offered adult status. Preindustrial youth "grew up on a series of separate timetables" (Kett, 1977, p. 42) that were largely influenced by family or household needs and resources. From data on Hamilton youth before industrialization, Katz observed greater uniformity in life pattern, relative to Kett's description, and a stage of semiautonomy between leaving home and marriage, one based on both employment and place of residence. "Young men and women frequently worked and lived as members of a household other than that of their parents" (Katz, 1975, p. 257)—generally households in the higher socioeconomic strata of the community. This stage of the early life course has been documented by other studies (see Little & Laslett, 1977; Bloomberg, 1974) on nineteenth-century communities in America.

Katz and Davey (1978) refer to the stage of semiautonomy as the "lost phase" of the life course, for it was gradually replaced in the course of industrialization by more prolonged residence in the parental home. A slight majority of Hamilton youth (aged 15 to 19 years) were living in nonparental residences as of 1851; 20 years later, this figure had declined to one-fourth of the males and one-third of the females. The median age at leaving home increased for young men from 17 to 22; for women, from 17 to 20. The practice of resident domestic service, which continued until late in the nineteenth century, accounts for the smaller change among young women. Four strands of evidence generally support Katz's (1975) claim that young men who boarded out experienced greater autonomy than those who remained in the family of origin:

- The more contractual basis of boarding, in contrast to the diffuse obligations of family life and parental surveillance.
- The link between boarding and employment—less than 10% of the boarders were employed by the household head.
- The concentration of school attendance and work for father among youth who resided at home, implying dependence on parental resources.
- A pattern of earlier marriage among boarders, when compared to family residents.

Overall, the stage of partial autonomy seemed to ease the tension between dependency and the obligations of adulthood (Katz, 1975): "Those men who left home were readier than those who remained to cross the boundary between child and adult" (p. 268).

Despite the change in residence between 1851 and 1871, little change occurred in age at entry into the labor market among boys and in the timing of marriage; women generally married by the age of 23, men by the age of 27. But with the extension of family residence, we see a pronounced decline in the prevalence of what might be called "idle" youth, those who were neither in school nor employed, a change reflecting increasing educational and economic opportunities. Nearly half of the 11- to 15-year-olds in 1851 and one-fourth of the 16- to 20-year-olds were neither enrolled in school nor working; the percentages were even greater among girls, leading Katz (1975) to conclude that,

> many adolescents must have roamed the city with little or nothing to do, a situation which provides an objective underpinning for the desire felt by adults in this period to devise institutions that would take adolescents off the streets. [P. 262]

Rising school enrollment markedly reduced this pool of youth during the first decade of educational expansion, followed by the impact of increasing job opportunities. Among 13- to 16-year-olds who were living at home (Figure 2), school and work recruited a larger proportion of boys in 1871 than in 1851; school attendance accounted for the major change in the status of girls. For this age group of girls, domestic service in other households represented the primary job opportunity.

During the early phase of industrialization in Hamilton, family rank or class became a more potent source of life-course differentiation in relation to residence, extended schooling, employment, and marriage. The sons and daughters of higher-status families remained at home for a longer period of time than youth from the lower strata (Katz & Davey, 1978). They were also more likely to continue their education through secondary school and to delay employment and marriage. Lower-status youth generally attended school on a more irregular basis, owing partly to family transience and needs. In leaving school for work at an early age, a good many of these youth undoubtedly played an important role in the economy of their families. Class differentials in schooling thus linked age-grading and class segregation; the world of secondary school was that of the sons and, to a lesser extent, the daughters of middle-class families.

This portrait of Hamilton youth shows (1) the decline of a life phase and practice that extended across class strata—that of young people between puberty and marriage living

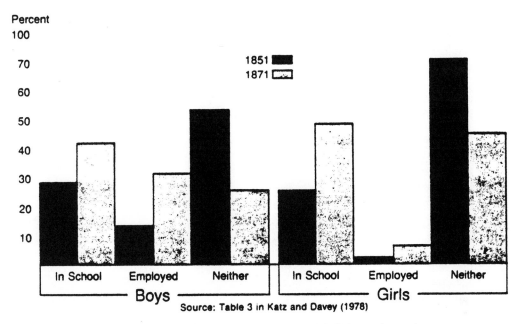

Figure 2. Work and school status among 13- to 16-year-olds living at home in Hamilton, Ontario, 1851 and 1871.

as members of other households and (2) an accentuation of class differentiation in the social worlds and life chances of youth. Many of the conditions we now ascribe to adolescence—features of institutionalized dependency—were emerging in the middle class of late-nineteenth-century Hamilton and other industrial communities. With workplace separated from the domestic unit and urban schools largely staffed by female teachers, prolonged family residence and education in the middle class placed male youth in a socialization environment managed by women—an environment too sheltered, some believed, from the male influences and real-world disciplines that make "big men of little boys" (Hantover, 1976, p. 117). This climate of "masculine anxiety" converged with the perceived dangers of idle, unruly youth in the lower class as a stimulus to middle-class support for adult-led organizations—Boys Clubs, YMCA, the Boy Scouts.

The Hamilton study brings us to the latter decades of the nineteenth century and to the question of how the transition to adulthood was altered by social changes of the twentieth century. If we think in terms of departure from home and the completion of schooling, educational upgrading over the twentieth century seems to indicate a more extended transition among contemporary youth cohorts when compared to the experience of youth in the nineteenth century. And yet, the downward trend in age at first marriage between 1900 and postwar America supports a different conclusion and even suggests a resemblance to Kett's description of preindustrial youth, straddling multiple timetables that varied greatly from one youth to another. Modell, Furstenberg, and Hershberg (1976) explored life-course change across this period through a comparison of two widely separated cohorts—white youth (male and female) in Philadelphia of 1880 (data from census manuscripts) and an all U.S. Census sample for 1970. A comparison of cohorts in different social units leaves much to be desired, but the authors concluded

from available evidence that the transition of adulthood among Philadelphia youth generally resembled a common pattern of late-nineteenth-century America. The rich contex-
tual detail of the Hamilton study is necessarily absent from this broad "then-and-now"
contrast. However, the study constitutes a pioneering effort to identify gross changes in
the early life course of youth and provides an empirical point of departure for more
focused explanatory research.

At both time periods, data were available on five life events or transitions:

- Exit from school.
- Entry into the labor market.
- Departure from home.
- First marriage.
- The establishment of an independent domicile.

Instead of dealing with the average timing of these events, Modell and associates (1976)
focused on their dispersion across age categories in the following concepts and operations:

- Prevalence—the proportion of a cohort that experiences a given transition in specific
  age categories.
- Timing—typical points of transition, such as when half a cohort has experienced an
  event.
- Spread—the span of time required for a given proportion of a cohort to pass
  through a transition.
- Age congruity—the degree to which the spread of transitions overlap.

All of the concepts are meaningful only on the aggregate or cohort level.

The concept of prevalence is based on the assumption that some individuals will not
experience a particular event, such as marriage. As one might expect, schooling shows the
greatest increase in prevalence, but contemporary youth more uniformly encounter all of
the transitions (except for work among females) when compared to the Philadelphia
population. On spread, or duration, of the transition within a cohort, the data show that
young men and women today generally take longer to complete their schooling, but they
also pass more quickly through the family transitions. Moving out of the parental household, marrying, and setting up an independent household occurs more rapidly now than
among late-nineteenth-century youth. With matters of timing in the picture, the early life
course of nineteenth-century youth differs from that of youth today in two major respects: (1) leaving school and work entry started earlier and required less time to complete and (2) the familial transitions were experienced later and consumed a larger
portion of the life span.

Over the past century, the combination of change in timing and spread has resulted in
a greater prevalence of overlapping transitions. Unlike the nineteenth-century pattern in
which members of a cohort typically left one status before entering another, the contemporary pattern shows a mixture of familial and non familial transitions. "A far larger
proportion of a cohort growing up today is faced with choices about sequencing and
combining statuses" (Modell, Furstenberg, and Hershberg, 1976, p. 29). But the com-
pression of transitions has not resulted in a helter-skelter response with the order of
events following a near-random pattern. The range of choice and action in the lives of
late-nineteenth-century youth has been replaced by a more tightly organized schedule of
contingent transitions to adult status. Early life transitions are more compressed and

contingent because they are more constrained by the scheduling imperatives of formal institutions. Control over these transitions has shifted from the family of origin, which allowed a wide measure of flexibility, to young people themselves and the generalized requirements of school and workplace. " 'Timely' action to nineteenth century families consisted of helpful responses in times of trouble; in the twentieth century, 'timeliness' connotes adherence to a schedule" (Modell, Furstenberg, and Hershberg, 1976, p. 30).

Missing from this analysis and interpretation is an explicit account of social change in the transitions of urban boys and girls from the middle and lower classes. Though working-class youth played an important role in family support within the uncontrolled economy of nineteenth-century America, this role bears little resemblance to that of the sons and daughters of upper-middle-class families at the time. Twentieth-century affluence increased the prevalence of this "favored" life situation among youth, liberating an expanding number from the pressing demands of family survival. It is this global change through multiple institutions that is most vividly described by the life-course changes reported by Modell, Furstenberg, and Hershberg (1976). The impact of major historical transformations that occurred between late-nineteenth-century America and the 1970s—especially the Great Depression and the two World Wars—as well as class and ethnic differences in life-course change have yet to be explored in detail. Winsborough (1975, 1976), for example, has observed the same historical trend toward overlapping transitions in the early life course of male cohorts from 1911 to 1941. He suggests that the anticipation of life disruptions associated with military service (see Hogan, 1976), especially during the post-1940 era of the draft, may have fostered greater "calculation about how to make the component transitions, an overcompensation for the time which may be lost, and a pressure to get on with the business of getting started in life before the ax falls" (Winsborough, 1975, p. 37).

Demographic records on events in the course to adulthood describe the patterning of one segment of the life span at different times and places, but they do not, in themselves, tell us what specific life paths or events meant to youth and the larger community. We can be certain that an extension of family residence and schooling in the latter half of the nineteenth century profoundly altered the social environment of young people, but a precise understanding of this environment and its developmental effects eludes our grasp with the historical documents at hand. Nevertheless, it is knowledge of these developmental outcomes that some historians regard as the ultimate objective of historical research on the family: to seek an understanding of family change and continuity in the lives of individuals (Greven, 1973, p. 11). Though folk literature (diaries, etc.) may offer valuable insights on the psychosocial dimensions of family life, its selective representations bear a highly problematic relation to the general population and to actual situations or behavior. Apart from this constraint, widely separated data points leave much to the imagination, as in the Hamilton study. We see Hamilton youth in 1851 and 1861, but not the differential experience of their families in the depression of the 1850s and its consequences on their upbringing. These observations illustrate some common data constraints that limit the possibilities of a life-course approach to the study of youth in historical times.

The impact of social change on youth is mediated by their proximal environments (family, school, peer groups, etc.), and one of the best opportunities to investigate this process is found in longitudinal archives that were initiated by child-study centers during the 1920s and 1930s. At the Berkeley Institute of Child Welfare (now Human Development, California), we see this development in the establishment of three longitudinal studies (Jones et al., 1971): the Oakland Growth Study—launched in 1930–1931, it followed children from northeastern Oakland, California, through the 1930s and up to the middle years of life ($N = 145$); the Guidance Study—selected infants who were born in Berkeley during 1928–1929 and investigated their course of development through annual measurements up to the end of World War II, approximately 180 members of the original core sample ($N = 214$) have participated in at least two adult follow-ups through 1970; and the Berkeley Growth Study—a small, intensively studied sample of children that corresponds in time frame with the Berkeley Guidance Study.

Over the past half century, these longitudinal projects have generated an impressive body of information on life-span development, though limited by neglect of life-course and historical experience. During the early 1960s, initial surveys of the Oakland archive alerted the author to the profound impact of the Depression on families and their offspring, to substantial variation in economic loss and adaptations, and, subsequently, to the design of a study on Depression hardship in the life experience of adolescents who entered the 1930s from the middle and the working classes (Elder, 1974). Research questions focused on the psychosocial effects of the Depression experience. Specification of this experience thus represented a first step toward identifying and explaining life outcomes of family deprivation during the 1930s. To what extent and in what ways did economic loss differentiate the social worlds of the Oakland adolescents? What were the social and psychological consequences of such variation? How were these early outcomes of Depression hardship expressed in the life course and in the adult personality? These questions established contexts in which to formulate models, using available theory and observation—models that specified plausible linkages between a family's deprivational status in the 1930s and its offspring's development. Notions of an event-structured life course acquired significance through efforts to sketch these interconnections between economic events of the 1930s and adolescent experience and between the latter and the adult years.

Prior to the Depression, middle- and working-class families in the sample were characterized by values and resources that had implications for their interpretation and response to economic deprivation. Middle-class families entered the 1930s with claims that placed them in a more vulnerable "psychic position" relative to income loss when compared to families in the lower strata, but they also occupied a position of relative advantage on problem-solving resources—knowledge, technical skills, material assets. Class position (as of 1929) entered the analysis by defining the cultural and economic context in which families worked out lines of adaptation to economic loss. Within the middle and working classes, the study compared families that differed in economic loss—the relatively nondeprived (less than 35% loss, 1929–1933) and the deprived (a classification that made allowances for a one-fourth drop in the cost of living at the time). The effects of deprivation were assessed within each class stratum according to a model that depicted the socioeconomic and psychological adaptations of the family to Depression hardship as the primary link between economic change, on the one hand, and the life experience and personality of the Oakland Study members, on the other.

With economic deprivation as the focal point, the investigation necessarily led to a variety of outcomes in the life course of the Oakland cohorts, a mode of inquiry that is well described as a "branching tree." Three hypothesized connections between family hardship and the adolescent emerged from the analysis:

1. *Change in the household economy*—drastic loss of income required new modes of economic maintenance, which altered the domestic and economic roles of family members, shifting responsibilities to mother (via employment, budgetary management) and the older children. Girls played a major role in household operations; boys contributed earnings from paid jobs.

2. *Change in family relationships*—father's loss of earnings and resulting adaptations in family support increased the relative power of mother, reduced the level and effectiveness of parental control, and diminished the attractiveness of father as a model.

3. *Social strains in the family*—resource losses, parental impairment, and status inconsistency enhanced the degree of social ambiguity, conflict, and emotional strain in the lives of family members.

These family conditions were associated with Depression hardship in both social classes and acquired developmental meaning in terms of the Oakland cohort's life stage. Members of the cohort were beyond the critical early stage of development and dependency when family losses occurred; they left high school in the late 1930s during economic recovery and initial phase of wartime mobilization. Unlike younger children, they were old enough to play important roles in the household economy and to confront future prospects within the context of Depression realities. In the lives of youth from deprived families, hard times generally lowered the social boundary of adulthood when compared to the life situation of youth from more privileged homes. Deprived youth, middle and working class, were more likely to be involved in adultlike tasks within the family economy, to aspire to grown-up status, and to enter the adult roles of marriage and/or work at an early age. Common psychic states observed in the course of adolescent development (e.g., self-consciousness, emotional vulnerability, desire for social acceptance) were more characteristic of boys and girls from hard-pressed families in both social classes, but we find little evidence of an enduring social or psychological disadvantage by the end of the 1930s. Family deprivation did not impair attainment in secondary school or lessen ambition, though it reduced prospects for education beyond high school among youth from the working class.

Soon after the Oakland boys left high school, they were called to military duty in World War II; all but a handful served two or more years. Though military service uniformly interrupted career beginnings in the cohort, the long arm of the Depression made a difference in event schedules and in the patterning of worklife, apart from the influence of class origin. Compared to the nondeprived, young men from hard-pressed families entered adulthood with a more crystallized idea of their occupational goals; they were more likely to delay parenthood, to establish their worklife at an early age, and, despite some handicap in formal education, managed to end up at midlife with a slightly higher occupational rank. Job security was uniquely important to men with a deprived background only under conditions of economic pressure and worklife problems. Despite the significance of work to men from deprived homes, they were more inclined than the nondeprived to stress family activity, to consider children the most important aspect of marriage, to emphasize the responsibilities of parenthood, and to stress the value of dependability in children. Personal aspects of Depression life are reflected in these preferences—the role of children in helping out, the importance of family support in time of crisis. From the vantage point of midlife, clinical ratings of health and self-evaluations show no adverse signs of growing up in the Great Depression, except perhaps among the offspring of working-class parents. On the whole, adulthood offered abundant gratification for men from deprived homes, and they were more likely than the nondeprived to regard these years as the best time of their life.

In life course and values, the Oakland women resemble the "ultradomestic" climate of the postwar years. However, a domestic life style is most pronounced among those women who grew up in deprived, mother-dominated families where they were involved in household responsibilities. During adolescence, these women were more inclined to favor marriage and family over a career when compared to women who were spared family hardships; they tended to enter marriage at an earlier age in the middle class; and they most frequently dropped out of the labor force after marriage or before the birth of their first child. Despite an educational disadvantage, the deprived were no less successful than other women in marrying college-educated men who made their way to the upper echelons of business and the professions. At midlife, family, children, and homemaking distinguished their priorities from those of the nondeprived, regardless of educational level or social position. From these gratifications to sound health, the adult years represented the best time of their lives, more satisfying by far than adolescence in the depressed 1930s and their memories of social exclusion, family burdens, and a controlling mother.

The full array of findings from this study inevitably raises questions concerning their generality, both in terms of a broader sample of Americans in the 1920–1921 cohort and the Depression's impact on other cohorts. The Oakland sample is small and its members were selected by criteria (e.g., permanence in the area) that ensured some degree of bias. The city of Oakland, its economic base, cultural institutions, and Bay Area locale, place other constraints on generalizations from the study. Generality is even more of a question when we turn to cohort variation. Successive cohorts encounter historical events at different points in the life course, which implies variations in adaptive potential and developmental outcomes. One might argue that the Oakland cohort occupied a "favored" position relative to events of the 1930s; in developmental age at the time of the economic crisis and in opportunities at the end of the decade. By contrast, younger cohorts experienced the crisis when they were more dependent on family nurturance and, consequently, were more vulnerable to family instability, emotional strain, and conflict. Family hardship came early in their lives and thus entailed a more prolonged experience, from the economic trough to the war years or departure from home. Issues of this sort led to the initiation of another longitudinal study of Depression hardship, one based on data from the Guidance archive at Berkeley—a study designed to parallel the Oakland project in analytic model, measurements (e.g., economic deprivation), and research foci. Members of the Berkeley Guidance Study were born in 1928–1929 and thus provide a sharp contrast with the Oakland cohort on life stage. Childhood in the prosperous 1920s preceded the Depression adolescence of the Oakland subjects, whereas the Berkeley children entered adolescence in the affluent and unsettled years of World War II, after a childhood shaped by economic deprivation and insecurity.

According to life-stage considerations, one would expect more adverse consequences from Depression hardship in the Berkeley cohort; preliminary analyses generally support this hypothesis on males (Elder & Rockwell, 1979). In the middle and working classes, Berkeley youth from deprived families held lower aspirations during wartime adolescence than members of nondeprived families (no difference in IQ); their scholastic performance turned sharply downward at this point, falling well below that of adolescents in more affluent homes. Despite expanding opportunities during the war, deprived boys were least likely to be hopeful, self-directed, and confident about their future, a dysphoric outlook most prevalent in the formerly hard-pressed middle class. This outlook is one element of a "dependency" syndrome that emerged from personality ratings in adolescence—personal and social inadequacy, a passive mode of responding to life situations, feelings of victimization, withdrawal from adversity, and self-defeating behavior. Aspects of this syndrome distinguished the behavioral course of adolescents who grew up in deprived families from that of youth who were spared such hardship, regardless of class origin.

The causal link between family deprivation in the early 1930s and adolescent personality included a continuing pattern of socioeconomic instability, with its distorting influence on family life—the emotional strain of resource exhaustion; loss of an effective, nurturant father; and an overburdened, dominant mother, anxiously preoccupied with matters of status and mere survival. The connection is most striking among deprived households in the middle class, especially when mothers sought gratification through the accomplishments of their sons. As of the 1930s, these mothers were most likely to have had a nonsupportive or impaired husband, a conflicted marriage, and lofty material aspirations. In fateful ways, wartime adolescence clearly bore the imprint of Depression experiences among some Berkeley youth.

The disadvantage of growing up in a deprived household continued into the postwar years, limiting formal education among the sons of both middle- and working-class parents and shaping a life course of relatively early work, late marriage, and military service. But records show a striking reversal in life experience by the middle years. Deprived men were likely to do far better in worklife than predictions based on their education. At midlife, their occupational attainment closely resembled that of men from nondeprived families. Marriage, work, and especially the "time out" provided by military service constitute plausible turning points in the lives of deprived men. These events offered a relatively independent, maturing experience, a chance to establish their own life course with minimal intrusion by parents. Between adolescence and midlife, deprived men achieved notable developmental gains (in self-esteem, assertiveness), though not sufficient to erase completely the inadequacies of the early years. Nevertheless, life had clearly improved since childhood and adolescence. From the vantage point of middle age, deprived men were most likely to regard adolescence as the very worst time of life and the years after 30 as a high point in their life.

Comparison of the Berkeley and Oakland men is risky at best, owing to differences in sample and locale. Nevertheless, the results to date identify suggestive cohort variations in the developmental and life-course effects of Depression hardship. In both cohorts, economic deprivation produced similar changes in the family (division of labor, family relationships, social strains), but their developmental effects vary in ways that generally conform to differences in life stage relative to Depression and war. By encountering such times at different points in life, the Berkeley and Oakland men have different stories to tell about childhood, adolescence, and adulthood. Worklife played a major role in enabling men in both cohorts to surmount at least some of the handicaps associated with family deprivation. Correlated developmental gains in the Berkeley cohort provide some clues to Jean Macfarlane's observation (1963) that nearly half of the "Guidance" men turned out to be more "stable and effective adults than any of us with our differing theoretical biases would have predicted . . ." (p. 338). A large proportion of the "most outstandingly mature adults in our entire group . . . are recruited from those who were confronted with very difficult situations and whose characteristic responses during childhood and adolescence seemed to us to compound their problems" (Macfarlane, 1964, p. 121). In retrospect Macfarlane (1963) cites two sources of error in the early predictions:

1. Overweighting the presumed negative influence of pathogenic aspects of development at the expense of recognizing the maturing benefits of hardship.

2. Insufficient awareness of the potential of adult independence and late development for changing the course of lives.

Needless to say, childhood and adolescence do not make a life.

Consistent with a "perspectives" theme, we have focused this concluding section on studies that illustrate the use of archival resources for tracing the effects of historical setting and change to the life course of youth. Breadth of coverage on historical times and topics (now available in book-length surveys [Gillis, 1974; Kett, 1977]) was sacrificed for a more intensive examination of studies that have applied a life-course perspective to aspects of social change in youth experience: early industrialization and institutional change—the Hamilton study of Canadian youth between 1851 and 1871; institutional change between late-nineteenth-century America and 1970—the study by Modell and associates of change in the transition of adulthood; and the Great Depression—a longitudinal investigation of family deprivation in the life course of development of two cohorts, with birthdates in the 1920s. However flawed, these studies constitute a new venture in the historical study of youth; their publication dates (1974–1976) bear witness to the early stage of development of this approach. Knowledge cumulation is beginning to occur on youth in nineteenth-century America and earlier times, but not in the twentieth century. We have learned very little about historical forces in lives, cohorts, and institutions since the 1920s. The archives of older longitudinal studies (e.g., the Terman gifted sample, the Fels Institute sample, and Grant samples, Harvard University) remain largely untapped by efforts to assess the impact of historical times and change in the course of adolescent and life-span development. Nevertheless, even a casual glance at the literature of recent decades indicates that much has been accomplished in bringing history to the study of youth.

Overview

Dominant and emerging perspectives offer a useful base from which to view the course of inquiry on adolescence and young people since the early decades of the twentieth century. Over this time period, two perspectives, developmental and social, have shaped perceptions of adolescence, theoretical concerns, and research. Adolescence has been defined by characteristics of the maturing organism (physical, cognitive, moral); by social criteria that specify the meaning of age categories and roles; and by the relation between developmental and social timetables. By the mid to late 1960s, we see evidence of a third perspective that viewed these timetables according to historical time and change, a perspective influenced by concepts of life-span development, greater understanding of age patterns in the life course, and the growth of archival studies on social change in youth experience. Two related developments emerged from this shift toward historical considerations and constitute central themes of this chapter: (1) the integration of three traditions of research and theory (developmental, social, and historical) in a life-course framework and (2) its application to studies of youth.

As a theoretical orientation, the life course is informed by three strands of theory and research that link age and time and, by association, life history and social history:

1. Life, or developmental time, and its focus on the process of aging from birth to death—chronological or developmental age as an index of position in the aging process.

2. Social time in the age-patterning of social roles and events across multiple, interlocking career lines, which constitute the social life course.

3. Historical time, with birth-year defining location in the historical process and membership in cohorts that may vary according to composition (social, cultural, psychological), size, and ecological setting.

Renewed attention to the latter dimension in the 1960s gave fresh visibility to the interdependence of life history and social history as well as to the variable nature of psychological development and institutions in the course of social change. Three general premises in the life-course approach illustrate this perception in current research:

1. The implications of historical change vary according to the developmental and social age of individuals and cohorts at the point of change.

2. The meaning of an historical event is derived in part from the life histories that individuals and cohorts bring to the situation—from life histories influenced by social change and differential location in class, ethnic, and residential subgroups.

3. Historical conditions are variable at points in time and in whether and how they are experienced by particular individuals and cohorts.

The remarkable growth of historical studies of youth since the 1960s represents one aspect of what some have called the "new social history" on the lives of ordinary people. This work has played a major role in the evolution of a life-course perspective through documentation of historical variations and their implications for the lives of young people. Moreover, some historical research has addressed issues and employed concepts that are part of a life-course approach: the interplay of youth cohorts and social institutions under conditions of economic and demographic change; youth cohorts as both consequence and vehicle of social change; life patterns among youth in relation to family, education, and economic change; and the timing and sequencing of events in the transition from childhood to adult status. For reasons of space and theme, only a small fraction of this research has been cited or reviewed, but even such limited coverage indicates something of the utility and necessity of an approach that links social history and the life course. From research on nineteenth-century American youth, we now have a clearer notion of what is distinctive of modern adolescence; for example, the lag between physical maturity and adult independence, long attributed to modern adolescence, was at least as characteristic of late-nineteenth-century youth. Though few studies have actually traced the effects of social change on the life course of youth, the evidence at hand tends to shift the burden of proof on assumptions of "developmental invariance" to the investigator.

In closing, it is fitting to return to John Seeley's trenchant criticism of the literature on adolescence as he perceived it during the early 1970s: the absence of a "sense of history" in which adolescence constitutes a point of articulation between historical time and the ontogenetic process. This criticism is well deserved by the literature through the mid-1960s as reviewed by Elder (1968); and one might be tempted to claim that it applies to contemporary research as well—historical considerations still rarely appear in studies of youth development and groups, life styles and status attainment (see Dragastin & Elder, 1975). However, significant change toward a historical perspective has occurred since the 1960s, even apart from developments in the field of history. We now have conceptual and methodological tools for studying youth according to historical time and the life span; in addition we have an expanding body of research that has put these tools to work on data archives. In potential, if not accomplishment, these developments suggest the possibilities of a historical perspective on adolescence.

Notes

1. Two developments in psychology warrant special notice: (1) the increasing emphasis on developmental studies that investigate transactions between the growing human organism and its changing environment, as expressed by the writings of Urie Bronfenbrenner in particular (1977); and (2) the evolution of a life-span developmental psychology that is focused on the assessment of antecedent-consequent relations in behavioral development from birth to death (Baltes & Schaie, 1973). Though both developments have much in common, including a life-span orientation, they represent outgrowths of issues and problem foci that are located at opposite ends of the life-span continuum—childhood in the case of Bronfenbrenner and the adult years or old age in the case of Baltes and Schaie. Greater sociological interest in historical and social influences on human development is associated with the emergence of a life-course perspective from the study of age (see Riley, Johnson, and Foner, 1972; Elder, 1975).

2. At the time, family sociologists were preoccupied with the evolution of the family as a more specialized unit in the social structure and with the intrafamilial consequences of this change for members. In conjunction with the 1930 White House Conference on Child Health and Protection, a survey of adolescents (*The Adolescent in the Family,* 1934) obtained evidence (more favorable personality adjustment of urban than rural youth) that was used to support the assumption that "loss of certain economic and other functions from the home makes possible the more harmonious organization of family life upon a cultural and affectional basis" (p. 7). The data were too superficially analyzed to support confidence in this finding; the assumption itself is suggestive of the limitations that grand theory on family change has for understanding the dynamics of family life.

3. Symptomatic of the concern over problems in the transition to adult status is the formation of the National Commission on Resources for Youth. The commission was established in 1967 by a small group of professionals who had "long been concerned with the well-being of youth. The decision to form a small organization was made as they discussed the difficulties young people face in making a constructive transition to adult life" (Ralph Tyler in "Foreword," *New Roles for Youth in the School and Community,* National Commission on Resources for Youth, 1974, p. viii). The role of schooling in this transition has been appraised by several independent reports, including that of the Presidential Science Advisory Commission (PSAC, 1973). In *Youth Policy in Transition* (1976), Michael Timpane and associates provide a thoughtful assessment of policy recommendations from the above reports in terms of available social science evidence, its knowledge base, limitations, and unknowns.

4. After reviewing the distorted knowledge on society that we have gained from synchronic social science, Peter Laslett (1977) concludes that "we do not understand ourselves because we do not yet know what we have been and hence what we may be becoming" (p. 5). Something of this appraisal is reflected in the deliberations of an international colloquium that was convened in September 1975, on the topic of adolescence in the year 2000 (Hill & Monks, 1977). At the outset of the colloquium, the severe lag in scientific knowledge on adolescence, past and present, was recognized and the participants dealt more with preferred models of the future than with specific predictions.

References

Abrams, P. The sense of the past and the origins of sociology. *Past and Present,* 1972, 55, 18–32.
Allmendinger, D. F., Jr., *Paupers and scholars: The transformation of student life in nineteenth-century New England.* New York: St. Martin's Press, 1975.

Andersson, B. E. *Studies in adolescent behavior.* Stockholm: Almquist & Wiksell, 1969.
Ariès, P. *Centuries of childhood,* trans. R. Baldick. New York: Vintage, 1965.
Bailyn, B. *Education in the forming of American society.* Chapel Hill: University of North Carolina Press, 1960.
Baltes, P. B. Longitudinal and cross-sectional sequences in the study of age and generation effects. *Human Development,* 1968, 11, 145–171.
———. Life-span developmental psychology: Some observations on history and theory. Presidential Address, Division 20 (Adult Development and Aging), American Psychological Association, San Francisco, August 1977.
Baltes, P. B. and Schaie, K. W. *Life-span developmental psychology: Personality and socialization.* New York: Academic, 1973.
Baltes, P. B., Cornelius, S. W., and Nesselroade, J. R. Cohort effects in developmental psychology: Theoretical and methodological perspectives. In W. A. Collins (Ed.), *Minnesota Symposium on Child Psychology* (Vol. II). Minneapolis: University of Minnesota, 1977.
Barker, G. and Gump, V. *Big school, small school: High school size and student behavior.* Stanford, Calif.: Stanford University Press, 1964.
Barker, R. *Ecological psychology.* Stanford, Calif.: Stanford University Press, 1968.
Bengtson, V. L. and Laufer, R. S. (Eds.). Youth, generations, and social change (Parts 1 and 2). *Journal of Social Issues,* 1974, 30 (2), (3).
Bengtson, V. L. and Lovejoy, M. C. Values, personality, and social structure: an intergenerational analysis. *American Behavioral Scientist,* 1973, 16, 880–912.
Bengtson, V. L. and Starr, J. M. Contrast and consensus: A generational analysis of youth in the 1970s. In R. J. Havighurst and P. H. Dreyer (Eds.), *Youth* (74th Yearbook, National Society for the Study of Education). Chicago: University of Chicago Press, 1975.
Berger, B. M. *Looking for America.* Englewood Cliffs, N.J.: Prentice-Hall, 1971.
Bloomberg, S. H. The household and the family: The effects of industrialization on skilled workers in Newark, 1840–1860. Paper presented at the Organization of American Historians, Denver, 1974.
Blyth, D. A., Simmons, R. G., and Bush, D. The transition into early adolescence: A longitudinal comparison of youth in two educational contexts. Revision of paper presented at the Biennial Meeting of the Society for Research in Child Development, New Orleans, March 1977.
Bowerman, C. E. and Kinch, J. W. Changes in family and peer orientation of children between the fourth and tenth grades. *Social Forces,* 1959, 57, 206–211.
Braungart, R. G. Youth and social movements. In S. Dragastin and G. H. Elder, Jr. (Eds.), *Adolescence in the life cycle.* Washington, D.C.: Hemisphere, 1975.
Bremner, R. (Ed.). *Children and youth in America: A documentary history* (3 vols.). Cambridge: Harvard University Press, 1970–1974.
Bronfenbrenner, U. Toward an experimental ecology of human development. *American Psychologist,* 1977, 32, 513–531.
Bühler, C. The curve of life as studied in biographies. *Journal of Applied Psychology,* 1935, 19, 405–409.
Carlsmith, L. Some personality characteristics of boys separated from their fathers during World War II. *Ethos,* Winter 1973, 1, 467–477.
Clausen, J. A. The life course of individuals. In M. W. Riley, M. Johnson, and A. Foner (Eds.), *Aging and society: A sociology of age stratification.* New York: Russell Sage, 1972.
Cohen, A. K. *Delinquent boys: The culture of the gang.* Glencoe, Ill.: Free Press, 1955.
Coleman, J. S. *The adolescent society.* New York: Free Press, 1961.
Cottrell, L. S. The adjustment of the individual to his age and sex roles. *American Sociological Review,* 1942, 7, 617–620.
Davis, K. Sociology of parent-youth conflict. *American Sociological Review,* 1940, 1, 523–535.
———. Adolescence and the social structure. *The Annals of the American Academy of Political and Social Science,* 1944, 236, 8–16.
Davis, N. Z. The reasons of misrule. In *Society and Culture in Early Modern France.* Stanford, Calif.: Stanford University Press, 1975.
Demos, J. *A little commonwealth: Family life in Plymouth Colony.* New York: Oxford University Press, 1970.

Demos, J. and Demos, V. Adolescence in historical perspective. *Journal of Marriage and the Family,* 1969, 31, 632–638.

Dennis, W. The adolescent. In Leonard Carmichael (Ed.), *Manual of child pscyhology.* New York: Wiley, 1946.

Dollard, J. *Criteria for the life history.* New York: Peter Smith, 1949.

Dollard, J., Doob, L. W., Miller, N. E., Mowrer, O. H., and Sears, R. R., *Frustration and aggression.* New Haven, Conn.: Yale University Press, 1939.

Douvan, E. and Adelson, J. *The adolescent experience.* New York: Wiley, 1966.

Dragastin, S. E. and Elder, G. H., Jr. *Adolescence in the life cycle.* Washington, D.C.: Hemisphere, 1975.

Eisenstadt, S. N. *From generation to generation.* Glencoe, Ill.: Free Press, 1956.

Elder, G. H., Jr. *Adolescent socialization and personality development.* Chicago: Rand McNally, 1968.

———. *Children of the Great Depression.* University of Chicago Press, 1974.

———. Adolescence in the life cycle. In S. Dragastin and G. H. Elder, Jr. (Eds.), *Adolescence in the life cycle.* Washington, D.C.: Hemisphere, 1975a.

———. Age differentiation and the life course. In A. Inkeles (Ed.), *Annual Review of Sociology,* Palo Alto, Calif.: Annual Reviews, 1975b.

———. Approaches to social change and the family. *American Journal of Sociology,* 1978, 84. (Special supplement)

Elder G. H., Jr. and Rockwell, R. W. Economic depression and postwar opportunity in men's lives: A study of life patterns and health. In R. G. Simmons (Ed.), *Research in community and mental health.* Greenwich, Conn.: JAI Press, 1979.

Erikson, E. H. Identity and the life cycle. *Psychological Issues,* 1959, 1.

———. *Insight and responsibility.* New York: Norton, 1964.

Fendrich, J. M. Activities ten years later: A test of generational unit continuity. *Journal of Social Issues,* 1974, 30, 95–118.

Finestone, H. *Victims of change: Juvenile delinquents in American society.* Westport, Conn.: Greenwood Press, 1976.

Flacks, R. *Youth and social change.* Chicago: Markham, 1971.

Furstenberg, F. F., Jr. *Unplanned parenthood: The social consequences of teenage childbearing.* New York: Free Press, 1976.

Garbarino, J. The historical and ecological correlates of school size: Shaping the adolescent experience. Unpublished manuscript, 1977.

Gillis, J. R. *Youth and history: Tradition and change in European age relations, 1770–present.* New York: Academic, 1974.

Goldstein, J. On being an adult in secular law. *Daedalus,* Fall 1976, 105, 69–87.

Goode, W. J. A theory of role strain. *American Sociological Review,* 1960, 25, 483–496.

Gordon, C. *The social system of the high school.* Glencoe, Ill.: Free Press, 1957.

Goulet, L. R. and Baltes, P. B. *Life-span developmental psychology: Research and theory.* New York: Academic, 1970.

Greven, P. J., Jr. *Four generations: Population, land, and family in colonial Andover, Massachusetts.* Ithaca, N.Y.: Cornell University Press, 1970.

———. Comments for the panel discussion on "Change and continuity in family structure." *The Family in Historical Perspective, An International Newsletter,* No. 5, Autumn 1973, 9–11.

Grinder, R. E. The concept of adolescence in the genetic psychology of G. Stanley Hall. *Child Development,* 1969, 40, 355–369.

Hall, G. S. *Adolescence: Its psychology and its relations to physiology, anthropology, sociology, sex, crime, religion, and education.* New York: Appleton, 1904.

Hampden-Turner, C. *Radical men.* Cambridge, Mass.: Schenkman, 1970.

Hantover, J. P. Sex role, sexuality, and social status: The early years of the Boy Scouts of America. Unpublished doctoral dissertation, University of Chicago, 1976.

Hareven, T. K. Family time and industrial time: Family and work in a planned corporation town, 1900–1924. *Journal of Urban History,* 1975, 1, 365–389.

———. *Transitions: The family and the life course in historical perspective.* New York: Academic, 1978.

Heyneman, S. P. Continuing issues in adolescence: A summary of current transition to adulthood debates. *Journal of Youth and Adolescence*, 1976, 5, 309–323.

Hill, J. P. and Monks, F. J. *Adolescence and youth in prospect*. Guildford, Surrey, England: IPC Science and Technology Press, 1977.

Hill, R. *Families under stress*. New York: Harper & Brs., 1949.

Hogan, D. P. The passage of American men from family of orientation to family of procreation: Pattern, timing, and determinants. Doctoral dissertation, University of Wisconsin, 1976.

Hollingshead, A. *Elmtown's youth*. New York: Wiley, 1949.

Hollingworth, L. S. *The psychology of the adolescent*. New York: Appleton, 1928.

Huston-Stein, A. and Baltes, P. B. Theory and method in life-span developmental psychology: Implications for child development. In H. W. Reese (Ed.). *Advances in child development and behavior*. New York: Academic, 1976.

Inglehart, R. *The silent revolution: Changing values and political styles among Western publics*. Princeton, N.J.: Princeton University Press, 1977.

Jennings, K. M., Allerbeck, K., and Rosenmayr, L. Value orientations and political socialization in five countries. Paper presented at the Workshop on Political Behavior, Dissatisfaction, and Protest, Louvain-La-Nueve, April 8–14, 1976.

Jones, H. E. The adolescent growth study: I. Principles and methods, II. Procedures. *Journal of Consulting Psychology*, 1939, 3, 157–159: 177–180.

Jones, M. C., Bayley, N., Macfarlane, J. W., and Honzik, M. P. *The course of human development*. Waltham, Mass.: Xerox, 1971.

Jordan, W. D. Searching for adulthood in America. *Daedalus*, Fall 1976, 105, 1–11.

Kaestle, C. F. and Vinovskis, M. A. Education and social change in nineteenth-century Massachusetts: Quantitative studies. Final Research Report, National Institute of Education, December 1976.

Kagan, J. A conception of early adolescence. *Daedalus*, Fall 1971, 100, 997–1012.

Kandel, D. B. and Lesser, G. S. *Youth in two worlds: United States and Denmark*. San Francisco: Jossey-Bass, 1972.

Katz, M. B. *The people of Hamilton, Canada West: Family and class in a mid-nineteenth-century city*. Cambridge: Harvard University Press, 1975.

Katz, M. B. and Davey, I. F. Youth and early industrialization in a Canadian city. *American Journal of Sociology*, 1978, 84. (Special supplement)

Keniston, K. Youth as a stage of life. *American Scholar*, 1970, 39, 631–654.

———. Psychological development and historical change. *The Journal of Interdisciplinary History*, Autumn 1971, 2, 329–345.

Kett, J. F. *Rites of passage*. New York: Basic Books, 1977.

Kuhlen, R. G. Social change: A neglected factor in psychological studies of the life span. *School and Society*, 1940, 52, 14–16.

Laslett, P. Age at menarche in Europe since the eighteenth century. *The Journal of Interdisciplinary History*, 1971, 2, 221–236.

———. *Family life and illicit love in earlier generations*. New York: Cambridge University Press, 1977.

Linton, R. Age and sex categories. *American Sociological Review*, 1942, 7, 589–603.

Lipschutz, M. R. Runaways in history. *Crime and Delinquency*, 1977, 23, 321–332.

Lipset, S. M. *Rebellion in the university* (Rev. ed.). Chicago: University of Chicago Press, 1976.

Lipset, S. M. and Lowenthal, L. *Culture and social character*. New York: Free Press, 1961.

Lipsitz, J. *Growing up forgotten*. Lexington, Mass.: Lexington Books, 1977.

Little, M. and Laslett, B. Adolescence in historical perspective: The decline of boarding in 19th century Los Angeles. Paper presented at the American Sociological Meetings, Chicago, September 6, 1977.

Loewenberg, P. The psychohistorical origins of the Nazi youth cohort. *American Historical Review*, 1972, 76, 1457–1502.

Lüscher, K. Perspektiven einer soziologie der sozialisation—Die entwicklung der rolle des kindes [Towards a sociology of socialization—The development of the child's role], *Zeitschrift für Soziologie*, 1975, 4, 359–379.

Lynd, R. S. and Lynd, H. M. *Middletown*. New York: Harcourt, Brace and World, 1929.

Macfarlane, J. W. From infancy to childhood. *Childhood Education*, 1963, 39, 336–342.

———. Perspectives on personality consistency and change from the "Guidance Study." *Vita Humana*, 1964, 7, 115–126.

Magee, E. S. Impact of the war on child labor. *The Annals of the American Academy of Political and Social Science*, 1944, 236, 101–109.

Mannheim, K. The problem of generations. In P. Keckskemeti (Ed.), *Essays on the sociology of knowledge*. New York: Oxford University Press, 1952. (Originally published, 1928.)

Matza, D. Position and behavior patterns of youth. In R. Faris (Ed.), *Handbook of modern sociology*. Chicago: Rand McNally, 1964.

Mead, M. *Coming of age in Samoa*. Ann Arbor, Mich.: Morrow, 1928.

Merkl, P. H. *Political violence under the swastika*. Princeton, N.J.: Princeton University Press, 1975.

Meyer, J. W., Tyack, D., Nagel. J., and Gordon, A. Education as nation-building in America: Enrollments and bureaucratization in the American States, 1870–1930. Unpublished research paper, Boys Town Center, Stanford University, 1977.

Modell, J., Furstenberg, F. F., Jr., and Hershberg, T. Social change and the transition to adulthood in historical perspective. *Journal of Family History*, Autumn 1976, 1, 7–32.

Modell, J., Furstenberg, F. F., Jr., and Strong, D. The timing of marriage in the transition to adulthood: Continuity and change, 1860–1975. *American Journal of Sociology*, 1978, 84. (Special supplement)

Moller, H. Youth as a force in the modern world. *Comparative Studies in Society and History*, 1968, 10, 237–260.

Musgrove, F. *Youth and the social order*. Bloomington: Indiana University Press, 1965.

Muus, R. *Theories of Adolescence* (3rd ed.). New York: Random House, 1975.

National Commission on Resources for Youth. *New roles for youth in the school and community*. New York: Citation Press, 1974.

National Society for the Study of Education (NSSE). *Adolescence*. (43rd Yearbook, National Society for the Study of Education.) Chicago: University of Chicago Press, 1944.

———. In R. J. Havighurst and P. H. Dreyer (Eds.), *Youth*. (74th Yearbook, National Society for the Study of Education.) Chicago: University of Chicago Press, 1975.

Nelson, E. A. and Maccoby, E. E. The relationships between social development and differential abilities on the Scholastic Aptitude Test. *Merrill-Palmer Quarterly*, 1966, 12, 269–284.

Nesselroade, J. R. and Baltes, P. B. Adolescent personality development and historical change: 1970–1972. *Monographs of the Society for Research in Child Development*, 1974, 39 (1, Serial No. 154).

Neugarten, B. L., Moore, J. W., and Lowe, J. C. Age norms, age constraints, and adult socialization. *American Journal of Sociology*, 1965, 70, 710–717.

Parsons, T. Age and sex in the social structure of the United States. *American Sociological Review*, 1942, 7, 604–616.

———. *Social structure and personality*. New York: Free Press, 1964.

Parsons, T. and Platt, G. M. Higher education and changing socialization. In M. W. Riley, M. E. Johnson, and A. Foner (Eds.), *Aging and society: A sociology of age stratification*. New York: Russell Sage, 1972.

Plath, D. W. and Ikeda, K. After coming of age: Adult awareness of age norms. In T. R. Williams (Ed.), *Socialization and communication in primary groups*. The Hague: Mouton, 1975.

Platt, A. *The child-savers: The invention of delinquency*. Chicago: University of Chicago Press, 1969.

Presidential Science Advisory Commission, Panel on Youth. *Youth: Transition to adulthood*. Washington, D.C.: U.S. Government Printing Office, 1973.

Riesman, D. (with Glazer, N. and Denney, R.). *The lonely crowd*. New Haven, Conn.: Yale University Press, 1950.

———. *The lonely crowd*. New Haven, Conn.: Yale University Press, 1961. [Abridged edition with new preface]

Riley, M. W., Johnson, M. E., and Foner, A. *Aging and society: A sociology of age stratification*. New York: Russell Sage, 1972.

Ross, D. G. *Stanley Hall: The psychologist as prophet*. Chicago: University of Chicago Press, 1972.

Rothman, D.J. Documents in search of a historian: Toward a history of childhood and youth in

America. (Review of *Children and youth in America: A documentary history,* R. H. Bremner, Ed.) *The Journal of Interdisciplinary History,* Autumn 1971, 2, 367–377.

Ryder, N. B. The cohort as a concept in the study of social change. *American Sociological Review,* 1965, 30, 843–861.

Schaie, K. W. A general model for the study of developmental problems. *Psychological Bulletin,* 1965, 64, 92–107.

Schlossman, S. L. *Love and the American delinquent.* Chicago: University of Chicago Press, 1977.

Scott, J. W. and El-Assal, M. Multiversity, university size, university quality, and student protest: An empirical study. *American Sociological Review,* 1969, 34, 202–209.

Scully, M. G. Student protest in Europe: The motive is "fear." *The Chronicle of Higher Education,* April 4, 1977, p. 9.

Sears, R. R. Your ancients revisited: A history of child development. In E. Mavis Hetherington (Ed.), *Review of child development research.* Chicago: University of Chicago Press, 1975.

Seeley, J. R. Adolescence: The management of emancipation in history and life history. H. Silverstein (Ed.), *The sociology of youth.* New York: Macmillan, 1973.

Skolnick, A. The limits of childhood: Conceptions of child development and social context. *Law and Contemporary Problems,* Summer 1975, 39, 38–77.

Smith, D. S. Parental power and marriage patterns: An analysis of historical trends in Hingham, Mass. *Journal of Marriage and the Family,* 1973, 35, 419–428.

Smith, D. S. and Hindus, M. S. Premarital pregnancy in America 1640–1971: An overview and interpretation. *Journal of Interdisciplinary History,* Spring 1975, 5, 537–570.

Stinchcombe, A. L. *Rebellion in a high school.* Chicago: Quadrangle, 1964.

Stolz, L. *Father relations of war-born children.* Stanford, Calif.: Stanford University Press, 1954.

Tanner, J. M. *Growth and adolescence* (2nd ed.). Springfield, Ill.: Thomas, 1962.

Thernstrom, S. Yankee city revisited: The perils of historical naivete. *American Sociological Review,* 1965, 30, 234–242.

Thomas, W. I. and Znaniecki, F. *The Polish peasant in Europe and America* (Vols. 1 and 2). Chicago: University of Chicago Press, 1918–1920.

Timpane, M., Abramowitz, S., Bobrow, S. B., and Pascal, A. *Youth policy in transition.* Santa Monica, Calif.: Rand Corporation, 1976.

Trow, M. The second transformation of American secondary education. *International Journal of Comparative Sociology,* 1961, 2, 144–166.

Turner, R. H. *The social context of ambition.* San Francisco: Chandler, 1964.

Tyack, D. B. *The one best system: A history of American urban education.* Cambridge: Harvard University Press, 1975.

Waller, W. *The sociology of teaching.* New York: Wiley, 1965. (Originally published, 1932.)

White House Conference on Child Health and Protection. *The adolescent in the family.* New York: Appleton-Century, 1934.

Winsborough, H. H. Statistical histories of the life cycle of birth cohorts: The transition from schoolboy to adult male. Paper presented at the Conference on Social Demography, University of Wisconsin, Madison, July 15–16, 1975.

———. The transition from schoolboy to adult: Accounting for change in the process. Paper presented to a Seminar on "The Life Cycle as a Demographic Perspective," at the Annual Meeting of the Population Association of America, Montreal, Canada, April 1976.

Yankelovich, D. *The new morality: A profile of American youth in the 70s.* New York: McGraw-Hill, 1974.

Zachry, C. Preparing youth to be adults. In *Adolescence.* (43rd Yearbook of the National Society for the Study of Education, Part I.) Chicago: University of Chicago Press, 1944.

2. Archetypal Patterns of Youth

Youth constitutes a universal phenomenon. It is first of all a biological phenomenon, but one always defined in cultural terms. In this sense it constitutes a part of a wider cultural phenomenon, the varying definitions of age and of the differences between one age and another.[1] Age and age differences are among the basic aspects of life and the determinants of human destiny. Every human being passes through various ages, and at each one he attains and uses different biological and intellectual capacities. At each stage he performs different tasks and roles in relation to the other members of his society: from a child, he becomes a father; from a pupil, a teacher; from a vigorous youth, a mature adult, and then an aging and "old" man.

This gradual unfolding of power and capacity is not merely a universal, biologically conditioned, and inescapable fact. Although the basic biological processes of maturation (within the limits set by such factors as relative longevity) are probably more or less similar in all human societies, their cultural definition varies from society to society, at least in details. In all societies, age serves as a basis for defining the cultural and social characteristic of human beings, for the formation of some of their mutual relations and common activities, and for the differential allocation of social roles.

The cultural definitions of age and age differences contain several different yet complementary elements. First, these definitions often refer to the social division of labor in a society, to the criteria according to which people occupy various social positions and roles within any society. For instance, in many societies certain roles—especially those of married men, full citizens, independent earners—are barred to young people, while others—as certain military roles—are specifically allocated to them. Second, the cultural definition of age is one important constituent of a person's self-identity, his self-perception in terms of his own psychological needs and aspirations, his place in society, and the ultimate meaning of his life.

Within any such definition, the qualities of each age are evaluated according to their relation to some basic, primordial qualities, such as vigor, physical and sexual prowess, the ability to cope with material, social, and supernatural environment, wisdom, experience, or divine inspiration. Different ages are seen in different societies as the embodiments of such qualities. These various qualities seem to unfold from one age to another, each age emphasizing some out of the whole panorama of such possible qualities. The cultural definition of an age span is always a broad definition of human potentialities, limitations, and obligations at a given stage of life. In terms of these definitions, people

S. N. Eisenstadt, "Archetypal Patterns of Youth," *Daedalus* 90 (1961). Reprinted by permission of *Daedalus,* Journal of the American Academy of Arts and Sciences, "Youth: Change and Challenge," 90, 1961, Boston, Massachusetts.

map out the broad contours of life, their own expectations and possibilities, and place themselves and their fellow men in social and cultural positions, ascribing to each a given place within these contours.

The various qualities attributed to different ages do not constitute an unconnected series. They are usually interconnected in many ways. The subtle dialectics between the unfolding of some qualities and the waning of others in a person is not a mere registration of his psychological or biological traits; rather, it constitutes the broad framework of his potentialities and their limits throughout his life span. The characteristics of any one "age," therefore, cannot be fully understood except in relation to those of other ages. Whether seen as a gradually unfolding continuum or as a series of sharp contrasts and opposed characteristics, they are fully explicable and understandable only in terms of one another. The boy bears within himself the seeds of the adult man; else, he must as an adult acquire new patterns of behavior, sharply and intentionally opposed to those of his boyhood. The adult either develops naturally into an old man—or decays into one. Only when taken together do these different "ages" constitute the entire map of human possibilities and limitations; and, as every individual usually must pass through them all, their complementariness and continuity (even if defined in discontinuous and contrasting terms) become strongly emphasized and articulated.

The same holds true for the age definitions of the two sexes, although perhaps with a somewhat different meaning. Each age span is defined differently for either sex, and these definitions are usually related and complementary, as the "sexual image" and identity always constitute basic elements of man's image in every society. This close connection between different ages necessarily stresses the problem of transition from one point in a person's life to another as a basic constituent of any cultural definition of an "age." Hence, each definition of age must necessarily cope with the perception of time, and changes in time, of one's own progress in time, one's transition from one period of life to another.

This personal transition, or temporal progress, or change, may become closely linked with what may be called cosmic and societal time.[2] The attempt to find some meaning in personal temporal transition may often lead to identification with the rhythms of nature or history, with the cycles of the seasons, with the unfolding of some cosmic plan (whether cyclical, seasonal, or apocalyptic), or with the destiny and development of society. The nature of this linkage often constitutes the focus round which an individual's personal identity becomes defined in cultural terms and through which personal experience, with its anguish, may be given some meaning in terms of cultural symbols and values.

The whole problem of age definition and the linkage of personal time and transition with cosmic time become especially accentuated in that age span usually designated as youth. However great the differences among various societies, there is one focal point within the life span of an individual which in most known societies is to some extent emphasized: the period of youth, of transition from childhood to full adult status, or full membership in the society. In this period the individual is no longer a child (especially from the physical and sexual point of view) but is ready to undertake many attributes of an adult and to fulfill adult roles. But he is not yet fully acknowledged as an adult, a full member of the society. Rather, he is being "prepared," or is preparing himself for such adulthood.

This image of youth—the cultural definition of youth—contains all the crucial elements of any definition of age, usually in an especially articulated way. This is the stage at which the individual's personality acquires the basic psychological mechanism of self-regulation and self-control, when his self-identity becomes crystallized. It is also the stage at which the young are confronted with some models of the major roles they are supposed to emulate in adult life and with the major symbols and values of their culture and community. Moreover, in this phase the problem of the linkage of the personal temporal transition with cosmic or societal time becomes extremely acute. Any cultural definition of youth describes it as a transitory phase, couched in terms of transition toward something new, something basically different from the past. Hence the acuteness of the problem of linkage.

The very emphasis on the transitory nature of his stage and of its essentially preparatory character, however, may easily create a somewhat paradoxical situation. It may evolve an image of youth as the purest manifestation and repository of ultimate cultural and societal values. Such an image is rooted first in the fact that to some extent youth is always defined as a period of "role moratorium," that is, as a period in which one may play with various roles without definitely choosing any. It does not yet require the various compromises inherent in daily participation in adult life. At the same time, however, since it is also the period when the maximum identification with the values of the society is stressed, under certain conditions it may be viewed as the repository of all the major human virtues and primordial qualities. It may then be regarded as the only age in which full identification with the ultimate values and symbols of the society is attained—facilitated by the flowering of physical vigor, a vigor which may easily become identified with a more general flowering of the cosmos or the society.

The fullest, the most articulate and definitive expression of these archetypal elements of youth is best exemplified in the ritual dramatization of the transition from adolescence to adulthood, such as the various *rites de passage* and ceremonies of initiation in primitive tribes and in ancient civilizations.[3] In these rites the pre-adult youth are transformed into full members of the tribe. This transformation is effected through:

1. a series of rites in which the adolescents are symbolically divested of the characteristics of youth and invested with those of adulthood, from a sexual and social point of view; this investment, which has deep emotional significance, may have various concrete manifestations: bodily mutilation, circumcision, the taking on of a new name or symbolic rebirth;

2. the complete symbolic separation of the male adolescents from the world of their youth, especially from their close attachment to their mothers; in other words, their complete "male" independence and image are fully articulated (the opposite usually holds true of girls' initiations);

3. the dramatization of the encounter between the several generations, a dramatization that may take the form of a fight or a competition, in which the basic complementariness of various age grades—whether of a continuous or discontinuous type—is stressed; quite often the discontinuity between adolescence and adulthood is symbolically expressed, as in the symbolic death of the adolescents as children and their rebirth as adults.

4. the transmission of the tribal lore with its instructions about proper behavior, both through formalized teaching and through various ritual activities; this transmission is combined with:

5. a relaxation of the concrete control of the adults over the erstwhile adolescents and its substitution by self-control and adult responsibility.

Most of these dramatic elements can also be found, although in somewhat more diluted forms, in various traditional folk festivals in peasant communities, especially those such as rural carnivals in which youth and marriage are emphasized. In an even more diluted form, these elements may be found in various spontaneous initiation ceremonies of the fraternities and youth groups in modern societies.[4] Here, however, the full dramatic articulation of these elements is lacking, and their configuration and organization assume different forms.

The transition from childhood and adolescence to adulthood, the development of personal identity, psychological autonomy and self-regulation, the attempt to link personal temporal transition to general cultural images and to cosmic rhythms, and to link psychological maturity to the emulation of definite role models—these constitute the basic elements of any archetypal image of youth. However, the ways in which these various elements become crystallized in concrete configurations differ greatly from society to society and within sectors of the same society. The full dramatic articulation of these elements in the *rites de passage* of primitive societies constitutes only one—perhaps the most extreme and articulate but certainly not the only—configuration of these archetypal elements of youth.

In order to understand other types of such configurations, it is necessary to analyze some conditions that influence their development. Perhaps the best starting point is the nature of the social organization of the period of adolescence: the process of transition from childhood to adulthood, the social context in which the process of growing up is shaped and structured. There are two major criteria that shape the social organization of the period of youth. One is the extent to which age in general and youth in particular form a criterion for the allocation of roles in a society, whether in politics, in economic or cultural activity—aside from the family, of course, in which they always serve as such a criterion. The second is the extent to which any society develops specific age groups, specific corporate organizations, composed of members of the same "age," such as youth movements or old men's clubs. If roles are allocated in a society according to age, this greatly influences the extent to which age constitutes a component of a person's identity. In such cases, youth becomes a definite and meaningful phase of transition in an individual's progress through life, and his budding self-identity acquires content and a relation to role models and cultural values. No less important to the concrete development of identity is the extent to which it is influenced, either by the common participation of different generations in the same group as in the family, or conversely by the organization of members of the same age groups into specific, distinct groups.

The importance of age as a criterion for allocating roles in a society is closely related to several major aspects of social organization and cultural orientation. The first aspect is the relative complexity of the division of labor. In general, the simpler the organization of the society, the more influential age will be as a criterion for allocating roles. Therefore, in primitive or traditional societies (or in the more primitive and traditional sectors of developed societies) age and seniority constitute basic criteria for allocating social, economic, and political roles.

The second aspect consists of the major value orientations and symbols of a society, especially the extent to which they emphasize certain general orientations, qualities, or types of activity (such as physical vigor, the maintenance of cultural tradition, the achievement and maintenance of supernatural prowess) which can be defined in terms of broad human qualities and which become expressed and symbolized in specific ages.

The emphasis on any particular age as a criterion for the allocation of roles is largely related to the concrete application of the major value orientations in a society. For instance, we find that those primitive societies in which military values and orientations prevail emphasize young adulthood as the most important age, while those in which sedentary activities prevail emphasize older age. Similarly, within some traditional societies, a particular period such as old age may be emphasized if it is seen as the most appropriate one for expressing major cultural values and symbols—for instance, the upholding of a given cultural tradition.

The social and cultural conditions that determine the extent to which specific age groups and youth groups develop differ from the conditions that determine the extent to which age serves as a criterion for the allocation of roles. At the same time, the two kinds of conditions may be closely related, as we shall see. Age groups in general and youth groups in particular tend to arise in those societies in which the family or kinship unit cannot ensure (it may even impede) the attainment of full social status on the part of its members. These conditions appear especially (although not uniquely[5]) in societies in which family or kinship groups do not constitute the basic unit of the social division of labor. Several features characterize such societies. First, the membership in the total society (citizenship) is not defined in terms of belonging to any such family, kinship group, or estate, nor is it mediated by such a group.

Second, in these societies the major political, economic, social, and religious functions are performed not by family or kinship units but rather by various specialized groups (political parties, occupational associations, etc.), which individuals may join irrespective of their family, kinship, or caste. In these societies, therefore, the major roles that adults are expected to perform in the wider society differ in orientation from those of the family or kinship group. The children's identification and close interaction with family members of other ages does not assure the attainment of full self-identity and social maturity on the part of the children. In these cases, there arises a tendency for peer groups to form, especially youth groups; these can serve as a transitory phase between the world of childhood and the adult world.

This type of the social division of labor is found in varying degrees in different societies, primitive, historical, or modern. In several primitive tribes such a division of labor has existed,[6] for example, in Africa, among the chiefless (segmentary) tribes of Nandi, Masai, or Kipsigis, in the village communities of Yako and Ibo, or in more centralized kingdoms of the Zulu and Swazi, and among some of the Indian tribes of the Plains, as well as among some South American and Indian tribes.

Such a division of labor likewise existed to some extent in several historical societies (especially in city states such as Athens or Rome), although most great historical civilizations were characterized mainly by a more hierarchical and ascriptive system of the division of labor, in which there were greater continuity and harmony between the family and kinship groups and the broader institutional contexts. The fullest development of this type of the social division of labor, however, is to be found in modern industrial societies. Their inclusive membership is usually based on the universal criterion of citizenship and is not conditioned by membership in any kinship group. In these societies the family does not constitute a basic unit of the division of labor, especially not in production and distribution, and even in the sphere of consumption its functions become more limited. Occupations are not transmitted through heredity. Similarly, the family or kinship group does not constitute a basic unit of political or ritual activities. Moreover, the general scope of the activities of the family has been continuously diminishing, while various specialized agencies tend to take over its functions in the fields of education and recreation.

To be sure, the extent to which the family is diminishing in modern societies is often exaggerated. In many social spheres (neighborhood, friendship, informal association, some class relations, community relations), family, kinship, and status are still very influential. But the scope of these relations is more limited in modern societies than in many others, even if the prevalent myth of the disappearance of the family has long since been exploded. The major social developments of the nineteenth century (the establishment of national states, the progress of the industrial revolution, the great waves of intercontinental migrations) have greatly contributed to this diminution of scope, and especially in the first phase of modernization there has been a growing discontinuity between the life of the children, whether in the family or the traditional school and in the social world with its new and enlarged perspectives.

Youth groups tend to develop in all societies in which such a division of labor exists. Youth's tendency to coalesce in such groups is rooted in the fact that participation in the family became insufficient for developing full identity or full social maturity, and that the roles learned in the family did not constitute an adequate basis for developing such identity and participation. In the youth groups the adolescent seeks some framework for the development and crystallization of his identity, for the attainment of personal autonomy, and for his effective transition into the adult world.

Various types of youth organizations always tend to appear with the transition from traditional or feudal societies to modern societies, along with the intensified processes of change, especially in periods of rapid mobility, migration, urbanization, and industrialization. This is true of all European societies, and also of non-Western societies. The impact of Western civilization on primitive and historical-traditional peoples is usually connected with the disruption of family life, but beyond this it also involves a change in the mutual evaluation of the different generations. The younger generation usually begin to seek a new self-identification, and in one phase or another this search is expressed in ideological conflict with the older.

Most of the nationalistic movements in the Middle East, Asia, and Africa have consisted of young people, students, or officers who rebelled against their elders and the traditional familistic setting with its stress on the latters' authority. At the same time there usually has developed a specific youth consciousness and ideology that intensifies the nationalistic movement to "rejuvenate" the country.

The emergence of the peer group among immigrant children is a well-known phenomenon that usually appears in the second generation. It occurs mainly because of the relative breakdown of immigrant family life in the new country. The more highly industrialized and urbanized that country (or the sector absorbing the immigrants) is, the sharper the breakdown. Hence, the family of the immigrant or second-generation child has often been an adequate guide to the new society. The immigrant child's attainment of full identity in the new land is usually related to how much he has been able to detach himself from his older, family setting. Some of these children, therefore, have developed a strong predisposition to join various peer groups. Such an affiliation has sometimes facilitated their transition to the absorbing society by stressing the values and patterns of behavior in that society—or, on the contrary, it may express their rebellion against this society, or against their older setting.

All these modern social developments and movements have given rise to a great variety of youth groups, peer groups, youth movements, and what has been called youth culture. The types and concrete forms of such groups varies widely: spontaneous youth groups, student movements, ideological and semipolitical movements, and youth rebellions connected with the Romantic movement in Europe, and, later, with the German youth movements. The various social and national trends of the nineteenth and twentieth centuries have also given impetus to such organizations. At the same time there have appeared many adult-sponsored youth organizations and other agencies springing out of the great extension of educational institutions. In addition to providing recreative facilities, these agencies have also aimed at character molding and the instilling of civic virtues, so as to deepen social consciousness and widen the social and cultural horizon. The chief examples are the YMCA, the Youth Brigades organized in England by William Smith, the Boy Scouts, the Jousters in France, and the many kinds of community organizations, hostels, summer camps, or vocational guidance centers.

Thus we see that there are many parallels between primitive and historical societies and modern societies with regard to the conditions under which the various constellations of youth groups, youth activities, and youth images have developed. But these parallels are only partial. Despite certain similarities, the specific configurations of the basic archetypal elements of the youth image in modern societies differ greatly from those of primitive and traditional societies. The most important differences are rooted in the fact that in the modern, the development of specific youth organizations is paradoxically connected with the weakening of the importance of age in general and youth in particular as definite criteria for the allocation of roles in society.

As we have already said, the extent to which major occupational, cultural, or political roles are allocated today according to the explicit criterion of age is very small. Most such roles are achieved according to wealth, acquired skills, specialization, and knowledge. Family background may be of great importance for the acquisition of these attributes, but very few positions are directly given people by virtue of their family standing. Yet this very weakening of the importance of age is always connected with intensive developments of youth groups and movements. This fact has several interesting repercussions on the organization and structure of such groups. In primitive and traditional societies, youth groups are usually part of a wider organization of age groups that covers a very long period of life, from childhood to late adulthood and even old age. To be sure, it is during youth that most of the dramatic elements of the transition from one age to another are manifest, but this stage constitutes only part of a longer series of continuous, well-defined stages.

From this point of view, primitive or traditional societies do not differ greatly from those in which the transition from youth to adulthood is not organized in specific age groups but is largely effected within the fold of the family and kinship groups. In both primitive and traditional societies we observe a close and comprehensive linkage between personal temporal transition and societal or cosmic time, a linkage most fully expressed in the *rites de passage*. Consequently, the transition from childhood to adulthood in all such societies is given full meaning in terms of ultimate cultural values and symbols borne or symbolized by various adult role models.

In modern societies the above picture greatly changes. The youth group, whatever its composition or organization, usually stands alone. It does not constitute a part of a fully institutionalized and organized series of age groups. It is true that in many of the more traditional sectors of modern societies the more primitive or traditional archetypes of youth still prevail. Moreover, in many modern societies elements of the primitive archetypes of youth still exist. But the full articulation of these elements is lacking, and the social organization and self-expression of youth are not given full legitimation or meaning in terms of cultural values and rituals.

The close linkage between the growth of personality, psychological maturation, and definite role models derived from the adult world has become greatly weakened. Hence the very coalescence of youth into special groups only tends to emphasize their problematic, uncertain standing from the point of view of cultural values and symbols. This has created a new constellation of the basic archetypal elements of youth. This new constellation can most clearly be seen in what has been called the emergence of the problems and stresses of adolescence in modern societies. While some of these stresses are necessarily common to adolescence in all societies, they become especially acute in modern societies.

Among these stresses the most important are the following: first, the bodily development of the adolescent constitutes a constant problem to him (or her). Since social maturity usually lags behind biological maturity, the bodily changes of puberty are not usually given a full cultural, normative meaning, and their evaluation is one of the adolescent's main concerns. The difficulty inherent in attaining legitimate sexual outlets and relations at this period of growth makes these problems even more acute. Second, the adolescent's orientation toward the main values of his society is also beset with difficulties. Owing to the long period of preparation and the relative segregation of the children's world from that of the adults, the main values of the society are necessarily presented to the child and adolescent in a highly selective way, with a strong idealistic emphasis. The relative unreality of these values as presented to the children—which at the same time are not given full ritual and symbolic expressions—creates among the adolescents a great potential uncertainty and ambivalence toward the adult world.

This ambivalence is manifest, on the one hand, in a striving to communicate with the adult world and receive its recognition; on the other hand, it appears in certain dispositions to accentuate the differences between them and the adults and to oppose the various roles allocated to them by the adults. While they orient themselves to full participation in the adult world and its values, they usually attempt also to communicate with this world in a distinct, special way.

Parallel developments are to be found in the ideologies of modern youth groups. Most of these tend to create an ideology that emphasizes the discontinuity between youth and adulthood and the uniqueness of the youth period as the purest embodiment of ultimate social and cultural values. Although the explicitness of this ideology varies in extent from one sector of modern society to another, its basic elements are prevalent in almost all modern youth groups.

These processes have been necessarily accentuated in modern societies by the specific developments in cultural orientations in general and in the conception of time that has evolved in particular. The major social developments in modern societies have weakened the importance of broad cultural qualities as criteria for the allocation of roles. Similarly, important changes in the conception of time that is prevalent in modern societies have occurred. Primordial (cosmic-mythical, cyclical, or apocalyptical) conceptions of time have become greatly weakened, especially in their bearing on daily activities. The mechanical conception of time of modern technology has become much more prevalent. Of necessity this has greatly weakened the possibility of the direct ritual links between personal temporal changes and cosmic or societal progression. Therefore, the exploration of the actual meaning of major cultural values in their relation to the reality of the social world becomes one of the adolescent's main problems. This exploration may lead in many directions—cynicism, idealistic youth rebellion, deviant ideology and behavior, or a gradual development of a balanced identity.

Thus we see how all these developments in modern societies have created a new constellation of the basic archetypal elements of youth and the youth image. The two main characteristics of this constellation are the weakened possibility of directly linking the development of personality and the personal temporal transition with cosmic and societal time, on the other hand, and with the clear role models derived from the adult world, on the other.

In terms of personality development, this situation has created a great potential insecurity and the possible lack of a clear definition of personal identity. Yet it has also created the possibility of greater personal autonomy and flexibility in the choice of roles and the commitment to different values and symbols. In general, the individual, in his search for the meaning of his personal transition, has been thrown much more on his own powers.

These processes have provided the framework within which the various attempts to force youth's identity and activities—both on the part of youth itself and on the part of various educational agencies—have developed. These attempts may take several directions. Youth's own activities and attempts at self-expression may first develop in the direction of considerable autonomy in the choice of roles and in commitment to various values. Conversely, they may develop in the direction of a more complete, fully organized and closed ideology connected with a small extent of personal autonomy. Second, these attempts may differ greatly in their emphasis on the direct linkage of cultural values to a specific social group and their view of these groups as the main bearers of such values.

In a parallel sense, attempts have been made on the part of various educational agencies to create new types of youth organizations within which youth can forge its identity and become linked to adult society. The purpose of such attempts has been twofold: to provide youth with opportunities to develop a reasonably autonomous personality and a differentiated field of activity; and to encompass youth fully within well-organized groups set up by adult society and to provide them with full, unequivocal role models and symbols of identification. The interaction between these different tendencies of youth and the attempts of adult society to provide various frameworks for youth activities has given rise to the major types of youth organizations, movements, and ideologies manifested in modern societies.

These various trends and tendencies have created a situation in which, so far as we can ascertain, the number of casualties among youth has become very great—probably relatively much greater than in other types of societies. Youth's search for identity, for finding some place of its own in society, and its potential difficulties in coping with the attainment of such identity have given rise to the magnified extent of the casualties observed in the numerous youth delinquents of varying types. These failures, however, are not the only major youth developments in modern societies, although their relatively greater number is endemic in modern conditions. Much more extensive are the more positive attempts of youth to force its own identity, to find some meaningful way of defining its place in the social and cultural context and of connecting social and political values with personal development in a coherent and significant manner.

The best example in our times of the extreme upsurge of specific youth consciousness is seen in the various revolutionary youth movements. They range from the autonomous free German youth movements to the less spectacular youth movements in Central Europe and also to some extent to the specific youth culture of various more flexible youth groups. Here the attempt has been made to overcome the dislocation between personal transition and societal and cultural time. It is in these movements that the social dynamics of modern youth has found its fullest expression. It is in them that dreams of a new life, a new society, freedom and spontaneity, a new humanity and aspirations to social and cultural change have found utterance. It is in these youth movements that the forging of youth's new social identity has become closely connected with the development of new symbols of collective identity or new social-cultural symbols and meanings.

These movements have aimed at changing many aspects of the social and cultural life of their respective societies. They have depicted the present in a rather shabby form; they have dubbed it with adjectives of materialism, restriction, exploitation, lack of opportunity for self-fulfillment and creativity. At the same time they have held out hope for the future—seemingly, the not very far off future—when both self-fulfillment and collective fulfillment can be achieved and the materialistic civilization of the adult world can be shaken off. They have tried to appeal to youth to forge its own self-identity in terms of these new collective symbols, and this is why they have been so attractive to youth, for whom they have provided a set of symbols, hopes, and aims to which to direct its activities.

Within these movements the emphasis has been on a given social group or collectivity—nation, class, or the youth group itself—as the main, almost exclusive bearer of the "good" cultural value and symbols. Indeed, youth has at times been upheld as the sole and pure bearer of cultural values and social creativity. Through its association with these movements, youth has also been able to connect its aspiration for a different personal future, its anxiety to escape the present through plans and hopes for a different future within its cultural or social setting.

These various manifestations have played a crucial part in the emergence of social movements and parties in modern societies. Student groups have been the nuclei of the most important nationalistic and revolutionary movements in Central and Eastern Europe, in Italy, Germany, Hungary, and Russia. They have also played a significant role in Zionism and in the various waves of immigration to Israel. Their influence has become enormous in various fields, not only political and educational but cultural in general. In a way, education itself has tended to become a social movement. Many schools and universities, many teachers, have been among the most important bearers of collective values. The very spread of education is often seen as a means by which a new epoch might be ushered in.

The search for some connection between the personal situation of youth and social-cultural values has also stimulated the looser youth groups in modern societies, especially in the United States, and to some extent in Europe as well—though here the psychological meaning of the search is somewhat different. The looser youth groups have often shared some of the characteristics of the more defined youth movements, and they too have developed an emphasis on the attainment of social and cultural change. The yearning for a different personal future has likewise become connected with aspirations for changing the cultural setting, but not necessarily through a direct political or organized expression. They are principally important as a strong link with various collective, artistic, and literary aspirations aimed at changing social and cultural life. As such they are affiliated with various cultural values and symbols, not with any exclusive social groups. Thus they have necessarily developed a much greater freedom in choice of roles and commitment to values.

Specific social conditions surround the emergence of all these youth groups. In general, they are associated with a breakdown of traditional settings, the onset of modernization, urbanization, secularization, and industrialization. The less organized, more spontaneous types of youth organization and the more flexible kind of youth consciousness arise when the transition has been relatively smooth and gradual, especially in societies whose basic collective identity and political framework evince a large degree of continuity and a slow process of modernization. On the other hand, the more intensive types of youth movements tend to develop in those societies and periods in which the onset of modernization is connected with great upheavals and sharp cleavages in the social structure and the structure of authority and with the breakdown of symbols of collective identity.

In the latter situation the adult society has made many efforts to organize youth in what may be called totalistic organizations, in which clear role models and values might be set before youth and in which the extent of choice allowed youth is very limited and the manifestations of personal spontaneity and autonomy are restricted. Both types of conditions appeared in various European societies and in the United States in the nineteenth and early twentieth centuries, and in Asian and African societies in the second half of the twentieth century. The relative predominance of each of these conditions varies in different periods in these societies. However, with the progress of modernization and the growing absorption of broad masses within the framework of society, the whole basic setting of youth in modern society has changed—and it is this new framework that is predominant today and in which contemporary youth problems are shaped and played out.

The change this new framework represents is to some extent common both to the fully organized totalistic youth movements and to the looser youth groups. It is connected mainly with the institutionalizing of the aims and values toward the realization of which these movements were oriented, with the acceptance of such youth organizations as part of the structure of the general educational and cultural structure of their societies.

In Russia youth movements became fully institutionalized through the organization of the Komsomol. In many European countries the institutionalizing of youth groups, agencies, and ideologies came through association with political parties, or through acceptance as part of the educational system—an acceptance that sometimes entailed supervision by the official authorities. In the United States, many (such as the Boy Scouts) have become an accepted part of community life and to some extent a symbol of differential social status. In many Asian and African countries, organized youth movements have become part of the nationalistic movements and, independence won, have become part of the official educational organizations.

This institutionalizing of the values of youth movements in education and community life has been part of a wider process of institutionalizing various collective values. In some countries this has come about through revolution; in others, as a result of a long process of political and social evolution.

From the point of view of our analysis, these processes have had several important results. They have introduced a new element into the configuration of the basic archetypal elements of youth. The possibility of linking personal transition both to social groups and to cultural values—so strongly emphasized in the youth movements and noticeable to some extent even in the looser youth culture—has become greatly weakened. The social and sometimes even the cultural dimension of the future may thus become flattened and emptied. The various collective values become transformed. Instead of being remote goals resplendent with romantic dreams, they have become mundane objectives of the present, with its shabby details of daily politics and administrations. More often than not they are intimately connected with the processes of bureaucratization.

All these mutations are associated with a notable decline in ideology and in preoccupation with ideology among many of the groups and strata in modern societies, with a general flattening of political-ideological motives and a growing apathy to them. This decline in turn is connected with what has been called the spiritual or cultural shallowness of the new social and economic benefits accruing from the welfare state—an emptiness illustrated by the fact that all these benefits are in the nature of things administered not by spiritual or social leaders but, as Stephen Toulmin has wittily pointed out, "the assistant postmaster." As a consequence, we observe the emptiness and meaninglessness of social relations, so often described by critics of the age of consumption and mass society.

In general, these developments have brought about the flattening of the image of the societal future and have deprived it of its allure. Between present and future there is no ideological discontinuity. The present has become the more important, if not the more meaningful, because the future has lost its characteristic as a dimension different from the present. Out of these conditions has grown what Riesman has called the cult of immediacy. Youth has been robbed, therefore, of the full experience of the dramatic transition from adolescence to adulthood and of the dramatization of the difference between present and future. Their own changing personal future has become dissociated from any changes in the shape of their societies or in cultural activities and values.

Paradoxically enough, these developments have often been connected with a strong adulation of youth—an adulation, however, which was in a way purely instrumental. The necessity of a continuous adjustment to new changing conditions has emphasized the potential value of youth as the bearers of continuous innovation, of noncommitment to any specific conditions and values. But such an emphasis is often couched in terms of a purely instrumental adaptability, beyond which there is only the relative emptiness of the meaningless passage of time—of aging.[7]

Yet the impact on youth of what has been called postindustrial society need not result in such an emptiness and shallowness, although in recent literature these effects appear large indeed. It is as yet too early to make a full and adequate analysis of all these impacts. But it should be emphasized that the changes we have described, together with growing abundance and continuous technological change, have necessarily heightened the possibility of greater personal autonomy and cultural creativity and of the formation of the bases of such autonomy and of a flexible yet stable identity during the period of youth.

These new conditions have enhanced the possibility of flexibility in linking cultural values to social reality; they have enhanced the scope of personal and cultural creativity and the development of different personal culture. They have created the possibility of youth's developing what may be called a nonideological, direct identification with moral values, an awareness of the predicaments of moral choice that exist in any given situation, and individual responsibility for such choices—a responsibility that cannot be shed by relying on overarching ideological solutions oriented to the future.

These new social conditions exist in most industrial and postindustrial societies, sometimes together with the older conditions that gave rise to the more intensive types of youth movements. They constitute the framework within which the new configuration of the archetypal elements of youth and the new possibilities and problems facing youth in contemporary society develop. It is as yet too early to specify all these new possibilities and trends: here we have attempted to indicate some of their general contours.

Notes

1. A general sociological analysis of the place of age in social structure has been attempted in S. N. Eisenstadt, *From Generation to Generation* (Chicago: The Free Press of Glencoe, Illinois, 1956).

2. The analysis of personal, cosmic, and societal time (or temporal progression) has constituted a fascinating but not easily dealt with focus of analysis. For some approaches to these problems, see *Man and Time* (papers from the Eranos Yearbooks, edited by Joseph Campbell; London: Routledge & Kegan Paul, 1958), especially the article by Gerardus van der Leeuw. See also Mircea Eliade, *The Myth of the Eternal Return*. Translated by W. R. Trask. New York: Pantheon Books, 1954 (Bollingen Series).

3. For a fuller exposition of the sociological significance of initiation rites, see Mircea Eliade, *Birth and Rebirth* (New York: Harper & Brothers, 1958) and *From Generation to Generation* (n. 1).

4. See Bruno Bettelheim, *Symbolic Wounds, Puberty Rites and the Envious Circle* (Chicago: The Free Press of Glencoe, Illinois, 1954).

5. A special type of age groups may also develop in familistic societies. See *From Generation to Generation* (n. 1), ch. 5.

6. For fuller details, see *From Generation to Generation*, especially chs. 3 and 4.

7. For an exposition of this view, see Paul Goodman, "Youth in Organized Society," *Commentary*, February 1960, pp. 95–107; and M. R. Stein, *The Eclipse of Community* (Princeton: Princeton University Press, 1960), especially pp. 215ff.; also, the review of this book by H. Rosenberg, "Community, Values, Comedy," *Commentary*, August 1960, pp. 150–157.

3. Psychological Development and Historical Change

Most efforts to marry psychology and history have ended in divorce or outright cannibalism. In the hands of psychologists and psychiatrists, psychohistorical works have traditionally concentrated upon the psychopathology of great men. Those few historians influenced by psychoanalysis have sometimes insisted that historical movements were "nothing but" repetitive reenactments of the basic themes of *Totem and Taboo*. For their part, the majority of historians and depth psychologists have been rightly skeptical of the usefulness of an approach that left one unable to understand how great men differed from psychiatric patients and did scant justice to historical events of interest primarily because they were *not* literal repetitions of the past. Until the last decade, most psychohistorical inquiries must be judged a failure from both a psychological and a historical point of view; despite the advocacy of distinguished historians like Langer, the union of history and depth psychology languished.[1]

In the last decade, inspired largely by the work of Erikson, new and potentially more fruitful kinds of psychohistorical inquiry have opened up.[2] Erikson's studies of Gandhi and Luther have shown that some of the insights of psychoanalysis can be applied to great men without reducing them to bundles of neurotic urges. In the works of psychiatrists like Lifton, Coles, and others, we see a new interest in the unifying psychological themes that unite historical movements as different as Southern school desegregation and the atomic bombing of Hiroshima. In the studies of younger historians like Demos or Hunt, we find a new sophistication in applying modern psychodynamic insights to the study of childhood and the family in other epochs.[3] To be sure, no one, least of all the authors of these works, would claim that a final psychohistorical "synthesis" has been achieved, much less that there exists a solid body of method or theory that can be taught to the novice psychiatrist, historian, or psychologist. Psychohistory is more than anything else a series of questions that cannot be answered by psychology or history alone. But the possibilities of fruitful psychohistorical collaborations seem brighter today than ever before.

The relationship between historical and psychological change is one of the problems that has most frequently attracted those interested in a collaboration between these fields. In the theoretical work of men like Reich, Fromm, and Riesman, as in anthropological studies of culture contact between nonliterate and "advanced" societies, we find a growing body of observation and theory concerning the relationship of historical and psycho-

Kenneth Keniston, "Psychological Development and Historical Change," reprinted from *The Journal of Interdisciplinary History* 2 (1971): 329–45, with permission of the editors of *The Journal of Interdisciplinary History* and the M.I.T. Press, Cambridge, Massachusetts. Copyright © 1971, by the Massachusetts Institute of Technology and the editors of *The Journal of Interdisciplinary History*.

logical change.[4] It is now clear, for example, that when so-called "primitive" peoples come into contact with more technologically advanced societies, there generally results not merely the adoption of new mores and technologies, but the erosion of the traditional culture and the demoralization of a whole people. From such studies have come the concepts of national character, social character, or modal personality—concepts which, whatever their limitations and imprecision, help us understand and explain the observable and regular differences between men in distinct cultures and distinct historical eras.[5]

Most theories of national character or modal personality originated in the effort to understand psychological and cultural change—be it the rise of Fascism or the impact of modernization upon primitive societies.[6] But, paradoxically, these theories turned out to be far more useful in explaining historical inertia and cultural stability than in clarifying the mechanisms of change. For theories of national character have depended almost entirely upon the related concepts of socialization and acculturation. These concepts in turn attempt to explain how it is that social norms and cultural symbols are transmitted from generation to generation through the family, educational institutions, and other institutions of cultural transmission. Since a "well-functioning" society is defined as one in which the young are "successfully" socialized and acculturated, the observable facts of social, cultural, and psychological change prove difficult to explain except as a consequence of "failures" in a key set of social institutions.

Stated differently, theories of national character and modal personality have tended to have an implicitly conservative bias, both ideologically and theoretically. As a result, they have proved particularly useful in explaining such phenomena as cultural disintegration, social anomie, and psychological disorientation. These concepts help us understand the high incidence of addiction, apathy, and retreatism among non-literate peoples confronted with cultures that are more technologically advanced. They help illumine the messianic cults that appear to flourish at just that point when an old culture is becoming moribund. But they have proved less useful in understanding those social and historical changes which, all things taken together, seem more constructive than destructive, more synthetic than disintegrative. They help little in understanding the undeniable advances in the human condition brought about by the Industrial Revolution, in explaining how men could make constructive political revolutions, or, for that matter, in clarifying *any* non-degenerative historical change.

But the intertwined concepts of socialization, acculturation, and modal personality do not exhaust the potential contribution of psychology in explaining historical change. Largely ignored so far in the study of historical change have been the emerging concepts of developmental psychology—a small but rapidly growing body of theories about the sequences of stages of human development, the conditions that foster or inhibit development in children, and the consequences of early development for adult roles, symbolizations, and values. I will here argue that, in the long run, developmental concepts are likely to prove more useful that concepts of socialization, acculturation, and national character in explaining historical change, and that the relationship between historical context and psychological development is far more intimate than we have heretofore suspected. Collaboration between developmental psychology and history will clearly require major accommodations from the practitioners of both fields, but the results should be a better understanding of both historical and psychological change.

Current Views of Human Development

Every epoch tends to freeze its own unique experience into an ahistorical vision of Life-in-General. Modern developmental psychology witnesses this universal trend. Despite recent advances in our understanding of human development, our psychological concepts have generally suffered from a historical parochialism that takes the patterns, timetables, and sequences of development prevalent among middle-class children in contemporary Western societies as the norm of human development. For example, many developmental psychologists, like most laymen, consider it fairly obvious that human life falls naturally into a set of stages that can properly be labeled infancy, the preschool years, childhood, adolescence, early adulthood, middle age, and old age—for these are the stages which we recognize and institutionalize in Western society, and virtually all research on human development has been conducted in America or Western Europe.

Historians or anthropologists, however, quickly note that these segmentations of the life cycle bear little if any relationship to the definitions of life stages in other eras or cultures. During almost any previous historical era in Western societies, the life cycle has been thought to consist of different stages than those we now acknowledge; in virtually every other contemporary culture, as well, the stages of life are quite differently defined. To attend seriously to these facts requires us to reexamine the assumptions of developmental psychology, and, in so doing, to open the door to a new possibility of collaboration between historians and developmental psychologists.

The reasons for the relative neglect of historical and cultural evidence in the study of development must be understood if this neglect is to be remedied. First among these reasons, of course, is the traditional excuse of psychology: It is a new field. It has in fact proven extraordinarily difficult to understand the complexities of human development even in one subculture of one society: understanding the development of upper-middle class American, French, Swiss, German, and English children is far from complete. How much more difficult, then, it is to study development in non-Western societies, much less in other historical eras.

Yet in addition to the infancy of developmental psychology, there are conceptual and ideological factors that have prevented our attending to historical and anthropological data. First is the generally unspoken assumption that we really *need* not examine development in any other place or time than our own, since the laws, sequences, and stages of development transcend both culture and history in their universality.[7] Once this assumption is openly stated, it is revealed as parochially acultural and ahistorical. But it is often simply taken for granted in many developmental theories. It is further supported by the widespread psychological assumption that the innate "thrust" of human development is so intense that development cannot be stopped by any "merely" cultural or historical factor. This assumption, in turn, is bolstered by the widespread conceptual confusion between biologically-determined physiological maturation, socially-defined age-grading, and real psychological development—all of which are considered equally inevitable. To open the way for a closer connection between develomental psychology and historical inquiry, we must therefore engage, however briefly, in an analysis of concepts that will challenge this presumption of the inevitability of development.

If we ask what we mean by psychological development, we clearly do not mean simply the accumulation of new facts, the strengthening or weakening of preexisting characteristics, or the repetition of previous attainment. What we can loosely call "quantitative" changes in human behavior are not necessarily developmental. The facts that old people often become more rigid with age, that American girls learn to skip rope more rapidly in the early school years, or that children's vocabulary enlarges with age are not truly developmental changes.

Nor is psychological development equivalent to physical growth or physiological development—that is, to maturation. Maturational changes are indeed virtually universal and inevitable, barring the grossest of insults to the organism. In all cultures, the brain of the child develops rapidly during the first two years of life, although gross malnutrition may slow or impair that development. The historical milieu may influence the age of menarche, but it does not prevent the onset of menstruation. In all societies, children pass through puberty, with important changes in their appearance, capacities, and general behavior. Maximal skeletal size is everywhere reached in the early twenties. And, in all eras, the vitality of early adulthood is followed by a progressive decline in physical strength that culminates in old age and death. Yet no one of these changes automatically *entails* developmental change. Maturation may, indeed perhaps usually does, promote or permit psychological development, but it need not. Both folk wisdom and clinical studies indicate that there are physically mature individuals with the psychology of children, and precocious biological children who possess adult developmental characteristics. In a phrase: Maturation and development are empirically correlated, but not *necessarily* related. The virtual inevitability of physiological maturation therefore does not demonstrate the inevitability of psychological development.

A second universal is socially-defined age-grading. A few societies or sub-societies have been or are rigidly age-graded:[8] e.g., classical Spartan society, some modern East African and Melanesian societies, or modern Western school systems. In most other societies, age-grading is somewhat looser: Age cohorts are less sharply demarcated. But, in all societies there are socially-defined differences in what is expected of the young and the old, the infant and the adult, the adult and the elder. In every known society the special status of the dependent and nursing infant is somehow acknowledged. It is also probably universal that societies distinguish the infant-child under the age of six or seven from the older child and/or adult. Every society, too, acknowledges that there is a stage or stages of life which are those of the fullness of life. The blessings and/or curses of old age are recognized. Admittedly, all societies do not divide up the life cycle in precisely the *same* way: On the contrary, they differ enormously in their definition of life stages, of the ages at which new stages begin, and in the substance of their expectations about age-appropriate behavior. But all societies do segment the life cycle in *some* way, and all societies apply formal and informal sanctions to ensure that people will "act their age." Thus, although the content of age-graded expectations varies with culture and history, the general process of age-grading is universal.

But neither maturation nor age-grading is equivalent to psychological development in the precise sense in which I will define this term. It is clearly possible to possess the social status of an adult but the mentality of a child. It is equally possible to have the body of an adult but the psychological development of a child. Psychological development, then, is related to both maturation and socialization, both of which may at times stimulate or prevent development, but neither of which is identical to development.

What do we mean by psychological development?[9] It can be defined as a process of qualitative change in functioning, in relationship to the world, or to oneself. To qualify as true development, this change must be age-correlated and synthetic—that is, it must involve moving to a progressively "higher" level of functioning, to a new level of organization that in general does not completely negate lower levels but tends to incorporate them. For example, the child who apprehends the grammar and vocabulary of his language, and thus learns to speak, does not lose his capacity to babble and imitate. The adolescent who moves beyond primitive identification with his parents to the more complex syntheses of identity formation described by Erikson still retains the capacity for identification.[10] The child who moves from the world of concrete operations to the hypothetical-deductive world of formal operations still remains capable of concrete operations.[11] Genitality, as defined by Freud, does not entail the disappearance of pregenital sexuality, but rather its inclusion and subordination in a genital orientation. In each case, lower levels of development tend to be subsumed as "special cases" in the next higher level of organization.

Psychological development is also essentially irreversible. This does not mean that regressions, recapitulations, reenactments, and reversions to earlier stages cannot occur in the course of development. On the contrary, most developmental theories find a place for such regressions within their theory. But *essential* irreversibility means that regression to a level is in some sense different from the first experience of that level: e.g., "regressed" behavior tends to be identifiably different; after regression (but not before) it is possible to "leapfrog" levels so as to resume development at the point from which one regressed, and so on. By stressing the sequentiality and essential irreversibility of development, we merely stress that development proceeds in a regular way through stages, each of which constitutes a prerequisite for the next. Stated schematically, Stage B cannot occur before Stage A, while Stage B is in turn prerequisite for Stage C. Each level thus builds upon the preceding one and is the building block for the one that follows it.

To define further the concept of development or the precise sequences of development would involve controversies and complexities irrelevant to this discussion. What is important is that psychological development as here defined is closely related to social age-grading and physiological maturation, but is not identical to either. In the study of socialization to age-grades we find valuable understanding of the matrix within which development occurs, the catalysts that tend to spur it, and the obstacles that may obstruct it. But an account of social expectations about age-appropriate behavior is not an account of development. Similarly, physiological maturation may be a prerequisite for developmental change or it may be a catalyst for development. But it does not automatically produce psychological development.

The Contingency of Human Development

These distinctions between socialization to age-grades, maturation, and development enable us to focus more sharply upon the *contingency* of human development. Most developmental theorists have tended to take for granted—or even to allege—that human development is virtually inevitable, barring any but the most traumatic insults to the individual's personality. This assumption springs partly from blurring the distinctions I have just made. For since maturation and socialization are indeed virtually inevitable, if development is not distinguished from them, then development, too, must be inevitable.

Thus, despite an accumulating body of research that demonstrates the possibility of irreversible retardations, slowings, arrests, fixations, lags, or foreclosures in development, the logical conclusion has not been drawn, nor have its implications been explored.

In fact, our present understanding suggests that the *extent* of human development is dependent upon the bio-social-historical matrix within which the child grows up; some developmental matrices may demonstrably retard, slow, or stop development; others may speed, accelerate, or stimulate it. We have traditionally seen the human life cycle as an escalator onto which the infant steps at birth and along which he is carried until his death. The view I am proposing here is that human development is instead a very rough road, pitted with obstructions, interspersed with blind alleys, and dotted with seductive stopping places. It can be traversed only with the greatest of support and under the most optimal conditions.

In order to carry the discussion further with any precision, it is now necessary to distinguish between "development-in-general" and development within specific "lines" or sectors of growth. Developmental theories can be roughly grouped on the basis of this distinction: some deal primarily with development in general or broad life stages (Freud, Erikson, Sullivan), while others deal with developmental changes in precisely defined areas of functioning (Piaget, Kohlberg, Perry).[12] It was Anna Freud who first pointed out that what we loosely call "development" in fact consists of a series of changes within distinguishable "developmental lines" or sectors of functioning.[13] Today developmental diagnosticians of childhood define separately the levels attained by each child in a variety of distinct sectors: e.g., fine motor, cognitive, gross motor, interpersonal, affective, defensive-adaptive, verbal-speech, etc.[14] Any global judgment of overall developmental level is based upon a profile derived from sector-specific evaluations. Thus, if we are to speak precisely about the factors that promote an individual's development, we must specify which sectors or lines of development we are talking about.

This apparently technical point is especially relevant to the cross-cultural and historical study of development. For historical or cultural conditions which may stimulate development in one sector of life may well fail to stimulate it or actually retard it in other sectors. For example, many social critics today argue that a narrow kind of cognitive development is over-stimulated in modern Western societies at the expense of affective and interpersonal development, which are in turn retarded. Freud believed that precocious sexual development tended to retard intellectual development. And it is probably possible to stimulate or over-stimulate some sectors of growth but to understimulate, neglect, or suppress others. The "intellectually precocious, emotionally immature" child in Western societies is a case in point.

Thus, if we are to compare different historical epochs or different cultures from a developmental perspective, we must not merely compare how they define the overall stages of life and study the extent to which individuals actually pass through these global stages, but we must examine specifically how a given cultural and historical context affects each of many specific sub-sectors of human development.

Furthermore, only when we have distinguished between sectors of development does the precise influence of the environmental matrix upon development become truly clear. For example, during the past two decades, the study of children in extreme situations has shown that they may "fail to develop" unless defined environmental conditions are present. The most dramatic examples of developmental failure come from studies of infants institutionalized in antiseptic, hygienic, but impersonal "childrens' homes." The conditions of infant care in such institutions—multiple mothering, unresponsiveness to the child's indications of distress and pleasure, lack of sensory stimulation, and so on—produce specific developmental arrests or retardations in virtually all children subjected to these conditions. Some such children die of extreme reactions to minor physical illnesses; others develop a lethal apathy called marasmus. Those who survive physically are often grossly retarded. And those who live to adulthood tend to be diagnosed as amoral sociopaths.

Until recently, the blame for these developmental failures was laid at the door of heredity: The children who ended up in foundling homes were considered constitutionally defective. But research has made clear that the damage is not done by constitution, but by environment. And research by Provence and Lipton, which carefully distinguishes between development in distinct sectors, has helped pinpoint the areas in which early developmental arrest appear to be irreversible.[15] If the children in question are placed in normal foster homes at approximately the age of two, they soon make up most of the lost ground with regard to cognitive development, speech, and gross motor development. But, in other areas, retardation appears enduring: Such children seem never to develop the full capacity for deep personal relationships, for imaginative fantasy, or for the physical grace characteristic of children brought up from birth in natural or foster homes. Each of these fundamental qualities appears to be contingent upon a certain kind of environmental matrix in early life.

The barbarity of "modern" foundling homes is so extreme that if such conditions were societally universal, they would probably produce psychological deformations so extreme that no society could survive for long. In an enduring society, infants can take for granted most of the conditions they need in order to develop. Indeed, as a preliminary hypothesis, we might suggest that until about the age of six or seven, society has relatively little leeway in what it provides children: If the society is to survive, it must provide adequate stimulation—adequate "emotional and cognitive nutriments"—for the infant to become a child. Thereafter, however, we can speculate that the relative contingency of development upon the matrix in which it occurs seems to increase, and we begin to discover a series of truly developmental changes that may or may not occur. For example, Inhelder and Piaget have described at length the development of the capacity for formal operations: i.e., the ability to generate hypotheses and deduce their conclusions regardless of whether or not these conclusions are empirically true.[16] The capacity for formal operations is the capacity for logical-deductive thought. With this capacity, the intellect breaks free from the concrete world into the realm of hypotheses, ideals, and contra-factual conjectures. Upon this cognitive capacity, Piaget insists, philosophies, systems of scientific thought, utopias, and man's awareness of his historicity are based.

With Piaget's well-bred middle-class Swiss youths, the capacity for formal operations emerges at around the age of puberty. And, despite Piaget's *pro forma* acknowledgement that environment plays a role in the development of this capacity, he has associated formal operations firmly with early adolescence. But other studies have questioned this association. In some subcultures and in some societies, including our own, numerous adults seem to lack this capacity.[17] One study of American adolescents from "culturally deprived" backgrounds found that when the capacity for formal operations developed at all, it generally emerged well after puberty.[18] One may further question whether this capacity is likely to emerge at all in non-literate societies. In brief, here is a specific human potential which appears *not* to be actualized in certain environments, but to be crucially dependent upon the catalysts of the surrounding matrix.

Kohlberg's studies of moral development give a still more unequivocal example of developmental levels that are *not* reached by most men and women in American society, or for that matter in any society that has been studied.[19] Kohlberg argues that moral development may proceed from what he calls the preconventional and conventional levels, occurring during childhood and early adolescence, to post-conventional levels. These post-conventional levels are developmental in the precise sense defined above: They are essentially irreversible, sequential, age-related, and synthetic. But Kohlberg's empirical work indicates that the great majority of young Americans, like their parents, do not in fact pass beyond the conventional stage of moral reasoning. The precise psychological and cultural matrix that promotes the development of post-conventional moral reasoning remains largely a matter for speculation.[20] But what seems clear is that Kohlberg has identified measurable stages of moral development which the great majority of Americans do not reach. Research in other cultures suggests that elsewhere these stages are reached even less frequently.[21]

We as yet know very little about the precise sequences of development in each of the areas of human growth that can be distinguished.[22] It will doubtless take decades before we have begun to fill in the chart of human development, much less to understand the impacts of different environmental matrices upon distinct sectors of development. But what we do now know consistently supports the hypothesis that human development, from infancy onward, is contingent upon the characteristics of the environmental matrix.

Life Stages and Developmental Profiles

This hypothesis, if correct, has important implications for the study of historical change. For, in general, members of any given society in any given historical epoch tend to share a highly similar developmental matrix. It follows that, despite the variations in human development generated by constitutional and idiosyncratic differences, there should be important constancies in the *modal developmental profile* of adults. Put differently, people in any given society or sub-society tend to resemble each other not only because they have internalized the same roles (socialization) and the same symbols and values (acculturation), but also because they have "leveled off" at approximately the same point in their development in each of the sectors of human growth.

In the past, we have learned to analyze how children internalize shared social roles and how they incorporate common cultural symbols and values. Now we should begin to examine the environments of children, adolescents, and adults in terms of their selective impact on the unfolding of development potentials. We may discover, for example, that certain societies like our own place immense stress upon some kinds of cognitive and intellectual development, while they deemphasize other sectors of development—for example, motoric development and the early development of responsibility. If this is true, then we will require a concept like "modal developmental profile" to characterize the developmental attainments of the average individual in any subculture, society, or historical epoch.

If these hypotheses and concepts prove useful, they may open the possibility of new ways of examining the family, the life cycle, and the phenomenology of human experience in other historical eras. My argument implies that we have been too quick to assume that human development in other societies and other historical eras proceeds in a manner essentially similar to development in our own society. In our rush to reject the arrogance of the nineteenth century vis-à-vis the "savage native," we have been too quick to assume a complete identity of experience between modern man and ancient man, technological man and pre-literate man. In our acceptance of cultural relativism in the realm of values, we may have confused values with facts, generating a twentieth-century pseudo-egalitarianism which is little more than the ethnocentric assumption that all men are "basically" like Western industrialized men. Developmental psychologists have helped us to remember how profoundly different from our own are the mental processes and conceptual maps with which the small child approaches the world. Working together, developmental psychologists, historians, and anthropologists may now help us to recall how profoundly different has been the human experience of growing up in other societies and other times—and how different, as a result, was the inner experience and mind-set of adults in other places and eras.

It may clarify the view I am proposing to consider several problems which might be illumined by this approach. Consider, for one, the observation by anthropologists studying some pre-literate societies and by historians studying earlier eras that the life stage of adolescence has not always been formally recognized or acknowledged. Since puberty obviously occurs in all societies, these same scholars have generally assumed that adolescence as a psychological stage has also occurred, and have devoted their main investigative effort to explaining why so obvious a milestone in human development was not formally noted. But the point of view introduced here suggests a different interpretation. It may well be that adolescence as a stage of psychological development occurs only under specific conditions like those which obtain in modern Western societies. In other societies or historical eras, puberty is therefore not followed by anything like what we consider an adolescent experience.[23]

To state this general hypothesis in its most extreme and provocative form: Some societies may "create" stages of life that do not exist in other societies; some societies may "stop" human development in some sectors far earlier than other societies "choose" to do so. If, therefore, a given stage of life or developmental change is not recognized in a given society, we should seriously entertain the possibility that it simply does not occur in that society. And, if this is the case, then in societies where adolescence does not occur many of the psychological characteristics which we consider the results of an adolescent experience should be extremely rare: For example, a high degree of emancipation from family, a well-developed self-identity, a belief system based upon a reexamination of the cultural assumptions learned in childhood, and, perhaps, the cognitive capacity for formal operation.

Let us consider a second example. Elkins has drawn an analogy between what he terms the "Sambo" mentality prevalent until recently among black American slaves and their nominally free descendents and the particular mentality observed amongst the inmates of concentration camps.[24] Elkins' hypothesis focuses upon the impact of extreme and traumatic degradation upon adult personality; he disregards almost completely the posssible effects upon children of growing up under the conditions prevalent in slave quarters on North American plantations. As a result, the major intellectual problem in Elkins' formulation is how to explain why the trauma of the middle passage was communicated from generation to generation over so many centuries.

Even with our present limited knowledge of the effects of gross cultural deprivation, illiteracy, discontinuity of mothering, lack of sensory stimulation, and so on, we can readily supplement Elkins' theory by informed speculations about the catastrophic effects upon child development (and, therefore, upon adult personality) of the conditions in which children born into slavery were reared. Such conditions should predictably lead to a dulling of adult cognitive capacities, to resignation, apathy, and indifference, and to a "survival mentality" which stresses manifest acquiescence and covert resistance.

An even more speculative example of the possible connection between developmental and historical concepts may follow from the observations of Ariès, qualified by the later studies of Hunt, concerning the characteristics of child development in sixteenth- and seventeenth-century France.[25] Ariès argues that the concept of childhood as a separate stage of life was unknown during the Middle Ages. Only in the sixteenth and seventeenth centuries, and, initially, only for a small elite, was a separate stage that followed infancy but preceded adulthood socially acknowledged and sanctioned in age-graded schools. If we leap from this datum to the theories of Erikson concerning childhood as a stage of life, we find that the developmental "task" of childhood in Erikson's terms is the achievement of a sense of "industry," which Erikson relates to such human qualities as skill, a sense of workmanship, an absence of feelings of inferiority, and a sense of vocational competence. We might argue that in the absence of a stage of childhood, the psychological quality of industry simply did not develop on a mass scale, and that its absence thus helps to explain the absence of the motivations necessary for an entrepreneurial, capitalistic-industrial society. Perhaps only as childhood was recognized on a mass scale and as a larger proportion of the population therefore developed a sense of industry could capitalism and large-scale industrialization proceed. Such an explanation might help us define the developmental component in the complex relationship between capitalism, Protestantism, and the work ethic.

A variety of other topics might be illumined by the application of developmental concepts. We might ask, for example, how the historical extension of literacy changes the cognitive development and social behavior of those who can read. Does it enable them to deal more effectively with complex political questions? Does it make them more susceptible to mass totalitarian movements? Does literacy help the individual attain the detachment from admired but defeated political figures which is necessary in a democracy if the opposition is gracefully to concede defeat? Or does it lay the groundwork for the ideologization of political and social controversy? Or we might ask whether, after the fall of the Roman Empire, the matrix of child development changed so that children of succeeding generations attained a less advanced cognitive level than that which characterized the aristocracy in Rome, with the result that original thought ceased for several centuries throughout most of Western Europe and the Mediterranean.

Finally, turning to our own era, I have elsewhere argued at greater length[26] that a good part of the untoward restiveness of affluent, educated young people today must be understood as a consequence of a massive historical change in the developmental matrix. Among other things, this new matrix promotes the individualization of moral judgments and the relativization of truth. One consequence is that a large minority of a youthful generation is unable, for better and for worse, to accept on faith previous moral evaluations or uncritically to accept traditional ways of viewing the world. These new mind-sets are not simply matters of the recurrence of perennial generational conflict. On the contrary, to understand fully the emergence of an oppositional youthful counter-culture in the most technologically advanced nations of the world, we must begin to examine how the drastically altered historical conditions of the twentieth century (extended mass education, widespread affluence, exposure to other cultures, threat of holocaust) have in turn changed the modal matrix of human development, "producing" on a mass scale a kind of questioning, restless youth who, if he existed at all in the past, was always part of a tiny and exceptional minority.

In urging that we examine the psychological effects of wide-scale historical changes in the developmental matrix, I am not proposing that we abandon more familiar and traditional modes of psychological and historical inquiry. The concept of national character or modal personality, for example, has emerged from scathing criticism scarred but still useful in the understanding of historical continuity and change. Developmental concepts are in no sense a panacea either to the psychologist or the historian. My only claim is that they may help us understand better the processes by which socio-historical change produces psychological change, and by which psychological change on a mass scale may in turn generate social and political transformations. And, if developmental psychology and historical inquiry can move toward a closer accommodation, we may be less inclined to impose our own culturally ethnocentric and historically parochial world-views and mind-sets upon the experience of those in other cultures and historical eras.

Notes

1. William L. Langer, "The Next Assignment," *American Historical Review,* LXIII (1968), 285–286.
2. See especially Erik H. Erikson, *Young Man Luther: A Study in Psychoanalysis and History* (New York, 1958), and *Gandhi's Truth: On the Origins of Militant Non-Violence* (New York, 1969).
3. See especially Robert Jay Lifton, *Thought Reform and the Psychology of Totalism: A Study of "Brainwashing" in China* (New York, 1961); *Death in Life* (New York, 1967); Robert Coles, *Children of Crisis: A Study of Courage and Fear* (Boston, 1967); Joel Kovel, *White Racism: A Psychohistory* (New York, 1970); Robert Liebert, *Radical and Militant Youth: A Psychoanalytic Inquiry* (New York, 1971); John Demos, *A Little Commonwealth: Family Life in Plymouth Colony* (New York, 1970); David Hunt, *Parents and Children in History: The Psychology of Family Life in Early Modern France* (New York, 1970).
4. Wilheim Reich, *The Mass Psychology of Fascism* (New York, 1946); Erich Fromm, *Escape from Freedom* (New York, 1941); David Riesman, *The Lonely Crowd* (New Haven, 1950); Margaret Mead, *New Lives for Old: Cultural Transformation* (New York, 1956).
5. For a critical review of the concept of national character, see Alex Inkeles and Daniel J. Levinson, "National Character: The Study of Modal Personality and Socio-Cultural Systems" in Gardner Lindzey and Elliot Aronson (eds.), *Handbook of Social Psychology* (Cambridge, Mass., 1968).
6. Daniel Lerner, *The Passing of Traditional Society: Modernizing the Middle East* (New York, 1964).
7. Sigmund Freud's uncompromising views about the biologically-based universality of the developmental sequences are well known. Jean Piaget's acknowledgment that environmental factors play a role in determining the rate of development has always been largely *pro forma*, since he has never defined or studied these environmental differences.
8. On the sociology of age-grading, see S. N. Eisenstadt, *From Generation to Generation* (Glencoe, 1956).
9. The following account draws heavily upon Bärbel Inhelder, "Some Aspects of Piaget's Approach to Cognition" in *Monograph of the Society for Research in Child Development,* XXVII (1962), 19–33; Laurence Kohlberg, "Stage and Sequence: The Cognitive-Developmental Approach to Socialization," in David A. Goslin (ed.), *Handbook of Socialization Theory and Research* (Chicago,

1969). For a more general discussion of concepts of development, see Dale B. Harris (ed.), *The Concept of Development: An Issue in the Study of Human Behavior* (Minneapolis, 1957).

10. Erik H. Erikson, *Identity: Youth and Crisis* (New York, 1968).

11. Bärbel Inhelder and Jean Piaget (trans. Anne Parsons and Stanley Milgram), *The Growth of Logical Thinking from Childhood to Adolescence* (New York, 1958).

12. For an authoritative summary of the psychoanalytic view of development, see Otto Fenichel, *The Psychoanalytic Theory of Neurosis* (New York, 1945), Chs. IV–VI. Erikson's views are summarized in his "Identity and the Life Cycle," *Psychological Issues,* I (1959), 18–164; Harry Stack Sullivan, *The Interpersonal Theory of Psychiatry* (New York, 1953). The best general introduction to Piaget's immense body of work remains John H. Flavell. *The Developmental Psychology of Jean Piaget* (New York, 1963). For Kohlberg's views, see Kohlberg, "Stage and Sequence," and "The Child as a Moral Philosopher," *Psychology Today,* II (1968), 25–30; William G. Perry, Jr., *Forms of Intellectual and Ethical Development in the College Years* (New York, 1970).

13. *Normality and Pathology in Childhood: Assessments of Development* (New York, 1965).

14. See, e.g., the elaborate forms used to assess early child development by Sally Provence and her colleagues at the Developmental Unit of the Child Study Center at Yale Medical School.

15. See René Spitz, "Hospitalism," *The Psychoanalytic Study of the Child,* I (1945), 53–75; John Bowlby, *Maternal Care and Mental Health* (Geneva, 1951); Sally Provence and Rose C. Lipton, *Infants in Institutions* (New York, 1962).

16. *Growth of Logical Thinking.*

17. Flavell, *Developmental Psychology of Jean Piaget,* 399.

18. Martin P. Deutsch, Remarks at Research Conference, Dept. of Psychology, Yale Medical School, 1968.

19. "Child as a Moral Philosopher."

20. Kenneth Keniston, "Student Activism, Moral Development and Morality," *American Journal of Orthopsychiatry,* XI, (1970), 577–592.

21. Kohlberg, "Child as a Moral Philosopher."

22. Stuart T. Hauser, *Black and White Identity Formation* (New York, 1971), demonstrates marked identity foreclosures in black working-class adolescents. Research done in other cultures also suggests different rates and patterns of development that depend on the socio-cultural matrix. See Patricia M. Greenfield and Jerome S. Bruner, "Culture and Cognitive Growth," in Goslin, *Handbook;* Jerome S. Bruner, Rose S. Olver, and Patricia M. Greenfield, *Studies in Cognitive Growth* (New York, 1967), especially Chs. 11–14; Flavell, *Developmental Psychology of Jean Piaget,* 379–402; John Jay and Michael Cole, *The New Mathematics and an Old Culture: A Study of Learning among the Kpelle of Liberia* (New York, 1967).

23. Some observers of development after puberty have argued that "adolescence," as commonly defined, is extremely rare in American society as well: see Edgar Z. Friedenberg, *The Vanishing Adolescent* (New York, 1962); Elizabeth Douvan and Joseph Adelson, *The Adolescent Experience* (New York, 1966); Daniel Offer, *Psychological World of the Teenager: A Study of Normal Adolescent Boys* (New York, 1969). These works may be interpreted either to indicate a wide-spread "foreclosure" of development in early adolescence or to indicate that the concept of adolescence has been incorrectly defined.

24. Stanley M. Elkins, *Slavery: A Problem in American Institutional and Intellectual Life* (Chicago, 1968).

25. Philippe Ariès, *Centuries of Childhood: A Social History of Family Life* (New York, 1962); Hunt, *Parents and Children in History.*

26. Kenneth Keniston, "Youth as a 'New' Stage of Life," *The American Scholar,* XXXIX (1970), 631–654.

4. Documents in Search of a Historian: Toward a History of Children and Youth in America

By exploring a new area of investigation, like the history of childhood and youth in America, we are forced to confront fundamental issues. What do we need to know if we are to write such a history? What issues must be resolved before we can determine whether the subject merits the attention of historians? What are the critical questions that must be answered if such categories are to become central to historical analysis?

First, and most obvious, do age groups in fact have histories? Have fundamental changes occurred in the experiences of children and youth from the colonial period to the present? Although at first the inquiry may seem a bit forced (surely something must have happened to them between 1607 and 1971), the matter is far from clear. There may be no way, for example, to trace changes in patterns of parental discipline. In the seventeenth century some fathers were lenient, others harsh; in the twentieth, the same holds true. Or take the question of youth culture. It is perfectly possible that seventeenth-century youths banded together with the same self-consciousness and frequency as did their urban counterparts several hundred years later. Because the *concept* of adolescence was invented only at the end of the nineteenth century is no indication that the *actual* experience of the young had changed. It is also unclear as to whether there have been shifts in the ages at which the young left home, took their first job, underwent religious initiation, adopted adult clothing, or married. As Philip Greven recently noted, it seems that the young left their father's household at about the same age in colonial Andover, Massachusetts as in post-Civil-War Union Park, Chicago.[1]

If changes did occur, however, what influences promoted them? What forces shaped the nature of childhood and youth? Were demographic shifts decisive? Did a reduction in the rates of infant mortality revolutionize parental attitudes and practices? Did the movement from farm to village to town to city prompt adults to adopt new styles of child-rearing, or encourage the child to assume a different stance toward the community? Were the most significant variables economic, with industrialization standing as a major divide in the history of childhood? Or did military organizations, educational theories, religious enthusiasm, or some combination, cause major shifts?

Equally important is an understanding of the significance of the stage of pre-adulthood in causing historical change. Do the young provoke change or reflect it? Is this notion a dependent variable which is interesting but ultimately of secondary importance

David J. Rothman, "Documents in Search of a Historian: Toward a History of Children and Youth in America," a review of *Children and Youth in America: A Documentary History,* ed. Robert H. Bremner (Cambridge, Mass.: Harvard University Press, 1970–71) vol. 1. Reprinted from *The Journal of Interdisciplinary History* 2 (1971):367–77, with permission of the editors of *The Journal of Interdisciplinary History* and the M.I.T. Press, Cambridge, Massachusetts. Copyright © 1971, by the Massachusetts Institute of Technology and the editors of *The Journal of Interdisciplinary History.*

to the historian's story, or an independent variable that is crucial to his analysis? What does a study of childhood attempt to explain? Is it a collection of trivia, or does it uncover elements essential to a history of society?

The books reviewed here touch on some of these points, but they are too few in number to answer many questions, and too flawed intellectually to stand as models. Wishy's *The Child and the Republic*[2] is an exercise in intellectual rather than social history. Using child-rearing literature and childrens' books, Wishy focuses exclusively on the "debate about child nurture," between 1830 and 1900, and not on the child himself. He finds changes in attitudes, but fails to present a convincing explanation for the changes, or an understanding of their implications. Nor does he inform us about the actualities of childhood in these years, which puts us in the position of trying to recreate the battle of Gettysburg by reading only Karl von Clausewitz.

Certainly we cannot fault Demos' *A Little Commonwealth*[3] for not trying to recreate the actualities of childhood. His examination of family life in the Plymouth colony is based upon the designs and architectural remains of the houses and their furnishings, demographic data, styles of dress, and the content of wills; much of the argument depends on psychological theory. But his observations are admittedly speculative, and his results are so thin and inconclusive that they intensify a nagging fear that a history of childhood may well be impracticable.

Demos describes the typical environment surrounding the newborn infant: "for his first year or so a baby had a relatively comfortable and tranquil time" (134). To support this idea, he notes that the houses were usually small, the clothing light, and the infants breast-fed.[4] But these same facts lead just as easily to an opposite conclusion: Since the household was small and the mother burdened with many duties, the infant always seemed underfoot: breast feeding was rushed and impersonal, at the mother's convenience. The noise level in the house was high (with people working, eating, playing, and visiting), so that the baby slept fitfully and was frequently startled; when he added his own cries to the din, he was perfunctorily moved or attended to.

Demos then describes the dramatic consequences of weaning between the infant's first and second year, generally compounded by the probable arrival of a second child, and a new paternal insistence, backed by social and religious doctrines, on breaking the child's will. Demos posits, through Erikson's theories on aggression, a pattern of indulgence-severity in infancy that affected adult behavior. The result of this childhood syndrome was that Plymouth's citizens were prone to take each other to court with incredible regularity. But might it not be that other siblings took an increased interest in the growing infant, so that in fact the household was more pleasant for him as he matured? And the resorting to courts could be explained by any number of other influences including the need to rely upon formal mechanisms to settle disputes because comity was important. Many historians have experienced that middle-of-the-night panic when contemplating how thin a line sometimes separates their work from fiction. But on this score the study of childhood seems especially nerve-racking, threatening to turn us all into novelists.

A third approach to the field may be found in Sennett's *Families Against the City*,[5] which utilizes quantitative data on family size and social mobility. Analyzing manuscript census data between 1850 and 1880 for Chicago's Union Park, Sennett contends that a decline in family size led to internal family tensions that ultimately weakened the sons' ability to master the external environment. Yet the quantitative data are often skimpy (in that Sennett generalizes from a handful of cases), several of his procedures are dubious (as when he sets up a "traditional" upper middle-class extended family from one diary), the thoroughness of his research is questionable (surely there were some voluntary associations in Union Park, and the schools must have exerted some influence), and we are finally asked to accept the idea of an injurious small family dynamic without a shred of internal supporting evidence. Even if one grants that children from smaller families were not upwardly mobile, that their fathers actually behaved as Sennett claims they did—in that they were jealous of their children and unable to guide them intelligently in life choices—the entire hypothesis remains speculative. There is less reason to believe that one of Union Park's larger families—typically bigger because a maiden aunt lived with it—would have helped a youngster to adjust. The data are on one side, and the child in the family on the other—with no connection between them.

Despite the many methodological and substantive difficulties apparent in the literature, historians are understandably reluctant to quit the field. It seems too important. Well aware of the work in other social science disciplines in which childhood in particular and socialization in general is so crucial an element, they cannot help but wonder about the effects of childhood and family training on the structure of past societies, and about the changes that have occurred. Given the vast bibliographies compiled in psychological, anthropological, and sociological research, historians would have to be intellectual recluses to avoid pursuing the subject. The unprecedented energy now being devoted to social history also makes this area a prime candidate for investigation. If, to date, failures outnumber advances, that would seem to be the price for asking new questions.

The newest and in many ways most ambitious venture in this area is a documentary history, *Children and Youth in America,* compiled under the direction of Robert Bremner. Volume I, upon which I will focus here, takes the subject from 1600 to 1865. Volume II, whose appearance is imminent, will bring the story to 1932, and Volume III will come to the present. This is no ordinary gathering of documents. The size of Volume I alone makes that obvious—813 double-columned pages of handsomely printed text. Most of the space goes to the documents themselves, but introductions to the various sections and subsections of the book put the material into context.

The project was funded by the Children's Bureau, with the specific charge to update Grace Abbott's *The Child and the State* (Chicago, 1947;2v.). Helping Bremner were three associate editors, a five-man executive committee, two editorial assistants, thirty-one research assistants, and thirty-six advisers. Given the obviously large expenditure of energy, one approaches the volume with keen anticipation. It might well supply a broad structure and interpretation, bringing some coherence to the study of the child. To be sure, its mandate was more limited, but surely the project intended to do more than add a few recent documents to Abbott's book.

Bremner's preface defines the focus of the volume narrowly: The collection will not treat the history of children and youth in America, but the history of public policy toward them. The differentiation is certainly intellectually valid, and one can trace public policy without entering directly into the actualities of family life or child behavior. But Bremner does not maintain this distinction. The premises underlying the organization of the volume, as well as the substance of many of the documents reprinted, reveal a major concern with the experience of the family and the child in America.

The scope and perspective of the volume emerge clearly in its periodization. Bremner divides the story into three stages. First, between 1600 and 1735, the child was the subject not the citizen of the family. The father was master and the child was to serve both him and the state. Child-rearing practices were rigid, intended to secure the immediate and complete submission of the child to parental will. By 1735, however, in practice but not in theory, New World conditions had undermined this scheme. Following the interpretations of Handlin and Bailyn,[6] Bremner argues that the wilderness and the availability of land quickly began to liberate the child from external controls. Then, in the next period (1735–1820), the child, although still officially subject to family authority, increasingly practiced the doctrines of self-help, independence, and self-interest. He became more and more autonomous, and concomitantly the family's influence weakened. The trends evident in the era of settlement continued to gather momentum under the influence of Enlightenment thought, the Great Awakening, the American Revolution, and the spread of the idea of progress. Each of these elements encouraged the intellectual acceptance of the child as worthy and promoted the social conditions under which he could exercise a wide degree of initiative. Even the nascent industrialism of New England worked to the same end, with the mills decreasing still further the power of the family. What the wilderness began the factories continued. Sensing a possible discrepancy in treating industrialism as part of a story of child liberation, Bremner notes that "one can only speculate on the impact of factory labor on the independence of child workers. The meager wages earned went into the family pocket." Still, he insists, "the factory experience occasionally produced experts at an early age" (148).

In the third period, 1820 to 1865, the child was part of a society undergoing extensive political and social change whose sum effects, Bremner concedes, were varied and elusive. "No brief formula adequately explains or summarizes the varieties of family and child life that existed in the United States by the early nineteenth century." What did the slave child, immigrant child, slum child, frontier child, and plantation child have in common? Yet, after issuing this warning, Bremner elaborates the line of argument developed earlier. Labeling this section "The American Child," he contends that for the middle classes the principles of individualism, *laissez-faire,* and democracy permeated not only the economy, the government, and the church, but the family as well, with revolutionary results. "The Western world had not seen the like of the American family before," or the like of the American child. He was, in essence, "a new creature," the culmination of 200 years of New World history. Having once been the subject of the family, the child was now "independent, individualistic." The family which had once treated him as a servant now made his welfare its preeminent goal (343–346).

The critical assumption underlying this framework is that there was an appropriate, convenient, and beneficial match between the evolution of American society and the family. In this interpretation the family reflects without distortion the triumph of freedom and democracy that transformed other institutions. The history of the child is the victory of liberty over dictatorship, of opportunity over rigidity, and of initiative over authority. The child is the quintessential American, and no other story better exemplifies the triumph of republicanism. The decline of the father's influence in the household coincides with the decline of the prerogatives of the crown and the royal governor in politics. They all represented unbridled and autocratic authority at the top of hierarchical structures, and all of them succumbed to republican principles and a fluid social order. The only lamentable fact is that not all social classes were equally affected: Indian, immigrant, and slave children did not share in these changes—just as their parents did not enjoy the same political or social privileges as native-born whites. Nevertheless, for the middle classes—those Americans who were not immigrants, or red, or black—the story of the child is the story of liberation and one worthy of celebration.

But the problem is that we have gone far beyond this facile and triumphant interpretation in our study of other institutions. Apply the key elements in the family framework to politics or economics, and its simplifications become immediately apparent. An equivalent argument in political history would suggest that the seventeenth-century colonies took the first steps to liberty (the Puritan charter? Bacon's Rebellion?), that developments proceeded predictably and smoothly into the 1700s leading inevitably to the victory of republican principles first in the Revolution, and then by steady stages through the Jacksonian period. The economy ostensibly followed an identical course: State authority in the marketplace began to weaken in the seventeenth century and declined still further in the eighteenth; *laissez-faire* triumphed, again smoothly and predictably, in the nineteenth. Although these contentions are not without some basis in historical reality, and are not completely unreasonable, modern scholarship has made our sense of them far more complex. Few serious researchers would insist that these developments emerged without major conflicts; nor would they be so certain that political and economic developments were ultimately to the best interests of everyone in the society, that there were only gains, no losses. Were Jacksonians the great democrats? Was colonial Massachusetts a middle-class democracy? The matter is more complex and major qualifications are in order. Yet the history of children and youth is in so rudimentary a state that what passes as too simplistic in other areas here remains the basic structure of interpretation. The field, by a measure of equivalency, is still in the hands of a George Bancroft.

But not altogether. For all of the weaknesses and methodological limitations of the recent studies, several do highlight the inadequacies of traditional interpretations. The work of Greven is a case in point.[7] Meticulously tracing the transfer of land in colonial Andover, he attempts to use the resultant data to interpret father-son relations. He remains very much on the outside looking in, recreating family dynamics from external behavior. The links between the deeding or willing of land and the exercise of personal authority in the household are weakly forged since substantive evidence is lacking. Nevertheless, Greven does make clear that the interests of fathers and sons frequently diverged, and that a fundamental tension over the transfer of land pervaded these colonial families. Moreover, he argues persuasively that the father's authority did not automatically or rapidly decline in the 1600s. Although it had probably weakened by the mid-1700s, the decisive element was not the munificence of life in the New World but the growing shortage of town land. Crowded settlements rather than open wilderness may have reduced paternal prerogatives.

The image of family life that emerges from the Demos and Sennett studies also points to conflict and maladaptation. Demos argues that family training in Plymouth (e.g., the vacillation between permissiveness and rigid discipline for the infant) did not prepare the child well for community life. As adults, citizens were constantly at odds with one another. And, if his contentions remain speculative, they still undermine the facile assumption that family dynamics conformed to social needs in the colonial period.

Sennett's work is perhaps the most self-conscious attack on the notion that the American family served its children and its society well. He vigorously disputes the idea of the functionalism of the nuclear family. And although he is more polemical than convincing, his work does stand as an important corrective to the bland and equally unsubstantiated optimism inherent in the traditional viewpoint.

The more one reads in this field, the more apparent it becomes that the history of childhood and youth is central to the study of social change. The many documents that Bremner collects are filled with pertinent information, and he and his assistants have made extraordinary efforts to bring to light relevant archival and published sources. They have reprinted fascinating excerpts from the original records of the New York House of Refuge and included little-known but important selections on early factory life from the papers of Samuel Slater. They have also been acutely aware of the fate of minorities. Moreover, the kinds of materials they omit—descriptions or pictures of artifacts, and demographic data—are available elsewhere. Ultimately, all of these documents will find historians. Almost certainly the new works will devote greater attention to the dysfunctional elements, to the conflict of interests, and to the tensions in the story. Precisely at the points of stress and opposition, childhood and youth become germane to an analysis of social change.

Among the problems that most demand a new perspective is the exercise of parental authority. Bremner and others connect a decline in the influence of the parent to the democratization of American society; ostensibly everyone acquiesced in the change for it fitted so well into other developments. Bremner delights in the story of Frederick Marryat, a visitor to the U.S. in the Jacksonian period, who witnessed an incident in which an American child steadfastly refused to obey his parents; his father's reaction was to inform Marryat that the boy was "a sturdy republican," all the while "smiling at the boy's resolute disobedience" (344).

But, in fact, the interaction between the young, the family, and the community provoked much greater strain and dissension than this interpretation allows. In the colonial period, and lasting well into the 1700s, family and community were so intertwined that one cannot talk of children escaping parental authority without considering whether this also meant a rejection of community values. The family's charge was to make children serviceable to their generation and God-fearing Christians, and to fulfill such wider obligations as boarding the poor, educating and caring for apprentices, and managing delinquents. So what does it mean to describe a gradual weakening of parental influence in the colonial years? The child practiced self-help and self-interest, declares Bremner. But the other side of the coin may have been a disregard of the general welfare for narrow private ends. We must recognize that such change would have been controversial, and that the community and the parents would have done battle with the young over it. Coercion, conflict, and a divergence of goals might have been more integral to these events than grand celebration.

Indeed, there is much evidence to suggest that paternal authority had not simply withered away by the end of the Jacksonian period. Perhaps the most obvious manifestation of its survival appears in the lower-class families of both immigrants and natives. The interests of the father and the child clearly diverged, and the father usually won. The youngster's self-interest dictated a fairly lengthy schooling period, while the father preferred an immediate cash return and put him to work as quickly as possible. The father's victory brought a greater accumulation of property to the family, but a life in unskilled or semi-skilled jobs to the youngster.

In the middle classes, too, parental authority may have maintained itself through a shift in tactics. The manipulation of the child, rather than his outright coercion, became more prevalent in Jacksonian America—and this change was not a necessary concomitant of democracy warranting the fulsome applause of historians. We cannot assume that every remark in a child-rearing manual recommending affection represents progress for the child or for the society. The normative literature of the period insisted that strict obedience be the ultimate goal of parental training, but now authors had a wider variety of fresh strategies to recommend before resorting to the rod. Although they counseled greater displays of affection than their eighteenth-century counterparts, they were no less insistent on denying the child autonomy.

Even more compelling is the evidence pointing to a war between the community and the young, which contradicts any simple notion of a neat fit between the child and the state. The spread of common schools, the erection of houses of refuge, the multiplication of orphan asylums, and the nature of college training did not necessarily indicate improvements and reforms. The coercive elements in the pre-Civil-War common schools, both in practice and in concept, are so obvious that it is a testimony to the strength of democratic ideology that historians could ignore them for so long. An element of social control runs through almost everything that Horace Mann wrote. The houses of refuge and orphan asylums were an overt attempt to infantilize the young, to put delinquents, vagrants, and the homeless into a rigid and disciplined environment where they would acquire the obedience that their parents had failed to inculcate. Behind these institutions was the assumption that any manifestation of public disorder in the young was evidence of future depravity. The behavior that a later generation (G. Stanley Hall's) would diagnose as part of a stage of youthful storm and stress, and therefore to be tolerated, was labeled deviant and suppressed by Americans in the Jacksonian period. Universities were also more intent on socializing the young than educating them—and were not particularly successful in either task. To judge from all of these materials, it is hardly accurate to posit a fundamental harmony between the family, the community, and the young.[8]

Other crucial shifts occurred, but their import is lost when historians focus so exclusively on the theme of family democratization. It seems that many institutions affecting the young, from the school to the church to the reformatory, were more carefully and precisely age-graded in the Jacksonian period than before. Traditional interpretations view this phenomenon as evidence of an increasing sensitivity to the various stages of childhood and youth, and another step in the rise of child welfare. But there is a darker side that should not be so completely ignored. Age-grading may have been part of an effort to lock-step the child into rigid and predetermined modes of behavior. The change looked not to his benefit, but to the rationalization of childhood so that behavior would become more predictable and manageable. This altered perspective raises questions about the ideology and reality of social order and disorder, and leads to the general issue of social change. As soon as one drops the assumption that innovation equals reform, that men of good will invariably took the next and logical step to maximize child welfare— that the history of the child in America is one of uninterrupted progress—then this field becomes even more critical for the social historian.

Similarly, one cannot assume that the norms set down in the child-rearing literature or actually inculcated by the family were invariably appropriate for community needs. Is there not enough evidence of friction and maladaptation in American society to make historians skeptical? Was the emphasis on rigid training, order, obedience, rote learning, and bell-ringing punctuality in the schools and asylums of the period, and to some degree in the families as well, necessarily functional for all social classes? It is true that we lack social and psychological theories that unambiguously relate childhood experiences to adult behavior—but our ignorance still makes it at least as appropriate to search for discontinuities as well as neat matches.

It may be difficult for historians to perceive the family as a coercive institution or the community as warring on its young. And perhaps this is not the essential component of the American story. But if we do not explore this theme, if we insist on making progress the exclusive ingredient in our analyses, we are certain to be left with more questions than answers.

Notes

1. An interesting conference at Princeton University in April, 1971, organized by John Gillis and devoted to childhood and youth, was the occasion for these remarks. The conference also helped me to conceptualize many of the issues raised here.

2. Bernard Wishy, *The Child and the Republic: The Dawn of American Child Nurture* (Philadelphia, 1968).

3. John Demos, *A Little Commonwealth: Family Life in Plymouth Colony* (New York, 1970).

4. *Ibid.*, Ch. 9.

5. Richard Sennett, *Families Against the City: Middle Class Homes of Industrial Chicago, 1872–1890* (Cambridge, Mass., 1970).

6. See Oscar Handlin's opening chapter in James M. Smith (ed.), *Seventeenth Century America: Essays in Colonial History* (Chapel Hill, 1959); Bernard Bailyn, *Education in the Forming of American Society: Needs and Opportunities for Study* (Chapel Hill, 1960). For an elaboration of this point, see David J. Rothman, "A Note on the Study of the Colonial Family," *William and Mary Quarterly,* XXIII (1966), 627–634.

7. Philip J. Greven, Jr., *Four Generations: Population, Land, and Family in Colonial Andover, Massachusetts* (Ithaca, N.Y., 1970).

8. These themes emerge in Stephan Thernstrom, *Poverty and Progress: Social Mobility in a Nineteenth Century City* (Cambridge, Mass., 1964); Michael B. Katz, *The Irony of Early School Reform: Educational Innovation in Mid-Nineteenth Century Massachusetts* (Cambridge, Mass.,1968); Oscar and Mary Handlin, *The American College and the American Culture: Socialization as a Function of Higher Education* (New York, 1970). They are also elaborated in my study, *The Discovery of the Asylum: Social Order and Disorder in the New Republic* (Boston, 1971).

PART II.

Early America: The Colonial Beginnings

Introduction

In Part II, we move from approaches to historical cases as we confront the "infancy" and "childhood" of growing up in America. Key issues and questions, we shall see, relate to the European origins of early American society; and the influence—accepted or debated—of Philippe Ariès's seminal contribution in his *Centuries of Childhood* is especially marked. Ariès argued that childhood did not emerge as a distinctive phase of growing up until the rise of major elements of modernity in early modern Europe; he tied its appearance to class, cultural, and family formations and an increased divergence between family and community with a key role to the development of educational institutions. This, for example, John Demos accepts in his interesting psychological excursion into early Plymouth Colony. Confronting the same historical experience, however, Ross Beales, Jr., expresses his skepticism about the views of both Ariès and Demos as he offers an alternative formulation for us to ponder.

Equally important is the question of the exceptionality or uniqueness of the (colonial) American experience. Did, many historians ask, the confrontation with the wilderness stimulate a novel social structure, cultural formation, and political sensibility with growing up transformed from its European background; or, to the contrary, were the European, especially the English, patterns central to the formation of early American culture and society with family forms and patterns of growing up at the core of that process? Consider not only the variations presented—by place within the colonies as well as by historical time, social class and background, and, especially, by gender—but also the importance of a comparative approach: with the "Old World" and between different areas of the developing "New World."

In a very important sense, the six essays of this section point to a much more subtle process of intersecting forces making for a complex blend of changes and continuities. Here we may sense: (1) the range of interactions and forces that impinge upon and shape patterns of growing up; (2) the kinds of sources that historians have turned to and the uses made of them; (3) the searches for a historical baseline (or baselines) from the colonial period from which to assess changes throughout American history; (4) the prominence of psychological approaches—and differences among them, and of demographic and quantitative analysis in this body of research; (5) the extent of transformation (and continuity, too) and of variation within the century and a half of colonial "beginnings." Compare the northern and southern patterns as well. Especially significant are the diverse contributions of church and religion, family and community, and variations in individual life chances especially as they are conditioned by demographic and economic factors. To what extent can we speak of growing up—of childhood, adolescence, and/or youth—in this set of contexts? To what extent are common versus divergent paths of growing up apparent? What difference did colonial conditions make? What issues bring agreement and which ones stimulate sharp disagreement? On what basis may we choose among them to grasp the underlying patterns and experiences of growing up in this time and place?

Demos and Beales offer instructively rich but different interpretations of children in New England. Consider their conceptualizations, frameworks, assumptions, evidence, and arguments. From the southern colonies, Walsh and Daniel Blake Smith offer contrasts to New England and to each other. The first four essays offer an important opportunity for close comparison of different approaches to and interpretations of similar historical developments. The last two raise enormously consequential questions about the nature of family life, gender, and incipient social class difference.

Daniel Blake Smith, Philip Greven, Jr., and Daniel Scott Smith enable us to move from the seventeenth-century origins of social forms and their implications for growing up to the eighteenth century and colonial societies beginning to mature. These three essays are marked by their respective and often revealing focuses on familial affection and psychology, religious motivations and pressures, and demographic-economic interactions. Each has implications for the ways in which we might view the key connections tying growing up to family change and social change and the fundamentally historical nature of growing up itself. Each offers a different model of research and interpretation for readers to compare and evaluate. Where then are the origins of growing up in America? Where lies the distinctiveness of the colonial era? What traditions and legacies would undergird the next two "centuries of growing up"? What connections might relate the growing up of Americans to the maturity of their society and their polity and individual with new national quests for autonomy, maturity, and independence?

5. Developmental Perspectives on the History of Childhood

Among the shifting currents of scholarly inquiry it is possible to discern a growing interest in the study of childhood in times past. A number of historians have undertaken detailed research into particular aspects of this subject; some of their projects are now complete, others are still in progress.[1] The major professional organizations have recently included such work in the programs of their annual meetings, and, in March 1970, the first conference devoted entirely to the investigation of "childhood and youth in history" was held at Clark University in Worcester, Massachusetts.

The sources of this trend are many and complex. But, as often happens in such cases, a single book seems to have exerted a very special influence. I refer to the seminal work of Ariès.[2] Few recent studies are better known, and there is no need to summarize the contents here. Nor is there space to enter the controversy that has arisen over some particular parts of the book. But it may be worthwhile to examine briefly the kind of approach to the study of childhood that Ariès so brilliantly seems to represent.

In analyzing childhood across a span of nearly a millennium, Ariès illuminated a vast territory of social and intellectual history. He examined with great imagination portraits of children, medical treatises on the care of infants, pedagogical tracts, toys and games, and a variety of other materials, in order to reveal certain core elements of medieval and early modern society, and of the transition between the two. It is clear, however, that he has concentrated not so much on the actual life-experience of children in the past as on the prevalent attitudes *toward* and *about* these children. His work is founded on the important and incontrovertible assumption that much can be learned about a culture by investigating the way it regards its young. In this sense, *Centuries of Childhood* is primarily about adults—those who commissioned and painted the portraits, wrote and read the medical treatises, and designed and maintained the schools. By extrapolating from Ariès one can imagine a whole range of detailed studies with the same underlying purpose. Attitudes toward childhood become, then, a kind of yardstick for measuring historical trends of the most profound consequence. And work of this type exhibits an obvious resemblance to other studies of basic cultural attitudes: attitudes toward death, for example, or love, or nature.

Here is a vitally important area of inquiry—and an area, too, in which much work remains to be done. This essay, however, will deal with *another* form of the study of childhood—related, and yet significantly different in both purpose and method. There is no easy way to designate this approach, for it has scarcely been contemplated, let alone attempted by historians before now. But what I have in mind is an effort to find certain underlying themes in the experience of children in a given culture or period in order to throw some light on the formation of later personality.[3] The approach assumes the ironic truth that "the child is father to the man"; it also assumes that each culture fosters the development of certain dominant character traits or styles. It requires, in short, something like the concept of "modal personality," which has shaped a very broad range of anthropological and psychological studies.[4]

It is well to bring the anthropologists directly into this discussion, for they have long elaborated many of the chief theoretical issues. There is no way to summarize all of the relevant literature; but perhaps the most valuable work, from the standpoint of historians, is associated with the so-called "culture and personality" school, in which names like Abram Kardiner, Ralph Linton, Margaret Mead, Clyde Kluckhohn, and George P. Murdock might reasonably be joined—and with important contributions from the side of psychology by men like Erik Erikson, Henry Murray, and T. W. Adorno. Kardiner's formulation of the issues is especially clear, and is useful here by way of example. He defines modal personality as "that constellation of personality characteristics which would appear to be congenial with the total range of institutions comprised within a given culture."[5] And he divides the institutions into two broad categories. "Primary institutions" are the major force for shaping personality; but they also have an important influence on other aspects of culture—political and economic systems, mythic and religious belief—which he terms "secondary." Chief among the "primary institutions" are customary practices and commitments in the area of child-rearing. To be sure, the Kardiner definitions have been criticized by other anthropologists,[6] and the priorities implied in the terms "primary" and "secondary" seem especially questionable. Kluckhohn and Murray present a more cautious viewpoint, stating simply: "The members of any organized group tend to manifest certain personality traits more frequently than do other groups."[7]

Every practitioner of the "culture and personality" approach has perforce made certain assumptions about human psychology; and in practice much of this work has been deeply infused with one form or another of psychoanalytic theory. It seems likely, in my opinion, that most serious historical inquiry along these lines will be similarly organized. At any rate, it seems clear that we will need *some* theoretical viewpoint from which to approach the subject. This requires emphasis since virtually all prior comment by historians has implied a static, largely undifferentiated model of childhood. We have settled for general notions on the order of "Puritan children were subjected to severe and repressive discipline," or "slave parents regarded their children with considerable indifference."[8]

Moreover, the source materials bearing on the history of childhood form a large, diverse, and fairly inchoate mass. Simply in order to organize them, one must find some principles for distinguishing the important from the trivial—the events which strengthen, or expand, or inhibit, or traumatize the growing personality from those which leave no lasting impression. In this sense I am urging a "developmental" approach to the subject, and it is indeed from developmental psychology that we may borrow some further procedural guidelines.

Broadly speaking, there are two different but interrelated ways of carving up our materials. One may be called "vertical," since it examines the child's development through time, and the other "horizontal," in that it separates out the different areas of the child's experience.

The "vertical" dimension requires a theory of "phases" or "stages" through which the individual proceeds from his first days of life to full maturity. (Indeed, such theory should logically extend to the adult years, and even to death itself, though this is not of direct concern in the present context.) One valuable contribution of this type—and, in my opinion, the *most* valuable—is Erikson's developmental model of the "eight stages of man."[9] "Basic trust vs. mistrust," "autonomy vs. shame and doubt," "initiative vs. guilt," "industry vs. inferiority," "identity vs. role diffusion": here, according to Erikson, are the critical periods in the life of every young and growing person. The stages are not, of course, rigidly programmed across the board, and no two individuals experience them in exactly the same way. Nonetheless, each one presents certain vital "tasks" that cannot really be avoided: indeed, each one involves a measure of "crisis" that is rooted in common psycho-social determinants.

If we take this kind of theory seriously, we are obliged to investigate how a culture manages on its own terms to distinguish between different periods of childhood. We cannot be content with knowing that discipline was generally harsh, or that parents were often indifferent to their young. We must try to determine whether such tendencies were more manifest at one stage of development than another, whether there was a kind of uneven curve of repressiveness or indifference with visible peaks and valleys over time.

But even this is not enough. We must also ask whether repressiveness, or indulgence, or indifference was more effective in some areas of the child's experience than in others. Most cultures do make certain distinctions among the various human instincts, drives, emotions—however they may be named and defined. A good theoretical picture of these issues can be found in the work of the cross-cultural anthropologists Whiting and Child. Their studies are organized around a five-part division of child development, including sex, aggression, dependency, orality, and anality.[10] They have applied this scheme in the analysis of more than fifty contemporary cultures around the world, and a similar effort might well be made by historians.

Once we are committed in this direction, however, some new difficulties arise. There are many varieties of theory available in the developmental field, and it is difficult to reconcile or choose among them in a systematic way. Erikson may strike some of us as being particularly useful, but others may well form a different set of preferences. I believe, however, that the use of almost *any* developmental model—any serious attempt to differentiate among the varied experiences of childhood on either a "vertical" or a "horizontal" basis—will represent progress for the historian.

Let us consider some substantive ideas about one particular historical setting as a way of exemplifying the larger, "developmental" approach. The ideas presented in the next few paragraphs are based entirely on materials left by those seventeenth-century "Puritans" who founded the colonies of New England. There is no intention here to produce a rounded view of Puritan culture—nor is there space to provide the appropriate sort of documentation. But, hopefully, these comments will serve to characterize a certain way of thinking about historical problems, and to reveal both the gains and the drawbacks inherent in such an approach.

Here, then, are some tentative conclusions about particular aspects of Puritan practice in the treatment of infants and very young children. For the sake of clarity they are separated into seven distinct statements:[11]

(1) All infants were breast-fed for the first twelve to sixteen months of life.

(2) The clothing of infants was light and loosely fitted; there is no evidence in early American materials of the custom of swaddling.

(3) Very young infants often slept in the bed of one or both of their parents. Later they might be transferred to a cradle, or in some cases, to a trundle-bed shared with one or more older siblings.

(4) Their immediate surroundings were animated, warm, and intimate. Puritan families tended to be quite large,[12] and most infants would have from the start a number of siblings. At the same time, the houses of this period were small, with most daytime activities being confined to the room known as the "hall." One imagines, therefore, an infant lying in a cradle, which is set near the fireplace for warmth, and with a variety of familiar shapes and faces moving constantly around him. This is, to some degree, conjectural, but there is a fit about it all that seems persuasive. In short, we may conclude that for the first year or so, the Puritan child had a relatively comfortable and unrestricted mode of life. But consider what followed.

(5) As previously noted, breast-feeding ended after twelve to sixteen months. We know little enough about the usual manner of weaning in this culture, but there is fragmentary evidence to suggest that it may have been quite abrupt. Apparently in some instances a bitter substance was applied to the breast so as to curb the infant's wish to suckle. And certain mothers may actually have left the household for a few days in order to make a clean break. Particularly suggestive in this connection is the appearance of weaning as a metaphor in a wide range of Puritan literature. Experiences of misfortune and disappointment were often described as "weaning dispensations," and obviously this usage was meant to convey a poignant sense of loss.

(6) When the child was about two, a new baby would arrive. Most Puritan mothers gave birth at remarkably regular intervals of twenty-two to twenty-six months. The reason for this was the powerful contraceptive influence of lactation. We can, thus, recognize that for many infants in this culture the second year of life was bounded by experiences of profound loss—at the beginning by the loss of the breast (with all that this implies for *emotional* as well as physical sustenance), and at the end by the loss of the mother's special care and attention.

(7) Puritan writings which deal in some direct way with child-rearing share one central theme: The child's inherent "willfulness" must be curbed—indeed, it must be "broken" and "beaten down"—as soon as it begins to appear.[13] All other aspects of character development are dependent on this procedure. Here, for Puritans, lay *the central task* of parenthood; and, in a profound sense, they regarded it as involving a direct confrontation with "original sin."

None of the extant literature specifies the precise age at which such will-training should begin, but most likely it was some time during the second year. For this is the age when every child becomes, for the first time, able to express his own wishes in an organized and effective way. He develops a variety of motor skills: he walks and runs, and he rapidly improves the coordination of hand and eye. He begins to learn speech. And, more generally, he becomes acutely aware of the difference between "I" and "you," "mine" and "yours." Even under the mildest sort of disciplinary regime there is bound to be some degree of conflict with authority, parental or otherwise, for a significant part of the child's new assertiveness is expressed as anger and aggression. This, after all, is the phase which Benjamin Spock discusses under the general rubric "the terrible twos."

And what does the psychologist have to say about it? For Erikson, this is the second of the major developmental stages, the one in which the central task is the formation of "autonomy." "This stage," he writes, "becomes decisive for the ratio between love and hate, for that between freedom of self-expression and its suppression. From a sense of *self-control without loss of self-esteem* comes a lasting sense of autonomy and pride." Moreover, while the goal of this stage is "autonomy," its negative side—and its specific vulnerability—is the possible fixation of lasting shame and doubt. It is absolutely vital that the child receive support in "his wish to 'stand on his own feet,' lest he be overcome by that sense of having exposed himself prematurely and foolishly which we call shame, or that secondary mistrust, that 'double-take' which we call doubt."[14]

Let us return now to the Puritans, in order to pull together these varied materials on their child-rearing patterns. We have, first, a period of perhaps twelve months when the infant is for the most part treated indulgently—followed, in the second year of life, by weaning, by the arrival of a younger sibling, and by a radical shift toward a harsh and restrictive style of discipline. It is necessary to emphasize, above all, the last of these events, since, in Erikson's terms, the determination to crush the child's will is nothing less than an effort to deprive him of a chance to develop a lasting and confident sense of autonomy.

Clinical experience would argue that these patterns must have exerted a profound influence on all of the people who lived through them. Our next task is to survey some of the larger areas of Puritan life in which such influence can be discerned. Let us consider the whole field of interpersonal behavior—the style of relating to one another that was characteristic of this culture. It presents, in fact, a strikingly two-sided aspect. On the one hand, the Puritans placed a tremendous emphasis on the value of harmony, unity, and concord: one could cite as evidence literally countless sermons, essays, official decrees, and pronouncements. At the level of aspirations, nothing was more important for these people.[15] On the other hand, if one examines in detail the actual record of life in these communities—through various court and personal records—one discovers an extraordinary atmosphere of contentiousness and outright conflict. "Harmony" was always the preeminent value; yet, in trying to attain it, the Puritans constantly disappointed themselves. There is no paradox here; there is only the core of a pervasive ambivalence, something that was deeply rooted in the people themselves. To a very considerable degree, the inner life of Puritanism turned on a kind of axis between the opposite poles of conflict and conciliation, anger and love, aggression and submissiveness. And *all* of this, I suggest, is a plausible outcome of the pattern of childhood experience as previously described.

Moreover, we must attempt to assess the specific causes of the many conflicts in which Puritans became enmeshed, and the manner in which such conflicts were resolved. Disputes over boundaries were a constant source of trouble in these communities—boundaries between one man's land and his neighbor's, or often between whole townships that were adjacent to one another. A second, closely-related category of actions involved "trespass" of some sort; and here, too, the court cases are very numerous. More generally, many cases in which the immediate problem was something else—debt, or theft, or breach of contract—seem to have been experienced *emotionally*, by those directly involved, as a form of personal "trespass." We may conclude, in short, that "boundaries" were an immensely potent issue for Puritan culture—and that this, in psychological terms, was tightly bound up with the question of autonomy.

We can also investigate these patterns from the *negative* side of the Eriksonian model, recalling that the reverse of autonomy is the distress created by deep inner trends of shame and doubt. Consider the large number of slander and defamation cases in the records which reveal an extreme sensitivity to the threat of public exposure and humiliation. Some of the most common forms of punishment imposed by legally-constituted authorities in these settlements were sitting in the stocks, branding, or being forced to wear badges of infamy. It seems clear that the pain which these punishments inflicted was above all due to the element of shame. As to Erikson's notion of "doubt," once again the Puritans appear to make a striking fit. Traditionally, of course, they have been pictured as smug, dogmatic, self-righteous, and intolerant—and indeed they often did wear this appearance. But how deeply did it penetrate? If one reads a few of the spiritual diaries and autobiographies left by Puritans with this question in mind, something very much like "doubt"—doubt of their faith, of their "standing" in the eyes of God—emerges as the primary *leit-motif* of such documents. If they sometimes acted smugly and self-satisfied, this was perhaps a kind of false front—a defense against profound inner anxieties from which they could never truly escape.

Here we have made a direct contact with their religious experience, and this might well be a particularly fruitful field in which to develop the same line of analysis. Let us consider for a moment some of the most familiar imagery of Puritan belief: the God who was by turns infinitely loving and overwhelmingly angry, and a God, too, who had the very special power to "see" every human action, no matter how secret, and to make the sinner feel deeply shamed; Heaven pictured as the place of total harmony, Hell as the place of everlasting strife; a moral universe in which each man was to struggle to achieve his personal salvation, though God had already entirely predestined the outcome of that struggle. It is tempting, indeed, to regard Puritan religious belief as a kind of screen on which all of their innermost concerns—autonomy, shame, doubt, anger—were projected with a very special clarity.

In order to become persuasive, these interpretations will require an extended treatment, much more so than is possible here. Therefore I propose, in conclusion, simply to point out some of the strategic and theoretical problems that are likely to arise in any analysis of this sort. We must be careful not to underestimate them.

There is, in the first place, an obvious need for work on the other developmental stages besides the earliest ones—work that finally presents childhood as a long and continuing sequence of growth and change. Character is not fixed at age two or three; later socialization is also of major consequence. With respect to the Puritans, one can surmise that there was much in the experience of later childhood to reinforce the training of the first few years. Any overt display of aggression or willfulness would elicit a stern parental response. Shaming was employed as a disciplinary technique, to an extent that directly enhanced the early sensitivities in this area.[16] The religious education of young persons stressed their utter dependence on God, their need to obliterate all traces of selfhood in order to become worthy of salvation. Traditional folklore underscored these lessons; stories of witchcraft, for example, conveyed with particular vividness the aura of danger that clung to manifestly hostile behavior.[17] There was also the general influence imparted by observing one's elders engaged in countless everyday transactions with each other—in which, of course, the same themes were repeatedly elaborated.

We need not contend, therefore, that all of Puritan culture was determined by traumas occurring during the second year of life, or that there is a simple "linear" connection between autonomy issues in early childhood and later adult behavior. At the same time we can believe that what happened during the second year was critical in the development of these people—that "autonomy" was *the* characteristic Puritan conflict, and that all of this was reflected in a variety of important social and cultural forms.

But are there not other, preferable explanations for the same range of phenomena? Perhaps we should look instead to certain features of Puritan social structure or political process—fields of inquiry with which historians are generally more familiar and more comfortable. It might be argued, for example, that chronic quarreling over boundaries resulted from the entirely "natural" concerns of peasants and yeomen in an overwhelmingly agricultural society. But this interpretation seems dubious for two reasons. First, there are many agricultural societies in which boundaries are not nearly so troublesome an issue; and, second, the empty lands of the New World should, from a practical standpoint, have lessened any competitive pressures of this type.[18]

Another sort of alternative explanation might be developed from our data on shame. Perhaps the frequency of trials for slander and defamation should be viewed as a necessary concomitant of life in little communities. Where so much human interchange was on a face-to-face basis, a man would have to protect his good reputation in order to obtain rewarding work and social contacts. There is substantial merit in this idea, but it need not be construed as opposed to a more psychological mode of explanation. Indeed, these two factors, the psychological and the practical, lock neatly together. One can even see a measure of gain for the people who endured such a harsh system of discipline: When they emerged as adults, they were conditioned to respond to precisely those cues which would ensure their practical welfare. In this respect, Puritan child-rearing was functionally appropriate to the wider Puritan culture.

But to use the word "Puritan" is simply to beg some further questions. How widely should such interpretations be applied? What groups of people can they reasonably be made to cover? We may agree perhaps that the above analysis treats real problems and issues in the lives of New England Puritans of the seventeenth century. But are we concerned here *only* with New England Puritans? Or can the same patterns be found among New Englanders in general, among settlers in other parts of the colonies, among Puritans in both the Old World and the New, among all English-speaking people—or, indeed, throughout all of "Western civilization" in early modern times? In short, the problem is to determine the extension of a particular line of analysis in terms of both historical time and cultural space. Until there is good comparative data on other communities from roughly the same period, we cannot be sure to what extent Puritan child-rearing and Puritan personality development were, in fact, distinctively Puritan.

There are, finally, some special methodological problems in this kind of study: They are not by any means insurmountable problems, but it is best to be explicit about what they involve. There is, first, a style of "proof" or "verification" which may seem somewhat novel when set against traditional canons of historical scholarship. We have, on the one hand, certain information about the prescribed method of disciplining young children, and, on the other, certain information about adult behavior in this society—court cases, methods of punishment, statements of ultimate value, and styles of religious concern. The connection between these two matters is not something that we can follow along a visible chain of evidence. Indeed, we can scarcely link them at all except through a process of analogy and inference, and the basis for this process is what we know from clinical experience in our own time. Moreover, because we are dealing in inference, there is a sense in which each side of the sequence confirms the other. That is: if Puritan adults were especially concerned about "boundaries" and "trespass," and especially vulnerable to shame, then we can say that they *must* have been roughly treated at an early age for their assertive and aggressive strivings. Similarly, if handled this way in childhood, then they *must* have behaved more or less as described later on. This may sound like circular reasoning to the historian—but not to the psychologist, who can adduce countless clinical observations to verify the correlation of the critical variables. It is, after all, less a case of circularity, and more a matter of internal consistency.

The second problem can be presented in the form of a warning. Historians are, officially at least, well aware of the pitfalls created by their own bias; but it is sometimes unclear as to how serious they are about this. In any event, the study of childhood and the family, the exploration of the whole inner world of human personality, is particularly open to various forms of projective distortion—vastly more so, for example, than the study of political, economic, or diplomatic history. Political bias or intellectual preferences are relatively easy to recognize and deal with. But the kinds of psychological baggage that we all carry within us—the outcome, in large part, of our own experience as children, as siblings, and as parents—are both much more powerful and much less conscious.

Yet the gains made possible by adopting a developmental approach remain substantial. What I hope I am doing in my own research is reinterpreting, or at least reordering, some of the most significant elements in early American life; and a similar strategy could certainly be applied in the analysis of other historical periods and other cultures. In the effort to make this strategy work, the study of childhood necessarily assumes a central place. It serves to bring into view certain themes which may not have been clearly recognized before, and, more broadly, it adds analytic depth to the entire research enterprise. We might refer once again to the distinction suggested earlier between the two basic types of approach to our subject. In the first instance we can point to Ariès, and no doubt many others who will be following the course he has marked out—scholars who study the child as a kind of mirror which focuses and reflects back cultural themes of central importance. But in the second instance—what I have been trying to outline here—something else is involved: The child becomes not just a mirror, not only the creature, but also the creator of culture, and, in this sense, a dynamic force in his own right.

Notes

1. See, for example, David Hunt, *Parents and Children in History: The Psychology of Family Life in Early Modern France* (New York, 1970); Bernard Wishy, *The Child and the Republic: The Dawn of Modern American Child Nurture* (Philadelphia, 1967); Robert H. Bremner, *et al.*, *Childhood and Youth in America* (Cambridge, Mass., 1970–71), I–II.

2. Philippe Ariès (trans. Robert Baldick), *Centuries of Childhood: A Social History of Family Life* (New York, 1962).

3. A book which *does* foreshadow many of the concerns of this paper is David M. Potter, *People of Plenty: Economic Abundance and the American Character* (Chicago, 1954), esp. Ch. 9. See also Hunt, *Parents and Children in History,* Chs. 6–9.

4. For an excellent summary of this work, see Alex Inkeles and Daniel J. Levinson, "National Character: The Study of Modal Personality and Sociocultural Systems," in Gardner Lindzey and Elliott Aronson (eds.), *The Handbook of Social Psychology* (Reading, Mass., 1969; 2nd ed.), IV, 418–506. See also Milton Singer, "A Survey of Culture and Personality Theory and Research," in Bert Kaplan (ed.), *Studying Personality Cross-Culturally* (New York, 1961), 9–90.

5. Abram Kardiner, *The Individual and His Society* (New York, 1939), 24.

6. Some of these criticisms are outlined in Inkeles and Levinson, "National Character," 424–425.

7. Clyde Kluckhohn and Henry A. Murray (eds.), *Personality in Nature, Society, and Culture* (New York, 1962; rev. ed.), 57. On this general topic see also Anthony F. C. Wallace, *Culture and Personality* (New York, 1961). It is not necessary in this paper to enter the controversy over the proper meaning, and usage, of the concept of "modal personality." I am willing for present purposes to accept a very minimal definition, such as the one quoted above from Kluckhohn and Murray.

8. These statements—not actual quotations—are intended to represent viewpoints widely prevalent in previous historical literature.

9. The best summary of this scheme is in Erik H. Erikson, *Identity and the Life Cycle* (New York, 1959), 50–100.

10. See John W. M. Whiting and Irvin L. Child, *Child Training and Personality: A Cross-Cultural Study* (New Haven, 1953). Erikson's model also lends itself to a "horizontal" breakdown, since each of the eight stages involves a "task" that is of lasting importance throughout an individual life.

11. These matters are presented at greater length in John Demos, *A Little Commonwealth: Family Life in Plymouth Colony* (New York, 1970), esp. 46–49, 131–144.

12. Completed families in colonial New England averaged roughly eight children apiece. For a detailed analysis of this point, see Demos, *A Little Commonwealth,* 68–69, 192; Philip J. Greven, Jr., *Four Generations: Population, Land, and Family in Colonial Andover, Massachusetts* (Ithaca, 1970), 30–31, 111–112.

13. See, for example, certain statements in Robert Ashton (ed.), *The Works of John Robinson* (Boston, 1851), i, 246–247. See also Cotton Mather, "Some Special Points, Relating to the Education of My Children," reprinted in Perry Miller and Thomas H. Johnson (eds.), *The Puritans* (New York, 1963), II, 724–727.

14. Erikson, *Identity and the Life Cycle,* 63.

15. This aspect of Puritan life has been the subject of two recent studies: Kenneth A. Lockridge, *A New England Town: The First Hundred Years* (New York, 1970); Michael Zuckerman, *Peaceable Kingdoms* (New York, 1970). These authors have brilliantly portrayed the *ideal* of community in early New England—and to this extent I am much in their debt. My own analysis, however, diverges somewhat from theirs in finding a large amount of actual conflict-behavior among the individual people in question.

16. Note the following attributed to John Ward, in Cotton Mather, *Magnala Christi Americana* (Hartford, 1853), I, 522: "Of young persons he would himself give this advice: 'Whatever you do, be sure to maintain shame in them; for if that be once gone, there is no hope that they'll ever come to good." In his essay, "Some Special Points, Relating to the Education of My Children," Mather writes: "I cause them to understand, that it is an *hurtful* and a *shameful* thing to do amiss. I aggravate this, on all occasions; and lett them see how *amiable* they will render themselves by well doing. The *first chastisement,* which I inflict for an ordinary fault is, to lett the child see and hear me in an astonishment, and hardly able to beleeve that the child could do so *base* a thing, but beleeving that they will never do it again" (725–726). The shaming effects of this procedure are impossible to miss.

17. See John Demos, "Underlying Themes in the Witchcraft of Colonial New England," *The American Historical Review,* LXXV (1970), 1311–1326.

18. This point can be clarified by exploring the contrary case as well. If the concern with boundaries is to be explained in terms of *psychological* functioning, then it is quite plausible that the whole issue should have been sharpened by the literally "unbounded" character of the American wilderness.

6. In Search of the Historical Child: Miniature Adulthood and Youth in Colonial New England

"I shall miss the little grown-ups—were there no children in those days?"[1] This question about an eighteenth-century portrait of four American children essentially states the widespread scholarly and antiquarian view of children in colonial America. Not only is it assumed that colonial Americans treated their children differently than we do today, but it is also believed that they regarded their children as "miniature adults" and recognized no stage of development like twentieth-century adolescence. While this essay does not suggest that colonial Americans treated their children as we treat ours, it does conclude that notions of "miniature adulthood" and the absence of adolescence in colonial New England are, at best, exaggerations.

Much of the myth of miniature adulthood stems from the belief that children in colonial portraits appeared old and dressed like their parents. Until the Revolution, writes Alice Morse Earle, "as soon as a boy put on breeches he dressed precisely like his father—in miniature."[2] According to Arthur M. Schlesinger, "the older generation as late as Independence still displayed its basic assumption that children were miniature adults by continuing to dress the young like little grownups. . . . The vital distinction between youth and age as yet remained unrecognized."[3] Monica Kiefer finds that eighteenth-century children occupied "a submerged position in an adult setting"; only through the child's "gradual emergence" from that status would he come to occupy "a place of honor as a cherished social entity." Like other observers, she concludes that, "as children of Colonial times were expected to behave like adults, they quite logically wore clothes appropriate for the role."[4] Michael Zuckerman also states that there was "no clear distinction between child and adult" in eighteenth-century Massachusetts. Children in Puritan portraits are "only scaled-down adults," who wear both wigs and the same clothes as their parents. "If clothes do not make the man," he asserts, "they do mark social differentiations; a distinctive mode of dress for children never developed before the Revolution." New Englanders did not believe that children had "distinctive needs and desires," and children were therefore given "no distinctive places or roles." Eighteenth-century Massachusetts children "did not live separated from the society in a protected preserve of carefree innocence; they were part of a single undifferentiated community."[5]

Accounts of childhood in early America are marked by condescension, sentimentality, and even blank incomprehension. In describing Cotton Mather's admonitions to his daughter, Earle confesses, "I hardly understand why Cotton Mather, who was really very gentle to his children, should have taken upon himself to trouble this tender little

Ross W. Beales, Jr., "In Search of the Historical Child: Miniature Childhood and Youth in Colonial New England," *American Quarterly* 27 (1975): 379–98, with the permission of the *American Studies Association*. Copyright 1975, American Studies Association.

blossom with dread of his death." None of Earle's concern for Mather's "tender little blossom" appears in her discussion of Nathaniel Mather, whose diary contains the admission, "Of the manifold sins which then I was guilty of, none so sticks upon me as that, being very young, I was *whitling* on the Sabbath-day; and for fear of being seen I did it behind the *door*. A great *reproach* of God! a specimen of that *atheism* I brought into the world with me!" For Earle, "it is satisfactory to add that this young prig of a Mather died when nineteen years of age."[6]

Certain that modern parents know best how to rear children, authors like Earle believe that their knowledge is an appropriate standard by which to judge other cultures and eras. They insist that colonial child-rearing practices were not only incorrect but also harmful. Arthur W. Calhoun thus emphasizes the ill effect of "precocity" on children. The seventeenth century was "an age of precocity," which was encouraged in America by Puritan theology and a scarcity of labor. Parents' "zeal for education," for example, "overstimulated and forced baby minds"; the churches encouraged "infantile conversion"; and, in economic life, children were overworked and exploited. In Calhoun's judgment, the Puritans failed "to make the child appear valuable or noteworthy to himself or others." Such a "curtailment of infancy" was both a "distortion" of and "a crime against childhood."[7]

Sandford Fleming argues that in Puritan society "children were regarded simply as miniature adults, and the same means and experiences were considered as suitable for them as for those older." This view of children resulted partly from the general attitudes of a society which lacked the benefits of modern psychology. Furthermore, Puritan theology "had banished the child, and classed everyone indiscriminately, infants and those of maturity, as sinners who were in urgent need of being saved from hell." The necessity of encouraging early conversions was particularly unfortunate in the century after the Great Awakening, when an "overdependence" on revival methods caused the "child mind" to develop "wrong" and "perverted" ideas of God. Indeed, the emotional excesses of revivalism "could hardly fail to do permanent physical, mental and spiritual injury to many of the children wrought upon."[8]

John Demos finds that childhood in Plymouth Colony lasted a short, but crucial, six to eight years. Although a child's first year was "relatively comfortable and tranquil," his second year was likely to be traumatic. Not only would he be weaned and later be confronted by the birth of a rival sibling, but his parents, heeding the repressive advice of minister John Robinson, would seek to crush his "assertive and aggressive drives." As Robinson warned, "surely there is in all children . . . a stubbornness, and stoutness of mind arising from natural pride, which must, in the first place, be broken and beaten down." Demos suggests that this early childhood experience, in which the desire for "autonomy" was beaten down, instilled a lasting sense of "shame and doubt" in the Puritan character. As a result, adult life in Plymouth Colony was characterized by numerous personal conflicts and court cases, especially incidents involving slander, defamation, and fear of public exposure.

At about six to eight years of age, a child in Plymouth Colony became, in effect, a "miniature adult." Clothing symbolized this new status: previously dressed "in a kind of long robe which opened down the front," boys and girls now dressed very much like their parents. This implies "a whole attitude of mind," in which "there was no idea that each generation required separate spheres of work or recreation. Children learned the behavior appropriate to their sex and station by sharing in the activities of their parents."

Six- or seven-year-olds began "technological" training, the boys perhaps working with their fathers at planting or fencemending, the girls helping their mothers with the cooking, spinning, or candlemaking. There may also have been some academic training, including more intensive religious instruction. The pattern of age at apprenticeship and service in other families also leads Demos to stress the years from six to eight, "the most common age for such arrangements."

Children's religious experiences also suggest miniature adulthood, for whole families attended the same church services, and "the young no less than the old were expected to digest the learned words that flowed from the pulpit." While nineteenth-century conversions typically occurred among young people in their teens, "no similar pattern" was found at Plymouth. In fact, many conversions apparently took place well before puberty. "Perhaps, indeed, a religious 'crisis' can more reasonably be connected with the whole matrix of changes customary for children at the age of about six to eight." Thus, with the evidence converging on this early age, it is likely that "the culture attached a very special importance to this particular time of life. Further 'proof' is lacking, but perhaps it was now that children began to assume the role of little adults."

After these crucial years, the development of the child was relatively smooth. "The way to maturity appeared not as a cliff to be mounted in a series of sudden and precarious leaps, but as a gradual ascent the stages of which were quite literally embodied in the many siblings variously situated along the way." Adolescence was not the turning point that it is today, for "at Plymouth the 'teens' formed a period of relatively calm and steady progress toward full maturity." Courtships began during this stage of development, and following marriage, "the later years of life in Plymouth Colony brought, in most cases, no new departures of a major kind."[9]

Joseph F. Kett agrees with Demos's findings with respect to adolescence. "Verbal distinctions between childhood and youth" were "practically nonexistent in the seventeenth century and still rare in the eighteenth." While there were numerous references to "youth" as early as the seventeenth century, the Puritans used "youth" as a noun rather than as a concept. Thus, their sermons commonly "mixed up children, youth, young people, and young men." Indeed, even if they experienced adolescence in a social sense, seventeenth-century "Puritans would have had difficulty coming to terms with it," for they viewed life as a highway rather than as a series of stages.[10]

Substantial agreement thus exists among authors who discuss attitudes toward children and adolescents in colonial New England. That New Englanders regarded and treated their children as miniature adults is, in C. John Sommerville's words, "one of the hoariest shibboleths."[11] Similarly widespread is the belief that there was no stage in human development comparable to today's adolescence.

Recently, however, David E. Stannard has suggested that "there is no real evidence to support the contention that in 17th century New England, as in 15th and 16th century France, there was little or no distinction between children and adults." He notes, for example, that Puritan journals, autobiographies, histories, and family manuals make "clear distinctions between adults and children well into their teens" and that the law definitely discriminated "between acceptable behavior and appropriate punishment for children, post-adolescent youths and adults."[12] Stannard's observations are confirmed by an examination of the language New Englanders used to describe the "ages of man," by legal distinctions among age groups, and particularly by religious thought and practice.

Colonial New Englanders included both children and youth in the "ages of man," with youth extending from the early teens well into the twenties. When Gilbert Tennent preached in Boston in 1741, he used four familiar chronological divisions in addressing his audience: "old" and "*aged Persons*"; "*middle-ag'd People*, of thirty Years old and upwards"; "*my younger Brethren*, of fourteen Years and upwards"; and "*little Children*, of six Years old and upwards."[13]

Tennent's age-groups approximated the concept of the "ages of man" held by New Englanders. These ages included old age, middle age, youth, childhood, and sometimes infancy. Anne Bradstreet, for example, wrote "Of the Four Ages of Man," while Ellis Gray spoke of the "Old, and the middle Aged, the Young and little Children." Samuel Moody included "infancy" when he warned that "Judgment shall be Universal with respect to Persons, *viz.* Youth as well as Children and Infants below them, and Middle, with Old Age above them. . . ." Jonathan Edwards advised "every one that is yet out of Christ, and hanging over the Pit of Hell, whether they be old Men and Women, or middle Aged, or young People, or little Children, now [to] hearken to the loud Calls of God's Word and Providence." William Cooper also addressed "MANY of you *Children*, you *Young People*, you that are *middle aged*, and you that are *old*. . . ."[14]

Edwards placed the upper limits of childhood at fourteen when he described the revival of 1735 at Northampton. It had been unusual for children to be converted, but now, he reported, "near thirty were to appearance so wrought upon between ten and fourteen years of age, and two between nine and ten, and one of about four years of age. . . ." Thomas Shepard also saw the early teens as a dividing point. When his fourteen-year-old son was admitted to Harvard College in 1672, Shepard urged him to "Remember . . . that tho' you have spent your time in the vanity of Childhood; sports and mirth, little minding better things, yet that now, when come to this ripeness of Admission to the College, that now God and man expects you should putt away Childish things: now is the time come, wherein you are to be serious, and to learn sobriety, and wisdom in all your ways which concern God and man." While young Shepard ended his childhood at fourteen, Cotton Mather dared call himself a "youth" at thirty-one. "I am willing now," he told an audience of young people, "at an Age thus far Extending, to conclude my own *Youth*, with one Affectionate Endeavour more" to encourage youthful piety.[15]

The early teens were recognized as special years in other aspects of Puritan culture. The laws of Massachusetts, for example, established fourteen as the age of discretion in cases of slander. (Neighboring Plymouth Colony set the "age of discretion" at sixteen for slander and lying.) Fourteen was also the age for "chusing of Guardions." Sodomists were to be executed, but if one party was forced to commit sodomy or was under fourteen, he was only "seveerly punished."[16]

The "ages of man" and the different ages of legal responsibility might be dismissed, however, as mere conventions that had no real social meaning. Such an argument might be especially persuasive with respect to the law because of Puritan attempts to institute Mosaic law in New England. But another area of New England culture—religious thought and practice—provides abundant evidence to confirm the patterns of language and law described above.

Historians like Calhoun, Fleming, and Demos argue that Puritans treated the young and old equally and encouraged early conversion experiences. "The young no less than the old," writes Demos, "were expected to digest the learned words that flowed from the pulpit." John Cotton would have disagreed. "Bring them to Church," he urged, "and help them to remember something, and tell them the meaning of it, and take a little in good part, and encourage them, and that will make them delight in it." This suggests that because children's capacities were limited, loving parents should take care that children understood at least something. William Williams later warned that "because of the weakness of their Understandings, and narrowness of their Capacities, in their younger Years, Pains must be us'd to convey Truth in such a manner as they may be able to *conceive* of it, and not meerly learn Things by rote."[17]

Puritan descriptions of the age-groups from which God was most likely to call His elect show that infants and children were not miniature adults. God would not, of course, restrict His call to any one age-group. "Should God call onely children, middle aged men, or old men onely," explained Thomas Hooker, "then men would conceive that there were something in the persons that moved him to this, either the weakenesse of the child, or else the innocencie thereof did move God to shew mercy thereunto, or else that God did delight in the strength or in the gifts and parts of a young man, or if he should call men in their old age onely, then men might thinke that their experience and gravitie did move God to call them onely." God called "some in all ages and at all times, some young ones chosen, and some refused, some old men called, and others cast aside." The selection of some for salvation and others for damnation resulted not from particular men's natural qualities but "from the freenesse of God's mercy."[18]

Despite its freeness, God's mercy was extended to some groups more often than to others. "Some are called in their youth, some in their middle age, some in their old age, some in their tender yeares, some in their riper age, some old, some young, but this is most true that those whom God doth call it is most commonly in their middle age before they come to their old age." According to Hooker, the middle age "hath better Materials . . . wherein, or whereupon the frame of Conversion may be erected, or imprinted by the stamp of the Spirit."[19]

The special fitness of middle age for conversion followed naturally from the attitude summarized by John Norton: "Though knowledg may be without grace, yet there can be no grace without knowledg." Infants were incapable of the knowledge that preceded grace. "In Infancy," explained Hooker, "a man lives a life little other than the life of a Plant, or Beast, feeding and sleeping, growing and encreasing; or else he takes up himself with delights of outward objects most agreeable to his Sences." This did not mean that God would not save infants, but rather that His manner of converting them was special. "Calling," said Norton, "is either extraordinary, as in Elect Infants, dying in their Infancy: or ordinary." Thus, in John Cotton's view, children were "capable of the habits and gifts of grace from their first Conception . . . , and the reason is, as soon as capable of sin, capable of grace." Hooker noted that there was "a number of children" whom it was God's purpose to save "according to election." They were to be saved, however, not because they were children but while they were children, for "all the men in the world are either vessels of mercy, or vessels of wrath, according to the good will of God." The operation of God's grace on infants was "extraordinary in mans account," but Hooker cautioned against curiosity, "for secret things belong to God," and man should be content to know "that some children are elected, and God will sanctifie them, and glorifie them; but the number, and manner, I leave that."[20]

A child who lived through infancy could exercise his understanding little more than an infant. In Hooker's opinion, a child of ten or twelve lived "the life of a beast," and it was "almost impossible" for him "to consider of the mysteries of life & salvation." In his "tender yeares" a man had "such a weake understanding" that he could "hold nothing." If a child was told of the wonders of salvation, it was "impossible unless God workes wonderfully that hee should receive them." However, when a man arrived at "the ripenesse of his yeares, from 20. years until he come to be 40. or thereabouts," Hooker believed, "the Understanding begins to shew it self in her operations: Invention is then most quick to apprehend, the Judgment to discern, Memory to retain, and the Affections tenderest and nimblest to imbrace any thing offered, and most pliable to be wrought upon." At this age "a man is able to conceive and partake of the things of grace, and fadom [*sic*] them, and the power of his understanding comes on whereby he is able to embrace them." The middle years were therefore "the fittest time that God should bestow his graces upon a man."[21]

Puritan ideas about the age-groups from which God called His elect were borne out in practice. At Dorchester, Massachusetts, for example, in the period 1640–1730, only thirty-four (8.9%) of the 382 new communicants whose ages are known were under the age of twenty; only three, all girls, were under seventeen (one each at age thirteen, fifteen, and sixteen). In the same years, 202 (52.9%) of the new communicants were in their twenties, and ninety-four (24.6%) were in their thirties.[22] At New Haven, in the years 1685–1739, only fifty-four (7.9%) of the 681 new communicants whose ages are known were younger than twenty.[23] Data from eighteenth-century Andover and Norton, Massachusetts, and Norwich and Woodbury, Connecticut, reveal the same pattern.[24] One must conclude, therefore, that the most famous conversion of the eighteenth century, that of four-year-old Phebe Bartlet of Northampton, was a remarkable exception.[25]

Provisions for catechizing children in the churches at Dorchester and Norwich also indicate that the Puritans treated children and youth differently. At Dorchester in 1672, the minister compiled a list of "all children & servants that weer under any famely government in order to catechising or some other way of instruction." The names for 1672 did not survive, but the church records do contain a list of catechumens for 1676. Males aged thirteen to twenty-eight are separated from the younger males, designated "Children from 12 et infra" and as young as seven. The list of "young Maids," aged seven to thirty-one, is not so explicitly divided, although there are spaces between ages twelve and thirteen and between ages eight and nine. The church at Norwich decided that "all the Males who are eight or nine years of age, shall be presented before the Lord in his Congregation every Lords Day to be Cate[c]hised, until they be about thirteen years in age." At thirteen, the boys and girls attended "the Meeting appointed in private for their instruction," and they continued to meet as long as they lived "under Family Government of Parents or others" or until they became full communicants.[26]

Communion presupposed a degree of knowledge that children could not achieve. "Children are not capable sabjects [*sic*] of the Lords Supper," wrote John Cotton. "For receiving whereof, the Apostle requireth wee should examine and judge our selves." Among "men of years, the Spirit . . . worketh faith by the hearing of the Word, and by revealing and tendering Christ as the al-sufficient and onely way of life." Aware that individuals matured at different rates, Puritan thinkers did not set an arbitrary age when individuals might be said to arrive at the "years of understanding." As early as 1643, Richard Mather recognized the problem of "how long Children should be counted under age." He noted that the New England churches had no occasion to look into the question. "Onely this we thinke, that one certaine rule cannot be given for all, whereby to determine how long they are under age, but according as God gives experience and maturity of naturall understanding, and Spirituall; which he gives sooner to some then unto others." Mather was somewhat more specific a number of years later when he asked, "*Till what age shall they* [children] *enter into Covenant with their Parents, whether sixteen, twenty-one, or sixty?"* He answered that "as long as in respect of age or capacity they cannot according to ordinary account, be supposed to act in a matter of this nature for themselves, so long they shall enter in by means of their Parents covenant, because whilst they are children and in their minority, they are not otherwise capable of covenanting: When adult, they are to covenant in their own persons." Thirteen years of age was not too old for a child to be included in his parents' covenant, for Ishmael (Genesis 17:25) had been "admitted to the Seal by his Fathers covenant at thirteen years of age." Nevertheless, Mather cautioned, in "the bounding of adult and in-adult age, depending upon the judgment of prudence, much is to be left unto the discretion of Officers and Churches in this case."[27]

Charles Chauncey agreed with Mather on this point. "It cannot be concluded," he wrote, "that all persons are to be looked upon as adult at the very same age, some persons coming to years of discretion before others; and some . . . having weaker parts and less means of instruction then others have, therefore we see not how there can be any *particular time* fixed when all *persons* shall be accounted adult, (or of age) to answer for themselves at this or that age, but a latitude must be allowed in this case."[28]

At Northampton, the congregation of Richard Mather's son, Eleazer, sought to "come to som[e] de[ter]mination respecting the continuing [or] expiring of the state of minority," but did not find it "limited in Scripture to any perticular yere or tyme." They therefore followed Richard Mather's advice and voted that "the fixing of Adult, and not Adult age bee left to the wisdome, discretion and judgment of the Elders of the Church from tyme to tyme, and as they upon tryall and Examination of the Ability and capacity of each person respectively shall determine them to bee in that state either of Adult or inadult, accordingly shall Such persons bee accounted and walked towards by this Church."[29]

Solomon Stoddard, Eleazer Mather's successor, departed significantly from the Mathers' point of view. Stoddard came to believe that the sacrament of the Lord's Supper was a "converting ordinance" that should not be restricted to God's visible saints; it should rather be offered to the regenerate and to the unregenerate alike with the expectation that it would help bring the latter to Christ. But Stoddard did not follow his doctrine to its logical conclusion, for it was said that he permitted only those who were "Civilized & Catechized above 14 years old" to come to the Lord's Table.[30] He thus demanded good behavior, knowledge of doctrine, and a minimal age. In discarding an older conception about the purposes of the Lord's Supper, he also discarded a flexibility in assessing the age when individuals arrived at years of understanding. It was certainly easier to classify a person as "adult" or as "inadult" merely by his age than to examine the ability and capacity of each person under fourteen, but one wonders whether this decision did not reflect a certain loss of spiritual energy, perhaps a waning of piety, that led to a less personal treatment of each soul. Put in slightly different terms, Stoddard's open communion and the arbitrary restriction of communion to persons over fourteen can be viewed as movement away from Puritanism's sect-like qualities toward an increasingly church-like form of religion.

Not all churches made such arbitrary distinctions among persons of different ages. At Barnstable, for example, the church baptized a sixteen-year-old boy "by vertue of his fathers Covenant bec[ause] upon examination, before the Elders & divers brethren of the Church thereto appointed, hee was Judged An Inadult person though 16 years old when his father Covenanted." Another case was that of Jane Bump, who, "being about fourteen or 15 years old, was examined, & being one of the family & looked upon in her minority, was Baptised." The minister declared seventeen-year-old John Howland "to be adult" and "that he could not baptize him on his mothers faith but finding In him Such pious dispositions declared that he Could baptize him on his own faith and Covenant." The members of the church agreed that John was "a Subject of baptism," but since "this was a new Case" and the members could not agree on the reasons why he should be baptized, they concluded that "this Instance [was] not to be made a precedant In time to Come." Jedidiah Lumbert's eighteen-year-old son was baptized at the West Parish of Barnstable "by vertue of his fath[er's] Covenant, for upon examination of him before the elders of the Church, he appeared not of maturity to act for himself," and "therefore he was Judged an In[adult?] & received baptism as one In minority."[31]

At Chelmsford, the church decided in 1657 that children might be baptized if they were under the age of fourteen or fifteen when their parents became communicants. Six years later, it was agreed that the minister and at least one other church member were to examine the knowledge and spiritual experience of children who had grown to years of discretion. As a result of this examination, some children were taken into communion, but others were found to have a better memory than a real understanding of doctrine. In this case, the age of discretion was probably regarded as sixteen years, for in 1666 the church agreed on a course of catechism for all persons under sixteen. Unmarried men over sixteen were given special treatment: they had the choice either of publicly demonstrating their knowledge of religion or of attending the catechism classes.[32]

These kinds of records confirm the practice of what men like Richard Mather and Charles Chauncy held in theory: that there was no set age at which a person might claim, merely by virtue of accumulated years, a new standing in the church. Recognition that an individual had arrived at years of understanding or at years of discretion depended on an examination of that understanding or discretion. Even Stoddard's church required an examination, for a person who sought communion had to be both fourteen and "Civilized & Cathechised." Persons under fourteen, regardless of their precocity, were automatically excluded from communion; persons over fourteen were only conditionally eligible for communion.

Language, law, and religious thought and practice thus suggest that New Englanders, far from regarding children as "miniature adults," recognized their immaturity. But what about individuals who were no longer children? Did "youth" in colonial New England in any sense resemble twentieth-century adolescence? "The adolescent as a distinct species," writes F. Musgrove, "is the creation of modern social attitudes and institutions. A creature neither child nor adult, he is a comparatively recent socio-psychological invention, scarcely two centuries old."[33] In contrast to this viewpoint, S. N. Eisenstadt observes that

> however great the differences among various societies, there is one focal point within the life span of an individual which in most societies is to some extent emphasized: the period of youth, of transition from childhood to full adult status, or full membership in the society. In this period the individual is no longer a child (especially from the physical and sexual point of view) but is ready to undertake many attributes of an adult and to fulfill adult roles. But he is not yet fully acknowledged as an adult, a full member of the society. Rather, he is being "prepared," or is preparing himself for such adulthood.[34]

Eisenstadt's generalization is applicable to colonial New England, where the stage of development, commonly called "youth," resembled today's "adolescence."

In physiological terms, adolescence is the biological and sexual maturation of a child, extending from puberty to the achievement of full reproductive capacity. In a broader sense, adolescence includes both sexual maturation and the social and psychological development of the individual. Sociologically, adolescence has been described as "the transition period from dependent childhood to self-sufficient adulthood." It ends with the attainment of full adult status within the limits prescribed by one's culture, class, and sex. Adolescents and children are thus distinguished from adults by the adult activities from which they are excluded: for example, marriage and the rearing of families; economic self-sufficiency; participation in the political life of the community to the extent that their sex and station permit. Psychologically, adolescence "is a 'marginal situation' in which new adjustments have to be made, namely those that distinguish child behavior from adult behavior in a given society." Chronologically, adolescence continues "from approximately twelve or thirteen to the early twenties, with wide individual and cultural variations."[35]

The transition from the dependence of childhood to the self-sufficiency of adulthood was not made suddenly in early New England. This can be seen, for example, in the individual's gradual assumption of the legal rights and obligations of adulthood. Massachusetts children over sixteen, "and of sufficient understanding," were to be executed if they cursed or struck their parents. Likewise, "a stubborn or REBELLIOUS SON, of sufficient years & understanding (*viz*) sixteen years of age," risked capital punishment for incorrigible disobedience. Another law provided that "the minoritie of women in case of marriage shall be till sixteen years." Although Plymouth youths were eligible for militia service at sixteen, "noe single persons under twenty yeares of age either children or servants" could vote in "milletary concernments." In Massachusetts, twenty-one was the age both for "passing away of lands, or such kinde of hereditaments, or for giving of votes, verdicts or sentences in any civil courts or causes," and for making "Wills & Testaments & other lawfull Alienations of their lands and estates." A statute of limitations affecting inheritances in Plymouth Colony permitted minors to bring suit within five years of reaching twenty-one. Finally, in the town of Barnstable in Plymouth Colony, a person had to be either twenty-four years old or married in order to share in a division of the town lands.[36]

"Where land was abundant and labor at a premium," writes Bernard Bailyn, "it took little more to create a household than to maintain one. Material independence was sooner or later available to every energetic adult white male, and few failed to break away when they could." Oscar and Mary F. Handlin assert that "the passage of the child to adulthood ceased to be a gradual progression through well-defined stages and became a single great leap away from home."[37]

Recent studies show that Bailyn and the Handlins overestimate the ease with which the economic self-sufficiency of a separate household might be attained. "A man ready to marry," observes Kenneth A. Lockridge, "did not just go out and get a job; he prepared a farm of his own to support his family or else he made sure that he could expect to inherit the family home and acres."[38] The creation of a household, contrary to Bailyn's premise, often must have required considerable labor, parental assistance, and capital outlay. Land had to be acquired, cleared, and fenced; buildings, however rough in the first years, had to withstand New England winters; animals and tools, as well as household utensils and furnishings, were also needed.

Philip J. Greven, Jr.'s study of the first four generations in Andover, Massachusetts, documents the slowness with which sons achieved economic independence. The key to independence was land, and fathers often retained until death legal title to the lands on which their sons were settled. Those sons who purchased their shares of the paternal estate were more often than not "mature men rather than youths just out of adolescence or in their early twenties." Some sons, particularly in the third and fourth generations, did choose to leave Andover, and their fathers often helped them to achieve autonomy relatively early.[39]

Patterns of apprenticeship in New England also suggest that a "youth" of thirteen or fourteen would not assume autonomous economic status for several years. In the seventeenth century, according to Edmund S. Morgan, a boy typically chose his calling between the ages of ten and fourteen. Most apprenticeships required seven years of service to a master and lasted until the age of twenty-one.[40] Thus, while an individual made an early choice of his life-long occupation, his actual economic independence was delayed seven years while he learned the skills of his calling. And even if he were fully trained at the age of twenty-one, it is unlikely that a young man would have had the capital or connections necessary to establish his economic independence.

Political rights also came slowly. In Plymouth Colony, the revised laws of 1671 established twenty-one years as the earliest age at which a man might become a freeman. John Demos finds no "set age" at which men became freemen, for his sample of sixty adult males achieved that status between twenty-five and forty. "This privilege and responsibility . . . was perhaps the last in the series of steps leading to full adult citizenship in the community." Delayed political adulthood followed naturally from the economic qualifications for freemanship and late economic adulthood.

Marriage was closely connected to economic independence, for marriage presupposed the ability to provide for a family. Parents played an important role in their child's choice of a spouse, for successful courtship, at least in the seventeenth century, depended on the parents' directing influence, good will, and skill in negotiating a marriage settlement. Like the ability to earn a living, marriage was often delayed until the middle twenties and later.[41]

"The most sensitive register of maturity," writes Greven, "is the age at marriage, since the responsibilities and duties involved in the establishment of a new family suggest the recognition that the married couple were ready to function as adults."[42] This insight is confirmed by other evidence. The provisions for catechizing at Norwich and Dorchester took special notice of unmarried non-communicants, who were apparently required to receive religious instruction either until they became communicants or until they married and set up independent households. The laws of Plymouth Colony also accorded special recognition to the married *vis-à-vis* the unmarried. A married man under the age of twenty could presumably vote in "milletary concernments," while his single counterpart could not. Finally, at Barnstable a single male had to wait until the age of twenty-four in order to share in a division of the town lands, while a married male under twenty-four was eligible for a share.

From these varied data emerge a picture of a prolonged "adolescence" or "youth" experienced by young people in colonial New England. Youth, in Benjamin Colman's words, was a "chusing time."

> Now O Young People is *your chusing time,* and commonly your *fixing time,* and as you fix it is like to last. Now you commonly chuse your *Trade;* betake yourselves to your business

for life, show what you incline to, and how you intend to be imploy'd all your days. Now you chuse your *Master* and your Education or Occupation. And now you dispose of your self in *Marriage* ordinarily, place your *Affections,* give away your hearts, look out for some *Companion* of life, whose to be as long as you live. And is this indeed the work of your Youth?[43]

For today's adolescent, at least in his idealized type, this "chusing time" presumably provides the opportunity to try out a number of life styles or roles, for the choices are abundant and the pressures for early decision are often not great. In this respect, adolescence has been called a "moratorium," during which the adolescent is dependent on parents and society, yet free from significant responsibilities. As a result, the adolescent in an age-stratified society is likely to be part of a peer-group based on age and having its own distinctive "culture."

In colonial New England, the range of choices open to youth was narrow, particularly outside Benjamin Colman's Boston, and decisions tended to be irrevocable: "as you fix it is like to last." As Demos points out, "the professional and 'artisan' classes were relatively small" in seventeenth-century Plymouth, "and the vast majority of the populace was engaged simply in farming. In the typical case, therefore, the choice of a calling was scarcely a choice at all; instead it was something assumed, something everywhere implicit in the child's surroundings and in the whole process of growth." Kenneth Lockridge suggests that "most men showed the typical peasant's satisfaction with the *status quo*. It worked for his father and for his father before him, why tinker with success? Why, especially when it could be dangerous?"[44] In addition to having limited choices, sons—to say nothing of daughters—were heavily dependent upon their parents both in timing and in making their choice of education or occupation, economic independence, and marriage. Under such circumstances, a son's bold assertion of independence from his parents or adoption of an alien life style was surely difficult if not unthinkable. Neither the desire nor the ability existed.

This is not to say, however, that elements of a distinctive youth "culture" did not exist in colonial New England. Ministers' descriptions of youthful behavior before and after the revivals of the eighteenth century reveal a deep strain of anxiety about the apparent collapse of family government and a rejoicing that the revival had prompted a measure of youthful self-control and reformation. Jonathan Edwards, for example, reported that there was "a time of extraordinary dullness in religion" just after the death of his grandfather, Solomon Stoddard. "Licentiousness for some years greatly prevailed among the youth of the town," many of whom were "very much addicted to night-walking, and frequenting the tavern, and lewd practices, wherein some, by their example exceedingly corrupted others." The youth "very frequently" gathered "in conventions of both sexes, for mirth and jollity, which they called frolics," and in which they often spent "the greater part of the night . . . without any regard to any order in the families they belonged to: and indeed family government did too much fail in the town." The Northampton revival of late 1734 and 1735 radically changed the behavior of the town's young people. The conversion of a young woman, "one of the greatest company-keepers in the whole town," was "almost like a flash of lightning, upon the hearts of young people all over the town, and upon many others." As Edwards looked back on the revival, he expressed the hope that those young people who were "on other accounts most likely and considerable" had become "truly pious and leading persons in the ways of religion." Similarly "those that were formerly looser young persons are generally, to all appearance, become true lovers of God and Christ, and spiritual in their dispositions."[45]

This pattern of youthful reformation was repeated frequently during the Great Awakening. At Somers, Connecticut, "those *Youths* that delighted themselves in Frolicking and Mischief" were reported to "have wholly left it off" and reputedly found "more Pleasure and Satisfaction in serving GOD, than ever they did in the Ways of *Sin and Satan*." The young people of Halifax, Massachusetts, abandoned "all Frolicking and Carousing, and merry Meetings" and now "took more delight in going to a Meeting than ever they did to a Frolick." The minister of Wrentham rejoiced that the "*young People*" had "generally and voluntarily *done* with their *Frolicking* and *merry Meetings*" and bitterly lamented the time they had wasted in such pursuits. Even "some of the *late Ring-leaders* of their Merriment" shared these sentiments. The Awakening at Bridgewater convinced many of the young "of the Sin of spending away Days & Nights in Singing and Dancing, and other youthful Sins, which they were much addicted to before, and greatly delighted in." As a result they stopped "their youthful Practices, of Singing, Dancing, Company-keeping, which before they esteemed lawful Recreations, and took abundance of Pleasure in."[46]

These and other accounts of pre-revival patterns of youthful behavior—night-walking, frolicking, company-keeping, carousing, merry-meeting, dancing and singing—suggest that there were elements of a separate youth "culture" at least in eighteenth-century New England. If this culture was not so sharply separated from the adult world as today's adolescent "cultures," the explanation may be that Puritan youth did not live in as highly an age-stratified society as today's adolescents. This is probably the source of Arthur W. Calhoun's alarm at Puritan "precocity." Puritan hagiography includes accounts of children who learned their letters and catechism at remarkably early ages. Moreover, it was not unusual at Harvard and Yale for brothers of different ages to be in the same class, or for a class to contain members whose ages ranged from the early teens to the twenties.[47]

It thus appears that in colonial New England, childhood was not succeeded by "miniature adulthood" but by "youth," a lengthy transitional period preceding adult status. During this "chusing time," when the young were expected (in Thomas Shepard's words) to "putt away Childish things," the youth remained dependent on his elders for his education, for his choice of and training in a calling, and for the material means, usually land, which would support a family. While this dependence carried with it a measure of parental control, it also provided a moratorium, a freedom from adult responsibilities, during which the elements of a youthful "culture" might emerge.

What do these findings suggest about the history of family life in America? On the one hand, as Stannard argues, the Ariès paradigm of French parent-children relationships is not applicable to the American experience. In part, this may arise from America's relatively short history, and therefore the Ariès model can be tested only in the context of the longer Anglo-American experience. On the other hand, recent investigations suggest that the Ariès paradigm may not apply to England and may not even be wholly correct in terms of the French experience.[48] In any event, historians must re-examine parent-child and inter-generational relationships from the earliest American settlements through the nineteenth century. Recent studies offer some outlines of a new, possibly American paradigm. Greven's study of Andover shows that first-generation fathers exercised remarkably strong and enduring control over their sons' lives. If this relationship existed elsewhere, perhaps we can attribute it not only to an abundance of land but also to a high degree of religiosity among the first-generation settlers. The weakening of patriarchalism in successive generations would fit not only into the narrowing economic base of farming communities but also into the weakening or dilution of religious zeal, the "declension" which Perry Miller has so masterfully analyzed. The slackening of parental discipline, one symptom of the declension, gave the younger generation more latitude to develop their own "culture," which at times might seem very much at odds with parental authority. Both Marion L. Starkey and John Demos, for example, identify a structural conflict between generations in Salem Village in 1692.[49] Although their interpretations of the sources of this conflict are markedly different, does not the conflict itself partly reflect the development of a youthful "culture" not subject to parental supervision and control?

The most startling manifestation of weakened parental control can be seen in the dramatically increasing rates of pre-marital pregnancies which occurred from the late seventeenth to the mid-eighteenth century. Equally dramatic, however, were the decreasing rates of pre-marital pregnancies that took place a century later.[50] When the New Lights of the 1740s observed an apparent reformation of manners and morals among the youthful converts of the Great Awakening, their rejoicing was perhaps premature, for, at best, the reformation may have affected only the new converts. Nineteenth-century revivalists were more successful than their predecessors, for early conversions were expected and widespread and may have contributed to an alteration in pre-marital sexual behavior—at least among middle-class Protestants. The submergence or temporary denial of adolescent sexuality may have prepared the way for the "discovery" of adolescence in the late nineteenth and early twentieth centuries, as well as the mistaken belief that earlier generations treated their children as miniature adults. As a result, the idea of "miniature adulthood" must be seen, not as a description of social reality, but as a minor chapter in the history of social thought.

Notes

1. Alice Morse Earle, *Child Life in Colonial Days* (New York: Macmillan, 1899), p. 50.
2. Ibid., p. 62.
3. Arthur M. Schlesinger, *The Birth of the Nation: A Portrait of the American People on the Eve of Independence* (New York: Knopf, 1968), p. 25.
4. Monica Kiefer, *American Children Through Their Books, 1700–1835* (Philadelphia: University of Pennsylvania Press, 1948), pp. 1, 94, 225.
5. Michael Zuckerman, *Peaceable Kingdoms: New England Towns in the Eighteenth Century* (New York: Knopf, 1970), p. 73. None of these publications systematically examines either children's clothing or portraiture. One suspects that little precise information will be gleaned from such sources, for neither extant clothing nor portraits reveal everyday styles. Any extensive examination of portraits must take into account Philippe Ariès's finding with respect to French children: *"The first children's costume was the costume which everybody used to wear about a century before, and which henceforth they were the only ones to wear."* Ariès, *Centuries of Childhood: A Social History of Family Life*, trans. Robert Baldick (New York: Random House, 1962), p. 57.
6. Alice Morse Earle, *Customs and Fashions in Old New England* (New York: Scribner's, 1896), pp. 13, 15.
7. Arthur W. Calhoun. *A Social History of the American Family from Colonial Times to the Present* (Cleveland: Bobbs-Merrill, 1917), I, 105, 107, 108, 110, 111.
8. Sandford Fleming, *Children and Puritanism: The Place of Children in the Life and Thought of*

the New England Churches, 1620–1847 (New Haven: Yale Univ. Press, 1933), pp. 16, 60, 66, 67, 153, 188.

9. John Demos, _A Little Commonwealth: Family Life in Plymouth Colony_ (New York: Oxford, 1970), pp. 69, 134–36, 138–40, 142, 146, 182. See also John Demos, "Developmental Perspectives on the History of Childhood," _Journal of Interdisciplinary History,_ 2 (1971), 315–27, and Joseph E. Illick, "Child-Rearing in Seventeenth-Century England and America," in _The History of Childhood,_ ed. Lloyd deMause (New York: Psychohistory Press, 1974), pp. 303–50. In his most recent discussion of the family, Demos emphatically states, _"Colonial society barely recognized childhood as we know and understand it today."_ "The American Family in Past Time," _American Scholar,_ 43 (1974), 428.

10. "Adolescence and Youth in Nineteenth-Century America," _Journal of Interdisciplinary History_ 2 (1971), 285–86.

11. "Bibliographic Note: Toward a History of Childhood and Youth," _Journal of Interdisciplinary History,_ 3 (1972), 446 n.25.

12. "Death and the Puritan Child," _American Quarterly,_ 26 (Dec. 1974), 457–59.

13. Gilbert Tennent, _The Righteousness of the Scribes_ . . . (Boston: J. Draper for D. Henchman, 1741), p. 16.

14. _The Works of Anne Bradstreet,_ ed. Jeannine Hensley (Cambridge, Mass.: Harvard, 1967), pp. 51, 64; Ellis Gray, _The Fidelity of Ministers_ . . . (Boston: G. Rogers for M. Dennis, 1742), p. 20; Samuel Moodey [_sic_], _The Vain Youth Summoned_ . . . (Boston: Timothy Green, 1707), p. 7; Jonathan Edwards, _Sinners in the Hands of an Angry God_ . . . (Boston: S. Kneeland and T. Green, 1741), p. 24; William Cooper, _One Shall Be Taken_ . . . (Boston: T. Fleet for D. Henchman, 1741), p. 21. See also George Whitefield, _The Lord Our Righteousness_ . . . (Boston: S. Kneeland and T. Green, 1742), pp. 26–28, and Perry Miller, "Jonathan Edwards' Sociology of the Great Awakening," _New England Quarterly,_ 21 (1948), 62–66.

15. Jonathan Edwards, _A Faithful Narrative of the Surprizing Work of God_ . . . (London: printed for John Oswald, 1737), in _The Great Awakening,_ ed. C. C. Goen, _The Works of Jonathan Edwards,_ 4 (New Haven: Yale Univ. Press, 1972), p. 158; Colonial Society of Massachussetts, _Publications,_ 14 (1913), 193; Cotton Mather, _Early Religion_ . . . (Boston: B. H[arris] for Michael Perry, 1694), p. 2.

16. _The Laws and Liberties of Massachusetts Reprinted from the Copy of the 1648 Edition in the Henry E. Huntington Library,_ intro. by Max Farrand (Cambridge, Mass.: Harvard, 1929), pp. 1, 5, 35; _Records of the Colony of New Plymouth in New England,_ ed. Nathaniel B. Shurtleff and David Pulsifer (Boston: W. White, 1855–1861), XI, 63.

17. John Cotton, _A Practical Commentary, or An Exposition with Observations, Reasons, and Uses upon the First Epistle Generall of John_ (London: R. I. and E. C. for Thomas Parkhurst, 1656), p. 102; William Williams, _The Duty and Interest of a People_ . . . (Boston: S. Kneeland and T. Green, 1736), pp. 63–64.

18. T[homas] H[ooker], _The Unbeleevers Preparing for Christ_ (London: T. Cotes for A. Crooke, 1638), p. 195; Thomas Hooker, _Application_ . . . (London: Peter Cole, 1656), p. 266.

19. Hooker, _Unbeleevers,_ p. 198; Hooker, _Application,_ p. 268.

20. John Norton, _The Orthodox Evangelist_ . . . (London: John Macock for Henry Cripps and Lodowick Lloyd, 1654), "The Epistle Dedicatory," and p. 130; Hooker, _Application,_ p. 268; John Cotton, _A Practical Commentary,_ p.100; Hooker, _The Covenant of Grace Opened_ . . . (London: G. Dawson, 1649), pp. 24–25.

21. Hooker, _Unbeleevers,_ pp. 199–200; Hooker, _Application,_ p. 268.

22. Based on data in the _Records of the First Church at Dorchester in New England, 1636–1734,_ ed. Charles Henry Pope (Boston: Geo. H. Ellis, 1891), and in genealogical materials cited in Ross W. Beales, Jr., "Cares for the Rising Generation: Youth and Religion in Colonial New England," Diss., Univ. of California, Davis, 1971, pp. 244–46.

23. Based on data in the _Historical Catalogue of the Members of the First Church of Christ in New Haven, Connecticut (Center Church), A. D. 1639–1914,_ comp. Franklin Bowditch Dexter (New Haven: The Church, 1914).

24. Philip J. Greven, Jr., "Youth, Maturity, and Religious Conversion: A Note on the Ages of Converts in Andover, Massachusetts, 1711–1749," _Essex Institute Historical Collections,_ 108

(1972), 119–34; J. M. Bumsted, "Religion, Finance, and Democracy in Massachusetts: The Town of Norton as a Case Study," *Journal of American History,* 57 (1971), 817–31; Gerald F. Moran, "Conditions of Religious Conversion in the First Society of Norwich, Connecticut, 1718–1744," *Journal of Social History,* 5 (1972), 331–43; James Walsh, "The Great Awakening in the First Congregational Church of Woodbury, Connecticut," *William and Mary Quarterly,* 3d ser., 28 (1971), 543–62.

25. On Bartlet, see Edwards, *Faithful Narrative,* in *The Great Awakening,* ed. Goen, pp. 199, 205.

26. *Records of the First Church at Dorchester,* ed. Pope, pp. 67, 183–85; James Fitch, *An Explanation of the Solemn Advice . . .* (Boston: S. Green for I. Usher, 1683), p. 69.

27. John Cotton, *The Grounds and Ends of Baptisme . . .* (London: R. C. for Andrew Crooke, 1647), pp. 16, 129; [Richard Mather], *Church Government and Church-Covenant Discussed . . .* (London: R. O. and G. D. for Benjamin Allen, 1643), p. 22; [Richard Mather], *A Discussion Concerning Church-Members and Their Children . . .* (London: J. Hayes for Samuel Thomson, 1659), p. 13.

28. Charles Chauncy, *Anti-Synodalia Scripta Americana . . .* (London, 1662), p. 23.

29. Northampton Church Records, Feb. 2, 1668 (microfilm, Forbes Library, Northampton, Mass.).

30. James P. Walsh, "Solomon Stoddard's Open Communion: A Reexamination," *New England Quarterly,* 43 (1970), 110, quoting Edward Taylor's MS Notebook (Massachusetts Historical Society).

31. Barnstable, Mass., West Parish, Church Records, Jan. 18, 1683 (Massachusetts Historical Society), "Scituate and Barnstable Church Records," *New England Historical and Genealogical Register,* 10 (1856), 349.

32. *The Notebook of the Reverend John Fiske, 1644–1675,* ed. Robert G. Pope, Publications of the Colonial Society of Massachusetts, 47 (Boston: The Colonial Society of Massachusetts, 1974), pp. 110, 186, 200.

33. F. Musgrove, *Youth and the Social Order* (Bloomington, Ind.: Indiana Univ. Press, 1965), p. 13. See also John Demos and Virginia Demos, "Adolescence in Historical Perspective," *Journal of Marriage and the Family,* 31 (1969), 632–38.

34. S. N. Eisenstadt, "Archetypal Patterns of Youth," *Daedalus,* 91 (1962), 30.

35. Rolf E. Muuss, *Theories of Adolescence,* 2d ed. (New York: Random House, 1968), p. 4. See also David Matza, "Position and Behavior Patterns of Youth," in *Handbook of Modern Sociology,* ed. Robert E. L. Faris (Chicago: Rand McNally, 1964), p. 192.

36. *The Laws and Liberties of Massachusetts,* pp. 1, 6, 12; *Records of the Colony of New Plymouth,* XI, 219, 225; George D. Langdon, Jr., "The Franchise and Political Democracy in Plymouth Colony," *William and Mary Quarterly,* 3d ser., 20 (1963), 519, citing Barnstable Town Records, I (Town Offices, Hyannis, Mass.).

37. Bernard Bailyn, *Education in the Forming of American Society: Needs and Opportunities for Study* (Chapel Hill, N.C.: Univ. of North Carolina Press, 1960), p. 23; Oscar Handlin and Mary F. Handlin, *Facing Life: Youth and the Family in American History* (Boston: Little, Brown, 1971), p. 17.

38. Kenneth A. Lockridge, "The Population of Dedham, Massachusetts, 1636–1736," *Economic History Review,* 2d ser., 19 (1966), 343.

39. Philip J. Greven, Jr., *Four Generations: Population, Land, and Family in Colonial Andover, Massachusetts* (Ithaca, N.Y.: Cornell Univ. Press, 1970), pp. 75, 126, 132, 135 (quotation), 222–23.

40. Edmund S. Morgan, *The Puritan Family: Religion and Domestic Relations in Seventeenth-Century New England,* rev. ed. (New York: Harper, 1966), p. 68.

41. Demos, *Little Commonwealth,* p. 148, 152–57, 193; Lockridge, "Population of Dedham," p. 330; Greven, *Four Generations,* pp. 33, 35, 118, 120, 206, 208.

42. Greven, *Four Generations,* pp. 31–32. See also S. N. Eisenstadt, *From Generation to Generation: Age Groups and Social Structure* (Glencoe, Ill.: Free Press, 1956), pp. 30–31, and Peter Laslett, *The World We Have Lost* (New York: Scribner's, 1965), p. 90.

43. Benjamin Colman, *Early Piety Again Inculcated . . .* (Boston: S. Kneeland for D. Henchman and J. Edwards, 1720), p. 33. See also William Cooper, *Serious Exhortations . . .* (Boston: S. Kneeland and T. Green for J. Phillip and J. Edwards, 1732), p. 10.

44. Demos, *Little Commonwealth*, p. 147; Lockridge, "Population of Dedham," p. 344.

45. Edwards, *Faithful Narrative*, in *The Great Awakening*, ed. Goen, pp. 146, 149, 158.

46. *The Christian History, Containing Accounts of the Revival and Propagation of Religion in Great-Britain & America*, ed. Thomas Prince, Jr. (2 vols.; Boston, 1743–45), I, 241, 260–61, 398–99, 409.

47. The average age of entering students in the Yale College classes from 1702 to 1739 was 16.4 years. Six students were under the age of seventeen at graduation (the youngest being fifteen), while three were graduated at twenty-eight. Richard Warch, *School of the Prophets: Yale College, 1701–1740* (New Haven: Yale Univ. Press, 1973), p. 254. On the mixing of different ages in English and French schools, see Lawrence Stone, *The Crisis of the Aristocracy, 1558–1641* (Oxford: Clarendon, 1965), p. 681, and Ariès, *Centuries of Childhood*, p. 239.

48. Natalie Zemon Davis, "The Reasons of Misrule: Youth Groups and Charivaris in Sixteenth-Century France," *Past and Present*, 50 (1971), 41–75; Steven R. Smith, "The London Apprentices as Seventeenth-Century Adolescents," ibid., 61 (1973), 149–61, and "Religion and the Conception of Youth in Seventeenth-Century England," *History of Childhood Quarterly*, 2 (1975), 493–516.

49. Marion L. Starkey, *The Devil in Massachusetts: A Modern Enquiry into the Salem Witch Trials* (New York: Knopf, 1949), and John Demos, "Underlying Themes in the Witchcraft of Seventeenth-Century New England," in *Colonial America: Essays in Politics and Social Development*, ed. Stanley N. Katz (Boston: Little, Brown, 1971), pp. 113–33.

50. Daniel Scott Smith and Michael S. Hindus, "Premarital Pregnancy in America, 1640–1971: An Overview and an Interpretation," *Journal of Interdisciplinary History*, 5 (1975), 537–70. See also James A. Henretta, *The Evolution of American Society, 1700–1815: An Interdisciplinary Analysis* (Lexington, Mass.: Heath, 1973), pp. 132–34.

7. "Till Death Us Do Part": Marriage and Family in Seventeenth-Century Maryland

The fabric of family life in seventeenth-century Maryland took on a markedly different texture from that found in either Old or New England. It has been argued that in Elizabethan and Stuart Britain parents had great and long-lasting influence over their children's lives. The head of the household exercised patriarchal authority over other members of the family and especially over his children, who often did not achieve economic independence until well after they reached majority. Paternal control was most evident in the father's dominant role in his children's marriages. In order to marry, a child had to have not only his parents' consent but also their economic support in the form of a marriage settlement. The choice of a mate was not just a matter of individual preference; the parents were the final arbiters of when and whom their children would marry.[1]

Englishmen who immigrated to New England were able to transfer these same patterns of behavior with relatively little disruption. They soon established and then maintained stable families and orderly communities in which fathers retained traditional authority over their children. Late marriages of men and women in strict birth order, delays in the transference of real and personal estates from fathers to sons, and residence of married children on their father's lands were characteristic of many New England families in the seventeenth century and much of the eighteenth.[2]

In contrast, immigrants to the Chesapeake experienced an immediate and profound disruption in the patterns of family life, first in the selection of their mates, then in family politics, and finally in relationships with their children. As a result, traditional family arrangements were much less successfully transplanted there in the seventeenth century.

Differing demographic experience in New England and in the Chesapeake was undoubtedly one of the most important causes of the apparent differences in family life. Immigrants to the Puritan settlements included larger numbers of women and children, and they more often arrived in family groups. In addition, a much smaller proportion of the immigrants were bound laborers. Since New Englanders not only had a greater opportunity to marry but also outlived their fellows in Maryland, they raised more children. These larger families, combined with the reduction in immigration after the first decade, allowed the native-born population to dominate New England society much earlier than in Maryland, where families were smaller and significant numbers of immi-

Lorena S. Walsh, " 'Till Death Us Do Part': Marriage and Family in Seventeenth-Century Maryland," reprinted from *The Chesapeake in the Seventeenth Century,* ed. Thad W. Tate and David L. Ammerman (Chapel Hill: University of North Carolina Press, 1979, for the Institute of Early American History and Culture, Williamsburg, Virginia), 126–52. Copyright © 1979, by the University of North Carolina Press. Reprinted with permission of the Institute and Press.

grants arrived over a longer period of time. Consequently, the northern colonies more rapidly succeeded in recreating the characteristics of a settled community.

The situation in Maryland was different. A majority of the immigrants who ventured their lives in the tobacco colony were young and single, and they married late. Nearly three-quarters of them arrived as indentured servants, and neither men nor women servants were free to marry until their terms were completed. Additional years were often required to accumulate the capital necessary to establish a household. Immigrant women in Maryland usually married in their mid-twenties, and men seldom wed before their late twenties. Perhaps even more significant—since New Englanders were also late to marry—was the lack of women. Because male immigrants outnumbered female by as much as three to one, many men remained single; over one-quarter of the men who left estates in southern Maryland in the second half of the seventeenth century died unmarried.[3]

Not only did the immigrants marry late, they also died very young. A man who came to Maryland in his early twenties could expect to live only about twenty more years. By age forty-five this man and many of his companions would be dead. Native-born sons fared only slightly better than their fathers. A boy reaching majority in southern Maryland before 1720 had only about twenty-five more years to live. In contrast, men reaching age twenty in the Plymouth Colony in the same period could expect to live an additional forty-eight years.[4]

The life cycle of growing up, marrying, procreating, and dying was compressed within a short span of years in seventeenth-century Maryland. Most marriages were of brief duration. One-half of the unions contracted in one Maryland county in the second half of the century were broken within seven years by the death of at least one of the partners. As a result, families were small; most couples had only two or three children.

This situation did not change significantly until rather late. Although native women married very early—between sixteen and nineteen—and were likely to bear one to two more children than had their immigrant mothers, families remained small. In the first place, immigrants constituted a majority of the population until the end of the century. Moreover, because there continued to be fewer women than men in the colony, most native-born men married only two and a half years earlier than their immigrant fathers. Since women who raised large families usually had two or more husbands, the number of children per couple remained small. Wives were twice as likely to survive their husbands in Charles County, Maryland, between 1658 and 1705 than were husbands to survive their wives. In addition, three widows married again for every widower who remarried.[5]

These various demographic features had far-reaching effects on marriage and family relationships in the Chesapeake. However much the new immigrants may have attempted to recreate traditional procedures and norms, they found it impossible. Old World social structure and institutions were inevitably disordered in the process of transferring them across an ocean, and when combined with extreme demographic disruption, this circumstance forced alterations in the forms of marriage, in sexual mores, and in the kinds and degree of control exercised by the family.

Marriage and Family Politics

Unlike the New England Puritans, whose religious philosophy called for retention of a traditional patriarchal family structure but with a reinterpretation of the character of marriage and divorce, settlers in Maryland demonstrated no desire to reform either the laws or the attitudes about marriage then prevalent in England. Whenever conditions permitted, they followed the five steps indicated by Edmund Morgan as necessary to a proper marriage in England—espousals, publication of banns, execution of the espousal contract at church, celebration, and sexual consummation.[6]

Often, however, the austerity of a recently settled area caused some of the steps to be eliminated. As in England, all marriages were recognized as valid "that had been consummated in sexual union and preceded by a contract, either public or private, with witnesses or without, in the present tense or the future tense."[7] Espousals were probably the first step and were then frequently followed directly by the last, sexual consummation of the marriage.[8] Banns were published only irregularly until after 1696, and, with the scarcity and sometimes complete absence of clergy in a colony that banned public support of religion, very few marriages, especially those of non-Catholics, were solemnized by a minister. Before justices of the peace were authorized to perform marriages, many couples simply married themselves, signifying their union by some customary ceremony such as breaking a piece of silver between them.[9]

Marriage celebrations were apparently uncommon in the seventeenth century; there are almost no records of wedding feasts until after 1700. A marriage in St. Mary's County in 1676 was thus described: "One Charles Fitzgeferis went Over St. Mary's River to St. Inegoes to be married to one Ann Townsend in Company . . . with John Sikes, John Miller, and William Wheret, and . . . they came back againe the same day to the house of the said John Sikes and there Beded as Man and Wife and from that time passed as man and wife."[10]

Giles Tomkinson, a planter, expressed very well the prevailing conception of a marriage when, in November 1665, he came to the Charles County Court to refute the charges of Constable Thomas Gibson, who "Accuseth a woman living at Gils Tomkinsons to bee illegitimately got with child":

> The sayd Gils Tomkinson affirmeth in open Court that shee is and was befor the Getting of her with Child his lawfull wiffe and Confeseth himself the father of the Child shee now Goeth with and hear in Open Court alleageth that his marriage was as good as possibly it Coold bee maed by the Protestants hee beeing one because that befor that time and ever since thear hath not bin a protestant minister in the Province and that to matrimony is only necessary the parties Consent and Publication thereof befor a lawfull Churchman and for their Consents it is Apparent and for the worlds satisfaction they hear publish themselves man and wife till death them doe part.[11]

Maryland colonists of marriageable age were peculiarly lacking in family ties. Most had come as indentured servants, and even among the free immigrants there were few family groups. When the immigrants left Europe, their break with their families was usually complete. Few of them expected ever to return to the Old World, and probably there was little communication with relatives left behind. In addition, when many immigrants came to marry, questions of property were irrelevant. An ex-servant had accumulated through his own hard labor whatever estate he brought to a marriage, and thus he was not obliged to ask anyone's consent to its disposition.

Parental control over native-born men and women in Maryland was not significantly greater than that of the immigrant generation. Because most parents died before their children reached marriageable age, native-born men and women in Maryland also frequently married without parental consent. Stepparents or guardians could prevent their

Table 7.1. **Marital Status and Life Cycle of Southern Maryland Decedents, 1658–1705**

Date	Total No. Male Decedents	No. Single	No. Married	No. Widowers	No. Unknown	Life Cycle 1	2	3	4	5
1658–1669	158	50	85	21	2	88	15	3	1	3
1670–1679	380	125	209	45	1	197	21	10	4	21
1680–1689	380	111	231	33	5	187	23	18	7	46
1690–1699	459	95	285	50	29	211	46	26	6	97
1700–1705	294	55	170	49	20	105	38	28	5	72
Total	1671	436	980	198	57	788	143	85	23	239

Key to life cycles:
1. has been married, all children under 18
2. has been married, some children under 18, some children over 18
3. has been married, all children over 18
4. not number 1
5. cycle unknown

Source:
A study of Maryland inventories, "Social Stratification in Maryland, 1658–1705," being conducted by P.M.G. Harris, Russell Menard, and Lois Green Carr under the auspices of the St. Mary's City Commission and with funds from the National Science Foundation (GS-32272).

charges from marrying before they were of age but could not control what they did afterwards. Up to the 1690s, most men did not marry until several years after the age of inheritance, at which time their own fathers had often been dead for some years. Thus the wishes of a man's parents infrequently entered into his decision about when and whom to marry.[12]

Somewhat more control was exercised over women, since they married much earlier than men. Because of community distaste for child brides, most guardians refused to allow, or the court instructed them to prevent, girls marrying much below the age of fourteen.[13] Orphaned women, however, generally became free to order their lives when they reached the age of inheritance—sixteen—making relatively short the period in which others could restrict their freedom to marry.[14]

Seventeenth-century marriages were unusual in other ways. Frequent disparity in the age and status of the partners characterized many unions. Often, a man marrying for the first time was ten years older than his bride. When widowed, a woman might choose a second husband no older and perhaps younger than herself. Since many unions were broken by the early death of one of the partners, second marriages were frequent. Single men often married widows with a charge of children, and some single girls chose husbands with families by earlier wives. If both husband and wife had previously married, they were each likely to have custody of underaged offspring by their first spouses.[15] Age differences and conflicts arising from the presence of both natural children and stepchildren in the same household must have heightened tensions within a marriage.

Lack of family ties, unsettled New World conditions, and the pressures of the sex ratio all contributed to a milieu of relative sexual freedom in seventeenth-century Maryland. One result was a high rate of bridal pregnancy, especially among immigrants. In a register of marriages and births for seventeenth-century Somerset County, more than a third of the immigrant women whose marriages were recorded were pregnant by the time of the ceremony. Such a high rate of bridal pregnancy—two to three times that of many contemporary English parishes—is testimony to the extent of social disruption. There is little evidence that the community objected to this kind of sexual freedom; no presentments for bridal pregnancy appear in any of the Maryland courts.[16]

Native-born women also shared in this freedom, although to a lesser degree than their mothers. Preliminary research suggests that in the seventeenth century about one out of five Maryland-born brides was pregnant when she married. Lack of parental control was a contributing element. Orphaned girls were apparently particularly vulnerable to pre-marital conceptions; initial study indicates an even greater frequency of bridal pregnancy among women whose fathers had died during their minority.[17]

While not approved by the community, other kinds of sexual freedom persisted after marriage. Both the lax marriage laws and the freedom of movement to another colony or back to England provided the unscrupulous with opportunity for bigamy.[18] Sarah Youn-ger related that Alexander Younger, "pretending himself to bee a person free to marry being a widdower did persuade . . . her to marry him" and then took all her goods, including her children's portions, sold the land, and left for England with the proceeds. Two neighbors testified that they happened to meet Younger in London, where he introduced them to his English wife and maintained that in Maryland, Sarah was "only his Whore."[19]

The large measure of freedom that native-born children enjoyed when marrying in Maryland was as much a result of historical accident as of deliberate policy on the part of parents. In instances where parents survived until their children were of marriageable age, they tried to direct their children's marriages much as parents in New England did. Where substantial amounts of property were involved, it was essential that the prospec-tive couple obtain their parents' consent. Sons and daughters of wealthy families, unlike many of their compatriots, could not simply marry at will. After giving consent, their parents or guardians negotiated the terms of the marriage contract, and dissatisfaction with the share offered by one of the parties could prevent a match.[20]

A surviving parent, whether affluent or of more ordinary circumstances, customarily bestowed a "portion" of his property on his children when they married and also might help the couple by extending them credit with which to buy household goods. Although not many deeds of gift at marriage were recorded, there are other indications that children customarily received their shares of their father's estate at this time. Married children were frequently granted only token bequests in their father's will, often with the notation that they had already received their due portions; gifts previously made to married offspring often were confirmed but not augmented by the will.[21] Also, in cases where a father died intestate, the county courts were ordered to determine, before apportioning the estate, which orphans had been "advanced by the Dec[ease]d in his Lifetime" and which had yet received nothing.[22] The effect of these practices must have been to give surviving parents considerable influence over their children's choice of mates.

Parents might provide for their own future maintenance as part of the marriage settlements for their children. This was uncommon simply because few parents lived long enough to see their offspring married. One who did was Christopher Kirkly, a joiner, who made over all his estate, including forty acres of land, a house, livestock, household goods, and debts receivable, to his daughter, Susannah, when she married John Vincent in 1705/6. In return he was to have "Meat Drinck washing and apparrell in the same manner and noe worse than the said John Vincent himself his heires Executors or Administrators (according to his or their ability) shall Eate Drinck or Weare." Kirkly reserved for himself one chamber, a bed, a gun, the use of a horse, his workshop and joiner's tools, and all the tobacco and money he could make from carrying on his trade.[23]

Since few parents lived to see their children married, the question of whether or not they tried to control the lives of adult offspring by retaining economic sanctions after children wed is relevant in but a few instances. Surviving parents apparently did not try to maintain such controls. Fathers did not often retain title to lands that constituted an adult son's portion, and in the few cases where land on which a son was already seated was bequeathed by will, it appears that the son had only recently reached twenty-one.[24]

Because the woman was usually younger and her parents thus more likely to be alive when she married, the wife's parents more often gave advice or intervened in a marriage than the husband's. Her family might, for example, look after her and her husband's interests in case of inheritance. Robert Cager, Jr., was "near 21 and married" when Henry Hyde, the executor of his father's will, made his final account. The account "was first Read unto the said heire and his wifes father and Brothers then present in Court and the same was Immediately delivered unto the said Robert Cager and the heire, and notice given by the Judge heereunto him and his wifes relations . . . that they had liberty to except to the said account." Cager decided to approve the account after deliberation with his father- and brothers-in-law.[25]

Recognizing the likelihood of an early death, parents might attempt to control their children posthumously. Some fathers, prompted by a desire to provide for their widows and to keep their families together, did seek to order their children's futures through their wills. Edward Bowles, for example, gave his son Edward his entire estate, with the proviso that Edward maintain his mother in the family home "with Sufficient meat, drink, and apparrell with one room to herself and a good bed and chest."[26] If one child were of age, the father might require that he allow the younger children to live with him, so long as they remained unmarried and worked. Robert Marston received all his father's land, but with the restrictions that his two younger brothers were to live and work with him and that he would maintain them to age eighteen and his sister Elizabeth to sixteen. He was also to support another sister, Mary, then of age, so long as she was single and kept house for him.[27] A wealthier planter bequeathed his sons substantial acreage on the frontier but stipulated that they not leave their mother to settle on it until they reached age twenty-five.[28]

Restrictions on a child's future freedom of action by his parents through their wills were, however, the exception, not the rule. In the majority of cases, a father sought to give his children as much freedom as possible to order their lives after his decease, apparently feeling that flexibility rather than rigid control would best protect his children's interests in an uncertain future. This emphasis on freedom rather than on regulation was the result of a fear (often well-grounded) of the treatment the children might receive at the hands of subsequent stepfathers or guardians. Sons were frequently made of age by will at seventeen or eighteen and sometimes as young as sixteen. Richard Jones, for example, willed that his son was "to enjoy the benefit of his Estate in his own hands and to bee free from all servitude at the age of sixteen either from his mother or any other person."[29] An arrangement that allowed a measure of both freedom and regulation was often employed. A father would direct that his sons could act only with the consent of their guardians until age twenty-one but that they should work "for themselves" (that is, enjoy the proceeds of their labor) at age eighteen. In this way, the length of time a boy labored for someone else would be minimized. The boy could gain experience at making his own living and begin adding to his estate, while still enjoying the legal protection and the advice of a guardian.[30]

Precisely because he could not foresee the future, a man sometimes maximized his children's future options by providing one or more alternative arrangements for his family after his death. For instance, he might will that the children were to remain with their mother when she remarried, so long as their new stepfather did not mistreat them, or, in the event that he did, they were to be removed to the household of a guardian. A way of protecting both widow and child, if the child was nearly of age, was to bind the child to his mother until he reached majority or until she died. If the mother lived, she could look after the child's welfare and in return might be at least partially supported out of the proceeds of his labor. However, if she should die before the child reached majority, he would then be free and would not have to continue working for a stepfather after his mother's death.[31]

If the threat of early death and resulting disruptions to family life affected the kinds and amount of control that seventeenth-century Maryland fathers sought to exercise over their children, these circumstances also influenced the ways in which husbands regarded their wives. The kinds of provisions that dying husbands made for their widows must reflect to some degree the position that married women occupied in family politics. In St. Mary's and Charles counties over the seventeenth century nearly three-quarters of married male testators left their widows with more than the dower the law required, a husband frequently giving his wife all or a major part of the estate for her life and usually making her his executor. This is an indication of great trust indeed, considering that the men knew that their widows were highly likely to remarry. By the standards of the time, most Maryland wives received highly favorable property settlements and were accorded an unusually influential role in managing the estate and in bringing up the children.[32]

Because a woman could not legally own property or make any contracts while married, it was essential that before remarrying, a widow safeguard her own and her children's estate while she was still *feme-sole* and free to act. Some prudent widows deeded shares of the deceased husband's estate to their children before remarrying in order to protect the children's inheritance.[33] In other cases, the marriage contract specified in detail what the second husband had to pay to the children of his wife's first marriage as their portions of their father's estate.[34] Such measures were clearly advisable in view of the speed with which remarriage frequently took place. The offspring of less prudent widows often suffered from their mother's failure to safeguard their interests.[35]

It is impossible to determine whether marriages in Maryland in this period were more or less happy than marriages in other periods and locations. That difficulties did occur is clearly demonstrated in the court records. Adultery, continual and violent quarreling, and desertion signaled the factual if not the legal end of a marriage.[36] There is ample evidence as well of other problems that might not end a marriage but that would make living together difficult: disputes over the estates of the respective partners, disagreements about the upbringing of children, and personality conflicts between husband and wife.

In Maryland, as in England, there was no divorce. Separations could be obtained in the event that the marriage contract was broken. When Robert Robins charged his wife with adultery, the couple decided to separate. Before the county clerk they "did make this their Particular declaratione": "I Robert Robins doe hearby disclayme my wife Elizabeth Robins for ever to acknowledge her as my wife and I doe hear oblige myself and everie one from mee never to molest or trouble her any further." Elizabeth made the same declaration, with the additional promise that she would not ask Robert "for maintainance or any other necessaries."[37]

Separation with maintenance by the husband might be ordered by the court in cases of extreme and prolonged incompatibility. Suits of this sort were unusual. Most couples resolved their marital difficulties by other means than legal proceedings. Anne Hardy, the wife of a Charles County justice, did resort to the courts. In 1702 she, "upon a difference betweene her and her Husband petitions that shee with her Children may be permitted to live upon her Owne Land and to be allowed a Sufficient maintenance to Subsist upon." In this instance two of the justices were appointed to try to compose the couple's differences. The two continued to quarrel, however, disagreeing particularly about the treatment and discipline of Anne's children by a former husband. In 1703 she complained of Hardy's "harsh and ill usage of her Children and desires they may be taken away from him and that they may all be bound out to trades." She finally petitioned in 1706 that "through his harsh and Ill Usage shee is not able to Live and Cohabitt with him and Therefore Desires with the approbation of the Court Shee may Live from him and that the Court would Order her A competency for a Separate Maintenance." Hardy agreed to a separation and "propounds to Allow her fifteen hundred pounds of Tobacco [about £5] Yearly and Every Yeare Dureing her natural Life and Doth promise and Engage to Deliver her her necessary Utencills of Cloathing and as shee is now Possest with According to the Degree of his wife." This "mutual agreement of boath partyes" was approved by the court.[38]

More frequently, unhappy spouses sought to escape unwelcome marriages by simply running away. Anthony Smith, for example, was reported in 1691 as having "absented himselfe from his sd wife Martha and hath left her destitute of any way of releiveing herselfe or to gett her livelyhood." In 1699 Elizabeth Johnson, in desperation, for several months "absented herselfe from Dan: Johnson then her husband and having noe place of Residence or abode Bt wandering from place to place," sought shelter from various neighbors.[39]

In many instances couples turned to relatives and neighbors rather than the courts when they encountered marital problems. Neighbors, for example, intervened on St. Clement's Manor in 1659 when Clove Mace came to the house of his neighbor John Shanks, "beinge bloudy and said that Robin Coop and his wife were both upon Him." Shanks asked another neighbor, John Gee, to go with him to Mace's house. Shanks "asked her [Mrs. Mace] to come to her husband and shee replyed that hee had abused Robin and her and . . . John Shancks gott her consent to come the next morning and Robin up to bee freinds with her . . . husband but hee would not bee freinds with her but the next night following they were freinds."[40] Wives, especially, could probably expect little sympathy from an all-male court that had a special interest in preserving the authority of husbands and fathers. Many women, trapped in unhappy marriages, probably just endured the situation.

From evidence about matches that failed, it can be deduced that colonists considered normal and exclusive sexual union, peaceful cohabitation, and economic support of the wife by the husband the minimal duties that spouses must perform. Testimony about the more positive ingredients of a marriage are more rarely encountered. A 1719 case of contested administration, however, provided an explicit discussion of contemporary attitudes about marriage.

The case involved Kenelm Cheseldyne, a substantial landowner, who died in 1718, naming his wife, Mary, as administratrix of his estate. Cheseldyne had, in fact, never married the woman with whom he had been living. At Mary's request, a number of neighbors testified that they believed that she and Cheseldyne had been man and wife because Cheseldyne had behaved in ways that defined the manner of a husband, not a paramour.[41]

The Cheseldynes' problems arose because, about 1712, they had "Marryed in private," without banns, license, clergyman, justice, or witnesses, after Mary, then the Widow Phippard, was pregnant, and possibly not until after the birth of the child. Although Cheseldyne asserted that "shee was his Lawfull wife" as much as any other man's, proof of Cheseldyne's marriage depended solely on their word and on community acceptance.

John Greaves testified about why he considered the couple married. He related that while he was constable he had gone to arrest Mary Phippard at Cheseldyne's because she had recently borne an illegitimate child. Cheseldyne had forewarned him "from taking her away at his perrill for that he would give his oath that there was not any such person as Mary Phippard," claiming Mary as his wife and declaring the child legitimate. Because Cheseldyne had always acknowledged Mary as his wife and because neighbors had believed they were married, Greaves had also accepted the union.

Sarah Turner, the midwife who had delivered the three children of Kenelm and Mary, testified that they were man and wife because "the said Cheseldyne particularly was at the birth of the second and seemed very fond of the child and [Mary]. . . . Chesldyne called her his wife and took care of her as such and Owned the Children."

Benjamin Reeder, a neighbor, had inquired of Cheseldyne's kinsman, John Coode, whether or not they were married. Coode had assured him that they had been married in private. Reeder had then believed that they were, and he testified that "afterwards . . . Cheseldyne came with her publickly to Church and helped her off and on her Horse and shewed her the respect due to a wife."

Another neighbor, Thomas Bolt, once went to Cheseldyne's house, and found him "walking in his Hall with one of the Children he had by [Mary] . . . in his Armes and in discours about a certaine Mr. Donaldson who had been [at the house] but a small time before and was angry about [Mary's] . . . giving the said Donaldson's Child Indian Bread in boiled Milk . . . Cheseldyne sayd that he thought his wife knew what was best for children for says he our own Children Eat the same."

The conception of a husband expressed by these neighbors was that he always acknowledged his wife, that he appeared with her in public, that he showed affection and respect for her, and that he supported her in a condition commensurate with his means. A husband also owned the children born of the union, showed affection toward them, and cared for them. In addition, he acknowledged his wife's joint authority in their upbringing.

Bringing Up Children

Colonists in seventeenth-century Maryland bore children and brought them up through the early years much as they themselves had been born and brought up in the Old World. In later childhood and adolescence, however, familiar patterns often broke down. Because at least one of a child's natural parents so often died early, the community was forced to take on responsibilities for the support, supervision, and education of children that had traditionally been carried out by the family. Not entirely prepared for the role so suddenly thrust upon it, the community was far from completely successful in carrying out these responsibilities.

Babies were born in the home, usually with the help of a midwife.[42] The husband was probably customarily at hand; the explanation of "his wife being neare Delivery" regularly excused men from jury duty and other official business.[43] He might be joined by his nearer neighbors as soon as they heard the delivery was in progress. They apparently went to the house in order to be among the first to view the new arrival and to celebrate the event with a round of drink.[44] When a minister was available, the infant was normally baptized within two months, otherwise baptism would be delayed until a minister arrived in the neighborhood.[45]

Infants were breast-fed, and if for some reason the mother could not nurse, a neighbor with milk to spare was hired to help nourish the baby. One such negotiation was recorded. John Ashbrooke related: "Mr. Arthur Turner came to this Deponent's house on the 25th of October last past hee Sat him downe by the table, and this Deponants wife Sukling her owne Child upon the left breast, the sayd Turner Sitting by Sayd unto this Deponants wife, Roase I see thow hast good Store. I Sir Replyed this Deponants wife. So I have thanke Godd for it whearupon the sayd Turner Sayd hee had a Child that wanted it to which this deponant Sayd, Sir, if in Case you have I coold wish it had as much as my wife coold Spaer it."[46] Infants were occasionally also nourished by other means. Turner had previously approached Marie Dod about nursing the child, and she "answered Shee coold not for Shee thought She was with child herself but if hee woold have it drie nurst she woold doe her best endeavor for it."[47]

For the first two or three years of their lives, children were probably attentively cared for. Petitions for aid from the county levy to help maintain orphan infants attest to "the trouble I have with such an one," and "the Trouble of my hous with 2 small children [twins about a year and a half old] washing Lodgeing Combeing, Pickeing, nurseing and fostering them one whole yeare."[48] Until a child was able to walk well, it was carried in the arms of one of the parents when they went abroad, and very young children were probably frequently picked up and fondled. Women are often recorded as going out "with their infants in their arms," and a father was described as "walking in his Hall with one of the Children . . . in his Armes."[49]

The line between infancy and childhood was crossed at age three. A child was likely to be weaned sometime at the beginning of the second year, and a new baby might be expected by the end of it.[50] One or both of these events apparently signified the transition from the status of infant to that of "little adult." A child's chances of surviving to maturity also improved about the third birthday. This fact was reflected in public policy. The county courts authorized payment from public taxes to persons who cared for orphans without estates until they were two years old. Thereafter orphans, in theory, paid for their maintenance through their own labor. Clearly, a child of three or four would not be able to do much work, so the custom of public payments for early care must have taken into account a high infant death rate. The chances of a baby not living to repay the costs of its care were apparently so great that public compensation was necessary to induce a couple to take charge of an orphaned infant. Conversely, masters were willing to accept the risk for children above age three.[51]

From an examination of period inventories something can be learned about the material conditions in which children were raised. It appears that whatever toys children may have had were homemade and of so little worth that they were never valued. Since most houses were quite small, usually just one or two rooms, children generally slept with their brothers and sisters in the same room as their parents or in a loft above. Most children were provided with but one new suit of clothes and a pair of shoes and stockings per year. They might in addition be given combs, and boys perhaps received pocket knives. There was little in a typical merchant's stock that was designed specifically for the young, aside from clothing, which, except in the case of infants, apparently differed from that of adults merely in size. Probably the single treat that a parent might ever purchase for his children at the store would be a little sugar.[52]

Usually the only valuable thing children possessed was livestock. Frequently a father would register a separate livestock mark for each child, and when his stock gave birth he would present the child with an animal of his own. Grandparents, uncles and aunts, and godparents might also give a favorite child livestock. Gifts of animals were the seventeenth-century equivalent of opening a bank account or purchasing a savings bond for a child today.[53]

The most frightening aspect of childhood in the seventeenth century must have been the genuine uncertainty of the future. Most children could expect that at least one, or perhaps both, of their parents would die before they were old enough to care for themselves. In southern Maryland between 1658 and 1705, 67 percent of married or widowed male decedents left all minor children, while only 6 percent left all adult children.[54] Hence, in the best of circumstances, minor orphans would have to adjust to a new stepparent and subsequently learn to live with stepbrothers and sisters. The potential for conflict was great in situations where children of more than one marriage lived together in a family. Each parent naturally tended to favor his own children and to discriminate against those from a partner's previous marriage. Parental favoritism only heightened conflicts between stepchildren already competing for their parents' attention and affection.

Complaints of ill treatment by stepparents were legion. Margaret O'Daniell protested about her stepfather, Thomas Denton: "Your pet[itione]r after her father's decease, lived with . . . Thomas Denton about 9 yeares as his servant working for him at the Hoe, as hard as any servant, and when hee saw, shee would marry, hee put her off, without any clothes or shift to her back, that was good for anything, soe that her husband was forced to buy her necessaries, and now refuseth to give her anything of her fathers estate or her owne."[55] Stepparents sometimes went so far as to try to rid themselves entirely of stepchildren. Thomas Price was presented in 1696 "by the Information of Hannah Price his wife for selling a child of the sd Hannahs which shee had by another Husband in the Colony of Virginia."[56] Enough suspicion was aroused by the death of Katherine Lee that her stepmother was accused, but later acquitted, of poisoning her.[57]

Although the county court acted to remove children from the custody of patently abusive stepparents, it firmly maintained the stepparent's right to compensation for raising another's offspring. Almost every orphan was expected to work to some degree for his maintenance, since by law only the income from his inheritance—not the principal—could be used for the child's upbringing. In this period few estates were large enough to so support an orphan.[58]

Mothers who were unable to remarry quickly or otherwise support their orphans had no choice but to put the children out. For example, Mary Empson, age four, was given to another family to raise, in return for four cows, because her mother was too poor to keep her after her father died. Often, a remarried woman sought to buy back the children she had been forced to bind out after the death of her first husband. Fatherless children were put out to others often while quite young. Their only advantages over other servants were that they could not be sold to other masters and that the mother was sometimes able to mitigate treatment and conditions of labor and to stipulate that they receive some education.

The fate of children who lost both parents might be even worse. Seldom were there surviving relatives to take them in. Unless they had a large estate, the county court bound them out to labor for someone else until they reached majority.[59] The court was responsible for overseeing the treatment of all orphans, and each year a special jury inquired into their welfare. If children were mistreated or their property embezzled, the court was supposed to place them with other masters or guardians.[60]

The experience of the Watts children in St. Mary's County tells much about the standards of care expected as well as about abuses. William Watts died in 1678, two years after his wife, leaving three sons: Charles, eight, William, six, and Edward, four. The children's grandfather protested in 1682 about the treatment accorded them by their acting guardian, Gerrard Slye, the executor of Watts's estate: "I never know any bastard Children in the Province soe used as to victualls and Cloathes and Labour as his Grand Children. . . . They have noe manner of Cloathes but such Raggs and old Clouts that scarce would cover their nakedness and those given them by the charity of others and as to victualls nothing allowed this present year but salt and hominy and half a bull for meate amongst all the family."

A laborer, Richard Craine, added further testimony. Captain Slye had given him the eldest Watts son at age ten to work for half a share. Craine told Slye the boy was not able to perform such labor, as did John Sheppard, the cooper, but Slye replied that their estate would not maintain them and that if Craine would not take the boy, he would put him to another quarter. So Craine worked Charles for two years and for the last year had worked the next youngster at planting corr. and suckering tobacco. For clothes, Craine testified, the last year the two eldest had a yard of linen apiece and a pair of shoes and stockings and the youngest only an ozenbuck frock, "so that for the most part of this Last yeare they were almost quite naked only a paire of drawers apice that this deponent made them of Sacking Cloath."

One neighbor swore "that they were putt to unreasonable Labour supposing them to have been bastard Children much more orphants that had an Estate left them." A stranger to the quarter testified that, when he had asked who the naked and ragged children were, a woman had told him that the children were put to hard work, had little or no clothes, "and were saddly beaten and abused by the overseer as tyed up by the hands and whipt." The Chief Judge of Probate agreed that the orphans "have not the Common Care had of them as is usuall for planters to have of their meanest Serv[an]ts or Slaves" and recommended that the county court put them in their grandfather's custody.

There were delays, however, and not until two years later were the children finally put in their grandfather's hands.[61]

This sad history shows that the community expected orphans to be at least minimally clothed and fed. Second, it suggests that there was some concept of "children's work." Witnesses stated that expecting a ten-year-old to raise a crop half the size of that grown by an adult was "unreasonable." The older boy must have been performing tasks in the field more laborious than those performed by the younger—planting corn and suckering tobacco. Perhaps these latter jobs were among those regularly assigned to young children. Third, flogging of children was clearly not an accepted method of discipline. Fourth, it was expected that orphans be accorded different treatment depending on the size of the estate left them. Bastard children could expect nothing beyond minimal maintenance. Legitimate children with no estates were accorded a higher status than the illegitimate but probably were given little more in the way of food and clothing and were also expected to work to cover the costs of their care. Orphans with inheritances were supposed to be better maintained and apparently were required to work less. Such children were to "be kept from Idleness," but they were not to be "Kept as Comon Servants" working continually at routine tasks.

Because of the real uncertainty of a parent's survival, the choice of godparents for his child was an important decision. The practice of naming godparents was probably most common in southern Maryland among Catholic families, who had greater access to the sacrament of baptism, but Protestant couples named them also. The godparent promised to see that the godchild was brought up in the natural parents' religion, and should the child be orphaned, this promise could theoretically include raising and educating the child. Many godparents took these duties very seriously. Frequently they made some gift to their godchildren in their lifetime such as a cow, horse, or sheep; others left livestock or some personal belonging in their wills. In the event that a man had no children of his own, he might will a substantial portion of his estate to his godchildren. When one or both parents died, a child's godparents might provide a home and some education; because of the special interest that godparents might take in orphans, county courts often preferred to bind the children to their godparents rather than to more indifferent masters.[62]

Of course, the lives of all orphans were not so dismal as those in some of the preceding illustrations. Neighbors, family friends, or other relatives might supply kindness and support. Nevertheless, the wicked stepfather and the brutal master of today's "fairy stories" were often real persons in the lives of seventeenth-century Maryland children.

There are suggestions that, among boys at least, something of an adolescent crisis may have occurred. Not all children exhibited the "dutifull behavior" expected of them. Especially in families where the father had died, teenaged sons argued with their parents, sought to escape from work and from the authority of others, spent their inheritances imprudently, and got into scrapes with the law.

Older men often commented on the lack of industry and self-discipline they saw in younger charges. A father complained that his stepson, age seventeen, "takes to idle company, absents himself from the house and endeavours to get his freedom."[63] Another man described his future stepson as "a young Wilde and dissulute person much given to Company Keeping and of such as are debouched and rude fellows, and that hee is uncapable of managing his own estate left by his father being Considerable but living up and downe, or to and fro the County one weeke in one place and a fortnight in another letting his estate fall to Ruine and decay for want of Management."[64] William Dent willed that his children have their estates in Maryland delivered to them at age seventeen, but admonished, "I will not have any of the boys to have their Moneys in England till twenty one yeares to the intent that if they Take loose and Idle Courses here which Godde for bidd they may have one after game more to play by which time they may see their former folly and amend."[65] Since girls generally assumed adult roles earlier than their brothers, there was less time for conflict with parents to develop. For a girl, marriage frequently proved an easy escape from an unhappy home situation.

The education that children received was supposed to suit their station, and might be practical or academic or both. Apprenticeship was a common method of educating children in many places, but as practiced in southern Maryland in the seventeenth century, it was mainly a means for teaching trades, including planting, to orphans. Until the late 1690s very few fathers bound out their children; when families were not broken up by the early death of the father, both sons and daughters were kept at home. Rather, it was the widows who insured that their orphaned sons were cared for and taught how to earn a living through apprenticeship and that their orphaned daughters were provided for by binding them out to learn housekeeping.[66] Unlike the New England area, where nonagricultural trades developed, the labor-intensive, staple crop economy of the Chesapeake offered no rationale for apprenticing children to trades when their labor was needed in the family's fields.

The criterion of an academic education was the ability "to read distinctly in the Bible." Usually it was expected that children could achieve this proficiency with two years of instruction.[67] Literate parents frequently taught their own children to read or perhaps sent them to another relative for instruction. A schoolmaster might then be employed in the home for six months to a year to teach writing or accounting. Generally the latter instruction was reserved for boys. After being taught to read, girls were put to sewing "and Such other Education as is suitable for Woomen." Less frequently, both boys and girls might also be sent for a season or so to a boarding school. Such an education served two purposes. It conferred an advantage in making a living, and it enabled the child to gain a firsthand knowledge of the Bible.[68]

The age at which children received their education varied widely. Thomas Dickinson's father willed in 1673 that his son, then age sixteen, should have two years' schooling and then be put to work. Robert Cole's five children ranged in age from five to twelve years when they were first instructed. William Hawton directed that his godchild, Richard Smoot, have two years' schooling at age seven or eight. Clearly there was a danger that children who received their education when quite young might "forgett their learning" before they came of age unless parents or guardians saw that their lessons were periodically reviewed.[69]

The paucity of education so often noted in the colonial South was probably as much a result of a short life expectancy as it was of the absence of towns and the low density of settlement. Parents often did not live long enough to oversee their children's education or to teach them whatever they themselves knew. Guardians, stepparents, or masters were not likely to have the same interest in seeing that a child was educated as would his own parents. Toward the end of the century, it was more and more often stipulated in indentures that an orphan receive some education, usually that boys be taught to read and write and that girls learn to read distinctly from the Bible.[70] Unless the mother lived long enough to enforce the contract, however, the children frequently may not have gotten the specified instruction. If an apprentice complained to the courts that he had not received the education to which he was entitled by his indenture, he was frequently awarded monetary compensation instead of remedial instruction.[71]

Even when an orphan could be educated out of the proceeds of his own estate, his guardian might not attend to it. Colonel John Courts complained about the situation of his godson, John Warren, the orphan of a wealthy Charles County planter and justice of the peace. Warren's father and two subsequent guardians had died during his minority, and he was then in the custody of the widow of the second guardian, who, Courts maintained

> is but a woman and I believe has a great deale of business of her own to mind. . . . [Warren was being] brought up to nothing but idlenesse, swearing and all other ill vices. She hath pretended to put him to schoole to Mr. Potter about 4 months agoe after that shee heard that I did intend to move the Court about him; I will testify that hee has not been att schoole above fifteene days in the four months. . . . [Courts promised to] keepe him close to schoole untill I have learned him to read and write a legible hand and to cast account as farr as the Rule of Three, and after soe done to learn him to know how to gett his living and that hee shall have the same in dyett lodging and apparrell as well as my owne Children or little worse.[72]

Of course, neglect of education was not so serious a matter then as now. Many of those children who received no education at all prospered as adults. Literacy was not necessary for economic success. Nevertheless, in Maryland, as in England, most of those who held positions of real power had at least a minimal education.[73] From the period of first settlement, parents were concerned that their children be "brought up in Civility good litterature and the feare of God," but the struggle just to stay alive often made this goal impossible to achieve.

By the turn of the century, demographic conditions were changing. Immigration to the Chesapeake slowed after 1700, a substantial number of native-born children were coming of age, and many single men were leaving the settled regions of southern Maryland for areas that offered more opportunity. Thus the proportion of men and women was becoming more equal. More men were able to marry, and they often could do so by the time they reached majority. The age at marriage for women remained low, and as a result the birthrate increased and native-born finally outnumbered immigrant in the population. Life expectancy also increased somewhat for those born after 1700.[74]

As a consequence of a longer life span and a more uniformly early age at marriage, many more parents lived to raise their children to maturity and to see them married. In addition, when one or both parents did die before their children were of age, in a society in which the majority were native born, kin were much more often present.[75] Eighteenth-century orphaned minor children usually had uncles, step-uncles, aunts, cousins, older siblings or step-siblings, or other relations under whose oversight they might fall. Previously, many a father, fearing the consequences of his early death for his family, had given his children as much freedom as possible to control their lives after his demise. By the early eighteenth century, parents were more often able to reassert control over the lives of their maturing offspring.

Family life in colonial Maryland throughout the seventeenth century had in contrast been gravely affected by the extreme demographic disruption that occurred in the process of transplanting Old World population and civilization to the New. In concert, unbalanced sex ratios, various economic impediments to early marriage, and short life spans virtually guaranteed that marriages would be brief and that often the futures of the offspring born to these unions would be uncertain. In these circumstances traditional controls over sexual behavior and marriage formation broke down, as did to a great extent patriarchal authority over wives and children. Fathers who survived to see their children become adults often tried to direct their children's lives in a traditional manner, but few lived that long. The majority died while their children were still minors, and while some responded to anxiety about their family's future by attempting to restrict their children's subsequent careers, others reacted by bequeathing their offspring a large measure of freedom. So long as immigrants continued to predominate in the population, family life continued to be brief, soon broken by the early death of one or both of the parents, and usually unreinforced by the presence in Maryland of other kin. Consequently the community had to take on major responsibilities for the support, supervision, and education of a good proportion of the first generation of children born in the colony. In human terms, the initial costs of peopling Maryland had been high indeed.

Notes

1. Peter Laslett describes this view in *The World We Have Lost* (New York, 1965), 3–4, 18–21, 78–79, 150–151, 173. See also Lawrence Stone, *The Crisis of the Aristocracy, 1558–1641* (Oxford, 1965), chap. 11, and Christopher Hill, *Society and Puritanism in Pre-Revolutionary England* (New York, 1964), chap. 13.

2. Philip J. Greven, Jr., *Four Generations: Population, Land, and Family in Colonial Andover, Massachusetts* (Ithaca, N.Y., 1970), chaps. 4, 6, 8, 9; Daniel Scott Smith, "Parental Power and Marriage Patterns: An Analysis of Historical Trends in Hingham, Massachusetts," *Journal of Marriage and the Family,* xxxv (1973), 419–428.

3. Russell R. Menard, "The Growth of Population in Early Colonial Maryland, 1631–1712," manuscript report, St. Mary's City Commission, Hall of Records, Annapolis, Md., 1972; Menard, "Immigration to the Chesapeake Colonies in the Seventeenth Century: A Review Essay," *Maryland Historical Magazine,* lxviii (1973), 323–329; Menard, "Immigrants and Their Increase: The Process of Population Growth in Early Colonial Maryland," in Aubrey C. Land, Lois Green Carr, and Edward C. Papenfuse, eds., *Law, Society, and Politics in Early Maryland* (Baltimore, 1977); Lorena S. Walsh, "Charles County, Maryland, 1658–1705: A Study of Chesapeake Social and Political Structure" (Ph.D diss., Michigan State University, 1977), chap. 2. For a good general discussion of the effects of unbalanced sex ratios, see Roger Thompson, *Women in Stuart England and America: A Comparative Study* (London and Boston, 1974), chap. 2.

4. Lorena S. Walsh and Russell R. Menard, "Death in the Chesapeake: Two Life Tables for Men in Early Colonial Maryland," *Md. Hist. Mag.,* lxix (1974), 211–227; Maris A. Vinovskis, "Mortality Rates and Trends in Massachusetts before 1860," *Journal of Economic History,* xxxii (1972), 184–213.

5. Menard, "Economy and Society in Early Colonial Maryland" (Ph.D. diss., University of Iowa, 1974), chap. 4; Walsh, "Charles County," chap. 2. The pattern of marriage survivorship in England may have been different. Among the aristocracy between 1558 and 1641 husbands were more than twice as likely to survive their wives. Stone, *Crisis of the Aristocracy,* 619–623.

6. Edmund S. Morgan, *The Puritan Family: Religion and Domestic Relations in Seventeenth-Century New England,* rev. ed. (New York, 1966), 30–32. A study of family life in 17th-century Maryland is severely handicapped by the complete absence of literary sources; one must rely almost entirely on scattered information found in court records. The discussion that follows is based largely on manuscript materials available at the Hall of Records, Annapolis, Md. The series primarily used are the Charles County Land and Court Records for the years 1658 to 1705 and Testamen-

tary Proceedings for the same years. Materials from later volumes of the Testamentary Proceedings, from Wills, from Provincial Court records, and from Provincial Court Papers are also used.

7. Morgan, *Puritan Family,* 31.

8. The binding nature of espousals is illustrated by the fact that an intended marriage gave the surviving partner the right to administer the other's estate and to be guardian of the deceased's children. Testamentary Proceedings, xɪɪB, 71–73, xɪv, 140.

9. William Hand Browne *et al.,* eds., *Archives of Maryland* . . . (Baltimore, 1883–), xlɪx, xxiii, 42–43, 84–85, xlɪ, 456–457; Charles County Court, E#1, 145; Somerset County Deeds, IKL (Marriage register). Registration of marriage was still uncommon in the middle of the eighteenth century. In 1786 an Anglican minister, Rev. Henry Addison, stated, "If the rule was Established here that no marriage should be deemed valid that had not been registered in the Parish Book it would I am persuaded bastardize nine tenths of the People in the Country." Montgomery County Land Records #3(C), 330.

10. Provincial Court Deeds, PL#6, 265. This argument from negative evidence seems more valid in the light of, first, abundant evidence about funeral dinners in the 17th century, in contrast to almost none about wedding celebrations, and, second, frequent reference to both in 18th-century sources. In addition, the kinds of evidence presented in court as proof of the validity of a marriage changed. Most 17th- and early 18th-century proofs were similar to the example given in the text; continued cohabitation and community acceptance of the union were the main evidence submitted. By the mid-18th century, proofs of marriage usually began by describing the wedding ceremony and subsequent celebration. For example see Montgomery County Land Records #3(C), 326–331. Widows' applications for Revolutionary War pensions contain many such descriptions. See Revolutionary War Pension series, National Archives. The two latter sources were brought to my attention by Allan Kulikoff.

11. Charles County Court, B#1, 492.

12. Table 7.1 confirms that one-quarter of men leaving inventories in southern Maryland between 1658 and 1705 died without ever marrying and that, of those who married, at least two-thirds left families in which all the children were under 18.

13. Charles County Court, P#1, 240; Testamentary Proceedings, xvɪɪ, 206.

14. Charles County Court, B#1, 355–356; Testamentary Proceedings, xvɪ, 269, xvɪɪ, 51.

15. Walsh, "Charles County," chap. 3. For a similar observation (not elaborated) about the structure of 17th-century French families, see Elizabeth Wirth Marvick, "Nature versus Nurture: Patterns and Trends in Seventeenth-Century French Child-Rearing," in Lloyd deMause, ed., *The History of Childhood* (New York, 1974), 288.

16. Russell R. Menard, "The Demography of Somerset County, Maryland: A Preliminary Report" (paper presented at the Conference on Early American Social History, Stony Brook, New York, June 1975), contains the information on bridal pregnancy. The observation on presentments for bridal pregnancy was supplied by Lois Green Carr. For rates of English premarital pregnancy see P.E. H. Hair, "Bridal Pregnancy in Rural England in Earlier Centuries," *Population Studies,* xx (1966–1967), 233–243, and N. L. Tranter, "Demographic Change in Bedfordshire, 1670–1800" (Ph.D. diss., University of Nottingham, 1966), 244, reported in J. D. Chambers, *Population, Economy, and Society in Pre-Industrial England* (London, 1972), 75.

17. Menard, "Demography of Somerset County, Maryland."

18. Morgan, *Puritan Family,* 31.

19. Provincial Court Deeds, WRC#1, 122–123. See also Browne *et al.,* eds., *Archives of Maryland,* xxv, 13, 22–24, 42, 140; Testamentary Proceedings, xɪv, 29–30; Provincial Court Papers, St. Mary's County, *Wildman v. Wildman,* 1718.

20. Charles County Court, S#1, 111; Z#1, 42–49; Browne *et al.,* eds., *Archives of Maryland,* lɪɪɪ, 631.

21. Charles County Court, F#1, 182–183; Q#1, 2–3; Testamentary Proceedings, xɪɪɪ, 331–332; Wills, ɪɪɪ, 475, ɪv, 40, v, 91, vɪ, 251, vɪɪ, 11, xɪ, 199, 381.

22. Lois Green Carr, "County Government in Maryland, 1689–1709" (Ph.D. diss., Harvard University, 1968), 352–353.

23. Charles County Court, Z#1, 227–228; K#1, 131–133; Provincial Court Deeds, WRC#1, 211–213.

24. Wills, ɪɪ, 78, vɪɪ, 71, 268; Testamentary Proceedings, vɪ, 269. For instance, John Lewgar

wrote from London in 1663 to promptly assign to his son John a warrant for 1,000 acres, "which land I hear is since layd out for my sone John and hee hath entered upon it." Charles County Court, B#1, 110.

25. Testamentary Proceedings, VI, 323–324.

26. Wills, I, 87.

27. *Ibid.,* VI, 271.

28. *Ibid.,* 241.

29. *Ibid.,* 201. See also 177, VII, 320, 393.

30. *Ibid.,* IV, 189, XIII, 157; Charles County Court, X#1, 251.

31. For instance, see Charles County Court, D#1, 99; A#2, 259; Wills, V, 82, 167.

32. Lois Green Carr and Lorena S. Walsh, "The Planter's Wife: The Experience of White Women in Seventeenth-Century Maryland," *William and Mary Quarterly,* 3d Ser., XXXIV (1977), 542–571.

33. Testamentary Proceedings, XIV, 14–20, 116–117, XVII, 29–31; Charles County Court, V#1, 160; Provincial Court Deeds, WRC#1, 439.

34. Testamentary Proceedings, VI, 63–65, XVII, 29–31; Charles County Court, A#1, 216–217; B#1, 78; C#1, 270–271; P#1,180; Q#1, 39.

35. Testamentary Proceedings, XIII, 1–2.

36. See Morgan, *Puritan Family,* chap. 2, and John Demos, *A Little Commonwealth: Family Life in Plymouth Colony* (New York, 1970), chap. 5.

37. Charles County Court, A#1, 4, 39.

38. *Ibid.,* A#2, 5, 250; B#2, 242–243. See Carr, "County Government," 189.

39. Charles County Court, C#1, 80; E#1, 96, 99; R#1, 279–280; Testamentary Proceedings, XIII, 458–462.

40. Browne *et al.,* eds., *Archives of Maryland,* LIII, 628.

41. Testamentary Proceedings, XXIII, 349–377.

42. Charles County Court, A#1, 37–39, 225–227, 269; D#1, 4; S#1, 297–298; X#1, 51; Testamentary Proceedings, XXIII, 363.

43. Charles County Court, A#2, 81, 164.

44. *Ibid.,* A#1, 37; Testamentary Proceedings, XXIII, 363.

45. Charles County Court, F#1, 244; K#1, 11–12, P#1, 208, 210, 211; Q#1, 11; Y#1, 143; Testamentary Proceedings, V, 348.

46. Charles County Court, A#1, 35, 38.

47. *Ibid.,* 38.

48. *Ibid.,* I#1, 230; X#1, 303; Y#1, 13, 130.

49. *Ibid.,* A#1, 4, 32; B#1, 145–150; Testamentary Proceedings, XXIII, 365–366.

50. Demos, *A Little Commonwealth,* 135–136. See also Alan Macfarlane, *The Family Life of Ralph Josselin, A Seventeenth-Century Clergyman: An Essay in Historical Anthropology* (Cambridge, 1970), 87–88, and appendix A, for a similar example of the effect of breast-feeding on birth intervals.

51. Carr, "County Government," 346–347; Charles County Court, A#1, 37; C#1, 244; F#1, 13; H#1, 105, 242; I#1, 124, 230–231; K#1, 84; L#1, 71; Y#1, 143; B#2, 3. A child was able to produce substantial returns by his labor beginning between ages eight and ten. Testamentary Proceedings, XIIB, 238–254; Provincial Court Judgments, DSC, 55–56; Charles County Court, E#1, 81. Apparently Englishmen shared similar expectations for children, at least those of the poorer classes. Locke in his *Report for the Reform of the Poor Law* (1697) proposed that "working schools" be set up for poor children between the ages of three and fourteen so that "from their infancy [they] be inured to work.... " Quoted in Joseph E. Illick, "Child-Rearing in Seventeenth-Century England and America," in deMause, ed., *History of Childhood,* 341.

52. Testamentary Proceedings, VI, 118–146; Inventories and Accounts, WB#3, 718; XXV, 390, XXII, 99. See Laslett, *World We Have Lost,* 105, for the similar condition of children in England.

53. See, for example, Charles County Court, A#1, 66, 110, 138; B#1, 111, 243; D#1, 5, 6; E#1, 34, 101.

54. "Social Stratification in Maryland, 1658–1705," a study of Maryland inventories conducted by P.M.G. Harris, Russell R. Menard, and Lois Green Carr under the auspices of the St. Mary's City Commission and with funds from the National Science Foundation (GS-32272).

55. Testamentary Proceedings, IX, 512–515.

56. Charles County Court, V#1, 1.

57. *Ibid.*, P#1, 123.

58. *Ibid.*, B#2, 129; F#1, 199; Browne *et al.*, eds., *Archives of Maryland*, LXII, 302; Wills, IV, 313; Carr, "County Government," 340–347. In this period an orphan was defined as a child whose father had died. The mother could be the guardian only if she could give the bond required to ensure payment of the child's portion, and she was accountable to the court for the condition of the child and his property. If she remarried and was then *feme covert,* the new husband was required to give bond, or else the court would appoint other guardians, at least to care for the property.

59. Charles County Court, A#1, 145; M#1, 221; V#1, 310; Y#1, 78, 100; A#2, 131, 260, B#2, 141; Testamentary Proceedings, VIII, 355; Carr, "County Government," 345.

60. Charles County Court, I#1, 259. For a discussion of the jurisdiction and functioning of the orphans' court in Maryland, see Lois Green Carr, "The Development of the Maryland Orphans' Court, 1654–1715," in Land, Carr, and Papenfuse, eds., *Law, Society, and Politics.*

61. Testamentary Proceedings, XIIB, 238–254, XIII, 135–139. For similar cases see Testamentary Proceedings, X, 312–313, XVII, 122.

62. *Ibid.*, A#1, 95; E#1, 132; P#1, 195; S#1, 402; V#1, 126; Y#1, 16, 311; Z#1, 160; Testamentary Proceedings, IV, 9–10, XIIB, 71–73, XIV, 21–23; Wills, I, 379, II, 102, III, 638, VI, 93, 181, 342, XI, 377.

63. Charles County Court, B#2, 129.

64. Testamentary Proceedings, IX, 174–178.

65. Wills, III, 475–480.

66. Walsh, "Charles County," chap. 3.

67. Charles County Court, A#1, 16–17; Y#1, 209, 311; A#2, 306; B#2, 129, 174; Wills, IV, 201, VI, 93, XI, 199; Inventories and Accounts, XIIIB, 122.

68. Testamentary Proceedings, VI, 118–146; XIIB, 71–73; Charles County Court, A#1, 13–14; G#1, 1; S#1, 430; X#1, 130, 343; Y#1, 16, 176, 311; A#2, 386; B#2, 5; Wills, IV, 189, XII, 14.

69. Wills, I, 182–186, II, 78, XI, 377; Testamentary Proceedings, VI, 118–146.

70. See, for example, Charles County Court, K#1, 209; S#1, 402; V#1, 126, 164, 310, 454; X#1, 130; Y#1, 35, 129, 209, 340.

71. Charles County Court, S#1, 402; V#1, 410; X#1, 50, 375; B#2, 175; Carr, "County Government," 344.

72. Charles County Court, Y#1, 311–312.

73. Russell R. Menard, "From Servant to Freeholder: Status Mobility and Property Accumulation in Seventeenth-Century Maryland," *WMQ,* 3d Ser., XXX, (1973), 47, 56–57; Laslett, *World We Have Lost,* 19, 65–66.

74. Walsh, "Charles County," chap. 2; Menard, "Growth of Population." The fall in age at marriage was dramatic. Men born in the 1670–1679 cohort married at a mean age of 26, while those born in the 1680–1689 cohort married at a mean age of 20. Those born in 1690–1699 married at a mean age of 22. An improvement in life expectancy in the 18th century is demonstrated in the unpublished research of Paul G. E. Clemens of Rutgers University and in Allan Kulikoff, "Tobacco and Slaves: Population, Economy, and Society in Eighteenth-Century Prince George's County, Maryland" (Ph.D. diss., Brandeis University, 1976), chap. 3.

75. An increase in kin ties is demonstrated in preliminary analysis by the St. Mary's City Commission of early 18th-century St. Mary's County wills and in biographical studies of county decedents who left inventories.

8. Autonomy and Affection: Parents and Children in Eighteenth-Century Chesapeake Families

Most parents in eighteenth-century Virginia and Maryland were deeply attached to their children and they structured family life around them. Such an assertion could not be confidently made about parental conduct in much of the pre-industrial West. For as historians of childhood have pointed out, until the very recent past children played a distinctly secondary role in the family; they were valued chiefly for the labor they would eventually provide the household economy.[1] In well-to-do families of Chesapeake society, however, the presence of infants and small children was an important source of pleasure and diversion, providing a central emotional focus in the life of the family. Indeed, the child-centered family which became commonplace in the nineteenth century first emerged in these planter households of the eighteenth century. The following discussion of childhood in the eighteenth-century Chesapeake suggests that child-rearing in this plantation culture bore a closer resemblance to that in modern society than in the "world we have lost."

The world of family and kin that surrounded a new-born child in Chesapeake society usually offered a warm, affectionate environment for his development.[2] Indeed, an "increase in the family" brought considerable pride and elation to parents and kin. The paternal self-pride engendered at childbirth is suggested in the praise Thomas Davis gave St. George Tucker at the birth of Tucker's daughter in 1779. Davis was excited "at learning my much-esteemed, Thy amiable Fanny had escaped the Danger of Child-Birth and had presented to my Friend such a lovely Image of himself."[3] James Parker was away from home when his daughter Susan was born in the winter of 1777, but he wrote affectionately of his new baby girl, "The Summer Duck": "God bless the Dear little [one] how I long to hold it to my heart."[4]

Parents arranged christenings and baptisms—usually within a few weeks after birth—to bring kin and friends together in celebration of parenthood.[5] These ceremonies, held in private homes in most cases, were often quite festive affairs with dinner and dancing. Relatively small crowds of perhaps a dozen or so kin and close friends usually attended.[6] William Byrd went to the christening of the Reverend Charles Anderson's son in 1709 where, according to Byrd, everyone dined and danced well into the evening. Anderson, Byrd noted, "was beyond measure pleased with the blessing God had sent him."[7] Philip Fithian, plantation tutor for Robert Carter of Nomini Hall, reported in 1773 that christenings were "one of the chief times for Diversion here."[8] Godparents were announced on these occasions; parents frequently chose a brother or sister or close family

Daniel Blake Smith, "Autonomy and Affection: Parents and Children in Eighteenth-Century Chesapeake Families," reprinted from the *Psychohistory Review* 6 (1977–78): 32–51, with permission of Human Sciences Press, Inc., New York, New York, copyright © 1977–78.

friend as symbolic guardians of the child. For some men, such as Presbyterian James Gordon of Orange County, a child's baptism carried a significant religious meaning. Gordon named his son Nathaniel at the baptismal ceremony in September of 1762 and later recorded in his diary a solemn wish for his son's spiritual fate: "O, may the Lord grant that he be a Nathaniel, indeed: the gift of God, and his name written in the Book of Life."[9]

A child's first important experience in the world comes in his relationship with his mother or nurse, especially in the feeding process.[10] In this earliest stage of development, until about age two, a child is mainly concerned with the simple but essential tasks of "getting" and "taking," as Erik Erikson has suggested. His success in this incorporative mode of behavior depends in part on parental willingness and ability to provide the nourishment a child needs and demands. And most important, the nursing bond significantly influences a child's earliest perceptions about the trustworthiness of the people around him.[11]

Studies of childhood suggest that children in the pre-industrial West often failed in their crucial efforts at "getting" and "taking." Many remained underfed and left in the hands of mothers and nurses who distrusted their "primitive" demands for survival. Seventeenth-century European parents were ambivalent about children whom they felt obligated to protect, but who were also, they believed, "demanding and dangerous little animals."[12] As a result of these tensions, the relationship between nurses or mother and child in early modern Europe resembled more a struggle than a cooperative effort. Mothers, especially after a difficult delivery, viewed breastfeeding as a debilitating experience, one in which an infant drained a mother of her vital substances for his own survival. Some mothers feared that breastfed children might transmit to them some dreaded disease.[13] Consequently, most women who could afford it put their children out to nurse, despite the advice of physicians that an infant would thrive best when nourished by his own mother. Moreover, poorly prepared solid food was often fed to children before they were fully able to digest it. High infant mortality rates of between 20 and 30 per cent for seventeenth-century Europe reflect in part this low level of maternal care of children.[14] It was not until the mid-eighteenth century that critics of child care in England and France became effective in encouraging maternal nursing.[15]

In the colonial Chesapeake maternal nursing was probably the most common form of infant feeding. Little is known about parent-child relations in Virginia and Maryland during the seventeenth century because of the scarcity of personal documents such as family papers and diaries. The fragmentary evidence that does exist, however, indicates that mothers probably breastfed their children. Nonetheless, infant and childhood mortality rates remained extremely high, perhaps as high as 40 per cent, because of an endemic malarial environment which prevailed in the early Chesapeake. Infants frequently received from diseased mothers a short-term immunity to malaria which allowed many of them to survive infancy, only later to succumb to the disease as small children when their immunity had worn off.[16]

In the eighteenth century, even though a larger number of families could afford to hire wet nurses, most women, barring illness, seem to have continued to nurse their own children. One woman in 1780, for example, was reported to be "too weakly to Suckel her little Girl—and is Obliged to Put it out to nurse."[17] In sharp contrast to parents in early modern Europe who feared that infants communicated diseases to those who nursed them, parents in the eighteenth-century Chesapeake worried more about children becoming ill from their contact with sick mothers. For instance, Margaret Parker of Norfolk, Virginia, in 1771 wrote to her husband that their infant boy had "Sucked the fever from me I believe." "I was obliged to get a woman to Suckle him a while till I get my milk again which the fever dried up."[18] Other women nursed their infants despite the pain and inconvenience.[19] Breastfeeding, many women believed, ruined the shape of the breasts and doubtless some women hesitated to nurse their children for this reason.[20] The experience of Mary Dulaney of Maryland, however, suggests that a mother's affection for a child could outweigh such concerns. A friend noted that Mary breastfed her infant boy despite her fear that "her good looks may be injured by nursing her fine son. . . ."[21]

Maternal love, though, was not always the central motivation for mothers who decided to nurse their own children. Given the discomfort of frequent pregnancies and the danger and violent pain associated with childbirth—especially in the eighteenth century—some mothers chose to nurse their offspring because the lactation period tended to delay conception.[22] Landon Carter certainly felt that this was the strategy of his daughter-in-law in 1770 when, according to him, she continued to breastfeed her baby girl despite being sick herself. Carter complained that:

> The poor little baby Fanny is every time to share her Mamma's disorder by sucking her, and this because she should not breed too fast. Poor children! Are you to be sacrificed for a parent's plesure? I have been a Parent and I thought it murder and therefore hired nurses or put them out.[23]

Despite Carter's protest, his granddaughter "little Fanny" continued "to suck the poizon" from her mother's "morbid breast."[24]

In exceptionally wealthy and large families (of perhaps 10 or more children) mothers sometimes relied on nurses—both black and white—to breastfeed some of their children.[25] Philip Fithian noted this practice in 1773. "I find it is common here for people of Fortune to have their young Children suckled by the Negroes!" Mrs. Carter, who had given birth to 13 children, told Fithian that "wenches have suckled several" of her infants.[26]

Fithian, however, was speaking of a very small minority of women—only those with great wealth and burdened by huge families, like Mrs. Carter. Most mothers, except when seriously weakened by childbirth or sickness, nursed their own infants—often out of strong maternal sentiment. As a result of this natural maternal nursing bond, deep emotional attachments were established between mothers and children. And as a child gained confidence in the accessibility of his mother as an attachment figure, his anxiety and fear about the world around him declined.[27] It was from such an early atmosphere of maternal warmth that planters' children developed a strong measure of self-confidence and independence.

The weaning process, however, threatened to disrupt the close ties between a child and his nurse or mother. Sometime in their second year children were removed from their secure source of nourishment. Weaning was critical in the child's first efforts toward autonomy which normally characterize the second year of life.[28] It proved to be a difficult time for parents too, for they worried incessantly about children becoming ill during this uncertain stage of development.

Parents separated children from the breast at different times in early modern Europe and America. In the seventeenth and eighteenth centuries, children in England and

France were weaned at around 24 months, and often abruptly among wealthy families.[29] Parents in colonial America appear to have allowed for a more gradual weaning, but began the process earlier, which suggests that they encouraged an earlier sense of autonomy in the child than their European counterparts. In seventeenth-century Plymouth and the colonial Chesapeake, the scattered evidence indicates that weaning began between twelve and eighteen months.[30] A starchy mixture of flour and milk such as gruel or pap was introduced into the child's diet sometime in the first year to begin to accustom him to eating solid food. Mothers often dabbed mustard, pepper or some bitter substance on their breasts to discourage the child from nursing.[31]

Weaning was particularly trying on parents since many probably felt ambivalent about separating the child from his mother's breast. Parents were clearly relieved when weaning was accomplished without pain or illness. In September of 1728 Dolly Jones was reported to have "weaned herself," at age one. As her nurse explained to Dolly's mother, she "won't touch the breast when offered her, which I think you'll have no reason to be sorry for, but it was first occasioned by her being kept from it when she took the bark, but she never seemed to desire it."[32] Mothers or nurses clearly controlled the weaning process. Frances Tucker, her husband noted, had gone to Port Royal, Virginia, in the spring of 1784 where she was "weaning our last little Brat."[33]

Parents also found teething a difficult period in the child's early development. It was an event that usually signalled the beginning of weaning, for mothers stopped breast-feeding near the time that children began cutting teeth—at the end of the first year.[34] Teething brought on a period of pain and sickness which left parents and kin fearful and anxious. William Prentis, for example, worried that his one-year-old son John had the same "disease" that all of his children had developed the year they were weaned: "a disorder in the bowels, and cutting of Teeth."[35] In 1725 Elizabeth Pratt empathized with her suffering two-year-old son: "poor Billy has been pulled down by his hard breeding of teeth."[36] And Martha Jefferson Carr was anxious to hear whether her fourteen-month-old granddaughter Martha Terrell had "got safely through the worst of her teething."[37]

Teething concerned parents and kin mainly because of the physical discomfort children experienced during this period. The biting stage also represented an important test of the child's basic trust in the nurturant and protective attitudes of his parents. For teething compelled the child to bite to ease the pain just as the mother was beginning to withdraw the breast.[38] But as we have seen, parental sensitivity to the difficulties children faced during weaning and teething probably helped to create a trusting relationship between a mother and her child.

Anyone who reads through the family letters and diaries from the eighteenth-century Chesapeake will discover a welter of evidence of parental tenderness and affection toward yound children.[39] These sources clearly suggest that children were not treated as depraved beings whose willfulness and sense of autonomy had to be quashed by age two or three—as children were apparently seen in early Plymouth.[40] Rather, parents in Virginia and Maryland during the eighteenth century seemed to delight in the distinctively innocent, playful childhood years of their offspring. Parents and an assortment of kin—grandparents, uncles, aunts and cousins—who frequently helped in child-rearing were usually quite fond of children and considered them pleasant diversions. Indeed, as we shall see, family and kin often indulged young children and granted them considerable freedom.

It is not likely that during the seventeenth century children enjoyed such a prominent place in Chesapeake households. Because of oppressive infant and child mortality rates and a short life expectancy in early Virginia and Maryland, parents probably invested less of their emotional life in their children than did eighteenth-century parents. When infants or children died, parents—especially fathers—showed little emotion or deep concern.[41] Moreover, Protestant religious thought, which stressed the inherently sinful and inferior condition of children, shaped the character of family life in the seventeenth century. Fathers remained emotionally detached from infants and small children, insisting on the child's acceptance of self-control and obedience to paternal authority.[42]

In the increasingly secular culture of eighteenth-century Virginia and Maryland, which was committed to an expanding tobacco economy based largely on slave labor, religious values rarely intruded into family life and child-rearing, especially in Anglican planter households.[43] As a result, Chesapeake parents felt free to stress more of the positive, pleasurable capacities of children. Indeed, the personal documents of eighteenth-century Chesapeake families, especially after mid-century, reveal a familial and social environment in which children were often the centerpiece of family affection. Mothers and fathers and kin, at least in well-to-do families, lavished attention on their children. One father from Queen Anne's County, Maryland, for example, was reported to be "Excessively fond of his Daughter a fine sprightly girl."[44] Richard Tilghman confided to a friend in 1763 that his three-year-old daughter Anna Maria was "the plaything of the family."[45] James and Margaret Parker struggled to avoid spoiling their young son. "I endeavour as much as possible to [guard] against it," Margaret wrote her husband in 1765, "but find it requires more resolution than I am mistress of to help doting on him."[46] When away from their families, fathers almost always asked to be remembered to their children. While staying in Williamsburg in the fall of 1755, George Braxton told his wife to "Give little Molly a thousand kisses for me."[47] St. George Tucker was particularly fond of his children and stepchildren. His letters to his wife Frances during his service in the Revolution suggest the pleasure he derived as a parent. "Remember me with a Tenderness Truly Parental to my Boys," he wrote Frances, "and let Patty and Maria be assured I am neither unmindful nor indifferent in regard to them." Tucker, like many parents, used affectionate nicknames for his children. "My poor little Monkies are insensible to all that a parent can feel for them."[48]

Parents were diverted by, rather than impatient with, the nonsense language and "childish" behavior of their offspring. Jane Swann wrote to her uncle of the satisfying moments she and her husband spent with their four-year-old girl. Their daughter, she said, was "very lively and full of Inocent Prattle with which She often pleasantly amuses her Father and my Self. May the almighty preserve her long with us."[49] Surrounded by the familiar and attentive faces of parents and kin, children provided their caretakers with uninhibited and seemingly irrational behavior which was unacceptable in the adult world. The experience of Eliza Custis as a child growing up in Virginia in the 1770s demonstrates vividly that children were welcome diversions to their parents.

> I can now remember standing on the table when not more than 3 or 4 years old, singing songs which I did not understand—while may father and other gentlemen were often rolling in their chairs with laughter—and I was animated to exert myself to give him delight—The servants in the passage would join their mirth, and I holding my head erect, would strut about the table to receive the praises of the company, my mother remonstrated in vain—and her husband always said his little Bet could not be injured by what she did not understand

that he had no Boy and she must make fun for him, until he had—he would then kiss her to make his Peace, and giving me a Nod my voice which was uncommonly powerful for my age resounded through the rooms, and my Mother who could not help laughing, used to retire and leave me to the gentlemen, where my fathers caresses made me think well of myself.

Custis's treatment of Eliza, at least in her retrospective view, suggests that he was asking of Eliza what most parents expected of their children: to give pleasure and comfort in return for parental tenderness and nurture.[50]

For Thomas Gilpin of Maryland in the 1790s proper child-rearing involved a close friendship between parents and children. Parental participation in a child's world of play, he believed, encouraged sound character and virtuous conduct in the child as he matured. Gilpin's wife observed that her husband took great pleasure in cultivating "a freedom and sociability with his Tender offspring in order to Unite Fillial Obedience with [paternal?] affection in the Closest tyes of Friendship which he often used to say was the surest way for Parents to Secure the affection of their Children." According to his wife, Gilpin spent a lot of time with the children, often giving them "little Inocent amusements to keep them in from the street and out of others [pernicious?] Company and would often be one of their party himselfe thereby discovering the great pleasure that their little Inocent Company and Diverting Actions Afforded him." This kind of intimate, parent-child relationship, Gilpin assumed, helped a child to choose proper "Friends and Confidents and none was so proper as their Parents."[51] By this affectionate form of paternal child-rearing, planters like Thomas Gilpin nurtured a sense of deference and duty in their children without resorting to authoritarianism or coerced obedience. Respect and filial devotion came much easier to sons secure in the knowledge that their parents, especially their fathers, derived pleasure from their presence.[52]

Childhood had clearly become a distinctive period in the minds of Chesapeake parents and kin during the eighteenth century.[53] The presence of grandparents was extremely influential in shaping these child-centered families. The short expectation of life in the seventeenth-century—to about the mid-forties among adult men and women—precluded the development of an elderly generation and a large body of supporting kin. Indeed, family life in the early Chesapeake was often limited to contact between two generations—and with such high death rates these relationships usually proved to be rather short-lived as the profusion of step-parents and orphans in this period suggests.[54] If relationships between parents and stepchildren in modern families are any guide to the past, then many of these seventeenth-century Chesapeake households, filled with half- and step-brothers and sisters, may have been unable to develop strong emotional ties within the family.[55] With the improvement in life expectancy during the eighteenth century—to about the mid-fifties for adult men—family relationships among three generations became commonplace.[56] As a result, by mid-century planters frequently sent their children to stay with grandparents and other relatives where they were often indulged and fondly cared for.

Family letters from this period allow us to glimpse the quality of kin attachments to children. Six-year-old Betty Pratt spent much of the fall of 1728 with her aunt who admitted to Betty's mother that she was receiving too much attention. "She is exceedingly fondled at [the] other House, more than I think, is necessary tho she manages herself with it better than one cou'd expect from a Child of her age."[57] Charles Carroll of Annapolis was particularly attached to his granddaughter Molly Carroll, the daughter of Charles Carroll of Carrollton. He ended almost every letter to his son or daughter-in-law with affectionate expressions for Molly, such as: "I long to kiss my little Gran-daughter."[58] Carroll sent her gifts—once a pocketbook, purse and money—and when she received them, Carroll instructed his son to "tell her I sent it."[59] Children and their grandparents sometimes exchanged pictures—or "miniatures," which were usually placed in a locket—or other personal items as permanent expressions of their affection and kinship.[60] In 1784, Henry Tucker, Sr., sent his granddaughter Nancy Tucker a lock of his hair which, as he told his son, he hoped would please her—"the device is paternal affection."[61]

Despite the pleasure parents and kin clearly derived from young children, they approached child-rearing with serious purposefulness. They expected to develop in their offspring powers of self-discipline which, parents believed, would produce self-reliant, independent adults. And it was the warm, nurturant attitudes of Chesapeake parents which we have described above that allowed them to shape children into dutiful sons and daughters.

Parents were especially mindful of developing powers of self-sufficiency and strength in their children. They applauded but rarely demanded precocity in their children, unlike seventeenth-century Anglo-American parents who sought to hurry children out of their childhood dependency.[62] Still, initial signs of mobility and autonomy, suggested in early efforts at walking and talking, attracted close attention from observant parents. Lucy Terrell, according to her grandmother, Martha Jefferson Carr, "prattles Everything she hears," and was "very spritly." Years later, Mrs. Carr expressed the same interest in another granddaughter, one-year-old Martha Terrell. She was anxious to see "little Martha's attempts to prattle and to see her shuffling across the room."[63] Frances Randolph was equally proud of her daughter "Mopsey," who "talks *prodigiously*. She will walk in a fortnight."[64]

Parents took a special interest in the early muscle control and coordination of their sons, who were especially encouraged to move about on their own. The observations of Thomas Jones are revealing in this connection. In July of 1728 Jones reported at length to his wife, Elizabeth, then visiting relatives in England, on the growth and character of their three children. Lusty, exuberant children clearly appealed to Jones. His youngest son, two-year-old Tom, particularly pleased him, for, as Jones noted, "he runs about the house, hollows and makes a noise all day long and as often as he can, gets out of Doors." Tom's father was keenly aware of the boy's progress in walking. After returning from a trip, Jones noticed the "great alteration in the use of his Feet in so short a time, and I believe [he] is as forward in that as most children of two years old." Taking his first tentative steps became a lesson in self-sufficiency for young Tom: "when he falls I order him not to be taken up by which means he takes it patiently, unless he hurts himself pretty much." Young Tom was a less remarkable talker, however, which seemed to bother his father somewhat: "he is very backward with his tongue, I use him to pa-pa; and Ma-ma, and in a morning he say (not Tea) but Tee, and sometimes mo' which is all the improvement he has made that way; he grows Tall and is a fine Boy."[65]

To encourage a hardy constitution in children, parents followed the advice of John Locke by dressing them in loose-fitting clothes and allowing them plenty of time in the open air.[66] Locke's prescriptions for early child care seem to have been in the mind of one father who, while away from home on business, inquired about his son's upbringing: "How goes the dear little thing. Do you permitt Charles to run half-naked as he should do, feed him on Mush Milk &c, do you sufficiently correct his little [fancy?] faults, keep him in due Subjection toward his little [servant?] . . . ?"[67] During early childhood boys and girls were dressed alike in distinctively children's clothing—a kind of long robe which opened down the front to provide unrestricted movement. A pair of ribbons hanging from the back of the gown, which was used in the seventeenth century to support children in their early ambulatory efforts, became simply an ornament of child's dress by the eighteenth century. Girls wore more confining clothes, especially the stays placed on the neck to promote straight posture. By age six or seven boys were put into breeches and shirts, perhaps symbolic of their first step toward manhood.[68]

The goal of most eighteenth-century Anglo-American parents was to develop honest, republican virtues of self-discipline and self-reliance in their children. Child-rearing literature since the late seventeenth century advised parents to inculcate these values as early as possible in their offspring, perferably in infancy or early childhood, when a child's character and temperament were most pliable and susceptible to parental guidance.[69] Parental authority should be moderate in nature, Locke argued, a strategic combination of indulgence—to gain a child's lasting affection and gratitude—and firm discipline—to insure obedience and a continuing sense of duty to his parents. Punishment was most effective when administered through shame, rather than through whippings—which, at best, produced only a temporary remedy. Only by inducing an apprehension of parental displeasure and shame early in a child's life could parents instill habits of obedience and self-control.[70]

While Chesapeake parents in general seem to have adopted many features of this child-rearing style—especially its emphasis on developing hardy, self-reliant children—parent-child relationships in this eighteenth-century agrarian society took on a form different from what Locke and other critics would have advised. The wide open nature of the plantation environment—uncrowded with an abundant supply of land and free of many of the vices of the cities—allowed planters to raise their children under more optimistic and permissive assumptions about childhood and parental conduct. Obedience and respect for parental authority remained important for the development of strong character and stable family life, but Chesapeake parents placed considerably more emphasis on developing a child's, especially a son's, freedom of movement and sense of personal autonomy.

Chesapeake households were often complex units with servants and kin living on the plantation, making constant parental supervision of children unnecessary. Indeed, one senses from the letters and diaries of the period, that children were allowed—perhaps encouraged—to explore their immediate environment with little parental supervision. While visiting his friend Colonel Eppes in February of 1711, William Byrd was asked to help locate a small child who had just learned to walk but had wandered off from his little friends. "All the people on the plantation were looking for it," Byrd explained, "and I went likewise to look [for] it and at last found it, for which the women gave me abundance of blessings."[71] Parents clearly admired rambunctious, energetic children to whom they seemed to have given the run of the planation. Margaret Parker reported to her husband that their young son was doing well, as he had been "imployed all day making bonfires."[72] One woman who went to see her cousin noted that her cousin's two children, a two- and three-year-old, "were fighting on the carpet, during the whole visit."[73]

Children thrived on companionship and vigorous play with other children, parents believed; confining them at home weakened their important instinct for sociability. White and black children often mingled freely on the plantation, relatively unsupervised by parents.[74] Parents and kin did become concerned when children missed opportunities for companionship in their early years. One man, fretting over the limited social contacts his eight-year-old nephew had with other boys, complained that it "is not so proper for a boy to be under so much Confinement; and to live so remote without any Company."[75]

Not only did young children experience considerable freedom of movement on the plantation, but they also lived under few parental restraints to their conduct. Parents and kin, at least in middle and upper class families, apparently made little effort to stifle childhood willfulness and self-assertion. To be sure, overt disobedience was not countenanced, but parents did not attempt as a matter of principle to root out autonomous behavior in young children—in sharp contrast to Anglo-American parents in the seventeenth century. Paternal indulgence—anathema to Locke and other child care advisors—appears far more frequently in the records than concern for strong discipline in the family.[76] William Byrd, for example, stood up for this three-year-old daughter Evie when his wife forced the child "to eat against her will."[77] Thomas Jones seemed almost pleased that his young nephew Frederick "Strutts around the House and is as Noisy as a Bully." Jones's sister-in-law commented on his excessive fondness for his two-year-old son Tom. Tom's boisterous behavior, she noted

> is enough to distract all about him except his papa and to him I believe all his noys is musick if he can't have and do everything he has a mine to he is ready to tare the house down, but if Nanny has opertunitys, she will bring him to better order before you return.[78]

The presence of uncles and aunts, grandparents, and other kin, who sometimes stayed with a family for weeks or months at a time, probably lent an even more permissive tone to Chesapeake family life. Disciplining a child was largely a father's responsibility, so relatives who helped care for children tried to avoid this aspect of child-rearing. Instilling a sense of shame or guilt in disobedient children came hard for Rachel Cocke, an aunt of the Jones children. Mrs. Cocke had grown so close to one of her nieces who often visited her that she could not bring herself to chastise the girl for telling lies, "for all I can do I cant make her think there is any harm in a ly if she is not found out in it, nor can I be angry with her if she does it so innocently." Despite her fondness for her niece, Mrs. Cocke eventually succeeded in shaming her into compliance:

> . . . if she thinks I'm angry in good earnest she's sadly frightened and falls to beging my pardon and promises never to do so again and I do assure her that she is one of the most orderly, best children that ever was borne.[79]

Committed to the principle of self-sufficiency, Chesapeake parents tried to avoid crushing the assertive instincts of children. Rather like modern parents, planters employed reason and parental affection to control unruly behavior in their offspring. As a result, parental discipline was often accomplished by negotiation and bargaining rather than by a show of authority. Thus, one finds a father like Thomas Jones explaining to his wife how he had managed to win an argument with his ten-year-old son. "Saturday after you went, Tom and I had some difference, but I got the better. Since which he has been a very orderly good Boy and is very good Company."[80] Other parents offered rewards as incentives for orderly conduct. Lewis Joynes asked that his daughter Susanna "be a good girl and I will bring her a Book and a Thimble." Susanna's younger brother Jack, age five, was likewise instructed "to be a good Boy and not go near the Steers and I will not forget his great coat."[81]

The relatively permissive and nurturant environment that parents and kin seem to have provided infants and small children in the eighteenth-century Chesapeake shaped children's perceptions about parental authority and the larger society. The evidence from the personal documents of planter families, fragmentary as it is, suggests that fathers, far from remaining indifferent to young children, entered their affective world very early on, perhaps earlier than fathers do in modern families.[82] Thus children, especially sons, may have absorbed paternal values and feelings of affection long before reaching the age— usually after six or so—when paternal guidance became more explicit. Recent psychological studies of parent-child relationships demonstrate that children are more likely to adopt the behavior of nurturant models than those who are indifferent to them.[83] The strong ties of affection and filial duty which bound many children to their parents in the eighteenth-century Chesapeake—often until the parents' deaths—were in part rooted in the close emotional regard that fathers, as well as mothers, displayed toward them during childhood. In short, many planters appeared to have gained the life-long gratitude and respect of their children more out of paternal fondness during childhood than out of early assertions of authority and coerced obedience.

That fathers took such an early, affectionate interest in their offspring probably encouraged a strong sense of emotional security in their children. Parents seem to have offered themselves more as a collective unit for nurturance and discipline than as a sharply differentiated one in which mothers provided the affection while fathers distanced themselves as stern disciplinarians. In the absence of clashing child-rearing styles, children could form a clearer, more secure self-identity.[84] It does not strain the evidence to suggest that the independence training Chesapeake parents gave their children provided the psychological roots for the generations of strong-willed planter gentry who rose to such political prominence in Revolutionary America.[85]

The nature of child-rearing in planter families also encouraged children very early in life to sense the meaning of the world beyond the immediate family. From infancy on, children were introduced to a network of grandparents, uncles and aunts, and in-laws who helped in the child-rearing process. Young children were not confined at home with their parents, but lent out freely to relatives whom they sometimes visited for weeks or months at a time. Because of this early experience with other planter families, children could perceive their parents, especially fathers, as immediate representatives of a "known community of adults" with whom they could easily identify.[86] A supporting web of kin helped ease the transition from childhood to adulthood in this plantation society.

Notes

1. Much of this new work on the history of childhood can be found in the pages of *The Journal of Psychohistory,* whose editor, Lloyd deMause, appears obsessed with discovering child abuse or neglect in times past. For a statement of his position, see DeMause, ed., *The History of Childhood* (New York, 1974), 1–73. In *The Making of the Modern Family* (New York, 1975) Edward Shorter sees a shift toward better maternal care in Europe beginning in the mid-eighteenth century.

2. This should be contrasted with the comparative indifference with which infants were received in much of the seventeenth-century West. See, *ibid.,* 168.

3. Thomas Davis to St. George Tucker, October 3, 1779, Tucker-Coleman Papers, Earl Gregg Swem Library, College of William and Mary.

4. James Parker to Margaret Parker, March 24, 1777, Parker Family Papers, Colonial

Williamsburg Research Center. See also, Molly Tilghman to Polly Tilghman, October 6, 1787, Hollyday Family Papers, Maryland Historical Society, Baltimore; Robert Innes to St. George Tucker, March 25, 1783, Tucker-Coleman Papers; Richard Tilghman to Abraham Tilghman, March 15, 1750, "Letters of the Tilghman family, 1697–1764," *Maryland Historical Magazine* (hereafter *MHM*), XXXIII (1938), 167.

5. Robert Rose Diary, October 8, 1749, Alderman Library, University of Virginia; Louis B. Wright and Marian Tinling, eds., *The Secret Diary of William Byrd of Westover, 1709–1712* (Richmond, 1941), 249. (Hereafter cited as *Byrd Diary, 1709–1712*.)

6. Francis Taylor Diary, June 16, 1799, November 2, 1796, Alderman Library, University of Virginia; Robert Rose Diary, October 8, 1749; Jack P. Greene, ed., *The Diary of Colonel Landon Carter of Sabine Hall, 1752–1776* (2 vols., Charlottesville, Va., 1965), I, 376–7; *Byrd Diary, 1709–1712*, 2; "The Journal of James Gordon of Lancaster County, Virginia," *William and Mary Quarterly* (hereafter cited as *WMQ*), 1st. ser., XI (1903), 9, 232.

7. *Byrd Diary, 1709–1712*, 2.

8. Hunter Dickinson Farish, ed., *Journal and Letters of Philip Vickers Fithian, 1773–1774* (Williamsburg, Va., 1943), 47.

9. "Journal of James Gordon," 9.

10. According to Peter L. Giovacchini, "the early mothering experience is the most important single relationship in the child's life." See Giovacchini, "The Submerged Ego," *Journal of the American Academy of Child Psychiatry*, III (1964), 439.

11. Erik Erikson, *Identity, Youth and Crisis* (New York, 1968), 96–9.

12. See David Hunt, *Parents and Children in History: The Psychology of Family Life in Early Modern France* (New York, 1970), 123.

13. *Ibid.*, 105.

14. Elizabeth Wirth Marvick, "Nature Versus Nurture: Patterns and Trends in Seventeenth-Century French Child-Rearing," in deMause, ed., *The History of Childhood*, 263–6, 282–3; Hunt, *Parents and Children,* 122. See Edward Shorter's compilation of infant and childhood mortality rates for early modern Europe, *The Making of the Modern Family*, 202–3.

15. Bogna W. Lorence, "Parents and Children in Eighteenth-Century Europe," *The Journal of Psychohistory,* II (1974), 1-30; *The Works of Dr. John Tillotson* (3 vols., London, 1728), I, 488–9. By 1780 a substantial proportion of aristocratic women in England were breastfeeding or dry nursing their own children. See Randolph E. Trumbach, "The Aristocratic Family in England, 1690–1780: Studies in Childhood and Kinship" (unpublished Ph.D. dissertation, The Johns Hopkins U., 1972), 90.

16. Lorena S. Walsh, " 'Till Death Us Do Part': Marriage and Family in Maryland in the Seventeenth Century," in Aubrey C. Land, Lois Green Carr, and Edward C. Papenfuse, eds., *Law, Society, and Politics in Early Maryland: Essays in Honor of Leon Radoff* (Baltimore, 1977); Darrett B. and Anita H. Rutman, "Of Agues and Fevers: Malaria in the Colonial Chesapeake," *WMQ*, 3rd ser., XXXIII (1976), 31–60; Rutman and Rutman, " 'Now-Wives and Sons-in-Law': Parental Death in a Seventeenth-Century Virginia County," in Thad W. Tate and David Ammerman, eds., *The Chesapeake in the Seventeenth Century: Essays on its Euramerican Society and Politics* (Chapel Hill, N.C.: University of North Carolina Press, 1979); Daniel Blake Smith, "Mortality and Family in the Colonial Chesapeake," *Journal of Interdisciplinary History,* VIII (1978), pp. 403–27.

17. Anne Tucker to St. George Tucker, April 13, 1780, Tucker-Coleman Papers. See also Frances Tucker to Frances Bland Tucker, June 16, 1783, *ibid; Carter Diary*, I, 345, II, 765.

18. Margaret Parker to James Parker, 1771, Parker Family Papers.

19. Francis Taylor Diary, April 23, 1790; Molly Tilghman to Polly Tilghman, January 29, 1789, "Molly and Hetty Tilghman Letters," *MHM*, XXI (1926), 232–3.

20. Trumbach, "The Aristocratic Family in England," 57–9; John Rendle-Short, "Infant Management in the Eighteenth Century with Special Reference to the Work of William Cadogan," *Bulletin of the History of Medicine*, XXXIV (1960), 114.

21. Catherine Belt to Mary Dulaney, May 2, 1802, Dulaney Papers, Maryland Historical Society, Baltimore.

22. For a discussion of the effect of lactation on delaying conception, see A. Perez, "First Ovulation after Childbirth: The Effect of Breastfeeding," *American Journal of Obstetrics and Gynecol-*

ogy, CXIV (1972), 1141–7; J. K. Vanginneken, "Prolonged Breast Feeding as a Birth Spacing Method," *Studies in Family Planning,* XI (1974), 201–6.

23. *Carter Diary,* II, 511.

24. *Ibid.,* II, 512, 515. Some men may have opposed maternal breastfeeding because of medical objections to nursing women engaging in sexual intercourse. See Joseph E. Illick, "Child-Rearing in Seventeenth-Century England and America," in deMause, ed., *The History of Childhood,* 310; Hunt, *Parents and Children,* 106–7; Trumbach, "The Aristocratic Family in England," 89.

25. The decision to put infants out to nurse could probably be correlated—if enough evidence were available—with growing family size and high economic status. See Marvick, "Nature versus Nurture," 266.

26. Farish, ed., *Journal and Letters of Fithian,* 52. Jonathan Boucher considered the practice among Maryland's elite of slaves nursing white children "a monstrous Fault." Boucher to Rev. John James, August 7, 1759, "Letters of Jonathan Boucher," *MHM,* VII (1912), 6.

27. See John Bowlby, *Attachment and Loss* (2 vols., New York, 1969 and 1973), I, 308, II, 335, 362.

28. John Demos, *A Little Commonwealth: Family Life in Plymouth Colony* (New York, 1970), 136; Alan Macfarlane, *The Family Life of Ralph Josselin: A Seventeenth-Century Clergyman* (Cambridge, England, 1970), 87–8.

29. Illick, "Child-Rearing in Seventeenth-Century England and America," 309; Trumbach, "The Aristocratic Family in England," 95–6; Marvick, "Nature Versus Nurture," 275–6.

30. Demos, *A Little Commonwealth,* 136. Middle class families in modern America wean their children at around six months. See John W. M. Whiting and Irving L. Child, *Child Training and Personality* (New Haven, 1953), 70–1.

31. Illick, "Child-Rearing in Seventeenth-Century England and America," 309.

32. Rachel Cocke to Elizabeth Jones, September 17, 1728, Jones Family Papers, Library of Congress.

33. Thomas Tudor Tucker to St. George Tucker, April 14, 1784, Tucker-Coleman Papers.

34. See Macfarlane, *Family Life of Ralph Josselin,* 87–8.

35. William Prentis to Joseph Prentis, July 28, 1801, Prentis Papers, University of Virginia.

36. Elizabeth Pratt to William Pratt, September 7, 1725, Jones Family Papers.

37. Martha Jefferson Carr to Richard Terrell, October 11, 1794, Carr Family Papers, University of Virginia. For other examples of parental concern over the teething problems of children, see Theodorick Bland, Jr., to John Randolph, September 14, 1770, Bland Papers, Virginia Historical Society, Richmond; Elizabeth Holloway to Elizabeth Jones, June 27, 1751, Jones Family Papers; and *Byrd Diary, 1709–1712,* 125.

38. Erik H. Erikson, *Childhood and Society* (New York, 1963, 2nd. ed.), 248.

39. One historian of eighteenth-century American childhood, however, maintains that children appeared as little more than afterthoughts in the letters of their parents. See John F. Walzer, "A Period of Ambivalence: Eighteenth-Century American Childhood," in deMause, ed., *The History of Childhood,* 359. The evidence from the eighteenth-century Chesapeake suggests a different conclusion.

40. Demos, *A Little Commonwealth,* 136–8. Philip J. Greven, Jr., finds continued suppression and control of child autonomy throughout the seventeenth and eighteenth centuries. See Greven, ed., *Child-Rearing Concepts, 1628–1861: Historical Sources* (Itasaca, Ill., 1973), 4.

41. Even in the early eighteenth century one finds evidence of religious fatalism—or rationalization—in response to infant and child death. The following comment was made in the *Gentlemen's Magazine,* in 1740: "It is a wonderful Part of the Providence of God that so many little creatures seem to be born only to die. . . . God, who does nothing in vain, has wise ends no doubt, and Purposes worthy of Himself to serve in any by the Birth of Infants who seem born only to die." Quoted in Ivy Pinchbeck and Margaret Hewitt, *Children in English Society* (London and Toronto, 1969), II, 301–2. For an extensive discussion of familial attitudes toward death, see Daniel Blake Smith, "Family Experience and Kinship in Eighteenth-Century Chesapeake Society" (unpublished Ph.D. dissertation, University of Virginia, 1977), chapter six.

42. Illick, "Child-Rearing in Seventeenth-Century England and America," 323, 325. A good example of seventeenth- and early eighteenth-century religious opinion on childhood comes from the widely read essays of Benjamin Wadsworth. In "The Nature of Early Piety" [*A Course on*

Sermons on Early Piety (Boston, 1721), 10] Wadsworth described the sinful character of newborn children:

> Their Hearts naturally, are a mere nest, root, fountain of Sin, and wickedness; an *evil Treasure* from whence proceed *evil* things, viz. *Evil Thoughts, Murders, Adulteries* &c. Indeed, as sharers in the guilt of *Adam's* first Sin they're *Children of Wrath by Nature,* liable to Eternal Vengeance, the Unquencheable Flames of Hell. But besides this, their Hearts (as hath been said) are unspeakable wicked, estrang'd from God, enmity against Him, eagerly set in pursuing Vanities, on provoking God by actual Personal transgressions, whereby they merit and deserve greater measures of Wrath.

43. In my reading of letters and diaries of Chesapeake families, I have rarely seen any mention of religious instruction for children. The Reverend Devereux Jarratt noted an irreligious tone in most planter households, though pointing out his own parents' interest in family religion. "The Autobiography of the Reverend Devereux Jarratt, 1732–1793," *WMQ,* 3rd. ser., ix (1952), 356, 363–4. Only two other instances of family religious instruction could be found in extant letters and diaries. The Reverend Robert Rose occasionally read prayers to his family "& a few others." Diary of the Reverend Robert Rose, September 29, 1749. In the 1770s Robert Carter Nicholas apparently taught his daugher Elizabeth the principles of the established church "with strictness, if not bigotry." Quoted in Victor Golladay, "The Nicholas Family in Virginia" (unpublished Ph.D. dissertation, University of Virginia, 1973), 172. A systematic sampling of wills in York and Albemarle County, Virginia, in the eighteenth century revealed that less than 5 per cent of all testators made reference to, or provision for, religious instruction in the family. Dissenter families doubtless showed more concern for religion in the home than Anglican parents. See, for example, the discussion of sermons and family prayers in the presbyterian household of James Gordon, "Journal of James Gordon," 4, 218. Almost all sermons to planter audiences and Anglo-American advice literature emphasized the need for religious child-rearing. See, for example, Benjamin Wadsworth, *The Well-Ordered Family* (Boston, 1719, 2nd. ed.); Samuel Davies, *Little Children Invited to Jesus Christ* (Hartford, 1766), a sermon preached in Hanover County, Virginia, May 8, 1758; John Witherspoon, *A Sermon on the Religious Education of Children* (Princeton, 1789).

44. Richard Lloyd to James Hollyday, June 14, 1756, Hollyday Family Papers.

45. Richard Tilghman III to the Rev. P. Crump, (after June 1763), "Letters Between the English and American Branches of the Tilghman Family," 173. In 1791 Thomas Jefferson told his daughter Mary Jefferson Randolph that he hoped his granddaughter "will make us all, and long, happy as the centre of our common love." Thomas Jefferson to Mary Jefferson Randolph, May 31, 1791, in Sarah N. Randolph, *The Domestic Life of Thomas Jefferson* (New York, 1939), 202.

46. Margaret Parker to James Parker, March 31, 1765, Parker Family Papers.

47. George Braxton to Mrs. Braxton, November 16, 1755, in Frederick Horner, *The History of the Blair, Banister and Braxton Families: A Collection of Letters* (Philadelphia, 1898), 131. See also, Sarah Cary to Betsy Braxton, October 20, 1781, *ibid.,* 58.

48. St. George Tucker to Frances Tucker, March ? 1781, Tucker-Coleman Papers. See also in this collection, St. George Tucker, to Frances Tucker, March 13, June 28, 1781, Frances Tucker to St. George Tucker, February 1780, March 24, 1781. See also Richard Terrell to Lucy Terrell, November 26, 1793, Carr Family Papers; William Byrd to Mrs. Otway, October 2, 1735, "Byrd Letters," *Virginia Magazine of History and Biography,* xxxvi (1928), 119–120.

49. Jane Swann to Thomas Jones, October 19, 1743, Jones Family Papers.

50. "Self-Portrait, Eliza Custis, 1808," *Virginia Magazine of History and Biography,* lxi (1953), 93–4. See also, *Carter Diary,* ii, 861–2, 1149; Charles Carroll of Annapolis to Charles Carroll of Carrollton, June 19, 1772, Carroll Family Papers, Maryland Historical Society, Baltimore. Children's birthdays were often remembered by their parents, who paid special attention to them on these days. See, for example, *Byrd Diary, 1709–1712,* 60, 483. Parents sometimes entertained their children. Thomas Bolling, while visiting Byrd's house in 1740 "entertained the children with his tricks." M. Tinling and Maude H. Woodfin, eds., *Another Secret Diary of William Byrd of Westover, 1739–1741* (Richmond, 1942), 79.

51. Mrs. Gilpin to Joshua Gilpin, 1796? Thomas Gilpin Letterbook, University of Virginia.

52. The emotional security of children in father-dominated households—as in the Chesapeake—has been studied by psychologists, but always with the assumption that the deference and sense of

duty children showed toward their father grew out of a fear of him and developed into a castration complex. I am suggesting that planters nurtured strong superegos in their sons, but under a rewarding, affectionate form of paternal discipline, not through authoritarianism. See T. Benedek, "Fatherhood and Providing," in E. Anthony and T. Benedek, eds., *Parenthood: Its Psychology and Psychopathology* (Boston, 1970), 167–184. This close contact and emotional bond between a planter and his son helped to gradually dissolve the boy's symbiotic bonds with his mother and to give him an accurate idea of his physical skills, responsibilities and values as a male in society. See Tess Forest, "The Paternal Roots of Male Character Development," *Psychoanalytic Review,* 54 (1967), 86–7.

53. New England parents may have viewed childhood in the same way. See Ross W. Beales, Jr., "In Search of the Historical Child: Miniature Adulthood and Youth in Colonial New England," *American Quarterly,* XXVII (1975), 379–98. However, Beale's study, like so many investigations of childhood in pre-industrial America, focuses almost exclusively on sermons, family manuals, and other normative advice literature. A close study of the personal documents of the family—letters, diaries, reminiscences, and wills—probes more deeply and accurately into actual child-rearing values and practices.

54. On the near absence of grandparents in th seventeenth-century Chesapeake, see Smith, "Mortality and Family in the Colonial Chesapeake"; Rutman and Rutman, " 'Now-Wives and Sons-in-Law' "; Walsh, "Marriage and Family in Seventeenth-Century Maryland." That grand-parenthood had become a widespread phenomenon by the last quarter of the eighteenth century is reflected in the calculations Allan Kulikoff has made from the census for Prince George's County, Maryland, in 1776. In that year 49 per cent of all children under age 4, 44 per cent between age 5–9, and 40 per cent between 10–14, had at least one living grandparent. See Kulikoff, "Tobacco and Slaves: Population, Economy, and Society in Eighteenth-Century Prince George's County, Maryland" (unpublished Ph.D. dissertation, Brandeis University, 1976), 58.

55. See Charles E. Bowerman and Donald P. Irish, "Some Relationships of Stepchildren to their Parents," *Marriage and Family Living,* 24 (1962), 113–121.

56. Kulikoff, "Tobacco and Slaves," 439.

57. Rachel Cocke to Elizabeth Pratt, September 17, 1728, Jones Family Papers.

58. Charles Carroll of Annapolis to Charles Carroll of Carrollton, December 5, 1770. See also, same to same, April 2, June 3, August 8, 1771; June 12, September 2, 1772, Carroll Family Papers.

59. Same to same, April 8, 1773, *ibid.*

60. Richard Henry Lee to Thomas Lee Shippen, January 17, 1785, in James C. Ballagh, ed., *The Letters of Richard Henry Lee* (New York, 1970), 322.

61. Henry Tucker, Sr. to St. George Tucker, August 21, 1784, Tucker-Coleman Papers. Horatio Belt confessed to the same kind of affection toward his grandchildren. He told his wife in 1783 to "give my love" to his grandsons "for in spite of my reason I cant help loving them." Belt to Catherine Belt, September 30, 1783, Dulaney Papers.

62. Illick, "Child-Rearing in Seventeenth-Century England and America," 312.

63. Martha Jefferson Carr to Richard Terrell, May 18, 1793, October 11, 1794; same to Lucy Terrell, August 9, 1794, March 28, 1796, Carr Family Papers.

64. Frances Randolph to St. George Tucker, March 22, 1781, Tucker-Coleman Papers. See also Charles Carroll of Annapolis to Charles Carroll of Carrollton, July 21, 1779, Carroll Family Papers. While away in France, Jefferson asked frequently about his granddaughter Anne Randolph. He hoped that she "grows lustily" and he instructed his daughter Mary to "learn her to run about before I come." Thomas Jefferson to Mary Jefferson Randolph, May 8, 31, 1791, in Randolph, *The Domestic Life of Thomas Jefferson,* 200, 202.

65. Thomas Jones to Elizabeth Jones, July 8, 1728, Jones Family Papers. See also Henry Tucker, Jr. to St. George Tucker, November 4, 1782, Tucker-Coleman Papers.

66. James Axtell, ed., *The Educational Writings of John Locke* (Cambridge, 1968), 123–4.

67. James Parker to Margaret Parker, March 8, 1776, Parker Family Papers.

68. Alice Morse Earle, *Childlife in Colonial America* (New York, 1899), 41–4, 55–8; William Nelson to John Norton, August 14, 1767, in Frances Norton Mason, ed., *John Norton and Sons Merchants of London and Virginia (Being the Papers from their Counting House for the Years 1750 to 1795* (Richmond, 1937), 32; Philippe Ariès, *Centuries of Childhood: A Social History of Family Life* (New York, 1962), 51–8.

69. A firm show of parental authority, Locke suggested, should begin early in the child's life but diminish as he matured: "If you would have him stand in Awe of you, imprint it *in his infancy:* and as he approaches more to a Man, admit him nearer to your Familiarity: So shall you have him your obedient Subject (as is fit) whilst he is a Child, and your affectionate Friend, when he is a Man." Axtell, *Educational Writings of Locke,* 145.

70. *Ibid.,* 154–5; Richard Allestree, *The Ladies Calling* (London, 1673), 48, 50. The most provocative study of Anglo-American child-rearing literature is in Daniel Calhoun, *The Intelligence of a People* (Princeton, 1973), 134–205. See also Edwin G. Burrows and Michael Wallace, "The American Revolution: The Ideology and Psychology of National Liberation," *Perspectives in American History,* VI (1972), 260–1. There are, however, serious difficulties in trying to understand child-rearing practices based on advice literature. For a perceptive analysis of these problems, see Jay Mechling, "Advice to Historians on Advice to Mothers," *Journal of Social History,* IX (1975), 44–63.

71. *Byrd Diary, 1709–1712,* 307. Byrd's young son William attended church by himself and frequently left the plantation with his playmates. See Tinling and Woodfin, eds., *Another Secret Diary,* 122–3, 130, 148.

72. Margaret Parker to James Parker, c. 1770, Parker Family Papers.

73. Molly Tilghman to Polly Tilghman, 1783 or 1784, "Letters of Molly and Hetty Tilghman," 33. See also Henry Hollyday to James Hollyday, September 22, 1754, Hollyday Papers; Frances Tucker to St. George Tucker, April 1787, Tucker-Coleman Papers; *Carter Diary,* II, 661–2.

74. Farish, ed., *Journal and Letters of Fithian,* 82, 94; Henry Hollyday to James Hollyday, May 17, 1777, Hollyday Papers; Karen Dawley, "Childhood in Eighteenth-Century Virginia" (unpublished Master's Thesis, University of Virginia, 1972), 25.

75. Henry Pratt to Elizabeth Jones, December 27, 1731, Jones Family Papers.

76. To counter the tendency of mothers and servants to become excessively fond of children, Locke emphasized the need for firm paternal discipline. Otherwise children would never learn the essential lesson of self-control. Calhoun, *The Intelligence of a People,* 141.

77. *Byrd Diary, 1709–1712,* 180–1.

78. Rachel Cocke to Elizabeth Jones, September 17, 1728, Jones Family Papers. See also, Thomas Jones to Elizabeth Jones, November 10, 1736, *ibid.*

79. Rachel Cocke to Elizabeth Jones, September 17, 1728, Jones Family Papers. See also Jean Blair to Mary Blair, October 14, 1769, in Horner, *The History of the Blair, Banister and Braxton Families.*

80. Thomas Jones to Elizabeth Jones, September 17, 1736, Jones Family Papers.

81. Lewis Joynes to Anne Joynes, November 4, 1788, "Joynes Family Letters," *Virginia Magazine of History and Biography,* LVI (1948), 149–50.

82. Fred Weinstein and Gerald Platt, *The Wish to be Free: Society, Psyche and Value Change* (Berkeley and Los Angeles, 1969), 191–92, 295–97.

83. Philip Slater has pointed out in a thoughtful essay that "the internalization of paternal values tends to occur to the degree that nurture and discipline come from the same source." Slater, "Parental Role Differentiation," in Rose L. Coser, ed., *The Family: Its Structures and Functions* (New York, 1974), 270. See also, Justin Aronfreed, "The Concept of Internalization," in David A. Goslin, ed., *Handbook of Socialization Theory and Research* (Chicago, 1969), 283, 307.

84. Weinstein and Platt also argue that this early internalization of parental values, characteristic of pre-modern societies, produced a "superego structure" that made independent behavior difficult, if not impossible. Their position, it seems to me, is much too narrowly conceived, for I am suggesting that close paternal involvement early in a child's life can lead (as I believe it did in the eighteenth-century Chesapeake) to an independent, self-sufficient personality structure in children. See Weinstein and Platt, *The Wish to be Free,* 178–92.

85. For a similar view of the "contractual" arrangement between parents and children in eighteenth-century America which fostered a psychology of liberation in the household and in Anglo-American relations, see Burrows and Wallace, "The American Revolution," 255–67.

86. Slater, "Parental Role Differentiation," 266–71.

9. Youth, Maturity, and Religious Conversion: A Note on the Ages of Converts in Andover, Massachusetts, 1711–1749

In my recent book on families in colonial Andover, Massachusetts, *Four Generations,* I argued that the families established by the first generation of settlers in the mid-seventeenth century proved to be remarkably rooted to the community throughout the lifetimes of the first and second generations, that fathers in both the first and second generations were patriarchs who used their lands to control the lives and fortunes of their sons.[1] I also argued that many of their sons remained economically dependent upon their fathers long after their adolescence and youth and well into the years which we normally associate with maturity, adulthood, and autonomy—the late twenties and the thirties. These patterns of family relationships of fathers and sons continued to shape the lives of the third generation as well, so that patriarchalism remained a dominant characteristic of family life and experience for males during the first three decades of the eighteenth century. In view of the fact that men delayed their marriages on the average until the age of twenty-seven during this period, and in view of the further delays in achieving their own economic independence owing to the continued possession of the land by their fathers, I argued that maturity came late for Andover men during the latter part of the seventeenth century and the early decades of the eighteenth century. The evidence which I used was entirely secular, and it was extremely reticent as far as the emotional or the personal experiences and feelings of the men themselves were concerned. The only evidence which might permit further insights into their inner lives was the evidence from the churches, of those persons who acknowledged the covenant and thus placed themselves under the watch of the churches, and those who experienced conversion and then joined in full communion.

From such an analysis of the lives of men in Andover during this period of the early eighteenth century, we ought to be able to anticipate some of the emotional and psychological consequences of lives of delayed independence and long-delayed maturity and thus, in effect, to predict some of the basic characteristics of their religious experiences. This would presume, of course, that the religious lives corresponded closely to the secular lives of the people involved, an assumption which I adhere to and believe will be fully supported in time by the analysis of the religious experiences, and especially the conversion experiences, of eighteenth-century New Englanders. Given the known facts about these men's lives, we ought to be able to rule out the likelihood of frequent psychological crises among sons during their childhoods, and more important, during their years of adolescence and youth.[2] Sons usually remained a part of their parental households until

Philip J. Greven, Jr., "Youth, Maturity, and Religious Conversion: A Note on the Ages of Converts in Andover, Massachusetts, 1711–1749," reprinted from the *Essex Institute Historical Collections* 108 (1972): 119–34, by permission of the Essex Institute, Salem, Massachusetts.

long after their teen-age period had passed and well into their twenties. In effect, a son continued to be a child, or to have a relationship with his father which was dependent upon submissive, dutiful behavior, and acquiescence to the authority and the judgements of the father. This would have continued unchanged and unchallenged during the entire period of a man's youth. The son thus would have little opportunity as a youth in his early twenties to establish his own personal identity independent of his role as dutiful son and child. Particularly in the families where the sons expected to become farmers like their fathers, the relationships of fathers and sons would be sustained well into the twenties and often into the thirties owing to the economic, as well as the filial, dependence of sons upon fathers. Their conversions, therefore, ought not to take place between the years of sixteen and twenty-six, which Jonathan Edwards identified as the period of youth in the mid-eighteenth century, but much later.[3] The question must therefore be asked: when, in fact, did people experience conversion?

Answers to this question can be derived from an analysis of the membership records of the churches in both the North and the South parishes of Andover between 1711, when the town was divided into two parishes and South Parish Church was formed, and 1749.[4] The records of the First, or North Parish, Church contain membership lists of persons entering the church in full communion between 1686 and 1711, listed without dates of entry, and between 1711 and 1749 (as well as later) listed annually, with actual dates of entry given in many instances. Not until 1727 are persons owning their baptismal covenants recorded in the North Church records, however, and even then relatively few names are listed. In the South Parish Church, the membership records list both persons owning the covenant, and thus joining in half-way status, and those entering the church in full communion, with the dates of their entry. With the use of additional genealogical data from the *Vital Records of Andover* it is thus possible to compute the ages at which men and women joined both churches, and thereby to compare the experiences of persons in two churches within a single community over a period of almost half a century.

In order to evaluate the starkly quantitative data which emerges from the analysis of membership lists, however, some understanding of the attitudes and beliefs of their ministers and the actual practices of both churches with regard to entry into the churches is essential.[5] The First, or North Parish, Church, was headed by Reverend Thomas Barnard between 1682, when he was ordained as co-pastor with Reverend Francis Dane, and 1718 when he died. The following year, his son, John Barnard, was ordained as his successor, and continued as pastor until his own death in 1757, thus providing the North Church with a remarkable degree of familial continuity in the ministry for more than seven decades. The church evidently did make a distinction between members in full communion (considering them to be persons who had experienced a satisfactory degree of saving grace and who thus could be considered regenerate) and persons who merely acknowledged their baptismal covenants, thus placing themselves under the watch and care of the church. While John Barnard was theologically orthodox, he evidently was less rigid and demanding than his fellow minister in the South Parish. In a sermon delivered in 1728 before a group of young men, Barnard noted that "Piety is not a Flower that grows in natures Garden; that you can't of your selves come into the Sentiments and Dispositions of Piety; that its God alone, who must work in you both to will and to do," a position which maintained orthodoxy while, in tone at least, suggesting a more benign approach to grace than the rigidly Calvinist. "Be willing," he said, "to be beholden to free Grace, for the whole of your Salvation."[6] In 1739, he warned that "There are many that live under the Gospel, who deceive themselves; their Hope of Salvation is without a Foundation. Too many think they have saving Grace, when they have none."[7] Barnard thus believed in the necessity for regeneration, and was not an Arminian in creed. But no evidence has survived to indicate anything about the actual practices of his church with respect to the testing of regenerative experiences as a prerequisite for membership.

Evidence for the South Parish Church, governed firmly and continuously for sixty years (1711–1771) by Reverend Samuel Phillips, is far more abundant, thanks to both the printed and the manuscript sermons by him preserved for this period. Phillips certainly was "a Gentleman" of a "Calvinistick turn," as Reverend Thomas Foxcroft described him in a letter of 1744.[8] He firmly believed in the orthodox doctrines of election and predestination, original sin, and regeneration. He maintained the necessity for a sharp distinction between a church of saints and a church open to all men, and the South Parish Church accordingly examined the experiences of regeneration recounted by men and women seeking membership in full communion, although it permitted their relations to be written and read to the church by the minister, prior to voting on their admission.[9]

Much of Phillips' energy and time was consumed with exhortations to his congregation to seek their salvation, to use the appointed means, and to await the gift of free grace essential to their regeneration or conversion. But the experience of regeneration, according to Phillips, was not necessarily a decisive, highly emotional, and exceedingly intense inner transformation. "Man does not at once come to be perfect in goodness," he said in a sermon in 1716. "But gradually, therefore there are means appointed for our growth in Grace."[10] In 1727, he continued to urge his congregation to seek grace and to come into full communion, assuring them that he was persuaded that "you can do much more than you do" and that "Our Gracious God is not wont to deny the Holy Spirit, to such as ask for Him; and continue to seek Him." He wanted people to take communion, but cautioned that "I am not about to perswade you to come to the Lord's Table, before you have reason to hope, that you are passed from death to life." Men must be regenerated before they can covenant with God. "Yet, I don't say, that they must be strong in the Grace which is in Christ Jesus, before they come to Communion; No; for, such who have sanctifying Grace, tho' but in a low measure; have a right to this Privilege; because their Hearts are right with God."[11] In 1738, he reasserted this position in almost identical words, indicative of his persistent attempts to reassure his congregation of their ability to seek grace and assurance of their personal election, and thus to participate in the church as full members.[12]

In 1741, he urged men "to hold fast" to "the Doctrine of Original Sin" and to "that of the Necessity and Nature of the New-Birth" as well as of "Justification by Faith."[13] After the Great Awakening, he gave a sermon on the New Birth in early 1748 strikingly similar to many of the fervent New Light sermons of earlier years, exhorting his congregation on "the necessity of the new Birth" without which "no man is a true member of the church of Christ on Earth." He urged men "to be Diligent in the use of all proper means that we may get into such a State [regenerate] very Quickly. That which is a matter of absolute necessity and without which we are undone, we can't be too Sollicitous to obtain." Regeneration, he said, gives men "Such a Byass to their wills as Disposes them to Submit to Christ with all willingness." Those who remained unconverted he consoled by saying that "Many, very many have been born again probably, as bad as you, yea and doubtless many more shall and for ought you know, you among others." Five months previously, he had denounced half-way members of his and other churches, telling them that God "abhors half-way Christians," and will damn all but full Christians.[14] Without conversion, there could be no salvation. Samuel Phillips, at least, had never believed otherwise.

For both John Barnard and Samuel Phillips, the first decades of their ministries proved to be the most successful in terms of the number of new admissions of members in full communion to their respective churches (see Tables 9.1 and 9.2). In the North Parish, Barnard's father had had between two and six new members in full communion annually between 1711 and 1718. In 1720, the year after his ordination, John Barnard received ten men and eleven women into full communion, with nineteen additional members the following year. The great earthquake of 1727 produced the largest influx of new converts into the North Church during the first half of the century: seventy-two in 1727 and eighty-seven in 1728. The next seven years were lean ones, with between three and seven new members annually, but in 1736, the year in which the diphtheria epidemic struck Andover, thirty-eight new members were added, followed by another thirty in 1738, the year of the greatest mortality in Andover's colonial history. No great influx occurred during the period of the Great Awakening of the early 1740's, however, indicative of the resistance of Barnard's church to the revival. In the South Parish, Samuel

Table 9.1. **Number of Members in Full Communion in the North Parish Church, by Decades**

| Years | Male | | Female | | Total |
	Number	Percent	Number	Percent	
1686–1710	78	40.6	114	59.4	192
1711–1719	35	41.2	50	58.8	85
1720–1729	98	39.2	152	60.8	250
1730–1739	42	35.9	75	64.1	117
1740–1749	37	42.0	51	58.0	88
1750–1759	24	34.3	46	65.7	70
1686–1759	314	39.2	488	60.8	802
1711–1759	236	38.7	374	61.3	610

Table 9.2. **Number of Members in Full Communion in the South Parish Church, by Decades**

| Years | Male | | Female | | Total |
	Number	Percent	Number	Percent	
1711–1719	76	47.2	85	52.8	161
1720–1729	42	27.8	73	72.2	115
1730–1739	24	35.8	43	64.2	67
1740–1749	17	36.2	30	63.8	47
1750–1759	32	40.0	48	60.0	80
1711–1759	191	40.6	279	59.4	470

Phillips added a total of one hundred and twenty-six new members in full communion to his newly formed church between 1711 and 1719, in addition to the original thirty-five men and women who formed the initial membership in 1711. In 1727, he added twenty-two new members, and in 1728 an additional forty-one. In 1731, however, he noted sadly in his record book, "Alas! No Addition this year," a complaint which he renewed for the next two years as well. In 1736, though, he added twenty-three new members in full communion, but only two in 1738. During the 1740's, his new additions remained few in number, for the awakenings shaking other communities were not to be seen in the two parishes of Andover. For those who remained in Andover, conversion had become increasingly rare during the 1740's.

From the membership records of both the North and South Parish Churches, it is evident that the number of men and women experiencing conversion varied considerably over time, and especially that the decades of the 1730's and the 1740's were periods of declension. What is not apparent from these records, yet is even more startling, are the changes in the ages—and thus of the points in the life cycles—of the men and women who experienced conversion and who could enter these churches in full communion. A comparison of the ages at which people entered the churches in full communion between 1711 and 1729, and again between 1730 and 1749, reveals some remarkable changes in the characteristics of the conversion experiences of Andover's population.

Since the South Parish Church used the half-way convenant, which was a means of publicly acknowledging one's desire for Christian fellowship but which also signified that a person had not yet experienced regeneration, the ages at which men and women owned the covenant provide a clue to the earliest points in their lives at which they were willing to come formally under the care of the church[15] (see Tables 9.3 and 9.4). Except for the years 1711–1719, when the average age of men and women owning the covenant was high, the ages at which men and women acknowledged their baptismal covenants remained surprisingly constant. The average age of women owning the covenant between 1711 and 1729 was 20.7 years, and 20.3 years between 1730 and 1749. During the period 1711–1729, half of the women were between the ages 12 and 19 at the time of owning the covenant, with ¾ owning the covenant before reaching the age of 25. Most women thus acknowledged their baptismal covenant either before or shortly after marriage, since the average age of marriage for third-generation women, most of whom

Table 9.3. **Number of Persons Owning the Covenant (Half-way Members) in the South Parish Church, by Decades**

	Male		Female		
Years	Number	Percent	Number	Percent	Total
1711–1719	34	54.8	28	45.2	62
1720–1729	63	50.4	62	49.6	125
1730–1739	39	47.6	43	52.4	82
1740–1749	78	56.1	61	43.9	139
1750–1759	69	48.3	74	51.7	143
1711–1759	283	52.0	268	48.0	551

Table 9.4. **Average Age of Persons Owning the Covenant in the South Parish Church, 1711–1749**

Years	Male		Female	
	Number	Average Age	Number	Average Age
1711–1719	27	26.1	18	27.3
1720–1729	42	22.5	47	18.1
1730–1739	32	23.2	36	19.8
1740–1749	61	22.1	44	20.8
*	*	*	*	*
1711–1729	69	23.9	65	20.7
1730–1749	93	22.4	80	20.3

married during this period, was 24½ years. During the period 1730–1749, 85 percent of the women who owned the covenant did so between the ages of 15 and 24. For men, the average age was slightly higher than for women: about 24 years between 1711 and 1729, and about 22½ between 1730 and 1749. In both periods, men owned the covenant about three years before marriage on the average. Nearly 22 percent of the men owned the covenant between the ages of 12 and 19 during both periods, 55 percent owned the covenant between the ages of 12 and 24 from 1711 to 1729, and 72 percent did so at these ages from 1730 to 1749. Only 5 men owned the covenant after reaching the age of 30 during the period 1730 to 1749. In general, both women and men owned the covenant after 1720 while still youths.

While the proportions of men and women owning the covenant in the South Parish were nearly equal over the period from 1711 to 1759, the admissions to membership in the church in full communion were proportionately higher for women than for men: three women for every two men overall, and nearly three-to-one during the 1720's. In the North Parish, the proportion of women to men was roughly the same from 1711 to 1759. Women experienced regeneration more often than men throughout this period in both churches (see Tables 9.1 and 9.2). They also were converted at appreciably younger ages than men during the period 1711–1729, when the average ages of conversion for women in both parishes ranged between 7.5 and 9.4 years less than for men. Just as the ages of owning the covenant were higher between 1711 and 1719 than in subsequent decades, so too were the average ages of conversion of women in both parishes higher than later (see Table 9.4). Between 1711 and 1729, the average age at the time of entry into full communion for women was 26.7 years in the North Parish, and 28.8 years in the South Parish; during the next two decades, 1730–1749, the average ages dropped in both parishes—to 20.8 years in the North Parish and to 24.0 in the South Parish. In the South Parish, 80 percent of the female converts entering the church between 1711 and 1719 were already married, whereas less than half were married when converted during the 1720's and 1730's. Similarly, in the North Parish, 30 of the 36 female converts during the period 1711–1719 were already married, whereas between 1720 and 1729, 61 of the 96 were unmarried when converted, and between 1730 and 1739, 30 of the 38 converts were also unmarried. During the period 1711–1729, teen-age conversions were rare in both parishes: only 15 out of 98 in the South Parish (the youngest being 11 years old), and 36 out of 132 in the North Parish. Between 1730 and 1749, there were 9 teen-

Table 9.5. **Average Age at Time of Entry into Full Communion in the North and South Parish Churches, 1711–1749**

	NORTH PARISH CHURCH				
	Male		Female		
					Average Difference in Ages of Males and Females
Years	Number	Average Age	Number	Average Age	
1711–1719	32	39.2	36	31.7	7.5
1720–1729	75	34.2	96	24.8	9.4
1730–1739	27	27.0	38	20.0	7.0
1740–1749	29	25.6	29	21.9	3.7
*	*	*	*	*	*
1711–1729	107	35.7	132	26.7	9.0
1730–1749	56	26.3	67	20.8	5.5
	SOUTH PARISH CHURCH				
1711–1719	52	39.1	50	31.1	8.0
1720–1729	33	34.7	48	26.3	8.4
1730–1739	17	25.1	32	23.0	2.1
1740–1749	12	27.3	22	25.6	1.7
*	*	*	*	*	*
1711–1729	85	37.4	98	28.8	8.6
1730–1749	29	26.0	54	24.0	2.0

age conversions in the South Parish out of a total of 54 female conversions, and 35 out of 67 in the North Parish—a very high proportion indeed. In both parishes, women tended, after 1720, to be converted at relatively young ages.

The ages of conversion of men differed significantly from the ages of women in both parishes between 1711 and 1729. In the North Parish, only four men converted in their teens (the youngest being 15) and in the South Parish only one man converted while still in his teens (aged 18). In both parishes, more than ¾ of the men were converted after reaching the age of 25 years. In the South Parish, ⅔ of the men were 30 years or older when they experienced regeneration and joined the Church in full communion; in the North Parish, 44 percent of the men joining in full communion were 35 years or older. The range in ages of male converts in the South Parish during this period was between 18 and 87, and in the North Parish between 15 and 78. The average age of regeneration for men converted between 1711 and 1719 was about 39 years in both parishes, an extraordinarily late age for conversions; between 1720 and 1729, the average age of conversion in both parishes was still in the mid-30's. For the average man conversion thus usually occurred nearly a decade *after* marriage. In both parishes, adolescent conversions were exceedingly rare, youthful conversions were fairly uncommon, and the great majority of men experienced regeneration as adults. In view of their ages, it is vividly clear that the sermons being given both by Barnard and Phillips to encourage youthful conversions must have been mostly in vain.

The striking differences in the religious experiences and the religious behavior—evident in the ages of the converts—of women and men in Andover between 1711 and 1729 indicates that their life experiences also must have differed significantly, with women reaching maturity sooner than men, as their younger ages at marriage and at conversion both testify. The extraordinarily late ages of conversion for men in this period

Table 9.6. **The Age at Full Communion of Men in the North and South Parish Churches, 1711–1749**

Ages	North Parish		South Parish	
1711–1719	Number	Percent	Number	Percent
1–14	0	0.0	0	0.0
15–24	6	18.8	3	5.8
25–34	8	25.0	20	38.5
35–44	6	18.8	15	28.8
45–59	10	31.2	8	15.4
60–100	2	6.2	6	11.5
	32	100.0	52	100.0
1720–1729				
1–14	0	0.0	0	0.0
15–24	16	21.3	6	18.2
25–34	30	40.0	16	48.5
35–44	17	22.7	3	9.1
45–59	5	6.7	5	15.2
60–100	7	9.3	3	9.1
	75	100.0	33	100.1
1730–1739				
1–14	0	0.0	0	0.0
15–24	16	59.3	11	64.7
25–34	7	25.9	5	29.4
35–44	1	3.7	0	0.0
45–59	3	11.1	1	5.9
60–100	0	0.0	0	0.0
	27	100.0	17	100.0
1740–1749				
1–14	0	0.0	0	0.0
15–24	14	48.3	6	50.0
25–34	12	41.4	3	25.0
35–44	2	6.9	2	16.7
45–59	1	3.4	1	8.3
60–100	0	0.0	0	0.0
	29	100.0	12	100.0

is further evidence of the fact that maturity for men came late in this period. Their ages of conversion, like their ages of marriage and the ages at which sons gained their economic independence from their fathers, point to the same conclusion: that childhood and youth were not periods of stress and crisis in the lives of men in early-eighteenth-century Andover. As we ought to expect, therefore, conversions reflected the long-delayed maturity of men, and indicate that whatever personal crises took place affected men who were already adults, as far as their ages were concerned. Their ages of conversion are mute, but striking, testimony to the emotional and psychological transformations of men who still were boys in their middle thirties.

The next generation, however, reached maturity much sooner and at appreciably younger ages than had the third generation. Thus we find that the ages of marriage of

Table 9.7. **The Age at Full Communion of Women in the North and South Parish Churches, 1711–1749**

Ages	North Parish		South Parish	
1711–1719	Number	Percent	Number	Percent
1–14	0	0.0	0	0.0
15–24	8	22.2	17	34.0
25–34	17	47.2	20	40.0
35–44	8	22.2	7	14.0
45–59	3	8.3	4	8.0
60–100	0	0.0	2	4.0
	36	99.9	50	100.0
1720–1729				
1–14	8	8.3	1	2.1
15–24	49	51.0	27	56.3
25–34	26	27.1	11	22.9
35–44	10	10.4	5	10.4
45–59	1	1.0	3	6.3
60–100	2	2.1	1	2.1
	96	99.9	48	100.1
1730–1739				
1–14	6	15.8	0	0.0
15–24	29	76.3	28	87.5
25–34	1	2.6	2	6.3
35–44	0	0.0	2	6.3
45–59	2	5.3	0	0.0
60–100	0	0.0	0	0.0
	38	100.0	32	100.1
1740–1749				
1–14	0	0.0	0	0.0
15–24	25	86.2	12	54.5
25–34	2	6.9	8	36.4
35–44	2	6.9	1	4.5
45–59	0	0.0	1	4.5
60–100	0	0.0	0	0.0
	29	100.0	22	99.9

fourth-generation men dropped by an average of two years, their economic independence from their fathers was gained at younger ages, and their lives in general reflected a cycle of development which indicated that they were autonomous and independent of their fathers and families sooner than previous generations had been. With the emergence of the fourth generation on the scene in Andover during the 1730's and 1740's, there ought to have been some equally significant changes in the characteristics of their religious experiences and especially in their ages of conversion. Given the other changes in the process of maturity evident in the lives of the fourth generation, we ought to expect their conversions to occur at earlier ages than in the previous period. Was this actually the case?

In the North Parish, the average age of conversion for men dropped from 35.7 years for the period 1711–1729 to 26.3 years for the period from 1729 to 1749. In the South Parish, the average age of conversion for men dropped from 37.4 years for the period 1711–1729 to 26 years for the period 1730–1749—a remarkably similar pattern within the two churches of Andover, and a rather astonishing change in ages of conversion. In neither parish, however, were any males converted before the age of 15, but none of the conversions occurred after the age of 60 either. In the North Parish, more than half of the conversions took place between the ages of 17 and 24 (53.5 percent), with 82 percent occurring *before* the age of 30, and only 12.5 percent occurring at 35 years or more. In the South Parish, nearly 60 percent of the conversions occurred between the ages of 16 and 24, and close to ¾ of the conversions (72.4 percent) occurred before the age of 30. Whereas nearly half of the conversions had occurred at 35 years of age or later during the earlier decades, during the 1730's and 1740's only 14 percent of the conversions oc-curred that late. Since the ages at which men acknowledged the covenant did not change significantly between these two periods, 24 and then 22½, the age of conversion is the principal religious indication of fundamental changes in the life cycle and development of men. During the period in which the fourth generation was reaching maturity, therefore, their conversions were occurring much sooner than had been the case earlier. In effect, men were maturing earlier and gaining their independence as young men rather than as middle-aged men. Their religious experiences confirm the inferences from the other sources.

The ages of conversion dropped for women as well as men during the period 1730–1749 in both parishes: from 26.7 years to 20.8 years in the North Parish, and from 28.8 years to 24.0 years in the South Parish. During the 1730's, one girl of 8 years joined the North Church in full communion, and one of 10 years, but the overwhelming majority were between 14 and 24 years of age. During the 1740's, neither parish had girls under 14 years of age joining in full communion. The youngest female convert in the South Parish between 1730 and 1749 was 17. What is most notable is that conversion even for women in Andover was still not primarily a phenomenon of the teen-age years, but it had become most definitely a phenomenon of youth, the period of life between 16 and 26 years. Since fourth-generation women in Andover were marrying during these decades at an average age of 23 years, their conversions closely accompanied their experiences of becoming wives and mothers, those points in their own life cycles which most clearly signified their own coming to maturity as young women.

Two conclusions from this preliminary survey of data on conversions seem inescap-able: that the ages at which men and women converted in the eighteenth century were *not constant,* and that the experience of conversion itself was closely associated with the process of maturity. The later the age of conversion, on the average, the more delayed the process of maturing itself must have been. When the average ages of conversion de-creased, a fundamental change in the developmental process itself must have taken place. If this is so, and for Andover, at least, I am convinced that it is, then perhaps we will have discovered that the age of conversion is a major key to the developmental cycles of individuals in eighteenth-century New England, and one which might enable us to begin to unlock some of the many secrets about their personalities and their lives. It is one vital clue to those points in the lives of men and of women when they faced a crisis of autonomy and of maturity, which they expressed through religious experience. Until now, I thought that the age of marriage provided us with the most sensitive index of maturity, and the delayed ages of marriage of men, especially, were symptomatic of a society and an economy which prevented the early maturity and independence of men.[16] Yet now I am convinced that the age of conversion actually may be an even better index of the age of maturity, for as the Andover data reveal, the variations in ages of conversion were far greater than were the variations in ages of marriage. By computing the ages at which men and women experienced conversion, we will have an extraordinarily useful key to the developmental cycles and the whole process of maturing—a process of individual development of an emotional and psychological nature which ordinarily is unrecoverable from the evidence which survives. By seeing that the age of conversion does *not* necessarily correspond to the years of adolescence, we will begin to see when and how people have reached maturity, and gained their own personal autonomy, or lost it again by the very experience of conversion itelf, and thus be able to probe dimensions of their lives which have not yet been explored.

Notes

1. Philip J. Greven, Jr., *Four Generations: Population, Land, and Family in Colonial Andover, Massachusetts* (Ithaca, N.Y., 1970). An earlier version of this essay was presented at the Conference on Childhood and Youth in History held at Clark University, Worcester, Mass., March 19–21, 1970.

2. John Demos, in his study of families in seventeenth-century Plymouth, also finds that "one looks for signs of a difficult adolescence in the sources from the period, and looks in vain," but suggests instead that "Many Puritan conversions seem to have occurred well before puberty" and that "Perhaps . . . a religious 'crisis' can more reasonably be connected with the whole matrix of changes customary for children at the age of about six to eight." *A Little Commonwealth: Family Life in Plymouth Colony* (New York, 1970), p. 146. As in so many other ways, Andover's experience was quite different.

3. See the excerpt from Jonathan Edwards' letter of November 12, 1743, in the *Christian History*, reprinted in Joseph Tracy, *The Great Awakening: A History of the Revival of Religion in the Time of Edwards and Whitefield* (Boston, 1842), pp. 194–195. He speaks of "the *children* that were under sixteen years of age" but of the "*young people*" between sixteen and twenty-six years (italics added).

4. The records of the North Parish Church, originally Congregational but now Unitarian, are in the Journal of Church Matters, Baptisms, and Weddings, kept by Rev. Thomas Barnard, Rev. John Barnard, and Dr. Symmes from 1687 to 1810, located in the North Andover Historical Society. The records of South Parish Church members are in Rev. Samuel Phillips' Record Book, kept in an Andover bank vault.

5. For an excellent general discussion of Andover's early church history, see Sarah Loring Bailey, *Historical Sketches of Andover . . . Massachusetts* (Boston, 1880), pp. 410–516.

6. John Barnard, *Piety Described, and Early Religion Recommended, In A Sermon Preach'd to a Society of Young Men, October 15th, 1727* (Boston, 1728), p. 87.

7. John Barnard, *The Expectation of Man Disappointed by the Great God* . . . (Boston, 1739), pp. 4–5. A few sermons by Barnard are to be found in the Simon Gratz Collection, Historical Society of Pennsylvania, Philadelphia.

8. Rev. Thomas Foxcroft to Rev. Samuel Phillips, Boston, letter of October 10, 1744 (Historical Society of Pennsylvania, Philadelphia).

9. See Samuel Phillips, *A Word in Season* (Boston, 1727), pp. 121–122.

10. Samuel Phillips, sermon, September 16–23, 1716, in Simon Gratz Collection, HSP. All contractions have been expanded and italics omitted in all questions.

11. Phillips, *Word in Season,* pp. 70–71, 80, 89.

12. Samuel Phillips, *The Orthodox Christian: Or, A Child Well Instructed in the Principles of the Christian Religion* . . . (Boston, 1738), pp. 104–105. Also see pp. 130–132 for a copy of the covenant read upon entry into full communion.

13. Samuel Phillips, *Soldiers Counseled* (Boston, 1741), p. 51.

14. Phillips, sermons, August 30, 1747, and January 17, 1747/8, Gratz Collection, HSP.

15. For fascinating comparative data for seventeenth-century New England churches, see Robert G. Pope, *The Half-Way Covenant: Church Membership in Puritan New England* (Princeton, 1969), pp. 208–238, 279–286. J. M. Bumsted's essay, "Religion, Finance, and Democracy in Massachusetts: The Town of Norton as a Case Study," *Journal of American History,* LVII (March 1971), 817–829, is superb. His data on ages of conversion for males are strikingly similar to the Andover data, with the average age of men entering full communion prior to 1740 being 39.7 years, dropping to 29.9 years during the revival (p. 828).

16. See Greven, *Four Generations,* pp. 31–33.

10. Parental Power and Marriage Patterns: An Analysis of Historical Trends in Hingham, Massachusetts

Perhaps the central conceptual issue in the sociology of the family is the relationship of modernization to family structure. Paradoxically the theoretical significance of this problem has not engendered an empirical preoccupation with the details of the transition from "traditional" to "modern" family structure. For sociologists, as Abrams (1972:28) puts it, "the point after all was not to know the past but to establish an idea of the past which could be used as a comparative base for the understanding of the present." While historians often implicitly use a conception of the modern family as a baseline for their researches into the past, formally at least they attempt to relate the family to the culture and other institutions of an historical period. Only rarely have either group of scholars actually measured the dimensions of change by analyzing data over a long time interval. Thus the element of change in family structure has been more usually assumed or inferred from casual comparisons of past and present than consciously measured and analyzed. A great chasm persists between the theoretical perspective on the family and modernization (see Smelser, 1966:115–117, for a concise summary) and a limited body of empirical evidence more often qualifying or denying these relationships (for example, Furstenberg, 1966; Lantz *et al.,* 1968; and Laslett and Wall, 1972) than supporting or extending them.

The problem of the connection between modernization and family structure may be conveniently divided into three analytically distinct areas—the relevance of the family for the structuring of other institutions, the role of the family in shaping individual lives, and finally the significance to the individual of the family he is born into (family of orientation) for the one he creates by marriage (family of procreation). Since the historical trends in the first two areas have presumably seemed so obvious, systematic empirical data have not been collected and analyzed to establish the precise dimensions and timing of change. In the first instance the modern family is not as quantitatively important for the organization of other structures—economic, political, and social.[1] What influence the modern family exerts in these areas is indirect, exerted either through early socialization and personality formation or mediated by intervening institutions. Male occupational status in modern America, for example, is related to the family of orientation mainly through the provision of education, not by direct parental placement. Few families today control jobs which can be given to their children (Blau and Duncan, 1967:131–133). Having less of an instrumental role, the family is now a specialized institution providing nurture and affection for both children and adults. Perhaps the best historical study of the transformation in this second area is the impressionistic classic of Ariès (1962) which

Daniel Scott Smith, "Parental Power and Marriage Patterns: An Analysis of Historical Trends in Hingham, Massachusetts," reprinted from *Journal of Marriage and the Family* 35 (1973): 419–28, by permission, © 1973, National Council on Family Relations, 1910 West County Road B, Suite 147, St. Paul, Minnesota 55113.

delineates the social separation of the family from the community and the emergence of the psychological centrality of the child in the conjugal family. Since this interpretation now rests on changes in ideals and lacks adequate behavioral support, more historical analysis is required to determine the extent of this shift. It is possible, for example, that emotional or expressive ties between parents and children have been essentially invariant over the course of American history. These affective relationships may appear to have increased historically only because of the separation of instrumental activities from the family.

Although not necessarily more significant than the changes in the first two areas, the relationship between the family of orientation and the family of procreation has often been considered to be the central issue in the modernization of the family. Davis (1949:414–418), in fact, has argued that this distinction is the most adequate key to understanding other variations in family structure. If the family newly created by marriage is dominated by pre-existing families of birth, then households are more likely to be extended in structure, marriages are more likely to be arranged and will take place at earlier ages, intrafamilial relationships will tend to be authoritarian, etc. Despite Parsons later disclaimer that his well-known analysis (Parsons, 1943) was mainly concerned with the isolation of the family from other social structures and his acceptance of the Litwack-Seeman critique as complementary not contradictory, he was not deterred from elaborating his earlier argument. The substance of the debate on extended kinship in modern American society continues precisely on the quantity and nature of interaction between married couples and their parents (Parson, 1965). Historians as well have concentrated on this question, usually employing the classic extended-nuclear dichotomy to summarize their findings. Greven (1970) has argued that by withholding land fathers in seventeenth century Andover, Massachusetts, were able to exercise considerable power over their adult sons. Once land had become relatively scarce in the early eighteenth century, they found it more difficult or less desirable to do so. More recently an entire volume of papers has been devoted to crushing the proposition that extended *households* ever were a significant element in western society, at least since the middle ages (Laslett and Wall, 1972).[2]

The Historical Problem

In a decade review of research on modern American kinship, Adams (1970) has suggested that the most recent work is moving beyond debate and description to the more significant tasks of specification, interrelation, and comparison. This change of emphasis is as important for historical as for contemporary studies, even though an adequate, empirically based, systematic description of the historical evolution of the relationship between the family of orientation and the family of procreation does not presently exist. Despite the fact that it is always easier to decry than to remedy scholarly failures, this absence should be a challenge rather than an obstacle for historians. Much of the critical evidence regarding the extent and kind of interaction between parents and adult children is, of course, unwritten. Despite their interest in the same substantive issues, historians inevitably are forced to employ different methods than sociologists. Yet there are serious problems in the interpretation of historical evidence on the family.

While a body of literary comment on ideal family relationships does exist, it becomes progressively more biased toward higher social strata as one moves farther back into the past (Berkner, 1973). Furthermore, the relating of historical information about ideals to actual behavior is not easily accomplished (Goode, 1968:311–313). Since literary sources are available, relatively inexpensive to exploit, and suggestive concerning the more subtle aspects of family interaction, it would be foolish to dismiss them as biased and unreliable. It would be equally risky to base the entire history of the American family on these sources. What appears to be crucial at this point for a reliable descriptive history of the American family is the development of series of quantitative indicators for various aspects of family behavior.

On both theoretical and historical grounds the idea that a shift from the centrality of the family of orientation to the family of procreation has occurred within the time span of American history may be questioned. American history, it is often argued, lacks a "traditional" or "premodern" period. If modernization and the transformation of the family from extended to nuclear are related, one would not expect to find evidence for it within the three and one-half centuries of American history. The classic polarities of sociological theory are often used by historians to contrast America with England or as a literary device to highlight rather small shifts over time. Still, the dominant theme in American historiography is "uniqueness" and this peculiar quality of the American experience is linked to the various characteristics of modernity. Ideal types, of course, describe no particular empirical realities. Since these classic dichotomies emerged from the attempt to understand the transformation of western society in the nineteenth century, their empirical relevance surely ought to be as much in the analysis of the history of western development as in the explanation of cross-cultural differences. If the discussion of historical change in the family is to progress, the selection of terms is less important than the precise specification of the extent of change along the theoretical continuum.

Some important aspects of the nuclear, conjugal, or family-of-procreation-dominant family system such as neolocal residence, undoubtedly have been dominant since the earliest American settlement in the seventeenth century (Goode, 1970a:xvi). Other significant historical continuities such as the priority given to nuclear as against extended kin (Demos, 1970: 181) may also be present. If change is to be detected in an area of known continuity, a specific, well-defined problem and subtle and discriminating measures of change are required. The relative centrality of the family of orientation versus the family of procreation can be examined from various angles. Marriage formation, however, is probably the most crucial since it is the point of transition for the individual. Transitions involving decisions are inevitably problematic. Furthermore, marriages produce records for nearly the entire population, not just for atypical elites. Thus a substantial data base exists for historical analysis. If the American family has undergone substantial historical change, it should be reflected in the conditions of marriage formation. Were, in fact, the marriages of a significant segment of the American population ever controlled by parents at any point in our history? Parents today are, of course, not irrelevant in the courtship and marriage formation process. The earlier, "traditional," pattern of control should be direct rather than indirect, involve material rather than psychological relationships, and involve power exercised by parents in their own interest at the expense of the children.

A shift in the control of marriage formation is clearly to be expected by the sociological theory of family modernization.[3] Confident, if vague, statements exist describing the emergence of a non-parentally controlled, participant-run courtship system within the time span encompassed by American history (Reiss, 1964:57–58; Stone, 1964:181–182).[4] Yet Reiss presumably relies on literary evidence in his broad summary and Stone on the decidedly atypical experience of the English aristocracy. Furthermore, the shift specified is subtle—from a parental choice, child veto system in the seventeenth century to its converse by the late nineteenth or early twentieth century. Given the particularistic relationship between parents and children, choosing and vetoing choices may not be a constitutional system but instead an ongoing process of action and reaction.

Method and Sample

The dead, of course, cannot be subjected to surveys. The extent of parental power in courtship and marriage formation cannot be directly measured. Inherently the concept has a certain diffuseness and multidimensionality. Parents, for example, could determine the actual choice of spouse, they could determine the age at marriage but not name the partner, or they could merely structure indirectly the range of acceptable spouses. The actual process of decision making and bargaining is forever lost to the historian of ordinary people. If the dead cannot be interviewed, they can be made to answer questions if various consequences of the larger issue of parental control over marriage can be explicitly formulated. This is possible through the construction of long-term series of indices which are logically associated with the operational existence of parental control. Unlike the possibilities available in direct interaction with respondents, these indices inevitably lack meaning in an absolute, substantive sense. Conclusions must rest not just on one measure but on the conformity of various indicators to some pattern. Quantitative measures, whatever their limitations, have the great advantage of providing consistent information about change over time—the great question in the sociological history of the family and the most severe limitation of literary source materials.

Since the expected transition to a participant-run courtship system allegedly occurred between the seventeenth and late nineteenth century, either comparable data sets separated by more than a century or a long continuous series seem appropriate. For sociological purposes the former would be sufficient since a test of the change is all that is required. For historical analysis the time-series approach is better suited since the timing and pace of the transition are equally interesting. If the change did occur, was it gradual or concentrated in a few decades as a result, say, of the American revolution or the inception of rapid economic growth.

The larger study from which the ensuing data derive covers the social and demographic experience of the population of one Massachsetts town over a quarter-millennium (Smith, 1973). Economically, this period—1635 to 1880—encompasses the shift, mainly after 1800, from agriculture to commerce and industry. Demographically, it includes the transition from a fertility level which was high by west European standards to the below replacement reproduction rates of the mid-nineteenth century (Smith, 1972a; Uhlenberg, 1969). The basic methodological technique of the larger study was family reconstitution—essentially statistical genealogy (Wrigley, 1966). Records of births, deaths, intentions to marry, marriages, and wealth data from tax lists were combined into family units for analysis. Various series of comparable data extending over the two centuries were constructed to measure change in demographic, familial, and social behavior. By examining differences in the timing of changes in these indicators, the history of the evolution of the population and social structure can be interpreted (Furet, 1971). Every decision about research design necessarily involves a price. Although long-term trends and change can be studied by this approach, the conclusions strictly must be limited to the population of the town of Hingham. Furthermore, primarily because of migration, nearly one-half of the families could not be fully reconstituted. Although wealth is inversely related to outmigration after marriage, this distortion only marginally affects most indicators. Since the wealth-bias is fairly consistent over time, trends are affected to a lesser degree than levels for any particular cohort.

Evidence

In early New England, as in the pre-industrial West generally, marriage was intimately linked to economic independence (Wrigley, 1969:117–118). As a result, age at marriage and proportions never-marrying were higher in western Europe than in other cultural areas (Hajnal, 1965). Since the late marriage pattern tended to reduce fertility, European societies had less of a dependency burden from non-productive children; the easy mobility of the young, unmarried adult population may also have facilitated the transition to modern economic growth. Arguing in theoretical terms, one historical demographer has suggested that mortality level was also an important mechanism in the determination of marriage age. Higher mortality would open up opportunities for sons who then could marry earlier than if their fathers survived longer. The growth of population was thus controlled by the countervailing forces of mortality and marriage age (Ohlin, 1961).

These central demographic characteristics of west European societies can be used to formulate a test of the extent of paternal economic power. Since newly married sons were not incorporated into the paternal economic or living unit, marriage meant a definite transfer of power intergenerationally. The transfer might be eased by custom, limited by paternal retention of formal title to the land, and moderated by continuing relations along non-instrumental lines. However, fathers inevitably had something to lose—either economic resources or unpaid labor services—by the early marriage of their sons.[5] One might expect, therefore, that sons of men who die early would be able to marry before sons of men who survive into old age. By law male ophans inherited at age twenty-one and were thus economically free to marry. On the other hand, if fathers either could not or would not exercise such control, no differential in marriage age should exist between these two groups of sons.

Over two centuries of the study 60 years was the approximate mean age of fathers at the time of marriage of their sons. For the three cohorts of sons born to marriages up to 1740, Table 10.1 shows a differential of 1.6, 1.6, and 2.0 years in the predicted direction between sons whose fathers died before age 60 and sons whose fathers survived that age. For sons born to marriages formed after 1740 and especially after 1780, the "paternal power" effect is greatly diminished. While one and one-half to two years may appear to be a small difference, this gap is wider than that between the marriage ages of first and

Table 10.1. **Differential in Marriage Age of Sons by Age at Death of Fathers**

| Period of Fathers' Marriage Cohort | Age at marriage of sons by age at death of fathers: | | Difference |
	Under 60	60 and over	
1641–1700	26.8 (64)	28.4 (142)	+1.6
1701–1720	24.3 (30)	25.9 (130)	+1.6
1721–1740	24.7 (38)	26.7 (104)	+2.0
1741–1760	26.1 (43)	26.5 (145)	+0.4
1761–1780	25.7 (42)	26.8 (143)	+1.1
1781–1800	26.0 (71)	25.8 (150)	−0.2
1801–1820	25.7 (93)	26.5 (190)	+0.8
1821–1840	26.0 (42)	25.9 (126)	−0.1
1641–1780	25.73(217)	26.89(664)	+1.16
1781–1840	25.86(206)	26.11(466)	+0.25

Note: Sample size of sons whose marriage ages are known in parentheses.

younger sons or between sons of wealthy and less wealthy parents (Smith, 1973). Nor should an extreme differential be expected. Fathers had a cultural obligation to see their children married although it was not in their short-run self-interest. The most meaningful interpretation of the magnitude of the differential depends on comparison with results obtained from reconstitution studies of English population samples.

Since the meaning of this differential is inferential, this index cannot by itself confirm the argument that parents significantly controlled the marriage of their sons. An additional aspect of the relative centrality of the family of orientation in a society is a concern for the preservation of the line at the expense of a coexistent desire to provide for all children in the family. Inasmuch as the number and sex composition of surviving children are not completely certain and economic circumstances are not perfectly forecast, this tension is essentially insoluble for individual families (Goode, 1970b:125–126). By favoring only one son, families could help to maintain the social continuity of the family line. Although strict primogeniture did not obtain in Massachusetts, the eldest son was granted a double share in intestacy cases before the egalitarian modification of the law in 1789. Fathers, however, were not legally required to favor the eldest son. They had a free choice between an emphasis on lineage or giving each child an equal start in life. If common, this limited form of primogeniture should have an influence on the social origins of the spouses of first and younger sons. Having more resources eldest sons should be able, on the average, to marry daughters of wealthier men. In seventeenth century marriage contracts the wife's parents provided half as much as the husband's for launching the couple into marriage (Morgan, 1966:82). In order to test the influence of birth order on marriage chances, Table 10.2 compares the quintile wealth status of fathers and fathers-in-law who were living in Hingham at the earlier date to men who were taxed by the town at the later date. While these nonmigratory requirements limit and perhaps bias the sample, the differences are quite dramatic. First sons taxed on the 1680, 1779, and 1810 property lists were roughly twice as likely as younger sons to have a father-in-law who was in a higher wealth quintile than their own father. They were similarly only half as likely as younger sons to have a father-in-law who was poorer than their own father. Birth order was thus an important determinant of the economic status of the future spouse and influential in determining the life chances of men during the colonial period.[6]

A radical change is apparent for men on the town tax lists of 1830 and 1860. Birth order in the nineteenth century exerted no significant effect on the relationship between the relative wealth of father and father-in-law. Instead of a gradual diminution in paternal power, as was apparent in the effect of father's survival on the marriage age of sons, a decisive break is apparent.[7] While the measure in Table 10.1 involves the operation of paternal power on the individual level, primogeniture reflected in Table 10.2 is more a social constraint on the "freeness" of marriage choice. Apparently it was easier for all fathers to discriminate automatically against younger sons than it was for individual fathers, after the middle of the eighteenth century, to postpone the age at marriage of their own sons. The change evident in both indicators relating to the marriage process of sons is consistent with the larger hypothesis of a shift away from the dominance of the family of orientation in the family system.

The distinction between individual and social aspects of parental control is also apparent for daughters as well as sons. Traditionally in western society women have been more subject than men to parental control, particularly in the area of sexual behavior. Although penalties for premarital fornication were assessed equally against both parties, colonial New England did not escape this patriarchal bias. As a symbolic example geographically-mixed marriages usually occurred in the hometown of the bride, suggesting that the husband had to receive his wife from her father. Post-marital residence in these cases, however, was more often in the husband's town. Although the Puritan conception of marriage as a free act allowed women veto power over the parental choice of the husband, marriages in the upper social strata were arranged through extensive negotiations by the parents (Morgan, 1966:79–86). In short the existing evidence points to a pattern intermediate between total control of young women by their parents and substantive premarital autonomy for women. The historical question, once again, is not either-or but how much? Were women, in fact, "married off," and was there any change over time in the incidence of this practice? Direct evidence does not exist to chart a trend, but a hypothetical pattern may be suggested. If parents did decide when their daughters could and should marry, one might expect them to proceed on the basis of the eldest first and

Table 10.2. **Relationship of Wealth Status of Fathers and Fathers-in-law of First and Younger Sons**

Tax list date for:		Percentage of men whose fathers-in-law were in:						
		Same quintile as father		Higher quintile than father		Lower quintile than father		
Fathers and fathers-in-law	Sons	1st	younger	1st	younger	1st	younger	N
		%	%	%	%	%	%	
1647—1680		25	29	58	29	17	43	26
1749—1779		30	33	44	26	25	41	94
1779—1810		26	30	55	27	18	43	117
1810—1830		36	27	30	36	34	37	139
1830—1860		34	35	34	30	32	34	138

so on. Passing over a daughter to allow a younger sister to marry first might advertise some deficiency in the elder and consequently make it more difficult for the parents to find a suitable husband for her. If, on the other hand, women decided on the basis of personal considerations when (and perhaps who) they should marry, more irregularity in the sequence of sisters' marriages should be expected.

Table 10.3 demonstrates a marked increase in the proportions of daughters who fail to marry in order of sibling position after the middle of the eighteenth century. Because of the age difference among sisters most will marry in order of birth. Since women may remain single for reasons independent of parental choice, *e.g.,* the unfavorable sex ratio in eastern Massachusetts in the second half of the eighteenth century, the measure which omits these cases (left column of Table 10.3) is a more precise indicator of the trend. However, the increasing tendency in the eighteenth and particularly the nineteenth century for women to remain permanently single is certainly consistent with an increasing absence of strong parental involvement in the marriage process of their children. More and more women in the late eighteenth and early nineteenth century were obviously not being "married off." Suggesting the obvious point that their marriages were controlled more directly through the power fathers had over economic resources, a similar index of sons marrying out of birth order shows no secular trend.

Just as primogeniture relates to the intergenerational transmission of economic resources, so too does the relationship of parental wealth to the marriage age of daughters. If wealth transmission by marriage were important in the society, then parents obviously would have greater direct control over their daughters than if women were expected to provide no resources to their future husbands. If daughters brought economic resources to the marriage, then one would naturally be sought after by other families as being the

Table 10.3. Percentage of Daughters Not Marrying in Birth Order in Relationship to Those at Risk

Periods when daughters are marriageable	Spinsters excluded		Spinsters included	
	%	N	%	N
1641–1650 to 1691–1710	8.1	86	11.2	89
1701–1720 to 1731–1750	11.6	138	18.4	147
1741–1760 to 1771–1790	18.2	176	25.1	191
1781–1800 to 1811–1830	14.9	214	24.9	245
1821–1840 to 1861–1880	18.4	298	24.7	320

Note: In a family with n known adult sisters, there are n−1 possibilities for not marrying in birth order, *e.g.,* an only daughter cannot marry out of order, two daughters can marry out of order in only one way, etc. The interpretation of this measure is dependent, of course, on the assumption (true until the early nineteenth century) that the mean interval separating living sisters remains constant. With the fall in marital fertility during the nineteenth century, the gap between sisters increases. Since daughters who never marry obviously do not marry in order of birth, the left column excludes and right column includes these women.

more desirable marriage partners for their sons. The higher level of demand should mean that daughters of the wealthier would marry at a younger age than daughters of the less wealthy. If, on the contrary, property transfer and marriage were not intimately connected, then the class pattern of female marriage age would conform to male class career patterns. Market conditions rather than the behavior of individual actors can be assessed by examining the differential by wealth in the female age at first marriage. For daughters born to marriages formed in Hingham between 1721 and 1780 there is a perfect inverse relationship between paternal wealth and marriage age. Once more there is evidence for a significant role of the family of orientation in structuring marriage patterns. This wealth pattern is dramatically reversed for daughters born to marriages between 1781 and 1840. The stability in the mean marriage age (bottom row of Table 10.4) masks the divergent class trends. Daughters of the wealthy married later in the nineteenth century, while daughters of the less wealthy married at a younger age than before.[8] The slight positive relationship between wealth and male marriage age becomes much stronger during the nineteenth century as well. Nothing could be more suggestive of the severing of direct property considerations from marriage.

During the nineteenth century, then, daughters were not property exchanged between families. Nineteenth century marriage, in contrast to the preceding two centuries, was between individuals rather than families. Parents, of course, continue to play an important role in structuring the premarital environment of their children (Sussman, 1953). Their role today is presumably more indirect and their influence is more psychological than instrumental. What may be conceded in principle may be denied in practice. The extent of parental resources and the age of the children are key determinants of the efficacy of parental power. One could argue that the historical shift has been not the disappearance of parental power but its limitation to the earlier phases of the life cycle of the child. On the symbolic-ideological level the shift, albeit incomplete, toward the recognition of the child's independence from his family of orientation is apparent in child-naming patterns.[9]

The decline of parental involvement in marriage formation is also suggested by the decrease in the proportion of marriages involving couples who were both residents of the town. One may presume that parents were more knowledgeable about, and hence more influential in, marriages to children of other families in the town. Between 59.6 per cent

Table 10.4. **Age at Marriage of Daughters by Wealth Quintile of Fathers**

| Wealth quintile class of father | Daughters born to marriages of | | | | Change in mean age |
| | 1721–1780 | | 1781–1840 | | |
	Age	N	Age	N	
Richest 20 per cent	23.3	99	24.5	114	+1.31
Upper-middle 20 per cent	23.5	98	24.4	179	+0.96
Middle 20 per cent	23.6	110	22.1	172	−1.47
Lower-middle 20 per cent	24.5	92	23.1	159	−1.37
Poorest 20 per cent	24.5	57	22.9	135	−1.63
Fathers not present on extant tax list	22.7	37	23.0	96	+0.30
Totals	23.7	493	23.3	855	−0.37

and 71.8 per cent of all marriages in decades between 1701–1710 and 1791–1800 involved two residents of Hingham; by 1850–1853, only 48.2 per cent of all marriages, by 1900–1902 only 32.0 per cent and finally by 1950–1954, a mere 25.8 per cent were both residents of the town. Improved transportation and communication in the nineteenth and twentieth centuries, of course, modify the magnitude of this trend. Once again, the shift is in the predicted direction and it occurs at the time—the first half of the nineteenth century—consistent with changes in the other indices.

Conclusions

At least in the area of parental control over marriage, significant, documentable historical change has occurred in American family behavior. These are difficulties, of course, in extending the findings of a local study to the entire American population. The trend in the family parameter which has been best-documented on the national level, fertility, is consistent with the more detailed evidence on the families of Hingham. From the early nineteenth century onward American marital fertility has been declining. With a level of fertility lower than the national average in 1800, New England was the leader in the American fertility transition (Grabill *et al.*, 1958:14–16; Yasuba, 1962: 50–69). What the sequence of change in the Hingham indicators suggests is an erosion and collapse of traditional family patterns in the middle and late eighteenth century *before* the sharp decline in marital fertility began. In the seventeenth and early eighteenth century there existed a stable, parental-run marriage system, in the nineteenth century a stable, participant-run system. Separating these two eras of stability was a period of change and crisis, manifested most notably in the American Revolution itself—a political upheaval not unconnected to the family (Burrows and Wallace, 1972).[10]

Articles which begin with a capsule or caricature of a theoretical perspective and then proceed to a narrow body of empirical evidence typically conclude that the theory fails to explain the data adequately. Only criticism and revisionism represent *real* scholarly contributions. Only covertly does this study follow that format. Substantively, the empirical measures presented above for the population of Hingham, Massachusetts, confirm, if more precisely define and elaborate, the conclusions and interpretations of Smelser, Goode, Reiss, and Stone. It is perhaps revisionist in the sense that the current state of the field is confused because of the great gap separating a bold and sweeping theory of change and the evidence which would support it. A systematic history of the American family can be reconstructed if sociological theory, long-run series of quantitative data, and historical imagination in devising subtle measures of change are combined. The vulgar notion of a drastic shift from "extended" to "nuclear" families had to be exposed and rejected in order to generate historical research. The equally simple-minded opposite extreme of the historical continuity of the conjugal family is just as fallacious both on historical as well as the better-known sociological grounds. American *households* may always have been overwhelmingly nuclear in structure, but household composition is a measure of family structure—not the structure of the family itself. Historians love complexity—the tension between change and continuity over time. Unravelling this complexity is the particularly challenging task for scholars working in the history of the family.

Notes

1. While it is undoubtedly true, for example, that more members of the Virginia House of Burgesses in 1773 had fathers who served in that body than United States Congressmen of 1973 whose fathers were also congressmen, no quantitative evidence exists to determine the magnitude of these changes. Perhaps more importantly, it is not certain how family status "worked" to get men into office in the colonial period—whether through deference to the family name or through arrangement by the class of elite families. Nor has the relative importance of wealth and family status in political recruitment been determined. Determination of the timing of the shift away from family domination of office would be of considerable historical importance. Trends in this area are not necessarily linear. Harvard students, for example, were ranked by their ability in the seventeenth century, but their family status counted in the eighteenth (Shipton, 1954). The fathers of 16 per cent of the U.S. Senators of 1820 had held political office, 8 per cent in 1860, 12 per cent in 1900 and 19 per cent in 1940 (Hoogenbloom, 1968:60). Although the numbers involved are very small to be sure, perhaps the final phase of the system in which office was a concomitant of social prestige and the emergence of politics as a specialized profession is reflected in this cycle. In the economic area nineteenth century entrepeneurial capitalism may be closer in terms of the linkage between family and property to medieval feudalism than to twentieth century corporate capitalism (Bell, 1961:39–45).

2. The relevance of household composition data to the nuclear-extended dichotomy pertains only to three-generation households. Although servants were an important addition to pre-industrial western households and lodgers to nineteenth century urban-industrial households, these nonkin additions were *in* but not *of* the family. Other kin also resided in households but their presence is probably chiefly due to demographic failure elsewhere—orphanhood, widowhood, and spinsterhood.

3. According to Smeiser (1966:117), for example, "In many traditional settings, marriage is closely regulated by elders; the tastes and sentiments of the couple to be married are relatively unimportant. . . . With the decay of extended kinship ties and the redefinition of parental authority, youth becomes emancipated with respect to choosing a spouse."

4. The necessary imprecision of Reiss' succinct summary reflects the dearth of hard historical evidence: "The seventeenth century saw the working out of a solution. Romantic love had spread to much of the populace (but almost exclusively among couples who were engaged. . . . The parents were still choosing mates. . . . By the eighteenth century the revolt had secured many adherents and was increasingly successful, so that by the end of the nineteenth century, in many parts of Europe and especially in America, young people were choosing their own mates and love was a key basis for marriage. The revolution had been won!" (Reiss, 1964:57–58).

5. John Winthrop, the leader of the great Puritan migration of 1630, was partially influenced to leave England by his declining economic status resulting from launching three of his sons with substantial gifts of land that cut his own holdings in half (Morgan, 1958:43).

6. This empirical conclusion contradicts the conventional interpretation of the social insignificance of primogeniture in colonial America (Bailyn, 1962:345; Keim, 1968:545–586). Earlier studies, however, have only shown that all sons generally got some property, not *how much* each one actually received. Wills lack a monetary value for the bequests making direct measurement impossible. In Virginia younger sons often received land in less-developed (and presumably land of less value) frontier areas while first sons got the home plantation. More generally historians who have analyzed inequality in colonial America have thought in terms of industrial society and have thus ignored sources of *intrafamilial* inequality. No published studies exist comparing the actual life experiences of first and younger sons in early America. In England, of course, the differential treatment accorded to first and younger sons was of considerable economic, social, and political importance (Thirsk, 1969).

7. The use of primogeniture may actually have increased in the early and mid-eighteenth century as the supply of land within settled areas declined. This trend has been documented for the town of Andover, Massachusetts (Greven, 1970:131–132), and on a broader cross-cultural basis the relationship between land scarcity and impartible inheritance has been suggested (Goldschmidt and Kunkel, 1971).

8. Although the data are unreliable because of an absence of information on the marital status of many daughters, the same shift occurred in the class incidence of permanent spinsterhood. In the

eighteenth century the daughters of the wealthier strata were most likely to marry; in the 1781–1840 period, daughters of the wealthier were most likely to remain spinsters.

9. Some 94.4 per cent of families formed before 1700 with three or more sons and 98.5 per cent with three or more daughters named a child for the parent of the same sex. For families formed between 1841 and 1880 with the same number of boys or girls (to control for declining fertility), the respective figures are 67.8 per cent and 53.2 per cent. The decline in parent-child name sharing and especially the more rapid decrease in mother-daughter name sharing reflects the symbolic fact of the ultimate separation of children, especially girls, from their family of birth. The persistence of kin-naming in the nineteenth and twentieth centuries simultaneously confirms the continuing importance of kinship in modern American society (Rossi, 1966; Smith, 1972b).

10. Trends in premarital pregnancy—very low mid-seventeenth and mid-nineteenth century levels, high mid- and late eighteenth century rates—support this periodization of family change (Smith and Hindus, 1971).

References

Abrams, Philip
  1972 "The sense of the past and the origins of sociology." Past and Present 55 (May): 18–32.
Adams, Bert N.
  1970 "Isolation, function, and beyond: American kinship in the 1960's." Journal of Marriage and the Family 32 (November):575–597.
Ariès, Phillipe
  1962 Centuries of Childhood. A Social History of Family Life. Tr. by Robert Baldwick. New York: Knopf.
Bailyn, Bernard
  1962 "Political experience and enlightenment ideas in eighteenth-century America." American Historical Review 67 (January):339–351.
Bell, Daniel
  1961 "The breakup of family capitalism: on changes of class in America." Pp. 39–45 in Daniel Bell, The End of Ideology. New York: Collier.
Berkner, Lutz K.
  1973 "Recent research on the history of the family in Western Europe." Journal of Marriage and the Family 35 (August).
Blau, Peter and Otis Dudley Duncan
  1967 The American Occupational Structure. New York: Wiley.
Burrows, Edwin G. and Michael Wallace
  1972 "The American Revolution: the ideology and practice of national liberation." Perspectives in American History 6:167–306.
Davis, Kingsley
  1949 Human Society. New York: Macmillan.
Demos, John
  1970 A Little Commonwealth: Family Life in Plymouth Colony. New York: Oxford.
Furet, Francois
  1971 "Quantitative history." Daedalus 100 (Winter):151–167.
Furstenberg, Frank F., Jr.
  1966 "Industrialization and the American family: a look backward." American Sociological Review 31 (June):326–337.
Goldschmidt, Walter and Evalyn Jacobson Kunkel
  1971 "The structure of the peasant family," American Anthropologist 73 (October):1058–1076.
Goode, William J.
  1968 "The theory and measurement of family change." Pp. 295–348 in Eleanor Bernert

Sheldon and Wilbert E. Moore (eds.), Indicators of Social Change. New York: Russell Sage Foundation.

1970a   World Revolution and Family Patterns. New York: Free Press Paperback.

1970b   "Family systems and social mobility." Pp. 120–136 in Reuben Hill and Rene Konig (eds.), Families in East and West. Paris: Mouton.

Grabill, Wilson H., Clyde V. Kiser, and Pascal K. Whelpton
1958   The Fertility of American Women. New York: Wiley.

Greven, Philip J., Jr.
1970   Four Generations: Population, Land, and Family in Colonial Andover, Massachusetts. Ithaca: Cornell.

Hajnal, J.
1965   "European marriage patterns in perspective." Pp. 101–143 in D. V. Glass and D. E. C. Eversley (eds.), Population in History. London: Edward Arnold.

Hoogenbloom, Ari
1968   "Industrialism and political leadership: a case study of the United States Senate." Pp. 49–78 in Frederic Cople Jaher (ed.), The Age of Industrialism in America. New York: Free Press.

Keim, C. Ray
1968   "Primogeniture and entail in colonial Virginia." William and Mary Quarterly 25 (October):545–586.

Lantz, Herman R., Margaret Britton, Raymond Schmitt, and Eloise C. Snyder
1968   "Pre-industrial patterns in the colonial family in America: a content analysis of colonial magazines." American Sociological Review 33 (June):413–426.

Laslett, Peter and Richard Wall (eds.)
1972   Household and Family in Past Time. Cambridge: Cambridge University Press.

Morgan, Edmund S.
1958   The Puritan Dilemma: The Story of John Winthrop. Boston: Little, Brown.
1966   The Puritan Family. New York: Harper Torchbooks.

Ohlin, G.
1961   "Mortality, marriage, and growth in preindustrial populations," Population Studies 14 (March):190–197.

Parsons, Talcott
1943   "The kinship system of the contemporary United States." American Anthropologist 45 (January–March):22–38.
1965   "The normal American family." Pp. 31–50 in Seymour Farber, Piero Mustacchi, and Roger H. Wilson (eds.), Man and Civilization: The Family's Search for Survival. New York: McGraw-Hill.

Reiss, Ira L.
1964   Premarital Sexual Standards in America. New York: Free Press Paperback.

Rossi, Alice S.
1965   "Naming children in middle class families." American Sociological Review 30 (August):499–513.

Shipton, Clifford K.
1954   "Ye mystery of ye ages solved, or, how placing worked at colonial Harvard and Yale." Harvard Alumni Bulletin 57 (December 11):258–263.

Smelser, Neil J.
1966   "The modernization of social relations." Pp. 110–122 in Myron Weiner (ed.), Modernization: The Dynamics of Growth. New York: Basic Books.

Smith, Daniel Scott
1972a   "The demographic history of colonial New England." Journal of Economic History 32 (March):165–183.
1972b   "Child-naming patterns and family structure change: Hingham, Massachusetts, 1640–1880." Unpublished paper presented at the Clark University conference on the family, social structure, and social change.
1973   "Population, family and society in Hingham, Massachusetts, 1635–1880." Unpublished Ph.D. dissertation, University of California.

Smith, Daniel Scott and Michael S. Hindus
    1971   "Premarital pregnancy in America, 1640–1966: an overview and interpretation." Unpublished paper presented at the annual meeting of the American Historical Association.

Stone, Lawrence
    1964   "Marriage among the English nobility." Pp. 153–183 in Rose Laub Coser (ed.), The Family: Its Structure and Functions. New York: St. Martin's Press.

Sussman, M. B.
    1953   "Parental participation in mate selection and its effects upon family continuity." Social Forces 32 (October):76–81.

Thirsk, Joan
    1969   "Younger sons in the seventeenth century." History 54 (October):358–377.

Uhlenberg, Peter R.
    1969   "A study of cohort life cycles: cohorts of native born Massachusetts women, 1830–1920." Population Studies 23 (November):407–420.

Wrigley, E. A.
    1966   "Family reconstitution." Pp. 96–159 in E. A. Wrigley (ed.), An Introduction to English Historical Demography. New York: Basic Books.
    1969   Population and History. New York: McGraw-Hill.

Yasuba, Yasukichi
    1962   Birth Rates of the White Population of the United States, 1800–1860. Baltimore: Johns Hopkins.

First Transitions, 1780 to 1870

Introduction

Part III, "First Transitions," traversing the nearly one hundred years from the late eighteenth through the first two-thirds of the nineteenth century, constitutes—along with Part IV—what might well be viewed as the heart of this volume and of its own conceptualization of the transformations at the center of the historical experiences of growing up. With the seven essays that make up this section, we cover a lengthy period and also encounter a widening sphere of diverging patterns, whether we choose to view them in terms of the shifts in historical time, geographic location, gender, social class, race, or ethnicity, in whatever combination, as these emerging factors were felt on the shaping and the reshaping of the principal paths of growing up. Indeed, in these experiences and in this period, we confront fundamentally the "adolescence," early as it might be deemed, of growing up in America.

From the late eighteenth century, major transformations in social relations and social forms—stimulated in large measure by the impacts of an emerging and maturing market and commercial capitalist economy, and the responses of differently situated men and women to it—reshaped American society. This was an epochal process, as broad and subtle in its implications and consequences as it was uneven and irregular in its timing and impacts. Part and parcel of the making of "modern society," it intertwined changes in social thought and theory, family forms and relations, community, modes of production and livelihoods, formation of middle and working classes, and social policy and social institutions. Individually and collectively, they all contributed to the redefining and increasingly differentiated processes of growing up. In that process, the norms—and sometimes the facts, too—of child rearing and childhood, adolescence (in terms increasingly familiar to us today), and youth were reformed. The seeds of modern social relations, policies, and expectations all lay here. For example, the maternal role in family and child rearing, the notions of family sanctity, transformed relations of youthful dependency, strategic use of such institutions as schools, increased division of labor by gender all develop in new, distinctive ways. There should be no doubt of the significance of this period in the history of growing up.

The seven essays, presented in approximately chronological order, encapsulate much of this key experience. They take us from rural New England in the early throes of social change to the lives of Afro-American slaves, the streets of the nation's major metropolis, early commercial and industrial cities, and the worlds of men and women of the middle and the working classes. Their comparison and contrast is virtually demanded by the reader who seeks to make sense of the range of transformations.

Kett and Cott locate the beginnings of change. Kett considers the irregularity and inconsistency of patterns of growing up especially with respect to young men and their relations to family, school, and work in rural New England. In an inquiry that compares nicely with Greven's essay in Part II, Cott focuses on young women and their heightened conflicts in modes and means of maturity through the lens of the evangelical revival of the Second Great Awakening. Here we capture the stirrings of change in common contexts and are able to contrast the challenges to and responses of the sexes.

Thomas Webber takes us into the revealingly contrasting—but not in every respect—world of the plantation slave quarter. In this comparative perspective, the struggles and strategies of the bound population emerge with an exceptional importance and poignancy. Issues of choice and opportunity confront those of restriction. From the Afro-American world—and its similarities but key differences—we journey with Carroll Smith-Rosenberg into the separate spheres of middle-class girls and women and ponder the evolution of gender differences and their implications for the reshaping of growing up. The comparative demand here is a multiple one: with earlier patterns of female development, with that emerging among men of the same class (Mary Ryan's equally ethnographic inquiry pairs nicely with Smith-Rosenberg's), and, finally, with the rich reconstruction of the "street life" courses of the poor women and children of New York City. Katz and Davey, from a Canadian urban and early industrial perspective, offer an overall interpretation of the transformations of growing up in that setting as well as highlight the opportunities that quantitative research may bring to these issues.

The interplay throughout this section is in terms of class formation, economic development, lives (and sources too) public and private. Stansell, in particular, suggests the special implications that class-cultural differences represented in terms of the meanings and implications that middle-class and laboring-class experiences had for each other just as they diverged even more from each other. In turn, the key questions reflect these issues: roles of family and community, private and public, intersections of social thought and social experience, shifting patterns of policy and institutions and their framing of growing up's parameters, and the nature of sex, class, ethnicity, and location in shaping increasingly familiar paths, conflicts, patterns of growing up—and new relations of dependency for the young and consequent "problems" for family, community, and society writ large.

11. Growing Up in Rural New England, 1800–1840

A concern with the adolescent has been a distinctive feature of twentieth-century social thought. Psychologists and others have written books on the teen years as frequently as nineteenth-century theologians turned out concordances of the Bible. Whole journals have been devoted to the psychological and social significance of adolescence. Professional writers on youth have enjoyed successful careers, while youth culture has become so pervasive that it is often dominant over adult culture. All of this presupposes the existence of typical adolescents, so that one can generalize from the experience of a sample group to that of untested groups. We assume that street-corner society in Brooklyn is like street-corner society in Cicero, that the Grosse Point teenager shares common experiences with the Mamaroneck teenager. Few early adolescents work; the great majority attend school of a special type, the high school. There they are segregated by age with peers, exposed to similar subjects, and expected to engage in carefully regulated and age-graded pursuits, whether cheerleading or sports, proms or debating.

Nothing remotely resembling this pattern existed in early nineteenth-century America. The experience of growing up differed, often profoundly, from one youth to the next. There was no set age for leaving school, leaving home, or starting to work. Variations among regions were at least as deep-seated as those among classes or individuals. The dominance of regional variation arose from two sources: the differing character of work demands and opportunities in settled and in frontier areas, and the immense discrepancy among the kinds of schooling available in the Northeast, the South, and the West. These variations often had an intensely personal application. The boy who started to grow up in New England might find himself at the age of ten in Ohio and at fifteen in Michigan. His attachment to his family would be the only constant factor as he was ruthlessly ushered from one setting to the next.

The pattern of random experience, however, could extend just as readily to the family itself. Families were constantly being disrupted by the death of one or both parents, not simply because of higher mortality from disease, but also because of the length of time which usually elapsed between the birth of the first and the last child. A man who fathered his first child at 25 might not father his last until he was 40 or even 45. It was a statistical probability that the father would be dead before the youngest child reached maturity. The frequency of being orphaned in the early nineteenth century had a personal as well as a demographic significance, for it meant that the plans laid by youth were subject to drastic shattering by chance.

All of these factors make it difficult to reconstruct the experience of growing up in the

Joseph F. Kett, "Growing Up in Rural New England, 1800–1840," reprinted from *Anonymous Americans*, ed. Tamara K. Hareven (Englewood Cliffs, N.J.: Prentice Hall, (1971): 1–16. Copyright © 1971. Reprinted by permission of Prentice-Hall, Inc., Englewood Cliffs, New Jersey.

early nineteenth century. Even if we confine our attention to New England between 1800 and 1840 and exclude from consideration sons of the very rich and the very poor, we only assuage the problem. The most typical experience of any child in the early nineteenth century was coming into contact with death before he reached the age of five. Although writers in the period did not produce a significant body of literature on the teen years, they did often talk of childhood and youth, indicating that they were conscious of some model experiences, and thereby tempting the historian to explore the nature of growing up.

Feminine Control in the Early Years

Very early in the nineteenth century a consensus emerged in published literature to the effect that the first five or six years of childhood were primarily the mother's responsibility. These were the years of "infancy," not in its modern connotation of reference to suckling babes, but used more broadly to indicate the years of maternal control of the child. The same literature which affirmed the preeminent role of the mother insisted on two corollaries: the need to pay attention to little children, and the superiority of moral suasion over corporal punishment in discipline.[1]

In all likelihood, the simple conditions of farm life did more to reinforce than to frustrate the accomplishment of the prescribed regimen. Although mothers were busy managing large families and cooking meals for husbands and field hands, they could expect and command assistance from older daughters for these tasks. During the winter, moreover, the workload for all parties eased and more time could be found for children. In the summer, especially in the busy hours before noon (the time of the principal meal), children under eight were usually sent to district schools, which functioned virtually as nurseries in the planting, haying, and harvesting seasons. Summer schools, which usually served three- to eight-year-olds, were taught by women, and never acquired the unsavory reputation for disorder which marked the winter schools. The absence of older boys in summer sessions meant that discipline for younger children could be mild, an extension of approved family discipline.

District School and Discipline

The first of many jarring discontinuities involved in the experience of growing up usually came not in "infancy" but between the ages of six or eight to twelve, and was an outgrowth of new experiences in school, work, and, often, religion. After the age of eight or nine, boys customarily attended only winter schools, being kept at home to work on the farm in summer. The transition to winter school was, in a fundamental way, abrupt.

District schools in the winter bore little resemblance in either composition or discipline to summer sessions. Prior to the 1840's, the former were usually taught by men of all ages and temperaments. Some were college students, some academy students, and others were local farmers who had advanced to the rule of three, if little beyond. Differences among the pupils were even greater. Most winter schools included "large boys" of

16 and 17, and many had young men of 18 or 20. The majority of pupils, however, were between 8 and 15. Sometimes efforts were made to seat the smaller children separately, but they would still be in the same room with older boys, since no effective grading system existed outside of large cities before 1840.[2]

Available evidence suggests that disorderly conditions were the norm in winter schools. Even progressive educators and reformers attached primary importance to the establishment of order. School was occasionally broken up by the "carrying out" of the schoolmaster. Although such complete dismantling was rare, chaos, or a measure of order purchased by brutal discipline, was common. Discipline itself consisted in a combination of corporal punishment and humiliation, especially the latter. There was nothing in theory to exempt younger boys from this regimen, but in practice schoolmasters had to focus on the teenagers who, by all accounts, made the most trouble. This preoccupation gave a random quality to the kind of discipline experienced by the younger boys. But such discipline could be as unsettling as systematic chastisement. Autobiographers frequently commented on the shame they felt when they were first singled out for correction, for severe discipline occasionally administered was likely to produce a more profound sense of shame and guilt than the daily drubbing to which the older boys became inured.[3]

Early Piety

If the years of seven and eight were significant as the time when most boys started to attend winter schools, these years had importance in other respects as well. At about the age of seven a boy was expected to begin work on the farm. How much he would do was dependent on a host of factors including his size, the number and age of his male siblings, the health of his father, and the size of the farm. Whatever the variables, however, direction in his daily routine now came both at school and work from older boys or men.

The third experience which occurred with some regularity between the ages of eight and twelve was the commencement of religious anxiety. Religious instruction began earlier, just after infancy, but most autobiographers traced the start of personal religion to the period between eight and twelve. At times, especially among girls, religious conversion took place this early, but the expectation, at least up to the 1840's, was that conversion would come later. At eight or nine children were expected to evince no more than "early piety" and to become subjects of "hopeful conversion."[4] Early piety usually involved lying awake most of the night in anxiety about salvation, a morbid fear of death, and a tendency to meet together with peers, sometimes in district schools, in prayer meetings. This is the syndrome which emerges in autobiographies of evangelicals, and considerable evidence points to its spread among those who never went on to become ministers.[5] Some of it was undoubtedly due to the intense desire of most boys between eight and twelve for peer group acceptance. Contemporary skeptics put forward a version of this argument, attributing early piety to mere "sympathetic enthusiasm," but there was also an aspect of solitary introspection to it not explicable in terms of any current developmental model.

Although peer group pressure is not an altogether satisfactory explanation for the prevalence of morbid piety among children in early nineteenth-century New England, other leads are available. The kind of regimen of guilt and shame to which most schoolchildren were exposed could produce feelings of inadequacy which led to juvenile religious anxiety. Early nineteenth-century New England Calvinism, moreover, took a paradoxical approach to childhood. Children were told that they were damned unless converted, that they had to repent, but that they could not do so without divine aid. Finally, they were told that such assistance was not likely to come before the age of 17 or 18.[6] The approved practice in much of New England before 1840 was to usher children into religious anxiety but not to let them out. To take an apt if anachronistic analogy, children from 8 to 17 or 18 were put into a kind of moral pressure cooker.

Children of the Wealthy

There were, naturally, differences among classes in the experience of growing up. Children of moderately wealthy or well-educated parents were less likely to be exposed to the district school's winter session. Instead, they were sent to private schools or academies where classes were smaller, the curriculum much more difficult, and discipline more regular. The regimen of moderately wealthy children was not softer but more consistent, for all academies stressed punctuality, and, at least within a given term, regular attendance. After 1840 the school reform movement had the effect of bringing practices in public schools more in line with those of private schools, but the gap in the previous period between the discipline of boys who, for whatever reason, never went beyond district schooling, and those who were exposed to private schools and academies was substantial. In a general way, this represented a class difference.[7]

The years from eight to twelve comprised a unit in the lives of most boys, marked primarily by the commencement of work and winter schooling and often by the start of religious anxiety. Neither idleness nor leaving home was an ingredient of this unit. An artisan's son was likely to work in the shop, close to his father or an older brother. A farmer's boy would follow the plough and perform odd jobs around home. Both would be sent to district schools in the winter. There were exceptions, coming, oddly enough, at opposite ends of the social ladder. Children of poor people were often sent away to work, because they could not easily be incorporated into the family routine. When the father did not own his own shop or farm, it was difficult for him to find a suitable place for his son close to home, even though such a father would need all the money a son could earn. Similarly, children of ministers or of wealthy parents were often sent away to school at extremely early ages. Wealthy mill owners and manufacturers, who were not, as a rule, great believers in prolonged schooling, often put their sons into the family factory at eight or nine, making them child laborers. Length of dependency did not correlate neatly with rising social class. In fact, there seems to have been an inverse correlation. Children of wealthy parents were thrust out into the world at an earlier age than sons of middle-class farmers. Thus, one encounters 16-year-old sons of merchants traveling to St. Petersburg as supercargo and being taken in as partners of the firm at 19.[8] In the course of the nineteenth century a reaction to this did take place, and by 1900 the sons of the rich usually enjoyed a more protected and sheltered upbringing than did the sons of the middle classes. But this reaction had little effect before 1840.

Dependency and Discontinuities

It is difficult to say exactly when the period of total dependency ended, simply because youthful experiences in the early republic were not determined in any precise way by numerical age. Still, sometime after the age of 12 and before the age of 15 or 16, middle-class boys passed into a new stage of semidependency. Sons of artisans and small manufacturers were likely to be apprenticed, sometimes to their fathers, sometimes to relatives, sometimes outside the family altogether. Those who were not apprentices in theory were usually apprentices in fact, having entered machine shops or mills to learn the routine. The pattern does not seem to have involved continual employment at the same position until 21, but rather a moving from job to job or apprenticeship to apprenticeship. Thus, while tradition sanctioned a lengthy apprenticeship to occupy the remaining years of minority, social conditions facilitated short-term apprenticeships with frequent removals.[9]

Sons of farmers experienced a different pattern. They were likely after the age of 12 or 14 to be withdrawn from winter schooling and encouraged to seek employment or possibly advanced schooling away from home during the winter. Late spring, summer, and early fall would find them back on the farm again, thus completing the cycle of homeleaving and homecoming. Although there was an element of regularity in the summer employment of farm boys, their winter occupations had little consistency. Some clerked in country stores, others went to academies, others found employment in such winter work as lumbering. Although many stopped attending winter school between 12 and 14, there was nothing to stop them from resuming attendance at 16 or 17.[10]

Whether one is discussing sons of artisans or small manufacturers or sons of farmers, there were certain discontinuities which beset the life experiences of teenagers in early nineteenth-century New England regardless of occupation or parentage. The first of these was between school and work. In the twentieth century work normally follows a period of schooling, but in the early nineteenth century the relationship was less definite. Many apprentices had the right to a month or two of annual schooling stipulated in their contracts with masters, and farm boys often managed to snatch a few months of schooling in the winter. Two aspects of the school experience of teenagers might be noted. First, prior to the middle of the century, there seems to have been little understanding that teenagers might need a type of discipline different from that given to younger children. If there was any difference of emphasis in pedagogical thought, it was that older boys were more unruly and hence greater effort had to be made to break their wills. Second, in virtually all types of school (including colleges), few efforts were made before 1840 to segregate pupils by age. Pupils of 15 or 16, both in academies and common schools, were likely to be grouped with much younger children in classes and exposed to a more severe version of the same type of discipline experienced by the eight- or nine-year-olds. Quite obviously, the adult roles which teenagers often played in one part of the year were followed by demands for childish submission during the rest of the year.

The major educational innovation of the late eighteenth and early nineteenth century, the New England academy, dramatically accentuated these tendencies. Although the academy offered a valuable opportunity for intermediate education between the district school and the college, academy students were subject to many of the same anomalies as district school pupils. One encountered in academies, as in winter district schools, students of eight or nine to 20 or 25 years of age, with the concentration falling in the 10- to

20-year-old category.[11] Teenagers were constantly matched first against children and then against mature men.[12] We sometimes indulge in a stereotype of nineteenth-century boyhood which postulates that boys were then exposed much more than now to the company of adults. The stereotype has an element of truth, but older men were also periodically classified with children. Like the experience of work, the academy experience presented boys with alternating demands, now for childish submission, now for adult responsibility.

The fact that many boys had already worked for a number of years before attending academies accentuated the anomaly. This accounted for the unusual age distribution of academy students; for some attendance at the academy was the first departure from home, for others it represented a respite from job demands. Moreover, for nearly everyone, attendance at academies did not exclude the performance of useful work during part of the year. Attendance usually fell off in the winter as students went out to teach or labor, and again in the summer, when any strong male, boy or adult, could command high wages on the farm. The academy was a form of seasonal education to complement the seasoned labor pattern of an economically active but preindustrial society. Academy pupils thus experienced the same odd shifting from dependent to independent to dependent status which characterized the lives of boys who never attended school beyond the age of 12.

The critical constituent of the teen years was, therefore, an endless shifting of situations—home to work, work to school—in a society in which discipline was determined not so much by numerical age as by situation. Flogging was much less common in academies and colleges than in common schools, yet pupils in the latter were often older than students in either of the former. Similar factors dominated the experience of work. Because of rapid economic change in New England in the early nineteenth century, boys often had to give up one type of employment to learn a new trade; one could be nearly self-sufficient at 14 and an apprentice at 16. This was especially true of farm boys, who often did not enter apprenticeships until their late teens after years of semi-independent manual labor in winters, but it was also at least partly true of sons of artisans. Although the institution of apprenticeship no longer existed in its Elizabethan form, it still involved a master-dependent relationship, with the latter receiving low wages for the duration. The pattern of discontinuity was not only horizontal, between work and school, but vertical, between types of work and types of schooling.[13]

A second tension in the lives of teenagers was between their desire for ultimate independence and the fact of their semidependence. Because of the new economic opportunities created by the beginnings of industrialization and by territorial expansion, many teenagers were largely self-supporting. Even those who sought higher education in the academies could probably earn enough in the winter and summer months to pay the meager tuition demands. There were even instances of boys becoming factory overseers at 16 or 17. But traditional assumptions about maturity persisted, assumptions which thus ran counter to the new economic forces. Although the latter made possible an earlier independence than ever before, the former still provided that a boy became a man at the age of 21. Before that age he was conceived of as a piece of property under obligation to work for his father. Even where there were more sons than could possibly be settled on family land, as was often the case in New England, fathers could usually use their sons' labor in the late spring, summer, and early fall. There was no easy or consistent resolution of this problem. A few boys simply left home at 15 or 16, never to return; a few stayed on the farm until 25 or later. For most, however, the critical period came between 17 and 21. By the age of 17, many youths had acquired enough capital to launch themselves in the world, and saw that there was no future for them on the farm. If a father resisted his son's demands for independence, the likeliest solution was for the son to make a cash payment to the father in lieu of his services, thus in effect ending the contractual relationship.[14]

A final, and central, ingredient of the teen years in the early nineteenth century was religious crisis, which was often followed by conversion. Evangelical clergymen involved in the Second Great Awakening in the early 1800's noted time and again the frequency of religious conversion among "youth" or the "young people." There had been some fore-shadowing of this in the Great Awakening of the eighteenth century, although young converts at that time were more likely to be in their late 20's than in their teens. In the early nineteenth century, by contrast, a pattern of teenage conversion began to emerge. It is impossible to compute the average or median age of conversion, and it would be pointless, since some individuals experienced a religious crisis in their teens without going through conversion, and others experienced conversion without a religious crisis. A huge number of published autobiographical conversion narratives of the nineteenth century, however, point to the predominance of conversions between the ages of 15 and 21.[15]

Teenage Conversions

Conversion narratives emphasized three themes. Two were traditional—the idleness and sinfulness of the convert's past life and the appeal of conversion as a decisive break with the past. But a third theme was relatively novel in the early nineteenth century: the importance of a sudden, quick transformation. Although seventeenth-century Puritans had emphasized a gradual conversion experience, the distinctive feature of early nineteenth-century thought, encapsulated in the doctrine of regeneration or rebirth, was that one could experience the turning point in an instant.[16]

Given this rhetoric of the Second Awakening, it is possible to locate at least one factor in the experience of middle-class New England boys which would dispose them to evangelical conversion. Enough has been said to indicate that the need to make choices was, perhaps as never before, incumbent on every youth. The beginnings of industrialization, the spread of commercialization, increasing pressure on the available land, and proliferation of educational opportunities for teenagers gave the experience of maturation novel dimensions. But the religious dimension of choice was no less important. In seventeenth-century Massachusetts the principal sects had been Congregationalism and Anglicanism. Dissenters such as Baptists and Quakers could be isolated in places such as Rhode Island. From 1750 on, however, the number of dissenters increased, and arguments and even fistfights among dissenters and between dissenters and the orthodox became more common. By 1820 even small villages in New England were likely to have, besides the "standing order," a number of free-will Baptists, Methodists, and Universalists.[17]

The extravagant claims of each sect only further necessitated the importance of making a choice. In his autobiography, Joseph Smith, who had grown up in Vermont but moved to western New York state—the so-called burnt-over district which was to be the scene of extraordinary religious commotion in the years 1820–1845—drew a revealing portrait of small-town religious excitement:

> Indeed, the whole district of country seemed affected by it, and great multitudes united themselves to the different religious parties, which created no small stir among the people, some crying, "Lo, here!" and others, "Lo, there!" Some were contending for the Methodist faith, some for the Presbyterian, and some for the Baptist. . . . During this time of great excitement my mind was called up to serious reflection and great uneasiness. . . . In process of time my mind became somewhat partial to the Methodist sect and I felt some desire to be united with them, but so great were the confusion and strife among the different denominations that it was impossible for a person young as I was and so unacquainted with men and things, to come to any certain conclusion who was right and who was wrong. . . . In the midst of this war of words and tumult of opinions, I often said to myself, what is to be done? Who of all these parties are right; or are they all wrong together? If any one of them be right, which is it, and how shall I know it?[18]

Smith, only 15 at the time, resolved his crisis with the discovery of the Book of Mormon and the launching of a new religion. While his resolution was atypical, the kind of anxiety he expressed at confrontation with religious choice found expression elsewhere.

In one sense religious choice was part of the larger pattern of choice; in another sense it held forth to the convert the lure of finality. Although many lapsed after making a religious identification, in theory religious choice was absolute. Therein lay part of its appeal to the young, for it was the choice to end all choices in a society in which young people were subjected to an apparently endless sequence of role changes.

The Turbulence of Adolescence

In the twentieth century a variety of factors have conspired to make the teen years difficult. The evidence indicates that they were also turbulent in early nineteenth-century New England, but for different reasons. The significance of adolescence today lies in its following a protected and sanitized period of childhood and in the forced economic inactivity of teenagers. Neither of these conditions was present in the early nineteenth century. Although attitudes toward childhood were changing in the direction of sentimentality, social conditions scarcely permitted sealing off the cares of adulthood from the life of the child. One might illustrate this by taking so simple yet pervasive a concern as death. People generally did not die in hospitals in early nineteenth-century New England, but in homes, right in front of the family. Although intense religious anxiety often marked the teen years, religious concern, the so-called early piety, was expected to begin before the age of 12. In the experience of work, a farm boy of nine or ten toiled in the field alongside his older brother of 14. Many aspects of adolescent life were thus simply extensions of patterns launched in late childhood.

Although adolescence as we know it did not exist in 1820, boys did experience an intermediate period between childhood and adulthood. An opposing view is sometimes presented. The period of dependency, it is asserted, was very short in the early nineteenth century. Boys left home and became men at 15, if not earlier, and thus scarcely experienced a period of youth. It is true that the period of total dependency was brief, but the intermediate stage of semidependency was often lengthy. However, even the period of semidependency was getting shorter after 1750. Research on the seventeenth century has indicated that boys commonly stayed around the homestead until their middle 20's.[19] Between about 1750 and 1820, pressure on the land and availability of attractive alternatives to following the plough were operating to end the period of semidependency in the late teens. But the very fact that the period of semidependency was shortening made it even more turbulent. As long as young people were not expected to make important decisions until they reached 21, semidependency had more chronological than psychological content; it was long but not critical. One could have dependency without youth, without a time of erratic indecision. In this sense, youth hardly existed in the seventeenth century, even though the period of semidependency was long. It did exist by the early nineteenth century, largely because of the contraction of the outer limits of semidependency.[20]

What effect did the kind of experience described have on the attitudes of those who went through it? It would be ridiculous to suppose that it had any uniform effect; personalities differed as much in the nineteenth century as they do in the twentieth. But Americans born between 1800 and 1840, especially those born in New England, were more prone than any previous generation to assign importance to boyhood and youth. Two themes in their romanticization of boyhood did have a traceable connection to the actual experience of growing up: the idea that such a boyhood was free, and that it encouraged initiative or individualism.[21] It was free, not because parents or teachers were indulgent, but because the social institutions which came to bear on youth had a loose and indefinite character. An economically active but largely preindustrial society allowed boys, and adults, a footloose life. The cycle of the seasons rather than the time clock or an office manager regulated the routine of work. Home authority could be severe, when one was home, but a great deal of time was spent outside the home. Discontinuity of experience, frustrating in one respect, was liberating in another, since it meant that no single regimen had to be submitted to for long.

Finally, the experience of growing up in New England between 1800 and 1840 did encourage initiative. There were abundant opportunities but no fixed experiences which automatically led the young to success. One had to respond to and make the best of a complicated situation. What writers in the late nineteenth century had to say about the early initiative nurtured by a rural boyhood certainly had its fanciful elements. Whole segments of society—Negroes, women, paupers, and immigrants—were excluded from even the opportunity of making a choice, and the mere presence of choice did not ensure that those who could choose would make the right choices. Moreover, an ability to make choices was a precondition, even if not a guarantee, of success in life.

Notes

1. John and Virginia Demos, "Adolescence in Historical Perspective," *Journal of Marriage and the Family*, XXXI (November 1969), 632–633; Bernard Wishy, *The Child and the Republic: The Dawn of Modern American Child Nurture* (Philadelphia, 1968), Part I.

2. Warren Burton, *The District School as It Was* (Boston, 1833), 118–123; George Moore, Diaries, ms., 4 vols., Harvard College Library, I, *passim*.

3. John T. Trowbridge, *My Own Story with Recollections of Noted Persons* (Boston, 1903), 40–42; Heman Dyer, *Records of an Active Life* (New York, 1886), 9.

4. Elias Smith, *The Life, Conversion, Preachings, Travels and Sufferings of Elias Smith* (Boston, 1840); *Autobiography of Adin Ballou* (Lowell, Mass., 1890), 31; Raphael Pumpelly, *My Reminiscences* (2 vols., New York, 1918), I, 14–15.

5. Henry C. Wright. *Human Life: Illustrated in My Individual Experiences as a Child, a Youth, and a Man* (Boston, 1849), 96; Catherine E. Beecher, *Religious Training of Children in the School, the Family, and the Church* (New York, 1864), 133–136; Joseph Packard, *Recollections of a Long Life*, ed. Thomas J. Packard (Washington, D.C., 1902), 48.

6. Packard, *ibid.*, 48.

7. *Reminiscences of Neal Dow: Recollections of Eighty Years* (Portland, Me., 1898), Chap. 2; Octavius B. Frothingham, *Recollections and Impressions, 1822–1890* (Boston, 1891), 20.

8. J. D. Van Slyck, *New England Manufacturers and Manufacturing* (2 vols., Boston, 1879), II, 693, 700.

9. *Ibid.*, I, 371–372, II, 641–642; Thomas V. Sullivan, *Scarcity of Seamen* (Boston, 1854), 5–6.

10. Richard C. Stone, *Life-Incidents of Home, School and Church* (St. Louis, 1874); *Memoir of the Life and Religious Experience of Ray Potter* (Providence, 1829), 22–23.

11. *Catalogue of the Officers and Students of Phillips Exeter Academy, 1783–1883* (Boston, 1883). The same pattern prevailed at other academies.

12. Hiram Orcutt, *Reminiscences of School Life: An Autobiography* (Cambridge, Mass., 1898), 25–26.

13. Van Slyck, *New England Manufacturers*, II, 519, 554–557, 606–608, 617.

14. For examples of buying time, see Van Slyck, *New England Manufacturers*, I, 264–266; Jason Whitman, *A Memoir of the Rev. Bernard Whitman* (Boston, 1837), 34. The assertion that the critical period came between 17 and 21 is based partly on this author's strong impression gained from autobiography and partly on two surveys I have made. The first is from Van Slyck, *New England Manufacturers*. I have charted the early careers of 200 of the 350 manufacturers listed. All were born between 1785 and 1840, with the great majority between 1800 and 1830. All were raised in New England. Sixty-seven of the 200 were sons of farmers and another 19 were sons of farmers who had some other identifiable occupation. It should be added that the sample is biased toward short dependency, since, by definition, all the subjects left the homestead. Of the 67, 40 left between the ages of 17 and 21; of the remainder, only three left after their twenty-second birthday. Sons of farmers with some other identifiable occupation were more likely to leave home to enter an apprenticeship or a factory at an earlier period. Nine of the 19 left before the age of 17.

The second survey derives from a festival held in Boston in 1849 by the "Sons of New Hampshire," a fraternal organization; see *Festival of the Sons of New Hampshire, . . . Nov. 7, 1849* (Boston, 1850). Appended to the speeches is a list of some 1,500 New Hampshire boys who came to Massachusetts before 1849. The majority came between 1830 and 1849. The list gives, besides names and occupations, places of birth and the years in which the subjects came to Massachusetts. Working with local histories and death records I have ascertained the year of birth of 150 of the sons. The data indicates that those who left home were most likely to do so after their seventeenth and before their twenty-second birthday.

15. William W. Woodward, ed., *Surprising Accounts of the Revival of Religion in the United States of America, . . .* (n.p., 1803), 12, 44, 231; Joshua Bradley, *Accounts of Religious Revivals in Many Parts of the United States from 1815 to 1818* (Albany, N.Y., 1819); Daniel W. Fisher, *A Human Life: An Autobiography with Excursions* (New York, 1909), 58.

16. Reuben Smith, *Truth without Controversy: A Series of Doctrinal Lectures, Intended Principally for Young Professors of Religion* (Saratoga Springs, N.Y., 1824), Lecture IX. The doctrine of regeneration originated in the Great Awakening.

17. Orestes A. Brownson, *The Convert: or, Leaves from My Experience* (New York, 1857), 9.

18. *A Brief History of Joseph Smith, the Prophet, by Himself* (Salt Lake City, 1910), 6–8.

19. John Demos, *A Little Commonwealth: Family Life in Plymouth Colony* (New York, 1970), Chap. 10; Philip J. Greven, Jr., *Four Generations: Population, Land, and Family in Colonial Andover, Massachusetts* (Ithaca, 1970), 126, *passim*.

20. The appearance of a number of advice books aimed at youth after 1830 indicated the growing popular awareness of the critical nature of youth. See Demos and Demos, "Adolescence in Historical Perspective," 634.

21. John Albee, *Confessions of Boyhood* (Boston, 1910); B. M. Hall, *The Life of Rev. John Clark* (New York, 1856), 21.

12. Young Women in the Second Great Awakening in New England

In the first several decades of the nineteenth century, New England churches experienced a "Great Awakening." Converts appeared in Congregational, Presbyterian, Methodist, and Baptist churches in town after town beginning in the late 1790s, a time when revival seemed desperately necessary to churchmen and some lay persons. Calvinist piety and religious intensity had been undermined throughout the eighteenth century by worldly engagement, rationalism, and deism. The War for Independence had diverted attention away from religious salvation toward political survival. After the turmoil of the Revolutionary period, the membership and vitality of New England churches were at a low ebb.[1] New England pastors were further worried by the example and influence of "godless" revolutionary France,[2] and some began a campaign of countersubversion marked by vigorous preaching and encouragement of any sign of religious revival.[3] Their successes, reported in evangelical magazines, inspired other congregations to seek their own religious awakenings. After a first wave of revivals in New England towns between 1798 and 1801, revival peaks recurred every two to five years until the 1830s.[4]

A conspicuous feature of the second Great Awakening (the first having been during the 1740s in New England) was the predominance of female converts. There were at least three female converts to every two male converts between 1798 and 1826, according to the Reverend Ebenezer Porter's estimate in 1832.[5] An examination of women's attraction to evangelical preaching and religious commitment at this time should illuminate women's attitudes and self-perceptions, while providing some reasons for revival successes. Women's diaries and correspondence, and ministers' published accounts of the revivals, furnish the historical sources. Modernization theory and developmental psychology supply perspectives that allow the analysis of religious choices in the context of a more inclusive model of human behavior.

Although the second Great Awakening occurred episodically and under the aegis of ministers of several denominations, the revivals appear to have been remarkably uniform. New England ministers consistently preached, and "hopeful converts" accepted, what they acknowledged as "soul-humbling doctrines" or "hard sayings": the doctrines of "the divine sovereignty—the holiness, extent and inflexibility of the moral law—human depravity—our entire dependence on God—the special agency of the Holy Spirit in conviction and conversion—and mere grace through Jesus Christ as the Mediator."[6] This was Calvinist doctrine. New England Calvinism in the eighteenth century, however, in

Nancy F. Cott, "Young Women in the Second Great Awakening in New England," reprinted from *Feminist Studies* 3, no. 1–2 (1975): 15–29, by permission of the publisher *Feminist Studies,* Inc., c/o Women's Studies Program, University of Maryland, College Park, Maryland 20742.

its struggle against skepticism, deism and rational Christianity, had begun to admit elements of the Arminian heresy—the doctrine that an individual's actions could affect his or her salvation. Revival preaching in the second Great Awakening stressed this idea by focusing on the necessity of active repentance. As the Reverend Increase Graves of Bridport, Vermont, explained, individuals were obliged "to do all they are able, just as much as if they could save themselves by their own works." The Reverend Ebenezer Porter aptly labeled this prevalent strain of preaching "doctrino-practical."[7]

According to ministers' reports, conversions during the second Great Awakening were restrained and serious, with "scarcely a single instance . . . of over-heated zeal, or flight of passion."[8] The main vehicles of the revivals were prayer or singing meetings and other group conferences, held in churches, schools, or homes, and usually segregated by age and sex. In prayer meetings, individuals expressed their religious anxieties or convictions extemporaneously, often inducing listeners to blurt out similar feelings. The Reverend Ammi Robbins described the impact that an individual profession of faith had in Norfolk, Connecticut in 1798:

> Numbers who had as yet remained unmoved, when . . . they beheld many of their intimate companions—a husband—a wife—a brother—a sister—a parent—a child—a near friend—a late jovial companion, with sweet serenity, solemnly giving up themselves to the Lord . . . they were pierced through, as it were, with a dart. They often went home full of distress, and could never find rest or ease until they had submitted to a sovereign God.[9]

Other features promoted repeated comment in revival after revival. The converted were neither self-assertive nor self-righteous—they expressed humility, and continued in self-doubt. Conversion usually came not as a lightening bolt, but through a gradual struggle.[10] And although ministers delighted in unexpected conversions of lifelong infidels, they had to report that the best subjects for conversion were young persons who had been reared in families of some piety.[11]

The most striking and consistent characteristic of the second Great Awakening was the youthfulness of its participants. Again and again ministers noted that religious concern and conversion occurred first and most frequently among youths. "Youth" was an inexact term, generally applied to those between twelve and twenty-five, but sometimes restricted to those between twelve and eighteen, or between twelve and twenty.[12] Most of the youths affected by the revivals were female. In revivals in Plymouth, Torrington, Bristol, and Norfolk, Connecticut, and in Lenox, Massachusetts, in 1798–1799, almost two-thirds of the converts were female. In Canton, Connecticut in 1805–1806, and in Farmington, Connecticut in 1826, the reporting ministers said the conversions occurred "chiefly" among females. And Reverend Ebenezer Porter, as mentioned, estimated that three-fifths of the converts in the New England revivals between 1798 and 1826 were female.[13]

Young women, then, made up the largest single age and sex grouping in these revivals. "Young" women usually meant unmarried women, since the average age at marriage was about twenty-two to twenty-three.[14] In the absence of detailed community studies and investigations of church registers, it is impossible to determine the exact social base of the Awakenings, or to figure the proportional relation that female converts bore to the population at large. Contemporary documents give the impression, however, that a broad middle range of the population was affected. Young female converts ranged from mill workers to students at selective female academies.[15] Were there circumstances peculiar to the lives and prospects of young unmarried women at this time that might make them especially susceptible to religious "awakening"?

In the decades following the American War for Independence, the removal of New England's economy from its agricultural and household base was perceptible in the rising density of population, the multiplication of nonfarming occupations, the expansion of commerce, and the beginnings of industrialization. Rationalization and specialization occurred. Commercial and market orientation appeared in the farm population in the forms of specialized agriculture, wage-earning (both in farm labor and in "given-out" industry), and greater reliance on cash purchase of household goods. Even before large-scale industrialization took place, a household economy in which families produced all the goods they needed was displaced by a market economy.[16]

These developments affected young unmarried women's work more noticeably than they affected married women's work. Married women's work in the preindustrial household economy included organization and management of the household, care of children, and domestic manufacture. Young unmarried women also contributed to the preindustrial economy in several ways: they performed general household work in their own families, or were hired out to do the same for pay in other families; they helped out in a family shop; at home they did varieties of handiwork, such as knitting and lace-making, and sold or exchanged their products; by the mid-eighteenth century they taught summer sessions of school. Their chief employment, however, was spinning, weaving, and needlework in their homes and also in the employ of other families.[17] As compared to matrons' work, young unmarried women's household work lay more exclusively in textile manufacture. Economic development in New England decreased the importance of this domestic manufacture. The textile industry was the first machine industry in New England. Spinning machinery was introduced in 1789; and when the power loom was installed in Waltham, Massachusetts in 1814, all the processes of turning raw fiber into finished cloth were first united under one factory roof.[18] The industrialization of spinning and weaving, virtually completed by 1830 in New England, was the single greatest factor affecting young women's work.

It is important to recognize that economic development—especially the decline in household manufacture—disrupted the daughter's usual place in the household before it disrupted the mother's. While the wife/mother's life continued to be defined (and consumed) in household management and rearing of children, the daughter's household contribution sank from vital to marginal significance. The *predictability* of the daughter's relation to and function in the family faltered. The decline of household manufactures compelled many young women to seek paid employment outside the family, to reproduce in cash their former domestic usefulness. Early textile mill operatives, almost all of them between fifteen and thirty years old, were women who followed their traditional occupation to their new locations, the factory. The textile industry from its start employed vastly more women than men.[19] Other paid employments open to young women were industrial piece work, sewing for individuals, and schoolteaching in summer sessions of public schools or in the growing number of academies. None of these employments was permanent or exclusive. Young women combined or alternated among them; for instance, some factory workers taught school part of the year.[20] Female academies attracted students who had new leisure time or a need for education.

In the search for training and income, many young women of this period experienced relative mobility and variety of experience. The scope of action opened to them enlarged but so did the uncertainty and insecurity. In contrast to the "settled" lives of married women, unmarried women's circumstances were—in the language of the day— "unsettled." For a wide middle range of the young female population, a predictable role in the household economy had ended. Their experience now very likely included repeated change—of work, of place, of associates. Their economic alternatives frequently required them to leave home and board with unfamiliar people in strange towns— perhaps in a succession of towns. The pursuit of work, or support, or education, strained their ties to family and native home. Educational experiences and certain employments also tended to emphasize rootless, age-peer relationships. Young women boarding together looked to each other for sympathy and emotional support, and in some cases this worked to devalue family ties. Teen-aged Rebeccah Root, for example, felt depressed after she left Hartford, Connecticut, where she had shared school and revival experiences with her friends Harriet Whiting and Weltha Brown. Back at home, she wrote to Weltha, "here is Mama but I cannot say anything to her although the best of Mothers, My sisters feel differently from me therefore cannot participate in my feelings I often think if I could see you or Harriet a few moments I should feel much more contented."[21]

Young women who did not enjoy secure places and predictable occupations in their families may also have had difficulty envisioning their future roles. Although the normative role for adult women was that of wife and mother, several factors may have complicated young women's expectation of this role for themselves. One was the surplus of women over men of marriageable age in the populous eastern towns of New England.[22] Perhaps even more important, a cultural focus on romantic love bloomed in the late eighteenth century, contemporaneously with a heightened perception of marriage as a commercial transaction. These developments accompanied a greater freedom of marital choice from parental management, and an increased separation of the conjugal pair from the larger kinship network.[23] In some young women's discourse, a fine distinction appeared between giving one's *hand* in marriage and giving one's *heart*. Mary Orne Tucker of Haverhill, Massachusetts, for instance, twenty-six years old and four years married, recognized that marriage could be a "galling chain": "*souls* must be *kindred* to make the bands silken; all other I call unions of *hands*, not *hearts*,—I rejoice that the knot which binds me was not tied with any mercenary feelings, and that my *heart* is under the same sweet subjection as my *hand*." Some young women expressed a preference for "single blessedness" above a less than ideal marriage. Some spinsters attributed their lifelong singleness to their high romantic ideals, which no man could actually approximate.[24]

Customarily, a woman could not choose her mate, but could only respond to an offer of marriage. As the importance of parents in arranging marriages declined, the power of young men in choosing wives increased and the leverage of marriageable young women decreased further.[25] Yet marrying was the most important step a woman would take: her marriage would probably determine her residence, her economic status, her acquaintances.[26] Women were aware, as well, that a wife's role prescribed subjection and obedience to her husband. A "Hint to a New-Married Sister" composed by a Connecticut woman in 1819 included the warning, "Now you have left your parents wing,/ Nor longer ask their care./ It is but seldom husbands bring/ A lighter yoke to wear."[27]

During the years of the second Great Awakening, then, it was likely that young women's experience contained one or more disorienting elements. It could include disruption of traditional domestic usefulness, uncertainty about means of financial support, separation from family, substitution of peer-group for family ties, unforeseen geographical relocation, ambiguous prospects for and attitudes toward marriage, and hence an insecure future. To be unable to anticipate marriage with equanimity was an occupational as well as emotional hazard, because wife/motherhood was the major occupation as well as status for adult women. It seems that the process of change that made social and economic functions more complex, rational, and specialized in New England brought young women uncertainty rather than opportunity; it brought them indeterminacy with little power to exercise personal choice. The commercialization and rationalization of the economy in this period made men's economic dominance, and women's economic dependence on men, more salient. Because there were severe social and economic constraints on women's means to earn money, the release of young women from their productive domestic roles did not transform them into economic individuals competing equally with men in the marketplace.[28] The gap between opportunities available to women and to men appears to have widened, as does the gap between personal decision making powers exercised by women and by men.[29] For young men, economic and social developments in this period created new opportunities and in the process added uncertainties; for young women, who were shut out from economic initiatives, such developments created insecurity without a compensating new range of choice.

In other words, women and men experienced the impact of modernization in different ways. I use the word modernization to mean the development of "the institutional concomitants of technologically induced economic growth."[30] In the economic sphere modernization implies rationalized production, mobilization of available resources, specialization, and increased scale and integration of the economy. In the social and political spheres it implies analogous developments toward rational, functional, and integrated structures: expanded political participation, centralization of authority, and movement away from small, isolated, traditional communities with ascriptive or hereditary hierarchies toward one large (national) society with common and cosmopolitan values.[31]

In the United States, decisive modernization was under way within fifty years following the War for Independence. Moreover, American men seem to have exhibited by this time a modern personality type, one animated by secular, rational, and cosmopolitan values, demonstrating openness to new experience, abandoning reliance on hierarchical authority, and adopting initiative rather than passivity or resignation in the face of difficulties;[32] It is open to question, however, whether the same forces that were "making men modern" in the post-Revolutionary generation were also "making women modern." Women were largely shut out from speculative business ventures and popular politics, the two main avenues leading men to exhibit "modern" characteristics. The "calculating, dynamic approach to economic life and social mobility" which Richard D. Brown points to as a central manifestation of the modern personality in America did not apply to women, because of their economic and social subordination to men. Women could not take part in republican politics where the rule of deference to officeholders was replaced with ideas of popular will and public service.[33] Women were socialized to remain deferential to their traditional authority figures—men (especially husbands). They were taught to be passive and resigned, and were expected to exhibit self-renunciation rather than self-assertion.[34]

Yet societal modernization certainly affected women's roles and expectations. It may have had a crucial impact on young women in the process of establishing their adult identities, at just the age that so many responded to revival appeals. Erik Erikson's analysis of the psychosocial stage of adolescence is very useful here. Erikson says the "task" of adolescence is identity formation, "the selective repudiation and mutual assimilation of childhood identifications and their absorption in a new configuration." The child's observation of ordered social roles in and outside the family gives her a set of expectations regarding her future roles; but, Erikson observes, cultural and historical change can prove "traumatic to identity formation: it can break up the inner consistency of a child's hierarchy of expectations."[35] The lack of predictability in young women's economic resources and marriage prospects in the first decades of the nineteenth century may thus have made identity formation problematic for them.

In Erikson's view, the ego's specific tasks in adolescence are to defend against newly intense bodily impulses, to match important "conflict-free" achievements with work opportunities, and to put childhood identifications together in a way that is unique and yet accords with accepted social roles. Adolescents are eager "to be inspired by 'ways of life,'" Erikson maintains, and so are attracted by the "ideological potential of a society." Erikson also suggests a distinction between types of adolescent experience that seems pertinent to the differential impact of modernization on male and female youth:

> In any given period in history . . . that part of youth will have the most affirmatively exciting time of it which finds itself in the wave of a technological, economic, or ideological trend seemingly promising all that youthful vitality could ask for.
>
> Adolescence, therefore, is least "stormy" in that segment of youth which is gifted and well trained in the pursuit of expanding technological trends, and thus able to identify with new roles of competency and invention and to accept a more implicit ideological outlook. Where this is not given, the adolescent mind becomes a more explicitly ideological one, by which we mean one searching for some inspiring unification of tradition or anticipated techniques, ideas, and ideals.[36]

Early nineteenth-century adolescent males were, in general, better trained "to identify with new roles of competency and invention" in a time of rapid modernization, and to accept the modern ideology implicit in these roles, than were females, who looked for a "more explicitly ideological" framework such as that offered by religious conversion. This does not exclude the possibility that young male converts in the second Great Awakening were also attempting to resolve anxieties about their adult roles. Although their childhood identifications and the causes of their indeterminacy would have differed from young women's, religious conversion may have served analogous purposes for them.[37]

More detailed examination is in order to explain how conversion could provide young women with ideological ballast useful to stabilize their lives and identities. First of all, the "doctrino-practical" approach of the second Great Awakening allowed individuals to take an initiative in their own salvation. In bright contrast to the uncertainties that young women encountered in most pursuits and prospects, ministers proposed repentance and resignation of all to God as conscious choices that would affect their temporal and eternal salvation. Yet, the religious choice was actually a surrender—to God's will. One minister likened the sinner's obstinate heart in relation to God to a garrison surrounded by an army. "Many a garrison has been unable to *stand out,* and *resist;* but who ever heard of one that had not *power* to *surrender!!*"[38] The submission required of those who were to be saved was consistent with female socialization, but this submission was also an act of initiation and assertion of strength by female converts. Conversion set up a direct relation to God's authority that allowed female converts to denigrate or bypass men's authority—

to defy men—for God. The appeal of this proposed religious choice may have been especially strong for young women because, as Erikson has emphasized, adolescent identifications urgently "force the young individual into choices and decisions which will . . . lead to commitments for 'life.' "[39]

Just as the doctrine of the revivals intersected at vital points with young women's needs, the means used to propagate revivals suited young women's predilections. Prayer meetings gave young women opportunity for public expressions of anxiety, and offered the sympathy and support perfectly attuned to the peer relationships they relied on at work or at school away from home. These small group meetings also put effective pressure on participants to become converts. Characterized by restraint, such practices did not frighten away "respectable" girls as the more exuberant Methodist practices frightened young Nancy Thomson in 1806:

> I attended a campmeeting at Sharon. I went praying that God would awaken and convert my companions but was very fearful that the exercises would be so alarming to my tender feelings that I should appear indecent and I thought If I could obtain religion in a still way without much ado I would be glad to do it but would rather remain without this blessing than to lose my strength or cry out as some did.[40]

The experience of Lucinda Read, as revealed in her diary, was probably typical. Oldest child of ten in a farming family of Greensboro, Vermont, she taught the summer session of a local school when she was seventeen, then departed from home the following January, in 1816, to spend a year with relatives in Farmington, Connecticut. After a few weeks in Farmington, she was sent by her uncle to an academy in Canton, Connecticut, where she boarded with a family. In Canton she began to attend "young female conferences" and to berate herself for not believing, seeking, and attaining grace. Four years earlier she had rejected a hope of conversion as specious. After hardly a week in the revival movement at Canton, however, she expressed religious convictions and felt she had experienced conversion. Thereafter she called Canton the place of her "second nativity."[41]

Conversion brought the young person a "new birth" into an extensive family of "sisters" and "brethren"—a family that promised to be more secure than her original family. As ministers noted, young converts tended to have had some religious upbringing, so their conversion suggested the persistence of childhood identifications that received support from sources outside the family. Achievement of secure identity in adolescence, according to Erikson, requires some form of recognition from society or from subsocieties. The young individual should "be responded to and be given function and status as a person whose growth and transformation make sense to those who begin to make sense to [her]." The community of professing Christians supplied precisely this response to the young believer. Converts were well aware of revivals occurring in towns other than their own, and this served to reaffirm their sense of membership in a growing camp. The support of other female converts particularly encouraged in young women the peer-group loyalties that Erikson has called an important part of testing and reinforcing identity formation.[42]

Conversion during a revival also proved a satisfying ideological commitment, supplying a person with an inspiring "way of life."[43] Providing both an immediate and a long-term purpose, conversion could resolve young women's uncertainties about the future. To summarize the meaning of her conversion in 1808 at age nineteen, Nancy Thomson of Connecticut wrote, "I made religion the principal business of my life." Likewise

Lucinda Read vowed, upon her conversion, to devote all of her thought and action to God and righteousness.[44] Conversion did not mean complacency. The Reverend William Sprague advised ministers to impress young converts "with the consideration that *if they have really been renewed, they are just entering on a course of labor and conflict.*"[45] One could never rest in certainty of salvation. But the convert's otherworldly concern could provide a source of fortitude in this world.[46]

As opposed to the vagaries encountered in social and economic pursuits, the Christian's struggle was comprehensible, its consequences were well-defined, and a supportive community echoed the individual's experience. Evangelical religion made each proselyte a proselytizer as well. The propagators of nineteenth-century orthodox religion acted on the notion that the best defense is a good offense. Lucinda Read, who was boarding with her students' families while she taught school, after her conversion, wrote in her diary: "Oh that my duty were plain while residing in an irreligious Family. Must I usurp the conversion and introduce religion in the midst of levity? Or must I try to engage the attention of the family individually and say something upon the all-important concerns of the soul: the never-dying immortal soul which they are selling for paltry pelf?"[47]

The revival demanded individual commitment in its central question, "What shall you do to be saved?" The community of converts offered supportive recognition to the person who repented and sought grace. The church required "fidelity" and an ideological stance against "infidelity." Conversion promised not only a lifetime's work in religious struggle, but also a loyal peer-group with whom to share it. For young women whose growth to adulthood in a period of modernization was marked by disruption and uncertainty, these elements together comprised a persuasive argument for forming a religious identity.[48] While evangelical Christianity confined women to private religious roles, sex-specific propriety, and subordinate public status, it also brought them vital strength and purpose that found confirmation among their peers. The reasons supporting young women's conversions during the second Great Awakening suggest why Christian identity was fundamental to the definition of "womanhood" through the nineteenth century.

Notes

1. Cf. William Warren Sweet, *Revivalism in America* (New York: Charles Scribner, 1944), p. 117: "[In post-Revolutionary America] religious and moral conditions of the country as a whole reached the lowest ebb tide in the entire history of the American people"; and Sydney E. Ahlstrom, *A Religious History of the American People* (New Haven: Yale University Press, 1972), p. 365: "The revolutionary era was a period of decline for American Christianity as a whole. The churches reached a lower ebb of vitality during the two decades after the end of hostilities than at any other time in the country's religious history." Lawrence Cremin, *American Education: The Colonial Experience* (New York: Harper Torchbooks, 1970), p. 493, concurs that Sweet's estimate that twenty to twenty-five percent of the New England population were church members in 1760 seems fair or a little high.

2. The Rev. Nathan Perkins of West Hartford, Connecticut, for example, in 1798 attributed the errors and heresies of recent years to the corruption of morals during the American Revolution, to revolutionary events in Europe, and to the number of atheistic and infidel publications released "by the votaries of MODERN PHILOSOPHY, and the NEW THEORIES of liberty and equality." Quoted in William Wallis Woodward, *Surprising Accounts of the Revival of Religion, in the United States of America* . . . (Philadelphia: the author, 1802), p. 117.

3. The best known of the New Divinity men were Samuel Hopkins of Newport, R.I., Stephen West of Stockbridge and Nathaniel Emmons of Franklin, Mass., and Ebenezer Porter, Asahel Hooker, Azel Backus and Abel Flint of Connecticut. Charles R. Keller, *The Second Great Awakening in Connecticut* (New Haven: Yale University Press, 1942), pp. 26, 33.

Richard D. Birdsall, in "The Second Great Awakening and the New England Social Order," *Church History* 39 (1970): 358, sees the first stage of the revivals as "the expression of intense religious feelings coming from solitary individuals and building into numerous close though temporary communities," and the second stage as "a kind of consolidation and crystalization of this spirit, in which the clergy rather than the people played the more active role."

4. Charles Keller notes revival peaks in 1798–1801, 1805–1806, 1807–1808, 1812, 1815–1816, 1818, 1820–1821, and 1825–1826: *Second Great Awakening*, pp. 37, 42.

5. Ebenezer Porter, *Letters on Revivals of Religion* (Andover, Mass.: Revival Association, 1832), p. 5. Women constituted the majority of New England church members from about the middle of the seventeenth century onwards. See Edmund S. Morgan, "New England Puritanism: Another Approach," *William and Mary Quarterly* 3rd ser., 18 (1961): 236–42; Darrett Rutman, "God's Bridge Falling Down—'Another Approach' to New England Puritanism Assayed," *William and Mary Quarterly* 3d ser., 19 (1962): 408–21; and Mary Maples Dunn, "Colonial Women and Religion: Quaker and Puritan Compared," paper delivered at the Second Berkshire Conference on the History of Women, Cambridge, Mass., October 26, 1974. Nevertheless, the great influx of female converts during the second Great Awakening requires explanation. Donald Mathews, "The Second Great Awakening as an Organizing Process," *American Quaterly* 21 (1969): p. 42, and Whitney R. Cross, *The Burned Over District* (New York: Harper Torchbooks, 1965), esp. pp. 84–89, have noted the potential significance of the disproportionate numbers of female converts during these revivals. In the first Great Awakening of the 1730s–1740s, according to Cedric Cowing, "Sex and Preaching in the Great Awakening," *American Quarterly* 20 (1968): 624–44, male converts brought the sex ratio to parity in New Light churches.

6. The Rev. Alexander Gillet, regarding the revival in Torrington, Connecticut, 1798–1799, quoted in Bennet Tyler, *New England Revivals, as they existed at the close of the eighteenth and the beginning of the nineteenth centuries. Compiled principally from narratives first published in the Connecticut Evangelical Magazine* (Boston: Sabbath School Association, 1846), pp. 90–91. See also Keller, *Second Great Awakening*, pp. 29–30, 204, 366–67; William B. Sprague, *Lectures on Revivals of Religion . . . with an Appendix, consisting of letters from . . . [many ministers]*, 2d ed. (New York: Daniel Appleton, 1833), p. 238, 271; and Ebenezer Porter, *Letters*, p. 15.

Ahlstrom, *Religious History*, p. 417, notes that before Western, Methodist, and "New School" practices took hold, the second Great Awakening in New England broadcast simple and uniform doctrine: God's absolute sovereignty, man's total depravity, Christ's atoning love.

7. Graves was quoted in an account of the Bridport revival of 1813–1814 in Tyler, *N. E. Revivals*, pp. 366–67. Porter, *Letters*, pp. 13, 15, explained that the doctrino-practical approach stressed "the entire alienation of the sinner's heart from God;—his voluntary, inexcusable, and yet certain rejection of the gospel, till his heart is subdued by divine influence; his complete obligation, as a moral agent, to repent, and do all that God requires of him, and to do it immediately; his need of an infinite Saviour to make atonement for him, for an infinite Sanctifier to renovate him, and take away his only obstacle to obedience, the guilty opposition of his heart; and his dependence on free grace through faith to justify and save him."

Cf. William McLoughlin's summary of the idea of "compliance with the terms of salvation," introduced by the New Divinity pastor Nathaniel Taylor: "The process of conversion thus became a shared act, a complementary relationship. Man striving and yearning; God benevolent and eager to save; the sinner stretching out his hands to receive the gift of grace held out by a loving God. This belief in man's free will or his partial power to effect his own salvation had in earlier Calvinist days been condemned as the heresy of Arminianism. For this reason most nineteenth-century ministers preferred to call themselves Evangelicals," (*The American Evangelicals 1800–1900* [New York: Harper Torchbooks, 1968], p. 10).

8. Thomas Baldwin, *A Brief Account of the Late Revivals of Religion in a Number of Towns in the New-England States* (Boston, Manning and Loring, 1799), p. 6. See also Woodward, *Surprising Accounts*, pp. 8, 11, 25; Joshua Bradley, *Account of Religious Revivals in Many Parts of the United States from 1815 to 1818* (Albany, New York: G. J. Loomis and Co., 1819), pp. 30, 40, 51–53;

Tyler, *N. E. Revivals,* pp. 57–58. In fact, this claim appears in almost every revival account of the period, intending, no doubt, to disarm critics who associated revivals with "enthusiasm." Did the minister-reporters "protest too much"? The absence of accusations of enthusiasm, and honest admission of a few instances of over-zealous behavior, suggest that the ministers were reporting the circumstances fairly.

9. Quoted in Tyler, *N. E. Revivals,* pp. 186–87; also in *New England Tracts, No. 1; Narratives of Reformations, in Canton and Norfolk, Connecticut, in four letters* (Providence, Barnum Fields, n.d.), p. 16.

For a description of prayer meetings by an opponent of them, see Menzies Rayner, *A Dissertation upon Extraordinary Awakenings* (New Haven: Herald Office, 1816), pp. 43–51.

10. Tyler, *N. E. Revivals,* pp. 76, 148, 159, 189; Porter, *Letters,* p. 35. Part of this emphasis was probably due to ministers' desire to ward off criticism of enthusiasm.

11. Tyler, *N. E. Revivals,* pp. 197, 209, 318, 342, 357; Sprague, *Lectures,* p. 114; Porter, *Letters,* p. 5. Many ministers joined Ammi Robbins in recognizing and exploiting the influence a person's conversion could have on other members of her or his family; e.g., Woodward, *Surprising Accounts,* pp. 7, 238–42; Tyler, *N. E. Revivals,* pp. 186–87; *New England Tracts,* p. 16.

12. See Tyler, *N. E. Revivals,* pp. 24–27, 55, 84, 93, 120, 155, 196, 284–86, 322, 339, 356; Sprague, *Lectures,* pp. 272, 295; Porter, *Letters,* p. 6; Woodward, *Surprising Accounts,* pp. 7, 12, 18, 22; Baldwin, *Brief Account,* pp. 4, 5, 7; Bradley, *Account,* pp. 13–22, 26–29, 34–35, 36–38, 38–41, 41–42, 49–50, 51, 53–59, 65–77, 85–95, 130–32.

The largest pool of possible converts obviously consisted of youths. There were also reasons of self-interest and church-interest that would have led ministers to emphasize the youth of their new professors. Convention of young persons promised most for the future stability of church and society, and contradicted the notion that orthodox doctrines were old-fashioned and irrelevant to post-Revolutionary America. Nevertheless it is unlikely that ministers exaggerated the role of youths, because such claims were also subject to the accusation that young people were volatile and susceptible to enthusiasms, and their professions of faith often specious.

Joseph Kett has written about "youth" (male) in New England in "Growing Up in Rural New England, 1800–1840," in *Anonymous Americans: Explorations in Nineteenth-Century Social History,* ed., Tamara K. Hareven (Englewood Cliffs, N.J.: Prentice-Hall, 1971), pp. 1–16, and "Adolescence and Youth in Nineteenth-Century America," in *The Family in History,* eds., Theodore K. Rabb and Robert I. Rotberg (New York: Harper Torchbooks, 1973), pp. 95–110.

13. Tyler, *N. E. Revivals,* pp. 95, 84–85, 187, 155, 322–32; Sprague, *Lectures,* p. 295; Porter, *Letters,* p. 5.

14. On age of marriage in this period, see Robert V. Wells, "Quaker Marriage Patterns in a Colonial Perspective," *William and Mary Quarterly* 3d ser., 29 (1972): 418–21; and Bernard Farber, *Guardians of Virtue; Salem Families in 1800* (New York: Basic Books, 1972), pp. 41–43.

15. E.g., Catherine Sedgwick reported to her brother in a letter of September 15, 1833, from Lenox, Massachusetts, "We have had the religious agitators among us lately—They have produced some effect on the factory girls & such light & combustible materials—." Sedgwick, a Unitarian, objected to evangelical religion. CS to Robert Sedgwick, Sedgwick Collection, Massachusetts Historical Society.

See also Almond H. Davis, *The Female Preacher, or Memoir of Salome Lincoln* (Providence, R.I.: J.S. Mowry, 1843), the memoir of a Massachusetts factory worker who became a Freewill Baptist preacher.

Numerous conversions at such academies as Miss Pierce's in Litchfield, Connecticut, indicated that middle-class and elite group responded to revival appeals. A student at Miss Pierce's in 1814–15 wrote to a friend about the success of revival meetings in Litchfield, "We trust that more than half the school have been made the subjects of renewing grace." Abigail Bradley to Eliza Nash, September 14, 1815, Bradley-Hyde Collection, Schlesinger Library.

16. See Percy Wells Bidwell, "The Agricultural Revolution in New England," *American Historical Review* 26 (1920): 683–702; David Montgomery, "The Working Classes of the Pre-Industrial American City," in *New Perspectives in American History,* eds., Stanley Katz and Stanley Kutler, 2d ed. (Boston: Little-Brown, 1972), I, pp. 222–37; Douglass C. North, *The Economic Growth of the United States, 1790–1860* (New York: W. W. Norton, 1966), pp. 156–77; and Nancy F. Cott, "In

the Bonds of Womanhood: Perspectives on Female Experience and Consciousness in New England, 1780–1830," (Ph.D. dissertation, Brandeis University, 1974), chapter 1.

17. See Cott, "In the Bonds," pp. 11–19.

18. The first manufactories, established during the 1760s in major American cities, were merely places of business to collect yarn spun and cloth woven by women in their homes by traditional hand methods. Then, by the 1780s, some employers put spinning wheels and looms on their own premises, and hired women to work them there. In general, at this stage a small number of women were employed on the premises, and a much larger number worked at home. After the introduction of spinning machinery, and the subsequent spread of spinning mills, these circumstances were reversed. Spinning became a machine industry more than two decades before weaving did. The first factories produced yarn only, not cloth. With the introduction of the power loom, weaving also became a factory rather than a domestic occupation. See Edith Abbott, *Women in Industry* (New York: D. Appleton, 1918), pp. 36–39, 41–47; and Rolla M. Tyron, *Household Manufactures in the United States 1640–1860* ([1917] New York: Augustus M. Kelly, 1966), pp. 274–77.

19. Abbott, *Women in Industry,* pp. 89–90, 121.

20. Ibid., p. 119; Lucy Larcom, *A New England Girlhood* ([1889] New York: Corinth Books, 1961), p. 223. For examples of women who spent their youth pursuing various means of economic support see *The Life and Letters of Mrs. Emily C. Judson,* ed., A. C. Kendrick (Boston: Gould and Lincoln, 1861), pp. 15–26, and Davis, *The Female Preacher.*

21. Rebeccah Root to Weltha Brown, August 7, 1815, Weltha Brown Correspondence, Schlesinger Library.

According to operatives like Lucy Larcom, Harriet Hanson Robinson, and the contributors to the Lowell magazines, work in the Lowell-area mills also emphasized age-peer relationships among operatives.

22. There was a surplus of women above age sixteen in the eastern counties of Massachusetts from the latter part of the eighteenth century. See the 1764–1765 census in *Early Census-Making in Massachusetts,* ed., J. H. Benton, Jr. (Boston: Boston University Press, 1905). David Montgomery reports that the sex ratio in Massachusetts in 1810 was 103 (women) to 100(men) for the age group 16–45; for the age group over 26 it was 107 to 100. The sex ratio in Boston was 127 to 100 "Working Classes," pp. 235–36.

23. Data assembled by Daniel Scott Smith indicate a shift toward individual autonomy and away from parental control in marriage choice beginning markedly during the Revolutionary period. "Parental Power and Marriage Patterns—An Analysis of Historical Trends in Hingham, Massachusetts," *Journal of Marriage and the Family* 35 (1973): 419–28. See Herman R. Lantz, *et al.,* "Pre-Industrial Patterns in the Colonial Family in America: A Content Analysis of Colonial Magazines," *American Sociological Review* 33 (1968): 413–26, on the existence of romantic love ideals by the late eighteenth century. See also Ian Watt, "The New Woman: Samuel Richardson's *Pamela,*" in *The Family: Its Structure and Functions,* ed., Rose Laub Coser (New York: St. Martin's Press, 1964), pp. 269–72, on the implications of freeing the conjugal pair from the larger family network.

24. Manuscript diary of Mary Orne Tucker, April 17, 1802, Essex Institute Library, Salem, Massachusetts. Eliza Chaplin of Salem asserted in 1820 that she would never give her hand without her heart, having as she did a romantic ideal of the perfect mate. "Rather than be subject to the 'eternal strife,' which . . . prevails . . . where minds are 'fettered to different moulds,' " she said, she would "ever remain in 'single blessedness' and deem it felicity thus to live." Eliza Chaplin to Laura Lovell, July 26, 1820, Chaplin-Lovell correspondence, Essex Institute Library.

Cf. Mrs. A. J. Graves (pseud.), *Girlhood and Womanhood* (Boston: T. H. Carter, 1844), p. 210; and Catherine Sedgwick's musing, at 45, that her rejections of marriage offers may have been because "romantic imaginative persons formed a *beau ideal* to which nothing in life approximated near enough to satisfy them." Manuscript diary of Catherine Sedgwick, May 24, 1834; Massachusetts Historical Society.

25. A nineteen-year-old of Maine wrote with sarcasm in 1802 on this point, "We ladies, you know, posess that 'sweet pliability of temper' that disposes us to enjoy any situation, and we must have no choice in these things till we find what is to be our destiny, then we must consider it the

best in the world." Eliza Southgate to Moses Porter, May 1802, reprinted in *Root of Bitterness: Documents of the Social History of American Women,* ed., Nancy F. Cott (New York: E. P. Dutton, 1972), p. 109. "There are more blanks than prizes in the matrimonial lottery," Mary Orne Tucker admitted in her diary, April 28, 1802.

26. Cf. the opinion of an eligible bachelor—a student at Litchfield Law School in 1820—who felt that the advantage in marital choice should be on the woman's side, "because the contract is so much more important in its consequences to females than to males—for besides leaving everything else to unite themselves to one man they subject themselves to his authority—they depend more upon their husband than he does upon the wife for society & for the happiness & enjoyment of their lives—he is their all—their only relative—their only hope—but as for him—business leads him out of doors, far from the company of his wife . . . & then it is upon his employment that he depends almost entirely for the happiness of his life." Journal of George Younglove Cutler, 1820, quoted in *Chronicles of a Pioneer School,* ed., Emily Vanderpoel (Cambridge, Mass.: Harvard University Press, 1903), p. 196. With increased migration of population out of New England after 1800, the likelihood multiplied that marriage would remove a young woman from her native place, family, and friends, and make her husband's influence on her life all the more salient.

27. Manuscript journal of Lucy Beckley, 1819, Connecticut Historical Society.

28. Women's wages were generally about one-fourth to one-half as high as men's for comparable work. See Abbott, *Women in Industry,* pp. 76n, 157, 192, 262–316, 249.

29. See Gerda Lerner, "The Lady and the Mill-Girl: Changes in the Status of Women in the Age of Jackson," *Mid-Continent American Studies Journal* 10 (1969): 5–15, for a discussion of the relative status-deprivation felt by some middle-class women circa 1820–1840.

30. The phrase is that of Peter L. Berger, Brigitte Berger, and Hansfried Kellner, *The Homeless Mind: Modernization and Consciousness* (New York: Random House, 1973), p. 10. I would also adopt their caution that there are "reciprocal relations of causality" between "the technological transformation of the economy, and the gamut of modern institutions," and that "the great transformation could not have taken place without antecedent processes that were neither technological nor economic (as, for example, religious and ethical interpretations of the world)." Modernization is a loaded word, since it has usually been used to indicate the superiority of the industrialized West over the Third World, while implying that all social values and structures accompanying modern industrial capitalism are positive goods. I intend to use the word modernization without these connotations, if possible.

31. My summary of the model of modernization relies on Richard D. Brown, "Modernization and the Modern Personality in Early America, 1600–1865: A Sketch of a Synthesis," *Journal of Interdisciplinary History* 2 (1972): 201–202. See also E. A. Wrigley, "Modernization and the Industrial Revolution in England," *Journal of Interdisciplinary History* 3 (1972); North, *Economic Growth,* esp. pp. 156–77; William N. Chambers, *Political Parties in a New Nation* (New York: Oxford University Press, 1963), pp. 14–15, 95–96, and, on the implications of modernization for women's roles, Cott, "In the Bonds," Chapters 1 and 2.

32. Other "modern" characteristics are readiness to form opinions about distant or abstract problems; belief that one can conquer one's environment rather than being dominated by it; orientation toward the present and future rather than the past; and adoption of time-discipline, scheduling, and planning ahead as ways to organize life. Alex Inkeles, "Making Men Modern: On the Causes and Consequences of Individual Change in Six Developing Countries," *American Journal of Sociology* 75 (1969): 210, and "The Modernization of Man," in *Modernization: The Dynamics of Growth,* ed., Myron Weiner (Voice of American Forum Lectures, 1967), pp. 153–57. For the application of the concept of modern personality to American history, see Brown, "Modernization and Modern Personality," pp. 201–222.

33. On these aspects of "modern" behavior, see Brown, "Modernization and Modern Personality," pp. 216–19. See David H. Fischer, *The Revolution of American Conservatism* (New York: Harper Torchbooks, 1965) on the general theme of the decline of political deference between 1790 and 1815.

34. Cf. Hannah More's advice, which echoed through subsequent American tracts: "Girls should be led to distrust their own judgment; they should learn not to murmur at expostulation; they should be accustomed to expect and to endure opposition. It is a lesson with which the world will not fail to furnish them; and they will not practice it the worse for having learnt it the sooner.

It is of the last importance to their happiness, that they should early acquire a submissive temper and a forbearing spirit" (*Strictures on the Modern System of Female Education,* 9th ed. [London: A. Strahan, 1801], I, pp. 183–84.

35. Erik H. Erikson, *Identity: Youth and Crisis* (New York: W. W. Norton, 1968), p. 159. Erikson's theoretical model of the life cycle is valuable for this analysis despite the fact that it is implicitly more male than androgynous. Erikson intends his analysis to apply to the *human* personality, and does use some case studies of females to illustrate his general points about adolescence and identity.

36. Ibid., pp. 128–30, 156.

37. On young men in the second Great Awakening, cf. Lois Banner, "Religion and Reform in the Early Republic: The Role of Youth," *American Quarterly* 23 (1971): 677–95.

38. Quoted in Porter, *Letters,* p. 16.

39. Erikson, *Identity,* p. 155.

40. "A Short Sketch of the life of Nancy Thomson," written c. 1813, manuscript included in the diaries of Nancy Thompson [*sic*] Hunt, Connecticut Historical Society. On the contribution of Methodist measures to Congregational and Presbyterian revival practice in the Northeast before Finney, see Richard Carwardine, "The Second Great Awakening in the Urban Centers: An Examination of Methodism and the 'New Measures,' " *Journal of American History* 59 (1972): 327–41.

41. Manuscript diary of Lucinda Read, 1815–1816, Massachusetts Historical Society, esp. entries for January 19; February 1, 23, 25, 27; March 23, 1816.

42. Erikson, *Identity,* pp. 156, 132–33. For an example of converts' correspondence noting revivals in other towns, see Rebeccah Root to Weltha Brown, April 1829, Weltha Brown Correspondence.

43. Erikson maintains that "fidelity" or "the search for something and somebody to be true to," is "in the center of youth's most passionate and most erratic striving" (*Identity,* pp. 233, 235).

44. Thomson, "Short Sketch," and Lucinda Read diary, March 30, 1816. Cf. Birdsall, "Second Great Awakening," p. 357: "From this new and brief community a new sense of individual and social possibility could develop; for the individual was no longer existing in the broad and somewhat abstract social pattern of the formal law with its universal prescription of what was criminal and what was not, but rather within a community of belief in which he was encouraged to make a decision that would be a positive organizing principle for his own life. For this instant he experienced a radical freedom—in which he could make a personal decision and this in a new community of mutual concern."

45. Sprague, *Lectures,* p. 151.

46. Professing faith implied earthly self-denial, but for sufficient cause; as one female convert confided to another, "I long to become 'crucified to the world, that the world may become crucified to me.' The greatest joy of a christian is, that while he is in the world he is out of it" (Rebeccah Root to Weltha Brown, September 27, 1816, Weltha Brown Correspondence).

47. Lucinda Read diary, September 20, 1816.

48. An example of the consoling power of a religious identity may be seen in the case of Rachel Stearns, of Greenfield, Massachusetts. Descended from solidly respectable New England families, she nevertheless endured financial stringency from her youth as a result of her father's early death. In the mid-1830s, when she was in her early twenties, she pursued a variety of types of work—sewing, teaching—and seemed to suffer a sense of isolation and class displacement as one of the genteel poor. In 1835 she deserted her family's traditional Congregationalism and became a Methodist convert, though this set her off even more from her relatives. In her diary she recorded the encouragement she gained from the Methodist doctrine of God's perfect love, and the sole happiness she found in feeling that she was living for God and in Christ: "Yes, through the grace and mercy of God, it is possible that *I,* the 'self-willed' 'obstinate' 'head-strong' and at the same time 'inefficient' 'shiftless' and 'ill-tempered' *Rachel,* that girl whose very name conveys the idea of the essence of ugliness, and who added to all her other faults, pride and self-conceit, who conscious that this long catalogue of evil things applied to her by her friends did not apply in its full extent, thence concluded that some of them knew, and that she was in reality very good superior to most people, Yes, *this girl, this Rachel,* may live to fear God without committing sin" (Rachel Willard Stearns diary, September 14, 1836, volume 6, Stearns Collection, Schlesinger Library; see also entries for May 3, July 19, November 15, 19, 1835).

13. The Setting: Growing Up in the Quarter Community

Dese all my fader's children,
Dese all my fader's children,
Dese all my fader's children,
Outshine de sun.
Allen, *Slave Songs*

For the black children of the quarter community the world of their home plantation was, for all intents and purposes, the entire world of their personal experience. Within its confines they encountered nearly all the physical and material realities of their childhoods and acquired the knowledge, attitudes, values, and skills with which they learned to view the world and make sense of their relationship to it.[1]

The physical condition and appearance of the cabins and other buildings that comprised the slave quarters depended greatly on the wealth and inclination of the plantation owner. On plantations of moderate size, where there was only one quarters, the cabins would be built several hundred yards away from the "great house" of the owner's family, near a spring and a ready supply of fuel from the nearby woods.[2] Commonly slaves wanted their cabins out of sight and hearing of the great house. "When left to themselves," writes Julia Harn, the daughter of a Georgia planter, "they wanted their cabins in some secluded place, down in the hollow, or amid the trees, with only a path to their abode."[3] On large plantations of more than seventy or eighty slaves, two sets of cabins were often built: an "upper quarter," near the more distant fields, and a "lower quarter," closer to the great house.

By the time of the last three decades of slavery the typical slave cabin consisted of one large room.[4] Most often they were constructed of wood logs daubed with mud and sticks "made perfectly tight with mortar, with hog or cow hair worked in to make it stick in the crevises."[5] An ex-slave interviewed by the Fisk project remembers that when the dirt between the logs in the cabin he lived in as a slave would fall off, "you could look out and see the snow falling. Sometimes you would get up out of your warm bed and the side towards the wall would be full of snow."[6] On the Georgia seacoast the houses were often build with tabby, "a plaster of burned oyster shell, lime, and sand applied to a wattle surface; the roof was shingled with cypress or pine, and there was a chimney. . . ."[7] Louis Hughes, who was born a Virginia slave in 1832, describes a fairly typical slave quarters:

> Each cabin was about fourteen feet square, containing but one room, and was covered with oak boards, three feet in length, split out of logs by hand. These boards were not nailed on, but held in their places by what were termed weight-poles laid across them at right angles.

> There were in each room two windows, a door and a large, rude fireplace. The door and
> window frames, or facings, were held in their places by wooden pins, nails being used only in
> putting doors together.[8]

On the large Louisiana plantation where Charley Williams grew up, "De quarters was a
little piece from de big house, and dey run along both sides of de road dat go to de fields.
All one-room log cabins, but dey was good and warm, and everyone had a little open
shed at de side whar we sleep in de summer to keep cool."[9] The small cabin on a Virginia
plantation in which Austen Steward lived as a child had an earthen floor, small openings
in the walls for windows, a stick and mud chimney and "the whole was put together in
the rudest possible manner."[10]

Most slave cabins had holes in the walls with wooden shutters for windows, which
had the disadvantage, according to Margaret Nillin of Texas, of letting "flies in durin' de
summer an' col' in durin' de winter. But if you shuts dat window dat shut out de light."[11]
In the Mississippi slave cabin where Austin Parnell was raised the problem was not so
much letting in the light as keeping out the rain and snow.

> I laid in bed many a night and looked up through the cracks in the roof. Snow would come
> through there when it snowed and cover the bed covers. We thought you couldn't build a
> roof so that it would keep out rain and snow, but we were mistaken. Before you would make
> a fire in them days, you had to sweep out the snow so that it wouldn't melt up in the house
> and make a mess.[12]

Another problem with many of the cabins was that the mud-and-sticks-chimneys would
catch fire. According to Richard Carruthers, who lived as a slave in Texas, the log cabins
of the quarters "burned down oftentimes. The chimney would catch fire, 'cause it was
made out of sticks and clay and moss. Many the time we would have to get up at
midnight and push the chimney away from the house to keep the house from burnin'
up."[13]

On some plantations, households with many children were permitted to add a second
room to their cabins. "My mother had so many children she had to have two rooms,"
recollects a Fisk informant. "It had old-fashioned windows that you would shut, no glass
at all. There was a fireplace in each room that would come out on the inside. We called
that the hob, and we chillen would climb on it sometimes."[14] In other quarters, cabins
with two rooms with a chimney built between them was the rule for everybody.[15] Rarely
would a cabin have more than two rooms although the cabin where Alec Pope lived in
Georgia "had two rooms on de fust flo' and a loft up 'bove whar de boys most gen'ally
slep' and de gals slep' downstairs."[16] On the Georgia plantation where Georgia Baker
grew up, "De long, log cabins what us lived in was called 'shotgun' houses 'cause dey had
three rooms, one behind the other in a row lak de barrel of a shotgun. All de chillun slept
in one end room and de grown folkses slept in de other end room. . . . Gals slept on one
side of de room and boys on de other in de chillun's rooms."[17] Olmsted reported even
larger slave houses made of boards on some of the Virginia plantations of the James
River. In these, up to eight families occupied what Olmsted observed to be "ornamental"
structures each having its own "distinct sleeping-room and lock-up closets."[18] By the
account of Jacob Stroyer, who lived as a slave on the large Singleton plantation in South
Carolina, in such multi-family dwellings anyone "accustomed to the way in which the
slaves lived in their cabins could tell as soon as they entered whether they were friendly or

not, for when they did not agree the fires of the two families did not meet on the hearth, but there was a vacancy between them, that was a sign of disagreement."[19]

The furnishings of the quarter cabins were generally very simple, consisting of home-made chairs, tables, and beds which could be cleaned easily and scoured with sand. In most cabins the beds were constructed in a corner "with one leg out and the two walls supporting the other sides."[20] Celeste Avery, an ex-slave interviewed in Georgia, remembers that "The beds were bottomed with rope which ran backward and forward from one rail to the other. On this framework was placed a mattress of wheat straw. Each spring the mattresses were emptied and refilled with fresh wheat straw."[21] Sometimes instead of cords, boards were used for support and mattresses might be filled with cotton, moss, leaves, or occasionally, feathers.[22] Addie Vinson, whose parents were both fieldhands on the Georgia plantation of Peter Vinson, recalls how she "laked dem matt'esses 'cause when de chinches got too bad you could shake out dat straw and burn it, den scald de tick and fill it wid fresh straw, and rest in peace again."[23] During the day the trundle beds on which the children slept were pushed under the big bed. "You would get it out at night, and the children would sleep in it, and in the morning you would push it back under the big bed. They had one room, and had everything in the one room, and they did that to save space."[24]

Other cabin furnishings included shuck-bottomed chairs, a wooden table, and tallow candles or lamps made out of fat lightwood torches.[25] Often boxes were used for everything from bureaus and chairs to storing food.[26] Even the most sparsely furnished cabin contained a wooden bench, a broom made of straw or corn shucks, and various cooking utensils. Gourds which slaves grew of many sizes had, as Robert Shepherd, who lived as a slave on the Echols plantation in Oglethrope County, Georgia, informs us, equally as many purposes. "Us loved to drink out of gourds. Dere was lots of gourds raised every year. Some of 'em was so big dey was used to keep eggs in and for lots of things us uses baskets for now. Dem little gourds made fine dippers."[27] Most slaves also possessed at least one big wooden water bucket and perhaps an even larger wash barrel. The most prominent aspect of many cabins was the large fireplace.

> De fireplaces was a heap bigger dan dey has now, for all de cookin' was done in open fireplaces den. 'Taters and cornpone was roasted in de ashes and most of the other victuals was biled in de big old pots what swung on cranes over de coals. Dey had long-handled fryin' pans and heavy iron skillets wid big, thick, tight-fittin' lids, and ovens of all sizes to bake in. All of dem things was used right dar in de fireplace. Dere never was no better tastin' sompin t' eat dan dat cooked in dem old cook-things in open fireplaces.[28]

Many slaves did much of their cooking in a large three-legged black pot nicknamed "the spider."

In general, both the black people of the quarters and the white authorities took care to insure that the cabins were clean and sanitary. On his South Carolina plantation, ex-Governor James H. Hammond scheduled elaborate spring and fall house cleanings. "The houses were to be emptied and their contents sunned, the wall and floors were to be scrubbed, the mattresses to be emptied and stuffed with fresh hay or shucks, the yard swept and the ground under the house sprinkled with lime. Furthermore, every house was to be whitewashed inside and out once a year. . . . "[29] Basil Hall, a widely traveled Englishman who visited the United States in 1827 and 1828, observed that the cottages of the quarters were "uncommonly neat and comfortable, and might have shamed those of many countries I have seen."[30] Though there were many exceptions (as on the Butler Island plantation of Fanny Kemble's husband, where she described the cabins as "filthy and wretched in the extreme"[31]) as a general rule the self-interest of both slave and owner prescribed that most cabins be clean and of crude comfort.

Near to their cabins many quarter residents cultivated a garden truck patch.[32] From his study of slavery in Kentucky, Ivan McDougle concludes that in Kentucky "as in Virginia, the slave was permitted to have a little 'truck-patch' of half an acre or more, where he could raise any crop that he desired. In Kentucky these small plots of ground were nearly always filled with sweet potatoes, tobacco and watermelons."[33] On some plantations slaves were allowed a chicken yard and sometimes even a pigsty.[34] According to Kate Stone, whose mother owned a cotton plantation in northeast Louisiana of over 150 slaves. "It was a very lazy 'cullud pusson' who did not raise chickens and have eggs."[35] Many slaves also owned their own dogs.[36]

Besides household cabins the quarters of the large plantations often contained a number of work houses—a tannery, wash house, smithy—a "children's house" or "nursery," a "sick house," and a bachelor quarters where unmarried males lived together.[37] Many contemporary descriptions of such quarters relate that they gave the appearance of a "thriving little village."[38] Ben Brown lived as a slave for more than twenty-five years on a large Virginia plantation where "De log cabins what we live in on both sides de path make it look like a town."[39] On some plantations the quarter cabins were arranged in a circle. Clayton Holbert recalls that he and the other slaves on a large plantation in Tennessee "usually had a house of their own for their families. They usually built their houses in a circle, so you didn't have to go out the door hardly to go to the house next to you."[40] Harriet McFarlin, who was the slave of Colonel Jesse Chaney in both Texas and Arkansas, gave this description of the slave quarters to her interviewer:

> Colonel Chaney had lots and lots of slaves, and all their houses were in a row, all one-room cabins. Everything happened in that one room—birth, death, and everything, but in them days niggers kept their houses clean and their door yards too. These houses where they lived was called "quarters." I used to love to walk down by that row of houses. It looked like a town, and late of an evening as you'd go by the doors you could smell meat a-frying, coffee making and good things cooking.[41]

Not all quarters, to be sure, were this neat and orderly. On some plantations the slave cabins were put up without plan, whenever the need arose and no attempt was made to give them a neat appearance.

It was in a physical setting such as this, within their mother's cabin, that the children of the quarters were born. Attended at first by only an experienced slave midwife, it was not long before they became a part of the natural commotion and human interaction of a household which sheltered, fed, slept, and provided for many of the human needs and wants of any number of individual slaves. Although the census records show that an average of between five and six slaves occupied slave cabins, quarter children at birth often became part of a household circle that contained, besides their parents and siblings, grandparents, aunts, uncles, cousins, and adopted children whose parents had died or been sold, or who had themselves been sold. John Brown, who was born on a large Virginia plantation where his mother was a fieldhand, reports, for instance, that his household included his mother, her three "natural children," and her three stepchildren, and his cousin and her children in a second room.[42]

Whatever the living arrangements of her cabin home, for the first few weeks the newborn slave child was the center of attention and concern. On most plantations the baby's mother was allowed from two weeks' to a month's "lying-in time" during which she was permitted to rest from her work in the fields and devote her time entirely to her new child. For the first seven days the child and her mother, on many plantations, were attended frequently by the midwife.[43] Depending on plantation rule and regulation, the child's father was allowed to visit his wife and child as soon as news of the arrival carried to the fields.

The day after delivery, if it was fairly clear that the baby was a healthy one, a stream of friends and relations would come to congratulate the mother, meet the new member, and issue judgement upon his health, beauty (or lack of it) and possible future. Thus, for example, a child born with a caul, "a veil over his face," might be thought to be gifted with the ability to see haunts and spirits.[44] A child born with a long or a large head might be marked to become a wise man.[45]

In addition, the new baby might receive a visit from the overseer, the mistress of the great house, or from the master himself checking out his new property. Sometimes, though infrequently, the white slaveowner named new quarter babies. Most often slaves were named by their parents, usually after an immediate family member or a member of an enlarged blood-kin group.[46] The date of the quarter child's birth was marked by the seasons or some important event. "Children often ask their parents their age," writes Henry Watson, who was born a slave in Virginia in 1813. "The answer is, 'this planting corn time you are six, eight or ten,' just as it may happen to be. . . ."[47]

Thus, the first weeks of the child's life brought him in contact with many of the prominent plantation personalities, both white and black, and were, by and large, weeks of peaceful companionship with his mother during the day and playful interaction with other family members at night. Well wrapped in a blanket and kept warm in a cradle before the fire or in his mother's bed; well fed from his mother's milk; and well cared for by any number of family members whose own sleep and peace depended on his quiet contentment, his life was a continual round of eating, sleeping, and physical comforting.

After the month or so of lying-in time was over and her mother returned to full-time work in the fields, the new child was most often cared for during the day at the plantation nursery. At the nursery the children of the quarters were tended by one or two women too old to work in the fields who were assisted by the older brothers and sisters of the infants. If a child had no older siblings mature enough to care for her, one of her older cousins was often appointed to the job.[48] On some plantations the general supervision of the nursery would be placed in the hands of some younger woman who had displayed a talent or an interest in the job. Occasionally, if an infant had a grandmother whose work days had passed, she would be cared for at her grandparents' cabin.

The actual nursery building (or "nurse house" or "chilluns' house") was an enlarged cabin that contained most often both a sleeping room and a room for playing and eating.[49] In the sleeping room, rows of cradles were arranged for the infants too young to crawl around on the floor or outside in the yard. Outside there was usually a fenced-in yard where the toddlers could crawl in safety. Often during the hot days of summer, the cradles would be placed outdoors in the shade. The number of children cared for at the nursery varied according to the size of the plantation's slave population. On the typical large plantation the proportion of nonworking children to the rest of the slave population seems to have varied around thirty-three percent.[50]

Whether he was being cared for at the nursery, at his grandparents' cabin, or in his own home by one of his older sisters or brothers, the child's mother would be released from work to come and suckle him two or three times during the work day. On most plantations the nursing schedule allowed a feeding in the morning before the mother left for the fields, another about ten, a third at lunch time around twelve, a fourth at three, and a fifth upon mother's return from the fields at dark.[51] Most quarter mothers suckled their children for at least a year and often longer. Amanda McCray, who grew up a slave on the large Florida plantation of Redding Parnell, recalls that, "It was a common occurrence to see a child of two or three years still nursing at the mother's breast."[52]

On those occasions when work was being done in fields too far away from the quarters to permit quick travel between field and nursery, suckling babies would often be carried to the fields, where they would be left in the shade at the end of the row, secured in a hammock-like cradle between two trees, or wrapped securely upon their mother's backs.[53] Jeff Bailey, an ex-slave from Arkansas, recounts being told that as a baby he was carried to the fields where, while he was sleeping in the cotton basket, all the cotton would be placed in the basket around him.[54]

As the black child was weaned, her mother's milk was supplemented with cow's or goat's milk and "the liquor from boiled cabbage, and bread and milk together."[55] The older children who were still too young to work would be served lunch and sometimes breakfast at the nursery, or at the "cook house." The fare consisted chiefly of whatever was being prepared to be carried to the fieldhands.[56] A picture of meals at one quarter cook house is provided by William L. Dunwoody, who was born a slave in South Carolina in the year 1840:

> After the old folks among the slaves had had their breakfast, the cook would blow a horn. That would be about nine o'clock or eight. All the children that were big enough would come to the cook shack. Some of them would bring small children that had been weaned but couldn't look after themselves. The cook would serve them whatever the old folks had for breakfast. They ate out of the same kind of dishes as the old folks.
> Between ten and eleven o'clock, the cook would blow the horn again and the children would come in from play. There would be a large bowl and a large spoon for each group of larger children. There would be enough in each group to get around the bowl comfortably. One would take a spoonful of what was in the bowl and then pass the spoon to his neighbor. His neighbor would take a spoonful and then pass the spoon and so on until everyone would have a spoonful. Then they would begin again, and so on until the bowl was empty. If they did not have enough then, the cook would put some more in the bowl. Most of the time, bread and milk was in the bowl; sometimes mush and milk. There was a small spoon and a small bowl for the smaller children in the group which the big children would use for them and pass around just like they passed around the big spoon.
> About two or three o'clock, the cook would blow the horn again. Time the children all got in there and et, it would be four or five o'clock. The old mammy would cut up the greens real fine and cut up meat into little pieces and boil it with cornmeal dumplings. They'd call it the pepper pot. Then she'd put some of the pepper pot into the bowls and we'd eat it. And it was good.[57]

Lunsford Lane, who was the slave of William Helm in Prince County, Virginia, remembers how greedily he and his friends fell upon the pot-liquor and corn-meal balls that had been mixed together, poured into a large common tray, and served to them in the middle of the yard.[58] In the Georgia quarters where Malhalia Shores grew up on the plantation of Jim Jackson, the children did not eat out of a common tray. "We had our plates and cup and took it to the pot and they put some victuals in 'em, then we went and et where we pleased."[59] The younger children in many quarters ate with their hands. The older ones used clam, oyster, or mussel shells, spoons whittled from wood, gourds, or pewter spoons if they were provided with them.[60] Fanny Kemble noticed that many of the children, and older folks, often ate and talked "squatting down upon their hams."[61]

Besides their regular food fare, many children were given various ingredients to make them grow strong and healthy. The favorite elixir of the quarter community seems to have been different kinds of herbal teas, although garlic and asefetida were used commonly also. Charlie King and his brothers and sisters who lived on the large plantation of John King in Merriwether County, Georgia, started every day with a swig of burnt whiskey.[62] Many children were also adorned with charms and greegrees to ward off diseases.

The clothing of most quarter children was a single garment made of varying types of cloth which fitted like a long shirt reaching to the ankles. "Boys until they got up large enough to work wore little slips," relates a Fisk informant. "We called them shirts; they'd sew it up like a sack and cut a hole in the neck for your head to go through, and you wore that till you were ten or twelve years old. There was not much difference in the dress of girls and boys."[63] Robert Anderson's clothes during childhood in Green County, Maryland, were typical of those worn by many slave children.

> The clothes that I wore did not amount to much, just a one piece dress or gown. In shape this was more like a gunny sack, with a hole cut out in the bottom for me to stick my head through, and the corners cut out for arm holes. We never wore underclothes, not even in the winter, and a boy was ten or twelve years old before he was given a pair of pants and a shirt to replace the sack garment. We never had more than one at a time, and when they had to be washed we went naked until they had dried. When the garment had been worn until it would no longer hold together, or hold a patch, it was discarded and cut up for carpet rags, and another garment handed out. When one·child outgrew a gown it was handed down to someone smaller. The fit was immaterial, because there was no shape to these one piece garments, other than that of a sack. Sometimes old sacks were used to make these garments for the smaller children. One of these garments was made to last a year, and sometimes longer.[64]

Perhaps the chief complaint made against these shirts by the slaves was that when first worn their coarseness scratched and irritated the skin. Charles Lucas, who was raised in Loudon County, Virginia, recalls being "kept mostly at the quarters until twelve or thirteen, wearing nothing in the summer but a course crocus shirt. Many a time have I taken it by the two ends, and pulled it round a post to break down the sticks."[65]

In the cold weather of winter some quarter children put on two of these gowns if two were to be had. Occasionally a child was lucky enough to own a yarn undershirt or some yarn drawers which buttoned down over the knees to ward off the cold.[66] Plantation authorities rarely handed out shoes for children. "On frosty mornin's when I went to de spring to fetch a bucket of water," recollects Will Sheets, "you could see my feet tracks in de frost all de way dar and back."[67] Hats for children were also an infrequently indulged luxury, though they were sometimes fashioned by a skillful friend or relative from bullrushes or the bark of trees.[68] In general, plantation owners left it to quarter parents to clothe those children too young to work. "Little children," as one former slave recalls somewhat bitterly, "wore what their parents put on them."[69] In most quarters the clothes were washed on Wednesdays or Saturdays. In Alabama where Mingo White spent much of his childhoood, "Wash day was on Wednesday. My mammy would have to take de clothes about three-quarters of a mile to de branch where de washin' was to be done. She didn't have no washboard like dey have nowdays. She had a paddle what she beat de clothes with. Everybody knowed when wash day was 'cause dey could hear de paddle for about three or four mile. 'Pow-pow-pow,' dats how it sound."[70]

As the children of the quarters were weaned and began to crawl and toddle about, they spent much of their time playing with the other black children of the nursery. On many plantations the quarters contained a fenced-in yard where the children could play in safety.[71] Their activities depended greatly upon the energy and inclination of the older children or "nurses" watching them. At the nursery of a South Carolina rice plantation Olmsted observed "a number of girls, eight or ten years old . . . occupied in holding and tending the youngest infants. Those a little older—the crawlers—were in the pen, and those big enough to toddle were playing on the steps, or before the house. Some of these, with two or three bigger ones, were singing and dancing about a fire they had made on the ground. . . . I watched for half an hour, and in all that time not a baby of them began to cry; nor have I ever heard one, at two or three other plantation-nurseries which I have visited."[72]

Occasionally a nursery teacher would organize an imaginative routine of games and activities for her children. Susan Eppes, whose father owned a large Florida plantation of over three hundred slaves, tells of one such woman, Aunt Dinah, who ran her nursery "like the kindergarten of today" and whose "inventive brain kept the children always busy." She told stories, demonstrated how animals could be made from potatoes, orange thorns, and a few feathers, and helped her pupils "set table" with mats made of the green leaves of the jonquil, cups and saucers of acorns, dishes of hickory hulls and any gay bit of china they could find; and had them bake mud pies in a broken stove. She also helped them dress up as flowers and taught them to make decorations with chains of china blossoms and long strings of chinquapins. She even encouraged them to catch "Mammy Doddles" and terrapins to be kept in the nursery as pets.[73]

In most nurseries, however, the children, especially the older ones, were left to their own devices. Their time was spent largely playing among themselves and roaming through the fields and woods of the plantation.

Whatever their activities during the day, upon the return of the older folks from the fields, the children would return to their own cabins for the evening meal. Evening chores were begun while supper was being prepared; the younger children would gather fuel for the fire and bring in water from the well. In Sam Aleckson's quarters, as in many, there was a spring between the big house and the quarters from which the slaves got their drinking water. "Every afternoon a long line of children might have been seen with 'piggins' on their heads, taking in the supply for the night."[74] An ex-slave of the Fisk survey recalls going "to the spring to get water, with a bucket on top of my head, and one in each hand."[75] At least one of the older girls usually helped with the cooking and the other children worked in the truck patch.

After dinner, which in the summer would often be cooked and eaten outside around a fire, other chores were completed. Children of both sexes helped with washing, sewing, repairing furniture, and working in the garden. Often children were called upon to help their mother with the spinning. Fannie Moore, an ex-slave from South Carolina, recalls helping her mother spin enough thread every night to make the four cuts required by the white folks.

Why sometime I never go to bed. Have to hold de light for her to see by. She have to piece quilts for the white folks too. Why, dey is a scar on my arm yet where my brother let de pine drip on me. Rich pine was all de light we ever had. My brother was a-holdin' de pine so's I can help mammy tack the quilt and he go to sleep and let it drop.[76]

Henry Cheatam, who was born a slave in 1830 near West Point, Mississippi, relates how he and his brothers and sisters would take off their "one-piece suit made outen ausenberg" and wash it and sleep while it dried.[77] Often children themselves were washed at night in big wooden wash tubs. Randel Lee, who lived as a slave in South Carolina, remembers how after a bath he "would sit a few minutes with his feet held to the fire so they could dry," as his mother rubbed "grease under the soles of his feet to keep him from taking cold."[78] The children's hair was usually combed with the card that was used for spinning. "That wouldn't get the lice out, but it would make it feel better. They had to use larkspur to get 'em out; that would always get the lice out of your head."[79]

On pleasant evenings after the chores had been completed, the older children were often allowed by their parents to play outside or to visit the cabins of their friends.[80] Frank Gill remembers how the people of his Mississippi quarters put "a big light out in de backyard" so that the children could play together at night.[81] Often the children sat around listening as the entire community brought their benches and chairs outside and sat around telling stories and singing songs. Occasionally, the older children, if they were considered mature enough to be trusted, were allowed to participate in the more clandestine nocturnal activities of the quarter community. Often the older male children, and sometimes the girls, accompanied their elders on moonlit hunting and fishing expeditions. As they grew older still, quarter children began attending their community's feasts of stolen food prepared deep in the woods, unsanctioned dances, voodoo ceremonies, and meetings of the clandestine congregation.

Most especially, nights were times of quiet family pleasures. Separated from their children for the entire, long workday, quarter parents took advantage of the night to play with and talk to their children. Often children would lie in bed and listen to the old folks sing or tell stories as they worked or simply sat around the fire. Jack Island, an ex-slave from Arkansas, tells of watching the women spinning: " . . . ah'd lie dar a while an' watch 'em spin den ah'd go tuh sleep ergin, and leave 'em spinnin'!"[82] Davenport remembers how he and his brothers and sisters used to gather nuts in the woods and steal potatoes so their family could eat them at night. "At night when de work was all done and de candles was out us'd set 'round de fire and eat cracked nuts and 'taters. Us picked out de nuts with horseshoe nails and baked de 'taters in ashes. Den Mammy would pour herself and her old man a cup o' wine."[83]

In most slave cabins, especially in cold weather, the fireplace was the center of family gatherings. Mary Reynolds, an ex-slave from Louisiana, relates how the slaves would "bring in two-three big logs and put them on the fire, and they'd last a week."[84] Olmsted described the not untypical scene he witnessed on a Mississippi plantation:

During the evening, all the cabins were illuminated by great fires, and, looking into one of them, I saw a very picturesque family group: a man sat on the ground making a basket, a woman lounged on a chest in the chimney corner smoking a pipe, and a boy and two girls sat in a bed which had been drawn up opposite to her, completing the fireside circle. They were talking and laughing cheerfully.[85]

Sometimes if it was very cold the entire household might sit around the fire the entire night. "De 'possum in his hollow, de squirrel in his nest, and de rabbit in his bed, is at home," observes Charles Davis of South Carolina. "So de nigger, in a tight house with a big hot fire, in winter, is at home, too."[86]

On most nights those slaves who had beds slept in them and those who had no beds slept on straw in front of the fire. One white observer wrote that slaves invariably would sleep "with the head to the fire. They will wrap their blankets around the head and the shoulders, or creep, head foremost into a bag or sack. . . ."[87] In many quarter cabins the small baby's cradle was placed in front of the fire at night. In others, it was the custom for children from one to three years of age to sleep in the big bed with their parents or one of the other grown-ups.[88] Dosia Harris of Georgia recalls that though many children slept on the floor she slept in a bed with her grandma.[89] Often one big bed would be built for all the children, who would sleep in it "crosswise." "It was plum' full in cold weather."[90]

Sundays and holidays were also times when the children of the quarters could participate in, or observe, family and community activities or merely play with their friends and relatives. On many plantations the children were not required to attend either the Sabbath schools or the worship services organized by the plantation whites for their slaves. Charles Colcock Jones, a white Presbyterian minister, lamented that "Negro children do not enjoy the advantages of a preached gospel; for the custom is, where no effort is made to alter it, for the children to remain at home on the Sabbath."[91] On some plantations the children did attend the white organized church services with their parents and many children attended Sabbath schools established especially for them.

Besides church, the Sunday activities of most quarters involved singing and story-telling, various games and athletic contests, and visiting among friends and relatives. For children with fathers who lived on neighboring plantations Sunday was especially important as the one day father was most certain to be able to visit.

Holidays, especially Christmas, crop-lying-in-time, the Fourth of July, and Easter were also times of family and community interaction which provided special meaning and excitement for quarter children. It was during evenings, Sundays, and holidays that the children of the quarters became acquainted with the structure, the style, and the leading personalities of their quarter community. Through their common experiences they learned the ways in which their community operated, how it made common decisions, planned secretive events, provided for common physical and recreational needs, and generally organized itself to be as independent as possible from the whims of the white personalities and the strictures of plantation rule and regulation.

Looking back on their childhood experiences, many of the men and women of the slave narratives cite the period up to the time when they were forced to become an institutionalized part of the white man's work force as the happiest time in their lives under slavery. Indeed, it is not uncommon for one of the autobiographers to recall that he was six, eight, or even fourteen before he began to realize the ramifications of what it might mean to be a slave. Frederick Douglass was seven before he had his "first introduction to the realities of the slave system."[92] Sam Aleckson was seven or eight, and it took the sale of his mother and two sisters before it dawned on him that his condition was not as good as that of any boy in the country. "With kind parents, two sweet little sisters, and every boyish wish gratified, the improbability of my succession to the presidential chair never once occurred to me."[93] J. Vance Lewis writes of his childhood in Louisiana: "As a barefoot boy my stay upon the farm had been pleasant. I played among the wild flowers and wandered in high glee over hill and hollow, enchanted with the beauty of nature, and knew not that I was a slave and the son of a slave."[94] Lunsford Lane offers the following testimony:

> On the 30th of May, 1803, I was ushered into the world; but I did not begin to see the rising of its dark clouds, nor fancy how they might be broken and dispersed until some time afterwards. My infancy was spent upon the floor, in a rough cradle, or sometimes in my mother's arms. My early boyhood in playing with other boys and girls, colored and white, in the yard, and occasionally doing such little matters of labor as one of so young years could. I knew no difference between myself and the white children; nor did they seem to know any in turn.[95]

This is not to suggest, however, that all, or even most, quarter children experienced idyllic childhoods. Besides the fights, cruel jokes, mishaps and punishments experienced within the quarters itself, the reality of life within the larger context of the white-controlled slave population touched most children and clouded even the most carefree of childhoods. Although direct contact with whites was infrequent for the child born and raised in the quarters, it was sometimes marked by harsh interaction. A. J. Mitchell recalls that when his master, Jack Clifton of Arkansas, was displeased with any of the children, he would "make us younguns put our head 'tween his legs and put that strap on us."[96] Often the relationship between the children of the quarters and the children of the white household was less than the harmonious one described by Lane. On the Maryland plantation where James Pennington lived as a slave child the "tyranny" of his master's two sons "early embittered" his life. Not only were James and his older brother "required to recognize these young sirs as our masters, but they felt themselves to be such; and in consequence of this feeling, they sought to treat us with the same air of authority that their father did the older slaves."[97] Pennington also describes the tyranny and abuse of the overseers. "These men seem to look with an evil eye upon children. . . . They seem to take pleasure in torturing the children of slaves, long before they are old enough to be put at the hoe, and consequently under the whip."[98]

Some slaves experienced a sudden traumatic event which directly touched their child-hoods. Douglass was taken from his beloved grandmother.[99] Charlotte Martin's brother was whipped to death for taking part in a series of secret religious ceremonies.[100] Josiah Henson saw his father appear one day with a bloody head and a lacerated back. "His right ear had been cut off close to his head, and he had received a hundred lashes on his back. He had beaten the overseer for a brutal assault on my mother, and this was his punishment."[101] William Wells Brown remembers watching his mother being whipped for tardiness in going to the fields and how "the cold chills ran over me, and I wept aloud."[102] Other children saw their friends divested of a finger for attempting to learn to read, escapees tortured, and grandparents put off the plantation and told by the white authorities to fend for themselves.

Despite these "darker clouds" which overcast the early childhood years, few slave children seem to have realized the full significance of their slave status until their slave training began in earnest. On many large plantations those children destined to become fieldhands were left to grow strong and healthy until between the ages of ten and fourteen.[103] H. C. Bruce asserts that the custom in Virginia was not to put young blacks to work in the field before they had reached age thirteen.[104] On the South Carolina plantation where Peter Clifton grew up the rule for the older slaves was: " 'Wake up de slaves at daylight, begin work when they can see, and quit work when they can't see.' But they was careful of de rule dat say: 'you mustn't work a child, under twelve years old, in de field.' "[105] Sally remarked that "It is policy to leave the slaves to grow and strengthen, unfatigued by labor, until they are old enough to be constantly occupied, as a colt is left unshackled, with free range of the pastures, until the 'break-in' time comes."[106]

Many planters did, however, begin the "breaking" process before the slave child was strong enough to do a full-hand's work. Most quarter children between the ages of six and ten were given miscellaneous chores around the plantation. They tended sheep, milked cows, gathered firewood, toted water, helped with the cooking, assisted at the nursery, swept the yard, ran errands, and generally did whatever little jobs were needed done from moment to moment. Henry Johnson, who was raised "all over the state of Virginia," recalls that "when I was a little bit of a fellow, I used to pack water to twenty-five and thirty men in one field, den go back to de house and bring enough water for breakfast de next morning. When I got a little bigger, I had to take a little hoe and dig weeds out of de crop."[107] Tom Baker of Alabama also describes the work of a water boy:

> I was a water boy for fifty fiel' han's dat worked in de sun all day long, an' I hadda carry many a bucket from de spring. It was a long walk—one fiel' ober from where most of dem was workin'. De spring run down between some willow trees an' it was powerful cool down dere in de shade. I use to lie on da moss an' let my bare belly git cool an' put my face in de outlet of de spring an' let de water trickle over my haid. Jus' about the time I get a little rest one of dem niggers would call:"Water boy! Bring dat bucket!" Den I grab up de bucket an' run back out in de hot sun."[108]

On what appears to have been a minority of plantations, children were given jobs to keep them busy most of the time. Jacob Branch of Texas recounts that he and the other children of his quarters were put to work as soon as they could toddle. "First us gather firewood. Iffen it freezin' or not us have to go to toughen us up. When us get l'il bigger us tend de cattle and feed hosses and hogs. By time us good sprouts us pickin' cotton and pullin' cane. Us ain't never idle."[109] Booker T. Washington, who grew up in Franklin County, Virginia, asserts with a touch of sadness that there was no period in his life that was devoted to play.

> From the time that I can remember anything, almost every day of my life has been occupied in some kind of labor; though I think I would now be a more useful man if I had had time for sports. During the period that I spent in slavery I was not large enough to be of much service, still I was occupied most of the time in cleaning the yards, carrying water to the men in the fields, or going to the mill, to which I used to take the corn, once a week, to be ground.[110]

Usually between the ages of ten and fourteen young blacks were forced to begin actual field work, though at first they were assigned special tasks. On the Mississippi plantation where Louis Hughes worked as a slave, children between the ages of nine and twelve, and women still suckling infants, were given the job of gathering the first bales of cotton from the lower part of the stalk where it opened months before the rest was ready for picking.[111] On tobacco plantations one of the principal jobs of the younger children was to pick worms off the tobacco leaves.[112]

As they grew older and stronger, children of the fields would be given regular but smaller tasks. Olmsted observed that all fieldhands "are divided into four classes, according to their physical capacities. The children beginning as 'quarter-hands,' advancing to 'half-hands,' and then to 'three-quarter hands'; and finally, when mature and able-bodied, healthy and strong, to 'full-hands.' "[113] Henry Waldon, describing how he and his sister worked one row on a Mississippi plantation, explains that "The two of us made a hand."[114] On many plantations an older fieldhand was assigned to teach the children how to do field work. Clayton Holbert relates that on the plantation in Tennessee where he learned to work as a fieldhand, "They always had a man in the field to teach the small boys to work, and I was one of the boys."[115] Andrew Moss, who received his slave training in Georgia, remembers how he was taught to stack his hoe at the end of the day's work and to chop with a little hoe which had a handle about the length of his arm. "I've walked many a mile, when I was a little feller, up and down de rows, followin' de grown folks, and chopping with de hoe round de corners where de earth was soft so de little 'uns could hoe easily."[116] Mary Reynolds tells how she held the hoe very unsteadily when an old woman was first put in charge of teaching the children of her Louisiana plantation how to "scrape the fields." "That old woman would be frantic. She'd show me and then turn 'bout to show some other little nigger, and I'd have the young corn cut clean as the grass. She'd say, 'For the love of God, you better larn it right, or Solomon will beat the breath out of you body.' Old Man Solomon was the nigger driver."[117]

By the time they had become full-fledged fieldhands, the young blacks of the quarters, whatever their individual childhood experiences, came face to face with the stark reality that the white world held them as slaves, and intended to use its power to make them behave like ones. "When I began to work," writes Lunsford Lane, "I discovered the difference between myself and my master's white children. They began to order me about, and were told to do so by my master and mistress. . . . indeed all things now made me *feel,* what I had before known only in words, *that I was a slave.* Deep was this feeling, and it preyed upon my heart like a never dying worm."[118] Many young slaves, like Frederick Douglass, began "to inquire into the origin and nature of slavery. Why are some people slaves and others masters?"[119]

How individual slaves answered these questions depended greatly upon their own unique personalities and upon the nature of the experiences and personal interactions they had encountered in the plantation environment. In drawing their own personal conclusions, however, most slaves were not left entirely to their own devices. Both the white society and the quarter community had a great stake in their answers and had long since deliberately begun to attempt to influence the nature of the values, attitudes, and understandings with which slaves struggled—both to understand themselves and to make sense of the world in which they lived.

Notes

1. In some quarter communities, probably the exceptions, the older children would be allowed to visit neighboring plantations. Older slaves and to some extent young house servants had greater intercourse with people and places off the home plantation.

2. Frederick Law Olmsted, *A Journey in the Seaboard Slave States, with Remarks on Their Economy* (New York: Dix and Edwards, 1856), p. 111.

3. Julia E. Harn, "Old Canoochee-Ogeechee Chronicles," Georgia Historical Chronicles, XVI (June, 1932), 149. This desire on the part of the slaves often fitted right in with the desires of their owners who did not wish to have the noise and structures of the quarters spoil the peace and beauty of the great house. The houses of the house servants were often whitewashed and closer to the

great house, "so the white folks," according to one ex-slave, "could get to them easy if they wanted them; and they had to have it that way to keep from spoiling the looks of the big house." Fisk Collection, *Unwritten History of Slavery; Autobiographical Account of Negro Ex-Slaves* (Nashville: Social Science Institute, Fisk University, 1945). (Hereafter noted as Fisk, *Unwritten. . . .*)

4. Genovese says that by the 1850's the great majority of slave cabins were at least sixteen by eighteen feet and housed on the average five to six slaves. Eugene D. Genovese, *Roll, Jordan, Roll: The World the Slaves Made* (New York: Pantheon Books, 1974), p. 524.

5. James Battle Avirett, *The Old Plantation: How We Lived in the Great House and Cabin Before the War* (New York: F. Tennyson Neeley, 1901), p. 46. Avirett, an Episcopalian minister, grew up on his father's large North Carolina plantation.

6. Fisk, *Unwritten* . . . , p. 10.

7. Ralph Betts Flanders, *Plantation Slavery in Georgia* (Chapel Hill: The University of North Carolina Press, 1933), p. 152.

8. Louis Hughes, *Thirty Years a Slave: From Bondage to Freedom. The Institution of Slavery as Seen on the Plantation and in the House of the Planter* (Milwaukee: M. E. Haferkorn, 1897), pp. 25–26.

9. Charley Williams in Rawick, ed., Oklahoma, VII(1), p. 334.

10. Austen Steward, *Twenty-two Years a Slave and Forty Years a Freeman, Embracing a Correspondence of Several Years While President of the Wilberforce Colony* (Rochester, New York: W. Alling, 1857), p. 13.

11. Margaret Nillin in Rawick, ed., Texas, V(3), p. 152.

12. Austin Penn Parnell in Rawick, ed., Arkansas, X(5), pp. 263–64.

13. Norman R. Yetman, ed., *Life Under the "Peculiar Institution": Selections from the Slave Narrative Collection* (New York: Holt, Rinehart and Winston, 1970), p. 52.

14. Fisk, *Unwritten* . . . , p. 13.

15. Jaspar Battle in Rawick, ed., Georgia, XII(1), p. 63.

16. Alec Pope in Rawick, ed., Georgia, XIII(3), p. 172.

17. Georgia Baker in Rawick, ed., Georgia, XII(1), p. 39.

18. Olmsted, p. 111.

19. Jacob Stroyer, *Sketches of My Life in the South* (Salem: Newcombe and Gauss, 1898), pp. 44–45.

20. William Brown in Rawick, ed., Arkansas, VIII(1), p. 320. See also Hattie Ann Nettles in Rawick, ed., Alabama, VI, p. 297.

21. Celeste Avery in Rawick, ed., Georgia, XII(1), p. 22.

22. Cull Taylor in Rawick, ed., Alabama, VI, p. 364.

23. Addie Vinson in Rawick, ed., Georgia, XIII(4), p. 99.

24. Fisk, *Unwritten* . . . , p. 33.

25. Willis Dukes in Rawick, ed., Florida, XVII, p. 121. Also, Isaam Morgan in Rawick, ed., Alabama, VI, p. 283.

26. Julia E. Haney in Rawick, ed., Arkansas, IX(3), p. 152.

27. Yetman, p. 267.

28. Benny Dillard in Rawick, ed., Georgia, XII(1), p. 289.

29. Ulrich B. Phillips, *American Negro Slavery: A Survey of the Supply, Employment and Control of Negro Labor as Determined by the Plantation Regime* (Baton Rouge: Louisiana State University Press, 1966), p. 267.

30. Captain Basil Hall, *Travels in North America, in the Years 1827 and 1828*, Vol. 3, Third edition (Edinburgh: Robert Cadell, 1830), p. 181.

31. Frances Anne Kemble, *Journal of a Residence on a Georgia Plantation in 1838–1839* (New York: Alfred A. Knopf, 1961), p. 69. (Originally published in 1863.)

32. See, for example, Victoria Clayton, *White and Black under the Old Regime* (Milwaukee: The Young Churchman Company, 1899), p. 22.

33. Ivan E. McDougle, *Slavery in Kentucky 1792–1865* (Westport, Connecticut: Negro Universities Press, 1970), p. 73. (Originally published in 1918.)

34. See Phillips, *American Negro Slavery* . . . , p. 253.

35. Sarah Katherine Stone Holmes, *Brokenburn: The Journal of Kate Stone 1861–1868,* ed. John Q. Anderson (Baton Rouge: Louisiana State University Press, 1955), p. 6.

36. See Genovese, *Roll, Jordan, Roll . . .* , p. 488.

37. Shade Richards in Rawick, ed., Georgia, xIII(3), p. 203.

38. Sam Aleckson, *Before the War and after the Union. An Autobiography* (Boston: Gold Mind Publishing Company, 1929), p. 28. See also Kemp Plummer Battle, *Memories of an Old-Time Tar Heel* (Chapel Hill: University of North Carolina Press, 1945), p. 121. Henry James Trentham in Rawick, ed., N. Carolina, xIV, p. 364.

39. Ben Brown in Rawick, ed., Ohio, xVI, p. 11.

40. Clayton Holbert in Rawick, ed., Kansas, xVI, p. 2.

41. B. A. Botkin, ed., *Lay My Burden Down: A Folk History of Slavery* (Chicago: University of Chicago Press, 1945), pp. xi–xii.

42. John Brown, *Slave Life in Georgia: A Narrative of the Life, Sufferings, and Escape of John Brown, a Fugitive Slave, Now in England* (London: W. M. Watts, 1855), p. 2. Brown's father lived on a neighboring plantation.

43. Phillips, *American Negro Slavery . . .* , p. 264. A high mortality rate for both whites and blacks was a fact of life, although the slave rate does seem to have been significantly higher than that of whites. See Kenneth M. Stampp, *The Peculiar Institution: Slavery in the Ante-Bellum South* (New York: Vintage Books, 1956), pp. 318–21.

44. Works Projects Administration, *Drums and Shadows: Survival Studies among the Georgia Coastal Negroes* (Athens: University of Georgia Press, 1940), p. 29. (Hereafter noted WPA, *Drums and Shadows. . . .*)

45. Duncan Gaines in Rawick, ed., Florida, xVII, p. 136.

46. See Herbert G. Gutman, *The Black Family in Slavery and Freedom 1750–1925* (New York: Pantheon Books, 1976), pp. 185–201. From his study of the slave family Gutman concludes that slaves named their children most frequently after father, dead siblings, grandparents, aunts and uncles, and sometimes great-aunts and great-uncles, in that order. Whereas sons, especially first or second born, frequently had their father's name, daughters almost never had the name of their mother. Gutman also suggests, on admittedly inconclusive data, that grandparents may have played a prominent role in the naming process.

For a discussion of how slaves blended names of African origins with anglicized versions, see Genovese, *Roll, Jordan, Roll,* pp. 449–50.

47. Henry Watson, *Narrative of Henry Watson, a Fugitive Slave. Written by Himself* (Boston: Bela Marsh, 1848), p. 5. See also, H. C. Bruce, *The New Man: Twenty-nine Years a Slave, Twenty-nine Years a Free Man. Recollections of H. C. Bruce* (York, Pa.: P. Anstadt and Sons, 1895), p. 11.

48. Yetman, p. 104. Sometimes, though infrequently, the children would be tended by an older man as in Harry Smith's quarters where the little slaves were "raised and nursed by an old colored negro, named Uncle Paul." Harry Smith, *Fifty Years of Slavery in the United States of America* (Grand Rapids, Michigan: Western Michigan Printing Company, 1891), p. 34.

49. For a description of typical nurse houses see: Estella Jones in Rawick, ed., Georgia, xII(2), p. 346; and Hughes, p. 44.

50. This estimate has been made from statistics of particular plantations given in the following sources: Phillips, *American Negro Slavery . . .* , p. 230, 244; Ulrich Bonnell Phillips and James David Glunt, eds., *Florida Plantation Records from the Papers of George Noble Jones* (St. Louis: Missouri Historical Society, 1927), pp. 538, 547–49, 556–71; Hall, Vol 3, p. 218; Olmsted, *Seaboard . . .* , pp. 57–58; and Mary Ross Banks, *Bright Days in the Old Plantation Time* (Boston: Lee and Shepard, 1882), pp. 143–44. Fogel and Engerman, using more comprehensive data, concur in this estimate at least for cotton plantations. See Robert William Fogel and Stanely Engerman, *Time on the Cross. The Economics of American Negro Slavery* (Boston: Little, Brown and Company, 1974), p. 42.

51. Dicey Thomas in Rawick, ed., Arkansas, x(6), pp. 290–92. Phillips reports that Hammond's rules allowed mothers "forty-five minutes at each nursing to be with their children. They return three times a day, until their children are eight months old—in the middle of the forenoon, at noon, and in the middle of the afternoon; till the twelfth month but twice a day, missing at noon; during the twelfth month at noon only. . . ." Phillips, *American Negro Slavery . . .* , p. 264.

52. Amanda McCray in Rawick, ed., Florida, xVII, p. 213. See also, Genovese, *Roll, Jordan, Roll . . .* , pp. 498–99.

53. Charles Ball, *Fifty Years in Chains* (New York: Dover Publications, 1970), p. 151. (Originally published in 1837.) John Thompson, *The Life of John Thompson, a Fugitive Slave: Containing His History of Twenty-five Years in Bondage, and His Providential Escape. Written by Himself* (Worcester: by the author, 1856), p. 17. Sara Colquitt in Rawick, ed., Alabama, VI, p. 87.

54. Jeff Bailey in Rawick, ed., Arkansas, VIII(1), p. 87.

55. Hughes, p. 43. Cornelia Robinson in Rawick, ed., Alabama, VI, p. 332.

56. On Hammond's plantation they were to have "hominy and milk and corn bread," for breakfast; "for dinner, vegetable soup and dumplings or bread; and cold bread or potatoes were kept on hand for demands between meals. They were also to have molasses once or twice a week. Each child was provided with a pan and spoon in charge of the nurse." Phillips, *American Negro Slavery . . .* , p. 226.

57. Yetman, p. 104. Ben Brown recalls the bread of his slave days: "Sometimes we got wheat bread, we called dat 'seldom bread' an' cohn bread was called 'common' becos we had it ev'ry day." Brown in Rawick, ed., Ohio, XVI, p. 11.

58. Lunsford Lane, *The Narrative of Lunsford Lane, Formerly of Raleigh, North Carolina* (Boston: by the author, 1842), p. 13.

59. Mahalia Shores in Rawick, ed., Arkansas, X(6), p. 155.

60. George Strickland in Rawick, ed., Alabama, VI, p. 359; Frank Cannon in Rawick, ed., Arkansas, VIII(2), p. 1; Estella Jones in Rawick, ed., Georgia, XII(2), p. 346.

61. Kemble, p. 64.

62. Charlie King in Rawick, ed., Georgia, XIII(3), p. 19.

63. Fisk, *Unwritten . . .* , p. 56.

64. Robert Anderson, *From Slavery to Affluence. Memoirs of Robert Anderson, Ex-Slave* (Steamboat Springs, Colorado: The Steamboat Pilot, 1927), p. 56.

65. Benjamin Drew, ed., *A North-Side View of Slavery, the Refugee: or the Narratives of Fugitive Slaves in Canada* (Boston: John P. Jewett, 1856), p. 105.

66. Yetman, p. 105.

67. Will Sheets in Rawick, ed., Georgia, XIII(3), p. 239. Often children wrapped their feet in bagging sacks to help keep warm. See Lewis Favor in Rawick, ed., Georgia, XII(2), p. 320.

68. Elisha Doc Garey in Rawick, ed., Georgia, XII(2), p. 4. John Cade, "Out of the Mouths of Ex-Slaves," *Journal of Negro History,* Vol. XX (1935), p. 298.

69. Fisk, *Unwritten . . .* , p. 255. For a notable exception to this general rule see Susan Smedes, *Memorials of a Southern Planter* (Baltimore: Cushings and Bailey, 1887).

70. Yetman, pp. 312–13.

71. Waters McIntosh in Rawick, ed., Arkansas, X(5), p. 20.

72. Olmsted, *Seaboard . . .* , pp. 424–25.

73. Susan Bradford Eppes, *The Negro of the Old South: A Bit of Period History* (Mason, Georgia: J. W. Burke, revised copyright, 1941), pp. 67–68.

74. Sam Aleckson, p. 77. A "piggin" was a wooden bucket.

75. Fisk, *Unwritten . . .* , p. 298.

76. Yetman, p. 227.

77. Henry Cheatam in Rawick, ed., Alabama, VI, p. 67.

78. Randel Lee in Rawick, ed., Florida, XVII, p. 199.

79. Fisk, *Unwritten . . .* , pp. 110, 115.

80. Georgia Baker in Rawick, ed., Georgia, XII(1), p. 46.

81. Frank Gill in Rawick, ed., Alabama, VI, p. 150.

82. Uncle Jack Island in Rawick, ed., Arkansas, IX(3), p. 380.

83. Yetman, p. 71.

84. Botkin, p. 121.

85. Frederick Law Olmsted, *A Journey in the Back Country* (London: Sampson Law, Son and Company, 1860), p. 142.

86. Charles Davis in Rawick, ed., South Carolina, II(1), p. 250.

87. Lewis W. Paine, *Six Years in a Georgia Prison. Narrative of Lewis W. Paine, Who Suffered Imprisonment Six Years in Georgia, for the Crime of Aiding the Escape of a Fellow-man from that State after He Had Fled from Slavery* (New York: for the author, 1851), p. 128. The feeling that the head

was the most important part of the body to keep warm was also noticed by Fanny Kemble, who observed that even on warm nights the babies were wrapped in swarthing with one or more caps on their heads but nothing on their feet. Kemble, pp. 69, 128.

88. Minnie Davis, in Rawick, ed., Georgia, xii(1), p. 254.

89. Dosia Harris in Rawick, ed., Georgia, xii (2), p. 105.

90. Allen Sims in Rawick, ed., Alabama, vi, p. 343; Malindy Maxwell in Rawick, ed., Arkansas, x (5), p. 59.

91. C. C. Jones, *The Religious Instruction of the Negroes in the United States* (New York: Negro University Press, 1969), pp. 114–15. (Originally published in 1842.) Charlie Smith's explanation for this occurrence on his plantation was that the older children needed to take care of the babies while the old folks were at church. Charlie Smith in Rawick, ed., Georgia, xiii (3), pp. 275–76.

92. Douglass, *Life and Times . . .* , p. 33.

93. Sam Aleckson, p. 113.

94. J. Vance Lewis, *Out of the Ditch: A True Story of an Ex-Slave, by J. Vance Lewis* (Houston: Rein and Company, 1910), p. 8.

95. Lane, pp. 2–3.

96. A. J. Mitchell in Rawick, ed., Arkansas, x(5), p. 104.

97. James W. C. Pennington, *The Fugitive Blacksmith; or, Events in the Life of James W. C. Pennington, Pastor of a Presbyterian Church, New York Formerly a Slave in the State of Maryland, United States,* Third Edition (Westport, Conn.: Negro University Press, 1971), p. 2. (Reprint of the 1850 edition.)

98. *Ibid.,* pp. 2–3.

99. Douglass, *Life and Times . . .* , pp. 30–33.

100. Charlotte Martin in Rawick, ed., Florida, xvii, p. 166.

101. Josiah Henson, *The Life of Josiah Henson, Formerly a Slave, Now an Inhabitant of Canada* (Boston: Arthur D. Phelps, 1849), p. 1.

102. William Wells Brown, *Narrative of William Wells Brown, a Fugitive Slave, Written by Himself* (Boston: Anti-Slavery Office, 1847), p. 16.

103. The training of house servants began much earlier.

104. Bruce, p. 24.

105. Yetman, p. 58.

106. Aunt Sally, *Aunt Sally; or, the Cross the Way to Freedom. A Narrative of the Slave-Life and Purchase of the Mother of Reverend Isaac Williams, of Detroit, Michigan* (Cincinnati: American Reform Tract and Book Society, 1858), p. 27.

107. Yetman, p. 182.

108. Tom Baker in Rawick, ed., Alabama, vi, p. 17.

109. Yetman, p. 40.

110. Booker T. Washington, *Up from Slavery* (New York: Dell, 1965), pp. 17–18. (Originally published in 1900.)

111. Hughes, p. 31.

112. John Brown, p. 12. James Davis in Rawick, ed., Arkansas, xiii(2), p. 109.

113. Olmsted, *Seaboard . . .* , p. 433.

114. Henry Waldon in Rawick, ed., Arkansas, xi (7), p. 16.

115. Clayton Holbert in Rawick, ed., Kansas, XVI, p. 1.

116. Yetman, p. 232.

117. Botkin, p. 120.

118. Lane, pp. 7–8.

119. Douglass, *Life and Times . . .* , p. 50.

14. The Female World of Love and Ritual: Relations between Women in Nineteenth-Century America

The female friendship of the nineteenth century, the long-lived, intimate, loving friendship between two women, is an excellent example of the type of historical phenomena which most historians know something about, which few have thought much about, and which virtually no one has written about.[1] It is one aspect of the female experience which consciously or unconsciously we have chosen to ignore. Yet an abundance of manuscript evidence suggests that eighteenth- and nineteenth-century women routinely formed emotional ties with other women. Such deeply felt, same-sex friendships were casually accepted in American society. Indeed, from at least the late eighteenth century through the mid-nineteenth century, a female world of varied and yet highly structured relationships appears to have been an essential aspect of American society. These relationships ranged from the supportive love of sisters, through the enthusiasms of adolescent girls, to sensual avowals of love by mature women. It was a world in which men made but a shadowy appearance.[2]

Defining and analyzing same-sex relationships involves the historian in deeply problematical questions of method and interpretation. This is especially true since historians, influenced by Freud's libidinal theory, have discussed these relationships almost exclusively within the context of individual psychosexual developments or, to be more explicit, psychopathology.[3] Seeing same-sex relationships in terms of a dichotomy between normal and abnormal, they have sought the origins of such apparent deviance in childhood or adolescent trauma and detected the symptoms of "latent" homosexuality in the lives of both those who later became "overtly" homosexual and those who did not. Yet theories concerning the nature and origins of same-sex relationships are frequently contradictory or based on questionable or arbitrary data. In recent years such hypotheses have been subjected to criticism both from within and without the psychological professions. Historians who seek to work within a psychological framework, therefore, are faced with two hard questions: Do sound psychodynamic theories concerning the nature and origins of same-sex relationships exist? If so, does the historical datum exist which would permit the use of such dynamic models?

I would like to suggest an alternative approach to female friendships—one which would view them within a cultural and social setting rather than from an exclusively individual pscyhosexual perspective. Only by thus altering our approach will we be in the position to evaluate the appropriateness of particular dynamic interpretations. Intimate

Carroll Smith-Rosenberg, "The Female World of Love and Ritual: Relations between Women in Nineteenth-Century America," reprinted from *Signs* 1 (1976): 1–29, © 1976, University of Chicago Press, by permission of the University of Chicago Press.

friendships between men and men and women and women existed in a larger world of social relations and social values. To interpret such friendships more fully they must be related to the structure of the American family and to the nature of sex-role divisions and of male-female relationships both within the family and in society generally. The female friendship must not be seen in isolation; it must be analyzed as one aspect of women's overall relations with one another. The ties between mothers and daughters, sisters, female cousins and friends, at all stages of the female life cycle constitute the most suggestive framework for the historian to begin an analysis of intimacy and affection between women. Such an analysis would not only emphasize general cultural patterns rather than the internal dynamics of a particular family or childhood; it would shift the focus of the study from a concern with deviance to that of defining configurations of legitimate behavioral norms and options.[4]

This analysis will be based upon the correspondence and diaries of women and men in thirty-five families between the 1760s and the 1880s. These families, though limited in number, represented a broad range of the American middle class, from hard-pressed pioneer families and orphaned girls to daughters of the intellectual and social elite. It includes families from most geographic regions, rural and urban, and a spectrum of Protestant denominations ranging from Mormon to orthodox Quaker. Although scarcely a comprehensive sample of America's increasingly heterogeneous population, it does, I believe reflect accurately the literate middle class to which the historian working with letters and diaries is necessarily bound. It has involved the analysis of many thousands of letters written to women friends, kin, husbands, brothers, and children at every period of life from adolescence to old age. Some collections encompass virtually entire life spans; one contains over 100,000 letters as well as diaries and account books. It is my contention that an analysis of women's private letters and diaries which were never intended to be published permits the historian to explore a very private world of emotional realities central both to women's lives and to the middle-class family in nineteenth-century America.[5]

The question of female friendships is peculiarly elusive; we know so little or perhaps have forgotten so much. An intriguing and almost alien form of human relationship, they flourished in a different social structure and amidst different sexual norms. Before attempting to reconstruct their social setting, therefore, it might be best first to describe two not atypical friendships. These two friendships, intense, loving, and openly avowed, began during the women's adolescence and, despite subsequent marriages and geographic separation, continued throughout their lives. For nearly half a century these women played a central emotional role in each other's lives, writing time and again of their love and of the pain of separation. Paradoxically to twentieth-century minds, their love appears to have been both sensual and platonic.

Sarah Butler Wister first met Jeannie Field Musgrove while vacationing with her family at Stockbridge, Massachusetts, in the summer of 1849.[6] Jeannie was then sixteen, Sarah fourteen. During two subsequent years spent together in boarding school, they formed a deep and intimate friendship. Sarah began to keep a bouquet of flowers before Jeannie's portrait and wrote complaining of the intensity and anguish of her affection.[7] Both young women assumed nom de plumes, Jeannie a female name, Sarah a male one; they would use the secret names into old age.[8] They frequently commented on the nature of their affection: "If the day should come," Sarah wrote Jeannie in the spring of 1861, "when you failed me either through your fault or my own, I would forswear all human friendship, thenceforth." A few months later Jeannie commented: "Gratitude is a word I should never use toward you. It is perhaps a misfortune of such intimacy and love that it makes one regard all kindness as a matter of course, as one has always found it, as natural as the embrace in meeting."[9]

Sarah's marriage altered neither the frequency of their correspondence nor their desire to be together. In 1864, when twenty-nine, married, and a mother, Sarah wrote to Jeannie: "I shall be entirely alone [this coming week]. I can give you no idea how desperately I shall want you. . . ." After one such visit Jeannie, then a spinster in New York, echoed Sarah's longing: "Dear darling Sarah! How I love you & how happy I have been! You are the joy of my life. . . . I cannot tell you how much happiness you gave me, nor how constantly it is all in my thoughts. . . . My darling how I long for the time when I shall see you. . . ." After another visit Jeannie wrote: "I want you to tell me in your next letter, to assure me, that I am your dearest. . . . I do not doubt you, & I am not jealous but I long to hear you say it once more & it seems already a long time since your voice fell on my ear. So just fill a quarter page with caresses & expressions of endearment. Your silly Angelina." Jeannie ended one letter: "Goodbye my dearest, dearest lover—ever your own Angelina." And another, "I will go to bed . . . [though] I could write all night—A thousand kisses—I love you with my whole soul—your Angelina."

When Jeannie finally married in 1870 at the age of thirty-seven, Sarah underwent a period of extreme anxiety. Two days before Jeannie's marriage Sarah, then in London, wrote desperately: "Dearest darling—How incessantly have I thought of you these eight days—all today—the entire uncertainty, the distance, the long silence—are all new features in my separation from you, grevious to be borne. . . . Oh Jeannie. I have thought & thought & yearned over you these two days. Are you married I wonder? My dearest love to you wherever and *who*ever you are."[10] Like many other women in this collection of thirty-five families, marriage brought Sarah and Jeannie physical separation; it did not cause emotional distance. Although at first they may have wondered how marriage would affect their relationship, their affection remained unabated throughout their lives, underscored by their loneliness and their desire to be together.[11]

During the same years that Jeannie and Sarah wrote of their love and need for each other, two slightly younger women began an odyssey of love, dependence and—ultimately—physical though not emotional, separation. Molly and Helena met in 1868 while both attended the Cooper Institute School of Design for Women in New York City. For several years these young women studied and explored the city together, visited each other's families, and formed part of a social network of other artistic young women. Gradually, over the years, their initial friendship deepened into a close intimate bond which continued throughout their lives. The tone in the letters which Molly wrote to Helena changed over the years from "My dear Helena," and signed "your attached friend," to "My dearest Helena," "My Dearest," "My Beloved," and signed "Thine always" or "thine Molly."[12]

The letters they wrote to each other during these first five years permit us to reconstruct something of their relationship together. As Molly wrote in one early letter:

> I have not said to you in so many or so few words that I was happy with you during those few incredibly short weeks but surely you do not need words to tell you what you must know. Those two or three days so dark without, so bright with firelight and contentment within I shall always remember as proof that, for a time, at least—I fancy for quite a long time—we might be sufficient for each other. We know that we can amuse each other for

many idle hours together and now we know that we can also work together. And that means much, don't you think so?

She ended: "I shall return in a few days. Imagine yourself kissed many times by one who loved you so dearly."

The intensity and even physical nature of Molly's love was echoed in many of the letters she wrote during the next few years, as, for instance, in this short thank-you note for a small present: "Imagine yourself kissed a dozen times my darling. Perhaps it is well for you that we are far apart. You might find my thanks so expressed rather overpowering. I have that delightful feeling that it doesn't matter much what I say or how I say it, since we shall meet so soon and forget in that moment that we were ever separated. . . . I shall see you soon and be content."[13]

At the end of the fifth year, however, several crises occurred. The relationship, at least in its intense form, ended, though Molly and Helena continued an intimate and complex relationship for the next half-century. The exact nature of these crises is not completely clear, but it seems to have involved Molly's decision not to live with Helena, as they had originally planned, but to remain at home because of parental insistence. Molly was now in her late twenties. Helena responded with anger and Molly became frantic at the thought that Helena would break off their relationship. Though she wrote distraught letters and made despairing attempts to see Helena, the relationship never regained its former ardor—possibly because Molly had a male suitor.[14] Within six months Helena had decided to marry a man who was, coincidentally, Molly's friend and publisher. Two years later Molly herself finally married. The letters toward the end of this period discuss the transition both women made to having male lovers—Molly spending much time reassuring Helena, who seemed depressed about the end of their relationship and with her forthcoming marriage.[15]

It is clearly difficult from a distance of 100 years and from a post-Freudian cultural perspective to decipher the complexities of Molly and Helena's relationship. Certainly Molly and Helena were lovers—emotionally if not physically. The emotional intensity and pathos of their love becomes apparent in several letters Molly wrote Helena during their crisis: "I wanted so to put my arms round my girl of all the girls in the world and tell her . . . I love her as wives do their husbands, as *friends* who have taken each other for life—and believe in her as I believe in my God. . . . If I didn't love you do you suppose I'd care about anything or have ridiculous notions and panics and behave like an old fool who ought to know better. I'm going to hang on to your skirts. . . . You can't get away from [my] love." Or as she wrote after Helena's decision to marry: "You know dear Helena, I really was in love with you. It was a passion such as I had never known until I saw you. I don't think it was the noblest way to love you." The theme of intense female love was one Molly again expressed in a letter she wrote to the man Helena was to marry: "Do you know sir, that until you came along I believe that she loved me almost as girls love their lovers. *I know I loved her so.* Don't you wonder that I can stand the sight of you." This was in a letter congratulating them on their forthcoming marriage.[16]

The essential question is not whether these women had genital contact and can therefore be defined as heterosexual or homosexual. The twentieth-century tendency to view human love and sexuality within a dichotomized universe of deviance and normality, genitality and platonic love, is alien to the emotions and attitudes of the nineteenth century and fundamentally distorts the nature of these women's emotional interaction.

These letters are significant because they force us to place such female love in a particular historical context. There is every indication that these four women, their husbands and families—all eminently respectable and socially conservative—considered such love both socially acceptable and fully compatible with heterosexual marriage. Emotionally and cognitively, their heterosocial and their homosocial worlds were complementary.

One could argue, on the other hand, that these letters were but an example of the romantic rhetoric with which the nineteenth century surrounded the concept of friendship. Yet they possess an emotional intensity and a sensual and physical explicitness that is difficult to dismiss. Jeannie longed to hold Sarah in her arms; Molly mourned her physical isolation from Helena. Molly's love and devotion to Helena, the emotions that bound Jeannie and Sarah together, while perhaps a phenomenon of nineteenth-century society were not the less real for their Victorian origins. A survey of the correspondence and diaries of eighteenth- and nineteenth-century women indicates that Molly, Jeannie, and Sarah represented one very real behavioral and emotional option socially available to nineteenth-century women.

This is not to argue that individual needs, personalities, and family dynamics did not have a significant role in determining the nature of particular relationships. But the scholar must ask if it is historically possible and, if possible, important, to study the intensely individual aspects of psychosexual dynamics. Is it not the historian's first task to explore the social structure and the world view which made intense and sometimes sensual female love both a possible and an acceptable emotional option? From such a social perspective a new and quite different series of questions suggests itself. What emotional function did such female love serve? What was its place within the hetero- and homosocial worlds which women jointly inhabited? Did a spectrum of love-object choices exist in the nineteenth century across which some individuals, at least, were capable of moving? Without attempting to answer these questions it will be difficult to understand either nineteenth-century sexuality or the nineteenth-century family.

Several factors in American society between the mid-eighteenth and the mid-nineteenth centuries may well have permitted women to form a variety of close emotional relationships with other women. American society was characterized in large part by rigid gender-role differentiation within the family and within society as a whole, leading to the emotional segregation of women and men. The roles of daughter and mother shaded imperceptibly and ineluctably into each other, while the biological realities of frequent pregnancies, childbirth, nursing, and menopause bound women together in physical and emotional intimacy. It was within just such a social framework, I would argue, that a specifically female world did indeed develop, a world built around a generic and unself-conscious pattern of single-sex or homosocial networks. These supportive networks were institutionalized in social conventions or rituals which accompanied virtually every important event in a woman's life, from birth to death. Such female relationships were frequently supported and paralleled by severe social restrictions on intimacy between young men and women. Within such a world of emotional richness and complexity devotion to and love of other women became a plausible and socially accepted form of human interaction.

An abundance of printed and manuscript sources exists to support such a hypothesis. Etiquette books, advice books on child rearing, religious sermons, guides to young men and young women, medical texts, and school curricula all suggest that late eighteenth-

and most nineteenth-century Americans assumed the existence of a world composed of distinctly male and female spheres, spheres determined by the immutable laws of God and nature.[17] The unpublished letters and diaries of Americans during this same period concur, detailing the existence of sexually segregated worlds inhabited by human beings with different values, expectations, and personalities. Contacts between men and women frequently partook of a formality and stiffness quite alien to twentieth-century America and which today we tend to define as "Victorian." Women, however, did not form an isolated and oppressed subcategory in male society. Their letters and diaries indicate that women's sphere had an essential integrity and dignity that grew out of women's shared experiences and mutual affection and that, despite the profound changes which affected American social structure and institutions between the 1760s and the 1870s, retained a constancy and predictability. The ways in which women thought of and interacted with each other remained unchanged. Continuity, not discontinuity, characterized this female world. Molly Hallock's and Jeannie Fields's words, emotions, and experiences have direct parallels in the 1760s and the 1790s.[18] There are indications in contemporary sociological and psychological literature that female closeness and support networks have continued into the twentieth century—not only among ethnic and working-class groups but even among the middle class.[19]

Most eighteenth- and nineteenth-century women lived within a world bounded by home, church, and the institution of visiting—that endless trooping of women to each other's homes for social purposes. It was a world inhabited by children and by other women.[20] Women helped each other with domestic chores and in times of sickness, sorrow, or trouble. Entire days, even weeks, might be spent almost exclusively with other women.[21] Urban and town women could devote virtually every day to visits, teas, or shopping trips with other women. Rural women developed a pattern of more extended visits that lasted weeks and sometimes months, at times even dislodging husbands from their beds and bedrooms so that dear friends might spend every hour of every day together.[22] When husbands traveled, wives routinely moved in with other women, invited women friends to teas and suppers, sat together sharing and comparing the letters they had received from other close women friends. Secrets were exchanged and cherished, and the husband's return at times viewed with some ambivalence.[23]

Summer vacations were frequently organized to permit old friends to meet at water spas or share a country home. In 1848, for example, a young matron wrote cheerfully to her husband about the delightful time she was having with five close women friends whom she had invited to spend the summer with her; he remained at home alone to face the heat of Philadelphia and a cholera epidemic.[24] Some ninety years earlier, two young Quaker girls commented upon the vacation their aunt had taken alone with another women; their remarks were openly envious and tell us something of the emotional quality of these friendships: "I hear Aunt is gone with the Friend and wont be back for two weeks, fine times indeed I think the old friends had, taking their pleasure about the country . . . and have the advantage of that fine woman's conversation and instruction, while we poor young girls must spend all spring at home. . . . What a disappointment that we are not together. . . ."[25]

Friends did not form isolated dyads but were normally part of highly integrated networks. Knowing each other, perhaps related to each other, they played a central role in holding communities and kin systems together. Especially when families became geographically mobile women's long visits to each other and their frequent letters filled with discussions of marriages and births, illnesses and deaths, descriptions of growing children, and reminiscences of times and people past provided an important sense of continuity in a rapidly changing society.[26] Central to this female world was the inner core of kin. The ties between sisters, first cousins, aunts, and nieces provided the underlying structure upon which groups of friends and their network of female relatives clustered. Although most of the women within this sample would appear to be living within isolated nuclear families, the emotional ties between nonresidential kin were deep and binding and provided one of the fundamental existential realities of women's lives.[27] Twenty years after Parke Lewis Butler moved with her husband to Louisiana, she sent her two daughters back to Virginia to attend school, live with their grandmother and aunt, and be integrated back into Virginia society.[28] The constant letters between Maria Inskeep and Fanny Hampton, sisters separated in their early twenties when Maria moved with her husband from New Jersey to Louisiana, held their families together, making it possible for their daughters to feel a part of their cousins' network of friends and interests.[29] The Ripley daughters, growing up in western Massachusetts in the early 1800s, spent months each year with their mother's sister and her family in distant Boston; these female cousins and their network of friends exchanged gossip-filled letters and gradually formed deeply loving and dependent ties.[30]

Women frequently spent their days within the social confines of such extended families. Sisters-in-law visited each other and, in some families, seemed to spend more time with each other than with their husbands. First cousins cared for each other's babies—for weeks or even months in times of sickness or childbirth. Sisters helped each other with housework, shopped and sewed for each other. Geographic separation was borne with difficulty. A sister's absence for even a week or two could cause loneliness and depression and would be bridged by frequent letters. Sibling rivalry was hardly unknown, but with separation or illness the theme of deep affection and dependency reemerged.[31]

Sisterly bonds continued across a lifetime. In her old age a rural Quaker matron, Martha Jefferis, wrote to her daughter Anne concerning her own half-sister, Phoebe: "In sister Phoebe I have a real friend—she studies my comfort and waits on me like a child. . . . She is exceeedingly kind and this to all other homes (set aside yours) I would prefer—it is next to being with a daughter." Phoebe's own letters confirmed Martha's evaluation of her feelings. "Thou knowest my dear sister," Phoebe wrote, "there is no one . . . that exactly feels [for] thee as I do, for I think without boasting I can truly say that my desire is for thee."[32]

Such women, whether friends or relatives, assumed an emotional centrality in each other's lives. In their diaries and letters they wrote of the joy and contentment they felt in each other's company, their sense of isolation and despair when apart. The regularity of their correspondence underlines the sincerity of their words. Women named their daughters after one another and sought to integrate dear friends into their lives after marriage.[33] As one young bride wrote to an old friend shortly after her marriage: "I want to see you and talk with you and feel that we are united by the same bonds of sympathy and congeniality as ever."[34] After years of friendship one aging woman wrote of another: "Time cannot destroy the fascination of her manner . . . her voice is music to the ear. . . ."[35] Women made elaborate presents for each other, ranging from the Quakers' frugal pies and breads to painted velvet bags and phantom bouquets.[36] When a friend died, their grief was deeply felt. Martha Jefferis was unable to write to her daughter for three weeks because of the sorrow she felt at the death of a dear friend. Such distress was not unusual. A generation earlier a young Massachusetts farm woman filled pages of her diary with her grief at the death of her "dearest friend" and transcribed the letters of condolence other women sent her. She marked the anniversary of Rachel's death each year in her diary, contrasting her faithfulness with that of Rachel's husband who had soon remarried.[37]

These female friendships served a number of emotional functions. Within this secure and empathetic world women could share sorrows, anxieties, and joys, confident that other women had experienced similar emotions. One mid-nineteenth-century rural matron in a letter to her daughter discussed this particular aspect of women's friendships: "To have such a friend as thyself to look to and sympathize with her—and enter into all her little needs and in whose bosom she could with freedom pour forth her joys and sorrows—such a friend would very much relieve the tedium of many a wearisome hour. . . ." A generation later Molly more informally underscored the importance of this same function in a letter to Helena: "Suppose I come down . . . [and] spend Sunday with you quietly," she wrote Helena " . . . that means talking all the time until you are relieved of your latest troubles, and I of mine. . . ."[38] These were frequently troubles that apparently no man could understand. When Anne Jefferis Sheppard was first married, she and her older sister Edith (who then lived with Anne) wrote in detail to their mother of the severe depression and anxiety which they experienced. Moses Sheppard, Anne's husband, added cheerful postscripts to the sisters' letters—which he had clearly not read—remarking on Anne's and Edith's contentment. Theirs was an emotional world to which he had little access.[39]

This was, as well, a female world in which hostility and criticism of other women were discouraged, and thus a milieu in which women could develop a sense of inner security and self-esteem. As one young woman wrote to her mother's longtime friend: "I cannot sufficiently thank you for the kind unvaried affection & indulgence you have ever shown and expressed both by words and actions for me. . . . Happy would it be did all the world view me as you do, through the medium of kindness and forbearance."[40] They valued each other. Women, who had little status or power in the larger world of male concerns, possessed status and power in the lives and worlds of other women.[41]

An intimate mother-daughter relationship lay at the heart of this female world. The diaries and letters of both mothers and daughters attest to their closeness and mutual emotional dependency. Daughters routinely discussed their mother's health and activities with their own friends, expressed anxiety in cases of their mother's ill health and concern for her cares.[42] Expressions of hostility which we would today consider routine on the part of both mothers and daughters seem to have been uncommon indeed. On the contrary, this sample of families indicates that the normal relationship between mother and daughter was one of sympathy and understanding.[43] Only sickness or great geographic distance was allowed to cause extended separation. When marriage did result in such separation, both viewed the distance between them with distress.[44] Something of this sympathy and love between mothers and daughters is evident in a letter Sarah Alden Ripley, at age sixty-nine, wrote her youngest and recently married daughter: "You do not know how much I miss you, not only when I struggle in and out of my mortal envelop and pump my nightly potation and no longer pour into your sympathizing ear my senile gossip, but all the day I muse away, since the sound of your voice no longer rouses me to sympathy with your joys or sorrows. . . . You cannot know how much I miss your affectionate demonstrations."[45] A dozen aging mothers in this sample of over thirty families echoed her sentiments.

Central to these mother-daughter relations is what might be described as an apprenticeship system. In those families where the daughters followed the mother into a life of traditional domesticity, mothers and other older women carefully trained daughters in the arts of housewifery and motherhood. Such training undoubtedly occurred throughout a girl's childhood but became more systematized, almost ritualistic, in the years following the end of her formal education and before her marriage. At this time a girl either returned home from boarding school or no longer divided her time between home and school. Rather, she devoted her energies to two tasks: mastering new domestic skills and participating in the visiting and social activities necessary to find a husband. Under the careful supervision of their mothers and of older female relatives, such late-adolescent girls temporarily took over the household management from their mothers, tended their young nieces and nephews, and helped in childbirth, nursing, and weaning. Such experiences tied the generations together in shared skills and emotional interaction.[46]

Daughters were born into a female world. Their mother's life expectations and sympathetic network of friends and relations were among the first realities in the life of the developing child. As long as the mother's domestic role remained relatively stable and few viable alternatives competed with it, daughters tended to accept their mother's world and to turn automatically to other women for support and intimacy. It was within this closed and intimate female world that the young girl grew toward womanhood.

One could speculate at length concerning the absence of that mother-daughter hostility today considered almost inevitable to an adolescent's struggle for autonomy and self-identity. It is possible that taboos against female aggression and hostility were sufficiently strong to repress even that between mothers and their adolescent daughters. Yet these letters seem so alive and the interest of daughters in their mothers' affairs so vital and genuine that it is difficult to interpret their closeness exclusively in terms of repression and denial. The functional bonds that held mothers and daughters together in a world that permitted few alternatives to domesticity might well have created a source of mutuality and trust absent in societies where greater options were available for daughters than for mothers. Furthermore, the extended female network—a daughter's close ties with her own older sisters, cousins, and aunts—may well have permitted a diffusion and a relaxation of mother-daughter identification and so have aided a daughter in her struggle for identity and autonomy. None of these explanations are mutually exclusive; all may well have interacted to produce the degree of empathy evident in those letters and diaries.

At some point in adolescence, the young girl began to move outside the matrix of her mother's support group to develop a network of her own. Among the middle class, at least, this transition toward what was at the same time both a limited autonomy and a repetition of her mother's life seemed to have most frequently coincided with a girl's going to school. Indeed education appears to have played a crucial role in the lives of most of the families in this study. Attending school for a few months, for a year, or longer, was common even among daughters of relatively poor families, while middle-class girls routinely spent at least a year in boarding school.[47] These school years ordinarily marked a girl's first separation from home. They served to wean the daughter from her home, to train her in the essential social graces, and, ultimately, to help introduce her into the marriage market. It was not infrequently a trying emotional experience for both mother and daughter.[48]

In the process of leaving one home and adjusting to another, the mother's friends and relatives played a key transitional role. Such older women routinely accepted the role of foster mother; they supervised the young girl's deportment, monitored her health and introduced her to their own network of female friends and kin.[49] Not infrequently women, friends from their own school years, arranged to send their daughters to the same school so that the girls might form bonds paralleling those their mothers had made. For years Molly and Helena wrote of their daughters' meeting and worried over each others' children. When Molly finally brought her daughter east to school, their first act on reaching New York was to meet Helena and her daughters. Elizabeth Bordley Gibson virtually adopted the daughters of her school chum, Eleanor Custis Lewis. The Lewis daughters soon began to write Elizabeth Gibson letters with the salutation "Dearest Mama." Eleuthera DuPont, attending boarding school in Philadelphia at roughly the same time as the Lewis girls, developed a parallel relationship with her mother's friend, Elizabeth McKie Smith. Eleuthera went to the same school and became a close friend of the Smith girls and eventually married their first cousin. During this period she routinely called Mrs. Smith "Mother." Indeed Eleuthera so internalized the sense of having two mothers that she casually wrote her sisters of her "Mamma's" visits at her "mother's" house—that is at Mrs. Smith's.[50]

Even more important to this process of maturation than their mother's friends were the female friends young women made at school. Young girls helped each other overcome homesickness and endure the crises of adolescence. They gossiped about beaux, incorporated each other into their own kinship systems, and attended and gave teas and balls together. Older girls in boarding school "adopted" younger ones, who called them "Mother."[51] Dear friends might indeed continue this pattern of adoption and mothering throughout their lives; one woman might routinely assume the nurturing role of pseudomother, the other the dependency role of daughter. The pseudomother performed for the other woman all the services which we normally associate with mothers; she went to absurd lengths to purchase items her "daughter" could have obtained from other sources, gave advice and functioned as an idealized figure in her "daughter's" imagination. Helena played such a role for Molly, as did Sarah for Jeannie. Elizabeth Bordley Gibson bought almost all Eleanor Parke Custis Lewis's necessities—from shoes and corset covers to bedding and harp strings—and sent them from Philadelphia to Virginia, a procedure that sometimes took months. Eleanor frequently asked Elizabeth to take back her purchases, have them redone, and argue with shopkeepers about prices. These were favors automatically asked and complied with. Anne Jefferis Sheppard made the analogy very explicitly in a letter to her own mother written shortly after Anne's marriage, when she was feeling depressed about their separation: "Mary Paulen is truly kind, almost acts the part of a mother and tries to aid and *comfort me,* and also to *lighten my new cares.*"[52]

A comparison of the references to men and women in these young women's letters is striking. Boys were obviously indispensable to the elaborate courtship rituals girls engaged in. In these teenage letters and diaries, however, boys appear distant and warded off—an effect produced both by the girl's sense of bonding and by a highly developed and deprecatory whimsy. Girls joked among themselves about the conceit, poor looks or affectations of suitors. Rarely, especially in the eighteenth and early nineteenth centuries, were favorable remarks exchanged. Indeed, while hostility and criticism of other women were so rare as to seem almost tabooed, young women permitted themselves to express a great deal of hostility toward peer-group men.[53] When unacceptable suitors appeared, girls might even band together to harass them. When one such unfortunate came to court Sophie DuPont she hid in her room, first sending her sister Eleuthera to entertain him and then dispatching a number of urgent notes to her neighboring sister-in-law, cousins, and a visiting friend who all came to Sophie's support. A wild female romp ensued, ending only when Sophie banged into a door, lacerated her nose, and retired, with her female cohorts, to bed. Her brother and the presumably disconcerted suitor were left alone. These were not the antics of teenagers but of women in their early and mid-twenties.[54]

Even if young men were acceptable suitors, girls referred to them formally and obliquely: "The last week I received the unexpected intelligence of the arrival of a friend from Boston," Sarah Ripley wrote in her diary of the young man to whom she had been engaged for years and whom she would shortly marry. Harriet Manigault assiduously kept a lively and gossipy diary during the three years preceding her marriage, yet did not once comment upon her own engagement nor indeed make any personal references to her fiancé—who was never identified as such but always referred to as Mr. Wilcox.[55] The point is not that these young women were hostile to young men. Far from it; they sought marriage and domesticity. Yet in these letters and diaries men appear as an other or out group, segregated into different schools, supported by their own male network of friends and kin, socialized to different behavior, and coached to a proper formality in courtship behavior. As a consequence, relations between young women and men frequently lacked the spontaneity and emotional intimacy that characterized the young girls' ties to each other.

Indeed, in sharp contrast to their distant relations with boys, young women's relations with each other were close, often frolicsome, and surprisingly long lasting and devoted. They wrote secret missives to each other, spent long solitary days with each other, curled up together in bed at night to whisper fantasies and secrets.[56] In 1862 one young woman in her early twenties described one such scene to an absent friend: "I have sat up to midnight listening to the confidences of Constance Kinney, whose heart was opened by that most charming of all situations, a seat on a bedside late at night, when all the household are asleep & only oneself & one's confidante survive in wakefulness. So she has told me all her loves and tried to get some confidences in return but being five or six years older than she, I know better. . . ."[57] Elizabeth Bordley and Nelly Parke Custis, teenagers in Philadelphia in the 1790s, routinely secreted themselves until late each night in Nellie's attic, where they each wrote a novel about the other.[58] Quite a few young women kept diaries, and it was a sign of special friendship to show their diaries to each other. The emotional quality of such exchanges emerges from the comments of one young girl who grew up along the Ohio frontier:

> Sisters CW and RT keep diaries & allow me the inestimable pleasure of reading them and in turn they see mine—but O shame covers my face when I think of it; theirs is so much better than mine, that every time. Then I think well now I *will* burn mine but upon second thought it would deprive me the pleasure of reading theirs, for I esteem it a very great privilege indeed, as well as very improving, as we lay our hearts open to each other, it heightens our love & helps to cherish & keep alive that sweet soothing friendship and endears us to each other by that soft attraction.[59]

Girls routinely slept together, kissed and hugged each other. Indeed, while waltzing with young men scandalized the otherwise flighty and highly fashionable Harriet Manigault, she considered waltzing with other young women not only acceptable but pleasant.[60]

Marriage followed adolescence. With increasing frequency in the nineteenth century, marriage involved a girl's traumatic removal from her mother and her mother's network.

It involved, as well, adjustment to a husband, who, because he was male came to marriage with both a different world view and vastly different experiences. Not surprisingly, marriage was an event surrounded with supportive, almost ritualistic, practices. (Weddings are one of the last female rituals remaining in twentieth-century America.) Young women routinely spent the months preceding their marriage almost exclusively with other women—at neighborhood sewing bees and quilting parties or in a round of visits to geographically distant friends and relatives. Ostensibly they were to receive assistance in the practical preparations for their new home—sewing and quilting a trousseau and linen—but of equal importance, they appear to have gained emotional support and reassurance. Sarah Ripley spent over a month with friends and relatives in Boston and Hingham before her wedding; Parke Custis Lewis exchanged visits with her aunts and first cousins throughout Virginia.[61] Anne Jefferis, who married with some hesitation, spent virtually half a year in endless visiting with cousins, aunts, and friends. Despite their reassurance and support, however, she would not marry Moses Sheppard until her sister Edith and her cousin Rebecca moved into the groom's home, met his friends, and explored his personality.[62] The wedding did not take place until Edith wrote to Anne: "I can say in truth I am entirely willing thou shouldst follow him even away in the Jersey sands believing if thou art not happy in thy future home it will not be any fault on his part. . . ."[63]

Sisters, cousins, and friends frequently accompanied newlyweds on their wedding night and wedding trip, which often involved additional family visiting. Such extensive visits presumably served to wean the daughter from her family of origin. As such they often contained a note of ambivalence. Nelly Custis, for example, reported homesickness and loneliness on her wedding trip. "I left my Beloved and revered Grandmamma with sincere regret," she wrote Elizabeth Bordley. "It was sometime before I could feel reconciled to traveling without her." Perhaps they also functioned to reassure the young woman herself, and her friends and kin, that though marriage might alter it would not destroy old bonds of intimacy and familiarity.[64]

Married life, too, was structured about a host of female rituals. Childbirth, especially the birth of the first child, became virtually a *rite de passage,* with a lengthy seclusion of the woman before and after delivery, severe restrictions on her activities, and finally a dramatic reemergence.[65] The seclusion was supervised by mothers, sisters, and loving friends. Nursing and weaning involved the advice and assistance of female friends and relatives. So did miscarriage.[66] Death, like birth, was structured around elaborate unisexed rituals. When Nelly Parke Custis Lewis rushed to nurse her daughter who was critically ill while away at school, Nelly received support, not from her husband, who remained on their plantation, but from her old school friend, Elizabeth Bordley. Elizabeth aided Nelly in caring for her dying daughter, cared for Nelly's other children, played a major role in the elaborate funeral arrangements (which the father did not attend), and frequently visited the girl's grave at the mother's request. For years Elizabeth continued to be the confidante of Nelly's anguished recollections of her lost daughter. These memories, Nelly's letters made clear, were for Elizabeth alone. "Mr. L. knows nothing of this," was a frequent comment.[67] Virtually every collection of letters and diaries in my sample contained evidence of women turning to each other when facing the frequent and unavoidable deaths of the eighteenth and nineteenth centuries.[68] While mourning for her father's death, Sophie DuPont received elaborate letters and visits of condolence—all from women. No man wrote or visited Sophie to offer sympathy at her father's death.[69]

Among rural Pennsylvania Quakers, death and mourning rituals assumed an even more extreme same-sex form, with men or women largely barred from the deathbeds of the other sex. Women relatives and friends slept with the dying woman, nursed her, and prepared her body for burial.[70]

Eighteenth- and nineteenth-century women thus lived in emotional proximity to each other. Friendships and intimacies followed the biological ebb and flow of women's lives. Marriage and pregnancy, childbirth and weaning, sickness and death involved physical and psychic trauma which comfort and sympathy made easier to bear. Intense bonds of love and intimacy bound together those women who, offering each other aid and sympathy, shared such stressful moments.

These bonds were often physical as well as emotional. An undeniably romantic and even sensual note frequently marked female relationships. This theme, significant throughout the stages of a woman's life, surfaced first during adolescence. As one teenager from a struggling pioneer family in the Ohio Valley wrote in her diary in 1808: "I laid with my dear R[ebecca] and a glorious good talk we had until about 4[A.M.]—O how hard I do *love* her. . . ."[71] Only a few years later Bostonian Eunice Callender carved her initials and Sarah Ripley's into a favorite tree, along with a pledge of eternal love, and then waited breathlessly for Sarah to discover and respond to her declaration of affection. The response appears to have been affirmative.[72] A half-century later urbane and sophisticated Katherine Wharton commented upon meeting an old school chum: "She was a great pet of mine at school & I thought as I watched her light figure how often I had held her in my arms—how dear she had once been to me." Katie maintained a long intimate friendship with another girl. When a young man began to court this friend seriously, Katie commented in her diary that she had never realized "how deeply I loved Eng and how fully." She wrote over and over again in that entry: "Indeed I love her!" and only with great reluctance left the city that summer since it meant also leaving Eng with Eng's new suitor.[73]

Peggy Emlen, a Quaker adolescent in Philadelphia in the 1760s, expressed similar feelings about her first cousin, Sally Logan. The girls sent love poems to each other (not unlike the ones Elizabeth Bordley wrote to Nellie Custis a generation later), took long solitary walks together, and even haunted the empty house of the other when one was out of town. Indeed Sally's absences from Philadelphia caused Peggy acute unhappiness. So strong were Peggy's feelings that her brothers began to tease her about her affection for Sally and threatened to steal Sally's letters, much to both girls' alarm. In one letter that Peggy wrote the absent Sally she elaborately described the depth and nature of her feelings: "I have not words to express my impatience to see My Dear Cousin, what would I not give just now for an hours sweet conversation with her, it seems as if I had a thousand things to say to thee, yet when I see thee, everything will be forgotteen thro' joy. . . . I have a very great friendship for several Girls yet it dont give me so much uneasiness at being absent from them as from thee. . . . [Let us] go and spend a day down at our place together and there unmolested enjoy each other's company."[74]

Sarah Alden Ripley, a young, highly educated woman, formed a similar intense relationship, in this instance with a woman somewhat older than herself. The immediate bond of friendship rested on their atypically intense scholarly interests, but it soon involved strong emotions, at least on Sarah's part. "Friendship," she wrote Mary Emerson, "is fast twining about her willing captive the silken hands of dependence, a dependence so sweet who would renounce it for the apathy of self-sufficiency?" Subsequent letters became far more emotional, almost conspiratorial. Mary visited Sarah secretly in her room, or the two women crept away from family and friends to meet in a nearby woods. Sarah became jealous of Mary's other young woman friends. Mary's trips away from Boston also thrust Sarah into periods of anguished depression. Interestingly, the letters detailing their love were not destroyed but were preserved, and even reprinted in a eulogistic biography of Sarah Alden Ripley.[75]

Tender letters between adolescent women, confessions of loneliness and emotional dependency, were not peculiar to Sarah Alden, Peggy Emlen, or Katie Wharton. They are found throughout the letters of the thirty-five families studied. They have, of course, their parallel today in the musings of many female adolescents. Yet these eighteenth- and nineteenth-century friendships lasted with undiminished, indeed often increased, intensity throughout the women's lives. Sarah Alden Ripley's first child was named after Mary Emerson. Nelly Custis Lewis's love for and dependence on Elizabeth Bordley Gibson only increased after her marriage. Eunice Callender remained enamoured of her cousin Sarah Ripley for years and rejected as impossible the suggestion by another woman that their love might some day fade away.[76] Sophie DuPont and her childhood friend, Clementina Smith, exchanged letters filled with love and dependency for forty years while another dear friend, Mary Black Couper, wrote of dreaming that she, Sophie, and her husband were all united in one marriage. Mary's letters to Sophie are filled with avowals of love and indications of ambivalence toward her own husband. Eliza Schlatter, another of Sophie's intimate friends, wrote to her at a time of crisis: "I wish I could be with you present in the body as well as the mind & heart—I would turn your *good husband out of bed*—and snuggle into you and we would have a long talk like old times in Pine St.—I want to tell you so many things that are not *writable*. . . ."[77]

Such mutual dependency and deep affection is a central existential reality coloring the world of supportive networks and rituals. In the case of Katie, Sophie, or Eunice—as with Molly, Jeannie, and Sarah—their need for closeness and support merged with more intense demands for a love which was at the same time both emotional and sensual. Perhaps the most explicit statement concerning women's lifelong friendships appeared in the letter abolitionist and reformer Mary Grew wrote about the same time, referring to her own love for her dear friend and lifelong companion, Margaret Burleigh. Grew wrote, in response to a letter of condolence from another woman on Burleigh's death: "Your words respecting my beloved friend touch me deeply. Evidently . . . you comprehend and appreciate, as few persons do . . . the nature of the relation which existed, which exists, between her and myself. Her only surviving niece . . . also does. To me it seems to have been a closer union than that of most marriages. We know there have been other such between two men and also between two women. And why should there not be. Love is spiritual, only passion is sexual."[78]

How then can we ultimately interpret these long-lived intimate female relationships and integrate them into our understanding of Victorian sexuality? Their ambivalent and romantic rhetoric presents us with an ultimate puzzle: the relationship along the spectrum of human emotions between love, sensuality, and sexuality.

One is tempted, as I have remarked, to compare Molly, Peggy, or Sophie's relationships with the friendships adolescent girls in the twentieth century routinely form—close friendships of great emotional intensity. Helena Deutsch and Clara Thompson have both described these friendships as emotionally necessary to a girl's psychosexual development. But, they warn, such friendships might shade into adolescent and postadolescent homosexuality.[79]

It is possible to speculate that in the twentieth century a number of cultural taboos evolved to cut short the homosocial ties of girlhood and to impel the emerging women of thirteen or fourteen toward heterosexual relationships. In contrast, nineteenth-century American society did not taboo close female relationships but rather recognized them as a socially viable form of human contact—and, as such, acceptable throughout a woman's life. Indeed it was not these homosocial ties that were inhibited but rather heterosexual leanings. While closeness, freedom of emotional expression, and uninhibited physical contact characterized women's relationships with each other, the opposite was frequently true of male-female relationships. One could thus argue that within such a world of female support, intimacy, and ritual it was only to be expected that adult women would turn trustingly and lovingly to each other. It was a behavior they had observed and learned since childhood. A different type of emotional landscape existed in the nineteenth century, one in which Molly and Helena's love became a natural development.

Of perhaps equal significance are the implications we can garner from this framework for the understanding of heterosexual marriages in the nineteenth century. If men and women grew up as they did in relatively homogeneous and segregated sexual groups, then marriage represented a major problem in adjustment. From this perspective we could interpret much of the emotional stiffness and distance that we associate with Victorian marriage as a structural consequence of contemporary sex-role differentiation and gender-role socialization. With marriage both women and men had to adjust to life with a person who was, in essence, a member of an alien group.

I have thus far substituted a cultural or psychosocial for a psychosexual interpretation of women's emotional bonding. But there are psychosexual implications in this model which I think it only fair to make more explicit. Despite Sigmund Freud's insistence on the bisexuality of us all or the recent American Psychiatric Association decision on homosexuality, many psychiatrists today tend explicitly or implicitly to view homosexuality as a totally alien or pathological behavior—as totally unlike heterosexuality. I suspect that in essence they may have adopted an explanatory model similar to the one used in discussing schizophrenia. As a psychiatrist can speak of schizophrenia and of a borderline schizophrenic personality as both ultimately and fundamentally different from a normal or neurotic personality, so they also think of both homosexuality and latent homosexuality as states totally different from heterosexuality. With this rapidly dichotomous model of assumption, "latent homosexuality" becomes the indication of a disease in progress—seeds of a pathology which belie the reality of an individual's heterosexuality.

Yet at the same time we are well aware that cultural values can effect choices in the gender of a person's sexual partner. We, for instance, do not necessarily consider homosexual-object choice among men in prison, on shipboard or in boarding schools a necessary indication of pathology. I would urge that we expand this relativistic model and hypothesize that a number of cultures might well tolerate or even encourage diversity in sexual and nonsexual relations. Based on my research into this nineteenth-century world of female intimacy, I would further suggest that rather than seeing a gulf between the normal and the abnormal we view sexual and emotional impulses as part of a continuum or spectrum of affect gradations strongly effected by cultural norms and arrangements, a continuum influenced in part by observed and thus learned behavior. At one end of the continuum lies committed heterosexuality, at the other uncompromising homosexuality; between, a wide latitude of emotions and sexual feelings. Certain cultures and environments permit individuals a great deal of freedom in moving across this spectrum. I would like to suggest that the nineteenth century was such a cultural environment. That is, the supposedly repressive and destructive Victorian sexual ethos may have been more flexible and responsive to the needs of particular individuals than those of mid-twentieth century.

Notes

1. The most notable exception to this rule is now eleven years old: William R. Taylor and Christopher Lasch, "Two 'Kindred Spirits': Sorority and Family in New England, 1839–1846," *New England Quarterly* 36 (1963): 25–41. Taylor has made a valuable contribution to the history of women and the history of the family with his concept of "sororial" relations. I do not, however, accept the Taylor-Lasch thesis that female friendships developed in the mid-nineteenth century because of geographic mobility and the breakup of the colonial family. I have found these friendships as frequently in the eighteenth century as in the nineteenth and would hypothesize that the geographic mobility of the mid-nineteenth century eroded them as it did so many other traditional social institutions. Helen Vendler ("Review of *Notable American Women, 1607–1950*, ed. Edward James and Janet James," *New York Times* [November 5, 1972]: sec. 7) points out the significance of these friendships.

2. I do not wish to deny the importance of women's relations with particular men. Obviously, women were close to brothers, husbands, fathers, and sons. However, there is evidence that despite such closeness relationships between men and women differed in both emotional texture and frequency from those between women. Women's relations with each other, although they played a central role in the American family and American society, have been so seldom examined either by general social historians or by historians of the family that I wish in this article simply to examine their nature and analyze their implications for our understanding of social relations and social structure. I have discussed some aspects of male-female relationships in two articles: "Puberty to Menopause: The Cycle of Femininity in Nineteenth-Century America," *Feminist Studies* 1 (1973): 58–72, and, with Charles Rosenberg, "The Female Animal: Medical and Biological Views of Women in 19th Century America," *Journal of American History* 59 (1973): 331–56.

3. See Freud's classic paper on homosexuality, "Three Essays on the Theory of Sexuality," in *The Standard Edition of the Complete Psychological Works of Sigmund Freud,* trans. James Strachey (London: Hogarth Press, 1953), 7: 135–72. The essays originally appeared in 1905. Prof. Roy Shafer, Department of Psychiatry, Yale University, has pointed out that Freud's view of sexual behavior was strongly influenced by nineteenth-century evolutionary thought. Within Freud's schema, genital heterosexuality marked the height of human development. (Schafer, "Problems in Freud's Psychology of Women," *Journal of the American Psychoanalytical Association* 22 [1974]: 459–85).

4. For a novel and most important exposition of one theory of behavioral norms and options and its application to the study of human sexuality, see Charles Rosenberg, "Sexuality, Class and Role," *American Quarterly* 25 (1973): 131–53.

5. See, e.g., the letters of Peggy Emlen to Sally Logan, 1768–72, Wells Morris Collection, Box 1, Historical Society of Pennsylvania; and the Eleanor Parke Custis Lewis Letters, Historical Society of Pennsylvania, Philadelphia.

6. Sarah Butler Wister was the daughter of Fanny Kemble and Pierce Butler. In 1859 she married a Philadelphia physician, Owen Wister. The novelist Owen Wister is her son. Jeannie Field Musgrove was the half-orphaned daughter of constitutional lawyer and New York Republican politician David Dudley Field. Their correspondence (1855–98) is in the Sarah Butler Wister Papers, Wister Family Papers, Historical Society of Pennsylvania.

7. Sarah Butler, Butler Place, S.C., to Jeannie Field, New York, September 14, 1855.

8. See, e.g., Sarah Butler Wister, Germantown, Pa., to Jeannie Field, New York, September

25, 1862, October 21, 1863; or Jeannie Field, New York, to Sarah Butler Wister, Germantown, July 3, 1861, January 23 and July 12, 1863.

9. Sarah Butler Wister, Germantown, to Jeannie Field, New York, June 5, 1861, February 29, 1864; Jeannie Field to Sarah Butler Wister November 22, 1861, January 4 and June 14, 1863.

10. Sarah Butler Wister, London, to Jeannie Field Musgrove, New York, June 18 and August 3, 1870.

11. See, e.g., two of Sarah's letters to Jeannie: December 21, 1873, July 16, 1878.

12. This is the 1868–1920 correspondence between Mary Hallock Foote and Helena, a New York friend (the Mary Hallock Foote Papers are in the Manuscript Division, Stanford University). Wallace E. Stegner has written a fictionalized biography of Mary Hallock Foote (*Angle of Repose* [Garden City, N.Y.: Doubleday & Co., 1971]). See, as well, her autobiography: Mary Hallock Foote, *A Victorian Gentlewoman in the Far West: The Reminiscences of Mary Hallock Foote,* ed. Rodman W. Paul (San Marino, Calif.: Huntington Library, 1972). In many ways these letters are typical of those women wrote to other women. Women frequently began letters to each other with salutations such as "Dearest," "My Most Beloved," "You Darling Girl," and signed them "tenderly" or "to my dear dear sweet friend, good-bye." Without the least self-consciousness, one woman in her frequent letters to a female friend referred to her husband as "my other love." She was by no means unique. See, e.g., Annie to Charlene Van Vleck Anderson, Appleton, Wis., June 10, 1871, Anderson Family Papers, Manuscript Division, Stanford University; Maggie to Emily Howland, Philadelphia, July 12, 1851, Howland Family Papers, Phoebe King Collection, Friends Historical Library, Swarthmore College; Mary Jane Burleigh to Emily Howland, Sherwood, N.Y., March 27, 1872, Howland Family Papers, Sophia Smith Collection, Smith College; Mary Black Couper to Sophia Madeleine DuPont, Wilmington, Del.: n.d. [1834] (two letters), Samuel Francis DuPont Papers, Eleutherian Mills Foundation, Wilmington, Del.; Phoebe Middleton, Concordiville, Pa., to Martha Jefferis, Chester County, Pa., February 22, 1848; and see in general the correspondence (1838–49) between Rebecca Biddle of Philadelphia and Martha Jefferis, Chester County, Pa., Jefferis Family Correspondence, Chester County Historical Society, West Chester, Pa.; Phoebe Bradford Diary, June 7 and July 13, 1862, Historical Society of Pennsylvania; Sarah Alden Ripley, to Abba Allyn, Boston, n.d. [1818–20], and Sarah Alden Ripley to Sophia Bradford, November 30, 1854, in the Sarah Alden Ripley Correspondence, Schlesinger Library, Radcliffe College; Fanny Canby Ferris to Anne Biddle, Philadelphia, October 11 and November 19, 1811, December 26, 1813, Fanny Canby to Mary Canby, May 27, 1801, Mary R. Garrigues to Mary Canby, five letters n.d., [1802–8], Anne Biddle to Mary Canby, two letters n.d., May 16, July 13, and November 24, 1806, June 14, 1807, June 5, 1808, Anne Sterling Biddle Family Papers, Friends Historical Society, Swarthmore College; Harriet Manigault Wilcox Diary, August 7, 1814, Historical Society of Pennsylvania. See as well the correspondence between Harriet Manigault Wilcox's mother, Mrs. Gabriel Manigault, Philadelphia, and Mrs. Henry Middleton, Charleston, S.C., between 1810 and 1830, Cadwalader Collection, J. Francis Fisher Section, Historical Society of Pennsylvania. The basis and nature of such friendships can be seen in the comments of Sarah Alden Ripley to her sister-in-law and long-time friend, Sophia Bradford: "Hearing that you are not well reminds me of what it would be to lose your loving society. We have kept step together through a long piece of road in the weary journey of life. We have loved the same beings and wept together over their graves." (Mrs. O. J. Wister and Miss Agnes Irwin, eds., *Worthy Women of Our First Century* [Philadelphia: J. B. Lippincott & Co., 1877] p. 195).

13. Mary Hallock [Foote] to Helena, n.d. [1869–70], n.d. [1871–72], Folder 1, Mary Hallock Foote Letters, Manuscript Division, Stanford University.

14. Mary Hallock [Foote] to Helena, September 15 and 23, 1873, n.d. [October 1873], October 12, 1873.

15. Mary Hallock [Foote] to Helena, n.d. [January 1874], n.d. [Spring 1874].

16. Mary Hallock [Foote] to Helena, September 23, 1873; Mary Hallock [Foote] to Richard, December 13, 1873. Molly's and Helena's relationship continued for the rest of their lives. Molly's letters are filled with tender and intimate references, as when she wrote, twenty years later and from 2,000 miles away: "It isn't because you are good that I love you—but for the essence of you which is like perfume" (n.d. [1890s?]).

17. I am in the midst of a larger study of adult gender-roles and gender-role socialization in America, 1785–1895. For a discussion of social attitudes toward appropriate male and female roles,

see Barbara Welter, "The Cult of True Womanhood: 1820–1860," *American Quarterly* 18 (Summer 1966): 151–74; Ann Firor Scott, *The Southern Lady: From Pedestal to Politics, 1830–1930* (Chicago: University of Chicago Press, 1970), chaps. 1–2; Smith-Rosenberg and Rosenberg.

18. See, e.g., the letters of Peggy Emlen to Sally Logan, 1768–72, Wells Morris Collection, Box 1, Historical Society of Pennsylvania; and the Eleanor Parke Custis Lewis Letters, Historical Society of Pennsylvania.

19. See esp. Elizabeth Botts, *Family and Social Network* (London: Tavistock Publications, 1957); Michael Young and Peter Willmott, *Family and Kinship in East London,* rev. ed. (Baltimore: Penguin Books, 1964).

20. This pattern seemed to cross class barriers. A letter that an Irish domestic wrote in the 1830s contains seventeen separate references to women and but only seven to men, most of whom were relatives and two of whom were infant brothers living with her mother and mentioned in relation to her mother (Ann McGrann, Philadelphia, to Sophie M. DuPont, Philadelphia, July 3, 1834, Sophie Madeleine DuPont Letters, Eleutherian Mills Foundation).

21. Harriet Manigault Diary, June 28, 1814, and passim; Jeannie Field, New York, to Sarah Butler Wister, Germantown, April 19, 1863; Phoebe Bradford Diary, January 30, February 19, March 4, August 11, and October 14, 1832, Historical Society of Pennsylvania; Sophie M. DuPont, Brandywine, to Henry DuPont, Germantown, July 9, 1827, Eleutherian Mills Foundation.

22. Martha Jefferis to Anne Jefferis Sheppard, July 9, 1843; Anne Jefferis Sheppard to Martha Jefferis, June 28, 1846; Anne Sterling Biddle Papers, passim, Biddle Family Papers, Friends Historical Society, Swarthmore College; Eleanor Parke Custis Lewis, Virginia, to Elizabeth Bordley Gibson, Philadelphia, November 24 and December 4, 1820, November 6, 1821.

23. Phoebe Bradford Diary, January 13, November 16–19, 1832, April 26 and May 7, 1833; Abigail Brackett Lyman to Mrs. Catling, Litchfield, Conn., May 3, 1801, collection in private hands; Martha Jefferis to Anne Jefferis Sheppard, August 28, 1845.

24. Lisa Mitchell Diary, 1860s, passim, Manuscript Division, Tulane University; Eleanor Parke Custis Lewis to Elizabeth Bordley [Gibson] February 5, 1822; Jeannie McCall, Cedar Park, to Peter McCall, Philadelphia, June 30, 1849, McCall Section, Cadwalader Collection, Historical Society of Pennsylvania.

25. Peggy Emlen to Sally Logan, May 3, 1769.

26. For a prime example of this type of letter, see Eleanor Parke Custis Lewis to Elizabeth Bordley Gibson, passim, or Fanny Canby to Mary Canby, Philadelphia, May 27, 1801; or Sophie M. DuPont, Brandywine, to Henry DuPont, Germantown, February 4, 1832.

27. Place of residence is not the only variable significant in characterizing family structure. Strong emotional ties and frequent visiting and correspondence can unite families that do not live under one roof. Demographic studies based on household structure alone fail to reflect such emotional and even economic ties between families.

28. Eleanor Parke Custis Lewis to Elizabeth Bordley Gibson, April 20 and September 25, 1848.

29. Maria Inskeep to Fanny Hampton Correspondence, 1823–60, Inskeep Collection, Tulane University Library.

30. Eunice Callender, Boston, to Sarah Ripley [Stearns], September 24 and October 29, 1803, February 16, 1805, April 29 and October 9, 1806, May 26, 1810.

31. Sophie DuPont filled her letters to her younger brother Henry (with whom she had been assigned to correspond while he was at boarding school) with accounts of family visiting (see, e.g., December 13, 1827, January 10 and March 9, 1828, February 4 and March 10, 1832; also Sophie M. DuPont to Victorine DuPont Bauday, September 26 and December 4, 1827, February 22, 1828; Sophie M. DuPont, Brandywine, to Clementina B. Smith, Philadelphia, January 15, 1830; Eleuthera DuPont, Brandywine, to Victorine DuPont Bauday, Philadelphia, April 17, 1821, October 20, 1826; Evelina DuPont [Biderman] to Victorine DuPont Bauday, October 18, 1816). Other examples, from the Historical Society of Pennsylvania, are Harriet Manigault [Wilcox] Diary, August 17, September 8, October 19 and 22, December 22, 1814; Jane Zook, Westtown School, Chester County, Pa., to Mary Zook, November 13, December 7 and 11, 1870, February 26, 1871; Eleanor Parke Custis [Lewis] to Elizabeth Bordley [Gibson], March 30, 1796, February 7 and March 20, 1798; Jeannie McCall to Peter McCall, Philadelphia, November 12, 1847; Mary

B. Ashew Diary, July 11 and 13, August 17, Summer and October 1858, and, from a private collection, Edith Jefferis to Anne Jefferis Sheppard, November 1841, April 5, 1842; Abigail Brackett Lyman, Northampton, Mass., to Mrs. Catling, Litchfield, Conn., May 13, 1801; Abigail Brackett Lyman, Northampton, to Mary Lord, August 11, 1800. Mary Hallock Foote vacationed with her sister, her sister's children, her aunt, and a female cousin in the summer of 1874; cousins frequently visited the Hallock farm in Milton, N.Y. In later years Molly and her sister Bessie set up a joint household in Boise, Idaho (Mary Hallock Foote to Helena, June [1874?] and passim). Jeannie Field, after initially disliking her sister-in-law, Laura, became very close to her, calling her "my little sister" and at times spending virtually every day with her (Jeannie Field [Musgrove], New York, to Sarah Butler Wister, Germantown, March 1, 8, and 15, and May 9, 1863).

32. Martha Jefferis to Anne Jefferis Sheppard, January 12, 1845; Phoebe Middleton to Martha Jefferis, February 22, 1848. A number of other women remained close to sisters and sisters-in-law across a long lifetime (Phoebe Bradford Diary, June 7, 1832, and Sarah Alden Ripley to Sophia Bradford, cited in Wister and Irwin, p. 195).

33. Rebecca Biddle to Martha Jefferis, 1838–49, passim; Martha Jefferis to Anne Jefferis Sheppard, July 6, 1846; Anne Jefferis Sheppard to Rachel Jefferis, January 16, 1865; Sarah Foulke Farquhar [Emlen] Diary, September 22, 1813, Friends Historical Library, Swarthmore College; Mary Garrigues to Mary Canby [Biddle], 1802–8, passim; Anne Biddle to Mary Canby [Biddle], May 16, July 13, and November 24, 1806, June 14, 1807, June 5, 1808.

34. Sarah Alden Ripley to Abba Allyn, n.d., Schlesinger Library.

35. Phoebe Bradford Diary, July 13, 1832.

36. Mary Hallock [Foote] to Helena, December 23 [1868 or 1869]; Phoebe Bradford Diary, December 8, 1832; Martha Jefferis and Anne Jefferis Sheppard letters, passim.

37. Martha Jefferis to Anne Jefferis Sheppard, August 3, 1849; Sarah Ripley [Stearns] Diary, November 12, 1808, January 8, 1811. An interesting note of hostility or rivalry is present in Sarah Ripley's diary entry. Sarah evidently deeply resented the husband's rapid remarriage.

38. Martha Jefferis to Edith Jefferis, March 15, 1841; Mary Hallock Foote to Helena, n.d. [1874–75?]; see also Jeannie Field, New York, to Sarah Butler Wister, Germantown, May 5, 1863, Emily Howland Diary, December 1879, Howland Family Papers.

39. Anne Jefferis Sheppard to Martha Jefferis, September 29, 1841.

40. Frances Parke Lewis to Elizabeth Bordley Gibson, April 29, 1821.

41. Mary Jane Burleigh, Mount Pleasant, S.C., to Emily Howland, Sherwood, N.Y., March 27, 1872, Howland Family Papers; Emily Howland Diary, September 16, 1879, January 21 and 23, 1880; Mary Black Couper, New Castle, Del., to Sophie M. DuPont, Brandywine, April 7, 1834.

42. Harriet Manigault Diary, August 15, 21, and 23, 1814, Historical Society of Pennsylvania; Polly [Simmons] to Sophie Madeleine DuPont, February 1822; Sophie Madeleine DuPont to Victoria Bauday, December 4, 1827; Sophie Madeleine DuPont to Clementina Beach Smith, July 24, 1828, August 19, 1829; Clementina Beach Smith to Sophie Madeleine DuPont, April 29, 1831; Mary Black Couper to Sophie Madeleine DuPont, December 24, 1828, July 21, 1834. This pattern appears to have crossed class lines. When a former Sunday school student of Sophie DuPont's (and the daughter of a worker in her father's factory) wrote to Sophie she discussed her mother's health and activities quite naturally (Ann McGrann to Sophie Madeleine DuPont, August 25, 1832; see also Elizabeth Bordley to Martha, n.d. [1797], Eleanor Parke Custis [Lewis] to Elizabeth Bordley [Gibson], May 13, 1796, July 1, 1798; Peggy Emlen to Sally Logan, January 8, 1786. All but the Emlen/Logan letters are in the Eleanor Parke Custis Lewis Correspondence, Historical Society of Pennsylvania).

43. Mrs. S. S. Dalton, "Autobiography," (Circle Valley, Utah, 1876), pp. 21–22, Bancroft Library, University of California, Berkeley; Sarah Foulke Emlen Diary, April 1809; Louisa G. Van Vleck, Appleton, Wis., to Charlena Van Vleck Anderson, Göttingen, n.d. [1875], Harriet Manigault Diary, August 16, 1814, July 14, 1815; Sarah Alden Ripley to Sophy Fisher [early 1860s], quoted in Wister and Irwin (n. 12 above), p. 212. The Jefferis family papers are filled with empathetic letters between Martha and her daughters, Anne and Edith. See, e.g., Martha Jefferis to Edith Jefferis, December 26, 1836, March 11, 1837, March 15, 1841; Anne Jefferis Sheppard to Martha Jefferis, March 17, 1841, January 17, 1847; Martha Jefferis to Anne Jefferis Sheppard, April 17, 1848, April 30, 1849. A representative letter is this of March 9, 1837 from Edith to

Martha: "My heart can fully respond to the language of my own precious Mother, that absence has not diminished our affection for each other, but has, if possible, strengthened the bonds that have united us together & I have had to remark how we had been permitted to mingle in sweet fellowship and have been strengthened to bear one another's burdens. . . ."

44. Abigail Brackett Lyman, Boston, to Mrs. Abigail Brackett (daughter to mother), n.d. [1797], June 3, 1800; Sarah Alden Ripley wrote weekly to her daughter, Sophy Ripley Fisher, after the latter's marriage (Sarah Alden Ripley Correspondence, passim); Phoebe Bradford Diary, February 25, 1833, passim, 1832–33; Louisa G. Van Vleck to Charlena Van Vleck Anderson, December 15, 1873, July 4, August 15 and 29, September 19, and November 9, 1875. Eleanor Parke Custis Lewis's long correspondence with Elizabeth Bordley Gibson contains evidence of her anxiety at leaving her foster mother's home at various times during her adolescence and at her marriage, and her own longing for her daughters, both of whom had married and moved to Louisiana (Eleanor Parke Custis [Lewis] to Elizabeth Bordley [Gibson], October 13, 1795, November 4, 1799, passim, 1820s and 1830s). Anne Jefferis Sheppard experienced a great deal of anxiety on moving two days' journey from her mother at the time of her marriage. This loneliness and sense of isolation persisted through her marriage until, finally a widow, she returned to live with her mother (Anne Jefferis Sheppard to Martha Jefferis, April 1841, October 16, 1842, April 2, May 22, and October 12, 1844, September 3, 1845, January 17, 1847, May 16, June 3, and October 31, 1849; Anne Jefferis Sheppard to Susanna Lightfoot, March 23, 1845, and to Joshua Jefferis, May 14, 1854). Daughters evidently frequently slept with their mothers—into adulthood (Harriet Manigault [Wilcox] Diary, February 19, 1815; Eleanor Parke Custis Lewis to Elizabeth Bordley Gibson, October 10, 1832). Daughters also frequently asked mothers to live with them and professed delight when they did so. See, e.g., Sarah Alden Ripley's comments to George Simmons, October 6, 1844, in Wister and Irwin, p. 185: "It is no longer 'Mother and Charles came out one day and returned the next,' for mother is one of us: she has entered the penetratice, been initiated into the mystery of the household gods, . . . Her divertissement is to mend the stockings . . . whiten sheets and napkins . . . and take a stroll at evening with me to talk of our children, to compare our experiences, what we have learned and what we have suffered, and, last of all, to complete with pears and melons the cheerful circle about the solar lamp. . . . " We did find a few exceptions to this mother-daughter felicity (M.B. Ashew Diary, November 19, 1857, April 10 and May 17, 1858). Sarah Foulke Emlen was at first very hostile to her stepmother (Sarah Foulke Emlen Diary, August 9, 1807), but they later developed a warm supportive relationship.

45. Sarah Alden Ripley to Sophy Thayer, n.d. [1861].

46. Mary Hallock Foote to Helena [winter 1873] (no. 52); Jossie, Stevens Point, Wis., to Charlena Van Vleck [Anderson], Appleton, Wis., October 24, 1870; Pollie Chandler, Green Bay, Wis., to Charlena Van Vleck [Anderson], Appleton, n.d. [1870]; Eleuthera DuPont to Sophie DuPont, September 5, 1829; Sophie DuPont to Eleuthera DuPont, December 1827; Sophie DuPont to Victorine Bauday, December 4, 1827; Mary Gilpin to Sophie DuPont, September 26, 1827; Sarah Ripley Stearns Diary, April 2, 1809; Jeannie McCall to Peter McCall, October 27 [late 1840s]. Eleanor Parke Custis Lewis's correspondence with Elizabeth Bordley Gibson describes such an apprenticeship system over two generations—that of her childhood and that of her daughters. Indeed Eleanor Lewis's own apprenticeship was quite formal. She was deliberately separated from her foster mother in order to spend a winter of domesticity with her married sisters and her remarried mother. It was clearly felt that her foster mother's (Martha Washington) home at the nation's capital was not an appropriate place to develop domestic talents (October 13, 1795, March 30, May 13, and [summer] 1796, March 18 and April 27, 1797, October 1827).

47. Education was not limited to the daughters of the well-to-do. Sarah Foulke Emlen, the daughter of an Ohio Valley frontier farmer, for instance, attended day school for several years during the early 1800s. Sarah Ripley Stearns, the daughter of a shopkeeper in Greenfield, Mass., attended a boarding school for but three months, yet the experience seemed very important to her. Mrs. S. S. Dalton, a Mormon woman from Utah, attended a series of poor country schools and greatly valued her opportunity, though she also expressed a great deal of guilt for the sacrifices her mother made to make her education possible (Sarah Foulke Emlen Journal, Sarah Ripley Stearns Diary, Mrs. S. S. Dalton, "Autobiography").

48. Maria Revere to her mother [Mrs. Paul Revere], June 13, 1801, Paul Revere Papers,

Massachusetts Historical Society. In a letter to Elizabeth Bordley Gibson, March 28, 1847, Eleanor Parke Custis Lewis from Virginia discussed the anxiety her daughter felt when her granddaughters left home to go to boarding school. Eleuthera DuPont was very homesick when away at school
in Philadelphia in the early 1820s (Eleuthera DuPont, Philadelphia, to Victorine Bauday, Wilmington, Del., April 7, 1821; Eleuthera DuPont to Sophie Madeleine DuPont, Wilmington, Del.,
February and April 3, 1821).

49. Elizabeth Bordley Gibson, a Philadelphia matron, played such a role for the daughters and
nieces of her lifelong friend, Eleanor Parke Custis Lewis, a Virginia planter's wife (Eleanor Parke
Custis Lewis to Elizabeth Bordley Gibson, January 29, 1833, March 19, 1826, and passim
through the collection). The wife of Thomas Gurney Smith played a similar role for Sophie and
Eleuthera DuPont (see, e.g., Eleuthera DuPont to Sophie Madeleine DuPont, May 22, 1825; Rest
Cope to Philema P. Swayne [niece], West Town School, Chester County, Pa., April 8, 1829,
Friends Historical Library, Swarthmore College). For a view of such a social pattern over three
generations, see the letters and diaries of three generations of Manigault women in Philadelphia:
Mrs. Gabrielle Manigault, her daughter, Harriet Manigault Wilcox, and granddaughter, Charlotte
Wilcox McCall. Unfortunately, the papers of the three women are not in one family collection
(Mrs. Henry Middleton, Charleston, S.C., to Mrs. Gabrielle Manigault, n.d. [mid 1800s]; Harriet
Manigault Diary, vol. 1; December 1, 1813, June 28, 1814; Charlotte Wilcox McCall Diary, vol.
1; 1842, passim. All in Historical Society of Philadelphia).

50. Frances Parke Lewis, Woodlawn, Va., to Elizabeth Bordley Gibson, Philadelphia, April
11, 1821, Lewis Correspondence; Eleuthera DuPont, Philadelphia, to Victorine DuPont Bauday,
Brandywine, December 8, 1821, January 31, 1822; Eleuthera DuPont, Brandywine, to Margaretta
Lammont [DuPont], Philadelphia, May 1823.

51. Sarah Ripley Stearns Diary, March 9 and 25, 1810; Peggy Emlen to Sally Logan, March
and July 4, 1769; Harriet Manigault [Wilcox] Diary, vol. 1, December 1, 1813, June 28, and
September 18, 1814, August 10, 1815; Charlotte Wilcox McCall Diary, 1842, passim; Fanny
Canby to Mary Canby, May 27, 1801, March 17, 1804; Deborah Cope, West Town School, to
Rest Cope, Philadelphia, July 9, 1828, Chester County Historical Society, West Chester, Pa.;
Anne Zook, West Town School, to Mary Zook, Philadelphia, January 30, 1866, Chester County
Historical Society, West Chester, Pa.; Mary Gilpin to Sophie Madeleine DuPont, February 25,
1829; Eleanor Parke Custis [Lewis] to Elizabeth Bordley [Gibson], April 27, July 2, and Septem-
ber 8, 1797, June 30, 1799, December 29, 1820; Frances Parke Lewis to Elizabeth Bordley
Gibson, December 20, 1820.

52. Anne Jefferis Sheppard to Martha Jefferis, March 17, 1841.

55. Peggy Emlen to Sally Logan, March 1789, Mount Vernon, Va.; Eleanor Parke Custis
[Lewis] to Elizabeth Bordley [Gibson], Philadelphia, April 27, 1797, June 30, 1799; Jeannie
Field, New York, to Sarah Butler Wister, Germantown, July 3, 1861, January 16, 1863, Harriet
Manigault Diary, August 3 and 11–13, 1814; Eunice Callender, Boston, to Sarah Ripley
[Stearns], Greenfield, May 4, 1809. I found one exception to this inhibition of female hostility.
This was the diary of Charlotte Wilcox McCall, Philadelphia (see, e.g., her March 23, 1842 entry).

54. Sophie M. DuPont and Eleuthera DuPont, Brandywine, to Victorine DuPont Bauday,
Philadelphia, January 25, 1832.

55. Sarah Ripley [Stearns] Diary and Harriet Manigault Diary, passim.

56. Sophie Madeleine DuPont to Eleuthera DuPont, December 1827; Clementina Beach
Smith to Sophie Madeleine DuPont, December 26, 1828; Sarah Faulke Emlen Diary, July 21,
1808, March 30, 1809; Annie Hethroe, Ellington, Wis., to Charlena Van Vleck [Anderson],
Apppleton, Wis., April 23, 1865; Frances Parke Lewis, Woodlawn, Va., to Elizabeth Bordley
[Gibson], Philadelphia, December 20, 1820; Fanny Ferris to Debby Ferris, West Town School,
Chester County, Pa., May 29, 1826. An excellent example of the warmth of women's comments
about each other and the reserved nature of their references to men are seen in two entries in Sarah
Ripley Stearn's diary. On January 8, 1811 she commented about a young woman friend: "The
amiable Mrs. White of Princeton . . . one of the loveliest most interesting creatures I ever knew,
young fair and blooming . . . beloved by everyone . . . formed to please & to charm. . . ." She
referred to the man she ultimately married always as "my friend" or "a friend" (February 2 or April
23, 1810).

57. Jeannie Field, New York, to Sarah Butler Wister, Germantown, April 6, 1862.

58. Elizabeth Bordley Gibson, introductory statement to the Eleanor Parke Custis Lewis Letters [1850s], Historical Society of Pennsylvania.

59. Sarah Foulke [Emlen] Diary, March 30, 1809.

60. Harriet Manigault Diary, May 26, 1815.

61. Sarah Ripley [Stearns] Diary, May 17 and October 2, 1812; Eleanor Parke Custis Lewis to Elizabeth Bordley Gibson, April 23, 1826; Rebecca Ralston, Philadelphia, to Victorine DuPont [Bauday], Brandywine, September 27, 1813.

62. Anne Jefferis to Martha Jefferis, November 22 and 27, 1840, January 13 and March 17, 1841; Edith Jefferis, Greenwich, N.J., to Anne Jefferis, Philadelphia, January 31, February 6 and February 1841.

63. Edith Jefferis to Anne Jefferis, January 31, 1841.

64. Eleanor Parke Custis Lewis to Elizabeth Bordley, November 4, 1799. Eleanor and her daughter Parke experienced similar sorrow and anxiety when Parke married and moved to Cincinnati (Eleanor Parke Custis Lewis to Elizabeth Bordley Gibson, April 23, 1826). Helena DeKay visited Mary Hallock the month before her marriage; Mary Hallock was an attendant at the wedding; Helena again visited Molly about three weeks after her marriage; and then Molly went with Helena and spent a week with Helena and Richard in their new apartment (Mary Hallock [Foote] to Helena DeKay Gilder [Spring 1874] [no. 61], May 10, 1874 [May 1874], June 14, 1874 [Summer 1874]. See also Anne Biddle, Philadelphia, to Clement Biddle [brother], Wilmington, March 12 and May 27, 1827; Eunice Callender, Boston, to Sarah Ripley [Stearns], Greenfield, Mass., August 3, 1807, January 26, 1808; Victorine DuPont Bauday, Philadelphia, to Evelina DuPont [Biderman], Brandywine, November 25 and 26, December 1, 1813; Peggy Emlen to Sally Logan, n.d. [1769–70?]; Jeannie Field, New York, to Sarah Butler Wister, Germantown, July 3, 1861).

65. Mary Hallock to Helena DeKay Gilder [1876] (no. 81); n.d. (no. 83), March 3, 1844; Mary Ashew Diary, vol. 2, September–January, 1860; Louisa Van Vleck to Charlena Van Vleck Anderson, n.d. [1875]; Sophie DuPont to Henry DuPont, July 24, 1827; Benjamin Ferris to William Canby, February 13, 1805; Benjamin Ferris to Mary Canby Biddle, December 20, 1825; Anne Jefferis Sheppard to Martha Jefferis, September 15, 1884; Martha Jefferis to Anne Jefferis Sheppard, July 4, 1843, May 5, 1844, May 3, 1847, July 17, 1849; Jeannie McCall to Peter McCall, November 26, 1847, n.d. [late 1840s]. A graphic description of the ritual surrounding a first birth is found in Abigail Lyman's letter to her husband Erastus Lyman, October 18, 1810.

66. Fanny Ferris to Anne Biddle, November 19, 1811; Eleanor Parke Custis Lewis to Elizabeth Bordley Gibson, November 4, 1799, April 27, 1827; Martha Jefferis to Anne Jefferis Sheppard, January 31, 1843, April 4, 1844; Martha Jefferis to Phoebe Sharpless Middleton, June 4, 1846; Anne Jefferis Sheppard to Martha Jefferis, August 20, 1843, February 12, 1844; Maria Inskeep, New Orleans, to Mrs. Fanny G. Hampton, Bridgeton, N.J., September 22, 1848; Benjamin Ferris to Mary Canby, February 14, 1805; Fanny Ferris to Mary Canby [Biddle], December 2, 1816.

67. Eleanor Parke Custis Lewis to Elizabeth Bordley Gibson, October–November 1820, passim.

68. Emily Howland to Hannah, September 30, 1866; Emily Howland Diary, February 8, 11, and 27, 1880; Phoebe Bradford Diary, April 12 and 13, and August 4, 1833; Eunice Callender, Boston, to Sarah Ripley [Stearns], Greenwich, Mass., September 11, 1802, August 26, 1810; Mrs. H. Middleton, Charleston, to Mrs. Gabrielle Manigault, Philadelphia, n.d. [mid 1800s]; Mrs. H. C. Paul to Mrs. Jeannie McCall, Philadelphia, n.d. [1840s]; Sarah Butler Wister, Germantown, to Jeannie Field [Musgrove], New York, April 22, 1864; Jeannie Field [Musgrove] to Sarah Butler Wister, August 25, 1861, July 6, 1862; S. B. Raudolph to Elizabeth Bordley [Gibson], n.d. [1790s]. For an example of similar letters between men, see Henry Wright to Peter McCall, December 10, 1852; Charles McCall to Peter McCall, January 4, 1860, March 22, 1864; R. Mercer to Peter McCall, November 29, 1872.

69. Mary Black [Couper] to Sophie Madeleine DuPont, February 1827, [November 1, 1834], November 12, 1834, two letters [late November 1834]; Eliza Schlatter to Sophie Madeleine DuPont, November 2, 1834.

70. For a few of the references to death rituals in the Jefferis papers see: Martha Jefferis to Anne

Jefferis Sheppard, September 28, 1843, August 21 and September 25, 1844, January 11, 1846, summer 1848, passim; Anne Jefferis Sheppard to Martha Jefferis, August 20, 1843; Anne Jefferis Sheppard to Rachel Jefferis, March 17, 1863, February 9, 1868. For other Quaker families, see Rachel Biddle to Anne Biddle, July 23, 1854; Sarah Foulke Farquhar [Emlen] Diary, April 30, 1811, February 14, 1812; Fanny Ferris to Mary Canby, August 31, 1810. This is not to argue that men and women did not mourn together. Yet in many families women aided and comforted women and men, men. The same-sex death ritual was one emotional option available to nineteenth-century Americans.

71. Sarah Foulke [Emlen] Diary, December 29, 1808.

72. Eunice Callender, Boston, to Sarah Ripley [Stearns] Greenfield, Mass., May 24, 1803.

73. Katherine Johnston Brinley [Wharton] Journal, April 26, May 30, and May 29, 1856, Historical Society of Pennsylvania.

74. A series of roughly fourteen letters written by Peggy Emlen to Sally Logan (1768–71) has been preserved in the Wells Morris Collection, Box 1, Historical Society of Pennsylvania (see esp. May 3 and July 4, 1769, January 8, 1768).

75. The Sarah Alden Ripley Collection, the Arthur M. Schlesinger, Sr., Library, Radcliffe College, contains a number of Sarah Alden Ripley's letters to Mary Emerson. Most of these are undated, but they extend over a number of years and contain letters written both before and after Sarah's marriage. The eulogistic biographical sketch appeared in Wister and Irwin (n. 12 above). It should be noted that Sarah Butler Wister was one of the editors who sensitively selected Sarah's letters.

76. See Sarah Alden Ripley to Mary Emerson, November 19, 1823. Sarah Alden Ripley routinely, and one must assume ritualistically, read Mary Emerson's letters to her infant daughter, Mary. Eleanor Parke Custis Lewis reported doing the same with Elizabeth Bordley Gibson's letters, passim. Eunice Callender, Boston, to Sarah Ripley [Stearns], October 19, 1808.

77. Mary Black Couper to Sophie M. DuPont, March 5, 1832. The Clementina Smith–Sophie DuPont correspondence of 1,678 letters is in the Sophie DuPont Correspondence. The quotation is from Eliza Schlatter, Mount Holly, N.J., to Sophie DuPont, Brandywine, August 24, 1834. I am indebted to Anthony Wallace for informing me about this collection.

78. Mary Grew, Providence, R.I., to Isabel Howland, Sherwood, N.Y., April 27, 1892, Howland Correspondence, Sophia Smith Collection, Smith College.

79. Helena Deutsch, *Psychology of Women* (New York: Grune & Stratton, 1944), vol. 1, chaps. 1–3; Clara Thompson, *On Women,* ed. Maurice Green (New York: New American Library, 1971).

15. Privacy and the Making of the Self-Made Man: Family Strategies of the Middle Class at Midcentury

Voluntary association did not suddenly fade from the American scene after 1845. In commemoration of the Union victory on July 4, 1865, the spirit of association paraded down the streets of Utica in full regalia. Fifteen lodges, at least one temperance society, and five fire companies joined the patriotic procession. The typographical union, the carmen, and the cabinetmakers filed into the streets just as in decades past. They were joined by some newer contingents as well. Five associations composed of immigrants and Roman Catholics entered the line of march to give a more cosmopolitan tone to the celebration of the nation's birthday. Even the growing proletariat was welcomed into this parade of associations. The Utica press reported that the "operatives of the Cotton and Woolen factories" marched in a body. It would seem that at least in the jubilant spirit of the Fourth of July the distinctive fragments of an increasingly complicated urban society, with its ethnic complexity and industrial sector, could still come together to form a pastiche community.[1]

A closer look at some of the marching units in 1865, however, reveals some important nuances in this ritual of community solidarity. Those fire companies, for example, were no longer voluntary associations but rather an assemblage of paid public servants. Behind them in the parade came another curious innovation, a wagon carrying thirty-six young women, chosen, we are told, for their fair faces and fine proportions, each one carrying the insignia of a state in the Union. These harbingers of municipal bureaucracies and beauty pageants suggest a subtle but important shift in the organization of urban society. Once the whole town was knit casually together by face-to-face bonds and alliances; now new sorts of social glue were required: first, an expansion of the formal public sector as illustrated by the city fire department and, second, a recourse to symbolic modes of social cohesion such as a carload of local beauties who represented some abstract notion of national unity.

Further evidence of a quiet transformation in Utica's social order can be spied *between the lines* of the Fourth of July procession—in the segments of the population that were conspicuously absent from the patriotic procession. No Protestant association or reform group made a public appearance. Neither did the growing ranks of the new middle class; neither professionals nor clerks formed themselves into a marching unit. The absence of these groups, which had played such a prominent role in the associated life of the canal era, would seem to be deliberate and self-conscious. Six years earlier the minister of the Utica Presbyterian Church made this observation about the participants in the Thanksgiv-

Mary P. Ryan, "Privacy and the Making of the Self-Made Man: Family Strategies of the Middle Class at Midcentury," reprinted from her *Cradle of the Middle Class: The Family in Oneida County, New York, 1790–1865,* 145–85, copyright © 1981, Cambridge University Press, with the permission of Cambridge University Press.

ing Day parade, a town festival originally instituted to commemorate the traditions of New England Protestants. "There were the working and laboring classes of our city who had little time for enjoyment and the time of most of them was for this world. If they knew the joys and pleasures that flowed from pure religion how sweet would be their rest at night—when the tasks of the day are done."

In this pastor's opinion, parades were an amusement of the lower classes and manual workers and an illegitimate one at that. Respectable people celebrated Thanksgiving in the church and at home, not in the public streets. A few years later a parishioner of the same church, Lavinia Johnson, observed the Thanksgiving Day parade from the quiet of her parlor. To Mrs. Johnson, such rituals served only "to draw the rabble of the city." She was particularly shocked to find females participating in this unseemly public activity. "Why can't women stay at home," she asked. "Poor women, and try to make home comfortable and take care for their children?"[2] Just a few decades earlier, the women of Lavinia Johnson's congregation had taken to the streets on a variety of evangelical missions and won the reputation of noisy, prying, intrusive busybodies. Now they withdrew into their private homes and shunned public rituals, including such Yankee traditions as Thanksgiving Day and the Fourth of July.

Varieties of Social Retreat: Domesticity, Privacy, and the Self-Made Man

This apparent retreat into a private world was endorsed by a voluminous body of popular literature that historians have labeled the "cult of domesticity."[3] The literate middle-class population of Utica had subscribed to the ideology of domestic privacy for some time. In 1837 a local publication entitled the *Young Ladies' Miscellany* enunciated the most central proposition of the cult of domesticity when it prescribed that "woman lives best, and most powerfully in the private role, where the historian yet seldom penetrates—in the causes of events, which he seldom deeply investigates and in the modes of action which he seldom finds."[4] By midcentury the middle-class man as well as his wife was being enticed into the same darkened corner of history. The popular literature of the 1850s courted men away from their male associations—from taverns, political clubs, lodges—into the feminine world of the home. *A Voice to the Married,* published locally, told the husband to regard his home as "an elysium to which he can flee and find rest from the stormy strife of a selfish world."[5]

This privatizing trend was articulated not only in the feminine ideology of the cult of domesticity but in a more masculine mode as well, the doctrine of the "self-made man." *A Voice to the Married* did not advise young men to form themselves into associations, neither unions nor mutual benefit associations. The author postulated instead that "a good character must be formed, it must be *made*—it must be built *by our individual exertions*" (emphasis mine). Popular literature at midcentury directed a responsible breadwinner, no less than a loving mother, into a narrowing social universe, one even more solitary than privacy—the domain of the self, the individual, of "manly independence."[6]

Both the cult of domesticity and the mythology of the self-made man were built on the assumption that the household was no longer the place of production, the locus of breadwinning. For most native-born Uticans with middle-range occupations and above, this assumption was correct. According to the listings in the *City Directory,* professionals, white-collar workers, and even prosperous artisans and shopkeepers left home each day for an office, store, or workshop that was detached from their place of residence. Some writers and domestic architects would like to deepen and widen the moat between home and the workplace by relocating middle-class families in bucolic settings on the outskirts of the city itself. At least some of Utica's husbands and fathers had begun this diurnal shuttle before the Civil War. Lavinia Johnson described such a practice in this account of her daughter's living arrangement one summer: "Will will come in the stage every morning to his business and Mary will meet him every night at the carriage in New Hartford to take him to their abode."[7] Such families seemed so determined to secure domestic privacy and isolation that they would fend off both society and history by retreating along the back roads of American economic development into quiet rural villages like New Hartford.

This reverence for quiet, seclusion, and privacy was usually portrayed in popular literature as a reflexive reaction to repellent developments outside the household. *Mother's Magazine* repeatedly warned women to protect their children from the "contamination of the streets." The newspapermen of Utica hardly encouraged their readers to regard the public thoroughfares as a safe and comfortable habitat. By the 1850s calls for "law and order" were front-page news. The *Morning Herald,* for example, ran a regular column entitled "Crimes and Casualties," which, with perverse exuberance, enumerated railroad, steamboat, and industrial accidents, as well as bloodcurdling acts of personal violence— murder, arson, infanticide, and rape. The scene of such atrocities was usually a hostile city street. In 1861 the *Herald* reported the fate of a woman who asked a passerby for directions to the railroad station: attempted rape by four men. In this incident and countless other grisly crime reports, the newspapers of Utica seemed to advertise the streets of their city as alien and threatening social spaces.[8]

But certainly this is something of a libel against the city at midcentury and, conversely, an exaggeration of the quiet and harmony of the American home. The local press also recounts copious examples of convivial social life outside the household. This was the era of Sunday-school picnics, ice-cream socials, and civic baseball games, as well as Fourth of July celebrations. With a population under twenty-five thousand in 1865, Utica's streets were not yet open territory for rapacious criminals. That case of attempted rape, for example, ended with protective interference by observant neighbors. Furthermore, the newly appointed law enforcement officers found more cases of violence within the city's domestic spaces than on the streets. Then, as now, wife beating was the most common violent crime.[9]

When middle-class writers or women like Lavinia Johnson vacated the streets and retreated into the private home, they were responding to more subtle changes in urban social life, to the transformation, rather than the breakdown, of the social order. First of all, the native-born Protestant was reacting to the increasing heterogeneity of the local population. Lavinia Johnson returned bewildered from the nearby railroad station: "Such a crowd of people together and most all strangers to each other, so many strangers."[10] Strangers to Lavinia Johnson were often members of diverse, but internally cohesive, new groups within the local population. Uticans gathered together, for example, in twenty-eight different churches in 1855. What disturbed the likes of Mrs. Johnson was not social and religious anonymity but the fact that the largest such institution brought together Roman Catholics, not her fellow Protestants. The inundation of Utica by

Catholics was a result of increasingly massive immigration beginning in the late 1840s and coming more often from Ireland and Germany than from England or Canada. By 1845, 40% of the city's residents and a full 60% of the local heads of households were foreign-born. It was a stream of alien ways and foreign tongues (not criminals) into the streets of Utica that caused the native-born middle class such apprehension.

The streets of the city at midcentury were no longer bordered by a smooth line of small shops and houses. The urban horizon was now broken by more massive commercial and industrial enterprises. The steam textile factories founded in the late 1840s were joined by three large garment works in the next decade, each employing four hundred workers or more. The 1860s witnessed the sudden growth and industrialization of the local shoe industry. The largest such factory contained some eighty sewing machines and could produce 150,000 pairs of boots annually.[11] Even Genesee Street was invaded by these relatively gargantuan enterprises. William Stacy's Dry Goods Store at number 104 was enlarged to stock a prodigious array of goods, including, for example, the forty-two different items of personal and home furnishings advertised in a single newspaper notice. Gaffney's Cheap Irish Stores, The China Emporium, and the warehouses of Lord and Taylor and G. W. Muir of New York City flooded Genesee Street with commodities and transformed retailing into such a bustling and impersonal process that shoplifting became a serious local problem. The mass of goods, hum of machinery, and hordes of workers, often of foreign birth, could not but impress older residents of Utica with the qualitative and disquieting changes that were occurring in their community.

The larger scale and greater complexity of urban life was apparent in Utica's political structure as well. A diverse population of more than twenty thousand people could hardly settle their differences and make public policy on a face-to-face basis. Only the small villages of Oneida County, such as Whitesborough and New Hartford, held town meetings after 1850. Utica had long since resorted to an elected town council and employed an increasing number of salaried, appointed officials—city engineers, policemen, and overseers of the poor. Nothing better demonstrated the impersonal quality of public life than this charge to police officers written into the city charter of 1862. "Each policeman shall acquire such knowledge of the inhabitants within his beat as to enable him at once to recognize them. He shall also strictly watch the conduct of all persons of known bad character." Utica's citizenry had abjured their responsibility to know and assist their neighbors and had foisted it off on a paid public official who operated within a bureau of the municipal government.[12] In other respects, the people of Utica saw political authority pass entirely out of local jurisdiction. After all, Utica was linked only by the impersonal threads of representative government and party politics to the decisions made in Washington and at Fort Sumter that held the power of life or death over the young men of the town in the 1860s. The preoccupation with privacy had developed in tandem with the enlargement, remoteness, and increasing formality of this public sphere.

All these permutations in urban social life were etched into an engraving of Utica dated 1850.[13] A local artisan named Lewis Bradley portrayed Bagg's Square as the hub of a busy urban scene, placed just to the rear of the primary symbols of the city's commercial and now industrial growth: the Erie Canal and the Utica and Syracuse Railroad. The urban space that radiated out from Bagg's Square was punctuated eleven times by bellowing smokestacks, which dwarfed the fewer, more diminutive church spires. In the far western corner of the panorama, not far from the textile factories, stood the grandiose columns of the New York State Lunatic Asylum, its massive granite a fitting symbol of the power and remoteness of the public sphere. Around these icons of industrial production and public life, Bradley assembled, almost as an afterthought, a largely undifferentiated sea of private dwellings. Most appeared to be two-story one- or two-family houses, except for larger barrackslike residences near the factories. Bradley bothered to depict only two central streets, which cut through this maze of buildings like narrow shaded caverns. The human figures who occupied these streets, furthermore, were either formally attired and were on public display or appeared to be passing briskly through commercial arteries toward some more important destination. Gone were the casual poses, rustic costumes, and leisurely postures favored by the artists who set their easels in Bagg's Square during the canal era. The urban ambience had been transformed into a more massive and formally organized social space, one that arranged social life into private and public sectors.

Lewis Bradley sketched a cool, massive alabaster urban scene. It did not, however, suggest a threatening urban jungle. Neither this sketch nor the social reality of Utica at midcentury justifies the sometimes hysterical urgency with which popular writers advised retreat into a private and individualized world. The reasons for this nervous stance toward the city must be located within the immediate experience of middle-class, native-born Protestants. The decade before the Civil War was especially difficult for the old middle class of Utica, the small producers and retailers who once waxed in the abundant opportunities of the canal era. This sector of the occupational structure employed a shrinking proportion of the local population after 1845. Between 1845 and 1856 the relative ranks of both the shopkeepers and craftsmen were reduced almost by half.

The history of shoemaking during this period illustrates the predicament of the old middle class. Cordwainers in Utica, as in cities throughout the Northeast, saw the value of their skills and business steadily decline as shoemaking became a fully mechanized factory operation. As late as 1860 the Utica economy accommodated considerable numbers of master shoemakers with capital investments in four figures and a handful of skilled workers in their service. By 1870, however, the solid middling ground of the shoemaking craft had eroded and in its stead stood, on the one hand, massive factories with capital investments of up to $130,000, and, on the other, the small shops and idle benches of shoe-repair men. A worker in Reynolds Shoe Factory might well earn a wage that was comparable to, or even higher than, that of the artisan shoemaker, yet he had clearly surrendered the cherished privileges of the old middle class: title to his own productive property, his own tools, and his own control of the pace and conditions of work.[14] Simultaneously, the journeyman or apprentice shoemaker saw his prospects of becoming an independent artisan diminish apace. Half the cordwainers of 1828 eventually opened small businesses of their own; less than 5% were so fortunate in the 1860s. With the establishment of large garment factories in Utica, the city's hatters and tailors could contemplate the same unhappy fate.

Utica's retailers felt a similar pressure at midcentury, exerted by competition from larger local department stores and the aggressive merchandising of New York wholesalers. Many of the city's shopkeepers were dealt a fatal blow by the Panic of 1857. The records of the Mercantile Agency reported twenty-six outright failures that year and double that number by 1860, complete with sheriff's sales and bankruptcy proceedings; countless other firms quietly "closed up" or "went out of business." The dimensions of the crisis were indicated by the report for the firm of Murdock and Andrews: "Only jewelers in Utica that did not fail during the panic." All these failing fortunes were clearly implicated in the machinations of a complex market system that reached far beyond Utica. The nationwide scope of the panic as well as more intimate business experiences made this patently clear. For example, when Utica's prominent Presbyterian businessman Spencer Kellogg closed his store in 1857, the Mercantile Agency attributed his failure to unsound investments in New York City. The critical link in the disastrous downturn in the national business cycle was Kellogg's own son, of Bliss and Kellogg, New York.[15]

The telescope of family and generational history magnifies the predicament of the old middle class at midcentury. Small-businessmen who were struggling to keep their own firms solvent were particularly hardpressed to put their progeny on a sound economic footing within the middling sort. Of all the wills processed in Utica after 1850 a mere five witnessed the transfer of a store or workshop to a second generation. The records of the Mercantile Agency also contain paltry testimony to the family networks of small-business men. Between the 1840s and the 1860s the proportion of family partnerships was reduced to one-fourth its former size. Of the 331 businesses reported on between 1860 and 1865, only 10 noted that a son had followed in his father's footsteps. Most of the sons of the old middle class who would come of age in Utica at midcentury could expect to be unceremoniously catapulted into the status of a self-made man.

Just what these young men would make of themselves remained, however, an open and anxious question. A self-made man was by no means assured of being a rich man, for the ranks of large merchants, financiers, and manufacturers accommodated less than 3% of Utica's adult males. Meanwhile, a place within the old middle class, among artisans and shopkeepers, was becoming harder to find and less comfortable to inhabit. The positions in the factories, although they often paid relatively good wages, were insecure and did not attract many native-born youths. Certainly the ranks of day laborers were without allure and, like factory jobs, were given over largely to the foreign-born or their children. More seductive and accessible than any of these occupational niches were posts within the new middle class, chiefly the professions or white-collar jobs. Although white-collar employment was one of the most rapidly growing sectors of the local job market, it could hardly be called booming. In fact, the increase in such positions did not quite keep up with the growth of the population. Clearly, midcentury was a sober time for middle-class families, a time of special anxiety about the economic prospects of the rising generation and a time, perhaps, to withdraw into the private home to assay the prospects ahead.

However, a middle-class family crisis does not translate automatically into a process of privatization. Something more was at work than an instinct to withdraw from an uncertain and threatening world into some familiar space full of loving kin. A more complete explanation of the impulse for privacy must be sought, first of all, within the increasingly individualized nature of middle-class occupations themselves. The corporate, collective aspects of the household economy and the master artisan's retinue of journeymen and apprentices had by the 1850s become overwhelmed by the imperatives of maximizing individual gain in a competitive market. A producer or retailer turned inward to his personal resources, his ability to manage labor, manipulate credit, and set prices in such a way as to outdo his competitors. The newer components of the middle class were more severely cut off from any economic collectivity. A professional or white-collar worker relied increasingly on his own skills, be they as lawyer or bookkeeper, with which to barter for his livelihood. In the more impersonal economic networks of the growing and industrializing city, furthermore, it was incumbent upon members of both the old and the new middle classes to demonstrate their own finely tuned aptitudes for business, to display, if not the financial wizardry of an entrepreneur, at least the prudence, honesty, and good sense of a reputable small merchant. Not even inherited wealth could exempt a modern-day businessman from these requirements. Consider the case of James Stocking who, despite all the riches and reputation of his father, Samuel, was dismissed by the Mercantile Agency as "a rich man's son who has been a pretty wild chap. He never was educated to economy."[16] In sum, a kind of geological shift gently quaked beneath the formerly more solid ground of the middling sort, casting asunder the old associational and collective forms and elevating more highly individuated, more private, concerns and imperatives.

Although the processes of individuation and privatization both turn in the same inward direction, away from more expansive social relationships, they are by no means one and the same thing. The doctrine of privacy venerated not the isolated individual but rather a set of intense and intimate social relations, essentially those of the conjugal family. Privacy was a social construction, in other words, and, as a consequence, the product of concrete historical actions. An unusually exuberant history went into the definition of the private sphere. In the crucible of revivals and reform associations, the men and women of Utica had elaborated an array of new social relationships and services and then earmarked them as the responsibility of families. The reforms favored by the old middle classes during the canal era were particularly innovative and productive, contributing to the private sphere such social functions as a new method of childrearing, new standards of self-control, new bourgeois values such as temperance and sexual restraint. In short, privacy had been sketched out in sufficient detail before midcentury so as to constitute a palpable set of social relations and functions. Accordingly, it was more than the last refuge of beleaguered individuals fleeing a hostile environment. It exerted its own positive social pull and had many concrete advantages to present to confused men and women. In fact, the associations of the thirties and forties had adumbrated a sequence of private activities that might guide the middle classes out of their predicament at midcentury.

Midcentury Utica, in sum, was at an intricate confluence of social and historical changes: Steady advances in the scale and capitalization of industrial production, shifts in the middle ranges of the occupational structure, and alterations in the social and political arrangement of the city converged with the associational legacy of innovative family forms. The consequences of these commingled forces can be sorted out in several ways: as the divergence of private and public life, as the separation of male and female spheres, as the emergence of a cult of domesticity and the parallel masculine ideal of the self-made man. I have chosen to draw out one salient strand in this complex historical fabric, the process whereby the native-born Protestant members of the middle class learned to work within the private sphere to maintain their own positions in the social structure and to provide similar comforts for their progeny. What follows should not be construed as a systematic, causal analysis of class formation. It does, however, identify a sequence of family practices typical of the native-born Protestants who would, in a period of major economic changes, maintain middle-range positions in the local social structure. The rest of this chapter, then, will describe some strategies whereby the American middle class reproduced itself in an industrializing society.

The Birth and Rearing of Victorian Children

These strategies began with biological reproduction itself. A look at the completed family size of mothers in their fifties in the year 1865 (and hence whose fertility cycle began in the 1830s) indicates that native-born parents had begun to rationalize the process of reproduction at an early date. This generation of women would bear on average only 3.6 children as opposed to a mean score of 5.8 for those twenty years older and 5.08 for those only ten years their seniors. In other words, an abrupt drop in the fertility of the native-born women of Utica occurred during the heyday of the canal era. The parents of these smaller families had already forestalled and reduced the problems of reproducing the middle class. At least they would have to worry about placing only one or two sons on the ladder to comfort and respectability.

It is not entirely fallacious to impute such conscious fertility control to the native-born men and women who began their families in the thirties and forties. The determination of native-born couples to intervene in the natural rate of procreation is underscored by the contrasting fertility rate for foreign-born females, who on the average bore two more children than did the natives and continued to bear children until later in life (a difference of two to three years by one inexact measure of the mother's age at last birth). More telling perhaps is the fact that native-born women of every age group mothered fewer children than their foreign-born counterparts. Women in their twenties reported a mean number of births of .612, compared with 1.04 for immigrant mothers. Native-born women in their thirties and forties also maintained fertility rates substantially lower than foreigners, having given birth on the average to 2.3 and 3.2 children, respectively. The determination of native-born women to control births throughout their fertility cycle is further evidenced by the longer intervals between the ages of their resident children. An average interval of 5.1 years for native-born women as opposed to 3.5 for the Irish and 3.5 for women born in Germany is suggestive of deliberate methods of prolonging the period between conceptions.

These prudent procreators had at their disposal a variety of methods of limiting births—withdrawal, abstinence, sundry folk potions and patent medicines, and abortion. James Mohr has argued convincingly that before it was thoroughly outlawed late in the nineteenth century large numbers of middle-class women resorted to abortion for this purpose. An advertisement in the *Utica Observer* dated 1833 explicitly recommended one patent medicine as an abortifacient. In 1834, however, the Oneida County Medical Society expelled a physician for performing an abortion and New York State legally restricted this method of fertility control soon thereafter.[17] Still, advice on abortion was hidden away in the fine print of the local advertising pages at midcentury. Advertisements for female pills often contained less than cryptic messages about abortion, warnings, for example, that certain portions should be shunned by pregnant women as they invariably caused miscarriage. A testimonial for Golden Female Pills dated 1856 claimed to be a miracle drug indeed, guaranteed to "prevent pregnancy."[18] Although female pills were ineffective methods of contraception, their existence, like all the references to abortion, testified to the fact that large numbers of women were painfully anxious to control their reproduction but were, as yet, without any reliable prophylactics.

The evangelical and reformist tradition of Utica had, however, recommended one very reliable, if Draconian, method of reducing family size: sexual control to the point of abstinence. Historians such as Daniel Scott Smith and Linda Gordon have argued that sexual abstinence, as enforced by pure womanhood, was one not insignificant means of curtailing births within the Protestant middle class.[19] Certainly one would expect that this method had its partisans and practitioners in Utica. The members of the Female Moral Reform Society had installed refined standards of female purity at the center of local culture by the late 1830s and supplied an elaborate rationale for sexual abstinence. It is also very likely that this ideology influenced the private relations and reproductive strategies of the middle class. At any rate, the standard of female purity was generally accepted by Utica's Protestant middle class at midcentury when native-born fertility had been put securely in check. Sexual matters had been relegated beyond the pale of polite conversation. Sometimes even family intimates were reticent about such topics. For example, Lavinia Johnson and her daughter did not broach the delicate issue of pregnancy until labor pains had begun. When an occasional church trial raised such unseemly issues, the details were veiled in feminine delicacy. One Elizabeth Dudley managed only to blushingly confess to the Whitestown session meeting that she had "allowed herself to be seduced." The *Oneida Whig,* meanwhile, let it be known that any attempt to educate women on these subjects, as proposed by the veteran moral reformer Paulina Wright, was an affront to femininity.[20]

Although Victorian purity may have been a code word and rationale for sexual control within marriage, it is unlikely that this was the sole method of limiting family size or that contraception was the unilateral practice and concern of females. There is direct evidence that men took an interest in birth control and had their own devices whereby to achieve it. Male culture, in fact, was the receptacle of some of the most explicit injunctions to keep families small. A businessman could even have been denied a loan on the grounds that he had sired an exorbitantly large family. The crudest expression of this norm was issued by the Mercantile Agency, along with an ethnic slur. The agency's records predicted the business failure of one German shoemaker with the report that "there are too many little Dutchmen around to make ends meet." A native-born man who failed to conform to this notion of the ideal family size could also see his credit denied on the grounds that he had a "large and expensive family."[21] Suitably prudent artisans and shopkeepers could resort to one ancient method of staving off such criticism, one that required considerable self-control but not utter self-denial, that is, coitus interruptus. Whether achieved by abortion, ordained by female purity, or controlled by masculine rationality, and more likely by some combination of the three, the curtailment of fertility involved an exacting, tense, and deeply internalized family strategy. It resided awkwardly at the most intimate connection of men and women.

Once birth had occurred, however, the process of social reproduction was increasingly delegated to females. Well before midcentury it was clear that the mother's control over the socialization of infants and children had been expanded and extended. Writings on childhood education during the 1820s were still a bit confused about the gender of the primary agent of socialization. Both Methodists and Presbyterians used male adjectives even when they described a mother's responsibilities, employing such curious phrases as "paternal love" or "paternal instructions." By 1833, however, *Mother's Magazine* regarded the transfer of parental obligations from male to female as a fait accompli: "The character of the man or woman is substantially laid as early as that period when the father is engaged in the bustling affairs of life." Through the remainder of childhood and until male children had entered that bustling world in their own right, mothers were placed in charge of shaping the character of the next generation. In this aspect of social reproduction, women were even admonished to dispense with that hackneyed but flaccid method of invoking paternal discipline, the warning "wait until your father comes home."[22]

With this change in the gender of the primary parent came a wholesale transformation in the preferred method of infant socialization, one recognized once again by *Mother's Magazine* as early as the 1830s. *Mother's Magazine* introduced its readers to this new method with a fictional rendition of an outdated and ineffective method of discipline employed by a woman called Mrs. F. "When they are little," said Mrs. F. of her children, "I suffer them to take their own way, so I think it is useless to attempt to control a child much before the age of six." As her son William grew more "passionate" with the approach of that fearful date in the old chronology of childhood, Mrs. F. awaited the right moment to begin a course of discipline in earnest. She swung into action when William violently attacked his sister. "After this Mrs. F. undertook to conquer her little son. A whip was placed on the chimney in the sitting room; and this, with the dark closet where he was told ugly creatures would catch him, frightened William into decent behavior while in the presence of his mother." In her absence, however, he was willful, disobedient, and, as any reader of *Mother's Magazine* could surmise, doomed for a tragic and wicked youth. The editor of *Mother's Magazine* categorized the mother who employed this childrearing method as follows: "An interesting woman, a kind neighbor and active in her religious profession. She was in society what many women are, useful and respectable." As a mother of the new era, however, she failed utterly, for she neglected her foremost maternal duty, "cultivating a knowledge of her own Heart." With this cool indictment of what might well have been one of the "principal women" of the socially active evangelical church, the *Mother's Magazine* banished the old methods of will-breaking from the modern and respectable home.[23]

A few years later the editors of *Mother's Monthly Journal* offered a detailed example of a more reliable method of dealing with stubborn and willful three-year-olds. After observing the child's birthday with prayer and fasting, the mother explained to the little girl, "in the simplest language, the sacrifices she was making in her child's behalf," all the while "caressing her affectionately." The clincher came when the mother told her daughter that she had abstained from eating for a full day in order to save her child from that "evil disposition that was destroying her happiness." At this the child reformed immediately, saying, "Well, ma, if you will go down and take something to eat, I will henceforth be a good girl." Another model mother had demonstrated the same foolproof method in the pages of *Mother's Magazine* five years before. This mother described to her little son the course of action she preferred to take in cases of disobedience. Eschewing corporal punishment or material reward, she greeted misbehavior with emotional withdrawal. "I would not smile upon you, I should not receive your flowers, but should have to separate you from my company." The fictional son responded appropriately: "Mother I should rather have your sweet kisses, and your pleasant smiles than ten rolls of gingerbread. I could not be happy if you did not love me." The practice of love withdrawal and the device of maternal martyrdom were two sides of the same coin, a method of socialization that used the child's close emotional ties to the mother as a pawn in a game of conformity and passivity. An anonymous mother writing to the *Mother's Magazine* described her strategy this way: "Why does an infant love its mother better than any other friend? Because her voice is gentlest, her eye beams with fondest affection; she soothes his little sorrows, and bears with his irritability with the tenderest and untiring patience. These silken threads are harder to burst than the iron chains of authority."[24] Put simply, love had vanquished force and authority, the female had replaced the male, in the social relations of childrearing.

To be effective, however, this method of discipline would require more than a sudden act of will-breaking at some specified age. It necessitated routine and intense maternal vigilance. One correspondent of *Mother's Magazine* illustrated this imperative of material socialization by recounting exact episodes of maternal discipline that recurred at age four months, six months, seven months, twelve months, fifteen months, eighteen months, twenty-seven months, and, supposedly, ad infinitum. A local poet put the matter more simply when he enjoined the model mother "to mark [her child's] growth from day to day." Soon the temporal bounds of motherhood reached their absolute limit: "Every day and every hour the mother is with her child." Something of the rigor of the maternal role was indicated by the "Maxims for Mothers" issued by the Utica Maternal Association. Some fifty in number, they included such bland injunctions as "teach each child to cultivate kind feelings and to do good" and "endeavor to make your child punctual at all appointments." Other maxims were introduced by the conjunction "if" and called for a finer sense of maternal strategy: "If a child asks a favor examine the propriety for granting or denying the request before you decide, and abide by the answer you first give unless there is an obvious reason for altering it." In the end, almost every aspect of the child's behavior should be monitored by the ever-attentive mother. Even the most routine physical care of infants and children, their feedings, diet, and attire, was now invested with moral as well as material meaning.[25]

Just what all this maternal supervision was designed to accomplish was seldom stated in any detail. At times the goal of maternal care seemed merely to keep order in the house, to make for polite, quiet, obedient children underfoot. Yet assumptions about the long-term socialization of children and the process of social reproduction clearly underlay this regimen. Nineteenth-century theories of childrearing identified the enduring consequences of maternal care by a moral rather than a sociological term, the awesome word *conscience*. One of the first appearances of the word *conscience* in Utica occurred in the *Evangelical Recorder and Gospel Advocate,* which defined the novel expression this way: "God has implanted a monitor within called conscience which warns against all sinful indulgence. Though he does but whisper, his language is clear and strong. He makes the bosom flutter and beat high with anxiety when the mind is directed to deeds of daring iniquity." One need not look very far to find more mundane sources of the pangs of conscience. The very same issue of this Universalist magazine contained an essay entitled "Early Impressions and Habits Formed in Infancy and Youth," a standard euphemism for the mechanisms of maternal socialization.[26]

Countless essays in both the religious and secular press advocated the same loving methods of installing parental values deep in the child's personality, at some psychological space called conscience. *Mother's Magazine* exposed the parental origins of conscience in such titles as "The Necessity of Cultivating the Conscience in Early Life." The Maternal Association of Utica put the point of conscience directly to children in this maxim: "Always act as if your parents were invisibly present." All the gentle admonitions and sly manipulations of maternal socialization conspired to equip children with sensitive consciences. This faculty would operate as a kind of portable parent that could stay with the child long after he left his mother's side and journeyed beyond the private sphere out onto the streets and into the public world. The values that this elaborate system was designed to implant in the child's personality are almost too mundane and obvious to recount: the usual array of petit bourgeois traits—honesty, industry, frugality, temperance, and, preeminently, self-control. Already in the 1830s, during the infancy of the young adults of the Civil War era, the literate native-born Protestants of Utica had worked out a set of strategies for the reproduction of a middle-class personality. In the process they defined the upper as well as the lower boundaries of the middle class, for the model child was infused not with the spirit of a daring, aggressive entrepreneur but with, rather, that of a cautious, prudent small-business man.

The mother's method of socialization was not, however, capable of training the progeny of native-born Protestants for specific occupational roles. The members of the Maternal Association might inculcate the virtue of frugality, but they were ill-prepared to teach bookkeeping, marketing, or shoemaking. In an increasingly privatized home, denuded of productive tasks, middle-class mothers could, at best, merely simulate the activities of adult breadwinners. In 1837 the members of the Baptist Maternal Association explored this strategy by asking, "Is it proper to supply our children with toys? If so, what kind of toys should they have?" To the first question the editors of *Mother's Monthly Journal* gave an emphatic yes, and in the following issues they offered more detailed instructions about the use of toys in inculcating good work habits. For boys, they recommended "hammers and hatchets"; for girls, there were such occupations as "dressing dolls" and "mimicry of housekeeping." This, of course, was only make-believe work, designed to have "a semblance of the sober activities of business." The *Mother's Monthly Journal* also advised, however, that a little bit of actual labor would not be amiss. A few exercises in sewing "might be instructed with pleasure and profit to both sexes."[27] Clearly, the profit was collected in moral rather than monetary currency. Whatever work had occurred in this idealized childhood contributed to building character in individual sons and daughters, not to the material support of the family.

The extended moratorium on productive labor was most troublesome for male children. Females, after all, could continue to act as assistant housekeepers or were, at least, in a position to observe the performance of their mothers in the role of adult female. Boy children, however, were increasingly distanced from the roles of their fathers. Their remoteness may account for the fact that boys were often described as restless inhabitants of the private domain. In a story appearing in the *Mother's Monthly Journal* in 1838 a little boy voiced his discontent: "Oh, how I wish I were grown-up! If I were as tall as father I would be happy." Another article dated 1842 and entitled "Boys!" exposed an alarming breach between mothers and boys. 'Who can love boys!' says one mother—"They are awkward, ugly things, always in the way and always in mischief! they are neither companions nor pets.' " Boys themselves, according to this account, heartily reciprocated these sentiments: "They are ungrateful to their mothers and indifferent to their sisters."[28]

Clearly, something had to be done to help families navigate more smoothly through this awkward later stage of male childhood, that problematical period called boyhood. The tactic of the mother's magazines of simply drawing the bonds of love ever closer as the child grew older could not solve the problem of vocational training. A sounder strategy might be to construct some intermediary world between the home and the labor force, one that could more adequately prepare boys for entry into economic adulthood. In other words, boys needed schools.

In the fourth decade of the nineteenth century a movement was already under way in Utica to establish the school as a social base for boyhood. Before that decade a few dame schools offered an erratic education to those who could pay for it, and public schools operated briefly on the Lancaster plan, which attempted to instruct more than two hundred pupils at a time. In 1830 some prominent Utica citizens, including Stephen Van Rensselaer, Fortuce C. White, and Hiram Denio, attended a meeting of the Friends of Education, convened in Utica to publicize the wretched conditions of the New York State schools: the impossibly large class size, the untrained teachers, poor facilities, and sporadic sessions. It was reported that some of the state's schools closed their doors arbitrarily for as long as nine months a year. The same meeting resolved to investigate the number of children between the ages of three and fifteen who were enrolled in common schools throughout the state, inquiring at the same time whether or not the beginning of schooling should not be postponed by a few years. The concerned fathers called for a common school system that would "keep pace with the age in its improvements" and prepare youngsters to "calculate their own profits in the world, and promote the limited views of their own individual interest." By 1830 Utica's city fathers had pointed to the need for the systematic preparation of young children for adult life in their commercial habitat. Concomitantly, they appealed for the systematic, long-term placement of children within educational institutions. They had begun, in sum, to rationalize the social life of children between the ages of five and sixteen—to convert it into the world of the schoolboy.[29]

By midcentury these goals had to a large extent been met. According to the New York State Census for 1845, the majority of children between the ages of five and sixteen were enrolled in schools. The figure stood at almost 80% in Whitestown and at 69% in Utica. More than 90% of Whitestown's schoolchildren were enrolled in public institutions. The comparable figure for Utica, which by this time had a number of parochial schools as well, was 52%. Utica's public schools were now more than purely custodial institutions. They were an increasingly efficient and bureaucratized educational system under the supervision of the city school commissioners. In 1842 the annual visiting committee found the local schools in exceptionally good order. The progress within the fourth school, once "virtually the prison of the disorderly ruffians" of the poorest ward of the city, particularly pleased the commissioners.[30] "Now the well-trained teacher ran the school with 'commendable emulation' which inspires the youth to orderly behavior, and stimulates them to the work of improvement." The city's private schools were also becoming a more highly structured social universe for children. The Whitestown Seminary included a "juvenile department" for children between the exact ages of six and ten. Whether private or public, the schools of the mid-1840s and beyond imposed a systematic order on the daily activities of youngsters, measuring off their young lives by classes, semesters, and the hours of a school day. Even this habitat of childhood was supervised by women, however. As of 1855, all twenty-six of Utica's public-school teachers were females. At the margins of academic life, meanwhile, mothers stood guard, having been advised to be at home when their offspring returned from school.

Some lacunae inevitably emerged between the diurnal and seasonal jurisdictions of the school and the home. It was in between these two social spaces that the more raucous activities of boyhood transpired. The term *boy* was often synonymous with prankster in the pages of the Utica press. The notable exploits of Utica boys included digging holes in the unpaved streets to trip passersby and stocking the butcher's sausage machine with exorbitant proportions of garlic. These idle youths could also pass the time in more structured play. Organized sports had become the essence of "Fun for the Boys" in the 1850s, when one's carefree youth could be relieved forever on the sandlot. In the summer of 1860 the *Utica Evening Telegraph* reported that "everybody of the masculine gender, young, middle-aged, and old is seized with the fever of playing base-ball and cricket."

For the "boys" under the age of sixteen, this playtime often mimicked adult roles and responsibilities. The 1840s saw boyish equivalents of many adult social groupings. The Cadets of Temperance, for example, were junior even to the "Sons" in the ranks of that reform group. The next decade brought the formation of political groups that were even junior to the young men's parties of the Jacksonian era. Boys as young as fourteen could affiliate with the Democrats as members of the Little Giants and face off against their miniature Republican opponents, the Wide Awakes. These juvenile parties were hardly serious political institutions. Their chief function seems to have been to march through the streets around election time carrying the banners and shouting the praises of the candidates selected by their elders in the party.[31] At about the same time, another curious expression of boys' culture emerged on the Utica scene. The early 1850s had seen the proliferation of the "boys' press," a variety of newspapers edited, published, and printed by children between the ages of twelve and fifteen.[32] In every way, from their logotypes to their subscription rates, these postage-stamp newspapers tried to imitate their adult models. They even engaged in juvenile parodies of misogynist humor and ethnic slurs.

The tiny pages of the boys' press also offered abundant testimony to the puerility of this youth culture. The papers bore such names as the *Star,* the *Sun,* the *Diamond,* the *Eagle.* The serious reporting and adult prose of the editors were frequently interrupted by an observation such as: "Horse chestnuts are fine things to pelt girls with." The boyishness of these publications becomes more starkly apparent when they are placed alongside the serious products of an apprentice printer only a generation before. In this contrast lies the distinct character of boyhood; rather than participating in productive activities even at the level of the apprentice, the youngsters of the 1840s and 1850s were practicing for adulthood in a make-believe world all their own. The editors of the boys' press were quite aware of the transitory and playful nature of their activities. They observed knowingly that their peers were under the delusion that a three-cent cigar could make a boy a man. They even concocted their own designation of the temporal parameters of boyhood: "Boys should remember that they will soon be men and that it is between the ages of 12 and 18 that character is finally formed for good or for ill."

Boys into Breadwinners

At some time during this period of the life cycle, the male children of Utica would have to take a giant step beyond boyhood and onto the lowest rungs of economic manhood by earning some portion of their support. Under the age of fifteen, according to the 1855 census, less than 4% of the males of Utica listed an occupation. Those who had entered the labor force at this early age, furthermore, were rarely apprentices embarking on serious and specific training for their life's work. Only two-tenths of 1% of the employed males of the city claimed apprentice as their occupational title. The juvenile worker by midcentury was more likely to hold a very marginal economic position, such as that described in this advertisement dated 1839: "Situation wanted—young lad eleven years old who would be willing to do almost anything for his board and clothing—would be good for doing errands, etc."[33] Soon after the age of fifteen, however, young men became a significant component of Utica's occupational structure. The public schools closed their doors to most youth around this age, and the *City Directory* listed all males aged seventeen and over among the "employed persons and household heads" of the city. At this point the ability of native-born parents to reproduce the middle class would be put to its crucial test: Now their sons would pass the midpoint of their teens and seek an occupation outside the private world of the home and beyond the cloistered space of the school.

The ever-garrulous local informant Emily Chubbuck chose the age of seventeen to designate the threshold of economic adulthood. In a story entitled *Allen Lucas,* Chubbuck encapsulated the timing and tension of youth in this image:

> "Seventeen years old today!" said Allen Lucas as he seated himself on a large stone, half embedded in the thick golden moss and the other half descending into the water—and in seventeen more I shall be a man, my character formed, my habits fixed, my destiny in the world decided—a busy man in this busy world, independent of control, of guidance, doing whatever I like and answerable for everything. Thirty four years! The very meridian of life."[34]

Poor Allen Lucas contemplated straddling the world of childhood and manhood for a full seventeen years. Yet he had his ultimate goal squarely in view. He had his task set out for him by the popular ideology of his age. He was, as Chubbuck's subtitle proclaimed it, on the path of the "Self-Made Man, or Life as It Is." Emily Chubbuck was hardly alone in celebrating this notion of the self-reliant American youth. The Oneida County press held it as one of its most cherished clichés. One of Utica's booteries, for example, advertised its wares especially to those trusty lads who wished to stand on their own two feet rather than step into their father's shoes. The newspaper editors of Utica customarily added a titillating fillip to the doctrine of the self-made man, the prospect of rising from rags to riches. In the midst of the Panic of 1857, the *Utica Evening Telegraph* cited the happy case of Thomas Maynard who had arrived in the city twenty years before with a half dollar in his pocket and had become one of the city's wealthiest merchants.[35]

For a young man to "make himself," be the final product rich or poor, was simply making a virtue of necessity in the world where Emily Chubbuck grew up and where she situated the story of *Allen Lucas.* Allen was the third son of Reuben Lucas, "a small and honest simple farmer who being always watchful and industrious contrived at the end of the year to balance account without saving a penny." Allen was not in line to inherit the family farm, nor could he expect his father to pay his way through school, college, or professional training. The education of a second character, the fiercely ambitious Robert May, was financed by his family but at an exorbitant domestic cost. Robert's father mortgaged his farm, his mother lost her health, his sisters forfeited their prospects of marriage, all to put him through college and law schol. Robert was a selfishly made man but still a relatively autonomous one. No less than Allen Lucas, he achieved an occupational status that was all his own, completely distinct and separate from that of his father.[36]

For all the contrasts in their character and worth, Allen Lucas and Robert May followed similar paths out of farm families and away from the old middle class. Both began to give earnest consideration to their life's work in their mid-teens, but neither arrived at his occupational destination until after age thirty. Both ultimately found themselves within the professional sector of the new middle class, Robert as a lawyer and Allen as an architect. Both gave their single-minded attention for upwards of a decade to building what could be loosely called a career, proceeding slowly upward through the ranks of a single carefully chosen occupation. Finally, both Allen Lucas and Robert May deferred the social and sexual gratification of marriage until their career goals were well within sight. "Allen Lucas remained a bachelor until he was more than thirty years of age, and, by industry and economy, he had amassed a little fortune." Robert May also postponed marriage, and even then subordinated his personal preferences to his career goals, choosing as his wife the daughter of a politician whose influence he coveted. As Chubbuck portrayed it, a large portion of the male life cycle, approximately from the ages of fifteen to thirty, would be devoted to pursuit of a comfortable economic status and would transpire in a vast domestic lacuna, remote from the parental home and antecedent to matrimony.[37]

In some features this fictional account of the making of the new-middle-class man is remarkably similar to the outlines of the male life cycle extrapolated from the manuscript census schedules of 1855 (which will be detailed as this chapter proceeds). First of all, the native-born youth of Utica began to file into the labor force roughly according to Chubbuck's timetable. Three out of five males between the ages of fifteen and twenty had secured some kind of job. Second, many of these young workers were, according to one interpretation of local mythology, "self-made." Like Allen Lucas and Robert May and endless Horatio Alger characters, a significant proportion of the young men who came of age at midcentury obtained positions in the social structure that differed from their father's generation. For example, whereas only about 6% of Utica's middle-aged household heads filled white-collar posts in 1855, 16% of the city's young men had secured such positions. At the same time, the proportion of young men within artisan occupations was more than 15% below that of their elders. Chubbuck seemed clairvoyant in yet another respect. The majority of native-born men, like Chubbuck's characters, were tardy about marrying, with large numbers of them waiting until their thirties to begin families of their own.

On another score, however, Chubbuck was considerably wide of the statistical mark. Although unmarried, the young men of the 1850s were rarely homeless. Forty percent of the native-born males between the ages of fifteen and thirty and the majority of those who had secured white-collar or professional occupations were living with their parents. By 1865 a full 60% of the native-born youths were living under the parental roof. Simultaneously, the practice of boarding became increasingly uncommon. Only 29.7% of the native-born youths were boarders in 1855 and a mere 11.1% in 1865. Even the once restless and roving clerks had become more domesticated by midcentury. As of 1860 almost 40% of them, double the ratio of a decade earlier, were living with kinsmen, usually their fathers or mothers. Young native-born shopkeepers and artisans were becoming equally attached to their parental homes: 25% to 35% remained there into their twenties. Extended residence under the parental roof was the favorite strategy of native-born youth and the middle class in particular, for the vast majority of immigrants (88%) and of unskilled workers (90%) lived apart from their parents by the time they reached their twenties. Continuing residence with parents tarnished the luster of a young man's self-made image. It suggests that parents still could exercise considerable care and authority over adult children and, accordingly, that obtaining middle-class status was not just a matter of self-creation: It was also the culmination of a parental strategy.

Prolonged residence in the family of origin could influence the occupational status of native-born youth in a variety of ways. It was associated, first of all, with delayed entry into the labor force. As of 1855, 43.5% of all native-born youth between the ages of fifteen and twenty had not yet secured an occupation. This contrasts markedly with the figure of 28.4% for the foreign-born. Native-born fathers of the new middle classes were the most likely of all to forestall the employment of their sons. Of the professional and white-collar fathers with adult children living at home, 80% kept their progeny out of the labor force. Although only about half of Utica's artisan and shopkeeping fathers followed suit, they, too, were more likely than the foreign-born and unskilled fathers to harbor children above the age of fifteen. Some of these home-bound youths were simply basking in the salubrious home influences recommended by childrearing theorists who would prohibit children "from encountering prematurely the seductive wiles that the wicked world will be sure to throw around them." Others were pursuing some form of education preparatory to their ultimate entrance into the world of work.[38]

In the absence of any precise information about school attendance in Utica, it is impossible to determine the relationship between delayed employment and extended education. Abundant impressionistic evidence exists, however, to indicate that native-born parents, particularly those on the margins of the new middle class, were well aware of the advantages of prolonged formal schooling. A fair proportion of the wills probated in Oneida County at midcentury made explicit provisions for the continuing education of their sons. The stipulations of some of these wills suggest that parents perceived education as a substitute for the family property whereby fathers of the past settled an economic status directly on their progeny. Charles A. Mann, a wealthy merchant and prominent financier, left his estate in trust until each of his children had reached the vintage age of twenty-five. His rationale was as follows: "I wish my children to be well educated and to be brought up to some useful profession or business with true habits of industry and economy which I consider more valuable than all the wealth I can give." Utica's ever-sagacious Sophia Clarke also wrote this familiar strategy into her last will and testament, leaving to her son Erastus, "the benefits of a liberal education and of acquiring a profession by means of which, with use, industry, and economy, he can support himself and his family comfortably." To Sophia Clarke, the makings of middle-class status (such as the legal careers of both her husband and her son) consisted not in a stock of cash, tools, goods, or real estate, but in training acquired at secondary schools or colleges.[39]

The groundwork for such a family strategy had been laid in the 1830s. Erastus Clarke, Jr., for example, would complete his secondary education at the Utica Free Academy, an institution that his father had helped to found during the canal era. The educational innovations of that era had been multiform and ingenious. In addition to public primary schools and academies, the 1830s gave birth to some less conventional educational experiments. Prime among these was the Oneida Institute, "a manual labor school," which operated in Whitestown during the canal era. Here was truly a school for self-made men. Students at the Oneida Institute, usually the sons of farmers and mechanics, many of them considerably older than the typical college or high-school student, labored in fields and workshops maintained by the school in order to support themselves. The Oneida Institute, yet another example of the more volatile youth associations of the canal era, spawned its own reformist fervor, which was led by such illustrious alumni as Theodore Dwight Weld.[40]

By midcentury, however, the Oneida Institute had sold out to a more conventional boarding school called the Whitestown Seminary. This secondary school was a way station for youth, neatly tucked under the extended eaves of the parental roof. Parents, not students, most often arranged and financed secondary education at midcentury. The staff of the Whitestown Seminary instructed mothers and fathers to "state very frankly and fully your wishes in reference to the studies, the intellectual and moral training of children, so that the teachers may feel at liberty to give you all the information which an intelligent and considerate parent desires when entrusting a son or daughter to the authority of strangers." The school, in turn, obligingly assumed the role of surrogate parent. Its official policy stated that if students failed to "govern themselves in accordance with precepts of sound morality," "energetic and decided measures" would be taken. In addition, the catalogue of Whitestown Seminary assured parents that every residential building would contain a supervising parent to act in loco parentis. Whether a young man attended a boarding school like Whitestown Seminary or a public high school such as the Utica Free Academy, he did not escape adult surveillance nor assume total self-direction. In the 1850s even the Democratic press, once the outspoken champion of dauntless independent youth, advised that children who remained at home and were supported by their parents, regardless of age, were obliged to respect, honor, and obey their mothers and fathers.[41]

The secondary schools of the 1850s did not open up a very direct route toward economic independence. The academies and seminaries were designed primarily for college preparation. The classical programs at Whitestown Seminary and the Utica Free Academy provided little vocational education per se, and aspiring professionals were obliged to go on to college and postgraduate training in law, medicine, or the ministry. The teacher training programs instituted by Oneida County secondary schools in the fifties and sixties proved most attractive to females. A commercial program developed by Whitestown Seminary in 1865 might have been more appealing to young men in search of white-collar jobs. Still, only a minority of even the sons of the native-born middle class could count on formal secondary education as an entree into professional or white-collar careers. It is unlikely that secondary education was much more prevalent at midcentury than it was in 1845, when in all of Utica there were only 140 high-school students and 33 collegians.[42]

Vocational training for the middle class was largely an informal, on-the-job, and catch-as-catch-can process. Aspirant clerks and bookkeepers could, for example, make use of a growing body of self-help literature. Until the late 1820s they were dependent upon *Daboll's Schoolmaster's Assistant* and its primitive set of instructions in merchandising, including demonstrations of barter and rudimentary commercial concepts. For example, Daboll defined "loss and gain" as follows: "A rule by which merchants and traders discover their profits and losses in buying and selling their goods; it instructs them how to rise or fall the price of their goods so as to gain or lose so much percent." Daboll's homespun economics was superseded in 1829 by the first Utica printing of *Preston's Manual on Book-keeping*, which contained directions for calculating interest on sums that went into six figures and advised ambitious youths to consider such modern business issues as "what is meant by the term Capital Stock?"[43] By the 1860s the young men of Utica could also enhance their business credentials by taking a short course at one of the city's commercial and bookkeeping schools.

Acquiring training for white-collar, professional, and mercantile careers were expensive in both time and money, and much of this cost was born by middle-aged parents. Many parents were unwilling or unable to make these sacrifices at a difficult stage in the family cycle. The families of the old middle class, both shopkeepers and artisans, clung quite tenaciously to the old expedients of the household economy by accumulating the earnings of young adult children in a common pool. According to the 1855 census, for example, the majority of households headed by craftsmen still counted on their children over fifteen to be gainfully employed. They included families like that of Daniel Harrington, a machinist, fifty years of age. Harrington had at least nine children, aged five to twenty. Four of them were in the labor force, all in manual jobs, as weavers, spinners, and tailors.

Other families more often those headed by professional and white-collar workers but occasionally those headed by members of the old middle class as well, organized the labor of their adult children in such a way as to foster better prospects for their sons. Take the case of Warren Armes, a native of Rhode Island, who was also a machinist of fifty years of age. The Armes household was more typical of the middle class at midcentury: It contained only four children, neatly spaced in age, between seven and twenty-one years. The oldest male child, Henry Armes, was seventeen and already on his way to the new middle class, having secured a job as a clerk. At the same time, Henry's elder sister, Harriet, was working as a tailoress and his mother made a sizable contribution to the family income by taking in two boarders. This consolidated income allowed the Armes family to purchase a house valued at $1,000 and might have contributed to the educational advantages that went into Henry's qualification for the job of clerk. This collective and comfortable income boded well for the younger Armes children, who were likely to enjoy the leisure, the family resources, and the education that went into middle-class careers.

The occupational pattern of the Armes family was routine within the households of the native-born new middle class. Children of white-collar and professional fathers were the latest to enter the work force, the longest to remain with their parents, probably the most highly educated, and hence the most expensive to rear. The relatively ample income[44] of professional and white-collar fathers no doubt eased these families through the difficult stage of the life cycle, but still the making of a middle-class son entailed effort, planning, and sacrifice. It was often women, moreover, who assumed a major portion of such labor and responsibility. Contrary to common assumptions, the native-born middle-class women of the Victorian Era were not entirely disdainful of paid employment. Although only a small minority ever listed an occupation with the census taker, native-born middle-class wives were more likely than the spouses of immigrants to enter the paid labor force. In 1865 the proportion of native-born working wives had grown appreciably, and the wives of white-collar workers reported occupations in considerable strength of numbers. In fact, about 1 in 7 of the latter held a job.

Neither were the daughters of the native-born middle class all that shy of employment outside the home. In fact, the employment of females, be they mothers or daughters, was relatively common among the native-born. Female workers were found in 14% of the households headed by natives, as opposed to a figure of 13% for the households of immigrants. Craftsmen were the least reluctant to employ women outside the home: 1 in 5 households of the native-born skilled workers contained a gainfully employed female. Yet even the nonmanual middle class endorsed women's paid labor with some enthusiasm, for 15.4% of the households of professional men sent a kinswoman into the labor force. Finally, it was the native-born middle-class household that was most likely to take in boarders, yet another source of household income. One in four native-born households resorted to this female mode of enhancing the family's economic well-being. Although conscious motivation cannot be imputed to heads of these complex household economies, it is very tempting to see a kind of trade-off at work here. On a small scale, middle-class native-born families seemed to be substituting the labor of wives and sisters for the employment of sons, who could therefore prepare at their leisure for higher-status jobs. Regardless of the motivation of individuals, however, the native-born middle-class households typically organized the labor of their members in such a way as to allow for the prolonged support and assistance of young adult males.

By remaining at home through the earlier years of their economic adulthood, the sons of the native-born middle class reaped social and psychological as well as material rewards. The family of origin was there to assist a young man in both securing a job and parlaying it into a secure, perhaps lucrative, career. This combination of parental influences is evidenced in the correspondence of a Utica physician named Horatio Dryer. Dryer invested considerable thought and energy in the career prospects of his son. "I am disposed to let Bob try for business," he wrote. "It will stimulate him to do something for himself. I have very little encouragement of getting a place here for him in a hardware store with a very fine man and one of the best businessmen I have ever met."[45] Paternal measures such as Dryer's (exposed only by a rare collection of letters) might have been a common way of securing a job in the mid-nineteenth century. At the same time, Horatio Dryer's plans for his son were more intricate than simply finding a place of employment. Dryer strived to "stimulate" his son's self-sufficiency and scrutinized the business skills as well as the payroll of his prospective employer. In other words, middle-class parents like Dryer were acutely conscious of the intangible aspects of career success and gave considerable thought to the best way to provide their sons with a legacy of skills and aptitudes as well as capital.

Another prominent father of Oneida County carried this parental awareness and its attendant anxiety to its extreme. The letters that passed between Hugh White, Jr., and his son William, that is, between the second and third generation of Whitestown's founding family, reveal the paternal vigilance demanded in a new era. At the time this correspondence began, the founder's grandson was not situated on a farm adjacent to his father's. Rather, William White was away at college, preparing to assume some undetermined economic role commensurate with the illustrious history of his family. Hugh White, Jr., did not, however, launch the third generation off into the world alone. He wrote his son long letters every week or oftener and demanded the same in return: "If you will sit down in the evening and write not only what has been done during the day, but give a statement of things in general, it will be very acceptable to me and make no innovation upon your scholarly pursuits." In Hugh White's mind, the parent's role in the socialization of children did not end when a young man left for college. He continued to oversee his son's conscience, stating, for example, that "it is exceedingly gratifying and adds largely to my peace and comfort to feel sure in the personal morals of my sons." His paternal jurisdiction extended to cultivating orderly habits and self-discipline as he presented William with an ascetic, indeed compulsive, work schedule.[46]

Hugh White's most assiduous campaign was to prepare his son for the world he would enter after graduation, the dangerous habitat of the businessman. And here the confidence of Whitestown's patriarchal lineage seemed to falter. Father and son encountered particularly sticky ethical questions when it came to business matters. On the one hand, proper business morality was simple. Hugh White assured his son that "the direct, straight-forward, manly course; open, frank candid, is the only one which will give either you or me any real satisfaction." At the same time, the world-weary father alerted William to the absence of such virtues among many of his business colleagues. He warned that every man must be "an expert in the observation of men, which ever quality of the soul it may be, always awake to note the good and evil around you." The cause of Hugh White's cynicism had been revealed in a few earlier letters when he described the caliber of men he caballed with in the railroad industry: "Cunning and unscrupulous men resort to all and any means and expedience for success. Open, honest, and manly proceedings will not serve them . . . rather, intrigue, treachery, and corruption."[47]

Just how much benefit William White derived from these parental admonitions is open to question. The tenor of Hugh White's letters often conveyed anxiety and trepidation rather than confidence. He kept his son posted on seemingly endless sequences of "pecuniary troubles" and a wide array of accompanying physical maladies. One business setback, the senior White confided, "affected my stomach to such a degree that now all such trouble seems to center there deranging my digestive organ." Hugh White was plagued in his stomach, his back, and his head, which ached "almost to madness." He gave the impression that all these pains were the routine occupational hazards of the adult world his son was soon to enter. Armed with all this knowledge of the insidious machinations of capitalism's higher circles, young William White went back to the old family farm upon graduation from college. Not even the management of an agricultural enterprise, however, was left to the young man's discretion. Hugh White continued to send his son regular instructions on everything from planting potatoes to hiring a cook. The case of the White family proves that neither physical distance nor intergenerational occupational mobility need sever the cord of support and advice between father and son.[48]

This same family correspondence described very weak bonds between a young man and his mother. Mrs. White occasionally appended a note like this to her husband's letter to their son: "I would just like to say that you are thought of continually by your affectionate mother." On other occasions her husband might report "your mother says she can't think of nothing, ain't that rich?" The White family was probably the exception rather than the rule in this regard. The packets of letters sent to parents by Civil War soldiers, for example, were more often addressed to mothers than to fathers. Sons' correspondence with their mothers was full of the more prosaic details of everyday life and particularly replete with requests for victuals, socks, and medicines. At the same time, mothers' epistles were steeped in concern for the character and morality of the young men. Mrs. Mary Perry wrote to her son this homiletic note: "My very dear boy, take good care of yourself, keep out of temptation, avoid bad company, try and do good. My dear Win, once more be a good boy, don't forget your Mother who thinks of you when the rest of the folks are asleep. Much love and kisses to yourself." Young Perry reciprocated with regular letters to his "dear homely mother," "Dear Ma," "Dear Mammy." The rare correspondence between fathers and sons was typically more stilted and instrumental. When asked to dictate a last epistle to his father, a dying boy reputedly lisped, "Tell him to send me money."[49]

At the same time, the homey warmth of maternal influence was not entirely unrelated to financial matters. Maternal sympathy might provide more reassurance to a young businessman than did the nervous twitches of Hugh White. Maternal admonitions to live soberly and prudently could also prove effective financial advice for aspirants to more routinely middle-class jobs in the 1850s and 1860s. The influence of early maternal education often retained its efficacy after sons had entered the male world of business. In 1837, for example, the Utica Maternal Association had discussed "How are we to teach our children to be prudent and economical?" One member of the association, Mrs. Julia Merrill, left the mark of such rearing in the ledger of the Mercantile Agency, a decade later when her son was described as "Honest, Industrious, Small Means."[50]

The citation of the virtues inculcated by maternal associations within the credit records was not mere coincidence: It represented the real matrilineal ties that were woven throughout the male life cycle. The importance of maternal influence was given further expression in the wills of Oneida County. The majority of wills probated between 1845 and 1865 transferred the whole of the father's estate directly to the wife and mother. This stipulation testified, first of all, to the ability of women to dispense the smaller estates that consisted of consumable rather than productive property, that is, cash and household furnishings rather than farms and workshops. Second, it was based on the increasing importance of maternal socialization rather than on property or vocational training in determining the economic status of children. The will of Lewis Bailey made this reasoning explicit: Bailey granted his full estate to his wife, "praying that she may have wisdom from on high given her to train up her children in the fear of the Lord which will be better for them than all the wealth of the Indies."[51] This expanding maternal role opened yet another avenue through which the family of procreation continued to exert its influence until quite late in the life cycle of its male offspring.

The family was not the sole source of emotional and moral support for young men in the industrial era. Associations of young men continued to assume an important role in Utica life in the 1850s and 1860s. The youth associations of this era, however, came more and more to resemble surrogate homes. The Young Men's Association had disbanded in the mid-1840s. Its successor, the Young Men's Christian Association, founded in 1859, was designed as a kind of halfway home for young men recently uprooted from the parental family. The association appealed to "kind friends, these fathers and sisters and mothers," for funds. Its library was touted as a refuge for "many half-homeless wanderers in these streets." The once-bold banner of independent youth faded into an image of pitiful waifs: "Many a young man in this city of yours," went one appeal from the YMCA, "spends his days at work, perhaps in some mechanics shop, or mill, or office, or in your stores, [and] when night has come has nowhere else to go, for at the best the little room he calls his own is no *Home* to him."[52]

The YMCA was not the only men's association that identified itself in these domestic terms. The Order of Oddfellows, which flourished in the 1850s, also cloaked itself in the rhetoric of an ersatz home and constructed benign and cozy lodges where controversial reform associations once stood. "Odd" fellows were simply domestic anomalies, solitary men, whom "business, pleasure, or necessity call far away from the homes of their youth, and the society of their heart—unknowing whither they are going, or what may befall them in a land of strangers."[53] The literary associations, as well as the lodges, of the 1850s and 1860s aimed to provide emotional support for these uprooted men and boys. The Phoenix Society, composed of students at Whitestown Seminary, met to "promote kindly feeling," dispense "good cheer," and, incidentally, to exercise talents for public debate. The young members eschewed subjects that might provoke partisan rivalry and debated instead rather innocuous issues, such as the merits and the methods of the self-made man. Favored topics of the Phoenix Society debates included "Does education make a man more independent than wealth?" "Is corporal punishment in the schools to be tolerated?" and "Does success in life depend more upon a man's own exertion than upon the circumstances attending to his life?" These young men did not seem particularly restless under the limitations and constraints of their student status. Rather, they stepped gingerly toward their public and adult roles. Within the protective fellowship of the debating society, for example, a young man could advance cautiously from the "first embarrassing and stammering speech" toward the "ease, grace, and self-possession" required of an adult man. The members of the Phoenix Society, like Oddfellows and members of the YMCA, were not as eager as the youth of the canal era to assert their manliness in social, economic, and political life. One member captured the trepidation of youth at midcentury in this description of graduation from secondary school: "stepping from the routine of schoolboys, to mingle in life's sterner scenes, on the stage of action."[54] In sum, the sons who came of age in Utica during the decade before the Civil War seemed more conservative, more patient, and more attached to domesticity, be it their parents' homes or the YMCA.

All this parental assistance, both material and psychological, seemed to be paying off at midcentury. In 1855 and 1865, according to the census, the majority of the native-born workers of Utica maintained positions within the old or the new middle class, either as artisans, shopkeepers, professionals, or white-collar workers. Only 12% of the city's native sons were found among unskilled or factory laborers, where immigrants abounded and where more than one-fourth of all adult males found employment. The younger generation of the native-born, furthermore, had become particularly well situated, advancing steadily into the newer sectors of the middle class. Only a small and probably insignificant proportion of the young native-born workers had, in the face of the encroaching obsolescence of some artisan occupations, moved into factory jobs. A far larger number became white-collar workers or professionals. A comparison of the occupational status of the two different age cohorts, young men between fifteen and thirty and household heads with children fifteen and over, demonstrates a definite generational shift in the pattern of middle-class employment. Of the younger men, 21% were employed in the skilled manual trades, as opposed to 37.5% of their elders. Within the white-collar and professional sector, on the other hand, the relationship was reversed, as young men outranked the old by more than 2 to 1.

Comparing the occupational achievement of young workers who were still residing at home with that of household heads presents a similar contrast. Home-bound youths were especially apt to shun artisan and shopkeeping jobs as well as the new working-class positions opening up in the city's factories. The occupational magnet of the new middle class was especially powerful to these young men. More than 40% of the young men who resided with parents, as opposed to 28% of the native-born heads of household, had found employment in high-level, nonmanual jobs, chiefly professionals or white-collar workers. The class background of the clerks who appeared in the *City Directory* of 1860 illustrates the pattern of generational occupational change. Of those clerks who resided with their kinsmen in 1860, 16% maintained the same white-collar status as the household head. The bulk of the remainder, however, came from the households of the old middle class: 37.7% made their homes with relatives who were shopkeepers and 29.5% with artisans. Of those remaining, 11.5% boarded with kinsmen who were unskilled laborers. This suggests that there was considerable motion within the middle ranges of the occupational structure of Utica. The movement was particularly strong in a horizontal and intergenerational direction, as the sons of artisan and shopkeeper fathers shifted to professional and white-collar stations within the American middle class. Sons who continued to reside with their fathers as they embarked on economic adulthood had especially good chances of making the lateral movement from the old to the new middle class. Through the extended residence of young sons and a variety of attendant parental services, the family helped to ensure the reproduction of the middle class, even if it required horizontal movement from skilled manual to white-collar jobs.

Domestic Dénouement

It would be foolish to attribute a young man's occupational accomplishments entirely to the efforts of his parents. Although hardly a pure incarnation of self-reliance, the native-born youth assumed some self-direction and invested abundant self-control in his career. By staying prudently and frugally under the parental roof, for example, a young man denied himself the social gratification of marriage and heading his own household. Native-born males were especially slow to embark on wedded life. Only 18% were married in the age group twenty to twenty-four; a bare majority, 50.4%, were married in the age group twenty-five to twenty-nine. (The comparable figures for immigrants in the respective age groups were 34.1% and 66.3%.) The new middle class was most obdurate about delaying matrimony. Only 35.3% of the white-collar workers in the age group twenty-five to twenty-nine were married; among professionals, the parallel figure was a paltry 26.7%. If maternal socialization and Utica's history of sex reform had left any imprint on the character of these young men, singleness would ordain celibacy as well. By postponing marriage and passing by Utica's infamous "nymphs du pave," a native-born youth enacted his own heroic strategy of achieving middle-class status.

By so doing, he also acted on the advice of domestic writers. According to *A Voice to Youth,* the prudent and responsible young man would not marry until he was capable of supporting a family "in circumstances of comfort," predictably at age twenty-four or twenty-five at the earliest or as late as thirty. The quintessential circumstance of comfort, a single-family dwelling to which the youthful household head held the title, was seldom obtained before the age of thirty. In the meantime, a young man was expected to maintain a delicate imbalance between his sexual needs and his career objectives, postponing gratifications of the former to enhance the latter. Something of the tortuous quality of this regimen was expressed in the correspondence between Hiram Denio, a prominent Utica attorney, and his wife-to-be, Ann Pitkin of Connecticut. The timing of this courtship, although it transpired in the 1830s, corresponds with that of the professional men of the 1850s. Denio was already twenty-eight years old when he proposed to Ann Pitkin; by their wedding day, he was almost thirty. He had been a practicing lawyer and boarder of long standing when he finally set off on a trip through Connecticut in search of a wife. Over the course of months, Denio gingerly approached his favorite, proceeding from a chilly formality to the most ardent romance. On the eve of his engagement, Denio wrote to Ann Pitkin: "My heart beats audibly and I can hardly hold my pen." Once he had won the hand of his favorite, however, Denio's thoughts turned more somber. After seeking out a commodious home in which he and his bride could board, he had second thoughts. Convinced of the value of domestic privacy, Denio decided to purchase a modest home of his own. From then on he fretted and grumbled about the expense of setting up housekeeping and burdened his bride-to-be with complaints that he was "depressed" about professional matters.[55]

Meanwhile, Ann Pitkin was not exactly devil-may-care about the approach of matrimony. She took pains to interrogate her suitor about the soundness and sobriety of his character. She asked pointedly in one of her first epistles just how much liquor Denio had consumed during his social rounds on New Year's Day.[56] Women like Ann Pitkin, in keeping with the caveats of popular writers, proceeded toward the altar in a cautious and calculating manner, aware that their own middle-class comfort would hinge on the temperate character and business habits of their mates. The prospective bride was not, however, completely helpless in this regard. She was repeatedly advised that she could use her allure as a marital and sexual partner to lead young men along the path to morality and middle-class competence. As one Utica publication put it: "That hope which aims at a beloved partner—a family—a fireside—will lead its possessor to activity in all his conduct. It will elicit his talents, and urge him to his full energy and probably call in the aid of economy."[57] Again the cult of domesticity and the arbiters of local economy recommended similar family strategies. In 1855, for example, one report of the Mercantile Agency based its optimistic forecast for a young businessman on the following observation: "has been pretty wild but recently married and will probably be more steady now."[58] Ideally, then, marriage transformed this salubrious female influence over male passions from mothers unto wives.

The formation of the second-generation, middle-class household lies largely outside the temporal bounds of this study. There is considerable suggestive evidence, however, that many of the young men of the 1850s would find a secure footing in the middle class. The census taken immediately after the Civil War indicates that males aged thirty to thirty-nine held occupational titles that were quite similar to those obtained by men in their twenties ten years earlier. A light increase in the number of unskilled workers was balanced by an expansion of the elite. The distribution of occupations in later age groups retained a similar resilient, middle-class shape. The records of the Mercantile Agency took note of a handful of "industrious young men, formerly clerks," who rose to considerable wealth. Andrew Ketchum who appeared as a clerk in the *City Directory for 1850* illustrates a more modest middle-class mobility. By 1870 he was self-employed as a music dealer. Ketchum was not, however, typical of his cohort, less than 30% of whom rose from clerks to proprietors of their own business. Other clerks of 1850, like A. A. Bogue and B. F. French and 1 in 5 of their peers, still retained the same occupation in 1870. More than one-third of the clerks of 1850 claimed loftier occupational titles twenty years later, like bookkeeper, accountant, cashier, or salesman. They remained, however, hired nonmanual employees, that is, white-collar workers. One Joshua Church, for example, advanced from clerk to secretary in 1870, and William Coffin had become the treasurer of the woolen factory. Their peer and fellow clerk George Knapp, advanced to the position of a bookkeeper by 1870 but by a more circuitous route, having in the interim tried his hand as a combmaker. Regardless of the erratic and variable place of their careers, these tenacious white-collar workers, a majority of the clerks who began their careers at midcentury, testify to the slow emergence of a quasi-permanent new middle class; being a clerk was no longer the monopoly of young men but an occupation that could endure through a large portion of the male life cycle.

With occupational stability came entrenched domesticity for the native-born middle class. After a few years of boarding, be it with parents or strangers, most clerks listed a private home address in the *City Directory*. By the time they reached middle age, the majority of Utica's native-born household heads owned their own dwelling houses. The modest but comfortable homes of the middle classes were concentrated in the fourth ward of the city, just to the east of the commercial hub and across town from the major factories and their immigrant workers. Typically, the artisans and shopkeepers of the fourth ward could boast of owning a home worth somewhere between $1,000 and $2,000. An advanced white-collar worker, such as P. W. Rogers, bank cashier, had real estate worth $4,000. These single-family dwellings, perhaps ornamented with a ginger-bread trim popularized by such domestic architects as Andrew Jackson Downing and stuffed with the bulky mahogany furniture and rococo iron stoves hawked by local merchants, gave a material expression and sense of permanence to the middle-class status of their owners. In turn, such evidence of domestic sobriety continued to serve as moral collateral in the marketplace. The mercantile agent smiled at a "man of family" of any age. Domestic impropriety could still bring his frown and withdraw his credit. The Mercantile Agency gave Urial H. Kellogg a bitter lesson in home economics in 1852. Kellogg, formerly a clerk with good family connections, had been described as a "careful small businessman." After about five or six years of modest and wholesome living, Kellogg bought a dwelling house for his growing family. This expense, according to the Mercantile Agency, "detracted from his capital in business" and led to a prediction of bankruptcy. Sure enough, one year later Urial Kellogg went out of business.[59] Other businessmen incurred the disapproval of the Mercantile Agency for being too extravagant in spawning children. A large family, for a modest businessman, was considered a profligate waste of resources. Once again, the middle class was reminded to exercise self-control and continue even into middle age the exacting regimen necessary to the maintenance of their class position.

In the meantime, the parents who had supervised the first stage in the cycle of reproducing the middle class were reaching middle age. This epoch in the middle-class family cycle was not clearly demarcated in social or biological time. There was no mass retirement at some specified age like sixty-five. The rate of unemployment began to rise as men entered their fifties, but still more than 90% of all men in this age group remained on the job. Of the men over sixty, 80% still listed an occupation with the census taker. Neither do the records of the Mercantile Agency leave any perceptible evidence of a uniform age of retirement. On the one hand, a man like Jason Davis, age unspecified, ran a business from 1859 to 1871, at which time he was described simply as "used up." On the other hand, there was the career of John Tunbridge who had, over the years, built up his painting and blazing business into a modest fortune worth $10,000. At age seventy-one, the Mercantile agent found him "still good and active." The work and retirement of Edward B. Paine tells yet another story. At age sixty-four he had been in business twelve years, still remained at the status of journeyman, and was reputed to be living "from hand to mouth." Two years later he was declared "too old to work."[60] The work history of middle-class men at midcentury was not neatly ordered into the advancing ranks of a clearly measured and predictable career. It ended as it had begun with ambiguous timing and a firm but never certain, not quite self-assured, foothold in the middle class.

Most of the native-born men of Utica could rely, however, on domestic security through the remainder of their life cycles. Three out of four of them headed their own households even as they passed the age of sixty. Four out of five could count on having a wife by their side as they passed into old age. The minority of elderly men who were widowed and no longer headed their households, furthermore, was taken in by their adult children. More than 30% of native-born women in their sixties (who were far more likely than their mates to be widowed in old age) took up residence with their children. Not until after the Civil War, when the Sisters of Charity and later some benevolent Protestant women established homes for the aged, did the city of Utica provide any institution exclusively for the care of older citizens. Many indigent immigrant elders would, of course, be carted off to the poorhouse, but few native-born residents ever met this fate. Most of them spent their declining years nestled in private homes, in the company of kin and insulated from the public sphere. A few privileged elders in the community ended their lives in quiet contemplation. One founding father of the town, Judge Ezekiel Bacon, devoted his old age to writing verses. In a volume entitled *Vacant Hours,* Bacon bid this adieu to life:

> Shed no tears
> Have not a groan
> But pass on quickly
> And leave me alone.[61]

The men who completed their lives in Utica and Whitestown in the 1850s and 1860s had lived through one of the most unsettling eras in the nation's history. Most had traveled afield of the homes of their own boyhood and had watched an industrial city grow up where there once had been a few scattered farms, shops, and churches. The sons who survived them and remained in Oneida County lived out a quieter and smoother life cycle. These young men of the 1850s and 1860s spent large portions of their life searching for an economic anchor and awaiting entry into conjugal homes of their own. For the native-born middle class, careful nurture in infancy, as well as the accompanying moral education, could be extended through boyhood and even into young adulthood when large numbers returned from their first jobs to the comfort and warmth of their paternal and maternal homes. When native-born youth of the fifties and sixties finally left the parental nest, after perhaps a short interlude of boarding, they would be restored to domestic protection. They would be insulated again by womanly solace and nurture, now dispensed by a wife rather than a mother. Most would live out their lives with their spouses as the head of their own households. Thus the mid-nineteenth century may have cut the family off from economy and workplace, but it hardly set workingmen adrift in an anomic and friendless world. The breadwinners of Utica were always sustained by a network of familial relations. In this lies the essential irony of nineteenth-century individualism. The vaunted autonomy and egotism of the nineteenth-century male was not a monument to self-reliance. Quite the contrary, it was conceived, cultivated, pampered, and protected within a revitalized American home.

In retrospect, it seems that the native-born residents of Utica, New York, had carried through an elaborate and largely successful strategy for reproducing the middle class. Their story is not a dramatic case of upward mobility but rather a sustained battle to maintain middle-range occupations for themselves and their children. As Utica began to industrialize, the native born evaded the clutches of the factories, avoided unskilled day labor, kept skilled trades and small shops afloat, and in significant numbers entered the ranks of professionals and white-collar employees. The sequence of tactics that they employed to this end can be summarized as follows. Prescient native-born couples began in the 1830s to limit their family size, thereby concentrating scarce financial and emotional resources on the care and education of fewer children. Second, as indicated by the popular childrearing literature circulated through Utica beginning in the 1830s, native-born Protestant parents initiated methods of socialization designed to inculcate values and traits of character deemed essential to middle-class achievement and respectability. Next, native-born parents tended to keep their children within the households of their birth for extended periods, often until their sons were well over twenty years of age. By this strategy, mothers and fathers prolonged their moral surveillance and material support of the second generation even as it advanced out of the home into the labor force. At the same time, the parental generation had created the educational institutions and financed the schooling that qualified their children for more skilled and lucrative occupations. As a result of these parental strategies, the native-born youth of the 1850s not only secured middle-class jobs but also circumvented the declining segments of the old middle class and won a foothold in white-collar occupations. It was quite late in the family cycle, then, that the leadership of the household passed on to the second generation. The young men of the 1850s married late, steered a relatively steady course through the labor force, and partially repaid their parents at the end of their lives by taking widowed mothers and a few stray widowers into their homes. Clearly, neither the ties between the generations nor the links between the household and the labor force had been severed by the advances of industrialization in Utica, New York.

They did, however, take a radically different form. The members of the household were no longer meshed together by common productive property and shared work experience. In the urban middle-class setting, at least, family bonds were woven of deliberate strategies—decisions, for example, to finance an education or take in a boarder at a critical time in the family cycle. The ties between the generations were knit of more intangible materials of affection, self-sacrifice, guilt, and all the mysterious machinations of conscience. Moreover, the generational balance of family relations had shifted on its axis somewhat. Where the son of a farmer, artisan, or shopkeeper had once been a major source of household labor, he was now often a drain on family resources, especially if he had designs on the occupations of the new middle class, which required high investment in training and accrued highly individualized rewards of professional and white-collar careers. Finally, it should be noted that much of private labor, intelligence, and energy that reproduced and re-created the middle class at midcentury was expended by women, especially the mothers who cared for infants, socialized children, bestowed moral influence upon breadwinners, took in boarders, and even entered the labor force in their own right—all helping to maintain or advance the status of the men in their families. Such women have appeared in this chapter largely as the nurturers of male careers, the selfless supporters of self-made men. Their role in the home and in the social order is far more complex than this and far more integral to both society and economics. The sphere of the middle-class woman requires a chapter unto itself.

Notes

1. *Utica Morning Herald,* July 28, 1865.

2. Lavinia Johnson, "Diary," Aug. 8 and Aug. 17, 1859, OHS [Oneida Historical Society, Utica, N.Y.—Ed. note].

3. See Nancy F. Cott, *The Bonds of Womanhood* (New Haven, Conn., 1977); Kathryn Kish Sklar, *Catharine Beecher* (New Haven, Conn., 1973); Mary P. Ryan, "American Society and the

Cult of Domesticity, 1830–1860," doctoral dissertation (University of California at Santa Barbara, 1971).

4. *Young Ladies' Miscellany,* August 1842, 2.

5. John Mather Austin, *A Voice to the Married* (Utica, 1841), 38.

6. John Mather Austin, *A Voice to Youth* (Utica, 1838), 61, 64.

7. Johnson, "Diary," Dec. 15, 1859.

8. *Utica Morning Herald,* Jan. 16, 1861.

9. "Court Warrants," 1849, Uticana Collection, OHS.

10. Johnson, "Diary," Aug. 15, 1859.

11. *United States Census of Manufacturers,* Manuscript Schedules (Utica, 1860).

12. "Ordinances of the City of Utica, 1863" (Utica, 1863), 40–1.

13. Lewis Bradley, *Sketch of Utica, 1850,* Munson-Williams-Proctor Institute, Utica.

14. *United States Census of Manufacturers,* Manuscript Schedules (Utica, 1850, 1860, 1870). Clyde Griffen and Sally Griffen, *Natives and Newcomers* (Cambridge, Mass., 1978); Bruce Laurie, Theodore Hershberg, George Alter, "Immigrants and Industry: The Philadelphia Experience 1850–1880," in *Journal of Social History,* Winter 1975, 219–26.

15. Murdock and Andrews, Mercantile Agency Records, 1859; Spencer Kellogg, Mercantile Agency Records, 1857.

16. James Stocking, Mercantile Agency Records, 1951.

17. James Mohr, *Abortion in America: The Origins and Evolution of Public Policy* (New York, 1978), 34–5.

18. *Utica Observer,* Jan. 1, 1833; *Utica Daily Gazette,* Sept. 27, 1856.

19. Linda Gordon, *Woman's Body, Woman's Right: A Social History of Birth Control in America* (New York, 1976); Daniel Scott Smith, "Family Limitation, Sexual Control, and Domestic Feminism in Victorian America," in *Feminist Studies* 1, No. 3–4 (1973), 40–57.

20. Johnson, "Diary," April 2, 1859.

21. J. H. Shroder, Mercantile Agency Records, 1864; Michael McQuade, Mercantile Agency Records, 1854.

22. *Utica Magazine,* Sept. 23, 1827, 101; *Mother's Magazine,* March 1833, 36; Ann Kuhn, *The Mother's Role in Childhood Education: New England Concepts, 1830–1860* (New Haven, Conn., 1947).

23. *Mother's Magazine,* October 1833, 151–7.

24. *Mother's Monthly Journal,* February 1838, 26–7; *Mother's Magazine,* February 1833, 22–6.

25. *Mother's Monthly Journal,* February 1838, 26–7; *Utica Patriot and Patrol,* Oct. 10, 1820; *Mother's Magazine,* April 14, 1833, 95; "Maxims for Mothers," "Maxims for Children," unbound leaflets, 1840, Maternal Association of Utica.

26. *Evangelical Magazine and Gospel Advocate,* Sept. 26, 1829, 97–8.

27. *Mother's Monthly Journal,* April 1838, 30.

28. Ibid., 49–52; March 1838, 425; September 1842, 129–31.

29. "Proceedings of a General Convention of Friends of Education Held at Utica" (n.p., n.d.), 7, 8, 17.

30. Calculations based on the *New York State Census of 1845; Oneida Whig,* Sept. 20, 1842.

31. See, for example, the *Utica Morning Herald,* Nov. 5, 1860.

32. Copies of the boys' newspapers have been preserved in the local history collection of the Utica Public Library.

33. *Oneida Whig,* March 28, 1839.

34. [Emily Chubbuck Judson] *Allen Lucas, the Self-Made Man or Life as It Is* (Utica, 1843), 100–03.

35. *Utica Daily Gazette,* Dec. 14, 1848; *Utica Evening Telegraph,* Sept. 16, 1859.

36. [Judson], *Allen Lucas,* 12, passim.

37. Ibid., 149–50, 174, passim.

38. *Mother's Monthly Journal,* April 1838, 449–52; August 1839: The census measurement of residence in the parental home fails to acocunt for all the Utica natives who left the city entirely. A comparison of the population born in Oneida County with the number of teen-agers of local birth in subsequent census reports suggests that such migration was not excessive, perhaps accounting for only 1 in 5 sons.

39. Will of Charles A. Mann, 1860, Vol. 16; Will of Sophia Clarke, 1855, Vol. 14, WBOC [Will Books, Oneida County, Oneida County Court House, Utica, N.Y.—Ed. note].

40. "First Report of the Trustees of the Oneida Institute of Science and Industry" (Utica, 1828), 8–9; "A Voice from the Oneida Institute," July 1843, 5–12; "Third Report of the Trustees of the Oneida Institute of Science and Industry" (Utica, 1831).

41. "Catalogue of the Officers and Students of Whitestown Seminary for the Year Ending March, 1855" (Utica, 1855), 16; "By-Laws of the Utica Academy" (Utica, 1838); *Utica Daily Observer,* May 18, 1858.

42. "Catalogue of the Officers and Students of Whitestown Seminary, 1865" (Utica, 1865), 32; *New York State Census of 1845.*

43. *Daboll's Schoolmaster's Assistant Being a Plain Practical System of Arithmetic Adapted to the United States* (Utica, 1829), 138, 140; Lyman Preston, *Preston's Manual on Book-Keeping, or, Arbitrary Rules Made Plain* (New York, 1829).

44. The earliest available figures (1890s) indicate that white-collar workers earned twice the wages of manual workers; see Robert Burns, "The Comparative Economic Position of Manual and White Collar Employees," *Journal of Business* 27 (1954): 257–68.

45. Horatio Dryer to Harriet Dryer, April 10, 1856, Dryer Family Papers, New York Historical Society.

46. Hugh White, Jr., to William F. White, May 23, Oct. 17, Oct. 27, 1857, William Mansfield White Papers, OHS.

47. Hugh White, Jr., to William F. White, Feb. 16, 1852, Oct. 15, 1854, Sept. 25, 1858.

48. Hugh White, Jr., to William F. White, March 2 and July 30, 1855.

49. Mary Perry to Winifield Perry (n.d.), Winifield Perry Papers, OHS; Mrs. Eliza Baker to Mrs. Ellen Gridley, June 1, 1862, Gridley Family Papers, OHS.

50. *Mother's Monthly Journal,* August 1837, 127; Bradford Merrill, Mercantile Agency Records, 1844.

51. Will of Lewis Bailey, Vol. 12, 1857, WBOC.

52. Anson J. Upson, "An Address Delivered at the First Anniversary of the Young Men's Christian Association of Utica New York" (Utica, 1859), 24, 25; Allen S. Horlick, *Country Boys and Merchant Princes: The Social Control of Young Men in New York* (Lewisburg, Pa., 1975); Paul Boyer, *Urban Masses and Moral Order in America, 1820–1920* (Cambridge, Mass., 1978), 109–20.

53. A. B. Grosh, "Odd-Fellowship: Its Character and Tendency" (Utica, 1843), 17.

54. "Records of the Whitestone Seminary Phoenix Society," Ms, April 25, May 9, May 25, June 14, June 27, Oct. 3, 1856; May 1, 1857; June 4, 1858; May 20, 1859, Whitestown Collection, OHS.

55. Hiram Denio to Ann Pitkin, Nov. 17, 1827, Oct. 5, 1828; Denio Collection, OHS.

56. Ann Pitkin to Hiram Denio, April 12, 1828, Denio Family Papers, OHS.

57. *A Book for the Millions: The Home Miscellany or Book of Gems, Original and Selected* (Utica, 1857), 19.

58. Sayre and Tucker, Mercantile Agency Records, 1855.

59. Urial Kellogg, Mercantile Agency Records, 1849.

60. Jason Davis, Mercantile Agency Records, 1871; John Turnbridge, Mercantile Agency Records, 1870; Edward B. Paine, Mercantile Agency Records, 1869.

61. Ezekiel Bacon, *Vacant Hours* (Utica, 1845), 60.

MICHAEL B. KATZ

IAN E. DAVEY

16. Youth and Early Industrialization in a Canadian City

In this essay we ask a straightforward question: Did the stages in the lives of young people alter during early industrialization? To attempt an answer, we shall compare the major dimensions in the experience of young people within one city prior to and during early industrialization. In particular, three broad issues frame our inquiry into specific patterns of residence, education, work, and marriage and into the way in which class and ethnicity affected the shape of experience. Those three issues are the universality of adolescence, the relations between parents and children, and the social consequences of public education. We begin with the issues.

Three Issues

Youth, S. N. Eisenstadt (1965) argues, exists everywhere. No society fails to recognize the years between the onset of puberty and the arrival of adulthood as a separate and special phase within the life cycle. Human biology overrides cultural distinction; though we call it adolescence, others have recognized the same period by other names. In her argument for the recognition of youth in early modern France, Natalie Davis (1975) has stressed the same point. She portrays peer groups of young people sanctioned by cultural tradition playing well-defined and important roles, especially in the charivari through which they enforced community morality and vented political protest. In less sophisticated terms the assumption that something called adolescence exists as a fixed, biological, and psychological phase underlies much social policy. In educational reform, to take one policy area, it has shaped the attempt to design and redesign secondary schools. Educators have rarely asked, however, if adolescence itself need be taken as a given.

A few historians have raised the question, nonetheless. John and Virginia Demos (1969) have argued that Americans invented adolescence in the 19th century. And Frank Musgrove (1965, chaps. 3 and 4) has credited Europeans with its discovery in roughly the same period. At its simplest, then, the issue is who is right: Has a distinct stage in life which may be called youth or adolescence always been with us? At a more general level, however, the question becomes the malleability of the life cycle. To what extent do technology, economic organization, social order, and cultural tradition shape the manner in which irreducible aspects of human biology find expression during the lives of particular people?

Two examples should prove the legitimacy of the question. All physically normal people mature sexually. But the age of menarche in women has declined steadily during past centuries. Though puberty comes as always, its onset is variable, dependent on factors only imperfectly understood; through some mechanism historical forces have affected human biology to alter the timing of stages in the lives of women. Similarly, the forces that have increased longevity have made common a new phase in the life cycle: the extended period that couples now have to spend alone together after all their children have left home (Laslett 1973; Wells 1973). Clearly, it is reasonable to suppose that the stages in human lives are at least partially a product of forces other than biology, that the life cycle itself has a history.

Industrialization has had a bad press among students of the family; that makes the second issue which underlies this essay especially important. Industrialization, in a common argument, seriously weakened the family: the city, the factory, poverty, and the loss of communal controls eroded the stability in the relationships of family members with each other. As a result, working-class families lost their coherence: marital bonds loosened, parental influence declined, kin ties dissolved, and young people rejected the authority and discipline of the home for the freedom and dissipation of the city.[1]

In his study of 19th-century Lancashire, the most sophisticated contemporary investigation of the "disorganization hypothesis," Michael Anderson (1971) both challenges and supports these customary views. The operative principles of family life shifted from normative to calculative as people moved from farm to city, he argues. Though they derived solid benefit from family relations in the country, it was tradition and the weight of community opinion that prescribed and enforced customary ties between kin. Within the city old customs gave way; only those relationships perceived as useful in the short run were likely to be maintained. Industrial people looked upon the family as a marketplace in which a complicated set of exchanges took place. Only if the bargain would prove worthwhile were they willing to maintain strong ties with kin. Nonetheless, strong kinship networks did persist in industrial cities. The reason why, according to Anderson, is that they proved of solid benefit to most people: young couples took in grandmothers who baby-sat while wives went to work, kin networks offered access to employment, and so on. When youngsters perceived family relations as onerous, when, for instance, they felt their parents charged too much for room and board, they either bargained or left. Yet, despite the availability of alternatives and the pressures of urban life, kin frequently dwelled together, young married people frequently settled near their parents, mothers loved and cared for their children, and, overall, the industrial family retained a remarkably orderly shape.

Not all historians would agree that Anderson correctly located the dynamic of family life within an exchange theory. In *The Making of the Modern Family,* Edward Shorter (1975), for one, offers a strikingly different (though not totally incompatible) version of family history. For him the origins of modern society (which he traces to the development of market capitalism) set off an upsurge in individualism, a restless casting off of traditional customs, including conventional marriage, which stressed practical and economic advantage rather than individual inclination. Starting with the popular classes in mid-18th-century Europe, young people began to marry for love, and modern industrial society swept over the West in a wave of romantic sentiment. From one point of view, the rise of romance weakened the family by melting the bonds of authority between parent and child. At the same time, if Shorter is right, for the first time it brought husbands and wives together on the basis of love, channeling attention inward toward their relations with each other and with their children. A great swell of domesticity accompanied the egoistic surge of romantic love and elevated the importance, even sanctity, of home, which it cut asunder from community. Men deserted their male cronies in the pubs for the hearth; kin replaced neighbors in the social and emotional life of ordinary people. According to Shorter, in the long run industrialization strengthened the family as a domestic unit consisting of husband, wife, and children, even as it weakened the family as a system for the perpetuation of property.

The nub of the difference between Anderson and Shorter, by implication, lies in the relations between parents and children. If Anderson is right they became attenuated, explosive, and, in a general sense, weaker. If Shorter should be correct the parent-child relationship should have become more intense, enmeshed in a complex web of sentiment, guilt, and dependence rather than in an audit of mutual benefit. This is the problem on which we must try to shed some light.

One institution, especially, affected relations between parents, children, and society in the industrial era. That, of course, was school. As we all know, during the last century and a quarter young people in Western countries have spent increasingly long periods of their lives in school. The question is, What difference did it make?

Once, it was more or less assumed that the extension of public education had increased equality of educational opportunity and reduced the barriers that social class had erected in the paths of young people. Earlier historiography portrayed 19th-century school promoters and their creations in noble colors: enlightened humanitarians waging a disinterested struggle to extend and preserve democracy against the forces of reaction. Revisionist historians have discolored this portrait. It is no longer possible to ignore the influence of social class, the fear of cultural diversity, and the conservative impulse inherent in educational promotion; the problem rests more in its result. Here the data have been less decisive.[2]

The question can be put simply: Did the extension of educational facilities reinforce or alter existing patterns of social stratification? Did the educational state counteract the inequities of the industrial state with which it more or less simultaneously emerged? Traditional educational historiography would answer yes: albeit imperfectly, public schools gradually have lessened the association between the social origins and destinations of modern citizens. Revisionists, to the contrary, would argue that schools have regulated the amount of social mobility quite carefully and reinforced the structure of inequality in North American society. Though we can cast only a tiny amount of illumination on a vast and complex issue, our findings do support one point of view on this question quite substantially more than the other.

The history of the life cycle of young people between puberty and marriage, the relations between parents and children, the results of schooling—these are the three large issues which underlie our investigation of the way in which the experience of young people changed in one city during its early industrialization. We shall present the data, lay out their major patterns, and then return, at the end, to the relation between what we have found and these more general questions. First, however, it is important to describe briefly the nature of the data and the setting from which they derive.

Early Industrialization in Hamilton

This essay rests on data drawn from a study of family and society in Hamilton, Ontario, during the latter half of the 19th century. The complete 1851, 1861, and 1871 manuscript censuses of the city (population 14,000; 19,000; 26,000) have been coded and put into machine-readable form. The assessment rolls for each census year and for 1881 as well as a variety of other sources also have been coded. Some of these sources have been joined together in order to compile detailed information on individual people within and across time periods. The sources and methods of the project have been discussed elsewhere. Here it is our intention simply to point in a general way to the nature of the information on which our interpretation draws.[3]

Hamilton forms a particularly good setting for a study because it began the transition from a commercial to an industrial city between 1851 and 1871. An instant city which grew from a few thousand in the mid-1840s to 14,000 by 1851, it served as the center of a prosperous agricultural region. With a fine harbor, the creation of which had spurred its growth, Hamilton's supporters hoped their city would rival and even surpass Toronto as the leading port in Canada West (Ontario). Thus, in its heyday as a commercial city, little industry existed in Hamilton. Most manufacturing took place in small shops, while land speculation and trade comprised the dynamic aspects of the city's economy.[4]

The population which swelled the size of the city, it is critical to note, came mainly from Great Britain. In 1851 and 1861 only about nine of every 100 adult male household heads had been born in Canada West. Most of the rest came from Ireland, Scotland, and England, with a smattering from the United States and a few from other, scattered places. Until the depression of the late 1850s immigrants continued to pour into commercial Hamilton. During these years the city fathers undertook the modernization of the city's transport system, public services, and educational facilities. The city council invested heavily in a railroad, which started operation in the early 1850s; lit the streets with gas lamps; authorized the construction of an elaborate waterworks; and radically reconstructed the institutions of formal education, creating in the process, for those times, a remarkably modern and progressive school system.

The efforts of the city fathers were not wholly disinterested, for they had invested their own funds heavily in the railroad, waterworks, and gas company. Thus, their decision to overcommit the city's funds is understandable if not condonable. When the depression of the late 1850s struck the city its effect was severe, reducing the population and driving the city to bankruptcy as its investments proved shaky. By 1861, however, the crisis had passed, and a period of recovery, which in fact became another sustained boom lasting into the early 1870s, had begun.

However, Hamilton did not recover as a commercial city. Toronto's entrepreneurs strung out the Grand Trunk Railway straight through Hamilton's hinterland, ruining the city's prospects of overtaking its rival as the major center of trade for the region. In these circumstances, the city's promoters realized that the future required industrialization, which they actively began to promote as an economic policy.

They were remarkably successful. For, by 1871, when an industrial census was taken, Hamilton had emerged as a modest but unmistakable industrial center.

Why, it might be asked, could the city industrialize quickly? Though the answer is not entirely known, at least its main outlines appear reasonably clear. First, the city's leading citizens clearly wanted to industrialize quickly; the motivation, thus, existed. Second, entrepreneurs had access to capital markets in both Britain and the United States, which undoubtedly made it relatively easy to raise money quickly. Third, the technology of industrialization already existed in other countries and could be imported without much difficulty. Fourth, the railroad had created an adequate transportation system linking together a solid domestic market dependent at the time on imported manufactured goods. Fifth, the infrastructure of heavy industry existed in the workshops of the Great Western Railway. Sixth, and critically, for reasons that will become evident later, there existed in the city a supply of cheap, mobile labor, both male and female, ready and eager to enter industrial employment.[5]

As might be expected, industrialization increased the size of the city's firms: in 1851, 24% of the labor force worked in establishments that employed 10 or more people; by 1871 that proportion had increased to 83%. The new firms varied greatly in their organization and technology, but a significant fraction of the largest employed steam-driven machinery. The most modern and consistently mechanized sector was the metal industry: foundries, three sewing-machine factories, a rolling mill, one large agricultural implement firm, and the yards of the Great Western Railway. Within the other large sector of the economy, the apparel industry—clothing, hats, shoes—firms of a variety of sizes coexisted. The largest of these used sewing machines rather than steam power and employed women much more frequently than other industries. Throughout the city small firms and sweated labor in homes continued to flourish. Indeed, the pace of industrialization remained uneven. Industrial growth did not destroy the city's commercial role. Rather, it added to its economic functions, and Hamilton remained an important center of commerce (Katz 1975c).

In many accounts the development of textile mills is synonymous with early industrialization. This, emphatically, was not the case with Hamilton. No textile manufacture of any substance took place within the city during this period. The absence of textiles, moreover, created crucial differences between the economy of Hamilton and that of other early industrial cities, such as Preston, England, studied by Michael Anderson. For textile manufacture utilized very substantial numbers of women, including ones who were married, and young children. In Hamilton, though women (as we shall describe below) exchanged domestic service for industrial work (see Tables 16.1C and 16.1F), they did not remain employed after marriage, and there is no evidence that large numbers of young children toiled in factories (Katz 1975d).

Irregularity and insecurity comprised the two dominant features of the industrial work experience in Hamilton, and in most other cities as well. Neither condition was new, though some men within Hamilton argued that they had become increasingly acute during early industrialization. It is hard, of course, to evaluate the testimony of elderly men trying to make a case, in this instance before the Royal Commission on Capital and Labour. Nonetheless, evidence from a variety of sources does support their claim that—whatever their curve of intensity—irregularity and insecurity scarred the lives of workers. In both the commercial and early industrial city work took place within a system of structured inequality buffeted by the vagaries of seasonal demand and capitalist economic cycles. Worse almost than low wages were the inability to predict the number of days on which work would be available and the vulnerability of workers to arbitrary firing, falling profits, and business failure. Mechanization added the anxiety that younger, relatively untrained workers would flood the labor market, dilute wages, and weaken the precarious hold established artisans had on their jobs.[6]

We dwell on irregularity and insecurity because they shaped working-class life and, in so doing, created a rhythm echoed in the lives of young people and in the relations between family, class, and school.

The rest of this essay concerns patterns that can be detected within the lives of young people. We turn now to a fairly detailed examination of the changing nature of youth: where young people lived, when they began to work, which ones went to school, and when they married. We begin with fairly broad patterns that cut across social and ethnic, though less often sexual, divisions and then turn our attention to the way in which class and culture altered the behavior of young men and women during the transition to industrial capitalism in one Canadian city.

Dimensions of Youth

Residence

During the early years of industrialization young people changed their residence patterns. Earlier, young people customarily had left their parents' homes when they had found work; in the early industrial city they remained there far more frequently during the initial years of employment, often, we suspect, until they married. This was a shift of major importance. When young people had moved away from their parents' homes they usually had not lived by themselves or with groups of friends. On the contrary, they had moved in with other families, dwelling as boarders, relatives, or servants—quasi members of other households. This experience formed a distinct stage in the life cycle that virtually disappeared during industrialization. For not only in Hamilton, but practically everywhere that historians have looked, membership in one or more households for a prolonged period of time between puberty and marriage was ubiquitous.[7]

We call this lost phase of the life cycle "semiautonomy" because young people had exchanged the complete supervision of their parents for a relatively more autonomous, though still watchful, relation with another household. The argument that life within another household represented a relatively more autonomous existence than life with parents rests on assumptions that have been detailed elsewhere (Katz 1975e, chap. 5). Here we are concerned less with the relative degree of autonomy than with, as will be clear later, other consequences of the greatly prolonged residence of children in the home of their parents.

Table 16.1 provides data to support these contentions. In 1851, one-half of the young men in Hamilton had left home by the age of 17; in 1861, one-half did not leave until the age of 21 and, in 1871, until 22. In 1851, 24% of the 20-year-old men lived at home; that proportion rose to 54% in 1861 and 61% 10 years later. By the latter year, 27% of the 25-year-old young men lived at home compared with 14% and 19% in the two earlier decades, respectively. We shall discuss marriage age in some detail later. Here, however, it is relevant to point out that throughout the period it was unusual for a young man to marry before his mid-twenties.

Those young men not living at home were primarily boarders in another household (see Table 16.1B). At least 40% of all young men between the ages of 17 and 25 in 1851 lived as boarders; by 1871 that proportion had dropped substantially from 43% to 15% of the 17-year-olds and from 50% to 32% of the 23-year-olds, to take but two examples. To what extent, we must ask, were these figures—especially for 1851—an artifact of the heavy immigration of young, unmarried men into the city? The question is enormously difficult to answer. Evidence from Buffalo, New York, in 1855, does show that young men who were boarders had lived in the city for markedly fewer years than those who

Table 16.1. **Household Status, Employment, and School Attendance of Young People, Hamilton, Ontario, 1851, 1861, 1871**

A. Living with Parents (%)

Age	Male			Female		
	1851	1861	1871	1851	1861	1871
12	77	81	94	74	86	86
13	86	83	93	75	80	85
14	75	80	89	56	71	84
15	64	79	88	56	61	82
16	56	80	85	55	60	72
17	49	66	82	48	54	64
18	38	62	70	37	50	57
19	37	63	63	30	39	49
20	24	54	61	21	33	43
21	22	43	53	27	33	39
22	28	45	44	17	28	27
23	14	34	32	18	25	27
24	25	32	25	16	18	24
25	14	19	27	10	22	19

Source.—Entire population manuscript census for Hamilton, 1851, 1861, and 1871.
Note.—Percentages are rounded. Ages are in years in all tables.

	B. Male Boarders (%)			C. Female Servants (%)		
Age	1851	1861	1871*	1851	1861	1871
12	15	2	5	15	6	2
13	10	8	6	16	8	3
14	18	10	7	31	14	8
15	23	9	7	29	20	8
16	34	7	10	28	27	16
17	43	19	15	39	30	18
18	49	24	24	35	32	17
19	51	23	32	41	37	20
20	62	36	29	40	32	23
21	61	38	33	31	26	14
22	53	34	36	28	25	16
23	50	35	32	21	22	13
24	42	29	40	19	16	15
25	41	40	29	20	21	10

*Estimate of household status.

Table 16.1 (**Continued**)

D. Married or Widowed (%)

Age	Male			Female		
	1851	1861	1871*	1851	1861	1871
18	2	1	0	9	4	9
19	1	1	1	12	7	13
20	5	4	5	24	17	15
21	9	8	7	28	27	28
22	11	8	15	40	36	41
23	25	24	31	49	40	45
24	26	25	31	29	55	46
25	45	33	36	60	58	57
26	46	52	53	71	72	63
27	55	60	54	76	79	66
28	64	64	60	79	79	71
29	63	66	74	80	77	78
30	60	70	65	83	80	80

*Estimate of household status.

E. Index of Marriage to Independent Household Status*

Age	Males			Females		
	1851	1861	1871	1851	1861	1871
18	1.5	.5	.3	1.5	1.3	1.3
19	1.0	.3	.7	1.4	1.5	1.1
20	1.3	1.5	.9	1.4	1.2	1.1
21	1.2	.9	.9	1.3	1.2	1.1
22	1.0	.8	1.1	1.2	1.2	1.1
23	.9	1.1	1.0	1.2	1.2	1.1
24	1.1	1.1	1.1	1.2	1.2	1.1
25	1.2	1.1	1.0	1.2	1.2	1.0
26	1.1	1.1	1.0	1.2	1.1	1.2
27	1.3	1.1	1.0	1.2	1.1	1.0
28	1.1	1.0	1.1	1.2	1.1	1.0
29	1.0	1.0	1.0	1.1	1.2	1.1
30	1.1	1.1	1.0	1.2	1.1	1.1

*For men: $\dfrac{N \text{ men married/widowed}}{N \text{ household heads}}$ for women: $\dfrac{N \text{ women married/widowed}}{N \text{ household heads/wives}}$

F. Proportion of Servants among Employed Females (%)*

Age	1851	1861	1871
13–16	87	92	68
17–20	80	87	54
21–25	73	69	47
Mean of means, ages 13–25	79	82	56

*Calculated as % female servants/%female employees × 100.

Table 16.1 (**Continued**)

G. Portion Employed (%)

	Males			Females		
Age	1851	1861	1871	1851	1861	1871
11	2	1	1	15	3	1
12	12	2	4	15	6	3
13	15	2	7	18	8	4
14	21	9	22	35	15	12
15	41	18	53	34	23	16
16	51	29	66	34	30	26
17	67	46	74	48	35	30
18	76	53	85	49	36	35
19	77	64	89	51	36	39
20	76	69	91	48	39	39
21	81	75	91	43	37	35
22	85	79	94	37	39	30
23	88	82	91	31	30	25
24	88	81	93	25	26	30
25	89	89	94	30	27	24
26	93	94	96	21	17	21
27	89	96	96	22	15	21
28	93	91	97	19	13	19
29	96	94	96	11	17	17
30	92	93	95	15	18	15

H. Attending School (%)

	Males			Females		
Age	1851	1861	1871	1851	1861	1871
3	1	1	1	0	2	1
4	4	5	8	4	3	7
5	22	20	42	11	13	38
6	30	45	70	29	43	61
7	49	64	85	40	57	79
8	52	70	86	41	72	85
9	57	74	89	46	75	84
10	45	77	90	47	75	90
11	55	75	85	42	60	83
12	42	73	81	31	65	81
13	37	75	62	33	59	67
14	29	51	48	20	54	53
15	17	37	26	15	42	36
16	11	27	17	8	22	18
17	7	17	8	5	11	9
18	3	12	2	0	6	4
19	4	3	1	2	4	3
20	3	2	0	0	1	0
21	1	1	0	0	1	0

dwelled with their parents. On the other hand, demographic estimates based on the population of Hamilton, though still crude, do make it plausible that the shifts in the proportions of young people at home represent real trends, not merely the processes of population movement. These estimates are supported by the fact that the proportion of young people to the entire population remained almost unchanged between 1851 and 1871.[8]

One other characteristic of boarders should be stressed. They did not distribute themselves randomly throughout the households of the city, nor did they live most often with those most in need of extra income. On the contrary, with the exception of widows, wealthier families had boarders substantially more often than poor ones. In 1851, for instance, 50.5% of the wealthiest 10% of households contained a boarder compared with 20% of the poorest fifth; in 1861 the proportions were 27.5% and 12.4%, respectively.

Few boarders (by one estimate 9% at most) could have been employees of the household head. Rather, their presence signified the persistence of an essentially noneconomic tradition: the oversight of a community's youth by the well-to-do. Boarding represented an essentially moral arrangement, and its subsequent associations with poverty marked a significant shift in the relation between family and community. For, by the late 19th century, boarding had become almost wholly an economic arrangement associated with the lower classes.[9]

Once boarding acquired its association with poverty, middle-class reformers—increasingly refracting social reality through the new ideal of the private family—began a campaign of denunciation. Boarding emerged in respectable eyes as a cause and symptom of family pathology, a lower-class disease to be cleansed with domesticity (Modell and Hareven 1973).

Although young men exchanged earlier habits of boarding for an increasingly long residence in the home of their parents, they did not start to work later in early industrial Hamilton (Table 16.1G). In 1851, one-half of the men had been employed by the age of 16; in 1871 one-half were working at the age of 15. Thus, the period between the onset of work and the departure from home had been extended in two decades from at most a year to about seven years, a radical shift.

The trends in the residential experience of young women paralleled those of men (Table 16.1A). In 1851 one-half of the young women had left home by the age of 17; in 1861 and 1871 that age had increased three years to 20. In 1851, 48% of 17-year-old women lived at home, a proportion which increased to 54% and 64% during each of the next two decades. Similarly, the share of 23-year-old women at home rose from 18% to 27% between 1851 and 1871. (The fact that women married about four years earlier than men meant that fewer of them lived with their parents during their early and mid-20s.)

A new phase had entered the life cycle: a prolonged period of time spent with parents between puberty and marriage. If we are right, this shift occurred wherever industrial capitalism developed. The reasons, however, remain somewhat obscure. Relatively large industries may have made it possible for young people to find work near home. They may have found it cheaper to live with parents than in lodgings, and parents surely welcomed the additional income provided by working children. More than that, as we observed, the older practice had represented not an economic arrangement but a tradition of paternalistic responsibility in which the leading members of communities assumed an active role in the socialization of the young. However, the blurred boundaries between family and community sharpened as part of the process of specialization that accompanied the development of industrial capitalism. The encroachment of the market upon the family separated home from workplace and prefigured the doom of domestic arrangements which reflected the social relations of an earlier economic order.

School

The prolonged residence of young people with their parents partially reflected increased school attendance. For, between 1851 and 1871 the proportion of young people at school rose within each age group. The figures that follow (Table 16.2) are based only upon young people living with their parents in order to eliminate any distorting effects that immigration patterns, orphanage, or other unusual circumstances might exert upon the underlying trends. (The experience of all young people is represented in Table 16.1G). Among the youngest group, age 5–6, school attendance increased from about a quarter to a half (24%–51.6%), with the largest increase in the second decade. At the same time attendance became nearly universal for children of ordinary school age (7–12), rising from 50.6% to 71.7% to 85.1% in 20 years.

In sharp contrast to the experience of younger children, attendance among the 13–16-year-olds followed a bell-shaped curve: it rose from 27.9% to 51.7% between 1851 and 1861, a startling leap, and then fell back to 45.8% 10 years later. The reasons for this peculiar pattern relate to the connection between schooling, work, and the state of the job market. The commercial city in 1851 offered people over the age of 12 or 13 little in the way of employment; their labor simply remained unnecessary. At the same time educational provisions, unsystematic and ungraded, were inappropriate for teenagers. During the 1850s, conscious of its educational backwardness, the city modernized its school system, primarily through the introduction of a Central School (see Davey 1975b), a remarkably progressive institution for its time. Thus, by 1861 young people could attend an age-graded secondary school.

During the same period, moreover, there had been virtually no increase in job opportunities. Indeed, the depression made the employment situation for young people bleak, and in these circumstances they turned to the schools. However, within the next decade employment opportunities for young people grew quite remarkably, and many, as we shall see, left school in order to take up jobs in newly expanded or developed industries.

Young men and women did not attend school equally. At every age (Table 16.2) in 1851 young men went to school more frequently: among 5–6-year-olds the relative proportions were 27.0% for males and 20.4% for females, and comparable disparities occurred at each age. By 1861, when the differences had lessened somewhat, young women age 13–16 went to school as often as young men, and, though men under the

Table 16.2. **Age-Sex Structure of School Attendance, Hamilton, Ontario, 1851, 1861, 1871, All Children Living with Parents (% Attending)**

	Male			Female			All		
Age	1851	1861	1871	1851	1861	1871	1851	1861	1871
5–6	27.0	29.6	53.8	20.4	26.5	49.3	24.0	28.0	51.6
7–12	54.1	72.6	85.7	46.5	70.8	84.5	50.6	71.7	85.1
13–16	30.1	51.5	42.6	25.6	52.0	49.4	27.9	51.7	45.8

age of 12 retained the edge, by 1871 young women age 13–16 had established a notable lead over men: 49.4% of them compared with 42.6% of men attended school.

The reason for the increased attendance of young women over the age of 12 rested, as in the case of men, in the job market. As industrial employment increased, young men could leave school and find work without very much difficulty. In fact, as we will show in some detail later, working-class teenage men actually went to school less often in 1871, after industrialization was under way, than they had 20 years earlier in the commercial city. Young men from affluent homes, who more often remained in school, probably saw in school the route to nonmanual work. Similarly, some young women from relatively affluent homes must have stayed in school because they had nothing else to do; others viewed school as the way to the newest nonindustrial occupation open to women, namely, teaching. And for some, schooling may have provided a moderately attractive alternative to domestic service, for there was very little work in industry available to women under the age of 16. Thus, the explanation for trends in school attendance lies partly in the labor market, which makes it appropriate to turn our attention to the question of work.

Work

Overall, early industrialization did little to alter the customary age at which young people began to work. Young men, as we observed earlier, seemed to enter the workforce on the average about one year earlier in 1871 than in 1851. During the depression of the late 1850s teenage employment had dropped, but with the return of prosperity and the expansion of industrial opportunities it had climbed well above its level in the commercial city: the employed 16-year-olds rose from 51% to 66% and 18-year-olds from 76% to 85%, both between 1851 and 1871 (Table 16.1G).

The increase, importantly, took place not only among all young men but also among those living with their parents (Table 16.3). For instance, the proportion of employed 13–16-year-olds dwelling at home rose from 14.9% to 31.7% between 1851 and 1871. This rough doubling supports our contention that young men had begun to live with their parents during their early working years.

Among women, employment trends were quite different (Table 16.3). The proportion of all young women in the city at work decreased slightly, though the share of those living with their parents and working did increase a bit, from, for example, 3.1%–6.3% of the 13–16-year-olds. Nonetheless, the proportion of employed 16-year-olds among all women in the city dropped from 34% to 26%; for 18-year-olds the decrease was from 49% to 35%, and for 20-year-olds from 48% to 39%, all between 1851 and 1871 (Table

Table 16.3. **Employment and School Attendance among Young People 13–16 Years Old Living at Home, 1851, 1861, 1871 (%)**

	Male			Female		
	1851	1861	1871	1851	1861	1871
In school	30.1	51.5	42.6	25.6	52.0	49.4
Employed	14.9	9.4	31.7	3.1	1.8	6.3
Neither employed nor in school	55.0	39.1	25.7	71.3	46.2	44.3

16.1G). Most employed young women worked as resident domestic servants, which is why the proportion of all women at work so greatly exceeds the proportion at work and living with their parents.

Before we turn more precisely to the sort of work young people did, we should consider the *combined* effects of increased school attendance and, in the case of men, increased employment opportunities. Together they raised the number of "occupied" young people in the city quite dramatically (Table 16.3). In 1851 a large proportion of idle youths, neither in work nor at school, roamed the streets of Hamilton. For instance, 55% of the 13–16-year-old young people living with their parents in 1851 were neither in work nor at school. With the introduction of expanded educational facilities and, then, industrial employment, that proportion dropped sharply to 39.1% in 1861 and 25.7% 10 years later. The proportion of "idle" young women decreased at the same time, from 71.3% to 46.2% to 44.3% (see Katz 1975*e*, chap. 5).

Trends within the city as a whole reflected those for young people living with their parents. The proportion of 15-year-old young men neither at work nor at school, for instance, dropped from 41% to 21% between 1851 and 1871, and in the same years the proportion of "idle" 18-year-olds dipped from 21% to 13%. Similar patterns marked the experience of younger teenage women: the proportion of "idle" 13-year-olds declined from 49% to 29% and of 14-year-olds from 45% to 25% while the share of young women 16 years of age and over neither at work nor school held relatively constant. The latter trend reflected the more limited job opportunities of women, even during industrialization.

The rise in the proportion of "occupied" young men had taken two stages: between 1851 and 1861 school attendance accounted for virtually all of the increase, and attendance itself reflected both newly expanded educational facilities and the lack of work for young men in the commercial city, a problem exacerbated by the depression but by no means unique to hard times. During the next decade, however, increased employment opportunities fostered by industrialization brought about the continuing rise in the proportion of young men who were "occupied."

It is worth dwelling for a moment upon the problem of idle youth. Contrary to popular impression, little paid, regular work outside the home existed for young men in cities prior to industrialization. No shortage of labor made it necessary to press boys into unskilled work, and formally structured, long-term apprenticeships had ceased to exist by the mid-19th century. Apprenticeship, in fact, had not operated in anything like its traditional form for many years. In Great Britain, the source of most of Hamilton's population, the Elizabethan Statute of Artificers, which prescribed rules for apprenticeship, had been ignored for a long period prior to its formal repeal in 1814. Thus, it was not industrialization that had undermined apprenticeship, but capitalism. Apprenticeship was incompatible with a system of wage labor which stressed the manipulation of mobile resources in order to maximize profit.[10]

Idle youths, it was widely and correctly believed, comprised a real and growing element in urban life, and young people adrift in commercial cities with few opportunities to earn money provided the clientele for the establishment of school systems across North America. At the same time, idle and underemployed youths formed the pool of cheap, mobile labor which, as we argued earlier, helped to make industrialization possible.

In contrast to the case of men, industrialization exerted more of an impact on the kind of work young women did rather than on the proportion employed. Its effect, that is, was primarily redistributive.[11] In the whole population, the proportion of women employed dipped slightly from 25.2% to 22.3% between 1851 and 1871. Most working women, about 97% or 98%, remained unmarried; thus we can use employment trends among women in general to reflect the work experience of the young women with whom we are particularly concerned here.

The major shift came in the proportion employed in domestic service, which decreased from 72% to 59% to 47% of all employed women between 1851, 1861, and 1871, respectively (Table 16.1F). At the same time the share of women employed in various sorts of industrial work rose to about one-third of all those employed. The women in industry, as one would expect, worked mainly in the apparel trades as dressmakers, milliners, tailors, and so on: between 1851 and 1871 the proportion of women in the apparel industry rose from 14% to 25%. Women who were neither servants nor dressmakers of some sort worked at a broad range of occupations—most notably teaching, which acquired its heavily feminine composition in these years (see Prentice 1975a).

Industrialization provided some women with an opportunity to leave domestic service. In retrospect, life as a seamstress in a 19th-century shop or factory appears uninviting; but to young women of the time it obviously represented an improvement over the confinement of life as a resident servant. The attraction probably did not lie in improved wages; without board and room included in their pay, young women may have been less well off as seamstresses than they had been as domestics. Rather, its relative independence and the opportunity it offered to work in a group of peers undoubtedly lured many young women to the often wretched life of a seamstress.[12]

The statistics here probably underestimate the extent of employment among young women. A great many women sewed at home under a piecework system and for the most part may not have listed themselves as employed on the census. Thus, the actual number of young women who earned some money in the needle trades undoubtedly exceeded the proportion given here. Furthermore, the employment pattern of women in Hamilton, it must be understood, cannot safely be generalized to all settings which industrialized in the 19th century. For Hamilton in this period did not have mills which manufactured cloth, and elsewhere the presence of a large textile industry appears to have produced markedly different employment patterns during early industrialization.[13]

Though young men had a wide variety of occupations in both the commercial and the early industrial city, they entered the newer, expanding sectors of the economy in disproportionate numbers. For instance, considering only young men living with their parents between 1851 and 1871, the proportion of those employed who worked as molders increased from 2.4% to 4.5% as machinists from 0.9% to 9.8%, and as clerks and bookkeepers from 7.1% to 16.0%. (Clerical occupations expanded very rapidly in both the commercial and the early industrial city.) Conversely, stagnating sectors or sectors of the economy adversely affected by mechanization did not attract very many young men: between 1851 and 1871 the proportion of shoemakers, for instance, dropped from 5.2% to 1.8% of young men working and living at home and, among all young men age 15–24, from 35% to 3%, an enormous decline.

The same patterns emerge from another point of view as well. Consider fathers who had working sons living at home (table 16.4); 66 of the men were in the metal trades compared with 170 of their sons; 133 of the men and 222 of their sons worked in commerce; 24 fathers and 86 sons were carpenters. At the same time, 96 fathers but only 52 sons worked in the apparel industry, and 204 fathers and only 123 sons were laborers. Young men, clearly, did not enter the workforce in a random fashion. They chose

Table 16.4. **Comparison of Distribution of Occupations by Sector among Fathers and Their Sons Living at Home, 1871**

Sector and Occupation	N		%	
	Father	Son	Father	Son
Primary:				
Agriculture	7	2	.7	.2
Extractive	14	7	1.4	.7
Secondary:				
Textile & leather	2	2	.2	.2
Apparel	96	52	9.7	5.3
Wood & wood products	31	42	3.1	4.2
Metal & metal products	66	170	6.7	17.2
Food & beverages	22	18	2.2	1.8
Luxury items	12	18	1.2	1.8
Other	51	130	5.2	13.1
Construction	142	97	14.4	9.8
Labor	204	123	20.6	12.4
Tertiary				
Commerce	133	222	13.4	22.4
Transport	58	51	5.9	5.2
Service	21	13	2.1	1.3
Domestic service	12	5	1.2	.5
Professions	26	8	2.6	.8
Education & government	43	23	4.3	2.3
Arts/culture	7	6	.7	.6
Unclassifiable	42	0	4.2	0.0
Total	989	989	. . .	. . .

expanding sectors of the economy and avoided those which were unattractive. Their ability to choose reflected the relatively favorable job market that confronted young men in the early industrial city. It makes their eagerness to leave school understandable.

Marriage

Youth, as we define it, ended with marriage. Unlike residence, school, and work, marriage patterns apparently changed very little during the early years of industrialization. More detailed work with parish registers (now in progress) may alter this conclusion somewhat, but on the basis of the information in the census there was little overall relation between early industrialization and the age of marriage.

Throughout the period, marriage retained its "European" pattern: that is, it was late. A selection of marriage registers between the late 1840s and the late 1860s put the average age of marriage for men at 27 and for women at 23. In 1855 age at marriage in Buffalo, New York—according to the census—was exactly the same. The census for Hamilton lists one-half of the men married by the age of 27 in 1851 and by 26 in 1861 and 1871 (Table 16.1D). Looked at another way, man appeared to marry a bit later during the depression of the late 1850s and very slightly earlier in 1871 than they had 20 years previously. For example, in 1851, 14.8% of the 21–23-year-olds were married compared with 12.6% in 1861 and 16.9% in 1871; during the same period the proportion of 24–26-year-olds married varied from 38.7% to 36.4% to 40.8% (Table 16.5).[14]

The experience of women differed somewhat (Table 16.1D). Half of the women, according to the census of 1851, had been married by the age of 25 in 1851, 24 in 1861,

Table 16.5. **Married Males by Occupational Rank within Age Groups: Hamilton, Ontario, 1851, 1861, 1871 (%, Rounded)**

Age and Occupational Rank	1851	1861	1871
21–23:			
1	13	14	13
2	9	9	10
3	17	12	17
4	28	29	18
5	17	34	38
All	14.8	12.6	16.9
24–26:			
1	54	38	33
2	37	32	32
3	43	43	42
4	31	47	56
5	52	54	56
All	38.7	36.4	40.8
27–29:			
1	54	53	55
2	49	52	56
3	67	71	64
4	71	74	63
5	70	75	68
All	60.5	61.4	61.5
30–32:			
1	64	68	52
2	79	71	65
3	74	77	79
4	57	77	76
5	68	86	85
All	68.4	72.7	74.0

and 25 again 10 years later. However, by 1871 fewer women in their late 20s had married than in either of the previous census years. In 1851, 76% of 27-year-old and 79% of 28-year-old women were married compared with 66% and 71%, respectively, 20 years later. This decline reflects the unbalanced sex ratios in the city, especially severe in the aftermath of the depression of the late 1850s when young, unmarried men often left. In 1871, for example, there were only 82 men for every 100 women age 25–29 within the city.

Once married, couples usually established their own households. In sharp contrast to the situation in Preston, England (Anderson 1971), very few young married couples in Hamilton did not live in their own homes either prior to or during early industrialization. Between 1851 and 1871 the proportion of young couples not living in independent households remained one in 10 (Table 16.1E). This difference between Hamilton and Preston probably reflected housing supply rather than cultural preference. For Anderson points out that a severe shortage of housing existed in Preston, whereas in Hamilton almost all families lived in single-family dwellings and cheap rental housing remained easily available. In this respect families in Hamilton were more like those that Lynn Lees (1969) found among Irish and English working-class people in London during the same period. For there, too, young couples generally lived by themselves once they had married. In Preston, too, unlike Hamilton, the textile industry employed a large number of married women who needed the babysitting service that a resident grandmother could provide (Anderson 1971).

Thus, the marriage patterns in Hamilton and London support the case Peter Laslett (1972) has made that the simple family household—the conjugal family dwelling alone without kin—remained the accepted and preferred domestic arrangement among people of British origin. Three circumstances in particular appear to have exerted enough influence to alter that pattern: (1) a housing shortage; (2) the need for someone to care for young children in areas where women worked in factories, particularly in textile towns; and (3) the presence of indigent kin in need of a home, a situation described particularly effectively by Crandall Shifflet (1975) for a Virginia county in 1880.

Class and Ethnic Variation in the Experience of Young People

Young people from all backgrounds began to stay at home longer and to go to school more often during early industrialization. However, the experiences of young people of different ethnic and class origins did differ significantly.

First of all, consider general distinctions apparent in 1871. In that year the census for the first time listed "origin," which makes it possible to distinguish the ethnic backgrounds of individuals born in Canada.[15] Women of Irish origin born in Canada remained at home longer than Irish-born Catholics. The proportion of each group working as resident domestic servants reflects that difference: 40% of the 15–17-year-old Irish-born Catholic women compared with 18% of Catholic women of Irish origin born in Canada. Conversely, among 9–11-year-olds only 43% of the former compared with 87% of the latter attended school. Finally, striking differences between the two groups of Irish Catholic women existed in marriage. A very low proportion, only half, of Catholic women of Irish origin born in Canada had married by their late 20s, an age higher than that of any other group. Perhaps they remained spinsters because they found it especially difficult to locate suitable marriage partners. But the resolution of this problem is unclear. Indeed, its solution must be part of the larger, still unresolved issue of the relative weight of improved economic position and cultural assimilation in the different behavior of Irish Catholic young women born in Canada.

Little ethnic difference existed among young men in the age of leaving home, though the Scottish stayed longer with their parents and married later. However, differentials similar to those among young women did exist in school attendance. Irish-born Catholic young men left school earlier than Catholics of Irish origin born in Canada: between the ages of 12 and 14, 36% of the former and 56% of the latter had attended school. Nonetheless, the Catholic rate among the natives remained low by comparison with other Canadian-born groups. For the most part, ethnic differences in school attendance reflected employment trends: Catholics born in Ireland more often started work between the ages of 12 and 14 than did others. However, by the time they reached the age of 15–17 little difference remained between Catholic men born on different continents.

Social rank affected the age at which young people left home. Of course, we have no direct measures of the occupations or wealth of the fathers of young men living as boarders, and conclusions must rest, consequently, on estimates developed through more indirect methods. If fertility and infant mortality were roughly comparable (and there is no reason now to believe that they were not), then we can compare the ethnic and class variation in the proportion of men of a given age (45 and over) who had children of a particular age (over 17) living at home with them. Using this measure, a linear relation (Table 16.6A) exists between the occupational rank of fathers and the length of time children remained at home. In the case of males the number of sons divided by the number of fathers was highest in the top occupational rank (1), 0.64; for rank 3 (primarily artisans) it was 0.50 and for rank 5 (generally laborers), it was lowest, 0.42. The same results exist for daughters and for all children together. Thus, it is clear that the children of more affluent fathers remained at home longest. Similarly, 43% of Irish Catholic men age 45 or over compared with 64% of Canadian Protestants, the most affluent group, had a child age 17 or more at home.

Table 16.6. **Adolescent Children 17 Years Old and Over at Home, by Ethnicity, Occupation, and Marital Status, 1871**

A. Married Male Household Heads Age 45 or Over: % with One or More at Home (N = 1,427)

	Sons (36%)	Daughters (32.5%)	Sons and Daughters (51.5%)
Occupational rank:			
1.	47.1	38.4	62.3
2.	39.0	38.2	56.9
3.	36.5	36.7	55.0
4.	31.5	23.1	38.9
5.	31.4	20.3	40.7
Other	50.0	50.0	50.0
Ethnicity of men:			
Irish Catholic	31.9	26.0	42.5
Irish Protestant	43.5	39.5	59.3
Scotch Presbyterian	37.6	36.5	55.3
Other Scotch	40.0	42.4	57.0
English Anglican	30.6	27.8	48.2
English Methodist	45.9	49.5	67.6
Other English	36.7	25.6	51.1
Canadian Protestant	52.0	34.7	64.0
Canadian Catholic	62.5	12.5	62.5
U.S. Nonwhite	34.8	21.7	39.1
Other U.S.	21.7	30.0	41.7
Other	30.4	21.4	40.2

B. Widows Aged 40 + with One or More at Home (N = 454)

Children:	
Sons	44.7
Daughters	42.3
Sons and daughters	64.5
Ethnicity of women:	
Irish Catholic	45.8
Irish Protestant	34.2
Scotch Presbyterian	41.7
English Anglican	57.1
English Methodist	42.3
Canadian Protestant	57.1

One factor cut across both class and ethnic divisions: namely, widowhood (Table 16.6B). More often than any others, children of widows remained at home, doubtless to assist their mothers. For instance, 64.5% of widows age 40 or more had a child age 17 or older at home compared with 51.5% of male household heads. And this distinction held within ethnic groups.

Children from ethnically or occupationally advantaged families stayed home somewhat longer than others. They usually went to school somewhat more often as well. However, school attendance is a complex subject, to which we must turn our attention separately.

For some reason, Canadian birth promoted school attendance among children, especially those 13–16 years old, from various ethnic backgrounds. The conclusions here rest on a multivariate analysis in which all other factors were held constant. In this analysis, Canadian-born teenage children of Irish parents were more likely to attend school than Irish-born children of Irish parents, and the same distinction existed among children of English and Scottish parents. The explanation for these distinctions remains unclear. It is not certain, for instance, whether attendance resulted from the early experiences of the child or from the fact that the presence of Canadian-born teenagers signified a prolonged residence in North America, which had altered the outlook and behavior of parents.

By 1871 ethnic distinctions had diminished in importance, and class counted for more. By then the main distinction in teenage attendance separated the Irish Catholic young people from the high attendance of Canadian Protestants, but these differences were mainly a product of class. (Among younger children the attendance of Catholics had increased quite dramatically with the opening of Catholic separate schools in the 1850s.) Though children of the well-to-do continued to attend school longer, children of the working class left as soon as industrial employment became available. This bifurcation in the behavior of young men of different social origins largely accounted for the increased influence of class on school attendance.

To be concrete, in 1861, 61.9% of the 15–16-year-old sons of men in the highest occupational rank attended school; 10 years later that proportion had increased substantially to 85.3%. Conversely, the proportion of 15–16-year-old sons of skilled artisans attending school dropped from 32.0% in 1861 to 14.7% a decade later, and the proportion of laborers' sons dipped from 20.0% to a mere 7.4%. Clearly, a bifurcation in the school experience of young men from different social classes had taken place (Table 16.7).

The multivariate analysis (specifically, multiple-classification analysis) supports these trends. For instance, as schooling became nearly universal between the ages of seven and 13, nonattendance became virtually random; the share of the variation in attendance explained by a variety of social and demographic factors consequently dropped from 23% to 8% for men between 1851 and 1871 and from 17% to 6% for women.[16] However, among older youths, age 13–16, who went to school far less often, attendance retained its clear relation to social structure. The proportion of variance explained in the attendance of 13–16-year-old men shifted from 42% to 17% during the 20-year period. More interestingly, occupation and wealth played the key role, as we would expect, though occupation emerged as the more powerful factor. The beta (roughly analogous to a partial correlation) between wealth and attendance (all other factors constant) was .30 in 1851 and .16 in 1871; the beta for occupation with attendance was .29 in 1851 and .24 two decades later, revealing a roughly constant relation.

Looked at another way, the probability that a 13–16-year-old son of a professional

Table 16.7. **Adolescent School Attendance and Occupational Rank of Parents,* Hamilton, Ontario, 1861 and 1871 (%)**

	Occupational Rank, Age 13–14	Occupational Rank, Age 15–16
	1861	
1:		
M	79.4(34)	61.9(21)
F	72.0(25)	50.0(18)
2:		
M	67.4(46)	51.1(47)
F	72.7(44)	42.1(38)
3:		
M	79.2(96)	32.0(103)
F	76.6(94)	50.0(74)
4:		
M	69.2(13)	33.3(15)
F	81.8(11)	25.0(4)
5:		
M	58.1(62)	20.0(60)
F	47.6(45)	19.6(46)
6:†		
M	51.4(37)	30.8(52)
F	52.6(38)	20.0(45)
	1871	
1:		
M	90.2(41)	85.3(34)
F	78.1(32)	70.0(40)
2:		
M	72.6(84)	33.3(60)
F	75.6(78)	32.8(64)
3:		
M	57.8(256)	14.4(150)
F	64.3(207)	31.5(178)
4:		
M	41.4(29)	8.7(23)
F	69.7(33)	21.6(37)
5:		
M	38.7(106)	7.4(68)
F	49.4(85)	16.7(54)
6:†		
M	32.2(59)	9.6(52)
F	60.7(56)	23.1(52)

Note.—*N*'s in parentheses.
*1 = highest, 5 = lowest.
† Primarily widows.

would attend school in 1871 was 76%; of a merchant, 74%; of a clerk, 52%. Contrast these with the probabilities of 45% for the sons of men in apparel trades, 32% for sons of semiskilled workers, and 31% for those of laborers.

Though not as influential as occupation or wealth, ethnicity also contributed to school attendance. In 1851, an Irish Catholic young man 13–16 years old was 31 percentage points less likely than a Scottish Presbyterian, 10 percentage points less than an English Anglican, and 27 percentage points less than a Canadian Protestant to attend school. For women the comparative probabilities were similar. By 1871 the ethnicity of a person's father mattered considerably less, and the most striking differences, as we observed above, existed between young people of similar ethnic origins born in Canada and abroad. For instance, the likelihood that the 13–16-year-old Canadian-born son of an Irish Catholic might attend school was 41% compared with 29% for young men born in Ireland. Among young men from English Anglican backgrounds the different probabilities were 39% and 29%; for those of Scottish Presbyterian origin, 44% and 35% for those born on either side of the Atlantic; and for the native-born sons of Canadian Anglicans, 48%. Obviously, Canadian birth had come to override almost all distinctions based upon the ethnic origins of parents. Indeed, in 1861 the 13–16-year-old Canadian-born son of a man born in Ireland was 18 percentage points less likely than the son of a Scottish-born man and 35 percentage points less likely than one of a man born in England to attend school. By 1871 those differences had dropped to 6 percentage points and nil, respectively.

Over time ethnicity became notably less important than class in the determination of the kind of work that young men entered. That work is especially interesting because it also explains the bifurcation in the school experience of young men from different social classes that occurred during early industrialization. For vertical social mobility between the occupation of fathers and their teenage sons remained quite limited. In 1871, for instance, 62.7% of sons of fathers in entrepreneurial occupations themselves had entered nonmanual jobs. Most of the rest were skilled artisans. At the same time, 77% of the sons of skilled artisans and about half of the laborers' sons remained in the same occupational rank as their parents. Significantly, industrialization increased the opportunity for sons of laborers to enter skilled trades, for the proportion jumped from 24% to 34%. Across all occupational levels, those young men not following their fathers' occupations often entered skilled trades: 28% of the sons of lower-level white-collar workers, 56.5% of sons of semiskilled workers, and, as we noted, 34% of the sons of laborers.

Only a few sons—almost 5% of laborers', 14.5% of semiskilled workers', and 11.8% of artisans'—managed to enter nonmanual work while still living at home. Thus, most sons continued to inhabit the manual or nonmanual occupational world of their fathers. Those who did move into a different occupational rank, and most of the sons of skilled workers, entered the manufacturing sector of the economy, for which extended formal education was not necessary. Indeed, this conclusion reinforces the general pattern of youthful employment described earlier: young men more frequently moved not only into trades but into the newer, expanding industrial opportunities. Their ability to find work in these industries in their early and mid-teens reveals the irrelevance of prolonged schooling to the type of employment to which they aspired. By contrast, sons of men in higher-ranking occupations may well have prolonged their schooling in order to take advantage of the expanded commercial opportunities available to young men of their class.

Once again, the results of a multiple classification analysis permit relationships to be stated with precision. The probability that the son of a professional living with his parents would enter either a professional or a commercial occupation remained quite uniform—all other factors held constant—at 61% in 1851, 67% in 1861, and 73% in 1871. During this period, similarly, the probability that the son of a man in a clerical position would enter nonmanual work varied only from 51% in 1851 to 52% 20 years later. A fortunate ethnic background could boost these probabilities substantially in 1851, by 34 percentage points if a young man's father was a Protestant of Canadian birth and by 10 percentage points if he had been born in Scotland to a Scottish Presbyterian father. By 1871, however, ethnicity had lost virtually all of its impact. The contribution of a native Canadian father had dropped to 9% and of a Scottish Presbyterian one to nil.[17]

At the other end of the social spectrum, sons of laborers remained more likely than any others to become laborers themselves, though, importantly, that probability declined, as the cross-tabular data should lead us to expect, from 56% in 1851 to 49% in 1871. Similarly, the probability that the son of a laborer would become a skilled worker rose from 26% in 1851 to 36% two decades later. Sons of skilled workers themselves, meanwhile, had only slightly decreased chances of entering artisanal jobs, a decline in probability from 86% to 78%. In either case, Irish Catholic ethnic origin had an unfavorable influence in 1851, though virtually none 20 years later. In 1851 Irish Catholic ethnicity raised the probability that a young man would become a laborer by 17 percentage points; in 1871 it lowered that chance by 1 percentage point, a negligible influence. Conversely, in 1851 Irish Catholic ethnicity lowered the probability of entering a skilled trade by 7 percentage points and raised it by 1 percentage point in 1871; while the influence of the same ethnic background on entrance into nonmanual work was to decrease the probability 5 percentage points and 2 percentage points at either end of the decades, respectively.

As another way of viewing the same trends, note that the likelihood that the son of a laborer would become a nonmanual worker was 7% in 1851 and, identically, 7% 20 years later, while the chance that the son of a clerk would be a laborer was 7% and 4% at each date, respectively, and that of the son of a professional or businessman, 3% and 4%.

Still, the structure of occupational inheritance was becoming somewhat looser over time. For the percentage of variance in son's occupation that could be explained by a group of social and demographic variables decreased quite sharply: among laborers from 57% to 35%, among artisans from 45% to 27%, and among nonmanual workers from 49% to 36%, all between 1851 and 1871. This decrease, actually, came about not so much through a lessened role for fathers' occupation as through the decreased influence of ethnicity. Compare the betas of fathers' occupation with sons' occupation with those for fathers' ethnicity over the 20-year period. For nonmanual occupation they were .58 and .49, for artisans, .61 and .45, and for laborers, .59 and .55. At the same time the betas for ethnicity were lower and dropped substantially: for nonmanual occupations from .19 to .11, for artisans from .20 to .14, and for laborers from .25 to a negligible .04. Clearly, class of origin continued to count heavily in the early job history of young men. However, ethnicity lost much of its clear association with class during early industrialization. This dissociation of class and ethnicity is of major importance to an interpretation of the history of social structure, but its exploration would lead us far from the subject of this paper. Here we must be content to emphasize that the pattern of variation in the experience of young people shifted significantly. In the commercial city ethnicity and class operated in a related though often independent fashion to shape the lives of young people; in the early industrial city the independent influence of ethnicity had become muted, while the influence of class origins remained virtually as strong as—and perhaps more visible than—ever. Thus the combination of two factors—the expansion of industrial jobs and the customary association between the occupation of fathers and sons— explains the bifurcation in male school attendance during early industrialization.

School attendance itself did virtually nothing to promote occupational mobility. Multivariate analysis of the relationship between occupations of fathers and sons among over 700 young men traced from 1861 to 1871 shows that, with other factors held constant, school attendance exerted no influence upon the occupation of young men.[18]

Interestingly, the relation between school attendance and social class differed somewhat for young women (Table 16.8). As in the case of men, the attendance of 13–16-year-old daughters of well-to-do families continued to increase, whereas by 1871 the attendance of young women from manual working-class families had declined slightly from its high point 10 years earlier. However, significant class differences existed in the school attendance of young men and women: the highest-ranking occupational groups sent more of their teenage sons than daughters to school; artisans, semiskilled workers, and laborers sent more daughters. For instance, in 1871, 90.2% of 13–14-year-old sons of men in rank 1 compared with 78.1% of their daughters attended school; for 15–16-year-olds the proportions were 85.3% and 70.0%, respectively. By contrast, 57.8% of the 13–14-year-old sons of artisans attended school in 1871 compared with 64.3% of their daughters; 7.4% of the 15–16-year-old sons of laborers attended, and 16.7% of their daughters.

For the most part these trends probably reflect, again, the labor market. Working-class children may have left school as soon as they found suitable employment; and sons may have found jobs more easily and earlier than daughters. For, as we noted earlier, very few industries employed young women under the age of 16.

Ethnic and class differences affected the kind of work young women as well as young men entered. Generally, Catholic women born in Ireland worked most often; and, overall, more foreign than Canadian-born women were employed. However, 57% of the 24–26-year-old Canadian-born women of Irish Catholic origin worked in 1871, a very high proportion that reflected their low marriage rate, to which we have already referred.

Though the proportion of women working as servants declined, the decrease was not uniform. First, age played an important role: older women more often found alternatives to domestic service. Among the Irish-born Catholic women, for instance, the proportion of working women who were servants in 1871 decreased from 100% of the 15–17-year-olds to 75% of the 18–20-year-olds to 70% of the 21–23-year-olds and 57% of the 24–26-year-olds. Among Canadian-born women of Scottish origin, to take another example, the proportion diminished from 61% to 31% between the 15–17- and 24–26-year-old women.

Age aside, Irish-born Catholics were by far most likely to be servants, roughly twice as likely as Canadian-born women of Irish Catholic origin. And, in general, foreign-born were more likely than native Canadian young women to live as resident domestics. Thus, in part at least, Irish Catholic and other foreign-born young women probably left school earlier than others because they were willing—or forced by economic necessity—to take jobs as servants.

The nature of work affected school attendance, thus, partially through shifts in the labor market and through the connection between occupation, class, and ethnicity. At the same time, it affected attendance through one of its fundamental characteristics, to which we pointed earlier, namely, its irregularity. In a very real sense, the rhythm of school and the rhythm of work reflected each other.[19]

Table 16.8. **Occupational Rank* and School Attendance by Sex, Ages 3–21, Hamilton, Ontario, 1871 (%)**

| | Occupational Rank and Sex | | | | | | | | | | | |
| | 1 | | 2 | | 3 | | 4 | | 5 | | Other† | |
Age	M	F	M	F	M	F	M	F	M	F	M	F
3–4	4.5	4.1	4.4	2.8	5.2	2.7	4.9	11.1	1.5	1.6	11.1	0
5–6	50.0	35.3	58.4	49.0	58.3	51.4	55.3	53.3	42.3	46.0	30.4	50.0
7–12	89.1	84.7	94.0	89.9	86.2	87.2	87.0	84.9	76.3	75.9	81.7	79.3
13–16	86.7	73.6	56.3	56.3	41.9	49.1	26.9	44.3	26.4	36.7	21.6	42.6
17–21	9.5	17.9	3.7	8.3	2.6	3.3	2.2	0	0	2.4	1.2	4.2
All	58.2	54.6	57.0	51.0	50.8	51.0	47.3	51.1	40.6	45.1	33.8	41.1
N	376	339	717	690	1,517	1,464	205	226	614	576	476	382

*1 = highest, 5 = lowest.
†Primarily widows.

No problem troubled mid- and late-19th-century schoolmen more than irregular attendance. Despite compulsory education laws, children simply did not go to school regularly, and the actual daily attendance always remained well below the number formally enrolled. In Hamilton, for instance, in 1872 barely half of the enrolled students attended each day. In part, attendance varied with the seasons, for obvious causes: it peaked in the fall, fell away during the winter, increased in the spring to about its fall level, and, finally, dropped off again during the summer. Though apparent in the attendance of children from all classes, this seasonal rhythm especially marked the behavior of working-class children. Thus, the statistics that show the children of both manual and nonmanual workers in school mask the probability that the middle-class child had attended for a longer period of time.

Obviously, the effects of irregular attendance modified the impact of school attendance. Although most children attended at some point during the year, it is doubtful that many went often enough to learn very much. Thus, though schooling appeared nearly universal, few children spent most of their days within a school.

Working-class children left school earlier and attended less regularly. In addition, within the schools themselves, our one piece of evidence shows, they remained disproportionately concentrated in the lower grades, doubtless partly a consequence of their irregular attendance. The introduction of age-grading had been a key 19th-century innovation, designed, according to its sponsors, to regulate and systematize the educational process. Whether intended or not, it served another purpose: to keep apart the social classes increasingly found within the same school.

Our evidence comes from the Hess Street School in Hamilton for the years 1889–91 (Table 16.9). Of the 2,874 students on the registers, 29.4% were in grade seven or above and 44% in the kindergarten and first three grades. Most of the students came from either lower-white-collar (17.8%), skilled (44.6%), or semiskilled (12.4%) families. Only 7.7% were children of laborers and 5.6% children of professionals or proprietors; the parents of 3.5% were widows.

Table 16.9. **Students of Hess Street School, Hamilton, Ontario, by Occupational Rank of Parents, 1889–91 (%)**

| Grade | Occupational Rank | | | | | | |
	1	2	3	4	5	Other (Widow)	Total
Kindergarten	8.8	21.3	13.8	12.9	13.6	11.8	14.6
1–3	28.8	22.9	28.0	36.0	43.6	14.7	29.6
4–6	23.1	20.0	24.7	25.6	29.5	24.5	26.3
7 +	39.4	35.8	33.5	25.6	13.2	49.0	29.4
Total	5.6	17.8	44.6	12.4	7.7	3.5	. . .
N's	160	511	1,283	356	220	102	2,632
	Age Range						
Kindergarten	5–6	4–7	4–10	4–7	5–7	5–7	4–10
1–3	6–10	5–14	4–13	5–12	5–14	5–12	4–14
4–6	8–14	7–14	7–14	7–14	7–15	8–14	7–15
7 +	9–17	10–16	10–16	10–16	9–15	10–16	9–17

Source.—Compiled from daily attendance registers, Hess Street Public School, 1889–91.

The distribution of children throughout the grades did not reflect the social composition of the school (Table 16.9). For the children of laborers were greatly underrepresented among students in the higher grades: 13.2% compared with 35.8% for children of professionals and proprietors. Conversely, 57% of the latter's children compared with only 37% of the former's were in the first three grades. Given these disproportions, the age range of children in various grades differed according to their social class. The ages of skilled manual workers' children in grades one to three, for instance, varied from four to 13 in contrast to six to 10 for those whose fathers were lower-level white-collar workers. It was unusual, in fact, for a working-class child to progress beyond grade six.

Schoolmen often attributed the poor achievement of working-class children to their irregular attendance. And they blamed that on the neglect, indifference, and carelessness of their parents. However, these moralistic explanations missed the point: the connection between the rhythm of work and the rhythm of school. Those factors which contributed to poverty and economic security—trade depressions, crop failure, transient work patterns, and seasonal unemployment—largely determined the irregularity of attendance in Hamilton and, indeed, throughout the province.

One of these factors deserves special mention. Virtually every recent quantitative study has underscored the transiency that characterized 19th-century society. Time and again not only young men but families were on the move. It is unusual to find more than 30% of the household heads in a 19th-century city present at both ends of the decade, and that figure grossly understates the total amount of movement, which, as Thernstrom and Knights (1971) have shown, exceeded the difference between any two census years by several times. Though 19th-century families from all social classes were people in motion, the poor moved most often. Inability to find work, seasonal unemployment, and economic depression all promoted the continual movement of working people from one place to another. And, of course, transiency militated against the regularity of school attendance. Many young people simply lived too short a time in any one place to attend school very often or very long.[20]

Marriage as well as school attendance increasingly reflected diverging social class responses to the creation of an industrial capitalist society. In 1851 not much difference existed in the marital patterns of men with different occupations, with the exception of clerks who, below the age of 30, were least likely to be married. However, by 1871 new distinctions had emerged: men in professional, commercial, and clerical occupations began to postpone marriage while laborers, very definitely, began to marry earlier (see Table 16.5). For instance, among 21–23-year-olds, 13% and 10% of men in nonmanual occupational categories had married compared with 38% of laborers; at the age of 30–32, 52% and 65% of the former and 85% of the latter had married. At the same time the marriage practice of skilled and semiskilled workers resembled that of the laborers more than the clerks, merchants, and professionals.

It is possible, of course, that occupational differences in marriage reflected cultural rather than class distinctions. The divergent ethnic structure of various occupations rather than social stratification may have created the patterns reported above. For, by and large, Irish Catholics were far more likely to be laborers than men from any other background. Multivariate analysis, however, enables us to discount this possibility (Table 16.10). The association of occupation with marriage remained consistently higher than that of any other variable, including birthplace, religion, and, in 1871, ethnic origin.

Table 16.10. **Probability of Marriage among Selected Occupational and Literacy Groups, 1851 and 1871, All Factors Constant, Hamilton, Ontario (Adjusted Deviations)**

Group	Age 21–23		Age 24–26		Age 27–29		Age 30–32	
	1851	1871	1851	1871	1851	1871	1851	1871
Occupation:								
High commercial	.05	.13	.60	.27	.63	.67	.70	.62
Clerical	.08	.11	.38	.30	.48	.59	.75	.65
Apparel, textile, leather	.27	.21	.48	.44	.60	.44	.73	.66
Metal trades	.19	.16	.39	.41	.75	.66	.95	.78
Construction	.20	.20	.50	.46	.67	.63	.75	.86
Labor	.16	.37	.50	.58	.66	.68	.70	.83
Literacy:								
Literate	N.A.	.17	N.A.	.41	N.A.	.61	N.A.	.74
Illiterate or semiliterate	N.A.	.35	N.A.	.29	N.A.	.95	N.A.	.89
Grand mean	.15	.17	.39	.41	.60	.62	.68	.74

Note.—Derived from multiple classification analysis with marriage partitioned into age groups as dependent variable. In 1851 factor variables were occupational group, religion, and birthplace; in 1871 they were occupational group, religion, birthplace plus origin, literacy. In each year age was covariate. All main effects significant at better than .05. N.A. = not available.

More striking, all other factors held constant, the likelihood that a laborer would marry early increased among younger men from 1 percentage point to 20 percentage points greater than the average probability among 21–23-year-olds and from 11 percentage points to 17 percentage points among 24–26-year-olds between 1851 and 1871. In 1871 the probability that a 21–23-year-old clerk would be married was 11% compared with 37% for a laborer; at the ages of 24–26 the likelihood of marriage was 30% for clerks and 58% for laborers. By contrast, if the men under comparison had been born in Ireland their likelihood of marriage would have been reduced by 5 percentage points and, if born in Ontario, by 2 percentage points, effects much less weighty than those associated with occupation.

Throughout the 1851–71 period clerks remained less likely to marry early than men with most other occupations: among 27–29-year-olds, for instance, a clerical occupation reduced the probability of marriage for a man, compared with the average, by 12 percentage points in 1851 and 1861 and by 3 percentage points in 1871. In the latter year, in fact, it was professionals who married latest: the probability of marriage for professionals age 27–29 and 30–32 was a hefty 26 percentage points and 24 percentage points less than the mean. Thus, all in all, the increasing influence of class on marriage came through the pronounced earlier marriage of laborers and a few other manual workers and the progressively later marriage of clerks and, especially, professionals. At the same time, no religion made any significant difference in marriage age, and only Scottish birth acted consistently and independently to retard the age of marriage.

One other factor, however, exerted a significant influence on marriage age in 1871: illiteracy. In three out of four age groups illiterates married earlier. An illiterate 21–23-year-old was 18 percentage points, a 27–29-year-old 33 percentage points, and a 30–32-

year-old 15 percentage points more likely to be married than someone who could read and write.

The relationships between age of marriage and other factors point to a difference of behavior within the groups most clearly demarcated in industrial capitalist society: the increasingly early marriage of the laborers and the illiterates reflects the proletarianization of the unskilled workforce.

Increasingly cut off from traditional communal restraints and rural practices, young laborers could enter the job market earlier than before, earn a living wage, and marry sooner than in a rural or nonindustrial urban setting. By contrast, aspiring clerks and professionals adopted a rational, calculative mode of behavior appropriate to their later age of entry into the job market, initial low wages, and precarious early careers. The difference in marriage patterns underscored the distinction between men who saw in their future careers rewards which made the postponement of marriage necessary and worthwhile and those who quite rightly believed that they would never earn enough to invest, or, indeed, more than today. Though forced to accept the discipline of industrial work habits and public education, workers nonetheless managed to evade some of the culture of capitalism. No amount of rhetoric could turn a job into a career or mask the fact that the man of 23 earned as much or more than one two-score years his senior. If saving and the postponement of pleasure made sense to the clerk or the professional, it had no foundation in reality for the early industrial laborer. And each man responded appropriately and realistically to his place in a shifting social and economic order.[21]

The Evidence and the Issues

We must now return to the start of this inquiry: How do the experiences of Hamilton's young people during early industrialization bear upon the general questions posed at the beginning of this essay? In Hamilton young people remained longer at home; went more often to school; and married at about the same age, or very slightly earlier. At the same time, ethnicity and class cut across these general trends: working-class young men and women welcomed the expansion of industrial opportunity; the former left school to work while the latter, whenever possible, left domestic service. And the emerging industrial proletariat married earlier than had laborers in the commercial city. How do these findings relate to the issues about adolescence, the stability of the family, and the effects of education with which we began?

Let us start with education. We asked if education counteracted the inequalities within the social structure of industrial society, especially by promoting social mobility. In the commercial city, gross educational inequalities existed; many poor children received almost no exposure to schooling. By contrast, during industrialization this situation changed dramatically; by 1871 schooling between the ages of seven and 12 had become nearly universal, and many more young people over the age of 12 attended. Did this development represent an increase in equality of opportunity? The answer clearly is no.

First, the economic benefits of school attendance accrue from the differential advantage it bestows. That is, two levels of educational attainment always coexist: that reached by most people and that by a fortunate minority. It is the distance between the two rather than their intrinsic qualities which counts. If only 5% of the population attends high school, it is a high school diploma which confers the first and greatest advantage in the search for employment. When everyone has graduated from high school, it is a B.A. that counts, and so on.

Although children of manual workers began to go to school more often and for longer periods of time in mid-19th-century Hamilton, the children of more affluent parents stayed at school for even more years. They preserved their lead and reaped the differential advantage of longer school attendance. Thus, the sheer increment in the number of years a working-class child attended did nothing to increase the tangible occupational benefit that he or she received from school.

More than that, the pattern and structure of school attendance undercut any potential benefits of formal education. For working-class children attended less regularly, and within schools they were more likely than affluent young people of the same age to be found in lower grades. Thus, they not only left earlier, but during the years they did attend, working-class children received less exposure to school and generally did not reach the highest educational levels within the city.

In these circumstances, schooling could not be expected to do very much to promote social mobility. Indeed, both the analysis of the influence of school attendance on occupation and our comparison of the occupations of fathers and children support this contention. Children of nonmanual workers generally entered nonmanual occupations. If schooling had become increasingly necessary for entrance into clerical or commercial jobs, then affluent parents used the expanded educational facilities to prepare their sons to retain their customary occupational advantage. Similarly, they most likely used the schools to prepare their daughters for the one genteel occupation just opening to women, namely, teaching.

Sons of manual workers, on the other hand, generally entered manual occupations. In many instances, nonetheless, their jobs probably were better than those of their fathers', especially in the case of young men who managed to enter the newer, more dynamic sectors of the economy or for the substantial proportion of laborers' sons who became skilled manual workers. However, education had not contributed to the occupational improvement that took place. Its unimportance is reflected in the fact that working-class boys began to leave school earlier in order to work. Clearly, this argues, employers did not require prolonged schooling. Thus, any improvement in the prospects of young men compared with those of their fathers should be credited to the expansion and industrialization of the economy rather than to the extension and modernization of schooling.[22]

Industrialization increased the job opportunities for young men. More than ever, they had the financial ability to leave home and fend for themselves. If industrialization worked as the disorganization hypothesis would lead one to expect, that is what should have happened. Ties between parents and children should have diminished; children should have dwelled at home less often and experienced increased friction in their relations with their parents.

It is difficult to measure the quality of relationships but easier to estimate their duration. We have seen that a massive increase in the length of time children lived with their parents accompanied early industrialization. Instead of leaving home when they found work, young people increasingly lived with their families for years, in many instances probably for a decade. Young people, we suspect, began to live at home longer than at any previous time in Western history.

This development is especially remarkable because, as Michael Anderson has pointed out, an increasing variety of alternatives existed within the city. Boarding had been a customary practice, and it would be no more difficult than before to arrange. And the development of nonfamilial lodging houses meant that a young person could live alone with far less supervision than under more traditional arrangements. Added to this were the relatively high wages paid to young people, which would allow men, at any rate, to support themselves. Given these circumstances, the prolonged residence of young people in the homes of their parents reflects a conscious choice, not an adaptation to necessity. Young people must have lived at home, at least partly, because they wanted to. Thus, it is reasonable to suppose that during early industrialization ties between parents and their teenage children actually grew stronger.

The presence of working children affected the economic condition of the family as a whole. The impact of industrialization upon the standard of living remains a fiercely contested issue; and there is even less evidence assembled in Canada than elsewhere on which to base a conclusion. From one point of view, workers testified that wages and security of employment decreased during the early stages of industrialization. From the other side, working-class home ownership increased and the proportion of the workforce in unskilled laboring jobs decreased. Whatever the experience of individual workers, no answer to the question of what happened to the standard of living will be adequate which does not account for the income of the entire family unit. We are not yet able to calculate the income units available to various families at different points in their life cycles prior to and during industrialization. Nonetheless, even at this point, it is reasonable to suppose that the income from employed, resident children increased the prosperity of working-class families for a substantial portion of their existence.[23]

The prolonged residence of children within the homes of their parents brings us, finally, to the third general issue: Did the life stages through which a young person passed begin to alter?

Our answer is yes. Earlier practices in Hamilton reflected the last gasp of a long-standing custom that cut across social classes. For centuries parents had customarily sent their children to live between puberty and marriage as a member of one or more households. During early industrialization this practice became even less common. By our contemporary standards, the years between puberty and marriage gradually assumed a more familiar cast. Young people spent most of their lives before marriage in the home of their parents.

Whether this new practice can be called adolescence hinges partly on a question of definition. The characteristic feature of adolescence as a concept is not its recognition of the years between puberty and marriage as special. Rather, the concept became current in the late 19th and early 20th centuries when social commentators found it necessary to coin a new phase to correspond to a new stage in the lives of young people. The prolonged dependency of young people upon their parents and their increased education in specialized age-segregated institutions formed the basis for adolescence. Adolescence, we would argue, may be defined as a phase of institutionalized dependency that came to characterize the experience of youth in the 19th century. It proceeded, as do many social changes, in an uneven fashion, first evident among the affluent, spreading—sometimes over fierce opposition—downward throughout the social ranks as working-class children began to attend high school and, eventually, college. Thus, perhaps the origins of behavior we have come to associate with adolescence lay not in puberty but in the reaction to dependency, in the curious new conflict between biological maturity and cultural childhood that 19th-century society inflicted upon its youth. Adolescence, as we know it, is a product of culture and of history.

Notes

1. For one among many contemporary views, see Hunter (1965, pp. 200–203); for an analysis of mid-19th-century Canadian anxiety about the relation of the family to industrialization, see Houston (1974, passim).

2. The recent literature on the history of education has been substantial. For Canada, see Houston (1974), Prentice (1975b), Graff (1975), Davey (1975a), and Katz and Mattingly (1975). For an interpretation of the American experience and a comment on recent literature in the field, see Katz (1975a, 1976).

3. On the background of the project and for a statement of its major conclusions through 1973, see Katz (1975e).

4. For a discussion of Hamilton's early history, see ibid.

5. For comments on the early industrialization of Canada, see Pentland (1959), and Gilmour (1970).

6. The problem of irregularity of work is discussed and documented in Davey (1975a, chap. 6).

7. Some of the evidence for this contention is summarized in Katz (1975e, chap. 5).

8. The Buffalo data came from a Multiple Classification Analysis of the New York Census of 1855 for Buffalo (coded by Lawrence Glasco). The results of this analysis of length of residence in the city are reported by Katz, Doucet, and Stern (1978). The proportion of adolescents in the population of Hamilton was as follows: the proportion of 15–19-year-olds to the total population shifted between 1851, 1861, and 1871 from 12% to 10.4% to 10.4%; that of males 15–19 to all males went from 10% to 9.7% to 9.6%, and of males 15–24 from 21% to 17.8% to 18.6%.

9. For an intriguing interpretation of a similar and related tradition, see Foster (1974, pp. 25–27).

10. Thompson (1963, pp. 544–45) is one place in which the repeal of the Statute of Artificers and related measures are discussed.

11. In this sense trends in Hamilton reflected quite exactly those described in Europe by Scott and Tilly (1975).

12. For a comment on the unwillingness of young women to enter domestic service, see the *Toronto Globe* (October 28, 1969).

13. For example, in Preston, England, as described in Anderson (1971).

14. The marriage registers are all those for Wentworth County preserved by the Registrar-General of Ontario for 1842–69, about 5,000 marriages in all.

15. Full tables showing the relations between life-cycle variables, sex, and ethnicity are in Katz 1975b.

16. We shall describe this multiple classification analysis fully in a forthcoming essay.

17. Katz will present the results of the analysis fully in a forthcoming essay.

18. The results of this analysis are presented fully in Working Paper no. 20 in *Social History Project*.

19. For documentation of this point and of the following paragraphs, see Davey (1975a, chaps. 5 and 6; 1978).

20. The literature on transiency is discussed in Katz (1975e, chap. 3) and in Katz, Doucet, and Stern (1978).

21. On the relation among industrialization, proletarianization, and a decrease in the age of marriage, see especially Levine (1977).

22. The most compelling recent argument for the role of schooling in perpetuating class relations is Bowles and Gintis (1976).

23. For an excellent collection of the principal statements on the controversy, see Taylor

(1975). Our suggestive piece of evidence about the ability of workers to modestly increase their capital during early industrialization is the increase in working-class home ownership in Hamilton between 1851 and 1881, an increase we suspect happened in many places.

References

Anderson, Michael. 1971. *Family Structure in Nineteenth Century Lancashire*. Cambridge: Cambridge University Press.

Bowles, Samuel, and Herbert Gintis. 1976. *Schooling in Capitalist America: Education and the Contradictions of Economic Life*. New York: Basic.

Davey, Ian E. 1975*a*. "Educational Reform and the Working Class: School Attendance in Hamilton, Ontario, 1851–1891. Ph.D. dissertation, University of Toronto.

———. 1975*b*. "School Reform and School Attendance: The Hamilton Central School, 1853–1861. Pp. 294–313 in *Education and Social Change: Themes from Ontario's Past*, edited by Michael B. Katz and Paul Mattingly. New York: New York University Press.

———. 1978. "The Rhythm of Work and the Rhythm of School." In *Egerton Ryerson and His Times*, edited by Neil McDonald. Toronto: Macmillan.

Davis, Natalie Z. 1975. *Society and Culture in Early Modern France*. Stanford, Calif.: Stanford University Press.

Demos, John, and Virginia Demos. 1969. "Adolescence in Historical Perspective." *Journal of Marriage and the Family* 31 (November): 632–38.

Eisenstadt, S. N. 1965. "Archetypal Patterns of Youth." Pp. 29–50 in *The Challenge of Youth*, edited by Erik H. Erikson. New York: Doubleday.

Foster, John. 1974. *Class Struggle and the Industrial Revolution: Early Industrial Capitalism in Three English Towns*. London: Weidenfeld & Nicolson.

Gilmour, James M. 1970. "Structural and Spatial Change in Manufacturing Industry: South Ontario, 1850–1890." Ph.D. dissertation, University of Toronto.

Graff, Harvey J. 1975. "Literacy and Social Structure in the Nineteenth Century City." Ph.D. dissertation, University of Toronto.

Houston, Susan E. 1974. "The Impetus to Reform: Urban Crime, Poverty, and Ignorance in Ontario, 1850–1875." Ph.D. dissertation, University of Toronto.

Hunter, Robert. 1965. *Poverty*. New York: Harper. Originally published 1904.

Katz, Michael B. 1975a. *Class, Bureaucracy, and Schools: The Illusion of Educational Change in America*. Expanded ed. New York: Praeger.

———. 1975b. "Early Industrialization and the Life Cycle." Working Paper no. 1 in *Social History Project*. Toronto: York University.

———. 1975c. "Early Industrialization." Working Paper no. 3 in *Social History Project*. Toronto: York University.

———. 1975d. "Early Industrialization and the Labour Force." Working Paper no. 5 in *Social History Project*. Toronto: York University.

———. 1975e. *The People of Hamilton, Canada West: Family and Class in a Mid-Nineteenth Century City*. Cambridge, Mass.: Harvard University Press.

———. 1976. "The Origins of Public Education: A Reassessment." *History of Education Quarterly* (Winter), pp. 381–407.

Katz, Michael B., Michael Doucet, and Mark Stern. 1978. "Migration and the Social Order in Erie County, New York, 1855." *Journal of Interdisciplinary History*, vol. 8, no. 3 (Spring).

Katz, Michael B., and Paul Mattingly, eds. 1975. *Education and Social Change: Themes from Ontario's Past*. New York: New York University Press.

Laslett, Peter, ed. 1972. *Household and Family in Past Time*. Cambridge: Cambridge University Press.

———. 1973. "Age of Menarche in Europe since the Eighteenth Century." Pp. 28–47 in *The Family in History*, edited by Theodore K. Rabb and Robert I. Rotberg. New York: Harper & Row.

Lees, Lynn. 1969. "Patterns of Lower-Class Life: Irish Slum Communities in Nineteenth-Century London." Pp. 359–85 in *Nineteenth Century Cities,* edited by Stephan Thernstrom and Richard Seanett. New Haven, Conn.: Yale University Press.

Levine, David C. 1977. *Family Formation in an Age of Nascent Capitalism.* New York: Academic Press.

Modell, John and Tamara K. Hareven. 1973. "Urbanization and the Malleable Household: An Examination of Boarding and Lodging in American Families." *Journal of Marriage and the Family* 35, no. 3 (August): 467–78.

Musgrove, Frank. 1965. *Youth and the Social Order.* Bloomington: Indiana University Press.

Pentland, H. C. 1959. "The Development of a Capitalistic Labour Market in Canada." *Canadian Journal of Economics and Political Science* 25 (4): 450–61.

Prentice, Alison. 1975a. "The Feminization of the Teaching Profession." *Histoire Sociale* 15 (May): 5–20.

———. 1975b. "The School Promoters: Education and Social Class in Mid-nineteenth Century Upper Canada." Ph.D. dissertation, University of Toronto.

Scott, Joan, and Louise Tilly. 1975. "Women's Work and the Family in Nineteenth Century Europe." *Comparative Studies in Society and History* 17 (1): 36–64.

Shifflett, Crandall A. 1975. "The Household Composition of Rural Black Families: Louisa County, Virginia, 1880." *Journal of Interdisciplinary History* 1 (Autumn): 235–60.

Shorter, Edward L. 1975. *The Making of the Modern Family.* New York: Basic.

Taylor, Arthur J. 1975. *The Standard of Living in Britain in the Industrial Revolution.* London: Methuen.

Thernstrom, Stephan, and Peter Knights. 1971. "Men in Motion: Some Data and Speculations about Urban Population Mobility in Nineteenth-Century Social History." Pp. 17–47 in *Anonymous Americans: Explorations in Nineteenth-Century Social History,* edited by Tamara K. Hareven. Englewood Cliffs, N.J.: Prentice-Hall.

Thompson, E. P. 1963. *The Making of the English Working Class.* New York: Random House.

Wells, Robert V. 1973. "Demographic Change and the Life Cycle of American Families." Pp. 85–94 in *The Family in History,* edited by Theodore K. Rabb and Robert I. Rotberg. New York: Harper & Row.

17. Women, Children, and the Uses of the Streets: Class and Gender Conflict in New York City, 1850–1860

On a winter day in 1856, an agent for the Children's Aid Society (CAS) of New York encountered two children out on the street with market baskets. Like hundreds he might have seen, they were desperately poor—thinly dressed and barefoot in the cold—but their cheerful countenances struck the gentleman, and he stopped to inquire into their circumstances. They explained that they were out gathering bits of wood and coal their mother could burn for fuel and agreed to take him home to meet her. In a bare tenement room, bereft of heat, furniture, or any other comforts, he met a "stout, hearty woman" who, even more than her children, testified to the power of hardihood and motherly love in the most miserable circumstances. A widow, she supported her family as best she could by street peddling; their room was bare because she had been forced to sell her clothes, furniture, and bedding to supplement her earnings. As she spoke, she sat on a pallet on the floor and rubbed the hands of the two younger siblings of the pair from the street. "They were tidy, sweet children," noted the agent, "And it was very sad to see their chilled faces and tearful eyes." Here was a scene that would have touched the heart of Dickens, and seemingly many a chillier mid-Victorian soul. Yet in concluding his report, the agent's perceptions took a curiously harsh turn.

> Though for her pure young children too much could hardly be done, in such a woman there is little confidence to be put . . . it is probably, some cursed vice has thus reduced her, and that, if her children be not separated from her, she will drag them down, too.[1]

Such expeditions of charity agents and reformers into the households of the poor were common in New York between 1850 and 1860. So were such harsh and unsupported judgments of working-class mothers, judgments which either implicitly or explicitly converged in the new category of the "dangerous classes." In this decade, philanthropists, municipal authorities, and a second generation of Christian evangelicals, male and female, came to see the presence of poor children in New York's streets as a central element of the problem of urban poverty. They initiated an ambitious campaign to clear the streets, to change the character of the laboring poor by altering their family lives, and, in the process, to eradicate poverty itself. They focused their efforts on transforming two elements of laboring-class family life, the place of children and the role of women.

There was, in fact, nothing new about the presence of poor children in the streets, nor was it new that women of the urban poor should countenance that presence. For centuries, poor people in Europe had freely used urban public areas—streets, squares, courts, and marketplaces—for their leisure and work. For the working poor, street life was

Christine Stansell, "Women, Children, and the Uses of the Streets: Class and Gender Conflict in New York City, 1850–1860," reprinted from *Feminist Studies* 8, no. 2 (1982): 309–35, by permission of the publisher *Feminist Studies,* Inc., c/o Women's Studies Program, University of Maryland, College Park, Maryland 20740.

bound up not only with economic exigency, but also with childrearing, family morality, sociability, and neighborhood ties. In the nineteenth century, the crowded conditions of the tenements and the poverty of great numbers of metropolitan laboring people made the streets as crucial an arena as ever for their social and economic lives. As one New York social investigator observed, "In the poorer portions of the city, people live much and sell mostly out of doors."[2]

How, then, do we account for this sudden flurry of concern? For reformers like the agent from the CAS, street life was antagonistic to ardently held beliefs about childhood, womanhood and, ultimately, the nature of civilized urban society. The middle class of which the reformers were a part was only emerging, an economically ill-defined group, neither rich nor poor, just beginning in the antebellum years to assert a distinct cultural identity. Central to its self-conception was the ideology of domesticity, a set of sharp ideas and pronounced opinions about the nature of a moral family life. The sources of this ideology were historically complex and involved several decades of struggles by women of this group for social recognition, esteem, and power in the family. Nonetheless, by midcentury, ideas initially developed and promoted by women and their clerical allies had found general acceptance, and an ideology of gender had become firmly embedded in an ideology of class. Both women and men valued the home, an institution which they perceived as sacred, presided over by women, inhabited by children, frequented by men. The home preserved those social virtues endangered by the public world of trade, industry, and politics; a public world which they saw as even more corrupting and dangerous in a great city like New York.[3]

Enclosed, protected, and privatized, the home and the patterns of family life on which it was based thus represented to middle-class women and men a crucial institution of civilization. From this perspective, a particular geography of social life—the engagement of the poor in street life rather than in the enclave of the home—became in itself evidence of parental neglect, family disintegration, and a pervasive urban social pathology. Thus in his condemnation of the impoverished widow, the CAS agent distilled an entire analysis of poverty and a critique of poor families: the presence of her children on the streets was synonymous with a corrupt family life, no matter how disguised it might be. In the crusade of such mid-Victorian reformers to save poor children from their parents and their class lie the roots of a long history of middle-class intervention in working-class families, a history which played a central part in the making of the female American working class.

Many historians have shown the importance of antebellum urban reform to the changing texture of class relations in America, its role in the cultural transformations of urbanization and industrialization.[4] Confronted with overcrowding, unemployment, and poverty on a scale theretofore unknown in America, evangelical reformers forged programs to control and mitigate these pressing urban problems, programs which would shape municipal policies for years to come. Yet their responses were not simply practical solutions, the most intelligent possible reactions to difficult circumstances; as the most sensitive historians of reform have argued, they were shaped by the world view, cultural affinities, conceptions of gender, class prejudices, and imperatives of the reformers themselves. Urban reform was an interaction in which, over time, both philanthropists and their beneficiaries changed. In their experience with the reformers, the laboring poor learned—and were forced—to accommodate themselves to an alien conception of family and city life. Through their work with the poor, the reformers discovered many of the elements from which they would forge their own class and sexual identity, still ill-defined and diffuse in 1850; women, particularly, strengthened their role as dictators of domestic and familial standards for all classes of Americans. The reformers' eventual triumph in New York brought no solutions to the problem of poverty, but it did bring about the evisceration of a way of urban life and the legitimation of their own cultural power as a class.

The conflict over the streets resonated on many levels. Ostensibly the reformers aimed to rescue children from the corruptions and dangers of the city streets; indeed the conscious motives of many, if not all, of these well-meaning altruists went no further. There were many unquestioned assumptions, however, on which their benevolent motives rested, and it is in examining these assumptions that we begin to see the challenge which these middle-class people unwittingly posed to common practices of the poor. In their cultural offensive, reformers sought to impose on the poor conceptions of childhood and motherhood drawn from their own ideas of domesticity. In effect, reformers tried to implement their domestic beliefs through reorganizing social space, through creating a new geography of the city. Women were especially active; while male reformers experimented, through a rural foster home program, with more dramatic means of clearing the streets, middle-class ladies worked to found new working-class homes, modeled on their own, which would establish a viable alternative to the thoroughly nondomesticated streets. Insofar as the women reformers succeeded, their victory contributed to both the dominance of a class and of a specific conception of gender. It was, moreover, a victory which had enduring and contradictory consequences for urban women of all classes. In our contemporary city streets, vacated, for the most part, of domestic life yet dangerous for women and children, we see something of the legacy of their labors.

Children's Uses of the Streets

Unlike today, the teeming milieu of the New York streets in the mid-nineteenth century was in large part a children's world. A complex web of economic imperatives and social mores accounted for their presence there, a presence which reformers so ardently decried. Public life, with its panoply of choices, its rich and varied texture, its motley society, played as central a role in the upbringing of poor children as did private, domestic life in that of their more affluent peers. While middle-class mothers spent a great deal of time with their children (albeit with the help of servants), women of the laboring classes condoned for their offspring an early independence—within bounds—on the streets. Through peddling, scavenging, and the shadier arts of theft and prostitution, the streets offered children a way to earn their keep, crucial to making ends meet in their households. Street life also provided a home for children without families—the orphaned and abandoned—and an alternative to living at home for the especially independent and those in strained family circumstances.

Such uses of the streets were dictated by exigency, but they were also interwined with patterns of motherhood, parenthood, and childhood. In contrast to their middle- and upper-class contemporaries, the working poor did not think of childhood as a separate stage of life in which girls and boys were free from adult burdens, nor did poor women consider mothering to be a full-time task of supervision. They expected their children to work from an early age, to "earn their keep" or to "get a living," a view much closer to the early modern conceptions which Philippe Ariès describes in *Centuries of Childhood*.[5] Children were little adults, unable as yet to take up all the duties of their elders, but nonetheless bound to do as much as they could. To put it another way, the lives of children, like those of adults, were circumscribed by economic and familial obligations. In this context, the poor expresssed their care for children differently than did the propertied classes. Raising one's children properly did not mean protecting them from the world of work; on the contrary, it involved teaching them to shoulder those heavy burdens of labor which were the common lot of their class, to be hardworking and dutiful to kin and neighbors. By the same token, laboring children gained an early autonomy from their parents, an autonomy alien to the experience of more privileged children. But there were certainly generational tensions embedded in these practices: although children learned independence within the bounds of family obligation, their self-sufficiency also led them in directions that parents could not always control. When parents sent children out to the streets, they could only partially set the terms of what the young ones learned there.

Street selling, or huckstering, was one of the most common ways for children to turn the streets to good use. Through the nineteenth century, this ancient form of trade still flourished in New York alongside such new institutions of mass marketing as A.T. Stewart's department store. Hucksters, both adults and children, sold all manner of necessities and delicacies. In the downtown business and shopping district, passers-by could buy treats at every corner: hot sweet potatoes, bake-pears, teacakes, fruit, candy, and hot corn. In residential neighborhoods, hucksters sold household supplies door to door: fruits and vegetables in season, matchsticks, scrub brushes, sponges, strings, and pins. Children assisted adult hucksters, went peddling on their own, and worked in several low-paying trades which were their special province: crossing-sweeping for girls, errandrunning, bootblacking, horseholding and newspaperselling for boys.[6] There were also the odd trades in which children were particularly adept, those unfamiliar and seemingly gratuitous forms of economic activity which abounded in nineteenth-century metropolises: one small boy whom a social investigator found in 1859 made his living in warm weather by catching butterflies and peddling them to canary owners.[7]

Younger children, too, could earn part of their keep on the streets. Scavenging, the art of gathering useful and salable trash, was the customary chore for those too small to go out streetselling. Not all scavengers were children; there were also adults who engaged in scavenging full-time, ragpickers who made their entire livelihoods from "all the odds and ends of a great city."[8] More generally, however, scavenging was children's work. Six- or seven-year-olds were not too young to set out with friends and siblings to gather fuel for their mothers. Small platoons of these children scoured neighborhood streets, ship and lumber yards, shops and factories for chips, ashes, wood, and coal to take home or peddle to neighbors. "I saw some girls gathering cinders," noted Virginia Penny, New York's self-styled Mayhew. "They burn them at home, after washing them."[9]

The economy of rubbish was intricate. As children grew more skilled, they learned how to turn up other serviceable cast-offs. "These gatherers of things lost on earth," a journal had called them in 1831. "These makers of something out of nothing."[10] Besides taking trash home or selling it to neighbors, children could peddle it to junk dealers, who in turn vended it to manufacturers and artisans for use in industrial processes. Rags, old rope, metal, nails, bottles, paper, kitchen grease, bones, spoiled vegetables, and bad meat all had their place in this commercial network. The waterfront was especially fruitful territory: there, children foraged for loot which had washed up on the banks, snagged in piers, or spilled out on the docks. Loose cotton shredded off bales on the wharves where the southern packet ships docked, bits of canvas and rags ended up with paper- and shoddy-manufacturers (shoddy, the cheapest of textiles, mades its way back to the poor in "shoddy" ready-made clothing). Old rope was shredded and sold as oakum, a fiber used to caulk ships. Whole pieces of hardware—nails, cogs, and screws—could be resold: broken bits went to iron- and brass-founders and coopersmiths to be melted down; bottles and bits of broken glass, to glassmakers.[11] The medium for these exchanges were the second-hand shops strung along the harbor which carried on a bustling trade with children despite a city ordinance prohibiting their buying from minors.[12] "On going down South Street I met a gang of small Dock Thieves . . . had a bag full of short pieces of old rope and iron," William Bell, police inspector of second-hand shops, reported on a typical day on the beat in 1850. The malefactors were headed for a shop like the one into which he slipped incognito, to witness the mundane but illegal transaction between the proprietor and a six-year-old boy, who sold him a glass bottle for a penny.[13] The waterfront also yielded trash which could be used at home rather than vended: tea, coffee, sugar, and flour spilled from sacks and barrels, and from the wagons which carried cargo to nearby warehouses.[14]

By the 1850s, huckstering and scavenging were the only means by which increasing numbers of children could earn their keep. A decline in boys' positions as artisans' apprentices and girls' positions as domestic servants meant that the streets became the most accessible employer of children. Through the 1840s, many artisan masters entirely rearranged work in their shops to take advantage of a labor market glutted with impoverished adults, and to survive within the increasingly cutthroat exigencies of New York commerce and manufacturing. As a result, apprenticeship in many trades had disappeared by 1850. Where it did survive, the old perquisites, steady work and room and board, were often gone: boys' work, like that of the adults they served, was irregular and intermittent.[15]

There were analogous changes in domestic service. Until the 1840s, girls of the laboring classes had easily found work as servants, but in that decade, older female immigrants, whom employers preferred for their superior strength, crowded them out of those positions. By the early 1850s, domestic service was work for Irish and German teenagers and young women. In other industrial centers, towns like Manchester and Lowell, children moved from older employments into the factories; New York, however, because of high ground rents and the absence of sufficient water power, lacked the large establishments which gave work to the young in other cities.[16] Consequently, children and adolescents, who two generations earlier would have worked in more constrained situations, now flooded the streets.

The growth of the street trades meant that increasing numbers of children worked on their own, away from adult supervision. This situation magnified the opportunities for illicit gain, the centuries-old pilfering and finagling of apprentices and serving-girls. When respectable parents sent their children out to scavenge and peddle, the consequences were not always what they intended: these trades were an avenue to theft and prostitution as well as to an honest living. Child peddlers habituated household entryways, with their hats and umbrellas and odd knickknacks, and roamed by shops where goods were often still, in the old fashion, displayed outside on the sidewalks.[17] And scavenging was only one step removed from petty theft. The distinction between gathering spilled flour and spilling flour oneself was one which small scavengers did not always observe. Indeed, children skilled in detecting value in random objects strewn about the streets, the seemingly inconsequential, could as easily spot value in other people's property. As the superintendent of the juvenile asylum wrote of one malefactor, "He has very little sense of moral rectitude, and thinks it but little harm to take small articles."[18] A visitor to the city in 1857 was struck by the swarms of children milling around the docks, "scuffling about, wherever there were bags of coffee and hogshead of sugar." Armed with sticks, "they 'hooked' what they could."[19] The targets of pilfering were analogous to those of scavenging: odd objects, unattached to persons. The prey of children convicted of theft and sent to the juvenile house of correction in the 1850s included, for instance, a bar of soap, a copy of the *New York Herald,* lead and wood from demolished houses, and a board "valued at 3¢."[20] Police Chief George Matsell reported that pipes, tin roofing, and brass doorknobs were similarly endangered.[21] Thefts against persons, pickpocketing and mugging, belonged to another province, that of the professional child criminal.

Not all parents were concerned about their children's breaches of the law. Reformers were not always wrong when they charged that by sending children to the streets, laboring-class parents implicitly encouraged them to a life of crime. The unrespectable poor did not care to discriminate between stolen and scavenged goods, and the destitute could not afford to. One small boy picked up by the CAS told his benefactors that his parents had sent him out chip picking with the instructions "you can take it wherever you find it"—although like many children brought before the charities, this one was embroidering his own innocence and his parents' guilt.[22] But children also took their own chances, without their parents' knowledge. By midcentury, New York was the capital of American crime, and there was a place for children, small and adept as they were, on its margins. Its full-blown economy of contraband, with the junk shops at the center, allowed children to exchange pilfered and stolen goods quickly and easily: anything, from scavenged bottles to nicked top hats could be sold immediately.

As scavenging shaded into theft, so it also edged into another street trade, prostitution. The same art of creating commodities underlay both. In the intricate economy of the streets, old rope, stray coal, rags, and sex all held the promise of cash, a promise apparent to children who from an early age learned to be "makers of something out of nothing." For girls who knew how to turn things with no value into things with exchange value, the prostitute's act of bartering sex into money would have perhaps seemed daunting, but nonetheless comprehensible. These were not professional child prostitutes; rather, they turned to the lively trade in casual prostitution on occasion or at intervals to supplement other earnings. One encounter with a gentleman, easy to come by in the hotel and business district, could bring the equivalent of a month's wages in domestic service, a week's wages seamstressing, or several weeks' earnings huckstering. Such windfalls went to pay a girl's way at home or, more typically, to purchase covertly some luxury—pastries, a bonnet, cheap jewelry, a fancy gown—otherwise out of her reach.

Prostitution was quite public in antebellum New York. It was not yet a statutory offense, and although the police harassed streetwalkers and arrested them for vagrancy, they had little effect on the trade. Consequently, offers from men and inducements from other girls were common on the streets, and often came a girl's way when she was out working. This is the reason a German father tried to prevent his fourteen-year-old daughter from going out scavenging when she lost her place in domestic service. "He said, 'I don't want you to be a rag-picker. You are not a child now—people will look at you—you will come to harm,' " as the girl recounted the tale.[23] The "harm" he feared was the course taken by a teenage habitue of the waterfront in whom Inspector Bell took a special interest in 1851. After she rejected his offer of a place in service, he learned from a junk shop proprietor that, along with scavenging around the docks, she was "in the habit of going aboard the Coal Boats in that vicinity and prostituting herself."[24] Charles Loring Brace, founder of the CAS, claimed that "the life of a swill-gatherer, or coal-picker, or chiffonier [ragpicker] in the streets soon wears off a girl's modesty and prepares her for worse occupation," while Police Chief Matsell accused huckster-girls of soliciting the clerks and employees they met on their rounds of counting houses.[25]

While not all girls in the street trades were as open to advances as Brace and Matsell implied, their habituation to male advances must have contributed to the brazenness with which some of them could engage in sexual bartering. Groups of girls roamed about the city, sometimes on chores and errands, sometimes only with an eye for flirtations, or being "impudent and saucy to men," as the parents of one offender put it.[26] In the early 1830s, John R. McDowall, leader of the militant Magdelene Society, had observed on fashionable Broadway, "females of thirteen and fourteen walking the streets without a protector, until some pretended gentleman gives them a nod, and takes their arm and escorts them to houses of assignation."[27] McDowall was sure to exaggerate, but later witnesses lent credence to his description. In 1854, a journalist saw nearly fifty girls soliciting one evening as he walked a mile up Broadway, while diarist George Templeton Strong referred to juvenile prostitution as a permanent feature of the promenade in the early 1850s: "no one can walk the length of Broadway without meeting some hideous troop of ragged girls."[28] But despite the entrepreneurial attitude with which young girls ventured into prostitution, theirs was a grim choice, with hazards which, young as they were, they could not always foresee. Nowhere can we see more clearly the complexities of poor children's lives in the public city. The life of the streets taught them self-reliance and the arts of survival, but this education could also be a bitter one.

The autonomy and independence which the streets fostered through petty crime also extended to living arrangements. Abandoned children, orphans, runaways and particularly independent boys made the streets their home: sleeping out with companions in household areas, wagons, marketplace stalls, and saloons. In the summer of 1850, the *Tribune* noted that the police regularly scared up thirty or forty boys sleeping along Nassau and Ann streets: they included boys with homes as well as genuine vagabonds.[29] Police Chief Matsell reported that in warm weather, crowds of roving boys, many of them sons of respectable parents, absented themselves from their families for weeks.[30] Such was Thomas W., who came to the attention of the CAS; "sleeps in stable," the case record notes. "Goes home for clean clothes; and sometimes for his meals."[31] Thomas's parents evidently tolerated the arrangement, but this was not always the case. Rebellious children, especially boys, evaded parental demands and discipline by living on the streets full-time. Thus John Lynch left home because of some difficulty with his father: he was sent on his parents' complaint to the juvenile house of correction on a vagrancy charge.[32]

Reformers like Matsell and the members of the CAS tended to see such children as either orphaned or abandoned, symbols of the misery and depravity of the poor. Their perception, incarnated by writers like Horatio Alger in the fictional waifs of sentimental novels, gained wide credibility in nineteenth-century social theory and popular thought. Street children were essentially "friendless and homeless," declared Brace. "No one cares for them, and they care for no one."[33] His judgment, if characteristically harsh, was not without truth. If children without parents had no kin or friendly neighbors to whom to turn, they were left to fend for themselves. Such was the story of the two small children of a deceased stonecutter, himself a widower. After he died, "they wandered around, begging cold victuals, and picking up, in any way they were able, their poor living."[34] William S., fifteen years old, had been orphaned when very young. After a stay on a farm as an indentured boy, he ran away to the city, where he slept on the piers and supported himself by carrying luggage off passenger boats: "William thinks he has seen hard times," the record notes.[35] But the testimony garnered by reformers about the "friendless and homeless" young should also be taken with a grain of salt. The CAS, a major source of these tales, was most sympathetic to children who appeared before the agents as victims of orphanage, desertion, of familial cruelty; accordingly, young applicants for aid sometimes presented themselves in ways which would gain them the most favor from philanthropists. The society acknowledged the problem, although it claimed to have solved it: "runaways frequently come to the office with fictitious stories. . . . Sometimes a truant has only one parent, generally the mother, and she is dissipated, or unable to control him. He comes to the office . . . and tells a fictitious story of orphanage and distress."[36] Yet in reality, there were few children so entirely exploited and "friendless" as the CAS believed.

Not surprisingly, orphanage among the poor was a far more complex matter than reformers perceived. As Carol Groneman has shown, poor families did not disintegrate under the most severe difficulties of immigration and urbanization.[37] In the worst New York slums, families managed to keep together and to take in those kin and friends who lacked households of their own. Orphaned children as well as those who were temporarily parentless—whose parents, for instance, had found employment elsewhere—typically found homes with older siblings, grandparents, and aunts. The solidarity of the laboring-class family, however, was not as idyllic as it might seem in retrospect. Interdependence also bred tensions which weighed heavily on children, and in response, the young sometimes chose—or were forced—to strike out on their own. Step-relations, so common in this period, were a particular source of bad feelings. Two brothers whom a charity visitor found sleeping in the streets explained that they had left their mother when she moved in with another man after their father deserted her.[38] If natural parents died, step-parents might be particularly forceful about sending children "on their own hook." "We haven't got no father nor mother," testified a twelve-year-old wanderer of himself and his younger brother. Their father, a shoemaker, had remarried when their mother died; when he died, their stepmother moved away and left them, "and they could not find out anything more about her."[39]

Moreover, the difficulties for all, children and adults, of finding work in these years of endemic underemployment created a kind of half-way orphanage. Parents emigrating from New York could place their boys in apprenticeships which subsequently collapsed and cast the children on their own for a living. The parents of one boy, for example, left him at work in a printing office when they moved to Toronto. Soon after they left, he was thrown out of work; to support himself he lived on the streets and worked as an errand boy, news boy and boot black.[40] Similarly, adolescents whose parents had left them in unpleasant or intolerable situations simply struck out on their own. A widow boarded her son with her sister when she went into service; the boy ran away when his aunt "licked him."[41] Thus a variety of circumstances could be concealed in the category of the street "orphan."

All these customs of childhood and work among the laboring poor were reasons for the presence of children, girls and boys, in the public life of the city, a presence which reformers passionately denounced. Children and parents alike had their uses for the streets. For adults, the streets allowed their dependents to contribute to their keep, crucial to making ends meet in the household economy. For girls and boys, street life provided a way to meet deeply ingrained family obligations. This is not to romanticize their lives. If the streets provided a way to meet responsibilities, it was a hard and bitter, even a cruel one. Still, children of the laboring classes lived and labored in a complex geography, which reformers of the poor perceived only as a stark tableau of pathology and vice.

To what degree did their judgments of children redound on women? Although reformers included both sexes in their indictments, women were by implication more involved. First, poverty was especially likely to afflict women.[42] To be the widow, deserted wife, or orphaned daughter of a laboring man, even a prosperous artisan, was to be poor; female self-support was synonymous with indigence. The number of self-supporting women, including those with children, was high in midcentury New York: in the 1855 census report for two neighborhoods, nearly 60 percent of six hundred working women sampled had no adult male in the household. New York's largest charity reported in 1858 that it aided 27 percent more women than men.[43] For women in such straits, children's contributions to the family income were mandatory. As a New York magistrate had written in 1830: "of the children brought before me for pilfering, nine out of ten are those whose fathers are dead, and who live with their mothers."[44] Second, women were more responsible than men for children, both from the perspective of reformers and within the reality of the laboring family. Mothering, as the middle class saw it, was an expression of female identity, rather than a construction derived from present and past social conditions. Thus the supposedly neglectful ways of laboring mothers reflected badly not only on their character as parents, but also on their very identity as women. When not depicted as timid or victimized, poor women appeared as unsavory characters in the annals of reformers: drunken, abusive, or, in one of the most memorable descriptions, "sickly-looking, deformed by over work . . . weak and sad-faced."[45] Like prostitutes, mothers of street children became a kind of half-sex in the eyes of reformers, outside the bounds of humanity by virtue of their inability or unwillingness to replicate the innate abilities of true womanhood.

Reformers and Family Life

In the 1850s, the street activities of the poor, especially those of children, became the focus of a distinct reform politics in New York. The campaign against the streets, one element in a general cultural offensive against the laboring classes which evangelical groups had carried on since the 1830s, was opened in 1849 by Police Chief Matsell's report to the public on juvenile delinquency. In the most hyperbolic rhetoric, he described a "deplorable and growing evil" spreading through the streets. "I allude to the constantly increasing number of vagrants, idle and vicious children of both sexes, who infest our public thoroughfares."[46] Besides alerting New York's already existing charities to the presence of the dangerous classes, Matsell's exposé affected a young Yale seminar-ian, Charles Loring Brace, just returned from a European tour and immersed in his new vocation of city missionary. Matsell's alarmed observations coalesced with what Brace had learned from his own experiences working with boys in the city mission. Moved to act, Brace in 1853 founded the CAS, a charity which concerned itself with all poor children, but especially with street "orphans." Throughout the 1850s, the CAS carried on the work Matsell had begun, documenting and publicizing the plight of street children.[47] In large measure because of its efforts, the "evil" of the streets became a central element in the reform analysis of poverty and a focus of broad concern in New York.

Matsell, Brace, and the New York philanthropists with whom they associated formed—like their peers in other Northwestern cities—a closely connected network of secular and moral reformers. By and large, these women and men were not born into New York's elite, as were those of the generation who founded the city's philanthropic movement in the first decades of the century. Rather, they were part of an emerging middle class, typically outsiders to the ruling class, either by birthplace or social status.[48] Although much of the ideology which influenced reformers' dealings with the poor is well known, scholars have generally not explored the extent to which their interactions with the laboring poor were shaped by developing ideas of gentility: ideas, in turn, based upon conceptions of domestic life. Through their attempts to recast working-class life within these conceptions, this still-inchoate class sharpened its own vision of urban culture and its ideology of class relations. Unlike philanthropists in the early nineteenth century, who partook of an older attitude of tolerance to the poor and of the providential inevitability of poverty, mid-Victorians were optimistic that poverty could be abolished by altering the character of their almoners as workers, citizens, and family members. The reformers of the streets were directly concerned with the latter. In their efforts to teach the working poor the virtues of the middle-class home as a means of self-help, they laid the ideological and programmatic groundwork for a sustained intervention in working-class family life.

What explains the sudden alarm about the streets at midcentury? The emergence of street life as a target of organized reform was partly due to the massive immigrations of those years, which created crises of housing, unemployment, and crime. The influx of Irish and German immigrants in the 1840s greatly increased the presence of the poor in public areas. Thousands of those who arrived after 1846 wandered through the streets looking for housing, kin, work, or, at the least, a spot to shelter them from the elements. A news item from 1850 reported a common occurrence.

> Six poor women with their children, were discovered Tuesday night by some police officers, sleeping in the alleyway, in Avenue B, between 10th and 11th streets. When interrogated they said they had been compelled to spend their nights whereever they could obtain any shelter. They were in a starving condition, and without the slightest means of support.[49]

Indeed, severe overcrowding in the tenements meant that more of the poor strayed outside, particularly in hot weather. "The sidewalks, cellar doors, gratings, boxes, barrels, etc. in the densely populated streets were last night literally covered with gasping humanity, driven from their noisome, unventilated dens, in search of air," reported the *Tribune* several weeks later.[50]

The existence of the new police force, organized in 1845, also aggravated the reformers' sense of crisis by broadening their notions of criminal behavior. The presence of these new agents of mediation between the poor and the propertied shed light on a milieu which theretofore had been closed to the genteel. Indeed, the popularization of the idea of the dangerous classes after 1850 was partly due to publicized police reports and to accounts written by journalists who accompanied the police on their rounds. The "vicious" activities of the laboring classes were elaborated in such reports as Matsell's, published in pamphlet form for philanthropic consumption, and novelists' and journalists' exposés like those of Ned Buntline and Charles Dickens's description of Five Points in his *American Notes*.

The police also seem to have enforced prohibitions on street life with their own definitions of juvenile crime. Because conceptions of vagrancy depended on whether the police considered the child's presence in the streets to be legitimate, it is possible that some of the high number of juvenile commitments—about two thousand a year[51]—can be attributed to conflicting notions of the proper sphere of children. Brace was struck by the drama of children, police, and mothers in Corlear's Hook (now the Lower East Side). The streets teemed with

> wild ragged little girls who were flitting about . . . some with baskets and poker gathering rags, some apparently seeking chances of stealing. . . . The police were constantly arresting them as "vagrants," when the mothers would beg them off from the good-natured justices, and promise to train them better in the future.[52]

As for petty larceny, that at least some of the arrests were due to an ambiguity about what constituted private property was testified to by one New York journalist. The city jail, he wrote, was filled, along with other malefactors, "with young boys and girls who have been caught asleep on cellar doors or are suspected of the horrible crime of stealing junk bottles and old iron!"[53] As children's presence in the public realm became inherently criminal, so did the gleaning of its resources. The distinction between things belonging to no one and things belonging to someone blurred in the minds of propertied adults as well as propertyless children.

There were, then, greater numbers of children in the New York streets after 1845, and their activities were publicized as never before. Faced with an unprecedented crisis of poverty in the city, reformers fastened on their presence as a cause rather than a symptom of impoverishment. The reformers' idea that the curse of poor children lay in the child-rearing methods of their parents moved toward the center of their analysis of the etiology of poverty, replacing older notions of divine will.[54] In the web of images of blight and disease which not only reflected but also shaped the midcentury understanding of poverty, the tenement house was the "parent of constant disorders, and the nursery of increasing vices," but real parents were the actual agents of crime.[55] In opposition to the ever more articulate and pressing claims of New York's organized working men, this first generation of "experts" on urban poverty averred that familial relations rather than industrial capitalism were responsible for the misery which any clear-headed New Yorker could see was no transient state of affairs. One of the principal pieces of evidence of "the ungoverned appetites, bad habits, and vices"[56] of laboring-class parents was the fact that they sent their offspring out to the streets to earn their keep.

The importance of domesticity to the reformers' own class identity fostered this shift of attention from individual moral shortcomings to the family structure of a class. For these middle-class city dwellers, the home was not simply a place of residence; it was a focus of social life and a central element of class-consciousness, based on specific conceptions of femininity and childrearing. There, secluded from the stress of public life, women could devote themselves to directing the moral and ethical development of their families. There, protected from the evils of the outside world, the young could live out their childhoods in innocence, freed from the necessity of labor, cultivating their moral and intellectual faculties.[57]

From this vantage point, the laboring classes appeared gravely deficient. When charity visitors, often ladies themselves, entered the households of working people, they saw a domestic sparseness which contradicted their deepest beliefs about what constituted a morally sustaining family life.[58] "[Their] ideas of domestic comfort and standard of morals, are far below our own," wrote the Association for Improving the Condition of the Poor (AICP).[59] The urban poor had intricately interwoven family lives, but they had no *homes*. Middle-class people valued family privacy and intimacy: among the poor, they saw a promiscuous sociability, an "almost fabulous gregariousness."[60] They believed that the moral training of children depended on protecting them within the home; in poor neighborhoods, they saw children encouraged to labor in the streets. The harshness and intolerance with which midcentury reformers viewed the laboring classes can be partly explained by the disparity between these two ways of family life. "Homes—in the better sense—they never know," declared one investigating committee; the children "graduate in every kind of vice known in that curious school which trains them—the public street."[61] The AICP scoffed at even using the work: "Homes . . . if it is not a mockery to give that hallowed name to the dark, filthy hovels where many of them dwell."[62] To these middle-class women and men, the absence of home life was not simply due to the uncongenial physical circumstances of the tenements, nor did it indicate the poor depended upon another way of organizing their family lives. Rather, the homelessness of this "multitude of half-naked, dirty, and leering children"[63] signified an absence of parental love, a neglect of proper childrearing which was entwined in the habits and values of the laboring classes.

The Children's Aid Society

Although Brace shared the alarm and revulsion of reformers like Matsell at the "homelessness" of the poor, he also brought to the situation an optimistic liberalism, based upon his own curious and ambiguous uses of domesticity. In his memoirs of 1872, looking back on two decades of work with the New York laboring classes, Brace took heart from the observation that the absence of family life so deplored by his contemporaries actually operated to stabilize American society. Immigration and continual mobility disrupted the process by which one generation of laboring people taught the next a cultural identity, "that continuity of influence which bad parents and grandparents exert."[64] Brace wrote this passage with the specter of the Paris Commune before him; shaken, like so many of his peers, by the degree of organization and class consciousness among the Parisian poor, he found consolation on native ground in what others condemned. "The mill of American life, which grinds up so many delicate and fragile things, has its uses, when it is turned on the vicious fragments of the lower strata of society."[65]

It was through the famed placing-out system that the CAS turned the "mill of American life" to the uses of urban reform. The placing-out program sent poor city children to foster homes in rural areas where labor was scarce. With the wages-fund theory, a common Anglo-American liberal reform scheme of midcentury which proposed to solve the problem of metropolitan unemployment by dispersing the surplus of labor, the society defended itself against critics' charges that "foster parents" were simply farmers in need of cheap help, and placing-out, a cover for the exploitation of child labor.[66] At first, children went to farms in the nearby countryside, as did those the city bound out from the Almshouse, but in 1854 the society conceived the more ambitious scheme of sending parties of children by railroads to the far Midwest: Illinois, Michigan, and Iowa. By 1860, 5,074 children had been placed out.[67]

At its most extreme, the CAS only parenthetically recognized the social and legal claims of working-class parenthood. The organization considered the separation of parents and children a positive good, the liberation of innocent, if tarnished, children from the tyranny of unredeemable adults. Here, as in so many aspects of nineteenth-century reform, the legacy of the Enlightenment was ambiguous: the idea of childhood innocence it had bequeathed, socially liberating in many respects, also provided one element of the ideology of middle-class domination.[68] Since the CAS viewed children as innocents to be rescued and parents as corrupters to be displaced, its methods depended in large measure on convincing children themselves to leave New York, with or without parental knowledge or acquiescence. Street children were malleable innocents in the eyes of the charity, but they were also little consenting adults, capable of breaking all ties to their class milieu and families. To be sure, many parents did bring their children to be placed-out, but nonetheless, the society also seems to have worked directly through the children.[69] In 1843, the moral reformer and abolitionist Lydia Maria Child had mused that the greatest misfortune of "the squalid little wretches" she saw in the New York streets was that they were not orphans.[70] The charity visitors of the CAS tackled this problem directly: where orphans were lacking, they manufactured them.

Placing-out was based on the thoroughly middle-class idea of the redeeming influence of the Protestant home in the countryside.[71] There, the morally strengthening effects of labor, mixed with the salutary influences of domesticity and female supervision, could remold the child's character. Thus domestic ideology gave liberals like Brace the theoretical basis for constructing a program to resocialize the poor in which force was unnecessary. Standards of desirable behavior could be internalized by children rather than beaten into them, as had been the eighteenth-century practice. With home influence, not only childrearing but the resocialization of a class could take the form of subliminal persuasion rather than conscious coercion.[72]

Earlier New York reformers had taken a different tack with troublesome children. In 1824, the Society for the Reformation of Juvenile Delinquents had established an asylum, the House of Refuge, to deal with juvenile offenders. As in all the new institutions for deviants, solitary confinement and corporal punishment were used to force the recalcitrant into compliance with the forces of reason.[73] But Brace thought the asylum, so prized by his predecessors, was impractical and ineffectual. Asylums could not possibly hold enough children to remedy the problem of the New York streets in the 1850s; moreover, the crowding together of the children who were incarcerated only reinforced the habits of their class.[74] The foster home, however, with its all-encompassing moral influence, could be a more effective house of refuge. "We have wished to make every kind of religious family, who desired the responsibility, an Asylum or a Reformatory Institution . . . by throwing about the wild, neglected little outcast of the streets, the love and gentleness of home."[75] The home was an asylum, but it was woman's influence rather than an institutional regimen that accomplished its corrections.

This is an overview of the work of the CAS, but on closer examination, there was also a division by sex in the organization, and domesticity played different roles in the girls' and boys' programs. The emigrants to the West seem to have been mostly boys: they seem to have been more allured by emigration than were girls, and parents were less resistant to placing out sons than daughters. "Even as a beggar or pilferer, a little girl is of vastly more use to a wretched mother than her son," the society commented. "The wages of a young girl are much more sure to go to the pockets of the family than those of a boy."[76] Brace's own imagination was more caught up with boys than girls; his most inventive efforts were directed at them. Unlike most of his contemporaries, he appreciated the vitality and tenacity of the street boys; his fascination with the Western scheme came partly from the hope that emigration would redirect their toughness and resourcefulness, "their sturdy independence,"[77] into hearty frontier individualism.[78] Similarly, the agents overseeing the foster home program were men, as were the staff members of the society's much-touted Newsboys Lodging-House, a boardinghouse where, for a few pennies, news boys could sleep and eat. The Lodging-House, was, in fact, a kind of early boys' camp, where athletics and physical fitness, lessons in entrepreneurship (one of its salient features was a savings bank), and moral education knit poor boys and gentlemen into a high-spirited but respectable masculine camaraderie.[79]

Women were less visible in the society's literature, their work less well-advertised, since it was separate from Brace's most innovative programs. The women of the CAS were not paid agents like the men but volunteers who staffed the girls' programs: a Lodging-House and several industrial schools. The work of the women reformers was, moreover, less novel than that of the men. Rather than encouraging girls to break away from their families, the ladies sought the opposite: to create among the urban laboring classes a domestic life of their own. They aimed to mold future wives and mothers of a reformed working class: women who would be imbued with a belief in the importance of domesticity and capable of patterning their homes and family lives on middle-class standards.

Yet it was this strategy of change, rather than Brace's policy of fragmentation, which would eventually dominate attempts to reform working-class children. The ladies envisioned homes which would reorganize the promiscuously sociable lives of the poor under the aegis of a new, "womanly" working-class woman. In the CAS industrial schools and Lodging-house, girls recruited off the streets learned the arts of plain sewing, cooking, and housecleaning, guided by the precept celebrated by champions of women's domestic mission that "nothing was so honorable as industrious *house-work*."[80] These were skills which both prepared them for waged employment in seamstressing and domestic service and outfitted them for homes of their own: as the ladies proudly attested after several years of work, their students entered respectable married life as well as honest employment. "Living in homes reformed through their influence,"[81] the married women carried on their female mission, reformers by proxy.

Similarly, the women reformers instituted meetings to convert the mothers of their students to a new relationship to household and children. Classes taught the importance of sobriety, neat appearance, and sanitary housekeeping: the material basis for virtuous motherhood and a proper home. Most important, the ladies stressed the importance of keeping children off the streets and sending them to school. Here, they found their pupils particularly recalcitrant. Mothers persisted in keeping children home to work and cited economic reasons when benefactresses upbraided them. The CAS women, however, considered the economic rationale a pretense for the exploitation of children and the neglect of their moral character. "The larger ones were needed to 'mind' the baby," lady volunteers sardonically reported, "or go out begging for clothes . . . and the little ones, scarcely bigger than the baskets on their arms, must be sent out for food, or chips, or cinders."[82] The Mothers's Meetings tried, however unsuccessfully, to wean away laboring women from such customary practices to what the ladies believed to be a more nurturant and moral mode of family life: men at work, women at home, children inside.

In contrast to the male reformers, the women of the society tried to create an intensified private life within New York itself, to enclose children within tenements and schools rather than to send them away or incarcerate them in asylums. There is a new, optimistic vision of city life implied in their work. With the establishment of the home across class lines, a renewed city could emerge, its streets free for trade and respectable promenades, and emancipated from the inconveniences of pickpockets and thieves, the affronts of prostitutes and hucksters, the myriad offenses of working-class mores and poverty. The "respectable" would control and dominate public space as they had never before. The city would itself become an asylum on a grand scale, an environment which embodied the eighteenth-century virtues of reason and progress, the nineteenth-century virtues of industry and domesticity. And as would befit a city for the middle class, boundaries between public and private life would be clear: the public space of the metropolis would be the precinct of men, the private space of the home, that of women and children.

In the work of the CAS female volunteers lie the roots of the Americanization campaign which, half a century later, reshaped the lives of so many working-class immigrants. The settlement houses of turn-of-the-century New York would expand the mothers' classes and girls' housekeeping lessons into a vast program of nativist assimilation. Female settlement workers would assure immigrant mothers and daughters that the key to decent lives lay in creating American homes within the immigrant ghettoes: homes that were built on a particular middle-class configuration of possessions and housekeeping practices and a particular structure of family relations. And, as in the 1850s, the effort to domesticate the plebeian household would be linked to a campaign to clear the streets of a ubiquitous, aggressive, and assertive working-class culture.

Neither the clearing of the streets nor the making of the working-class home were accomplished at any one point in time. Indeed, these conflicts still break out in Manhattan's poor and working-class neighborhoods. Today, in the Hispanic *barrios* of the Upper West and Lower East sides and in black Harlem, scavenging and street huckstering still flourish. In prosperous quarters as well, where affluent customers are there for the shrewd, the battle continues between police on the one hand, hucksters and prostitutes on the other. Indeed, the struggle over the streets has been so ubiquitous in New York and other cities in the last 150 years that we can see it as a structural element of urban life in industrial capitalist societies. As high unemployment and casualized work have persisted in the great cities, the streets have continued to contain some of the few resources for the poor to make ends meet. At the same time, the social imagination of the poor, intensified by urban life, has worked to increase those resources. All the quick scams—the skills of the con men, street musicians, beggars, prostitutes, peddlers, drug dealers, and pickpockets—are arts of the urban working poor, bred from ethnic and class traditions and the necessities of poverty.

Neither is the conflict today, however, identical to the one which emerged in the 1850s. The struggle over the streets in modern New York takes place in a far different context, one defined by past victories of reformers and municipal authorities. Vagrancy counts against children are now strengthened by compulsory school legislation; child labor laws prohibit most kinds of child huckstering; anti peddling laws threaten heavy fines for the unwary. Most important, perhaps, the mechanisms for "placing out" wandering children away from "negligent" mothers are all in place (although the wholesale breakdown of social services in New York has made these provisions increasingly ineffectual, creating a new problem in its wake). The street life of the working poor survives in pockets, but immeasurably weakened, continually under duress.

In more and more New York neighborhoods, the rich and the middle-class can walk untroubled by importunate prostitutes, beggars, and hucksters. The women gossiping on front stoops, the mothers shouting orders from upstairs windows, and the housewife habitués of neighborhood taverns have similarly disappeared, shut away behind heavily locked doors with their children and television sets. New York increasingly becomes a city where a variant of the nineteenth-century bourgeois vision of respectable urban life is realized. "NO LOITERING/PLAYING BALL/SITTING/PLAYING MUSIC ON SIDEWALKS IN FRONT OF BUILDINGS," placards on the great middle-class apartment houses warn potential lingerers. The sidewalks are, indeed, often free of people, except for passers-by and the doormen paid to guard them. But as Jane Jacobs predicted so forcefully two decades ago, streets cleared for the respectable have become free fields for predators. The inhabitants of modern-day New York, particularly women and children, live in a climate of urban violence and fear historically unprecedented save in wartime. In the destruction of the street life of the laboring poor, a critical means of creating urban communities and organizing urban space has disappeared. As the streets are emptied of laboring women and children, as the working-class home has become an ideal, if not a reality, for everwidening sectors of the population, the city of middle-class hopes becomes ever more bereft of those ways of public life which once mitigated the effects of urban capitalism.

Notes

Many colleagues commented on drafts of this essay. My thanks especially to the participants in the Bard College Faculty Seminar at which the paper was originally presented, and to my friends Ellen Ross, Judith Walkowitz, and Sean Wilentz.

1. Children's Aid Society (hereafter referred to as CAS), *Third Annual Report* (New York, 1856), pp. 26–27.

2. Virginia Penny, *The Employments of Women* (Boston, 1863), p. 317.

3. For the class character of the New York reformers, see Carroll Smith-Rosenberg, *Religion and the Rise of the American City: The New York City Mission Movement, 1812–1870* (Ithaca, N.Y.: 1971), p. 6. For a more recent and ambitious analysis of the class base of the evangelical reform movement, see Mary Ryan, *Cradle of the Middle Class* (Cambridge: Cambridge University Press, 1981).

4. The literature on antebellum reform is voluminous. Two of the most helpful books specifically treating New York are Thomas Bender, *Toward an Urban Vision: Ideas and Institutions in Nineteenth-Century America* (Lexington, Ky.: University Press of Kentucky, 1975); and Paul Boyer, *Urban Masses and Moral Order in America, 1820–1920* (Cambridge, Mass.: Harvard University Press, 1978).

5. Philippe Ariès, *Centuries of Childhood: A Social History of Family Life* (New York: Random House, 1965).

6. Penny, *Employments of Women*, pp. 133–34, 143–44, 150–52, 168, 421, 473, 484; William Burns, *Life in New York: In Doors and Out of Doors* (New York, 1851); Phillip Wallys, *About New York: An Account of What a Boy Saw on a Visit to the City* (New York, 1857), p. 50; CAS, *First Annual Report* (1854), pp. 23–24, *Seventh Annual Report* (1860), p. 16.

7. Penny, *Employments of Women*, p. 484.

8. Charles L. Brace, *The Dangerous Classes of New York and Twenty Years' Work Among Them* (New York, 1872), pp. 152–53.

9. Penny, *Employments of Women*, p. 444.

10. *New York Mirror* 9 (1831): 119, quoted in the I.N.P. Stokes Collection, New York Public Library, New York, p. 461.

11. Brace, *Dangerous Classes,* pp. 152–53; Penny, *Employments of Women*, pp. 122, 435, 444, 467, 484–85; Solon Robinson, *Hot Corn: Life Scenes in New York Illustrated* (New York, 1854), p. 207; CAS, *Second Annual Report* (1855), p. 36; See also Sean Wilentz's "Crime, Poverty, and the Streets of New York City: The Diary of William H. Bell 1850–51," *History Workshop* 7 (Spring 1979): 126–55.

12. *Laws and Ordinances . . . of the City of New York* (1817), p. 112.

13. Bell Diary, 25 November 1850.

14. See also *Daily Tribune,* 16 March 1850.

15. *Chants Democratic: New York City and the Rise of the American Working Class* (New York: Oxford University Press, 1983). In this respect as in many others, I am deeply indebted to Sean Wilentz for my understanding of New York history.

16. Victor S. Clark, *History of Manufactures in the United States,* 3 vols. (New York: McGraw-Hill Book Company, 1929). 1:351. For the lack of children's factory employment, see CAS, *Seventh Annual Report* (1860), p. 7.

17. The aggressive character of juveniles on the streets and the prevalence of juvenile petty theft is discussed in David R. Johnson, "Crime Patterns in Philadelphia, 1840–70," in *The Peoples of Philadelphia: A History of Ethnic Groups and Lower Class Life, 1790–1940,* ed. Allen F. Davis and Mark H. Haller (Philadelphia, 1973).

18. New York House of Refuge Papers, Case Histories, New York State Library, Albany, 12 June 1852.

19. Wallys, *About New York,* p. 43.

20. House of Refuge Papers, Case Histories, 3 April 1854, 14 March 1855.

21. "Semi-Annual Report of the Chief of Police," *Documents of the Board of Aldermen,* vol. 17, p. 1 (1850), pp. 59–60.

22. CAS, *Fifth Annual Report* (1858), p. 38.

23. Brace, *Dangerous Classes,* p. 120.

24. Bell Diary, 10 June 1851.

25. Brace, *Dangerous Classes,* p. 154; "Semi-Annual Report," p. 63.

26. House of Refuge Papers, Case Histories, vol. 1, case no. 61.

27. John R. McDowall, *Magdalen Facts* (New York, 1832), p. 53.

28. Allan Nevins and Milton Halsey Thomas, eds., *The Diary of George Templeton Strong,* 2 vols. (New York: The Macmillan Company, 1952), 2:57 (entry for 7 July 1851).

29. *New York Daily Tribune,* 3 June 1850.

30. "Semi-Annual Report," p. 65.

31. CAS, *Second Annual Report* (1855), p. 45.

32. House of Refuge Papers, Case Histories, 3 April 1854.

33. Brace, *Dangerous Classes,* p. 91.

34. CAS, *Fifth Annual Report* (1858), pp. 39–40.

35. CAS, *Second Annual Report* (1855), p. 45.

36. CAS, *Sixth Annual Report* (1859), p. 67.

37. Carol Groneman (Pernicone), "The 'Bloudy Ould Sixth': A Social Analysis of a New York City Working-Class Community in the Mid-Nineteenth Century" (Ph.D. dissertation, University of Rochester, 1973).

38. CAS, *Sixth Annual Report* (1858), pp. 67–68. Brace also notes the connection of step-parents and child vagrancy in *Dangerous Classes,* p.39.

39. CAS, *Fifth Annual Report* (1858), p. 61.

40. CAS, *Sixth Annual Report* (1859), p. 58.

41. CAS, *Fourth Annual Report* (1857), pp. 43–44.

42. See my essay, "Origins of the Sweatshop," in *Working-Class America: Essays in the New Labor History,* ed. Michael Frish and Daniel Walkowitz (Urbana: University of Illinois Press, 1982), for an extended treatment of this point.

43. New York State Census, 1855, Population Schedules, Ward 4, Electoral district 2, and Ward 17, Electoral district 3, MSS at County Clerk's Office, New York City; Association for Improving the Condition of the Poor, *Fifteenth Annual Report* (New York, 1858), p. 38.

44. Letter reprinted in Matthew Carey, "Essays on the Public Charities of Philadelphia," *Miscellaneous Essays* (Philadelphia, 1830), p. 161.

45. CAS, *Third Annual Report* (1856), p. 27.

46. "Semi-Annual Report," p. 58.

47. Miriam Z. Langsam, *Children West: A History of the Placing-Out System in the New York Children's Aid Society* (Madison, Wis., 1964).

48. Boyer, *Urban Masses,* stresses the role of charity work in providing status and fellowship for newcomers to the city. Brace was from a family of declining Connecticut gentry; Matsell was born into an artisan family, became a dyer by trade, and rose to prominence and fortune in the city through Tammany Hall politics. See Emma Brace, ed., *The Life of Charles Loring Brace . . . Edited by His Daughter* (New York, 1894); "George W. Matsell," *The Palimpsest* 5 (July 1924): 237–248.

49. *New York Daily Tribune,* 4 July 1850.

50. Ibid., 31 July 1850.

51. From "Reports of Commitments to First District Prison published in Commissioners of the Almshouse," *Annual Reports* (1850–60).

52. Brace, *Dangerous Classes,* p. 145.

53. George C. Foster, *New York in Slices: by an Experienced Carver* (New York, 1849), p.20.

54. Rosenberg, *Religion and the Rise of the American City,* pp. 3, 29.

55. New York Assembly, *Report of the Select Committee Appointed to Examine into the Condition of Tenant Houses in New-York and Brooklyn,* Assembly doc. 205, 80th sess., 1857, p. 12.

56. CAS, *Third Annual Report* (1856), p. 29.

57. The best works on nineteenth-century domesticity are Nancy F. Cott, *The Bonds of Womanhood: 'Woman's Sphere' in New England, 1780–1835* (New Haven: Yale University Press, 1977); Ann Douglas, *The Feminization of American Culture* (New York: Avon, 1978); Kathryn Kish Sklar, *Catharine Beecher: A Study in American Domesticity* (New Haven: Yale University Press, 1973).

58. Here I strongly disagree with the view of the sisterly relations between women charity workers and their almoners presented in Barbara Berg, *The Remembered Gate: Origins of American Feminism—the Women and the City, 1800–1860* (New York: Oxford University Press, 1975).

59. Association for Improving the Condition of the Poor, *Thirteenth Annual Report* (1856), p. 23.

60. New York Assembly, *Report of the Select Committee,* p. 20.

61. Ibid., p. 51.

62. Association for Improving the Condition of the Poor, *Fourteenth Annual Report* (1857), p. 21.

63. CAS, *Third Annual Report* (1856), p. 4.

64. Brace, *Dangerous Classes,* pp. 46–47.

65. Ibid.

66. CAS, *Sixth Annual Report* (1859), p. 9.

67. Figures are from Langsam, *Children West,* p. 64.

68. Michel Foucault has most forcefully analyzed this ambiguity. See *Madness and Civilization: A History of Insanity in the Age of Reason* (New York: Random House, 1973).

69. See the appendices in CAS, *Annual Reports* (1854–60).

70. Lydia Maria Child, *Letters from New York* (London, 1843), p. 62.

71. CAS, *Third Annual Report* (1856), p. 8.

72. This is similar to the shift in criminal law from corporal punishment to the more enlightened environmental techniques of the penitentiary. See Michael Ignatieff. *A Just Measure of Pain: The Penitentiary in the Industrial Revolution, 1750–1850* (New York: Pantheon, 1978).

73. Ibid.

74. CAS, *First Annual Report* (1854), p. 7; *Second Annual Report* (1855), p. 5. See also Boyer, *Urban Masses,* pp. 94–95.

75. CAS, *Second Annual Report* (1855), p. 5.

76. CAS, *Fifth Annual Report* (1858), p. 17.

77. Brace, *Dangerous Classes,* p. 100.

78. See Boyer, *Urban Masses,* pp. 94–107; and Brace, *Dangerous Classes,* pp. 98–99.

79. Brace, *Dangerous Classes,* pp. 99–105.

80. CAS, *Ninth Annual Report* (1862), p. 13. See also *First Annual Report* (1854), pp. 7, 9.

81. CAS, *Tenth Annual Report* (1863), p. 23; *Seventh Annual Report* (1860), p. 8.

82. CAS, *Eleventh Annual Report* (1864), p. 28.

Comings of Age, 1870 to 1920

Introduction

Part IV, "Comings of Age," continues the themes and threads from Part III into the next half century, and serves to link the nineteenth with the twentieth century. Essential for readers to examine are the intricate patterns of continuities and continuing transformations at the core of this history. These two sections, in key relations and reflections, constitute a linked whole of historical experience, but we need not exaggerate their overlap and slight their divergence to grasp those larger integrating patterns. For in this complex blend of commonality and divergence lie increasingly apparent historical contradictions—as well as major historical controversies—central to the development of modern childhood, adolescence, and youth. Indeed, in this period we see, from diverse perspectives, the arrival of the formal concept of adolescence and may relate it to its longer-term historical development.

The nature of the transformations—with their ranges, variations, and contradictions—emerges nicely in the first essay, "Social Change and Transitions to Adulthood in Historical Perspective" by historians Modell and Hershberg and sociologist Furstenberg. With aggregate data and sophisticated statistical manipulations, they offer an overview of the most recent century of growing up beginning with this period—and underscore the perhaps surprisingly complicated patterns of change and continuity. In so doing they challenge in important ways some present-day truisms. This essay also demands that we turn backward to assess the place and contribution of the prior experiences, as it offers a synthetic opportunity to get an overview of the larger, encompassing American experience of growing up.

Each of the other six selections takes us into the expanding parameters in which the differentiated and differentiating processes of growing up in a transforming society must be located. With Brenzel, we penetrate the walls of a landmark institution for "wayward girls" and consider the evolving place of gender distinctions—in fact and in theory—and of institutionalized life courses. The Massachusetts setting also stimulates questions about the extent of change over the century between this history and our own times. With West, the rough and ready world of western settlement and its salience for growing up emerges in the fascinating setting of Rocky Mountain mining towns. Here, again, the balance between similarity and difference, change and continuity, and implications of historical context for understanding the meaning and contributions of distinct patterns of growing up emerges with singular clarity.

Bodnar takes us into another new world, that of the immigrant realm in a Pennsylvania industrial town. Especially important, this case study compares different immigrant populations as to their traditions and the strategic adaptations that impinged, often powerfully, on the coming of age of the young. This should be compared with Cohen's data and understanding of two different ethnic groups—Italians and Jews—in the distinctive setting of the large metropolis; both in turn demand a look backward to the experiences reconstructed especially by Stansell and Katz and Davey. The roles of place, gender, and ethnicity (with its associations with social class, too) as they intersect with social norms and social institutions influenced historical variations as they lay the foundations for the twentieth century.

Macleod extends the journey into another novel sphere, that of the proliferating number of special voluntary societies, such as the Boy Scouts and its counterparts for younger children and for girls, which constituted such a significant aspect of evolving approaches to the dilemmas increasingly perceived to surround, indeed to permeate, growing up. Here we capture the roles of adult and class conflict with the young and may ponder their meaning for growing up and for the developing society. In an instructive parallel, Troen blends the demands and dilemmas of adolescent boys' work world and the response of educational reformers to it—a key round of reform—in the early twentieth century. The nature of that "discovery," as Troen terms it, contributes in forms of legislation, policy, and expectations to the twentieth century's elaborate extension and enforcement of dependency and transformation of the labor market, and to the central contradictions we continue to struggle with today.

In sum, the combined impact of these developments spanning the most critical periods in American social and economic development frames the transformations of growing up. Their plural nature, as reflected in this section's title, "Comings of Age," is one key to the historical puzzle; equally important is the expanding range of conflicts and contradictions as growing up is imperfectly reshaped in its relations to social change and complex responses to it. These materials offer a special opportunity to understand comparatively—in terms of time and place and of different groups of young persons—the central questions whose relevance continues to plague us in the late twentieth century.

JOHN MODELL

FRANK F. FURSTENBERG, JR.

THEODORE HERSHBERG

18. Social Change and Transitions to Adulthood in Historical Perspective[1]

Rules can be found in every society governing the passage to adulthood. In some social systems, this transition is sharply demarcated, highly routinized, and carefully coordinated, while in others, it is far less easy to chart the course through which social members come of age. Sociologists and historians have shown little taste for studying patterns of transition, relegating these problems to anthropologists or social psychologists instead. Remarkably little work has been done on the scheduling of critical life events in our society, and on the existence of and changes in social timetables (Neugarten, 1968). How such scheduling is articulated with the requirements of other social institutions, though a subject of some speculation, has been generally neglected as a topic for empirical investigation (Elder, 1975).

Although this paper explicitly addresses only the problem of youth, we regard the transition to adulthood as an illustrative case of a more general set of problems concerning how institutional constraints bear on the construction of the life course. The present paper may be seen as an exploratory study of some gross contrasts between youth "then"—in the late nineteenth century—and "now" in 1970. At the same time, it proposes a series of analytic distinctions and a methodology, the implications of which will be discussed more fully further on.

I. Youth and Uncertainty

Discomfort, even turmoil, commonly characterize the period we have come to call youth, a stage of life during which major transitions of status are accomplished. These transitions, no doubt, are stressful in themselves, but our appreciation of the turmoil of youth typically rests on assumptions about the fit between the transition period and the society within which it occurs. It is widely held that this fit has changed substantially since industrialization. Most commentators have argued that the period of youth has been moved later in the life course (Musgrave, 1965; Keniston, 1972), extended (Flacks, 1971; Panel on Youth, 1974), removed for better or for worse from meaningful contact with the adult world (Coleman, 1961; Berger, 1971), and experienced as meandering and arbitrary. They contrast this to a vision of the past in which youth was a relatively brief period (lacking even a name) of substantial and near adult responsibility (Demos and Demos, 1969).

John Modell, Frank F. Furstenberg, Jr., and Theodore Hershberg, "Social Change and Transitions to Adulthood in Historical Perspective," reprinted from the *Journal of Family History* 1 (1976): 7–33, by permission of JAI Press.

As is often the case, our historical image is the product of no research in particular, but is instead based on nostalgia and the need for a contrasting image to our concept of youth today. Happily, in recent years a genuine historiography has developed. Joseph Kett's (1971; 1973; 1974) description indicates that the experience of rural youth in the nineteenth century was surely different from what we see today. But it was anything but brief and consistently filled with adult-like responsibility.

Michael Katz' intensive study (1975) of family behavior in an mid-nineteenth-century Canadian city also finds growing up then to have been a qualitatively different process from what it has become. His lucid exposition is the fullest treatment now available. "Most young people," Katz maintains, passed through "a semi-autonomous state," having entered some adult statuses but not having completed the entire set of transitions. Katz finds, moreover, that the length of this period of life—or even its occurrence at all—was quite responsive to local economic conditions, becoming rarer among youths during time of economic stringency.

Kett's account indicates that even within narrower segments of the population, fixed and regular patterns of transition were not much in evidence, and points out several ways in which the life course of the pre-adult was far less predictable. Early life in nineteenth-century America might be said to be "disorderly" to borrow Harold Wilensky's (1968) characterization of some types of work careers. Youth was not a clearly progressive and irreversible status sequence, but was variable and seemingly capricious.

Many commentators on contemporary youth would dispute the claim that the transition to adulthood has become more orderly and predictable during the twentieth century. Some writers contend that it has now become more difficult to grow up because passage to adulthood has become *less* and not *more* clearly charted. Protracted schooling, economic dependency upon the family, and the complex nature of career decisions are taken as signs that the timing in the transition to adulthood has become more prolonged and the sequence of movement less clearly prescribed. Alienation follows from the lack of clarity; weak institutionalization rather than its excess is seen as a defect of American society today.

Needless to say, these varying interpretations are possible because we possess relatively little systematic information that bears directly upon the question of what kinds of changes have occurred in the organization of the life course. Indeed, we lack even a clear conceptual basis on which to conduct empirical inquiry, despite widespread agreement that the "latitude," "predictability," or "clarity" of the transition to adulthood may have varied over time.

Students of youth typically have stressed learning in their models of growing older. Gerontologists, by contrast, studying a population deemed progressively incompetent to perform their former tasks, have often seen growing older in terms of a reallocation of roles. Growing older, of course, empirically involves both learning and role allocation, at all ages. The gerontological perspective, however, should be appealing to those studying social change, since it suggests the inexorable but variable process of replacement, which the social demographer, Norman Ryder (1965; 1974) has identified as a main feature of "social metabolism." This bio-social process, Ryder argues, gives rise to a set of conventions for moving individuals in and out of social patterns.

The most enlightening statement of the nature of this problem, by Matilda Riley and her collaborators (1969; 1972), divides the social-metabolic process into two conceptually distinct though empirically overlapped processes: "allocation"—the role-assignment and exchange process as seen from the structural point of view, and "socialization"—the motivation and instruction of role occupants. The timing of any particular transition in our complex society is rarely a simple reflection of an age norm, but is rather the cumulative outcome of the allocational needs of the society (the whole set of roles available and their age-related definitions), the time required for adequate socialization for the performance of these roles, and individual volition. Social schedules, Riley and her collaborators argue, reduce dangerous conflicts and minimize incompetence. Age norms limit the field of contestants for desired positions to a manageable number of relatively well-prepared persons. Yet even if one accepts the premises, one need not necessarily endorse the assumption that this is desirable.[2]

The present paper has three purposes: (1) We wish to turn this gerontological-demographic perspective to the question of youth. (2) We will do so especially by examining the distribution, timing, and sequencing of a series of transitions, thereby suggesting the juncture between the societal perspective of allocation and the individual perspective of the career. And (3) we intend to do these things while developing the points historically, indicating thereby some long-term shifts in the meaning of "youth" in American society.

When we speak of the transition to adulthood, we are already dealing with a some-what artificial construct. It is an open question whether individuals in any given society hold a common notion of adulthood. We can be reasonably certain that at the present time there would be imperfect agreement among Americans about when and how some-one attains adult status in our society. One can, however, safely assume that both in the past and now, becoming an adult involves a *series* of changes in status which moves an individual from economic dependence upon parents or their surrogates to economic independence (or dependence upon a spouse), and from participation in the family of orientation to establishment of a family of procreation (or, far less commonly, to move out of the family of orientation into lifetime roles as spinster or bachelor). These events may not universally announce adulthood, but they certainly bear an overwhelming and apparent association with participation in the adult world. In our construction of the complex transition to adulthood, we shall center our attention on five particular transitions for which data are available: exit from school; entrance to the work-force; departure from the family of origin; marriage; and the establishment of a household.

II. Methods and Data

The purposes of this paper are exploratory, aiming to look at a large subject with a new perspective and fresh information. The data we press into service are admittedly crude, though, we think, not inadequate to the purposes to which they are put. The same might be said about the methods. Taken together, these cautions argue that only where findings are strong and mutually supporting can we speak with certainty. Though our arguments are ineradicably quantitative, they do not pretend to be precise or refined.

What little systematic information we possess on tempo and organization of the transition to adulthood has relied heavily on the methods devised by Paul Glick for depicting changes in the life cycle of Americans. Glick's life cycle approach presented a pioneering effort to describe the shifts which have taken place during the twentieth century in the spacing of critical family events such as marriage, childbirth, and family dissolution. Thus, for example, Glick was able to show that the domestic careers of women have become *increasingly concentrated* in the early portions of their lives, leaving a lengthy period of time within marriage after the last child has departed from the home (Glick and Parke, 1965; and see Wells, 1973, for a still longer historical sweep).

The application of the Glick method has brought some interesting findings to light, but it is a rough tool at best for characterizing the timing and arrangement of events over the life span. What Glick and his followers have done is to estimate mean ages at which certain events occur. These means taken in sequence are a convenient way of expressing years "of experience" in particular life cycle stages for the population taken as a whole. But if we wished to arrive at a typical life course by arranging these averages in chronological order, we would need to assume that all transitions take place at the mean age and that everyone undergoes all transitions.[3] Moreover, if variance is high (or changing) the notion of average intervals is highly suspect. Based on aggregate averages, the interval between entering marriage and setting up a household may be far smaller than when computed on the basis of individual experiences.[4] Or, a significant minority may delay household formation substantially, while for the majority it occurs simultaneously with marriage.

Throughout our analysis, we employ a rather simple quantitative device, the intent and assumptions of which should be discussed here. Our treatment of transitions differs from the usual "age-at" basis (seen most typically in examinations of marriage), for our concern is not so much with central tendencies as with dispersion in timing. Accordingly, our technique calls for the analysis of the *distribution* of ages at which members of a population make a given transition. But our data are not from a registration of life-course events for individuals (such as a marriage register). What we have, instead, is an enumeration of statuses occupied by individuals, classified by their age and sex (from a census). Our problem is to infer from this count what set of age-specific events might have produced it. We can do this by assigning equal sizes to all equally-bounded age groups, and by assuming that only transitional events (which are irreversible) account for changes in distribution of statuses within succeeding age-groups, not death or migration.[5]

A source of uncertainty in inferring timing from a momentary distribution of statuses by age is the fact that entry into many statuses does not preclude subsequent exit; many transitions are, to a degree, reversible. Our nomenclature prevents us from thinking a widowed or divorced person "unmarried," but one could never know from age-specific labor-force participation rates that for males the process of youthful attachment and senescent detachment from work often involves a shuttling in and out of the work force. Were we to examine this feature of status transitions, longitudinal data would be required to measure reversibility. In a real sense, however, reversibility is not relevant, for our concern is with binding transitions—what Howard Becker calls "commitment" (Becker, 1960). To marry is to incur obligations and relationships that are generally lasting. While a casual job may not impose permanent obligation, commitment to regular work (even if at casual labor) does, and such commitment undoubtedly occurs close to the time of entry to the labor force.

If we had uniform, smooth data on these statuses for single years of age for men and women separately for 1880 and 1970, we would have no computational problems with the data (given the above operational assumptions). But we do not. Whereas we have all-United States data for 1970 from the published census, only sometimes available with single-year-of-age detail, our data for 1880 are fresh tabulations from a large, every Nth sample of Philadelphia whites from the Federal Population Manuscript Schedules.[6] Wherever possible, we also present calculations based on age-by-status data available for other nineteenth-century American populations, for the sake of comparison. In the broad terms in which we cast our argument, these data validate the general applicability of our Philadelphia materials, though of course there are differences of detail.[7] Where interpolation is necessary, we have interpolated linearly, unless the result is absurd. Where we have had to smooth, we have used the simplest arithmetic methods that seemed to give reasonable figures. For the most part, we have been able to make our categories for 1880 line up pretty well with those for 1970, although we do not know precisely how often a person in the nineteenth-century census lacking an "occupation" was really out of the work force. There is no reason to believe, however, that the distribution by age is seriously biased.

As much as possible, we have tried to use techniques of data analysis which remain intuitively comprehensible, and to remain close enough to the data so that the approximateness of our procedures will not be forgotten. Thus, we rely heavily in Section III upon calculating the approximate ages at which increasing cumulative deciles of the population had completed certain transitions—when the first 10 percent were married, the next 10 percent, and so on—and deriving measures from this. These will be described in detail below. Only one measure could not be accomplished with this intuitive simplicity: the measure of the inter-relatedness of a pair of statuses. Here we required a measure which would be applicable across age-groups in which marginal distributions for each of the statuses varied widely; a measure of association in which the effects of *both* sets of marginal frequencies are eliminated. Accordingly, we have computed Goodman's λ for the interaction of the two variables.[8]

The concepts we are developing are, perhaps, more complicated than our measurements. This is especially the case because the thrust of our argument is moving toward seeing experience as *longitudinal* and understood in *cohort* form. The ideal ending-point of this inquiry would be a distribution of careers, which might be categorized by starting age, sequence of transitions, and intervals among transitions. To know this distribution of careers would permit us substantial insight into how they were constructed. But our data permit us only to compare cross-sections, in order to draw implications for patterns of events within individual life courses.[9]

The concepts we will introduce here are designed to begin to bridge our present capabilities and our ambitions. We shall discuss five dimensions of status transitions. A sixth, reversibility, has not been introduced for methodological reasons. Within certain logical limits, these several dimensions of status passage are independent of one another. In reality, however, they form a coherent configuration linked to other features of a social system. Of these five dimensions, the first three are simple, referring to a property of a single status transition. The last two are complex, referring to the interrelationship of two or more status transitions. All five measures are meaningful at the aggregate level of analysis only.

(1) The *prevalence* of a transition is the measure of the proportion of a population (ignoring mortality) which experiences a given transition. Some transitions are quite rare, others almost universal.

(2) *Timing,* when considered in the aggregate, refers to typical points in the life course at which transitions occur. We shall employ three measures of timing: the age at which

half the population has experienced the transition under question, and the ages at which the first and fifth deciles make the transition (the latter two based only on those who ever make the transition). Timing may be early or late.

(3) *Spread* is the period of time required for a fixed proportion in a population to undergo a particular transition. As our measure of spread, we use the central 80 percent of those who make the transition, but some other figure would be equally appropriate. A transition can have a brief or protracted spread.[10]

(4) The *age-congruity* of a pair of transitions refers to the degree of overlap of their spreads. A population will undergo a pair of congruous transitions over the same period. If the transitions are incongruous, the population first accomplishes one transition, then the next. This dimension is a joint property of a pair of aggregate distributions, and does not refer to the closeness in time of transitions of the individual level.

(5) *Integration,* on the other hand, is a summary measure of individual-level relationships. The dimension refers to the degree to which status transitions are contingent upon one another at the individual level, apart from their degree of age-congruity. (Without longitudinal data, we cannot measure directly the contingency of transitions, but we can measure the contingency of statuses. Goodman's λ, mentioned above, measures this interaction for narrow age-groups.) A pair of transitions may be consistently integrated or unintegrated, or its integration may vary with age.[11]

III. The Pace of Transition to Adulthood

In the analysis which follows, we take up several different ways of assessing whether the timetable for coming of age has changed. For each method of assessment, we shall consider the five events which we identified earlier as important transitions in the early life course.

Prevalence

We can assume even in the absence of data that a fraction of the population will not make certain transitions at any point in their lives. Some individuals (even ignoring mortality in youth or before) never enter and thus never leave school, never go to work, marry, or depart from the households of their families of origin. To the extent that these transitions have become more prevalent, we may conclude the social timetable of becoming an adult may have become more rigidly prescribed.[12]

Table 18.1 presents prevalence estimates for the five events at different points in time for males and females separately. Considering the fact that the census data from the nineteenth century are more likely to omit information, and hence fail to record occupancy of a status, the figures do not reveal striking differences. In both centuries most individuals attended school, entered the work force, married, and ultimately left their household of origin to establish one of their own. The drift of the figures, however, is toward generally greater prevalence.

Not surprisingly, the greatest difference occurs in the proportion showing up as school attenders. In the twentieth century, we discover that virtually all youth attend school at some age. The figure (99.7 percent) is identical for both males and females. The

Table 18.1. **Prevalence Spread, Timing of First and Fifth Deciles, and Population Median Timing of Transitions, by Sex, 1880 and 1970**

	Leaving School			Entering Workforce			Leaving Household of Origin			Marriage			Establishing Own Household		
	1880 Phila.	Other 19th C.	1970 US	1880 Phila.	Other 19th C.	1970 US	1880 Phila.	Other 19th C.	1970 US	1880 Phila.	Other 19th C.	1970 US	1880 Phila.	Other 19th C.	1970 US
Males															
Prevalence	86.6%	82.0%[a]	99.7%	b	97.9%[c]	95.4%	d	d,f	d	88.7%	93.7%[c]	93.7%	86.5%	85.9%[f]	86.4%
Spread	5.0	7.5	7.5	6.9	9.6	8.1	16.0		12.4	17.1	19.7	7.1	18.1		13.6
Timing: 1st decile	11.9	11.4	16.4	12.4	12.4	14.5	17.7		15.8	21.2	19.9	19.6	21.6		17.0
Timing: 5th decile	14.4	14.9	19.1	15.3	16.5	17.3	23.2		20.1	26.0	26.4	21.8	25.8		23.9
Timing: Median	g	g	g	15.7	16.6	17.5	g		g	26.8	26.9	22.3	27.7		25.7
Females															
Prevalence	88.0%	82.0%[a]	99.7%	b	42.3%[c]	58.3%	d	d,f	d	80.3%	92.9%[c]	93.0%	83.8%	81.3%[f]	90.1%
Spread	5.8	6.2	7.6	6.7	7.3	4.8	19.0		12.7	11.7	15.0	7.9	17.0		12.4
Timing: 1st decile	11.3	10.8	16.3	11.3	11.0	14.3	17.0		16.1	18.5	17.4	17.1	19.1		16.8
Timing: 5th decile	14.3	14.1	18.6	14.6	14.7	17.0	20.1		20.5	22.7	22.3	20.2	24.0		22.0
Timing: Median	g	g	g	never	never	19.8	g		g	25.0	23.0	20.5	25.7		23.8

[a] Selected areas of Dutchess County, New York. From Calhoun (1973:348).

[b] The prevalence figure for Philadelphia is probably somewhat low because a small number of rare occupations had not yet received a code at the time we made our calculations. Persons thus occupied were temporarily recorded as though not in the work force. Occurrence of these miscoded people was essentially random by age (though not by sex).

[c] All United States, 1890. U.S. Department of the Interior (1896:21).

[d] "Child" prevalence is a function of orphanhood, not of abandonment of child status in the process of becoming adult. In a trivial sense, everyone surviving his parents ceases being a "child." No figures are presented.

[e] All United States, 1890. U.S. Census Bureau (1906:832).

[f] Massachusetts, 1885. (Massachusetts, Bureau of Statistics of Labor, 1887, I, part I:482–83.) The unfortunately broad age groups available in this publication for household status by age and sex did not permit the calculation of sufficiently precise spread and timing figures to justify the enterprise. As nearly as can be seen, however, the figures conform to the Philadelphia nineteenth-century pattern, and diverge markedly from the twentieth-century pattern.

[g] The notion of half a population leaving a status which not all of them have ever occupied is self-contradictory. No figures are presented.

rates for the two sexes are similar, too, in the nineteenth century, but the figure is lower—between 80 and 90 percent. Again, we should caution the reader that the nineteenth century data undoubtedly understate the proportion of individuals who *ever* attended school, but even so, few would dispute the claim that what is today virtually universal was in the nineteenth century merely commonplace. In that sense, we now see greater uniformity in the process of growing up.

Entrance to the work force reveals a similar pattern for females though it is questionable whether gainful employment for women has been a relevant part of the transition to adulthood. In both centuries nearly all males—over 95 percent—enter the work force at some point, while by contrast the figures for females are dramatically lower. Given the temporary nature of female participation in the work force, at least up until the present era, we must regard these prevalence estimates with suspicion. Nevertheless, it does seem likely that a higher proportion of women in the nineteenth century never had another occupation than housewife.

Looking at the departure from home, again we find greater uniformity in the twentieth century. According to the 1970 census, there are ages when virtually everyone lives as a child in a family. The pattern in the nineteenth century suggests that even at very early ages (under eight), nearly a tenth of the sample were not living in the households of their parents, presumably the result of orphanhood, separation from both parents, or residence in more complex households which their parents did not head.

For the other two statuses which we examined, marriage and household headship, we discovered little or no variation in prevalence between the pattern of a century ago and the contemporary mode. Roughly the same proportion—over 90 percent—married at some point in the life course.[13] Males and females differed little in this respect. Headship rates were also almost identical over time. Again, our estimate certainly understates the actual prevalence, yet indicates that in both centuries at least 86 percent of surviving individuals in the population set up their own household at some point.

With the exception of female participation in the work force, the prevalence data presented in Table 18.1 indicate that both males and females today more uniformly experience the five transitions. While this fact in itself does not necessarily imply a greater degree of determinacy in the process of entering adulthood, it is at least consistent with this interpretation.

Spread

Many commentators on the problem of youth in contemporary society have remarked on the extended nature of the transition to adulthood. It seems to take longer to grow up today than it did in times past. We have examined this supposition by looking at the typical ages at which most individuals have entered adulthood, but we must also measure the length of the transition process as it occurred in both centuries. Here we are not referring to the time it takes any one individual to pass from childhood, but the period of years it requires for an entire cohort to make the transition. In short, we want to know how many years it takes a cohort to leave school, enter the work force, and so on.

The spread of the five transitions we are discussing—exit from school, entrance to the work force, departure from home, marriage, and establishing a household—changes a bit in the nineteenth century, but it is minor in comparison to the historical trends we shall discuss below. In other words, cohort behavior in the previous century was probably relatively stable.[14] A good deal of variation always occurs at the extremes—the points at which the transition begins and concludes—and, in order not to give undue weight to these two tails, we shall define the spread as the period it takes for 80 percent of a given population to achieve a particular transition. Since the prevalence figures are generally quite high at both periods, this causes no problem in comparing the transition spreads within or between periods.

As the figures in Table 18.1 reveal, the trend toward extended schooling is evident in the larger spread in the period during which the 1970 youth exit from school. It took 6.5 years for the central 80 percent of the population to complete the process of transition in 1970 whereas the comparable figure in nineteenth-century Philadelphia was only 4.3 years. Though the estimates of spread square with our intuitions about the prolongation of this transition, they are not quite as dramatic as we might have expected. Even in the nineteenth century, the transition from schooling was not sudden or abrupt in the sense that most individuals left school at just the same age. We have reason to believe that in certain localities, the transition was quite gradual; indeed, the spread was hardly different from what we find today. For example, in Dutchess County, New York in 1850, it took 7.5 years for the central 80 percent of the males to make the transition from schooling. Although schooling is more prevalent today and extends over a far greater proportion of the life span, the length of time required by individuals to depart from schooling was not very much more concentrated during the last century. Despite the greater institutional pressures to attend school today, the spread in the transition out of school has only been extended by about two years.

Turning to entrance to the work force, the historical trend in spread is less obvious, though Table 18.1 shows a slight increase for males. During the nineteenth century, the entrance to work revealed a great deal of variation. Some individuals had occupations listed while quite young, while others acquired them only in their late teens or early twenties. Nevertheless, it seems unlikely that the time required to enter the work force was more extended in the past than now. In fact, there is some indication that the spread for males decreased in the mid-twentieth century, as entrance was delayed by child labor legislation but not deferred to the extent that it is today by prolonged schooling and the inability of young people to find work. In other words, the transition may have been more concentrated in the near past than the more distant past, when economic conditions both prescribed and favored the entrance of young people into the work force.

In the three familial transitions, there is a clear trend in the evidence we have assembled. Unquestionably, it now takes *less* time for young people to move out of their parents' household, marry, and set up their own home. Among both males and females there is a decidedly shorter pattern of departure from the family of origin. This corresponds to a strikingly different spread in the period over which marriage occurred. For both sexes the period in which 80 percent of the population marry is about half as long as was once the case.[15] Finally, setting up a separate household also occurs with more alacrity. Young people complete this transition in about two-thirds the time it took a century ago.

The narrowing of the spread in the years that it takes youth to make the transition from the family of orientation to the family of procreation is unmistakable. Like the figures presented earlier on prevalence, these findings reenforce the notion that the passage to adulthood has become more determinate, at least in respect to the familial transitions. In contrast to a century ago, young people today are more likely to be similar to one another in the age at which they leave home, enter marriage, and set up their own households. The greater rapidity of this transition is somewhat inconsistent with our notion that the stage of youth has become more protracted, though it is consonant with the view that this period of life has become more routinized.

Timing

The question of whether or not the period of youth has become more prolonged during the twentieth century cannot be completely settled by our measure of spread. Transitions may be concentrated into fewer years, as we have found, but that period in which the transition occurs may come later in the life course. In other words, most individuals may not arrive as early even if the passage takes less time because, in effect, they begin the movement later. Thus, the timing of the entrance to adulthood may be independent of the length of the period in which the transition takes place.

Certainly, what we know about the extension of schooling supports the supposition that entrance to adulthood has been delayed. Formal education has become more protracted for most young people today as compared to their forbearers. Table 18.1 presents two sets of figures on the timing of the departure from school. The first is the age at which the first decile of the school population has left, broken down by historical period and sex. The second is the median point for leaving school, correcting for the fact that not all individuals in the population attend school. The figures in the table are all ages in years.

Regardless of which figure we examine, there is little doubt that the age of departure from school has risen dramatically during the past century. The median age of school departure for both males and females is roughly four-and-a-half years later today—19.1 in 1970 as compared to 14.4 in the nineteenth century. The same degree of variation is evident at the first decile.

It is easy to understand why so many observers have been persuaded that the extension of schooling has delayed the entrance to adulthood. Yet if we look at the other transitions, the picture is different. Not surprisingly, as schooling has lengthened, entrance to the work force has occurred later. The differences over time, however, are less than impressive. The census data reveal that entrance to the work force occurs only one to two years later today than it did in the latter part of the nineteenth century.

Clearly, there are certain problems in making these inferences. The concept and measurement of occupational status have changed, and, more importantly, the significance of entrance to the work force has altered. Part-time work may well have proliferated among youths. While we need to take note of these differences, we should not exaggerate them. Like their counterparts today, most working youth in the nineteenth century were not economically independent, but were contributing to the family economy. To be sure, their contribution may have been more substantial and more necessary than is now the case. Not only economic independence, but also the establishment of a family were portrayed in literary sources as essential components of adulthood in the late nineteenth century.[16]

As Table 18.1 reveals, the age pattern of family formation in the nineteenth century was markedly different from current practice. As implied by our figures on the spread, many individuals delayed departure from the home a century ago. Although the pattern of boarding and lodging was quite common, most young people did not leave home until their early 20s, several years later than is the custom today. Even more disparity is apparent at the extremes. A fifth of the young people in the nineteenth century remained in the household of their family of origin until their late 20s; this pattern is extremely unusual today.

Age of marriage changed even more over the time period we are studying. Whereas at the present time, most of those who eventually marry do so by their early 20s, a century ago a substantial proportion of the females and most of the males did not wed until their late 20s or early 30s. There are, of course, certain variations according to the time and region, but the figures presented in Table 18.1 point to distinctly different configurations from those today.

Underscoring these patterns of family formation are the data on household establishment. Again, we discover sharp contrasts in the age at which most individuals formed separate residential units. At the median point, this event occurred several years later in the previous century, and at the extremes the differences were far more pronounced. Frequently, household formation did not occur until the early 30s for nineteenth-century males, and a delay between marriage and the establishment of a separate household was frequent. During this period, the newlyweds resided in the home of parents or boarded with another family. From the source material we have examined, there is good reason to suspect that many young people did not feel prepared to marry until after they had discharged obligations to their family as well as accumulated some resources to support a family of their own. In that particular sense, the period of preparation for adult responsibility was extensive and often was characterized by a good deal of uncertainty.

We can summarize some of these differences by creating an overall measure of the period of youth, examining the time elapsed between the point when the first quintile passed through the first status transition (leaving school, or entering the work force) and the last quintile arrived at the final status transition—headship of a household. This measure reveals the degree to which the transition to adulthood has become more concentrated. For males, the period was reduced by a third, taking 21.7 years in 1880, but only 14.4 years in 1970. While most of this concentration resulted from a truncation of the *end* of the period of "youth" some is attributable to a slightly later point of entrance to "youth" today. For nineteenth century Philadelphia males, the period of youth extended from 12.6 years to 34.3 years. Their counterparts in 1970 entered youth at 14.2 and completed the series of transitions at 28.6. For females the duration was and is shorter (because it ends earlier) though the increase in concentration is nearly as great.

When looked at from this vantage point, it would be difficult to substantiate the position that growing up in contemporary America has become more problematic because it takes a longer period of time or because the expectations for becoming an adult are more blurred than was once the case. If anything, the information of the pacing of the transition to adulthood suggests that the process of growing up has become more prevalent, less prolonged, and more concentrated than it was a century ago.

IV. Complex Measures: Age Congruity and Integration

There are two additional measures—age congruity and integration—which can be used to discover whether the transition to adulthood has become increasingly determinate over the last century. Unlike the "simple" measures, which dealt with the different dimensions of each status transition separately, these complex measures deal with two status transitions considered in conjunction.

Age congruity indicates the degree of overlap between the spreads of two transitions. To provide a summary measure, we have constructed an index of age congruity (Table 18.2). A value of 0.00 indicates complete incongruity or no overlap between spreads. In such an instance, almost all members of a cohort have completed one transition before beginning the other. A value of 1.00 indicates the opposite, complete congruity or overlap of spreads, or the simultaneous occurrence of the two transitions.

In our discussion of the five statuses considered separately, we noted that although the proportion of persons experiencing the statuses (prevalence) remained roughly the same in both centuries, there were significant changes in the spread and timing of the transitions. Two major findings emerged: the two non-familial status transitions (school leaving and work force entry) started earlier in the nineteenth century (timing) and required slightly less time to reach completion (spread); second, the three familial transitions started later, and required considerably more years for completion.

Prior to these changes, significant age congruity for males and females was found in 1880 only in the three wholly familial or wholly non-familial type transitions. All six mixed pairs of transitions (involving statuses from both the non-familial and familial categories) were quite age incongruous, with the slight exception of work force entry and leaving home (0.14 for males and 0.08 for females). Logic suggests that shorter spreads in 1970 should have resulted in reduced age overlap, yet we find the opposite: shorter spreads in the twentieth century were accompanied by increased overlap in spreads. What explains this apparent paradox is that the changes in spread did not occur in a vacuum. The reduction in spreads was more than offset by changes in timing which moved the spreads toward each other.

The movement toward each other of spreads in the mixed-pair category was brought about by legislation affecting the spread and timing of school leaving and work force

Table 18.2. **Age Congruity of Transition Pairs, by Sex, 1880 and 1970**

	Males		Females	
	1880	1970	1880	1970
Nonfamily transition:				
School/work force	.76	.79	.93	.45
Family transitions:				
"Child"/marriage	.72	.73	.80	.77
Marriage/head-spouse	.66	.69	.77	.78
Mixed transitions:				
School/"child"	.00	.75	.01	.75
School/marriage	.00	.59	.00	.91
School/head-spouse	.00	.64	.00	.71
Work force/"child"	.14	.60	.08	.34
Work force/marriage	.00	.39	.00	.31
Work force/head-spouse	.00	.51	.00	.27

Computing formula: $\text{Congruity} = \dfrac{2 \times \text{years overlapped (central 80\%) between two transitions}}{\text{transition}_a + \text{transition}_b}$

Sources: See Table 18.1. All 1880 figures based on Philadelphia data.

entry, and economic forces, which affected the spread and timing of leaving home, marriage, and headship. Yet it is important to note that these same forces did not produce a significant increase by 1970 in the degree of overlap of wholly non-familial or of wholly familial pairs of transitions. These remained age-congruous to roughly the same extent as they had been in the last century. In summary, family transitions are now (as they were not a century ago) mixed with nonfamilial aspects of the complex transition to adulthood. No longer do youth segregate into distinct phases the entrance into the world of work climaxed by the entrance into the family world of adults. Graphs 1a and 1b show how the development of rather massive overlap between marriage and labor-force entrance has at least formally *complicated* the sequencing decisions faced by contemporary youths.

The changes in spread and timing, then, had the effect by 1970 of collapsing or concentrating the transition to adulthood into a smaller number of years situated earlier in life. These changes raise questions about the nature of the organization of the life course today. Life-course organization in the nineteenth century was substantially the product of age-congruity. Most members of a cohort left one status before any entered another. Individuals today are forced to make more complex career decisions in a briefer period of time because increased age-congruity, in theory, makes possible the holding of several statuses simultaneously. Considered in the abstract, increased age-congruity is not necessarily accompanied by greater determinacy in the life course. Age congruity only makes possible simultaneous occupancy of statuses; it does not by itself tell if or how status transitions will be coordinated with each other. We wish to learn, therefore, whether the process of decision making has become more helter-skelter or more orderly. Is the high degree of age-congruity today associated with a reduction in the determinacy of the path to adulthood; that is, with large numbers of individuals holding once incompatible statuses simultaneously?

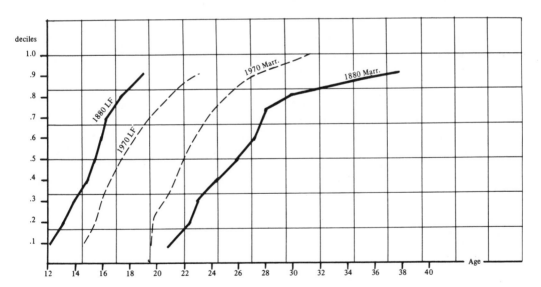

Graph 1A. Age at completion of first through ninth deciles: transition spread, work force, and marriage, males, 1880 and 1970.

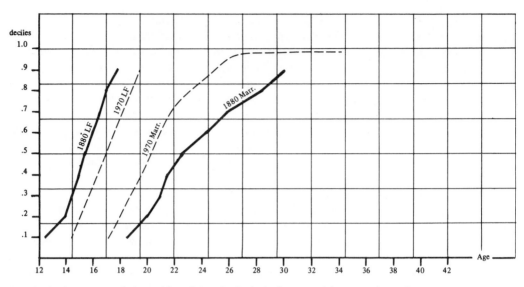

Graph 1B. Age at completion of first through ninth deciles: transition spread, work force, and marriage, females, 1880 and 1970.

This question bears directly on our understanding of the turmoil of youth today. To answer it we use a measure which we call *integration*. Here we are concerned with the degree to which *pairs* of statuses affect each other. Do they complement each other as do marriage and headship? conflict with each other as do school and marriage? or are they unrelated? Integration, in other words, indicates the degree of interaction—of contingency—between statuses.

To demonstrate how integration is measured, consider two age-congruous transition spreads, such as marriage and headship of household. Each of the variables is dichotomous (single/married and head/non-head) and can be displayed in a 2 by 2 table. Here we discover that statuses at given ages can be compatible or incompatible. Incompatibility is manifested by a cell frequency which is significantly below what would be expected from the marginal distributions for the incidence of the two statuses.

Our measure of integration is Goodman's λ. This measure indicates the degree to which cell frequencies in an N by N table can be explained solely by the interaction between two variables entirely apart from the size and distribution of either set of marginal frequencies. When λ is high, we can better predict holding of one status by knowing the holding of another. Since we have calculated λ values for specific ages, we are also able to see whether the interaction between statuses varied with age for each sex, and how this interaction changed between 1880 and 1970.

Let us now consider the interaction between status pairs in the three categories: non-familial, familial, and mixed. In the one non-familial pair (school leaving and work-force entry), being in school, as one would expect, consistently and strongly precluded labor force participation. (Graphs 2a and 2b portray this visually.)[17] While this was true in both centuries, the interaction was considerably stronger in 1880 than in 1970. This relationship weakened decidedly with age for both sexes in 1880, and for females in 1970.

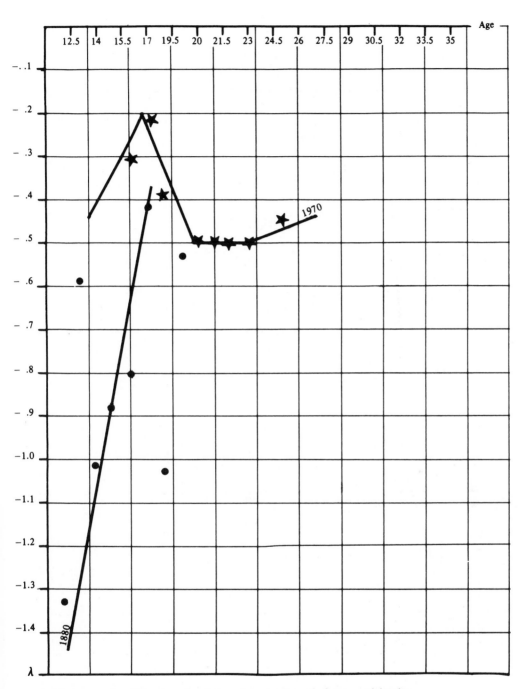

Graph 2A. Integration between school attendance and work force participation, males, 1880 and 1970. (Negative lambda indicates school attendance makes work force participation less likely.)

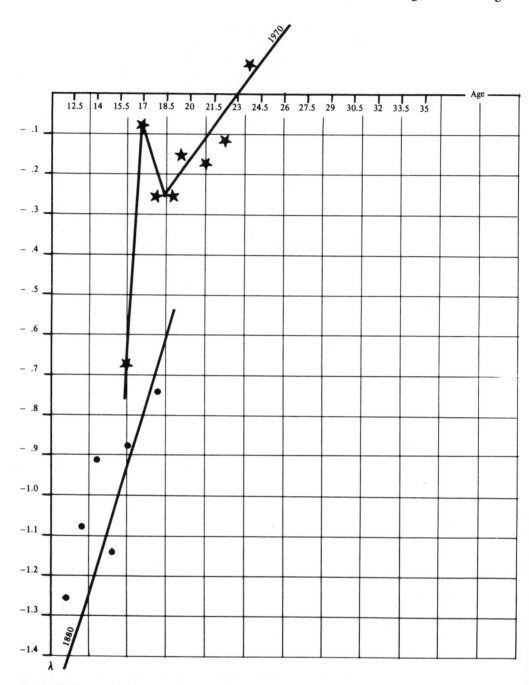

Graph 2B. Integration between school attendance and work force participation, females, 1880 and 1970. (Negative lambda indicates school attendance makes work force participation less likely.)

In the first familial pair of transitions, marriage and leaving home, we find a strong negative relationship; that is, knowing if someone was married increased significantly our ability to predict that he no longer resided in his parents' home. This was true in both centuries for both sexes, with contemporary patterns showing slightly greater predictive value. For the other wholly familial pair, marriage and headship, the two were related positively and strongly. Holding one status much increased the likelihood of holding the other; slightly more so in 1970 than in 1880. In addition, the interaction for males was sharply age-graded in both centuries, that is, predictive value declined with age, while for females the strength of the interaction increased until roughly 28–29, falling thereafter. In the instances noted above, both age-congruity and integration were found in both centuries, but while the degree of congruity remained constant over time, the degree of integration increased to an even greater peak in the twentieth century. We conclude that family decisions are highly orchestrated, especially through a very tight pattern of status integration.

Let us now consider the degree of integration found in the mixed category, among the six pairs each of which includes a non-familial and a familial status. The high congruity between school departure and marriage is one of the most dramatic instances of the increased complexity of transition to adulthood today.

Since this pair of transitions was age-incongruous in the nineteenth century, thus obviating the need for, or possibility of, integration, it is especially interesting to discover whether the transitions have by now become integrated. The two transitions might not now interact, even though they are simultaneous. What we in fact find to a significant degree is conflict between school and marriage in 1970 (though by no means so much as in some other pairs, like marriage and "child" family status). There is a striking difference between the sexes in integration: the degree of integration for women is generally twice as high as it is for men, though for both sexes λ declines steadily with age. For contemporary women (especially those at younger ages) school must be tightly meshed into the schedule of family transitions. For contemporary men, while school and marriage are still integrated, the greater instrumental worth of continued education to men means that more is to be gained by staying in school even when married. A common expression of this pattern is for a newly-married wife to leave school and go to work, in order to permit her husband to remain in school.

The nature of integration between headship and school, and its change over the century, is sufficiently like that between marriage and school departure that we need not discuss it at length. School attendance and departure from the family of origin is another question. Indeed, the patterns shown for this pair of transitions are as perplexing as any revealed by our data. What is especially striking is that lambda is generally low, and unstable over the relevant age ranges. In 1880, there is something of a predominance of positive λ values, indicating that those youth not yet departed from their parents' households (most often into statuses like "boarder" or "servant" rather than to headship) were more likely to be in school. But these positive figures were low. In 1970, the strongest generalization possible is that at the central transition ages, departure from family origin was almost unrelated to school attendance, although extreme ages show signs of a relationship. Residence at school may explain this in part.

Turning to the relationship between entrance into the work force and family transitions, it is important to remember that for women, work-force entry is by no means irreversible. Predictably, the patterns of integration break down quite differently by sex.

For males, "child" status in 1880 had a rather unstable integration with work-force participation. In 1880, at all ages but the youngest (where sons were *less* prone to work) the relationship is small and essentially insignificant. For females, the pattern is consistent both by age and over time: daughters were more likely to work than women who had left their families of origin. The degree of integration between the two statuses is roughly similar over time.

Among males, integration between marriage and work-force entrance was almost absent in 1880 (Graphs 3a and 3b). By 1970, a strong and significant positive relationship between marriage and work-force participation existed. The responsibilities of marriage typically include employment for men; a greater proportion of young men's work-force participation can now be attributed to marriage than was formerly the case. Our supposition is that work-force participation in 1880 was so general by the age when people began to marry that nonworkers were usually disabled or disinclined men, conditions rarely affected by a change in marital status.

Similar patterns can be seen in the other family and work-force transitions for males. Headship and work-force participation were to a great extent age-incongruous in 1880, but unlike the marriage/work force relationship just examined, even at that early date there are some signs that the statuses were contingent upon each other. By 1970, this relationship between the two appears to have become even stronger, and is consistently more impressive than the marriage/work force relationship. It would appear that the 1970 pattern was foreshadowed in 1880. Integration between work and family formation has been facilitated by institutional innovations. Thus, for example, for those in the work force, housing (rented as well as owned) is now easier to come by, making family headship more feasible.

Headship of household is the last of our transitions in sequence, and in that sense for males usually the culmination of a series of earlier moves. For women in 1880, by contrast, *departure* from the work force was often seen as the culmination of the transition to adulthood following marriage and household formation. Accordingly, in 1880, females displayed a strong integration between marriage and work-force participation, and between headship (most often "wife" status) and work-force participation, but in the *opposite* direction from that of males. The relationship, moreover, was remarkably stable across a wide band of ages. In 1970, major fragments of this convention remained, but it was not intact. The negative relationship is markedly weaker than in 1880, and is presently primarily at the younger ages. As women in 1970 entered their 30s, a new configuration took shape and a positive trend emerged between the married state and work-force participation.[18]

Leaving aside specific considerations, overall there is no doubt that the concentration of transition decisions in a briefer period of time has not resulted in a random or helter-skelter response. In contrast to the age-incongruity of the nineteenth century, an integrated mode has emerged in the twentieth century.

Conclusions

The burden of this paper has been to present evidence suggesting that over the last century there has been change in the pattern of the transition to adulthood. As a result,

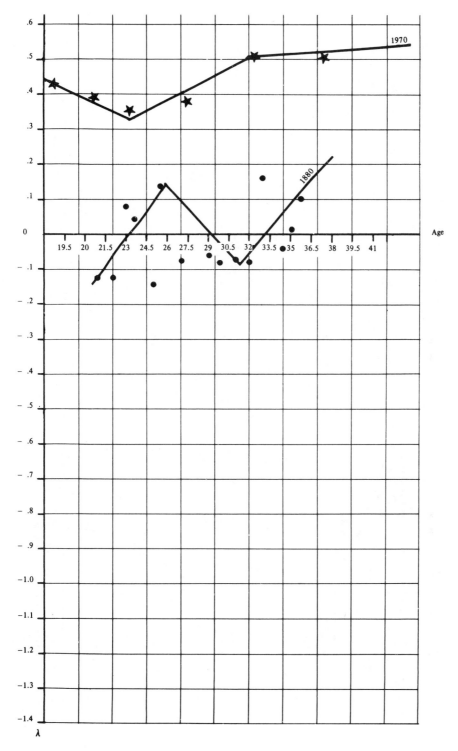

Graph 3A. Integration between marriage and work force participation, males, 1880 and 1970. (Positive lambda indicates marriage makes work force participation more likely.)

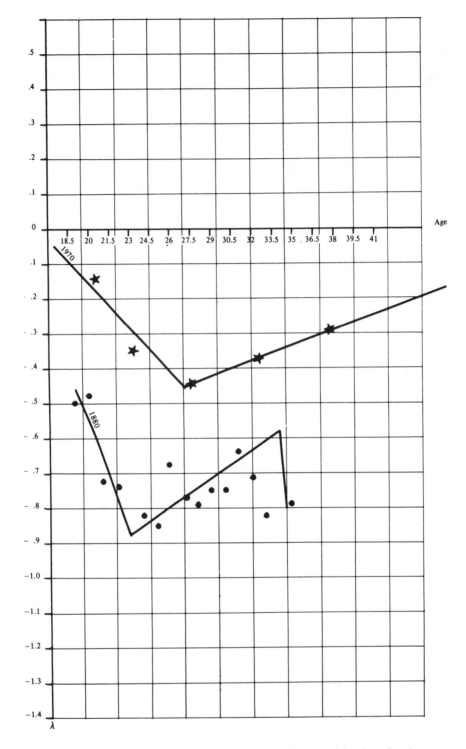

Graph 3B. Integration between marriage and work force participation, females, 1880 and 1970. (Positive lambda indicates marriage makes work force participation more likely.)

the early life course today is to an important degree organized differently, with different consequences for youth. Our quantitative evidence expands and refines Kett's argument that the broad latitude of choice that characterized growing up in the nineteenth century has been replaced today by a more prescribed and tightly defined schedule of life course organization. The prevalence of the usual transitions has increased somewhat, and for most of the transitions, the spread has narrowed, sometimes markedly. The relative timing of the several statuses—notably the moving together of the familial and the non-familial transitions—has created a situation of far greater age-congruity. A far larger proportion of a cohort growing up today is faced with choices about sequencing and combining statuses.

We can perhaps understand the slight increase of prevalence and the narrowing of spread as an aspect of the homogenizing over time of the regional, urban/rural, and ethnic differences in this country, each subgroup in the nineteenth century putatively living within its own age-graded system. Only further research into the sources of variation of age-norming can determine to what degree this was actually the case. Surely, however, young people today face more complex sequencing decisions, rendered stressful by their very individuation and preferential basis. Our use of the individual level Philadelphia data (regionally and ecologically homogeneous), demonstrates that the change in the mechanisms of life course organization from the age-incongruity of the nineteenth century to the integration of the twentieth century represents a real historical development.

The distinction between familial and non-familial transitions has appeared in all our discussions to this point. Our understanding of how growing up has changed is bound up with this dichotomy. Characteristics of familial and non-familial transitions, distinct from each other in the nineteenth century, today have become increasingly alike. They resemble each other in spread and timing, and they are more age-congruous and integrated with one another. No longer are the family transitions the predominately consequential ones: today school departure and work-force entry are far more important in shaping the subsequent work career than a century ago. And today the familial transitions are not so enduring as was once the case. In the nineteenth century, the family was a unique institution, standing alone; in the twentieth, it is one of many; or rather, one of the many in and out of which individuals have to thread their way.

The past century witnessed a radical alteration in the nature and functioning of the household economy as the family passed through its developmental cycle. Notable in regard to the transition to adulthood we are discussing has been a major change in the function of the labor of "dependents." In the nineteenth century, most urban American families were able to operate with a margin of comfort to the degree that they could count on a steady contribution from their laboring children of both sexes. A young man or woman in 1880 Philadelphia typically would enter the work force and contribute to a family income for about seven years (barring mortality). By contrast, the 1970 family economy depends upon husband and wife alone. Children, while they are briefly (2.5 years) of working age but still living with their parents, either spend the money they earn on consumption goods, or accumulate for their own subsequent families (usually by investing in their own education), rather than contributing their earnings to their families of origin.

Michael Anderson (1971) describes well the predictably unpredictable quality of nineteenth-century urban family life which made the family such a special institution. His focus, rightly we feel, is on the exigencies brought on by pre-modern urban morbidity and mortality, and by the narrow economic marginality which characterized family life as early industrialization transformed society. Sudden death, maiming accidents, frequent and extended layoffs, sickness, and other such devastating events made it essential for families to have a reserve of obligations to aid at times of such calamities. If the family, with its small knowledge and limited risk pool, were to perform as actuary, it needed the ability to call upon able members over many years. This period extended beyond what "youth" subsumes today and would be incompatible with current standards of adult independence.[19]

A major historical development of the past century has been the creation of nonfamilial responses to meet the material exigencies of life. Public health clinics, workmen's compensation, unemployment insurance, pensions, and the like have rendered life far more predictable and the risk-balancing role of the family far less important. At the same time, the affluence of industrial society has created a surplus that frees families from dependence on the labor of their "dependents." Individuals now find that their course to adulthood is far more involved than before with non-familial institutions, especially those concerned with training and occupation, and relatively free from familial obligations. In short, affluence has made participation in the family economy unnecessary and children have the luxury of leaving home earlier and hence can afford to set up their own family at a much earlier point in the life course. Here we are not arguing the desirability of an earlier schedule for family formation, but stating that what was once uncommon in the nineteenth century has today become more nearly normative.

It is important to bear in mind that the legislation which raised the ages of leaving school and entering the work force was *not* accompanied by other legislation governing the age-graded sequence of status decisions which constitute a social career. Indeed, if anything, to a larger extent than before, the career is for the individual to determine. Career decisions have in many cases become criteria for social evaluation, placing greater pressure on the individual to choose correctly.

Transitions are today more contingent, more integrated, because they are constrained by a set of formal institutions. The institutions with which individuals must increasingly deal call for and reward precise behavior. By contrast, the nineteenth-century family allowed for far greater latitude, providing individuals were prepared to satisfy their familial obligations. "Timely" action to nineteenth-century families consisted of helpful response in times of trouble; in the twentieth century, timeliness connotes adherence to a schedule.

Whatever the sources for the change in the mode of the transitions, it should be obvious enough that the shift to the contemporary pattern of allocation, the "integrated mode," has not been without stress. While we can make a case that in certain respects the current pattern of transition both allows more individual discretion and seems to display more articulation between statuses, the integrated mode does not in our way of thinking imply the reduction of strain. Growing up, as a process, has become briefer, more normful, bounded, and consequential[20]—and thereby more demanding on the individual participants.

Scholars who see today's period of youth as extended, normless, lacking bounds, and without consequential decisions are responding—we believe—not to its essential characteristics, but to the expressions of those experiencing the phase of life. They reflect rather than analyze turmoil.

Notes

1. The authors wish to thank the Center for Studies of Metropolitan Problems, NIMH, whose financial support (MH16621) has made possible the research of the Philadelphia Social History Project, of which this is a part.

2. That rigid schedules may be at the source of social-psychological problems is apparent from several of Bernice Neugarten's studies, which point to such consequences when individuals are forced to adhere to schedules they do not accept, or prove unable to conform to schedules they hold legitimate.

3. Peter Uhlenberg's alternative approach (1969, 1974) creates from demographic parameters a set of typical careers reflecting different experience, and estimates their prevalence in the population. Like the Glick approach, however, Uhlenberg's method makes nothing of the fact of *variance* in the timing of events.

4. This paradox depends on the possibility that for many persons establishing households precedes marriage.

5. For analogous inferences, well-established procedures are available, notably John Hajnal's (1953) method of estimating age at marriage directly from a single set of census data. Like Hajnal, we will make two assumptions: first, that the distribution of statuses by age has not been affected by rapid change; and, second, that in- and out-migration and mortality are not differential by the statuses we are considering. For purposes of simplicity (and since we are concerned with comparing distributions rather than determining absolute ages) we use a pair of techniques related to but distinct from Hajnal's "singulate mean age at marriage." To determine timing, we use a variant of Hajnal's "singulate median" age at marriage; and to get measures of the age-spread of the marriage transition, we use a crude "process of differencing" to estimate the number of marriages during each successive year of experience. Thus if 40 percent of 21-year-olds are still single but only 30 percent of the 22-year-olds, we can estimate that 10 percent of the population in question marries between 21 and 22 years of age.

6. The data are drawn from a far larger base collected by the Philadelphia Social History Project. Directed by Theodore Hershberg, the PSHP focuses on the impact which urbanization, industrialization, and immigration had upon: social and family structure; the formation and transformation of neighborhoods; the organization, mechanization, and journey-to-work; the development of an intra-urban transportation network; the spatial differentiation of residence, commerce, and industry; and patterns of migration and social mobility. Blacks (about 4 percent of the population) and members of households headed by persons outside of the United States, Ireland, and Germany (about 5 percent of the population) are omitted from our tabulations. The blacks introduced thorny problems of household definition we preferred to sidestep; the others omitted were for substantive reasons never a part of the Project sample.

7. We have been able to make the most thorough comparisons for marriage and work-force participation. In the former, Philadelphia's pattern of age by marital status essentially resembles that for Boston in 1845, Rhode Island in 1875, United States cities in 1890, and all United States in 1890. Philadelphia's age-pattern of work-force participation is similar to that for Massachusetts in 1885 and the United States in 1890. Finer analysis of the Massachusetts materials reveals that age at entrance to the work force did not vary widely there by urban/rural distinctions; while data from the United States census of 1910 shows minor differences in this regard. We feel entirely justified distinguishing "nineteenth-century" patterns (which Philadelphia shared) from "contemporary" ones. We include supplementary nineteenth-century material in Table 18.1, but for subsequent presentation of data, we rely on Philadelphia in 1880, since only for Philadelphia are our data uniform and useful for examining individual-level relationships.

8. The statistic is a by-product of the ECTA program for iteratively fitting different "models" to a given set of cell frequencies, and, for our purposes, are derived from the "fully-saturated" model in which all the marginal frequencies are determined by the given data.

9. Were the distribution of such careers known, we would of course know also the distribution of the component transition ages; but, equally obviously, the reverse is not the case. The connectedness of information about careers is considerably greater than that of information about a set of transitions examined singly.

10. Saveland and Glick (1969) anticipate our measure of "spread" in their discussion of marriage patterns, noting that by comparison with the American experience for the 1920–40 period, "the spread" of age at first marriage tended to become narrower by 1958–60." The authors draw no conclusions about trends, however, explaining the observed narrowing by the Depression.

11. These dimensions do not exhaust all aspects of the scheduling of transitions. For the moment, we should list two more dimensions: (1) *Reversibility,* already discussed, and (2) *Order,* referring to the time-sequence of two or more transitions, summed over a population. The order of a pair of transitions may be relatively fixed or relatively variable.

12. Unfortunately, census data from the nineteenth century, lacking retrospective items, do not indicate the proportion of individuals within a given cohort who ever went to school, worked, married, left home, or set up a separate household. Since some of these statuses are "reversible" it is difficult to ascertain exact prevalence estimates from cross-sectional data. As a rough approximation, we shall measure the prevalence by the maximum proportion achieving the transition in any age group. Needless to say, this is a conservative measure of prevalence because it does not take into account individuals who had achieved the transition by the age at which most other members of the population had "retired." Yet, it is most unlikely that these limitations do great violence to the comparisons we are drawing since in both instances we are relying on similar types of census material.

13. In reporting these differences, we are choosing to ignore the fact that at certain points the prevalence of marriage in the past was slightly lower. We prefer to disregard minor variations, concentrating instead on gross differentials.

14. While our "modern" picture could undoubtedly be improved by working out cohort-based figures really representing the experience of a given birth cohort, once again the differences would not be so substantial as to vitiate our major point: that the age-based organization of the process of transition to adulthood changed markedly over the century.

15. Carter and Glick (1970:78–80) note that "first marriages have (in the past few decades) been increasingly concentrated within a narrower range of years," and use an interquartile range of age at marriage as their measure. They concentrate, however, on the quantitatively less significant shift upward in the younger portion of marriages, explaining this hypothetically by "widespread expressions of disapproval of very young marriages." They ignore the more substantial foreshortening of the marriage transitions at the older end, and fail to consider the implications of the narrowing of the spread.

16. Six students under the direction of Frank Furstenberg examined a variety of forms of literature from the late nineteenth century—including marriage manuals, popular fiction, journalism, and sermons—seeking information about the timing of transitional events. The literatures (which shared a middle-class bias) included almost nothing about leaving school or entering the work force. The decision to leave the family of origin was discussed occasionally, as was also headship. Marriage was a favorite topic, a fact suggesting the importance of the event for the entrance to adulthood.

17. The trend lines are simply drawn in freehand between single-year-of-age observations to suggest a sense of orderliness. Economics of space preclude printing graphs for all relationships, and a simple summary measure has eluded our imaginations.

18. Whether or not the obscuring of a once-strong pattern of integration pointed to a general lack of integration of work-force departure and family formation, or whether instead it pointed to the presence of a pair (or more) of mutually effacing patterns in the population (a "liberated pattern" opposed to a "traditional feminine" pattern) cannot be discovered with the data at hand.

19. The other side of the coin, however, was a necessarily tolerant outlook upon individual and situational variation in behavior, unusually high by our current standards. The nineteenth-century family could ill-afford to exact precise behavior, since what it needed most was emergency backing. The study of transitions, seen in this light, fits neatly into our understanding of larger themes of family behavior.

20. The data below are excerpted from a remarkably rich table presented in Carter and Glick (1970: 107), based on 1960 census compilations. By controlling for age (men 45 to 54 years old only are included), educational background, occupational type, and race, we are enabled to document the assertion that timing has substantial consequences, though we cannot with single-observation data specify the routes. The table, at any rate, shows that age at first marriage, within a

single occupational stratum, has an effect on subsequent income twenty or more years later. Very crudely put, to marry early was about as consequential for income prospects as to marry late; and for this occupational stratum, the scheduling of marriage rightly was worth about as much as continuing on into high school, or entering college.

Mean Earnings in 1959 for White Men 45–54 Years Old Who are Operatives and Kindred Workers, by Educational Level and Age at First Marriage.

	Married 14–20	Married 21–26	Married 27–33	Married 34 +
0–8 years' education	$4384	$4658	$4600	$4339
Some high school	$5131	$5302	$5283	$4814
Finish high school	$5407	$5686	$5513	$5072
Some college	$5394	$6151	$5733	$5340

Bibliography

Anderson, Michael
    1971   Family Structure in Nineteenth Century Lancashire. Cambridge, England: The University Press.
Becker, Howard S.
    1960   "Notes on the Concept of Commitment." American Journal of Sociology 66:32–40.
Berger, Bennett M.
    1971   Looking for America: Essays on Youth, and Suburbia, and Other American Obsessions. Englewood Cliffs, N.J.: Prentice-Hall.
Boston
    1845   Census of the City of Boston, 1845.
Calhoun, Daniel Hovey
    1973   The Intelligence of a People. Princeton: Princeton University Press.
Carter, Hugh and Paul C. Glick
    1970   Marriage and Divorce: a Social and Economic Study. "Vital and Health Statistics Monographs," American Public Health Association. Cambridge: Harvard University Press.
Coale, Ansley J.
    1971   "Age Patterns at Marriage." Population Studies 25:193–214.
Coleman, James S.
    1961   The Adolescent Society. New York: Free Press of Glencoe.
Davis, James A.
    1972a   "The Goodman System for Significance Tests in Multivariate Contingency Tables." Unpublished paper, April, 1972. National Opinion Research Center, University of Chicago.
    1972b   "The Goodman Log Linear System for Assessing Effects in Multivariate Contingency Tables." Unpublished paper, June, 1972. National Opinion Research Center, University of Chicago.
Demos, John and Virginia Demos
    1969   "Adolescence in Historical Perspective," Journal of Marriage and the Family 31: 632–638.
Elder, Glen
    1975   "Age Differentiation and the Life Course." In Annual Review of Sociology, Palo Alto, California: Annual Reviews.
Flacks, Richard
    1971   Youth and Social Change. Chicago: Markham.
Glick, Paul C.
    1957   American Families. New York: Wiley.

Glick, Paul C. and Robert Parke
    1965   "New Approaches in Studying the Life Cycle of the Family." Demography 2:187–
    202.
Hajnal, John
    1953   "Age at Marriage and Proportions Marrying." Population Studies 7:111–136.
Katz, Michael
    1975   The People of Hamilton, Canada West. Cambridge: Harvard University Press.
Keniston, Kenneth
    1972   "Youth: a 'New' Stage of Life," In Thomas J. Cottle, ed., The Prospect of Youth.
    Boston: Little, Brown.
Kett, Joseph
    1971   "Growing up in Rural New England, 1800–1840." In Tamara K. Hareven, ed.,
    Anonymous Americans: Explorations in Nineteenth-Century Social History. Englewood
    Cliffs, New Jersey: Prentice-Hall, Inc.
    1973   "Adolescence and Youth in Nineteenth-Century America." In Theodore K. Rabb
    and Robert I. Rotberg, eds., The Family in History: Interdisciplinary Essays. New York:
    Harper & Row.
    1974   "Part I." In Panel on Youth of the President's Science Advisory Committee, Transi-
    tion to Adulthood. Chicago: University of Chicago Press.
Massachusetts, Bureau of the Statistics of Labor
    1887   Census of Massachusetts: 1885. Volume I, parts 1 and 2. ·
Musgrove, F.
    1965   Youth and the Social Order. Bloomington: Indiana University Press.
Neugarten, Bernice L., (ed.)
    1968   Middle Age and Aging: A Reader in Social Psychology. Chicago: University of
    Chicago Press.
Panel on Youth of the President's Science Advisory Committee
    1974   Transition to Adulthood. Chicago: University of Chicago Press.
Riley, Matilda White, Marilyn Johnson, and Anne Foner
    1972   Aging and Society. Volume Three: A Sociology of Age Stratification. New York:
    Russell Sage Foundation.
Riley, Matilda White, et al.
    1969   "Socialization for the Middle and Later Years." In David A. Goslin, ed., Handbook
    of Socialization Theory and Research. Chicago: Rand-McNally.
Ryder, Norman B.
    1965   "The Cohort as a Concept in the Study of Social Change." American Sociological
    Review 30:843–861.
    1974   "The Demography of Youth." In James S. Coleman, ed., Youth: Transition to
    Adulthood. Chicago: University of Chicago Press.
Saveland, Walt and Paul C. Glick
    1969   "First-Marriage Decrement Tables by Color and Sex for the United States in 1958–
    60." Demography 6:243–55.
Uhlenberg, Peter R.
    1969   "A Study of Cohort Life Cycles: Cohorts of Native Born Massachusetts Women,
    1830–1920." Population Studies 23:407–420.
    1974   "Cohort Variations in Family Life Cycle Experience of United States Females."
    Journal of Marriage and the Family 36:284–89.
United States, Bureau of the Census
    1906   Fifteenth Census of the United States: 1900. Special Reports. Supplementary Analy-
    sis and Derivative Tables.
    1972   Census of Population: 1970, Subject Report 4C, Marital Status.
    1973a   Census of Population: 1970, Subject Report 4A, Family Composition.
    1973b   Census of Population: 1970, Subject Report 4B, Persons by Family Characteristics.
    1973c   Census of Population: 1970, Subject Report 5A, School Enrollment.
    1973d   Census of Population: 1970, Subject Report 6A, Employment Status and Work
    Experience.

United States, Department of the Interior, Division of the Eleventh Census
1896   Special Report on the Statistics of Occupations.
Wells, Robert V.
1973   "Demographic Change and the Life Cycle in American Families." In Theodore K. Rabb and Robert I. Rotberg, eds., The Family in History: Interdisciplinary Essays. New York: Harper & Row.
Wilensky, Harold
1968   "Orderly Careers and Social Participation: The Impact of Work History on Social Integration in the Middle Mass." In Bernice L. Neugarten, ed., Middle Age and Aging: A Reader in Social Psychology. Chicago: University of Chicago Press.

19. Domestication as Reform: A Study of the Socialization of Wayward Girls, 1856–1905

In 1857, Bradford Peirce, superintendent of the first reform school for girls in North America, reported to the Massachusetts legislature on the role of female juvenile reform:

> It is sublime work to save a woman, for in her bosom generations are embodied, and in her hands, if perverted, the fate of innumerable men is held. The whole community, gentlemen, personally interested as they are in our success because the children of the virtuous must breathe the atmosphere exhaled by the vicious, will feel a lively sympathy for you, in your generous endeavors to redeem the erring mothers of the next generation.[1]

Peirce was echoing a pervasive point of view in mid-nineteenth-century America, that in one form or another, social stability rested on women. Women would set the moral and religious tone for family life,[2] and family life itself would counterbalance the effect of unchecked economic change and the new extremes of urban wealth and poverty. Mid-century reformers had two solutions to the dilemmas created by capitalist modernization and its effect on the American family. One was formal schooling, which was a public and collective antidote to the disorder and chaos of the new urban environment. The other was the private family, which would offer—in a phrase recently reappropriated—a haven from the world of work and urban problems.[3]

The increasing stress on the importance of the family as a refuge crystallized expectations of women. Now they were to remain in the home, tending and educating the younger children while their spouses and older children left daily for the workplace. In addition to nurturing children, they were to create a sanctuary against the evil of the outside world. As a result of these expectations, nineteenth-century society became irreversibly dichotomized into the domestic sphere and the workplace. Obviously, poor women were frequently unable to fulfill the stereotype of true womanhood, for their lives were shaped by the need to survive rather than by social prescription. Nevertheless, this view of women—as social saviors guarding home, hearth, and family morality—continued to be the cultural norm and provided the model for social theorists and policy makers, as well as for women of all classes.

Poor girls were of particular concern to the reformers, who believed that rehabilitation of juvenile offenders was both possible and necessary. As industrialization, urbanization, and immigration surged, poor, deviant adults seemed less likely to be rehabilitated and assimilated into the new society. As optimism for rehabilitating adults waned, reformers transferred their enthusiasm for rehabilitation to children, whose innocence made them attractive candidates for reform. Children of the urban poor, potential street urchins, threatened social order; their future had to be engineered to preserve society. Reformers believed that these children could be re-formed at an early and still malleable age by giving them an acceptable type of family life. The dual motives of juvenile reform were to save the child and preserve social order. These purposes were especially clear in the case of poor girls, who were considered potentially wayward—as vagrants and prostitutes. Saving the erring mothers of the next generation became vital.

In response to this pressing concern, reformers founded in 1856 the State Industrial School for Girls in Lancaster, Massachusetts. It was not only the first reform school of any kind for girls, but the first family-style institution in North America. Lancaster fused the twin nineteenth-century emphases on schools and families. Through the combination of schooling and reform, the girls at Lancaster would be saved so they could fill the appropriate female role within the family. Thus, reform ideology blended together the confused motives of benevolence and social control.

Once the school was established, it became apparent that reformist theories had to be adjusted to reality. Adhering to their belief in the family, reformers held steadfast in their efforts to train girls for the world of domesticity. The story of Lancaster is one of the changing definition of domesticity in the treatment of wayward girls. Although the school continued to train girls to fit into the domestic sphere, the emphasis narrowed from a total domesticity of surrogate family-style living and love, to an almost exclusive vocational training for domestic service.

What follows in this article is a social portrait of the reformers, the girls, and the school itself, in which we see vividly the expectations placed on women and changing but pervasive views of the role of domesticity. Studying Lancaster gives us access to fifty years of changing social theory about poor, wayward children, especially girls, and offers us a window on the past of the institutions we struggle to change today.

Methodology

Although historians have been interested in the lives of the poor and seemingly unimportant, they have found it exceedingly difficult to reconstruct the lives of the illiterate.[4] Until recently we assumed that many of the poor, especially poor women and children, had been lost to history. Now, material such as tax records, vital statistics, and census data as well as a more sophisticated use of computers has enabled social historians to write the history and to understand the lives of those previously forgotten. The Lancaster girls, the internal workings of the school, and reform thought are best understood by weaving quantitative and qualitative data together.

I have benefitted from the new historiography and, by using the original handwritten case records, have gained rich and carefully detailed information for every entrant, every fifth year for fifty years. By translating the data into a coding system, I marshalled certain facts about each girl: ethnicity, parental background, the family situation from which each girl entered Lancaster; her schooling, religious training, crime, complainant, behavior at the school, details of the indenture experience, and at least two "follow throughs," including place of residence and work subsequent to leaving the school. Many entries included a wealth of anecdotal materials about later events such as other employment, marriage, entrance into other institutions, or early death. I used indenture, employment, and place of residence to assess some of the school's outcomes.

Official statements made by the reformers of the day give us further information. Massachusetts state records contain many important discussions indicating attitudes toward crime, institutions, welfare, and causes of poverty and deviance. Legislative and other public documents of the Commonwealth, and early reports made by the Board of State Charities and Lancaster's trustees and superintendents contain much pertinent material. Some of the original diaries of the matrons and the budgets and personal records of the superintendent offer additional information. By concentrating on frequency distributions and cross tabulations, I have attempted to understand the interrelationships between all these variables.

The Establishment of Lancaster

Lancaster was an outgrowth of a widespread dialogue in Europe and North America that resulted in a series of institutional responses to capitalist modernization. As part of this ongoing transatlantic dialogue, state-appointed commissioners[5] went abroad to inspect institutions for juvenile reform. European reformers feared potential hordes of street urchins and, like their United States counterparts, combined a pressing need to control the urban poor with what they considered benevolent care for the deprived. The commissioners visited many schools, the most important of which included Das Rauhe Haus, Hamburg, Germany; École Agricole, Mettray, France; and Royal Philanthropic, Surrey, England. These European schools espoused environmental theories of crime and vagrancy, and sought to counter detrimental environmental conditioning through family-style institutional life. Therefore, in all these institutions, dependent and deviant children were brought to live in home-like cottages in which they were to be treated with the firm but loving guidance of a supervising adult. The children were to live and be reformed within this surrogate family, as all were considered potentially salvageable.

The antiurban bias of most nineteenth-century social theorists was evident in juvenile reform. These schools were located in rural settings where children were considered safe from the evil influences of big-city life. The pastoral environment was believed to be purifying, a healthy retreat enabling children to redeem their lost innocence. A combination of religious training and family-style living within these rural sanctuaries was to insure that they would become reliable working adults and responsible family members.

Having studied these institutions carefully and discussed juvenile reform theories with European reformers, the Massachusetts commissioners returned to the United States convinced that family-style juvenile reform institutions were appropriate for the first American reform school for girls. Yet nineteenth-century Americans did not want to borrow blindly from the Old World. They wanted a New World version of the European reformatories and, in characteristic American fashion, placed great emphasis on education. The commissioners were determined, therefore, to draw heavily on those aspects of European juvenile reform that seemed most applicable to their mission. They embraced the family-style reform as perfect for the reformation of young girls; they envisioned that in the cottages of the heterogeneous reformatory, girls could receive the common schooling held so precious by the reformers and would acquire the habits of domesticity deemed critical for them. However, the reformers were also determined to avoid those aspects of European institutions that seemed too punitive, lacking in educational value, or inappropriate for women. They therefore rejected, for example, military routine, harsh punishment, and overemphasis on vocational training.

The commissioners returned to Massachusetts at an auspicious time. Nineteenth-century Americans were reacting to the crisis of urbanization, modernization, and immigration by seeking to create institutions to mediate between older values and the consequences of modernization. Emerging cities with their large masses of poor and dislocated people, resulted in the loss of informal, familial, and community responsibility in which care for and control of the dependent and deviant traditionally occurred. Now, with towns swollen into cities, the same needy people were considered strangers; social reformers felt compelled to create new mechanisms to deal with them.

These reformers were, as a rule, driven by two motives: the hope of building a new social order, and the fear of social chaos. These motives were written into their reform innovations and characterized efforts to deal with strangers in their midst. It is important to note that Lancaster was an integral part of an institutional web[6] which had only partly begun to include reformatories, mental hospitals, public schools, orphanages, and various urban missions. In this light we can see Lancaster as part of an effort to care for and control the stranger—in this case, urban girls. This legacy was inherited from two sources: the egalitarian impulses which, in part, were inspired by the creation of America's democratic institutions and the common school movement.

The common school movement aptly illustrates the mixed motives of mid-century reform. Public schooling insured every child an equal education which would extend equality of opportunity to all children and teach them those habits of industry and morality considered important for responsible citizenship. By educating and socializing all children, reformers hoped to achieve social democracy and social order. Horace Mann, the father of the common school movement, articulated this dual purpose in his First Annual Report of 1837: "After the state shall have secured to all its children, that basis of knowledge and morality, which is indispensible to its own security; and after it shall have supplied them with the instruments of that individual prosperity, whose aggregates will constitute its own social prosperity; then they may be emancipated from its tutelage; each one to go whithersoever his well instructed mind shall determine."[7]

As a further effort to socialize and educate all children, the first state reform school for boys was opened in Westborough, Massachusetts, in 1847. Its purposes were to shelter those dependent and deviant boys who needed guidance beyond that offered by common schooling and to protect society from their potential evil. As Michael Katz discusses in *The Irony of Early School Reform*, a mechanism was creted to educate and correctly socialize those who chould not be reached by the regular process of common schooling.[8] In spite of the egalitarian rhetoric used to rationalize common schooling, however, the early reform school effort neglected girls. But the same view of children that led Horace Mann and others to promulgate common schooling for all children soon compelled reformers to offer the same reform opportunities to neglected and delinquent girls.[9] Mixed with this vision, however, was a growing concern that the family was faltering and the number of wayward girls was rising. It was, therefore, of immediate concern that girls, as future wives and mothers, be domesticated and reformed.

Given both their egalitarianism and commitment to common schooling, the reformers felt strongly that education had to be an integral part of the girls' reform program: they would learn to read and write as well as to perform household tasks and would receive rigorous religious training. Firm convictions of faith were motivational forces in the social activity of doing good for others less fortunate than oneself:

> Intellectual development exalts the moral, and although order and direct appliances may be necessary to complete its culture, still, when you open the avenues to knowledge and supply the mind with healthy food, it ceases to long after the garbage which works such mischief with those who have nothing else to feed on. The cultivation of *self-respect,* beside the inculcation and enforcement of those great moral truths which it is the business of society to develop and to cherish, should be carefully attended to.[10]

> The germ of all morality lies in self-respect; and, unless you have sufficiently stimulated and excited this, all your efforts will be as "sounding brass or a tinkling cymbal."[11]

The commissioners reported their thoughts in January 1855, and in the same year the Massachusetts legislature established the school they wanted. The legislative resolves pulled together four critical aspects of this new social experiment. First, Lancaster was to be created and operated on state initiative. Second, this school was a manifestation of a larger enthusiasm for social reform. Third, the school was to be a great social invention, combining the best of common schooling with training in the habits of work. Fourth, its program orientation stressed meeting the unique needs of women. The Resolves expressed the theory which governed the creation of Lancaster:

> The title of the Resolves under which the commissioners act is, "Resolves for the establishment of a State Reform School for Girls." *A State Reform School for Girls!* Every word is significant and suggestive. In the first place the institution established is to be a *state* school. . . . Its establishment and maintenance will certainly affect the material interest of every citizen; and its beneficial operation will as certainly it is hoped return a manifold recompense, purifying in its nature, into the bosom of society.

> In the second place, it is to be a *reform* school. . . . Its aim to be the means, under the divine providence and by the divine blessing, of reconstructing . . . of rebuilding . . . or re-forming. . . .

> In the next place, it is to be a reform *school.* It aims to accomplish its object in and upon its subject as *pupils.* It aims to enlighten the understanding, and to mend and regenerate the heart, by teaching the pupils what is true, and by training them to think and speak it, and by showing them what is good, and by leading them to act and do it. . . .

> And, finally, it is to be a school for *girls*—for the gentler sex. . . . This circumstance is an important one, and enters into and modifies the plan of building and arrangement of rooms, with all the details relating to employment, instruction, and amusement, and, indeed, to every branch of domestic economy.[12]

The principle of in loco parentis assured the Commonwealth that the Lancaster girls were indeed to be treated as if they were under the supervision of a wise parent. The matron served as a mother; each girl was to have her own room, and no more than thirty girls were to live in the same house. In keeping with the staunch mid-century belief in the potential goodness of all children, the girls were not separated either by age or alleged crime. The older girls would set an example for their younger sisters; the younger girls would serve as gentling influences on the older girls. Corporal punishment was no longer an acceptable means of discipline; firmness and love stood in its stead. The girls would be bound to their new home by cords of love rather than imprisoned by bars.

Both European and American reformers were caught in a struggle between utilitarian-

ism most clearly defined in Benthamite ideology and the romantic view of lost community idealized by nineteenth-century poets, especially Samuel Coleridge.[13] While the
utilitarians rationalized the growth and expedience of policies that resulted in the creation of social institutions and laissez-faire economic policies, the romantics yearned to
recover the pure and pastoral. Lancaster was to provide the perfect environment to
cleanse the girls, who were considered polluted by city life. The purity of natural living
would inspire the redemption and healthy growth of the potentially wayward child.

Lancaster was nestled in hilly farmland in a beautiful rural area of Massachusetts about
fifty miles west of Boston. A small stone chapel was built in the center of the grounds as a
symbol of the school's mission. The girls' living quarters reflected the two goals of the
founders. Each girl had her own room, although the size of the rooms and the layout of
the sleeping quarters made them appear cell-like. Yet, there was pleasant common living
and recreational space. Girls learned domestic skills in the ironing rooms in each cottage.
In spite of this homelike atmosphere, however, the square, red brick building appeared
less like the neighboring homes than the New England academies of the era. In this
institution the girls were to be sheltered, educated, and gently incarcerated.

The daily life at the school was based originally on a balanced three-tiered program
consisting of common schooling, religious observance, and domestic training. Life at
the school can best be described by looking at the "First Annual Report of the Superintendent":

> The chapel bell rings at six, at which time or before, the girls rise, and put themselves and
> their sleeping rooms in order, and prepare the breakfast; at seven this meal is eaten. House-
> work is attended to until nine, at which time the chaplain comes, to take the direction of the
> morning devotions. Labor holds as many as can be spared from domestic duties in the
> workroom until dinner; this occurs at twelve. School is held from half-past one until half-
> past four; supper at five; and sewing, knitting and reading in the work-room until evening;
> prayers at eight, after which the girls are dismissed for bed. During the day sufficient time for
> exercise is allowed in the open air.[14]

Regardless of the age at which the girls entered Lancaster, at sixteen they were to be
placed as indentured domestic servants. It was presumed that the moral and domestic
training received at Lancaster would ensure that they were well suited for their placements. Girls served these indentures under the jurisdiction of the state until age eighteen,
considered the age of majority. During their indentures, they performed household
duties within a supportive and supervisory household.

The probate court was empowered to sentence to Lancaster those girls it felt would
benefit from such a rehabilitative setting. Although they could be sent for both status
offenses, such as vagrancy, and more serious adult crimes, such as assault, more than
three-quarters of the girls had been accused of committing crimes considered morally
threatening to social stability. For the full fifty years under consideration, most of the
girls sent to Lancaster had been accused of stubborn, wayward, and potentially degenerate behavior; vagrancy, running away, and staying out late at night continued to be the
most frequent female juvenile crimes.

Given the structure of the school, there could only be a small group of girls in
residence at any one time. According to the Board of State Charities' Reports, the
number of girls in the school averaged between 90 and 120. On the average, there were
69 entrants per year. It is important to note that the small group of girls who came to
Lancaster had a great deal in common.

From 1856 to 1905, 75 percent of these girls were English-speaking, American-born, and very poor. Of the few who were foreign-born, almost all were Irish and therefore spoke English. Given the changes in immigration patterns around the turn of the century, it is not surprising that at that time a slightly larger proportion of the immigrant inmates were from non-English-speaking countries. Nevertheless, 85 percent of the girls still came from English-speaking countries, and the vast majority were native-born. A closer look at these girls' ethnic backgrounds indicates that most of them were the daughters of Irish Catholic parents. This is understandable, given the waves of immigration after the Irish potato famine of 1845. By the 1850s, more than half the population of Boston was foreign-born and most of these immigrants were poor Irish.[15] Therefore, it is safe to assume that their daughters were very poor indeed.

For these fifty years, Lancaster housed an almost equal number of Irish Catholic and Protestant American girls. It is considered unusual for such a large group of Catholics to be in a Protestant institution, except by force. Certainly by 1840, Catholics had issued public complaints against public schooling. In New York, for example, Catholic immigrants, through the efforts of Bishop Hughes, fought for public money to start their own schools. Catholic parents opposed the use of the King James version of the Bible, the lack of catechismal instruction in the classroom, as well as the Protestant insistence that schools be neutral. According to Carl Kaestle, many of the public school texts exacerbated this situation by containing anti-Irish slurs. In short, Catholics considered the neutral stance of the public schools to be, in effect, Protestant and, therefore, anti-Catholic.[16]

During the fifty years studied, 6 percent of the inmates were black. Although this figure is disproportionately high when compared to the number of Blacks in the state at that time, the black population was steadily growing as black families migrated from the South. They, like the Irish, were poor and dislocated, but there is no evidence that they were selected to be brought to the school in any way different from the other girls.

It is also striking that Lancaster consistently housed children whose parents spoke English. Since the majority of the girls had been born in the United States, we may also assume that their parents had been in this country long enough to internalize the social norms, to speak the language of the probate court, and ultimately to make use of the system in order to find shelter for their daughters. Throughout these fifty years, more than half of the girls, both Catholic and Protestant, were brought to the court by members of the own families. The complainant families seemed to have had in common a sense of desperation bred by poverty, unemployment, death, or physical uprooting.[17] That most of the complainants were family members undermines two popular assumptions: that reform schools were a malevolent plot of the state to take poor girls away from their families, and that Irish Catholic parents were extremely reluctant to place their children in a Protestant state institution.

Conventional wisdom assumed that state institutions, under the aegis of *parens patriae,* were legally sanctioned to take over child rearing because the natural parents were considered incapable. They were, therefore, considered enemies to families, especially to those destitute and foreign. Dickensian images of the heartless state hauling off weeping, protesting children from their humble, helpless parents are so ingrained that we are shocked to discover the extent of parental participation in a daughter's commitment to a state home.

As we have seen, Catholic parents exhibited great hostility toward institutions which they saw as undermining their own religious and ethnic identities. Understandably, their greatest hostility was directed toward schools and other institutions which cared for their young. Yet Catholics also brought their daughters to Lancaster.[18] It seemed that, when they were desperate, Lancaster was the only concrete help available to poor parents of difficult girls.

The evidence from the Lancaster School supports historians who consider most reform institutions as mechanisms for social control. However, the story of Lancaster suggests that our present understanding of the relationship between the state and the poor does not adequately account for the complicated web of relationships created among those involved. Given the benevolent impulses and the fears of the reformers, the seemingly inadequate supervision of the girls, and the desperation of poor parents, an inextricable triangular relationship emerged in the absence of any other welfare options. In large measure, the problem was the state's inability or unwillingness to offer more reasonable and less traumatic options for aid to the poor. Instead, parents were forced to take advantage of a punitive institution.

The story of Lancaster is not one of a dream come true. The Commissioners' lofty aspirations rapidly collided with social reality. In ways unanticipated by the reformers, the school had ties to social, political, economic, and institutional circumstances that would prevent it from becoming a rehabilitative utopia. Soon after Lancaster opened, the initial optimism of the trustees began to wane and, within a year, they began to doubt the feasibility of their scheme. Although the trustees continued to defend the innocence of childhood, their ambivalence grew, as demonstrated in the following passage:

> When the criminal desire has developed itself into the criminal act, the question is often asked, is there any prospect for permanent reformation? The answer will, of course, be greatly modified by the circumstances of age, previous social relations, strength of character, and their future position. In reference to the youngest cases, embracing even the astonishing premature age of twelve years, a glance upon their girlish faces will afford, in part, an answer to the question.[19]

The despair and frustration of the trustees and administrators was plain. Echoing the disillusionment expressed above, just slightly over a year later, another of Lancaster's trustees began to question heterogeneous groupings. He concerned himself with separating deviants from dependents. His rationale was a chilling harbinger of the policies to come. "This would enable us to separate those of a tender age from the older girls and to conduct, with a somewhat modified discipline, a department which might be considered *preventative,* anticipating temptation, and guarding the inmates from the peril of personal contact with the young offenders whose reformation is attempted in the other homes."[20]

By 1865 Lancaster was becoming less a place of loving familial guidance and more a place of punishment and incarceration. This was due to three interrelated factors: changes in reformist ideology, changes in the clientele, and changes in the school program itself. The Howe Sanborn Report, printed in the Annual Report of the Board of State Charities for 1865, indicated with frightening clarity the direction in which reform ideology was rapidly moving. This Report was concerned with the social burden of poor and deviant children and the elderly—those considered dependent. More important than this general concern, however, are the ideas found in the discussion of the "General Causes of the Existence of Dependents, Destructives, and the Like." Drunkenness was considered to reproduce weak stock, and there was also a strong suggestion of a new hereditarianism: evil tendencies were considered to be transmitted to children by parents inebriated at the time of conception. The report warned that the children of such a coupling could threaten social order.

Unlike the discussions of mid-century social theorists which blurred the distinctions between deviance and dependence in a sentimental judgment of all those who could and should be saved, less than fifteen years later analysis focused on the various causes of deviance. The concern shifted from saving children to classifying types of depravity. Although the authors of the report claimed to be confused about who was blighted irreversibly and who was redeemable, they revealed their hereditarian bias when they attempted to explain the difference between "lack of vital force" and "inherited tendencies." Mid-nineteenth century social theories had attributed juvenile dependency and deviance to poor environment and inadequate parents. Now the blame fell increasingly on the child, to whom the bad habits of parents had been directly transmitted.

At the same time that reform ideology was evolving toward a sterner hereditarian explanation for deviance, the age and supposed character of entrants also changed. Initially, girls between ages seven and sixteen were to be admitted to Lancaster. However, from its opening in 1856, most girls were pubescent—between fourteen and fifteen. The age of entrants steadily increased, so that by 1875 most of the entrants were between the ages of fifteen and sixteen and by 1895, they were between sixteen and seventeen.

The contrast between the sentimental attitudes of mid-century reformers, especially toward younger girls, and the harsher attitudes later in the century are reflected in the superintendents' reports. For example, both Sarah W. (1856) and Elizabeth B. (1880) were sent to Lancaster as "stubborn" girls, on the verge of deviance, but supposedly redeemable. However, the tone of Superintendent Bradford Peirce, writing in 1856, differs radically from that of Superintendent Marcus Ames, writing in 1880.

Sarah W., brought in for uncontrollable masturbation, was described as a "pretty little girl . . . who would be a substantial comfort to anyone who would carefully train her. . . .[21] Once it was discovered that she was suffering from erysipelas, a skin disease, rather than a need to "abuse herself," the state chose to keep her and thus be guaranteed that she would be properly trained. Bradford Peirce went on to describe her as "requiring medical attention and physical treatment."[22] It was unlikely that Sarah and girls like her would be considered incorrigible in 1856.

By 1880, however, girls were more likely to be described as Elizabeth B.: "Young as Lizzie is, her record is painfully bad. She has been off with bad men and to disreputable places on Charles Street."[23] Similarly, Winnifred C. is "unmanageable and disobedient; has been in bad company; appears hardened and utterly devoid of feeling or shame."[24] Certainly by 1890, Bradford Peirce's sensitive belief that the young "sinner" was to be pitied, loved, and redirected to a good life was replaced by the colder tone reserved for management of the unruly and depraved. The case report of Josephine C., the 1,557th entrant, reflected the officer's attitude toward newcomers to Lancaster: "[She] is said to be unchaste. Has not frequented houses of ill fame. She is not of average intelligence. Character of house not good. Father a drinking fiddler and her mother is deaf and dumb. Girl is on street. Stole a hat from a store in Holyoke. Her appearance indicates a want of teaching."[25]

This unfeeling tone colored reports for the next fifteen years. In 1905 the punitive voice of the superintendent can be heard in the description of Annie Elizabeth H.: "[She] is known to have been unchaste. Keeps low company. Out late at night. Character of home poor. Fa[ther] in H[ouse of] C[orrection] for drunkenness. Mother washes. These girls were found in a freight car with men. She has been immoral for some time."[26]

The Legislative Reports also systematically noted that the girls were harder and of a more "criminal" class, and now defined "criminality" in specifically female terms. The crimes reported at the boys' reformatory at Westborough were crimes which implied greater violence, and more damage to personal or public property. The more severe crimes for girls were those which suggested immorality, defined as wantonness and prostitution. No longer considered vulnerable to exploitation, girls now could be destructive of public morality. They were no longer seen as girls in need of protection or firmer, more loving supervision, but as threats to public safety in need of isolation and control.

The increase in the age of entrants, however, was affected by three legislated changes as well as by the emergence of new state reform institutions.[27] In 1871 the state passed a law which enabled the Board of State Charities to attend probate court and prevent younger and seemingly more innocent girls from going to Lancaster. The state could now intervene to separate the younger from older girls. This view countered the founders' conception of the family institution as a therapeutic environment. It was now important to save young girls from the potential harm resulting from exposure to older and more hardened girls. State policy now facilitated direct placement to help the young; direct placement was seen as less desirable for older girls. In 1871 other laws influenced the age composition at Lancaster. One determined that seventeen-year-olds could be sent to Lancaster. Another provided that girls of sixteen who were considered incorrigible or badly placed originally could be transferred to Lancaster from other institutions by the courts. Lancaster was rapidly becoming a dumping ground for older and tougher girls.

In 1886 the State Primary School at Monson opened.[28] The express purpose of this school was to care for young, destitute children. Younger girls who were originally to be sent to Lancaster were now to be sent to the Primary School. Although the Primary School closed in 1895, the age patterns at Lancaster remained relatively unchanged after that time.

While the original reform ideology of heterogeneous family-style life was debated until 1885, policy pressures and the working of the institutional web brought about the separation of younger from older girls long before the formal change in reform theory occurred. Segregation by age and character replaced the therapeutic vision of mid-century environmentalists and underlined an insistence on the permanence of taint. The state, through legislation, voiced its disbelief in the possibility of reclaiming innocence for everyone. It is difficult to evaluate the criminal character of these older girls, to determine whether they were, in fact, as the officers described them, harder. It is possible that they were more sexually experienced if only because they were older.

With the changes in age and supposed criminality of its clientele, Lancaster officials were forced to face pressing questions of management and control. Although, by 1877, hardened girls were being sent to Sherborn Reformatory for Women, as institution for adult female first offenders, the trustees of Lancaster felt that the increased number of hardened girls created a need for the school to have its own correctional department. The policy of transferring incorrigible girls to Sherborn sufficed when transfer was not a frequent necessity. By the 1880s, however, this policy was inadequate to handle the new clientele. The mid-century belief that "cords of love are stronger than chains of iron" and that "affection and attachment are more irresistible bulwarks than stone walls . . . that

iron and stone may restrain and confine the vicious, but they possess no healing properties for the morally diseased,"[29] was now undermined by the request for a more correctional measure. "Isolation or separate confinement, with or without work, as the case
may require, is conceded to be one of the most effective methods of bringing to a sense of
duty the insubordinate."[30]

With the new institutions for the very young and channels for shipping off the
unsuitable, Lancaster assumed a new role. In 1885, the trustees stated that "the Industrial School occupied a position more important than many it has held since its establishment. It is now a middle place between the care of the Board of State Charities and
a Reformatory Prison."[31] "The inmates are lodged in four separate family houses, each
with its own staff of officers. This division allows a careful classification within the
school, a classification depending upon the character and previous history of the girls,
and not upon age or conduct within the institution. As there is no promotion from
house to house, a perfect isolation is thus secured of those who might otherwise
contaminate the more innocent."[32]

A system to guarantee separation of girls by age and character was now in full
operation at Lancaster. This classification system formally acknowledged the acceptance
of the hereditarian argument for the causes of dependence and deviance. Older girls were
considered more tainted, harder, and less redeemable. Hereditarians argued that most
delinquent poor children suffered the "permanence of taint." In spite of this harsh
argument, some commitment to the ideas linking childhood and salvation continued.
Hope for some rehabilitation therefore, was reserved, but only for the very young. The
classification system also formally sanctioned a more punitive approach to older girls
whose characters were flawed. Girls would now be treated as cases, rather than as souls to
be redeemed. The work at Lancaster was to manage this classified system, making sure
that the girls were appropriately placed in the school. The loving family circle was a
forgotten dream.

Given all the factors influencing Lancaster's program—economic shifts, changing
social theory, different clientele, and internal school pressure—the school's officials kept
struggling to redesign a program suitable for both the social climate and the entrants.
Therefore, the appropriate roles of common schooling, domestic training, and placement were constantly debated. The success of Lancaster's program had depended upon
its healthy balance of religion, common schooling, and domestic training. This internal
program was to culminate in a successful indenture—one where the girls were to
perform satisfactorily as decent and self-respecting domestic servants. The indenture
period was the most vulnerable part of the program because it depended upon successful training at Lancaster and a welcoming climate and job market outside the school.
Flaws in the indenture system frequently resulted in efforts to redesign the school's
training program and educational curriculum. For example, in 1868 the program was
revised to include instruction in a wider variety of housekeeping skills to improve the
capacity for housework. The trustees saw in such increased versatility a greater guarantee to the girls that "[they would] readily find safe and respectable homes, liberal wages
and kind friends."[33]

Although domesticity was always the prime objective of Landcaster's program, the
increased stress on domestic training was now explicitly stated and justified as that aspect
of Lancaster's program most relevant to the attainment of true womanhood. The details
of this report read as a prescription for the happy lives of women:

Almost every woman is destined to have a leading or subordinate part in the management of a family. Preparation for the ready and intelligent performance of household duties, the lowest as well as the highest, is therefore, of the first importance. Now, as perfect cleanliness is essential to health of body and of mind and to cheerfulness, all the arts of washing and scouring should be early learnt and practised, so as to form and fix the habit of doing them well, throughly, rapidly, and willingly.[34]

The report than goes on to list explicitly the chores most closely linked to those deemed essential for women's happiness: " . . . these arts should include not only the washing of tables and dishes, but the scouring of floors, stairs, windows and walls, and of clothes, and especially of bedclothes, and bedsteads. These duties occur every day in every family. They should, therefore, be done methodically, and the habit of method and order should be insisted upon amongst the most important attainments."[35]

Common schooling, originally seen as an essential feature of Lancaster's program, become less important as the push for domestic science increased. By 1869 education at Lancaster largely had come to mean female vocational training. The zeal of Samuel Gridley Howe and Horace Mann for common schooling was swept under the carpet with domestic training.

In spite of the newly tailored curriculum, by 1875 the indenture system was in even greater danger. The number of indentures experienced by each girl had risen, so that as many as 15 percent of those girls who where indentured had more than three placements and a few had as many as five. It seemed that many Lancaster girls were not suitable for placement and that the school would have to refine its program in order to increase the girls' employability.[36]

By 1884 the program had diverged dramatically from its original plan. The 29th Annual Report discussed the constant change of inmates due to a new policy which placed out girls as soon as they seemed ready rather than when they reached sixteen. This new policy left more openings for new girls, and since the average length of confinement was short, the whole idea of family-style care was undermined; Lancaster became less a residence and place for reformation and more a place for expedient detention.

Because many of the girls were at Lancaster for only a short while, the trustees feared that the school would become a mere custodial institution. Therefore, they decided to speed up their training and enable the girls to earn a living within a domestic situation. If they did not comply, they were punished by being transferred to Sherborn Reformatory.

In one sense, the trustees' decision made sense; training for service all but insured the Lancaster girls employment. While employment opportunities for women expanded in the last two decades of the nineteenth century, domestic service continued to be the most available job for young women. In fact, the demand for domestic service increased as fewer women found jobs in service appealing. Many young women preferred to work in the mills and factories, away from the constant surveillance of the female employer. Moreover, many older immigrant and black women previously forced to live in as domestics preferred to live out and combine motherhood and work.[37] Given this demand, it is not surprising that the reformers chose to train Lancaster girls for domestic service. Not only was there a guaranteed market, but domestic service also continued the close and constant familial supervision of Lancaster. In many ways, the domestication of Lancaster girls continued beyond the school into domestic employment. This labor need continued well into the 1920s.

Regardless of this demand for domestics, several factors complicated the hiring of young women. One was that the marriage age had risen so that many young people remained at home longer. Given that more women had older daughters at home, it is possible that female heads of households would have been unwilling to have a non-American girl in the house. As Marcus Ames suggested, these women were no longer filled with mid-century benevolence; they were not anxious to extend their hospitality to the likes of a Lancaster girl. Rather, they wanted efficient and thorough work from their domestic employees. In addition, it seems likely that mothers might worry about the potential promiscuity between their older sons still at home, and young girls; any act which led to their stay in reform school was assumed to be evidence of previous promiscuity. Given the availability of jobs for Lancaster girls in domestic service as well as the bias of employees against girls who were untrained or in need of nurturance, the new policy seemed sensible. The affectionate domestic life of mid-century Lancaster became an artifact; in its stead was an expedient vocational training program.

The trustees recognized that Lancaster had become a school solely for rapid vocational training. The school was free of its mid-century conflicts; no longer did it claim to protect and reform deprived girls. Common schooling, once considered a critically important factor in the reformation of young girls, was no longer considered essential. Lancaster was finally adopting the type of British vocational program it had previously scorned. The shift in program, however, was part of a wider educational trend in which formal industrial education sought to prepare the poor and immigrant for jobs in the new industrial world.[38] At the same time, it was assumed that learning technical skills would train the whole child, that she would learn strong moral values as well as skills, and therefore be prepared to participate in the broader social world. Like common schooling, Lancaster's original program was no longer appealing.

Employment and Family Life

What impact did Lancaster have on the adult lives of its inmates? In keeping with nineteenth-century expectations for women, Lancaster girls were to live domestic, industrious, and morally upright lives. Although the founders did not anticipate that the girls would rise above their station, they hoped that would live respectably.

After leaving the supervision of the state, most Lancaster girls continued to live as the founders had hoped. Between 1856 and 1905, 75.6 percent of the girls lived with a family: parental, conjugal, in placement, or in Lancaster itself. From this group, 35 percent returned to their parents. The pattern emerging from these first follow-ups continued. Most girls remained within a family environment, usually with husbands in homes of their own. There continued to be a small number of girls living and working alone, but there was little to indicate that the majority of them were living dissolute lives.

It is dangerous to assume a cause-and-effect relationship between Lancaster's program and the subsequent lives of the girls. Lancaster may have provided no more than shelter for poor and difficult girls; it may have been little more than a way station for them. Or it may have functioned primarily as a job placement service. It is also likely that it offered slight comfort to some parents skidding from the lower class to the underclass.[39] Perhaps Lancaster prevented this fall for their daughters and returned them to society as poor but respectable women.

The inherent nature of women was presumed to be domestic. Lancaster's program was designed according to this stereotype and offered what was "natural" for the reformation of poor girls. The environmentalists blamed poverty and slum life for the unrestrained, and therefore unwomanly, behavior of the girls. Later, the hereditarians blamed vicious parents, especially mothers, for raising "unnatural" and tainted daughters. The definition of "natural" changed from a state of externally induced conditions to internal character weaknesses. Lancaster's job continued to be the domestication of girls so that they would be better able to fulfill their "natural" roles; regardless of changes in clientele of social theory, Lancaster's main objective did not change.

Conclusions

The story of Lancaster, its goals and program, tells us as much about the nineteenth-century view of women's roles in society as about the institution itself. Lancaster's primary objective was to domesticate girls who were considered potential deviants. In keeping with contemporary attitudes, it was especially important that women, as potential wives and mothers, be respectable, morally upright, and industrious.

Seemingly seductive women had always been feared and shunned as dangerous, uncontrolled, and lascivious. Now, renewed pressure to secure the family increased society's expectations of women. They were expected to insure social order, especially at a time when there seemed to be precious little of it. Lancaster's program, although initially claiming a great belief in the role of common schooling as crucial to reformation, increasingly became a domestic training program. Regardless of these changes, however, most of the girls left Lancaster to lead lives of domestic respectability. Although the ideology of reformation degenerated into little more than rhetoric, the school seemed successful because there was little evidence that Lancaster girls ended up in jail or on the streets. This program, however, perpetuated the class structure that was a major factor in the poverty of the girls' families. Few rose above their station and few skidded to the underclass or resorted to prostitution.

It is most important to remember that there were almost no options for poor parents. The story of Lancaster, therefore, is not just about a reform school, but also a drama about the devastating effects upon families of poverty and public charity. The story of Lancaster also offers an overarching view of reformers. In the fifty years covered by this study, the initial exuberance and optimism of the founders abruptly ended. In their stead came fatigue, disillusionment, pessimism, and anger. The early optimism of the founders changed partly because of changes in clientele, and partly because of economic changes and shifting trends in nineteenth-century social theories. In the end, we are left with many questions about the potential success of any social experiment over time. The trustees and state officials did not remain sensitive to Lancaster's success as a reform experiment, created from policies which attempted to accommodate the inherent ambivalence of the reformers—fear and benevolence. In an attempt to create a social institution that would protect and guide children, as well as incarcerate them for the public safety, the founders of Lancaster created an institutional experiment based on confused purposes. The school was to make restitution for the children's deprived family lives by offering them compulsory love.

Lancaster's story is a gloomy one, a tale of the decline of hopes for reform into a desire for social control. There is sufficient evidence that the institutional attempt to counter the unchecked forces of economic and technical change was not by itself sufficient. However, the story is not simply a revisionist parable of an elite imposing its will on the passive masses. It is a story of true mixed feelings and mixed results.

In 1980 historians, sociologists, and social policy analysts are questioning the beginnings of compulsory school attendance, and the growth of policies that have given the state increased jurisdiction over the lives of children, particularly those who are seen as receiving inadequate care from their families. These policies grew partly as a response to the needs of poor and potentially delinquent children in the nineteenth century and have ultimately touched the lives of all children. They are particularly relevant to policy makers currently in the process of formulating new programs for juveniles.

Today, we continue to face heartbreaking facts about the treatment of female delinquents. While the story of Lancaster is not totally unique either to the Commonwealth or to girls, parts of its history threaten to be repeated, especially in the new programs for the treatment of female juveniles. In 1973 Massachusetts took great pride in its bold and controversial policy to deinstitutionalize children. Soon after, the boys school at Westborough was closed amidst an almost celebratory event in which a cavalcade of cars and vans from the University of Massachusetts at Amherst "rescued" the last thirty-five inhabitants of the school. However, Lancaster remained partially occupied until 1976. Once again girls were neglected.[40] This suggests that, one hundred and twenty years later, fear still exists; the story of girls at Lancaster threatens to come full circle. Nevertheless attempts are now being made to avoid some of the mistakes we have seen in Lancaster's history. It is hoped that the story of Lancaster, and similar institutions, will prove valuable so that we can learn from the glaring errors of the past.

Notes

1. Bradford K. Peirce. 2AR. Public Document 16, 1857, p. 26.

2. Barbara Welter, "The Cult of True Womanhood," *American Quarterly* (1966), 151–174. In this article the author delineates the four qualities considered necessary for the ideal antebellum women: domesticity, submission, purity, and piety. It is obvious that even in postbellum America, Lancaster's founders were very much influenced by this ideology.

3. Christopher Lasch, *Haven in a Heartless World: The Family Besieged* (New York: Basic Books, 1977).

4. For a comprehensive example of this work, see Michael B. Katz, *The People of Hamilton, Canada West* (Cambridge, Mass.: Harvard Univ. Press, 1975); and Peter Laslett, *The World We Have Lost* (New York: Scribner, 1965).

5. The Fay Commission, headed by Francis Fay, a legislator, was appointed by the Massachusetts Legislature in 1854 specifically to begin plans for a state reform school for girls.

6. For a more detailed description of this movement, see Michel Foucault, *The Birth of the Clinic* (New York: Pantheon, 1973); Michel Foucault, *Discipline and Punish* (New York: Pantheon, 1977); Gerald N. Grob, *The State and the Mentally Ill* (Chapel Hill: Univ. of North Carolina Press, 1965); Gerald N. Grob, *Mental Institutions in America* (New York: Free Press, 1973); David W. Lewis, *From Newgate to Dannemora* (Ithaca: Cornell Univ. Press, 1965); Barbara Gutman, *Public Health and the State* (Cambidge, Mass.: Harvard Univ. Press, 1972); David Rothman, *The Discovery of the Asylum* (Boston: Little, Brown, 1971).

7. Lawrence A. Cremin, *The Republic and the School: Horace Mann on the Education of Free Men* (New York: Teachers College Press, 1957), p. 33.

8. Michael B. Katz, *The Irony of Early School Reform* (Cambridge, Mass.: Harvard Univ. Press, 1968), pp. 163–211.

9. Douglas E. Branch, *The Sentimental Years* (New York: Hill & Wang, 1965), pp. 289–318.

10. "Commissioner's Report," Massachusetts House Document 43, 1854, p. 6.

11. "Commissioner's Report," p. 34.

12. "An Act," Massachusetts House Document 43, 1854, p. 51.

13. F. R. Leavis, ed., *John Stuart Mill on Bentham and Coleridge* (New York: Harper & Row, 1950).

14. "First Annual Report of the Superintendent and Chaplain," Massachusetts *1AR* House Document 20, 1856, p. 35.

15. Oscar Handlin, *Boston's Immigrants* (New York: Antheneum, 1972); Malwyn A. Jones, *American Immigration* (Chicago: Univ. of Chicago Press, 1960); U.S. Dept. of Commerce, Bureau of the Census, *Historical Statistics of the United States: Colonial Times to 1970*, pp. 87–121.

16. Daniel Calhoun, ed., *The Educating of Americans: A Documentary History* (Boston: Houghton Mifflin, 1969), pp. 158–171; Carl F. Kaestle, *The Evolution of an Urban School System: New York City, 1750–1850* (Cambridge, Mass.: Harvard Univ. Press, 1973), pp. 148–158.

17. By using the occupational ranking scheme devised by Michael B. Katz in *The People of Hamilton, Canada West*, pp. 343–348. I was able to assess the fathers' occupational rank. The number of fathers who were dead, had deserted, or whose occupation was "uncategorizable" showed that the girls at Lancaster were from extremely poor homes. Those mothers who worked held exceptionally low-ranked jobs.

18. I calculated Irish or Irish-American girls as Catholics when the religion of the girls was not explicitly stated.

19. Massachusetts 2AR, Public Document 16, 1856, p. 14.

20. Massachusetts 2AR, House Document, 1857, p. 10.

21. Bradford K. Peirce, *First Handwritten Casebook,* 1856, p. 1.

22. Peirce, *Casebook,* p. 1.

23. Porter N. Brown, *Handwritten Casebook,* 1880, Case 1062.

24. Brown, Case 1070.

25. Mrs. L. Brackett, *Handwritten Casebook,* 1890, Case 1557.

26. Mrs. L. Brackett, *Handwritten Casebook,* 1905, Case 2751.

27. The following three acts brought about de facto classification. Sects. 8 and 10, Chap. 359, Acts of 1870, allowed the Visiting Agent of the Board of State Charities to attend trials and to oversee placement once the girls received their sentences. At the same time, Chap. 365, Acts of 1871, gave the Board the power of transfer of girls to Lancaster from other institutions. It also sanctioned the commitment of seventeen-year-olds to Lancaster.

28. Until 1872 the Primary School was really an adjunct to the Monson Almshouse. In 1872 the Primary School became independent of the Almshouse, sharing its trusteeship with the two reform schools. The increasing bureaucratization of the State Board of Charities eroded the informal mechanisms the founders felt necessary to work with these children. Bitter controversies arose over the education program and placement at Monson. In addition, hardened criminal children were placed with young destitute children. In 1886 the State Primary School at Monson was opened for the purpose of housing destitute and deprived young children; it was considered a preferable alternative to the Almshouse or reform school. The Primary School suffered the same fate at Lancaster, however. The legislature closed the school in 1895.

29. Massachusetts 4AR, Public Document 24, 1859, p. 6.

30. Massachusetts 22AR, to State Board of Health, Lunacy, and Charity, Public Document 20, 1877, p. 7.

31. Massachusetts 22AR, 1877, p. 14.

32. Massachusetts 32AR, to the State Board of Lunacy and Charity, Public Document 18, 1887, p. 14.

33. Massachusetts 13AR, to the Board of State Charities, Public Document 20, 1868, p. 2.

34. Massachusetts 13AR, 1868, p. 2.

35. Massachusetts 13AR, 1868, p. 8.

36. Massachusetts 19AR, to the Board of State Charities, Public Document 20, 1874, p. 8.

37. David M. Katzman, *Seven Days a Week* (Oxford: Oxford Univ. Press, 1978).

38. Barbara Brenzel and Walter McCann, "Education Technical," *Encyclopedia of Sociology* (Guilford, Conn.: Dushkin Press, 1974). For a more detailed and comprehensive account see Marvin Lazerson, *The Origins of the Urban Public School* (Cambridge, Mass.: Harvard Univ. Press, 1971); and Marvin Lazerson and W. Norton Grubb, eds., *American Education and Vocationalism* (New York: Teachers College Press, 1974).

39. Stephan Thernstrom, *The Other Bostonians* (Cambridge, Mass.: Harvard Univ. Press, 1973), pp. 45–75; Stephan Thernstrom, *Poverty and Progress* (Cambridge, Mass.: Harvard Univ. Press, 1964), pp. 150–152. Thernstrom describes static families. The girls at Lancaster seem to come from families like the ones Thernstrom describes as "unable to rise out of the most depressed impoverished segment of the manual laboring class."

40. Carol Peacock, "The Massachusetts Experiment: Towards Equal Services for Girls" (Boston: Dept. of Youth Services, 1978). I have also benefited from numerous conversations with Claire Donovan, former Superintendent of State Industrial School, Lancaster.

20. Heathens and Angels: Childhood in the Rocky Mountain Mining Towns

When thinking of the American frontier, most persons visualize a tapestry of cowboys, Indians, dance hall girls, cavalrymen, grimy miners, bewhiskered trappers, and sturdy homesteaders with their weathered wives. One figure, if he can be seen at all, usually has been pushed to the edges of this picture—the child. Historians have shared this bias. They have allowed blacks, ethnic minorities, and women a larger place in the story of the Far West, but readers of most historical works still will come away with the impression that the region was peopled almost entirely by adults.

This situation is especially striking because historians have begun to explore in detail the experience of childhood in Europe and the United States. They have given little attention, however, to the frontier.[1] The student curious about the process of growing up there will find only broad generalizations in a few older classics and recent surveys. In all these works, the story is told in much the same way. The frontier supposedly encouraged an emancipation of children within the family and in the world at large. The child took advantage of the many opportunities of the western economy, and he made his own way early by his own resources. In the pioneers' world, a more liberal spirit fostered in youth an independence of action and opinion. All this produced a new child—precocious, self-confident, and individualistic—whom newcomers and outside critics sometimes found profligate, disrespectful, and generally offensive.[2] Presumably these same sweeping statements held true everywhere on the frontier, whether Kentucky in the 1780s, Oregon in the 1850s, Comstock in the 1860s, a Kansas homestead in the 1870s, or a Montana ranch in the 1880s.

Clearly there is a need for studies of children and childhood in the many settings of the Far West. The mining towns of the Rocky Mountains offer one possibility. In this urban setting, society was somewhat more visible than on the plains and farmlands. Many mining camp newspapers, as well as diaries, journals, reminiscences, and travel accounts, have survived to illuminate day-to-day activities in the high country of Idaho, Montana, Colorado, Wyoming, Utah, New Mexico, and Arizona. These sources provide some insights into neglected aspects of life, including that of children, in this part of the western experience. Here at least a beginning can be made.

Historians have described many times the general characteristics of mining town society. Although women and families could be seen almost from the beginning, its transient population was dominated by young, unattached working men of many lands, and its social life was fitted mostly to their demands. If traditional institutions could be found at all, they had barely set their roots in the shallow mountain soil. It was a gathering of optimists and plungers, sprung up virtually overnight. The camp's spirit was

Elliott West, "Heathens and Angels: Childhood in the Rocky Mountain Mining Towns," reprinted from *Western Historical Quarterly* 14 (1983): 145–64, by permission of *Western Historical Quarterly*.

baldly acquisitive and its vices typically unashamed.[3] This environment helped shape the young as they made the passage from infancy to adulthood.

Of the conditions affecting the lives of children, one of the most obvious was the demand for labor. There was much to do in the camps and not enough persons to do it. Children of poorer families found employment outside the home to help put food on the table, but even at the upper economic levels the opportunity of income lured many young persons into the job market. The temptations began early. A visitor to Placerville, Idaho, in 1864 would have seen two brothers and their sister—the youngest age two and the eldest seven—working a small rocker beside a creek. At night their father would process their find with mercury.[4] Others of tender years panned for gold beside acquiescent placer miners, peddled their mothers' pies, and raised for sale cats to control the mice and pine squirrel population.[5]

Quite early the working lives of boys and girls began to diverge. A recent study emphasizes that the frontier was not a land of great occupational opportunity for women, most of whom found jobs doing for others what they did for their families—washing, cooking, cleaning, and making clothes.[6] Young girls learned this lesson quickly. From the more comfortable families to the poorest, they apparently were expected to work, but their efforts were confined to traditional tasks. Usually they helped care for younger brothers and sisters, swept and mopped, baked, hauled water, sewed, darned, and tatted.[7] Sometimes, however, death, abandonment, or other circumstances took the mother from the home, and since the older relatives usually had stayed behind in the East, daughters not yet in their teens faced far greater responsibilities. When her mother was blinded by lye while scrubbing a floor, for example, one girl of the camps took over the cooking and housework for her twelve older brothers. She was eight years old.[8] These child housewives learned as best they could the considerable skills needed to run a home. A ten-year-old who came with her father from Kansas to Silverton, Colorado, relied upon letters from her grandmother for instruction in tasks from sewing to making biscuits.[9] In any case, their work kept young girls close to the hearth.

Boys, on the other hand, found jobs that took them away from the influence of the home. Among the diaries and recollections of young boys, in fact, those that mention no outside work are the exception. By twelve or thirteen, many were performing the more menial tasks of the town—"forking" along the sluices, feeding pack mules, peddling bills, selling newspapers, washing dishes, and seeking out odd jobs.[10] Others took on remarkably difficult and occasionally perilous duties. "Pretty dangerous business, ain't it?" Walter Smith, age thirteen, wrote his mother from Tellurium, Colorado, where he was dodging rocks blown out by explosives, pounding out drills in a blacksmith shop, and throwing his ninety-five pounds behind a heavy miner's sledge in the tunnels. The brightest and most ambitious were given surprising responsibilities. As a clerk for a grocer in California Gulch, Colorado, the twelve-year-old Bennett Seymour often was left in charge of the store, and by the next year he was freighting goods for his boss from South Park. At thirteen, Charles Draper was so successful at selling books in Red Lodge, Montana, that a publishing house offered him an annual salary of $1,000 to serve as its field representative; at the same age, Willie Hedges, son of a Helena attorney and judge, received forty dollars a month as head of the capital's public library; and when only fourteen, another Montanan was running a ferry.[11]

Children, especially the boys, often seemed to take on the acquisitive, aggressive, economically individualistic values characteristic of the mining frontier. They shared in the gilded speculations and doomsaying. They followed the bitter labor disputes and commented learnedly on the depth of local mines, the quality of their ores, and the reliability of their financial returns.[12] The diary of fifteen-year-old Francis Werden suggests the sort of change that might have taken place in many youngsters under similar circumstances. Early in 1864 he arrived with his family in a Montana camp. At first he mentioned working as a cook and carpenter's helper, but quickly he began to show more independence and ambition in his choices of jobs. By the summer he was arranging to haul logs, carry dirt to the sluices and care for cattle. Then, on Christmas Day: "Today I stampeded [sic] off after a claim . . . (200 ft. each). I did not succeed in getting one. Heard tonight that they were made smaller so that gives me another chance."[13] In his impulsive optimism, this teenager could be mistaken for men twice (or four times) his age.

Other conditions in the mining towns shaped the experiences of children. In the more respectable events of public life, for example, there seems to have been little age segregation. Young and old mingled at town celebrations, political rallies, wedding receptions, fairs, dramatic performances, and even banquets of fraternal lodges.[14] The camps' most popular form of entertainment—a dance—brought together infants and old-timers under the same roof, and both boys and girls learned early the schottische and Virginia reel so they might take part. "It looked a little strange to see the married ladies hand their babies over to some friend while they went to dance," reported a newcomer to Summit, Montana, in 1866. "There was [sic] all ages present from the little ones of four months, little boys . . . , little girls, young ladies, married ladies old and young, and men of every age from 18 to 60."[15]

Apart from these activities, the many saloons, dance halls, brothels, and gambling houses stood out more prominently than in more settled communities. Children were bound to have some contact with the shadier recreations, if for no other reason than their own curiosity. But the land itself also played its part. In a town like Silver Plume, Colorado, or Atlanta, Idaho, strung out along a gulch or squeezed into a mountain valley, the land pressed together persons of all ages, classes, and moral persuasions.[16]

All this tended to draw the child into the world beyond the doors of his home, and contributing to these circumstances was yet another. Many parents, especially those below the economic elite of professionals and wealthy merchants, found it difficult to give close supervision to their sons and daughters. Most occupations took the father away from home, at least for much of the day. The high cost of living forced many mothers also to work, and those who did not found that ordinary household chores took more time under the demanding conditions of the new towns. Some children received even less attention, since a surprising number of single-parent households were found to be in the Rockies. Manuscript census schedules show, for instance, that one out of eight households with children in the camps of Lake County, Colorado, and Boise County, Idaho, in 1870 was headed by one parent, one out of five in Globe, Arizona, in 1880 and one out of four in Tombstone, Arizona, in the same year.[17] In the great majority of these cases, the mother, presumably widowed, divorced, or abandoned, faced the responsibilities of raising the children. Most of them seem to have found work as prostitutes or, more likely, at the difficult and time-consuming tasks of cooking, sewing, and cleaning.[18] How much time was left for care of youngsters can only be imagined. Finally, letters and diaries of the day sometimes mention children either orphaned or abandoned to their own resources, as well as runaways of eight or a dozen years, hiding out in the mountains or joining freighters and circuses passing through town.[19]

These facts of life—the chances for work, the frequent contact of young and old, the bawdy entertainments, the lay of the land, and the difficulties in overseeing children's lives—held one obvious implication for many adults. Young persons would grow up among influences that ranged from mildly disturbing to profoundly corrupting. One mother found Placerville, Idaho, "the hardest place to live upon principle I ever saw, and the young are almost sure to be led away."[20] Hers was a familiar complaint. She and others like her could see much evidence of changes for the worse among the young.

Some of these concerned personal habits, and from today's perspective they might seem relatively minor. Despite a severe whipping by his mother, for instance, a six-year-old in Creede, Colorado, refused to give up the cigarettes he had been smoking for a year, and he soon took up a pipe as well.[21] Children also adopted the colorful, but vulgar, western slang that offended conservative adults. "Must my little girl soil her sweet mouth with such words and expressions?" a mother wondered after listening to the vernacular of a neighborhood teenager. Unless she could send her daughter back to New England, she thought, the child would become a "fast western woman."[22] Worse was the awesome profanity learned from miners, freighters, and stage drivers. Many young boys, especially, swore as soon as they could talk, the wife of a Montana politician complained, and passed along their foul language to their playmates. The result was described by a Helena editor: "Parents are perhaps not generally aware of the profanity and obscenity indulged in by their hopeful offspring on the Broad Street sliding course. We have heard oaths and other disgusting language from the mouths of boys from five to ten years of age while running their sleds in front of our office, that would disgrace a Mormon pulpit."[23]

Children also acquired an outspokenness often associated with the West, and they offered comments and opinions that outsiders found impertinent and rude. When a small girl climbed onto the lap of her family doctor and remarked on his face's most prominent feature, for instance, her father gently reprimanded her. "Well, he has a big nose," came her reply. "I am not going to lie about it." Toddlers might intrude on the conversations of their elders to make jokes at the expense of the adults. The most solemn occasions were not spared these juvenile assaults. The Presbyterian minister George M. Darley recalled an "irrepressible" eight-year-old who impulsively joined the funeral procession of a Lake City, Colorado, saloonman. As Darley tried to deliver a few graveside remarks, the boy called alternately to the preacher and the widow, "When are you going to put that man in the hole?"[24]

Much more disturbing, children inevitably came into contact with the seamier details of life in the town. They gawked at the action in the local dance hall, ran errands for prostitutes, and came to know the sights, sounds, and even smells of plush bordellos and lowly cribs.[25] Nor did the ever-present gambling escape their attention. Men bet vigorously on the sidelines of children's marble-shooting matches and sledding contests, and youngsters in turn learned the basics of faro, keno, and poker. They followed closely the careers of the more flamboyant gamblers and placed bets on the number of wagons and oxen that would come down the street.[26]

Just as surely, some young persons crossed the line between observation and participation, and when enough of them did, their personal habits became to some a matter of public concern. An editor in Central City, Colorado, deplored the "ragged urchins" roaming the streets of his community like wild animals, and another in Montana complained of boys of eight to ten years lounging on the sidewalks, drinking in public, and loitering in dance halls and whorehouses.[27] Yet another journalist described with alarm and astonishment this vignette:

> A party of five chips off the old block whose ages varied from ten downward and whose height ranged from 3 feet 6 to 4 feet nothing in their stockings was pointed out to us last Sunday sitting on some boards engaged in playing poker. A young gentleman of some eight summers appeared to be losing as he brought down his knuckles violently on the board, exclaiming, "oh, h——l on it; I can't hold a pair," to which responded his companion of seven winter's growth: "Steady, old hoss, it's no use getting riled."[28]

Given sights like these, the prospects of public order when these unruly young boys grew a bit older were not comforting. In fact, groups of young toughs in some towns engaged in petty vandalism and harassed adults, particularly ethnic minorities and, above all, the Chinese.[29] Their pranks could get rough, even by frontier standards. Several New Mexican boys showered their town with rocks shot from an old cannon barrel, and on another occasion they set off a keg of black powder under the wagon of a man who had thrown them out of his skating rink. Fortunately, the victim escaped with only a broken arm.[30]

Anyone fearing that all was not well with the children might have turned for confirmation to one obvious place in the mining town—the schoolhouse. And there indications could have been found of the same personal vices, poor discipline, lack of respect, and unruliness reported on the streets. "Oh! dear how full is the experience of life of disagreeable things," an Episcopal minister wrote his wife of the dirty, gum-chewing students he saw in Montana.[31] The earliest school boards of Virginia City, Montana, saw a need to threaten with expulsion any children guilty of lying, profanity, vulgar language, cruelty, smoking, or chewing tobacco. Apparently there was some reason for the regulations, for the town's first public school teacher found her pupils to be "the worst set of children I ever saw or heard tell of," though she later softened her opinions.[32] Though she hesitated at first, a new principal of Fort Benton, Montana's schools turned to a rawhide whip her predecessor had left her in a desk drawer for some support.[33] Some educators thought even harsher methods were necessary. The Leadville, Colorado, board of education recommended the prosecution of one teacher for "shooting at scholars," and a Central, New Mexico, teacher kept a six-shooter strapped under his swallowtail coat to maintain order. Even then, one of the older boys in class struck this man from behind with a large chain, knocking him senseless. He soon abandoned teaching for the far safer profession of mining.[34]

In the evidence considered thus far, there is a pattern. It seems reasonable that the social environment of the mining town influenced the lives of its children; specifically, the effect appeared to threaten the contemporary standard of a "proper" childhood. By the late nineteenth century, childhood was considered more and more a unique period of human development requiring special treatment and consideration. These needs were to be satisfied by some community institutions, but above all by the home and the "true woman." In the home—a haven from the corrupting and jaded world of adults—the mother would provide the affection, basic education, and moral instruction essential to the transition from childhood to maturity.[35]

The reality probably matched this ideal rarely, if ever, elsewhere in the nation, but life in the mining towns seemed specially designed to weaken the bond between the child and his family and to shorten that time of protected dependence thought necessary to mold a young person's character for the good. Economic opportunities, as well as the excitement of life outside, drew young persons away from the home and into the world of adult work and play. These conditions influenced boys more than girls and sons and daughters of the poor more than those of the well-to-do, but they affected to some degree all children of the camps. Pushed or lured early into adult roles, young persons presumably would be shaped by the values of the marketplace and the temptations of the streets. Observers of the day often thought as much, and usually they did not like what they saw. Touring the Rockies in 1873, the Englishwoman Isabella Bird remarked: "One of the most painful things in the Western States and Territories is the extinction of childhood. I have never seen any children, only debased imitations of men and women, cankered by greed and selfishness, and asserting and gaining complete independence of their parents at ten years old. The atmosphere in which they are brought up is one of greed, godlessness, and frequently profanity."[36]

Was she correct? In fact, such conclusions should be drawn cautiously. As always, the alarming and the bizarre attracted unusual attention. More precisely, a chain-smoking, beer-swilling ten-year-old who cursed like a sailor tended to catch the public eye, but he was not necessarily typical. Moreover, literary tourists like Bird touched mainly the surface of town life; they seldom earned an understanding that came only with long and intimate exposure to the daily rhythms of those they saw on the streets. If a student today takes a closer look at the everyday lives of children in the camps, he can see at work other forces that balanced the ones already described. Some attention needs to be given to this evidence if a reasonably accurate picture is to be drawn.

One fact is of special importance: significantly fewer children lived in the mining towns than in most other communities of the nation. For a man or woman coming to the mountains in 1870 from Columbus, Ohio, for example, young people must have been a familiar and expected part of life, because about three out of every ten persons there (29.1 percent) were between five and eighteen years of age. The same could be said of virtually all towns and cities that sent immigrants to the Rockies, whether Maysville, Kentucky (30.9 percent), St. Joseph, Missouri (26.3 percent), Galena, Illinois (34.3 percent), Negaunee, Michigan (29.8 percent), Fishkill, New York (27.5 percent), or Reedy Church, Virginia (32.7 percent). But if an argonaut from any of these places had come to Fairplay, Colorado, he would have discovered that barely one in seven persons (13.1 percent) fell between those ages. Had he wandered during the next ten years to other towns, he would have found even fewer—one in ten in the camps of Idaho's Boise River basin and Globe, Arizona (10.3 percent and 10.7 percent), one in fourteen in Tombstone, Arizona, and Bannack, Montana (7.6 percent and 7.8 percent), and barely one in fifty in Beartown, Montana, and the diggings of Pinal County, Arizona (2.3 percent and 2.6 percent). Among the miners who sought the most remote recesses of the mountains, there were often no children at all to be found.[37]

If these statistics appear cold and dry, another fact should be kept in mind. Many among the adult majority missed, often desperately, the children they had left behind. Childless men and women fondly recalled younger brothers, sisters, nieces, nephews, and cousins, but the many fathers who had come west alone naturally suffered more. Reluctant to expose their wives and young ones to the rigors of the frontier, they were "batching it" while seeking their fortunes.[38] What were planned as brief separations had a way of turning into months, then years, as the search for riches went on, and still these men faced the same dilemma. "I cannot stay away from my little family . . . ," as one of them put it, "neather would I like to bring them hear."[39]

Their feelings are suggested in the romanticized images of children and the painful scenes of separation found in songs and poems of the mining frontier. The maudlin "Little Feller, Child of the Sunset Country" opened one volume of ballads, and the "Gold Seeker's Song" spoke for fifty-niners on their way to Colorado:

> Then farewell to sweethearts, and farewell to wives,
> And farewell to children, the joy of our lives . . .

An anonymous Idaho prospector in the 1860s left behind this scrap of verse:

> It was a hard thing to part from those little ones so gay
> That were playing in the yard around the door
> And my wife sobbed aloud as I started away
> Saying Farewell I'll see you no more.[40]

A visitor to Colorado estimated that the majority of mines in the new state were named after wives and children waiting for the return of their hopeful bonanza kings.[41]

The letters and journals of these men reveal their homesickness, guilt, and anxiety. They tell of staring for hours at pictures of their children, dreaming of them, and waking to fears of their illnesses and accidents.[42] And, as in this letter from a father on his way to Colorado, there is often a more basic fear that they themselves will be forgotten: "You must be good children and think about Pa."[43] Like the Virginia City, Montana, tin merchant who sent his youngest girl, Mattie, a ring he had made from his coat button, these men reached across time and space, however tentatively and symbolically, to touch their sons and daughters.[44]

These private feelings must be appreciated if one is to understand the lives of the children who did live in the mining towns. The evidence was all around. Whether bursting into tears at the sight of "the first baby I've seen in years," laying aside their picks and shovels to touch the hair of the first children in the diggings, or spontaneously giving boys and girls vials of gold dust and handfuls of coins, the men of the camps showed that by a law of emotional supply and demand, the value of young persons had increased.[45] The prominent part played by youngsters in public celebrations, especially the national and religious rituals of the Fourth of July and Christmas, hints as well at the enjoyment felt by adults at their presence.[46] In short, if some conditions encouraged the young to put their childhood quickly behind them, in other ways they were reminded that childhood was a special time with its own distinctive qualities, ones that were valued and sorely missed by the adult majority. By implication, childhood should be prolonged.

The scarcity of children may well have had other significant results. As noted above, conditions often left parents little time to watch over their sons and daughters. But on the other hand, some men and women, perhaps thinking of their own children or young relatives far away, played parents to children close at hand. Miners and freighters who worked beside young boys might introduce them to tobacco and salty language, but they might also teach responsibility, discipline, and honesty: "As I look back on it now," recalled a man of his childhood in Weaver, Colorado, "I realise how much those muleskinners, practically all of them unmarried, did to help our parents bring up a bunch of men. . . . A lot of things they taught us made us better boys."[47]

Adults without families could give more. The nineteenth century witnessed a growing recognition of the importance of affection and attention in the rearing of children. One rare autobiographical account of childhood on the mining frontier, Anne Ellis's *The Life of an Ordinary Woman,* shows how such nurturing might have come to some in the camps. Ellis tells of growing up in the small town of Bonanza in southern Colorado. Her father abandoned his family when she was four, and afterwards her mother married a miner who was a good provider, but "utterly without feeling." Young Anne grew up half-wild, wandering about the town and countryside. Her stepfather virtually ignored her, and her mother could give Anne and her five brothers and sisters only what time she could find within her exhausting schedule of work. Thus far, hers is the standard story of a neglected child of the camps. But throughout the account of her early years, Ellis writes warmly of a procession of other adults in her life—Si Dore, who fed her codfish and biscuits, made her a sled, and regaled her with hunting stories; "Picnic Jim," who took the Ellis brood on long raspberry-gathering expeditions; "Uncle Pomp," who bellowed out on request verses of "The Hat Me Father Wore" and blew clouds of pipe smoke into the infected ear of Anne's brother to ease his pain; Eli, a freighter and tinsmith who helped teach her how to cook; Lil, a notorious woman who often kept Anne overnight, joked and giggled with her, and read her "Peck's Bad Boy"; and nameless British remittance men, who introduced her to chocolate, orange marmalade, Worcestershire sauce, and the classics of English literature.[48] All of them lived without children of their own. Her memories suggest these adults—and probably many like them on the mining frontier—became in some ways surrogate parents. They could not provide much continuity and security, but they could give love, and they could help a child understand the bewildering world of grown-ups.

Those who looked only at the surface of town life would have missed more. If some adults mainly noticed children who worked and misbehaved, the youngsters themselves later would reminisce at least as often about lighthearted times of play. Moreover, their games typically were ones their parents had enjoyed. Their own grandchildren would find them familiar in later generations. Outside they built snow forts, sledded, and played hopscotch, hide-and-seek, snap-the-whip, London Bridge, run-sheep-run, and anti-I-over. Indoors they passed time with tic-tac-toe, tiddlywinks, and guessing games like "authors" and "cross questions and crooked answers."[49] These amusements were innocent enough by the standards of the day. Some aspects of children's lives may have changed in the mountains, but many of their recreations made the passage virtually intact.

Despite pressures upon it, furthermore, the family continued to play certain traditional roles. Many mothers and fathers, for instance, strove to preserve the culture of their past. Nowhere was this better demonstrated than in their extraordinary attempts to provide at least a rudimentary education for their young. Their efforts imply not only concern and affection for their offspring but also a view of childhood as a period with distinctive needs. Schooling at home was most apparent among the better-educated, more affluent families. Their sons and daughters often had access to extensive libraries brought west at great expense. The daughter of one judge could pull from the shelves volumes by Carlyle, Plato, Burns, Macaulay, Byron, and Thoreau.[50] More important than books, however, was the luxury of time. Wives of professionals and successful merchants did not have to work to supplement their husbands' incomes; they could spend hours each day directing the studies of their children.[51] They began early. The wife of a railroad official described a scene in her home: "You should see what a literary family we are this morning. While I am writing Eleanor is studying and printing her lesson and Katie is trying to follow her example and has established herself with a book at her little table and is muttering away at herself seemingly entirely absorbed in her task."[52] Eleanor was five years old, Katie two.

A closer look at the evidence, moreover, reveals a commitment to education among many poorer settlers at least as strong as their wealthier neighbors'. At daylight the parents might attend to their respective jobs, while the children spent the day largely on their own—working, roaming the hills, or playing among the tailings—but during the evenings these same boys and girls often learned from their mothers and fathers how to read, write, and cipher. The same Bennett Seymour mentioned above as a twelve-year-old grocer and freighter received basic instruction from his father by the light of tallow candles in California Gulch, while Charles Draper, the thirteen-year-old book salesman, spent his after-dinner hours reading history, geography, and a variety of books and magazines thrust upon him by his parents. A similar picture emerges from other reminiscences and memoirs. A day of panning in the placers or hitching up teams of horses might be followed by reading *The Merchant of Venice,* acting out a scene from *Henry VI,* or memorizing "The Battle of Sennacherib."[53]

An increasingly efficient publishing industry was producing far more books at prices far lower than before the Civil War. Consequently, as part of the larger educational impulse, parents with few other resources frequently made sure reading material was available for their young. The first woman to winter in Ouray, Colorado, brought a Bible, Rollins's *Ancient History,* and the complete works of Shakespeare to broaden her children's horizons. Others saved precious pennies so they might lessen their children's isolation with subscriptions to popular periodicals.[54] Even Anne Ellis, who prowled about town often without shoes, read from her family's treasured copy of Plutarch's *Lives* and borrowed works of Dickens, Scott, Zola, Sand, Kipling, and Dumas. "The greatest influence in my life has been books, good books, bad books, and indifferent ones," she would recall later.[55] Those with no books of their own might call on libraries, which appeared quite early in many towns. Within five years of its founding, Central City, Colorado, had a library association and reading room, as well as bookstores, and the small camp of Montezuma, Colorado, boasted a collection of more than three hundred volumes brought from Boston by a local mining company.[56]

As soon as they could, parents pressed for more formal education. Early subscription schools quickly gave way to school districts and tax-supported public instruction. For teachers, organizers utilized people who were available; parents in the new camp of Robinson, Colorado, hired the woman piano player in the local dance hall.[57] Many, however, came to their profession remarkably well prepared. An early Central City teacher later served as president of the University of Colorado, and another of Lake City, Colorado, went on to become chairman of the mathematics department of the University of Chicago. In fact, even in one-room log schoolrooms students often could expect instruction in a variety of subjects—the classics, mathematics, history, physiology, geography, literature, and the natural and "moral" sciences.[58]

Just how much the typical youngster was exposed to this education is difficult to determine. In the case of Idaho in the 1870s, between 48 and 74 percent of school-age children enrolled for terms that lasted four or five months.[59] But a much larger majority may well have attended classes at one time or another, for individuals often recall starting to school, then quitting to work for their families or themselves for a year or more, then returning to the schoolroom. Many apparently lived by this rhythm for several years. A rare school census of a Colorado camp shows twenty-one students ranging in age from six to nineteen, and enough older persons seem to have attended one Montana district that the clerk ordered those over twenty to pay a dollar a week.[60]

The point, first, is that most young persons may have gone to school rather erratically, but they took some advantage of education in the camps; and despite horror stories of disrespectful and violent students, instruction was traditional and reasonably good. Further, images of children in the streets and along the placers give a distorted impression, because in their education children and teenagers followed a pattern similar to that in other parts of their lives. They moved back and forth between the roles of children and adults. Upon arrival in Alder Gulch, Montana (later Virginia City), thirteen-year-old Raleigh Wilkerson shoveled gravel at the sluices and worked at other jobs. When he later moved to Helena, he returned to school to study trigonometry, geometry, Greek, and Latin and amused himself with sports and schoolyard games. "From being almost a man," he remembered later, "[I] became once more a boy."[61] He probably spoke for many others.

In this context should be noted also the attention given to the religious and moral instruction of children. Letters, diaries, and later memoirs often mention parents teaching their young the stories and lessons of the Bible in their homes and on steamboats and wagon trains on the way to the diggings. Sabbath schools appeared early, sometimes before organized secular education. Enrollment could be substantial. By 1866 in Central City, Colorado, nearly three hundred children attended classes sponsored by the Baptists, Congregationalists, and Methodists. Each of the three groups also had a library of several hundred volumes.[62] These figures do not mean children embraced the teachings of churches any more than school enrollments prove that students learned to read. But the establishment of classrooms and sabbath schools does show that community leaders recognized childhood as a time of life when youngsters should be partially separated from the adults for special attention and instruction.

Other scraps of evidence imply a closeness and affection within the family unseen in the descriptions of alarmed journalists and travelers. As usual, a disproportionate part of these documents comes from those at the top of the social order. The diary of the eleven-year-old Edna Hedges of Helena, Montana, for example, tells of family storytelling, camping, and long walks with her father, an attorney and probate judge.[63] But the poorer majority is not entirely unrepresented. Something, for example, might be made of the painstaking efforts of mothers to make simple toys for their youngsters and to fashion clothes from flour sacks, bed ticks, and canvas torn from walls of abandoned cabins.[64] In later years those who grew up in the camps recalled lengthy family discussions of problems and plans, as well as impromptu evening singing and concerts. The result might be a home like that discovered by a young wife near Denver in 1861. "This is the happiest family I have seen since I left my home," she told her diary. "There seems to be so much sympathy between the parents and children."[65]

These observations do not refute the ones noted above, but they do balance them and provide a larger perspective. The mining frontier undoubtedly did change somewhat the children who grew up there. They tended to go to work early and to internalize the acquisitive values of their elders. They picked up some colorful habits, took on more independent traits, and talked, and perhaps thought, a bit differently than many of their cousins elsewhere. Conditions appeared to deny some children the nurture and protection that the wisdom of the day expected of the family. But upon closer inspection, changes were not nearly so dramatic and wrenching as they might have appeared. Seemingly disparate parts of the experience of childhood in these towns—education and play in the home and in secular and sabbath schools, and the pampering and attention given children by the childless majority—all had two things in common. They represented a powerful momentum to implant on the frontier the values and institutions of the settlers' mother culture. And they rested on the assumption that childhood was a distinct, unique, and valued time of life. Because the unusual and the bizarre caught the eyes of observers, these aspects of life were easily overlooked. On balance, the family proved remarkably resilient in its new setting, and childhood was certainly not "extinct" in the diggings. Despite cries of alarm, not all parents and other adults were content to abandon the young to the gods of mammon and the vices of the streets.

The child's world, then, was one of ambivalence and contradiction. He received conflicting messages. He was urged to put aside childish things, yet he was petted and told that his status as a child was a precious one. His surroundings naturally taught him new habits, even as some elders demanded imitation of the manners and culture of their past. Now he was encouraged to join the grappling for wealth; now he was told to tend to his studies and moral betterment. Those two broad sets of influences are suggested by a diary entry of a twelve-year-old girl in Helena, Montana. It is a Sunday in 1865: "At two o'clock in the morning a highway Robber was hung on a large pine tree. After breakfast we went to see him. At ten o'clock preaching, at one o'clock a large auction sale of horses and cattle. At two o'clock Sunday school. At three o'clock a foot race. At seven o'clock preaching. The remainder of the time spent by hundreds of miners in gambling and drinking."[66]

Hanging corpses and sermons, Sunday school and drunken prospectors: no wonder this strange, contradictory world produced children some newcomers from the East found hard to understand. For elsewhere in the United States, the child's place in society was developing in quite a different way. The tendency between 1860 and 1900 was to segregate children and young people from adults and to ascribe to them their own needs and traits. First in child-rearing literature and eventually in the popular mind, the first twenty years of life were divided into increasingly distinct stages, each with its own characteristics and demands. Infancy and early childhood came to be seen as a time of innocence and natural morality that had to be protected from a corrupt and jaded older generation. During adolescence, young persons were to be trained for later life and integrated into adulthood gradually and deliberately. Because the virtues of youth were admired, even celebrated, it followed that childhood would be prolonged and young people given unusual protection and attention. The goal was one of an orderly and controlled transition from infancy to maturity. Reflecting these ideas were new organizations and institutions ranging from the YMCA, kindergartens, and the juvenile court system to the National Child Labor Committee and the Playground Association of America.[67]

The romanticization of youth and the founding of schools represent two obvious ways adults expressed these ideas in the towns of the Rockies. But this impulse in turn was blunted by changes among children encouraged by life in the camps. The result was a confusion of trends and influences. Interestingly, this situation seems to have resembled that of the nation at large at a previous time—the early nineteenth century. During that era of geographical expansion and the beginnings of rapid urbanization and economic growth, youngsters of from ten to fifteen years and even younger enjoyed remarkable freedom and occupational opportunities. They took part in activities and entertainments of their elders and moved rather easily and often across the blurred boundary separating their world from that of adults. Observers commented on their precocity, self-confidence, and arrogance. The child's place and role in society was shifting and imprecise. This uncertainty was part of a larger confusion of a dynamic and unsettled nation still building its basic institutions and stuttering to describe itself in its own distinctive tongue.[68]

If these impressions are accurate, then they represent a delicious irony. What some saw as new and sometimes disturbing may have been in one sense a survival of an older social tradition. In the mining towns, the older, uncertain relationship of the child to his society may have continued, as it was changing dramatically elsewhere. Here was an unusual wrinkle in the familiar interplay in the West of past and present, tradition and innovation. In any case, much more investigation is needed on this and other parts of the frontier if historians hope to understand the child—the most neglected figure in the story of westward expansion.

Notes

1. For a summary of work done thus far see N. Ray Hiner, "The Child in American Historiography: Accomplishments and Prospects," *Psychohistory Review,* 7 (1978), 13–23. A few anecdotal works on children in the West can be found. See, for example, Mary Anne Norman Smallwood, "Childhood on the Southern Plains Frontier, 1870–1910" (doctoral dissertation, Texas Tech University, 1975); Ruth Barnes Moynihan, "Children and Young People on the Overland Trail," *Western Historical Quarterly,* VI (July 1975), 279–94. Young persons have received some indirect attention from historians because of the recent interest in frontier women, but the emphasis still has been not on children but on child rearing and the place of sons and daughters in the lives of their mothers. For more recent examples see Julie Roy Jeffrey, *Frontier Women: The Trans-Mississippi West, 1840–1880* (New York, 1979); John Mack Faragher, *Women and Men on the Overland Trail* (New Haven, 1979); Joanna L. Stratton, *Pioneer Women: Voices from the Kansas Frontier* (New York, 1981).

2. An early statement of this view, and one upon which many later writers have relied, is Arthur W. Calhoun, *A Social History of the American Family from Colonial Times to the Present* (3 vols., New York, 1918), II, 51–77. Although he claims to describe children in all of the nation, many of his examples are drawn from the frontier. For more recent examples of this view see Richard A. Bartlett, *The New Country: A Social History of the American Frontier, 1776–1890* (New York, 1974), 361–63; Duane A. Smith, *Rocky Mountain Mining Camps: The Urban Frontier* (Lincoln, 1974), 23; Ronald C. Brown, *Hard-Rock Miners: The Intermountain West, 1860–1920* (College Station, Texas, 1979), 32–33.

3. For examples of these impressions see Hubert Howe Bancroft, *History of California, 1848–1859* (10 vols., San Francisco, 1888), VI, 221–28, 232–33, and ibid., *History of California, 1860–1890* (1890), VII, 698–700; Rodman Wilson Paul, *Mining Frontiers of the Far West, 1848–1880* (New York, 1963), 14–17, 164–66; Smith, *Rocky Mountain Mining Camps,* 16–28, 78–123.

4. Emma Jane Davison reminiscence, Idaho Historical Society. In this and all that follows, persons fifteen years and younger will be considered children.

5. Milton Barnhart reminiscence, SC 396, Montana Historical Society; Lizzie Moore Sisk reminiscence, Idaho Historical Society.

6. Jeffrey, *Frontier Women,* 124–26.

7. See Alice Lytle Weber reminiscence, Western History Collections, Denver Public Library; Mayme Guanella Sturm interview, Clear Creek County, Colorado Writers Project Collection, Colorado State Historical Society; Edna Hedges Diary, October 15, 1878, January 6, April 16, 18,

1979, folder 27, box 11, Hedges Family Papers #33, Montana Historical Society; Julia C. Stone Diary, July 3, 12, 31, August 6, 1865, Frank L. Stone Collection, Montana State University Library.

8. Mamie Rose Harbottle interview, #158, Pioneer Foundations Collection, University of New Mexico Library. See also Donald F. Danker, ed., *Mollie: The Journal of Mollie Dorsey Sanford in Nebraska and Colorado Territories, 1857–1866* (Lincoln, 1959), 145; Elizabeth E. O'Neill reminiscence, Mary Ann Busick Collection, Montana State University Library.

9. Mary Olive Gray interview, #161, Pioneer Foundations Collection.

10. The diaries of Wilbur E. and James Sanders, sons of the prominent Montana Republican Wilbur Fisk Sanders, mention practically no work. See folders 1–3, box 2, Sanders Family Papers, #47, Montana Historical Society. But by contrast, see Raleigh F. Wilkerson reminiscence, SC983, Montana Historical Society; Martin G. Wenger, *Recollections of Telluride, Colorado, 1895–1920* (Mesa Verde, Colorado, 1978); Cornelius Hedges to parents, April 18, 1868, folder 9, box 2, Hedges Family Papers.

11. Walter T. Smith to mother, May 30, 1878, June 6, 9, 16, 1878, Walter T. Smith Letters, Western History Collections, Denver Public Library; Bennett Seymour reminiscence, 13, Bennett Seymour Collection, #563, Colorado State Historical Society; Charles H. Draper reminiscence, SC642, Montana Historical Society; J. Milton Barnhart reminiscence, SC396, ibid.; Cornelius Hedges to parents, March 8, 1870, folder 11, box 2, Hedges Family Papers.

12. Mabel Barbee Lee, *Cripple Creek Days* (Garden City, 1958), 41; Wenger, "Recollections of Telluride," 25–27; Walter T. Smith to parents, July 15, 1878, Walter T. Smith Letters.

13. Francis H. Werden Diary, September 24, October 17, 28, November 10, 17, December 25, 1864, SC971, Montana Historical Society.

14. Edna Hedges Diary, December 10, 1878, January 18, 26, April 2, 1879, folder 27, box 11, Hedges Family Papers; Abigail Emigh reminiscence, G. Donald Emigh Collection, Idaho Historical Society; Anne Ellis, *The Life of an Ordinary Woman* (Boston, 1929), 36; Sara Jane Lippincott, *New Life in New Lands: Notes of Travel* (New York, 1873), 125.

15. Ellen Fletcher to Mary, October 14, 1866, Ellen Fletcher Letters, SC78, Montana Historical Society. See also Ellis, *Life of an Ordinary Woman*, 108–9, 126–27; Wilber E. Sanders Diary, January 20, 1875, folder 1, box 2, Sanders Family Papers.

16. For comments on the relationship of the structure of towns and their society in the Rockies see John W. Reps, *Cities of the American West: A History of Frontier Urban Planning* (Princeton, 1979), 457–522.

17. These figures are based on my own examination of original manuscript census schedules for the towns mentioned for 1870 and 1880.

18. Elizabeth E. O'Neil reminiscence, Mary Anne Busick Collection; Ellis, *Life of an Ordinary Woman*, 41, 82, 207–8, 218; Alice Lytle Weber reminiscence, 17–18, Western History Collections. Harriet Fish Backus, *Tomboy Bride* (Boulder, 1969), 183–85.

19. Estelline Bennett, *Old Deadwood Days* (New York, 1928), 196–97; Georgia Burns Hills, "Memories of a Pioneer Childhood," *Colorado Magazine,* 32 (April 1955), 115, 119; Danker, *Mollie,* 145; Jack Stockbridge interview, #402, and John Moses interview, #211, Pioneer Foundations Collection; *Caribou* [Colorado] *Post,* September 2, 1871.

20. Louisa [Walters] to "Dear Friends," May 17, 1865, Louisa Walters Letters, Idaho Historical Society.

21. Edwin Lewis Bennett, *Boom Town Boy* (Chicago, 1966), 40.

22. Elizabeth Fisk to mother, February 5, 1871, folder 4, box 6, Fisk Family Papers, #31, Montana Historical Society.

23. [Helena] *Montana Radiator,* February 24, 1866; James L. Thane, Jr., ed., *A Governor's Wife on the Mining Frontier: The Letters of Mary Edgerton from Montana, 1863–1865* (Salt Lake City, 1976), 102.

24. Elizabeth Fisk to Fannie, January 12, 1868, folder 12, box 5, Fisk Family Papers; Carrie Adell Strahorn, *Fifteen Thousand Miles by Stage* (New York, 1911), 66; George Marshall Darley, *Pioneering in the San Juan* (Chicago, 1899), 64–65.

25. Lizzie Moore Sisk reminiscence; Bennett, *Old Deadwood Days,* 23; Ellis, *Life of an Ordinary Woman,* 40–41; Bennett, *Boom Town Boy,* 27; Lee, *Cripple Creek Days,* 27.

26. Fiorello H. La Guardia, *The Making of an Insurgent: An Autobiography: 1882–1919* (New

York, 1961), 24–25; Walt Wilhelm, *Last Rig to Battle Mountain* (New York, 1970), 69–70; Lizzie Moore Sisk reminiscence; Bennett, *Old Deadwood Days,* 24, 139–40.

27. [Central City, Colorado] *Daily Miners Register,* June 18, 1863; [Virginia City] *Montana Post,* December 3, 1864.

28. [Virginia City] *Montana Post,* May 6, 1865.

29. Bennett, *Boom Town Boy,* 68; Ray Colwell reminiscence, 21–22, Western History Research Center, University of Wyoming; Brown, *Hard Rock Miners,* 33.

30. Jack Stockbridge interview, #387, and Wayne Whitehall interview, #502, Pioneer Foundations Collection, University of New Mexico Library.

31. Daniel Tuttle to "My own dear wife," August 27, 1867, Daniel Tuttle Letters, Montana Historical Society.

32. Madison County School District Rules and Regulations, Madison County School Records, ibid.; Sallie Herndon Diary, March 5, 1866, ibid.

33. Mary Johnstone Powers reminiscence, Montana State University Library.

34. Eugene Floyd Irey, "A Social History of Leadville, Colorado, During the Boom Days, 1877–1881" (doctoral dissertation, University of Minnesota, 1951), 320; Mrs. Victor Culberson interview, #125, Pioneer Foundations Collection, University of New Mexico Library.

35. Barbara Welter, "The Cult of True Womanhood: 1820–1860," *American Quarterly,* XVIII (Summer 1966), 150–74; John Demos, "The American Family in Past Time," *American Scholar,* 43 (Summer 1974), 422–46; Carl N. Degler, *At Odds: Women and the Family in America from the Revolution to the Present* (New York, 1980), 66–85.

36. Isabella Lucy Bird, *A Lady's Life in the Rocky Mountains* (London, 1879), 61–62.

37. These figures are based on a comparison of tables of numbers of school-age children in the published census of 1870 with my own tabulations from the original manuscript census returns from the following places:

1870	1880
Fairplay, Colorado	Tombstone, Arizona
Bannock, Montana	Globe, Arizona
Beartown, Montana	Pinal County, Arizona
Idaho City, Placerville,	
Centerville, and Pioneer, Idaho	

38. F. L. Kirkaldie to wife, July 7, 1864, September 15, 1867, F. L. Kirkaldie Letters, Montana State University Library; Thomas Conrad to Mary, January 1, 1865, folder 8, box 1, Thomas Conrad Papers, #30, Montana Historical Society.

39. C. S. Hinman to father et al., February 3, 1861, C. S. Hinman Letters, Western History Collections, Denver Public Library.

40. Robert V. Carr, *Black Hills Ballads* (Denver, 1902), 13–16; LeRoy R. Hafen, ed., *Colorado Gold Rush: Contemporary Letters and Reports, 1858–1859* (Glendale, California, 1941), 305; untitled song, G. W. Morse and George Liggett Papers, Idaho Historical Society.

41. Strahorn, *Fifteen Thousand Miles,* 229.

42. Thomas Conrad to Mary, October 2, 1864, folder 7, box 1, Conrad Papers; John D. Morrison, ed., "The Letters of David F. Spain," *Colorado Magazine,* 35 (April 1958), 84, 97; Henry H. Clark to brother, November 11, 1864, folder 1, H. H. Clark Collection, #24, Montana Historical Society.

43. Anonymous to Harry and Metta, n.d., Harry Faulkner Collection, Western History Collections, Denver Public Library.

44. Thomas Conrad to Mary, March 19, 1865, folder 8, box 1, Conrad Papers.

45. A. K. McClure, *Three Thousand Miles through the Rocky Mountains* (Philadelphia, 1869), 244; Hills, "Memories of a Pioneer Childhood," 113; Alice Griffin Buckley interview, Clear Creek County, Colorado Writers Project Collection, Colorado State Historical Society; Emma Jane Davison reminiscence; Ella Irvine Mountjoy reminiscence, Wiley and Ella Mountjoy Collection, SC545, Montana Historical Society; Mary E. Booth reminiscence, SC1492, Montana Historical Society.

46. Danker, *Mollie,* 132; Libeus Barney, *Letters from the Pike's Peak Gold Rush* (San Jose, 1959),

87–88; Elizabeth E. O'Neil reminiscence, Busick Collection; *Lake City Silver World* [Colorado], December 25, 1875.

47. Bennett, *Boom Town Boy,* 20–21.

48. Ellis, *Life of an Ordinary Woman,* 30–34, 58–59, 67–76, 100–102, 122–23.

49. Rhonda E. Steiner, "Children in Early Alder Gulch," ms. #268, Montana State University Library; Thane, ed., *Governor's Wife,* 115; Emma Teller Tyler reminiscence, Lynn Perrigo Collection, Western History Collections, University of Colorado Library; Mary L. Boatman reminiscence, SC444, Montana Historical Society; Edna Hedges Diary, December 31, 1878, folder 27, box 11, Hedges Family Papers.

50. Bennett, *Old Deadwood Days,* 47. See also Edna Hedges Diary, October 8, 1878, February 2, 11, March 16, 1879, folder 27, box 11, Hedges Family Papers.

51. Elizabeth Fisk to "the dear ones at Home," May 17, 1867, folder 10, box 5, Fisk Family Papers; Elizabeth Fisk to mother, March 22, 1875, folder 10, box 6, ibid.

52. Margaret Ferris to mother, September 10, 1880, Mrs. Eddy F. Ferris Collection, Montana State University Library.

53. Bennett Seymour reminiscence, 9, Seymour Collection; Charles H. Draper reminiscence; "Reminiscences of Early Days in Boise," Carolyn H. Palmer Collection, Idaho Historical Society; Sallie Davenport Davidson reminiscence, SC606, Montana Historical Society; Owen P. White, *A Frontier Mother* (New York, 1929), 87–89; Marvin Lewis, *Martha and the Doctor: A Frontier Family in Central Nevada,* ed. B. Betty Lewis (Reno, 1977).

54. Stella Fairlamb interview, #139, Pioneer Foundations Collection, University of New Mexico Library.

55. Ellis, *Life of an Ordinary Woman,* 122–24.

56. Nelle Frances Minnick, "A Cultural History of Central City, Colorado, From 1859 to 1880, in Terms of Books and Libraries" (master's thesis, University of Chicago, 1946), 30–72; Verna Sharp, "Montezuma and Her Neighbors," *Colorado Magazine,* 33 (January 1956), 16–41.

57. Hills, "Memories of a Pioneer Childhood," 123.

58. Alma C. Kirkpatrick reminiscence, SC940, Montana Historical Society; O. J. Goldrick, "The First School in Denver," *Colorado Magazine,* 6 (March 1929), 72–74; Frank Pierce Baird, "History of Education in Idaho through Territorial Days" (master's thesis, University of Washington, 1928), 31–65; Report of Superintendent of Schools, Lewis and Clark County, SC623, Montana Historical Society; Thomas Gray Thompson, "The Social and Cultural History of Lake City, Colorado, 1876–1900" (master's thesis, University of Oklahoma, 1961), 45; Hiram C. Hodge, *Arizona as It Is; or, The Coming Country* (Boston, 1877), 196–99; Louisa [Walters] to Emma, July 29, 1864, Walters Letters.

59. Baird, "History of Education," 77.

60. School Records, Montezuma, Colorado Collection, Colorado State Historical Society; Minutes, March 25, 1867, Madison County School District Collection, Montana Historical Society.

61. Raleigh F. Wilkenson reminiscence.

62. Louisa [Walters] to brothers and sisters, June 18, 1864, Walters Letters; Lizzie Moore Sisk reminiscence; Wilhelm, *Last Rig,* 63–65; Elizabeth Fisk to "the dear ones at Home," May 17, 1867, folder 10, box 5, Fisk Family Papers; Elizabeth Fisk to mother, March 30, 1873, folder 6, box 6, ibid.; Minnick, "Cultural History," 50–51; [Denver] *Rocky Mountain News,* June 15, 1866.

63. Edna Hedges Diary, September 22, 27, November 4, March 23, 1878, folder 27, box 11, Hedges Family Papers.

64. Ellis, *Life of an Ordinary Woman,* 42, 86–87; Jack Stockbridge interview; Mrs. Daniel Witter, "A Pioneer Woman's Story Written for Her Children," *The Trail,* 18 (August 1925).

65. The quotation is from Danker, *Mollie,* 157. See also La Guardia, *Making of an Insurgent,* 20; Ellis, *Life of an Ordinary Woman,* 83; Charles H. Draper reminiscence.

66. Julia C. Stone Diary, July 30, 1865, Stone Collection.

67. Joseph F. Kett, *Rites of Passage: Adolescence in America, 1790 to the Present* (New York, 1977), 111–211; John Demos and Virginia Demos, "Adolescence in Historical Perspective," *Journal of Marriage and the Family,* 31 (November 1969), 632–38; John Modell, Frank F. Furstenberg, Jr., and Theodore Hershberg, "Social Change and Transitions to Adulthood in Historical Perspective," Michael Gordon, ed., *The American Family in Social-Historical Perspective*

(New York, 1977), 192–219; Joseph M. Hawes, *Children in Urban Society: Juvenile Delinquency in Nineteenth-Century America* (New York, 1971); Ellen Ryerson, *The Best-Laid Plans: America's Juvenile Court Experiment* (New York, 1978); Dominick Cavallo, *Muscles and Morals: Organized Playgrounds and Urban Reform, 1880–1920* (Philadelphia, 1981); Bernard Bailyn, *Education in the Forming of American Society: Needs and Opportunities for Study* (Chapel Hill, 1960).
    68. Kett, *Rites of Passage*, 11–108; Rowland Berthoff, *An Unsettled People: Social Order and Disorder in American History* (New York, 1971), 214–17; David J. Rothman, *The Discovery of the Asylum: Social Order and Disorder in the New Republic* (Boston, 1971), 216–21.

21. Socialization and Adaptation: Immigrant Families in Scranton, 1880–1890

Sociologists and historians have debated the role of family structures in preparing children for life in industrial society. Talcott Parsons's classic interpretation of the nuclear family suggested that since familial roles were specialized, that is the father alone worked outside the family while the mother remained at home, a child gained a realistic view of the specialization of industrial society and of his own fragmented power.[1]

Parsons's faith in the ability of the isolated nuclear family to prepare children for their economic role in industrial society was not shared by historian Phillipe Ariès. With the period of childhood becoming increasingly longer and children being kept in retreat from the realities of the industrial world, Ariès felt that children not only acquired a sense of isolation but were deprived of valuable experiences in the adult world.[2]

In a test case of the Parsons-Ariès controversy, Richard Sennett attempted to discover the impact of family structure on the adaptation of children to urban-industrial life in Chicago. Sennett compared the work experience of sons from intensive nuclear families and, presumably, less intensive extended families. He discovered that sons from small, nuclear families had less favorable work experience. Sons from extended or less isolated families, however, were more successful and tended to move out of their neighborhood at a higher rate than sons from nuclear families who remained isolated in their traditional middle-class enclave, Union Park, and presumably took less economic risks or ventures.[3] Thus Sennett was forced to conclude, along with Ariès, that children from extended families were better able to adapt to the emerging bureaucratic order of work in the city than progeny from a more intensive and isolated background.

With the results of Parsons, Ariès, and Sennett's work in mind, this particular investigation seeks to study the experiences of two immigrant groups in an American industrial city in the decade of the 1880s. The choice of Irish and Welsh immigrants as subjects differs from Sennett's sample. The residents of Union Park were essentially middle class and native born. The Irish and Welsh of Scranton, on the other hand, were definitely working class and foreign born.

Such a sample provides another dimension, missing from Sennett's work, by which to view the adaptation of individuals and particularly children to urban-industrial society. The middle-class dwellers in Union Park in 1880 did not vary culturally to any significant extent. The Irish and Welsh newcomers to Scranton were from two distinctly different social backgrounds. The Irish were recent arrivals from a rural, largely premodern culture, whereas the Welsh were industrial workers arriving in Scranton already versed in industrial culture and society. It is this dimension, the impact of varying cultures on adaptation, which this essay hopes to add to the debate over the role of the family

John E. Bodnar, "Socialization and Adaptation: Immigrant Families in Scranton, 1880–1890," reprinted from *Pennsylvania History* 43 (1976): 147–62, by permission of *Pennsylvania History*.

structure and the preparation of children for adult careers. Indeed, in 1880, as well as today, the clash between preindustrial cultures and modern urban society continues.

By 1880 Scranton was typical of most smaller urban areas in the United States. Its population had grown from 35,092 in 1870 to 45,850 in 1880, a growth of 24 percent in a single decade. The ten years since 1870 had witnessed not only urban growth but industrial unrest. Hostilities between Irish and Welsh miners had erupted in 1871, and the railroad strike of 1877 had thrown the city into several days of turmoil. Such unrest may account for the fact that, although its population increased as a whole, the number of foreign born in Scranton had not changed at all between 1870 and 1880.[4]

Although Scranton was most prominently engaged in mining anthracite coal, it was by no means a one-industry town. In 1880 over 16,800 persons were working in Scranton in a wide variety of occupations. Of 8,177 workers listed in manufacturing and mining industries, 3,657 were classified as miners. While this was a significant amount, the city still had over 1,000 people employed as dressmakers and milliners in cotton, woolen, and silk mills. There were 500 men working as carpenters, 200 stone masons, 300 machinists, several thousand day laborers, 600 blacksmiths, 149 painters, and nearly 400 teamsters.[5]

A listing of industrial concerns in the city illustrates the diversity of Scranton's economic life. The Delaware, Lackawanna, and Western Railroad Company operated mining operations in Scranton's third, fifth, fifteenth, and twenty-first wards. The Hyde Park shaft and the Oxford shaft were located in the fifth ward, an area of heavy Irish and Welsh concentration. In addition to operations of the Delaware and Hudson Canal Company, Scranton contained the Lackawanna Iron Works, the Providence Stone Foundry, the Green Ridge Iron Works, Sauquiot Silk Manufacturing Company, Harvey's Silk Mill, Gallands Underwear Manufactory, the Lackawanna Carriage Works, the Scranton Glass Company, the Scranton Wood Working Company, and the Scranton Brass Works.[6] The fact that such diversity existed is crucial in understanding the later careers of Scranton's immigrant population. Alternatives existed outside the coal mines.

The diversity displayed by the city in its economic activity was also reflected in its population. Among the 15,857 immigrants in Scranton in 1880 were newcomers from Ireland, England, Wales, Germany, and Scotland. While a few Poles lived in Scranton in 1880, their numbers were still small. Some Poles lived on Pittston Avenue, but most seemed concentrated in the eleventh ward on Washington Street. The largest immigrant group, the Irish, were scattered throughout the city, while Welsh were heavily concentrated in the fourth and fifth wards in the section known as Hyde Park.[7]

The sample of Irish and Welsh immigrants compiled for this study resided essentially in the Hyde Park section of the city. Hyde Park, in fact, had once been a separate town which was eventually incorporated into Scranton. Many of the Welsh settlers in the city had previously worked in mining operations in Wales and now were usually employed in the Scranton mines. The Irish were similarly employed, except that a good deal of the Irish were mine laborers while the Welsh tended to occupy skilled-contract mining positions. While over 60 percent of the heads of Irish households were unskilled laborers in 1880, only 16 percent of the Welsh held such jobs. On the other hand, 45 percent of the heads of Welsh households were skilled workers (almost all contract miners) in 1880. A mere 15 percent of the Irish occupied such positions.[8]

Differences abounded between the Irish and Welsh. In addition to the labor troubles in 1871 and their contrasting occupational status, the Welsh carried a long-standing antipathy toward the Irish. One observer believed that such resentment even accounted for the Welsh being staunch Republicans since the Irish were prominently Democrats. Such resentment, in part, stemmed originally from the competition posed by cheap Irish migrant labor in South Wales since the 1820s and because of the "general bellicosity and rowdiness" of the Irish.[9]

Actually the Welsh were much more versed in industrial experience. South Wales, especially Glamorganshire and Monmouthshire, were extensively industrialized by the mid-nineteenth century. Coal had been mined for decades. Throughout the century, unskilled, agricultural labor from Pembrokeshire, Carmarthenshire, Brecknockshire, and Cardiganshire moved into the Welsh coal fields. North Wales had also experienced significant industrial development before 1880. By the mid-nineteenth century the summer migration of even seasonal Welsh laborers to English agricultural counties was frequently replaced by a winter migration to ironworks.[10]

A study undertaken by the British government in 1842 on the employment of children in mines clearly revealed the extent of industrialization in Wales. Children were sent to the mines usually between the ages of six and ten in South Wales. Often sons would work for their fathers in the mines as assistants and turn their wages over until age seventeen or marriage. Even adult and young women worked below ground in drawing coal to the surface and above ground in screening it.[11] It is not surprising, therefore, that in a sample of 300 Welsh immigrants arriving through the Port of Philadelphia between 1820 and 1906, 50 percent listed their occupations as either miner or collier.[12]

By contrast the Irish arriving in Scranton, except for a few who had previously worked in the mines of Wales, were largely from rural, preindustrial homes. Agricultural labor predominated in most Irish counties according to the 1871 Irish census. Moreover, in the few scattered mining areas of Ireland, child labor was scarce. The 1842 commission on child employment found neither children at work below ground in Ireland nor women occupied anywhere around mines. One investigation in Kilkenny and Queen's counties reported that, after inspecting a dozen different shafts, only men were found to be employed.[13] In Kilkenny in 1871 of 6,000 boys between the ages of ten and fifteen, only 1,000 were employed at all. An even smaller proportion of females were working before age fifteen.[14] The cultural differences between the premodern Irish and the industrialized Welsh were caught by a contemporary observer in Scranton in 1877:

> The Irish are more volatile. They do not practice much domestic economy. . . . On a long strike they have generally nothing laid by for the emergency. The Irish are fond of singing, dancing, and carousing. The saloons on Lackawanna Avenue have two rooms the front one for drinking, and back for dancing and general amusement. On the contrary, dancing is generally considered a heinous sin among the Welsh.[15]

The differences between the Irish and Welsh also extended into their respective family structures.[16] Scranton's Irish were more frequently found in extended family households than the Welsh. Eighty-three percent of the Welsh households contained only nuclear families while only 71 percent of the Irish households were nuclear. Extended families, that is those including kin outside the basic nuclear unit, were also more prevalent among the Irish. Whereas a mere 3 percent of the Welsh households contained kin beside the parents and children, 14 percent of the Irish families were extended. Both the Irish and Welsh tended to keep boarders or roomers in the same proportion.

Table 21.1. **Family Structure by Ethnicity, Scranton, 1880**[a]

	Welsh Households	Irish Households
Nuclear	83%	71%
Extended	3%	14%
Augmented	14%	15%
Number of Households	277	212
Number of Individuals	1,413	1,189

[a] A nuclear household was defined as one containing only a mother, father, and their children. An extended household included other kin outside the basic nuclear family unit. An augmented household contained boarders, roomers, or servants. In a few cases households were both augmented and extended. The figures are from the U.S. Census, 1880, manuscript schedules for Scranton.

The distribution of family structures in Scranton, moreover, was not vastly different from that found among immigrants in other urban centers. In London in 1851, for instance, 79 percent of all Irish households were nuclear, a slightly higher figure than for Scranton. In Patterson, New Jersey, in 1880, 73 percent of the Irish households were nuclear and nearly 74 percent of the British households. In the mining town of Shenandoah, Pennsylvania, in the same year, 73 percent of the Irish households sampled were nuclear.[17]

In London, Patterson, Shenandoah, and Scranton between 12 and 15 percent of all Irish households contained extended families. This consistency revealed even more gradually the unusually low amount of Welsh extended families in Scranton. As will become clearer throughout this essay, the Welsh nuclear family, thoroughly imbued in industrial ways, was a smoothly functioning economic unit by 1880.[18]

If Parsons's or Ariès's theory of the role of the family in preparing children for industrial society is to have any validity, differences should occur in the adaptation of youth from various family structures to Scranton's social milieu. Occupational and geographical mobility provide important indications of the degree of adaptation. Children reared in nuclear family situations, if Parsons's view is correct, should show higher upward mobility rates and lower geographical mobility (that is less transiency and more residential stability). On the other hand, if Ariès and Sennett are correct, sons reared in extended family situations should move up the occupational scale to a greater extent than those raised in "isolated" nuclear homes.

In Scranton occupational and geographical mobility was measured by taking all sons from the Irish and Welsh families under scrutiny and tracing their careers over a ten-year period from 1880 to 1890. Sons, who were first identified and categorized in the 1880 manuscript census, were then traced in Scranton city directories[19] for 1890 to determine any occupational shifts, and whether or not they still lived in the city. The sample of young men was traced by family structure and by ethnicity.

At first glance the data contained in Table 21.3 suggest that Parsons was correct. Irish and Welsh sons, when traced collectively, tended to experience more occupational mobility if they were raised in nuclear families. Only 20 percent of the Irish and Welsh sons

Table 21.2. **Family Structure in Selected Cities[a]**

	Welsh Scranton 1880	Irish Scranton 1880	Irish Shenandoah 1880	Irish Patterson 1880	British Patterson 1880	Irish London 1851
Nuclear	83%	71%	73%	73.1%	73.9%	79.38%
Extended	3%	14%	15%	13.6%	13.5%	12.35%
Augmented	14%	15%	12%	15.3%	14.6%	—

[a] Source: U.S. Census, 1880 for Scranton and Shenandoah. For Patterson see Herbert Gutman, "Work, Culture, and Society in Industrializing America, 1815–1919," *American Historical Review,* LXXVIII (June, 1973), 562. The London data can be found in Lynn Lees, "Patterns of Lower-Class Life; Irish Slum Communities" in *Nineteenth Century Cities,* ed. by Stephan Thernstrom and Richard Sennett (New Haven, 1969), 378.

Table 21.3. **Upward Mobility from Unskilled and Semiskilled Ranks by Family Structure: Irish and Welsh Sons, Scranton, 1880–1890[a]**

Family Structure	Number 1880	Persisting 1890	Upwardly Mobile
Nuclear	320	58%	34%
Extended	103	51%	20%

[a] Mobility is often computed as the rate of advancement from manual to nonmanual jobs. This would be misleading in Scranton, for instance, since skilled manual occupations such as contract miners were among the highest paid of all workers. Thus upward mobility here was defined as a shift from unskilled or semiskilled manual work to skilled-manual, or nonmanual occupations. See Seymour Lipset and Reinhard Bendix, *Social Mobility in Industrial Society* (Berkeley, Calif., 1959), 104–105.

who remained in Scranton between 1880 and 1890 attained upward movement. On the other hand, 34 percent of those sons, who were reared in nuclear families and who persisted throughout the decade, advanced.

The difference in persistence rates between sons from nuclear and extended families, while not varying as much as mobility rates, is suggestive. Children from extended families were more geographically mobile and therefore, remained in Scranton less. While 58 percent of the sons of nuclear families stayed in Scranton throughout the 1880s, only 51 percent of the children from extended Irish and Welsh families did so. Sennett found similar variations between nuclear and extended families in Union Park.[20] While he attributed the higher persistence rates of the children of nuclear families to a conservative desire on their part not to venture far from their homes in search of economic opportunity, in Scranton the higher persistence rates of mobile sons from nuclear families seem to reflect a greater degree of economic stability.

Family structure, however, is not the only variable to use when computing mobility rates. Upon closer inspection, the difference in mobility rates was significantly greater when ethnicity was employed as a variable rather than family structure. Among Welsh sons who remained in Scranton between 1880 and 1890, 39 percent were upwardly mobile. Only 21 percent of all Irish sons who remained in Scranton moved upward by

Table 21.4. **Upward Mobility from Unskilled and Semiskilled Occupations by Ethnicity: Irish and Welsh Sons: Scranton, 1880–1890**

Ethnicity	Number 1880	Persisting 1890	Upward Mobile
Welsh	220	66%	39%
Irish	203	43%	21%

Table 21.5. **Upward Mobility Rates of Irish and Welsh Sons from Nuclear Families, Scranton, 1880–1890**

	Number 1880	Persistence 1890	Upwardly Mobile
Welsh	180	74%	45%
Irish	142	50%	14%

1890. Significantly, a greater proportion of Welsh sons moved upward than sons from all nuclear families regardless of ethnicity. (See Table 21.5.)

The difference in persistence rates, moreover, was vastly more dissimilar when ethnicity rather than family structure was used as a variable. While 66 percent of the more stable Welsh remained in Scranton between 1880 and 1890, only 43 percent of the Irish did. This 23 percent differential was certainly larger than the 7 percent difference in persistence rates obtained when family structure was used as a variable.

The ethnic differences in mobility rates are even more striking when compared to family structure. Among sons from Welsh nuclear families only, the upward mobility rate was 45 percent. This figure suggests that sons of Welsh nuclear families enjoyed greater success than sons from all nuclear families. The upward mobility rate for sons reared in Irish nuclear families was a mere 14 percent, certainly well below the level of Welsh nuclear children and of children from all nuclear families. (See Table 21.5.) Persistence rates for sons of Welsh nuclear families (74%) were also not only higher than those of children from Irish nuclear families (50%) but for those of children from all family structures combined.[21]

If ethnic background was a greater determinant than family structure in preparing children for industrial society in late nineteenth-century Scranton, the question remains as to what factor, peculiar to the Welsh, accounted for their greater success. Certainly the Welsh antipathy toward the Irish may have hindered Irish occupational advances somewhat in the mines where the Welsh held key positions. But the Irish did make some advances in the mines by 1890. In addition more than one-half of all occupations in Scranton were in areas besides mining where the Welsh were considerably less influential. In other words, the Irish did have opportunities outside of the mines. The answer appears to surface in a comparison of child labor rates between the Irish and the Welsh. Such an examination not only suggests the reason for the greater stability and success of the Welsh but also qualifies certain suppositions posited by Ariès and Parsons.

A recent study of the American family observed that in 1870, with the rise of the factory and the city and the weakening of religious beliefs, parents were persuaded to keep their young sheltered longer. "A little postponement could prepare them better for the struggle of life," one observer wrote. "Perhaps a job at fourteen or sixteen or eighteen was too early."[22] In late nineteenth-century Scranton such an observation would have been grossly inaccurate. Child labor was not only pervasive but also vital to the survival of many families.

Indeed, children frequently provided an essential share of the family's income. In one study conducted by the Pennsylvania Department of Internal Affairs in 1881 of 142 workers and their families, in not one instance did the earnings of the father equal the entire earnings of the rest of the family for the year. And in many instances the father's earnings accounted for less than one-fourth of the family's yearly income. One anthracite miner with five children earned $80 in 1881, yet his total family income exceeded $800.[23]

The employment of boys in and around the mines was long a part of the coal industry. Occupying positions usually as slate pickers, mule drivers, and doortenders, "boy colliers" even established themselves in the industry's folklore. The ballads of Irish youth such as "Mickey Pick-Slate" who was crushed to death at the mines or "My Handsome Miner Boy" became known throughout the anthracite fields.[24]

Parents usually encouraged their children to work and often falsified their ages to obtain employment for them. Children in return were expected to turn their wages over to their parents. Tales abound of Welsh boys (along with their father) handing their wages over to their mother who usually handled the family finances. One investigator of the region went so far as to conclude that the bond between fathers and sons was hardly more than a relation of economic convenience.[25]

Girls, too, were sent off to work at an early age, especially in Scranton's silk mills. While less than 10 percent of all girls between the ages of thirteen and sixteen were working in the state of Pennsylvania in 1904, in Scranton nearly 33 percent of the girls in this age bracket were employed and in Wilkes-Barre some 26 percent were working. In fact over 55 percent of all employees in Scranton's textile mills in 1900 were under twenty-one.[26]

Irish and Welsh families in Scranton continually sent their youth into mines, mills, and trades.[27] While over 92 percent of the children in Chicago's Union Park section were *not* employed, Scranton boys, in particular, were sent to jobs around the mines usually by age

Table 21.6. **Employment of Male Children, Scranton, 1880**[a]

Age	Working	Welsh Home or School	Number
6–10	17%	83%	66
11–15	100%	0%	49
16–20	95%	5%	99
		Irish	
6–10	9%	91%	29
11–15	67%	33%	56
16–20	90%	10%	47

[a] Source: U.S., Census, 1880.

eleven. Seventeen percent of the Welsh males and 9 percent of the Irish males were working before age ten. (See Table 21.6.)

What is even more crucial in examining the percentages of children working is the notable differences between the Irish and Welsh. It has already been noted that child labor had been considerably more widespread in Wales than in Ireland.[28] Moreover, Welsh sons demonstrated a greater measure of upward mobility and residential stability than Irish sons.[29] What, in fact, occurred was that Welsh families exposed their sons to industrial life in greater numbers and at an earlier age than the Irish. Nearly twice the proportion of Welsh males were working before age ten as Irish boys. And between the ages of eleven and fifteen, amazingly, 100 percent of all Welsh males studied were gainfully employed. Among Irish youth in this category only 67 percent were working. After age sixteen more than nine out of every ten boys were working, regardless of ethnicity.[30]

Such differentials in child labor suggest why Welsh youths were enjoying greater success than the Irish. Unlike Parsons's model of isolated children in nuclear families, the Welsh, who tended to live in nuclear families, were not separating their youth from the realities of economic life. The socialization of Welsh children included greater exposure to adult occupations, thus giving Welsh boys valuable industrial skills. While the Irish were being forced to send their children to work to a greater extent than they did in Ireland, they still had not committed themselves to such practices as totally as the Welsh. The results of keeping children home longer on the part of the Irish appeared to be placing a disadvantage on Irish youth in the competition for economic success in industrial society.

Similar results were obtained when comparing Irish and Welsh females. Three times the proportion of Welsh girls were working before age ten as Irish girls. Between ages eleven and fifteen, 86 percent of the Irish girls were still at home or in school. Among Welsh girls ages eleven to fifteen, only 70 percent were still at home. Even after age sixteen, 18 percent more Irish girls remained at home than Welsh. (See Table 21.7.)

Finally, it should be pointed out that few married women in Scranton worked outside the home. Only 4 percent of the Welsh wives and 2 percent of the Irish held outside jobs. Wives remained at home to keep house, handle budgets, bear more eage earners, and keep the family intact. Fathers and their children provided the income which kept this efficient economic system running.

The results of the Scranton data do not confirm Sennett's and Ariès's view that the

Table 21.7. **Employment of Female Children, Scranton, 1880**

Ages	Working	Welsh Home or School	Number
6–10	15%	85%	40
11–15	30%	70%	31
16–20	80%	20%	36
Irish			
6–10	5%	95%	30
11–15	14%	86%	33
16–20	62%	38%	24

nuclear family was used as a refuge from the city and thus failed to prepare children for industrial life as well as extended families. No group in Scranton lived in nuclear families more than the Welsh. Yet, their children enjoyed more occupational success than Irish children who were more likely to be reared in an extended home. Even when Irish and Welsh children were taken collectively, those from nuclear families rose to a greater degree than youths from extended households.

Such conclusions, however, do not wholly substantiate Parsons. While children from nuclear families experienced greater success, the youth in Scranton's families could not be considered "isolated" or cutoff from industrial society. The Parsonian model did not predominate in late nineteenth-century Scranton. Both Welsh and Irish youth were exposed to industrial life at an early age. The fact that the Welsh family was more willing than the Irish to share its socialization role with economic institutions made the adaptation of Welsh children to industrial society more successful. The reluctance of the Irish, not far removed from preindustrial culture, resulted in greater transiency, less occupational advancement, and, presumably, more economic difficulties in adult life.

Family structure was less influential than socialization practices. The divergent socialization exhibited by Irish and Welsh families in Scranton reflected their respective historical experiences. The Irish in Scranton were premodern people whose family life had been relatively unaffected by industrialization. While they were gradually relinquishing their children to modern economic forces, they were not nearly as disposed to do so as the Welsh. The cultural background of each of America's immigrant groups must clearly be understood before the adaptation of newcomers to urban America is fully explained.

Notes

1. See Talcott Parsons and Robert F. Bales, *Family, Socialization and Interaction Process* (New York, 1955), 33–131; Talcott Parsons, *The Social System* (London, 1952), 170–180. See also C. C. Harris, *The Family* (New York, 1969), 98ff; M. B. Sussman, "The Isolated Nuclear Family: Fact or Fiction?," *Social Problems,* VI (Spring, 1959), 333–40.

2. Phillipe Ariès, *Centuries of Childhood,* trans. by Robert Baldick (New York, 1962), 405ff.

3. Richard Sennett, *Families Against the City, Middle-Class Homes of Industrial Chicago, 1872–1890* (Cambridge, Mass., 1970), 17, 178, 183. See also Sidney M. Greenfield, "Industrialization and the Family in Sociological Theory," *American Journal of Sociology,* LXVII (Nov., 1961), 312–14.

4. John P. Gallagher, "Scranton: Industry and Politics, 1835–1885" (unpublished Ph.D. dissertation, Catholic University, 1964), 170ff; Pennsylvania, Department of Internal Affairs, *Annual Report, Part III: Industrial Statistics,* XXXVII (1909), 209–17; Robert V. Bruce, *1877: Year of Violence* (Chicago, 1970), 295–99; J. P. Shalloo, *Private Police, with Special Reference to Pennsylvania* (Philadelphia, 1933), 82–84; Stephen Graham, *With Poor Immigrants to America* (New York, 1914), 128–34; Samuel C. Logan, *A City's Danger and Defense* (Scranton, 1887).

5. United States, Congress, 47th Cong., 2nd Sess., H.R. Doc. 42, *Statistics of the Population of the United States at the Tenth Census* (Washington, D.C., 1883), 903.

6. David Craft *et al., History of Scranton, Pennsylvania* (Dayton, Ohio, 1891), 277; Pennsylvania, Department of Internal Affairs, *Annual Report of Pennsylvania Department of Internal Affairs* (Harrisburg, 1909), 209–11.

7. The population distribution can be seen by a study of the U.S. Manuscript Census, 1880 for Scranton. See also *Scranton Times,* July 2, 1966, 8; July 7, 1891, 8; United States, *Reports of the*

Immigration Commission (Washington, D.C., 1911), VI, 254; Pennsylvania, Department of Internal Affairs, *Annual Report of the Pennsylvania Department of Internal Affairs* (Harrisburg, 1909), 217. In 1910 Scranton still had over 4,000 Welsh immigrants, over 5,300 Irish immigrants, 3,000 from England, 4,000 from Germany, 3,000 from Italy, 1,000 from Hungary, and over 8,000 from "Russia" who were mostly Poles and Jews. See United States, Bureau of Census, *Thirteenth Census of the United States, Abstract of the Census with Supplement for Pennsylvania* (Washington, D.C., 1913), 652–53.

8. The occupational distribution of the heads of households in 1880 was determined from the U.S. manuscript census:

Occupational Category	Welsh	Irish
Unskilled	16%	60%
Semiskilled	33%	15%
Skilled	45%	15%
Low Nonmanual	6%	11%
High Nonmanual	0%	0%
Number	277	212

The ranking of occupational categories was determined by a ranking of wage rates. While actual wage rates often varied from colliery to colliery in mining operations, the ranking remained unchanged. For more detailed information or wage rates, see Anthracite Coal Strike Commission, *Report to the President on the Anthracite Coal Strike of May–October, 1902* (Washington, D.C., 1903), 185–86. Pennsylvania, *Annual Report of the Secretary of Internal Affairs of the Commonwealth of Pennsylvania, Part III, Industrial Statistics, IV* (1875–76), 680, gives data on the Delaware and Hudson collieries in Scranton. An example of wage rankings used in this study is provided below.

Wage Rankings	
Occupation	Wage for 10 hour day
Skilled:	
Contract Miner	$2.50
Civil Engineer	$2.50
Mine Boss	$2.25
Mechanic	$2.25
Blacksmith	$2.20
Semiskilled:	
Fireman (railroad)	$1.87
Inside Mine Laborer	$1.80
Brakeman (railroad)	$1.78
Teamster	$1.50
Unskilled:	
Mule Driver	$ .75
Slate Picker	$ .75
Dumper	$ .75
Common Labor	$ .75

9. Alan Conway, ed., *The Welsh in America, Letters from Immigrants* (Minneapolis, 1961), 16; A. H. John, *The Industrial Development of South Wales, 1750–1850* (Cardiff, 1950), 68.

10. John, *Industrial Development of South Wales,* 63, 66; Dov Friedlander, "The Spread of Urbanization in England and Wales, 1851–1951," *Population Studies,* XXIV (Fall, 1970), 423–33; W. E. Minchinton, *Industrial South Wales, 1750–1914* (New York, 1969), 19–28; A. H. Dodd, *The Industrial Revolution in North Wales* (Cardiff, 1951), 361–64; John Saville, *Rural Depopulation in England and Wales, 1851–1951* (London, 1957), 100–103.

11. *First Report of the Commissioners on the Employment of Children, Mines* (London, 1842), 20–38; *Third Report of Commission of the Employment of Children, Young Persons, and Women in Agriculture, 1867* (London, 1870), 186; J. H. Morris and L. J. Williams, *The South Wales Coal Industry, 1841–1875* (Cardiff, 1958), 211–36; Eli Ginzberg, *Grass on the Slag Heaps: The Story of the Welsh Miners* (New York, 1942), 2–8.

12. The sample was compiled from passenger ship lists for the port of Philadelphia at the State

Library of Pennsylvania, Harrisburg. Most Welsh sampled arrived between 1845 and 1860. See also, Rowland Tappan Berthoff, *British Immigrants in Industrial America, 1790–1950* (New York, 1968), 48–49; David Jones, *Memorial Volume of Welsh Congregationalists in Pennsylvania* (Utica, 1934), 19–34, 44–45; W. S. Shepperson, *British Emigration to North America* (Minneapolis, 1957), 83.

13. *First Report of the Commissioners on Employment of Children, Mines*, 23, 36–37.

14. *Census of Ireland, 1871 Part I: Area, Houses, and Population, I: Province of Leinster* (Dublin, 1872–73), 360–81; Arnold Schrier, *Ireland and the American Immigration, 1850–1900* (New York, 1970), 72; Stephen Byrne, *Irish Emigration to the United States* (New York, 1873), 26–27.

15. P. E. Gibbons, "The Miners of Scranton," *Harper's New Monthly Magazine*, LV (November, 1877), 916–27; Herbert Gutman, "Work, Culture, and Society in Industrializing America, 1815–1919," *American Historical Review*, LXXVIII (June, 1973), 544ff.

16. Ariès, *Centuries of Childhood*, 405–15; Rudy R. Seward, "The Colonial Family in America: Toward a Socio-Historical Restoration of Its Structure," *Journal of Marriage and the Family*, XXXV (February, 1973), 58–70; Peter Laslett, *The World We Have Lost* (New York, 1965); John Demos, *A Little Commonwealth, Family Life in Plymouth Colony* (New York, 1970).

17. See table 21.2.

18. For a view that assesses family behavior in terms of a system rather than simply in terms of individuals see Walter R. Grove *et al.*, "The Family Life Cycle: Internal Dynamics and Social Consequences," *Sociology and Social Research*, LVII (January, 1973), 182–95.

19. *Williams' Scranton Directory*, 1890.

20. Sennett, *Families Against the City*, 180–83.

21. *Ibid.*

22. Oscar Handlin and Mary Handlin, *Facing Life: Youth and the Family in American History* (Boston, 1971), 150.

23. Pennsylvania, *Annual Report of the Pennsylvania Department of Internal Affairs, Part III: Industrial Statistics*, IV (1875–76), 830, X (1881–82), 76–80.

24. George Korson, *Minstrels of the Mine Patch, Songs and Stories of the Anthracite Industry* (Hatboro, Pa., 1964), 97–99. See also "A Miner's Story," *The Independent*, LIV (September, 1902), 1407–1410; Peter Roberts, *Anthracite Coal Communities* (New York, 1904), 24.

25. Owen R. Lovejoy, "Child Labor and Family Disintegration," *The Independent*, LXI (September, 1906), 750; Lovejoy, "The Extent of Child Labor in the Anthracite Coal Industry," *Annals of the American Academy of Political and Social Science*, XXIX (1907), 35–49; Pennsylvania, *Annual Report of the Pennsylvania Department of Internal Affairs* (1886), 46–47; Gibbons, "Miners of Scranton," 920. The needs of the family as a motive for sending children to work in the coal regions are discussed more fully in U.S., Dept. of Labor, *Child Labor and the Welfare of Children in an Anthracite Coal-Mining District* (Washington, D.C., 1922), 27–29. By the turn of the century it was estimated that nearly one-sixth of the employees in anthracite were children, including 19,000 slate pickers. See Francis H. Nichols, "Children of the Coal Shadow," *McClure's*, XX (February, 1902–03), 435–44.

26. Peter Roberts, "The Employment of Girls in Textile Industries of Pennsylvania," *Annals of American Academy of Political and Social Science*, XXIII (May, 1904), 435–37; Valerie K. Oppenheimer, "The Interaction of Demand and Supply and Its Effect on the Female Labor Force in the United States," *Population Studies*, XXI (November, 1967), 240; A. M. Maclean, "Life in the Pennsylvania Coal Fields, with Particular Reference to Women," *American Journal of Sociology*, IV (April, 1909), 335–36; Pennsylvania, *Annual Report of the Pennsylvania Department of Internal Affairs, Part III: Industrial Statistics*, XXII (1894), 152–59; Pennsylvania, Department of Labor and Industry, Bureau of Women and Children, *A History of Child Labor Legislation in Pennsylvania* (Harrisburg, 1928).

27. Sennett, *Families Against the City*, 90. A decade later Polish children in Scranton contributed substantially to the immigrant family income. *The Report on Condition of Women and Child Wage Earners in the United States, IV: The Silk Industry*, 61 Cong., 2nd Sess., Senate Doc. #645 (19 vols.; Washington, D.C., 1911), IV, studies over 800 immigrant families in Scranton and Wilkes-Barre. A representative sample of Polish families drawn from the report indicated the importance of child labor in family income.

Selected Polish Families Total Income for year, 1910	% Earned by Father	% Earned by Children
$ 459	91%	9%
544	70%	30%
920	69%	31%
557	83%	17%
973	56%	44%
599	90%	10%
740	88%	12%
801	52%	48%
798	64%	36%
785	57%	43%
1,150	50%	50%
1,062	75%	25%
1,082	59%	41%
861	42%	58%
632	35%	65%
Average $ 798	65%	35%

28. In sampling two Irish counties in 1871, child labor rates were considerably lower than found in Scranton. In 1871 in County Kilkenny 16 percent of all males and 10 percent of all females between ages ten and fifteen were gainfully employed. In the County of Carlow 17 percent of the males and 11 percent of the females between ages ten and fifteen were employed. See *Census of Ireland* 1871, 24–36, 360–81. For Wales see A. M. Carr-Saunders and D. Caradog Jones, *A Survey of the Social Structure of England and Wales* (London, 1927), 55–63.

29. Pennsylvania, Department of Labor and Industry, *A History of Child Labor Legislation*, 21. In 1880 only 13 percent of all children ages ten and fifteen were employed in the entire state of Pennsylvania.

30. Percentages were computed from the Manuscript Census, 1880 for Scranton. Most women did not marry until their late twenties, although Welsh girls tended to marry earlier than the more sheltered Irish:

	Ages of Married Women Scranton, 1880				
	21–25	26–30	31–35	36–40	Number
Welsh	17%	27%	22%	35%	160
Irish	10%	30%	36%	23%	110

22. Act Your Age: Boyhood, Adolescence, and the Rise of the Boy Scouts of America

The search for order and social control is a pervasive theme in recent writing on the Progressive era. Although bureaucratic and professional structures reshaped middle-class life, historians tend to assume that the most blatant social control was directed against the lower class.[1] But another imperfectly assimilated group was of equal concern to upper and middle-class adults: the rising generation of their own class. While some such adults sallied forth to impose social control upon the lower orders, others stayed inside the ramparts of the middle class and worked to keep the garrison loyal. The accepted first lines of control—family, church, and school—had enough gaps, it seemed, to need supplementing; and prominent among schemes to this end were character-building agencies. For boys, the main ones were the Boy Scouts of America and the junior department of the YMCA. Although these organizations have been neglected by historians, few Progressive-era innovations won more approbation from reformers and conservatives alike. Few won more participants either; for by 1921 the BSA had 16,910 Scoutmasters and 391,382 Scouts; YMCAs had 243,050 juniors.[2]

Loss of control was not the only adult concern; for the conditions of middle-class urban boyhood—sedentary pursuits, pervasive feminine influences, and prolonged dependency—also raised widespread fears that the boys were growing weak in physique and will power. Adding to these fears was a broad complex of middle-class anxieties about the corrupting and debilitating effects of urbanization and social change. In response to this battery of concerns, character builders proposed simultaneously to strengthen and control boys, making them manly yet keeping them dependent.

Historians have just begun to explore these themes with regard to Boy Scouting. Peter Filene and Jeffrey Hantover treat its sudden popularity as evidence of a middle-class masculinity crisis in the Progressive years: through Scoutmastership, white-collar employees could affirm their manliness. Joseph Kett considers control primary, citing boys' work agencies as manifestations of adult hostility to precocity, part of a cluster of late nineteenth-century innovations—youth groups, high school extracurricular activities, and organized college life—which preoccupied adolescents with functionless earnestness.[3]

Although Kett is right to stress the superficiality of turn-of-the-century strenuosity, adults in charge of middle-class boys felt genuinely torn between keeping them dependent and fostering manly strength. To do both seemed hard, given the traditional association of masculinity with free self-assertion; and the balance tipped towards control.

To understand how character builders tried to maintain control without sacrificing too much strength, we must be more specific than historians usually are about adult attitudes towards age differences among the young and also about the way boys grouped

David I. Macleod, "Act Your Age: Boyhood, Adolescence, and the Rise of the Boy Scouts of America," reprinted from the *Journal of Social History* 16 (1982): 3–20, by permission of the *Journal of Social History*.

themselves by age. Popular psychology and prolonged schooling had awakened Progressive-era adults to a lively concern that adolescence imperilled both adult authority and teenage strength of character. The character builders' response was to hold boys back and inculcate strengths characteristic of a more juvenile stage of development or else to see that boys went forward very, very cautiously.

This much, perhaps, we know already or at least suspect. But all too often historians writing on institutions for social control—whether asylums or schools or juvenile courts—have been content to establish, usually in the spirit of an exposé, that the self-professed reformers who set up the institution in question were bent upon controlling some hapless group of supposed beneficiaries. Historians have been much less willing or able to determine how those beneficiaries actually responded and whether the reformers' dreams of governing their behavior really came true. This article, too, begins by explaining the concerns of boys' workers and the ways in which they hoped to shape boys' lives. But then it goes on to examine the boys' reactions to Scouting and shows how in this case a massively popular and enduring project for voluntaristic social control failed to meet its originators' objectives.

Boys' workers tried to manage boys by manipulating their peer groups; but peer pressure cut two ways, causing boys to drop out as well as join. Thus Boy Scout and YMCA enrollments by age offer revealing evidence on a subject which often eludes historians of schools and other youth agencies: the reactions of young people in the mass. If large numbers participated at a given age, they must have been willing to accept continued supervision, eager to develop strength and skills, or at least satisfied with the recreation they got. But if—as happened—many dropped out by their middle teens, then clearly what adults offered them must have disappointed their expectations or affronted their sense of what self-respecting boys that age might do or submit to. Thus Scouting won preadolescent boys with its uniforms, achievement awards, and outdoor adventures. But it could not hold them long.

Boy Scouting was not the first major boys' work agency. The oldest, the Young Men's Christian Association, began in the 1850s, offering religious and social life to urban white-collar workers. Local Associations originally admitted boys of twelve or fourteen to full membership; but as young men tired of the small fry, YMCAs began in the 1870s and 1880s to form separate junior departments. Volunteers or part-time workers were in charge until about 1900, when rapid expansion led to the hiring of full-time boys' secretaries (the YMCA term for salaried staff), who ran sports, hobby clubs, and religious programs.[4]

Boy Scouting was founded in 1908 by Robert Baden-Powell, a British general and Boer War hero who set out to enliven church cadet corps with elements of army scouting and ended up by producing a complete program. Scouting freed Edwardian boys from stuffy surroundings and soothed fears that the Empire's future workers and soldiers were turning politically radical, morally degenerate, and physically soft. Echoes of Scouting's popularity soon crossed the ocean, and YMCA men supervised formation of the Boy Scouts of America in 1910. Though independent, the BSA carried over personnel and ideas from the Y. Under Chief Scout Executive James West, a lawyer whose child welfare work had won praise from Theodore Roosevelt, the BSA Americanized its rules and set age limits at twelve through eighteen. Paid executives ran a centralized bureaucracy; but the troops of boys were led by volunteer Scoutmasters, mostly young ministers, teachers, other professionals, businessmen, and clerks. Troops also had institutional sponsors, mainly churches and a few schools.[5]

"Boys' work" was a comprehensive term, encompassing not only Boy Scout and YMCA activities but also those of boys' clubs and many lesser organizations. What set YMCA and Boy Scout leaders apart from their counterparts in boys' clubs was their distinct favoritism towards older boys from good homes. Sons of business and professional men were most likely to become Scouts or YMCA juniors; those of lower-white-collar workers and skilled blue-collar workers joined less often; and sons of semiskilled or unskilled workers tended to stay away.[6] Like all boys' workers, YMCA and Scout leaders hoped to get boys off the streets and keep them busy. But they expected to do more: they saw themselves as character builders, believing that superior raw material—adolescent boys from good homes—would enable them to inculcate ideals and build the social reliability and all-around strength called for in the American Boy Scout oath: "1. To do my duty to God and my country, and to obey the scout law; 2. To help other people at all times; 3. To keep myself physically strong, mentally awake, and morally straight."[7] Theodore Roosevelt, the BSA's Chief Scout Citizen, epitomized the character builders' ideal of moralistic energy and forceful conventionality.

As every textbook writer knows, America underwent huge changes in the half century after the Civil War, changes which alarmed people whose moral and social frame of reference was the farm or small town and which ultimately spurred character builders to try to rebuild old strengths and virtues. As cities mushroomed, contemporaries lamented the steady drain of young people off the farms. In the evening light of nostalgia, rural communities appeared innocent, homogeneous places to grow up, whereas cities glared in the darkness of popular imagining as hellish centers of luxury and misery, where feverish debauch followed hectic work. To panicky observers, cities and their immigrant slums were like metastasizing cancers.[8]

Meanwhile, the nature of work—traditionally central to masculine identity and the building of character—was changing. Farming declined and urban work, with its shorter days and faster pace, did not offer the same safe, steady preoccupation for men and boys; instead, moralists feared, it fostered nervousness and drove men to vice. Though white-collar jobs proliferated, large corporations and other bureaucratic structures compelled a growing segment of the middle class to accept lifelong paid employment instead of manly independence.[9]

These social changes troubled character builders, boding enfeeblement and loss of social control. Ernest Thompson Seton, the famed nature writer who was the BSA's Chief Scout from 1910 to 1915, wrote that farmboys had once been "strong, self-reliant," yet "respectful to . . . superiors [and] obedient to . . . parents." But the rise of industry and growth of spectator sports had turned boys into "flat-chested cigarette smokers with shaky nerves and doubtful vitality. . . ." Luther Gulick, a specialist in physical education who revitalized YMCA boys' work in the 1890s and later helped found the Boy Scouts of America and the Camp Fire Girls, portrayed the urban middle class as unable to outbreed newcomers to the city and "pained to find that their children have less power and less vitality" than they themselves.[10] Without toughening, their sons would be outnumbered and undercut by immigrants.

Underlying Gulick's alarm was widespread fear of race suicide; the best people, in their own imaginings, faced submergence by inferior but hardier and more prolific immigrant stock. More generally, middle-class men feared loss of masculinity in an age of salaried dependence, soft living, and changing sex roles. To have women colleagues threatened the pride of male clerks and teachers; and women's rights undercut the simple equation of manliness with power.[11]

A popular anodyne was to fantasize escape into an energetic, all-male world, through western novels, sports, or camping out. Scouting's outdoor program led some clerks, teachers, and clergymen to become Scoutmasters to prove their masculinity.[12] But Scouting's tamed adventure appealed more directly to youngish boys; and for them it was sponsored fantasy to hold them in place.

In dealing with boys, after all, control remained basic. Freed of farm labor, urban boys were becoming an unsupervised leisure class. The BSA's James West spoke for most boys' workers when he complained that schools turned boys loose in midafternoon and that parental surveillance was weak. In small cities and towns, where Boy Scouting recruited best, the problem still looked manageable; but boys loitered about the streets and stables, and the growth of big cities in size and cultural hegemony made urban vices seem near enough. Parents needed little incitement to scent contagion and welcomed supervised recreation. Ideally, Scout leaders tried to root boys in a cohesive middle-class community. Locally, they set up supervisory councils of prominent men and tied boys to churches and schools through sponsored troops. Nationally, the BSA worked for conformity through citizenship training and insistent Americanism.[13]

It remains to explain why character builders focussed their response to social change exclusively on boys twelve through eighteen. Obviously, the socioeconomic situation of teenagers had changed. In the mid-1800s, farming and commerce gave many teenage boys employment, including promising white-collar jobs. Working long hours and living with parents, these boys remained under sustained adult surveillance. But as farming ceased to expand and industrial and commercial technology changed, full-time jobs for the early and middle teens dried up and those that remained led nowhere. High school enrollments rose from 110,000 in 1880 to 2,200,000 in 1920, as demand for educational credentials compelled ambitious teenagers to stay in school. Middle-class adults realized they must hold boys in check well past fourteen, the usual minimum age for entering high school but also for quitting school. Middle-class boys generally stayed on but were often bored and restless. Since high school extracurricular activities were still limited in the 1910s and grammar schools had next to none, character builders saw a need for programs to keep schoolboys safely occupied.[14]

Yet character builders worried that prolonged dependency exposed boys to effeminizing influences. They agreed that boys should stay under female control until age twelve, but then must begin to break free. As teenage boys ceased to work alongside men, however, women succeeded by default to the task of continuing supervision. Even in high schools, a majority of teachers were women, and character builders complained that schools geared their routine to the sedentary inclinations of girls. Sunday schools were worse, they charged. And when boys came home after school, father was away pursuing his career. Troubled by the conflict between dependency and vigor and by the guilty knowledge that men often ignored boys, character builders regarded home and mother with traces of misogyny. Edgar M. Robinson, a leader in YMCA boys' work, railed against "the boy who has been . . . so carefully wrapped up in the 'pink cotton wool' of an overindulgent home [that] he is more effeminate than his sister. . . ."[15] More constructively, character builders devised supervised, strenuous, sex-segregated recreation to keep boys dependent but energetic.

This dual concern was pronounced among Protestant churchmen, whose churches were embarrassingly short of males. Mid-nineteenth-century remedies had centered on winning young men; but as Sunday schools became the churches' main recruiting grounds, concern shifted towards a younger group. Young people's societies sprang up in the 1880s to accommodate church members too young for adult prayer meetings, but boys shunned the societies' dull gatherings. By 1900, membership was two thirds female and two thirds over age eighteen; and boys' workers attacked the societies as effeminate. Meanwhile, experience accumulated that Sunday schools lost three quarters or more of their boys between twelve and eighteen. So concern gravitated towards the early teens, where the exodus began.[16] To clergymen worried that the "boy problem" reflected their own or the church's lack of virility, muscular Christianity was a godsend; an enthusiast advised colleagues each to master "one athletic game so as to beat all the boys in the parish at it." Ministers adopted Boy Scouting with alacrity, comprising 29 percent of all Scoutmasters in 1912. More than half of all early troops were church-sponsored.[17]

Physical changes drew further attention to the early and middle teens; for at fifteen the average American boy of 1920 was more than two inches taller and fifteen pounds heavier than his counterpart of 1880. (Younger and older boys grew less.) In addition, the median age of pubescence declined—to about fourteen in the 1910s. Had character builders simply wanted stronger boys, they should have rejoiced, but fears for control made them apprehensive of boys who seemed outsized and oversexed. The BSA's James West said the "most difficult" ages were fourteen and fifteen.[18]

Dismay at physical and social changes among teenagers converged in hatred of precocity, an antipathy common among educated Americans.[19] Threatening loss of control and moral and physical degeneracy, precocity subsumed whatever moralists decried in urban youth: debility, nervousness, independence, and above all sexuality.

It is well known that respectable Victorian opinion condemned sexual indulgence; the Christian gentleman was "continuously testing his manliness in the fire of self-denial." So, too, was the Christian boy, for the belief was well established that masturbation entailed penalties ranging from debility to madness. Though less alarmist, the Boy Scout *Handbook* warned boys against loss of "the sex fluid . . . that makes a boy manly, strong, and noble."[20] Purity, in this view, was power—and thus essential if big business and mass immigration were eroding opportunity. *Scouting* magazine warned that a Scout must grow up "free from every blemish and stain—then and only then will he be fully equipped to . . . fight the battles of business life." Yet YMCA secretaries judged masturbation nearly universal among middle-class boys.[21] And character builders regarded coeducational high schools as hotbeds of precocity. H.W. Gibson, a leading YMCA boys' worker who wrote frequently for Boy Scout publications, blamed "unnatural, hot-house forcing," especially overpressure in the schools, "for the highly nervous and sexually passionate adolescents. . . ." According to Norman Richardson, an educator and Scout commissioner who taught a course in Scouting at Boston University, certain high schools rivalled "Sodom or Babylon" because sedentary schoolwork had replaced physical labor.[22]

The word adolescent—seldom used before the 1890s—gave character builders' worries a name. They got it from the famed psychologist G. Stanley Hall, who posited that growing children recapitulate human history, progressing upward as instincts implanted in past culture epochs emerge in sequence. In Hall's view, the boy from eight to twelve was an individualistic replica of an early pigmy. Then, after a massive infusion of new instincts, the adolescent emerged—similar to men of medieval times, imaginative, emotional, capable of idealism and altruism, but not fully mature. Echoing both antebellum expectations of teenage conversion and Victorian alarm at youthful sexuality, Hall depicted adolescence as promising yet dangerous. "The dawn of puberty . . . is soon followed by a stormy period," he warned, "when the very worst and best impulses in the human soul struggle against each other. . . ." His ideas rationalized hatred of precocity: since failure to assimilate new instincts meant "retrogression, degeneracy, or fall," adolescents must patiently live out their instincts and sublimate sexual drives into altruism and religious faith.[23]

Hall's hyperbolic portrait of adolescent *bouleversement* made it logical to concentrate character building then, when all was in flux and susceptibility to moral and religious idealism was at its peak. Yet many character builders thought the threat of adolescence outweighed the promise. Hall's picture of storm and stress confirmed fears that teenage boys—even those from good homes—were hard to control and liable to enfeebling degeneracy. Since character builders had no wish to hurry boys into danger, many looked to boyhood, which was implicitly preadolescent, as a safer model for the teens.

Two traditions were involved. One was the cloistered life of the English public schoolboy, which underlay Baden-Powell's conception of Scouting. Although older schoolboys wielded great power within their little world, they were kept basically dependent until their late teens. Such prolonged segregation from adult affairs charmed American observers; and as prep schools multiplied towards 1900, Americans shaped their own version of the schoolboy life.[24]

The home-grown tradition of American boyhood referred by the late 1800s to small-town lads aged six or eight to twelve or fourteen who foraged through the woods and frolicked at the swimming hole. Rural boyhood offered, it seemed, a moratorium during which boys could let off steam without threatening adults. Books on this sort of boyhood were popular, exploiting nostalgia for antebellum country life. The "real boy" in such tales played in an all-male world invaded only rarely by fussy mothers and timid girls; brimming with vigor, he was pure because he was energetic—and vice versa. Charles Dudley Warner claimed: "Every boy who is good for anything is a natural savage." In American stereotyping, Indians were violent but seldom lascivious; so too were preadolescent boys. Indeed, writers caught up in the turn-of-the-century celebration of energy lauded the boyish scrapes of famous men and professed to prefer boys with "life enough to get into mischief. . . ."[25]

To vigor and basic decency, writers of the early 1900s added virtues for an urban age, emphasizing the group context of boyhood and its amenability to adult control. Researchers inspired by Hall reported that boys from ten or twelve to fourteen, fifteen, or sixteen had an instinct to form gangs or tribes. Referring synonymously to "Boyhood or the Gang period," boys' workers concluded that the secret of control was to form artificial gangs or take over existing ones and rule through boy leaders. Chief Scout Seton compared this technique, formalized in Scouting's patrol system, to Britain's imperial policy of governing tribes through their chiefs.[26]

Interest in gangs reflected Progressive-era enthusiasm for cooperation and social concern. As service became a middle-class catchword and men went to work in large organizations, character builders looked to gang experience to teach boys rudimentary altruism and social conformity without compromising their masculinity. "Out among his peers God intends that he shall go," proclaimed William Byron Forbush, a student of Hall's and a leading writer on boys' work, "to give and take, to mitigate his own selfishness and to gain the masculine standpoint which his mother, his nurse, and his school-teacher cannot give. . . ."[27]

Conveniently, the gang age overlapped the years which Hall assigned to early adolescence, forming a bridge from childish individualism to adolescent altruism. Yet character builders held to Hall's belief that dramatic adolescent changes began about age twelve. They expected middle-class boys to be under fairly close adult control until that age, but then to be potentially troublesome. Accordingly, acting under YMCA influence, the BSA's organizers barred boys under twelve, lest they limit Scouting's "effectiveness in dealing with adolescent problems."[28] Even so, Scouting's answer to these problems was to encourage the boyish characteristics of gang-age boys and discourage the adolescent. In effect, the gang age carried aspects of small boyhood over into the early teens; by prolonging this sort of boyhood through the middle teens, Scout leaders hoped to give adolescent boys a refuge from female-infested, precocity-inducing situations.

YMCA boys' work and recapitulation-based theories of character building took root together. In the late 1890s, Luther Gulick, who had studied with Hall, enunciated a rationale for boys' work as the answer to adolescent problems. Under Edgar M. Robinson, who headed YMCA boys' work from 1900 to 1920, Hall's and Gulick's ideas became an ideology justifying rapid expansion of junior departments. Local YMCAs hired boys' work specialists who looked to knowledge of adolescence as their basis for professional status; the age range for juniors rose from ten to sixteen in the 1880s to twelve to eighteen after 1900; and membership grew rapidly.[29]

To serve this new constituency, boys' secretaries tried to arrange a supervised adolescence in which crises were mild and age brought measured doses of recognition and authority. They sought "decisions for Christian living" from the boys and enrolled more than a third in Bible classes. But conversion was not to be convulsive; it was the first of many "forward steps": join the church; do committee work; give up some bad habit.[30] Y men fought masturbation with purity talks and readings, but recognized the older boys' interest in girls and held occasional ladies' nights, urging respect for future wives and mothers. They also raised the problem of vocational choice, though their advice was undramatic: stay in school. Lest older boys chafe at dependency, secretaries portioned out authority to boys' cabinets and held other boys' conferences. By sponsoring an attenuated adolescence, in short, YMCA men tried to innoculate boys against adolescent turbulence, impurity, and independent-mindedness.[31]

At the same time, Y workers sought to prolong boyish vigor and work off sexual or other forms of energy, but in ways that older boys would accept. Special interest clubs adapted to boys' changing hobbies and summer camps satisfied any lingering "savage" instincts. But sports and gymnastics were the key to pleasing older boys; for team sports were fashionable in high schools by the 1910s, and basketball, the leading YMCA sport, was distinctly a high school boy's game.[32]

Whereas Y men tried to combine adolescent idealism with boyish activism, the BSA's answer to adolescent problems was simpler: extend boyhood and distract boys from adolescence. Baden-Powell had originally designed Scouting for boys as young as ten. In applying his program to boys twelve through eighteen, American Boy Scout leaders opted for delay and "preoccupation" as the remedy for adolescence. Chief Scout Executive James West said that Scouting "takes the boy . . . when he is beset with the new and bewildering experiences of adolescence and diverts his thoughts therefrom to wholesome and worthwhile activities." Fear of adolescent brooding led a camp committee to warn that during "the moody hours of twilight" Scouts were prone to "great thoughts" and must be kept busy. And Boy Scout officials shared the common belief that vigorous exercise would "short circuit" sexual impulses.[33]

Boyish activism suffused Scouting. The better troops hiked often and camped in summer. Good Scoutmasters packed the weekly meetings with instruction, drills, and games. And the heart of the official program was a hierarchy of awards to tap the schoolboy's gold star mania, building strength and skills and filling leisure time. To reach first class rank, boys passed tests on woodcraft, reconnaissance, and civic service skills; then they could earn specialized merit badges and amass 21 to become Eagle Scouts. Since promotion became the main criterion of success, Boy Scouts faced pressure to keep busy.[34]

Meanwhile, Boy Scout leaders skirted adolescent issues. A few merit badges explored vocations, but most were for hobbyists; and Scouting's woodcraft emphasis pointed away from careers. In order to please all faiths, the BSA left religious instruction to the churches; most Scoutmasters dodged the purity issue; and moral education came down to memorizing the Boy Scout Oath and Law, a chore which some Scouts skimped.[35] Boy Scout leaders made a serious effort to teach altruism through individual and group good turns. But rather than risk the passionate enthusiasm and unsettling introspection predicted by Hall, they reduced adolescent idealism to a commitment to conventional morality.

Basically, Scouting systematized patterns typical of youngish boys. Although new team sports were displacing older pastimes towards 1900, small boys still roamed the woods. In Cleveland in the 1910s, for instance, 45 percent of elementary schoolboys said they went hiking. But tastes changed as boys grew older: fewer hiked and more played baseball, basketball, and football. An 1896 study of Massachusetts schoolboys found that interest in hide-and-seek held steady until age thirteen and then fell off, whereas interest in ball games kept rising. And small-town high school boys, surveyed in the 1920s, almost all named a team sport among their favorite recreations, while only a third mentioned swimming and a fifth said hiking or camping. By 1920, team sports played a major role in boys' lives, one that increased with age; the highly publicized example of high school, college, and professional athletics was more than woodcraft and camping could match. Scouting had its own games, but they resembled those like hide-and-seek that small boys played. Though Boy Scouts importuned for the new team sports, BSA headquarters discouraged Scoutmasters from giving in, lest they compromise Scouting's uniqueness.[36] In effect, the BSA maintained a juvenile, somewhat old-fashioned form of boyhood.

To combat enfeeblement and bolster boyish pride, the BSA cultivated an air of determined masculinity, symbolized by awards for heroism, service alongside police at parades, and a uniform like the U.S. Army's. Women were barred even from supervisory committees. So it was no surprise that the BSA's Chief Scout Executive disliked the Girl Scouts and pressed them to change their name and program. West preferred the Camp Fire Girls, whose name suggested a stronger orientation towards hearth and home. As for the boys, some feared being called sissies if girls could also be Scouts. Young Boy Scouts wanted to avoid girls altogether; older ones would happily have met socially but sometimes balked at service projects on which they and Girl Scouts worked as equals.

Still, Girl Scouting troubled Boy Scout leaders more than it did the boys.[37] The leaders were trying to curb the boys' thoughts of independence while compensating them with a simulacrum of manliness. Scouting for girls unbalanced the trade-off.

How did boys react to Boy Scout and YMCA strategies? One need not accept the premise—fashionable in studying oppressed or neglected groups—that "youth makes its own history" to recognize that boys held a crude veto over character builders' plans, since they could always quit.[38] If revisionist historians of education have sometimes overstated its power for social control by confusing intentions with results, there is no reason to do so in the case of boys' work.

We must also realize that masculinity was not the same issue for boys as for men. Boys saw manhood at least as much in terms of age as sex role; they wanted the status, amusements, and autonomy they associated with growing older. When asked why boys left Sunday school, most boys replied that those of fifteen to twenty were "too old"; Sunday school was "kiddish." Far fewer said it was "only for girls." Even in relations with Girl Scouts, age was at issue, since girls could join at ten and that made Scouting seem juvenile, not just unmasculine.[39]

For boys turning twelve, the Scout program of woodcraft backed by badges was enticing: just to attend evening meetings was a step towards independence, while summer camp promised the first week ever away from mother. So young boys flocked to join; two thirds of all new Boy Scouts in the 1920s were twelve or thirteen.[40]

Yet runaway success with gang-age boys created problems, making it almost impossible to keep underage boys out and older ones in. Scoutmasters often admitted boys under twelve. Southerners claimed their boys matured faster; others simply found boys of ten or eleven eager to join and easy to lead.[41] But older Boy Scouts felt demeaned, as extended graded schooling, by herding students the same age into the same classroom, had made them very sensitive to age differences. The YMCA's E. M. Robinson considered three years the maximum age span for a cohesive group of boys. Since few Boy Scout troops were divided by age, most suffered from the Gresham's Law of boys' work: younger boys drive out the older ones. A dropout explained: "[W]e got a bunch of little kids in the troop and they wanted to be with us all of the time and we wanted to be by ourselves. And I guess we wanted to do different things."[42]

Baden-Powell's solution was to give older boys responsibility as patrol leaders; but the number of such offices was limited. Besides, Americans lacked the English faith in social hierarchy and would not give boys much authority. American Scoutmasters used simulated gangs as a thin disguise for direct control, reducing patrol leaders to monitors and seldom letting patrols hike or camp alone.[43]

Underlying American losses of older Boy Scouts was enormous annual turnover in membership. From 1915 to 1925, 47 to 65 percent of each year's Boy Scouts did not reregister the next year. The problem was not unique to Boy Scouting, for YMCA persistence rates were equally low; but since the BSA recruited mainly boys of twelve or thirteen, rapid turnover made for a shortage of Boy Scouts past fourteen or fifteen. The median age of quitting was 14.5 in 1921, and 78 percent left before reaching sixteen.[44] Current Scouts, of course, were younger still.

Boy Scouts quit for many reasons. Although some found badge work an exciting challenge—in 1921, one in 600 reached Eagle Scout and the proportion was rising—many showed little interest in promotion. At any given time, a majority were tenderfeet, the lowest rank. Boys who did not advance commonly dropped out; and BSA headquarters blamed Scoutmasters for not inspiring them to ambition. But some Boy Scouts found signaling and first aid dull, clamoring instead for sports and "fun."[45] The outdoor program appealed best to youngish boys. In fact, age predicted length of membership just as well as rank: the older a Boy Scout joined, the sooner he quit. Dropouts blamed accumulating dissatisfactions and distractions. In one survey, 25 percent mentioned the lure of sports, social life, or other duties; 14 percent each blamed poor leaders or the collapse of their troop; 12 percent said they got bored; 7 percent cited conflict with younger boys; and 28 percent gave other reasons.[46] Not all these motives were age-related, but many gained in force as boys grew older.

Scouting's symbolism caused problems too. The very term *Boy* Scout gave offense. E. P. Hulse, a BSA publicist, warned: "Kids of 15 down South when called 'boy' used to retort, 'If I'm a boy where did Jackson and Lee get their men?' " The uniform, which looked manly to twelve-year-olds, struck older boys as childish; and in high schools with R.O.T.C., girls ostracized Boy Scouts as juvenile imitators. Yet adults delighted in the uniform's juvenility; Frank Gray, a New Jersey Boy Scout executive, condemned "the boy who wants to dress up like a man" and urged Scoutmasters to "see that the boy is living a boy's life. . . ."[47]

The few older Boy Scouts from immigrant families faced added constraints. Just to walk their streets in uniform invited mockery or fights. And some Scout leaders—though not all—treated boys of immigrant stock as more juvenile than others the same age, making less effort to apply the patrol system and suspecting—in the words of a Scoutmaster at the Chicago Commons settlement house—that the full Scout program was "too hard and comprehensive for our Italian boys."[48]

At best, efforts to recruit and retain older boys came up against increased restiveness about age fourteen or fifteen. Of 47 Boy Scouts whom *Scouting* magazine advertised as runaways from home in the late 1910s, 8 were fourteen-year-olds and fully 19 were fifteen-year-olds, whereas just 1 was twelve and 3 were thirteen. These were extreme cases, to be sure, but ordinary boys also grew impatient around fourteen or fifteen; and part-time jobs, high school life, and girls began to compete for their time. Boy Scouts who quit school usually left Scouting as well, seeking autonomy or simply lacking free time. High school boys came under pressure to concentrate on sports and study.[49] They also met girls who looked on Boy Scouts as "little kids"—and by high school age, they cared. Yet Boy Scout leaders often regarded the "girl-struck boy" with distaste and discussed the "girl problem" in pathological terms, wondering how to cure boys "infected" with "girlitis."[50]

Clearly, Y men catered more to older boys, since they provided lots of sports, prescribed no uniforms, divided boys by age, and sought out high school and white collar working boys. By 1920, most YMCAs had a separate group for clerks and office boys; and Hi-Y clubs spread through the high schools. Because YMCA juniors were freer than Boy Scouts to choose their own activities—often paying fees separately for what they chose—older boys could pick what interested them. Most juniors signed up for gymnastics and sports (78 percent in 1920). They dodged vocational training, but otherwise showed an interest when Y men addressed adolescent problems. Although only one junior in fifteen professed conversion, large attendance at meetings for moral improvement, vocational choice, and religious decision-making suggested that boys wanted to assuage worries with some form of resolution. Some even found open condemnation of masturbation a relief.[51]

Evidence that adolescents responded favorably when adults addressed their problems and interests—as YMCA workers did—can be seen in the age difference between Boy Scouts and YMCA juniors. In the 1910s, a quarter of the YMCA boys held jobs; and by 1921, two fifths were high school students; whereas most Boy Scouts were still in grade school. In 1922, Trenton, New Jersey, had twice as many Boy Scouts as YMCA members among grammar school and junior high pupils, but nearly four times as many Y boys as Boy Scouts among senior high students. On average, Boy Scouts were younger than YMCA boys. A survey of rural and suburban counties in the early 1920s found a median age for Boy Scouts of 14.3, compared to 15.5 for YMCA juniors. Nationwide, the Boy Scouts' median age in 1919 was 13.8 and fewer than ten percent were sixteen or older. Fifteen years later, the median remained almost unchanged at 13.9, although 16.5 percent were sixteen or above. By contrast, the median age of YMCA juniors was about 15.0 and many were in their middle or later teens.[52]

In summary, the YMCA had fewer boys than Scouting, but a larger share of those who did enroll were adolescents, that is, well into their middle or late teens. The BSA enlisted many more boys of twelve and thirteen, but could not attract or hold many boys more than a year or two past the average age of male pubescence, then about fourteen. Even Sunday schools had more boys in their late teens.[53] So if Boy Scout leaders hoped to strengthen and control boys by extending boyhood and distracting them from adolescence, such hopes often went unfulfilled. To prolong the latency period by a controlled, somewhat contrived promotion of masculine vigor and activism proved harder than Boy Scouting's American organizers had foreseen.

Enrollments by age suggest limits, therefore, to adult success at voluntaristic social control; for the tug of war across the generations ended near a draw. The YMCA held older boys by adapting at least partially to their wishes, while the BSA won its triumphs with boys twelve or fourteen, a bit older than the age at which growing boys first clamored to join, but definitely younger than the BSA's early leaders would have preferred. Scouting appealed vividly to group tastes—in a sense, the peer culture—of boys ten to thirteen or fourteen. But by denying older boys the tokens of maturity and the fee-for-service autonomy of the YMCA, Scouting branded itself too juvenile for boys in their middle teens; and except for a few hardy souls devoted to the outdoors or Scout badge work, it lost them.

The pattern of Boy Scout attrition may seem familiar today. So may adult ambivalence towards adolescence and preference for the latency period, which have survived not only the collapse of Hall's theoretical underpinnings but also claims by scholars that adolescent upheaval is less dramatic or prevalent than Hall believed. But in this regard the 1900s and 1910s *should* seem somewhat familiar. For we cannot encompass the history of twentieth-century teenagers simply by saying that they have grown more restive and sophisticated. That may well be true; and adult anxiety may likewise have risen as adult authority has weakened. But concern about adolescents was sharp and increasingly explicit in the decades around 1900; and many of our would-be agencies of control date from that era. Furthermore, many of those institutions were—as agencies of control—partial failures from the start. I have concentrated upon middle-class boys' work, but one might make a similar argument regarding street boys' clubs, juvenile courts, perhaps even high schools.[54]

As schooling engulfed teenagers, they looked to recreation for self-assertion and some limited autonomy. Teenage boys had definite tastes and a jealous regard for status marks of increasing maturity, however factitious these became.[55] This does not mean there was a full-blown, self-conscious youth culture among middle-class teenage boys of the 1910s, though their removal from the mainstream of economic life met one precondition for the rise of modern youth cultures. By holding implicitly to certain roles for each age and sex they were forerunners of a sort, but not forerunners of a single youth culture. They were internally divided—as young people are to this day. Historians interested in masculine and feminine sex roles and in the changing context of adolescence must not forget that the young have not seen masculinity or youth whole; especially since the early 1900s, they have subdivided each condition by age as well as gender and social class and have acted in terms of those finer gradations.[56] To control them, adults have had to accede in part to their desires.

Such an adaptation to the tastes of different age groups eventually reshaped boys' work. In the 1920s, YMCA secretaries relaxed their preoccupation with adolescence and set up groups of Friendly Indians for boys under twelve. More reluctantly, American Boy Scout officials began Cubbing (the early term for Cub Scouting) for boys nine through eleven in 1930 and lowered the minimum age for Boy Scouts to eleven in 1949. Only in the late 1940s, though, with Explorer Scouting, did the BSA provide separate groups for older boys and emphasize accepted needs of adolescence such as vocational guidance and a social life with girls. Boys could join at fourteen or remain regular Scouts.[57]

The results suggest at first glance that the boys' downward pressure on age triumphed; for Cub Scouting mushroomed, while Explorer Scouting grew more slowly. Yet Scouting for older boys kept pace sufficiently that the ratio of Boy Scouts and Explorers fourteen and older to those aged twelve and thirteen changed little over the years. Furthermore, the proportion of American boys aged fourteen through seventeen enrolled in Scouting rose from 4 percent in 1919 to 9 percent in 1967. Since this increase reflected declining farm population, better organization by the BSA, creation of the Explorer program, and somewhat better recruitment among racial and ethnic minorities, it did not prove that traditional Scouting had grown more attractive to older boys. But neither did it show the movement losing ground.[58] Age patterns established early in the century proved remarkably stable.

With programs differentiated by age, the BSA eventually enrolled crowds of preadolescents. An observer might see in this a downward extension of institutionalized adolescence; but the basic Boy Scout program, though originally promoted in America in response to concern about middle-class adolescence, was only marginally adolescent in design and practice. Boys under age twelve had *always* wanted to join, and most left by fifteen or so. In recreation they set their own timetable; and efforts to alter that timetable work about as well today as in the 1910s.

Notes

1. E.g., Robert H. Wiebe, *The Search for Order, 1877–1920* (New York, 1967); Jerry Israel, ed., *Building the Organizational Society: Essays on Associational Activities in Modern America* (New York, 1972); Don S. Kirschner, "The Ambiguous Legacy: Social Justice and Social Control in the

Progressive Era," *Historical Reflections* 2 (1975): 69–88; Paul Boyer, *Urban Masses and Moral Order in America, 1820–1920* (Cambridge, Mass., 1978).

2. Boy Scouts of America, *Twelfth Annual Report . . . May 1, 1922,* H. Doc. 296, 67th Cong., 2d sess., 1922, p. 103; Young Men's Christian Associations of North America, *Year Book for the Year May 1, 1920 to April 30, 1921* (New York, 1921), 217, 232. Hereafter BSA; YMCA, *Year Book.*

3. Peter Gabriel Filene, *Him/Her/Self. Sex Roles in Modern America* (New York, 1975), 105–7; Jeffrey P. Hantover, "The Boy Scouts and the Validation of Masculinity," *Journal of Social Issues* 34 (1978): 184–195; Joseph F. Kett, "Curing the Disease of Precocity," in John Demos and Sarane Spence Boocock, eds., *Turning Points: Historical and Sociological Essays on the Family* (Chicago, 1978), 203–4; Joseph F. Kett, *Rites of Passage: Adolescence in America, 1790 to the Present* (New York, 1977), 173–211.

4. Howard Hopkins, *History of the Y.M.C.A. in North America* (New York, 1951); Edgar M. Robinson, *The Early Years: The Beginnings of Work with Boys in the Y.M.C.A.* (New York, 1950); David Macleod, "A Live Vaccine: The YMCA and Male Adolescence in the United States and Canada, 1870–1920," *Histoire sociale-Social History* 11 (1978): 5–25.

5. John Springhall, *Youth, Empire and Society: British Youth Movements 1883–1940* (London, 1977), 53–70. For an account of Boy Scouting's origins and early institutional history in America, see my *Building Character in the American Boy: The Boy Scouts, YMCA, and Their Forerunners, 1870–1920* (Madison, Wis., 1983).

6. Jeffrey P. Hantover, "Sex Role, Sexuality, and Social Status: The Early Years of the Boy Scouts of America" (Ph.D. diss., Chicago, 1976), 170, 182; "Survey Shows Value of Boy Scout Work," unidentified clipping, Aug. 1918, Charles Deere Velie Papers, Minnesota Historical Society, St. Paul; David Snedden, "New Light on the Scouts," *Work with Boys* 17 (1917): 258–59; "Classes of Working Boys," *Association Boys* 9 (1910): 252–56, 265–68.

7. BSA, *The Official Handbook for Boys* (Garden City, 1911), 14.

8. See, e.g., R. Richard Wohl, "The 'Country Boy' Myth and Its Place in American Urban Culture: The Nineteenth-Century Contribution," *Perspectives in American History* 3 (1969): 77–156; Boyer, *Urban Masses,* 65 and passim.

9. Daniel T. Rodgers, *The Work Ethic in Industrial America, 1850–1920* (Chicago, 1978), 1–39; Hantover, "Boy Scouts," 185–88; Filene, *Him/Her/Self,* 79–82; James R. McGovern, "David Graham Phillips and the Virility Impulse of Progressives," *New England Quarterly* 39 (1966): 352.

10. Ernest Thompson Seton, "The Boy Scouts in America," *Outlook* 95 (1910): 630; Luther Gulick, "Studies of Adolescent Boyhood," *Association Boys* 1 (1902): 149–150. See also R.S.S. Baden-Powell, *Scouting for Boys: A Handbook for Instruction in Good Citizenship,* rev. ed. (London, 1909), 192–95, 287–291.

11. David M. Kennedy, *Birth Control in America: The Career of Margaret Sanger* (New Haven, 1970), 42–45; Filene, *Him/Her/Self,* 77, 85–86; Hantover, "Boy Scouts," 188; McGovern, "Virility Impulse," 344–355.

12. Filene, *Him/Her/Self,* 105–7; Hantover, "Sex Role," 237–247. But cf. David R. Porter, "The Boys' Work Secretaryship," *Association Boys* 8 (1909): 51, for a suggestion that some men felt demeaned by working with boys instead of men.

13. See Henry S. Curtis, "The Boy Scouts the Salvation of the Village Boy," *Pedagogical Seminary* 20 (1913): 78–85; Clyde Brion Davis, *The Age of Indiscretion* (Philadelphia, 1950), 60; James West, "Scouting as an Educational Asset," in National Educational Association, *Addresses and Proceedings* 54 (1916): 1012; idem, "Training Young America for Citizenship" (speech, n.d.), in West File, BSA, National Headquarters, North Brunswick, N.J. Hereafter BSA, NHQ. In cities over 25,000 in 1920, there was an inverse correlation between city size and the ratio of Boy Scouts and YMCA juniors to boys aged 10–14 ($r = -.43$ and $-.48$ respectively). The BSA did even better in smaller places, but not in the open countryside.

14. Kett, *Rites,* 144–172; John Modell et al., "Social Change and Transitions to Adulthood in Historical Perspective," *Journal of Family History* 1 (1976): 7–32; Selwyn Troen, "The Discovery of the Adolescent by American Educational Reformers, 1900–1920: An Economic Perspective," in Lawrence Stone, ed., *Schooling and Society: Studies in the History of Education* (Baltimore, 1976), 239–251; Galen Jones, *Extra-Curricular Activities in Relation to the Curriculum* (New York, 1935),

1, 20–21; George E. Johnson, *Education Through Recreation* (Cleveland, 1916), 29, 34; U.S. Bureau of the Census, *Historical Statistics of the United States, Colonial Times to 1970* (Washington, 1975), 368–69; West, "Scouting," 1012; idem, "Training."

15. "Boys as Savages," *Association Boys* 1 (1902): 129. See idem, "The Adolescent Boy in the Sunday School," ibid. 10 (1911): 39–57; William Byron Forbush, *The Boy Problem*, rev. ed. (Boston, 1907), 33, 177; John L. Alexander, ed., *Boy Training: An Interpretation of the Principles that Underlie Symmetrical Boy Development* (New York, 1912), 111–133; H.W. Gibson, *Boyology, or Boy Analysis* (New York, 1918), 216–19; *Statistical Abstract of the United States, 1922* (Washington, 1923), 105.

16. See Ann Douglas, *The Feminization of American Culture* (New York, 1977); Ozora S. Davis, "The Endeavor Movement and the Boy," *How to Help Boys* 2 (Jan. 1902): 60; William Byron Forbush, "A Preliminary Study of the Condition and Needs of Societies of Christian Endeavor," *Work with Boys* 4 (1904): 114–125; Walter S. Athearn et al., *The Religious Education of Protestants in an American Commonwealth* (New York, 1923), 209–212; *Boys' Brigade Bulletin* 1 (Nov. 15, 1892), 7; Eugene C. Foster, *The Boy and the Church* (Philadelphia, 1909), 9; H.N. Morse and Edmund deS. Brunner, *The Town and Country Church in the United States* (New York, 1923), 164. On average, girls stayed longer in Sunday school.

17. Rev. H. A. Jump, letter in *Work with Boys* 6 (1906): 207. See Forbush, *Boy Problem*, passim; BSA, *Third Annual Report* (New York, 1913), 19.

18. BSA, *Official Report of the Third Biennial Conference of Scout Masters and Executives* (New York, 1924), 195. A compilation of studies shows that average height and weight at age 15 rose about 5½ inches and 33 pounds from 1880 to 1960, but only 3.75 inches and 13 pounds at age 10 and 1¼ inches and 16 pounds at age 20. My interpolation for 1920 draws on specific studies and is conservative. Howard V. Meredith, "Change in the Stature and Body Weight of North American Boys During the Last 80 Years," in Lewis P. Lipsitt and Charles Spiker, eds., *Advances in Child Development and Behavior,* Vol. 1 (New York, 1963), 70–114. On ages at puberty, see C. Ward Crampton, "Anatomical or Physiological Age Versus Chronological Age," *Pedagogical Seminary* 15 (1908): 230–34; Bird T. Baldwin, "A Measuring Scale for Physical Growth and Physiological Age," in National Society for the Study of Education, *Yearbook* 15; part I (1916): 11–16. On trends, see J. M. Tanner, *Growth at Adolescence,* 2nd ed. (Oxford, 1962), 153; Rolf E. Muuss, "Adolescent Development and the Secular Trend," *Adolescence* 5 (1970): 270–73. The belief that the age of puberty has declined rests mainly on reports of girls' ages at menarche. Vern L. Bullough, "Age at Menarche: A Misunderstanding," *Science* 213 (1981): 365–66, argues convincingly that Tanner has exaggerated the nineteenth-century decline in menarcheal ages.

19. Kett, "Precocity," 184.

20. Charles E. Rosenberg, "Sexuality, Class and Role in 19th-Century America," *American Quarterly* 25 (1973): 139; BSA, *Handbook,* 232. See also R.P. Neuman, "Masturbation, Madness, and the Modern Concepts of Childhood and Adolescence," *Journal of Social History* 8 (1975): 1–27.

21. "The Father's Duty to a Scout," *Scouting* 1 (Jan. 15, 1914): 5; Luther Gulick, "Sex and Religion," *Association Outlook* 7 (1898): 197–201.

22. Gibson, *Boyology,* 25; Norman E. Richardson and Ormond E. Loomis, *The Boy Scout Movement Applied by the Church* (New York, 1915), 123.

23. G. Stanley Hall, *Youth: Its Education, Regimen and Hygiene* (New York, 1906), 135; idem, *Adolescence: Its Psychology and Its Relations to Physiology, Anthropology, Sociology, Sex, Crime, Religion and Education* (New York, 1904), II, 72. See ibid., ix–xv and passim; John and Virginia Demos, "Adolescence in Historical Perspective," *Journal of Marriage and the Family* 31 (1969): 634–35; Kett, *Rites,* 221; Dorothy Ross, *G. Stanley Hall: The Psychologist as Prophet* (Chicago, 1972), 328–330.

24. See F. Musgrove, *Youth and the Social Order* (Bloomington, 1965), 56; Guy Lewis, "The Muscular Christianity Movement," *Journal of Health, Physical Education, Recreation* 37 (May 1966): 27. The men who most closely supervised Boy Scouting's transit to America in 1910 were E. M. Robinson, a Canadian; Ernest Thompson Seton, a British immigrant via Canada; and John L. Alexander, a Scots immigrant who wrote much of the early BSA handbooks.

25. Henry A. Shute, *The Real Diary of a Real Boy* (Boston, 1902); Charles Dudley Warner, *Being a Boy* (Boston, 1878), 198–99; Richardson and Loomis, *Scout Movement,* 208. See also Winthrop Jordan, *White Over Black: American Attitudes towards the Negro, 1550–1812* (Baltimore,

1969), 162–63; John H. Johnson, "The Savagery of Boyhood," *Popular Science Monthly* 31 (1887): 798; W. D. Howells, *A Boy's Town* (New York, 1890); E. T. Seton to W. I. Talbot, Apr. 12, 1905, Ernest Thompson Seton Papers, Seton Memorial Museum, Cimarron, New Mexico; Henry R. Sparapani, "The American Boy-Book: 1865–1915" (Ph.D. diss., Indiana, 1971), 1–34. An admirer traced Admiral Dewey's career from hooking apples to seizing the Philippines. "The Hero of Manila," *Leslie's Weekly* 86 (1898): 335.

26. BSA, *Handbook for Scout Masters* (New York, 1914), 107; Seton, "Boy Scouts," 631. On enthusiasm for gangs, see T. J. Browne, "The Clan or Gang Instinct in Boys," *Association Outlook* 9 (1900): 223–274; J. A. Puffer, "Boy Gangs and Boy Leaders," *McClure's* 37 (1911): 678; George Walter Fiske, *Boy Life and Self-government* (New York, 1912), 109, 150–166; Joseph Lee, *Play in Education* (New York, 1915), 350–379; Steven L. Schlossman, "G. Stanley Hall and the Boys' Club: Conservative Applications of Recapitulation Theory," *Journal of the History of the Behavioral Sciences* 9 (1973): 142–46; Dominick Cavallo, *Muscles and Morals: Organized Playgrounds and Urban Reform* (Philadelphia, 1981), 90–92.

27. Forbush, *Boy Problem,* 23. See also Theodore P. Green, *America's Heroes: The Changing Models of Success in American Magazines* (New York, 1970).

28. BSA, *Handbook for Scout Masters,* 28. See Luther Gulick, "Boys' Work Necessary," *Association Outlook* 8 (1899): 162. Overriding concern about adolescence was typical only of American character builders who concentrated on middle-class boys. Boys' club workers, by contrast, tried to keep lower-class boys of all ages out of trouble. Club memberships averaged 50% to 60% age 12 and under; and club spokesmen criticized the YMCA and BSA for neglecting preteenagers. For his part, Baden-Powell thought the English of all ages were degenerating; he sought young, malleable boys, initially as young as 10 or even 9. Through Forbush and other writers, he knew something of gang theories and American boys' work; but he gave no special heed to puberty and adolescence, though he loathed masturbation. American Boy Scout leaders criticized British Scouting for filling up with preadolescents. Thomas W. Chew, "The Boys' Club Viewpoint," *Association Boys* 3 (1904): 70–71; William R. Taylor, "Character-Making in the Brick Church Institute," *Work with Boys* 7 (1907): 112; *Darkest Chicago and Her Waifs,* n.v. (Jan. 1911): 20, in Chicago Boys' Club Papers, Chicago Historical Society; Baden-Powell, *Scouting for Boys,* 30, 196–97; S. A. Moffat, "Memorandum to Mr. West Regarding Boy Scout Movement in England" [c. 1914], Daniel Carter Beard Papers, Library of Congress; BSA, *Official Report of the Second Biennial Conference of Scout Executives* (New York, 1923), 366.

29. Macleod, "Live Vaccine," 12–15.

30. YMCA, *Year Book* (1921), 217; editorial note, *Association Boys* 8 (1909): 96.

31. H. Parker Lansdale, "A Historical Study of YMCA Boys' Work in the United States, 1900–1925" (Ph.D. diss., Yale, 1956); Macleod, "Live Vaccine," 16–19.

32. Jones, *Extra-Curricular Activities,* 12–29; Joel H. Spring, "Mass Culture and School Sports," *History of Education Quarterly* 14 (1974): 494; Johnson, *Education,* 57.

33. BSA, *Handbook for Scout Masters,* 73; James West, untitled speech, n.d., in West File, BSA, NHQ; Queens Council, N.Y., BSA, Report of the Camp Committee, 1919, in Beard Papers; Richardson and Loomis, *Scout Movement,* 215.

34. "Conference of Scout Masters, Feb. 2–3, 1917" (transcript at BSA, NHQ), 55–68; "Troop Meeting Programs," *Scouting* 7 (Aug. 21, 1919): 3–5.

35. "The Boy Scout Movement at Its Best," *American Youth* 3 (1914): 29; "National Conference of Scout Masters and Executives, Sept. 15–22, 1920" (transcript at BSA, NHQ), 510–537; H. Paul Douglass, *How Shall Country Youth Be Served? A Study of the "Rural" Work of Certain National Character-Building Agencies* (New York, 1926), 152–53.

36. Johnson, *Education,* 39, 51–73; T.R. Croswell, "Amusements of Worcester School Children," *Pedagogical Seminary* 6 (1899): 229–230; Edmund deS. Brunner et al., *American Agricultural Villages* (New York, 1927), 215; James West to Sidney Sigler, n.d., under Athletics in "Correspondence about Policies" (scrapbook at BSA, NHQ); "Conference . . . 1917," 298–99; Henry D. Shelton, "The Institutional Activities of American Children," *American Journal of Psychology* 9 (1898): 429.

37. William D. Murray, *The History of the Boy Scouts of America* (New York, 1937), 101–137; "The Resolutions," *Scouting* 8 (Apr. 22, 1920): 21; BSA, *Second Biennial Conference,* 354–363; Charles E. Strickland, "Juliette Low, the Girl Scouts and the Role of American Women" (paper at

Conference on the History of Women, St. Paul, Minn., Oct. 1977); Mary Aickin Rothschild, "A Girl Is to Guide: The Boy Scout-Girl Scout Controversy" (paper read to the History of Education Society, Chicago, Oct. 1978).

38. John R. Gillis, *Youth and History: Tradition and Change in European Age Relations, 1770–Present* (New York, 1974), ix.

39. Gibson, *Boyology,* 225; BSA, *Second Biennial Conference,* 363.

40. BSA, *Seventeenth Annual Report,* 1926, H. Doc. 93, 70th Cong., 1st sess., 1928, p. 171; "National Conference . . . 1920," 461.

41. H. E. Montague to James West, Apr. 22, 1911, in "Committee on Standardization" (scrapbook at BSA, NHQ), "Conference of Executive Officers, May 17–18, 1916" (transcript at BSA, NHQ), 303–314. See also B. F. Skinner, *Particulars of My Life* (New York, 1976), 86–89.

42. Emory S. Bogardus, *The City Boy and His Problems: A Survey of Boy Life in Los Angeles* (Los Angeles, 1926), 116; Edgar M. Robinson, "Age Grouping of Younger Association Members," *Association Boys* 1 (1902): 35. Because British Scouting openly admitted young boys, more than 70 percent of English Boy Scouts in the late 1910s were under age 14. P. Jacques Sevin, *Le Scoutisme,* 3ᵉ ed. (Paris, 1933), 158–59.

43. "Conference . . . 1916," 23–36; BSA, *Third Biennial Conference,* 179–194. American school prefects also had less authority than English. James McLachlan, *American Boarding Schools: A Historical Study* (New York, 1970), 281.

44. Bear in mind that these ages are for *quitting.* See BSA, *Report of the Commission on Scout Mortality and Turnover* (New York, 1922), 8; editorial notes, *American Youth* 16 (Feb. 1917): 6; 19 (Mar. 1920): 22; BSA, *Annual Reports.*

45. "What Are the Answers?" *Scouting* 4 (Aug. 1, 1916): 5; "A First Aid Criticism," ibid. 6 (June 15, 1918): 11. Tenderfeet: 1917—65%; 1925—54%; second class: 1917—23%; 1925—26%; first class: 1917—12%; 1925—20%. BSA, *Eleventh Annual Report,* 1920, S. Doc. 180, 67th Cong., 2nd sess., 1922, p. 44; BSA, *Sixteenth Annual Report,* 1925, H. Doc. 431, 69th Cong., 1st sess., 1926, p. 178.

46. This 1921 survey polled 707 boys. BSA, *Scout Mortality,* 20. See also BSA, *Third Biennial Conference,* 95–96; Mark M. Jones, *Report on a Survey of the Boy Scouts of America* (New York, 1927), 10, 25, 27.

47. E. P. Hulse to Daniel C. Beard, Feb. 7, 1920, Beard Papers; "Conference . . . 1917," 311. See also BSA, *Second Biennial Conference,* 189; "Why I Joined the Boy Scouts of America," *Scouting* 5 (July 15, 1917): 4.

48. Klaas Oosterhuis, report of Scout troop 24, July 15, 1924, Chicago Commons Papers, Chicago Historical Society. See also BSA, "Annual Meeting, 1915" (transcript at BSA, NHQ), 57; BSA, *Third Biennial Conference,* 191–93.

49. *Scouting,* 3–7 (May 1915–Dec. 1919). See "The Ranger," ibid. 6 (Sept. 1, 1918): 6; "Conference . . . 1917," 176–194, 298–301. Of 577 Indian Boy Scouts surveyed in 1920, just 15 percent had jobs; 4 percent had quit school. Athearn, *Religious Education,* 232.

50. Quotations: E. B. DeGroot, in BSA, *Second Biennial Conference,* 189; BSA, *Handbook for Scout Masters,* 106; Bogardus, *City Boy,* 114; "Retaining the Interest of the Older Scout," *Scouting* 6 (Feb. 1, 1918): 14.

51. E. M. Robinson, "Was This an Accident?" *American Youth* 4 (1915): 11–14; YMCA, *Year Book* (1921), 217.

52. In 1905, the median age of YMCA juniors in Buffalo, N.Y., was 15.2 and 29.6 percent were 16 or older. G. Barrett Rich, "The Boys' Work in Buffalo," *Association Boys* 4 (1905): 190. See YMCA, *Year Books* (1910–1921); Rotary Club and YMCA, *Some Salient Facts Gathered from Trenton's Boy-Life Survey* (Trenton, N.J., 1922), 9, 27; BSA, *Scout Mortality,* 16–18; Douglass, *Country Youth,* 69; Athearn, *Religious Education,* 289; Ray O. Wyland, *Scouting in the Schools: A Study of the Relationships between the Schools and the Boy Scouts of America* (New York, 1934), 71. For similar statistics, see BSA, *15th Annual Report,* 1924, H. Doc. 109, 69th Cong., 1st sess., 1926, p. 148; editorial note, *American Youth* 16 (Oct. 1917): 13.

53. Of 3,135 male pupils aged 12 through 18 in Indiana Sunday schools polled around 1920, 24.5 percent were 16 or older. Athearn, *Religious Education,* 224.

54. E.g., Frederic M. Thrasher, "The Boys' Club and Juvenile Delinquency," *American Journal of Sociology* 42 (1936): 66–80; Harold Finestone, *Victims of Change: Juvenile Delinquents in Ameri-*

can Society (Westport, 1976), 51. On views of adolescence, see Ross, *Hall,* 340. Of course, the targets of adult anxiety have shifted—from masturbation, say, to drugs—but the pattern of tension over teenage morals persists.

55. Boys and adults were at war over smoking before 1900.

56. See James S. Coleman, "Youth Culture," in idem et al., *Youth: Transition to Adulthood* (Chicago, 1974), 112–125; Herbert J. Gans, *The Levittowners: Ways of Life and Politics in a New Suburban Community* (New York, 1967), 207.

57. Will Oursler, *The Boy Scout Story* (Garden City, 1955), 176–77. By 1963, YMCAs had 556,775 boys and 180,612 girls aged 11 and younger; 234,849 boys and 96,955 girls 12 through 14; and 244,237 boys and 149,250 girls 15 through 17. YMCA, *Year Book* (1964).

25. A lingering Protestant affiliation and organizational handicaps, such as overreliance on large buildings, limited YMCA growth. YMCA boys' work never got such single-minded promotion as Boy Scouting; and it could not match Scouting's vivid, though narrow, appeal to any one age group.

58. The ratio of Boy Scouts and Explorers 14 and over to those 12 and 13 was 45 percent to 55 percent in 1919 and 43 percent to 57 percent in 1967. The median age of Boy Scouts and Explorers 12 and older in 1967 was 13.7 and 14.4 percent were 16 or older. See decennial U.S. census and BSA, *58th Annual Report,* 1967 H. Doc. 287, 90th Cong., 2d sess., 1968, p. 121. By 1974, there were 2,178,315 Cub Scouts; 1,678,003 regular Scouts; and 471,336 Explorers, a fifth of them girls (admitted since 1969). BSA, *Annual Report to Congress, 1974,* H. Doc. 94-118, 94th Cong., 1st sess., 1975, p. 4.

23. The Discovery of the Adolescent by American Educational Reformers, 1900–1920: An Economic Perspective

The first two decades of the twentieth century marked an important watershed for public education in the United States. For the first time, educators became concerned with adolescent dropouts and instituted curricular and legislative reforms designed to encourage them to remain in school and to coerce them if they hesitated. This constituted a fundamental break with the largely literary curriculum and voluntary attendance that characterized nineteenth-century education. The popularity of vocational courses and the effectiveness of new compulsory education laws caused the average duration of schooling to double between 1900 and 1920. As formal education came to have an increasingly important place in the lives of children, society placed significantly higher expectations and demands on it.[1]

Interest in teenagers became a widespread phenomenon and contributed to educational reform. Many noneducators sought to improve the social conditions affecting youth through legislative as well as educational programs. As recent scholarship has shown, the discovery of "adolescence" just before the turn of the century, primarily through the work of G. Stanley Hall, generated distinctive institutional responses to deal with the special problems of this stage of personal development. Although it is difficult to weigh the motives of educators, it is probable that psychologists and philanthropists offered additional reasons and rationales for extending and adapting educational institutions to meet the needs of the adolescent.[2] Nevertheless, this essay argues that the attention lavished on youth by educators was not so much a consequence of new psychological insights or of a newly sensitized social conscience as of a recognition of educators' responsibility to prepare future workers for a technological society. An examination of the shift in attitudes toward established patterns of school attendance at the turn of the century suggests that the primary and direct impetus for change derived from an appreciation that the urban economy had developed into a more advanced industrial phase and that, therefore, unschooled teenagers were becoming a liability to society and to themselves.

I

In the second half of the nineteenth century there was a continuum in the patterns of school attendance and a pervasive set of attitudes that sustained them. For example, an analysis of attendance in St. Louis discloses that schooling was nearly universal for

Selwyn K. Troen, "The Discovery of the Adolescent by American Educational Reformers, 1900–1920: An Economic Perspective," reprinted from *Schooling and Society: Studies in the History of Education,* ed. Lawrence Stone (Baltimore, Md.: Johns Hopkins University Press, 1976), 239–51, by permission of Johns Hopkins University Press.

children from ages eight through eleven, with an average attendance of three to four years. Children began to drop out around age twelve, so that by age sixteen less than 20 percent were still enrolled. Moreover, those who discontinued their education began their vocational careers immediately, with the exception of some girls who returned to the isolation and dependency of the home.[3]

Although their data revealed that the children of the higher occupational classes stayed in school longer, educators did not lament the failure of children of the poorer classes to remain, since even middle-class children had relatively abbreviated scholastic careers. And when the problems of elimination and retardation were systematically explored in St. Louis and elsewhere around the turn of the century, most investigators concluded that poverty was not the reason children dropped out. Rather, they faulted the curriculum for failing to sustain the attention of older students.

The figures on St. Louis are representative, for the underuse of educational opportunities was a national phenomenon. In 1898, William Harris, the United States commissioner of education, reported that of every one hundred students, ninety-five were in elementary schools, four in high schools, and one in post-secondary institutions. Harris interpreted these figures as a sign of success, for they suggested that public education was fulfilling its mandate to diffuse basic reading, writing, and computational skills. This attitude, which accurately reflected the sentiments of other educators and of the public at large, was based on the conception that the schools' prime responsibility was to impart to students the requisite tools with which to continue their education on their own after leaving school. Belief in the culture of self-help inevitably minimized the relationship between formal education and vocational preparation. Until a greater appreciation for such a relationship occurred, the curriculum was severely circumscribed—at least by present standards—and consequently, attendance was comparatively limited.[4]

What is most impressive as well as suggestive about nineteenth-century attendance is that it was voluntary. Compulsory education laws tended to confirm already existing levels of attendance rather than to bring in older students.[5] These laws, which were widely enacted outside the South in the post–Civil War period, generally stipulated twelve as the legal minimum age for terminating schooling and therefore did not result in increased attendance. Laws directed at those above that age rendered ineffective because of numerous loopholes—including easily invoked claims of poverty and literacy; meager statutory punishments, especially small fines; and the obligation of the state to prove that infractions were "willingly and knowingly committed."[6] In 1895, for example, a task force established by the state board of education in Massachusetts to investigate compliance with the law reported that parents still regarded the schooling of their children as strictly their own concern and violated the laws without fear of prosecution or fines.[7] In reviewing the efficacy of New York's 1874 legislation, the superintendent of public instruction commented: "It has failed to accomplish anything except subject itself to ridicule." The 1874 law was itself advertised as a reform of New York's fundamental compulsory education law of 1853.[8] Similarly, the Pennsylvania statutes went through periodic revisions without significant impact. The 1897 law permitted children aged thirteen to sixteen to work if they could produce a certificate attesting merely to the literacy expected of a third-grader. In fact, even these examinations were a farce, and for twenty-five cents a child could obtain the certificate enabling him to work.[9]

Child labor laws—which might have resulted in increased attendance, since they were directed at children twelve to fourteen—were also ineffective. A major shortcoming was the fact that the states invested limited resources in their enforcement. For example, Illinois's nationally respected inspector of factories and workshops, Florence Kelley, complained in 1896 that she had only twelve assistants with whom to police thousands of establishments throughout the state. In one year this corps traveled thousands of miles inspecting about 6,700 companies and more than 200,000 workers. The inspections were naturally superficial even in the places they were able to visit. The situation was only slightly better in Massachusetts, which at that time had thirty-three inspectors, and in New York, which had forty-four.[10]

Educators' lack of concern for adolescent dropouts was therefore unexceptional in a society that provided only for their most minimal protection. So long as teenagers were able to find gainful employment—and even unskilled work could be considered a necessary or valuable prelude to future advancement—there was insufficient pressure for change. Complacency was encouraged by the many vocational opportunities available in nineteenth-century cities. Children between twelve and sixteen found many openings in service occupations that required minimum skills and in laboring positions that demanded less than adult strength. Thus, large numbers were employed in factories, stores, and offices as cigar makers, messengers, cash boys or cash girls, delivery boys, stock clerks, wrappers, markers, inspectors, and the like. But the invention of cash registers, pneumatic tubes, paper-folding machines, and telephones—to suggest only the most obvious—necessarily made many of their jobs obsolete. An advancing technology had not only brought about the unemployment of legions of adolescents, but in so doing, had also undermined a basic premise of nineteenth-century education. A complete cataloguing and analysis of the consequences of technological change are beyond the scope of this paper. The examples that follow suggest the significance of the topic and the need for extended treatment.

II

Around 1900, department stores were the single largest employer of youths from ages twelve to sixteen in Chicago and among the most important in other major cities. The need of department stores for adolescent labor grew with the rapid development of these enterprises in the post–Civil War period. Although the jobs paid only about two dollars per week in the 1880s, they were desirable since they offered useful experience for future clerks and entrepreneurs. The most common position was that of cash boy or cash girl, which involved shuttling back and forth between the sales counter, cashier, and wrapping desk, carrying a basket containing the salesbook, money, and purchase. Sitting in tight-fitting uniforms on benches, these boys and girls were expected to respond immediately to the clerk's call of "Cash! Cash!" Their task was to take the money, merchandise, and sales slip from the clerk to an inspector for wrapping and checking, then rush to the departmental cashier to make change, and finally to return the package and the change to the salesclerk. The work was simple, essentially mechanical, and an easy prey to technological innovation.[11]

By the 1870s, one-third of the labor force of Macy's in New York was composed of cash girls; the same proportion worked as cash boys in the dry goods section of Marshall Field's in Chicago in the 1880s. In 1902, first Macy's and then Field's introduced the pneumatic tube, which eliminated a major portion of these employees' function. Macy's installed the most elaborate system, consisting in large fans which moved cash and slips, along with millions of cubic feet of air per hour, through eighteen miles of brass tubing to several hundred stations throughout the store. A network of horizontal and vertical conveyor belts was introduced at the same time for the movement of parcels, further reducing the need for human intermediaries.[12] Finally, the cash register, invented in 1878, had become sufficiently sophisticated by the turn of the century to further reduce need for cash boys by concentrating transactions at the counter where purchases were made.[13] Thus, the cash boys and girls who were members of a flourishing and numerous vocation in 1900 were virtually eliminated from modernizing department stores by 1905.

Although it is difficult to obtain figures for teenage office workers, it is clear that their numbers began to diminish at the same time. The growth of offices, as of department stores, in number and in size was one of the phenomena of a modernizing society. One raw indicator of this growth is the number of bookkeepers in the United States, which rose from 10,000 in 1880 to 250,000 by 1900.[14] Particularly in larger firms, managers attempted to gain greater control over operations and to cut costs by replacing personnel with newly invented machines which folded papers, addressed envelopes, affixed stamps, performed calculations, and assisted in bookkeeping. In addition, there were inventions which facilitated communications—typewriters, dictating machines, pneumatic tubes, and telephones. The result was a demand for a more highly skilled worker who was adaptable to the procedures of the modern office and capable of operating its machines. As a consequence, numerous unskilled teenage workers who ran errands in the late-nineteenth-century office were displaced by personnel trained to utilize the new apparatus.[15]

Further obstacles to workers below the age of sixteen arose in the early 1910s when disciples of Frederick Taylor applied his principles of scientific management to the office. Through the introduction of William Leffingwell's methods of "scientific selection," office workers were expected to pass psychological tests and to have acquired the kinds of skills that entailed attendance in a high school or a vocational secondary school. The application of Taylorism to the operations of the office led also to a scientific rearrangement of apparatus and personnel. The result was that in the early 1910s such companies as Curtis Publishing and Montgomery Ward, which employed hundreds of office workers, cut their staffs by half, with only the most skilled, and therefore the most schooled, remaining.[16]

The reports of factory inspectors in Illinois arond the turn of the century demonstrate that numerous other industries steadily lessened their dependence on workers under sixteen. Although the inspectors were willing to assume credit for the diminution of child labor, their reports also indicate that technology and more efficient organization produced the same end. The experience of the communications industry, as represented in telegraph and telephone companies, documents this process. In 1900, Western Union's downtown Chicago offices employed 189 boys between fourteen and sixteen, who composed 50 percent of the total work force. By 1906 there were only 64 boys, or 24 percent of all employees. During the same years, the company's total downtown work force declined from 375 to 267. These declines were precipitated by the rapid development of the telephone industry, which, requiring a higher level of skill, employed virtually no children under sixteen. As telephone wires interlaced the streets of Chicago, both the telegraph industry and the telegram delivery boys suffered, becoming casualties of technological advance.[17]

Children's jobs were especially vulnerable in industries where unskilled operations were taken over by machines. For example, in the tobacco industry many youngsters lost their jobs with the relative decline of cigars and the growth of the cigarette trade, which, beginning in the 1880s, became increasingly efficient through improvements in cigarette-making machines.[18] Occasionally, the inspectors themselves contributed to adolescent unemployment. In 1895, one inspector suggested a rearrangement of furnaces at the Illinois Glass Company in Alton, the single largest employer of children in the state, with the result that large numbers were forced out of work.[19] Indeed, so many advances were made in most types of manufacturing that Edith Abbott and Sophinisba Breckenridge, Chicago social settlement workers and leaders in the national struggle for legislation protecting children, admitted in 1917 that "the most convincing argument for the extension of child labor laws is to be found in the fact that at present there is so little demand for the labor of children under sixteen years of age that it is impossible for more than a small percentage of the children who leave school at the age of fourteen or fifteen to find employment."[20] Unlike the period before the turn of the century, leaving school after third or fourth grade was not the beginning of vocational experience or advancement; it led to unemployment.

III

Some educators had foreseen that literacy and a reliance on self-help were not adequate in a modern industrial society. Beginning in the 1870s, John Runkle, the president of M.I.T., and Calvin Woodward, a professor of engineering at Washington University in St. Louis, advocated instruction in Russian *sloyd*, a form of manual training. They established polytechnic high schools as adjuncts to their universities, with sloyd as a central feature of the curriculum. Amidst considerable debate, in which Calvin Woodward and William Harris were the leading opponents, manual training began to infiltrate the curriculum of the public schools in the 1880s.[21] It quickly gained sufficient backing so that in 1891 the National Education Association, the most important association of educators in the country, established a special unit, the Department of Industrial Education and Manual Training.

The growing acceptance of manual training marked the first step in what became a general movement to increasingly specific, industrially oriented courses. This departure from the traditional literary curriculum of the nineteenth century was directly related to an effort to retain the interest of children who ordinarily dropped out at age twelve. Woodward, in perhaps the first studies that focused on explaining why children did not attend school beyond the third or fourth grade, sought to end the complacency with which most educators viewed the massive exit of twelve- to sixteen-year-olds. For Woodward the attendance data was evidence of "a public calamity," and the departure of young teenagers from the schools was all the more lamentable since he felt it could be avoided. In his 1900 survey of major American cities, Woodward claimed that a small portion of this exit could be considered "a reasonable loss," attributable to "a certain death rate, a certain amount of pinching poverty, and a certain amount of incapacity which practically shuts out pupils." Concerned with identifying the causes for "abnormal withdrawals," he refused to grant that among most healthy and able children there was a genuine need to supplement family income as soon as possible, and labeled the claim of poverty merely an "excuse." The real reasons were that parents did not appreciate the value of more schooling and that children were bored with their classes. Sympathizing with these attitudes, he placed the ultimate blame on the schools. More specifically, he faulted neither teachers nor facilities, which he found good, but the curriculum.[22]

Woodward was not surprised that boys and girls became discontented after age twelve. Biological and psychological changes impelled them to engage in a more active life and made it difficult for them to submit to the sedentary and passive behavior demanded in the usual classroom. This was particularly true of boys, who "long to grasp things with their own hands; they burn to test the strength of materials and the magnitude of forces; to match their cunning with the cunning of nature and of practical men." Inevitably, the energies of these youths found expression in the streets or in the factory, office, and home. Manual training for boys and domestic science for girls was the answer, for these courses were "suited to their tastes." Moreover, Woodward suggested ways for assuaging the discontent of parents by showing them that schools could teach their children skills that would meet their needs as future wage earners. This, too, could be met by a new curriculum of a "more practical character" than the traditional literary one.[23]

Between 1900 and 1920, the problem of "elimination," as the phenomenon of early withdrawal was called, became the subject of numerous reports sponsored by city and state boards of education, the Russell Sage Foundation's Department of Child Hygiene, the National Committee on Vocational Education, and the United States Bureau of Education.[24] The studies generally focused on cities, although there was a widespread feeling that conditions were even worse in rural areas, where there were many pressures as well as opportunities for work and the resources for a more advanced education were limited. These studies were similar to Woodward's initial description of the problem and largely agreed with his findings as to its causes. The most comprehensive report, based on a survey of 318 cities, was produced in 1911 by George Strayer, a professor at Columbia University's Teachers College writing under the auspices of the Bureau of Education. It showed that the public schools lost one-half of their students between the ages of thirteen and fifteen. Strayer suggested that the solution was to create a differentiated curriculum that segregated the college-bound from those who would want or need to find work. He argued that "it is manifestly unfair to provide a rigid curriculum which leads straight to the college or university." To be truly democratic, the schools must offer each student "training which will best fit him for his life's work." The point of Strayer's study was to make a case for vocational training. Unlike Woodward, who had envisioned manual training as a part of a general curriculum from which all students might benefit, Strayer was typical of a current of opinion that advocated the abandonment of a common curriculum and favored the separation of youths into different tracks which assumed that large numbers of students would enter specialized vocational courses. Strayer had modified Woodward's earlier studies in another significant way. He wanted the schools to include all children, even those whom Woodward put into the category of "reasonable loss." He therefore called for special schools that would accommodate the "unusually deficient either mentally or physically," and applauded the movement to enforced compulsory education. Like most early-twentieth-century educators, Strayer joined reforms that would engender new, positive attitudes toward advanced schooling with legislative reforms that would coerce the unpersuaded.[25]

As with Woodward's studies, Strayer's was based on the assumption that more children would stay in school if the curriculum emphasized more practical studies. A large body of statistics confirmed Woodward's belief that the majority of children used poverty as an "excuse" for withdrawing from the schools. In 1910, for example, the Federal Investigation into the Condition of Woman and Child Wage-Earners offered the following analysis of "elimination":

Child's help desired though not necessary—27.9%

Child dissatisfied with school—26.6%

Child prefers to work—9.8%

Thus, about 65 percent of the children were potential students if parents and children could be persuaded that more schooling was worthwhile. Only 30 percent were in the category "Earnings necessary to family support" and 5.7 percent accounted for by "other causes," which included mental and physical problems. This commission's figure of 30 percent for children whose earnings were necessary for family support was about average, but higher than the 20 percent reported by the Public Education Association's study of New York in 1912 and the Douglas Commission's 24 percent for Massachusetts in 1906. Furthermore, investigators felt that these genuinely poor children were not necessarily lost to the schools, for they beliefed that if the value of education were sufficiently demonstrated, then poor families might be willing to make the sacrifices necessary to prolong their children's education. The net effect of these studies on educators was to convince them that with the appropriate reforms they could reach a very substantial number of youths.[26]

The necessity for doing so was buttressed by studies conducted during the 1910s on what children did upon leaving school. The most comprehensive survey, undertaken in Philadelphia, inquired into the vocations of 14,000 children. Of these, only 3 percent were in skilled positions. The same was true in surveys taken in Chicago and in Worcester, Massachusetts. These studies showed that the average wage of a child was $3.00 to $3.50, which was only one-third of that earned by adults. In addition, employment was of a temporary nature. In another series of studies conducted at the same time, it was shown that children tended to work at one job for only a few months. At Swift and Company of Chicago children worked an average of only three and a half months; in Hartford, Connecticut, they averaged two and a quarter jobs per year; and in Maryland, which compiled the best statistics, more than 50 percent of children under sixteen worked for two months or less, and 15 percent for only two weeks. Such investigations showed that children who left school, particularly for unskilled work, held a very insecure place in the job market. This meant that there was little likelihood for a steady, dependable income and—what was of great importance to educators—little opportunity to learn new skills. The career of the early dropout was marked by shiftlessness, unemployment, low skills, and low wages.[27]

Paul Douglas, a reformer and academic who later became senator from Illinois, best summed up in 1920 the work of the previous two decades. He described the experience of many children as drifting "from job to job, from industry to industry, still unskilled, and exposed to all the social and industrial evils which threaten adolescence." Typically, when the child matures to manhood, he finds that his position is vulnerable because of the incessant influx of younger unskilled workers into the labor force. The result is that he "finds himself one of the class of the permanently unskilled with the attendant low wages and unemployment of his class." As a final judgment, Douglas noted: "He had nothing to sell but his youth; he sold it, and received nothing in return." Surely, the press of family circumstances and the dissatisfaction with schooling had to be very great to sustain the willingness of tens of thousands of youths to confront these possibilities.[28]

These studies ultimately served to elaborate and make more precise a problem with which many educators around the turn of the century were concerned—the decline of apprenticeship. Woodward connected it with industrialization: "The invention of machinery and the use of costly machine tools so far modified and limited apprenticeship as to almost ruin it."[29] Manual training was his response to the problem. Most educators, however, preferred more specific vocational instruction. During the first decade of the twentieth century, a national movement of educators, businessmen, and organized labor successfully collaborated in such organizations as the National Society for the Promotion of Industrial Education and pressed for the inclusion of vocational courses in the public school curriculum. On a national level, their work resulted in the passage of the Smith-Hughes Act of 1917, which allocated federal funds for the first time on behalf of vocational training.[30]

The movement toward vocationalism is most clearly evidenced in the differences in emphasis of two influential studies commissioned by the National Education Association—the 1892 Report of the Committee of Ten, and the *Cardinal Principles of Secondary Education* of 1918. The 1892 statement, which was formulated by some of the most distinguished educators in the United States, was concerned with defining the curriculum of the high school so that there would be a better correspondence between its work and the uniform entrance requirements to which many of the nation's colleges had recently agreed. Commissioner of Education Harris, who wrote the section on the ideal high school curriculum, not surprisingly emphasized the traditional subjects of English, mathematics, geography, history, and foreign and ancient languages. There was no mention of manual training or vocational courses. Since the high school was thought of primarily as a necessary step leading to college, its courses of study was subordinated to the demands of the universities.[31] In 1918, the select committee organized by the National Education Association defined more broadly the function of the high school. Arguing that "a comprehensive reorganization of secondary education is imperative at this time," they stressed the need to readjust the curriculum to what they perceived to be a new social order by providing explicit instruction for work, leisure, home life, and citizenship. The result was the "comprehensive high school," which included a "differentiated curriculum" that was a direct repudiation of Harris's model in the Report of the Committee of Ten.[32]

The most radical departures stemmed from the committee's recognition of a public responsibility to offer specialized vocational training, for there had developed "a more complex economic order" characterized by "the substitution of the factory system for the domestic system of industry; the use of machinery in the place of manual labor; the high specialization of processes with a corresponding division of labor; and the breakdown of the apprenticeship system."[33] In the new order, the patterns of advancement and self-development that had applied in the relatively unschooled society of the nineteenth century no longer applied. By 1918, after a generation of agitation for practical studies and the evidence of numerous analyses on the problems of youth, the committee was ready to recommend that in addition to the usual literary courses, there should be agricultural, business, clerical, industrial, fine arts, and household curricula.

IV

The adoption of the *Cardinal Principles* signified less the setting of guidelines for the future than the ratification of innovations already undertaken in many urban systems and an accommodation to the preferences of teenage students. The diversification of the curriculum and the enactment of effective compulsory education legislation first affected such systems during the first decade of the twentieth century and resulted in a dramatic and immediate increase in the duration of attendance. Including in the work of the classroom that which formerly would have been acquired outside, schools became the surrogate for apprenticeship; and the movement to incorporate the adolescent and broaden the scope of instruction developed a powerful momentum. By 1910, about 90 percent of the children in the nation's five largest cities—Boston, Chicago, New York, Philadelphia, and St. Louis—were enrolled from ages seven through thirteen. By 1920, formal schooling extended to age fourteen, or a minimum of eight years of instruction, and almost 40 percent of the students continued through age sixteen (see Table 23.1). This represented a doubling of the extent of schooling that was usually attained twenty years earlier.[34]

The enlargement of the pool of students finishing the eighth grade also contributed to increased high school enrollments. While the creation of active corps of truant officers assured a large reservoir of potential students, it does not by itself explain the expansion of the high school, since compulsory attendance laws generally stopped short of forcing students to remain in school past the eighth grade. The major stimuli for the growth of the high school were probably the diminution of satisfactory work opportunities for teenagers and the attractiveness of the new courses. Whereas perceptions of vocational opportunities cannot be measured, the impact of the new curricula can be tested through the experience of individual systems.[35]

In St. Louis—which may be taken as representative of large, innovating urban systems—the high school population increased fivefold between 1800 and 1920. While

Table 23.1. **Percentage of Children Ages 5–20 Attending School in Boston, Chicago, New York, Philadelphia, and St. Louis, 1910 and 1920**

Age	1910	1920	Age	1910	1920
5	—	33.7	13	94.6	95.6
6	55.6	75.9	14	80.1	89.1
7	86.9	89.9	15	56.6	68.2
8	91.6	92.6	16	34.8	38.9
9	93.0	93.5	17	17.9	23.5
10	95.9	95.6	18	13.7	14.6
11	96.0	96.1	19	9.5	10.1
12	95.6	96.2	20	6.0	6.8

Sources: *Thirteenth Census of the United States, 1910*, 1: 1157–59; *Fourteenth Census of the United States, 1920*, 2: 1131–36.

some of this growth is explained by an expanding population, the real significance of this increase is that proportionately more students were continuing on in the higher grades. Only 3 percent of the total day population of students went on to high school in 1900; 7 percent were enrolled in 1910; and 11 percent in 1920. Further refinement of the schools' statistics shows that between 1900 and 1920 there was an important shift directly related to the new offerings in the distribution of the student body. Analysis of the programs pursued by senior class students reveals a decline in the popularity of classical and scientific courses, the mainstay of the old curriculum, and increased enrollment in the new programs—particularly in general studies, manual training, and the commercial course—which by 1920 attracted 77 percent of the students. The figures indicate that the appeal of the general and vocational courses, which were not necessarily related to college entrance, was very great, and that the curriculum of the previous decades had lost the interest of all but a minority of students.[36]

With the creation of innovative programs it became essential to advertise the new options and explain their values. Thus, vocational guidance followed almost immediately upon the introduction of vocational training. The initiation of such services also satisfied the contention of Woodward and other critics that early withdrawal would be diminished and attendance be improved if students and parents were informed of the kinds of skills necessary for success in an industrial society and of how schools could satisfy those requirements. Between 1900 and 1910, individual systems and state education boards established guidance departments which surveyed the local job market, suggested the kinds of courses necessary to fill local needs, and tried to persuade students to avail themselves of new opportunities. The close relationship between vocational training and vocational guidance was also evident on a national level. Shortly after the establishment in 1907 of the National Society for the Promotion of Industrial Training, members of that group called for a new association, which resulted in the organization in 1915 of the National Vocational Guidance Association.[37]

The schools were decisively transformed by the introduction of vocationally related programs. In order to meet the challenges of a changing economy, they assumed unprecedented responsibilities for the preparation of the young and became an intermediary between the emerging labor force and employers. The complementary strategies of an emphasis on practical instruction and effective compulsory attendance laws successfully overcame the relatively limiting definition of common schooling that had been championed by nineteenth-century educators. The crisis over adolescent attendance and its resolution had produced a far more broadly defined and socially engaged concept of schooling which marked a significant departure in the history of American education.

Notes

1. Basic studies in the development of secondary and vocational education include Edward A. Krug, *The Shaping of the American High School*, vol. 1, *1880–1920* (New York: Harper and Row, 1964) and vol. 2, *1920–1941* (Madison: University of Wisconsin Press, 1972); Marvin Lazerson, *Origins of the Urban School: Public Education in Massachusetts, 1870–1915* (Cambridge: Harvard University Press, 1971); and Joel Spring, *Education and the Rise of the Corporate State* (Boston: Beacon Press, 1972). The impact of curricular and legislative reforms on school attendance in a major city can be found in Selwyn K. Troen, "Defining Educational Change through Patterns of

School Attendance: The Case of St. Louis, 1850–1920" (Paper delivered at the Joint Meeting of the National History of Education Society and the Midwest History of Education Society, Chicago, 26 October 1973).

2. Dorothy Ross, *G. Stanley Hall: The Psychologist as Prophet* (Chicago: University of Chicago Press, 1972); John Demos and Virginia Demos, "Adolescence in Historical Perspective," *Journal of Marriage and the Family* 31 (1969): 632–33; Anthony M. Platt, *The Child Savers: The Invention of Delinquency* (Chicago: University of Chicago Press, 1969); and Joseph F. Kett, "Adolescence and Youth," in *The Family in History: Interdisciplinary Essays,* eds. Theodore Rabb and Robert Rotberg (New York: Harper and Row, 1971), pp. 95–110.

3. Selwyn K. Troen, "Popular Education in Nineteenth-Century St. Louis," *History of Education Quarterly* 13 (1973): 23–40.

4. William T. Harris, "Elementary Education," in *Education in the United States,* ed. Nicholas M. Butler (New York: American Book Company, 1900), pp. 79–94.

5. William Landes and Lewis Solmon, "Compulsory Schooling Legislation: An Economic Analysis of Law and Social Change in the Nineteenth Century," *Journal of Economic History* 32 (1972): 54–89; Moses Stambler, "The Effect of Compulsory Education and Child Labor Laws on High School Attendance in New York City, 1898–1917," *History of Education Quarterly* 7 (1968): 189–214.

6. Forest C. Ensign, *Compulsory School Attendance and Child Labor* (Iowa City: The Athens Press, 1921), pp. 231–51.

7. Ibid., p. 70.

8. Ibid., p. 121.

9. Ibid., p. 184.

10. *Fourth Annual Report of the Factory Inspectors of Illinois for the Year Ending December 15, 1896* (Springfield, Ill., 1897), p. 3.

11. Robert W. Twyman, *History of Marshall Field and Company, 1852–1906* (Philadelphia: University of Pennsylvania Press, 1954), p. 71; Ralph M. Hower, *History of Macy's of New York, 1858–1919* (Cambridge: Harvard University Press, 1943), pp. 196–98, 452–53.

12. Twyman, *Marshall Field,* p. 200; Hower, *Macy's,* pp. 324–25.

13. Isaac F. Marcosson, *Wherever Men Trade: The Romance of the Cash Register* (New York: Dodd, Mead, 1945), pp. 9, 164–68.

14. William H. Leffingwell, *Office Management: Principles and Practices* (Chicago: A. W. Shaw, 1925), pp. 824–33.

15. Leffingwell, *Office Management,* pp. 434–68.

16. William H. Leffingwell, *Scientific Office Management* (Chicago: A. W. Shaw, 1917), pp. 3–7. A survey conducted in eighteen cities during the 1930s demonstrates in typical job descriptions and requirements the extent to which technological advance had eliminated children under sixteen and those without schooling. See Dorothea de Schweintz, *Occupations in Retail Stores: A Study Sponsored by the National Vocational Guidance Association and the United States Employment Service* (Scranton, Pa.: International Textbook Co., 1937).

17. *Eighth Annual Report of the Factory Inspectors of Illinois for the Year Ending December 15, 1900* (Springfield, Ill., 1901), pp. 171–172; *Fourteenth Annual Report of the Factory Inspectors of Illinois for the Year Ending December 15, 1906* (Springfield, Ill., 1908), pp. 653–55. The figures are based on the records of the Chicago Telephone Company and Western Union, which were the largest in their respective industries. The same pattern held true for the smaller companies.

18. In Chicago, of total employees, the percentage of children under sixteen declined from 14.7 percent to 1.1 percent between 1896 and 1906 (*Fourth Annual Report,* p. 107; *Fourteenth Annual Report,* p. xxiv).

19. *Third Annual Report of the Factory Inspectors of Illinois for the Year Ending December 15, 1895* (Springfield, Ill., 1896), pp. 14–18.

20. Edith Abbott and Sophinisba P. Breckenridge, *Truancy and Non-Attendance in the Chicago Schools: A Study of the Social Aspects of the Compulsory Education and Child Labor Legislation of Illinois* (Chicago: University of Chicago Press, 1917), p. 324.

21. Berenice M. Fisher, *Industrial Education: American Ideals and Institutions* (Madison: University of Wisconsin Press, 1967), pp. 72–84; Arthur G. Wirth, *Education in the Technological Society: The Vocational-Liberal Studies Controversy in the Early Twentieth Century* (San Francisco:

Intext Educational Publishers, 1972), pp. 9–15; Calvin M. Woodward, *Manual Training in Education* (New York: Scribner and Welford, 1890), pp. 2, 41–51, 218–19, 264.

22. *Forth-sixth Annual Report of the Board of Education of the City of St. Louis, Mo., for the Year Ending June 30, 1900* (St. Louis, 1901), pp. 15–16.

23. Ibid., pp. 27–30.

24. An excellent survey of the literature is found in Paul Douglas, *American Apprenticeship and Industrial Education,* Columbia University Studies in Economics, History and Law, 955, no. 2 (New York: Longmans, Green and Co., 1921), pp. 85–108. Among the more noteworthy studies are *Report of the Commission on National Aid to Vocational Education,* House Docment 1004, 63rd Cong. 2d sess.; Luther Gulick and Leonard Ayres, *Why 250,000 Children Leave School: A Study in Retardation and Elimination in City School Systems* (New York: Charities Publications Committee [Russell Sage Foundation], 1909); George D. Strayer, *Age and Grade Census of Schools and Colleges: A Study of Retardation and Elimination,* United States Bureau of Education Bulletin no. 5, 1911 (Washington, D.C.: Government Printing Office, 1911). George S. Counts made major contributions to this field in the 1920s and 1930s; see his *Selective Character of American Secondary Education* (Chicago: University of Chicago Press, 1932).

25. Strayer, *Age and Grade Census,* pp. 11, 139–40.

26. *Report on Conditions of Women and Child Wage-Earners in the United States,* Senate Document 645, 61st Cong., 2d sess. (Washington, D.C.: Government Printing Office, 1910), 1: 46; Douglas, *American Apprenticeship,* pp. 89–90.

27. Douglas, *American Apprenticeship,* pp. 96–105.

28. Ibid., p. 85.

29. Calvin Woodward, "Manual, Industrial, and Technical Education in the United States," *Report of the Commissioner of Education for the Year 1903* (Washington, D.C.: Government Printing Office, 1905), 1: 1021.

30. Wirth, *Education in the Technological Society,* pp. 33–42.

31. "Report of the Committee of Ten on Secondary School Studies," *Report of the Commissioner of Education for the Year 1892–93* (Washington, D.C.: Government Printing Office, 1895), 2, pt. 3: 1457–64. For analysis of the setting and significance of the report, see Theodore R. Sizer, *Secondary Schools at the Turn of the Century* (New Haven: Yale University Press, 1964).

32. Commission on the Reorganization of Secondary Education, *Cardinal Principles of Secondary Education,* Bureau of Education Bulletin no. 35, 1918 (Washington, D.C.: Government Printing Office, 1918), pp. 7–8, 22.

33. Ibid.

34. There are many difficulties in obtaining statistics on attendance prior to the 1910 census, since they are compiled for age spans, such as five through thirteen or five through twenty, rather than by each age. The only means for establishing more complete statistics is to utilize the manuscript census. The results of the most extensive use of this procedure are reported in Troen, "Popular Education in Nineteenth-Century St. Louis."

35. National statistics on the popularity of various curricula are not available or not usable. The difficulties are (*a*) not all schools reported; (*b*) definitions of what constitutes a high school are not standardized; (*c*) not all high schools offered the new courses, thus biasing statistics when available; and (*d*) the modes of grouping courses into a curriculum also varied.

36. The same trend towards vocational courses was found in the evening classes, which underwent a similar expansion. A more complete analysis of student selections can be found in Selwyn K. Troen, "Defining Educational Change through Patterns of School Attendance." For a generalized discussion of the shift in student preferences, see Krug, *The Shaping of the American High School,* 2: 55–59.

37. Wirth, *Education in the Technological Society,* pp. 33–42.

24. Changing Education Strategies among Immigrant Generations: New York Italians in Comparative Perspective

At the turn of the twentieth century, two social investigators wrote admiringly about the Jewish immigrants they observed in New York's Lower East Side:

> The Jewish parent nearly always hopes his sons may become doctors, lawyers, teachers and merchants and he knows a thorough grounding in school must come during the early years.

They noted that the other large immigrant group which inhabited lower Manhattan, the Italians, provided quite a contrast with respect to the education of their children. "The Italian parent," reported the authors, "is satisfied if a child can just read or write. He (the Italian) is anxious that the child become a wage earner." Italians thus frequently took their children out of school as soon as possible, to put them to work.[1]

These observations were echoed by many others who wrote about immigrant life during the early decades of the twentieth century. Writers pointed to the low truancy rate among Jewish children in comparison to the Italians and noted the greater willingness of Jewish families to keep children in school during adolescence.[2]

What contemporaries observed during the early years of the century has been confirmed by the best available evidence we have on the educational achievement of first and second generation immigrants, a U.S. Census Bureau report of 1950 on ethnic groups in American cities. In 1950, the Bureau asked first and second generation Italians and Jews in New York and other cities how many years of school they had completed and reported the statistics by age cohorts. Approximately two times as many foreign born Jewish males who were over the age of twenty-five in 1950 had completed one year of high school as had the Italians; in the second generation, almost three times as many Jewish males had completed high school (See Table 24.1). The educational achievement of foreign born women of both groups was substantially below that of the males, but even in this case, approximately two times as many Jewish women had completed one year of high school. Among the second generation, three to four times as many Jewish women had completed high school (See Table 24.2).

In accounting for these patterns, both contemporary observers and later day scholars have emphasized the differences in the world views of Southern Italians and Eastern European Jews. Russian Jewish culture, with its appreciation of education, particularly for males, enabled these immigrants to benefit from American schools. And, because of their commitment to upward mobility, Jewish immigrants were anxious to invest in the future of their children, so that they could take advantage of opportunities in America.[3] By contrast, the Italian attitude towards schooling was just one more example of the

Miriam Cohen, "Changing Education Strategies Among Immigrant Generations: New York Italians in Comparative Perspective," reprinted from the *Journal of Social History* 15 (1982): 443–6, by permission of the *Journal of Social History*.

Table 24.1. **Number School Years Completed, Italian and Jewish Males, New York, 1950**

	Foreign Born				Native Born, Foreign Parentage			
	Age				Age			
	25–44		45+		25–44		45+	
Percent Completing School	*Italian*	*Jewish*	*Italian*	*Jewish*	*Italian*	*Jewish*	*Italian*	*Jewish*
One Year High School or More	36%	61%	12%	28%	60%	88%	29%	63%
Four Years High School or More	21%	44%	8%	20%	31%	72%	16%	47%
Median School Years Completed	8.5	10.9	5.6	8.1	10.1	12.7	8.4	11.4
Total in Population	N = 42,430	N = 20,218	N = 217,840	N = 148,290	N = 283,020	N = 156,755	N = 58,405	N = 52,995

Compiled from: U.S. Department of Commerce, Bureau of the Census, *United States Census of Population, 1950,* Vol. IV, Part 3A, *Special Reports, Nativity and Parentage* (Washington, U.S. Govt. Printing Office, 1954) pp. 283, 284.
*Area includes New York–Northeastern New Jersey Standard Metropolitan Area. (Also note: Many of the immigrants ages 45 and over were educated in Europe.)

Table 24.2. **Number School Years Completed, Italian and Jewish Females, New York, 1950**

| Percent Completing School | Foreign Born Age | | | | Native Born Age | | | |
| | 25–44 | | 45+ | | 25–44 | | 45+ | |
	Italian	Jewish	Italian	Jewish	Italian	Jewish	Italian	Jewish
One Year High School or More	27%	54%	7%	18%	55%	87%	20%	59%
Four Years High School or More	14%	36%	5%	12%	29%	69%	10%	40%
Median School Years Completed	8.2	9.7	4	5.8	9.6	12.4	8.2	10.5
Total in Population	41,530	27,215	117,210	143,335	292,955	170,870	58,045	53,465

Compiled from: U.S. Department of Commerce, Bureau of the Census, *United States Census of Population, 1950,* Vol. IV, Part 3A, *Special Reports,* pp. 283, 284. *Area includes New York–Northeastern New Jersey Standard Metropolitan Area. The data are used because they provide the best available information on our educational achievements, by cohorts for two generations of American immigrants. The Federal manuscript census schedules after 1900 are unavailable to the public; New York State did not conduct a census after 1925.

traditional culture of this Mediterranean peasantry, which like other non-modern societies placed little importance on investment for the future.[4]

The analysis which follows suggests that during the early decades of the twentieth
century Italian attitudes about the education of their children made quite good sense.
They were not merely a carry-over of traditional values, but reflected Italian efforts to
cope with the social realities of their lives in America. These circumstances were different,
in important ways, from those of American Jews and account, in large part, for the
differences between Italian and Jewish school patterns. By focusing on Italian school
patterns over the course of fifty years, this study also suggests that traditional attitudes
towards schooling were less deeply rooted than has previously been assumed. Throughout the period under study, commitment to the well-being of the family remained the
paramount goal for Italians. But within the parameters of that goal, Italians were pragmatic in their efforts to adapt to American life. They were quite willing to alter their
behavior with respect to the education of their children and they did so in a very short
time period. As social and demographic conditions changed for New York Italians at the
end of the Great Depression, so too did the work and school-patterns of their children.
By the 1940s and 1950s, we find important parallels in the educational patterns of young
Italians and Jews in New York City.

Many scholars writing about Southern Italians and American schooling have emphasized the importance of understanding that these immigrants came from a society which
placed little value on education.[5] Not only did time spent in school have negative consequences for the family because it would lose the child's labor on the land, but also Italian
parents felt that educational training had little to offer their offspring because the necessary skills needed for survival could be taught at home. Girls learned cooking, sewing,
gardening, housecare, and how to assist in harvesting crops from their mothers; boys
learned their trades, or how to farm, from fathers. Furthermore, because schools were
poorly financed and badly organized, the Italian state made little effort to enforce school
attendance on the part of its poor peasantry. Additionally, there were demographic
conditions which affected attitudes toward the education of children. Like many poor
people in the nineteenth and early twentieth centuries, Italian parents were not in a
position to consider investing in their children's future. High rates of infant and child
mortality encouraged high fertility, putting enormous financial strains on the family; the
older children had to be put to work as soon as possible.[6]

But if it is true that Italians did not arrive in New York with experiences enabling them
to appreciate education, it is also true that the real situation they faced in New York
reinforced these attitudes. Italian families adopted similar strategies with regard to schooling in New York largely because the problems they faced were similar.[7] Elsewhere I have
discussed at length the fact that just as in Europe, Italian children in New York lived in
families in which the earning capacities of the male household heads were quite low. The
largest proportion of males did unskilled labor, which was poorly paid, and most of the
jobs were vulnerable to seasonal fluctuation. In order to survive, all members of the
family were expected to contribute to the economic maintenance of the family, just as
they had done in Italy. Mothers generally did not work outside the home, but contributed income by tending boarders and by doing finishing operations at home for New
York's garment industry. Adolescent and young adult children also contributed to the
family income—boys worked as laborers, or, if they were lucky, followed their father's

trade; girls flocked to the garment factories which were so dominant in New York's economy. Children under fourteen years of age could not work in factories after the turn of the century, but daughters contributed to the family by assisting their mothers in homework tasks and domestic chores, while boys over age 12 peddled goods and shined shoes in the streets.[8] Hence, just as in Italy, time spent in school had negative consequences for the family because it diminished the ability of the child to contribute badly needed labor.

Demographic conditions in the New York Italian community reinforced negative attitudes about education. Although mortality for Italian children in New York was considerably lower than in their native land, the child mortality rate of 42.5 (children under five per 1,000 children) was still high, greater than any other group in the city.[9] The high mortality of children encouraged families to practice high fertility; it reinforced the lessons of past experience, which pointed to high fertility for all immigrant parents. The consequences of this high fertility strategy had not been so severe in late nineteenth-century Italy, because several children often would not survive. In the United States, they were greater, for more children were surviving. Hence Italian-American households were actually expanding in the early decades, and the strain on family resources was enormous; consumers had to be turned into wage-earners as soon as possible. In sum, economic and demographic conditions encouraged Italian parents to view their children as workers, rather than as students.

Data from census records and other government surveys indicate the extent to which opportunities for work acted as an incentive to pull children out of school. Analysis of a sample of families from the New York State census indicates that in 1905, 67 percent of the Italian males 14 and 15, who were out of school, were engaged in manufacturing, while another 17 percent worked in street trades, 4 percent in homework operations.[10]

The data also indicate that girls were pulled out of school because families needed their labor, not because, as has often been assumed, Italian parents wished to maintain a tradition of keeping adolescent women behind the protective walls of home.[11] A greater percentage of girls out of school (some 33 percent) was recorded as having no occupation. This makes sense when we consider the number of domestic duties which females could be expected to perform to alleviate the enormous demands on mothers. Along with non-paid labor, these girls could also help in homework operations—in the 1905 sample some 8 percent reported to the census taker that they did. But the largest group, 49 percent of the women ages 14 and 15 who were pulled out of school, were listed as employees in manufacturing shops.[12] And in 1925, 100 percent of the girls who were out of school were listed as workers outside the home, certainly evidence that Italians were quite willing to make use of their wage-earning abilities.[13]

For children under fourteen, who were supposed to be full time students, problems of truancy were greatest in neighborhoods where the girls were kept at home to do homework and care for young children and boys were sent out to do odd jobs. Lillian Wald conducted a study of schooling patterns among Italian homeworker families in East Harlem and found that of a group of 100 children doing homework, each had been absent on the average of 29.5 out of 89 school days in the year. On the other hand, in neighborhoods dominated by skilled workers, where mothers were not taking in work, officials found that Italian families were sending their children to school.[14]

Although Italians tended to think of their children as potential wage earners for the family, they did show appreciation for the value of some schooling, even in the early years of settlement. In the primary grades, children were taught to read, write and speak English, and to do simple arithmetic. Such skills were useful for the Italian community, and we have already seen that families sacrificed little in terms of wages by sending the young ones to school, because full time employment was not available to the young. Thus, it is logical to find that the majority of young children obtained some schooling.[15]

But in the case of Italian adolescents, schooling was hardly more valuable in New York than it was in Southern Italy. Most of these children, as indicated earlier, could expect to enter unskilled occupations which required little education. If the family could afford to forego their wages, schooling beyond the elementary grades for males was beneficial. Vocational training in secondary schools enabled some males to enter skilled jobs. And by the 1920s, a smaller number of second generation Italian males were obtaining white collar work.[16] The circumstances for females, however, rendered schooling even less valuable from the perspective of Italian families than was the case for males. With the skills they learned from kin, girls were fully prepared to contribute to the family, either within the home or outside. Schooling was not very helpful in enabling them to secure better paying, less dangerous or more stable work.

Social reformers often lamented the lack of ambition on the part of Italian girls who seemed uninterested in furthering their education so that they might gain better positions.[17] But they did concede that most often, Italian women had to take what they could get regardless of training.[18] An analysis of the female labor force in the men's garment industry, heavily dominated by Italian women, is suggestive of the problem. The U.S. Bureau of Labor obtained information on the earnings and educational achievement of 601 single women who were employed in the New York men's garment industry in 1910. Regression analysis reveals that the amount of completed schooling accounted for virtually none of the differences in the earnings of women.[19]

If schooling had little to offer most Italian families, it is also true that, just as in Southern Italy, immigrant families had little to fear from the legal authorities in New York if they wished to keep their adolescent children away from school. After 1910, when New York children were legally required to attend school between the ages of seven and fourteen, any employer who hired children under fourteen to do factory work was subject to penalty. With the increasing use of machinery in garment shops and the need to maintain production at a fast pace, such prohibition against employing young children made sense, not only from the point of view of dedicated reformers, but from that of manufacturers as well; as factory size increased and factories modernized, the number of young children employed in industry diminished.[20]

Young adolescents, however, could easily be put to work in factories—girls as clothing finishers, box packers and folders, candy wrappers; boys as machine helpers, carriers, runners in important New York industries dependent on cheap labor. Thus, although New York State boasted some of the most progressive school and child labor legislation in the country, the local municipal institutions did very little to block the efforts of immigrant parents to send their children to work.

During the progressive era, propelled by the efforts of welfare reformers, the New York legislature passed a series of laws to ensure that only fourteen and fifteen year olds who were both minimally educated and healthy could leave school to seek employment. But neither the Health Department, the government, nor the courts was willing to enforce the regulations. False papers certifying a child's age were available in immigrant neighborhoods, while physical examinations by the Health Department, if given at all, were most often cursory.[21]

Manufacturers who hired children without proper papers had little to fear, for the number of factory inspectors in New York was far too small to enforce regulations. And the city's police magistrates almost always refused to fine parents for allowing the youths to remain out of school, even if they had failed to obtain certification.[22] Finally, large segments of the educational bureaucracy itself, from administrators to teachers, wanted to be *rid* of as many immigrant pupils as soon as possible, because they viewed the students as unruly and uneducable. And so school officials at the local level regularly certified students they knew to be functionally illiterate, failing, and even under age.[23]

If reformers found it difficult to enforce laws regarding the employment of adolescents in factories, regulating the labor of younger children in homework operations was next to impossible, and it remained so until the 1930s. In 1913, for example, a law was enacted prohibiting the employment of children under the age of 14 in tenement manufacturing. It was difficult to enforce, mostly because a manufacturer could only be held liable if it could be proved that he actually *knew* a child was being employed illegally. Since this was almost never proved, the employer had little to fear, and the employment of children in homework flourished.[24] Some reformers understood that to combat absenteeism, the possibility for youngsters to earn money at home had to be removed. We must "compel the child's return to school," wrote Mary Van Kleeck in a 1909 report on Italian homeworkers in the artificial flower industry, "by preventing effectively the work which was the most important cause of her absence."[25] But reformers conceded the difficulties of their task, given the lack of law enforcement. Reporting on their investigations of Italian flower-makers, one settlement house report of 1915 admitted that:

> although a house would be visited and work stopped for a time, it was only a matter of months until a family would secure flowers from another factory. So well aware of this were most families that in the majority of cases, they made no attempt to hide the flowers.[26]

In actuality, adequate enforcement of child labor and compulsory school laws would have had disastrous consequences for the schools. Even as large a public school system as New York was not adequate to accommodate all the children in this rapidly growing city; rather than investing in an enormous growth of the school system, it was easier to set up a moderate expansion program, while sending thousands of extra youths into the labor market.[27]

Why, however, among these thousands of immigrant youth in the labor market, were there proportionately fewer Jewish children than Italian? Certainly, Jewish families did arrive in America better prepared to take advantage of schooling. While Jewish immigrants were poor, by and large, they came from the ranks of artisanal workers or small shopkeepers, both literate segments of the society.[28] This was particularly true of the Jews who emigrated after 1900. While 54 percent of the Italian immigrants told immigration officials between 1899 and 1910 that they could neither read nor write when they arrived, only 26 percent of the Jewish immigrants stated that they were illiterate.[29] Jewish adults had for years used their literary skills in their work and leisure lives, and in their political activities.[30] Naturally, they expected that their children would acquire such skills and encouraged their male children, in particular, to learn. And, according to the U.S. Immigration Commission, many foreign born Jewish children arrived in New York with a reading and writing knowledge of one language; thus, they could more easily learn to read and write English, at least in comparison to children who arrived with no such skills.[31]

But is important to understand that Jewish children could continue, even extend their pattern of educational achievement, because the social and economic conditions of the Jewish community in New York made it easier, in comparison to the Italians, for these families to think of their children as students, rather than wage earners. Thomas Kessner has shown that the immigrant Jewish population was better off economically than the Italian, largely because there was a greater proportion of skilled workers among the Jewish male population. Furthermore, in the late nineteenth century, Jewish males took advantage of their skills to gain a foothold in the expanding garment industry before the bulk of the Southern Italians arrived in the United States. Because a greater proportion of Jews had been small traders in Europe, they were more prepared than the Italians to take advantage of small-scale mercantile operations available in New York, and many did prosper.[32] And, because more Jewish mothers could afford to remain unemployed, fewer daughters had to forego schooling so that they could assist either in homework tasks or childcare.[33]

The difference in family size also made it easier for Jewish families to forego the earnings of their children. While Italians had the highest child mortality rate in New York City, the Russian Jewish rate of 24.9 was lowest.[34] The reasons for this difference are not clear, for both groups lived in poor housing and in highly congested neighborhoods. It may have been due to differences in diet, and the fact that in contrast to the Italian situation, health services were well entrenched in the Jewish community.[35] Finally, since fewer mothers did homework, fewer Jewish children were exposed to the health hazards involved.[36] Certainly, because more children survived in Jewish households, the pressure to control fertility was greater than in the Italian neighborhoods. A 1940 U.S. Census Bureau report on the fertility of immigrant women indicated that for the country as a whole, Jewish women bore fewer children than their Italian counterparts during the first three decades of the twentieth century.[37] Similarly, J. B. Maller, in his 1930 study comparing Italians and Jews in New York, found that along with lower infant mortality rates, Jewish neighborhoods evidenced lower birth rates. Maller also found greater school achievement among Jewish children.[38] With fewer youngsters to support, these families could more easily afford to invest in the future generation.

By the end of the Great Depression, however, schooling patterns among the Italians began to parallel those of the Jewish community. Children attended school more regularly and now female children, as well as males, were staying on into high school years.[39] These changes occurred not because Italians adopted middle-class values of individualism. Despite significant improvement in the economic status of Italian families over thirty years, they still remained, by and large, a working-class population; most males continued to work in blue-collar occupations.[40] Some improvement in the economic and social conditions of Italian families did have an effect on the lives of the females, as will be shown, but because they remained working-class, Italian families still depended on the contributions of all family members. However, important changes in the demographic structure of the Italian community and in the employment structure of New York affected the educational patterns of Italian-American children, particularly of daughters.

The demographic changes were among the most dramatic. By the later 1920s major decreases in infant and child mortality were noticeable, in large part a result of the decrease in child deaths due to diphtheria, measles and scarlet fever.[41] During the 1930's, while surveys of all neighborhood in New York City reported continual drops in infant and child mortality, the declines in Italian-dominated areas were even greater.[42] Comprehensive figures for the Italian populations in New York City are unavailable but while the infant mortality rate among Italians in the country as a whole was still above the average in 1920, by the mid 1930's it was almost identical to the figure for all Americans.[43]

What caused the decline in infant and child mortality among Italians in this period? No doubt, improvements in the Italian diet, especially for infants, was important.[44] Also, the increasing availability of modern medical care in New York, as the neighborhood health centers greatly expanded their services during the 1930s, ultimately had its effects.[45] As more children survived, the stage was set for parents to change their attitudes towards their children and to become receptive to new ideas about the value of education for both males and females. Growing numbers of surviving children increased the economic burden of the family, so the pressures to decrease fertility began to take effect. And the lower fertility strategy had spiraling consequences. With fewer children to support, it made more sense to invest greater resources, such as education, on each of the children. One good way to marshal resources was to have still fewer children.[46]

Fertility data for all Italians in New York after 1925 are unavailable, but information for all Italians in the United States and for some Italian neighborhoods in New York, indicates a dramatic drop at the end of the 1920s, and especially in the 1930s. A drop in fertility was common among all white American groups during the years of the Great Depression, as families tried to conserve resources during hard times, but for Italians, the drop was particularly striking.[47] And during the early post–World War II baby boom years, fertility among second generation Italian women remained low, in comparison to other Americans.[48] Clearly, Italian families were choosing to concentrate their resources on fewer children. For daughters, the change in family size may have had a particularly important effect. Fewer children meant that mothers' domestic burdens were lightened; since their daughters could more easily be spared away from home, parents were more likely to allow them to attend school.[49]

If demographic developments encouraged parents to invest in the education of their children, changes in employment opportunities for youngsters in New York removed one of the most important incentives for families to keep their offspring out of school. Homework in the garment and artificial flower industries, the two major employers of Italian mothers and girls, flourished during the early years of the depression. But under the New Deal governments of President Roosevelt and New York Governor Herbert Lehman, there were serious attempts to eliminate homework completely. This occurred in part as a response to the increased agitation by the men's and women's garment unions and because homework was an obstacle to New Deal plans for recovery.[50]

The first attempts to eliminate homework began as early as 1933 with the adoption of the federal National Industrial Recovery Act codes. When the National Recovery Act was struck down in 1935, the volume of homework increased sharply.[51] But the efforts to eliminate homework in New York were by no means over. In 1934, a revised state statute made it easier to prosecute garment manufacturers for the use of child labor on their products. The New York State Department of Labor was committed to the elimination of homework, and between 1936 and 1938 issued orders eliminating homework in the artificial flower and feather industry, the men's and boy's outer clothing industry and the men's and boy's neckwear industry.[52]

The new laws, combined with important union gains in the garment and artificial flower industries, had far-reaching effects on the homework operations in the Italian community. A study of the ethnic composition of the Amalgamated Clothing Workers of America in New York City found that between 1933 and 1937, Italian women had become the dominant group in the men's garment union; 81 percent of these females had been initiated into the union within those five years. "By far the largest proportion of this group," the report noted, "consists of finishers and fellers pursuing tasks within the shops that had formerly been accomplished in slum tenement flats as homework."[53]

The removal of work from the home virtually eliminated one important way for young Italian girls to do wage labor, and with it one of the most important factors which accounted for their widespread absence from school. Boys under age fourteen could still obtain jobs selling newspapers, but by the mid-1930s it was no longer possible for any 14- or 15-year-old to obtain factory employment. The imposition of the codes in 1934 had virtually established a sixteen-year-old minimum age for all New York industries engaged in interstate commerce. In 1935, the New York State legislature passed a new school attendance law, effective the following September, requiring New York children, with some exceptions, to remain in school until age 16.[54]

Committed to keeping children out of an economy which had no room for them, New York officials enforced this new law. It became much more difficult for underage children to leave the classroom. To house the enlarged school population, old continuation schools were converted into regular schools, and new schools were built. To fill the gap in the Italian neighborhoods, several parochial schools were also built and in ethnic communities, school curriculums were revised to encourage school attendance.[55] One Italian, writing for the WPA Federal Writers Project on Italian life in New York City in 1939, summarized the changes nicely:

> It must be admitted that (earlier) New York's truant officers did not always display the greatest zeal for gathering Italian children of school age. Politics may or may not have been responsible, but the fact is, most public schools in these (neighborhoods) were filled to overflowing. . . . The Catholic Church stepped in and set up parochial schools. . . . In recent years a number of public grammar and high schools, especially in the Italian neighborhoods have added courses in Italian.[56]

Thus, by the mid-1930's, Italian families in New York City were confronting a different situation from what they had found when they arrived in New York City. Although there was some opportunity for boys to work in the street, very little work was available for female children, and the state was now taking steps to keep adolescents in school as long as possible. In sum, the economic advantage in keeping girls away from school had practically been eliminated and the risk of sanctions against all children illegally out of school was greater than it had been before. In the case of the older adolescents, one clear reason that they remained in school during the depression was the lack of employment opportunities in New York factories.[57]

These negative factors cannot totally explain why truancy declined, or why Italian families in New York began to allow their daughters, in particular, to remain in school, even beyond the legal age of sixteen. It does not necessarily follow that because few jobs were available to women in the 1930s, adolescent females would automatically choose to spend their time in school. We know that today, despite the existence of legal sanctions against truants, there is widespread absenteeism among very poor and newly-migrant populations in the United States. The real question, therefore, is why Italian families came to appreciate the *value* of schools, and especially why they decided to keep daughters in school, often beyond the legal age. What did schooling have to offer?

During the early years of the century, schooling could do little to prepare Italian girls for adult life. Towards mid-century, major shifts in the female employment structure of New York City dramatically altered that situation. New York had been a major center for the production of consumer goods, but as the century progressed, the tertiary sector of the economy, rather than manufacturing, showed the largest gains. While manufacturing had dominated the female employment structure in New York at the turn of the century, by 1930 clerical work was the largest single category of women's work, occupying 30 percent of the city's female labor force; clerical and saleswork rose steadily in the next two decades.[58] To qualify for these jobs, Italian American women needed education. Clerical jobs required reading and writing skills, and the ability to do simple arithmetic. Almost all clerical jobs required high school training. And during the 1930's, commercial and business courses for young women in New York high schools expanded to meet the growing demand for white collar workers.[59]

Clerical jobs were attractive to working-class females for several reasons. White collar work offered women cleaner working conditions and better hours; in some cases, but by no means in all, they offered better pay. Perhaps the most important advantage of white collar employment was that it was more secure than factory work, less subject to seasonal fluctuation and generally less vulnerable to downturns in the business cycle.[60]

Italians could observe the advantages of clerical work on the basis of their own experiences. During the height of the depression, Italians saw that the small minority of clerical workers in their own communities were, as a group, better able to withstand the effects of the economic crisis than were the much larger number of factory workers. In one Italian neighborhood, for example, the level of unemployment increased for both female factory workers and clerical workers between 1930 and 1932. In both years, however, factory workers, as a group, suffered more lay-offs than clerical workers. In 1930, two times as many clerical workers were employed full time than was the case with factory workers; in 1932, three times as many clerical workers were employed. In a community so heavily dominated by blue collar workers, the favorable position of white collar workers must have been striking.[61]

In order for Italian families to change their attitudes about the value of education, of course, there had to be some indication that, in contrast to earlier years, white collar jobs were opening up for Italian women in New York. Indeed there was. First, native born Italian women had a better chance of being hired to do office work than did foreign born women, simply because they spoke English without a trace of foreign accent, and because they tended to look and behave more like native-stock Americans.[62] Secondly, as second generation Italian males began to organize their own small businesses, it became even easier for the females to obtain white collar jobs. A substantial number of Jewish women were found in office jobs in the early decades of the century, in part because of the abundance of small Jewish businesses which required clerical help. Jewish women found that it was just as hard, if not harder, for them to secure employment in large American corporations, but it was common to find Jewish females working as bookkeepers or clericals in garment businesses, or in small Jewish stores. By mid-century, Italian women as well were able to find jobs in business enterprises within their own community.[63]

During the New Deal years, government bureaucracies grew enormously, and these agencies became huge employers of ethnic women; this was particularly true in New York City, where ethnic voters were such an important element in political coalitions. Eventually, as the tertiary sector of the economy continued to expand, it became easier for ethnic women to obtain jobs even in the larger corporations.[64]

Table 24.3 indicates that by 1950, Italian women had entered the ranks of white collar work in large numbers. The U.S. Bureau of the Census reported that while only 8 percent of the first generation women were employed in clerical work, 40 percent of the second generation were employed in those jobs. Among the youngest group of second generation workers, females born between 1926 and 1936, 58 percent were employed in clerical occupations.

By contrast, over 50 percent of the second generation males still worked in blue collar jobs, as craftsmen, operatives or laborers, while only 17 percent of the males were employed in clerical jobs; adding the numbers who worked in professional jobs, and as managers and proprietors, we find 33 percent of the second generation males in white collar jobs, as opposed to 47 percent of the females. In the youngest age cohort, workers age 14 to 24, over 50 percent of the males were still working in blue collar jobs, and 31 percent were working in white collar jobs, as opposed to 62 percent of the females who were listed as white collar workers (See Table 24.3).

A comparison of the educational achievements of Italian-American men and women who were in the prime of their working lives in 1950, offers some insight into how the shifts in the employment structure affected Italian family behavior with respect to the education of their children. In the case of Italian-Americans born between 1900 and 1925, who were between the ages of 25 and 44 in 1950, the percentage completing high school was greater among the males than the females. In the younger categories, however, the gap between the educational achievement of the men and women narrowed and reversed; for second generation Italian-Americans born between 1926 and 1936, a greater percentage of females than males completed some high school (See Table 24.4).

If the level of education among Italian men and women is viewed as an index of traditional attitudes about male and female children, these results would be rather puzzling. While one might expect that the level of female educational achievement would rise as Italians became "Americanized," it seems unlikely that a culture presumably so prejudiced against the idea of *female* education per se would, in a matter of decades, *reverse* its age-old conviction and allow the females to equal and even *surpass* the achievement of their brothers. But if, as has been argued here, it was social circumstances which dictated whether or not Italian children attended school, the data are more understandable. When schooling was of little value to this working-class community, parents kept the children away; when schooling became essential for training girls to meet the needs of a changing job market, girls were sent to school. By contrast, many more manufacturing jobs were available for working class males, and after the depression men could earn relatively good wages, particularly if they were skilled laborers or worked in strongly unionized industries; hence, advanced education was less crucial.[65]

The difference in educational strategies for males and females suggests that while, as the revisionist historians have noted, high school training had little practical value for working class males, by the middle of the twentieth century it did serve a very practical purpose for working class females. In his study of a working class high school in the 1960s, the sociologist Arthur Stinchcombe found that the greater amount of rebellious behavior among working class males compared to the females could be attributed partly

Table 24.3. **Percent Occupational Distribution, First- and Second-Generation Italians, New York—Northeastern New Jersey Standard Metropolitan Area, 1950**

Occupations/Female	Foreign Born Age				Native Born Foreign Parents Age			
	14–24	25–44	45+	Total	14–24	25–44	45+	Total
Professional	3	4	2	2	3	5	4	5
Managerial & Proprietors	1	3	4	4	1	3	5	2
Clerical	28	12	4	8	58	31	19	40
Crafts	1	2	3	2	1	3	3	2
Operatives	62	73	80	77	31	51	58	44
Private Household	—	—	1	1	—	—	1	—
Service	2	3	4	4	3	4	7	4
Laborers	1	—	—	—	1	—	—	—
Not Reported	1	1	1	1	1	1	1	1
Total Number	3,285	14,925	13,510	51,720	64,395	97,310	14,955	177,250

Occupations/Male	Foreign Born Age				Native Born Foreign Parents Age			
	14–24	25–44	45+	Total	14–24	25–44	45+	Total
Professional	3	5	3	3	4	7	7	6
Managerial & Proprietors	4	12	14	13	3	11	16	10
Clerical	10	9	5	6	24	16	14	17
Craftsmen	21	25	24	24	18	22	22	22
Operatives	35	27	24	24	34	28	23	29
Private Household	—	—	—	—	—	—	—	—
Service	9	10	15	14	4	7	10	6
Laborers	16	10	15	14	11	8	7	6
Not Reported	—	—	—	1	—	—	—	1
Total Number	3,995	39,475	153,405	196,775	65,435	254,320	49,650	369,405

Source: U.S. Department of Commerce, Bureau of the Census, *United States Census of Population, 1950*, Vol. 10, Part 377, *Special Reports, Nativity and Parentage*, Washington, D.C. U.S. Government Printing Office, 1954, p. 234.
Numbers constituting less than one percent are recorded as blank (—). This table does not include farming categories which are well under one percent of the population.
Area includes New York City–Northeastern New Jersey Standard Metropolitan Area.

Table 24.4. **Number School Years Completed, Young Italians in New York, 1950**

Percent Completing School	Age Sex	Foreign Born						Native Born			
		14–24		25–44		14–24		14–24		25–44	
		M	F	M	F	M	F	F	M	M	F
One Year High School or More		52%	54%	36%	27%	75%	80%	80%	60%	60%	55%
Four Years High School or More		27%	27%	21%	14%	34%	39%	39%	31%	31%	29%
Median School Years Completed		9.3	9.4	8.5	8.2	10.8	11.2	11.2	10.1	10.1	9.6
Total in Population		N = 5,980	N = 6,735	N = 42,430	N = 41,505	N = 119,365	N = 126,325	N = 126,325	N = 283,028	N = 283,028	N = 292,955

Source: U.S. Bureau of the Census, *United States Census of Population, 1950*, Vol. IV, Part 3A, *Special Reports*, 284. Area includes New York–Northeastern New Jersey Standard Metropolitan Area.

to the fact that the boys saw little relationship between school tasks and their own futures; the girls, on the other hand, tended to view high school training as an entree to white collar jobs and were less likely to be alienated from the classroom.[66]

If we compare the pattern of educational achievement which emerged among Jewish men and women at mid-century, we find a startlingly similar result, suggesting that structural changes in the economy affected Jewish families in ways that paralleled the Italians. Among the older cohorts, those born between 1905 and 1925, males showed greater educational achievements than the women. Among the younger group of native-born Jewish Americans, born between 1926 and 1936, although a larger proportion of males completed college than among females, more *women* (67 percent) remained at least through high school than was the case with men (61 percent) (See Table 24.5). How might we account for this shift? In contrast to the Italian community, there were many white collar workers among Jewish men (see Table 24.6). However, many of the large number of white collar Jewish males in 1950 were small entrepreneurs and most of these occupations did not require formal education. Among second generation Jewish males, 27 percent were listed as manufacturers and proprietors, while only 19 percent were professionals and another 28 percent were clerical workers. In the case of second generation females, however, 63 percent were clerical workers and another 16 percent were listed as professionals. Among the youngest group of women 88 percent were clerical workers or professionals, in the case of males 56 percent were either clerical workers or professionals. Thus, as in the case of Italians, it is not surprising to find that in 1950, more Jewish women ages 14–24 held high school diplomas than did the men.[67]

These figures are only suggestive of the ways that structural changes in the economy might influence the educational patterns of Jewish men and women, but we do know that it was common in the Jewish community for women to help out in the family business by working as a bookkeeper or secretary.[68] And several recent inquiries among eastern European Jewish families suggest that the high-school-educated woman married to a wealthy but less-educated businessman is not an uncommon pattern among second generation adults, and is worthy of further inquiry.

This limited comparison has suggested that to the extent social, economic and demographic circumstances were different for Jewish and Italian families in New York so, too, were the educational patterns of their children. During the early decades of the twentieth century, the demographic and economic conditions in the Jewish community, as well as the skills which Russian Jews brought over from Europe, enabled them to invest in the education of their children to a greater extent than was the case with Italians. Yet it appears that the educational strategies of both groups were affected by changes in the urban economy. And the nature of those changes suggests that we might want to question the tendency of scholars to view educational patterns among immigrant groups as an index of traditional or modern values.

Both groups reversed an age-old pattern with respect to the education of their children; while both groups still continued to invest in higher education for males, among the younger cohorts in both groups in 1950, more women obtained at least a high school diploma. Age-old convictions about the "propriety" of education for males and females did not have to change in the course of about fifteen years for these new patterns to emerge. What seems more plausible is that parental attitudes about education changed not because their attitudes about females, males, or children in general changed, but because these parents had to adapt to changing social circumstances in an effort to do

Table 24.5. **Number School Years Completed, Young Jews in New York, 1950**

Percent Completing School	Age Sex	Foreign Born 25–44		Native Born 14–24*		25–44	
		M	F	M	F	M	F
One Year High School or More		61%	54%	89%	91%	88%	87%
Four Years High School or More		44%	36%	61%	67%	72%	69%
Median School Years Completed		10.9	9.7	12.4	12.4	12.7	12.4
Total in Population		N = 20,218	N = 27,215	N = 50,905	N = 52,735	N = 156,755	N = 170,870

Source: U.S. Bureau of the Census, *United States Census of Population, 1950*, Vol. IV, Part 3A, *Special Reports*, p. 283. Area includes New York–Northeastern New Jersey Standard Metropolitan Area.
*Less than 500 males and 500 females foreign born ages 14–24, therefore did not compute.

Table 24.6. **Percent Occupational Distribution, First- and Second-Generation Jews, New York, 1950**

Occupations/Female	Foreign Born Age				Native Born Foreign Parents Age			
	14–24	25–44	45+	Total	14–24	25–44	45+	Total
Professional	—	11	3	5	12	17	16	16
Managerial & Proprietors	—	9	13	12	3	8	14	—
Clerical	—	37	24	28	76	53	50	63
Crafts	—	2	2	2	—	1	2	1
Operatives	—	33	42	40	4	10	11	8
Private Household	—	1	2	2	—	—	—	—
Service	—	4	6	4	2	3	3	3
Laborers	1	—	—	1	—	—	—	—
Not Reported	—	1	2	1	—	—	2	1
Total Number		N = 7,850	N = 22,310	N = 30,400	N = 22,415	N = 45,395	N = 13,270	30,880

Occupations/Male	Foreign Born Age				Native Born Foreign Parents Age			
	14–24	25–44	45+	Total	14–24	25–44	45+	Total
Professional	—	13	8	9	14	20	16	19
Managerial & Proprietors	—	31	32	32	10	27	34	27
Clerical	—	19	13	14	42	27	25	28
Crafts	—	15	17	16	12	8	11	10
Operatives	—	18	24	23	15	10	12	12
Private Household	—	—	—	—	—	—	—	—
Service	—	3	4	4	3	3	3	3
Laborers	—	1	2	2	1	1	1	1
Not Reported	—	—	—	1	1	1	1	1
Total Number		N = 18,965	N = 115,255	N = 130,450	N = 22,755	N = 146,020	N = 42,725	216,310

Source: U.S. Bureau of the Census, *United States Census of Population*, Vol. IV, *Special Reports*.

Area includes New York City–Northeastern New Jersey Standard Metropolitan Area.
Foreign born Jews, ages 14–24, too few to enumerate.

what they had always done—to prepare their children with the proper skills so that they would survive, even succeed, as adults.

Notes

Earlier versions of this paper were delivered to the American Historical Association annual meeting, San Francisco, California, December 1978, and the Newberry Library Program in Family and Community History Conference on Women and Quantitative History, Chicago, Illinois, July 1979. Thanks to Claudia Goldin, Michael Hanagan, Molly Shanley, Mark Stern, Louise Tilly and Maris Vinovskis for comments and criticisms.

1. Kelly Durand and Louis Sessa, "The Italian Invasion of the Ghetto" (New York, 1909?), p. 10. (Reprint in the New York City Public Library collections.)

2. See, for example, Mary Van Kleeck, *Working Girls in Evening Schools* (New York, 1914); U.S. Immigration Commission, *The Children of Immigrants in School*, Vol. 4, S. Doc. 5074, 61st Cong. 2nd Sess. (Washington, 1911); Lillian Betts, *The Italians in New York,* University Settlement Studies, Vol. 1, No. 3 (1908); Caroline Ware, *Greenwich Village, 1920–1930* (Boston, 1935). J. B. Maller, "Vital Indices and their Relation to Psychological and Social Factors," *Human Biology* 5 (1933): 94–121. In his book on the Italian immigrant communities of Utica, Rochester and Kansas City, John Briggs suggests that the discrepancy in educational achievement between Italians and other groups has been exaggerated. According to Briggs, children of Italian households tended to begin school later than most children, at the legally required age of seven, rather than six, because it was in accordance with Southern Italian custom. Once they were in school, he contends, their attendance records were similar to other groups, but because they were over-age for their class, they, more so than other children, reached the age of fourteen without completing elementary school. See *An Italian Passage: Immigrants to Three American Cities, 1890–1920* (New Haven, 1978), pp. 225–238. My analysis of the school attendance patterns of Italian and Jewish children in New York City, suggests that the difference cannot be explained by the fact that Italian children tended to get a later start at school. Comparing the percentage of Italian and Jewish children in New York schools as recorded by the U.S. Federal Census of 1920 we find the differences for children age six to be quite small (less than 5 percent). Yet by age 14 and 15, 10–15 percent more of the Jewish children were in school than was the case with Italians. Data analyzed from the records of Walter Laidlaw, *Statistical Sources for the Demographic Study of Greater New York* (New York, 1922), four census tracts for Manhattan, sixteen tracts for Brooklyn. See also Michael Olneck and Marvin Lazerson, "The School Achievement of Immigrant Children, 1900–1930," *History of Education Quarterly* 14 (1974): 454–482.

3. See Olneck and Lazerson, "The School Achievement."

4. See Ware, *Greenwich Village*. See also Greenwich House, *Annual Reports,* 1916–1918; Van Kleeck, *Working Girls in Evening School;* Louise Odencrantz, *Italian Women in Industry* (New York, 1919), p. 255.

5. See for example, Leonard Covello, *The Social Background of the Italo-American School Child* (New York, 1967, c. 1944). See also Olneck and Lazerson.

6. On the patterns of mortality and fertility in Southern Italy, see Massimo Livi Bacci, *A History of Italian Fertility* (Princeton, 1977). Also see Robert Foerster, *The Italian Emigration of Our Times* (Cambridge, 1919), p. 95; on schooling in Southern Italy, see Miriam Cohen, "From Workshop to Office: Italian Women and Family Strategies in New York City, 1900–1950" (unpublished Ph.D. dissertation, University of Michigan, 1978), Chapter 2. On the relationship between high infant and child mortality and fertility strategies, see Charles Tilly, "Population and Pedagogy in France," *History of Education Quarterly* 13 (1973): 113–128. See also Charles Tilly, ed. "The Historical Study of Fertility," in *The Historical Study of Fertility* (Princeton, 1978); E.A. Wrigley, "Fertility Strategy for the Individual and the Group," also in Tilly, *The Historical Study of Fertility.*

7. John Bodnar makes a similar point about the role of peasant traditions in Slavic-American

communities. See "Immigration and Modernization: The Case of Slavic Peasants in Industrial America," *Journal of Social History* 10 (1976): 44–71.

8. See Miriam Cohen, "Italian American Women in New York City, 1900–1950: Work and School," in Milton Cantor and Bruce Laurie, eds., *Class, Sex and the Woman Worker* (Westport, Conn., 1978), pp. 120–43.

9. The child mortality rates by ethnicity, as reported by the New York City Health Department in 1915 were:

Austria/Hungary	26.3
Germany	32.3
Ireland	36.3
Italy	42.5
Russia/Poland	24.9
American*	40.0
All Manhattan	37.9

*Includes native whites of native parents, Black Americans. See New York City Department of Health, *Influence of Nationality Upon the Mortality of a Community,* Monograph Series No. 18 (November, 1917). Infant and child mortality does decline for Italian American families in the twentieth century, as will be discussed, but in the 1920's, the rates among Italians remain very high in comparison to the rest of New York City. In 1920 the rate among all Italians was 39.7, for the city as a whole, 30.8. See the U.S. Bureau of Commerce, Bureau of the Census, *Fourteenth Census of the United States,* 1920 (Washington, 1924), p. 513. See also the East Harlem Health Center, *Why East Harlem Needs Health Services,* 1924, p. 65, and John J. Gebhardt, *The Health of a Neighborhood: A Social Study of the Mulberry District* (New York, 1924), pp. 15, 19. On infant and child mortality in Italy, see Massimo Livi-Bacci, *A History of Italian Fertility* (Princeton, 1977).

10. Based on sample, New York State Manuscript Census, 1905. For detailed discussion of this data see Cohen, "From Workshop to Office," Chapter 5.

11. See, for example, Virginia Yans-McLaughlin, *Family and Community, Italian Immigrants in Buffalo, 1880–1930* (Ithaca, 1977), Chapter 7.

12. *Ibid.*

13. *Ibid.* New York State Census, 1925.

14. New York Factory Investigating Commission, *Public Hearings,* First Series, reprint from the *Preliminary Report of the New York Factory Investigating Commission* (October, 1911), pp. 1739, 1740. Also see Harriet M. Johnson, *The Visiting Teacher in New York City* (New York, 1916), pp. 4, 5.

15. An analysis of 1920 census tracts in Manhattan and Brooklyn in which Italian Americans (first and second generation) constitute over 90% of the population indicates that from 75 to 95% of the children ages 7–14 were enrolled in school. Data analyzed from the records of Laidlaw, *Statistical Sources for the Demographic Study of Greater New York,* four census tracts from Manhattan, sixteen tracts for Brooklyn analyzed. For detailed discussion of this data, see Cohen, "From Workshop to Office," Chapter 5.

16. On employment patterns for Italian males in New York City in the 1920's, see Cohen, "From Workshop to Office," Chapter 3.

17. See, for example, Louise Odencrantz, *Italian Women in Industry,* Chapter x.

18. *Ibid.,* p. 225.

19. A linear regression was calculated to see if an increase in schooling was correlated with an increase in earnings for these women. The correlation coefficient (R^2) revealed that only .04463 of the variance in earnings was correlated with educational achievement, and the results were significant at the .0 level. Calculated from survey data recorded in U.S. Congress, Senate, Bureau of Labor, *Report on Condition of Woman and Child Wage Earners in the United States,* Vol. 2: *Men's Ready Made Clothing,* S. Doc. 645, 61st Cong., 2nd Sess. (Washington, 1911), pp. 780–807.

20. See Jeremy Felt, *Hostages of Fortune: Child Labor Reform in New York State* (Syracuse, 1964), Chapter 4.

21. See *Ibid.,* Chapter 5. Also see New York City Department of Education, *Fourteenth Annual Report of the City Superintendent of Schools* (New York, 1912); New York, *Department of Labor, the Health of the Working Child,* New York State Department of Labor Special Bulletin No. 134 (Albany, 1924). From 1913 to 1923 approximately 2000 children were found, annually, working in factories without any employment papers. See New York, Department of Labor, *The Trend of*

Child Labor in New York State, Supplementary Report for 1923, New York State Department of Labor Bulletin No. 132 (Albany, 1924), p. 23.

22. See Felt, *Hostages of Fortune,* Chapter 4.

23. *Ibid.,* Chapter 5. Also see New York City Department of Education, *First Annual Report of the Director of Attendance* for the year ending July 31, 1915 (New York, 1916).

24. See Felt, *Hostages of Fortune,* p. 147; New York, *Preliminary Report of the Factory Investigating Commission,* Vol. 1, p. 86; New York, *Factory Investigating Commission,* Vol. 3 (Albany, 1913), p. 101. See also New York, *Second Report of the Factory Investigating Commission,* Vol. 3, pp. 104–108; Felt, *Hostages of Fortune,* pp. 149, 150.

25. Mary Van Kleeck, "Child Labor in New York City Tenements," *Charities and the Commons* (January 18, 1908), p. 6.

26. Greenwich House, *Annual Report,* 1916, p. 25. See also New York, *Second Report of the Factory Investigating Commission,* Vol. 3, pp. 104–108; see also, Felt, *Hostages of Fortune,* pp. 149, 150.

27. See Felt, *Hostages of Fortune,* Chapter 5. Also see New York, Factory Investigating Commission, *Public Hearings,* First Series, reprint from the *Preliminary Report of the New York Factory Investigating Commission* (October, 1911), testimony of Lillian Wald, pp. 1735–1746, and Lillian Betts, "The Italians in New York," p. 95.

28. See Thomas Kessner, *The Golden Door: Italian and Jewish Immigrant Mobility in New York City, 1880–1920* (New York, 1977); Moses Rischin, *The Promised Land, New York's Jews, 1870–1914* (Cambridge, 1963).

29. Note also that the figures for Jews included more women than the figures for Italians because the Italian migration was more male-dominated. See U.S. Immigration Commission, *Reports of the Immigration Commission,* Vol. 3, *Statistical Review of Immigration* (Washington, 1911), p. 84. Also, Thomas Kessner points out that the 26 percent figure for Jews probably represents the number of Jews who could neither read nor write Yiddish or Russian; almost all Jewish males could read Hebrew. See Kessner, *The Golden Door,* p. 41.

30. Many people have written about the importance of education for Jewish work life, leisure, and political life. See, for example, Irving Howe, *World of Our Fathers* (New York, 1976).

31. See U.S. Congress, Senate, *Reports of the Immigration Commission,* Vol. 26; *Immigrants in Cities,* Vol. 2, S. Doc. 338, 61st Congress, 2nd sess. (Washington, 1911), pp. 329–331. In his 1930 study of Italians and Jews in New York City, J. B. Maller found statistically significant differences between these groups both with respect to IQ's and rate of progress through the grades. While it is difficult to evaluate the meaning of I.Q. tests in 1930, as it still is today, it indicates that Jewish children were better prepared to benefit from the kind of education offered to these students. See J. B. Maller, "Vital Indices and their Relation to Social Factors."

32. See Kessner, *The Golden Door,* Chapters 2–4. Also see Cohen, "From Workshop to Office," Chapters 3, 4.

33. The U.S. Immigration Commission reported that among the Russian Jewish households they surveyed, 17 percent of the wives reported that they were at work, compared with 30 percent of the Southern Italians. See U.S. Congress, Senate *Reports of the Immigration Commission,* Vol. 26; *Immigrants in Cities,* Vol. 1, S. Doc. 338, 61st Congress, 2nd sess. (Washington, 1911), p. 228.

34. See figures, Footnote 9.

35. On American Jews and diet, see Moses Rischin, *The Promised Land,* p. 87. On the difficulties of getting Italians to take advantage of the medical services offered by New York philanthropists, see, for example, Lucy Gillett, *Adapting Nutrition Work to a Community* (New York, 1923).

36. Before 1900, Jews dominated homework in New York, but by 1911, their numbers had shrunk to about one-third of the work force and continued to decline as the community prospered and strong unions developed in the women's clothes industry and cigar manufacturing, where most Jews worked. See Felt, *Hostages of Fortune,* p. 141; Van Kleeck, "Child Labor in New York City Tenements," New York, Bureau of Women in Industry, *Homework in the Men's Garment Industry in New York and Rochester,* Bulletin No. 147 (Albany, 1956). It is probably the case that not only did the presence of strong unions work to eliminate homework; because fewer Jewish families were dependent on the homework industry for survival, it was easier to organize the community to fight homework. At any rate, this possibility is worth further study.

37. The number of children ever-born per 1000 ever-married Russian and Polish Jewish

immigrant women, as recorded in 1940 was 4.8 for ever-married women ages 65–74 in 1940, 3.7 for women ages 55–64, and 2.9 for women ages 45–54. All of these women, except for the last group, had passed their peak child bearing years (to age 44) by 1930. For Italian immigrant women, the figures are as follows: for ever-married women ages 65–74 in 1940, 5.4, for women ages 55–64, 5.2, for women ages 45–54, 4.7. See U.S. Department of Commerce, Bureau of the Census, *Census Population, 1940, Differential Fertility, 1940 and 1910* (Washington, 1942), Table 40. Also see Ira Rosenwaike, "Two Generations of Italians in America: Their Fertility Experience," *International Migration Review* 7 (1973): 276.

38. See Maller, "Vital Indices and their Relation," pp. 119–121.

39. See Leonard Covello, *The Social Background of the Italo-American School Child*, p. 286; Selma Berrol, "Education and the Italian and Jewish Community Experience," in Jean Scarpeci, ed., *The Interaction between Italians and Jews in America* (New York, 1975), pp. 31–41.

40. The job as unskilled worker ranked as the leading occupation for Italian males in 1935, and the numbers of unskilled workers was actually growing during the Depression, as more and more Italian men were thrown out of work and were forced to take whatever job they could find. See John J. Alesandre, *Occupational Trends of Italians in New York City*, Bulletin No. 6, Casa Italiana Educational Bureau (New York, 1935), p. 17. Also see Cohen, "From Workshop to Office," Chapter 3.

41. See East Harlem Health Center, *A Decade of District Health Pioneering* (New York, 1932), pp. 114, 116, 117. See also Cohen, "From Workshop to Office," Chapter 6.

42. See Committee on Neighborhood Health Development, *Handbook Statistical Reference Data, Ten Year Period, 1930–1940* (New York, 1944, 4th ed.) See in particular, information on infant and child mortality rates for Italian dominated health areas (where at least 80% of the inhabitants are either first or second generation Italians) in the East Harlem and Lower West Side Health Districts in Manhattan, and the Fort Greene and Red Hook Districts in Brooklyn, pp. 75, 91, 150, 151. For the city as a whole, see pp. 24, 25, 36.

43. See Massimo Livi Bacci, *L'Immigrazione L'Assimilazione Degli Italiani Negli Stati Uniti* (Milan, 1961), p. 86. See also Cohen, "From Worhshop to Office," Chapter 6.

44. See Dorothy L. Bovee and Jean Downes, "The Influence of Nutrition Education in Families of the Mulberry Area of New York City," *Milbank Memorial Fund Quarterly*, XIX (1941): 121–146.

45. The East Harlem and Mulberry District Health Centers, for example, did service many Italians by the late 1920's. By the end of the 1930's, health centers were serving Italians in all boroughs. See Committee on Neighborhood Health Development, *Handbook*.

46. This analysis draws on arguments presented in Charles Tilly, "Population and Pedagogy in France," pp. 113–128; Tilly, "Historical Study of Fertility"; E. A. Wrigley, "Fertility Strategy for the Individual and the Group." Among the poorest families, of course, there were fewer resources available to invest in children and thus the impetus to conserve them was not as great. Indeed, the fertility rates among the poorer families tended to be higher. But even among the poorer households, large numbers of small children were a great problem in twentieth-century New York because of legal prohibitions against factory work for the very young. Thus the need to limit the number of offspring was felt, to some degree, by all families. See Cohen, "From Workshop to Office," Chapter 3.

47. For example, the fertility ratio (number of children born per 1000 married women) among second generation Italian women ages 25–29 went from 2,276 in 1926 to 1207 in 1936; for women of native white stock, the ratio was 1420 in 1926, 1140 in 1936. See Massimo Livi Bacci, *L'Immigrazione*, pp. 65, 67. It is not clear if Livi Bacci has used all Italian women in determining fertility, or only married women with spouses. Livi Bacci estimated the population of Italian women for each year by using immigration records to estimate the number of women who migrated into the country each year, and life tables to estimate annual mortality. See his discussion in *L'Immigrazione*, pp. 62, 63 and Appendix B. Public Health data on New York fertility do exist for neighborhoods. For seven health areas in which the Italian population was 80% or more, the decline in birth rate was 1.5 between 1931 and 1940, for New York City as a whole, this decline was 1.3. See Committee on Neighborhood Health Development, *Handbook Statistical Reference Data*, pp. 74, 75, 89, 90, 150, 151, 158, 159, 11, 22.

48. Ever-married women of Italian stock who were between the ages of forty-five and fifty-four in 1960 reported that they had had an average of 2.1 children, all ever-married women of native

white American stock, ages 45–54 in 1960, reported an average of 2.3 children ever born. See Ira Rosenwaike, "Two Generations of Italians in America," p. 276.

49. It is also likely that improved health conditions not only encouraged greater investment in education through their effects on mortality rates. Children also were able to attend school more regularly because they suffered fewer illnesses than in earlier years. Ian Davey points out that in nineteenth-century Hamilton, absenteeism was particularly noticeable among working-class school children in the winter months, when they were likely to be suffering from childhood disease. See Ian Davey, "The Rhythm of Work and the Rhythm of School, Hamilton, Ontario in the Nine-teenth Century" (York University, 197?).

50. On the importance of labor unions to the New Deal coalition, see Sam Lubell, *The Future of American Politics* (New York, 1952), Arthur Schlesinger, Jr., *The Age of Roosevelt*, Vol. III, *The Politics of Upheaval* (Boston, 1960); William E. Leuchtenberg, *Franklin D. Roosevelt and the New Deal* (New York, 1963), Chapters 3 and 8. A good summary of the economic strategies of the Roosevelt administration appears in Leuchtenberg, *Franklin D. Roosevelt,* Chapter 4.

51. See Teper and Weinberg, "Aspects of Industrial Homework," p. 34; New York Department of Labor, *Homework in the Artificial Flower and Feather Industry.*

52. See Felt, *Hostages of Fortune,* pp. 151, 152.

53. Jacob Loft, "Jewish Workers in the New York City Men's Clothing Industry," *Jewish Social Studies* (1938): 61–77. There has been a recent resurgence of illegal homework in both the East Coast and West Coast areas. This development is made possible by the massive influx of new migrants and it is an index of the current weakness of the garment unions in the United States. They are having difficulty in holding the line in this troubled industry which tries to remain competitive with imports by using the cheapest available labor.

54. See Loft, "Jewish Workers," p. 126.

55. *Ibid.,* pp. 126, 127. See also Works Progress Administration, Historical Records Survey, Population file. (Municipal archives, New York City); New York City, Board of Education, *Youth in School and Industry, the Continuation School and Their Problems* (1933–34).

56. Works Progress Administration, Historical Records Survey, New York City Guide Files, Catalogue #3561, "Italians," Article 16, "Schools and Education," 1939, pp. 2, 3 (Municipal archives, New York City).

57. On this point, see Gwendolyn Berry, *Idleness and the Health of a Neighborhood* (New York, 1933), p. 21; Works Progress Administration, Historical Records Survey, Catalogue #3597 (Municipal archives, New York City).

58. See Personnel Research Foundation, *Occupational Trends in New York City: Changes in the Distribution of Gainful Workers, 1900–1930* (New York, 1936) Charts 1 and 2. See also U.S. Department of Commerce, Bureau of the Census, *Census Population: 1950,* Vol. 2, *Characteristics of the Population,* Part 32, New York State (Washington, 1952), pp. 266, 267, 269, 272, 273, 275. For more discussion of these changes, see also Cohen, "Italian American Women," in Cantor and Laurie, *Class, Sex and the Woman Worker.*

59. See Randolph C. Wilson, *Office Work as an Occupation* (New York, 1940), pp. 25, 29, 35, 40, 49.

60. In 1930, the U.S. Census reported that 10% of females in manufacturing jobs in New York City were unemployed; only 5% of female clericals were unemployed. See Personnel Research Foundation, *Occupational Trends in New York City,* Index, Fifteenth Census of the United States, Vol. II quoted. Today, clerical work still remains less vulnerable to economic downturns. Thus, *The New York Times* reported in November 1977 that women suffered lower rates of unemploy-ment during that recession because their jobs were disproportionately concentrated in the service and retail sectors of the economy, which continued to grow. The only major industry in which women's share of the jobs declined was in the durable goods manufacture sector. See "Women Said to Weather Recession," *New York Times,* November 2, 1977, p. 1.

61. Berry, *Idleness and the Health,* p. 80.

62. On the importance of proper personality characteristics and office decorum for female white collar workers, see Wilson, *Office Work as an Occupation.* See also Anne Valles, "Miss America Takes Shorthand: Job Manuals and the Changing World of Women and Work, 1900–55," senior thesis, Vassar College, Poughkeepsie, New York, 1979.

63. Thomas Kessner found 23.8 percent of the female offspring of Russian Jews to be em-

ployed in low white collar positions as early as 1905. See *The Golden Door,* p. 90. On the growth of small-scale Italian businesses, see Nathan Glazer and Daniel P. Moynihan, *Beyond the Melting Pot* (Cambridge, 1963), pp. 206, 207. Glazer and Moynihan write that the growth of Italian busi-nesses expanded a generation later than was the case for New York Jews, but had nonetheless made gains by mid-century.

64. On the enormous growth in demand for female clerical and sales workers in the twentieth century and its effects on the attitudes of employers, see Valerie Kincaid Oppenheimer, "Demo-graphic Influence on Female Employment and the Status of Women," *American Journal of Sociology* 78 (1973): 946–961. Also see Valerie Kincaide Oppenheimer, *The Female Labor Force in the United States,* Population Monograph Series, No. 5 (Westport, Conn., 1970).

65. Craft work, operative jobs, and laborer jobs accounted for 45 percent of the male work force in the New York-north-eastern New Jersey area, compared to 24 percent for females. See U.S. Bureau of the Census, *Census Population,* 1950, Vol. ii, Characteristics of the Population, Part 32, pp. 245–266.

66. See Arthur Stinchcombe, *Rebellion in a High School* (Chicago, 1964), Chapters 4 and 5. To what extent high school, itself, fostered new self-images for second generation women, or changed relationships between parents and children, is unknown and beyond the scope of this study. Available evidence suggests that commercial training for working class high schoolers was not designed to promote a sense of individuality. The ability to get along, discipline, adaptability and obedience were considered crucial characteristics of the attractive clerical worker whose job usually involved little self initiative. On these points, see Wilson, *Office Work as an Occupation;* Valles, "Miss America Takes Shorthand." These points are further developed in Cohen, "From Workshop to Office: Italian Women and Their Families in New York City, 1900–1950."

67. See U.S. Department of Commerce, Bureau of the Census, *United States Census of Popula-tion,* 1950, Vol. iv, Part 3A, *Special Reports, Nativity and Parentage* (Washington, 1954), p. 284.

68. See Charlotte Baum, Paula Hyman and Sonya Michel, *The Jewish Woman in America* (New York, 1976).

Framing the Present, 1920 to 1980

Introduction

Part V, "Framing the Present," ranging from about 1920 to the 1980s, takes material largely familiar to many readers, but places it in a novel context by locating it in its social-historical position. Confronting it from the frameworks and comparisons developed in the preceding pages facilitates our seeing the past half century or so in a new manner: as the outcome and consequence of a lengthy and intricate historical process. That, of course, need not diminish the distinctiveness we associate with the present century; rather, it mandates that we not consider it novel or unique solely as a result of viewing it in isolation from its development context. The often subtle but sometimes brash blend of change and continuity emerges freshly.

Similarly, the historical view combined with the present emphasis on variety and diversity of experience reflected in these selections warns against easy assumptions of convergence or increasingly homogeneous experiences of growing up; or of wholly alienated, restless, rebellious youth; conforming youth; idle youth; or isolated peer cultures of the young. Social scientists recently attempted to stress this in views that simply can no longer be credited. In contrast, the range and significance of recent experience flow from contextualized case studies that include several modern classics, such as Gans's urban villagers of Boston and Seeley's Crestwood Heights of Toronto.

In a creative piece of original research combining opinion polls with high school yearbooks and newspapers and earlier sociological work, Modell recaptures the flavor of the emergence of what sociologist Willard Waller termed "the rating and dating game." In the essay "Dating Becomes the Way of American Youth," John Modell illustrates that blend of commonality with divergence, continuity with change, and contradictions and psychosocial costs in culture and experience all so central to the emergence of twentieth-century youth culture and consumption. The focus here is on the 1920s.

The world of such superficial triviality seemingly clashes with the demands and dilemmas of the Great Depression's differential impacts on the children and youth of the next decade. Indeed, the task of grasping the terms of contrast while understanding their combined impact on so many among the young falls upon readers of these two pieces. So too does placing the household economy and its implications for those growing up during the Depression with earlier, historical forms of the family and household economy and its relevance for the terms of growing up. Perhaps most interesting and rich in its implications for this volume's overall concerns are the ways in which Elder reveals the very impacts of the Depression to be different for the young of families in different situations and for those of different ages when its effects were felt.

The worlds—typically presumed to be so quiescently outside the paths of major historical events—of family, neighborhood, and growing up in the 1940s and 1950s take on a renewed importance when we closely examine and juxtapose the lives of the growing generations in the distinctive but not unique communities of Boston's Italian West End "urban village" and Toronto's upper-middle-class "Crestwood Heights." Masterly studies by Gans and by Seeley and his associates capture realms of experience to which mass media recreations in the forms of TV series and movies have done a real disservice. These worlds of the young—especially when extended to and compared with Rubin's working-class and Stack's inner-city blacks of the 1960s and 1970s—remind us of the rich diversity of recent human developmental experience. Equally, they underscore the highly contradictory and costly (in human terms), but nonetheless historical, nature of each of these paradigmatic cases of growing up in modern America. The resourcefulness of families and the young themselves so often contrasts strikingly with the limits on their development and restrictions—so very different for different young persons—but seemingly always so different from what their potential might merit. The interplay between social norms and social change on the one hand and class, ethnic, race, and gender-conditioned paths of growing up on the other can only be understood in these kinds of historical dimensions.

In "Ambivalence: The Socialization of Women," finally, Bardwick and Douvan highlight the consequences that persist for young women. At this juncture, all readers must struggle to place and examine, as they evolve over the course of American history, the intersections of gender along with class, ethnic, race, and location—as they confront economic change, inequality, norms, policies, and institutions—all of them highlighted from a historically oriented framework. Change and continuity, similarities and divergences, conflicts and contradictions: the patterning of growing up as experienced in American history.

25. Dating Becomes the Way of American Youth

I never go with any girls,
I never make a date.
I'm never fussing on the squad
Or saying "ain't love great?"
I never take one to a dance,
The reason's plain to see.
I never go with girls because
The girls won't go with me.
—from *Minneapolis Central High News,* 1923

Dating was already becoming prescriptive behavior for urban high school students when a Minneapolis boy published this comic lament in his high school newspaper in 1923.[1] His nonfeasance was to be explained neither by simple preference on his part, nor by any characteristic of the dating system itself: only a personal flaw could explain why one did not date. In high school, if one hoped to be favorably recognized by one's peers, one dated—and this, if anything, was even truer for girls than for boys. "I am . . . considered not bad looking or a bad dresser. But somehow I just can't be popular either with boys or girls. I would love to, but I simply can't. I don't know what is the matter. All my girl acquaintances always talk about their beaus and dates, but I don't have any. I'm always by myself."[2] My essay seeks to elucidate the terms of the dating system in its early years, to discuss the reasons for and to describe the pattern of its spread, and to consider some of its cultural and personal implications.

I

"The outside world of today has no use for flimsy worshipers of petty idols such as 'popularity,' " thundered a Minneapolis Central High editorialist in 1923, but popularity was the universally understood term for what the great majority of high schoolers sought to a greater or lesser degree. Such editorial fulmination was, of course, to no avail. "Many individuals as soon as they attain 'popularity' turn down their friends of former days and never even seem to recognize them again," the editorial claimed, but at the same time other high-school editorialists were excoriating the tendency to cliquishness that evidently characterized their schools then as now.[3] Popularity and cliquishness were closely

John Modell, "Dating Becomes the Way of American Youth," reprinted from *Essays on the Family and Historical Change* (The Walter Prescott Webb Memorial Lectures, 17), ed. Leslie Page Moch and Gary D. Stark (College Station: Texas A & M University Press, for the University of Texas at Arlington, 1983), 91–126, by permission of Webb Memorial Lectures, University of Texas at Arlington.

related and tied closely to dating: both were parts of a new system of social relations governed informally but firmly by young people themselves. Not all youth saw dating in the same light, to be sure, even in the high schools. Material wherewithal made a difference, as we shall see; so also did cultural heritage. And asymmetries of gender roles were the armature around which the dating system evolved. But for the moment let us simply note that well before the adult world took much notice,[4] most boys and girls from their mid-teens on came to organize their social lives around an institution not of their elders' making, one that was to reorient—partially—the road to marriage.

The defining characteristic of the new dating system and, what is more critical, of the graduated series of dates that might lead to a closer relationship between young men and women was that a date was away from home, unchaperoned, and not subject to parental veto; it depended upon the free election of the participants. Certainly, *some* American boys and girls of the middle classes had coupled in every imaginable way without parental awareness before the turn of the century, but "dates" of this sort lacked the continuity and regularity that the full evolution of the dating system would permit after World War I. Under the older system, there was no normatively sanctioned way to get "serious" about someone without doing so at least occasionally at home and with parental approval. Chaperonage asserted parents' oversight of what boys and girls might do together, and the home visit assured girls' parents of some control over whom their daughters might be seeing. Both were important, and both vanished with dating, which substituted peer oversight. Not the occurrence of emotional or physical intimacy but the question of whose advice guided young people in developing heterosexual ties was the critical difference between dating and "keeping company," which it supplanted.[5]

When 1920s' parents asserted chaperonage or oversight, they were repulsed. The young unmarried woman "considers the whole matter a farce," reported an earnest "young matron" to her discussion group in 1922. She continued, "There is little respect for the chaperone, whose presence has no effect whatever upon the actions of the young people. The chaperone is considered mainly as a sop to the older generation."[6] And efforts to bring the date into the home in the face of the spread of commercial amusement and the prosperity to get to it proved hopeless gestures: "A mother [cannot] . . . oppose her in the progress of this affair which the girl takes so seriously. But one thing she can do; she can have the man or the boy, if it is only a boy, constantly invited to the house. When the girl compares him with her father or brothers he may fall short of the standards of taste or education which they maintain."[7] Parents shortly abandoned these checks as they surrendered the more direct aspects of their oversight of their adolescent children. A chapter in Emily Post's 1923 edition was titled "Chaperons and Other Conventions." By 1927, it was "The Vanishing Chaperon and Other New Conventions," and by 1937 "The Vanished Chaperon and Other Lost Conventions."[8] In 1932 a government advice pamphlet described the new pattern of youth behavior (including petting) as a "wholesome" abandonment of "Victorian" patterns, and a sensible aspect of mate selection. (The advice, to be sure, was somewhat in the van of public opinion on the petting issue.) The "crush," once the subject of utter condescension, had now to be seen as a valuable developmental episode, and dating as the occasion for mature choice.[9]

The date itself had a compelling logic quite distinct from that of prior forms: it was a step in an ongoing negotiation with rules defined and deviations punished by age peers. The logic of the date anchored it in pleasure and centered the choices it occasioned in the daters themselves (within limits imposed by the peer culture). The home visit or chaperoned dance, in essence, had been either purely sociable—part of a group occasion—or overtly related to courtship. The date might turn out to be either of these, or both, or something else again, but what it turned out to be depended upon how well the negotiation at its core went, a negotiation regarding immediate pleasure. By definition, boys planned and paid for "a good time" and asked of their girls a bit of physical intimacy. How a boy pled his case, how his date responded, and the future of the pair as a couple depended not only on the boy's sense of his investment and the girl's scale of values, but also on the public commitment each was willing to make to the other and their tastes for emotional intimacy.[10]

Petting, that delicate standoff between sensual indulgence and constraint, was almost universal in the sense that all daters petted at some time, but not in the sense that all couples petted. Graduated physical intimacy became an accepted part of lasting teen relationships, both a marker of affection and a spur to increased commitment.

Boys were assumed to be always on the lookout for some petting, but girls were assumed on the whole to get far less physical pleasure from the act itself.[11] Boys pursued; girls rewarded boys who were affectionate, restrained, and provided a pleasant time; girls rewarded boys moderately. Even when girls were fond of petting, they found that their peer group, curiously aided by boy gossip, stood in the way of their being too easy. Even for girls in love, peer pressure set limits to lovemaking. Thus, a high school girl noted in 1929: "The girl who permits liberties is certainly popular with boys, but her popularity never lasts very long with any one boy. You know the saying, 'Just a toy to play with, not the kind they choose to grow old and grey with.' "[12] Boys' behavior could be modified: "Even freshmen girls know . . . that a boy who considers himself a gentleman may have standards that vary according to those of the girl with whom he may be," wrote a high school dean of women.[13] Dating, thus, operated still within a double standard of sexual conduct that demanded of girls the strength to say no and the strength of mind to prevent matters from coming to such a pass.

The absolute good girl–bad girl dichotomy inherent in this code was shifted to permit more physical expression by girls, but if blurred somewhat, it was not eradicated. Dating was threatening to girls, even as it partially liberated their heterosexual expressiveness. With imperfect contraceptive knowledge, pregnancy was a lurking danger, certainly in view of the widespread assumption that sexual excitement was rapidly progressive for inexperienced girls as well as boys. "In that first, burning kiss Betty forgot everything except that Jack was her man, her mate, her lover," *True Confessions* reported in its first volume, and steadily thereafter.[14]

The terms of the dating exchange were widely understood among the young, but not uniformly. Petting was particularly often at the heart of misunderstanding, probably because it incorporated a partial revision of the deeply inculcated double standard.[15] Certain adolescents, like "Miss Dateless," found themselves essentially outside of the dating pool because they failed or refused to recognize that this fundamental exchange in dating was normatively governed and structured by a sense of the emotions appropriate to age and stage.

> I am 20 years old and, to use the slang expression, "hard up for dates." I am rather small, but have my share of good looks. I am inevitably cheerful, like sports of all kinds and like to talk of them. I am interested in good music. . . . But—I sit at home without the boys. I think one of the reasons is that I am not common enough. I let a boy know it if he gets fresh with me

and scratch him off my list. I use cosmetics, but sometimes look pale near some of these "clowns." However, they get "dates."[16]

Miss Dateless quite correctly blames her peer group for her unfortunate situation and expresses an alienation (carried by her use of the class term "common" and by her snide reference to "clowns") that hardly admits of much room for improvement. Letters from casualties of the dating system to lovelorn columnists are filled with evidence that they were condemned by their peers as "stuck up." Others, no doubt, simply petted, either out of anguish at being outsiders or out of anxiety at datelessness leading to matelessness. Dating, insofar as it encouraged at least somewhat spontaneous behavior in the negotiation that lay at its core, laid a cruel burden on those who were stiff and uncomfortable on dates—boy and girl alike, but more terrifyingly for girls because marriage was prescriptive for them. So also the impecunious boy and the ugly girl must suffer.

The remarkable (if problematic)[17] sexual histories collected by Alfred Kinsey and his associates permit us a close view of the historical role of this particular dynamic of the dating system. These data point to a distinct sexualization of noncoital (or precoital) relations between the pre–World War I and postwar adolescent cohorts—more striking, indeed, than the often remarked increase in premarital coitus also recorded. Among the men and women in the ever-married sample I employed, the 34 percent of women who achieved orgasm in petting in the older cohort increased to 60 percent among the first cohort that passed its adolescence in the "dating" era: for men, the increase was from an already high 64 percent to 71 percent. The particular datum—related closely to that on orgasm—that I will employ in my discussion is age at first petting. The Kinsey data here point to an increase from 29 percent to 43 percent of girls who petted "young" (before sixteen) and an increase from 41 percent of boys to 51 percent.

Dating (and petting), I have argued, was part of a new bargain between girls and boys, weakening parents' oversight but not resolving the asymmetries implied by the double standard. Early petters among the Kinsey respondents relatively often paid the price in family tension. Table 25.1 indicates that while perhaps one in five of the postwar adolescent cohort recalled tension with both of his or her parents during early adoles-

Table 25.1. **Proportions Reporting Conflict with Both Parents, by Sex, Cohort, and Age First Began Petting**

Cohort	Petted before 14 (N)	Petted 14–15 (N)	Petted 16–17 (N)	Petted 18 or older (N)
Women				
Born before 1910	18.5% (53)	29.6% (162)	17.0% (212)	19.1% (309)
Born 1910–1919	31.3 (96)	25.0 (212)	26.5 (260)	14.1 (170)
Men				
Born before 1910	16.4 (116)	14.6 (191)	23.0 (187)	18.0 (250)
Born 1910–1919	28.4 (141)	19.0 (226)	17.4 (201)	16.6 (151)

Source: Kinsey Sex Histories (ever-married whites only). See note 17.

Table 25.2. **Proportions Reporting "Many" Friends of the Opposite Sex at 16 or 17, by Sex, Cohort, and Age First Began Petting**

Cohort	Petted before 14	Petted 14–15	Petted 16–17	Petted 18 or older
Women				
Born before 1910	64.1%	61.7%	44.5%	32.5%
Born 1910–1919	69.4	59.8	41.7	20.8
Men				
Born before 1910	49.2	41.3	30.8	14.7
Born 1910–1919	57.0	48.6	32.6	13.0

Source: Kinsey Sex Histories (ever-married whites only).

cence,[18] the proportion was markedly higher (especially for the girls) among the early petters and lower among the late petters. The pattern was absent in the earlier cohort. The reason for the historical emergence of this pattern lies in the meaning of petting to 1920s' adolescents: it was at once a source of pleasure, a coin in the dating bargain, and a challenge to parental values. In participating in the dating system, boys and girls helped modify the existing pattern of values, giving more play to preference and less to received wisdom. Parents, rightly, recognized a behavior that bespoke a larger resistance to their authority and resented it.

For peers, too, petting was increasingly incorporated into a normatively relevant set of behaviors. To a far greater degree than parental disapproval, popularity with opposite-sex friends came to depend on comfort in petting and dating. Table 25.2 takes age at first petting as a crude reflection of being at ease with the evolved rules of the dating system and shows a striking relationship between such an easy accommodation and respondents' estimates of "how many (opposite-sex) friends and companions did you have . . . when you were 16 or 17." It is obviously impossible to sort out the direction of causality here: those who had petted were probably the more successful daters and possessed the qualities that made for popularity; those who were popular had the opportunity to pet. But there is no need to sort out the cause: the point is to note that in the dating era the relationship obtained for both boys and girls.

Popularity, as successful dating, depended not on particular attributes so much as on the ability to perform comfortably and enthusiastically within the peer group. When students selected their "most popular" peers (and in the "Senior Hall of Fame" compilations I have examined, "most popular" is always the honor atop the list), boys and girls adjudged "best looking," "classiest," "cutest," or "smartest" rarely were voted "most popular."[19] ("Most Studious" students never were.) Instead, the winners were outstandingly "courteous," "generous," and "thoughtful," were "busy looking," "100 per cent," filled with "class spirit," and just plain "best all-around." My sources do not reveal what derisory terms were applied to those who most apparently lacked such social ease. We can, however, be sure that for them the oversight of courtship by peers seemed a poor substitute for the parental role that had been abandoned.

The only serious historical account of the emergence of the dating system is that of the historian Paula Fass, whose recent *The Damned and the Beautiful* is a subtle view of the youth culture that emerged among collegians in the 1920s. Fass interprets dating as one among many of the accomplishments of a self-conscious generation, acting in part over and against its predecessors: "It was not caprice . . . that made them question traditional proprieties in sexual morality and in such areas as smoking, drinking, and dancing. These the young defined as the private sector, as a sphere for personal expression to be governed by need and taste rather than by law and morals. . . . The young knew that their patterns and attitudes provided a margin of difference between them and their elders, and gave them a vehicle for group cohesion."[20]

Oddly, perhaps inadvertently, Fass's explanation of dating in the 1920s abandons internal group factors for such macrosocial factors as mobility, commercial amusement, and an overall weakening of family authority. Moreover, while I find her description of the dating scene most persuasive and the notion of self-conscious youth compelling, two elements in her account demand reconsideration. First, her identification of youth with collegians leads her to overlook the fact that a dating system evolved simultaneously among high school students. This part of the system affected more people and coincided with the period of heterosexual awakening in participants' lives. Second, the generality of Fass's account of youth probably explains her mistaken assumption of a basic unity of interest within middle-class youth that denies that boys and girls had different things at stake in the development of dating.

Fass powerfully demonstrates that the symbols of generational revolt were preeminently borne by women and that they took the form of the narrowing of differences in the behaviors of the two genders: language, clothing, smoking, hairstyle, and social intercourse between the sexes, in the latter constituting a modest challenge to the double standard of sexual propriety.[21] If "freedom" or autonomy seemed to contemporaries to be at stake, in retrospect, youth—and young women in particular—seem to have proposed no fundamental changes in the moral order, only the lifting of limitations, based on age and gender, upon their own right to choose among conventional options. They challenged received definitions of authority, not morality, positioning themselves to take advantage of the alluring but hardly revolutionary range of new consumer choice created by the burgeoning economy.[22] If sex was now "as frankly discussed as automobiles or the advantage of cold storage over moth balls, why should our elders consider our interest in this subject a sign of unnaturalness or perversion? Should it not constitute the chief concern of those in whose hands the future generation lies?"[23] If young people in rejecting received courtship procedures rejected traditional romanticism, they by no means rejected marriage or marriage based on love.[24] The dating system, as they understood it, was an institutional framework to accomplish exactly this end.

The dating system suited boys well, but its establishment represented some inroads upon the double standard. The main architects of its code were girls.[25] Before dating, parents tended to construe strictly girls' obligation to enter marriage untainted by even a hint of scandal, and they supervised courting accordingly, limiting not only its occasion, but, to a degree, the set of eligibles. The boy who came calling had not only to be prepared to behave himself; he also had to pass prima facie muster as a boy who by reputation *would* behave himself. Under the double standard, however, boys' reputations were both subject to repair and of far less interest to their own families. Whereas girls had to be chosen by a boy and then gain parental permission to receive his attentions, boys had only to choose. The girls had more to gain by the establishment of dating, because the new version of the double standard that it put in place was considerably less restrictive to them than the one it replaced.

II

In the 1920s, as Fass argues, "the schools first and foremost gave youth a setting and a home, . . . [where] the society of peers flourished, enclosing the young in a world that was theirs by right of possession." Fass particularly intends to describe residential colleges, maintaining by a comparison that "the world of the high school was more circumscribed by adult supervision and regulation; . . . in the high school the peer group was one of a number of competing influences."[26] There is some truth to this, but Fass has not really looked at much high school evidence, and this points to a fully elaborated dating system. Moreover, high school rather than college included the ages at which boys and girls started seeking each other out.[27] It is a trifle difficult to imagine young people practicing parentally supervised "courting" through the high school years, but then regearing themselves emotionally for dating in college. And while we must grant Fass's important point about the relative strength of peer-group dominance at college as compared with high school, the high school subjected far more young people to an age-graded setting and encouraged the kind of peer-group activities that (as Fass suggests) created a controllable leadership structure among the students.[28]

The middle of the teenage spectrum rather than either end was most implicated in the sharp expansion of schooling in the 1920s smack in the middle of the high school years. The graph, comparing the proportion of unmarried boys and girls who attended school during 1920 and 1930, shows the focus of the expansion to be among sixteen- and seventeen-year-olds, for both sexes.[29] To be sure, college grew even more explosively than did high schooling in the 1920s in proportional terms. Between 1920 and 1930, B.A.s conferred increased by 152 percent while the number of high school diplomas awarded grew by a somewhat more modest 114 percent. In both college and high school the sex ratio of graduates evened out during the decade, women collegians approaching the number of men, boy high school graduates nearly equalling girls. Trends aside, colleges still enrolled and graduated far more men than women, but high schools had almost even sex ratios—a demography far more conducive to widespread dating than that in college.[30] Many college men had to import female companions ("townies"), whom they often sought to exploit sexually as "bad girls," in a setting lacking the near equality and peer group oversight of the evolving high school date, thereby emphasizing rather than mitigating the double standard.[31]

In the 1920s, age homogenization was a self-conscious policy of many high school administrators, accomplished even as the schools expanded rapidly and took in students from families that were close enough to the economic margin to require supplementary income from their children from time to time.[32] Nonpromotion increasingly was seen to encourage dropping out, and this seen as unfortunate; "social promotion" now suited educational and developmental theory. (Early promotion was far less common.) A dramatic example of the progress of age homogenization is found in the school system of Duluth, Minnesota. Among sixteen-year-olds attending Duluth public schools in 1920–1921, only 25.1 percent of the boys and 36.1 percent of the girls were in a single grade; five years of age homogenization brought these figures to 33.5 percent and 40.2 percent; by the mid-1930s they were up to 41.6 percent and 54.2 percent.[33] (The continued greater age homogenization of girls is explained by their greater trained capacity for regimentation, as at school, and by the greater pressure for boys to earn money.) Homogenization by age makes a great deal of difference to dating, since dating depended

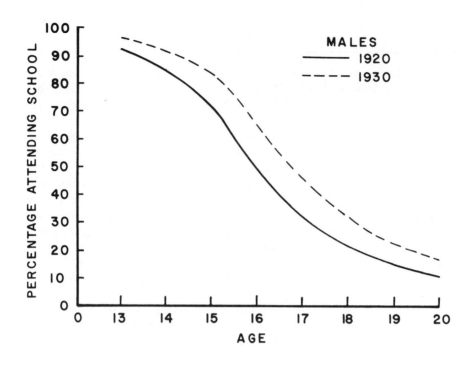

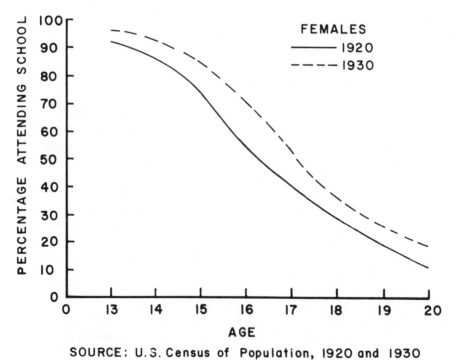

SOURCE: U.S. Census of Population, 1920 and 1930

Graph 25.1. Proportions of never-married boys and girls attending school, by single year of age 1920 and 1930.

upon freely entered short-term agreements between near equals, differentiated mainly by gender, and overseen by the opinion of mutually valued, interrelated sets of age peers. Age, with its correlated experience, earning capacity, and prestige was the kind of differentiator that could render too unequal the negotiation at dating's core. (In parallel with cultural expectations governing marriage, girls could date somewhat older boys.) Age homogenization limited exploitation and permitted the girls to move somewhat beyond the constrictive safety provided by adherence to the double standard.

The formal extracurricular life of the high school quickly came to be articulated with the interpersonal dynamics of the dating system. Quite early, many high schools instituted dances, in an effort of varying success to take the play away from commercial dance halls and road houses.[34] Too, "it is a well-known fact that club pins are an absolute necessity when a young man wishes to plight his time-enduring regard for some lady, but, even considering this, it ought not be necessary to have more than three or four."[35] Beyond visible symbols, word of mouth was powerful where everybody was likely to know everybody. "Why should we have so many idle gossipers in the school? . . . Much to our dislike we have many social groups and this lowers cooperation within the student body."[36] Gossip, of course, while lowering cooperation also regulated behavior—reassuringly for the most part, oppressively upon occasion. Trends in fashion were sharply defined and served to mark out those who qualified for the dating pool. A "bobbed hair census" at Little Falls (Minnesota) High in 1923 indicated the strength of fashion: in each of the four classes, more than three girls in four adopted this hair style, so rich in affirmation of modernity.[37] (Even among "sub-freshmen," 65 percent had already caught on.)

I do not propose even to speculate about when the institution of dating began. The records of behavior initiated by children are as spotty as for any literate group, and an institution that "just grew" found no chroniclers, much as it provides few pegs for the memory. Adolescent diaries for the twentieth century are surely not rare, but do not seem to be collected. What is documentable is that the elaboration of dating as a system began in the first quarter of the current century and spread with noteworthy rapidity from an initially urban and middle-class epicenter during the 1920s and 1930s. The circumstances of youth itself provide one key to this timing, as does also the rapid enlargement of consumer choice. An ideological element, too, played a part. The frankly—if guardedly—sexual quality of the date (and thereby of courtship incorporating the date) is consistent with "proper" behavior for boys and girls only after "the conspiracy of silence" governing sexual matters was challenged in the public areas and some consequences of the double standard of sexual morality called into question by highly respectable twentieth-century reformers and symbolically challenged by "new women."[38]

Dating spread remarkably quickly. In a San Jose, California, high school, two-thirds of the sophomore boys and three-quarters of senior boys were dating in 1930. Data collected in 1933 from a large sample of high school girls, oversampled among Catholic schools, found that half of the freshmen and 84 percent of the seniors had begun dating. An excellent study of an urban high school found that in 1941 virtually every boy had dated by his senior year, and all but 14 percent of the girls.[39] Burgess and Wallin presented data collected mainly from college students and graduates, pertaining to the late 1920s and early 1930s, which indicates that about one-third of both boys and girls dated by age fourteen, a bit more than two-thirds by sixteen, and virtually all by eighteen. A national, "faithfully balanced cross-section of high school students" in 1942 gave average estimates of 71 percent of the boys and 63 percent of the girls "necking" on dates, averaged over the four years of high school.[40]

Dating is almost universally identified as an urban pattern in its early years and not a rural one. A careful study of upstate New York rural girls in 1933 revealed that although the institution had definitely made its way into the countryside, it had done so rather tenuously. Thirty-three percent of the girls aged fifteen to seventeen had never yet dated, and an additional 49 percent did not yet date "consistently." Even at ages eighteen to twenty, 58 percent were not yet consistent daters, in addition to the 15 percent who still did not date at all. It is noteworthy that for each younger cohort of girls interviewed, dating had begun younger, as the institution diffused, but at the mid-30s alternative modes of mate selection were still in operation in the country.[41] These girls, when they dated, went to movies, dances, parties, and on motor rides, just as did urban youth. But where the rural families were less prosperous than families in upstate New York, rural social life devoted exclusively to youth was exceptionally truncated. In the countryside, parents' capacity to exercise close supervision was often too great; many farm youth were said to seek the city partly on this account. Urbanites brought up on the dating system described as "grim" the marriage that a farm girl might contract without "a chance to get out when she was a girl, to know more men," to find through dating "the singing joy that lightens daily burdens."[42]

Urban working-class youth seem to have had sufficient distance from parental oversight to erect a dating system, but other matters militated against it. Jane Synge's fine oral history accounts of family life during this period in Hamilton, Ontario, indicate that for working-class daughters parental oversight often extended no further than the initial permission to be called upon by the first boy or two. Thereafter, perhaps, courtships might ensue that were strangely "informal" and without recognizable stages: "Direct control was impossible since . . . most informants met their spouses-to-be at work and spent time with them on the way to and from work."[43] Yet working-class children could not control the time, place, or tempo of such contacts. They also lacked both the wherewithal for the "good time" dating asked of the boy and the effective, school-based, same-age peer group that oversaw behavior within the dating system. The sociological accounts of Donovan on waitresses, Thrasher on the boy gang, and Thomas on girl delinquents discuss nonmiddle-class milieus of the 1920s lacking in both material wherewithal and overseeing peer groups, in which dating in the sense we are discussing clearly does not organize heterosexual contact.[44] Whyte's Boston observations in the mid-1930s pointed out the continued existence of ethnic working-class settings in which assumptions about gender roles rendered dating inappropriate.[45] Even among less isolated high school students, impecunious boys operated at a real disadvantage in the dating system, a problem that was to become acute during the Depression, since the terms of the date still required the boy to *purchase* amusement for the couple.[46] In college, the "economic status" of boys (but not of girls) explained more than "looks" about how young they started dating, how often they dated, and how intimate they became with their dating partner. Girls, or course, needed to spend at least enough to keep up with clothing fashions.[47]

By the end of the Depression decade, dating was generally but not entirely diffused as a youth pattern and as an aspect of mate selection. The dating system was part of a larger set of behaviors in which youthful peer groups arrogated authority previously exercised by adults within the family. A remarkable youth survey conducted in 1939 asked about several of these symbolic areas of conduct (although, unfortunately, not very directly about dating), permitting us a suggestive view of the bounds of the youth culture at this date.[48]

Table 25.3 makes evident, first of all, that in 1939 both smoking (as an example) and differing with parents about opposite-sex friends were strongly dependent upon both age and gender. Large proportions of boys and girls eventually took up smoking as they grew up, but boys started earlier than girls and continued to smoke more commmonly. While smoking was generally considered a fitting thing for young men to do in 1939, for some girls it connoted a "racier" image than they desired. If girls were more restrained than boys in adopting cigarettes as a sign of self-determination, they were nevertheless considerably more likely than boys to report conflict with their parents about such issues as opposite-sex friends. Undoubtedly, the girls' answers here reflected real differences in the closeness of the scrutiny parents attempted to exercise over their activities, dating in particular. For both boys and girls, as they grew up, the tensions over this question were exacerbated. But girls were held to a higher standard.

Among boys, smoking (at any given age) varied rather little by father's occupational type (our indicator of the class of the family) and varied little, too, by the size of town or city in which the family lived. The rapid adoption of cigarettes was essentially ubiquitous for boys. For girls, the story was different. Most striking is the class difference: really, it is fair to say that among teenage girls, smoking (and probably dating) developed first in the middle class and to a degree remained particularly a middle-class habit. Middle-class girls were pretty nearly as likely to smoke at any given age as boys. But strong gender differences were present for blue-collar and farm families, which denied girls the freedom to smoke that they granted their sons. Girls, too, but not boys, were treated differently in city and countryside. Whether they lived in large or small city, town, or countryside, boys learned to smoke according to pretty much the same schedule. Girls, however, who commonly smoked if they lived in cities, smoked only rarely if they lived on farms, with intermediate-sized places arrayed appropriately in between. It was in the large city where girls developed and enforced upon their parents a peer code that incorporated the sophisticated gesture of smoking, a gesture that even in 1939 gained meaning in part from its similarity to the behavior of the boys and in part from the contrast it allowed them to make to their parents' generation (and to rural girls). I do not doubt but much the same pattern obtained with regard to aspects of the dating code itself.

If sophistication varied systematically, as we have seen was the case with smoking, we might well hypothesize that conflict with parents (as that about opposite-sex friends) varied in the same way. We have seen this to have been the case with regard to age, but that girls at once were less free in their behavior than boys and more often at odds with their parents. Table 25.3 indicates, moreover, that in the places and in the social categories in which girls were more sophisticated, a *smoother* accommodation with their parents had on the whole already been accomplished. The dating system here had already realized its potential of promoting cultural change. Blue-collar and white-collar parents of girls (as of boys) were equally likely to differ with their daughters over boyfriends. Despite the different pace at which peer norms affected girls' behaviors, parents of both social classes grew concerned to roughly the same degree as their daughters grew up. Farm parents, on the other hand, kept their daughters away from smoking rather successfully, evidently by a prickly and active oversight over their social activities more generally, especially at the younger ages. Nonfarm parents had settled into a truce with their children, an uneasy one

Table 25.3. **Smoking and Conflict with Parents over Opposite-Sex Friends by Sex and Age, by Father's Occupational Category, and by Town Size, 1939**

	Boys			Girls		
Group	14–15 (N)	16–17 (N)	18–19 (N)	14–15 (N)	16–17 (N)	18–19 (N)
Smoke regularly or occasionally (All)	23.6% (314)	44.8% (306)	66.0% (300)	9.0% (312)	21.0% (310)	44.2% (303)
Father's occupational type						
White collar	16.1 (112)	37.4 (115)	64.8 (128)	12.2 (123)	31.5 (127)	64.8 (125)
Blue collar	23.1 (136)	45.5 (134)	71.3 (101)	3.9 (128)	11.3 (115)	27.8 (97)
Farm	31.1 (45)	55.3 (38)	63.2 (57)	10.0 (40)	25.6 (39)	21.1 (57)
Town size						
1 million +	26.2 (42)	52.2 (46)	62.8 (43)	0.0 (40)	12.8 (39)	74.4 (43)
25,000–999,999	15.1 (86)	31.7 (82)	72.3 (83)	12.4 (89)	30.2 (86)	56.1 (82)
Town to 24,999	21.9 (73)	37.1 (70)	49.2 (63)	11.0 (73)	21.3 (75)	42.6 (68)
Rural	30.1 (113)	56.5 (108)	72.1 (111)	8.2 (110)	16.4 (110)	24.5 (110)
"Have different ideas from either one or both of your parents on (girl) (boy) friends" (All)	12.9 (310)	16.0 (301)	21.5 (298)	29.6 (314)	39.4 (307)	42.0 (298)
Father's occupational type						
White collar	9.0 (111)	11.4 (114)	21.3 (127)	29.0 (124)	37.3 (126)	42.7 (124)
Blue collar	15.7 (134)	19.4 (134)	23.3 (103)	25.6 (129)	36.8 (114)	39.6 (96)
Farm	22.2 (45)	14.3 (35)	19.6 (56)	41.5 (41)	55.1 (49)	46.4 (56)
Town size						
1 million +	7.3 (41)	15.2 (46)	11.4 (44)	23.1 (39)	30.0 (40)	36.6 (41)
25,000–999,999	16.3 (86)	9.8 (82)	26.2 (80)	31.1 (90)	32.1 (84)	36.6 (82)
Town to 24,999	8.6 (70)	20.3 (69)	23.8 (63)	24.7 (73)	40.0 (75)	41.2 (68)
Rural	17.7 (113)	18.3 (104)	20.7 (111)	33.9 (112)	48.1 (108)	48.6 (107)

Source: Roper Commercial Poll No. 15. Roper Center, University of Connecticut.

to be sure, that farm parents hadn't quite accepted yet—two decades after urban girls made gestures in the direction of what they saw as freedom. The tabulations by city size, likewise, indicate that in 1939 the further away one was from the sources of urban sophistication, the more likely was the clash of cultures between the generations.

Granted, the argument is inferential, but it seems safe to argue that a diffusion process spread the dating complex from middle to urban working-class families, and from city to countryside. For this, no doubt, we can credit the concurrent differential pace of the spread of age-homogenized high schools, the consumer culture, and "modern" values regarding sex and gender. The interrelated set of behavioral manifestations and redefinitions of personal feelings that dating entailed, permitting as they did girls to negotiate a somewhat more balanced set of gender relationships with their dates than their predecessors had received under their parents' protection, moved gradually through the American culture. One can easily imagine how a dating boy might teach a formerly nondating girl the rudiments, and how adolescent conversation could convey the essence of the institution. "Cora told me that I was a fool to high-hat Ben. He was a good, hard-working guy, she said, and would make a swell husband. But . . . I wasn't in any hurry to get married, and when I did, I wanted someone different from Ben," who was a repetitious, sexually unimaginative, and distinctly *cheap* date. In this 1931 confession, the narrator but not Cora had learned the middle-class dating code.[49]

III

Despite their substantially united front toward their parents' generation, boys and girls had by no means identical interests in the new dating scheme. The earlier female growth spurt provided a convenient sign for what contemporaries believed (and thereby encouraged) to be girls' earlier awareness of the opposite sex as objects of interest. Contemporary accounts of adolescent behavior had boys entering the high school ages still in a "gang stage," while girls had long before turned to "fancies . . . of men and boys, and of herself as the center of attraction and interest. . . . She becomes interested in dress and personal adornment . . . [and] ruin[s] her healthy skin with rouge and lipstick."[50] Girls, furthermore, more often than boys remained through high school graduation. If there were more girls in high school potentially to be seeking dates, so also higher proportions of them, particularly among the freshmen and sophomores, presumably hoped to date. Accordingly, girls sought to limit competition by defining its terms and to enlarge the pool of eligible boys. There was, of course, the alternative possibility for a girl to be a collegian's or an employed boy's "townie," but such a choice took the date outside its familiar negotiating balance and outside the supportive structure of peer-group gossip. Gossip and the clique system operated to limit the terms of competition among girls, most particularly by regulating the amount of physical gratification with which they could reward their dates: commonly such gossip took the form of "catty" statements that anyone could get boys by giving a good deal of sex (i.e., that this did not reflect true popularity). Meanwhile, the repeated jousting and chiding of the boy population in general (sometimes, happily for the historian, in the high school newspaper) served to bring marginal boys into the dating pool. Ritualized gender conflict was one of the most striking aspects of high school newspapers, and, one suspects, of peer-group activities more generally, when these supported the dating system.

Chiding served to educate boys to the proper ways of behaving toward girls, so that the rules of the dating system might be learned even by the more backward boys: "Boys, is it fair to make the girls come to a school entertainment unescorted? So far, I have not been to an entertainment without seeing three-fourths of the girls come without escorts. The most disgusting thing about it is, that the boys act as though they did not realize the predicament they've placed the girls in . . . . I believe the faculty should make a rule that no girls come to the parties unescorted and that no boy be admitted without a young lady."[51] Or: "What has come over the boys of this school? . . . Is it the lack of carfare? I am sure that we girls would be happy to supply that . . . instead of going home alone after 11 o'clock. Fewer girls will be allowed to attend parties at school, since they must return late alone. Just because a boy is gentleman enough to take a girl home, is no reason that he is in love with her. All we want is common courtesy, not husbands."[52] Boys must be taught the nonbinding quality of a date, to distinguish it from the courtship system that dating was replacing. The complaint was not misdirected, for an earnest correspondent responded in the next issue: "There are many reasons. Not that the young man has not the price of carfare, or is too stingy, but that the girls of to-day are too different from those of yesterday. He has not as yet become acquainted with their ways. It will take a long time unless the girls do their part and bring the boys out of that bashful state which is keeping them from mixing in with the girls and being treated as equals. Therefore, act as though you wanted to be taken home, and I am sure you will not be disappointed."[53]

"Bashful" was the word. Throughout the decade, female correspondents in all of these papers would resurrect it as an adjective of mild condescension addressed to the boys they hoped to recruit to the pool of dating eligibles: "As usual, only senior and junior girls are to be present, but boys of the lower classes are allowed to come. In that case the senior and junior girls must wait to be invited before they can attend. It would be unfortunate to have these girls left out and, weird as it may seem, the task of inviting them is up to the boys—bashful and otherwise. Let's have as many junior and senior girls asked as possible, boys."[54] "Stags" posed a problem, and girls pressed for the elimination of stags and the establishment of fixed-partner dates at school dances and no doubt elsewhere. For girls, the "Stag" arrangement and its attendant "cutting in" at dances was an invitation to humiliation or boredom and left all the power of decision making in the hands of boys, who not rarely looked after one another's interests and gave no thought to the wallflowers the system inevitably created. "Just fancy knowing that a boy is dancing past the stagline and waving a five-dollar bill behind your back as an offer to anyone who'll come and take you away!"[55] While in the dating system a girl had to wait on a boy's invitation, once an invitation was issued, a boy was bound (if imperfectly until the system was quite learned) to honor certain rules of conduct.

A correspondent to the *Minneapolis Central High News* in 1924 put the problem well: "What is a sunlite [informal daytime dance] for? Is it so the male population of the school can go and occupy one side of the room and the female population go and occupy another? There are the same few boys at every sunlite who won't dance—they just stand there. Why will a boy go to a girl's home and dance all evening and then not dance with her any place else? Is it that he doesn't consider her good enough? . . . May I have an answer to this question from some one of the 'Stags'?"[56] Why would some boys act in this fashion, and why would girls object to it? To understand this we need to take into consideration the ambiguous moral meaning of dance at the time. Dancing was one of the symbols of youth revolt, and in this symbolic meaning dancing was downright sexual. But between members of a generation who had grown up with such forms, the meaning of dancing was in the main recreation and structured sociability, but inherently suggestive and potentially explosive. Boys, as a group, found it in their interest to press dancing in a sexual direction, which suited girls' purposes insofar as the dancing served as a declaration of generational freedom; but for them the sexualization of dancing also inched the terms of the boy-girl negotiation that much closer to "going too far," at which point they had more to lose. The public nature of the high school dance, accordingly— aside from fueling the competitive element of the dating system—served girls' purposes ideally. Thus, perhaps, when the Alexandria (Minnesota) High School circulated in 1927 a questionnaire to its students regarding more parties and, for the first time, school dances, both boys and girls voted overwhelmingly for more parties, but boys only split evenly on dances, which girls supported by five to two.[57]

Probably far less important to girls than their partial escape from parental oversight was the right subtly to affirm in dating the sexual element in courtship, which value they shared (if not to the same extent) with boys. But even here, girls had something special at stake, because in dating physical pleasure was defined as properly a token of affection and commitment. Through dating, girls considerably before marriage could discover with boys patterns of emotional intimacy congruent with those the female subculture had long valued, but without ultimate commitment, physical or marital.[58] Nor need the task of finding a good mate be forgotten, for the dating system elaborated a series of stages that led toward engagement and beyond. The tender interpersonal qualities sought in a good date, while not identical to those of a good mate, were nevertheless among the desirable traits. For boys, of course, their date's good looks—and by the 1920s this would include the appearance of sexual awareness ("sex appeal" or "it")—ranked high. Dating was a negotiation between boys and girls, but one in which at least the physical component of girls' bargaining counters was seen as both dangerous and perishable. Pretty girls, with more occasion to attract the most eligible boys and to hone their social skills, married earlier and better. For those less favored by nature or less able to attain the prescribed appearance, dating was a less pleasant process.[59] Boys, after all, initiated dates. And the double standard allowed them a wider leeway in the kinds of pleasures they could seek from the opposite sex and gave them the leeway of a later preferred marriage age.

Occasionally rebelling verbally against "girls who have dates four or five out of the seven days of the week" and the "sort of contest" among girls "to see who can get the most dates in one week," boys accepted the new regime.[60] For them, it was something of a gain, in the sensual pleasures of petting, in the tenderness of occasional intimate conversation, in the articulation of "popularity" with the bumptiously democratic tone (and stratified structure) of the new, expanded, age-homogenized high schools. " 'It's just that I like to take her places,' explained one among the many suitors of Bette, the most popular date in the junior class. 'You're sure to have a good time with her. She's never a liability, you know that she'll be the belle of the ball. But really I'm not crazy about her.' "[61]

The developing internal logic of the date can be discerned in the statements of those whose dating experiences seemed to them imperfect enough that they wrote to newspaper advice columnists. In the broad shifts in vocabulary, usage, and assumptions in these published letters can be seen the progressive definition of the institution of dating as it spread.[62] Urban readers were still only somewhat familiar with dating in 1920, and even the simplest rules of the dating system were not generally well known. Doris Blake's early correspondents often asked about when boys might be and should be invited to girls' homes (reflecting the transition from the older courtship tradition); but it was the goodnight kiss that provided the most common perplexity at this early date. W. A. wrote Blake: "I am a girl seventeen years of age. I have been going with a young man three years my senior, whom I love and admire very much. . . . Is 11 o'clock too late to arrive home from a show or some other place? Is it all right to allow him to kiss me good night, even though we are not engaged?" (August 7, 1920). Within a few years, kissing would imply almost no commitment. But in 1920, many youth were genuinely uncertain about the role of physical pleasure in the dating relationship.

The growing recognition that dates by design incorporated an ambiguous mixture of physical pleasure and self-restraint did not by itself remove all the perplexities of daters. They had still to learn how to read the surface of the dating situation in a sophisticated fashion. R.S., for instance, couldn't fathom quite the implications of the behavior of the young man "that I care for." "He has declared his love for me also. But he goes to visit other girls and takes them to places and has never yet taken me anywhere. He's forever praising those girls. All this makes me doubt that he really cares for me. Do you think he does?" (December 27, 1920). R.S. simply does not know whether "caring for" is in any way articulated to the dating system, and, while she obviously perceives that there is such a thing as a "line," she lacks confidence in her ability to discern it in action.

The two 1920 correspondents just quoted presented their cases as individuals operating outside the peer context, and this is rather characteristic of the early letters. Dating, it would seem, early in its existence stranded relatively many people, who, uncomprehending, wrote to lovelorn columnists because they didn't know the rules. For whatever reason, their peer groups had seemingly failed to instruct them sufficiently. Shortly, however, a common complaint of the lovelorn was that their peers were all too much with them. Occasionally, the young women and men were troubled that other members of their peer group were in competition with them for the same dating partner, but more often they felt perplexed that for their partner the peer group's influence extended too far into the dating situation. Typically, the dating partner's inconstancy toward them was explained by such pressure. This was the case with "Heartbroken," a girl of sixteen, dating a boy of seventeen in 1925: "I love this fellow very much and I know he loves me. When we are at a party or at a dance he is always with me, and he always asks to take me home, and I let him. He is very nice, but when he is with a bunch of boys he just says hello and keeps right on going. I would like to know the reason for this (he is very bashful), because I love him. There are other boys whom I can go with, but I don't seem to take to any but him" (May 10, 1925). The use of "bashful" in this formulation is particularly instructive. "Heartbroken," more committed than her fellow to a unique emotional commitment, explains his responsiveness to his friends' groupishness as a social failing. Girls corporatively desired peer oversight of the dating system, but chided the limitations the clannishness of the boys imposed upon emotional commitment. (Sexual commitment, of course, was another matter again.)

Boys and girls did not agree entirely, but a rough peer consensus helped to define dating situations, to the considerable comfort of those involved. Symbol and gesture fitted into a changing youth code of dating that was nowhere written but was part of the oral tradition of youth, taught not by precept but in concrete cases. "I am 16, good looking and a good sport. A is 17, bashful, and not very good looking. His friends say he likes me" (Nellie K., April 29, 1925); "I am a young boy of 16 and am in love with a girl 5 months my junior. So far I have not told the girl anything but have confided in two of my boy friends. One of these boys went back and told her. As a result she was just a bit peeved" ("Troubled Nick," February 19, 1925).

Jealousy appeared increasingly often in the letters through this period, as the peer network—or, rather, the interlocking boy and girl peer networks—asserted a set of values and behaviors for dating. "I have known a boy for years and have been going with him for the last 14 months," wrote "Jealous" to Martha Carr in 1931. "I love him and I'm sure he likes me, but why on earth does he act so funny? He goes out with other girls and brings them where I can see them. He goes up to my friends' house [*sic*] and won't let them come down to my house. He takes one girl out and then asks her if she told me. I go out with others but I don't care for them. Tell me, is he just trying to make me jealous?" (October 5, 1931). Sexual jealousy, of course, may be a rather primal emotion, but in the case of the teenage lovelorn letters, it is not this kind of jealousy that crops up so often. Rather, jealousy was a sort of confused frustration, a product of divergent definitions of the two partners over the degree of articulation of the dating system with intimacy, on the one hand, and the peer popularity system, on the other. The publicness of the errant dating partner's behavior is striking in such letters: it is not failure in the inner resources of the heart that leads dating partners to write, but the inability to break free of the social snare in which they are enmeshed: "My friend's chum is keeping him away from me because my sister doesn't care to go out with him" ("Broken Hearted" to Blake, November 8, 1930).

Such shifts in the interpersonal dynamics of dating, as the institution evolved, did not fail to affect the emotional component of the institution and certainly not the way the emotions were conceptualized by those experiencing them. The reader of adolescent lovelorn letters from this period can hardly fail to observe the generally shallow connotation of the word "love." The notion, of course, was by 1920 carried into teenage courtship parlance through insipid romantic fiction of stage, screen, and print, so teenagers had good authority to feel love more transitorily. In the 1920 letters the vocabulary is limited to a few variant usages of "love," and occasional references to "care for." By 1925, the range of expression had widened a bit, with a new verb or two enlarging the capacity for discrimination, and a raft of new, conventionalized intensive adverbs suggesting a prescription not just to love, but to "love this girl dearly" (Luke to Blake, January 13, 1925).

Even such nonsense points to the capacity of the evolving dating system to instruct the emotions. By 1925, correspondents were being led to decide whether or not to assert a passionate relationship. "Troubled Sunny," in this vein, reasoned that "it must have been a case of love at first sight because as soon as I saw him I fell in love with him" (to Blake, May 14, 1925). The object of Sunny's affection said he felt the same way, but his continued talk of doings "with this blonde and that blonde" led Sunny to write Blake for help in defining the relationship. She explained, "He told me that the trouble with me is that I take things too seriously."

By 1930, even the brief letters to Blake indicate a concern for emotional precision. Connie wrote Blake (October 16, 1930) that her fellow "never told me he even cared for me." "Cared" is by now no synonym for love. "Doubtful" reported that her "fellow says he loves me. I like him as a friend" (to Blake, November 5, 1930). "Blue Peggy," seventeen years old, wrote that she felt left out because while "several of my girl friends have fellows and seem so in love," she herself "can't seem to get enthused" over her "several boy friends" (to Carr, September 17, 1931). In "Blue Peggy's" view, being "in love" was something one might be but at least should "seem" to be at seventeen, and that such a seeming might be approached through enthusiasm in dating, if only she could experience even that. In 1920, dating had to be subsumed to an emotional vocabulary developed under the romantic assumptions of "keeping company." By 1930, a considerably more modulated set of emotional responses was available, attuned to particular situations. One might even find uncensored cynicism, like that of the dialectically minded H.L., who had "found that the more a man spends on you [in dating], the more he likes you" (to Blake, October 31, 1930).

Dating took form. The letters mention an increasingly elaborate set of verbal categories and nonverbal symbols of dating affiliation—rings, pins, and peer-group insignia—and, even more significantly, of a more or less clearly differentiated set of dating stages. "Friend" and "fellow" were replaced by "boyfriend" and "girlfriend." The "keeping company" of the 1920 letters merged gradually into "going out." If "keeping company" still evoked the front porch, "going out" connoted going *out,* outside the immediate purview of watchful parents and outside assumptions regarding marriage as an explicit goal of the process. "Going out" implied one had somewhere to go.

In the 1930–1931 letters, "steady" relationships of one kind or another, including classic references to "going steady," virtually absent before, were quite common. Lacking such a defined stage, earlier daters like Tootsie had been confused: "I am a young girl of 17 and am really in love with a young man of 19. I have known him for over a year. We are not exactly engaged, but he has promised not to go with any other girls, nor I with any other boys. I am in a suburb now and am attending school. He goes to a university. I love this boy with all my heart. But some time it is such a temptation to go out with the boys" (May 25, 1925). A few years later, a metropolitan seventeen-year-old would have found no need to define her relationship with her young man residually. She would have known that going steady was easy to begin or terminate, combined clear behavioral prescriptions with undefined emotional commitment, and was only the boundary between casual dating and the steep and demanding road to marriage, not the first step on that road. Tootsie could have negotiated with her young man for gradually enhanced emotional intimacy without such risk of irrevocable sexual intimacy or premature marriage, possible in an overheated, unstable relationship of "not exactly" engagement.

IV

Boys' commitment to symmetrical affectionate relationships was no doubt limited, but a limited commitment was all that was needed to establish the particular rhythm of the dating system. Once in place, fueled in no small part by the sexual energies it brought into play, the dating system itself was consequential, a mechanism for a gradual shift in normative categories. One sixteen-year-old boy, for instance, was just barely able to retain the strongly engrained good girl–bad girl distinction: "The girls I know can be divided into two classes—passionate but dumb and frigid but intelligent. . . . I believe my desire for love is quite proper in view of the fact that it embodies no sexual relations. I really despise my friends who speak of all girls in terms of their flesh. Yet it seems impossible to find a girl who is both intelligent and human."[63]

The date, as a bargain, was unromantic even if affectionate. In dating, style mattered a great deal: performance was on the whole more important than the unmediated expression of feelings. Whereas both "crushes" and love affairs had been seen to be full of "idealization," the very ordinariness of dating placed practical limits upon the amount of romantic idealization that courtship could now support.[64] The success of the dating system encouraged a set of rules, rules of performance more than of feeling, rules that even young boys and girls could learn. Thus, Ernie, thirteen, stoutly denied in 1931 that "I want to call on girls and take them out," but admitted to having girlfriends and that in defiance of his parents' wishes he liked "to have friendly talks with girls over the telephone." "Every boy my age likes to have money to spend and to dress up," Ernie lectured Martha Carr (April 3, 1931).

Thus propelled, the whole schedule of dating was accelerated, especially as the prosperity of the post–World War II period permitted younger boys to gain access to the money a proper date required[65] and no doubt to learn to enjoy (with the help of peer-group games) the controlled but overt sexuality that was part of dating. By the postwar period, adolescents' parents as often as not had themselves dated. Most ordinarily, of course, normatively—and interpersonally—structured restraint outweighed sexual desire, but there can be little question that the success of the dating system placed a downward pressure on the age of marriage. The ideas about marital timing that had evolved among daters in the early decades of that institution's existence were realized after World War II.[66] Thereafter, material circumstances permitted a simultaneous lowering of the marriage age and a considerable prolongation of schooling, thus bringing dating and marriage into closer articulation.

For girls in particular these developments had alarming implications. When dating and marriage became closely linked in time, "popularity" became even more prescriptive for girls, and its attainment precluded for them ambitions that looked much beyond the confines of the peer group. Students understood this well: "To get dates you must be liked by the kids and to be liked you must take part in the activities around school. If you keep your nose in the book all of the time and don't show any interest in the other kids, you are not even considered as a prospect for dating."[67] Quantitative confirmation of the immediate impact of this orientation upon girls' lives is a major theme of James S. Coleman's classic *The Adolescent Society*, based on late-1950s data from high school students.[68] A researcher who reinterviewed these respondents in the mid-1970s found that high school dating frequency was one of very few prior variables that had a continuing impact upon women's adult lives, although it had but little upon men's. Popular girls had had relatively little educational ambition and had attained relatively little in the educational system. Instead, they had married young.[69] The dating system had permitted them considerable freedom of choice, but the end product of their choice was nevertheless sharply constrained by the asymmetries of contemporaneous marital roles. Thus constrained, women sought fulfillment in their children.[70]

Beginning with the wartime and continuing until the late 1950s marriage was followed by first childbirth more and more quickly and uniformly, as dating led more directly and uniformly to marriage and for women to a life substantially within the confines of that institution. For young men, as one would expect, early marriage was neither so closely related to dating career nor so consequential.[71]

This pattern did not hold. Women's age at first marriage rose in the 1960s; first childbirth became progressively postponed after marriage; and total fertility declined sharply.[72] Already by the 1960s, youth began dating later than they had a decade before. The term still exists, but it is far indeed from capturing as once it did what boys and girls do together.[73]

Notes

1. Tauno Pajari, "Who Doo," *Minneapolis Central High News,* January 25, 1923. I read about ten years each of six Minnesota high school newspapers, four from the Twin Cities and two from small cities outstate (in nonmetropolitan areas), all maintained at the Minnesota Historical Society.

2. "All Alone" to Doris Blake, "Doris Blake's Love Answers," *New York Daily News,* May 21, 1925.

3. *Minneapolis Central High News,* December 20, 1923; *Little Falls the Comet's Tail,* February 24, 1928; *St. Paul Central High Times,* April 4, 1925, and September 28, 1927; *Minneapolis Central High News,* December 15, 1925.

4. Scholarly observation of dating began with the inquiry into 1930s' college dating carried out by the sociologist Willard Waller. Although Waller described dating as a special case of dissipation, he nonetheless established the crucial point that it was peer supervised, rule-governed behavior. Waller, "The Rating and Dating Complex," *American Sociological Review* 2 (1937): 727–34; idem, *The Family* (New York: The Dryden Press, 1938), chap. 9; Michael Gordon, "Was Waller Ever Right? The Rating and Dating Complex Reconsidered," *Journal of Marriage and the Family* 43 (1981): 67–76; Samuel Harmon Lowrie, "Dating Theories and Student Responses," *American Sociological Review* 16 (1951): 334–340.

5. Gordon in "Was Waller Ever Right?" is more concerned with intimacy than with the system governing it, and therefore finds dating-like relationships in the nineteenth century.

6. Minutes of December 15, 1922, meeting, Chapter (Study Group) 13, Child Study Association of America, in Folder 282, Child Study Association Collection, Social Welfare History Archives, University of Minnesota.

7. Caroline Benedict Burrell, *Our Girls and Our Times* (Boston: W. A. Wilde Co., 1927), pp. 63–64.

8. Emily Post, *Etiquette* (New York: Funk & Wagnalls, 1923); idem, *Etiquette,* new and enlarged ed. (New York: Funk & Wagnalls, 1927); idem, *Etiquette* (New York: Funk & Wagnalls, 1937). The shifts between 1927 and 1937 are particularly revealing: "Ethically the only chaperon is the young girl's own sense of dignity and pride. The girl who has the right attitudes of character needs no chaperon—ever" (1927, p. 288). "From an ethical standpoint, the only chaperon worth having in this present day is a young girl's own efficiency in chaperoning herself. The girl who has been trained to appraise every person and situation she meets . . . needs no one to sit beside her and tell her what to do" (1937, p. 354). Post epitomized "the most important change in the whole chaperon situation" as "training is taking the place of protection" (p. 353), or the empowering of the adolescent girl within her own family or orientation.

9. D. C. Thom, *Guiding the Adolescent* (Washington, D.C.: U.S. Department of Labor, Children's Bureau, Publication No. 225, 1933), pp. 84–85; Theodore L. Smith, "Types of Adolescent Affection," *Pedagogical Seminary* 11 (1904): 178–203; Marion Dowd, "Concerning the Socio-moral Life and Behavior of the Adolescent," *Education* 49 (1928): 65–78; Eleanor Rowland Wembridge, "Suggested Improvements in Jane Doe and Her Boy Friend," *Survey* 61 (1929): 719–21; Eugenie A. Leonard and Margaret Bond Brockway, "Must a Girl Pet to Be Popular?" *The Parents' Magazine* 71 (June, 1932): 20; Henry F. Pringle, "What Do the Women of America Think about Morals?" *Ladies Home Journal* 54 (May, 1938): 14–15.

10. Waller, describing dating at the Pennsylvania State University, far more cynically and simplistically characterized the date as incorporating mutual exploitation, with prestige and "thrills" in view (*The Family,* chap. 9; "The Rating and Dating Complex").

11. For a classic expression of this belief see "A High School Boy Reveals Youth's Love Problems," *True Confessions* 12 (July, 1928): 34.

12. Quoted in Arthur Dean, "A Survey on Petting," *Journal of Education* 110 (1929): 414.

13. Jessie E. Gibson, *On Being a Girl* (New York: Macmillan, 1927), p. 141.

14. "The Danger Period," *True Confessions* 1 (August, 1922): 46.

15. The classic 1920s' exposition is Phyllis Blanchard and Carolyn Manasses' *New Girls for Old* (New York: The Macaulay Co., 1930). Theodore Newcomb's thoughtful conclusion that by the 1930s a "less compulsive and more spontaneous demonstration of affection between boys and girls" was common suggests the gradual accomplishment of this cultural change ("Recent Changes in Attitudes toward Sex and Marriage," *American Sociological Review* 2 [1937]: 662).

16. "Miss Dateless" to Martha Carr, "In My Opinion," *St. Louis Post-Dispatch,* October 31, 1931. And see the exchange between Doris Blake and H. Ann and Peggy, "Doris Blake's Love Answers," *New York Daily News,* October 28 and November 27, 1930. On the centrality of petting, see Robert S. Lynd and Helen Merrell Lynd, *Middletown* (New York: Harcourt, Brace, 1929), pp. 162–64.

17. For a thorough discussion of the statistical drawbacks to the Kinsey data, see the report of a committee appointed by the American Statistical Association: William G. Cochran et al., *Statistical Problems of the Kinsey Report on Sexual Behavior of the Human Male* (Washington: American Statistical Association, 1954). On the interviewing technique, see Alfred C. Kinsey, Wardell B. Pomeroy, and Clyde E. Martin, *Sexual Behavior in the Human Male* (Philadelphia: W. B. Saunders Company, 1948), chaps. 3–4, and Kinsey et al., *Sexual Behavior in the Human Female* (Philadelphia: W. B. Saunders Company, 1953), chap. 2. On theoretical assumptions, see Paul A. Robinson, *The Modernization of Sex* (New York: Harper & Row, 1976), chap. 2. For sample, interview, and the preparation of the public-use data tape, see Paul H. Gebhard and Alan B. Johnson, *The Kinsey Data: Marginal Tabulations of the 1938–1963 Interviews* (Philadelphia: W. B. Saunders Company, 1979), which includes tabulations of all variables separately for college and noncollege white males and females and for college black males and females. Dr. Gebhard was more than courteous in permitting me to use the galleys of this volume in making up the data tape I have used and in facilitating preparation of the tape.

I here treat the white informants only; there are too few blacks to treat separately, and to merge them would merely add to the heterogeneity of the sample without (because of the high degree of education of the blacks) adding to its representativeness. I have also excluded all never-married persons from tabulations presented here, in order to avoid very thorny problems in the sexual-career sequence data, related to the vast difference between the never-married (who are considerably over-sampled by Kinsey) and those who had married, and because (as Kinsey found) sexual careers typically accelerate as marriage approaches, quite apart from age-related effects. Obviously, my decision limits the use of these samples for estimating population parameters, but homogenizes the sample in a way that relationships of variable to variable can be seen more clearly. The data presented here use all married informants born before 1910 to represent those who went through adolescence before about 1920, and those born 1910–1919 to represent the first dating cohort of adolescents. The ideal cutoff date would have been a bit earlier, but because I wished to integrate the tabular materials created for the purposes of this paper with other work I am doing with these data, I stuck to the 1910 date I had earlier established. Clearly, I am pointing to the nature and direction of change, not trying to present accurate measurements of any given behavior for the entire population.

18. In my tabulations, this group included those respondents who answered other than "well" to *both* questions, "When you were 14 to 17, how did you get along with your father?" and " . . . with your mother?"

19. *Minneapolis Central High News,* April 26 and December 20, 1923; April 20, 1926; April 27, 1927. For contemporaneous confirmation of the centrality of such traits to popularity among high school–age children see the correlation matrices of personality traits in Caroline McCann Tyron, *Evaluations of Adolescent Personality by Adolescents,* monograph of the Society for Research in Child Development, vol. 4, no. 4 (Washington: National Research Council, 1939), chap. 2.

20. Paula S. Fass, *The Damned and the Beautiful* (New York: Oxford University Press, 1979), pp. 262–63, 324–25. Elsewhere, more persuasively, she explains other facets of youth behavior in the 1920s by group characteristics of youth, notably its segregation, enhanced material endowment, and institutional completeness.

21. Ibid.

22. Choice, wide and frequent, had come to dominate considerations of quality and price in consumer behavior. See, for example, Paul H. Nystrom, *Fashion Merchandising* (New York: The Ronald Press, 1932), p. 31. On the morally unsettling impact of consumer choice as proposed by "the passing show" of luxury and fashion, see William I. Thomas, *The Unadjusted Girl* (1923: reprint ed., New York: Harper Torchbook, 1967), p. 82. And, on the kinds of dilemmas radically enlarged choice posed for modern young people (especially girls), see Margaret Mead, "Adolescence in Primitive and Modern Society," in *The New Generation,* ed. V. F. Calverton and Samuel D. Schmalhausen (New York: The Macaulay Co., 1930), pp. 169–88.

23. Regina Malone, "Has Youth Deteriorated? II: The Fabulous Monster." *The Forum* 76 (1926): 29.

24. See, for example, Ernest R. Burgess, "The Romantic Impulse and Family Disorganization," *Survey* 57 (1926): 290–94; Alexander Black, "Is the Young Person Coming Back?" *Harper's Monthly* 149 (1929): 337–46; and, for the parents' perspective, see Jessica H. Cosgrave, "Romantic Love," *Good Housekeeping* 81 (November–December, 1928): 36.

25. The girls who did not prosper under the new system shortly became its victims. As early as 1924, a California high school dean of girls set up a program to help those girls (54 percent in her school, by her reckoning) who were left out. There were many reasons for failure, "yet it will be observed that all of these various types have something in common. The non-social individual centers all her thoughts and activity upon herself." (Note the contrast with the traits of the popular girl.) See Caroline Power, "The Social Program for the Unsocial High-School Girl," *School Review* 32 (1924): 773.

26. Fass, *The Damned,* pp. 129, 211. But see the small-town ethnography of "Age-Group Conflict and Our Changing Culture," by Earl H. Bell, a University of Nebraska sociologist, in *Social Forces* 12 (1933): 237–43. Bell casually drops the phrase "the period of dating and high school" (p. 238).

27. Phyllis Blanchard, *The Adolescent Girl* (New York: Moffat, Yard and Company, 1920).

28. A persuasive ethnographic account of high school as "a fairly complete social cosmos in itself" is found in Lynd and Lynd, *Middletown,* p. 211, and in chap. 6 generally.

29. I have assumed that almost no one was both married and attending school, which 1930 data suggest was quite the case. Eliminating the married directs our attention to the youth at risk of dating. Data are from the *Population: General Reports* volumes of the 1920 and 1930 U.S. censuses.

30. Note Waller's discussion of the relationship of sex ratio to exploitative dating in "Rating and Dating."

31. The operation of this structure is acutely explored in Winston Ehrmann, *Premarital Dating Behavior* (New York: Holt, 1959), pp. 143–62. For a review of dating in colleges in the 1920s, see R. H. Edwards, J. M. Artman, and Galen M. Fisher, *Undergraduates: A Study of Morale in Twenty-three American Colleges and Universities* (Garden City, N.Y.: Doubleday, Doran, 1928), chap. 5.

32. John K. Folger and Charles B. Nam, *Education of the American Population,* 1960 Census Monographs (Washington: U.S. Government Printing Office, 1967), pp. 8–9. For a fine, naive, contemporaneous expression of recent changes as they affected school life, see Olivia Pound, "The Social Life of High School Girls: Its Problems and its Opportunities," *School Review* 28 (1920): 50–56. On economic aspects of school prolongation, see Howard G. Burdge, *Our Boys* (Albany: State of New York, Military Training Commission, Bureau of Vocational Training, 1921), chaps. 13, 23.

33. Duluth, Board of Education, *Annual Report,* 1921, 1926, 1937. In New Bedford, Massachusetts, in 1922, only 21 percent of sixteen-year-old boys were found in a single grade, and only 26 percent of the girls; by 1930 these figures had increased to 38 and 39 percent, respectively (New Bedford, *School Report,* 1923, 1931).

34. Ella Gardner, *Public Dance Halls* (U.S. Department of Labor, Children's Bureau, Publication No. 189, 1929), pp. 36–49; and see M. V. O'Shea, *The Trend of the Teens* (Chicago: Frederick S. Drake and Co., 1920).

35. Editorial, *St. Paul Central High Times*, December 16, 1927. And see *Minneapolis South High Southerner*, April 13, 1921, letter from A.C.

36. *Little Falls the Comet's Tail*, February 24, 1928, editorial. Also see Lynd and Lynd, *Middletown*, pp. 162–64.

37. *Little Falls the Comet's Tail*, March 27, 1923.

38. John C. Burnham, "The Progressive Era Revolution in American Attitudes toward Sex," *Journal of American History* 59 (1973): 885–909; Mark Thomas Connelly, *The Response to Prostitution in the Progressive Era* (Chapel Hill: University of North Carolina Press, 1980).

39. In the San Jose study, only 30 percent of the senior boys dated as often as once a week. See Frederick T. Shipp, "Social Activities of High-School Boys," *School Review* 39 (1931): 771; Sister M. Mildred Knoebber, "The Adolescent Girl" (Ph.D. dissertation, St. Louis University, 1935), p. 162; Helen Moore Priester, "The Reported Dating Practices of One Hundred and Six High School Seniors in an Urban Community" (M.A. essay, Cornell University, 1941), p. 41.

40. Ernest W. Burgess and Paul Wallin, *Engagement and Marriage* (Philadelphia: Lippincott, 1953), p. 119; "The Fortune Survey," *Fortune* 26 (December, 1942). Almost identical findings for a somewhat similar sample are reported in John C. Flanagan, "A Study of Factors Determining Family Size in a Selected Professional Group," *Genetic Psychology Monographs* 25 (1942): 78.

41. Mildred B. Thurow, "Interests, Activities, and Problems of Rural Young Folk: I," in *Bulletin* 617 (Ithaca, N.Y.: Cornell University Agricultural Experiment Station, 1934): 34.

42. Paul H. Landis, "Problems of Farm Youth—a Point of View," *Social Forces* 18 (1940): 502–13; O. Latham Hatcher, *Rural Girls in the City for Work* (Richmond, Va.: Garrett and Massie for the Southern Women's Educational Alliance, 1930), pp. 52–53; "Dearly Desired," *True Romances* (March, 1941): 20.

43. Jane Synge, "The Way We Were: Farm and City Families in the Early Twentieth Century" (Unpublished manuscript, Department of Sociology, McMaster University, Hamilton, Ontario, n.d.), chap. 5 (quoted here by permission of the author).

44. Frances Donovan, *The Woman Who Waits* (Boston: Richard G. Badger, 1920), chaps. 17–19; Frederic M. Thrasher, *The Gang* (Chicago: University of Chicago Press, 1927), chap. 13; Thomas, *Unadjusted Girl*, chap. 3.

45. William Foote Whyte, "A Slum Sex Code," *American Journal of Sociology* 49 (1943): 24–29; and see Dorothy Reed, *Leisure Time of Girls in a "Little Italy"* (Portland, Oregon: Privately printed, 1932; Ph.D. dissertation, Columbia University, n.d.).

46. Emory S. Bogardus, *The City Boy and His Problems* (Los Angeles: Rotary Club of Los Angeles, 1926), pp. 44–45; Bell, "Age-Group Conflict," pp. 240–41; Nettie Pauline McGill and Ellen Nathalie Matthews, *The Youth of New York City* (New York: Macmillan, 1940), p. 315; Rachel Stutsman, *What of Youth Today?* (Detroit: Detroit Youth Study Committee, 1935), Table 28. In a peculiar way, some affectionate couples were pressed by Depression shortfalls toward a substitution of intimacy for amusement—that is, toward the substitution of a different kind of arrangement for the dating negotiation: "The boy I love doesn't come to see me any more because he hasn't any money. All I want is him." Dorothy to Doris Blake, *New York Daily News*, November 27, 1930.

47. Robert F. Winch, "Interrelations between Certain Social Background and Parent-Son Factors in a Study of Courtship among College Men," *American Sociological Review* 11 (1946): 335; idem, "Courtship in College Women," *American Journal of Sociology* 55 (1949): 273. A student protested that girls' excessive dependence upon fashion leaders had antidemocratic implications: "In the grade schools perhaps the difference in dress is not noted, but when a girl enters high school she is thrown in contact with girls of her classes who use the classroom as sort of a 'style show.' Many girls have left school because their parents were not able to dress them well enough to 'keep up' with the more fortunate few" (*Minneapolis West High Weekly*, April 11, 1919). And see Lynd and Lynd, *Middletown*, 162–64.

48. The Youth Survey, August, 1939, is Roper Commercial Poll No. 15, and is available at the archives of the Roper Center, University of Connecticut. The sponsor of the survey was the National Tea Bureau, a trade group that evidently sought to inquire into youth's attitudes toward tea drinking and how these fit into what we would call the youth culture. The questionnaire is rich in material on "reference groups" and on relationships with parents. For present purposes, we focus on just two items. Roughly equal numbers of boys and girls at each age and roughly equal

numbers of children at each year of age ten through nineteen were questioned in the survey, 3,139 altogether. I have excluded children under fourteen from the tabulations presented here as not germane to my inquiry and omitted those without clear answers to the questions tabulated. A memo from an Elmo Roper employee, dated 1968, in the Roper Center archives indicates that "most nationwide samples at that time were of the quota-type," with the quotas for age, sex, geographic distribution, and size of place. This indicates that the sample is not suitable for estimating national population parameters, but that relationships of variables are credible, which is what I seek. Note that the discussion here relates group-level not individual-level patterns.

49. "Play Girl of Coney Island," *True Confessions* 19 (August, 1931): 247.

50. Winifred Richmond, *The Adolescent Girl* (1925; reprint ed., New York: Macmillan, 1936), p. 53: cf. idem, *The Adolescent Boy* (New York: Farrar and Rinehart, 1933); and for an unconventional statement of the conventional understanding on this point, see Ben B. Lindsey and Wainright Evans, *The Revolt of Modern Youth* (New York: Boni & Liveright, 1925), chaps. 5 and 6. Linsey and Evans hold, on p. 66, that "the high-school boy is a much less dramatic figure than the high-school girl. Generally, she sets the pace, whatever it is to be, and he dances to her piping."

51. L.C. in *Minneapolis South High Southerner,* February 29, 1919.

52. "One of Them" in *Minneapolis South High Southerner,* October 27, 1920.

53. *Minneapolis South High Southerner,* November 18, 1920.

54. Letter of E.D., *St. Paul Central High Times,* March 26, 1926.

55. "We Are Bachelor Girls of 30," *True Confessions* 26 (June 1935): 38–39.

56. *Minneapolis Central High News,* November 13, 1924.

57. *Alexandria High Al-Hi-Nuz,* December 16, 1927.

58. Fass, *The Damned,* chap. 6, is splendid on the meaning of sexuality if a little underemphatic about the gender dialectic.

59. Glen H. Elder, Jr., "Appearance and Education in Marriage Mobility," *American Sociological Review* 34 (1969): 519–33; S. J. Holmes and C. E. Hatch, "Personal Appearance as Related to Scholastic Records and Marriage Selection in College Women," *Human Biology* 10 (1938): 65–76.

60. Russ Brackett, letter in *Minneapolis West High News,* May 2, 1924; and "One of the Many Sufferers," letter in *Little Falls the Comet's Tail,* February 11, 1930.

61. Quoted in Caroline B. Zachry, *Emotion and Conduct in Adolescence* (New York: Appleton-Century, 1940), p. 121. The study was conducted 1934–1939.

62. I do not propose a naive reading of these letters, nor any kind of quantitative treatment. Internal evidence points to regular editing (even apart from selectivity) by the columnists, and scuttlebutt suggests some fabrication; newspaper readerships were narrower than the full range of the population, and only readers possessing both a sense of moderate anguish and a yen for publicity would even consider writing. On the other hand, if the letters did not smack of verisimilitude, the advice proffered would be read as a parody of itself; and to judge from the generally sober (while distinctly adolescent) tone of the great majority of the letters examined that dealt with problems in the early stages of boy-girl relationships, adolescent readers were in fact reached. (That parodies appeared frequently in the high school newspapers attests to the intense, if ambivalent, readership interest within this age group.)

For the assessment that follows, I read perhaps some 650 letters to two lovelorn columnists in three time periods—1920–21, 1925, and 1930–31—choosing and transcribing for closer analysis 326 of these, roughly divided among the three dates. Doris Blake was a syndicated columnist (first as "Doris Blake's Answers," later as "Doris Blake's Love Answers") in the *New York Daily News,* a pioneer tabloid appealing to relatively unsophisticated readers. Blake's column was the earliest I found that employed the letter-and-reply format (as contrasted with Dorothea Dix's essay-with-quotations format). Blake truncated her letters, obviously, especially by 1930, but by then I also had Martha Carr's evidently local and nonsyndicated "In My Opinion" column from the *St. Louis Post-Dispatch,* a newspaper of far higher tone, unfortunately. Although Carr regularized grammar and spelling, she allowed her correspondents to ramble on at considerable length, which was quite a boon for my purposes.

63. Quoted in Zachry, *Emotion and Conduct,* pp. 389–90.

64. Waller's commitment to a conception of love in which idealization played a large part, I believe, blinded him to the affectionate element in dating and led him to believe that dating and courtship were wholly different activities. See Waller, "Rating and Dating"; Waller, *The Family,*

chap. 8. See also Clifford Kirkpatrick and Theodore Caplow, "Courtship in a Group of Minnesota Students," *American Journal of Sociology* 51 (1945): 114–25.

65. University of Michigan, Survey Research Center, "Adolescent Girls," mimeographed (n.p., n.d. [1956 or 1957], p. 134; John C. Flanagan et al., *The American High School Student* (Cooperative Research Project No. 635, multilith [Pittsburgh: University of Pittsburgh Project Talent Office, 1964], appendix tabulations of Q. 51).

66. John Modell, "Normative Aspects of American Marriage Timing since World War II," *Journal of Family History* 5 (1980): 210–34.

67. Quoted in John Richard Crist, "High School Dating as a Behavior System" (Ph.D. dissertation, University of Missouri, 1951), p. 153.

68. James S. Coleman, *The Adolescent Society* (New York: The Free Press of Glencoe, 1961).

69. Margaret Mooney Marini, "The Transition to Adulthood: Sex Differences in Educational Attainment and Age at Marriage," *American Sociological Review* 43 (1978): 498, 501.

70. This argument is based on intensive analysis of the textual materials in the more than one hundred questionnaires gathered from eighteen- and nineteen-year-old single women in 1955 as part of the first Growth of American Families Study. Alice Robbin of the University of Wisconsin Program and Data Library has been most generous with her time in helping me gain access to these documents.

71. Alan E. Bayer, "Early Dating and Early Marriage," *Journal of Marriage and the Family* 30 (1968): 632; Paul Ronald Voss, "Social Determinants of Age at First Marriage in the United States" (Ph.D. dissertation, University of Michigan, 1975), pp. 239–48.

72. The best demographic account of this trend is in Amy Ong Tsui, "A Study of the Family Formation Process among U.S. Marriage Cohorts" (Ph.D. dissertation, University of Chicago, 1978), especially pp. 92, 102, 160. A discussion of the voluntary aspects of this demographic change is found in John Modell, Frank F. Furstenberg, Jr., and Douglas Strong, "The Timing of Marriage in the Transition to Adulthood: Continuity and Change, 1860–1975," in *Turning Points,* ed. John Demos and Sarane S. Boocock (Supplement to *American Journal of Sociology* 84 [1978]: S138–42). For the impact of early marriage on women, see Larry Lee Bumpass, "Age at Marriage as a Variable in Socioeconomic Differentials in Fertility" (Ph.D. dissertation, University of Michigan, 1968), pp. 149–50.

73. James V. Scanlon, *Self-reported Health Behavior and Attitudes of Youths 12–17 Years,* Vital and Health Statistics, Series 11, No. 147 (Washington, D.C.: U.S. Department of Health, Education and Welfare, 1975), p. 73; Robert C. Sorensen, *Adolescent Sexuality in Contemporary America* (New York: World Publishing, 1973), pp. 108–15; Melvin Zelnik, John F. Kantner, and Kathleen Ford, *Sex and Pregnancy in Adolescence,* Sage Library of Social Research, Vol. 133 (Beverly Hills, Calif.: Sage Publications, 1981), p. 44.

26. Children in the Household Economy

> It was an enormously hard life. . . . But there was also a sense of great satisfaction in being a child with valuable work to do and, being able to do it well, [able] to function in this world.
>
> —Margot Hentoff, *New York Review of Books*[1]

The roles that children assumed in the economy of deprived families are an integral aspect of two adaptive strategies. Deprived families both curtailed expenditures and developed alternative sources of income. The first strategy orients the family unit toward a more labor-intensive economy in which some goods and services formerly purchased in the marketplace are acquired through family labor. Food preparation, making clothing, and home repairs are examples. These activities and particular sources of income, such as boarders, generally increase the utility of children's labor. This applies to girls in particular, since most household tasks are traditional aspects of the homemaker's role.

Family efforts to supplement income include activities in which children earn money on jobs in the community. Apart from parental demand or encouragement, this activity is a logical response to personal needs and an awareness of family requirements. However, economic options were limited for the Oakland children. They were still enrolled in school and were too young during the early years of the Depression to obtain permits enabling full-time employment. Part-time jobs for children offered low wages, but they were relatively plentiful in Oakland during the 1930s. Examples include newspaper carrier, baby sitter, janitorial assistant, store clerk, and delivery agent. According to cultural prescription, boys are more likely than girls to have taken economic roles.

The involvement of children in the household economy is not by itself an indication of accelerated entry into the adult world, though it would imply a downward extension of adultlike responsibilities in the Great Depression. The act of managing substantial tasks in the home and community is more compatible with the work orientation of the young adult than with the "irresponsible" theme of youth culture,[2] a mass phenomenon that emerged after the depressed 30s. In the latter half of this chapter, we shall compare children from nondeprived and deprived families on behavior patterns that reflect an orientation toward the realities of adult life, as expressed in the sex-differentiated world of the 30s: mature judgment in the handling of money; dependability; social independence among boys and domestic concerns among girls; an interest in the company of adults and a desire for adult status.[3]

Glen H. Elder, Jr., "Children in the Household Economy," reprinted from his *Children of the Great Depression*, 64–82, copyright © 1974, University of Chicago Press, by permission of the University of Chicago Press.

Children's Economic and Domestic Roles

Children's roles in the household economy were explored in a series of questions that were asked of mothers in the 1936 interview. The most severe phase of economic hardship had passed at this point, although deprivational conditions persisted well into the second half of the 30s. The interview was timely in relation to the children's capacity to make significant contributions to family maintenance. They were old enough in the mid-30s to handle demanding jobs away from home and parental supervision.

Two-fifths of the children were employed in part-time jobs, according to their mothers. Over half of the boys held at least one paid job compared to a fourth of the girls. In measuring the performance of household tasks, we included selected chores and questions dealing with the child's response to them. Unlike employment, which includes some measure of quality control, the quality of household assistance is not necessarily indicated by assigned chores. In the data, however, measures of assistance and quality of response were sufficiently related to warrant including both in a single index. Five items were used: three dealt with the performance of chores (cares for room, helps with cooking, and helps with odd jobs around the house), and two indicated the child's response (helps without being reminded and grumbling). An affirmative response by mothers to at least three of the items was defined as a measure of involvement in household chores. Though most children in the sample were involved, this pattern of activity was especially common among girls (82% vs. 56% among boys).

Employment and domestic tasks were related to economic deprivation in both the middle and working class, with boys tending to specialize in the former and girls in the latter. Since class differences were negligible, only the effects of economic loss and father's work status are shown in Table 26.1. The one point where social class made a difference in these results appears in the prevalence of employed girls among deprived families in the working class (44% vs. 16% of all other girls in the sample). Variations in task specialization by economic conditions are most pronounced among boys. Forty percent of the boys from deprived families were engaged in a paid job, and did not have responsibilities in the home. By contrast, most working girls also managed tasks in the

Table 26.1. **Children with Economic and Domestic Roles, by Sex of Child, Economic Deprivation, and Father's Work Status**

Economic Deprivation and Father's Work Status	Percentage of Boys and Girls with Work and Domestic Roles[a]			
	Employment		Domestic Chores	
	Boys	Girls	Boys	Girls
Nondeprived	42 (37)	16 (26)	69 (37)	56 (26)
Deprived				
Employed	57 (21)	19 (20)	46 (21)	92 (20)
Unemployed	72 (25)	43 (27)	43 (25)	89 (27)

Note. Percentages were statistically adjusted for the effects of social class (1929) in a multiple classification analysis. The correlation of employment and chores with social class was less than .08 in parametric and nonparametric measures of association (r, Kendall's tau_c). A comparison of nondeprived and deprived groups in each sex and task group yielded the following results: work role—boys ($x^2 = 5.0$, 1 df. $< .05$) and girls ($x^2 = 1.5$, ns.); chores—boys ($x^2 = 5.3$, 1 df. $< .05$) and girls ($x^2 = 12.4$, 1 df. $< .01$).
[a] The parenthetical figure beside each percentage represents the number of cases on which the percentage was computed.

home, and over 90 percent of the girls from deprived families made some contribution to the family economy—domestic, economic, or both. At the other extreme were girls from nondeprived homes, a large number of whom lacked any obligation to household operations or employment. Forty-two percent were not engaged in either activity.

One consequence of a decremental change in family status and resources is to heighten children's awareness of parental investments which made possible the goods and services they had formerly taken for granted. These include the effort and skills which provide income for the family unit, as well as the labor involved in homemaking and child care. Economic scarcity brought out the reciprocal aspects of consumption which entail obligations to others. Especially in middle-class families, deprivation generally changed one-sided dependency regimes, in which parents indulged their offspring's desires, to an arrangement where children were expected to demonstrate more self-reliance in caring for themselves and family needs. From qualitative data on the Oakland families, we find that change in parental roles typically preceded a shift in responsibilities to the children. Examples of this change are suggested by parental preoccupation with financial problems and alternative sources of income, by father's unemployment and departure from the family in order to find a job outside the community, by parental illness resulting from the emotional stress of family hardships, and by the inability of parents to provide money for the children's school expenses, clothes, and social activities. These conditions often placed children in responsible positions within the home and challenged them to take on some of the burdens in family maintenance.

While most working boys held only one job, some were involved in two or more enterprises. As an example, one boy from a hard-pressed, middle-class home delivered newspapers, made ashtrays which he peddled on the street, and helped his mother around the house while his father was searching for a job in Los Angeles. Another youngster washed dishes in the school cafeteria and supervised the work of six delivery boys after school. Six of the Oakland children coupled work in their father's business with occasional paid jobs in the community. A common pattern among working girls entailed baby-sitting for neighbors and employment in local stores or businesses.[4] Particularly in severely deprived families, a portion of the children's earnings was used for basic expenditures.

We have interpreted the relation of children's activities to economic deprivation as a consequence of labor and economic needs in the deprived family. An important element in household needs is whether mother was employed. Maternal employment tends to increase both opportunities and the need for children's assistance in household operations.[5] Since working mothers were most prevalent in deprived families, this adaptation may account in part for the domestic activities of girls in these households. In fact, boys and girls with employed mothers were more likely to have domestic responsibilities than other youth (an average percentage difference of 13, with deprivation controlled). Though boys from deprived families were more apt to have a job than domestic tasks, working boys were not more prevalent in the families of working mothers. As a supplementary source of income, the employment of mother may have lessened the economic incentive of children to get a job. In any case, the data show no positive effect of mother's work on the work status of boys and girls.

Economic loss occurred in the context of cultural and social factors which have different implications for the role of children. Family culture, for instance, may advocate responsible roles for children or express no position on this matter. Two value standpoints on children's roles are suggested by the entrepreneurial ethic of self-employed fathers and the traditional family beliefs of foreign-born parents. As likely subscribers to the Protestant ethic, fathers in entrepreneurial occupations should be in favor of hard work and economic activity on the part of their sons. Other aspects of this value orientation include individual responsibility, thrift, and self-denial. In traditional family cultures, work experience and domestic tasks are generally regarded as virtuous activity for children, and tasks are assigned according to sex role—employment for boys and household chores for girls.

More than any other social attribute of the family, number of children has direct consequences for labor and economic needs in the household. As the number of children increases, household operations must expand, caretaking and parenting become more demanding and less available for each child, and financial resources per member are reduced. In the large family, older children commonly assume adult tasks which are usually managed by parents in small families[16]. The labor-intensive economy of large families thus resembles that of deprived households. In terms of children's roles, the large deprived family should differ markedly from the small nondeprived family.

Children in entrepreneurial families were more likely than any other youth to have sex-typed roles, but this effect is entirely due to economic conditions in these families. Foreign parentage and family size do have some effect on children's roles which is independent of economic conditions, and both of these factors are related to deprived status. However, they do not account for the effects of deprivation on children's activities.

The belief that children are obliged to carry their share of responsibilities in the home was a common theme in interviews with foreign-born mothers. In a Swedish family the children were described as "having borne their share of responsibility in a capable manner," despite very trying circumstances. The mother made a special point of assigning tasks to even the youngest child, a five-year-old. A similar attitude was expressed by a first-generation mother from Eastern Europe. Each of her four children had some task in the home, and all were expected to help each other. These attitudes generally correspond with the household role of girls in the families of foreign-born parents. Even with economic deprivation controlled, these girls were more likely to have domestic responsibilities than girls with native-born parents (a difference of 14 percent). Other than this result, foreign parentage had a weak negative effect on the work status of girls and was only slightly related to the roles of boys, both economic and domestic.

The most significant effect of family size is seen in the work role of boys. Two-thirds of the boys with three or more siblings were employed, in comparison to 44 percent in smaller families. The proportion of girls with tasks in the home also increased from small to large families, but the difference is not as large (17 percent). Neither social class nor economic deprivation had an appreciable effect on these results, though differences in activity were most striking between children in large deprived and small nondeprived families. Over three-fourths of the boys in the former group were employed, compared to one-fourth in the latter group. The contrast in domestic involvement among girls is equally pronounced (from 88 to 47 percent).

In deprived families we find no evidence that the eldest child was more likely to earn money or help in the home than younger siblings, and this result did not vary between two-child and larger families. Available evidence does suggest, however, that the eldest child generally had greater responsibility in the household. In fact, some mothers explicitly noted that they expected their eldest daughters to assume a supervisory role with respect to housework and the younger children. One of these girls, with three younger brothers, was described by her mother as carrying much of the responsibility for running the household. That younger siblings make a difference in responsibility is most clearly seen in the special case of the only child. Even in the most deprived circumstances, only children were less frequently employed and involved in the home than members of larger families.

In review, two conditions are particularly noteworthy as determinants of the roles children played in both household and work setting: economic deprivation and a large family. Economic loss generated labor and financial needs which favored the involvement of girls in home operations and of boys in work roles, and led to parental adaptations (such as mother's employment) which enhanced the value of children's efforts in the household economy. Since maternal employment was not a potent source of children's domestic roles ($r = .12$), it is a relatively weak link between this activity and deprivation, but it is theoretically important as an example of interdependence in the family. Change in the mother's role initiates change in the household role of children. We should note that information on the work status of mother was available in 1934 and not two years later when data were collected on children's roles. While the 1934 data may provide a reasonable estimate of mother's employment in 1936, any error would necessarily attenuate the effect of this adaptation on household operations and children's responsibilities therein.

Next to economic deprivation, a family of three or more children is the most significant predictor of sex-typed roles among boys and girls. On the work experience of boys, the main effect of family deprivation is stronger than that of family size (betas of .29 and .22) and is even more pronounced on the domestic roles of girls (betas of .32 and .13).[7] The pressures and needs of a large family would seem to be greatest under deprived circumstances, and yet we find little evidence of such variation. Number of children had no appreciable effect on children's roles under deprived conditions, and economic loss did not have a stronger effect on children's activities in large families.

Throughout this analysis we have used the family system as a frame of reference for interpreting the economic roles of children in deprived families. According to this perspective, children sought jobs in response to economic needs and pressures in the family. Their perception of family circumstances is the untested link in this account since we do not have direct evidence on how or whether objective economic loss was expressed in the subjective world of the Oakland children. In some cases, the actual extent of family hardship may not have been recognized. A disparity of this sort could explain why a number of boys did not have jobs in the most severely deprived families.

Under deprived conditions, we would expect the personal needs or desires of children to be associated with their perception of the family situation. Awareness of family hardship is implied in the outlook of children who felt deprived of spending money and desired greater control over their life situation. For boys, in particular, gainful employment is a logical outlet for these motivational orientations in situations of economic hardship, and the data generally show this connection between family deprivation and economic activity. Very briefly, we find that aspirations on spending money that exceeded the perceived economic status of age-mates were most common among boys from deprived homes in the middle and working classes, and clearly distinguished the gainfully employed from boys who did not have jobs, regardless of family deprivation. Likewise, boys with a deprived background and those with a job were most likely to be described as ambitious in social aspirations during the high school years; trained clinicians rated them highest on the desire to control their environment by suggestion, persuasion, or command. Even among the economically deprived, this desire was most characteristic of boys with jobs.[8]

From the data at hand, we do not know for certain whether economic or mastery aspirations led to or developed out of work experience. There is sufficient reason to claim that employment was prompted by a sense of financial deprivation, but one could argue that money-making endeavors increased economic desires. Both outcomes are likely. Also, the developmental experience of work supports the assumption that jobs both expressed and reinforced the mastery desires of boys from hard-pressed families.

Children's Tasks as a Developmental Experience

A common folk belief in rearing children defines household tasks and jobs as a valuable apprenticeship for the realities of adult life. The presumed benefits of this experience include sound work habits, reliability, judgment, and, in the case of household obligations, an awareness of the needs of others. Work roles in the community also entail independence from family, and provide experience in self-direction. As applied to children from deprived families, this interpretation describes an adult-oriented form of upbringing. The other side of these activities points to the interpersonal costs of children's contributions, to the restriction of social experiences, playful leisure, and experimentation which are normally characteristic of modern adolescence. In addition to these social costs, the following outcomes of task experience have particular relevance for personality and adult values: judgment and values concerning the use of money; dependability and industry; and social independence, with emphasis on freedom from parental control.

Paid employment away from home generally offers experience in learning the value of money and skills in managing income. There is some evidence that children who are made aware of economic problems in the family and earn their own money are likely to act responsibly in financial matters.[9] Though involvement in household operations should increase awareness of family hardships, judgment on economic matters may be more contingent on how spending money is obtained. Are children paid for doing chores or do they receive money as needed? The latter offers minimal experience in handling money.

Conditions in deprived families presented children with a moral challenge that called for their best effort, reliable and energetic. Though most studies of children in affluent times have not found support for the developmental value of tasks in the home, economic and labor needs in deprived families created urgent, realistic, and meaningful demands which were not in any sense contrived. In this respect there is a suggestive resemblance between the role of children in deprived families and farm households. Labor needs are real and meaningful on the family farm, the jobs are demanding and adultlike, and children seem to take their responsibilities seriously. In both types of families the labor of children has value and consequence for the family unit as a whole.

Most paid jobs in our study placed children in a situation that required independence from the family and self-direction, while domestic obligations drew them more completely within the family circle. In the context of economic hardships, the emancipating influence of a job should be most evident among boys, since they were more often employed than girls, especially in jobs requiring some measure of independence. In addition to their consequence for family dependence and parental supervision, household activities are a significant mode of domestic upbringing for girls, an apprenticeship in homemaking. Compared to the daughters of nondeprived parents, girls from deprived homes can be expected to rank higher on family dependence and domestic interests.

An empirical test of these relations is presented below, beginning with sources of financial judgment.

Financial Judgment

Apart from family need and values, wisdom in spending and saving money is dependent on practical experience with financial matters. When a child has his own sum of money to manage, an ill-considered expenditure has direct consequences for him and, especially in deprived households, for the family as a whole. Personal funds may be acquired by paid jobs, whether in the work setting or home, or by a regularly scheduled allowance. Unlike these sources or money, the practice of giving money to children according to need (as determined by parents) fosters economic dependence. As shown below, economic dependence was more characteristic of girls than of boys, owing partly to the roles they assumed in the household economy. But more noteworthy is the negative effect of economic dependence on financial judgment.

For the total sample, economic support which offered some measure of autonomy on financial matters was more common in the experience of boys than of girls. Two sources of data were used in the analysis: the 1936 interview with mothers and a self-report questionnaire completed in 1937. Mothers were asked whether they gave their offspring an allowance and paid them for doing chores. Information on whether money was received according to need was obtained from the questionnaire. Forty-six percent of the boys were given an allowance, 20 percent were paid for doing chores, and 25 percent received money according to need. A smaller proportion of girls received an allowance and were paid for helping in the home (40% vs. 10%), while a majority were given money upon a determination of their need (61%). As might be expected, middle-class parents were more apt to give their offspring spending money than were lower-status parents, an average difference of 16 percent.

Parental support was highly contingent on whether the child held a job, and thus varied by deprivational conditions mainly among boys. This result reflects conditions which motivated employment—economic need and the inability or unwillingness of parents to provide spending money. Boys from deprived families in both social classes received less support from parents—as an allowance, pay for chores, or when needed—than members of nondeprived homes, but the difference is largely explained by their work status. An allowance and economic support by need were less common among working than among unemployed youth (30% vs. 66% and 15% vs. 39%). Most boys in nondeprived families were engaged in household chores, and slightly more than a third were paid for their labor.[10]

If economic dependence on parents restricts practical experience in the use of money, this deficit should be most evident in the financial responsibility of girls. Only a small proportion were employed, and those who only helped their parents were seldom paid for their efforts. Especially in deprived families, girls with domestic responsibilities were more often given money when needed than an allowance, and very few working girls received any money from their parents.

In the 1936 interview, mothers were less likely to attribute responsibility in the use of money to daughters than to sons. Seventy-six percent of the boys were described as both saving their money and spending it wisely, in comparison to 64 percent of the girls. Good judgment in the use of money is correlated with deprived status among boys (a difference of 21 percent between nondeprived and deprived groups), but does not vary by either class or deprivation among girls (differences of less than 7 percent). Neither class background nor economic loss proved to be as influential as an allowance and job in determining the mothers' evaluation.

To assess the main effects of an allowance and task experience, we included these factors in a multiple classification analysis which statistically controlled both social class and deprivation. Three factors (characteristically present = 1, not present = 0) were constructed from patterns of employment and domestic chores: employed, only chores in the home, and neither role. Boys and girls were combined in the analysis since the results did not vary by sex of child. Children who received an allowance were more often perceived by their mothers as financially responsible than other children (82% vs. 60%), but this effect is less than that of employment and domestic chores. Eighty-seven percent of the employed were viewed as financially responsible, in comparison to 38 percent of the children who lacked obligations. Between these extremes were youth who only carried responsibilities in the household (66%).

Do these variations in financial judgment have any significance beyond the adolescent world of the study children? in their economic behavior as adults? Unfortunately, we do not have adequate *prospective* evidence of such effects. Available data is restricted to the practice of saving money. From data collected in the 1958 interview, we were able to identify variations in the regularity of savings. Approximately 70 percent of the respondents saved money on a regular basis. Class origin, family deprivation, employment status in 1936, and mother's evaluation of financial judgment were all analyzed in relation to the above index of economic behavior, with adult status controlled. While none of these factors was predictive among women, men who saved their money were most likely to have been reared in a deprived family, to have had a job, and to have been judged responsible in the use of money as an adolescent. Of these three factors, the most significant predictor was employment. Eighty percent of the men who earned money in the 30s reported a saving program, compared to 54 percent of those who did not have a job.

However fragile the evidence, a large number of the study members are convinced that hardship in the Depression has made a difference in their financial outlook. They tend to use the Depression as an explanation for their behavior. In the words of a young white-collar worker, hardships in the 30s made him "realize that money doesn't always come so easy. It makes you just a little conservative in spending money, especially in spending it beyond your means." Such explanations are of little value as a guide to the formative origins of economic attitudes, but they do provide a rationale for conduct and may have social significance for the young as object lessons. A survey of 171 undergraduates at the University of California, Berkeley, during the fall of 1965 indicates that parental memories of the Depression's impact are frequently communicated to children as moral lessons.[11]

Dependability and Industry

The tasks children performed in the Depression can be viewed in terms of the behavior they required. In varying degree, paid jobs call for punctuality, courtesy, thoroughness, and obedience to superiors. If jobs in the household or work setting entailed some measure of dependability and industry, were these patterns of behavior generalized to other situations? Were children who engaged in these activities perceived by adults outside the family as relatively dependable and energetic?

As measures of this behavior, we selected three scales from the 1937 Situation Ratings. Each scale was constructed from the averaged and standardized ratings of staff members at the Institute of Child Welfare who observed the children in social activities and school affairs. As described by their characteristic behavior, the three scales are: dependable—"assumes responsibilities and performs them reliably, is conscious of the rights of others"; resists authority—"deliberately breaks rules, refuses to comply with requests of person in charge, resists authority"; industrious—"energetic, concentrated effort displayed in activity."

Boys in domestic or work roles were not distinguished by their dependability or resistance to authority, and neither of these ratings were correlated with economic deprivation or class position. However, industry was attributed most often to working boys, and was also related to deprived status ($p < .01$). The effect of deprivation is largely due to its relation to employment, and diminished to insignificance with the latter controlled.[12] Economic hardship is a plausible stimulus of energetic behavior, as suggested by Bakke's research on children in deprived families, but it is also likely that jobs were more often found by the industrious. Furthermore, the time required by the job, coupled with the usual requirements of school, family, and friends, would place a premium on energetic activity.

Girls in deprived families were judged slightly higher on dependability and industry than members of nondeprived households, but neither this difference nor the effects of social class were statistically reliable. An explanation for this outcome is seen in the observed behavior of girls in domestic and work roles. Those who only helped out in the home were most prevalent in deprived families, and their observed behavior closely resembled that of girls who lacked obligations. The main contrast occurs in relation to girls who were doubly committed, those with domestic responsibilities and a paid job. They were rated substantially higher on both dependability and industry.

A work-oriented life style is most evident in the behavior of girls who assumed roles in both household and work setting. Are their social characteristics more a consequence of factors related to economic loss or of socialization in a lower-status family? Employment was mainly restricted to girls from deprived families, and two-thirds of the working girls were members of working-class families. However, dependability and industry were equally characteristic of employed girls in both social classes.

Another way of looking at the behavioral effects of task experience in the Depression is to take the respondent's viewpoint. Did responsibilities enhance the importance of dependability and industry? To explore this question, we must turn to the adult years for data on behavioral preferences. A questionnaire administered to members of the study (1964) included a list of sixteen attributes of children's behavior, including that of dependability. They were asked to check the three attributes which they considered most desirable in a teen-age boy and girl. In line with our expectation, men who valued dependability were most likely to have grown up in a deprived family, and a majority earned their own money as teen-agers. Even with adjustments made for family and adult status, 52 percent of the men from deprived families favored dependable behavior in a boy and girl, compared to 26 percent on the nondeprived. This effect proved to be much greater than that of employment during the Depression. Neither economic loss nor roles in the household economy were prominent in the behavioral preference of women.

In retrospect, the premise that task experience selectively conditions behavior and values rests on assumptions which may not be valid for the social roles assumed by some members of the Oakland study. One of these assumptions concerns the duration and demand character of tasks in the home and work setting, neither of which were directly measured. As in the case of occupational roles, the behavioral impact of tasks in the preadult years is likely to vary directly with both of these conditions. Without empirical support, we have also treated the domestic and work activities of children in 1936 as if they were characteristic of their adaptations to economic hardship throughout most of the Depression decade. A detailed history of these activities is clearly needed to provide a developmental measure of task experience.

Social Independence and Domestic Values

As adaptive responses to economic deprivation, gainful employment and domestic involvement differ in their apparent consequence for social independence. The former reponse implies some measure of autonomy and responsibility outside the family, especially for boys, while the latter function among girls entails activity in the home and domestic constraints.

There are two aspects of social independence in the preadolescent and adolescent years which need to be distinguished: the freedom to select same-sex friends, places, and times for social activity; and the freedom to associate with members of the opposite sex, as in dating, socializing with boys and girls in the evening, and attendance at unchaperoned parties. Since boys lag behind girls in heterosexual interests and development, the most appropriate index of social independence for sex-group comparisons is one which is not restricted to interaction with the opposite sex. In the 1936 interview with mothers, this form of independence was indexed by answers to a question on participation in social activities on school nights. Degree of independence in heterosexual activities was measured by replies to whether the child associated with boys and girls on weekend evenings. Affirmative responses to each question were defined as an indication of social independence. Girls were most likely to associate with groups of boys and girls on weekend evenings, while boys were more often involved in activities on school nights.

Social independence is related to deprived status among boys in the middle and working classes. This relationship is strongest for school-night activities, and is partly a function of employment and its liberating influence. Boys from deprived families were likely to have a job ($r = .33$), and both family deprivation and a job are similarly related to involvement in extrafamilial activities on school nights ($r = .21$). In a regression analysis (which defined deprivation and family status as givens), the direct effect of deprived status proved to be stronger than its indirect effect through unemployment (betas = .20 vs. .15). Even though low-status parents generally supervise their offspring less closely than parents in the middle class, class background did not make a difference in the social liberties of boys.

In size and consistency, deprivational conditions had less of an effect on the social independence of girls. Within the middle class, girls from deprived families were more rather than less likely to associate with peers in the evening, but the only meaningful difference occurs in heterosexual activities. This result is contrary to our expectation, cannot be attributed to economic or domestic roles, and differs from the effect of deprivation among the working-class girls. In their group, social independence is most prevalent among the nondeprived, and especially among those who had no obligation in the family or work setting. Approximately half of the girls who did not have role obligations engaged in social activities on school nights, compared to a fourth of the girls who earned money and assisted their parents in the household. The size of this difference, which accounts for the effect of deprivation, most likely reflects the burden assumed by girls who performed both economic and domestic roles.

This difference in the working class also shows up in the leisure time and social experience of girls, according to the reports of mothers (1936). Girls and even boys from the deprived working class ranked lower on free time and social experience than other groups in the sample—the nondeprived working class and both deprivational groups in the middle class. While most children were described as having adequate opportunities for social contacts and hobbies, this was least true for members of deprived families in the working class (68% vs. 86%). Similar differences appear on the interviewer's rating of free or play time and of the variety and suitability of friends. These variations are at least consistent with the constraints and pressures of life in the most deprived sector of the working class, but they do not emerge in staff observations of the study children in social situations. Neither economic hardship nor responsibilities produced differences in the observed popularity of boys and girls. These data do not support the assumption that family deprivation and children's responsibilities imposed severe limitations on social experience. [See also chapter 6 of Elder, *Children and the Great Depression* (Chicago: University of Chicago Press, 1974)—Ed. note.]

Up to this point we have defined employment as a causal link between family hardship and the social independence of boys. There is an alternative interpretation, however, which has not been ruled out. As an outgrowth of economic burdens in the family, social independence may have preceded and increased the likelihood of employment. According to this perspective, the boys who found jobs were more self-reliant and liberated from traditional family constraints than other youth. The important question, then, is whether differences in social independence preceded or followed the point at which they were hired for the first time. If we assume that this point occurred no earlier than the seventh or eighth grade, we can test this question by using data from questionnaires which were administered in junior and senior high school.

In each time period, identical questions were asked on whether the respondent resembled a young person who is allowed by his parents to stay out late at night, is able to go places without permission, and is permitted to associate with friends in the absence of adult supervision. Since the items were interrelated, scores on the five-point scales (ranging from one "low" to five "high") were summed to provide a single indicator for each period. As one might expect, degree of independence increased sharply between the two time periods among boys in the sample ($\overline{X}$s = 6.8 vs. 11.4). Girls reported less social freedom than boys, but they also acquired more liberties during these years ($\overline{X}$s = 5.8 vs. 10.1).

In junior high, economic conditions did not make a significant difference in the social freedom of either boys or girls, and there is no evidence that boys who later obtained jobs were more liberated from parental constraints at this time than other youth. On the contrary, the former group reported slightly less independence than the latter, and similar results were obtained among girls (an average difference of .53). In high school, however, boys who reported the greatest amount of social freedom were generally members of deprived families, and a majority held jobs. Of these two factors, employment most strongly influenced degree of independence and accounted for the influence of economic deprivation. On the average, boys who earned money on jobs reported more independence ($p < .05$), and showed much lower stability in this respect from early adolescence than the unemployed. This difference in stability and its relation to work experience is shown by correlations between the two measures of social independence among the employed and unemployed ($r = .25$ vs. .52). The largest gains in social freedom were experienced by boys who obtained jobs.

In high school, girls who reported a high degree of independence were not distinguished by deprived status, class position, or role in the household economy. Economic deprivation did have a slight negative effect on reported independence among working-class girls, and parental limitations were correlated with domestic involvement. These variations were too small, however, to be statistically reliable.

Up to this point, the data on social independence are mainly consistent with our expectations on boys in the Depression. All of the evidence suggests that economic loss and work roles tended to free boys from the traditional restraints of parental control. While most girls responded to family hardship by assuming household responsibilities, this adaptation had little consequence for their dependence on the family or parental control, with the possible exception of girls from working-class homes. But apart from the issue of parental control, involvement in household operations has implications for social learning in the role of homemaker. These implications include exposure to domestic models and values. Were girls from deprived families more inclined to favor domestic interests and the role of homemaker than members of nondeprived homes?

To investigate this question we used measures of domestic interests which were based on a vocational questionnaire in the high school period (the Strong Vocational Interest Inventory). From this inventory we obtained two measures of domestic interests: a single item which asked whether the respondent favored only marriage and the homemaker role, a career, or both lines of activity; and a clinical assessment of the relative strength of domestic and career interests, based on profiles in the inventory.[13] Since very few girls were characterized by a predominant career orientation, the main comparison is between those who preferred domestic activity and those who showed a combination of career and family interests.

Domestic interests were associated with economic deprivation and household obligations, but only among girls from middle-class families, a subgroup which is less conservative on sex-role behavior than the working class. Both indicators of role preference showed this result. Two out of three girls from deprived families in the middle class preferred domestic activities to a career (the single item), a preference level which is well above that of girls in nondeprived households (38 percent). In this social class, girls who favored the domestic role were more likely to be involved in household operations than other girls, but the difference (21 percent) is not large enough to account for the effects

of economic deprivation. Sixty-eight percent of the working-class girls in both deprivation categories chose family over career interests, and domestic obligations made relatively little difference in this preference.

As seen in these findings, the context in which economic conditions influenced the
girls' values and social freedom is specified by their social class. Traditional family values
are less prevalent in the middle class than among families of lower status, and the
reinforcing effect of family hardship in domestic socialization occurred only among girls
from the middle class. Economic deprivation tended to increase the resemblance of
middle- and working-class girls on family interests. If the responsibilities of working-class
girls were heavier and more time-consuming than tasks managed by girls in the middle
class, this would help explain the results on social independence. Economic hardship and
domestic activity restricted the social freedom of girls only in the working class.

The Downward Extension of Adultlike Experience

Roles in the household economy of deprived families are not by themselves an indication of accelerated entry into the adult world, but in the Depression they were performed
in a sex-differentiated context which placed unusual responsibilities on the young. Early
emancipation from family constraints, a preference for dependability, and maturity in the
management of money are at least consistent with this interpretation of Depression
influences among boys; and so are the dependability and domestic inclination of girls.
But we need more direct evidence of this orientation toward adult life, such as an
indication that children from deprived households were most likely to seek out and
associate with adults and to show an interest in growing up rapidly. Traditionally, the
apprenticed young display this mode of social development, and we discern basic elements of apprenticeship in the life situation of the Depression children.

If the years between childhood and adult status take the form of preparation, they
represent a developmental phase in which experience has direct consequences for subsequent activity. The young learn by doing as they engage in the occupational ways and
constraints of adult life. For the Oakland children, economic deprivation in the 30s
increased the common involvement of mother and daughter in household operations,
and encouraged economic activity which often placed boys in a responsible position to
nonfamily employers. To a considerable extent, adolescents from deprived families were
engaged with adults in conjoint activities of mutual significance. From the standpoint of
adult orientation, economic roles in the community have special significance as a mode of
exposure to nonfamily adults. In an important sense, the transference of attachment from
parents to nonfamily adults represents a step toward adulthood, a movement away from
the particularistic world of family and kin.

As a general measure of adult orientation, we used a staff rating of adult-oriented
behavior in school-related situations (drawn from the Situation Ratings, 1937): seeks
adult company—"seeks out adults in preference to children in a group. Hangs around
adults making frequent bids for attention. Identifies with adults and is very cordial to
them." In the various settings where the behavior observations were made, adults included teachers, playground supervisors, visitors, and the staff observers.

Children from deprived families and the working class were most likely to be described as adult-oriented, as were those who held jobs. But the most significant factor is gainful employment. Boys and girls who were employed showed much greater interest in adults and spent more time with them in school-related activities than other children ($p < .01$).[14] Even within the deprived group, working youth were rated higher on affiliation with adults than the unemployed. Interest in adults was neither more nor less prevalent among children who were committed to responsibilities in the home.

A variety of factors may lead children to seek the company and attention of adults outside the family, apart from shared activity. These include the need for a parent-surrogate (resulting from family turmoil, rejection) and a desire to be recognized as an adult. One might expect this desire to be characteristic of youth who favored the company of adults—and some evidence of this relation does appear in the data. Boys and girls from economically deprived families were most likely to aspire to grown-up status.[15] This aspiration is related to low family status, but it was most prevalent among deprived children within each social class. In these data, at least, the goal of adult status is very much a function of family hardship. The greater the hardship, the more prevalent the goal.

According to our analysis, the roles children performed in the economy of deprived families paralleled traditional sex differences in the division of labor, and oriented them toward adult ways. Economic hardship and jobs increased their desire to associate with adults, to "grow up" and become an adult. This adult orientation is congruent with other behavioral correlates of roles in the household economy, including the responsible use of money (as perceived by mothers), energetic or industrious behavior, dependability and domesticity among girls, and the social independence of boys.

If "coming of age" was accelerated by economic hardships, did this developmental course entail a premature closure of identity and role preference? In what ways, if any, did the adultlike experience of children shape their options, decisions, and life course as they moved into the early and middle years of adulthood? Two additional types of adaptation in the Depression bear upon these questions: adjustments in family relations, including roles in decision making, and the psychological response of children to family change, status ambiguity, and stress. Economic loss required new adaptations in family maintenance that involved both parents and children.

Notes

1. Epigraph: From Margot Hentoff's review of Laura Ingalls Wilder's "Little House Books" ("Kids, Pull Up Your Socks: A Review of Children's Books," *The New York Review of Books,* 20, April 1972, p. 15). Wilder's story of Laura Ingalls, beginning with her early childhood in a pioneer family (circa 1860s) may appear to have little relevance to the experience of urban children in the Depression. But there are some important similarities, as we shall see. On social roles, children in deprived families had more in common with Laura Ingalls than with contemporary children in affluent families, a point implied in Hentoff's thoughtful question: "How, in *this* world, are we going to be able to give the young back their sense of worth?" (p. 15).

2. See Talcott Parsons, "Age and Sex in the Social Structure of the United States," in C. Kluckhohn and H. A. Murray, eds., *Personality in Nature, Society, and Culture,* 2d ed., rev. (New York: Knopf, 1953), pp. 269–81.

3. A durable belief in research on work roles assumes that tasks shape behavior. However, empirical knowledge on this problem is still every rudimentary. For provocative work in this area, see Breer and Locke, *Task Experience as a Source of Attitudes* (1965).

4. Systematic information on type of job, hours, and wage was not obtained from the Oakland children or from their parents. As a result, we are unable to determine the prevalence of examples cited in this paragraph.

5. In a cross-cultural study, Minturn and Lambert found that a child receives strong pressures to assume responsibility if his mother is making a contribution to the family economy. *Mothers of Six Cultures* (1964), p. 271. See also Prodipto Roy, "Adolescent Roles: Rural-Urban Differences," in Nye and Hoffman 1963, pp. 165–81.

6. James H. S. Bossard, *Parent and Child* (Philadelphia: University of Pennsylvania Press, 1953), chapter 6. A relation between pressures to assume responsibilities and size of family was found by Minturn and Lambert (1964), p. 271.

7. All four variables in this standard regression analysis are dichotomies; economic deprivation, nondeprived vs. deprived; family size, less than three children vs. three or more; work experience for boys, yes vs. no; and domestic chores for girls, scores of 0–2 vs. 3–5. Deprivation and family size are correlated .33 and .30 with boys' work, and .42 and .16 with girls' chores.

8. All reported differences by family deprivation and work status are statistically significant at the .05 level. Economic aspirations were indexed by an item on the junior high questionnaire which asked the respondents whether they wanted to have more spending money than their classmates (a gradient scale with scores ranging from 1 to 5). Desire for control was indexed by the average ratings of trained judges who read observational and self-report materials in the high school period on each child in the sample. Values on the scale range from 1 to 5.

9. Esther E. Prevey, "A Quantitative Study of Family Practices in Training Children in the Use of Money," *Journal of Educational Psychology* 36 (1945): 411–28.

10. The economic support of boys in nondeprived families is similar in this respect to that of urban boys in Straus's study (1962). In both groups, over a third received pay for doing chores around the house.

11. Glen H. Elder, Jr., "The Depression Experience in Family Relations and Upbringing," unpublished manuscript, spring 1966.

12. It is most unlikely that the observers' rating of industrious behavior was influenced by knowledge of the boys' work status. All the Situation Ratings were based on observed behavior in school-related activities.

13. The classification was performed by Dr. Barbara Kirk, director of Counseling Center, University of California, Berkeley. Four categories were used: strongly domestic, probable domestic, mixed domestic-career, career. The first two categories defined a preference for the domestic role.

14. For both sexes, mean scores on adult orientation are 52.4 for the employed and 46.1 for the unemployed categories.

15. Desire for adult status was indexed by a question in the junior high questionnaire: "Do you want to be a grown-up man or woman?" A majority of the children gave an affirmative response (67 percent), and the percentage increased by family hardship. In terms of percentage difference, the effects of class and deprivation are identical (14 percent).

JOHN R. SEELEY
R. ALEXANDER SIM
E. W. LOOSLEY

27. Age in Crestwood Heights, Toronto, Ontario

Age is the child of time. Every society inescapably takes count of age in the distribution of rights and duties, in the attribution of characteristics and status. The distinctions that are made are various, but it seems safe to say that in no society are the distinctions carried further than in the one under study. Just as some societies have a dozen or more different terms for an arrow or a natural object that has unusual importance for them, so, in this society, one might say that terms for age grades—especially for children—are carried almost to the ultimate refinement. Not only is there, in effect, a sub-society of four-year-olds, as distinct from five-year-olds, for the children but there is very nearly a science of the four-year-olds as against a science of the three-year-olds for the adult. And not only a science, but a system of expectations and a system of obligations as well.

Up to Two: Birth and Earliest Dependence

The planning which we have seen as characteristic of Crestwood Heights extends, of course, even to the advent of a child. Parents usually "arrange" to have children as they do to make a trip to Europe or to buy a new car; and this prior, deliberate choice is made possible and nearly sure by adequate contraceptive devices and knowledge. If, as often happens in other areas of Crestwood life, carefully laid plans miscarry, and a child is conceived without the element of forethought, the tendency is to regard the event as an accident which must be accepted with good grace. No Crestwood mother would admit ordinarily that her child was unwanted, since love and security norms now receive such emphasis.[1]

Birth in Crestwood Heights, and the pregnancy which precedes it, introduce a cultural situation which the child will continue to meet in his progress towards maturity. In our modern society with its intricate division of labor, it is not surprising that the advice of a medical specialist is sought to confirm the fact and supervise the process of the pregnancy. He is the first of a series of experts or specialists to whom the Crestwood couple will refer their problems connected with child-rearing. The link between the family and the non-familial institutions, with their attendant experts, begins to be elaborated at this early point.

The obstetrician cares for the woman throughout her pregnancy, prescribing in detail her diet, hours of rest, exercise, weight, attitudes, and expectations as to the development of the embryo. He is also responsible for the delivery of the child, in a downtown hospital, and for the care of the mother while in hospital.

The hospital birth, at a distance from home and family, provides another symbol: from the beginning, individualization is mapped out as a pattern of life in Crestwood Heights. As soon as he leaves his mother's body, the child is launched upon the first of a series of separations from her. He is cared for in the hospital nursery, and its staff regulates his first contacts with his mother. The scientific and antiseptic setting assures the physical survival of both mother and child, but it rarely takes into account the mother's anxieties and emotions, particularly lively at the birth of the first child. In the words of a Crestwood mother:

> It all depends on how busy they are. If the nursery isn't too crowded and the nurses have more time, you see your baby oftener. But when Billy and Tom [her twins] were born, I was sure I didn't see Tom for days. They kept bringing in Billy for feeding. I knew the difference between them right away and I told them, but they were too busy to pay much attention. I got quite frantic about it.

It is evident that this mother's anxiety, ill or well founded, was not allayed.

Since independence is essential for the achievement-in-isolation which is highly valued by the culture, the significance of the hospital delivery for the later character of the adult can scarcely be over-emphasized. As has been pointed out by Margaret Mead,[2] the feeling-contact of child with mother in the first months and years of life is an important determinant of personality. The Crestwood Heights mother, in order to give birth to a child, is separated from her family. The infant is separated from his mother for most of the hours of his first days of life; his physical contacts are alternated between the mother and the efficient, crisply starched nurses. In the cluster of practices surrounding birth, the Crestwood mother and child would seem thus to be impressed immediately and deeply with the cultural concept that each has a separate and isolated identity: the mother at the conscious level, the infant at the deep feeling-nexus of existence, not yet touched by reason.[3] At the moment of birth, they take the first step in a long process of "psychic weaning" which will end finally in the breaking of all ties of dependency between them; this break will in turn enable the child, later, to repeat the same cycle with his own children.[4]

The relationship of the Crestwood child to his mother is of particular importance, especially in the earliest phases of his development, since the father may be absent for long times, or at least for long working days. This relationship is also reinforced because the family is a separate unit, rather than an integral part of a larger family system as it would be in another culture or another era.

Yet the child must continue to learn, at this early stage, to accept substitutes for his mother, and she must learn to share the responsibility for her child with others. The nurse is but one of a series of women who now come and go within the family circle: the baby-sitter, the cleaning woman, the housekeeper who may come for a week or two after the mother's return from the hospital, the occasional friend or relative who may assume brief responsibility for the child.[5] Such substitution is inevitable in the Crestwood cultural pattern. The busy mother, who must run the house without the aid of a maid, entertain for husband and friends, attend meetings, and have "outside interests," is literally compelled to ration strictly her physical contacts with her child.[6] Thus in early infancy preparation continues for achievement-in-isolation, for the individual pursuit of materialistic goals in which the human relationships must often be subordinated.

The two roles the mother is called on to play, which bring her now close to and now away from the child, are difficult to accept and practise, particularly in the child-centered culture of Crestwood Heights which emphasizes love and emotional security for the child. Her position is, of course, the more difficult because there is no universally agreed set of rules for child-rearing. In patriarchal family organization there were clearly defined rules, but in the more democratic family organization of Crestwood Heights, there are many paths from which to choose.

Besides, there are no clear-cut norms as to what is expected, no absolute measuring sticks to serve as a guide. The child who is two this year is not expected to be exactly like the child who was two last year; attitudes are required to be always flexible and "expectations" are constantly changing. What is constant is the expectation that expectations will change.

Because of the mother's uncertainty, her sense of responsibility towards the child increases. Because practices constantly change, she tends to seek advice and help from sources outside the family. A pediatrician will advise in matters of health. A vast amount of printed material is available to the highly literate Crestwood mother. In the women's magazines she is confronted with innumerable articles on child care written by convincing experts. These present opinions on topics ranging from the proper nutrition for her baby to the best means of "developing in a positive way the mental health of her child." Many of the articles are by professionals, but she is also bombarded by the statements of other persons, representing commercial and business interests: the toymakers,[7] the manufacturers of special foods and clothing for children. Each has a word of advice for the mother—or of censure. Each suggests something she should "buy," something which is calculated, if not guaranteed, to contribute to her child's welfare. There are also her friends, with whom she can exchange notes on the height, weight, walking ability and so on of her children and with whom she can search for solutions to the "problems" which confront her.

These innumerable recommendations do not, however, supply the mother with definite instructions. Their often contradictory directives only add to her uncertainty amid the changing patterns of her culture.[8]

The modern stress on physical, intellectual, and emotional growth coexists, as Allison Davis has said,[9] with a necessity to teach respect for property. The Crestwood home, as has been pointed out, usually contains expensive decoration and household equipment, easily damaged or destroyed by small exploring fingers. From the moment he can toddle, the Crestwood child, not confined to a nursery or "picked up after" by a servant, encounters a series of instructions about the articles he may not touch, the flower he may not pick in his own or a neighboring garden, the dress or suit he must not dirty, the dangerous road on which he may not play.[10] Despite the prevalent view that too early and too severe toilet training may be "traumatic" for the child, many a Crestwood mother, given the setting of her immaculate home, is virtually compelled to focus attention upon this training. Broadloom is particularly incompatible with permissiveness in toilet training. To some considerable degree, therefore, the child is not free to explore and manipulate his material environment but is hampered by necessities growing out of the equally strong value placed upon the sacredness of property in this culture. The modified goals for this stage of the child's socialization seem to be the achievement of some independence and motor co-ordination within the narrow limits of the handling of gadgets and toys; property values and the very real dangers of traffic-crammed streets restrict his freedom to examine his immediate surroundings more fully.

In his first two years the child has become accustomed to his own crib and playpen, to the toys cannily designed to amuse and improve him; he has also become accustomed to an absence of long physical contact with his mother, and to prohibitions respecting many things which have a fascination for him at this period.

Three, Four, Five: First Ventures Beyond the Family

Around the age of three, the Crestwood Heights child may make his first direct and prolonged contact with a newly recognized child-rearing institution, the Nursery School. Even before this first important venture into the wider community, the child may have had many "experiences" outside the home (for example, intervals at the summer cottage and with relatives at a distance; meals eaten in restaurants; visits to the pediatrician and dentist; trips with the family by car or by airplane; or, more rarely, a period alone with a brother or sister at a summer camp), but nursery school is likely to be the first place in which he has spent any length of time completely separated from his mother and from a familial environment.

The function of the nursery school, it is commonly thought, is to reinforce the child's emotional and physical independence of his mother, and to teach him social and physical skills under trained professional supervision and in contact with those of his own age. From the mother's viewpoint, the nursery school provides, in addition, responsible care for the child, and guides him along tested and therefore culturally approved lines of development.

Crestwood Heights has its own nursery school, supported on a voluntary basis by parents in the community. There are also many other, privately owned, nursery schools in adjacent Big City, a number of them on "The Crest" or at the outer edges of the Heights. Not by any means all parents wish or can find accommodation for their pre-schoolers, but for the busy, educated Crestwood mother, sending her child to nursery school seems to be emerging as a norm.

There is nevertheless frequently ambivalence in the mothers who send a child to nursery school. Some mothers relinquish their children reluctantly to nursery school, and do so only because they believe it will be beneficial to them: it is thus common to hear a mother say that both she and her child benefit from being apart for some part of the day. Others, under the conflicting pressures of the care of small children and their other responsibilities—express relief—"I can hardly wait until Jackie is ready for Nursery School"—though the admission is frequently made with doubt or guilt.

Attendance at a private nursery school usually entails the assumption of some responsibility by the parents; sometimes volunteer service is expected or required; sometimes attendance at a parent education group is made a condition of the child's admission; sometimes service on a board of directors is requested. The privately administered nursery school, therefore, tends to interpenetrate the child's home, and to influence considerably parental methods of child care.

Crestwood parents who support and patronize nursery schools expect three returns for their time and money. First, they hope the child will learn how to "get along with" other children of his own age group, for, even at the age of three, four, or five, getting along amiably with peers is considered of great importance. Second, they hope he will become more independent of his parents, particularly of his mother, with whom the closest ties have been forged. Third, they hope that the nursery school personnel will give them "solutions" for the "problems" of child-rearing which they have encountered. Parents who thoroughly believe in the value of the nursery school hope to acquire up-to-date information which will enable them "to become better parents."

Nursery school theory, which emphasizes the emotional and physical development of the child in a permissive atmosphere, is implemented in a setting of abundant play material and equipment. The child is presented with a wide choice of activity, which is carefully scaled to his size and motor ability: chairs, for instance, are always small, and scissors have blunt ends. The choices offered—between plasticene, poster paint, jungle gym, record player, big blocks or toys—give him considerably more freedom[11] than he finds in his own home, whose furnishings and equipment are not adapted in the same way to his age level.

Evidence of the achievement of independent behavior in the nursery school is sought not only in the child's initiative in the exploration and use of his new environment, but also in his ability to adjust to the absence of his mother (if he cannot easily renounce his claims on his mother, *both* are likely to be regarded as "problems"), and to the presence of other children. This adjustment is measured largely by his capacity to "co-operate" with other children, and to accept the light rein with which the supervisor presides over the children's purposeful play. In the name of co-operation he is expected to learn to control his aggressive impulses.[12] The nursery school is the first agency which impresses upon the child these cardinal middle-class demands. In his society, skills are also stressed, and they are similarly emphasized in the nursery school which is an ante-room to it: the child learns simple dances, and how to manipulate materials. The overriding concern, however, is with skills in human relations, and these will be exhibited in "co-operative" play under firm but amiable adult leadership.

The nursery school child learns in his contacts with the adult staff (if he has not previously done so) that the adult time is strictly rationed where he is concerned. He must learn to share the teacher as well as the toys and play materials with his peers; again this necessity prepares for later expectations of his society. He must learn to terminate a project such as play at the sand tables when "it is time" in the routine for rest or song, or a trip to the toilet. As one would expect, the average attention-span for a three-year-old child, established by measurement or the supervisor's judgment, cannot coincide with the individual child's rhythm of attention and change. Nursery school helps him to take his cues from the group rather than from his own immediate predilections and inclinations.

Because of the situation in the Crestwood Heights family, this newer institution, the nursery school, is becoming more and more firmly established. It meets a definite need. In view of the varied roles played by adults in the culture, it is becoming essential that the child should, as soon as possible, learn to function in roles of his own. The mother, given the many activities which she is expected to carry on within the home and in the community, must be freed periodically from the care of her children. Failing a paid Nanny or a willing neighbor or relative, a substitute must be found. Through the nursery school experience, then, the mother takes another important step in the direction of delegating a responsibility which the circumstances of her life hinder her from retaining: the responsibility for her child's socialization. The nursery school teacher, who is thought to have none of the mother's emotional involvement with the child, is considered able to teach him to let go his emotional dependence on his mother, and to redirect this freed energy towards good relationships with children of his own age—who, in most cases, would not be available to the child in his own family circle, anyway. The cultural expectation is that the child will seem to be drawn into the society from the outside, rather than pushed out into it from the family nest. Individual differences determine how far this smooth and harmonious merging with peers under sympathetic and tolerant adult guidance will proceed.

Six to Twelve: Institutions Share the Child

By the time the Crestwood child is five, the age for kindergarten, the basic pattern of his social behavior has been relatively set, chiefly by his experiences in the home, and at the nursery school if he has attended one. When the child graduates from nursery school,[13] he enters the state-supported school system, the most important, or second most important, institution for socialization in Crestwood Heights. The nursery school, which afforded a transition-stage for both child and parent, is now succeeded by an institution which will to a large extent regulate the life of the Crestwood child for the next thirteen or fourteen years.

Here, in the school, the long-sustained training of the child for his adult roles has its serious beginnings. Here, achievement-in-isolation gradually will take on real and earnest meaning for the child who must, year after year, increasingly adapt himself to the pace of the school program.

Probably the most marked feature of the Crestwood Heights school system to an outsider from another culture would be its division into grades by age, and even within the age grades, into "achievement levels." Despite its garden-like décor, Crestwood Heights reveals in the organization of the school strictly urban characteristics. It has a pattern markedly different from that of an Eskimo group teaching a boy the rudiments of hunting, or from that of the one-room rural school. Because of sheer pressure of numbers, the Crestwood school is compelled to sort the children into groups, on the basis of intelligence and performance, with a corresponding rough equivalence in chronological age. Thus the child at any one age level in the school may be conscious that there are other levels above him and perhaps below. In the one-room school, the set of requirements in other grades is part of each day's experience. In Crestwood Heights, the child is cut off from the other grades and the separation heightens a sense of mystery, difference, and, it seemed to at least one observer, anxiety. The "Grade" becomes an important means for the child's definition of self and others in his environment. An inescapable conclusion of the child's experience in the school system is his realization that the ladder leading to an adult career is exceedingly long.

For the child coming into the school system for the first time there may be many adjustments to make. Although the material environment of the nursery school and the kindergarten may appear similar—both have well-modulated light, space, movable furniture, toys—there are many differences.

Unlike the nursery school, which often is held in a home, a reconverted house, or a church hall, the kindergarten occupies one or two rooms in a building which also houses other school grades. One of the first facts the kindergarten child will assimilate in his new setting is that he belongs to the lowest group in the school hierarchy. Not infrequently, first-graders on the school playgrounds will yell at these newcomers, "Nyah! Nyah! Kindergarten babies!" This kind of expression is common, the peer opposition to the school's principle of "letting the child accept himself happily" at each stage of his school experience.

Thus the kindergarten child in his contact with older children in the school system recognizes early that there are innumerable stages ahead of him, in so long a vista that he can envisage neither the whole nor the end result towards which these stages are intended to move him. His horizons suddenly widen. He sees for himself that there are big boys and girls who are important in school affairs. Instead of a familiar group of adults, there is the loud-speaker system, relaying the voice of the Principal from his distant office to the kindergarten. Although the kindergarten child may have a warm relationship with his one, or perhaps two, teachers, he senses the larger world of the school, spreading out from his own classroom—a world from which his mother, his father, and his brothers and sisters are regularly excluded. Unlike nursery school, this school will bring him each year, as he advances through the grades, to another teacher, if not another peer group, and he realizes intuitively that continuous readjustment will be necessary. He listens to the conversation of older childen. This teacher is "cross," that teacher is "nice" or "pretty" or "easy." Even very young children, as well as those in the higher grades, have all the teachers minutely classified. Fears and hopes are organized around these adult figures and the fictions or facts associated with them, and this complex is connected with incentives and strivings. "If you do good, you get into Miss T.'s class; all the other kids have to go to. . . . " Thus, if Miss T. is desired as a teacher, incentives are sharpened by anxiety."[14]

Whereas the nursery school child is encouraged to explore his environment, freedom of movement for the kindergarten child is necessarily more limited. The larger school building may at first seem overpowering. The child soon learns that there are certain areas he may not enter. He cannot, for instance, use the teachers' door. He must not play or linger in the halls. There is a certain manner of proceeding to the playground. No pupil goes into the building before a certain time. In an astonishingly short space of time the newcomer has absorbed these taboos.[15] Indeed the rules stressed by the school may become more binding than those prevailing in the home. One mother, for example ruefully told how the whole family had been forced to change its toothbrushing habits at the insistence of a kindergarten child.

The kindergarten resembles nursery school in its atmosphere of permissiveness, but there are certain subtle differences which are reflected to the child in the teacher's attitudes. The kindergarten and its teacher are related to the larger bureaucratic structure of the educational system. She must meet the standards of the Department of Education; her work is supervised by the Principal, and evaluated by visits from the Inspector of Schools. In addition, the public school teacher is strongly encouraged to improve her professional qualifications if she wishes to enjoy regular promotions or progress towards higher positions in the educational hierarchy. These are strains to which the nursery school teacher is not usually so subject.

The position of the public school teacher as a figure in the whole complex school system, affects her role as a parent-surrogate. Because of the self-contained program of the nursery school, the teacher and her volunteer helpers may be viewed by the small child more as he regards his own mother. Or, in the absence of close relatives beyond the parents and one or two other children, which is the case in the majority of families, it is not too difficult for the child to envisage the nursery school teacher as a kindly but firm aunt, interested in his play, or as a guide on many expeditions to new and fascinating experiences. In contrast, the elementary school teacher cannot be divorced in the child's mind from the more rigid structure of the public school, whose disciplinary methods reach, even though mediated by personal warmth and kindliness, to the kindergarten level. In the mind of the child in the early grades, the teacher is backed with all the authority of the system, no matter how gentle or permissive her demeanor.

At the elementary school level, the teacher, as the sole adult with direct responsibility for roughly thirty to forty children, must be shared by the class to a much greater extent than the nursery school supervisor, who, with her assistants, usually deals with fewer children.[16] Children at this age struggle—in reality or fantasy—for a disproportionate share of such attenuated attention as the teacher can give.

The public school teacher, too, enters the family orbit in a way quite unlike that of the nursery school supervisor. When the nursery school is a community venture like the one in Crestwood Heights, the teacher may either be a member of the community or an outside professional, but, in either case, the contact with the parent is close and informal. The nursery school teacher advises the parents on child-rearing problems, but it does not lie in her power to "pass" or "fail" the child. Emotional and social development, together with evidence of certain motor skills, do count to a certain extent in reckoning achievement at nursery school, but chronological age remains the dominant criterion for passing out of it.

With the change to the public school, mental age and performance in school tasks tend to become the standards for advancement from one grade to the next, though emotional and social development also receive careful attention in the assessment of the child's "readiness" to progress through the school system. The child's "intelligence" is determined by scientific tests, administered under the school's jurisdiction (the results are the knowledge of the school alone), and this information controls to a large extent the rate of the child's advance. At the kindergarten level in Crestwood Heights schools, particular care is taken to give the parents a detailed and scientific profile of the child, and, in addition, informal sessions are held with the parents about the child's progress and development. The information is generally given a great deal of weight by the parents, even when they disagree with the conclusions, since it is backed by the authority of the educational system and presented by a recognized professional, one who has in her sphere of responsibility, moreover, the power to advance or to retard the child's progress up the educational ladder. Thus instead of being somewhat like a partner in responsibility, as was the case with the nursery school child, the parent assumes a far smaller role in the educational enterprise of the public school. With the increasing complexity of the school system and the increasing formality of the curriculum, however much the school may wish to involve the parent, the teacher's role becomes more professional, and the role of the parent becomes much more that of a "layman."

The elementary grades are composed of both boys and girls, and instruction is the same for both. The teacher is usually a single woman, although men and married women are welcomed to the teaching staff in Crestwood Heights. The teacher's professional role is in contrast with the approved feminine role of a woman: wife and mother within a family circle. But because of her professional status, the female teacher represents for many Crestwood mothers an ambition which has been extinguished.

The girl in the elementary school may experience some ambivalence about her projected female cultural role. She is, as she progresses in the school system, more and more cut off from smaller children unless she has younger brothers and sisters. Unlike the daughter in a lower-class family, she does not have charge of these younger siblings while the mother works, nor is she in position to mix with or help teach the children of an earlier grade, as she might be in the rural school. The Crestwood Heights girl, nevertheless, has a more prolonged and more intimate relationship with the mother than has the boy. Her difficulty in the home and in the elementary school is more to experience sufficient "maleness" in contact with male teachers and with her own father. She must depend upon relationships with her brothers, or boys in her own age group, for much of her knowledge of masculinity in the culture.[17]

The boy is likewise largely deprived of a male model with which to identify himself in the elementary school setting and thus learn at first hand the masculine role in the culture. And he does not have the same opportunity as the girl for finding an image within the home, since the father plays his major masculine role outside it. Almost his only alternative, apart from male teachers and camp and Scout leaders, is afforded by his male school mates, who are in the same psychological position as himself. But the boy finds, as does the girl with female teachers, that his occasional male teachers and the Principal stand in partial or even marked contrast to the masculine values for the male role in his culture. The boy, even more than the girl, is therefore thrust into a dependency upon the peer group for his masculine models, and this group, in turn, has a tendency, in upper middle class culture, to select as its model the athletic hero or the currently popular movie or TV star.

Because of the complexity of the culture, there cannot be, for either boy or girl, one composite male or female image to serve as a guide in learning the expected cultural roles. The school, while it gives instruction in the *knowledge* essential for the main cultural roles, cannot, because of the very nature of its structure, offer at the elementary school level the emotional experience of close relationships between adults and children, which will lead to the identification by which adult cultural roles may be internalized. The school system has made attempts in this direction through its counselling services, but at this initial stage the whole complex matter of role-learning through emotional association rests primarily with the family.[18]

It is nevertheless largely the age-graded nature of the school, in concurrence with the existing social structure of the family, which determines the *means* by which the child learns his cultural roles. And this pattern is for the most part set in the early grades. The school experience, then, cuts across the socialization process initiated in the family. The parents, anxious for the child's "maturity" and "independence," relinquish much of their jurisdiction over him to this institution. The organization of the school, with large classes under one teacher,[19] throws the child into the beginning of long contact with his peer group, although he may orient himself in the general structure of the school to those above or below him.

The school, however, is not the only institution which, through age-graded activities, assists in the socializing of the child in this period of his life. The summer camp (which now accepts children of nursery school age as well as those up to and including the teens), is a supplement of the school in this respect. The age-graded structure of the school is somewhat relaxed in the more informal camp setting, but the division of the children according to chronology is generally closely adhered to. The influence of the camp social system is considerable in shaping the child's concept of cultural roles. The camp affords a communal existence, at some physical distance from the home, which allows for a closer emotional relationship between adult leaders and the children in their charge. Moreover, since the parents are, of course, not present except on visitors' days, the prevailing values of independence and maturity can be stressed by the counsellors.

Camp, unlike school, is not compulsory, but there is a widespread feeling that "camp is a good thing." Among the reasons most frequently given by parents for sending children is their desire for the child to have broader group experiences with a peer group and for him to develop social and physical skills; neither of these can be secured, it is felt, in the home situation.

The step from home to summer camp is a more difficult one for the child than the transition from home to school, since he lives entirely in the camp orbit. One of several letters written to her mother by a nine-year-old during her first summer at camp suggests the strain:

> Camp Birch Bark,
> August 15, 1951.

Dear Mommy,

I still want to go home but if you don't want me to come I'll stay here. If I'm staying here I want some ink for my pen and some staishenairy and envolopes. But please may I come home on visitor's day. Today we went for a boat ride. I really want to come and if I don't I'll come back a reck. The food here tasts horrible. I really want to go hom. Please let me.

> Love,
> Linda.

Other institutional groupings lead the child of this age grade away from dependence exclusively on his own family. There are, for instance, church-sponsored groups for both Jewish and Gentile children. Many of the Jewish children enter the Hebrew school, where preparation is begun in the age level between five and twelve for a ceremony symbolizing adulthood: Bar-Mitzvah for the boy, and a corresponding, but more recently invented, ceremony for the girl. Although there is not the same religious uniformity among Gentiles, children still receive less formal, but nevertheless highly ritualized, preparation for Confirmation, for First Communion, or for joining the church.

Children between the ages of eight and twelve are eligible to enter the lowest ranks of such organizations as the Girl Guides or the Boy Scouts, and many children become Cubs or Brownies around the age of eight or nine. These groups too are graded by age, and a highly developed and internationally accepted series of symbols marks the child's passing from one age grade to the next, stressing as criteria for progress, factual knowledge, motor skills, and social qualities.

In addition to participating in the institutional activities enumerated above, the five- to twelve-year-old must learn many individual and social skills. This is the age at which adults consider it desirable to begin instruction in piano or some other musical instrument, in figure skating, swimming, eurhythmics, dramatics, art, and for girls, in dress and general appearance. It is not uncommon for a five-year-old to have had her first "permanent," and for slightly older girls to "plan" their clothes with their mothers.[20]

What is noticeable in the life of the age group between five and twelve is not only the high degree of institutionalized activity at this level, but also the nature of the experiences to which children are introduced at this early age, despite the view, also part of the culture, that "the place for the small child is with his own mother in his own home."[21] There would seem to be an important relationship between these two emphases in this age period—the network of organized activity with the peer group, outside the home, and the tendency to push to an ever earlier period the beginning of activities formerly associated with an older age group. Dating and mixed parties and kissing games begin at the age of eleven or twelve, if not earlier. Such activities lead to fears on the part of parent and teachers alike (and these also express some of the values of the society) lest sex experience occur "too early" for the children.[22] Adults are, however, committed to the notion that both sexes should learn to adjust to each other by boy-girl participation in extra-curricular activities; the school therefore attempts a careful regulation of those activities under its jurisdiction, and so also do the other related institutions in the community. The tightly filled time-schedule of the Crestwood Heights child thus serves also as a protective device, not only in adolescence, but as early as this five-to-twelve period.

A schedule of activities such as the Crestwood Heights child follows enables the parent to know where he is and what he is doing, and at the same time it offers preparation for the work habits of later life which enable the doctor, or lawyer, or business executive to put in long, arduous hours; these are essential if the material living standard of Crestwood Heights is to be maintained or improved. Punctuality and "responsibility" are the qualities which are highly emphasized in this context. Throughout the five-to-twelve period the "responsibilities" of the child are increasingly stressed as his skills develop: responsibility for doing his lessons, for helping around the home, for spending a small allowance of money which is gradually increased with his age. "Responsibility" in regard to a wide range of behavior is frequently the theme at Home and School meetings.

It is, thus, in the five-to-twelve year stage that serious formal steps are taken to develop in the child the qualities which are felt to be the prerequisites for success in adult occupational and social life. And it is the school, with its carefully graded system of education, its facilities for assessing the intellectual potentialities of the child, its authority to advance or to hold him back in his progress through the grades of the system, which is the most potent single institution in the society for teaching him the social roles which anticipate adult status. Compelled by law to attend school until the age of sixteen, the child is subject to its influences for the major portion of his time during the greater part of the year. Peripheral institutions support the school in its task of socialization, and one, the Home and School Association, attempts to include the parents in this process. And more and more, in Crestwood Heights, the child is institutionalized in his leisure hours as well, both through the school and otherwise.

Perhaps the most outstanding feature of the Crestwood Heights culture is becoming increasingly evident: the degree to which secondary groups are assuming responsibility for virtually the whole socialization process. As a result—or prerequisite—the Crestwood Heights child must learn very early how to function in secondary groups, which, as he grows older, will come to claim more and more of those areas of the personality once reserved for relationships with the primary group, and even those once thought private or open only to sacred scrutiny. The family is still necessary to ensure the launching of the child into the society, as it were, but its traditional social function is widely shared with other institutions, in the endeavour to procure early and radical emancipation from the family of orientation. It is largely in the time span between five and twelve that the psychological and social groundwork is laid for this particular type of functioning in society.

The child in Crestwood Heights does not "just grow up," loved and nurtured but unnoticed. As one might expect, in a society where time and the child are major preoccupations, where preparation for a career is emphasized, where health is seldom forgotten, an elaborate system to observe and evaluate the growth of the child has been perfected. The school offers the most obvious model for this system. Through its grades the child is made to pass, experiencing a succession of stages, each of which commences with ignorance and ends in a tested and classified level of competence and achievement. Other institutions follow this lead: summer camp, the special schools, the church and synagogue, Boy Scouts and Girl Guides, all practise a similar system of age grading. Within the home, in one respect, age grading is not so easily observed since each member is supposedly equal under the affectionate tutelage and watchfulness of the parents. But, in another respect, it is the family which mediates the age grading system through which the child is sent. Changes in dress and deportment, changes in obligation and privilege are supervised, and often initiated, by parents; they are frequently synchronized with the actual physical changes in the child and with his position in the extra-familial grades through which, as a normal growing child, he must pass.

It is important to note that this age grading creates a system of status which permits the recognition of physical growth and performance in the child. The "normal" child, so far as age grading is concerned, maintains a balance as he "grows in wisdom and stature." That child tends to become a problem who is too big for his age, or "too large for his hat." Each of the status levels is, as noted in discussion of the roller-coaster in the chapter on "Time," a "life" in itself. An entire book could be devoted to the genetic pattern of childhood development through these grades: each grade has its initiatory or birth phase, and passes thence through maturity and full competence to graduation and "death" rites, as a new status is won and a new initiation awaits. Perhaps in a rapidly changing society the norms of behavior and structure are too fluid to justify more detailed description, but the child's social development and physical growing in Crestwood Heights should be seen in relation to age grading.

Thirteen, Fourteen, Fifteen: Early Adolescence

It will already be clear that socialization in Crestwood Heights is by no means a steady, harmonious progression. It involves, as we anticipated in discussing "Time," many sharp breaks and new beginnings to which the child has been working since Grade I, and especially the new beginning which culminates with high school entrance. In many cultures, the physical transformation of puberty coincides with social recognition of adult status, but this is not the case in Crestwood Heights where children remain in prolonged economic dependence. Moreover, the temporal coincidence, for many children, between the onset of puberty and the sudden transfer from the top grade of the elementary school to the bottom grade of the Junior High School is often productive of heightened stress.

This transition between childhood and what we might call "youthhood" is considered so difficult that the "Junior High School" has, indeed, been devised to help spread the adjustment over three years. The period in question is, however, marked by the child's growing consciousness of what his culture expects of him, a consciousness not evident to the same degree in preceding stages.

The preoccupations of the children in this age group (as revealed, for instance, in the free discussion of the Human Relations classes) indicate focal points in the socialization process. Concern centers around dating, summer work, choice of vocation, and sex roles; and considerable questioning of adult values may be discerned. The expectations of parents and teachers for academic achievement, for social skills, for "responsibility," are intensified at this age level. The child, in his turn, exerts a corresponding pressure upon himself since he has now more or less thoroughly internalized these cultural expectations.

In their new situation, the children have a number of behavior patterns to learn. The question of male-female sexual roles, and the difficulty of learning these roles, were again made evident in the Human Relations classes.

> On one occasion a boy suggested a discussion on "whether or not the male sex is superior." Here the male role, emphasizing creativity in intellectual and technical spheres, physical strength, status in the social structure, and authority, was held up as the norm for superior and culturally approved behavior for both boys and girls alike. Girls were judged by some boys as inadequate in measuring up to these requirements—although they admitted that women might possibly compete with men even in physical strength (e.g., as truck drivers or women wrestlers); only two boys advanced the view that each sex had its own duties and responsibilities, and that, therefore, the whole argument was futile. One boy accused women of "remaining in the home" and "refusing to take chances" and yet another boy added the comment "housework isn't hard—I've tried it!" [laughter]—a direct devaluation of the traditional female role.
>
> In this particular discussion, the girls were decidedly on the defensive. There was only the slightest hint that there might be a female role, differing from the male role in that it is biologically determined, when a girl commented that "women mature earlier than men." One girl, in refuting a boy's allegation that "housework is easy," did appear to resent this male view of the female role.
>
> Girls were clearly weighing their own role against that of the male—and the female role, in its traditional sense of childbearer and homemaker, was found wanting by both boys and girls. From the children's conversations, it is evident that neither boy nor girl expects to be ready for the adult sex roles for many years—which lends a note of unreality and uncertainty to such discussions.

In the adult character of Crestwood Heights, there appears to be a growing convergence between types of social behavior once more clearly distinguished as male and female. Differences in social aspects of the male and female roles which were previously defined on the basis of biological difference alone, appear to be lessening in Crestwood Heights. This allows women to share more fully in the intellectual and rational orientation towards life, while the men are expected to participate in home and child-rearing functions formerly relegated to the mother. The conflicts raised in the Human Relations classes over the uncertain definition of the female role, in particular, are symptomatic of the shifts in social personality of both men and women.

No sustained effort is made by any Crestwood institution outside the family to teach the girl the arts of child care and homemaking. However, another ingredient in the female role is being strengthened; great emphasis is now being laid on physical attractiveness. At Junior High level, preoccupation with "glamor" begins to emerge, although girls of an earlier age are also concerned with appearance and dress. Both boys and girls esteem physical attractiveness highly, and recognize the importance of grooming and clothing. Although the boys expressed some hostility (based on the ultimate expense to the male) towards female competition in dress, the girls were almost unanimous that "glamor" was an integral part of the female role. Physical strength and intelligence, qualities which the girls also try to emulate, denote masculinity at this age.

Clothing, for both boys and girls of this age, becomes an important symbol of changing status. In one discussion the children branched off into talk of clothes and lipstick:

> One girl said that in Grade VI and still a bit in Grade VII, their clothes were tunics and frilly sorts of things, but that in Grade IX they got into longer skirts and smarter clothes—more grown up—and they started to use lipstick. The researcher asked about the boys. They gave a picturesque description of boys' graduation into drapes, key chains, loud shirts, and fancy shoes.

The children appear to follow the lead of the peer group rather than that of the teacher or parent where dress and appearance are concerned, and the models seem to be TV and movie stars, or others provided by the mass communication media. That clothing and general appearance contribute largely to the adequate playing of the sex roles at this age is most evident.

Tied in with the learning of the sex roles at this stage is the dating pattern, which now definitely crystallizes after its first appearance at the previous age level.

In the twelve- to fifteen-year-old group, much concern is expressed over the choice of one partner. Although some children still voice a preference for group activities, there is an increasing trend towards what might be called "trial monogamy." The boys in Grade IX showed some uncertainty about assuming their masculine role in regard to dating, and questions arouse about how far in advance an invitation should be given for a dance or a party. Though both boys and girls agreed that the choice of partner is the responsibility of the boy, some of the boys felt that the present system is financially unfair to them. It is evident that the economic dependence of children in the culture bears more heavily on the boys than on the girls, since the former feel that their prerogative of choosing a partner, an integral part of the male role in Crestwood Heights, is limited by this dependence.

A subtle distinction seems to exist between dating and friendship. As Caroline Tryon has demonstrated,[23] various criteria are used by adolescents to evaluate the *quality* of the relationship between girls and girls, between boys and boys, and between girls and boys. Within the wider term of friendship as it is understood in Crestwood Heights, the terms "boy friend" and "girl friend" underline the importance of the sex differential in relationships which imply some degree of permanency. The term "date" appears to highlight the qualities of physical attractiveness and glamor upon which the choice of sex partner is based in a culture permeated by the value of "romantic love." The "date" or "dates" symbolize the initial stage in the pattern of mate selection; with the prolongation of the adolescents' economic dependence on the parents, this stage later tapers off into "going steady" with a "girl friend" or "boy friend," without the expectation either of eventual marriage or even of relative permanency.

The report of a thirteen-year-old girl expresses the "friendship" pattern, which, she states, changes between Grades VII and VIII:

FRIENDS: What I do with them: Grade 7 went to movies, stag parties. Grade 8 go on dates—to movies—to parties—skating—skiing.

Then in a separate section, she adds:

How I pick boys: looks, personality, don't show off, sex appeal (good in sports). Girls: loyalty, uncattish, trustworthy, personality, kindness, etc.

In another discussion on "friendship," the question of money entered:

Peter indicated that "not all people have money, but all have friends." Another boy remarked that a wealthy person can have a television set and can always find friends who want to listen in. Johnny asked: "What is meant by a true friend? Some are parasites and do not wish to contribute anything to the friendship." Shirley felt that selfish people do not have friends, but if people use their money to help others, they will have more friends. Linda said that everyone wants to have friends and rich people buy friends if they do not get them any other way. Tom suggested that those who are friends only when you have money are not true friends. In reply to a question from one student as to how you could know which are true friends, Margie thought the best way was to lose your money and then see who stood by you. Johnny remarked "life is a mirror"; in your friends, you look for intellectual and social companionship, so choose your friend on your own level. Two or three boys now spoke of those friends who pretend to be loyal, but as soon as they find you have run out of money, they only grudgingly offer to help. The researcher threw a question, "What do you look for in a friend?" Moira replied, "People I can talk to seriously, have a good time with, share things with and get along well with."

"Dating" and "friendship," it would seem, are different, but the above discussion indicates uncertainty and shifting relationships in the area of friendship as well as in dating. In view of the many and subtle nuances of relationship between boy and girl in this group, and of friendships between members of the same sex, it is far from easy to learn sex roles, or to achieve the "maturity" expected of the pre-adolescent.

The choice of occupation presents another set of problems to the children in this age grade. During the years in Junior High, both boy and girl are expected to decide whether they wish to proceed to university, to take a business or commercial course, or to enter technical school. In practice, however, there is not much choice for the Crestwood Heights child, for there is a strong pressure on him from all sides to "elect" a university education. It is mostly those who cannot make the requisite academic grades, or those few who are going into business immediately upon leaving high school, who consider alternatives to university.

Although boys and girls in the school system are given almost identical academic training, future occupation is considered a more important question for the boy, since it is tacitly assumed that the girl will pursue a career only until she marries. Thus the boy, even in Junior High, fully realizes that he will ultimately become the breadwinner of a family, a role which demands intensive and prolonged training for a vocation. The hostility sometimes shown by boys of this age towards girls, ostensibly because of their competitive taste in clothes and their alleged tendency to coax a boy into spending more money than he actually possesses, may be a kind of protest against the demands of the male occupational role; it may also, of course, express restiveness under prolonged dependence upon the family.

The girl is "interested too" in an occupational role, but to a less degree than the boy, since she sees that women, for example, her mother and her mother's women friends, are not gainfully employed, although they may have been before marriage. The meaning of "occupation" for the girl is essentially different from what the boy understands by the term. For her, as for the boy, an occupation confers a sense of social worth; but in the case of the woman, the full stamp of cultural approval is given only if she later achieves husband and children. (The achievement of matrimonial and parental roles is of course important too for the male.) But the value for the girl of an occupation as a safeguard against the possible impermanency of marriage cannot be overlooked; its utility in this respect is alleged by the more outspoken women as a justification for it, over and above the mandate to self-fulfillment.

For both boy and girl, the question of future occupation is intertwined with the values of "responsibility" and "independence" stressed by parents and teachers alike. Summer jobs are viewed by the children both as chances to learn responsibility and independence, within or beyond the family circle, and as badges of impending adult status.

In the following discussion, all shades of feeling about work were expressed in a Human Relations class. There was obvious ambivalence. The Crestwood Heights culture, while it stresses the value of responsibility for its children, also expresses a strong collective feeling that the years of childhood should be as carefree as possible, and this view is mirrored in the children's conversation:

> Kitty Tailor thought it was good for girls to go to C—— Inn and such places to work. It was good experience for girls to be on their own, to make their own decisions, learn how to get along with other people. Marilyn G. thought that two months' work made you somewhat independent in buying clothes and meeting people. A boy thought one might work to earn a hockey glove or some such things; otherwise he could go to camp. A boy thought that girls might work since they get married and someone else would support them anyway, but there was no point in boys working too soon! Bill said that most of the group spent the summer at cottages and they do not want to come home and go to work. Wilma S. said she wanted to work after five years of camp and four of boarding schools; she was "sick of it." She thought they'd get more experience in getting along with people if they worked. Milton C. said a boy might work into a good job through summer work; he might work in a department store and so work his way up to a good position in later life. Dave J. said some people worked through the summer to pay their way through college. It was pointed out that some kids couldn't afford to go to camp; camp and cottage depended on the financial status of the family. It would be up to the individual student to decide whether he should work. One boy said cynically that if the kids in the room got a job they'd not hold it for two weeks. Tom S. said it was all right just now to talk about jobs, but they'd not be so keen on working when the temperature was in the eighties. Cameron McN. said he was tired of camp last year, so he got a job, a tough job where he worked different hours. He'd like to get a job again this year, but he'd want a different job, such as trucking, where you'd see the countryside, have fun, and get paid for it. Linda B. said she'd like to go to camp. She mentioned a canoe trip she'd made from camp to C—— Inn. She said the girls working there weren't too happy—they have small girls' sleeping quarters and aren't allowed in some parts of the establishment. Leonard H. said he'd like to hitchhike this summer; you couldn't get a better education than by hitchhiking. Sam said that if people wanted to go to camp, they could get a job right now and save enough money to pay for it. Meg M. thought it wasn't fair of parents to insist on their children going to the cottage, even though it was the only time when a good many fathers saw anything of their children.
>
> Boris G. said some parents let their children eat whenever they wanted to, but when they went to camp they had to eat at mealtime or starve! One boy felt going to camp was good experience; if one were going into the Army, learning to obey rules would be valuable. Dan L. observed that two months away from girls didn't hurt anyone! Someone said that at school you were with your parents; if you got a job you'd be away from parents. The researcher inquired further, asking about dependency on parents. Alex D. said he tried to solve his own problems, even if his parents were in the next room. He felt that one needn't be

dependent on parents, even if one lived with them. As for an easy life at the cottage, he'd learned that you couldn't sleep if you had younger brothers. Cameron McN. said he'd learned all the camp routine—canoeing, shooting with bow and arrow, etc., and now he'd rather meet adults. While working last year, he'd been sworn at, ordered about, worked from eleven to four A.M. and met all sorts of guys. Then he had stayed a week at a guy's cottage. This chap, he said, isn't out of diapers yet and doesn't go around with anyone and runs to his mother for everything. Marilyn said that not everyone had money to go to camp. She thought that if parents couldn't send their children to college, the children should work and pay their own way, as their brother, a dentist, had done. It wasn't necessary to go away to work; you could get a job in the city. Wilma S. objected to Cameron's statement, saying not many were tied to their mother's apron strings. Said she, "We aren't exactly sick of parents but. . . . " In his speech, Cameron said he'd not take any job—only one he liked. Boris inquired how he'd find such a job; he'd had jobs he disliked. Paul said if Boris didn't know what kind of a job he liked he couldn't very well go on looking for it. Leonard H. thought summer work was a good way to try out different jobs, e.g., law office, city newspaper. A boy spoke again of scouting, saying in response to Wilma's two hundred dollar estimate, that you needn't go to such a "ritzy," expensive camp. Other camps were better, for you were more on your own.

It is evident from the foregoing that in this age group some were discussing from actual experience, but many were projecting their ideas into a new area when talking about summer jobs. The boys seem particularly concerned about summer jobs in relation to adult status. Girls express some desire to work, but this seems chiefly a gesture towards independence from the family. A boy verbalized the cultural expectation that girls will work only up to the time of marriage.[24] Considerable ambivalence is expressed in the camp-cottage versus work argument. One boy shows interest in work as an opportunity to escape from limitations of social class; a girl reveals the contrary view, that summer work as a waitress puts one outside one's own class, a disadvantage which one does not find with camp.

It is interesting at this point to note that the children (like many of the women) may have only a hazy picture of the family's financial standing, and that, because of this, they cannot approach the job situation realistically. Throughout the children's debate, the element of choice in the decision to work or not to work is evident and striking. Such a choice does not confront the lower-class child who must begin to earn as soon as he is able.

With closer approximation to adulthood, in chronological if not always in social and emotional terms, the children of Crestwood Heights are found in the process of weighing and internalizing some of the adult values of the community. Norms of behavior as established by parent and school were frequently questioned in the Human Relations classes. Male reactions center around the status symbol of the car; smoking, another badge of adult status; parental controls, exemplified in expectations that the boy will be in by a certain hour; and the boy's financial dependence on the family.

The car is an item of great importance in Crestwood Heights. The boy, even before he reaches the age of fifteen, wants a driver's licence and access to the family car (or cars) since these are the accolade of adult male status; he commonly has not the economic ability to buy a car of his own. But although he desires freedom in the use of the car, he is also inclined to cast some blame on the parents if an accident occurs, and does not generally wish to assume responsibility either for the use of the car or for its financing. Girls do not appear to express the same concern about the use of the car, although a boy's ability to provide transportation will generally give him a higher rating as a date.[25]

Although the children seem to want freedom from parental controls, it is evident that in the case of a car this is a "difficult" demand. There are many variations of opinions among the parents as to the degree of freedom advisable at each age for the boy, to whom the car is such a vital symbol, when it is a question of sharing the car or cars between parents and children. Their problem is complicated by the fact that the car in North American culture generally, is recognized as a symbol of sexual freedom. It cannot be denied that the automobile has revolutionized sexual behavior on this continent. Freedom to drive the family car *alone* assumes even greater importance for the male adolescent since the privilege carries with it at least the possibility of sexual expression uncontrolled by direct adult supervision.

Since many Crestwood parents of both sexes smoke themselves, there does not seem to be as much conflict about this for either boys or girls; and smoking apparently does not carry the connotation it once did in regard to male adult status. A Human Relations discussion with a Grade VIII class in Junior High illustrates:

> They then started to talk about smoking. They admitted that boys smoke a bit from the time they are in Grade VI, but in Grade VIII they do it openly walking home from dances, etc. They said that boys do it to show off to the girls. The researcher then asked if they thought smoking was really a sign of growing up, and one boy said "No . . . " because boys that were really getting grown up didn't smoke, because they wanted to keep their wind for sports.
>
> Beryl S. says that if she were a mother, she'd want her children to smoke at home, not on the street corners; she thought girls might start to smoke at seventeen or eighteen, boys at fifteen or sixteen.

Girls appear to accept smoking as both a female and a male prerogative, but make some distinction on a sex basis about the age at which one may begin.[26] It is interesting to note that, though in a previous discussion the girls claim an earlier maturity than boys, they indicate a two-year difference here, and put themselves in the junior position. The school, it would seem, takes a stricter stand than do parents in the home: smoking by students on or near school property or during school hours is forbidden, ostensibly as a fire precaution or to avoid public criticism of the school.

The regular allowance of money given by parents is another topic for frequent discussions in the Junior High Human Relations classes. As in the case of the car, money to spend as one wishes is a sign of adult status, but the chances to earn it are limited. Boys and girls substantially agree that an allowance is necessary in this age group, but are quite divided as to how it should be obtained.

> Sam began the discussion by saying that smaller boys don't need so much allowance because they can get to shows more cheaply. Another said that some boys are more mature in taste, and so need more allowance: a boy should get enough allowance to get practice in spending it. One girl felt an allowance should be big enough to include everything but clothes. Another girl said that they should get an allowance, and a job if the allowance isn't big enough, but they shouldn't take an allowance for granted. A girl objected to this, saying that the student's chief job was to get through school, not to hold down jobs, and if she did this, parents would be satisfied. A boy, Angus, and a girl, felt that allowances should be conditional upon doing work around home. Leonard said his parents gave him what he needed; he felt less money was wasted in this way than if he were receiving a regular allowance. A girl expressed the idea that an allowance should be considered from the viewpoint of training for later life; the student will learn the value of money through management of an allowance; if all the allowance is not spent, that part should be saved.
> . . . A boy said that if you had to learn how to spend money, you may as well do it on

your parents' money, so an allowance is a good thing. A girl felt money might be wasted through unwise choice; it was also suggested that parents could buy more cheaply as they might get things wholesale. A girl pointed out that parents aren't anxious for their children to be too independent. A boy felt it was necessary for boys to have an allowance so they could learn to budget their incomes. A girl felt it was necessary and important for girls to have a clothing allowance, but not for boys. This remark brought strong protests and many boys were anxious to speak on the question. It was felt that one couldn't generalize; it would depend on the parents' income. One boy felt an allowance helped develop a sense of responsibility; boys could save if they had a purpose in mind, such as a gift for Mother's Day. A girl pointed out that boys' styles change too, so they do need a clothing allowance. One boy, Angus, felt that boys needn't worry so much as girls about being in style. Said he, "Baldheaded fat men will get along all right, but a baldheaded fat woman won't get far!" He said if he were going to pick a girl, he'd pick a nice one, but of three nice girls, he'd pick the most stylish one . . . hence girls need a clothing allowance more than boys. A girl opposed the clothing allowance, saying they could get experience in handling money from their regular allowance, but they needed to know how to choose before being given a clothing allowance.

. . . As the class was going out, the boy who had suggested the topic came up to the researcher and said he hadn't a clothing allowance but he picked out the clothes he wanted, and then took his parents down to see them. "Dad didn't like these drapes," said he, glancing with obvious admiration at his trousers, "but I got them anyway."

Here again, it is obvious that the expectations of parents that the child become "responsible" and "independent" while at the same time he is financially dependent on them, create considerable confusion in the minds of many adolescents about the possession and spending of money. Money, a potent symbol of adult status, is usually given to the child in the form of an allowance, but there seems to be little uniformity in the amount or in the directives about how it should be spent. Few children appear to have money which they are completely free to spend without any adult supervision.

Although the children voice the opinion that money is of the utmost importance, and that the wise and responsible spending of it is both a sign of and a preparation for adult status, they also express some feelings about receiving money which they have not earned; this sentiment is shared by the parents.[27] As one researcher put it:

In connection with "spoiling," I got the impression that a majority of children would subscribe to the following views:
   (a) Most Crestwood Heights children are spoiled.
   (b) It is difficult to avoid being spoiled if you are wealthy.
   (c) There is nothing the child can do to prevent being spoiled, if he is wealthy.
   (d) The fault lies largely with the parents.
   (e) It is a bad thing to be spoiled.[28]

This summary in its very succinctness reveals how the difficulties experienced by the child in living up to the expectations of both parents and the school for "responsibility" and "independence" amplify in an environment which largely eliminates necessity for striving in this direction.

The children in Junior High expressed certain clearly defined attitudes of this age period towards school, which for them is beginning to assume somewhat the same seriousness as the career for the adult. As one child expressed it (in the quotation below) "school isn't just preparation for life, it *is* life."[29] While the children seem to recognize that school connotes work, discipline, and a certain degree of impersonality (the "home-room" teacher has by now given way to subject-specialists), they also display regrets for the vanished freedom and emotional security of early childhood.

Sally C. pointed out that kindergarten and primary school children don't dislike school, but rather enjoy it. Norman F. thought that children liked school until they got to higher grades where they had to work. Fred O. felt that worry about examinations caused pupils to dislike school. Betty Joan G. thought some children were spoiled at home, and so they resented discipline at school. . . .

. . . Sally G. thought children naturally would dislike school since in preschool days they had freedom and toys but in school they had to sit in classes and do as the teacher said.

. . . Morris S. felt that students should enjoy their school life because later on they had to assume great responsibilities and not enjoy life any more.[30] It was suggested by Sally G. that when adults talk about school days being the happiest days of their lives, they do so because they have forgotten the unhappy times and remember only the fun they had at school, dances, sports, etc. Fred O., in response to Sally's suggestion that the more education one had, the better equipped one was for life, pointed out that school isn't just preparation for life, it *is* life.

In the twelve-to-fifteen year level, therefore, the child himself, for the first time becomes seriously aware of what the society demands of him, if he is to become adult. Both home and school impose high standards of performance. The child, at the same time, must adjust to the demands of his peer group, which frequently run counter to those of parents and of teachers. At this age, too, the child must form the heterosexual relationships which later lead to courtship and marriage. The achievement-in-isolation theme of the culture deepens and strengthens, as the child is expected to achieve more and more in the competitive academic life which leads to university entrance. Self-reliance must be developed through experience at the summer camp, or, more rarely, the part-time job. The girl, while expected to prepare for a career of her own, must also assimilate the idea of renouncing it for marriage; and the boy must, in the absence of close or clearly identified masculine models, learn what it means to play a man's role in the society. These are the difficult tasks of early adolescence.

Sixteen to Nineteen: Dependent Independence

The emphasis for this particular age level in Crestwood Heights works to deepen and strengthen even further the trends noted for the previous stage. This period is character-ized by a more intense experience with the peer group, experience which contributes to and is a manifestation of conflict between age group and parental standards.[31]

The arguments about fraternities and sororities in high school are but one manifesta-tion of this conflict, and they may be selected for the purposes of illustration. Fraternities and sororities prove to be lingering thorns in the sides of both parents and teachers. They have been defended ably by the children when under adult attack. Fraternities and sororities, say the adolescents, give a sense of belonging and acceptance, which they have been *taught* is important to their well-being. And as for tolerating the principles of racial tolerance and equality, the children demonstrate that the same breach is present in many of the parents' clubs after which their own youth associations are patterned. Fraternities and sororities continue to exist despite criticism, providing for the children groups in which they are relatively free to formulate their own standards. These groupings are closed to adult supervision—which disturbs the parents and teachers, despite the stress they lay on responsible and independent action.

On the whole, though, the general pattern of this age group, as it is evident in the life history documents, seems to be one of acceptance of the adult values and way of life. Yet there are other evidences of a kind of rebellion somehow possible within the general frame of reference, set by adults, during this transitional period between childhood and adult life.

Contributions of senior students to the High School magazine reveal some criticisms of adult standards and behavior, as well as some comment on conventional values and current happenings at school and in the world about. Two issues, taken at random, for the years 1949–50 and 1950–51, were examined carefully. Fiction and articles were concerned with a variety of topics, often treated satirically. Four articles discussed general popularity and loss of it; two emphasized pleasant social manners as the criteria for successful human relationships; one definitely associated popularity with the possession of high social status and wealth. Three dealt with international understanding and the threat of war; three criticized the economic system; one was about racial prejudice towards a Negro business man. In one article, a boy penetratingly criticized life in the city, comparing it to that of a rat on a garbage dump. In a story with a slight flavor of Somerset Maugham, the writer treated of the marital infidelity of a middle-aged woman. An essay satirized the high standards required in English classes. A final humorous article described a program of dieting, which was circumvented by a secret craving for chocolate (equated with alcoholism). The level of sophistication in these writings is high; the understanding of the "grown-up" world, acute and penetrating; the tone, moralistic. Rebellion was expressed in the fantasy content of some of these contributions, but one might expect on the evidence of the foregoing to find "rebels" in this age group.

It is rare, however, to find Crestwood young people who act out the rebellion expressed in such fantasy. During the research, only a few such cases came to the attention of the observers. One was that of a young adult, who had continued to live at home, although receiving a salary from a downtown job. This young man went to visit relatives on one of the Channel Islands, and found life there so congenial that, after evaluating the experience in comparison with Crestwood Heights, he returned to the island to earn his living in a situation where it is extremely difficult to secure comparable monetary rewards.

The more general pattern is exemplified by a girl whose rebellion was within the framework of acceptance of the general patterns of the culture. Her rebellion-within-dependence took the form of graduate study, for which her father paid, in Europe. Despite her strong protestations that she wanted freedom from her family above all else, she returned to her Crestwood Heights home and continued her course of specialization, at the same time studiously avoiding all conformity with her family's wishes about social life.

Even these two persons were a little older than the high school group. Again we come back to the fact that the Crestwood Heights adolescent is still economically dependent upon his parents during this period of rebellion. It is true that from an early age he has been given an allowance, usually increased in direct proportion to his age, and that he may have earned money of his own from summer or part-time work. Yet he knows that he cannot approximate his father's income until long after he has completed high school and subsequent vocational preparation. So feelings of rebellion and desire for greater independence are generally subdued in favor of the path that leads to the career in the manner approved by the society.

Adult attitudes to the child's growing independence are also mixed. Father, in particular, would appear to expect the boy to undergo a period of "roughing it" on the way up, in imitation of his own initial struggles.[32] To "have it too easy" is definitely considered as a danger; but to encourage the child to make any real break with his family and its protections and comforts at this time would be considered a courting of even greater peril.

It is evident that adolescence in Crestwood Heights implies by no means a smooth and easy acceptance of adult values. The reports of Human Relations classes, the conduct of children meeting parent groups, and clinic records[33] all attest to a high degree of independent thought during this period. It appears that once again the pressure of cultural circumstances militates against the translation of this independence into deliberate rebellion. A cultural solution at this age level appears to be participation in fraternity or sorority, where the child achieves solidarity, where he has the support of his peers in evading some of the adult expectations, and where he may have a brief respite from the strenuous maturation process of which he is the object. Although the adolescent may seriously question race discrimination and exclusiveness, to the point of suggesting reform, he is by no means disposed, as we have noted, to give up exclusive fraternities and sororities, which are important and perhaps necessary social defences at his age.

While the peer group is assuming ever greater importance in the adolescent's environment, the world of school still bulks large, although it is soon to be discarded for university. The school in Crestwood Heights recognizes the fact that it must soon relinquish the child for higher education. Its concept of responsibility and maturity demands that he "reach autonomy in the direction of his own life, tolerance, individuality, knowledge, and judgment." In actual practice, however, the school does not delegate to the student at this stage anything like complete responsibility for his academic work or action. Marks and passing of examinations are too important in the achievement of academic or vocational success—one fundamental reason for the school's existence. Each school, too, is part of a competitive system and it measures *its* success in terms of the academic standing of its graduates.

The major solution of the Crestwood school to this well-recognized dilemma is the "Senior Plan" for Grade XIII. A general meeting of the Collegiate Home and School unit was devoted to an explanation and discussion of this plan. Mr. E. told the parents:

> Grade XIII students have been consulted about this. They were asked how they thought the school could prepare them for life after high school. . . . They met in small groups to discuss "how they could accept responsibility and act more grown up." They approached their task with extreme caution. There was no feeling that "now we are free and can do what we like!" They asked themselves such questions as "Are we old enough to handle this freedom?" They made up a list of suggestions for Grade XIII teachers. These were gone over to see how far they would be practicable. One was that if a student were absent, there need be no note from home. Then they felt that study form was not a good place for Grade XIII. This meant that they were being treated as having no responsibility. A study room was set up for Grade XIII, a special room to which they could go or not, as they pleased. In this room there was no supervision. Then, detention was considered childish. Those who needed detention should have help or advice, not just punishment; they had not "outgrown childish tricks." When students were late, the real objection was that they disturbed twenty other students and the teacher. The penalty should be that the latecomer miss the class. "We," said Mr. E., "went on to consider safeguards." The plan was just a halfway step to the future.
>
> 1. No student was to be on the Senior Plan unless he wanted to be. If it is the wish of either the student or the parents, he may be excluded.

2. New students in the school are not included. They come without the preparation or background of the other students and have not been in the school long enough to know what it is all about. This gives a chance to get a line on a new student. . . . The first report card, which comes at the end of October, usually gives this.

3. There is an advisory council to operate the plan. It is made up of two students from each of the four Grade XIII classes and the four home room teachers . . . the council will watch the progress of each Grade XIII student. The "failures" will be called before the council and asked why it happened. If necessary, help would be offered; but if improvement were not forthcoming, the council would notify the staff, who would take the student off the plan.[34]

This plan is a departure from the more stereotyped pupil-teacher relationship; it places a strong emphasis on the acceptance of responsibility for progress upon the students themselves. The weight of peer-group opinion is organized to safeguard its successful operation. At the same time, the teachers and the Principal, whose ultimate responsibility it is, are there in the background to ensure the maintenance of academic standards.

In the area of social adjustment, the school, as well as the peer group, expects the child to be a "joiner." A true criterion of belonging to the teen-age culture would appear to be membership in such an organization as the fraternity or sorority. The school, too, provides organizations for its extra-curricular program. To help the student in his general social adjustment, it appoints teacher-counsellors. As Mr. M. of the Collegiate explained:

> The students in the schools need to feel they had friends among the teachers, to whom they could go with any problems that bothered them. . . . Miss P. was doing this type of work with the girls and Mr. C., who was also responsible for sports, was working with the junior boys, as well as two others. Thus the schools had a complete team of people. Each student would find one of the four a helper and friend to whom he would naturally turn.

The school is here attempting, in the meeting of students' problems, to increase the number of face-to-face relationships which are difficult to maintain in an institution with such a large student body.

The school tries to maintain a balance between extra-curricular activities and school work, and to spread the executive responsibility as widely as possible among the students, but here again with large numbers there are difficulties:

> It was explained that, at a meeting of teachers, the extra-curricular record of the student was checked against his results [academic]. They could deal only with extreme cases. At the June staff meeting, it was the job of the counsellors to get hold of the students who hadn't been doing enough in extra-curricular activities. It was done on a class and a personal basis. They had never been able to set a definite limit to the number of activities a student could participate in. They had been trying to spread out responsibility, and had had some success in having students with one position refuse others, if offered. . . . there was a "professional executive type" in the school. They could run things, but there were others with plenty of ability too.
>
> Mr. Y. said that in the preparatory school especially, they were trying to develop club activities, an hour a week, where the student could join some club under the sponsorship of a teacher.
>
> Mr. N. went on to elaborate on the extra-curricular activities. If the student failed in even one exam at Christmas, his extra-curricular activities were checked. If the case was an extreme one, the parents were notified. . . .

The promotion on the part of the school staff of extra-curricular activities indicates the importance assigned to them in this phase of school adjustment. However, when it is a question of priority, the school work essential for academic or vocational success comes first. Students who are members of the basketball team, for example, will be put off the team if they cannot pass all their term examinations.

On the one hand, therefore, the school expects mature students, responsible for the direction of their work and social activities. On the other hand, if the student fails to keep these demands in what is considered a proper balance, the teacher is still vested with sufficient authority to regulate them for him.

Thus the Crestwood child arrives on the threshold of adulthood extremely sophisticated in certain ways, such as intellectual ability and emotional independence. He is less adept, in all likelihood, at the actual tasks of adult life than is his rural counterpart, who if he is a farm boy has assumed different kinds of responsibilities as he encounters with his father situations which allow practical learning. The Crestwood child has been constantly urged by his parents and teachers to become mature and responsible, but the culture has not provided many opportunities to become either in reality. Both boy and girl of this age understand more or less clearly what is required of them in the years ahead. The boy usually is more definite about his future plans than is the girl. She sees marriage as a goal, and her years at university are considered a useful interval and sometimes as a means of acquiring a husband.

Here, then, at a peak of the socialization process, as mediated by the family and the school, the Crestwood Heights boy and girl must be left. But ahead will be many new learnings and relearnings, for, sensitive to their changing culture as they are, they can only terminate such learning at death.

Notes

1. Clinic cases drew enough such reluctant admissions, however, to suggest that many children were unwanted—planned for or not.
2. M. Mead, *Male and Female: A Study of the Sexes in a Changing World* (New York: William Morrow & Co., 1949), pp. 51–160.
3. This situation is in marked contrast with that existing in many a primitive society, where the newborn infant is differentiated only slowly from the mother and the kinship group closely surrounding him.
4. In the Crestwood culture, " . . . the nuclear family is dependent for its (temporary) persistence and institutionally required dissolution on a process of socialization which allows children as well as parents to do without each other." K. D. Naegele, "Hostility and Aggression in Middle Class American Families" (Doctor's dissertation, Department of Social Relations, Harvard University, 1952), p. 142.
5. Even where a maid or housekeeper is employed full time, she seldom remains long, seldom assumes the supportive role of a "Nanny."
6. From the child-rearing experts she has learned the great importance attached to this physical contact, both for good and for ill. Too much may bind the child to her forever and restrict his psychosexual development; too little may make him insecure and "mentally ill" as an adult. Cf. J. R. Seeley, "Bali-like treatment of children in Crestwood Heights."
7. Advertisements for a well-known line of educational toys stress the value of "learning while playing."
8. See M. Mead, *And Keep Your Powder Dry: An Anthropologist Looks at America* (New York: William Morrow and Co., 1942).
9. W. A. Davis and R. J. Havighurst, *Father of the Man: How Your Child Gets His Personality* (Boston: Houghton Mifflin Company, 1947), pp. 171–172, 207.
10. Children at a later stage of growth, in the Project-sponsored Human Relations classes in the Crestwood schools, expressed resentment that there was "no place to play" in Crestwood

Heights. The slum child, also an urban resident, would not make the same complaint, since he aggressively takes over the whole of his neighborhood as play space.

11. The freedom, of course, always entails careful supervision, and follows upon the selection by adults of what is considered workable and appropriate for the nursery school group.

12. The afore-mentioned "messy" materials—clay, plasticene, finger paint—as well as play-acting, may serve as outlets for the "sublimation" of aggression not allowed expression in other areas.

13. A photograph in a local newspaper bore the following caption: "TOTS GRADUATE. Wearing caps and gowns are 27 five-year-olds in front of Marillac Social Center's school in Chicago for graduation from Tiny Tots Town into kindergarten. Children are prepared for kindergarten in Tiny Tots Town." *Globe and Mail* (Toronto), September 1, 1952, p. 8. In the nursery school, the child talks of "juniors" and "seniors," just as later in kindergarten he talks of the "older children," the "younger ones," or contemptuously of "babies," and even of "failing."

14. If she is desired as a teacher, but not as a person, conflict may be set up early in grade school between desires for "success" and desires for comfort. Desire for success bulks large for even the kindergarten child; pupils in the earliest grades fearfully discuss the possibility of "failure." (Father's comment on his child's behavior, while a pupil at Birch Prep.)

15. One mother reported that during his first months at kindergarten her small son fell into a puddle on his way to school. Since he had no other snow suit, his mother drove him to school in his wet suit, with the intention of handing him over immediately to his teacher. The child worried all the way to school: "Mr. A. [the Principal] won't *let* you in the school! I *have* to stay outside and play until the bell rings!" His mother attempted to explain that rules did not matter in an emergency, but her remarks had no effect whatever. When she stopped the car in the school yard, the child tried to run away. A group of children gathered in consternation, asking "What's wrong, B.?" The mother felt most hard-hearted as she propelled B. into the school. His teacher happened to be passing. She took in the situation at once, and escorted B. into the classroom to take off his wet clothes. A few months previously, the child (a nursery school product) would not have objected to entering the school at any hour, with or without an adult, as his mother emphasized.

16. Since adult approval is the most potent incentive towards learning acceptable patterns of social behavior, particularly at this age level, the size of classes, increased by the high post-war birth-rate, would appear to have some direct bearing on the socialization process.

17. That this happens early is witnessed by the comment of a little kindergarten girl to her teacher after being pushed by a male class-mate, "Miss X., some boys are just *born* babies!"

18. The description of a first-year Crestwood Heights university student (female) of student-teacher relationships at the collegiate level underlines the difference between the elementary and secondary schools: "It requires little or no effort on the part of the student to become a good friend of one of his teachers. He does not have to be a member of this particular teacher's class. The student need only be registered in the school. Of course, as in any relationship, he must have the desire to become friends with an individual. And if this desire is latent, more than likely the teacher or teachers will find it and do more than their share to initiate the friendship. Often a certain teacher can become a second mother or father to the pupil. This is a wonderful experience, so long as the teacher's importance to the boy or girl is secondary to that of his parents. A student feels free to discuss practically every aspect of his life with his teacher. He will learn to confide in his teacher and to consider him as one of his very close friends. I myself developed such a relationship with one of my teachers. After school was over, providing I had no meeting or game to attend, I would go into his classroom and talk to him for hours, as I would with a good friend. This friendship grew from my first year in high school until now. Although I no longer attend collegiate, I try to keep in touch with my teachers and I miss their companionship very much." This would appear to be more an experience of adolescence (and even then somewhat uncommon) than that of the age group five-to-twelve.

19. Contrast the situation in Birmingham, England, where there are four teachers to every thirty children in the nursery classes attached to Infants' Schools. *Globe and Mail* (Toronto), April 10, 1953, p. 6.

20. One researcher reported a conversation with a Crestwood Heights mother in which she described how her five-year-old daughter would lay out at bed-time the dress and accessories to be worn the next day. If a hair ribbon happened to be rumpled, the child would iron it. Cf., also, reference above (note 13) to news photography of pre-school children in caps and gowns at Marillac Social Center nursery school, Chicago.

21. It is important also to note the rapid tempo of the planned activities of the child in this age group. The time diaries, kept for research purposes on an hourly basis by children in grades throughout the school system, demonstrate a tightly-packed series of organized activities; spontaneous play is minimal.

22. In a Human Relations class (Grade VI) this topic came up for discussion: ". . . there was more talk about the game and with much giggling. R. told that it was Spinning the Bottle. Evidently there is some kissing connected with it. They are only supposed to kiss on the hand, but some of the boys kissed right up the arm to the cheek! It was out! This was the game about which there were so many guilt feelings. Someone suggested that they should plan their parties and avoid this game."

23. C. M. Tryon, "Evaluations of Adolescent Personality by Adolescents," in *Child Behavior and Development: A Course of Representative Studies,* ed. R. G. Barker, J. S. Kounin, and H. F. Wright (New York: McGraw-Hill Book Company, Inc., 1943), pp. 545–566.

24. It should be noted, however, that women's work in the home, which may actually be more laborious, is not "work" to the boys and men. If the psychological criterion for work is used (i.e., effort or negatively toned tension) both boys and girls are destined to "work" nearly all their lives in both work and leisure portions of the day.

25. An interesting detail is that children themselves do not want parents to teach them to drive. This view was presented in a Human Relations class: "Most children don't want their parents to teach them to drive. Parents expect too much—they're too impatient. There was a chorus of 'That's right!' " This attitude is evident not only about learning to drive, but about many other skills which children would prefer to acquire from someone else other than the parents. Almost anyone else will do, even a person of less competence. It is also curious that women, by their own wish, would rather be taught to drive by someone other than a husband or male relative; they express first preference for a commercial service. The inner meaning of this disposition is conjectural. At least, it helps to open a profitable market to the male expert, even though it gives cause for understandable male jealousy in the husband.

26. Here again is the tendency, in the face of the universally accepted and perhaps unfounded belief that females mature earlier than males, to permit boys earlier access to adult privileges such as smoking and heterosexual experience. It was a girl who blandly put forward this view in the discussion quoted. The same girl will, in all likelihood, concurrently or later, fight a desperate ideological battle for equality of male and female.

27. In a discussion parents gave recognition to the favored position of these children: "Mrs. J. wondered if the parents weren't to blame for not giving the children enough responsibility. Everything was given to them—they didn't have to work for a thing. . . . Mrs. P. said: 'They don't even want anything very badly.' 'Perhaps this is because they get things before they even know they want them,' Mrs. J. replied."

28. The researcher might have asked what "spoiling" means since, of course, it is a more nebulous concept than the above ideas connote.

29. This is, of course, a third- or fourth-hand parroting of one of the distinguishing views of "progressive" educators.

30. This statement is overwhelmingly significant, in view of the strenuous efforts made by family and school to ensure glad acceptance of responsibility as one important means to the good and happy life.

31. Cf. T. Parsons, "Age and Sex in the Social Structure of the United States," in *Personality in Nature, Society and Culture,* ed. C. Kluckhohn and H. A. Murray (2nd ed., New York: Alfred A. Knopf, 1953), pp. 365–367; and M. Mead, "Administrative Contributions to Democratic Character Formation at the Adolescent Level," *ibid.,* pp. 665–666.

32. "Imitation" is here used in its strictest sense. The boy must not repeat the father's *real* struggles with their real benefits, and losses. His efforts can have only symbolic reference to the earlier trials experienced by the father in much the same way as the candyless Lent is now but an attenuated shadow of the original forty-day fast. Indeed, this whole mechanism of imitation might be termed "participant magic."

33. Several children "ran away" in the course of the five-year Project, mostly girls! At least two "escaped" more realistically and permanently, one to Britain, the other to Palestine.

34. Note that "freedom" needs triple or quadruple consent: pupil, staff, peers, and parents.

28. The Family: Peer Group in the Urban Village

In the West End, children come because marriage and God bring them. This does not mean that West Enders believe children to be caused by God, but that the Catholic Church opposes birth control, and that this is God's wish. There is some planning of conception, either through the use of the church-approved rhythm method, or, more rarely, through contraception. But while the sale of contraceptives is illegal in Massachusetts, this does not preclude their acquisition. West Enders, however, do reject their use—or at least talking about their use—on religious grounds. The major method of family planning seems to be ex post facto. Should the wife become pregnant after a couple has had what they deem to be enough children, she may attempt to abort herself, using traditional methods that she has learned from other women. If the attempt fails, as it probably does in many cases, the new child is accepted fatalistically—and usually happily—as yet another manifestation of the will of God. Even so, families are smaller among second-generation Italians than among their parents. The couple with six to eight children, which seems to have been prevalent among the first generation, now has become a rarity. A large family is still respected, however, because children themselves are still highly valued.

The fact that children are not planned affects the way in which parents relate to them, and the methods by which they bring them up. Indeed, American society today is characterized by three types of families: the *adult-centered*—prevalent in working-class groups—run by adults for adults, where the role of the children is to behave as much as possible like miniature adults; the *child-centered*—found among families who plan their children, notably in the lower middle class—in which parents subordinate adult pleasures to give the child what they think he needs or demands; and the *adult-directed*—an upper-middle-class pattern—in which parents also place low priorities on their own needs, in order to guide the children toward a way of life the parents consider desirable.[1]

In the lower middle class of the present generation, husband and wife are likely to have finished high school, perhaps even the same one. This shared background helps them to communicate with each other, and creates some common interests, although much spare time is still spent with peers of the same sex. The most easily shared interest is the children, and the parents communicate best with each other through joint child-rearing. As a result, this family is child-centered. Parents play with their children—which is rare in the working class—rear them with some degree of self-consciousness, and give up some of their adult pleasures for them. Family size is strongly influenced by educational aspirations. If the parents are satisfied with their own occupational and social status, and feel no great urgency to send their children to college, they may have as many children as possible. For each child adds to their shared enjoyment and to family unity—at least while the children are young. Sometimes, the child will dominate his parents unmercifully, although child-centered parents are not necessarily permissive in their child-rearing. Rather, they want the child to have a happier childhood than they experienced, and will give him what they believe is necessary for making it so. One of their child-centered acts is the move to the suburb, made not only for the child's benefit, but also to make their child-rearing easier for themselves, and to reduce some of the burdens of child-centeredness. They give the child freely over to the care of the school, and to organizations like the Scouts or Little League, because these are all child-centered institutions.

Among college-educated parents, education and educational aspirations shape family life. College education adds immeasurably to the number of common interests between husband and wife, including activities other than child-rearing. Consequently, these parents know what they want for their children much more clearly than does the child-centered family, and their relationship to the children is adult-directed. Child-rearing is based on a model of an upper-middle-class adulthood characterized by individual achievement and social service for which parents want the child to aim. As a result, the child's wants are of less importance. Such parents devote much time and effort to assuring that the child receives the education which will help him to become a proper adult. For this purpose, they may limit the size of their families; they will choose their place of residence by the quality of the school system; they will ride herd on the school authorities to meet their standards; and, of course, they will exert considerable pressure on the children to do well in school.[2]

The West End family is an adult-centered one. Since children are not planned, but come naturally and regularly, they are not at the center of family life. Rather, they are raised in a household that is run to satisfy adult wishes first. As soon as they are weaned and toilet-trained, they are expected to behave themselves in ways pleasing to adults. When they are with adults, they must act as the adults want them to act: to play quietly in a corner, or to show themselves off to other adults to demonstrate the physical and psychological virtues of their parents. Parents talk to them in an adult tone as soon as possible, and, once they have passed the stage of babyhood, will cease to play with them. When girls reach the age of seven or eight, they start assisting the mother, and become miniature mothers. Boys are given more freedom to roam, and, in that sense, are treated just like their fathers.

But while children are expected to behave like adults at home, they are able to act their age when they are with their peers. Thus, once children have moved into their own peer group, they have considerable freedom to act as they wish, as long as they do not get into trouble. The children's world is their own, and only within it can they really behave like other children. Parents are not expected to supervise, guide, or take part in it. In fact, parent-child relationships are segregated almost as much as male-female ones. The child will report on his peer group activities at home, but they are of relatively little interest to parents in an adult-centered family. If the child performs well at school or at play, parents will praise him for it. But they are unlikely to attend his performance in a school program or a baseball game in person. This is his life, not theirs.[3]

Schoolteachers and social workers who dealt with West End children often interpreted the family segregation patterns from a more child-centered perspective, and assumed that the parents had lost interest in their children or were ignoring them. But this is not the case. At home, they are still part of the family circle, and continue to play their assigned roles. In fact, West End children continue to attend family gatherings at ages at which middle-class children are usually excused from them. They also sit in on social gatherings from which middle-class children might be excluded altogether. But then West Enders do not make the same distinctions between family and social gatherings, since they usually involve the same people.

There are parents among the West Enders who do ignore their children, and take no interest in them. Usually, these are people who for one reason or another are incapable of playing a parental role, and most West Enders consider them to be immoral, or pathological.

The departure of the children from home to peer group functions to support the adult-centered family. When the adults have complete authority over what goes on in the home, the children's need to behave like children must take place outside the view of adults. In the case of an acculturating ethnic group, the segregation of children and adults also reduces some of the conflict that would otherwise result from culture clashes between the children and the parents. At the same time, the children are able to bring home some of the dominant American culture patterns, and thus to act as an acculturating influence on the parents.

The children's movement into the peer group proceeds gradually, with the latter taking up more and more of their time as the children become older. As already noted, boys are allowed more freedom than girls, but when girls reach their teens, they also move into peer groups outside the home, performing their household functions grudgingly. Although parents would like to keep the girls closer to home, they find it difficult to fight the peer group attractions that draw their daughters out of the household. By adolescence, then, children spend little time in the parental home.

Mothers do attempt to teach their departing children rules of proper behavior, namely, the rules of the adult-centered and routine-seeking home, and urge them to adopt these in peer group activities. During this time, however, the child is also learning what are called the rules of the street, that is, those of the peer group. Thus, for some years, parents fight the ascendancy of street rules over home rules, especially if the former appear in his behavior at home. When a boy reaches the age of ten or twelve, however, parents feel that he is now responsible for his own actions. If he gets into "trouble," through behavior bringing him to the attention of the police or the priest, the blame must be attached to the influence of bad companions. Having done their best by urging him to follow home-rules, parents hope that he will do so. Should he fail to do so, however, the consequences are ascribed fatalistically to his peer group and his own moral failings. But whereas parents are concerned about the results, they neither feel the same responsibility for the child that is found in the middle-class family, nor develop the same guilt feelings should he get into trouble.

Interestingly enough, the home-rules that are preached to the child differ little from those held by the middle class. Mothers are more likely to be routine-seeking than action-seeking, and their desire for stability creates values which are also found in the middle class. The extent to which these rules are enforced, however, varies between action-seeking and routine-seeking or mobile families. The former, for instance, seem to surrender earlier, with less resistance to the child's inevitable adoption of the rules of the street. Moreover, the child himself reacts differently to the enforcement of these ideals. The child of a routine-seeking family, discovering that there are home rules and street rules, soon learns therefore to act accordingly in both places. In an action-seeking family, however, the child learns that the rules which the parents preach and those which they themselves practice diverge sharply. Thus he is more likely to reject the preached rules, and behave according to the street rules both at home and on the street.

The predominant method of child-rearing is punishment and reward. Children are punished when they misbehave, and rewarded—though not always—when they are obedient. Punishment is both physical and verbal: mothers slap and beat their children, tell them not to do this or do that, and threaten to tell their fathers when they come home. Indeed, to a middle-class observer, the parents' treatment often seems extremely strict and sometimes brutal. There is a continuous barrage of prohibitions and threats, intertwined with words and deeds of rewards and affection. But the torrents of threat and cajolery neither impinge on the feelings of parental affection, nor are meant as signs of rejection. As one mother explained to her child, "We hit you because we love you." People believe that discipline is needed constantly to keep the child in line with and respectful of adult rules, and that without it he would run amok.

West Enders raise their children impulsively, with relatively little of the self-conscious, purposive child-rearing that is found in the middle class. Parents tell their child how they want him to act without much concern about how he receives their message. They do not weigh their words or methods in order to decide whether these are consistent with earlier ones, or with the way they want to raise their child. Since the child is viewed as a little adult, parents do not think much about how he reacts qua child. Nor do they worry whether too strict a punishment or too permissive rewarding will have subsequent detrimental consequences. Even while they are conscious of the possibility of children being "spoiled," especially by relatives, they mean by this only that the child may get more attention than is compatible with an adult-centered family system.

Impulsive child-rearing is possible because West-Enders are not concerned with *developing* their children, that is, with raising them in accordance with a predetermined goal or target which they are expected to achieve. Unlike adult-directed or even child-centered families, West Enders have no clear image of the future social status, occupational level, or life-style that they want their children to reach. And even when they do, they do not know how to build it into the child-rearing process.

West Enders want for their children what they want for themselves—a secure existence as persons who are both accepted and somewhat envied members of their family circle and peer group. They hope that their children will seek a better education and obtain a better job than they, but the children are not pushed hard toward this goal. If a child does not achieve the parental wishes, he is pressed no further. Indeed, the parents' greatest fear is that the child will become a "bum." The worry about downward mobility is stronger than any desire for upward mobility. Consequently, the major hope is that in education, occupation, and general status, the child will not fall below that of his peers.

The impact of these child-rearing patterns on the child himself is less confusing than one might imagine. As the child learns largely by imitation, parents often try to behave as models—in censoring their own profanity, for example. But as they cannot long keep up such behavior, the child soon learns what is considered normal. He accepts the unending mixture of physical or verbal reward and punishment in the same way. Public reactions, of course, are no index to possible deeper impact, but judging by what is visible to the observer, the child is guided by the torrent of words to avoid behavior that results in punishment. He pays less attention to the rest of what is said. He reacts similarly to the verbally stated norms which he is asked to follow, but which he sees are being violated by his parents and the world around him. The child, thus becoming aware of the inconsistencies between word and deed, soon learns that what people say is less significant than what they do. Although he neither rejects the words, nor the norms they state, he quickly learns to dichotomize between what is and what ought to be.

These conclusions not only color his later life, but many of them stand him in good stead. The child learns the morality imbedded in the stated rules, but seems to internalize little of it. Instead, he accepts it as an ideal guide by which to judge the reality he faces, and to measure the deviation between the two. This allows him to justify his own failure to act in terms of the ideal, and to develop a protective cynicism, especially toward the stated norms of the outside world. In turn, this skepticism protects him from the deprivations and disappointments he encounters as a member of a low-income population. But it also blinds him to people's good intentions. When such intentions might result in desirable innovations, his failure to respond to them other than cynically often deprives him of the benefits offered by the outside world.[4]

The child's pragmatic outlook impresses him with the need to obey authority that can implement power and to ignore that which cannot. The dichotomy between word and deed allows him to develop a posture of respect for authority and the cunning to subvert it for his own aims. At first, he uses this to negotiate between the conflicting rules of street and home. Later, it will allow him to develop strategy to maneuver through the intricate mixture of words and deeds in the peer group. Words, he learns, are meant to impress people, but deeds and only deeds count.[5]

The Mother's Role in Child-Rearing

As noted previously, child-rearing is the mother's function; the father provides mainly the formal discipline. The father is also a behavior model for the male child, and, as in all cultures, the boys learn male behavior by watching him and other males in the family circle. The mother also refers to the father as a model of masculinity, and identifies him with male authority as well. More important, she frequently reminds the boy that he is male, and lets him know when his behavior deviates from what she considers to be properly masculine. In this, she is supported by other male and female members of the family circle. Mothers and aunts will point out instances of the slightest "girlish" or "sissy" behavior even in the men that the boy sees. In one family, for example, the reluctance of one of the men to watch the fights on television, and his interest in dramatic programs was interpreted as a deficiency in maleness, and pointed out as such to the boys in the family. Mothers also become as much concerned as fathers when their boys are called sissies by their peers. Sometimes, boys may be punished with taunting signs of femaleness. For example, I was told that when students in the West End parochial school forgot to wear ties, the nuns punished them by making them wear bows in their hair.

A number of observers of working-class life have pointed out that the mother's dominance in child-rearing and the lack of a consistently present male figure in the household can result in the boys' concern about their maleness and a tendency toward latent and overt homosexuality.[6] Although West End adolescents exhibit similar behavior, it cannot be attributed to the absence of the father from the home.

Actually, what matters is not the husband's physical presence but his family role, and how this is interpreted by the mother. In the Negro population, described by Walter Miller, long-term male employment instability, coupled with the availability of stable employment for Negro women and the long history of matriarchy in Negro society, have practically pre-empted the male's family role. Thus, he is often a weak or absent father, for he may desert the family when he is unemployed, or he may be asked to leave by the woman. Under such conditions, the mother becomes the dominant member of the family, and has little respect for the man—or men—around her.[7] The children not only see evidence of male weakness, but are also exposed to the mother's never-ending complaints of male failure.

Among the West Enders, however, the man is not usually weak. Italian peasant society was always patriarchal, and, although there are many families in which the woman is actually stronger than the man, the nominal power is still acknowledged to belong to him. Yet, while the men have suffered layoffs and unemployment in periods of national or local depression, there has been no history of continuous unemployment. When full-time jobs have been scarce, West Enders seem to have found some part-time employment, often with relatives who were better situated than they. Even in times of unemployment, however, Italian men have been less likely to abdicate from the household, either through desertion or breakdown. As a result of all these conditions, women have not needed to turn against their husbands, or men in general, as has been the case in the Negro population. Moreover, as I noted earlier, the women themselves are active in supporting by word and deed the authority of the father, and in urging the child to act in ways defined as male by Italian culture.

Many Italian men, of course, do evince the kind of vanity regarding their physical and sexual powers, and the concern with their physical appearance and dress that is usually identified with latent homosexuality. But whether or not this display of male vanity is always an index of homosexuality—as is often the case in middle-class culture, where such displays are out of the ordinary—cannot be answered conclusively by the data collected in the West End. It should be noted, however, that in a low-status, uneducated population whose life proceeds largely within a relatively cohesive primary group, individualistic behavior by men and women alike is normally expressed in personal and verbal display. This, in fact, is the main way of expressing individualism. Consequently, observers from a culture that provides a variety of opportunities for individualistic behavior may thus be culture-bound in their unilateral identification of display with homosexuality.

Even so, instances of latent as well as overt homosexuality can be found. Indeed, among a small group of action-seeking young men whom I observed sporadically, joking and semi-serious accusations of homosexual desires or escapades were often expressed. Their conversation dealt even more frequently, however, with heterosexual adventures. While these men had little respect for women, they spoke only in the most deferential tones about their mothers. Perhaps they had experienced the maternal overprotection that has been suggested as a cause of latent homosexuality.

Maternal overprotection seems to be found in families in which the father is unreasonably authoritarian toward his children. Adult West Enders, who sometimes described their fathers as having been excessively strict, explained that, since they were immigrants, they could not understand or tolerate the children's American ways. Under these conditions, mothers protected their children as much as they possibly could from severe paternal punishment, by lying to their husbands about the children's activities and hiding their misdeeds. This may well have led to the maternal veneration and paternal hatred expressed by some West End men, especially among the action-seekers.

From Adolescence to Adulthood

As the child grows into an adolescent, he is home less and less often, until parents begin to think of him—and, to a lesser extent, her—as only a boarder in the home.[8] Relationships with parents become more tenuous, and often result in conflict. For while the child has some difficulty in conforming to the rules of the adult-centered household, the adolescent finds it much harder. The source of conflict may be found in the changes in family structure and family concept that accompany acculturation. In Italy, and among the immigrants, there was no such concept as adolescence. Childhood, as noted earlier, was a brief period, which ended about or even before the age of ten. From then on, the young person occupied an adult economic role, but remained in the household, contributed to the family income, and obeyed the patriarchal regulations until he married. In America, where compulsory school attendance lengthened the period of functional childhood, the immigrants had some difficulty in accepting the American concept of a longer childhood, and often felt that their children should leave school to go to work.[9]

Second-generation parents have accepted the need for education through high school, but they—like their own parents—have continued to maintain the traditional demand that within the household the child must obey parental rules. The adolescent, however, does not accept the traditional pattern. He feels that he too has reached adulthood, and that the household should respect his own style of life.

The West End adolescent, as noted before, is alive only with his peer group; outside it, he exists as a quiet and almost passive individual. With adults, he is likely to be lethargic and sullen, seeking always to minimize contact with them. In the peer group, however, the style of life is one of action-seeking. Much of the conflict between adolescent and adult therefore is that between the action-seeking and the routine-seeking patterns.

In the adolescent peer group, manifesting the episodic search for action in an almost pure, ideal-typical form, life alternates between killing time and searching for action. Some of it takes place right within the group, in a dialectic of conformity and competitiveness through which the individual realizes himself. Most satisfying, however, is the search for action by the group as a whole. In this activity the adolescent achieves a kind of personal autonomy that he gets nowhere else. "Action" generates a state of quasi-hypnotic excitement which enables the individual to feel that he is in control, both of his own drives and of the environment. Also, it allows him to forget that he is living in a routine-seeking world, where "they," that is, the routine-seeking adults, make and enforce most of the rules. As previously noted, this state may be achieved through a card game, an athletic contest, a fight, a sexual adventure, or through an attack on the adult world. Whereas most of these attacks are in the nature of petty mischief—taunting adults, stealing fruit from a push cart, writing angry exclamations on public walls, or breaking windows in an empty building—some are more serious, and are defined by the adult world as delinquency. There was some disagreement about the amount of delinquency in the West End; city officials claimed that it was high, while West Enders and the local police insisted it was low. I encountered little evidence of delinquency while I lived in the West End.

Many explanations have been offered as to the causes of adolescent delinquency. Bloch has argued that it results from the tensions of the transitional adolescent stage; Walter Miller, that it is simply an expression of lower-class cultural values such as toughness, the search for excitement, and maleness; and Matza and Sykes, that it implements leisure values pursued also by the middle class—which the latter is unwilling to admit or recognize.[10] Cohen, and Cloward and Ohlin have stressed the gap between aspirations and reality.[11] Cohen argues that delinquency is an overcompensation against middle-class goals that the lower-class child cannot implement because of social and economic deprivation. Cloward and Ohlin propose a similar hypothesis but describe the goals not as middle class but as "conventional." Finally, Paul Goodman explains delinquency as protest against the unwillingness of adults to give teenagers a viable function in the society.[12]

The behavior of West End adolescents would suggest that there is some truth in all of these hypotheses. The strains between teenagers and adults, noticeable in relationships with adults, were most often expressed by sullen withdrawal. As already indicated, school officials in the West End pointed out that in school their charges were unexpectedly quiet and well-behaved. Outside the school, however, the teenagers expressed the kinds of cultural values that Miller has identified. Some of their doings that differ little from the hell-raising activities of middle-class groups—notably school fraternities—were more noticeable to the adult world because West Enders, like other working- and lower-class groups, could not carry them on behind the closed doors of fraternity houses. Most of the time, they had to meet on street corners, in tenement hallways, settlement houses, or in and around the small soda-shops and groceries that dot areas like the West End. After vacancies began to increase in the area, some of the groups set up "cellar clubs"— clubrooms located in a basement, an empty store, or apartment that could be rented cheaply. The clubroom, obtained if the group had money to pay the rent, was vacated when the money ran out, at which time the group returned to the corner. Within the cellar clubs the activities were not too different from those of a fraternity house: card-playing, stag conversation, and informal weekend dances, with beer, whiskey, and profanity flowing freely.[13] After hours, individuals might return for sex play. While the police did keep an eye on the clubs, they intervened only if the neighbors complained, or in cases of extreme drunkenness and violence. When the groups had no clubrooms, they frequented the settlement houses on "club nights," but restrained themselves in activities and language to conform more to the routine-seeking culture.

Of course, all adolescents, whether they be middle class or working class, are at times attracted to mischief and vandalism, although their desires are not always expressed in action. Generally speaking, such activities are directed against the institutions that the mischief-makers feel to be most oppressive at the moment, especially those from another social stratum. Thus, whereas middle-class adolescents are more often aggressive toward the police, working-class ones leave the police alone, and direct their energies toward the school or the recreation center. In the West End, for example, there was considerable breakage of windows, but mostly in the schools and only rarely in stores or in the hospital. The adolescents did not like the police, but they were not aggressive toward them. Conversely, the police were not as hostile toward them as they are in some middle-class communities I have observed, where the resident has a higher status than the policeman. The working-class teenager probably will do more damage than the middle-class mischief-maker. Moreover, he carries it out with a toughness that makes it more visible and more threatening to the larger society, and he does seek out middle-class institutions as a target.

There is no doubt that the West End teenager's withdrawal in school and his protest against the routine and aims of the school are based on a gap between aspirations and reality. Indeed, some of the after-school destructiveness is a more active form of expressing this gap. My impressions of West End teenagers would suggest that their protest is directed less against middle-class values than against what Cloward and Ohlin call conventional ones—what I identify as the values of the routine-seeking society—some of which overlap working and middle class. But there is no indication that West Enders are seeking either the goals usually sought by middle-class children, or, for that matter, the manly, manual, and craftsmanlike-forms of work proposed by Goodman. In early, or even late, adolescence, they have not thought seriously about their future as adults, and, since the peer group does not encourage career aspirations, they are not yet anticipating the trauma of low-status employment and the dead-end job. Rather, they want the material appurtenances of modern life—especially cars and spending money—and they want to be freed from the routine-seeking society which "bugs"—or imposes on—them. Yet, at home, school, church, and in public recreation facilities, action-seeking is strictly forbidden to them. Their protest, then, is directed diffusely against the parental and adult demand for conformity to routine as defined by adults.

Why should teenagers be addicted to the action-seeking life style? The main reason, perhaps, lies in their inability to accept routines that adults propose to them, and their lack of any self-defined routine as a substitute. For this reason the most important adult routine, that of school, is anathema to many. Emerging from homes in which learning has not been encouraged, they have been brought up in such a way that their attention span is very short. This makes studying and learning difficult. Moreover, the school—a middle-class institution—seeks to train them for a way of life that in many ways is diametrically opposed to the one which they have so far experienced. Also, they are being taught by women, which, especially after the onset of puberty, can be an insult—if not a threat, to maleness. But, if school has no meaning, there are no other functions which society permits them to perform. Moreover, as the peer groups in which they gather have no substantive function, they must therefore find things to do in a world hedged by adult restrictions. As a result, adolescent groups represent a form of the leisure class, sharing some of the ways of the departed aristocratic leisure class but lacking the power, status, and resources that would legitimize such behavior.[14] This is not to imply that adolescents would necessarily welcome the opportunity to pursue routines developed on their own. Action-seeking episodes are, after all, a source of fun and excitement, as well as an opportunity for exploring one's identity as an individual and group member.

Yet no explanation of adult behavior or delinquency can ignore the fact that these patterns do cease abruptly with marriage. Although it was difficult to determine numbers, few West Enders graduated from adolescence to a career in crime. Moreover, many West Enders did regret their lack of interest in school, and their failure to graduate from high school, as soon as their occupational function in society had been established. Consequently, the transitional nature of this behavior and the close relationship it bears to the adolescents' lack of viable function in the society cannot be ignored in theories of adolescent conduct.

Although the teenage way of life seems to coincide more often with the action-seeking than with the routine-seeking values, there is, of course, considerable variety among teenage groups. Some are embroiled in continuous conflict with the adult world, and it is they who become most visible to the middle-class eye. More participate—at least part of the time—in school and in settlement house activities, and thus are on the way to becoming routine-seekers. A rare few become middle class in the way in which the school and settlement house want all of them to be. Thus, the teenager may choose from a variety of groupings although the choice does become numerically more limited toward the middle-class end of the scale.

While the teenage groups were sexually segregated, girls' groups in the West End met near the corners where the boys hung out. Occasionally, the two groups joined forces for an evening outing. Likewise, girls were invited to weekend dances at the male cellar clubs—usually those girls who were attached to the boys' group in a more or less steady, though informal, arrangement. These were group get-togethers. But the hold of the group is so strong that only rarely did the boy have an individual date. West Enders noted that boys rarely left the group for a girl, and that a male group seldom broke up because of conflicts over a girl. They did indicate, however, that female peer groups were much less stable, and often collapsed if two girls became interested in the same boy. If a boy should leave the group for a girl, he is likely to be accused of disloyalty, and must either give her up or leave the group. I am distinguishing here between a date with a "good girl" who may be a potential wife, and the continuous search for sexual relations with compliant "bad girls." It is dates with the former that result in accusations of desertion. Dating the latter, however, is a much sought after experience. It is a form of action that is subsequently described to the group—with proper embellishment—and provides a source of conversation many times over.

Eventually, as group members reach the end of their teens, boys will leave to court, and at that time many of the peer groups break up. Subsequently, new ones form among those boys who are not yet ready to get married, and those who may never marry.

Marriage is a crucial turning point in the life of the West End boy. It is then that he must decide whether he is going to give up the boys on the corner for the new peer group of related siblings and in-laws—a decision related to and reflected in his choice of a mate. If he marries one of the girls who has hung nearby on the same corner, he may interrupt the life on the corner only during the early months of marriage. Should he fall in love with a girl who has spent her adolescence closer to the family, he is likely to move into a family circle on marriage. He may even be attracted to a mobile girl who wishes to leave the peer group society entirely. But should he fail to agree with her, his married life is likely to be marked by ambivalence and marital tension. This is one instance where the lack of communication between men and women is a real drawback in married life. In most cases, the West Ender leaves the corner on marriage, and from then on participates in a not altogether different peer group existence in the living room and kitchen of his own home.

That the man may or may not make the move from the corner to the apartment is one index of his future choice between routine and action, and is evaluated as such by West Enders. Indeed, routine-seeking people feel that adult men who return to the corner "never grow up," and remain adolescents. There is considerable truth in this observation, for the boys who stay with the corner and the episodic life are continuing adolescent, or what Bennett Berger calls youthful, patterns.[15] They are apt to participate only sporadically in married life and continue as long as possible to maintain the attitudes and values they held during adolescence.

Needless to say, life on the corner is often routine, and the meetings of the family circle are interrupted by weekly nights out in male company. Moreover, even in the family circle the search for action is not given up, but frozen in time. Much of the talk is given over to recalling exciting episodes of adolescence and early adulthood that are relived vicariously, over and over again.[16]

This emphasis on the past is not only nostalgia, but an index to the real importance that childhood and adolescence have in the life of the West Ender. As these were the times when he was most alive, when things happened, and when he could make things happen, his adventures are remembered fondly as pranks, and are retold frequently, if only to show that the person has not really given in to the requirements of responsibility or to the routine. The stories reinforce the belief that one can fight back, outsmart, and even defeat the outside world. Adolescence is also a period of achievement, especially for the talented boy. Thus, within the small world of the neighborhood, he may have been the best boxer, baseball player, or the most successful gambler, and as an adult he will bring out trophies, pictures, and other evidence of his past accomplishments.

Childhood and adolescence are also the time when enduring friendships are made.[17] Some of these, which last for the rest of the person's life, are maintained alongside the friendships that exist between brothers and other relatives. I was constantly amazed at the continued contact which adults maintained with the people whom they had known as children or adolescents. Not all of these become friends, but they do remain acquaintances for life, and, when they meet, childhood events are recalled with pleasure. Most of the adult friendships outside the family circle are established in childhood and adolescence, and probably outnumber those formed during adulthood. Of course, this is encouraged by the fact that West Enders are not mobile, and that most of them will occupy a similar social—as well as physical—space throughout their lifetime. Consequently, they are likely to have enough in common to remain friends. The converse was brought out by one West Ender who told me that he had had a number of close Jewish friends in childhood, but that he had lost them in adolescence, as they went off to a college preparatory high school and he did not. Because of the lack of mobility among most of the Italian West Enders, ties between childhood friends remained strong even when one moved out of the West End, especially since the move usually was to a neighborhood easily accessible to, and in continuing contact with, the West End.

Although the adults limited their reverence for adolescent behavior mainly to the nostalgic memories, they did occasionally indulge in activities that resembled adolescent ones in deed and spirit. For example, they gambled behind the priest's back in church organization meetings, went on sprees that wreaked havoc with the family budget, or enjoyed a stag night out on the town. And while they did not recognize them as regressions into adolescence, these adventures were talked about in such a way as to suggest that they do bear some similarity to adolescent behavior.[18]

Middle-class observers of working-class life around the turn of the century often described their adult subjects as child-like or happy like children. Some of these interpretations reflected the cultural difference and the social distance between a reserved Yankee middle class and a less inhibited working class. They also were meant—or at least reported—in a somewhat patronizing fashion. But they seem to have had some truth to them, in that they did touch on the strong identification with childhood and adolescence that is found much less among the middle class. Obviously, West End adults are neither childlike, nor are they children, but as they do place such great emphasis on the early years, an outsider might possibly arrive at this conclusion.

Observers of working-class life, here and in the underdeveloped areas, have called attention to the fact that for girls, the high point of life is adolescence—especially the courting period—and that they age quickly after marriage and childbearing, becoming old and passive much earlier than do middle-class women. Although men go through much of the same rapid cycle, their greater freedom of movement all through life does reduce this difference between adolescence and adulthood. They also age somewhat more slowly unless their work is so strenuous as to drain them physically.

Rapid aging was more prevalent among the immigrants than it is among the West Enders, since life is no longer a constant struggle for survival for the men, or an endless succession of childbirths for the women. It is still true, however, that for the West Ender—and perhaps for all working-class people—childhood and adolescence are the most gratifying phases of life, and that adulthood only rarely attains the same level. Conversely, the middle-class adult—and especially the upper-middle-class one—is likely to view the periods prior to adulthood as less happy times, with real fulfillment found only as family and the career are firmly established. I am not implying that adult life is a period of dull decline for the West Ender. The absence of interest in a career, the lack of identification with work, the fatalism about deprivation inflicted by the outside world, and the vitality of peer group life—all combine to minimize feelings of resignation and decline, perhaps more so among Italians than among other working-class groups.

Notes

1. S. M. Miller and Frank Riessman have used similar terms—parent-centered and child-centered—to distinguish working-class families from middle-class ones in "The Working-Class Subculture: A New View," *Social Problems,* vol. 9 (1961), p. 92. For a different typology of family organization, using somewhat the same terms, see Bernard Farber, "Types of Family Organization: Child-Oriented, Home-Oriented, and Parent-Oriented," in Arnold Rose, ed., *Human Behavior and Social Processes,* Boston: Houghton Mifflin, 1962, pp. 285–306.

2. For an example of what I call adult-directed child-rearing, see J. Seeley, R. Sim, and E. Loosley, *Crestwood Heights,* New York: Basic Books, 1956, especially Chaps. 7–9.

3. Covello reports that immigrant Italians criticized their children for participating in such childish activities as school sports, and tried to prevent their playing. They were expected to behave like grown adults by the time they reached the age of eight, and to have outgrown the need for play. Leonard Covello, "The Social Background of the Italo-American School Child," Unpublished Ph.D. Dissertation, New York University, 1944, p. 467.

4. This creates problems in community participation and in relationships with the outside world generally.

5. Thus, words are used as means to an end, rather than as conceptual tools. This may explain why the Italian-American community has produced so few analytically inclined intellectuals, but a larger number of critical and moralizing polemicists. For they also have come out of working-class parental backgrounds similar to those of the West End.

6. See, for example, Walter B. Miller, "Lower Class Culture as a Generating Milieu of Gang Delinquency," *Journal of Social Issues,* vol. 14, No. 3 (1958), pp. 5–19, at p. 9.

7. *Ibid.*

8. Most of the analysis that follows concerns the adolescent boy; adolescent girls are harder to talk to in a society like the West End, and their activities are less visible to the male observer.

9. The cultural conflict over the school is described fully—and skillfully—by Covello, *op. cit.*

10. Herbert Bloch and Arthur Neiderhoffer, *The Gang,* New York: Philosophical Library, 1958. Walter B. Miller, "Lower Class Culture as a Generating Milieu for Gang Delinquency," *op. cit.*; David Matza and Gresham Sykes, "Juvenile Delinquency and Subterranean Values," *American Sociological Review,* vol. 26 (1961), pp. 712–719.

11. Albert Cohen, *Delinquent Boys: The Culture of the Gang,* New York: The Free Press of Glencoe, 1955; Richard A. Cloward and Lloyd E. Ohlin, *Delinquency and Opportunity,* New York: The Free Press of Glencoe, 1960. These hypotheses are in turn based on Durkheim's and Merton's work on anomie.

12. Paul Goodman, *Growing Up Absurd,* New York: Random House, 1960.

13. The girls, having no cellar clubs, had to meet on the corner or in tenement hallways.

14. Edgar Friedenberg, *The Vanishing Adolescent,* New York: Beacon Press, 1959, especially Chap. 1.

15. Bennett M. Berger, "On the Youthfulness of Youth Cultures," Urbana: University of Illinois, 1961, mimeographed. He makes a distinction between adolescence and youthfulness, noting that young people who conform to the routines set by the adult world are hardly youthful, and that adults may continue the behavior pattern falsely identified as limited to adolescence.

16. The Italian ability to recollect past events vividly has also been noted by G. Lolli, E. Serriani, G. Golder, and P. Luzzatto-Fegiz, *Alcohol in Italian Culture,* New York: The Free Press of Glencoe and Yale Center of Alcohol Studies, 1958, p. 65.

17. For a similar observation among the North End "corner boys," see William F. Whyte, Jr., *Street Corner Society,* Chicago: University of Chicago Press, 1943; 2nd ed., 1955, p. 255.

18. This behavior is not restricted to the West Ender, but can, at some time, be found among all classes.

29. And How Did They Grow in the Working-Class Family?

> Life was mean and hard. My parents didn't have a lot to give us, either in things or
> emotions. [*Guiltily.*] I don't blame them; they couldn't help it. They did their best,
> but that's just the way it was. They were young, and their lives weren't any fun
> either. They were stuck together by their poverty and their five kids.
>
> —Twenty-seven-year-old beautician,
> second from the youngest in a family of five

Over and over, that's the story—a corrosive and disabling poverty shattered the hopes
and dreams of their young parents, and twisted the lives of those who were "stuck
together" in it. Flight is, of course, one way in which people try to get "unstuck"—
sometimes symbolically in alcohol, sometimes literally in divorce or desertion. Thus, of
the people I met, 40 percent had at least one alcoholic parent, usually but not always the
father;[1] almost as many were children of divorce or desertion;[2] and 10 percent spent part
of their lives in institutions or foster homes because their parents were unable, unwilling,
or judged unfit to care for them.

And how did they grow, the children of these families?

With pain:

> One of the first things I remember was when the police came in the middle of the night and
> they dragged us out of bed. [*Struggling to hold back tears.*] God, we were scared, my sister and
> me; we couldn't stop crying. I don't know where my parents were. I never saw my father
> again; he was always drunk anyway. And my mother, I don't know where she was, maybe
> she was working or something. They took us to juvenile hall that night, and we didn't get to
> go home for nine years.
>
> —Thirty-four-year-old housewife,
> the oldest in a family of two children

. . . with bitterness:

> I don't remember much about my father; he left when I was about six. The one thing I
> remember very well is that he used to beat us with a coathanger.
>
> Twenty-eight-year-old warehouseman,
> the middle child in a family of five

. . . with loneliness:

> When I was eight my parents got divorced, and I lived with my mother. She went out a lot.
> She went dancing, and she had lots of boyfriends. A lot of the time I didn't see her for two or
> three or four days. God, that was terrible because it was a time when I was absolutely
> terrified of being alone. And there I'd be—I'd come home alone; I'd take care of myself and

Lilian Breslow Rubin, "And How Did They Grow?" reprinted from her *Worlds of Pain: Life in the Working-Class Family,* 23–48. Copyright © 1976 by Lilian Breslow Rubin. Reprinted by permission of Basic Books, Inc., Publishers.

put myself to bed. And I'd get up the next morning and wash and dress and go to school. I wandered around the streets by myself a lot in those days, partly because I was so afraid to be in the house alone, but also there was nothing to do.

—Thirty-year-old short-order waitress
from a family where she was an only child

. . . with anger:

I ran away from home four or five times before I turned seventeen and finally stayed away. And they didn't come looking for me none of the time. The first time after I came back, my dad just walked in and beat me up. Another time when I ran away, the dude who was running the juvenile hall sent my family a telegram, and told them that I was there, and that they should come and get me. They sent back word that they should find me a job because they didn't have no more time for me.

—Thirty-four-year-old sheet-metal worker
from a family of six

. . . with rebelliousness:

I was always in a lot of trouble. In fact, I was considered incorrigible, and I was sent to juvenile hall and made a ward of the court when I was thirteen.

—Twenty-nine-year-old welder,
the second child in a family of five

. . . with resignation:

We never did have a lot of money; it was always a rough go. We got our clothes from the Goodwill, and there wasn't a lot of food around, you can bet. They both did their best, but it just wasn't enough. But I'm not complaining. Life is what you make it, and we always made the best of it. We had fun, too. I remember we'd go out and ride around sometimes, just little things like that were very nice. You can't have everything, you know.

—Twenty-five-year-old houswife,
the next to the youngest in a family of four

For most, the memories of childhood and the family are some tortured combination of all these feelings, and more—most notably guilt at allowing their expression and denial that any negative feelings exist at all. In fact, this guilt and denial was, for me, one of the most puzzling issues I encountered. Why, I kept asking myself, are these articulate people so distant from the sources of childhood pain and anger? Why is it necessary for them to deny so much of it? In the professional middle-class world in which I have lived for so many years, one encounters exactly the opposite response—young adults, encouraged by the psychotherapeutic milieu that pervades their culture, expose and examine the pain of childhood and the anger that accompanies it seemingly without end.

Could it be that these currents in the culture are so alien from working-class conscious-ness? I doubted it. For a variety of reasons—first among them, the cost, but also fears about being defined as "crazy," and the reluctance to probe the past that I observed—the women and men of the working class do not often seek out psychotherapy. But they are aware of its existence and of some of the basic premises on which it rests. In interview after interview, I heard the evidence of that psychological awareness—especially as it was expressed in their concerns about communication in interpersonal relationships and the kind of parenting they are offering to their own children.

What then? Why do we hear so much anger expressed by the middle-class child of the "committee" mother?

My mother was always busy—too busy for us. At least that's the way it felt when I was little. She was always out doing her thing—worrying about the poor people or the black people and on one damn committee to save the world or another. I used to be jealous of those people because she didn't seem to spend nearly as much time worrying about me or caring that I felt lonely or scared.

—Thirty-one-year-old housewife,
the oldest in a family of two

. . . and so little anger expressed by the working-class child of the mother who left home, husband, and children for another life:

My mother never meant to leave us. She loved us. But she was young; and she wanted to have fun, too. It was really my grandmother's fault. She was my father's mother, and she lived with us. She made my mom's life miserable. My mom couldn't even paint the walls of her own bedroom the color she wanted without my grandmother interfering.

Even on the issue of a mother who works outside the home, there often are differences between the ways in which a child in a professional middle-class home experiences that:

I always hated it that my mother worked. She didn't have to. She could have stayed home and taken care of us like other mothers did.

. . . and the experience of the child in a working-class family:

My mother worked on and off all the years we were growing up. It was a hard life for her having to work and take care of all of us at the same time.

No complaints from the working-class child. What sense would it make? Mother worked because she had to—the crucial difference, it seems, in a child's understanding and experience of a working mother.[3] Children in all families frequently are "lonely or scared," or both. But the child in the working-class family understands that often there's nothing his parents can do about it. They're stuck just as he is—stuck with a life over which they have relatively little control.

In a family where all the material necessities and most of the comforts and luxuries are taken for granted, a child can feel angered and rejected by a father who "works all the time," by a mother whose energy is directed into the kind of volunteerism that engages so many women in the professional middle class, by the one who *chooses* a career. But how can poor children justify or rationalize those feelings when they know that father works two jobs to keep a roof over their heads and food on the table; that mother does dull, demeaning, and exhausting work just to help make ends meet? When the same father gets drunk or violent; when the mother "takes it," joins the father in this behavior, or, once in a great while, simply runs away, a child's condemnation doesn't come easily. However imperfectly articulated or understood, children in such families sense the adults' frustration and helplessness. Their own hurt notwithstanding, assigning blame to parents makes little sense to these children. Their anger either is turned inward and directed against self—in childhood, "if only I were somehow different or better, this life wouldn't be happening to me"; or projected outward or directed against other, less threatening objects—in adulthood, "the country would be better off if we let those welfare bums starve." But always the source of the anger is kept distant from consciousness, as this dialogue with a thirty-four-year-old truck driver, one of three children, illustrates:

Tell me something about what life was like in your family when you were growing up?
Oh, I don't know what to say. It was a happy family.

Well, can you tell me something about it—like what kind of people were your mother and father?

My father was an alcoholic, so I don't know. My mother probably should have gotten a divorce, but I think she stayed married because of the kids; and probably because she didn't have any job skills and everything like that.

It must have been difficult to grow up with an alcoholic father then, huh?

[*Reluctantly*] Yeah. I remember my mother going down to the bar after he got paid when I was twelve, thirteen, fourteen and pleading for money to go pay the bills. But once she got down there to the bar, she'd go in and sit with him and drink beer, too. [*Quickly and defensively.*] But I don't want you to get the idea she was an alcoholic, because she wasn't. She'd just sit there and drink beer with him, that's all.

When I was a lot younger—a real little kid—I remember sitting in the car outside the bar for a long time waiting for them to come out. Sometimes I remember we would go in and ask them when they were coming home, and they'd give us a nickel or a dime to get rid of us. Then we'd go back and sit in the car. It got cold out there, and we'd be so hungry.

That sounds like it must have been a painful time for you?

Oh, I don't know. We didn't know any better; it was okay. I suppose the worst part was having to sit down there when you're a little kid and you're cold and hungry, and your mother and father are still sitting in the bar. That's the worst part. Sometimes though, they'd let us come in and we'd sit in a corner and drink Coke, and we'd try to be quiet so nobody would see us or notice us. Those times were better. At least we could be close to them and see what was going on.

But listen, I don't want you to get the idea that my mother was an alcoholic, too, because she wasn't. Anyhow, I don't think it's right for kids to go around blaming their parents for things they couldn't help. So I don't blame them none. They loved us and they brought us up the best they could; so you can't blame people for doing the best they can, can you?

Yes, there it is—"I don't think it's right for kids to go around blaming their parents for things they couldn't help"—a comment which, in various versions, I heard again and again.

For all children, life often feels fearful and uncontrollable. When a child's experience suggests that the adults on whom he must depend for survival have little control as well, his fears of being unprotected and overwhelmed are so great that he must either deny and repress his experience or succumb to his terror. Given those alternatives, most people rely on the mechanisms of denial and repression, for to succumb is to threaten life itself. No wonder our truck driver ends the conversation, as did so many others, with the insistent statement that "it's better to forget about things that bother you."

I don't know why I even got to thinking about these things. It don't do no good. I tell my kids all the time—it's better to forget about things that bother you; just put them out of your mind, otherwise you'll just be sitting around feeling sorry for yourself all the time. Just put those things out of your mind is what I tell them, just like I did; then they won't get to you.

But, one might wonder, isn't this an unusual family history? Isn't it true that in most families, no one drinks too much; that wives and husbands live together, raise their children together, and grow old together? The answer: yes, but barely. Among the 100 working-class men and women I met, only 54 percent of the families into which they were born were without some elements of instability—alcoholism, divorce, desertion—for some part of their lives. That means that 46 percent suffered one or more of those experiences some time during their childhood. It is that temporary quality of both the stability and instability in so many families that is noteworthy. Life changes, depending upon circumstances outside personal control. A lay-off, a serious illness in the family, an accident, a death—such events can thrust a stable family into instability for a while.

Similarly, a job that pays enough to meet the bills and live with some minimum comforts can mean, for some, the shift from instability to stability.

Even in the most consistently stable families, however, the first and fundamental fact of most of their lives was that they were poor. Not one person, even those from the most solid and integrated homes, failed to mention growing up poor—some worse off than others, to be sure, but all whose dominant experience of childhood was material deprivation.

It matters little that these families may not have been poor by some arbitrary definition set by a governmental agency. What counts is the experience of the people who lived those lives. For them, the deprivation was real—real when they knew parents had trouble paying the rent, when they didn't have shoes that fit, when the telephone was shut off, when the men came to take the refrigerator away. That fact alone colors every dimension of life and, for both parents and children, contributes powerfully to a world filled with pain, anger, fear, and loneliness—a world over which neither has much control.[4] Small wonder, then, that few adults from working-class families look back over those early years with the "Oh-to-be-a-child-again" fantasy so often heard among middle-class adults. Small wonder, too, that the working-class young grow up so fast while an extended adolescence—often until the mid-twenties and later—is the developing norm in much of the professional middle class. Such a moratorium on assuming adult responsibilities is a luxury that only the affluent sector of the society can afford.

Thus, at least intermittent poverty was the common experience of the children growing up in most of these working-class families. But there are differences in how their parents adapted to that primary fact of life. Some families struggled desperately and, most of the time, successfully remained among the "respectable" poor. Others gave up the fight and, more often than not, escaped their pain in drinking, violence, or desertion. Observing these patterns recently, one writer labeled them as the "settled-living" and "hard-living" lifestyles—a distinction that I will use as well because it rests on differences in family lifestyle and avoids some of the negative connotations of so many characterizations of working-class life.[5]

Like all such typologies, however, this one, too, should be labeled, "Approach with Caution," for at best it is only an approximation of reality. Thus, several things should be clear. First, the hard-living–settled-living styles represent two extremes rarely found in their pure states; elements of each are often found in the other. Second, just as many settled-living men and women may experience some aspects of hard-living in their own lives as they try to grasp and hold the American dream, so most hard livers of one period are settled livers in another. Third, in almost every settled-living family, there are hard-living brothers, sisters, or cousins who, while scorned, are omnipresent and painful reminders of the precariousness of the settled-living lifestyle—of the fact that at any moment external life forces might push even the most determinedly settled-living family off its course.

These terms, then, speak more to the ethos of a family rather than to a hard-and-fast reality, more to the dominant tone of life than to the day-to-day experience. The daily, weekly, even monthly experience may change at any given time. But what remains in the consciousness in adulthood is the sense of how things were, the sweep of life rather than its detail.

For just over half the families I met, that "sense of how things were" suggests the settled-living lifestyle—families that were characterized by stable work histories:

My dad had been working for the same company, on the same job for the last thirty years. Times were bad sometimes. He was laid off a lot. After the union came, there were strikes. But he's still proud of the fact that they always hired him back.

. . . stable families:

I guess they must have had problems, everybody does. But my folks always seemed to get along okay, and if there was trouble, none of us kids knew about it.

. . . a sense of rootedness:

I grew up in the same neighborhood and in the same house. It was the family's pride and joy that we always had a roof over our heads, and one that we owned.

They were cautious, conservative, church-going, and if they drank, they did so with moderation. Their children were dressed neatly and attended school regularly—at least in the elementary grades. They were brought up strictly to mind their manners, and subject to a very rigid discipline:

My folks, especially my father, made us toe the line, not like kids today. When my brother got out of line, my father nearly killed him. Actually, I guess I'm not sure how much good it did, because he kept getting into trouble.

Like it or not, the men went to work every day:

My father was always proud of the fact that he never missed a day's work and was never late. I mean, it doesn't count when he was laid off. He brought us up to respect work, too, and to be responsible and reliable.

. . . and the women kept house and children in shining order:

My mother was always cleaning or scrubbing or washing and ironing. It seems like I can hardly remember her doing anything else. Oh yes, she cooked, too.

In contrast to the settled lives, there were the hard-living families—just under half the people I met who recalled families that were characterized by fathers with chaotic work histories:

My father did so many things, I can't just tell you his occupation. I guess he was a painter, but he did a lot of other stuff, too. It seemed like most of the time, he was out of work.

. . . unstable family relations:

Something was wrong with my mother by the time I was born. She got sick—psychologically sick, I guess. She just didn't take care of us; and sometimes she'd just disappear. We—my sister and me—we ran wild until I was about nine. I didn't go to school; I couldn't read and write. My mother either wasn't there or couldn't take care of us. My father knew what was going on, but he didn't seem to care. He just got drunk all the time.

. . . violence:

When my father got drunk, he'd get mean and pick on whoever was around. When I was about twelve, he came home roaring drunk one night and picked me up like a sack of potatoes and threw me right across the whole room. My mother stood there and watched, and she never did a thing.

. . . a general rootlessness:

We moved around a lot. Sometimes we were evicted, but sometimes we just moved; I'm not sure why. I went to ten, maybe twelve, schools by the time I dropped out of high school; that was in the tenth grade.

. . . and alcoholism—the tragic consequences of which were experienced repeatedly by many of the children growing up in these families. At best, it meant poverty and dislocation as father moved from job to job with long periods of unemployment in between:

My dad had trouble holding a job because of his drinking. I guess he wasn't what you'd call a reliable worker. When he didn't work, things would really get tough. We were even evicted from where we lived one time.

At worst, it meant the total disruption of the family, as this story from a thirty-five-year-old woman, the middle child in a family of three, illustrates:

When I was three or so, my mother and father were separated and I was taken as a ward of the court. My father was an alcoholic; he still is a drunk. So he couldn't take care of us. I don't know exactly why they took us from my mother. She was pretty young at the time. Maybe she couldn't handle all the responsibility by herself. She probably wanted to have some fun, too.

I grew up partly in juvenile hall, partly in a children's home up north, and partly in a Salvation Army home for kids nobody wants. My mother and grandmother would come up to visit us once in a while—not often, just a couple of times a year. Not my father; we didn't see him again for years.

I used to tell my mother how I hated it in that home and how I wanted to go home with her, but she would tell me that until she had a good home to bring us to, they wouldn't let her take us home. So we just had to stay there.

It sounds as if those were painful years?

Yeah, it wasn't much fun. I hated everybody. I guess I made my life pretty miserable for everybody around me because I thought I'd been mistreated. Being little, you get ideas like that, I guess.

I was about eleven when my mother remarried and we got to live with her again. But by then, all of us didn't fit into the family anymore. We didn't get along with each other; my brothers and I used to fight something terrible. And we didn't get along with my stepfather. He drank a lot, too. It's funny, after all those years, and my mother marries another man who drinks. And then [*hesitating and reddening with embarrassment*], he used to make passes at me, and I couldn't stand it. I hated him, and I hated my mother because she didn't do anything about it. I don't know, maybe she didn't know; maybe she did.

Finally, we all just took off. My older brother joined the service; and I and my younger brother kept running away. Each time I'd run away, they'd catch me and put me back in juvenile hall again. So I spent all those years going back and forth between juvenile hall and home. All I could think of was getting out of that house. As soon as I turned eighteen, I just up and got married. I just had to get away from them all—my family, my parole officer, all of them; and that was the only way I could.

The hard-livers are, in some fundamental way, the nonconformists—those who cannot or will not accept their allotted social status. They are the women and men who rebel against the grinding routine of life; the dulling, numbing experience of going to the same mindless job every day; of struggling with the same problems of how to feed, clothe, and tend the children without adequate resources; of fighting an endless and losing battle with roaches, rats, sore throats, and infected ears. But rooted in the individualistic ethic of American life, the rebellion does not take the form of some constructive collective action directed at changing the social system. Rather it is a personal rebellion against what are experienced as personal constraints.

Thus, the explosive episodes of drinking and violence, the gambling away of a weeks' wages, the unexplained work absences (Why explain? Who would understand not showing up for that lousy job when the fish are running?), and the sudden, angry quittings. All these may make life harder in a family. But the ability to say "take your damn job and shove it" makes a man feel like a man again, at least for the moment. He can stand tall, at least until he faces the reality that his wife and children won't eat so well next week. He can defer dealing with that reality by getting drunk.

But even for the settled-living families, life was precarious—uncertain and unpredictable. Fathers who were unemployed or underemployed—out of work or working for wages which left the family just this side of wanting—were the norm:

Tell me something about what life was like in your family when you were growing up.

A thirty-seven-year-old woman, the second child in a family of four, recalls:

It was a good family, not like a lot of others we saw. My folks cared a lot, and they were always trying. But it seems no matter how hard they tried, something went wrong, and we'd get behind. We were dirt poor most of my life. There were always money problems; sometimes there wasn't even enough food.

It seemed like every three months my father was on strike or laid off. [*Laughing.*] I guess that's an exaggeration, but he really was on strike a lot. He was a laborer in construction, and he couldn't afford to be off work like that. Maybe the guys higher up got something out of the strike—you know, the carpenters and plumbers, and those workmen—but people like my dad just lost pay. They never could make it up.

Sometimes, too, there was violence—the angry explosions of people who feel entrapped:

The family was okay. I mean, my father worked steady, and they both tried their best. But life was plenty hectic. My father worked in the mines, and there wasn't much money. There were ten of us kids, and even though for that town we lived in a big house, it certainly wasn't large enough for all of us. So there was a lot of abrasive contact all the time.

The folks had their knock-down drag-outs, and it seemed like us kids were always caught in the middle. My father would take after my mother, and then she'd come after us. There was so much violence in that house. [*Pauses thoughtfully for a moment, then adds*] I was just thinking, most of that violence happened in the winter time when we were crowded together in that house and couldn't get out. At least in the summer, we could all be outside and get away from each other a little bit.

—Thirty-year-old ironworker

Of course! Poverty and crowded living conditions go together, making a fertile breeding ground for the violent acting out of the anger, the frustration, and the pain of being defined and defining oneself a failure. For the settled livers are, at bottom, the conformists—those who have bought into the system, who believe in the ethic of hard work, who believe in the American myth that everyone can pull themselves up by their bootstraps if only they have the will and the brains. What, then, are such people to say to themselves when they don't succeed? They *know* they have the will. There's little left but to accept that they don't have the brains—a devastating self-image from which all people must seek periodic relief and surcease.

This is one of the most destructive of "the hidden injuries of class" about which Richard Sennett and Jonathan Cobb write so compellingly.[6] Most of the time, the settled livers tend to deal with this injury to personal dignity by containing their anger and pain. But in their effort to bind their wounds—to restore dignity and affirm self—they redefine success so that it is more compatible with the modest accomplishments, and they accumulate possessions as the visible symbols of their achievements and status.[7] Often, however, it's not enough; it doesn't work. Some find the respite they need in angry explosions, some in deep withdrawals. Again and again, the men and women I met recall parents, especially fathers, who were taciturn and unresponsive:

> My father was a very quiet man. He almost never talked, even when you asked him a question. He'd sit there like he didn't hear you. Sometimes, an hour later (it was like he'd come out of a spell), he'd look at you and say, "Did you want something?" Most of the time, he just didn't know you were there.
>
> —Thirty-one-year-old steelworker,
> the middle child in a family of three

A twenty-five-year-old woman, the oldest in a family of two, recalls:

> My father never seemed to talk or be part of the family. The only thing I can remember that he enjoyed was working in his garden. He'd come home, eat, and go out in the yard almost every night of the year, even when it was raining. Otherwise, he'd just sit quiet for hours, like he wasn't there or something.

It's true that fathers in the professional middle-class homes may also be recalled as silent, as not "part of the family." But none of the adults who grew up in those homes recall the kind of brooding, withdrawn quality that so often describes the experience in a working-class home. The child of a professional father may recall that he was "always working even when he was home"; that he was "preoccupied a lot"; or that he "always seemed to have something on his mind." But that same person is also much more likely than his working-class counterpart to remember some ways in which fathers participated in family life, even if only to recall the dinner hour as a time for family conversation. Preoccupation, then, would seem to be the most remembered quality about fathers in professional families; withdrawal, the most vivid memory in working-class families.

This, then, is some part of the experience of life as it was lived day-by-day—sometimes chaotic and unpredictable, always difficult. If that was their present, what did the future look like to the children in these families?

When you were little, what did you think you'd like to do or be when you grew up?

A hard question for most people from poor homes—one that focuses sharply on the limitations that poverty exacts upon the futures of its victims. Listen to this thirty-two-year-old appliance repairman, the middle child in a family of seven:

> We were maybe one step above what you would call white trash. If we thought about it at all, we would have considered ourselves lucky to get through high school. Most of the kids in the family didn't do that.
>
> There was no demand on any of us for any goal. You see, my father wasn't an educated man. He was taken out of school when he was nine, and him not having an education, it kept him from seeing a lot of hopes for his kids. He can hardly write his own name, even now. Oh, I guess he didn't want us to be just ordinary laborers like he was, but it wasn't ever talked about. Like, going to college was never discussed. It never occurred to me to think about it. That was something other kids—rich kids—did. All I knew was that I'd have to work, and I didn't think much about what kind of work I'd be doing. There didn't seem much point in thinking about it, I guess.

In fact there not only "wasn't much *point* in thinking about it," there was no *way* to think about it. For in order to plan for the future, people must believe it possible to control their fate—a belief that can only be held if it is nourished in experience. That seldom happens in working-class life. Instead, for most, the difficult realities of their lives often limit their very ability to envisage a future. Indeed, it is precisely that inability that most sharply distinguishes the consciousness of the working class from that of the more privileged classes.

For the child—especially a boy—born into a professional middle-class home, the sky's the limit; his dreams are relatively unfettered by constraints. In his earliest conscious moments, he becomes aware of his future and of plans being made for it—plans that are not just wishful fantasies, but plans that are backed by the resources to make them come true. All around him as he grows, he sees men who do important work at prestigious jobs. At home, at school, in the neighborhood, he is encouraged to test the limits of his ability, to reach for the stars.

For most working-class boys, the experience is just the reverse. Born into a family where daily survival is problematic, he sees only the frantic scramble to meet today's needs, to pay tomorrow's rent. Beyond that it's hard for parents to see. In such circumstances, of what can children dream?

The authors of one famous study argue, in fact, that such boys face "a series of mounting disadvantages"—that is, poverty, lack of education and vocational guidance, no role models in prestige occupations, no personal contacts to help push a career along—all come together to create an inability to plan for the future and form a vicious circle from which few ever escape.[8] It is in this process that the class structure is preserved—as if in ice—from generation to generation.

It should be clear by now that the lack of planning to which I refer is not due, as some social scientists insist, to some debilitating inability of the working class to delay gratifications; indeed, there seem to be precious few available to delay.[9] Rather in the context of their lives and daily struggles, looking either backward or forward makes little sense; planning for the future seems incongruous. Consequently, work life generally is not planned; it just happens. A thirty-six-year-old refinery worker, the oldest of four children, recalls:

> I didn't think much about it. I just kind of took things as they came. I figured I knew I'd work; I worked most of my life. I started working at real jobs when I was fourteen. I worked in an upholstery place then. I used to carry those big bolts of material, and keep the workers supplied with whatever they needed, and I kept the place clean. That gave me a good idea of what work was all about. There wasn't much point in dreaming. I guess you could say in my family we didn't—maybe I should say couldn't—plan our lives; things just happened.

And from a thirty-three-year-old truck driver who grew up in a series of foster homes, we hear:

> In the kind of life I lived, you didn't think about tomorrow. I didn't know where I'd be tomorrow, so how could I plan for it? In fact, I don't think I knew *how* to make plans. I wasn't even so sure about today. Tomorrow just didn't exist; it didn't have any reality.

To the degree that either men or women could answer questions about their hopes for the future, the answers were largely in the realm of fantasy[10]—for the boys: a cowboy, a pilot, a star athlete. But not one man ever recalled thinking of, let alone planning for, a professional career. With fathers, uncles, and neighbors largely in marginal jobs, there were no live models of any other kind of work. Mostly the men say they just expected to grow up, get married, and work just as their fathers had. Even the modest wish to become a policeman takes on the color of an unattainable fantasy. A twenty-eight-year-old machinist, from a family of four children with an intermittently employed father, recalls:

> I dreamed I wanted to be a policeman, but I just never followed through with it.
>
> *Why was that?*
>
> I really didn't think I was smart enough, I guess. I knew you had to go through three, maybe four, years of college. And I don't know, I just kind of let it go.
>
> Even if I *had* thought I was smart enough for college, there was no way I ever thought about going to college. I guess the really big dream was just to get out of high school and get a job. Things were tough at home. I wanted more than anything else to get some money in my pockets so I could do something, have some fun once in a while. Now I can't figure out why I thought working was such a big deal. But how can you know things like that when you're a kid?

Among the women, a few recall girlhood dreams of being a model or an actress, but most remember wanting only to marry and live happily ever after:[11]

> I never had any goals to be anything, except I always figured I'd get married and have kids, and that would be enough for anybody.

The dream of the knight who comes to sweep her off her feet:

> I used to fantasize a lot about boys, and I'd dream that one day somebody would come on his white charger and we would fly off and live happily ever after in a vine-covered cottage.

. . . or the prince who rescues Cinderella from ashes and cruelty, was alive and vital for most of these young women when they were children:

> When I was about eight or so, I went to live with my oldest brother. I had to clean the house and do all the hard work there, and their own daughter didn't do nothing. Then, if we both got new shoes and she wore hers out faster than I did (and she always did), they gave her mine and I had to wear my old ones. I used to sit in that house and dream about how some day some wonderful man who looked like a prince would come and take me away, and how we'd live happily ever after.

It's not that the girls from middle-class homes dreamed such different dreams. But along with the marriage fantasy, there was for them some sense of striving for their own development. Even if that were related to enhancing marriage prospects (that is, with a college education a girl can make a "better match"), some aspiration related to self existed alongside it. And, in fact, for those middle-class women, marriage came much later since it was deferred until after college. Moreover, once these girls left home for college, they had at least some of the freedom and autonomy young people so deeply desire while, at the same time, they were engaged in an activity that brings status and respect from both family and peers.

For most young working-class girls, on the other hand, getting married was—and probably still is—the singularly acceptable way out of an oppressive family situation and into a respected social status—the only way to move from girl to woman.[12] Indeed, traditionally among girls of this class, being grown up *means* being married. Thus, despite the fact that the models of marriage they see before them don't look like their cherished myths, their alternatives often are so slim and so terrible—a job they hate, more years under the oppressive parental roof—that working-class girls tend to blind themselves to the realities and cling to the fantasies with extraordinary tenacity. For in those fantasies there remains some hope:

Things were so ugly in my family—my father drunk and in a rage, hitting one of us or beating my mother up. My mother worked most of the time. She had to because Daddy couldn't, seeing as how you could never know when he'd be drunk. She'd come home and fix supper, then we'd all sit around and wait and wait. Finally, Mom would give us kids our supper. Eventually my father came home, and if he was drunk, he'd storm around. Maybe he'd knock the pots off the stove and make a holy mess. Or maybe he'd take out after one of us or my mother.

When I think about it now, it sounds crazy, but honestly, the worse things got at home, the more I used to dream about how I was going to marry some good, kind, wise man who would take care of me; and how we'd have beautiful children; and how we'd live in our nice house; and how we'd always love each other and be happy.

Not so crazy, when one realizes that there were no models in their lives of women who do interesting or rewarding work; indeed, few models of women who do anything but endure:

I used to get mad at my mother because she'd just stay there and take anything my father dished out. She wouldn't protect herself and she wouldn't protect us kids. My father would rant and rave like a maniac; he would get very irrational and had a lot of brute strength.

But now I think back and I understand her better, and I think maybe I shouldn't have been so mad at her then. She was just as scared as I was, I guess. He used to hit her, too, and shove her around plenty; a lot more than he shoved me around. And when he's so much bigger and stronger, and you got four kids to take care of, what's a woman supposed to do?

"When he's so much bigger and stronger . . . what's a woman supposed to do?" A good question: one it only recently has occurred to social scientists, male or female, to ask.[13] Yet even small girls in many working-class homes already know that men's greater strength is one source of male domination over women.

When the mother worked outside the home, it was a hard, tedious, often demeaning job from which she returned home tired and angry and with yet another day's work before her as she picked up her household chores:

My mom did domestic work, and it always seemed like she never stopped working. She'd come home and clean the house, and cook dinner, and clean up the clothes, and fix our lunches for the next day. It seemed like no matter what time you woke up at night when we were little, Mom was still up doing something—ironing or something. When we got older, we kids helped some, but there was always more for her to do, it seemed.

And you know, she was never late with a meal. We ate at five-thirty every night of our lives. My father came home at five, and he got cleaned up and had a beer; then we ate. My mother always taught us that you shouldn't keep a man waiting for his supper after a hard day's work. You know, it's only recently that I began to realize that she worked hard all day, too, and nobody *ever* made supper for her. No wonder she was always in a bad mood.

Sometimes, of course, children—especially girls—were expected to take over those chores. One thirty-six-year-old cannery worker, mother of three and married for twenty years, recalls her life, her fantasies, and the paucity of alternatives:

My mom worked on and off when we were growing up. There were five of us kids, and the house we lived in was crowded and a mess all the time. My older sister and I were expected to keep things up—you know, cleaning and picking up, doing the dishes, watching the younger kids, keeping them clean, all that stuff. And let me tell you, doing the wash in those days was a lot different than now. We did it the hard way; I mean, boiling the water and scrubbing the clothes on one of those old-fashioned wash boards. You know, the kind you don't ever see anymore.

And during those years, what did you think you'd like to do or be when you grew up?

All I wanted was just to grow up and get out of there. I used to dream about how I'd grow up and get married and live in one of those big, beautiful houses like they show in the magazines—you know, magazines like *House Beautiful*. God, all the hours I spent looking at those magazines, and dreaming about how I would live in one of those houses with all that beautiful furniture, and everything just right; and how my husband would come home at night; and how I'd look beautiful waiting for him; and how the kids would be pretty and good; and how we'd all be happy together.

Life turns out a lot different in the end, doesn't it? [*Looking down at her hands folded in her lap and speaking softly, shyly.*] I guess you'll think I'm silly, but I still look at those magazines and dream about that life.

Once in a while, a woman did perceive some alternatives, but the circumstances of her life combined with her experiences at school to push her back into her "place."[14] Witness the story of a twenty-five-year-old mother of three who grew up in a family where both parents were alcoholics, and whose memories of childhood are dominated by images of fighting, drunken parents, squabbling siblings, and appalling poverty:

I started working when I was about twelve as a kind of live-in baby-sitter–housekeeper for a family with three little kids. That family was my fantasy; they gave me a kind of an idea of what a different kind of life could be like. You know, it was like they gave me an idea of something I could work for. It was like because of them I knew there was something better going on somewhere.

Given that, what did you think you'd like to do or be when you grew up?

I was a good student, and somehow I could lose myself in school. And I used to love some of my teachers; they knew so much, and everybody treated them with respect. So I used to dream about wanting to be a teacher.

I used to dream about having a family, too; I mean, I dreamed about having children. But it's funny, I never thought about getting married, just about my being a teacher. I actually was in college prep in high school, even though my counselor didn't think it was such a good idea because there was nobody to help me through college.

Then, when I was going into the twelfth grade, my father got sick and went to the hospital. My counselor told me then that she didn't think I would have the strength to go through with going to college all by myself. So she got me a scholarship. It wasn't much of a scholarship; it was to a beauty college instead of to a real college. [*Sadly.*] I don't know; I guess she was right. Anyway, she was sure she was, so I did what she told me. And then, not long after that—I was seventeen—I got married.

In most families, there was only enough money for daily necessities, sometimes not even for those. Yet, interestingly, even where financial need was compelling, it usually was the boys who *had* to work. For the girls, it was often elective; most stayed home and prepared for the life of a housewife. One twenty-eight-year-old woman, now married ten years with three chldren and employed throughout most of her marriage in a variety of part-time occupations, sums it up neatly:

My brother had to work after school, but I didn't. I never wanted to work, and I didn't have to. After all, boys *have to* learn how to work, but it doesn't make much difference if girls don't learn how because they're going to get married and won't have to.

And so the myth persists. Despite the fact that as long ago as 1960, 60 percent of all the women in the labor force were married, and over 30 percent of all married women living in intact families worked, most girls and their families still believed that they wouldn't "have to."[15] Just as today, even in the face of their own experiences when they work throughout most of their married years, most women define that as "temporary."

The boys, on the other hand, went to work early, partly to help the family:

Things were slim around the house; sometimes there wasn't enough food. By the time I was thirteen, I was working—doing all kinds of odd jobs. We needed the money.

. . . partly to get some pocket money for themselves:

It wasn't any fun not having any money for extras like other kids had. If you wanted something for yourself, or some money so you could have some fun, you just had to go out and get it. And that's what I did. I knew my way around, and by the time I was fourteen, I had my first real job in a lumber yard. After that I always had at least a little money so I could hang around with the guys and do things with them.

. . . and partly because it was one of the ways in which their families prepared them to meet future responsibilities:

We learned young to honor work. That's what it was about in my family—work, all work. I suppose I'm glad about that now, because I see a lot of people who don't know how to work. But on the other side, I didn't like it much then. I didn't have any freedom. I saw other kids my age going out, doing things after school; you know, having fun. [*Pauses uncomfortably.*] And well, I had to go to work.

By the time I was fourteen, I had two jobs. I worked in a bakery from two A.M. until school started. Then I came home and changed my clothes, and I went to school. Then I came home again and changed my clothes again, and I went to work in a gas station.

I'm not complaining, mind you, because now I see that it was good for me. If I didn't have that kind of training, I'd be a lot worse off than I am today. I'm making a good living now, and I know how to take care of myself and my family. My old man knew what he was doing when he made sure I'd grow up and appreciate the value of money and work. It's just that kids don't know that when it's happening to them, because then all they want is to go out and have some fun.

—Thirty-one-year-old mechanic,
father of two, married nine years

Were there no tales of happy childhoods? The answer: very few. There are always a few good memories, some families less troubled, more loving than others; but happy childhoods: no. Often people implored, even commanded me, to believe they had happy home lives as children. I tried. I told myself that as an observer from the professional middle class, I couldn't understand what would make a working-class child happy. But that didn't make sense. I recalled my own impoverished background. Yes, there were happy moments—an ice cream cone, a small toy, an infrequent and unexpected family outing, a rare approving remark from a harassed, frightened, and overburdened mother, a few cents occasionally to spend as I would and the exquisite agony of making a choice.

But those were isolated moments, not descriptive of the warp and woof of my life. The dominant memories of childhood for me, as for the people I met, are of pain and deprivation—both material and emotional, for one follows the other almost as certainly as night follows day.

Parents who must meet each day with worry and fear are too preoccupied with the existential and material realities of life to have much left in the way of emotional support for their children. To them, it often seems the deepest possible expression of love just to do what they must to keep the family together. "You're lucky you're not in an orphanage," my widowed mother would remind me angrily—or at least so it seemed to my child's ears. And with terror I thought, "I am," even as I hated her for the threat. Today, I know it was a statement of her love—hard for a child to experience, but true nevertheless.

There's pain in such acknowledgments, and a terrible sense of disloyalty—even for me—to parents who did their best in a world where the cards were stacked against them. So we try to tell ourselves—and even more, to tell strangers—it wasn't so bad. But no matter how hard we try, it comes out "bad." The people I met tried; and I tried to help them:

Tell me some of the good things you remember about growing up in your family.

Most often the question was met with a series of halting attempts to enumerate the "good" memories. Usually, the conversation limped to an uncomfortable end:

We used to go out for a ride on Sunday sometimes. It was nice to be all together in the car.

. . .or:

I remember my father coming home sometimes and taking us all down to the railroad station to watch the trains. I liked that. I liked being with him.

But the car rides didn't happen often, and this father at least usually came home too drunk to go to the railroad station—those things had already been said with passion and force. This new information seemed insubstantial—to them as well as to me—born of a sentimental yearning to rewrite history so as to protect self and parents from exposure:

Tell me some of the good things you remember about growing up in your family:

Struggling thoughtfully with the question, one thirty-five-year-old machinist spoke more openly than most—a poignant truth that applied to most of the others as well:

It's hard to remember the good things as if they were a real part of my life because they didn't happen most of the time. I'm trying to think about whether we were happy or not, and it's hard. I can't say because I don't think we even thought about things like that in those days.

These, then, are the early experiences of the women and men who fill the pages of this book; the story of the families of the families I met. For all, even the most settled livers, life was often mean and hard—hanging in a delicate balance, easily upset. For in a society not committed to the full employment of its work force, work often was not available to the men, and parents could not adequately clothe or care for their children. Thus, even where children recall a loving, stable home, they also recall at least periods of unemployment, poverty, and deprivation.

Such periods take their toll on family life—on the self-image of the man as the "responsible" head of the household, on his self-respect, and, indeed, on the respect accorded him in the family. For if the men and women in these families accept the belief that anybody can make it if he has the brains and the will, then the man who can't must be seen as lacking—a failure. In a society where the roles in the family are rigidly fixed and stereotyped according to sex—where it's *his* job to support the family, *her* job to feed and tend it—the man who cannot perform his assigned task is stigmatized, both by himself and by those around him.

Thus, whether settled- or hard-living, most of the working-class adults I spoke with recalled childhoods where, at best, "things were tight" financially. They recall parents who worked hard, yet never quite made it; homes that were overcrowded; siblings or selves who got into "trouble"; a preoccupation with the daily struggle for survival that precluded planning for a future. Whether they recall angry, discontented, drunken parents, or quiet, steady, "always-there" parents, the dominant theme is struggle and trouble. These realities not only reflect the past, but dominate the present—consciously or unconsciously underpinning the alternatives children can perceive, the choices they make, and the way they play out their roles in the new families they form as adults.

Notes

1. Although well aware of the problems of defining alcoholism, I use the word here because that is the way my respondents described what they saw in their families. Under any circumstances, from the evidence they presented, there is little doubt that they were describing problem drinkers according to the generally accepted definitions in the field. See, for example, Plaut (1967:137–38) who describes problem drinking as "a repetitive use of beverage alcohol causing physical, psychological, or social harm to the drinker or to others."

While the 40 percent problem drinkers reported here seems shockingly high, the figure actually is congruent with findings from national studies which sampled the household population—that is, which excluded the institutionalized, the homeless, and the skid-row derelicts. For example, in several such national samples in which the researchers also controlled for class, Don Cahalan and his associates (1967) found that among men aged twenty-one to fifty-nine, one half reported some drinking problem within the last three years, and one third had some fairly severe problems during that period. Their findings lead them to conclude, moreover, that "men of lower social status have more severe problems, and a higher ratio of interpersonal problems to alcohol intake." And, further, that "the primary independent correlates of drinking problems appear to be socio-economic status, large city residence, age, childhood deprivations, race, and religion." All together, then, the findings of their very comprehensive work support my own, and suggest that the proportion of problem drinkers in all strata of the population is even higher than the gross national statistics suggest, and highest among those at the lower levels of the socio-economic order. See also U.S. Department of Health, Education, and Welfare (1971:28) which presents an occupational breakdown of drinking patterns. Among male manual workers who drink at all, 25 percent of the craftsmen, 36 percent of the semi-skilled, 28 percent of the service workers, and 27 percent of the laborers are classified as heavy drinkers.

2. Presently, over half the teenage marriages in the United States end in divorce. Schoen (1975) examined the California divorce statistics for 1969 and found a strong inverse relationship between the age at first marriage and the likelihood of divorce—that is, the lower the age at first marriage for both males and females, the higher the chance that the marriage would end in divorce. Thus, the California divorce rates imply that three out of seven first marriages undertaken by males between eighteen and twenty-five and females between sixteen and twenty-four will end in divorce. For those who marry at the lower end of these age ranges, however, the risk of divorce is *twice as great* as it is for those who marry at the higher end of the ranges.

The proportion of such young marriages is highest among those who do not go to college, which generally means young people of the working class. Shostak (1969:175) writes: "Oriented toward early marriages, the blue-collar accommodators are heavily represented among the half-million or more seventeen-year-old young women who marry before their eighteenth birthday, a bloc equal to 25 percent of all seventeen-year-old females. They are also disproportionately found among half of all young women who marry before they are twenty years of age." If this is true of the present generation about which Shostak writes, it probably was even more true a generation ago before the boom in college attendance in all sectors of the population.

Among the respondents in this study, the median age of the women at *first marriage* was 18.1. Given the trend data—that is, the increase in the median age at first marriage over the last two decades (U.S. Bureau of the Census, 1974:66)—it is a reasonable assumption that their mothers generally were married somewhat younger. Indeed, often enough, by way of explaining a divorce or a mother who left her children, I was told that, "My mother was just a kid herself when she got married—only fifteen."

3. In no way are these words intended to give support and legitimacy to the traditional role divisions in the family. They are simply a statement of fact about the structure of family relations— that is, given women's traditional role in the family, *they* are likely to take the heat of a child's anger, to be blamed when a child feels less than adequately nurtured and loved. If the structure of roles in the family were changed so that men had the primary nurturing tasks, then it would be fathers instead of mothers who would be the source of disappointment and the target of hostility.

4. For a poignant, first-hand story of life in such a family, see Sharon Isabell's (1974) autobiographical novel. Also Cottle (1976) for a compelling account of a mother and child's ambivalent love-hate feelings toward each other—the mother, because she can't protect her child from the pain and suffering of poverty; the child, because she wants that protection so desperately yet understands her mother's inability to give it to her.

5. Howell (1973). Others have made parallel and equally useful distinctions. Bernard (1966) speaks of the "externally adapted" and the "acculturated"; Gans (1962) describes the "action seekers" and the "routine seekers"; Rainwater (1970) distinguishes between the "expressive' and the "instrumental" lifestyles; and Shostak (1969) makes the tripartite distinction among the "rebels," the "accommodators," and the "achievers." Rather than add another set of terms to those that already exist, I have chosen to use Howell's "hard-living–settled-living" distinction primarily because his referent is families while, except for Bernard (1966), the other work cited here refers to individuals, usually to men. Shostak (1969:169–184) does have a brief chapter entitled, "Blue-Collar Daughters" in which ". . . particular attention [is] paid to the vast bulk of white urban daughters of blue-collarites who appear to be accommodators—now and forevermore." Forever is, of course, a very long-term prediction.

6. Shostak (1969:54–57) remarking upon the same phenomenon, writes: "Blue-collarites begin and end the workday with the knowledge that their employ could hardly have less status. . . . They may earn enough to 'command respect,' but the low blue-collar origins of their high earnings may undermine both their self-esteem and the respect they command from others."

7. Sennett & Cobb (1973:171–172) insist that "no more urgent business in a life can exist than establishing a sense of personal dignity." In this society, they argue, the quest for personal dignity is at the root of consumerism. "In consuming . . . men are not trying to keep capitalism alive, nor have they arrived at that identification with the Establishment that Marcuse depicts." Rather, their consuming behavior is in the interest of "personal restoration." Ironically, these "manifold acts of personal restoration added to one another . . . become transformed into a force that keeps the wounding society powerful."

8. Lipset and Bendix (1964:197–199). In an early but still relevant study, Hollingshead (1949:267–287) analyzes the ways in which family influence and prestige (or lack of it) determine job prospects for adolescents. Cf., also Blau and Duncan (1967); Goyder and Curtis (1975); Rogoff (1953).

9. For the seminal article on the deferred gratification pattern, see Schneider and Lysgaard (1953). Miller, Riessman, and Seagull (1965) offer an excellent critique. For the related literature on the culture of poverty, see Coser (1969); Davis (1946); Hyman (1953); Knupfer (1947); Lewis (1968); Liebow (1966); Miller (1958); Moynihan (1965); Riessman (1962). Criticisms of culture of poverty theory are to be found in Billingsley (1968); Carper (1968); Coles (1968); Gans (1968); Gladwin (1967); Lewis (1967); Mackler and Giddings (1967); Miller and Riessman (1964, 1968); Rainwater (1966, 1970); Rainwater and Yancy (1967); Riessman (1966); Rodman (1965); Valentine (1968, 1971).

10. For others who have observed the unrealistic fantasy-like aspirations of lower-class adolescents, see Danserau (1964); Furstenberg (1971); Hollingshead (1949); Howell (1973); Kerchkoff (1972); Kohn (1969); Lipset and Bendix (1964); Nagasawa (1971).

11. Cf. Komarovsky (1962); Rainwater, Coleman, and Handel (1959); Shostak (1960).

12. Komarovsky (1962:24–26) also points to the "marriage as liberation" theme in the lives of working-class youth, both female and male.

13. See Collins (1971); Gillespie (1972).

14. In a case study of a high school, Cicourel and Kitsuse (1963) present a vivid account of

how *routine* decisions of school guidance and counseling personnel reinforce and perpetuate the existing class distinctions. Greer (1972), confronting the persistent American myth that schools are the primary agency of upward mobility, argues that the real achievement of the schools in America has been their ability to train children to accept the prevailing class structure and their fate as workers in the industrial system. Katz (1968, 1971, 1975), analyzing the roots of educational reform movements, also digs beneath the ideology to show the same reality. Wilson and Portes (1975) also challenge those studies which argue for the primacy of family influence and attitudes and other social psychological variables in determining educational attainment. Instead, their examination of a national sample shows that "personal influences and subjective orientations are of less significance than the structural effects of parental resources and the bureaucratic evaluation of ability."

For other expositions of the ways schools serve the class structure of America, see Bowles (1972); Bowles and Gintis (1973, 1976); Clark (1965); Coleman, et al. (1966); Dennison (1969); Dentler, et al. (1967); *Harvard Educational Review* (1969, 1973); Hentoff (1966); Herndon (1965); Hollingshead (1949); Jencks, et al. (1972); Kozol (1967); Leacock (1969); Miller and Riessman (1968); Parenti (1973); Rist (1970); Rosenthal (1973); Rosenthal and Jacobson (1968); Rubin (1972); Schafer, et al. (1970); Schrag (1968); Sexton (1964); Stein (1971); U.S. Commission on Civil Rights (1967).

15. The figures cited here are taken from the U.S. Bureau of the Census (1974:340). See also Dahlstrom and Liljestrom (1971); Myrdal and Klein (1956); Peterson (1967); U.S. Department of Labor, Women's Bureau (1968).

References

Bernard, Jessie. (1966) *Marriage and Family Among Negroes*. Englewood Cliffs, N.J.: Prentice-Hall.

Billingsley, Andrew. (1968) *Black Families in White America*. Englewood Cliffs, N.J: Prentice-Hall.

Blau, Peter M. and Duncan, Otis D. (1967) *The American Occupational Structure*. New York: John Wiley.

Bowles, Samuel. (1972) "Getting Nowhere: Programmed Class Stagnation." *Society* 9(1972):42–49.

Bowles, Samuel and Gintis, Herbert. (1973) "I.Q. in the U.S. Class Structure." *Social Policy* 3 (1973):65–96.

Bowles, Samuel and Gintis, Herbert. (1976) *Schooling in Capitalist America*. New York: Basic Books.

Cahalan, Don; Crisin, Iris; and Crossley, Helen. (1967) *American Drinking Patterns*. Report No. 3. Publication of the Social Research Group, George Washington University, Washington, D.C.

Carper, Laura. (1968) "The Negro Family and the Moynihan Report." In *Poverty: Views from the Left*, ed. Jeremy Larner and Irving Howe. New York: William Morrow.

Cicourel, Aaron V. and Kitsuse, John. (1963) *The Educational Decision-Makers*. Indianapolis: Bobbs-Merrill.

Clark, Kenneth. (1965) *Dark Ghetto*. New York: Harper and Row.

Coleman, James, et al. (1966) *Equality of Educational Opportunity*. Washington: U.S. Government Printing Office.

Coles, Robert. (1968) *Children of Crisis*. New York: Delta Books.

Collins, Randall. (1971) "A Conflict Theory of Sexual Stratification." *Social Problems* 19:3–21.

Coser, Lewis A. (1969) "Unanticipated Consequences of Liberal Theorizing." *Social Problems* 16:263–272.

Cottle, Thomas J. (1976) "Angela: A Child-Woman." *Social Problems* 23.

Dahlstrom, Edmund and Liljestrom, Rita. (1971) "The Family and Married Women at Work." In *The Changing Roles of Men and Women*, ed. Edmund Dahlstrom. Boston: Beacon Press.

Danserau, H. Kirk. (1964) "Work and the Teen-Age Blue-Collarite." In *Blue-Collar World,* ed. Arthur Shostak and William Gomberg. Englewood Cliffs, N.J.: Prentice-Hall.

Davis, Allison. (1946) "The Motivation of the Underprivileged Worker." In *Industry and Society,* ed. by William F. Whyte. New York: McGraw-Hill.

Dennison, George. (1969) *The Lives of Children.* New York: Vintage.

Dentler, Robert A., et al. (1967) *The Urban R's.* New York: Praeger.

Furstenberg, Frank F., Jr. (1971) "The Transmission of Mobility Orientation in the Family." *Social Forces* 49.

Gans, Herbert J. (1962) *The Urban Villagers: Group and Class in the Life of Italian-Americans.* New York: Free Press.

Gans, Herbert J. (1968) *People and Plans.* New York: Basic Books.

Gillespie, Dair. (1972) "Who Has the Power? The Marital Struggle." In *Family, Marriage, and the Struggle of the Sexes,* ed. Hans P. Dreitzel. New York: Macmillan.

Gladwin, Thomas. (1967) *Poverty USA.* Boston: Little, Brown.

Goyder, John C. and Curtis, James E. (1975) "A Three-Generational Approach to Trends in Occupational Mobility." *American Journal of Sociology* 81 (1975): 129–138.

Greer, Colin. (1972) *The Great School Legend.* New York: Basic Books.

Harvard Educational Review, eds. (1969) *Equal Educational Opportunity.* Cambridge, Mass.: Harvard University Press.

Harvard Educational Review, eds. (1973) *Perspectives on "Inequality: A Reassessment of the Effect of Family and Schooling in America."* Cambridge, Mass.: Harvard University Press.

Hentoff, Nat. (1966) *Our Children Are Dying.* New York: Viking.

Herndon, James. (1965) *The Way It Spozed to Be.* New York: Simon and Schuster.

Hollingshead, August B. (1949) *Elmtown's Youth.* New York: John Wiley.

Howell, Joseph T. (1973) *Hard Living on Clay Street.* Garden City, N.Y.: Anchor Books, 1973.

Hyman Herbert H. (1953) "The Value Systems of Different Classes: A Social Psychological Contribution to the Analysis of Stratification." In *Class, Status, and Power,* ed. Reinhard Bendix and Seymour Martin Lipset. New York: Free Press.

Isabell, Sharon. (1974) *Yesterday's Lessons.* Oakland, Calif.: Women's Press Collective.

Jencks, Christopher, et al. (1972) *Inequality: A Reassessment of the Effect of Family and Schooling in America.* New York: Basic Books.

Katz, Michael B. (1968) *The Irony of Early School Reform: Educational Innovation in Mid-Nineteenth Century Massachusetts.* Cambridge, Mass.: Harvard University Press.

Katz, Michael B. (1971) "The Present Moment in Educational Reform." *Harvard Educational Review* 41 (1971):342–359.

Katz, Michael B. (1975) *The People of Hamilton, Canada West: Family and Class in a Nineteenth-Century City.* Cambridge, Mass.: Harvard University Press.

Kerchkoff, Alan. (1972) *Socialization and Social Class.* Englewood Cliffs, N.J.: Prentice-Hall, 1972.

Knupfer, Genevieve. (1947) "Portrait of the Underdog." *Public Opinion Quarterly* 11 (1947):103–114.

Kohn, Melvin. (1969) *Class and Conformity.* Homewood, Ill.: Dorsey Press.

Komarovsky, Mirra. (1962) *Blue-Collar Marriage.* New York: Vintage Books.

Kozol, Jonathan. (1967) *Death at an Early Age.* Boston: Houghton Mifflin.

Leacock, Eleanor Burke. (1969) *Teaching and Learning in City Schools.* New York: Basic Books.

Lewis, Hylan. (1967) "Culture, Class and Family Life Among Low-Income Urban Negroes." In *Employment, Race, and Poverty,* ed. Arthur N. Ross and Herbert Hill. New York: Harcourt, Brace, and World.

Lewis, Oscar. (1968). *La Vida.* New York: Vintage Books.

Liebow, Elliot. (1966) *Tally's Corner.* Boston: Little, Brown.

Lipset, Seymour Martin and Bendix, Reinhard. (1964) *Social Mobility in Industrial Society.* Berkeley: University of California Press.

Mackler, Bernard and Giddings, Morsley G. (1967) "Cultural Deprivation: A Study in Mythology." In *The Urban R's,* ed. Robert A. Dentler. New York: Praeger.

Miller, Walter B. (1958) "Lower Class Culture as a Generating Milieu of Gang Delinquency." *Journal of Social Issues* 14:5–19.

Miller, S. M. and Riessman, Frank. (1964) "The Working-Class Subculture: A New View." In

Blue-Collar World, ed. Arthur Shostak and William Gomberg. Englewood Cliffs, N.J.: Prentice-Hall.

Miller, S. M. and Riessman, Frank. (1968) *Social Class and Social Policy.* New York: Basic Books.

Miller, S. M.; Riessman, Frank; and Seagull, Arthur. (1965) "Poverty and Self-Indulgence: A Critique of Non-Deferred Gratification Patterns." In *Poverty in America,* ed. Louis A. Ferman, et. al. Ann Arbor: University of Michigan Press.

Moynihan, Daniel P. (1965) *The Negro Family: The Case for National Action.* Publication of the U.S. Department of Labor, Washington, D.C.

Myrdal, Alva and Klein, Viola. (1956) *Women's Two Roles: Home and Work.* London: Routledge and Kegan Paul.

Nagasawa, Richard. (1971) "Social Class Differentials in Success Striving." *Pacific Sociological Review* 14 (1974):215–232.

Parenti, Michael. (1973) "Politics of the Classroom." *Social Policy* 4:852–872.

Peterson, Esther. (1967) "Working Women." In *The Woman in America,* ed. Robert J. Lifton. Boston: Beacon Press.

Plaut, Thomas F. (1967) *Alcohol Problems: A Report to the Nation.* New York: Oxford University Press.

Rainwater, Lee. (1966) "Crucible of Identity: The Negro Lower-Class Family." *Daedalus* 95: 172–216.

Rainwater, Lee. (1970) *Behind Ghetto Walls.* Chicago: Aldine Publishing.

Rainwater, Lee; Coleman, Richard P.; and Handel, Gerald. (1959) *Working-man's Wife.* New York: McFadden Books.

Rainwater, Lee and Yancey, William L. (1967) *The Moynihan Report and the Politics of Controversy.* Cambridge, Mass.: M.I.T. Press.

Riessman, Frank. (1962) *The Culturally Deprived Child.* New York: Harper and Brothers.

Riessman, Frank. (1966) "In Defense of the Negro Family." *Dissent* 13:141–144.

Rist, Ray C. (1970) "Student Social Class and Teacher Expectations: The Self-Fulfilling Prophecy in Ghetto Education." *Harvard Educational Review* 40:411–451.

Rodman, Hyman. (1965) "The Lower-Class Value Stretch." In *Poverty in America,* ed. Louis Ferman, et al. Ann Arbor: University of Michigan Press.

Rogoff, Natalie. (1953) *Recent Trends in Occupational Mobility.* Glencoe: Free Press.

Rosenthal, Robert. (1973) "The Pygmalion Effect Lives." *Psychology Today* 7:56–63.

Rosenthal, Robert and Jacobson, Lenore. (1968) *Pygmalion in the Classroom.* New York: Holt, Rinehart, and Winston.

Rubin, Lillian B. (1972) *Busing and Backlash: White Against White in an Urban School District.* Berkeley: University of California Press.

Schaefer, Walter E., et al. (1970) "Programmed for Social Class: Teaching in High School." *Trans-Action* 7:39–46.

Schneider, Lewis and Lysgaard, Sverre. (1953) "The Deferred Gratification Pattern: A Preliminary Study." *American Sociological Review* 18:142–149.

Schoen, Robert. (1975) "California Divorce Rates by Age at First Marriage and Duration of First Marriage." *Journal of Marriage and the Family* 37:548–555.

Schrag, Peter. (1968) *Village School Downtown.* Boston: Beacon Press.

Sennett, Richard and Cobb, Jonathan. (1973) *The Hidden Injuries of Class.* New York: Vintage Books.

Sexton, Patricia Cayo. (1964) "Wife of the 'Happy Worker.'" In *Blue-Collar World,* ed. Arthur Shostak and William Gomberg. Englewood Cliffs, N.J.: Prentice-Hall.

Shostak, Arthur B. (1969) *Blue-Collar Life.* New York: Random House.

Stein, Annie. (1971) "Strategies of Failure." *Harvard Educational Review* 41:158–204.

U.S. Bureau of the Census. (1974) *Statistical Abstract of the United States, 1974.* 95th ed. Washington, D.C.: U.S. Government Printing Office.

U.S. Commission on Civil Rights. (1967) *Racial Isolation in the Public Schools.* Washington, D.C.: U.S. Government Printing Office.

U.S. Department of Health, Education, and Welfare. (1971) *Alcohol and Health: First Special Report to the U.S. Congress.* Publication of the National Institute of Mental Health, Washington, D.C.

U.S. Department of Labor, Women's Bureau. (1968) "Working Wives—Their Contribution to Family Income." Publication of the U.S. Department of Labor, Wage and Labor Standards Administration, Washington, D.C.

Valentine, Charles A. (1968) *Culture and Poverty: A Critique and Counter Proposals.* Chicago: University of Chicago Press.

Valentine, Charles A. (1971) "Deficit, Difference, and Bicultural Models of Afro-American Behavior." *Harvard Educational Review* 41:137–157.

Wilson, Kenneth L. and Portes, Alejandro. (1975) "The Educational Attainment Process: Results from a National Sample." *American Journal of Sociology* 81:343–363.

30. Child-Keeping: "Gimme a Little Sugar"

The black community has long recognized the problems and difficulties that all mothers in poverty share. Shared parental responsibility among kin has been the response. The families I knew in The Flats told me of many circumstances that required co-resident kinsmen to take care of one another's children or situations that required children to stay in a household that did not include their biological parents.

Most of the adults involved in this study had been fostered at one time or another by kinsmen. Some of their own children are currently residing in the homes of kinsmen, or have been kept by kinsmen in the past. These alternatives enable parents to cope with poverty; they are possibilities that every mother understands.

People in The Flats often regard child-keeping[1] as part of the flux and elasticity of residence. The expansion and contraction of households, and the successive recombinations of kinsmen residing together, require adults to care for the children residing in their household. As households shift, rights and responsibilities with regard to children are shared. Those women and men who temporarily assume the kinship obligation to care for a child, fostering the child indefinitely, acquire the major cluster of rights and duties ideally associated with "parenthood."

Within a network of cooperating kinsmen, there may be three or more adults with whom, in turn, a child resides. In this cycle of residence changes, the size of the dwelling, employment, and many other factors determine where children sleep. Although patterns of eating, visiting, and child care may bring mothers and their children together for most of the day, the adults immediately responsible for a child change with the child's residence. The residence patterns of children in The Flats have structural implications for both the ways in which rights in children distribute socially and also the criteria by which persons are entitled to parental roles.

From the point of view of the children, there may be a number of women who act as "mothers" toward them; some just slightly older than the children themselves. A woman who intermittently raises a sister's or a niece's or a cousin's child regards their offspring as much her grandchildren as children born to her own son and daughter.

The number of people who can assume appropriate behaviors ideally associated with parental and grandparental roles is increased to include close kinsmen and friends. Consequently, the kin terms "mother," "father," "grandmother," and the like are not necessarily appropriate labels for describing the social roles. Children may retain ties with their parents and siblings and at the same time establish comparable relationships with other kinsmen. There is even a larger number of friends and relatives who may request a hug and kiss, "a little sugar," from children they watch grow up. But they do not consistently assume parental roles toward those children. Parental role behavior is a composite of many behavior patterns (Keesing 1969) and these rights and duties can be shared or transferred to other individuals.

Natural processes and the events of the life cycle create new child-care needs and new household alignments. It is not uncommon for young children residing in the homes of rather aging kin who become too old to care for them to be shifted to another kinsmen's home. At these times, the fostering parent often decides who is next in line to raise the child.

Loretta Smart, a forty-year-old Flats resident, was raised by her great-grandfather for the first five years of her life. "When I became five years old," Loretta told me, "my daddy just got too old to care for me. My mother was living in The Flats at the time, but my daddy asked my mother's brother and his wife to take me 'cause he really trusted them with me. I stayed with them and their three kids, but my mother came by and took care of us kids lots of times. When I was about nine years old my mother got married and from then on I stayed with her and her husband and he gave me his name."

Close kin may fully cooperate in child care and domestic activities during times when they do not live together. On the other hand, kin may actively assume a parental right in children, insisting upon joining a household in order to help in child care. Amanda Johnson's mother had a hard time keeping track of her three daughters even when they were pretty young. "My grandmother decided to move in with us to bring us up right. She was old then, on a small pension, and getting some help from her son. She stayed for about four years, but she and my mother didn't get on. They fought a lot. After my grandmother died, all our kin in The Flats was helping us out and we didn't want for nothing. One of my uncles kept us and fed us every Thursday and Sunday night when my mother worked, and another uncle got us all our clothing. We was really being kept good."

For many of the families I knew in The Flats, there were circumstances that required mothers and fathers to sleep in households apart from their children. A close look at the housing of children in homes that do not include their biological parents shows how misleading it is to regard child-keeping apart from residence patterns, alliances, and the interpersonal relationships of adults, and from the daily exchanges between kinsmen in the domestic network of the child.

The beginning of a new relationship between a man and woman, or the end of a marriage or consensual union, may cause a family to temporarily separate. Geraldine Penney left her husband because she was told that he had been "fooling around." "After that," she told me, "my family was really split in parts for a while. I sent my three oldest children to stay with my husband's aunt (husband's mother's sister), my middle girl stayed downstairs with my husband's mother, and my two youngest stayed here with my mother."

When a woman enters a new marriage or consensual relationship, occasionally she temporarily disperses her children among kin (Goody 1966; Midgett 1969). Soon after Flats resident Henrietta Davis returned to The Flats to take care of her own children, she told me, "My old man wanted me to leave town with him and get married. But he didn't want to take my three children. I stayed with him for about two years and my children stayed in town with my mother. Then she told me to come back and get them. I came back and I stayed."

Occasionally adolescents decide on their own that they want to live with a kinsmen other than the one with whom they are residing, and they have that option open to them. Boys, for example, who have maintained a close relationship with their natural father, may choose to go and live with him. Bernard Smith said that his father started buying him clothes when he was half grown. When Bernard was sixteen he decided to go and stay with his father because "he lived near the center of town." Bernard is twenty-five now, and even though he visits his mother nearly twice a week, he is still living with his father.

When a young girl becomes pregnant, the closest adult female kin of the girl, or of the unborn child, is expected to assume partial responsibility for the young child. Usually rights in such children are shared between the mother and appropriate female kin. If the mother is extremely young, she may "give the child" to someone who wants the child—for example, to the child's father's kin, to a childless couple, or to close friends. Lily Proctor ran away from home in Mississippi when she was fourteen. She ran off to Chicago and went to The Flats. The friends of kin from the South who took her in had two sons. She gave birth to the oldest boy's baby, but, Lily recalls, "I was in no way ready for a baby. The baby's grandmother [father's mother] wanted the baby, so I gave my baby to her and she adopted her as her own."

Children are sometimes given to non-kin who express love, concern, and a desire to keep the child. Oliver Lucas, a thirty-year-old Flats resident, lives with his mother and his sister and her children. Oliver and his kin have been raising his girl friend's child since she was a baby. "My girl friend had six children when I started going with her, but her baby daughter was really something else. I got so attached to that baby over about two years that when my girl friend and I quit, I asked if she would give the baby to me. She said fine, and my 'daughter' has been living with me, my mother, my grandmother, my sisters and brothers ever since. My daughter is ten years old now. She sees her mother now and then, and her father takes her to church with him sometimes, but our family is really the only family she's ever had."

Bonds of obligation, alliance, and dependence among kinsmen are created and strengthened in a variety of ways. Goods and services are the main currency exchanged among cooperating kinsmen. Children too may be transferred back and forth, "borrowed" or "loaned." It is not uncommon for individuals to talk about their residence away from their mother as a fact over which she had little or no control. For example, kin may insist upon "taking" a child to help out. Betty Simpson's story repeats itself with her own daughter. "My mother already had three children when I was born. She had been raised by her maternal great-aunt. After I was born my mother's great-aunt insisted on taking me to help my mother out. I stayed there after my mother got married and moved to The Flats. I wanted to move there too, but my 'mama' didn't want to give me up and my mother didn't want to fight with her. When I was fourteen I left anyway and my mother took me in. When my youngest daughter got polio my mother insisted on taking her. I got a job and lived nearby with my son. My mother raised my little girl until my girl died."

A mother may request or require kin to keep one of her children. An offer to keep the child of a kinsman has a variety of implications for child givers and receivers. It may be that the mother has come upon hard times and desperately wants her close kinsmen to temporarily assume responsibility for her children. Kinsmen rarely refuse such requests to keep one another's children. Likewise they recognize the right of kin to request children to raise away from their own parents (Goody 1966). Individuals allow kinsmen to create alliances and obligations toward one another, obligations which may be called upon in the future.

It might appear that the events described above contribute to a rather random relocation of individuals in dwellings, and a random distribution of the rights individuals acquire in children. But this is not the case. Individuals constantly face the reality that they may need the help of kinsmen for themselves and their children. As a result they anticipate these needs, and from year to year they have a very clear notion of which kinsmen would be willing to help. Their appraisal is simple because it is an outcome of calculated exchanges of goods and services between kinsmen. Consequently, residence patterns and the dispersing of children in households of kin are not haphazard.

Statistical Patterns

The responsibility of caring for children in The Flats is a kin obligation. It is not necessarily a role required of a single individual. Rights in children are delegated to kin who are participants in domestic networks of cooperation. In 1970 four-fifths of the children in The Flats were being raised by their mothers. One-fifth of the children were living with kinsmen rather than with their mothers.

Information on the frequency of fosterage collected from AFDC case histories in Jackson County shows that one-fifth of 694 dependent children were assigned to the welfare grant of a close female kinsman other than their mother. This means that the adult female responsible for the child is not the child's mother. Table 30.2 shows the frequency of fostering based upon AFDC case histories and the relationship of grantees to AFDC children on their grant and in their households.

These statistics on the frequency of fostering are in fact much lower than actual instances of child-keeping in The Flats. According to the AFDC case histories, 81 percent of the dependent children are being raised by their own mothers, and 18 percent by close female kinsmen. Grantees must claim that a dependent child is residing in their household in order to receive benefits for the child. But my personal contact with individuals whose case histories make up the statistical survey clearly shows disagreement between the record and actual residence patterns. Mothers temporarily shift the residence of their children in response to changes in their own personal relationships, or because of illness or pregnancy or housing problems. Dependent children, and the funds for these children, are dispersed into households of cooperating kinsmen. In the process of switching the residence of the children, mothers or grantees rarely report these residence changes to the welfare office.

Table 30.1. **Frequency of Child-Keeping, AFDC Data**

	Frequency	Percentage
Children raised by biological mother	559	81
Children raised by adult female kin	127	18
Children raised by non-kin	8	1
	694	100

Table 30.2. **Frequency of Child Keeping, AFDC Data**

	Frequency	Total	Percentage
Children raised by biological mother	559	559	81
Children raised by adult female kin:			
younger sibling	34		
sibling's child	34		
grandchild	24		
other kin	35	127	18
Non-kin	8	8	1
		694	100

The variance between the statistics and actual residence patterns is also demonstrated in detailed life histories of adults and children involved in the study. The residential life histories[2] of children show that at least one-third of the children have been "kept" by kinsmen one or two times during their childhood. Consequently the frequency of child-keeping in The Flats is higher than the AFDC statistics indicate. The lower limit of child-keeping in The Flats may be 20 percent, but the range of child-keeping is between 20 percent and 35 percent.

Important factors which show the relationship between patterns of child-keeping and the daily domestic organization of cooperating kinsmen are the age, status, and geographical location of the mothers of dependent children assigned to grantees who are not the child's mother. Field observations of 139 dependent children who are assigned to a grantee other than their mother revealed that practically one-half of those children's mothers generally resided in the same dwelling as their child. Many of those mothers were teen-agers when their first child was born. At the time of the survey only 6 percent of them were under eighteen. Table 30.3 shows the status and location of biological mothers whose dependent children werre assigned to AFDC grants of female kinsmen. According to the female kin now responsible for the children (Table 30.3), only 8 percent of the mothers had actually deserted their children. Three-fourths of the biological mothers of these children were living in The Flats at the time of the survey. They resided intermittently in the grantee's household, the household of a kinsman, or from time to time in a separate residence with male or female friends.

The examples above point to the confusion that can arise when statistical data is interpreted out of context. Statistical patterns do not divulge underlying cultural patterns. This confusion between statistics and cultural patterns underlies most interpretations of black family life.

Another clear example of this confusion is the assumption discussed earlier that black children derive all their jural kin through females. Widely popularized statistics on female-headed households have contributed to the classification of black households as matrifocal or matriarchal and to the assumption that black children derive nothing of sociological importance from their father. In fact, 69 percent of the fathers of AFDC children recognized their children by helping the children and their mothers out, and by providing the children with kinship affiliations. These children's father's kin assumed an active role in their nurturing.

Table 30.3. **Status and Location of Biological Mother**

Status and Location of Biological Mother	Frequency	Percentage
Married adult (over 18) Resides in grantee's house	34	24
Adult Lives in The Flats	34	24
Unmarried adult Resides in grantee's house	19	14
Mother deserted child	11	8
Married or unmarried minor Resides in grantee's house	9	6
Not ascertainable	32	24

Table 30.4. **Patterns of Child-Keeping, AFDC Data**

	Frequency	Percentage
Mother's kin	57	74
Father's kin	20	26
	77	100

The importance of the kinship links a child acquires through his mother and father is demonstrated in fostering patterns. Table 30.4, derived from the AFDC survey, shows the residence of children temporarily fostered in households of kinsmen at a given time.

Individual life histories reveal changes that have occurred in the residence of people in The Flats over the past fifty years. The data show the residence patterns of children fostered between 1925 and 1971. Table 30.5 shows residence patterns of children fostered in the households of kinsmen based on information derived from life histories of adults and children.

The ratio of children kept in the homes of kinsmen related through a child's mother or father is approximately the same in Table 30.4 and Table 30.5. Although the majority of children in this study lived with their mother or her kin, based on the statistical study of AFDC histories, one-fourth of the fostered children lived with their father's kin. Based on life histories, one-third of all children fostered are living with their father's kin.

When mothers apply for AFDC benefits for their dependent children, they are required to list, in order of rank, whom they expect to raise each of their children if they die or are unable to maintain custody of the child. The responses of mothers in Table 30.6 reflect their "expectations" regarding which kinsmen would be willing and able to raise their child.

When asked by welfare workers who they would expect to raise their child in the event of their own death, mothers of 228 children named their own blood relatives; mothers of 76 children named the child's father's kin. The agreement between the expectation of adult females regarding child-keeping and the statistical patterns of child-keeping over the life cycle is striking.

Table 30.5. **Patterns of Child-Keeping, Residence Histories**

	Frequency	Percentage
Mother's kin	43	69
Father's kin	19	31
	62	100

Table 30.6. **Child-Keeping Expectations, AFDC Data**

	Frequency	Percentage
Mother's kin	222	73
Father's kin	83	27
	305	100

The data obtained from AFDC case histories on the nurturing and fostering of children in The Flats, and from the life histories of people I knew well, suggest shared community expectations of rights and duties toward children. Both a child's mother's and father's socially recognized kinsmen are expected to assume parental rights and duties, and these expectations are borne out by actual events (Table 30.4 and Table 30.5). These predictable, stable child-keeping patterns provide a commanding contrast to the characterization of the black family life as "broken" and "disorganized."

Transactions in Parenthood

When and why kin can become "parents" is a matter of folk rights and duties in relation to children. The content of rights and duties in relation to children differs cross-culturally; residents in The Flats find it difficult to spell out particular rights and duties in children. The elaboration of rights pertaining to children is best elicited from observed scenes.

Scenes in which rights in children are in conflict must be analyzed in terms of the social context in which they occur. The social context of situations includes at least the following considerations: the participants present, the specific life histories of the participants, the socially meaningful occurrences, which preceded the event, and the rules which come into play. The scenes described below reflect tension or conflict among kinsmen over rights in children. These scenes provide a basis for identifying parental behaviors which may be shared.

The first scene takes place on the front porch of a house which Georgia and her three children share with Georgia's middle-aged Aunt Ethel and Ethel's boyfriend. Just before the incident occurred, Georgia and Ethel had fought over the division of housework and the utility bills. Aunt Ethel was angered by Georgia's lack of respect and her unwillingness to support her with the AFDC benefits Georgia received for her children. Georgia was willing to pay the rent but insisted that Ethel's boyfriend pay the utilities and that

Ethel take over more of the cooking and housework. Following the argument, Ethel's brother dropped by to visit. Ethel, her boyfriend, and her brother sat in the sunshine on the porch. Georgia and her children joined them. Georgia's daughter Alice was bothered by her first loose tooth. Alice continued whimpering on the porch as she had for most of the afternoon.

Scene One

Aunt Ethel yanked Alice's arm, drawing Alice nearer to her on the porch. Trouble over Alice's loose tooth had gone far enough. Ethel decided to pull the tooth. Without nudging it to see how loose it really was, Ethel fixed her fingers on the tooth and pulled with all her strength. Alice screamed with fear, kicked, and tried to bite her aunt. Alice's mother, Georgia, sat nearby, her tense body and bulging eyes voicing silent resistance to her aunt's physical act. After some moments of the struggle passed, a friend who happened to be visiting said, "Maybe the tooth isn't ready, Ethel," and Ethel let the child go. Georgia's tensed face and body relaxed as her daughter sprang into her arms in tears. Georgia turned to her friend, her eyelids lowered, expressing relief that her friend's quick words had stopped Ethel's performance.

Georgia had lived in the same household with her mother's sister Ethel for most of her life. Ethel helped Georgia's grandmother raise her. After her grandmother's death, Ethel assumed responsibility for Georgia. Georgia's mother lived close by, but she had nine other children to raise on her own. Ethel has been married twice, but she never had any children. She refers to Georgia as her daughter even though she did not become head of the household in which Georgia was raised until Georgia was thirteen. In recent years Georgia has been much closer to her mother than to her aunt. Nevertheless, Ethel regards Georgia's children as her own grandchildren.

Ethel's assertive behavior with regard to Alice was not an isolated event. In Georgia's presence, Ethel frequently demonstrates the right she holds to love, discipline, and even terrify Georgia's children. Ethel feels intense love, obligation, and bitterness toward Georgia's children. Not so long ago Georgia left her children with Ethel and ran off with a serviceman. When Georgia returned six months later she complained that Ethel had neglected her children, their clothes, their hair, and had not fed them well.

In the context of the previous fight between Ethel and Georgia, Ethel's action is partly a performance. Ethel is demonstrating the rights which she shares and may be expected to assume in relation to Georgia's children; rights she assumed when she forcefully attempted to pull Alice's tooth. She was angered by Georgia's arrogance just minutes before. In response, Ethel strongly asserted and strengthened the rights she has in Georgia's children, rights which she simultaneously shares with Georgia.

Commenting on the event to me, Georgia said, "Whatever happens to me, Ethel be the person to keep my kids. She already kept them once before. My mother, she ain't in no position to take them with all of her own, and I wouldn't have Aunt Flossie take them noway." But the episode disturbed Georgia. She didn't want to sit quietly and allow her child to be hurt, but she found herself powerless to act, considering her expectation that Ethel might be required to nurture her children.

The second scene takes place during a train ride to Chicago. It includes some of the same participants as those in the first scene. Kin to Ethel and Georgia rode the train together for a Fourth of July celebration with relatives. The group traveling together included Ethel's sisters Wilma and Ann, their children and grandchildren, and Georgia and her children—fourteen children in all.

Scene Two

The three sisters, Ethel, Wilma and Ann, sat toward the rear of the train, dressed fine for the occasion, ignoring the children's noise. Georgia sat across from them with her girl friend. A Coke bottle struck against the iron foot railing broke into pieces. Shrieks of laughter traveled from seat to seat where most of the small children—all cousins—were sitting together in the front of the train. Instantly Ethel walked forward to the front of the train by Wilma's young boy and began beating him harshly with her handbag. Then, showing she meant business, Ethel grabbed the boy next to the window who was laughing and gave him a few sharp slaps on the cheek. Wilma paid no attention to the cries of her two young boys. But when Ethel returned to her seat, Ann told her, "Don't you lay a hand on my granddaughter."

Throughout the trip Ethel shouted at, beat, and teased the children. Her sisters enjoyed the train ride and generally ignored the children. But Ethel's rights regarding each of her sister's children are not equivalent. From time to time, Ethel helped Wilma raise her children, including Georgia. Ethel has cared for or lived with Georgia's children for the past five years. Her rights in Wilma's and Georgia's children are recognized by both the mothers and the children. During the train ride, in the presence of her sisters and her niece, Ethel demonstrated her right to discipline the children of these kin. Likewise, the children observed the authority Ethel had over them.

On the other hand, Ethel's sister Ann had been married and was living fairly well. Ann was not an active participant in the domestic network of the sisters: she did not participate in the daily flow of exchanges among the sisters, and more often than not, Ann avoided exchanges of services which might obligate her to her sisters. Ann's daughters are self-supporting adults. It is quite unlikely that Ethel, Wilma, or Georgia would be expected or be required to raise Ann's granddaughters. In fact, Ann and her daughters consider themselves "better" than Ethel and Wilma. Usually Ann does not even allow her granddaughter to play with Wilma's children except for short periods of time. Rights over children come into conflict indicating who is excluded from parental rights in children. The third scene provides an example of who is not eligible to assume parental behavior patterns.

Vilda, Ann's daughter and Ethel's niece, had the opportunity to get a job she wanted. But she had to begin working immediately. Ann was working and Vilda had difficulty finding someone to care for her daughter Betty, who was four years old. She asked her cousin Georgia to take care of her daughter during the day and offered to pay her ten dollars a week.

Scene Three

Betty cried and put up a fuss at breakfast because she didn't want her mother to go to work, and she didn't want to stay at her Aunt Georgia's house. Betty said that Georgia beat her and yelled at her. Vilda and her mother, Ann, took the child to Georgia's house together that morning. They told Georgia that they didn't want her to yell or lay a hand on Betty.

This incident clearly communicated to Georgia that her cousin did not respect her and did not consider her an equal. Georgia made a big issue over this event to her friends and close kin. She said that Ann and Vilda were spoiling Betty and that "Betty was nothing but a brat." In turn, Georgia was unwilling to share rights in her children with Vilda and Ann. During the summer, at a large family barbecue with many kin and friends present, Georgia made this clear.

Scene Four

Georgia's daughter took a hot poker from the fire and ran after the younger children, threatening them. Ann quickly took the poker away from her niece and slapped her. Georgia jumped into the scene, grabbed her daughter from Ann and said, "You won't let me touch your granddaughter, so don't you tell my child what to do."

Although it is common for rights in children to be distributed among close female kin in The Flats, Scene Four shows that standards other than kin criteria are operative. Ann is not an active participant in the domestic network of her sisters; she and her husband are both employed and economically secure. Ann is the adult female kin least likely to be willing to accept responsibility for her nieces, nephews, and grandnieces and grandnephews.

Scenes One and Two are examples of circumstances in which a cluster of parental rights (the discipline of children, administering folk cures, and so forth) are shared by the biological mother along with eligible kin who are common members of her household. There are, however, circumstances in which clusters of rights and entailing behaviors are transferred from one individual to another. In these situations, mothers still retain their folk and legal right to acquire physical custody over the child if the right is disputed, the right to take their child as heir, and the rights of cognatic descent. But the major cluster of behavioral entailments of parenthood are shared or transferred to the woman currently raising the child.

Within the folk system of shared parental rights in children, time and intent play an important role. How long a child resides in a household apart from his mother may determine the extent to which the mother, in the eyes of the community, retains or transfers rights in the child to the responsible female. Likewise, whether the biological mother views the situation as a permanent or a temporary response to her personal problems is an important factor.

In Scene Five a young mother, Violet, married and moved to another state with her husband and her two youngest children by a previous union. She left her two older daughters with their grandmother (mother's mother), Bessie, because at the time the couple could not afford to take them along. Violet intended the situation to be temporary, but it lasted over seven months. Before Violet left the state she told Bessie not to let the children see their father. Violet feared that the father would try to acquire custody of the children by claiming that she had deserted them. After about seven months Violet learned through gossip that her children were spending a lot of time with their father and had been staying with him on weekends. She took the train back home as soon as she could in order to get her daughters and take them to her new home out of state.

Scene Five

Violet was angered by her mother's decision to let her granddaughters stay with their father every weekend. She told her mother, "You wasn't s'posed to let him see them." Bessie said to Violet, "You ain't doing nothing for your children—the children are lucky their father and his kin take an interest in them."

Two issues complicate this situation. While Violet was living in The Flats with her children, she was willing to have her children's father buy their clothes and take them places. At least once a month the children would spend the weekend with their father at his sister's house. But when the father began "keeping house" with a new girl friend, Violet became very jealous and told her friends, "The girl wants to take my babies from me."

The issue of paternity is a further complication in this scene. The father considered himself father only to Violet's oldest child. Violet told her second-born child that she and the oldest child had the same daddy. The father's kin showed much more concern and responsibility toward the oldest child and teased Violet, saying, "Soon, girl, you going to push all your children off on him." When Violet was in town she demanded that this man treat her two oldest children as his own. One time the second child became very emotionally upset when the father said to her, "I ain't your daddy." Violet was afraid that in her absence he would say it again, or hurt the child. Although Violet's mother was aware of both these issues, she decided that while she was responsible for her grandchildren, she would decide what was best for them. Bessie exercised the rights she acquired in her grandchildren when Violet left town and left her children.

The conflict between Violet and Bessie over this issue was so great that Violet returned to town to regain physical custody of her children. Late one winter evening, she rode the Greyhound bus into The Flats with winter coats for her two daughters. She took a cab to her mother's home, woke her daughters, put on their coats, and took the same cab back to the bus station. Within two hours Violet and her daughters were on their way out of town. The father had no knowledge of what had happened until several days later. He made no attempt to contact Violet.

Violet did not have enough money with her to buy tickets to travel out of the state. In fact, she only had enough money to buy one-way tickets to Chicago. She and her daughters took the bus to Chicago and she called one of her closest girl friends, Samantha, to pick them up at the bus station. Violet and her daughters stayed with Samantha and her three children for nearly a month.

Violet and Samantha considered themselves kin. They lived down the street from one another while they were growing up, attended the same schools, and dated boys who were close cousins or best friends. Five years ago, just after Samantha gave birth to her second child, she became very ill. Violet insisted upon "taking" Samantha's year-old son in order to help her.

Scene Six was told me by Violet three years after the event.

Scene Six

That day I went over to visit Samantha, I don't know how the good Lord tell me, since I hadn't been seeing her for some time. The last old man she had didn't like me, so I stayed away. He sure was no good. Left her right before the baby come.

I went over to her place. She had a small, dark little room with a kitchen for herself and those two babies. The place look bad and smell bad. I knew she was hurting. I took one look around and said to her, "Samantha, I'm going to take your boy." I hunted up some diapers and left the house with her year-old son. She didn't come by my place for over a month, but her younger sister brought me a message that Samantha was feeling better. A week or two later she came by to visit. Her boy hardly knew her. She came by more often, but she still seemed pretty low. I told her one day, "Samantha, I don't have any sons, just daughters, so why don't you just give me this boy." She said that if he didn't favor his father so much she'd let me keep him, but she was still crazy over that man. Her boy stayed with me three or four months, then she came and got him. Soon afterwards she moved to Chicago with her two kids and her new old man.

When friends in The Flats have good social dealings with one another they often call each other by kin terms and conduct their social relations as if they were kinsmen. Close kin form alliances with one another to cope with daily needs. Close friends assume the same style of dealing with one another. Samantha and Violet shared an exchange of goods and sevices over the years and lived up to one another's expectations. They obligated, tested, and trusted one another.

The exchange of children, and short-term fosterage, are common among female friends. Child-care arrangements among friends imply both rights and duties. Close friends frequently discipline each other's children verbally and physically in front of each other. In normal times, and in times of stress, close friends have the right to "ask" for one another's children. A woman visiting a friend and her children may say, "Let me keep your girl this week. She will have a fine time with me and my girls. She won't want to come back home to her mama." This kind of request among kin and friends is very difficult to refuse.

Temporary child-care services are also a means of obligating kin or friends to future needs. Women may ask to "keep" the child of a friend for no apparent reason. But they are, in fact, building up an investment for their future needs. From this perspective it is clear that child-keeping in The Flats is both an expression of shared kin obligations toward children and an important feature of the distribution and exchange of the limited resources available to poor people in The Flats.

The scenes in which conflicts arise between kin over rights in children provide a basis for pinpointing the patterns of rights and duties in relation to children in The Flats.[3] From the viewpoint of the white middle class the kinship term "mother" is an idealized combination of behavioral roles expected to be assumed by a single person (Keesing 1969). In striking contrast, the scenes just described are illustrations of a sharing among close kinsmen of obligations toward children.

Close female kinsmen in The Flats do not expect a single person, the natural mother, to carry out by herself all of the behavior patterns which "motherhood" entails. When transactions between females over the residence, care and discipline of children run smoothly, it is difficult to clarify the patterns of rights and duties to which kin and non-kin are entitled. But scenes in which these rights and duties come into conflict show which behaviors may be shared.

Keesing (1970b, p. 432) suggests that "where the division of behaviors usually performed by a single actor among two or more actors follows lines of cleavage established by and standardized in the culture, then we are dealing with separate 'social identities.' " Goodenough (1965, p. 3) has defined social identity as "an aspect of self that makes a difference in how one's rights and duties distribute with respect to specific others." A kin term such as "mother" entails a cluster of social identities which we will define as distinguishable social positions. A set of appropriate behavior patterns apply to each social position; and more than one person can occupy the same social position at the same time (Keesing 1969; 1970b). For example, if two or more women customarily assume behavioral roles toward individual children which could be performed by a single person, then these women occupy a social position which has behavioral entailments with respect to those children.

Scenes from the preceding section illustrate patterns of rights and duties toward children in The Flats and furnish examples of social positions which kinsmen occupy with respect to one another's children. As stated earlier, it is impossible to fully elaborate the rights and duties in children within a culture. But from scenes in which these rights come into conflict, some of the following more apparent social positions stand out (Keesing 1970b): provider, discipliner, trainer, curer, and groomer.

These social positions represent the composite of typical parental behaviors which may be shared primarily among a child's close female kinsmen. They are categories of behavior which have predictable, non-legal rights and obligations.

Economic providers are expected to share in providing subsistence and scarce goods, daily meals, food stamps, a bed, a blanket, clothes, and shoes. Discipliners (primarily women) are allowed to participate in the control of children. At their own discretion they may beat—usually with a green branch stripped of leaves—threaten, terrify, blame, or scare children for unacceptable social behavior. Trainers not only discipline but teach moral values and respect for adults. They instruct by example, teaching children the consequences of their acts. A girl is taught to sit like a lady—even a two-year-old would be slapped for sitting with her legs apart, or a three-year-old boy might be chastised for hugging or touching a two-year-old girl. The consequences are taught by trainers by harsh, clear example. One afternoon Ruby's four-year-old daughter and my son Kevin were bored from being kept indoors on a cold winter day. The four-year-old grabbed a book of matches from the kitchen and was lighting them one by one, and both children were blowing them out with great joy. Ruby and I were talking in the dining room. She saw what was happening, rushed over, and held a burning match to her daughter's arm, slightly blistering the skin. An adult, may, for example, yell at a noisy child, "I'll tear your eyes!", or "I'm going to beat your black ass until it's red as burning coals!" The older children often repeat such phrases in their discipline of the younger children. Curers provide folk remedies for physical ailments. They have the right to attempt to heal rashes with a little lye or detergent in the bath water, remove warts, pull teeth, and cure stomach ailments of children with "persnickety"—a pungent brew made from tobacco and added to the baby's milk. A groomer has the obligation to care for the children, wash clothing, and check the child's bodies for rashes and diseases. In addition to eligible adults, older females are also expected to groom younger children.

Adult females who share parental rights in children are recruited from participants in the personal domestic networks of the child's mother. This includes cognatic kin to the mother, the child, and close friends. Social roles such as that of provider were often shared; thus, responsibilities were seen to have composite elements and the various parts could be assumed by more than one individual. For example, a woman who lived next door to Ruby left her three children with her sister. The sister fed and clothed the children, took them to the doctor, and made all the other necessary decisions with respect to their lives. But the rights that eligible kinsmen or close friends share in one another's children are not equal. Other factors such as economics and interpersonal relationships within domestic networks come into play. In white middle-class families, on the other hand, few persons, not even kin, would be authorized or would feel free to participate in health care or disciplinary behavior with regard to children without specific permission or transfer (care of a child in case of a parent's illness), or except in the case of an emergency.

A detailed look at scenes from preceding sections provides important clues about eligibility.

Scene One. What factors underlie the mutual expectations that Ethel and Georgia share concerning Ethel's rights in Georgia's children?

1. Ethel raised Georgia and assumes grandparental rights in Georgia's children.

2. Ethel assumed full responsibility for Georgia's children when Georgia abandoned them and left town temporarily with a serviceman.

3. The behavior patterns which Ethel assumes with respect to Georgia's children are appropriate, independent of whether or not they are co-resident.

4. In the presence of others Ethel frequently exhibits the rights she shares in Georgia's children and Georgia acknowledges these rights.

It appears that Ethel is demonstrating the rights in which she shares and may be expected to assume in Georgia's children. Georgia's own words reinforce this interpretation: "Whatever happens to me, Ethel be the person to keep my kids."

Scenes two, three, four, and six illustrate that standards other than kin criteria effectively exclude individuals from assuming parental rights in children. Close friends who are active participants in domestic networks may be expected to "keep" children. On the other hand, relatives who are not participants in the domestic networks of kinsmen are not eligible to assume parental roles:

1. Ann was not a participant in the domestic network of her sisters.
2. Ann is excluded from parental rights in her sister's and niece's children.
3. Ann's sisters do not have parental rights in Ann's children or grandchildren.

These situations show that even siblings' rights regarding sister's children are not equivalent.

Kin and friends in domestic networks establish mutual ties of obligation as they bestow rights and responsibilities upon one another. As these responsibilities are met with satisfaction, the depth of the involvement between kinsmen and between friends increases. Simultaneously, females acquire reciprocal obligations toward one another's children and rights in them. As responsibilities toward specific children are amplified, females are ultimately allowed to occupy parental roles toward children which are recognized by both adults and children. When women consciously perform duties as provider, discipliner, trainer, curer, and groomer, then they have accepted the reality that they may be required to nurture these children. These are the women who are next in line to nurture and assume custody of the children to whom their obligations apply.

Our concern up to now has not been with motherhood itself, but with the criteria by which rights and duties in children distribute socially and may be delegated to other kinsmen. At this point it is necessary to take a close look at Goodenough's definition of jural motherhood:

> If we try to define jural motherhood by the kinds of rights and duties comprising it, we are in trouble, as the societies we have already considered reveal. For the ways in which rights in children distribute socially and the very content of the rights themselves vary considerably cross-culturally. We are dealing with a jural role, then, but can identify it cross-culturally not by its content but by some constant among the criteria by which people are entitled to this role (1970, p. 24).
>
> With the foregoing in mind, we may say that jural motherhood consists of the rights and duties a woman has claim to in relation to a child by virtue of her having borne it, provided she is eligible to bear it and provided no other disqualifying circumstances attend its birth (1970, p. 25).

Potential nurturers of children share or transfer non-jural rights in children in the process of child-keeping. Individuals do not acquire rights of motherhood in the temporary exchange of children. But some child-keeping situations which are intended to be temporary become permanent. And child-keeping can ultimately involve the transfer of rights in children.

There is no specific time period after which child-keeping becomes a permanent transfer of rights in the eyes of the community. The intentions which the jural mother makes public, the frequency of her visits, the extent to which she continues to provide for the child, and the extent to which she continues to occupy all of the social positions of parenthood are all factors in sanctions over rights in children.

Some mothers whose children are being kept by kin or friends eventually stop visiting and providing goods and services for their children. In such cases, the child-keeper may ultimately become the parent in the eyes of the community. Later attempts by the biological mother to regain custody of her child may be met with disapproval, threats, and gossip within the domestic group.

In the eyes of the community, individuals who acquire rights in children have the right to make decisions over the subsequent transfer of custody of the child. In one situation a great-grandfather "kept" his great-granddaughter for eight years. During this time the mother showed little concern for her daughter, and the great-grandfather came to be considered the child's parent. When the grandfather decided that he was too old to care for the child, the mother wanted the child back. But he decided to give custody to another relative whom he considered more responsible. The decision was supported by their kinsmen. As the daughter herself said, "I was staying with my great-grandfather for the first five years of my life, but he just got too old to care for me. My mother was living in The Flats at the time, but my 'daddy' asked my mother's brother and his wife to take me 'cause he really trusted them with me."

Folk sanctions concerning the transfer of rights in children are often in conflict with the publicly sanctioned laws of the state. The courts are more likely to award custody of a child to its biological mother rather than to other kinsmen. Individuals in The Flats operate within the folk and legal system. Mothers have successfully taken close kinsmen (their own mother or aunt, for example) to court in order to regain custody of their natural children. But such acts are strongly discouraged by people who regard children as a mutual responsibility of the kin group. Children born to the poor in The Flats are highly valued, and rights in these children belong to the networks of cooperating kinsmen.[4] Shared parental responsibilities are not only an obligation of kinship, they constitute a highly cherished right. Attempts of outside social agencies, the courts, or the police to control the residence, guardianship, or behavior of children are thwarted by the domestic group. Such efforts are interpreted in The Flats as attempts on the part of the larger society to control and manipulate their children.

Notes

1. Child-keeping corresponds to the general characterizations of fosterage (Carroll 1970; Goody 1966; Keesing 1970a; Sanford 1971). Keesing (1970a) and Sanford (1971) have defined fosterage as the housing of a dependent child in a household which does not include the mother or father. Carroll (1970) views fostering in more specific terms as a temporary obligation of kinsmen to take care of one another's children. Goody (1966) contrasts kinship fostering in crisis situations with the rights of kinfolk to take children and rear them apart from their own parents.

2. Residence life histories are detailed chronological accounts of the residence changes from birth to the present. For each residence change or change in household composition, I gathered data on: (1) the age of the person at the time of each residence change; (2) the situation which precipitated the move (context); and (3) the kinship links between members of each newly formed household.

3. This section reflects theoretical advances in the analysis of transactions in parenthood (Goodenough 1970) and role analysis (Goodenough 1965; Keesing 1969, 1970a, 1970b), and

stimulating discussions with Douglas Midgett and Norma Linton who are both engaged in research on patterns of child exchange.

4. Rivers (1924) makes a strikingly similar statement in his book *Social Organization*. He says that "A child born into a community with societies or clans becomes a member of a domestic group other than the family in the strict sense."

References

Carroll, Vern, ed. (1970) *Adoption in Eastern Oceania*. Honolulu: University of Hawaii Press.

Goodenough, Ward H. (1965) "Rethinking Status and Role." In *The Relevance of Models for Social Anthropology*, ed. M. Banton. London: Tavistock Press.

Goodenough, Ward H. (1970) *Description and Comparison in Cultural Anthropology*. Chicago: Aldine Publishing Co.

Goody, Esther. (1966) "Fostering of Children in Ghana: A Preliminary Report." *Ghana Journal of Sociology* 2:26–33.

Keesing, Roger M. (1969) "On Quibblings over Squabblings of Siblings: New Perspectives on Kin Terms and Role Behavior." *Southwestern Journal of Anthropology* 25:207–227.

Keesing, Roger M. (1970a) "Kwaio Fosterage." *American Anthropologist* 72(5):991–1020.

Keesing, Roger M. (1970b) "Toward a Model of Role Analysis." In *A Handbook of Methods in Cultural Anthropology*, ed. R. Cohen and R. Naroll. New York: Natural History Press.

Radcliffe-Brown, A. R. (1950) Introduction. In *African Systems of Kinship and Marriage*, ed. A. R. Radcliffe-Brown and C. D. Forde. London: Oxford University Press.

Rivers, W. H. (1924) *Social Organization*. New York: Knopf.

Sanford, Margaret Sellars. (1971) "Disruption of the Mother-Child Relationship in Conjunction with Matrifocality: A Study of Child-Keeping among the Carib and Creole of British Honduras," Ph.D. Dissertation, The Catholic University of America, Anthropology Studies, 19, Ms.

Schneider, David M. (1968) *American Kinship: A Cultural Account*. Englewood Cliffs, N.J.: Prentice-Hall.

JUDITH M. BARDWICK
ELIZABETH DOUVAN

31. Ambivalence: The Socialization of Women

"What are big boys made of? What are big boys made of?"

Independence, aggression, competitiveness, leadership, task orientation, outward orientation, assertiveness, innovation, self-discipline, stoicism, activity, objectivity, analytic-mindedness, courage, unsentimentality, rationality, confidence, and emotional control.

"What are big girls made of? What are big girls made of?"

Dependence, passivity, fragility, low pain tolerance, nonaggression, noncompetitiveness, inner orientation, interpersonal orientation, empathy, sensitivity, nurturance, subjectivity, intuitiveness, yieldingness, receptivity, inability to risk, emotional liability, supportiveness.[1]

These adjectives describe the idealized, simplified stereotypes of normal masculinity and feminity. They also describe real characteristics of boys and girls, men and women. While individual men and women may more resemble the stereotype of the opposite sex, group differences between the sexes bear out these stereotypic portraits. How does American society socialize its members so that most men and women come close to the society's ideal norms?

From infancy children have behavioral tendencies that evoke particular types of responses from parents, older siblings, and anyone else who interacts with the child. Such responses are a function of both individual values—whether the particular person values outgoing extroverted behavior, for example—and widespread social values of acceptable child behavior. Socialization refers to the pressures—rewarding, punishing, ignoring, and anticipating—that push the child toward evoking acceptable responses.

Comparisons between boys and girls in infancy and the earliest childhood years reveal modal differences between the sexes. Boys have higher activity levels, are more physically impulsive, are prone to act out aggression, are genitally sexual earlier, and appear to have cognitive and perceptual skills less well-developed than girls of the same age. Generally speaking, girls are less active physically, display less overt physical aggression, are more sensitive to physical pain, have significantly less genital sexuality, and display greater verbal, perceptual, and cognitive skills than boys.[2]

All impulsive, aggressive children are forced to restrain these tendencies since running away, biting, kicking, publicly masturbating, and other similar behaviors are injurious either to the child and his playmates or the pride of his parents. It is critically important to the development of sex differences that these tendencies are more typical of boys than of girls. In addition, girls' more mature skills enable them to attend to stimuli, especially from other people, more swiftly and accurately than boys.[3] Girls are better at analyzing and anticipating environmental demands; in addition, they have greater verbal facility. Girls' characteristic behavior tends to disturb parents less than boy's characteristic behavior. The perceptual, cognitive, and verbal skills which for unknown reasons are more characteristic of girls enable them to analyze and anticipate adult demands and to conform their behavior to adult expectations.[4] This all means that if the socialization demands made upon boys and girls were actually the same, girls would be in a better position to cope with the world than are boys.

While these differences in response tendencies would be sufficient to result in group differences between boys and girls, another factor adds to the probability of sex differences. Many characteristic responses are acceptable in girls, ranging from the very feminine through the athletic tomboy. For boys, neither the passive sissy nor the aggressive and physical "bad boy" are acceptable. From around the age of two to two and a half, when children are no longer perceived as infants but as children, more boys than girls experience more prohibitions for a wider range of behavior. In addition, and of special importance, dependent behavior, normal to all young children, is permitted for girls and prohibited for boys. Thus, girls are not encouraged to give up old techniques of relating to adults and using others to define their identity, to manipulate the physical world and to supply their emotional needs.[5]

When people find their ways of coping comfortable and gratifying, they are not motivated to develop new techniques which in the long run might be far more productive. All very young children are dependent on adults for their physical well-being and for the knowledge that they exist and have value. Girls' self-esteem remains dependent upon other people's acceptance and love; they continue to use the skills of others instead of evolving their own. The boy's impulsivity and sexuality are sources of enormous pleasure independent of anyone else's response; these pleasures are central to the early core-self. Negative sanctions from powerful adults against masturbation, exploration, and physical aggression threaten not only the obvious pleasures, but, at heart, self-integrity. Thus, boys are pressured by their own impulses and by society's demands to give up depending predominantly on the response of others for feelings of self-esteem. Adult responses are unpredictable and frequently threatening. Forced to affirm himself because of the loss of older, more stable sources of esteem, the boy begins, before the age of five, to develop a sense of self and criteria of worth which are relatively independent of others' responses. He turns to achievements in the outer and real world and begins to value himself for real achievements in terms of objective criteria.

On the other hand, neither the girl's characteristic responses nor widespread cultural values force her to give up older, more successful modes of relating and coping. Her sexuality is neither so genital nor so imperative,[6] but, rather, an overall body sensuality, gratified by affection and cuddling. Since girls are less likely to masturbate, run away from home, or bite and draw blood, their lives are relatively free of crisis until puberty. Before that girls do not have to conform to threatening new criteria of acceptability to anywhere near the extent that boys do. When boys are pressured to give up their childish ways it is because those behaviors are perceived as feminine by parents. Boys have to earn their masculinity early. Until puberty, femininity is a verbal label, a given attribute—something that does not have to be earned. This results in a significant delay in the girl's search for identity, development of autonomy, and development of internal criteria for self-esteem. Because they continue to depend on others for self-definition and affirmation and are adept at anticipating other people's demands, girls are conformist. Girls are rewarded by good grades in school, parental love, teacher acceptance, and peer belonging. As a result, girls remain compliant and particularly amenable to molding by the culture.[7]

Longitudinal studies which measure the same people from earliest childhood through adulthood reveal that some characteristics remain stable over the life span in both sex groups, while other traits change.[8] While activity level and the tendency to be extroverted or introverted are rather stable in both sexes, other dimensions like passivity-dependence and aggression may remain stable or change depending on sex. There are significant correlations over the life span for aggression in males and passivity and dependency in females; on the other hand, passivity and dependency in males and aggression in females show no consistency over the life span. These psychological dimensions change or remain constant depending on whether individual inclinations threaten idealized cultural concepts of masculinity and femininity.[9] Aggression in boys is permitted and encouraged and only the form is socialized; dependence and passivity in girls in permitted or encouraged, and only the form is altered. Sex differences in infancy and childhood are enlarged through socialization.

Schools are generally feminine places,[10] institutions where conformity is valued, taught largely by conformist women. The course content, the methods of assessing progress, and the personal conduct required create difficulties for boys who must inhibit impulsivity, curb aggression, and restrain deviance. The reward structure of the school system perpetuates the pattern set by relationships with the parents—boys are further pressured to turn to their peers for acceptance and to develop internal criteria and objective achievements; girls are further urged to continue the nondeviant, noninnovative, conformist style of life.

Girls are rewarded with high grades in school, especially in the early years of grammar school. What do girls do especially well in? What are they being asked to master? Grammar, spelling, reading, arithmetic—tasks that depend a great deal upon memorization and demand little independence, assertiveness, analysis, innovativeness, creativity.[11] The dependent, passive girl, cued into the affirming responses of teachers, succeeds and is significantly rewarded in school for her "good" behavior and her competent memorizing skills.

It appears that until puberty academically successful girls evolve a "bisexual" or dual self-concept. Both sexes are rewarded for achievement, especially academic achievement. Girls, as well as boys, are permitted to compete in school or athletics without significant negative repercussions. The girl who is rewarded for these successes evolves a self-concept associated with being able to successfully cope and compete. While there are no negative repercussions and there is a high probability of rewards from parents and teachers as long as her friends are similarly achieving, this girl will also feel normally feminine (although questions of femininity are probably not critically important in self-evaluation of prepubertal girls unless they are markedly deviant). With the onset of the physical changes of puberty, definitions of normalcy and femininity change and come precipitately closer to the stereotype. Now behaviors and qualities that were rewarded, especially successful competing, may be perceived negatively.[12] Femininity also becomes an attribute that has to be earned—this task is made crucially difficult because of the girl's ambivalent feelings toward her body.[13]

The maturation of the girl's reproductive system brings joy and relief, feelings of normalcy, and the awareness of sexuality. Simultaneously, in normal girls the physical changes are accompanied by blood and pain, the expectation of body distortion in pregnancy, the threat of the trauma of birth, and the beginning of sexual desirability. In addition, the physical changes of menstruation are accompanied by significant and predictable emotional cycles sufficiently severe to alter the perception of her body as secure or stable.[14] Simultaneously joyful and fearful, the young adolescent girl must begin to evolve a feminine self-concept that accepts the functions and future responsibilities of her mature body; at the same time these physical changes are cues for alterations in the demands made upon her by the culture.[15] From the very beginning of adolescence girls, as potential heterosexual partners, begin to be punished for conspicuous competing achievement and to be rewarded for heterosexual success. Socialization in adolescence emphasizes the use of the cosmetic exterior of the self to lure men, to secure affection, to succeed in the competition of dating. At the same time the girl is warned not to succeed too much: conspicuous success in competitive dating threatens her friendships with girls. She learns in puberty that she is likely to be punished for significant competition in either of her important spheres.

Thus, for a long time, even the girls who are competitive, verbally agressive, and independent can feel normal, but with the onset of puberty girls are faced with their first major crises: they must come to terms with and find pleasure in their physical femininity and develop the proper psychological "femininity." Since they are still primarily cued to others for feelings of esteem, and largely defined by interpersonal relations, under the stress of their evolving, incomplete feminine identity, most girls conform to the new socialization criteria. While girls characteristically achieved in grade school because of rewards for this "good" behavior from others (rather than for achievement's own sake), in adolescence the establishment of successful interpersonal relationships becomes the self-defining, most rewarding, achievement task.[16] When that change in priorities occurs—and it tends to be greatest in the later years of high school, and again in the later years of college—personal qualities, such as independence, aggression, and competitive achievement, that might threaten success in heterosexual relationships are largely given up.

While boys are often afraid of failing, girls are additionally afraid of succeeding.[17] The adolescent girl, her parents, her girl friends, and her boy friends perceive success, as measured by objective, visible achievement as antithetical to femininity. Some girls defer consciously, with tongue in cheek, but the majority, who were never significantly aggressive, active, or independent, internalize the norms and come to value themselves as they are desired by others. The only change from childhood is that the most important source of esteem is no longer the parents but the heterosexual partner.

The overwhelming majority of adolescent girls remain dependent upon others for feelings of affirmation. Unless in early life the girl exhibited the activity, aggression, or sexuality usually displayed by boys, and thereby experienced significant parental prohibitions, there is little likelihood that she will develop independent sources of esteem that refer back to herself. Instead, the loss of love remains for her the gravest source of injury to the self and, predictably, she will not gamble with that critical source of esteem.[18]

In the absence of independent and objective achievements, girls and women know their worth only from others' responses, know their identities only from their relationships as daughters, girl friends, wives, or mothers and, in a literal sense, personalize the world. When we ask female college students what would make them happy or unhappy, when would they consider themselves successful, both undergraduate and graduate students reply: "When I love and am loved; when I contribute to the welfare of others;

when I have established a good family life and have happy, normal children; when I know I have created a good, rewarding stable relationship."[19] During adolescence as in childhood, females continue to esteem themselves insofar as they are esteemed by those with whom they have emotional relationships. For many women this never changes during their entire lifetime.

Girls are socialized to use more oblique forms of aggression than boys, such as the deft use of verbal injury or interpersonal rejection. Their aggression is largely directed toward people whose return anger will not be catastrophic to self-esteem—that is, other females. In their relationships with their fathers and later with their boy friends or husbands, girls do not threaten the important and frequently precarious heterosexual sources of love. Instead, aggression is more safely directed toward other women with whom they covertly compete for love. In relationships between men, aggression is overt and the power relationships are clear; female aggression is covert, the power relationships rarely admitted. With the denial and disguise of anger, a kind of dishonesty, a pervasive uncertainty, necessarily creeps into each of a woman's relationships, creating further anxiety and continued or increased efforts to secure affection.

The absence of objective success in work makes girls invest in, and be unendingly anxious about, their interpersonal worth. Women use interpersonal success as a route to self-esteem since that is how they have defined their major task. If they fail to establish a meaningful, rewarding, unambivalent love relationship, they remain cued into the response of others and suffer from a fragile or vulnerable sense of self. Those who are secure enough, who have evolved an identity and a feeling of worth in love relationships, may gamble and pursue atypical, nontraditional, competitive, masculine achievements.

According to Erik Erikson, the most important task in adolescence is the establishment of a sense of identity. This is more difficult for girls than for boys. Because her sexuality is internal, inaccessible, and diffuse, because she feels ambivalent toward the functions of her mature reproductive system, because she is not punished for her impulsivity, because she is encouraged to remain dependent, a girl's search for her feminine identity is both complex and delayed. To add to her problems, she is aware both of the culture's preference for masculine achievements and of the fact that there is no longer a single certain route for achieving successful femininity. The problem grows ever more complex, ever more subtle.

In these affluent times middle-class girls are apparently not punished simply for being girls. They are not prohibited from going to college, seeking school office, or achieving honors. Marriage and maternity are held out as wonderful goals, not necessarily as inhibiting dead ends. Although girls are rewarded for conformity, dependence, passivity, and competence, they are not clearly punished for the reverse. Until adolescence the idea of equal capacity, opportunity, and life style is held out to them. But sometime in adolescence the message becomes clear that one had better not do too well, that competition is aggressive and unfeminine, that deviating threatens the heterosexual relationship.[20] Masculinity is clearly defined and earned through individual competitive achievement. For the girl overt freedoms, combined with cultural ambiguity, result in an unclear image of femininity. As a result of vagueness about how to become feminine or even what is feminine, the girl responds to the single clear directive—she withdraws from what is clearly masculine. In high school and increasingly in college, girls cease clearly masculine pursuits and perceive the establishment of interpersonal goals as the most salient route to identity.[21] This results in a maximization of interpersonal skills, an interpersonal view of the world, a withdrawal from the development of independence, activity, ability, and competition, and the absence of a professional work commitment.

The personality qualities that evolve as characteristic of the sexes function so as to enhance the probability of succeeding in the traditional sex roles. Whether you are male or female, if you have traditionally masculine personality qualities—objectivity rather than subjectivity, aggression rather than passivity, the motive to achieve rather than a fear of success, courage rather than conformity, and professional commitment, ambition, and drive[22]—you are more likely to succeed in masculine roles. Socialization enhances initial tendencies; consequently, relatively few women have these qualities.

Thus, the essence of the problem of role conflict lies in the fact that up until now very few women have succeeded in traditionally masculine roles; not only because of disparagement and prejudice, but largely because women have not been fundamentally equipped and determined to succeed. Some women's tragedy is their desire to succeed in competitive achievement and their contempt for the traditional role for which they are better equipped.

It is probably not accidental, therefore, that women dominate professions that utilize skills of nurturance, empathy, and competence, where aggressiveness and competitiveness are largely dysfunctional.[23] These professions, notably teaching, nursing, and secretarial work, are low in pay and status. The routes to occupational success for women are either atypical and hazardous or typical, safe, and low in the occupational hierarchy. (It is interesting to note that in the USSR where over 70 percent of the physicians are women, medicine is a low-status occupation.)

In spite of an egalitarian ideal in which the roles and contributions of the sexes are declared to be equal and complementary, both men and women esteem masculine qualities and achievements. Too many women evaluate their bodies, personality qualities, and roles as second-rate. When male criteria are the norms against which female performance, qualities, or goals are measured, then women are not equal. It is not only that the culture values masculine productivity more than feminine productivity. The essence of the derogation lies in the evolution of the masculine as the yardstick against which everything is measured. Since the sexes are different, women are defined as not-men and that means not good, inferior. It is important to understand that women in this culture, as members of the culture, have internalized these self-destructive values.[24]

What we have described is ambivalence, not conflict. Conflict is the simultaneous desire to achieve a stable and rewarding heterosexual relationship (and the rest of the female's traditional responsibilities and satisfactions) and to participate fully in competitive achievement and succeed. Conflict, in this sense, is understandable as a vying between traditional and nontraditional roles, between affiliative and achievement motives. (Most women resolve this potential difficulty by defining affiliation as achievement.) Ambivalence is clearly seen in the simultaneous enjoyment of one's feminine identity, qualities, goals, and achievements and the perception of them as less important, meaningful, or satisfying than those of men. Girls envy boys; boys do not envy girls.

The culture generally rewards masculine endeavors and those males who succeed—who acquire money, power, and status, who enjoy an easy and free sexuality, who acquire and produce things, who achieve in competition, who produce, who innovate and create. By these criteria, women have not produced equally. The contributions that most women make in the enhancement and stabilization of relationships, their competence and self-discipline, their creation of life are less esteemed by men and women alike. It is disturbing to review the extent to which women perceive their responsibilities, goals, their very capacities, as inferior to males; it is similarly distressing to perceive how widespread this self-destructive self-concept is. Society values masculinity; when it is achieved it is rewarded. Society does not value femininity as highly; when it is achieved it is not as highly rewarded.

Today we have a peculiar situation in which sex-role stereotypes persist and are internalized by adults and children, yet the labor force includes thirty-one million working women and the college population is almost half women.[25] The stereotype persists because there is always cultural lag, because few women achieve markedly responsible or powerful positions, and because the overwhelming majority of working women perceive themselves as working in order to benefit the family.[26] In general, working women do not see work as an extension of egocentric interests or as the fulfillment of achievement ambitions, but as another place in which more traditional motives are gratified.

Perhaps the percentage of the female population who have had at least some college and who have achieved and been rewarded in the educational system faces the most difficult problems. Some part of this population has evolved—normally and not as a compensatory function—self-concepts and motives that take for granted the value of marriage and maternity, but also include individuality, creativity, independence, and successful competitive achievement.[27] These characteristics become criteria by which the excellence of the self is measured. It is obvious that these characteristics are not highly functional within the traditional role, and moreover, cannot truly be achieved within the traditional female role. There would be no conflict if competitive achievement were the only aspect of these women's self-concept, but it is not. Characteristically, normal girls simultaneously put priority upon successful heterosexual relationships, which lead to the establishment of the nuclear family and traditional responsibilities.[28] Most girls effect a compromise, recognizing the hierarchy of their motivations and the appropriateness of their heterosexual desires. They tend to marry, work for a few years, and then start having babies. Inexperienced and unprepared, they tell themselves that the traditional role is creative and fulfilling. But creativity and fulfillment are hard to distinguish under the unending and repetitive responsibilities of diapers, dishes, and dusting. They tell themselves that when the children enter school they will reenter the labor force or the university. For these women, who have internalized the unequal evaluation of roles, who have developed needs to achieve, who have been rewarded because of their achievements, the traditional role is inadequate because it cannot gratify those nonnurturant, nonsupportive, nondependent, nonpassive aspects of the self.

Very few young women understand the very real limits upon achieving imposed by maternity, because they traditionally have had little experience with traditional role responsibilities before they marry. Typically, girls do not ask why there are so few female role models around who succeed in work while they have young children. While children are a real achievement, a source of joy and fulfillment, they are also time-consuming and energy-depleting, a major source of responsibility and anxiety. In today's child-centered milieu, with the decline of the extended family and the dearth of adequate child-care facilities, the responsibility for childrearing falls directly on the mother alone.

Success in the traditional tasks is the usual means by which girls achieve feelings of esteem about themselves, confidence, and identity.[29] In general they have continued, even as adults, to esteem themselves as they are valued by others; that source of esteem is interpersonal, best earned within the noncompetitive, nonaggressive traditional role. Without independent, objective competitive achievements, confidence is best secured within the traditional role—in spite of the priority given to masculine achievements. Whether or not the woman is achievement-oriented, her years of major childrearing responsibilities result in a decline in old work skills, a loss of confidence that she can work, a fear of failing within a competitive milieu that she has left. In other words, not only have specific techniques been lost or new data become unfamiliar, withdrawal from a competitive-achievement situation for a significant length of time creates the conviction that she is not able.

The very characteristics that make a woman most successful in family roles—the capacity to take pleasure in family-centered, repetitive activities, to sustain and support members of the family rather than pursuing her own goals, to enhance relationships through boundaryless empathy—these are all antithetical to success in the bounded, manipulative, competitive, rational, and egocentric world of work.[30] Because they are not highly motivated and because they are uncertain about what is normal or desirable, many women do not work. Even those who do continue to feel psychologically responsible for the maintenance of the family and are unwilling to jeopardize family relationships. Most work at jobs that contribute to family vacations, college fees, or the general family budget.[31] Even women who pursue a career or profession, rather than merely holding a meaningless job, assume the responsibility for two major, demanding roles. Rather than make this commitment, many women professionalize their voluntary or club activities, bringing qualities of aggression, competitiveness, and organizing skills to these "safer" activities.

Women tend not to participate in roles, or seek goals that threaten their important affiliative relationships because in those relationships they find most of their feelings of esteem and identity. This perpetuates psychological dependency which may be functional in the relationships but injurious to the self-concept of those who have internalized the values of the culture. Undeniably, it is destructive to feelings of esteem to know that you are capable and to be aware that you are not utilizing much of your potential.[32] The question of whether nontraditional success jeopardizes feelings of femininity has not yet been answered. Most women today would not be willing to achieve a greater success than their husbands. In this tradition-bound, sex-stereotyped culture, even though millions of women are employed, old values are internalized and serve as criteria for self-evaluation.

Neither men nor women entering marriage expect the sexes to share equally in privileges and responsibilities. Very few couples could honestly accept the wife's having the major economic responsibility for the family while the husband deferred to the demands of her work. Few individuals could reverse roles without feeling that he is not "masculine," and she is not "feminine."[33] Masculinity and femininity are aspects of the self that are clearly tied to roles—which role, how typical or deviant, how well accomplished, the extent of the commitment.

Yet a new reality is emerging today, for this is an era of changing norms. Although the unidimensional stereotype still persists and remains partially viable, it is also simplistic and inaccurate. Both men and women are rejecting the old role allocations which are exaggerated and costly because they push men and women into limited slots solely on the basis of sex. But an era of change results in new uncertainties and the need to evolve new clear criteria of masculinity and femininity, which can be earned and can offer feelings of self-esteem to both sexes.

The socialization model is no longer clear; in its pure form it exists primarily in media, less in life. Since almost half of American women work, the percentage rising with the rising level of education, it is clear that, at least for educated middle-class women, the simplistic stereotype is no longer valid. Similarly we find that more men are rejecting success as the sole source of esteem or masculinity. The male turning toward his family reflects his need not to be bound or limited by a unidimensional role model. For both sexes this is a period of change in which both old and new values coexist, though the visible norms derive from the old model. Today's college students seem to be more aware than the generation that preceded them of the consequences of role choice; they seem to be evolving a goal in which men are more nurturant than they were, while females are freer to participate professionally without endangering the male's esteem.

Both the work and the housewife roles are romanticized, since romanticism is enhanced when reality does not intrude. Women glorify work when and because they do not participate in it. Role conflict for women is largely a feeling of having been arbitrarily shut out from where the action is—a reaction to a romanticized concept of work and a reaction against the reality of the repetitive world of child care. Frustration is freely available to today's woman: if she participates fully in some professional capacity she runs the risk of being atypical and nonfeminine. If she does not achieve the traditional role she is likely to feel unfulfilled as a person, as a woman. If she undertakes both roles, she is likely to be uncertain about whether she is doing either very well. If she undertakes only the traditional role she is likely to feel frustrated as an able individual. Most difficult of all, the norms of what is acceptable, desirable, or preferable are no longer clear. As a result, it is more difficult to achieve a feminine (or masculine) identity, to achieve self-esteem because one is not certain when one has succeeded. When norms are no longer clear, then not only the "masculine" achieving woman but also the nonworking traditionally "feminine" woman can feel anxious about her normalcy, her fulfillment. Many women try to cope with their anxiety by exaggerating, by conforming to stereotyped role images. When one is anxious or uncertain about one's femininity, a viable technique for quelling those anxious feelings is an exaggerated conformity, a larger-than-life commitment to *Kinder, Küche, Kirche*. In this way a woman creates images, sending out clarified and exaggerated cues to others. Thus, the message is clear and she can be more certain that the feedback will assure her of her femininity.

It is easy to be aware of the discrepancy between the stereotyped norm and the reality. People are not simple. Whenever one sees a total investment or role adoption in its stereotyped, unidimensional form, one suspects a flight from uncertainty about masculinity or femininity. During a period of transition one can expect to see increasing numbers of women quelling anxiety by fleeing into a unidimensional, stereotyped femininity. As new norms gain clarity and force, more flexible roles, personalities, and behaviors will evolve. Role freedom is a burden when choice is available but criteria are unclear; under these circumstances it is very difficult to know whether one has achieved womanhood or has dangerously jeopardized it.

Notes

1. J. Silverman, "Attentional Styles and the Study of Sex Differences," in D. Mostofsky, ed., *Attention: Contemporary Studies and Analysis* (New York: Appleton-Century-Crofts, 1970); H. A.

Witkin et al., *Personality through Perception: An Experimental and Clinical Study* (New York: Harper, 1954); J. Kagan, "Acquisition and Significance of Sex Typing and Sex Role Identity," in M. L. Hoffman and L. W. Hoffman, eds., *Review of Child Development Research* (New York: Russell Sage Foundation, 1964), 1:137–167; L. M. Terman and L. E. Tyler, "Psychological Sex Differences," in L. Carmichael, ed., *A Manual of Child Psychology,* 2nd ed. (New York: John Wiley, 1954), ch. 19; E. Douvan and J. Adelson, *The Adolescent Experience* (New York: John Wiley, 1966).

2. Silverman, *op. cit.,* Terman and Tyler, *op. cit.;* R. Q. Bell and N. S. Costello, "Three Tests for Sex Differences in Tactile Sensitivity in the New Born," *Biologia Neonatorum* 7 (1964): 335–347; R. Q. Bell and J. F. Darling, "The Prone Head Reaction in the Human Neonate: Relation with Sex and Tactile Sensitivity," *Child Development* 36 (1965):943–949; S. M. Garn, "Roentgenogrammetric Determinants of Body Composition," *Human Biology* 29 (1957): 337–353; J. Kagan and M. Lewis, "Studies of Attention in the Human Infant," *Merrill-Palmer Quarterly* 2 (1965): 95–127; M. Lewis, J. Kagan, and J. Kalafat, "Patterns of Fixation in the Young Infant," *Child Development* 37 (1966): 331–341; L. P. Lipsitt and N. Levy, "Electrotactual Threshold in the Human Neonate," *Child Development* 30 (1959): 547–554.

3. Kagan and Lewis, *op. cit.;* Lewis, Kagan, and Kalafat, *op. cit.* In spite of this initial advantage which might be thought to lead, logically and inevitably to high-achievement investment, girls' socialization ends without realization of this early promise. J. Veroff, "Social Comparison and the Development of Achievement Motivation," in C. Smith, ed., *Achievement Related Motives in Children* (New York: Russell-Sage Foundation, 1969); pp. 46–101, suggests that the period of optimal generalization of the achievement motive is early, about the age of four or five. At this time girls are better at the truly critical tasks of speaking, comprehending, and remembering. But these accomplishments are taken for granted by children, who strive rather to tie shoelaces, ride bicycles, climb trees, and jump rope—all physical accomplishments. In other words, at the time when the motive for achievement is learned and generalized, the children themselves define physical tasks as important. Girls' greater cognitive and verbal skills do not, therefore, contribute to the development of a higher achievement motivation.

4. E. Maccoby, ed., *The Development of Sex Differences* (Stanford: Stanford University Press, 1966).

5. J. M. Bardwick, *The Psychology of Women* (New York: Harper & Row, 1971).

6. Helene Deutsch, *Psychology of Women* (New York: Grune & Stratton, 1944), vol. 1: K. Horney, "On the Genesis of the Castration Complex in Women," *International Journal of Psychoanalysis* 5 (1924):50–65.

7. Douvan and Adelson, *op. cit.*

8. N. Bayley, "Consistency of Maternal and Child Behaviors in the Berkeley Growth Study," *Vita Humana* 7 (1964):73–95; M. P. Honzik and J. W. MacFarlane, "Prediction of Behavior and Personality from 21 Months to 30 Years," unpublished manuscript, 1963; J. Kagan and H. A. Moss, *Birth to Maturity* (New York: John Wiley, 1962); E. S. Schaefer and N. Bayley, "Maternal Behavior, Child Behavior, and Inter-correlations from Infancy through Adolescence," *Monograph of the Society for Research on Child Development* 28 (1963), serial no. 87.

9. Kagan and Moss, *op. cit.*

10. H. S. Becker, "Social Class Variations in One Teacher-Pupil Relationship," *Journal of Educational Sociology* 25 (1952):451–465.

11. Maccoby, *op. cit.*

12. M. S. Horner, "Fail: Bright Women," *Psychology Today* 3 (November 1969):36.

13. Bardwick, *op. cit.;* E. Douvan, "New Sources of Conflict at Adolescence and Early Adulthood," in Judith M. Bardwick et al., *Feminine Personality and Conflict* (Belmont, Calif.: Brooks/ Cole, 1970).

14. M. E. Ivey and J. M. Bardwick, "Patterns of Affective Fluctuation in the Menstrual Cycle," *Psychosomatic Medicine* 30 (1968):336–345.

15. Douvan, *op. cit.*

16. J. G. Coleman, *The Adolescent Society* (New York: Free Press, 1961).

17. Horner, *op. cit.*

18. Deutsch, *op. cit.:* Douvan and Adelson, *op. cit.*

19. J. Bardwick and J. Zweben, "A Predictive Study of Psychological and Psychosomatic Changes Associated with Oral Contraceptives," mimeograph, 1970.

20. M. Komarovsky, *Women in the Modern World* (Boston: Little Brown, 1953).

21. *Ibid.;* R. Goldsen, M. Rosenberg, R. Williams, E. A. Suchman, *What College Students Think* (Princeton, N.J.: Van Nostrand, 1961); Coleman, *op. cit.;* N. Sanford, *The American College* (New York: John Wiley, 1962).

22. T. Parsons, "Age and Sex in the Social Structure of the United States," *American Sociological Review* 7 (1942): 604–616.

23. M. Mead, *Male and Female* (New York: William Morrow, 1949).

24. Bardwick, *op. cit.;* Mead, *op. cit.*

25. R. E. Hartley, "Children's Concept of Male and Female Roles," *Merrill-Palmer Quarterly* 6 (1960):153–163.

26. F. I. Nye and L. W. Hoffman, *The Employed Mother in America* (Chicago: Rand-McNally, 1963).

27. R. Baruch, "The Achievement Motive in Women: Implications for Career Development," *Journal of Personality and Social Psychology* 5 (1967):260–267.

28. Bardwick, *op. cit.*

29. Douvan and Adelson, *op. cit.*

30. D. L. Gutmann, "Woman and Their Conception of Ego Strength," *Merrill-Palmer Quarterly* 11 (1965):229–240.

31. Nye and Hoffman, *op. cit.*

32. G. Gurin, J. Veroff, and S. Feld, *Americans View Their Mental Health* (New York: Basic Books, 1960).

33. D. J. Bem and S. L. Bem, "Training the Woman to Know Her Place," based on a lecture delivered at Carnegie Institute of Technology, October 21, 1966, revised 1967.

Reflections on Past, Present, and Future

Introduction

Part VI, "Reflections on Past, Present, and Future," stands in lieu of any effort at overall conclusion. There can be no conclusion to the history of growing up; unless, of course, we ponder the extinction of humanity. Whatever the value of that particular exercise, this is not the place to undertake it. Instead, as we have learned to consider the present as the outcome of the past—never, of course, simply or directly—we turn to questions of alternative futures for growing up based on both past and present and contemporary responses to them.

Two essays contribute to this tentative ending. David Matza's seminal "Position and Behavior Patterns of Youth" represents a respected effort to make sense of the present, past, and the future. In that regard, as well as in assisting us to ask questions about today and tomorrow, it retains its usefulness. Readers will ask, How well does it continue to describe contemporary patterns since the time it was first written? To what extent is it now itself of primarily historical interest?

More current—in recency of publication and in faddishness—is Joshua Meyrowitz's "The Adultlike Child and the Childlike Adult: Socialization in an Electronic Age." Meyrowitz well represents a popular view today that stresses, based on access to electronic media and consumer culture (and slighting persisting class-cultural differences), a proclaimed "end of childhood," adolescence, and youth as we have known them. In the twist that Meyrowitz offers, an end to adulthood also seems to occur. Although I disagree with this point of view, and consider it deficient in far too many ways to state here, its currency and the ways in which it attempts to posit the "end of childhood" as at once a historical outcome and an outcome beyond history as we have known it merit its inclusion at the end of our journey. Readers will ask themselves the key questions of the argument's plausibility and persuasiveness and of its own place in the continuing history of growing up.

32. Position and Behavior Patterns of Youth

The surprising thing about youth is how little is known about it despite the considerable number of studies and essays on one or another of its aspects. One may learn a great deal about the correlates of different phases of adolescence or youth (Clausen & Williams, 1963), but he may still know very little directly about these self-same aspects. One knows something about the socialization processes by which children assume one or another youthful style, but considerably less about the variety, shape, and texture of the styles themselves. From the less empirical literature on youth, one may learn much about what is wrong with alleged characteristics of modern youth, but is not enlightened regarding the details of these characteristics and the particular youth to whom they presumably pertain. The present chapter will focus on the shape and texture of these youthful patterns and the position of youth on which the diversity of styles is presumably founded.

"Youth" is here used in a meaning broader than the usual connotation of "adolescence." It includes adolescence, but needs not culminate with the end of adolescence. Rightly or wrongly, adolescence has come to be associated with the teen-age years. Youth, however, may, under certain conditions, last well into the thirties or middle-age. Youth ends with the attaining of potentially self-sufficient adulthood. Adolescence has been similarly defined (Muuss, 1962, p. 4), but the word is usually less acceptable when used in such a broad scope. There is less reservation about conceiving of a 13-year-old youth. Such usage is not uncommon. Thus, the present conception of "youth" will be similar to that commonly used with reference to "adolescence"—the period between childhood and adulthood.

Youth is a period in the temporal ordering of society (Moore, 1963). It is a period whose beginning and end are more or less explicitly punctuated. As Ruth Benedict 1938), and other anthropologists after her, reminded readers, some societies make a great effort to celebrate and ritualize passage into youth and, subsequently, into adulthood. Other societies, however, are notorious for their lack of activity in these respects. Despite the great variability in the patency of the beginning and end of youth, all societies apparently conceive of the category (Eisenstadt, 1962, pp. 28–29) and manage to supply commonly understood *social indications* of onset and conclusion. These indications may themselves lack consistency and coherence, in which case they are *diffuse,* or they may coincide on a particular point in time, in which case they are *specific.*

Contemporary America tends to the lazy end of the spectrum, allowing the definitions of the beginning and end of youth to lie latent in common understandings and failing to supply a specific occasion on which diverse indications coalesce. But this should not be taken to mean that common understandings of the beginning and end of youth are

David Matza, "Position and Behavior Patterns of Youth," reprinted from *Handbook of Modern Sociology,* ed. R. E. L. Faris (Chicago: Rand McNally, 1964), 191–216, by permission of the editor, R. E. L. Faris.

lacking. The social indications of the start of youth in our society, and many others, have included publicly or privately visible aspects of biological pubescence (Ausubel, 1954; Lander, 1942; Muuss, 1962, pp. 19–23; Sarnoff, 1962, pp. 384–385). Moreover, the beginnings of youth are indicated in the partial subsiding of parental dominance and a concurrent license to utilize guardedly one's new sexual equipment in some pale or playful imitation of adult heterosexuality. Finally, in many modern societies the beginning of youth is indicated by a license—not a right—to engage in some imitation of adult work. Thus indicated, youth is a step, albeit a halting one, toward socially defined adulthood.

The conclusion of youth is obviously the assumption of adult status and, within the limits set by other prevalent systems of stratification, the ascription of first-class citizenship. With adulthood, one is at least a first-class subject within one's estate or caste and, at best, a first-class citizen in one's community. Excellent and persistent social indicators of the time at which the assumption of adulthood is warranted include the formation of new kinship ties by marriage, the begetting of children, the entrance into the labor force by taking or searching for full-time and permanent employment, and the establishment of a new and separate place of residence.

The conclusion of youth, like its beginning, may be obvious or latent, diffuse or specific, early or late. There is no avoiding this ambiguity and variability—both among and within societies (Muuss, 1962, pp. 8–10). If there are common understandings regarding when entry into and exit from youth take place, it is perhaps risky to rely too heavily on the variable propensities of societies explicitly to ritualize passage in accounting for stressful or tranquil youth. Common understandings of the general conditions of entry and exit may easily substitute for ritualized celebration in assuaging the anxiety presumably felt by youth who lack a concise date of graduation into one or another age grade. To suppose otherwise is to assume that rigid and meticulous social organization is somehow less productive of tension than are flexible and imprecise arrangements.

The Position of Modern Youth

Most analyses of youth have proceeded from a picture of their emergent position in modern society. The problems and potentialities of youth, both as seen from within and by ex-youth, derive from their position in society and their relations with adults. The consequences of the position of youth may be mediated through the special families encountered by them, and mollified or aggravated but not negated. The position of youth is the general circumstance within which adult agencies of variable character perform their work. Thus, any analysis of youth seems incomplete without a consideration of this position.

A common error in most portrayals of youth is an exaggeration of those aspects making for stress, turmoil, and, subsequently, for deviance and a variety of other psychic misfortunes. Literary essayists and positivist sociologists alike have shared in a common mood which stresses the sense in which growing up in the way preferred by adults is harder and more fraught with obstacles today than at some usually unspecified previous time (Coleman, 1961a; Goodman, 1960). Such a mood should immediately arouse suspicion since it partakes of the general, and for the most part unwarranted, intellectual gloom connected with the negative assessment of modernity (Grana, 1964). Moreover, a negative and pessimistic assessment of youth based on a purported degeneration of their position should be subjected to special scrutiny because of the common tendency of ex-youth to romanticize their own experiences and disparage those of succeeding cohorts.

Ameliorated Dependency

Youth is a dependent status (Parsons, 1962, pp. 110–111), which means that it suffers from special liabilities or penalties and enjoys special protections, indulgences, and privileges. The special status is most explicit in law, where youth receive special treatment and are subject to special provisions up to ages ranging from about 16 to the mid-twenties, depending on the particular jurisdiction and matter at hand. The dependent status of youth is also apparent in the special treatment and support accorded in other major institutions, ranging from the family to industry. Special provisions are often enacted in law (Abbott, 1938), but some are merely customary in character. The mere fact that someone is young grants him special treatment. This special treatment is a mixture of the sort of liability and indulgence that is generally characteristic of dependent status.

Sometimes youth are accorded special indulgence, sometimes special stringency. In either case dependency is a peculiar status. This status is best summarized in political rather than economic or social terms: It is a deficiency in citizenship (Marshall, 1950). Dependents are only limited citizens.

In what sense has the dependent status of youth been ameliorated? One important answer seems obvious and is implicit, though strangely only rarely explicit, in the many studies of child-rearing in America. The major secular drift described in these studies is a transformation of parental domination from reliance on physical coercion to one or another form of manipulation or persuasion. This drift has produced the profound amelioration inherent in the substitution of persuasion for brutality. Children today are protected from the coarsest physical forms of adult domination by both custom and law and, though not always effectively, from flagrant abuse by parents, teachers, and other officials. The secular trend and the increasing correspondence between the social classes were summarized by Bronfenbrenner:

> It is now a matter of scientfic record that patterns of child rearing in the United States have changed appreciably over the past twenty-five years. . . . Middle class parents especially have moved away from the more rigid and strict styles of care and discipline advocated in the early 1920's and '30's toward modes of response involving greater tolerance of the child's impulses and desires, free expression of affection, and increased reliance on "psychological" methods of discipline, such as reasoning and appeals to conscience, as distinguished from more direct techniques like physical punishment. . . . At the same time, the gap between the social classes in their goals and methods of child rearing appears to be narrowing, with working class parents beginning to adopt both the values and techniques of the middle class (Bronfenbrenner, 1961, p. 7).

Moreover, Bronfenbrenner (1961) indicated that the trend may be extended back to the early part of the twentieth century, suggesting that, at least during the present century, not merely cyclical variation is being witnessed. Bronfenbrenner based this judgment on a study of Californians reared in the early 1900's, and in the late 1920's and 1930's (Bronson, Katten, & Livson, 1959). Thus, according to Bronfenbrenner, the trend to greater reliance on persuasion and less on coercion has continued in the same direction from the early 1900's to the present.

The narrowing gap between the social classes continues to attract the attention of students of child-rearing. In one recent study, the results showed that the differences in the child-rearing patterns between working- and middle-class seem to have almost vanished (Kohn, 1959). The methods used in showing both the trend toward persuasion and in increasing similarity between the classes in the use of this technique may be challenged, but the challenge lacks credibility. The findings of these studies confirm the common sense and literary impression that persuasion has been replacing coercion.

The above trend is related to a tendency toward permissiveness, which has appeared within educational as well as family systems. Whatever the precise meaning attached to the term permissiveness, it indicates a rise in the indulgence granted young persons and a decrease in their liabilities and duties. There have, of course, been countertrends in permissiveness and the freedom of movement, choice, and action inherent in it, for instance, the instituting of curfew restrictions for youth in many large cities. These, however, have remained largely unenforced. Despite such countertrends, the secular trend toward permissiveness has hardly been reversed. Youth today enjoy greater indulgence of their freedom of choice and movement than formerly, and, in that measure, their status of dependency has been ameliorated.

The lessening of youthful dependency has been accomplished in a variety of other ways, each balancing the previously overwhelming liabilities and duties with newly granted protection and indulgence. Best seen in this light are such innovations as protective legislation and persistent restrictions on the conditions of child labor, the creation of special courts for juveniles, the emergence of the probation system which originally was mainly a special dispensation for minors, the progressive movement in education which was inspired and animated by a dedicated child-centeredness, and the considerable gains in financial allowance dispensed to youth by increasingly generous parents.

What have been the consequences of amelioration? A satisfactory answer is suggested by a reiteration of the fact that while dependency has been ameliorated, it still exists. Moreover, another answer is suggested by stressing the sense in which youth are a minority group (Friedenberg, 1959, p. 7; Friedenberg, 1963a, pp. 149–158). Minority can mean both a small fraction of a population and not having attained the age of maturity, blended in "minority group" as it pertains to ethnic fractions of the population. It is not that minors are treated as a fractional ethnic group; rather, ethnic fractions have been treated like minors.

Youth are not only *a* minority group. Symbolically, they are *the* minority group in that they have provided a paradigm for imputations and policy regarding disliked ethnic fractions. A conception of youth as a minority group suggests the probable consequences of the shift in position implicit in the amelioration of dependent status. Minorities whose dependence is lessened but not abolished manifest some standard features. The reaction of youth to improvement of their position has been partially similar to that of ethnic fractions. It has been different, too, since youth are a special kind of minority.

Young persons display considerable uncertainty and vacillation regarding their proper place in society. Amelioration, with the persistence of second-class citizenship, hardly leads to contentment and satisfaction; instead, it whets the previously undeveloped appetite for freedom and equality and makes some persons restless. This has been noted many times in the study of ethnic minorities and more generally disadvantaged sections of the population. Moreover, individuals whose dependency has been ameliorated come to forget their place in society, often because they no longer know what it is and neither do their majority benefactors. Thus, youth come to occupy a marginal status in society, and so it has been described by many writers. The incumbents of marginal position typically experience some measure of status anxiety. Irving Sarnoff described the marginality of youth:

> In our society . . . the adolescent is generally obliged to live for many years as a "marginal man." . . . That is, his social status is rather ambiguous, for he is considered neither an adult, nor yet a child; neither permitted to share the prerogatives of adults nor enjoy the irresponsibility of prepubescent childhood; neither taken completely seriously by adults nor ignored by them as they might ignore the antics of a young child . . . (Sarnoff, 1962, p. 392).

Kurt Lewin, too, in an earlier statement, attributed much of the tension of youth to their marginal position in society. Lewin, like Sarnoff and other recent writers, focused on the sense in which youth is currently marginal without sufficiently stressing the historical shifts which produced that legacy (Muuss, 1962, p. 90). Consequently, one often overlooks the fact that the ambiguity of youthful status emanates from an improvement, or amelioration, of position, rather than increased deprivation or degeneration.

A consequence of status ambiguity is a persistent uncertainty regarding the proper stance with which members of the minority are to interact with those of the majority, and the pathetic misunderstandings which normally attend uncertainty. For instance, the question of whether or not a youth knows his proper place is more important, and in some sense of greater social import to many adult law-enforcement officials than whether or not the youth has actually engaged in any violation of the law (Werthman & Piliavin, 1963). After this is established, interaction proceeds in one direction or another depending in some measure on the minority member's response to the query.

Place uncertainty may result in a higher predisposition to deviant modes of conduct in that it may generate hostility to the social order and its official agents or engender alienation from the norms and sentiments which regulate social behavior. While this is likely, one cannot be certain that place uncertainty will culminate in high rates of deviation, since many things obviously intervene between an affinity and an accomplished and registered act. Less conjectural is the idea that place uncertainty will result in greater *imputation of deviance* to minority members than to those of majority status.

Normally, place uncertainty means that official agents of the majority have a certain touchiness regarding the activities of those in minority position. They are touchy both because they suspect the minority of falling short of the standards of maturity and because they are uncertain regarding where they stand with their inferiors. The touchiness of adults is countered by a pushy show of youthful defiance, since many minority members mistake favors for rights and are resentful when reminded of their actual position. As a result of the mutual touchiness and the strained interaction which ensues, the chances of discovering and registering deviant acts are maximized. Moreover, given the wide latitude of youthful violations implicit in modern juvenile codes, police apprehension and subsequent citation for mere disrespect or other behavior unbecoming a person of minority status can and does occur. Given the circumstance of place uncertainty, police, like other adults, are apt to be highly sensitive to the respect accorded them by youth, and youth are apt to act in a way which is taken to be disrespectful. Thus, the initial imputation of deviant tendencies, coupled with the intensely touchy relations between the official registrars of deviance and youth, may serve to produce something of a self-confirming prophecy, especially if, as alleged by some sociologists, such reinforced imputations serve to structure self-conception and to shape the opportunities for association or affiliation (Becker, 1963; Lemert, 1951).

Place uncertainty and attendant difficulties are aggravated by the spiraling tendency by which expectations outrun realities. In another context, this has been termed the "revolution of rising expectations." Two forms of rising expectations may be distinguished, one rather unreasonable, the other quite reasonable and perhaps more common. The first, "runaway expectations," refers to a situation in which aspirant equals forget to surrender the indulgence and protection that befit them as ameliorated dependents but appear unseemly among first-class citizens. Women and youth are among the best examples of minorities which include persons who seem to aspire to more than full equality. Thus, for instance, some women desire deference and chivalry as well as freedom and equality. Some youth desire pampering and coddling as well as being treated as adults. Runaway expectations manifest themselves in an apparent ambivalence regarding equality and are a rather normal affliction among these special minorities that have been perpetually integrated in social circles which include majority members. An excellent instance of such a social circle is, of course, the family.

But however reasonable, the expectations of many women and youth surpass what is normally allowed. Their expectations are not runaway, merely galloping. An important aspect of "galloping youthful expectations" is implicit in Kingsley Davis' (1944) observation that the contemporary domination of the principle of merit results in tension and subsequent conflict. Davis felt that such a principle, when widely extended, provides a basis for intergenerational dispute regarding rightful incumbency in scarce positions and relative claims over scarce goods and services. Furthermore, the failure of such lofty principles to attain realization provides a setting for youthful resentment and a sense of injustice.

It is easy to exaggerate the proportion of youth who seriously experience such resentment. Though youth, like any minority, have their disgruntled and malcontented members, a large proportion of them accept the indulgence of adults and exhibit satisfaction instead of resentment. Thus, a third section, perhaps the largest, seems hardly touched by the rising expectations experienced by more obstreperous and thus visible youth. These are the staid and contented youth who have only recently begun to be noticed (Bealer & Willits, 1961; Danserau, 1961; Reiss, 1961). Such a contented type is most likely to appear and gain influence among minorities, like women and youth, who enjoy easy access to majority members. Moreover, the prominence of contented youth is especially enhanced by the unique feature of youthful minorities—the realistic expectation that with the passage of time majority status will be ascribed.

Youth are thus a minority who realistically look ahead to maturity and therefore majority. The conventionality of modern youth is mainly based on this aspiration to adulthood. The deviance is based on temporary minority status and the difficulties arising from touchy relations with adults. Moreover, youthful adherence to a variety of deviant forms is increased in the measure that adulthood must be achieved through adequate performance and conduct, rather than simply being gained with mere passage of time. Thus, youth who perform very badly in elementary or secondary schools are likely to have the realistic aspiration to adulthood interfered with and to that extent are less bound to convention. Such youth often engage in delinquent behavior. On the other hand, since youthful deviance is partially based on the prolonged period during which some are requested to exhibit patience and to continue as mere aspirants to majority status, it may not appear until the end of the long educational regimen—most notably in the American graduate school—and typically takes a bohemian or radical turn.

Prolonged Aspiration and Diversion

Statistics on years spent in school all show a consistent and sharp rise in the past century (Trow, 1961). One cannot, however, jump to the conclusion that increase in schooling produces a concomitant rise in the stressful condition of youth, at least until one knows what duration is subjectively considered "prolonged" by youth themselves. One may suggest that the duration of youth is subjectively prolonged when some youth believe that certain occupations warrant little preparation, or when they imply through sustained truancy, for instance, that whatever the theoretical value of educational preparation, it has failed to help them. Each of these states characterizes some sizable, though not necessarily major, segment of youth. However, overall satisfaction with the long period of youth may prevail despite the reluctance by some young persons to grant legitimacy to educational preparation. Youth is a period of remarkable contemporaneous engagements which serve to obscure the future. If these engagements of "youth culture" may divert youth from study, they may also divert them from their dissatisfaction with study taken as preparation for adulthood.

The long period and the tempo of American schooling provide the occasion for leisure and diversion as well as a period for aspiration and preparation. The long duration of education does not rest solely on the higher skill requirements of an advanced technology (Muuss, 1962). There is little doubt that education could proceed faster and consequently youths could be more quickly brought to adulthood. However, other values are involved. As Naegele suggested:

> We have increasingly come to expect childhood to be in some sense happy, light, carefree. Yet as childhood moves more and more into the province of the schools, we come to have various second thoughts as to this apparent light-heartedness. The debate about education is directly a debate about priorities and realities in adult life (Naegele, 1962, pp. 53–54).

Despite the second thoughts alluded to by Naegele, the persistence of the slow tempo of schooling, best symbolized by the summer vacation, indicates that the earlier ideas continue to dominate.

Second, our school system includes in its curriculum liberal, or impractical, subjects. Not all courses, or even most, are directed toward the technical proficiencies necessary for one or another career. Liberal education is an "inefficiency," but one that is more or less treasured by the professionals most immediately concerned with the school system. Thus, many courses taken in secondary school or college are valued by educational authorities on their own merits, rather than as a means to a job. A great assortment of interesting and otherwise worthwhile courses in the educational curriculum, with little or no relevance to any subsequent career, are offered because they contain the minimal aspects of the cultural heritage Americans wish to give to future citizens.

A third source of prolonged schooling may be found in occupational or professional rivalries. Occupations, especially those which are in close interaction with technical or staff professions, come to require higher and higher degrees of education partially to expedite the wielding of authority over those who are initially more educated or to achieve a greater measure of colleagueship with superior professions than currently exists. Thus, for instance, business executives "need" more education partially because they must legitimately supervise Ph.D. chemists, and social workers "need" more education partially because they wish to work on a collegial basis with psychiatrists. Each occupation desires to control its own entrance requirements. The time spent in school thus is only partially related to concern for the interests of youth.

Ameliorated dependence and prolonged aspiration and diversion combine to give youthful behavior its complex and markedly inconsistent character. The indulgences and freedom granted during youth produce a discontent and anxiety arising from a confused and often unrealized aspiration to equality, but they also permit a sort of frivolous euphoria. Similarly, the prolonging of education provides an opportunity for leisure or an occasion for boredom, frustration, and resentment. The peculiar combination of precocious resentment and leisured euphoria facilitates the third feature of the position of modern youth. The period of youth is only loosely integrated into the wider society. It is, in relative terms, a free sector in the social order.

Loose Integration and Partial Autonomy

The term alienation has served to obscure the obvious fact that integration in social systems is a matter of degree. Full alienation connotes, among other things, a feeling of sustained opposition to the system, but this feeling is not necessarily a feature of loosened integration.

Relative freedom from conventional controls initially follows from the normal subsiding of parental domination before the responsibility of self-support has appeared. Relative freedom is further facilitated by the social changes implicit in ameliorated dependence, the potentialities of prolonged and undemanding education, and the combination of resentment and euphoria elicited by these changes.

Eisenstadt (1951; 1962) suggested the general conditions under which youth groups are likely to emerge in society. He felt that they appear in societies in which the family is not directly linked to the productive sectors of the economy. Implicit in his theory is the idea that age periods during which the family subsides in importance and occupation has yet to appear are prone to the development of semiautonomous and relatively unregulated youth groupings.

Youth culture, more properly youth subculture, is neither clearly separated from adult conventions nor unified within itself. Youth subculture is not so separated from adult culture because it is manned by persons who in the past have been dominated by conventional families and look forward, or aspire, to subsequent entry into conventional life. Thus, the leisured diversions which make up much of the substance, temporary for each member, of youth subculture are themselves highly colored by activities and precepts which appear in adult life. Youth subculture is at least in part an adaptation of adult sentiments and practices to the special conditions of youthful existence (Elkin & Westley, 1955).

The integration of youth subculture and its separation from conventional adult life are both recognized in Coleman's *Adolescent Society* (1961), despite the fact that Coleman's main purpose was to document the fundamental separation. He related the separation to the "setting-apart" of children in the school system, to the tendency of schools to take on more and more in the form of extracurricular activities, and to the increased duration of education and training. Consequently, suggested Coleman, the adolescent is "cut off from the rest of society, forced inward toward his own age group, made to carry out his whole social life with others his own age" (Coleman, 1961a, p. 3). Most of the important interactions, according to Coleman, take place within the adolescent society. There are "only a few threads of connection with outside adult society" (Coleman, 1961). Coleman suggested that the basic cause of this separation may be found in the emergence and character of the school system. Thus, youth subculture, according to Coleman, is an unintended consequence of the organization of the school system. Youth have been placed in a collective context in which segregation from adult life has been imposed, and they have responded accordingly.

Whether separation is nominal or real, however, depends on the content of youth subculture. If a content different from that of the adult culture appears, one may speak of a separate youth subculture. If the substance of youth subculture is similar to that of adults, then despite the predominance of peer interaction one must exercise considerable caution in conceiving of a separate world of youth. Coleman's (1961a) findings—his data more than his interpretation—indicate a state of affairs somewhere between separation and integration. Coleman was, of course, aware of this, despite the main thrust of his argument which is toward the thesis of separation.

Youth subculture is intertwined with adult culture (Berger, 1963) and is highly pluralistic. Despite its connection with adult sentiments and its internally heterogeneous character, one may nevertheless note the existence of youth subculture and describe some of its manifestations. Youth subculture is by now a world-wide phenomenon, first occurring in advanced countries but increasingly apparent in emerging nations. Many perceptive observers have correctly stressed the central and initiating role played by American youth (Denney, 1962). Teen-age culture has been among the most important exports of the United States. To many Europeans, it has been a disturbing matter.

Youth relations, suggested Smith, "are largely informal and are composed of intimacy and sentiment" (E. Smith, 1962, p. 2). The subculture of youth is largely an informal system of highly localized and ephemeral units. It is for the most part not anchored in conventional formal organization, though portions of it may base their operation in one or another adult-sponsored house or area. There is some tendency to avoid adult supervision. Smith, relying heavily on Simmel's (1906, pp. 462–463) assertion regarding the universality of secrecy among youth, suggested the prevalence of youthful inclination to evade regular supervision.

> Solidarity and concealment . . . may be viewed as universal characteristics of youth culture. . . . The universality of secrecy suggests that youth will manifest varying degrees of withdrawal from adult socializing institutions. . . . The activities and interactions of youth will be hidden behind a veil of secrecy erected to escape the supervision and control of adults (E. Smith, 1962, p. 2).

Part of what youth are hiding must surely confirm the worst suspicions of their excluded elders; behind the veil they sometimes do disapproved of things. But there are at least two other sorts of activities that are concealed from adults.

First, youth, in a variety of ways, play at being adults. These games take many forms, some of which pay tribute to a public figure, some to members of private and intimate circles. One example of such activity consists of the playful conversion of informal and intimate ball-playing to out-and-out fantasies in which youthful players openly pretend before one another to be grown-up major league baseball stars. Only peculiar and specially defined adults are privy to public fantasies of this sort. Another example consists of the pretenses by which boys and girls act considerably more "grown up" than they and almost everyone else knows they are. Such aping of adults may be exhibited before peers, but to allow the conventional adult to observe would be embarrassing and in some circles an unpardonable admission of the respect accorded adulthood despite the frequent disclaimers. The staging of disdain of adulthood requires the obscuring of imitation and respect. Many adult observers, their vision being obstructed, have been deceived by the front.

Second, secrecy helps maintain the uncommitted character of youthful identity. Young persons toy with a variety of styles which they later discard. Even during engagement with a particular style, there frequently is little commitment to the precepts and practices underlying it. Publicity regarding identity, especially publicity which reaches conventional adults, minimizes the chances of playful engagement and maximizes the chances that character will be typed and lead to commitment.

Thus, seclusion upholds an inner secret of youth: fickle playing rather than commitment to identities. Conventional adults are likely to view the behavior implicit in one or another style completely out of context. They see it as harboring commitment, duration, and, thus, danger or a precocious closing of adolescence. Secrecy is therefore valuable to the youthful players since it minimizes the possibility that a temporary impression will endure as a stereotype.

The Pursuit of Identity

Adult identity is relatively focused and narrow. Presumably, men find identity in work, or, if work is too stultifying, perhaps in some seriously pursued avocation. Women invest their identity in kinship units, in the perceived occupational status of husbands, in their own roles as housewives, and in the character of their progeny. Increasingly, of course, women seek identity in an occupation or career. Youth, on the other hand, is the period of pursuit of *general* identity, a search which is simultaneously less intellectually demanding and more psychically tiring than that encountered during adulthood. Youth is engaged in self-discovery, except that it is not a self that is typically discovered but rather an already available style with which one's self can be comfortably associated. Identity here consists of generalized *preoccupations* instead of specific occupations (Eisenstadt, 1962; Erikson, 1950; Erikson, 1962; Muuss, 1962).

Because of the emerging position of youth, more or less stable identities have appeared within American life. These identities have grown into traditional styles which have been assumed and put aside by one cohort of youth after another. No style claims a majority of youthful adherence. Many youth vacillate among different identities, some of which will be discussed on the following pages, and most include in their wanderings shorter or longer stays in conventional amalgams which combine the features of analytically distinctive styles.

Scrupulosity

Scrupulosity is the most conformist of youthful styles. Among such persons, one finds little trace of the hedonism, expressiveness, and rebellion which presumably characterize youth culture. An expert on the incidence and forms of scrupulosity described it in the following way: "The term scrupulosity is well known to those devoted to pastoral work. . . . It may be taken to mean an unhealthy and morbid kind of meticulousness which hampers a person's religious adjustment" (Riffel, 1963, p. 39).

For the sociologist, however, the defining element of scrupulosity is the meticulous adherence to religious and moral precepts. Scrupulosity may take the form of meticulous avoidance of temptation, a studied devoutness unbecoming to frivolous youth, a serious-ness regarding church and parochial study, or a deeply introspective mentality. Whether such a style masks a deep emotional disorder, as is frequently alleged, is of little concern here, for almost all of the styles of youth to be described have been held by one writer or another to be the manifestation or symptom of a deep or transient disturbance. It remains to be shown, however, that abnormality is more representative of scrupulous youth than, say, the occasional athlete who turns out to be a pervert.

Scrupulosity, like most youthful styles, has a putative social base among students in the widespread system of Catholic parochial education. There is undoubtedly scrupulos-ity among youth who are devoted to other religious or secular faiths, but it is difficult to obtain information on these young people. Thus the present discussion must focus on Catholic scrupulosity.

The proportion of Catholic youth attending parochial school in America is high. Moreover, the proportion of those engaging in scrupulosity for longer or shorter inter-ludes is sufficiently large to make it an important youthful phenomenon. Numerically, scrupulosity seems of roughly the same order of magnitude as that youthful style at the other end of the spectrum which nowadays attracts so much public attention—juvenile delinquency.

Though it is obviously difficult to know with certainty the frequency with which youth take on the style of scrupulosity, there are a few studies which give a rough idea. The data reported in these studies seem unusually plausible since the conditions of true response are more or less built into the attributes of the style and the generally negative assessment it receives. Scrupulous persons, like delinquents, might have a motive to deny their condition, but, unlike delinquents, they cannot because of their scrupulosity.

Riffel summarized the few available reports on the frequency of scrupulosity:

> Though accurate figures on the extent of scrupulosity among Catholic adolescent students are hard to obtain, the data of several reports are available. Mullen (1927) reported in a study of 400 Catholic school girls that 26% of them admitted to habitual scrupulosity. A Fordham study (Riffel, 1958) corroborated this earlier report of Mullen. This study was based on 490 students divided between sophomore high school and sophomore college years. . . . Of the high school students, 26% admitted to current scrupulosity, but in college the number had declined to 14%. . . . Boys and girls were included in the sample and the percentage of boys admitting to scrupulosity was almost precisely the same as that for girls (Riffel, 1963, p. 42).

Even if one assumes no scrupulosity whatsoever among parochial students in other denominations, which hardly seems reasonable, and no scrupulosity whatsoever among nonparochial school youth, which is considerably more reasonable, he is still left with a national rate of scrupulosity of at least 2 or 3 per cent, which is of the same order of magnitude as that of juvenile delinquency.

Scrupulosity, like delinquency and most other styles of youth, varies in frequency by specific age within the time period of youth. Considerably higher proportions of high school than college youth assume this style. Riffel (1963) stressed the transitory quality of scrupulosity, though he was careful to avoid the common view that it is very short-lived. According to his findings, scrupulosity is a stylistic phase that is assumed and acted on for a year or two, then apparently dispensed for yet another. Some smaller proportion of young persons maintain scrupulosity for somewhat longer periods of time. Scrupulosity, like delinquency, seems to be a passing phase for certain kinds of youth and more or less impervious to correctional intervention. A few persons may develop commitment to the style or for other reasons maintain the identity into adulthood and perhaps even for a lifetime.

Studious Youth

Scholars and achievers, along with the scrupulous, are among the conforming youth. Studious youth conform because they are preoccupied by the official purpose of youth, aspiration and preparation, and for the same reason reduce their participation in diversion and leisure.

Preoccupation with officially-approved study accompanied by the reasonable anticipation of moral success during adulthood would seem calculated to achieve prestige. One might, therefore, expect studious youth to occupy the position of highest prestige among their peers. That they do not seems to be the general conclusion of most research. The findings of research are, in this case as in so many others, similar to those reached by less systematic commentators.

The position of studious youth is tenable, nevertheless, because the rewards and acclaim of scholastic achievement are large and established, though not perhaps as high and exclusive as we intellectuals might like. It is also tenable because studious youth are not so rare and isolated as to be unable to form cliques which function to insulate and protect members against the hostility or seduction emanating from nonstudious youth.

Implicit in the view that studious youth are vulnerable is the belief that they are so dispersed as to lack a demographic base for clique structure. This belief gives rise to the oft-expressed fear that initially studious youth run the danger of being discouraged by peers and anti-intellectual adults and thus deterred from serious enterprise. But if a delinquent subculture may flourish, why suppose that a studious subculture, nurtured as it is by official authority, cannot also survive. Surely, the demographic base is ample. For youth, both academically-oriented scholars and vocationally-oriented careerists (Clark & Trow, 1960), compose a demographic base for insulated and protective studious cliques. This does not mean they study together, though occasionally they may; rather, it means that they may support one another's studious propensities. Nor does this imply a separate studious sector within youth subculture. There is shifting from this style to others and vice versa though there is perhaps greater stable commitment to this studious style of youth than to other styles, because it is more adult-like in character, because its preoccupation is more securely linked to the realm of occupation, and because persistent performance—the amassing of a good and steady scholastic record—is a main criterion of success in this style.

Studious youth may hold to a tenable style despite the threats and seductions emanating from other styles and despite the ambivalence and uncertainty which studious youth themselves exhibit. Introspective ambivalence may be an essential and frequently misleading feature of the studious style. Thus, studious youth themselves are among the many critics of their style. They are often in the curious position of verbally wishing for the diversions which abound among the youth who surround them. But denunciation may have little effect on the tenacity with which they pursue study. They know that substantial rewards await scholastic performance. It is that realization that probably accounts for the hostility of nonstudious youth in the first place.

An impression of the proportion of youth who are in some measure oriented to studies may be found in Coleman's *Adolescent Society* (1961). He found that in large high schools about 6 per cent of the boys are identified by peers as scholars. Another 1 per cent are considered to be both scholars and athletes. In small high schools, a little less than 9 per cent are identified as scholars, and another 2 per cent are thought of as athlete-scholars. Moreover, the scholars are surrounded by many students whose attitudes seem generally sympathetic to studious enterprise (Coleman, 1961a, p. 147).

Coleman (1961a) suggested that occupational aspirations may be taken as indications of values, some of which provide supportive attitudes to the scholars. Thus, a favorable orientation toward an attractive representative of an occupation which requires conscientious study may indicate a supporting attitude toward scholarship.

The high school students in Coleman's (1961a) study were asked: "If you could be any of these things you wanted, which would you most want to be?" The available responses—jet pilot, nationally famous athlete, missionary, and atomic scientist—may be taken respectively as orientations to adventure, sports, morality, and scholarship. About 25 per cent chose atomic scientist. Even if one assumes that all who were identified as scholars chose atomic scientist, and surely many did not, he is left with more than 15 per cent of high school youth who, while not scholars, seem sympathetic to scholarship.

The secure status of studious youth and the tenability of the enterprise inherent in that status is indicated in many studies of youthful opinion. Though the interpretations convey a tone of complaint and an expressed wish that the status of studious youth were even higher, the findings themselves leave little doubt regarding their established position (Tannenbaum, 1962, Ch. 2). Coleman's (1961a) is one of many studies that legitimately stresses the preponderance of frivolous pursuits among youth, but in so doing minimizes the established and substantial minority given to studious concerns. The secure establishment of a studious style within the subculture is obscured by its minority positions, its failure to advertise its advantaged place, and the uncertainty and ambivalence with which the studious themselves hold to such a style. Partly, their ambivalence is a response to blandishments and taunts emanating from more diverted youth. Partly, however, the ambivalence is intrinsic to the studious style itself which, being less distracted by external diversion and more given to solitary study, is perhaps more prone to introspection and self-scrutiny. Some of the antistudious sentiment which abounds in opinion surveys of youth may actually emanate from studious youth themselves. The ambivalence may function to reduce the level of hostility directed toward the studious. Self-doubt is a mark of the intellectual which also appears among studious youth. It would be a mistake to suppose that the self-scrutiny and self-doubt of intellectuals, or studious youth, are tantamount to style- or self-rejection.

Tannenbaum's (1962) findings regarding the unfavorable attitudes of high school youth toward the studious are best seen in the light of the ambivalence maintained by youth who are themselves oriented in a studious direction. The students in Tannenbaum's sample were asked to respond in stereotypical fashion to eight adolescent types constructed by dichotomizing three attributes. The attributes were brillance, conscientiousness or studious effort, and sports-mindedness. The highest-regarded type was the brilliant, nonstudious, and sports-minded, while the lowest was brilliant, studious, and nonathletic. Between the two extremes, athletic orientation consistently attracted esteem while studious effort consistently repelled it. Thus far, there is nothing surprising in Tannenbaum's findings. Beyond this, however, he found virtually no relationship

> between character ratings and the respondent's own academic abilities . . . [or] the educational accomplishments of their parents. . . . Correlations hovered around zero . . . indicating that for the population studied, the value of information on intelligence and levels of parental education in predicting character ratings was negligible (Tannenbaum, 1962, p. 58).

This absence of any relation between the rating of the constructed character types and the background and performance of the raters was

> one of the most significant outcomes of the study. Even in the case of the brilliant-studious-non-athlete, rated significantly lower than any of the others, there was no evidence of higher regard shown by those who might identify more closely with this character on the basis of ability and dedication to school work (Tannenbaum, 1962, p. 58).

Tannenbaum (1962) felt that this may indicate a conformity on the part of studious youth to the atmosphere of anti-intellectualism current in high school. Whatever this finding *may* indicate, it surely demonstrates the persistence of a segment, in this case a large one, of studious youth, whatever their expressed attitude. Tannenbaum's study, as it happens, was of a middle-class high school in Brooklyn in which the student body was 75 per cent Jewish. Jews exemplify, perhaps better than any other American group, a culture which provides support for studious youth. The antistudious rhetoric of Jewish and other youth seems to be an element of the style of this group. It should not be confused with actual vulnerability to frivolous diversion or rejection of the studious effort implicit in the style.

Sports and Athletes

Sports are perhaps the most important of the conventional styles which divert attention from the officially defined purposes of youth. In the Coleman (1961a) study, the proportion of male youth identified by peers as athletes was slightly under 6 per cent in large schools. Another 1 per cent combined scholarly with athletic virtuosity. In small schools a little over 9 per cent were identified as athletes by peers. An additional 2 per cent were seen by their peers as coupling scholarly with athletic skill (Coleman, 1961a, p. 147).

The dominance of sports among American youth has drawn the attention of many observers. Typically, though not always, a disapproval of athletic dominance has accompanied the assertion of its central role in youth (Coleman, 1961a; Gorer, 1958; Laski, 1948). The major basis for this has been the claim that its seductive potency is so high that it diverts energy and attention from studies.

One of Coleman's (1961a) purposes in *Adolescent Society* was to document the prevalence of athletic orientation among high school youth and to designate the limited though large section of youth in which sports predominate.

High school boys were asked: "If you could be remembered here at school for one of the three things below, which one would you want to be?" Of the responses, 31.5 per cent of the boys chose brilliant student; 45.1 per cent, athletic star; and 23.4 per cent, most popular (Coleman, 1961a, pp. 28–29). The responses differ substantially from parental responses to the same question regarding their sons. Of the parents, 77 per cent would prefer boys to be remembered as brilliant students; 9 per cent as athletic stars; and 14 per cent, as the most popular student (Coleman, 1961a, pp. 32–33). Girls were asked: "Suppose you had the chance to go out with . . . [any of the following]. Which one would you rather go out with?" Of their answers 35 per cent said star athlete; 17 per cent, best student; and 48 per cent, best looking boy (Coleman, 1961a, pp. 30–31). Thus, if one grants the utility of such indicators, common sense impressions are supported. A strong case can be made for the predominance of sports among boys, the fact that this predominance is not especially reflected in parental sentiments and that athletic prowess has some limited appeal to girls.

Coleman, among others, tended to view this predominance as a problem or failing and suggested a remedy, or palliative, by intellectual contests to provide prestige for studious youth (Coleman, 1960, pp. 337–347; Coleman, 1961b, pp. 33–43). His desire to ameliorate the position of scholars led him to consider the meaning and appeal of sports among youth. He was forced to consider this question because he wished to provide a structural alternative to sports—something which performs the same variety of functions. The discussion of the basis of athletic appeal is interesting but incomplete. Thus, his suggested alternative, intellectual contests, remains unconvincing even if one shares the antiathletic bias implicit in Coleman's corrective approach, because intellectual contests do not fulfill the variety of functions performed by sports. Coleman was able to maintain the possibility of substituting intellectual for athletic contests because he ignored many other important functions performed by sports—functions which could not be served by intellectual contests.

Coleman's (1960; 1961b) discussion of the functions of sports and the basis of their appeal is essentially an elaboration of one of the points made by Waller (1932) in *Sociology of Teaching*. Waller's analysis of the appeal of sports is still the fullest and most perceptive attempt by a sociologist to answer the difficult question of the meaning of sports. Waller began, like Coleman, by noting the central role of athletics among youth. He said of the activities of youth within the educational system:

> Of all activities athletics is the chief and most satisfying. It is the most flourishing and most revered culture pattern. It has been elaborated in more detail than any other culture pattern. Competitive athletics has many forms. At the head of the list stands football, still regarded as the most diagnostic test of the athletic prowess of any school. Then comes basketball, baseball, track, etc. (Waller, 1932, pp. 112–113).

Waller went on to consider the basis of athletic pre-eminence:

> [We may also] account for the favorable influence of athletics upon school life in terms of changes effected in group alignments and the individual attitudes that go with them. It is perhaps as a means of unifying the entire school group that athletics seems most useful from the sociological point of view. There is a tendency for the school population to split up into its hostile segments of teachers and students and to be fragmented by cliques among both groups. . . . This condition [of potential conflict] athletics alleviates. Athletic games furnish a

dramatic spectacle of the struggle of picked men against the common enemy, and thus is a powerful factor in building up a group spirit which includes students of all kinds and degrees and unifies the teachers and the taught (Waller, 1932, p. 115).

This notion of athletics as a device for enhancing the unity or solidarity of schools was stressed by Coleman (1960; 1961a; 1961b). For Coleman, however, it was the sole basis of athletic appeal, whereas for Waller it was only one of a variety of bases.

Coleman concluded by contrasting the predicament of studious youth with the fortunate position of athletes. It is this contrast which stimulates Coleman's recommendation to promote intellectual contests by which studious youth, too, could serve as collective embodiments of scholastic unity.

> The outstanding student, by contrast, has few ways—if any—to bring glory to his school. His victories are purely personal ones, often at the expense of his classmates, who are forced to work harder to keep up with him. Small wonder that his accomplishments gain little reward, and are often met by such ridicule as "curve raiser" or "grind," terms of disapprobation having no analogues in athletics (Coleman, 1961a, p. 309).

By limiting his explanation of the appeals of sports to this single contribution, Coleman (1961a) was not driven to ask why athletics has emerged as *the* agency of school cohesion and therefore had little reason for exercising caution in commending intellectual contests as structural substitutes for football games. As soon as one considers other functions of sports and thus other bases of appeal, the case for intellectual contests is weakened and the case for the continued predominance of sports among youth is strengthened. These other functions are no more speculative, and no less, than the thesis which bases the appeal of sports on its service as a collective representation.

Many of the other possible social functions of sports are discussed by Waller (1932). Waller was able to capture some of the sense in which sports, but not intellectual contests, may exemplify masculinity, heroism, goodness, and danger and thus represent a tenable subject for drama and pageantry.

Waller stressed the contribution made by athletics in supporting an *adult-dominated* scholastic order. Athletic contests in many cases have emerged as increasingly routinized and institutionalized ways of channeling violent rivalries between towns, neighborhoods, and schools (Kittermaster, 1958, pp. 84–85; Rudolph, 1962, p. 378). Early athletic contests were frequently symbolic contests between fierce and violent rivals in which the conflict was increasingly limited by rules of the game and chosen representatives of each side. The routinization of violence in sports has never been quite complete in that there is a persistent tendency for uncontrolled violence to break through the limitations set by the rules, in the form of rough or dirty playing, and for the spectators to join the field of battle. Thus, the athletic contest may occasionally erupt into more total conflict, despite its long institutionalization. Normally, however, the official goal of civil order is well served by the routinized violence embodied in many athletic contests. The contest is still a fight in the crucial sense that physical force and prowess constitute essential elements of sports. The fight is controlled by the rules of the game—the instituted sanctions that attend flagrant violation—and, most important, by the limitation on participation to a few chosen representatives. Thus, as has been argued by some of its defenders, sports have played an important civilizing function. The peculiar and distinctive feature of sports is that it has maintained and encouraged physical force and strength while effectively controlling it.

Waller (1932) suggested the sense in which athletics have been a traditional means of social control. He also sensed the precariousness with which that purpose is served.

> Competition between schools in athletics comes to a focus on games. The game is in fact disguised war. There is a continual tendency for the game to revert to actual war.... Everyone treats the game as a fight, and thinks of it as a fight, except perhaps the referee. It is small wonder that the political order consisting of the rules and the referee to back them, is maintained with such difficulty and only by penalties which impose the direst disabilities upon the offenders. There is, it is true, a whole code of sportsmanship which arises from the conflict situation, a code which internalizes the rules and makes for the principle of fair play (Waller, 1932, pp. 113–114).

Thus, the appeal of sports among youth is enhanced by the fact that it is a forceful contest approved and even applauded by adults and the authorities among them. Sports have been traditionally viewed by adults as a means of stylizing and thus controlling violence. Moreover, athletics, and the associated codes of sportsmanship, have frequently been taken as the playground on which subsequently useful moral precepts are learned. This function can be exaggerated and idealized, but there is some correspondence between the moral demands of adult life and the particular code of sportsmanship prevalent in youthful games. A statement of correspondence or approximation need not be a mindless celebration of sports as character-building.

Waller (1932) suggested that athletics may expedite social control in yet another important sense. Athletes are, by the social definition of their endeavor, discouraged from engaging in many excesses which are commonly associated with youthful deviance. During the athletic seasons, athletes are enjoined to be "in training"; they are to refrain from smoking, drinking, staying out late, and other forms of dissipation which violate the expectations of adult authority and are seen by many as precursors to more serious delinquency. Whether such undesired precocious activity is always controlled by the Spartan requirements of training or whether such regimen is in fact necessary is of little consequence. What is important is that the athlete guided by its stern demands symbolizes the expectations of adults regarding clean-living among youth. Simultaneously, the high position awarded athletes serves to dramatize and glamorize the rewards of avoiding dissipation and other forms of early presumption of adulthood. In this way, as in others, the athlete is doing adult's work.

> Athletes may simplify the problem of police work in school. The group of athletes may ... furnish a very useful extension of faculty-controlled social order.... [There is] a close correspondence between athletic prowess and clean-living (Waller, 1932, pp. 116–117).

One final service of athletics warrants mention. There has never been any discernible *substantive similarity* between scholastic preparation and occupational goals. Substantive similarity is reserved for apprenticeship systems of preparation and for the small part of our scholastic system, usually in the performing arts or in graduate education, that has maintained important elements of apprenticeship. In almost all of a modern educational system there is little visible substantive connection between studying to be something and actually being that thing. There is formal connection, both direct and indirect, but the tasks of study and preparation bear little resemblance to concrete tasks in any particular occupation. Consequently, though adults expect youth to aspire, the very meaning of aspiration, and thus its impact, is obscure to youth. An important function of athletics is to make real the conception of aspiration.

Thus, sports links aspiration to diversion. Moreover, it joins youth to the adult social order in its functions as an agency of official social control. Athletics are the handmaiden of convention despite their harboring within them the spirit of exuberance, violence, prowess, freedom, and other attributes commonly imputed to youth. Thus, they are among the best examples of the social duplicity by which control is instituted through the illusion of autonomy. The substance of athletics contains within itself—in its rules, procedures, training, and sentiments—a paradigm of adult expectations regarding youth.

Like most actors who do important work for social systems and are paid in tenuous currency which is not always forthcoming, athletes are not as impressed with their lot as outsiders are. Thus, the high standing attributed to athletic youth does not necessarily result in a subjective feeling of satisfaction and contentment. The imagery of Saturday's hero is quite common among athletic youth, and in a variety of ways they display the same minority mentality as intellectuals or any other group which exists within a pluralistic system and feels its efforts insufficiently rewarded. Like others in their position, athletes are frequently more impressed with the liabilities of their enterprise than its more celebrated perquisites. These liabilities may include the humiliations of persistent defeat, grueling and dull periods devoted to practice and drill, the limitations on free and enjoyable leisure inherent in training regulations, the antiathletic biases of an influential and vocal minority of teachers and students—especially female—which often result in the dehumanizing stereotype of the "jock," the special fears concerning one's fortune after the typically very brief period of celebrity, and the very obvious dangers of incapacitating injury. Thus, the mood of those who maintain the athletic style may as much approximate that emanating from the demeaning ordeal of Sisyphus as that of Olympus.

Rebellious Youth

The final style of youth is a familiar one. Youth are generally known for rebelliousness, and, if one is careful to specify the small proportion who are rebellious, it is useful and informative to describe this contingent. Youth do seem more vulnerable to rebellious posture than either children or adults (Matza, 1961; Matza & Sykes, 1961). During the life cycle, maximum rebelliousness is generally reached during youth (Almond, 1954, pp. 218–220; Bernard, 1957, pp. 421, 444; Dunham & Knauer, 1954; Ernst & Loth, 1952; Lane, 1959, pp. 216–217; McCord, McCord, & Zola, 1959, p. 21; Parkinson, 1961, pp. 277–278; Parry, 1933, p. 2). This apparently holds for three forms of rebelliousness—delinquency, radicalism, and bohemianism.

Delinquency, radicalism, and bohemianism are forms of rebelliousness which apparently have a special appeal to youth. Each is a tradition that has distinct anticivil implications. Each is in some sense a threat to the stability and order of an on-going social system, though each threatens different aspects of that system. Delinquency does not denounce bourgeois property arrangements, but it clearly violates them. Moreover, the delinquent rejects bourgeois sentiments of methodism and routine, especially as they appear within the school system, which appears to be his major target of hostility. The bohemian's attitude toward property is typically one of condescending indifference, though he is appalled by the commercialization of art that he associates with property arrangements. His ire is reserved for the puritanical and methodical elements of the bourgeois ethos, especially as they pertain to personal and social relations. Moreover, the bohemian is typically antagonistic to recent trends in bourgeois society. He is opposed to the mechanized, organized, centralized, and increasingly collectivized nature of modern society, Capitalist, Socialist, or Communist. Radicalism, by contrast, envisages a less general denunciation. Particularly in the varieties of revolutionary Marxism, which represent the most important examples of modern radicalism, the primary focus of attack has been on the Capitalist system of economic domination, on the imperialist role allegedly played by such systems, and, most recently, on the threats to world peace presumably initiated or aggravated by Capitalist nations. The methodical, the puritanical, and, especially, the industrial aspects of the bourgeois order have been more or less embraced by most radicals.

Delinquency, radicalism, and bohemianism are most pronounced during youth, but they differ with respect to the specific age of vulnerability within youth. Since the duration of youth turns on the completion of schooling and preparation rather than chronology, it is not surprising that stage of education seems a more decisive point of division than chronological age. Youth who leave school earliest seem most vulnerable to delinquency. Delinquency is primarily a high-school-age phenomenon. Radicalism and bohemianism, especially in America, can be found in institutions of higher education. Its adherents are typically drawn from those whose education terminates during college, with the attainment of a bachelor's degree, or with some graduate work of indeterminable duration. Especially susceptible are persons whose studies are concentrated in areas without a clear-cut career route and without a demanding or exact curriculum. Bohemians seem so regularly concentrated in departments of English, art, and music that one is tempted to suggest that their real rebellion is not against society-at-large, but against the faculties in the respective departments and the standards of art they profess.

The modes of rebelliousness, furthermore, differ with respect to their ambitions. Delinquents have no designs on society; there is no desire on the part of delinquents to reconstruct society. Thus they are aberrant (Merton, 1961, pp. 725–727). Radicals, on the other hand, do wish to reshape society in the form of their own ideological predilections. Thus, they are the archetype of the nonconformist (Merton, 1961, pp. 725–727). Bohemians fall somewhere between, typically wishing to develop a private and insulated way of life, but rarely having any aspiration to convert the rest of society.

Finally, the modes of youthful rebelliousness differ with respect to assessments regarding their moral worth. In the case of delinquents, the judgments seem more or less to coincide with those belonging to conventional society (Sykes & Matza, 1957). There is no serious belief in either camp in the moral worth of the delinquent enterprise. There has been, however, considerable dispute regarding the moral value of radicalism and bohemianism. Many intellectuals attribute worth to each of these enterprises, and radicals and bohemians themselves, unlike delinquents, are convinced of the moral value of their doctrines and actions.

Beyond these general similarities and differences, each mode of youthful rebellion may be described separately, remembering that it is extremely unlikely that radicals, bohemians, and delinquents taken together and defined generously constitute even 5 per cent of the youthful population

Juvenile delinquency. There are many perceptive accounts describing the behavior of juvenile delinquents and their underlying sentiments. Perhaps no style of youth has been better covered and described (Bloch & Niederhoffer, 1958; Bordua, 1961; Cloward & Ohlin, 1960; Cohen, 1955; Cohen & Short, 1958; Finestone, 1957; Griffith, 1948; Kobrin, 1951; Miller, 1958; Shaw & Moore, 1931; Thrasher, 1936; Yablonski, 1962).

Although there have been important differences of opinion in the interpretation of this material and in the relative stress placed on various components, there has been some consensus on the content of delinquent values and sentiments.

The distinctive feature of the spirit of delinquency is the celebration of prowess. Each of the themes stressed in the delinquent tradition develops an aspect of the meaning of "prowess." First, delinquents are deeply immersed in a search for excitement, thrills, or "kicks." The approved style of life is an adventurous one. Activities pervaded by displays of daring and charged with danger are highly valued. The fact that an activity involves breaking the law and, thus, an eliciting of the game of "cops and robbers" is often the element that provides the air of excitement. "Kicks" or "action" may come to be defined as "any act tabooed by 'squares' that heightens and intensifies the present moment of experience and differentiates it as much as possible from the humdrum routines of daily life" (Finestone, 1957, p. 5). In courting danger and provoking authorities, the delinquent does not simply endure hazards; he creates them in an attempt to manufacture excitement. For many delinquents, "the rhythm of life fluctuates between periods of relatively routine and repetitive activities and sought situations of greater emotional stimulation" (Miller, 1958, pp. 10–11).

Second, to attain prowess is to seek and receive the material rewards of society while avoiding, in the manner of a leisure class, the canons of school and work with their implicit commitments to methodism, routine, and security. Delinquents commonly exhibit a disdain for "getting on" in the realms of school and work. Instead, there is a sort of aimless drifting or perhaps grandiose dreams of quick success.

The delinquent must be financed if he is to attain the luxury of the sporting life. Although some writers have coupled the delinquent's disdain of work with a disdain of money, it seems unlikely that money is renounced in the delinquent code; more likely, it is treated in a special but not unprecedented way. Money is valued, but not for purposes of a careful series of expenditures or long-range objectives. Money for the delinquent is a luxury. It is something to be attained in windfall amounts and subsequently squandered in gestures of largesse and other exhibitions of conspicuous consumption.

An age-old method of attaining such luxury income is gambling. Most of the other techniques involve victimizing others. Simple expropriation—theft and its variants— must be included, of course, but it is only one of a variety of ways of "scoring" and does not always carry great prestige in the eyes of delinquents (Finestone, 1957). Other forms of prowess include chicanery or manipulation, which may take the form of borrowing from gullible and sympathetic "squares" or more elaborate forms of hustling like exhorbitant initiation fees into otherwise defunct clubs; an emphasis on "pull," frequently with reference to obtaining a "soft" job assumed available only to persons with influential contacts; and the exploitation of females for gain.

A third theme running through the accounts of juvenile delinquency centers on aggressive masculinity. The code of the warrior, which in some ways the delinquent code reflects, calls for aggressive manliness, including reluctance to accept slights on one's honor (Margolis, 1960). The delinquent's readiness for aggression is particularly stressed in the analysis of juvenile gangs in slum areas of large cities. It is in such gangs that one finds the struggles for "turf," and, thus, it is in these cases that the applicability of the warrior code is most apparent. Cloward and Ohlin (1960) pointed out that one can be led into error by viewing conflict-oriented delinquents as typical of all delinquents. Yet the gang delinquent's use of honor, or "rep," and the proof of courage, or "heart," seems to express in extreme form the idea that aggression is a demonstration of toughness and, thus, masculinity. It is this idea which pervades delinquent thought.

Student radicalism. Relative to the many accounts of delinquency, there are few systematic descriptions of student radicalism in the United States (Iversen, 1959; Wechsler, 1953). Enough exists, however, to proceed with a tentative description of this tradition.

Radicalism among students did not begin in the decade of the thirties, although there is little question that it reached its height during that period. The Intercollegiate Socialist Society was organized in 1905, and in 1921 Calvin Coolidge decried student radicalism (Iversen, 1959, p. 13). Despite the internecine struggles within the revolutionary socialist movement since 1905, some aspects of the radical tradition have remained relatively stable.

First among the stable components is the vision of the apocalypse. This refers to "the belief that the evil world as we know it, so full of temptation and corruption, will come to an end one day and will be replaced by a purer and better world" (Shils, 1960, p. 59). This tradition has its origins in the apocalyptic outlook of the prophets of the Old Testament and has been passed down through the early Christians and adherents of heretical sects. Its modern recipients are "the modern revolutionary movements and above all the Marxian movements." The tradition is best reflected in "doctrinaire politics, or the politics of the ideal" (Shils, 1960, p. 60).

Whatever its general importance in revolutionary socialism, the politics of the ideal seems peculiarly well suited to the predispositions of youthful rebelliousness. This sort of politics seems consistent with Davis' description of youth's mixture of idealism and cynicism (Davis, 1949; Davis, 1944). In the politics of the ideal, perception and assessment become bifurcated with respect to idealism and cynicism. On this side of the apocalypse, one views and interprets events critically and cynically; on the other side, or in some contemporary foreshadowing of the future, one views and interprets events idealistically and generously.

The second component of the spirit of student radicalism is populism. "Populism is the belief in the creativity and in the superior worth of the ordinary people, of the uneducated and the unintellectual" (Shils, 1960, p. 60). Because of the central role of populism in modern radicalism, revolutionary movements have tended to equate the apocalypse with the liberation of the folk. The particular folk has varied: In the Russian social revolutionary movement, it was the peasant; in traditional Marxism, it was the industrial proletariat; in the anarchism of Bakunin, it tended to be the *Lumpenproletariat*. American student radicalism, largely unaware of these esoteric distinctions, has tended to lump these populist ideals together in a compote consisting of migrant farm workers, unskilled and semiskilled industrial workers, and Negroes.

Among students, the appeal of populism is not simply an outgrowth of traditional radical propensities. Just as the apocalyptic mentality has a special appeal to youth, so, too, does populism. Students have a special liking for populism because it is a vehicle for an effective attack on the professional authority and a way of defending against unflattering assessment of themselves. For the radical, and bohemian, too, a belief in populism allows students who perceive themselves as avant-garde to deflect the contrary judgments of academic elders.

A third component of the student radical spirit is evangelism, which is well suited to the exuberance and impetuosity characteristic of rebellious youth. Without it, radicalism would be too serious an enterprise to compete effectively for rebellious youth. Thus, evangelism seems as important in the bolstering of internal enthusiasm as in its alleged purpose of gaining new adherents. By encouraging excursion, it allows student radicals to stray from the dull routine of the radical enterprise (Wechsler, 1953) and challenges their capacities for argumentation, intimidation, persuasion, and seduction.

The substance of student radicalism is unconventional political action. Its round-of-life consists of taking stands on concrete issues, circulation of petitions, distribution of leaflets, sale of literature, raising funds, demonstrations and rallies, frequent meetings, discussions, debates, and the like. The mundane character of most of these activities is more or less obscured by the context within which they are viewed. This context is provided by the general characteristics of unconventional politics.

Radical politics is less attentive than conventional politics to the administrative bylaws which govern collegiate activity. Thus, elements of excitement and risk are introduced. Moreover, radical politics is revolutionary rather than simply reformist. This adds meaning and drama to concrete activities and provides a basis for vicarious excitement by requiring identification with actual revolutions taking place elsewhere. Furthermore, radical politics is ideological rather than "market" (Bell, 1960) politics, and, thus, a sense of moral superiority attaches to the activities of the enterprise. Finally, radical politics is year-round rather than seasonal, and so imparts a sense of urgency rarely apparent in conventional politics. In summary, each of the characteristics of unconventional politics conspires to transform the mundane to the extraordinary.

Bohemianism. Bohemianism is a socioartistic enterprise which appeared as a widespread phenomenon in the first part of the nineteenth century in France (Parry, 1933, p. ix). Since then it has spread to many parts of the United States. Despite indigenous sources in the United States and internal influences, the periods of rise and fall of American bohemianism have coincided fairly well with its cycles in France (Parry, 1933). "Beat," the most recent form of American bohemianism, is best viewed as a response to recurrent internal conditions, most notably postwar prosperity, as well as a reflection of developments on the French scene, especially the emergence of café existentialism.

The failure to understand the traditional character of bohemianism in selected American locales and to see its ebb and flow as a reflection of recurrent social process, internal and external, has been largely responsible for alarmist interpretations of beat. Beat has been viewed, alternatively, as a sign of incipient nihilist rebellion and a symbol of hedonistic withdrawal from public life. It has been interpreted as a symptom of some deeper malady and a dark foreboding of what is to come. Interpretations of this sort occur whenever deviant patterns are not viewed in their historical context (Sisk, 1961).

The first and major component of bohemianism is romanticism. Romanticism "starts with the appreciation of the spontaneous manifestations of the essence of concrete individuality. Hence it values originality . . . that which is produced from the 'genius' of the individual (or the folk), in contrast with the stereotyped and traditional actions of the philistine" (Shils, 1960, p. 57). The commitment to spontaneity and originality has had many manifestations among traditional bohemians, particularly in the graphic arts (Barrett, 1958; Rosenberg, 1959). Among beats, however, greater stress has been placed on development of originality and spontaneity in other art forms. Most notable among these have been the celebration of improvisation in modern jazz, poetry, and the novel. For this reason, among others, jazz and jazz musicians have occupied an exalted role in the beat realm. Kerouac, the most notable literary exponent of improvisation, has occupied a similarly exalted position (Kerouac, 1957; Kerouac, 1958a; Kerouac, 1958b).

The exaltation of spontaneity in artistic endeavor is reflected in the bohemian view of the folk. Bohemianism, like radicalism, has a distinctive form of populism, which is best termed "primitivism." Its authentic folk hero was, of course, the gypsy. Because of the gypsy's chronic unavailability, however, it was not long before the notion of primitive folk had expanded to include more available peoples. The closest approximation that could be found in urban society was the *Lumpenproletariat,* and it is this group that has occupied a central place in the bohemian's primitivist mystique (Malaquais, 1958). In the modern form of bohemianism, the idealized folk is the lower-class Negro (Mailer, 1957). The Negro, however, is not the first American ethnic group to be granted this dubious honor. East European Jews, too, have been perceived by previous bohemians as the incarnation of primitive folk (Parry, 1933, p. 35).

Closely connected to the celebration of the primitive is the tradition of dedicated poverty. "A neighborhood where the poor live, the poor who are resigned to their poverty, is the best environment in which to live 'the life.' This is a cardinal principle which the beat share with the bohemians of the past" (Lipton, 1959, p. 59). Although the dedication to poverty is, in part, a natural outgrowth of a commitment to primitivism, it is simultaneously a conscious way of avoiding the corrupting influence of the commercial world.

A final aspect of romanticism, consistent with primitivism, consists of a more or less complete rejection of bureaucratic-industrial society. This may be referred to as medievalism and is best described as an apocalyptic view without the apocalypse. Medievalism accepts the first part of the apocalyptic formula, man's fall from grace, but makes no provision, as in radicalism, for man's redemption.

The second component of the bohemian tradition is insistence on the expression of authentic inner feelings. Thus, bohemianism has been marked by an intense moodiness. Mood is not to be suppressed or obscured; rather, it is to be indulged, pursued, and exhibited. Mood is a crucial part of inner, or authentic, experience and, thus, deserves unhampered expression. Because of this dedication to the full expression of mood, bohemianism has always been somewhat perplexing to the outsider who expects some consistency of temperament to accompany a reasonably coherent viewpoint.

Bohemianism has long had two faces which, although often combined in the career of the same person, have been manifested in two roughly differentiated streams. There is frivolous bohemianism, reminiscent in many respects of aristocratic "dandyism," and there is morose bohemianism, initiated by Poe and popularized by Baudelaire (Parry, 1933, pp. 11–12). After Baudelaire, the two moods persist and are reflected in beat in the modern distinction between "hot" and "cool":

> By 1948 the hipsters, or beatsters, were divided into cool and hot. . . . The cool today is your bearded laconic sage . . . before a hardly touched beer in a beatnik dive, whose speech is low and unfriendly, whose girls say nothing and wear black. The "hot" today is the crazy talkative shining-eyed (often innocent and open-hearted) nut who runs from bar to bar, pad to pad, looking for everybody, shouting, restless, lushy, trying to "make it" with subterranean beatniks who ignore him (Kerouac, 1961, p. 73).

Thus, in the insistence on the authentic display of mood and in the development of frivolous and morose subtractions, bohemianism has pushed to the limits of human expression. It has had a manic and a depressive character.

Even for the morose, however, the solitary life receives little authorization in the bohemian view. The unfriendly, laconic sage in Kerouac's description had, after all, "made the scene." Bohemians must have "scenes," since bohemianism has always referred to a collecting of like-minded eccentrics (Lipton, 1959; Parry, 1933; Rigney & Smith, 1961).

Monasticism, which is the formation of insulated communities of adherents, is an explicit attempt on the part of bohemians to regain the sense of community which, according to their ideology, no longer exists in the broader society. The clubs, cafés, dives, or pads, which are their monasteries, are places where the bonds of familiarity can be assumed and, except for the danger of the police interloper, one hardly need "check out" a scene before feeling secure in it. Not all persons are welcome in the places of congregation. Bohemians are not evangelists; on the contrary, the newcomer must prove in a variety of ways that he belongs (Rigney & Smith, 1961).

Bohemians have long realized that both the unauthentic (pretenders or "phonies") and the outright conventional (tourists or "squares") are greatly fascinated by the bohemian life (Rigney & Smith, 1961, p. 181). But because of their stress on authenticity, bohemians have been guarded in their relations with phonies and squares. They are also dimly aware of the fate that, sooner or later, befalls all bohemias: The persistence with which the squares and phonies discover their haunts has meant that virtually no bohemian "monastery" can long survive.

The substance of bohemianism has two important and interrelated elements. First, there is the creation of unconventional art, which may be distinguished from the conventional variety in three major ways. It is disaffiliated from the major institutions which provide the machinery for the production and distribution of art. Among these institutions are the modern university, with its direct and indirect subsidization of the arts, and the modern industries of mass communication which deal commercially in art (publishing firms) and in commercialized art (advertising). Second, stylistic innovation is characteristic of bohemian art. In each of the arts, the bohemian has been an experimenter in new styles of expression.

The third feature of unconventional art applies to its subject matter. Bohemian art has frequently dealt with the forbidden, the censorable. In his attempt to plumb the depths of human existence, the bohemian has often been guilty of confusing or equating the two meanings of "depths." This equivocation was an outgrowth of the bohemian's peculiar style of populism in which authentic life coincides with primitive life, with life as it is lived in the lowest orders of society and the underworld. His own descent into the lowest orders, resulting from his dedicated poverty, allows him to extend the province of his subject matter in an important manner. If the bohemian feared the *Lumpenproletariat* or if he discovered that their behavior was not always censorable, he could always turn to what is, after all, the most frequent subject matter of bohemian art—bohemians.

This brings us to the second and interrelated element of the bohemian enterprise, the pursuit of unconventional personal experience. It is interrelated, because, whatever its motive among bohemians, it has persistently performed a crucial function for young, aspiring painters, poets, sculptors, and novelists. It has provided them with a subject matter to which to apply their variable talents.

In the pursuit of unconventional personal experience, there is no assurance of success. Some sorts of experience involve higher risks of failure than others—the pursuit of sexual conquest, for instance, is less likely to culminate successfully than is the use of alcohol to lessen inhibitions. Thus, a cataloguing of the forms of experience traditionally pursued by bohemians should not be mistaken for an accurate rendition of what bohemians typically do. More time seems spent in pursuit than in actual experience.

Two sorts of unconventional experience are pursued. First, there is the search for hedonistic experiences which overlap considerably with activities that are currently deemed illegal in the United States. These are generally nonvictimizing offenses and include such misdeeds as sexual excess, homosexuality, intemperate use of alcohol, disturbing the peace, use of narcotics, and speeding in automobiles. Since many of these activities held popularity among bohemians during the nineteenth century (Parry, 1933, p. 11), it should not be assumed that beats have attained new levels of hedonistic experience.

Second, there is a quest for transcendence which is closely related to the problem of creativity and represents an experimenting with the limits to which human perception may be pushed. It is as an attempt to transcend the mundane restrictions on human perception that can best be understood in three highly esoteric activities of the beats: religious mysticism as manifested in Buddhist meditation, or the "Zen kick" (Kerouac, 1958a); the flirtation with and acceptance of psychosis, or the "insanity bit" (Krim, 1960); and the hallucinogenic use of drugs (Lipton, 1959, p. 178).

Conclusion

The aim of this chapter has been to summarize and organize some of the accumulated sociological knowledge regarding youth by means of a description of a variety of styles of youth behavior. Many youth, of course, do not, during most of their young years, maintain these styles in a pure form. Most youth probably engage in conventional composites, which in varying mixes blend the styles of scrupulosity, scholarship, sports, and one or another mode of rebelliousness. These blends are so varied as to defy enumeration. Moreover, there are other styles about which very little is known.

References

Abbott, Grace, *The child and the state*. Chicago: Univer. of Chicago Press, 1938. **2** vols.

Almond, G. A. *The appeals of communism*. Princeton, N.J.: Princeton Univer. Press, 1954.

Ausubel, D. P. *Theory and problems of adolescent development*. New York: Grune & Stratton, 1954.

Barrett, W. *Irrational man*. New York: Doubleday, 1958.

Bealer, R. C., & Willits, Fern K. Rural youth: A case study in the rebelliousness of adolescents. *Ann. Amer. Acad. polit. soc. Sci.*, November, 1961, **338,** 63–69.

Becker, H. S. *Man in reciprocity*. New York: Frederick A. Praeger, 1956.

Becker, H. S. *The outsiders: Studies in the sociology of deviance*. New York: The Free Press of Glencoe, 1963.

Bell, D. *End of ideology*. Glencoe, Ill.: Free Press, 1960.

Benedict, Ruth. Continuities and discontinuities in cultural conditioning. *Psychiatry,* May, 1938, **1,** 161–167.

Berger, B. M. On the youthfulness of youth cultures. *Soc. Res.,* Autumn, 1963, **30** (3), 319–342.

Berger, B. M. Adolescence and beyond: An essay review of three books on the problems of growing up. *Soc. Probs.,* Spring, 1963.

Bernard, Jessie. *Social problems at midcentury*. New York: Dryden, 1957.

Bettelheim, B. The problem of generations. *Daedalus,* Winter, 1962, 68–96.

Bloch, H., & Niederhoffer, A. *The gang.* New York: Philosophical Library, 1958.

Bordua, D. Delinquent subcultures: Sociological interpretations of gang delinquency. *Ann. Amer. Acad. polit. soc. Sci.,* November, 1961, **338,** 119–136.

Boys' Club of America. *Needs and interest study of 11, 12, and 13 year-old boys club members,* 1963.

Bronfenbrenner, U. The changing American child. In E. Ginzberg (Ed.), *Values and ideals of American youth.* New York: Columbia Univer. Press, 1961. Pp. 71–84.

Bronson, W. C., Katten, E. S., & Livson, N. Patterns of authority and affection in two generations. *J. abnor. soc. Psychol.,* 1959, **58,** 143–152.

Brossard, C. *Who walk in darkness.* New York: New Directions, 1952.

Clark, B. R., & Trow, M. Determinants of college student subculture. Unpublished manuscript, Berkeley, Center for the Study of Higher Education, 1960.

Clausen, J. A., & Williams, Judith R. Sociological correlates of child behavior. *Child Psych., 62nd Yearb. nat. Societ. Stud. Educ.,* 1963, Part I.

Cloward, R. A., & Ohlin, E. E. *Delinquency and opportunity.* Glencoe, Ill.: Free Press, 1960.

Cohen, A. K. *Delinquent boys.* Glencoe, Ill.: Free Press, 1955.

Cohen, A. K., & Short, J. F. Research in delinquent subcultures. *J. Soc. Iss.,* 1958, **14,** (3), 20–37.

Cohen, A. K., & Short, J. F. Juvenile delinquency. In R. K. Merton & R. A. Nisbet (Eds.), *Contemporary and social problems.* New York: Harcourt, 1961. Pp. 77–126.

Coleman, J. The adolescent subculture and academic achievement. *Amer. J. Sociol.,* January, 1960, **65,** 337–347.

Coleman, J. *The adolescent society.* Glencoe, Ill.: Free Press, 1961.(a)

Coleman, J. Athletics in high school. *Ann. Amer. Acad. polit. soc. Sci.,* November, 1961, **338,** 33–43.(b)

Danserau, H. K. Work and the teen-ager. *Ann. Amer. Acad. polit. soc. Sci.,* November, 1961, **338,** 44–52.

Davis, A. Socialization and adolescent personality. In N. B. Henry (Ed.), *Adolescence, 43rd Yearb. nat. Societ. Stud. Educ.,* 1944. Part I.

Davis, K. Sociology of parent-youth conflict. *Amer. socio. Rev.,* August, 1940, **5,** 523–535.

Davis, K. Adolescence and the social structure. *Ann. Amer. Acad. polit. soc. Sci.,* November, 1944, **236,** 8–16.

Denny, R. American youth today. *Daedalus,* Winter, 1962, 124–144.

Dunham, W. H., & Knauer, M. E. The juvenile court and its relationship to adult criminality. *Soc. Forces,* March, 1954, **32,** 290–296.

Eisenstadt, S. N. *From generation to generation.* Glencoe, Ill.: Free Press, 1956.

Eisenstadt, S. N. Archetypal patterns of youth. *Daedalus,* Winter, 1962, 28–46.

Elkin, F., & Westley, W. A. The myth of adolescent culture. *Amer. sociol. Rev.,* December, 1955, **20,** 680–684.

Erikson, E. *Childhood and society.* New York: Norton, 1950.

Erikson, E. Fidelity and diversity. *Daedalus,* Winter, 1962, 5–27.

Ernst, M. L., & Loth, D. *Report on the American Communist.* New York: Holt, 1952.

Feldman, G., & Gartenberg, M. *The beat generation and the angry young men.* New York: Dell, 1958.

Finestone, H. Cats, kicks, and color. *Soc. Probs.,* 1957, **5,** 3–13.

Friedenberg, E. *The vanishing adolescent.* Boston: Beacon, 1959.

Friedenberg, E. The image of the adolescent minority. *Dissent,* Spring, 1963, **10,** 149–158.(a)

Friedenberg, E. The isolation of the adolescent. In W. C. Bier, S. J. (Ed.), *The adolescent: His search for understanding.* New York: Fordham Univer. Press, 1963. Pp. 11–20.(b)

Goodman, P. *Growing up absurd.* New York: Random, 1960.

Gorer, G. The all-American child. In B. Meltzer, H. Doby, & P. Smith (Eds.), *Education in society.* New York: Crowell, 1958. Pp. 53–58.

Grana, C. *Bohemian vs. bourgeois: French society and the Frenchman of letters in the nineteenth century.* New York: Basic Books, 1964.

Griffith, Beatrice. *American me.* Boston: Houghton, 1948.

Hess, R. D., & Goldblatt, Irene. The status of adolescents in American society. *Child Develpm.*, 1957, **28**, 459–468.

Hollingshead, A. B. *Elmstown's youth*. New York: Wiley, 1949.

Iversen, R. W. *The Communists and the schools*. New York: Harcourt, 1959.

Keniston, K. Social change and youth in America. *Daedalus,* Winter, 1962, 145–171.

Kerouac, J. *On the road*. New York: Viking, 1957.

Kerouac, J. *Dharma bums*. New York: Viking, 1958. (a)

Kerouac, J. *The subterraneans*. New York: Grove, 1958. (b)

Kerouac, J. The origins of the beat generation. In T. Parkinson (Ed.), *A casebook on the beat*. New York: Crowell, 1961. Pp. 68–76.

Kittermaster, R. Sport and education. In A. Natan (Ed.), *Sport and society*. London: Bowes and Bowes, 1958. Pp. 82–88.

Knowles, J. *A separate peace*. New York: Macmillan, 1960.

Kobrin, S. The conflict of values in delinquent areas. *Amer. sociol. Rev.*, 1951, **16**, 653–661.

Kohn, M. Social class and the exercise of parental authority. *Amer. sociol. Rev.*, June, 1959, **24**, 352–366.

Krim, S. The insanity bit. In Krim, S. (Ed.), *The beats*. Greenwich: Fawcett, 1960. Pp. 60–77.

Lander, J. The pubertal struggle against the instincts. *Amer. J. Orthopsychiatry*, July, 1942, **12**, 456–461.

Lane, R. E. *Political life*. Glencoe, Ill.: Free Press,1959.

Laqueur, W. Z. *Young Germany: A history of the German youth movement*. New York: Basic Books, 1962.

Laski, H. *American democracy*. New York: Viking, 1948.

Lemert, E. M. *Social pathology: A systematic approach to the theory of sociopathic behavior*. New York: McGraw, 1951.

Lipset, S. M. *Political man*. Garden City: Anchor, 1963.

Lipton, L. *The holy barbarians*. New York: Messner, 1959.

McClelland, D., Atkinson, J., Clark, R., & Lowell, E. *The achievement motive*. New York: Appleton-Century-Crofts, 1953.

McCord, W., McCord, Joan, & Zola, I. *Origins of crime*. New York: Columbia Univer. Press, 1959.

McIntosh, P. C. The British attitude to sport. In A. Natan (Ed.), *Sport and society*. London: Bowes and Bowes, 1958. Pp. 13–24.

Mailer, N. The white Negro. *Dissent,* Summer, 1957, **4**, 276–293.

Malaquais, Jean. Critique of "White Negro." *Dissent,* Winter, 1958 **5, 73–75.**

Margolis, J. Juvenile delinquents: Latter-day knights. *Amer. Schol.*, Spring, 1960, **29**, 211–218.

Marshall, T. H. *Citizenship and social class, and other essays*. Cambridge: Cambridge Univer. Press, 1950.

Matza, D. Subterranean traditions of youth. *Ann. Amer. Acad. polit. soc. Sci.*, November, 1961, **338**, 102–118.

Matza, D., & Sykes, G. Juvenile delinquency and subterranean values. *Amer. sociol. Rev.*, October, 1961, **26**, 712–719.

Merton, R. K. Social problems and sociological theory. In R. K. Merton & R. A. Nisbet (Eds.), *Contemporary social problems*. New York: Harcourt, 1961. Pp. 697–737.

Miller, W. Lower class culture as a generating milieu of gang delinquents. *J. soc. Iss.*, 1958, **14** (3), 5–19.

Moore, W. *Man, time and society*. New York: Wiley, 1963.

Muuss, R. E. *Theories of adolescence*. New York: Random House, Inc., 1962.

Naegele, K. Youth and society. *Daedalus,* Winter, 1962, 47–67.

Parkinson, T. Phenomenon or generation. In T. Parkinson (Ed.), *A casebook on the beat*. New York: Crowell, 1961. Pp. 276–290.

Parry, A. *Garrets and pretenders: A history of bohemianism in America*. New York: Covici-Friede, 1933.

Parsons, T. Age and sex in the social structure of the United States. *Amer. sociol. Rev.*, October, 1942, **7**, 604–616.

Parsons, T. Youth in the context of American society. *Daedalus,* Winter, 1962, 97–123.

Powers, E., & Witmer, Helen. *An experiment in the prevention of delinquency: The Cambridge-Somerville youth study.* New York: Columbia Univer. Press, 1951.

Reiss, I. L. Sexual codes in teen-age culture. *Ann. Amer. Acad. polit. soc. Sci.,* November, 1961, **338,** 53–62.

Remmers, H. H., & Radler, D. H. *The American teenager.* Indianapolis: Bobbs, 1957.

Riffel, P. A. Sex and scrupulosity. In W. C. Bier, S. J. (Ed.), *The adolescent: His search for understanding.* New York: Fordham Univer. Press, 1963. Pp. 39–51.

Rigney, F., & Smith, L. D. *The real bohemia.* New York: Basic Books, 1961.

Rosenberg, H. *The tradition of the new.* New York: Horizon, 1959.

Rudolph, R. *The American college and university.* New York: Knopf, 1962.

Sarnoff, I. *Personality dynamics and development.* New York: Wiley, 1962.

Shaw, C. R., & Moore, M. E. *The natural history of a delinquent career.* Chicago: Univer. of Chicago Press, 1931.

Shils, E. A. *The traditions of intellectuals.* In G. de Huszar (Ed.), *The intellectuals.* Glencoe, Ill.: Free Press, 1960. Pp. 55–61.

Simmel, G., The sociology of secrecy and of secret societies. *Amer. J. Sociol,* January, 1906, **II,** 441–497.

Sisk, J. P. Beatniks and tradition. In T. Parkinson (Ed.), *A casebook on the beat.* New York: Crowell, 1961. Pp. 194–200.

Smith, E. A. *American youth culture.* Glencoe, Ill.: Free Press, 1962.

Sykes, G. M., & Matza, D. Techniques of neutralization. *Amer. sociol. Rev.,* December, 1957, **22,** 664–670.

Tannenbaum, A. J. *Adolescent attitudes toward academic brilliance.* New York: Teachers' College, 1962.

Thrasher, F. M. *The gang.* Chicago: Univer. of Chicago Press, 1936.

Trow, M. The second transformation of American secondary education. *Int. J. comp. Sociol.,* September, 1961, **2,** 144–166.

Waller, W. *The sociology of teaching.* New York: Wiley, 1932.

Wechsler, J. A. *The age of suspicion.* New York: Random House, Inc., 1953.

Werthman, C., & Piliavin, I. Preadolescent delinquency as a relationship to authority. Unpublished manuscript, Berkeley, Center for the Study of Law and Society, 1963.

Yablonski, L. *The violent gang.* New York: Macmillan, 1962.

33. The Adultlike Child and the Childlike Adult: Socialization in an Electronic Age

In the first half of the twentieth century, childhood was considered a time of innocence and isolation, a time for children to be sheltered from the nasty realities of adult life. Not only were they dressed differently from adults, but there were separate "languages" for each, since certain words and topics—birth, death, sex, and money—were considered unfit for children's ears. In addition, there was a strict age-grading system, supported by the structure of the school, that designated what a child of any given age should know and do.

The last thirty years have seen a remarkable change in the image and roles of children. Childhood as a protected and sheltered period of life has all but disappeared. Children today seem less "childlike." They speak more like adults, dress more like adults, and behave more like adults than they used to. We might call this trend the "end of childhood." But that would tell only half the story, for without a clear sense of childhood, there can be no distinct notion of adulthood. Indeed, there are indications that many of the adults who have come of age within the last twenty years continue to speak, dress, and act much like overgrown children. What seems to be happening in our culture is an overall merging of childhood and adulthood. In this essay I shall briefly summarize recent changes in the social roles of children and adults and then explore the possibility that the changes are related in part to our shift from a "book culture" to a "television culture."

The Merging of Childhood and Adulthood

One of the clearest signs of differences in status in a culture is a difference in appearance and dress. The inferior status conferred on children was once clearly discernible in the way they were dressed—whether in knickers, sailor suits, or cartoon character T-shirts. What was significant was not *what* children wore but the fact that their clothing was different from that of adults. Today, a walk on any city street or in any park suggests that the era of distinct clothing for different age-groups has passed. Children dress in three-piece suits or designer dresses, and many adults look like "big children" in their jeans, Mickey-Mouse or Superman T-shirts, and sneakers. In fact, many adults these days wear such "playclothes" to their places of work—including the White House. In addition, new "uni-age" styles of dress have emerged. Designer jeans, which are worn by

Joshua Meyrowitz, "The Adultlike Child and the Childlike Adult: Socialization in an Electronic Age," *Daedalus* 113, 3 (Summer, 1984): 19–48. Reprinted by permission of *Daedalus,* Journal of the American Academy of Arts and Sciences, Cambridge, Massachusetts.

young and old alike, represent a synthesis of the playclothes of children with the high-fashion clothing styles of adults. There appear to be no limits to this trend since there are now even designer jean diaper covers on the market.

This may all seem to be only a surface phenomenon—merely similar costumes overlaid on very different social beings. Yet children and adults have also begun to behave more like one another. Their posture, sitting positions, and gestures are becoming more similar, and the sight of adults sitting cross-legged on the ground in public or playing "children's games" is no longer an unusual one. Indeed, the latest generation of play-things—video and computer games—are played avidly by both adults and children alike.

Age-related vocabularies and forms of language are also merging, with many slang words, phrases, obscenities, and grammatical constructions being shared across a wide spectrum of age-groups. Children are speaking more like adults, and vice versa. More-over, while children and adults may have always cursed in private, they now do so in front of one another. And the fact that, increasingly, children call adults—in many cases, their parents—by their first names is further linguistic evidence that the authority of adults in relation to children is disappearing.

It is no longer clear what topics should or should not be discussed with children. In any case, children now seem to know about once taboo topics before they are included in their home or school education. Sex- and drug-education programs, for example, seem to be after the fact, since they have been outpaced by the runaway increase in teenage sexual activity and drug abuse. Birth control, abortion, alcoholism, and suicide are now "children's issues,"[1] and many young children today express fears of nuclear holocaust.[2]

For children, the issue of birth was once clouded in the myths of storks and cabbage patches. Today, many children are routinely told about birth and are included in what hospitals now call the "family birthing process." In some cases—though still rare—children are invited to be present at the delivery of their siblings.[3]

Things are changing for adults, too. Education, career choice, and developmental stages were once discussed primarily in relation to children, but increasing numbers of adults are enrolling in adult education programs, changing careers in mid-life, and becoming concerned with their "life stages."

That adult psychological temperament may also be changing is evident, for example, in the attitudes of the "me generation," which can be viewed as adult manifestations of the egocentrism traditionally associated with children. In addition, surveys indicate that the sense of responsibility that adults traditionally had for children is shrinking. Parents are less willing to make sacrifices for their children, and the numbers of parents whose thoughts about the future include concerns about their children's aspirations is in sharp decline. Americans now rank cars above children as aspects of a "good life."[4] One consequence of the loss of the traditional parental perspective is more democracy in the home. There appears to be a greater sense of equality between children and parents, and parents today are more likely to confide in their children and to admit to their own anxieties, shortcomings, and failures.[5]

This homogenization of status finds its reflection in changes in the images of adults and children in entertainment. The Shirley Temple character of the past was merely a cute and outspoken child; child stars today, however, such as Gary Coleman, often play the roles of adult characters who are imprisoned in children's bodies, as did Brooke Shields not too long ago. Similar adultlike children now appear in children's literature.[6]

In the age of the "antihero," it is also difficult to find traditional adults in films or on television. Adult characters—including many of those portrayed by Diane Keaton, Burt Reynolds, Chevy Chase, and Elliot Gould—often have the needs and emotions of over-grown children. Not only are adults frequently outsmarted by children in today's television programs and motion pictures, but children are sometimes portrayed as more mature, sensitive, and intelligent (as in the motion picture *E.T.*).

The relative legal status of children and adults has also changed dramatically. In 1967, for example, the Supreme Court gave children the right to counsel, declaring that "neither the Fourteenth Amendment nor the Bill of Rights is for adults alone"; subsequent decisions have provided children with many adult legal rights.[7]

With the sharp increase in the number of minors who run away from home and refuse to return, courts are often faced with deciding between the rights of the children and the rights of the parents—and the balance of power is shifting toward the former. In more than twelve states, courts are now allowed to "emancipate" minors so that they can work and live apart from their parents. Connecticut, for example, allows sixteen-year-olds to "divorce" their parents and be treated legally as adults.[8] In California, freedom can be gained at age fourteen.[9]

The legal meaning of "child" has been further confused by the fact that children under the age of fifteen are increasingly committing "adult" crimes such as armed robbery, rape, and murder.[10] As a result, many states are moving away from special lenient treatment of juveniles. In 1978, for example, New York State passed a law that allows child-murderers over the age of thirteen to be tried as adults.[11] In 1979 the American Bar Association ratified a new set of standards for juvenile courts. Rather than being concerned with the child's "best interests"—the original rationale for the juvenile court system—the ABA suggested that children should be punished in proportion to the severity of their crimes.[12]

Conceptions of adult legal responsibility have also become clouded in recent years. The increasing use and discussion of the pleas of "*temporary* insanity" or "diminished capacity" as excuses for committing a crime in a moment of anger[13] suggest an attempt to legitimize temper tantrums for adults.

Even when the formal legal status of children and adults remains untouched, children have been accorded a new kind of respect from courts, medical institutions, and government agencies. Courts today are much more likely to consider a child's view in custody settlements, and children and adolescents are now often asked for consent before receiving medical or psychological assistance.[14] The new attitudes are reflected in New York City's decision to name two foster children—aged thirteen and sixteen—as full-fledged members of a city panel to improve foster care.[15] Such moves represent a trend away from the traditionally paternalistic belief that adults always know what is in the best interests of a child.

In some circles, children have come to be seen as another disenfranchised "minority," and the Children's Rights Movement has developed to aid children in their struggle for freedom.[16] While some of the recent attention to children's rights focuses on the "right" not to starve or be beaten (children's *welfare*), other advocates of children's rights have pushed for the full social, economic, and political participation of children in society (children's *liberation*). As a member of the latter camp, Richard Farson has argued passionately for basic "birthrights" for children to counter what he sees as the segregation and disregard of children and the systematic discrimination against them by adults.[17] Similarly, in *Escape from Childhood*, educator John Holt outlines a "bill of rights" for children. He proposes that the "rights, privileges, duties, [and] responsibilities of adult citizens be made *available* to any young person, of whatever age, who wants to make use of them."[18] Holt's "rights" include the right to work, to travel, to vote, to have privacy, to own property, to sign contracts, to choose sexual partners, to have one's own home, and to choose one's guardians.

Such proposals for "full equality" for children and adults may be farfetched, but they reflect the current trend in child-adult relations. The "child-saving movement" of the nineteenth and early twentieth centuries was a movement designed to meet the "special needs" of children and guarantee them the "rights to childhood"—in a sense, to segregate them. The current trend is toward reintegration of the rights and roles of children and adults.[19] Certainly, all children and adults do not and cannot behave alike, but there are many more similarities in behavior and social status than there used to be. The traditional dividing lines are gone.

Whether these changes are good or bad is difficult to say. Whether children's "escape from childhood" should be viewed as liberation or aberration, or a little of both, is not clear. For better or worse, though, childhood and adulthood, as they were once defined, no longer exist.

The Myth of Age-Determinism

One of the reasons the merging of childhood and adulthood has been difficult to observe—and once observed, still difficult to accept—is that there are so few intellectual models to account for it. One might expect to find a model in developmental psychology, but the dominant research and theory in this field has focused primarily on describing the capabilities of individuals at different ages or stages of development, with the greatest attention being paid to studying the factors that contribute to, or are associated with, age- or stage-related changes. Although a variety of differences *between* age groups have been identified, and the typical characteristics of people *within* given age groups have been described, what is usually taken for granted is the preexistence of distinct life stages such as "infancy," "childhood," "adolescence," "adulthood," and "old age." For the most part, the research in developmental psychology has not been geared toward studying factors that might change the social character of different periods of life.

The findings of developmental studies are usually reported in terms of developmental stages matched to age-ranges, and while a number of psychologists have explained the limited implications of findings stated in terms of ages,[20] their explanations are rarely included in popularized summaries of developmental research. Many parents, teachers, and others assume therefore that developmental research demonstrates that age itself naturally "determines" a child's behavior and the appropriate style of interaction between children and adults. The notion of "age-determined" behavior has been reinforced and extended by popular and scholarly publications on adult "life cycles," "seasons," and "passages." These works describe such periods as the "age-thirty transition" and the "age-forty crucible."[21]

In general, the idea of clear age-related "stages" of development appears to provide scientific support for our traditional distinctions in roles, rights, and responsibilities of people of different ages. Indeed, as interpreted by some, the developmental paradigm does not even allow for the view that dramatic changes in age-related roles are possible.[22] Yet, those who insist on the "naturalness" of our traditional conceptions of childhood and adulthood are basing their belief on a very narrow cultural and historical perspective. Childhood and adulthood have been conceived of differently in different cultures, and child and adult roles have varied even within the same culture from one historical period to another.

To see and grasp the current changes in age-related roles, we need to distinguish between the biological existence of children and the social construction of "childhood," and to separate the maturational reality of adults and the social roles of "adulthood." We can observe physiological development, and we can test the cognitive capabilities of people of different ages in specific times and places. It is much more difficult, however, to discover the limits of individual differences in social development, the extent to which cultural factors override or blur "actual" differences, or the degree to which observable psychological differences among people of different ages necessarily determine particular social roles. In many ways, children may always be children and adults may always be adults, but conceptions of "childhood" and "adulthood" are infinitely variable.

We have learned a great deal in our search for universal developmental stages, but such investigations are incomplete. Obviously, any description of *constants* in human development tends to overlook the many factors that would bring about wide-scale *change* in the definition of child and adult roles. Even a complete understanding of universal features of development (and of reasons for individual variation) would not necessarily tell us why age-related roles vary from culture to culture and within the same culture over time. To discover the processes through which changes in conceptions of childhood and adulthood take place, we must look beyond the sequence of *individual* development and examine larger social variables that influence the behavior of *all* people, regardless of age or developmental stage. One such variable is the "social-information matrix."

Socialization as Access to Information

One of the constituent elements of social status is access to social information: people of the same social status usually have access to similar social situations and to similar social information; people of different social statuses usually have access to different social situations and to different social information.[23] Distinctions in status, therefore, are often supported by separating people into different social and informational worlds: managers keep customers out of restaurant kitchens; the officers' club is off limits to enlisted personnel in the armed services; and in schools, students are usually excluded from faculty meetings. Without the maintenance of such distinctions, differences in status would also begin to blur.

The movement from one social status to another—whether child to adult, medical student to doctor, or any role to any other role—generally involves gaining admittance to the locations associated with the new status and learning the "secrets" of those who play that role.

Human development and age-related social roles, therefore, are not only based on physiological and cognitive growth, but also on what might be called specific "patterns of access to social information." Every stage of socialization involves both exposure to, and restriction from, social information. For example, we tell sixth-graders things we keep hidden from fifth-graders and keep hidden from sixth-graders things we will tell them when they become seventh-graders. Socialization, therefore, can be thought of as a process of gradual, or staggered, exposure to social information. Children are slowly walked up the staircase of adult information, one step at a time. A child's individual cognitive development may help in the climb, but it is not the only factor. The amount of information available at each step will also greatly influence the child's relative social status.

This analysis suggests that if a society is able to divide what people of different ages know into many small steps, it will be able to establish many stages or levels of childhood. Conversely, if a society does not have sharp divisions in what people of different ages know, there will be fewer stages of childhood. If we always taught fifth-, sixth, and seventh-graders in the same classroom, for example, we would have a very difficult time clearly dividing them into three different social statuses. The variations in social roles for people of different ages that characterize different historical periods, different cultures, and different subcultures may therefore be based in part on different patterns of "who knows what about whom."

By conceiving of socialization as a process related to "patterns of access to information," we are able to approach the study of media effects from a new perspective. While many studies have examined the effects of media *messages* on people at specific stages of socialization, very few studies have examined how changes in media environments may affect the structure of the socialization process itself. One way to do this is to look beyond specific messages and examine how different media may create different "situational geographies" for the worlds of childhood and adulthood.

By focusing below on the potential effects of a shift from "book situations" to "television situations," I do not mean to obliterate other explanations for recent changes in socialization or to dismiss the many factors that work to maintain traditional distinctions between childhood and adulthood. Certainly, the growing instability of marriages, economic issues, and many other variables contributes to recent changes; conversely, family traditions, religious beliefs, schooling, social class, and place of residence mute and channel many of the pressures toward merging age-related roles. I merely hope to show that changes in media may have much more to do with overall trends in conceptions of childhood and adulthood than is generally assumed.

Put differently, the subject of the remainder of this essay is not change in socialization and many of its possible causes; the subject is change in media and many of the ways such change may influence age-related roles. The analysis here should be interpreted the same way findings in an experiment on the effects of a chemical known to have been added recently to drinking water nationwide might be interpreted. This chemical may be found to increase heart rate and metabolism, for example, but such a fact does not mean that there are no other variables that may have similar effects, and it does not mean that there are no other drugs, foods, or family habits that might moderate or offset the effects of the chemical. The qualifier that must be used to defend the cause-effect linking in all experimental findings is "all other things held constant." The scholar using an analytical method must often use a similar disclaimer when studying the potential effects of a single variable. In what follows, I try to indicate the *direction* of television's effects on age-related roles—all other things held constant.

At Home in Television Land

At one time, what the young, preschool child knew about the world was determined primarily by where he or she lived and was allowed to go. The child's experience was often limited to the home and the surrounding area. As the child learned to read and gained proficiency in it, and as the area in which he or she was free to travel about expanded, the child gained access to the larger society—reading offering informational access, and travel physical access, to the world.

The family home has traditionally been portrayed as a protective and nurturing environment. In modern urban societies, however, the family home has functioned as a very *restrictive* environment as well, and in this way has limited the experiences of children. Charlotte Perkins Gilman, an early feminist writer, attacked the home as a prison, one that restricted both children and women from the outside world.[24] Even those who support the traditional function of the home recognize implicitly its limiting aspect. In *The Sociology of Childhood*, Oscar Ritchie and Marvin Koller note that the home is the child's "small world" and that the "family serves as a screen to the culture of its society and selects only those portions that it deems worthy of attention."[25] The child of course is not completely isolated from information about the outside world, but this information is generally filtered through parents and other adults who are allowed to leave the home freely. Because of the sharp limitations on the child's experience of social reality, Ritchie and Koller observe, visitors from the outside world often become a center of interest and fascination. "As a person who lives outside the child's home, the guest functions as a transmitter, bringing into the world of the child new ideas and information, and new and different opportunities for vicarious participation in the outside world."[26]

The "transmitter" metaphor is an interesting and significant one, revealing, as it does, a weakness in Ritchie and Koller's own description of the role of the family and home in socialization. They were writing in 1964, and should have realized that in over 90 percent of American households at that time, the home environment they describe was no longer restrictive, having already been transformed by a new and powerful transmitter—television. They note that "largely because parents control the situation, the child-guest relationship is likely to be a positive aspect of socialization."[27] Yet, the traditional family guest is invited, remains under family control, and acts as an adult filter on child information, while the guests who come through the television set are often uninvited visitors who broaden the child's informational world without the parents' full approval or control.

The impact of television on the redefinition of "home" is all but lost in the dominant message-oriented approach to the study of television. The focus on content rather than on situational structure has obscured the ways in which television bypasses the filters of adult authority and decreases the significance of the child's physical isolation in the home.

In one sense, it makes little difference whether children's programs reinforce the message that "adults always know best" or the message that "adults don't always know best," or whether a commercial tells children to buy a product themselves or to ask their parents to do it for them, since, regardless of the specific messages in programs and advertising, the pattern of information flow into the home has changed. While young children once received virtually all of their information about the outside world from their parents, television now speaks directly to them, with the result that power relationships within the family are partially rearranged. Television's messages have a significant impact—again, regardless of specific content—because they take children beyond the informational limitations once set by walls and parents.

Certainly, today's parents still control much of the atmosphere of the family home. Yet, while homelife was once the base of all the child's experiences, children who have television sets now have outside perspectives from which to judge and evaluate family rituals, beliefs, and religious practices. While parents could once easily mold their young children's upbringing by speaking and reading to children only about the things they wished their children to be exposed to, today's parents must battle with thousands of competing images and ideas over which they have little direct control. The influence of parents and family life continues to be seen, of course: children still differ markedly by class, religion, and ethnic background. But the family is no longer an all-powerful formative influence.

Very young children were once limited to the few sources of information available to them within or around the home: paintings, illustrations, views from a window, and what adults said and read to them. Now television escorts them across the globe even before they have permission to cross the street. One of the reasons many children may no longer seem to "know their place" is that they no longer *have* a place, in the sense of an isolated environment that largely restricts their access to adult situations and secrets.

"Children's Television"—There's No Such Thing

Access to television and access to books are two quite different things. Reading and writing involve an abstract code of arbitrary and semantically meaningless symbols. To read and write efficiently, these symbols must be memorized, practiced, and internalized. The complexity of print's code excludes very young children from virtually all communications in print. In a sense, print creates "places" where adults can communicate with one another without being overheard by children. Through books, adults can privately discuss things they may wish to keep hidden from young children. Furthermore, because reading involves a complex skill that is learned in stages, adults can control the information given to children of different ages by varying the complexity of the code in which books on various subjects are written. Because children must read simple children's books before reading complex adult books, print allows for the separation of people of different ages into different informational worlds.[28]

The varying complexity of the code in print not only serves to isolate children from adult situations, but works as well to isolate adults from children's situations. Children, for example, can be shielded from "adult" topics such as sex, crime, and death simply by encoding this information in long, difficult words and complexly written sentences. At the same time, however, the content of most children's books is so simple that adults find them uninteresting and would be embarrassed to be seen reading them. (Indeed, finding appropriate material to use in teaching illiterate adults to read is a major problem.) Children usually do not know what adults are reading, and adults (unless they are schoolteachers or parents who read books aloud to children) usually do not know what children are reading. With print, a society tends to be divided into many different information systems based on differences in the mastery of reading skills.

"Children's books" are special, then, for two significant reasons: they are the only type of books many children can read, and generally, only children read them. In this sense, children's literature is a kind of informational ghetto, both isolated and isolating.

There is no situational equivalent to a children's book on television. Television has no complex access code to exclude young viewers or to divide its audience into different age groups. Adult programs may present children with information they do not fully understand, and children's programs may contain childish content, but the basic code in which all programs are presented is similar for every television show: pictures and sounds. Unlike print, television's symbolic form resembles the things it represents. Television pictures—like all pictures—look like real objects and people; television speaks in a human voice. While children under the age of eleven or twelve may not fully understand television in an adult sense, they still find television accessible and absorbing. Children from two to five spend very little time staring at words and sentences in a book, but over the last few years, they have spent an average of between twenty-five and thirty-two hours a week watching television.[29]

In contrast to books, television programs have few, if any, "prerequisites." There is no set order in which programs must be viewed, because most programs require the same degree (or lack) of skill. One does not have to watch "Romper Room" before watching "Sesame Street"; one does not have to watch "The Muppets" before watching "Dallas." With television, there is no media filter to shield children from exposure to adult programs, and there is no simplistic visual style to bore adults when they watch children's programs. It is no surprise, then, that people of all ages tend to watch many of the same programs. In recent years, "Dallas," "The Love Boat," and "The Muppets" have been among the most popular programs in *all* age-groups in the country.[30] While the world of children's books can be insulated so that children are shown only an idealized view of life, television news and entertainment present to young children images of adults who lie, drink, cheat, and murder.

What is revolutionary about television, then, is not that it gives children adult minds, but that it allows the very young child to be "present" at adult interactions. Television removes barriers that once divided people of different ages and reading abilities into different social situations.

The widespread use of television, therefore, is equivalent to a broad social decision to allow young children to be present at wars and funerals, courtships and seductions, criminal plots and cocktail parties. Young children may not fully understand the issues of sex, death, crime, and money that are presented to them on television. Or, put differently, they may understand these issues only in childlike ways. Yet television exposes children to many topics and behaviors that adults have spent several centuries trying to keep hidden from them. Television thrusts children into a complex adult world, and it provides the impetus for them to ask the meanings of actions and words they would not yet have heard of, or read about, without television.

Not only are most children able to watch adult programming, but from the very beginning of the television era, they have *preferred* it.[31] According to one recent study, even the best available children's program cannot compete with adult programs for the child's interest.[32] Nevertheless, many parents naively continue to demand more "children's programming" on television or look forward to the more age-specific programming of cable, direct satellite-to-home broadcasts, and videodiscs. But a separate information system equivalent to the isolated world of children's books will not come into being simply by creating television programs that contain content traditionally thought suitable for children. Nor can it. There is, in fact, no children's television as distinct from adult television. There is simply "television."

The Television Doorway

Many of the physical characteristics of books serve as filters for the information made accessible to children. Each book is a distinct object that a child must acquire individually. If the book is not given to the child by a parent, the child must leave the house and borrow or buy it—usually from an adult. The special library cards given to children prevent them from borrowing adult books, and these books are often placed on shelves beyond a child's reach. Moreover, children have little knowledge of what books are available or where to get them.

As individual objects, books can be selectively chosen and selectively given to children. But television content is much more difficult to control. Once the child has access to a television set, he or she has direct access to everything that comes through it. The child does not have to go anywhere special to find a television program or necessarily ask any adult to see it. While the reading code and physical characteristics of books provide "automatic" constraints that require minimal parental intervention, effective censorship of children's television viewing would involve active and constant monitoring. With television, therefore, the important decision is whether to have a television set or not, whether to expose children to almost *all* of television's offerings or *none* of them.

Furthermore, because the child has not brought the specific program into the house, there is little guilt by association with a television program. For a child to buy a cheap novel or a "dirty book" and bring it into the house is to associate with its content; to watch such a television show is merely to view innocently what has been piped into the home (and what must be, from the child's perspective, implicitly sanctioned by the parents, who provide the television set, and by the larger society, which presents itself through this medium).

A child's book is like a guest in the house. It makes a "social entrance"; that is, it comes through the door and remains under at least nominal parental authority. As a physical object, it must be stored somewhere in the house—whether on a coffee table or under a mattress—and it can be discarded. The child's television set, in contrast, is like a new doorway to the home. Through it come many welcome and unwelcome visitors: schoolteachers, presidents, salesmen, police officers, prostitutes, murderers, friends, and strangers.

Parents who tackle the monumental task of censoring their children's television viewing are faced with at least two significant dilemmas. First, controlling viewing involves a conflict of values: protecting children versus allowing them to learn as much as they can. Parents once had to encourage children to read and learn. A good deal of the protection from adult information in books was taken care of automatically by the inherent features of print. Now parents find themselves in the uncomfortable position of actively intervening in the learning process of their youngsters. Parents must now try to evaluate the content of television and decide—often on the spot—whether their children can handle it.

Second, for parents to control their children's viewing of television very often means limiting their own. While a child has virtually no access to the books being read by adults in the same room, a television program being watched by adults in the room the child is in is accessible to the child. Many children are exposed to adult news, for example, because their parents watch the news during dinner.[33] To control children's viewing, therefore, parents must either limit their own or physically divide the family. The situation of course is further complicated when there are several children of different ages in the household.

The unique characteristics of books make it possible for adults to enforce the implicit rule, "Read what we want you to read about, not what we read about," but television offers little support for a like admonition. Reading, a family can stay together in a single room and yet be divided into different informational worlds. In households that have more than one television set, children and adults can be in different rooms and still be united into a single informational arena.

Exposing the "Secret of Secrecy"

There are many books for parents that discuss what books are suitable for children. This is essentially an adult-to-adult interaction that is closed to young children, and in fact, most children are even unaware that such books exist. With the help of such private adult "discussions," children were once shielded from certain topics such as sex, money, death, crime, and drugs, and shielded, furthermore, from the very fact that they were being protected. Print allowed for an "adult conspiracy."

This does not hold for television. It is true that television frequently offers advice to parents. Talk shows discuss children's television, and warnings are placed at the beginning of programs to let parents know that a program may contain material "unsuitable" for preteenagers. Yet, while the content is similar to that of books which give advice to parents about children's literature, the structure of the communication situation is radically different: television discussions and warnings are accessible to children. Ironically, then, such advice on television often cues children to programs they are not supposed to see and increases their interest in what follows. Even if such warnings are also heard by parents, and even if parents act to censor a program, parental control is nevertheless weakened because the control becomes overt, and therefore often unpalatable to both children and adults. Visible censorship is the weakest form of control.

Once television provides children with the certain knowledge that adult secrets concerning children exist, complete and immediate comprehension of adult behavior is of secondary importance. The knowledge that a secret exists is half the secret. Once its existence is revealed, claims that "I'm not supposed to tell you" or "It's a secret" generally lead to the demand for revelation. It is not necessary for television to reveal *all* of the secrets of adults; children already know a great deal about traditional adult roles just by knowing for certain that adults consciously conspire to hide certain things from them. Television, then, may have its greatest effect on children's knowledge and behavior when adults use television forums (such as talk shows) to discuss how to control television's effects on children.

Contrary to many claims, therefore, children's access to adult information through television is not simply the result of a lapse in parental authority and responsibility. Print provides many filters and controls that television by its very nature cannot. No matter what parents do, short of removing the television set altogether, the old information environment cannot be fully reinstated. And even if the set is removed from one child's home, there are certainly sets in the homes of friends and relatives.

Parents may be somewhat helpless in the face of television, but surely, regulation of what broadcasters are allowed to show on television will have a tremendous impact on what children know and learn. If, for example, only conservative programs such as "Little House on the Prairie" or "Leave It to Beaver" are permitted, and shows such as "One Day at a Time," "Different Strokes," and "Silver Spoons" are banned, won't children be provided only with the information traditionally given to them in books? Not necessarily.

Certainly, different programs have different effects. But the difference in impact is not as great or as simple as is generally assumed. While traditional shows such as "Leave It to Beaver" are, in manifest content, more conservative than newer programs such as "One Day at a Time," the two are, in one sense, very similar in terms of what they reveal to children about adult life.

Traditional distinctions between child and adult behavior depend not only on the restriction of what children know about adult topics such as sex, murder, death, and money, but also upon the restriction of what children know about adult *role-playing*. To borrow from the theater, traditional children's books presented children with an "on-stage" view of adulthood, wherein parents were all-knowing, calm, cool, and collected; children were never exposed to the "backstage" view of adulthood, wherein adults displayed doubts, anxieties, fears, childish behaviors, arguments, sexual activity, illness, *and* preparation for, and relaxation of, their parental roles.[34] Children, in fact, were shielded from the *knowledge* that such a backstage area even existed. They were presented with the onstage role as the reality. The secrecy surrounding the adult backstage not only kept children innocent, but also allowed adults to "stage" a very formal image of adulthood, since the larger an actor's rehearsal and relaxation area, the more formal and confident the performance.

Yet even traditional, conservative television programs tend to reveal a backstage (or perhaps a "sidestage") view of adulthood. Child viewers see adults moving from backstage to onstage, behaving one way when they are with their peers and another when they are with children. The parents are shown as cool and rational with their children, but when they are by themselves, they display doubts and anxieties, and agonize over "what to do with the kids."

While the child *portrayed* on traditional television shows may be innocent and sheltered, the child *watching* the programs sees both the hidden behavior and the process of concealing it from children. "Father Knows Best," for example, exposed child viewers to the ways in which a father and mother manipulate their behavior to make it appear to their children that they "know best." This view is very damaging to the traditional adult role.

The behavior in the revealed adult backstage may be idealized and fictionalized, but from a social dynamics perspective, what is significant is the revelation of the existence of the backstage itself. If nothing else, children are shown through traditional television programs that adults "play roles" for children. This is a dramatic discovery. Children old enough to understand basic deception learn that the behavior adults exhibit before them is not necessarily their "real" or only behavior. (It is no surprise that the generation which

grew up watching "Father Knows Best" and other traditional programs became so concerned with the issue of "credibility" and the gap between private and public behaviors.)

As a result of such views of adulthood, children may become suspicious of adults and
more unwilling to accept all that adults do or say at face value. Conversely, adults may feel
"exposed" by television, and in the long run, it may no longer seem to make as much sense
to try to keep certain things hidden from children. Indeed, traditional "adulthood" was not
something that simply developed as people grew older; it was also a behavioral style that
was supported by being able to hide many childlike behaviors in a private backstage area.
As television blurs the dividing line between the backstage and onstage areas of adulthood
in our culture, many childlike behaviors emerge into the new public adult role. Television's
exposure of the "staging of adulthood"—with its secret-keeping and secret of secrecy—
therefore undermines both traditional childhood naiveté *and* the all-knowing confident
adult role, and fosters the movement toward a uni-age behavioral style.[35]

Literacy and the "Invention" of Childhood and Adulthood

If television can alter the social meaning of childhood and adulthood, then it stands to
reason that these life stages, as they have been defined for many generations in our
culture, are not natural or necessary states of being. Indeed, the above arguments rest
heavily on the plausibility of the notion that our old views of childhood and adulthood
were dependent, at least in part, upon print and could not have existed in quite the same
way in a primarily oral society.

The history of childhood is a relatively new field, yet there is already striking, if
preliminary, support for the idea that our traditional concept of childhood was related in
great measure to printing. While the various studies of childhood point to many fluctua-
tions in attitudes toward children across time, country, class, and religion, one relatively
consistent theme that emerges is that of a major shift in attitudes toward children
beginning among some classes in the sixteenth century, the same century that saw the
spread of literacy and printing in the vernacular throughout Western Europe. Before that
time, little special attention was paid to children. From the sixteenth to the twentieth
century, however, children were increasingly isolated from adult society and perceived as
a separate group requiring special care, protection, and restriction.

In the best-known work on the subject, *Centuries of Childhood*,[36] Philippe Ariès advances the rather startling argument that childhood was "invented" in the sixteenth
century. According to Ariès, prior to that time, the notion of childhood as a separate time
of life simply did not exist. More precisely, age did not define social status or role. Once
past infancy, children began to participate in adult activities and learned about life
through direct experience.

Children often worked beside adults, drank in taverns with adults, went to war with
them, and shared their beds. Adults and children played the same games. Neither had a
distinct style of dress, and there were no topics, words, or activities from which children
were to be shielded. The few formal schools that existed (primarily to train clerics) were
not divided into separate classes, and it was not unusual for a ten-year-old to sit next to a
twenty-year-old in class. Young students lived where they could find lodging, bore arms,
drank, and gambled.

Ariès study is mostly of France, but his observations find their echo in other European countries. Lawrence Stone, for example, notes that before the sixteenth century, English children were often neglected or ignored by their parents, who sent them away from home when they were seven or eight, usually to work in the home of another family. The child's world was essentially that of the adult. Children saw deaths and executions, witnessed sexual activities, and often engaged in sex play themselves.[37] Thus, while children have always existed in the physiological sense, the preprint oral society of Western Europe accorded them few special social roles or behaviors.

Beginning in the sixteenth century, however, a new concept of children began to take hold; from relatively independent persons, they became weak, innocent beings in need of special care, love, discipline, and protection from evil. No longer were they to be exposed to violent and vulgar folktales as before, since they were now considered to be too innocent to share fully in "adult" information. Clerics began to demand that children should read only expurgated versions of the classics. Special etiquette books for children were printed, along with separate guides for their parents. The idea of supervising children at all times and restricting their wanderings and activities began to grow. Moralists began to speak against the mixing of ages in schools, and the school slowly evolved into a strictly age-graded structure. Precocity, which was once as valued as it was common, began to be seen as a dangerous disease. Children's ages more and more determined what they should know, where they could go, and what they could do.

Stone notes that the "innocence" of children, first discussed by humanists in the Renaissance, was quickly "interpreted as liability to sin,"[38] and Ariès suggests that childish innocence led to "safeguarding it against pollution by life."[39] But while children began to be protected from aspects of adult life, they were not at first isolated from death. For years, fear of death and eternal damnation were used to scare children into piety. Children were taken to see hangings and corpses, and encouraged to "convert" to Christianity before it was too late.

Later, the new attention paid to children would evolve into the more modern "maternal, child-oriented, affectionate and permissive mode."[40] The change occurred at different times in different countries, classes, and religions. But by the nineteenth century, the belief in "infant depravity" and the need for young children to undergo "conversions" to Christ were generally abandoned in favor of views of children as, at worst, morally neutral, and at best, angelic redeemers of adult sinfulness.[41]

Despite the varied treatment of children from the sixteenth through the early twentieth centuries, the entire period was set apart from both earlier periods and from present trends by an underlying consistency: children were seen as a distinct category of people to be isolated from the adult world and segregated in their own institutions and subculture. Why was this so? Why did this notion of children develop in the sixteenth century, and how can we account for its decline today?

There are, no doubt, multiple reasons for so fundamental a shift in the social conception of children, but the analysis presented here supports the view that the spread of printing and literacy may have been prime factors in the development of the "innocent" child. To share fully in the literate adult world, a child had to learn to read.

Many other features of the spread of childhood, as described by Ariès and other historians, support this analysis. Childhood as a separate period of life developed first among the middle and upper classes, as did literacy. Boys were thought of as children long before girls—perhaps because boys were sent off to school to learn to read and write, while their sisters stayed home and immediately took on the dress and tasks of adult women.

In the lower classes, which were for the most part illiterate, the new concepts of childhood took hold only much later. In the nineteenth century, many uneducated children worked in factories beside their parents. John Sommerville notes the irony that the nineteenth century saw both the heights and depths of childhood. As the children of the educated were being glorified with their own subculture of books and toys, the children of the poor and illiterate were providing the labor to support this subculture. Publishers, for example, hired children of the lower class to hand-tint engravings in the growing numbers of books for middle-class children.[42]

The increasing influence of books throughout the period led to changes in their form that reinforced the new belief in the distinctness of children. In the eighteenth century, children's books began to shift away from pedantic moral instruction and joyless drill to books of entertainment and unworldly play. A whole subculture for children developed: books and fairy tales, toys, birthday celebrations, and nursery rhymes. As education became more nearly universal in the late eighteenth and nineteenth centuries, childhood was extended to the lower classes. Children were sent to school at an earlier age and remained longer. Age-grading of both children and lessons became stricter and stricter.[43]

There are many implicit suggestions in the historical literature of the possible role of literacy in the increasing segregation of children and adults; it is therefore odd that most historians have nothing explicit to say about it. Stone notes that new approaches to children developed first among the most literate groups, but he attributes this to the openness of literate peoples to "innovations." Furthermore, while he suggests that the greater spread of literacy among men may have led to a decrease in the relative status of women, he fails to extend this argument to its obvious implications for the changing status of children and adults. Nevertheless, Stone does observe—without analysis—how a new concern over children's proper education led parents to "interfere" with children's freedoms in new ways.[44] And the general data presented by Stone and other historians suggest that the growth and spread of schooling was paralleled by a growing belief that certain things should be kept hidden from children.

Sommerville also provides some inadvertent clues to the role of literacy in the advent of childhood. He notes that before the spread of literacy, people of all ages enjoyed listening to what we today call nursery tales. "What has changed since then is that adults have 'grown up' and have left these stories to children. Partly, this has been the result of literacy, which develops man's critical abilities but shrivels his imagination. . . . It may be that adults were more childlike in the early years of the modern era."[45]

Elsewhere Sommerville notes that changes in community traditions occurred when "adults became too grownup and inhibited to take part in the songs, games, and dancing that had once bound the various age groups together."[46] Yet, while Sommerville briefly suggests that literacy is responsible for making adults less childlike, he neglects to consider the other side of the coin: that literacy may have made children seem less adultlike.

To my knowledge, the only historian who has explicitly linked literacy with the invention of childhood is Elisabeth Eisenstein. In her extensive analysis of the impact of printing on Western culture, she briefly suggests several ways in which printing fostered the age-grading of students and the separation of children and adults. The mechanical aspects of printing and the resulting potential for technical precision, she suggests, caused a general fascination with system, method, and *sequence*. Moreover, the growth of the printing industry allowed for segregation of markets and audiences. Some books began to be aimed only at teachers or parents, while "textbooks were newly designed to take students in sequence from the most elementary to the most advanced level of a given skill." Eisenstein suggests that new views of childhood may have been related to the significant transition from "learning by doing" to "learning by reading." "As a consumer of printed materials geared to a sequence of learning stages, the growing child was subjected to a different developmental process than was the medieval apprentice, plough-boy, novice or page."[47]

Printing and spreading literacy, says Eisenstein, also created a new way of "adult thinking" based on "cumulative cognitive advance and incremental change," that, in effect, created childhood by default. "Indeed the more adult activities were governed by conscious deliberation or going by the book, the more striking the contrast offered by the spontaneous and impulsive behavior of young offspring, and the more strenuous the effort required to remold young 'bodies and souls.' "[48]

These many clues to the link between literacy and the development of "childhood" and "adulthood" further support the argument that television may be a prime factor in the current evolution toward more homogenized adult/child roles.

The argument that different media of communication foster different conceptions of "childhood" and "adulthood" may at first seem facile and mystical. Yet is is logical to argue that similarity of social status is dependent upon ability to participate relatively equally in social interaction and that such participation depends on communication skills. In the primarily oral society of the Middle Ages, children may have been seen as less distinct from adults because by the age of seven or eight, children generally master the basics of speech. Printing and literacy may have given a boost to the Renaissance, but they also created a new and lasting dark age for the young and illiterate.

The medium of print removed the child from the adult world in a manner and to a degree inconceivable in an oral culture.[49] To learn what adults knew, to be able to join adult interactions in print, now required many years of schooling and training. Printing allowed for all-adult interactions in which parents and teachers could "privately" discuss how to treat children, what to teach them, and what to keep from them. It is no surprise, then, that the image of the weak and naive child should have developed alongside the growing impact of printing. Children were suddenly considered very "innocent," not immediately in the moral sense (which developed later), but in the sense of innocence of experience and knowledge. Conversely, adults gained in image and prestige as they were increasingly able to conceal their doubts, anxieties, and childish behaviors from children.

Of course, if television does undermine the traditional "staging of adulthood" that was fostered by print, then the undermining process must have begun with earlier media such as film and radio. Yet neither film nor radio has all of the characteristics that make television a potent merger of child and adult situations. While movies, like television, have an accessible audio/visual code, the child has to leave the home and travel through the adult world to pay for and see a movie. This precludes viewing by very young children, who spend many hours a week in front of the television set. Even for the older child, the choice to see a *particular* movie is quite distinct from the random flip-of-the-dial television-viewing that provides children with information they have not directly sought. Similarly, while radio is, like television, a new doorway to the home, its code is wholly aural and verbal; a listener needs to fill in the pictures based on *past experience*. This requirement obviously puts the inexperienced child at a disadvantage. Furthermore, radio's reliance on language often takes it to the realm of high-level abstractions that cannot easily be *pictured*. Television, on the other hand, tends to turn to the more tangible (and less impressive and mystifying) aspects of everyday social behavior.

With television today, the form in which information is transmitted in our society once again conspires against controlling what children know about adulthood and adult roles. Children still pass through a sequence of cognitive and physiological phases, but the social stages of information access have been blurred. In television, there is no set sequence in the level or type of information accessible. It bypasses the hierarchy of information access supported by stages of reading literacy and the age-specific grades of the school system. Indeed, the whole fascination with linear "sequences" and "stages" that printing encouraged seems to be disappearing from our culture.

While critics have attacked television for weakening children's willingness and ability to learn to read, television may undermine the *structure* of the traditional school system more than it undermines its particular lessons. The age-graded structure of the school not only gives children in each age-group certain information, but also consciously holds back information. Such a system cannot easily accommodate children who, through television or other sources, have gained access to social information in no particular pattern or sequence. While the school continues to have many valuable lessons to teach children, it can no longer assume that children who cannot read know little about adult behavior, and it cannot assume that even children in the early grades will be willing to accept the idealized and mythologized versions of reality that were designed for "innocent children."

As I said earlier, the effects of television are muted and shaped by many factors—religion, class, race, region, and education. In addition, the continuing importance of literacy in our culture places a limit on how homogenized childhood and adulthood can become. Yet the old sharp distinctions in the roles of people of different ages can no longer be maintained. Television has had a tendency to blur traditional distinctions in age-related roles by making it much more difficult for adults to maintain different informational and behavioral worlds for people of different ages. Just as we cannot clearly distinguish between the social statuses of students of different ages if we teach them all in the same classroom, neither can we make very sharp distinctions in status if we expose everyone to similar information through television.

Clear differences in social status often rely on lack of intimate knowledge of "the other." If the mystery and distance disappear, so do many formal behaviors. In the shared environment of television, children and adults know a great deal about one another's behavior and social knowledge—too much, in fact, for them to play out the traditional complementary roles of innocence versus omniscience.

Notes

This essay is based on a chapter of my book, *No Sense of Place: The Impact of Electronic Media on Social Behavior* (New York: Oxford University Press, 1985). These ideas were first developed in my doctoral dissertation completed at New York University in 1978 and made available through University Microfilms in 1979. This research was supported in its later stages by a Central University Research Fund grant from the Research Office at the University of New Hampshire and by a Summer Faculty Fellowship from the graduate school of the same institution.

1. For statistics on the rapid increase in teenage sexual activity, drug abuse, alcoholism, abortion, and suicide, see *Teenage Pregnancy: The Problem That Hasn't Gone Away,* by the Alan Guttmacher Institute (New York: Alan Guttmacher Institute, 1981); Lloyd D. Johnston, Jerald G. Bachman, and Patrick M. O'Malley, *Student Drug Use in America, 1975–1981* (Rockville, Md: Department of Health and Human Services, 1981); and "Adults are Failing, Not the Children," *USA Today,* February 1984.

2. William Beardslee and John Mack, "The Impact on Children and Adolescents of Nuclear Developments," in *Psychosocial Aspects of Nuclear Developments,* American Psychiatric Association Task Force Report no. 20 (Washington, D.C.: American Psychiatric Association, 1982), pp. 64–93.

3. For indications of the new attitude toward children and childbirth, see, for example, Tracy Hotchner, *Pregnancy and Childbirth: A Complete Guide to a New Life* (New York: Avon, 1979).

4. William Watts, "The Future Can Fend for Itself," *Psychology Today,* September 1981, pp. 36–48.

5. See, for example, the interview with Kenneth Keniston, director of the Carnegie Council study on children, "More Rights for Children: What an Expert Says," *U.S. News & World Report,* October 31, 1977, p. 33.

6. See, for example, Judy Blume, *Superfudge* (New York: Dutton, 1980).

7. Serena Stier, "Children's Rights and Society's Duties," *Journal of Social Issues* 34 (2) (1978): 48.

8. Lynn Langway et al., "A Nation of Runaway Kids," *Newsweek,* October 18, 1982, pp. 97–98.

9. Mark Blackburn, "Teen-Agers Leave Home—Legally," *The New York Times,* February 20, 1980.

10. Comparison of the FBI's 1951 and 1981 *Uniform Crime Reports for the United States and Its Possessions* (Washington, D.C.: Department of Justice) indicates a phenomenal increase over the last three decades in the proportion of arrests for murder (up 500 percent), robbery (up 1,750 percent), and rape (up 4,000 percent) that involve children under the age of fifteen—even as the corresponding Census Bureau reports, *Statistical Abstracts of the United States* (Washington, D.C.: U.S. Government Printing Office), indicate that the proportion of the population in that age-range has decreased. At least part of this apparent change in criminal acitivity may be attributable to a change in the *reporting* of crimes committed by children, but even such a trend would suggest a significant shift in conceptions of "childhood."

11. Linda Greenhouse, "Pragmatism Brings Changes in the Juvenile Justice System," *The New York Times,* February 18, 1979.

12. Ibid.

13. For a discussion of the current controversy over criminal responsibility and "irresistible impulse," see Willard Gaylin, *The Killing of Bonnie Garland: A Question of Justice* (New York: Simon & Schuster, 1982), pp. 245–71, and the chapter, "Criminal Intent and Responsibility," in John Monahan and Laurens Walker, *Social Science in Law: Cases, Materials and Problems* (Mineola, N.Y.: Foundation Press, 1985).

14. Stier, "Children's Rights and Society's Duties," p. 49.

15. Peter Kihss, "2 Children in Foster Care Named to City Panel to Improve System," *The New York Times,* June 11, 1979.

16. See, for example, Elise Boulding, "Children's Rights," *Society,* November/December 1977, pp. 39–43, and Marian Wright Edelman, "In Defense of Children's Rights," *Current,* April 1978, pp. 16–20.

17. Richard Farson, *Birthrights* (New York: Macmillan, 1974).

18. John Holt, *Escape from Childhood* (New York: Dutton, 1974), p. 18.

19. Ruby Takanishi, "Childhood as a Social Issue: Historical Roots of Contemporary Child Advocacy Movements," *Journal of Social Issues* 34 (2) (1978): 8–28.

20. In *Childhood: Pathways of Discovery* (London: Harper & Row, 1980), p. 53, for example, psychologists Sheldon and Barbara White note that age is "a profoundly unbiological fact about a child" that merely represents the number of times the earth has circled the sun since the child was born. Describing development in terms of age-ranges, then, is only an easy way of summarizing or averaging developmental changes; children of the same age often have very different abilities. The

Whites suggest that Piaget's age-related cognitive stages are the weakest part of his theory. "All the evidence shows that there are no sudden and total transformations in a child's thinking at any age." Other psychologists have pointed out the problems in *any* studies that describe behavior as a function of age. See, for example, Joachim F. Wohlwill, "The Age Variable in Psychological Research," *Psychological Review* 77 (1970): 49–64. As Wohlwill and others note, age is unlike other presumed behavioral "causes" in that a person's age is not something that can be manipulated by a researcher, and therefore the effects of age cannot actually be tested experimentally. Further, for many practical reasons, most developmental studies cannot even follow the lives of subjects over many years. Instead, within a short time period, people who are age X (four years old, for example), are compared to those who are age Y (nine years old). There is no direct evidence in such studies that in five years the four-year-olds will respond the way the nine-year-olds do now, or that the latter were similar to today's four-year-olds five years ago. The developmental *process* must be inferred, and serious mistakes are possible. As Ralph L. Rownow notes in *Paradigms in Transition* (New York: Oxford University Press, 1981), people were taught for many years that intelligence declined with age. But this belief was based on the results of intelligence tests given to people of different ages *at the same time*. The differences in scores were assumed to be related to age when they were probably due to economic and social change (pp. 90–91).

21. See, for example, Daniel J. Levinson et al., *The Seasons of a Man's Life* (New York: Knopf, 1978) and Gail Sheehy, *Passages: Predictable Crises of Adult Life* (New York: Dutton, 1976).

22. When I began speaking and writing about the merging of childhood and adulthood as part of my doctoral research in the mid-1970s, my observations and analyses were often greeted with hostility and ridicule, I was frequently lectured on the "naturalness" of childhood as "proven" in developmental research. In the last few years, the changes in childhood have become more numerous and explicit, and a number of others have written about them. David Elkind has described *The Hurried Child* (Reading, Mass: Addison-Wesley, 1981), Marie Winn has written of *Children without Childhood* (New York: Pantheon, 1983), and Neil Postman—one of the faculty sponsors of my doctoral dissertation—has described the *Disappearance of Childhood* (New York: Delacorte, 1982). But even these writers tend to view the current changes as negative distortions of "proper" child-adult roles.

23. For a discussion of the relationship between variable patterns of information flow and the variable structure of roles of group identity, socialization, and hierarchy, see chapter 4 of Meyrowitz, *No Sense of Place*.

24. *The Home*, reprint of 1903 edition (Urbana: University of Illinois Press, 1972), p. 75.

25. (New York: Appleton-Century-Crofts, 1964), pp. 86, 109.

26. Ibid., p. 103.

27. Ibid., p. 105.

28. There is of course, nothing inherent in print which *demands* that adults use books to shield children from certain information. It is possible, for example, to revise children's books and substitute sentences such as "See Mrs. Smith feed the children milk and cookies" with "See Mrs. Smith go to bed with the milkman." Yet print *allows* adults to control what and how much children know about adult situations. And general observation of social behavior suggests that when people can control access to private behaviors, they often do so. As television's exposure of adult secrets to children has bypassed the traditional censoring process, however, many authors have begun to include "adult" topics such as homosexuality, death, abortion, and prostitution in children's books.

29. See the 1980 to 1983 editions of the *Nielsen Report on Television* (Northbrook, Ill.: A.C. Nielsen Co.) for recent levels of child viewing.

30. Ibid., 1981, pp. 14–15.

31. For examples of early studies that demonstrated this point, see Robert Lewis Shayon, *Television and Our Children* (New York: Longmans, Green, 1951), p. 27, and Hilde T. Himmelweit, A. N. Oppenheim, and Pamela Vince, *Television and the Child: An Empirical Study of the Effects of Television on the Young* (London: Oxford University Press, 1958), pp. 13–15.

32. James G. Webster and William C. Coscarelli, "The Relative Appeal to Children of Adult vs. Children's Television Programming," *Journal of Broadcasting* 23 (1979): 437–51.

33. Charles Atkin found that about 30 percent of kindergarten through fifth-graders claimed they watch a national news program "almost every day." "Broadcast News Programming and Child Audience," *Journal of Broadcasting* 22 (1978): 47–61.

34. See Erving Goffman, *The Presentation of Self in Everyday Life* (New York: Anchor Books, 1959), for a "dramaturgical" analysis of social interaction. For an extension of the model to an analysis of the effects of changes in media on a wide spectrum of social performances, see Meyrowitz, *No Sense of Place.*

35. It would be possible, of course, for adults to choose to present on television only those programs that contain information available in traditional children's books. Yet, unlike books, television programs cannot be easily aimed at particular age groups. Adults must either abandon television to their younger children or share most of their programs with children of all ages. The decision of what to put on television, then, parallels the speech and behavioral decisions of a large family that lives in one room: to control what a child of one age experiences is also to control the experience of the other children and adults, and almost any information suitable for older children and adults exposes young children to "adult secrets."

36. *Centuries of Childhood: A Social History of Family Life* (New York: Vintage Books, 1962), translated by Robert Baldick.

37. *The Family, Sex, and Marriage in England 1500–1800* (New York: Harper & Row, 1977).

38. Stone, *The Family, Sex, and Marriage,* pp. 14, 174.

39. Ariès, *Centuries of Childhood,* p. 119.

40. Stone, *The Family, Sex, and Marriage,* p. 405.

41. Bernard Wishy, *The Child and the Republic: The Dawn of Modern American Child Nurture,* (Philadelphia: University of Pennsylvania Press, 1968), pp. 85, 108.

42. John Sommerville, *The Rise and Fall of Childhood* (Beverly Hills, Calif.: Sage, 1982), pp. 145, 160.

43. Ibid., pp. 136–47, 189–208.

44. Stone, *The Family, Sex, and Marriage,* pp. 449, 158, 216. For an analysis of the potential effects of literacy and electronic media on gender roles, see chapter 12 of Meyrowitz, *No Sense of Place.*

45. Sommerville, *The Rise and Fall of Childhood,* p. 136.

46. Ibid., p. 182.

47. Elisabeth L. Eisenstein, *The Printing Press as an Agent of Change: Communication and Cultural Transformations in Early Modern Europe,* 2 vols. (New York: Cambridge University Press, 1979), p. 432.

48. Ibid., pp. 432–33.

49. Of course, it is not the existence of literacy in and of itself that leads to "childhood" and "adulthood," but rather the increased possibilities that literacy affords for the *separation of adult and child information systems.* Because situation-separation is the key variable, we can see some evidence of distinctions in childhood and adulthood in various oral cultures where children are kept out of certain locations and discussions—but we do not see the division of childhood into thin year-by-year slices until the spread of literacy and the age-graded school. Conversely, even in literate societies, certain social conditions may override the distinctions in information systems that literacy makes possible. Thus, children were continued to be treated as "little adults" in many early American colonial settlements because harsh and primitive conditions made it difficult to isolate children. Similarly, childhood was "delayed" among the lower classes, not only by the slow spread of literacy, but also by crowded conditions and the lack of adult privacy. Childhood was also muted in many rural areas because children continued to work beside adults many hours a day and because the low density of the population often led to the mixing of ages in a one-room school.

Harvey J. Graff is a professor of history and arts and humanities at the University of Texas at Dallas. He earned his M.A. and Ph.D. degrees at the University of Toronto and the Ontario Institute for Studies in Education. His numerous publications include *The Literacy Myth: Literacy and Social Structure in the Nineteenth-Century City; Children and Schools in Nineteenth-Century Canada/L'école canadienne et l'enfant au dix-neuvième siècle; The Legacies of Literacy: Continuities and Contradictions in Western Society;* and many articles. A holder of National Endowment for the Humanities, American Council of Learned Societies, and Spencer Fellowships, he edits the Interdisciplinary Studies in History Series.

The manuscript was prepared for publication by Lois Krieger. The book was designed by Jim Billingsley. The typeface for the text and the display is Galliard. The book is printed on Warren's 1854 offset paper. The cloth edition is bound in Holliston Mills' Roxite Linen over binder's boards.

Manufactured in the United States of America.

Index

Abbott, Edith, 418
Abbott, Grace, 75
Abortion, 245
Abrams, P., 29, 156
Acculturation, 62
Achievement-in-isolation, 494–96, 512
Adams, Bert N., 157
Adolescence, adolescents: adulation/romanticization of, 59, 183, 379; archetypal image of, 50–60; athletics in, 597–601; bohemianism in, 601–2, 605–8; cohorts, 9–11, 21, 25–27; in colonial period, 94, 96–97, 102–6, 122; dating in, 453–72, 506–7, 528; defined, 102, 585–86; delinquency in, 13, 14, 57, 526–27, 601, 602–4, 629n; dependent status in, 514, 586–90; developmental/social themes in studies of, 15–18; emergence of concept of, xiii–xiv, 11, 73, 268; employment in, 251–62, 279–82, 296, 332, 333, 342, 416–18, 420–21, 431–32, 488–90, 508–9; and ethnicity, 284–90; family hardship in, 36–39, 478–92; fantasy/aspirations of, 541–42, 548n; financial judgment in, 484–85, 510–11; freedom to drive cars in, 509–10; friendships of, 506–07; generational analysis in studies of, 22–29; generational conflict in, 463–65, 513–14, 589; hatred of precocity in, 401, 402; historical times in studies of, 5–6, 13–40; identity formation in, 56–57, 190, 191, 572–73, 593; impact of industrialization on, 273–98; life-course perspective in studies of, 7–13, 22–23, 36–39; marriage in, 547–48n; in nineteenth century, 31–33, 175, 178–83, 251–54; organizations and movements of, 53, 54, 55, 56, 57–59, 397, 398–99, 400, 403–8, 512, 515; parenthood in, 28–29; peer influence in, 19–20, 52, 53–54, 457, 468–69, 514, 521, 525; prolonged, 590–91; as psychological stage, 69; radicalism in, 23–24, 25–27, 70, 601, 602, 604–5; religious conversion in, 104–5, 149–50, 181–82, 185–87, 190–92, 194n; residence patterns in, 31–32, 253–54, 257, 260–61, 273–78, 284–86, 296–97, 332, 334–35, 341; role models for, 55, 56, 58; school attendance in, 284, 286–88, 290–93, 330, 332, 338, 414–15; school departure in, 333, 334, 341, 415–16, 418–19, 420, 430; scrupulosity in, 594–95; semiautonomous stage in, 31–32, 103, 179, 182–83, 273–74, 277, 297, 326; smoking in, 463, 464, 510; social change in studies of, 29–40, 325–46; social

independence in, 487–90; socialization in, 504–16, 572–73; societal development in studies of, 18–21; and societal expectations, 511–12; studious, 595–97, 599; subculture of, 591–93; transition to adulthood in, 30–35, 49, 50–51, 54–55, 59, 101, 325–46, 490–91, 528–29; in working class, 525–28. *See also* Boyhood, boys; Men; Schools, schooling; Women, girls
Adolescence (Hall), 12
Adolescent Society, The (Coleman), 14, 19, 471, 591–92, 596, 597–98, 599
Adorno, T. W., 86
Adulthood: merging of childhood and, 612–15; television exposure of, 620–21, 623–24, 627–28; transitions to, 30–35, 49, 50–51, 54–55, 59, 101, 325–46, 490–91, 528–29, 585
Age: cultural definition of, 48–49; -grading, 64, 79, 459, 461, 493, 498, 501, 504, 626; of life transitions, 334–35; at marriage, 27, 33, 103, 124, 128n, 151–52, 153–54, 160–61, 186, 194n, 282–83, 293–95, 335, 471, 472, 547n; and role allocation, 51–52, 54. *See also* Cohorts
Age-congruity, in life transition, 34, 330, 336–37
Aggression: and delinquency, 603–4; female, 573; and socialization, 571
Alcoholism, parental, 532, 538, 547n
Allowance, payment of, 484–85, 510–11
Anderson, Michael, 269, 270, 296–97, 345–46
Anderson, Robert, 204
Apprenticeship, 103, 123, 179, 280, 308, 421
Ariès, Philippe, xi, xvi, 11, 70, 83, 86, 92, 105, 156–57, 304, 385, 392, 624–25
Art, bohemian, 607
Association for Improving the Condition of the Poor (AICP), 312
Attainment: and family hardship, 39–40; female, 572, 573–74, 575–76
Avirett, James Battle, 211n

Bacon, Ezekiel, 264
Baden-Powell, Robert, 398, 403, 405
Bailyn, Bernard, 11, 76, 102
Baltes, Paul, 22
Barker, Roger, 25
Barnard, John, 145–46, 147
Barnard, Thomas, 145
Beales, Ross, Jr., 83, 84
Beats, 605
Becker, Howard, 328